WILLA CATHER COLLECTION, EARLY NOVELS 1912-1922

Alexander's Bridge, O Pioneers!, The Song of the Lark, My Antonia, One of Ours

WILLA CATHER

This work reflects minor editorial revisions to the original texts.

Cover design created using Canva.com and reproduced pursuant to its free media license agreement. Cover art features the oil painting *The Song of the Lark*, 1884, by Jules Adolphe Breton (French, 1827-1906), courtesy of the Art Institute of Chicago, CC0 Public Domain.

CONTENTS

ALEXANDER'S BRIDGE

O PIONEERS!

THE SONG OF THE LARK

MY ANTONIA

ONE OF OURS

ALEXANDER'S BRIDGE

ALEXANDER'S BRIDGE

I.

LATE ONE BRILLIANT April afternoon Professor Lucius Wilson stood at the head of Chestnut Street, looking about him with the pleased air of a man of taste who does not very often get to Boston. He had lived there as a student, but for twenty years and more, since he had been Professor of Philosophy in a Western university, he had seldom come East except to take a steamer for some foreign port. Wilson was standing quite still, contemplating with a whimsical smile the slanting street, with its worn paving, its irregular, gravely colored houses, and the row of naked trees on which the thin sunlight was still shining. The gleam of the river at the foot of the hill made him blink a little, not so much because it was too bright as because he found it so pleasant. The few passers-by glanced at him unconcernedly, and even the children who hurried along with their school-bags under their arms seemed to find it perfectly natural that a tall brown gentleman should be standing there, looking up through his glasses at the gray housetops.

The sun sank rapidly; the silvery light had faded from the bare boughs and the watery twilight was setting in when Wilson at last walked down the hill, descending into cooler and cooler depths of grayish shadow. His nostril, long unused to it, was quick to detect the smell of wood smoke in the air, blended with the odor of moist spring earth and the saltiness that came up the river with the tide. He crossed Charles Street between jangling street cars and shelving lumber drays, and after a moment of uncertainty wound into Brimmer Street. The street was quiet, deserted, and hung with a thin bluish haze. He had already fixed his sharp eye upon the house which he reasoned should be his objective point, when he noticed a woman approaching rapidly from the opposite direction. Always an interested observer of women, Wilson would have slackened his pace anywhere to follow this one with his impersonal, appreciative glance. She was a person of distinction he saw at once, and, moreover, very handsome. She was tall, carried her beautiful head proudly, and moved with ease and certainty. One immediately took for granted the costly privileges and fine spaces that must lie in the background from which such a figure could emerge with this rapid and elegant gait. Wilson noted her dress, too,—for, in his way, he had an eye for such things,—particularly her brown furs and her hat. He got a blurred impression of her fine color, the violets she wore, her white gloves, and, curiously enough, of her veil, as she turned up a flight of steps in front of him and disappeared.

Wilson was able to enjoy lovely things that passed him on the wing as completely and deliberately as if they had been dug-up marvels, long anticipated, and definitely fixed at the end of a railway journey. For a few pleasurable seconds he quite forgot where he was going, and only after the door had closed behind her did he realize that the young woman had entered the house to which he had directed his trunk from the South Station that morning. He hesitated a moment before mounting the steps. "Can that," he murmured in amazement, —"can that possibly have been Mrs. Alexander?"

When the servant admitted him, Mrs. Alexander was still standing in the hallway. She heard him give his name, and came forward holding out her hand.

"Is it you, indeed, Professor Wilson? I was afraid that you might get here before I did. I was detained at a concert, and Bartley telephoned that he would be late. Thomas will show you your room. Had you rather have your tea brought to you there, or will you have it down here with me, while we wait for Bartley?"

Wilson was pleased to find that he had been the cause of her rapid walk, and with her he was even more vastly pleased than before. He followed her through the drawing-room into the library, where the wide back windows looked out upon the garden and the sunset and a fine stretch of silver-colored river. A harp-shaped elm stood stripped against the pale-colored evening sky, with ragged last year's birds' nests in its forks, and through the bare branches the evening star quivered in the misty air. The long brown room breathed the peace of a rich and amply guarded quiet. Tea was brought in immediately and placed in front of the wood fire. Mrs. Alexander sat down in a high-backed chair and began to pour it, while Wilson sank into a low seat opposite her and took his cup with a great sense of ease and harmony and comfort.

"You have had a long journey, haven't you?" Mrs. Alexander asked, after showing gracious concern about his tea. "And I am so sorry Bartley is late. He's often tired when he's late. He flatters himself that it is a little on his account that you have come to this Congress of Psychologists."

"It is," Wilson assented, selecting his muffin carefully; "and I hope he won't be tired tonight. But, on my own account, I'm glad to have a few moments alone with you, before Bartley comes. I was somehow afraid that my knowing him so well would not put me in the way of getting to know you."

"That's very nice of you." She nodded at him above her cup and smiled, but there was a little formal tightness in her tone which had not been there when she greeted him in the hall.

Wilson leaned forward. "Have I said something awkward? I live very far out of the world, you know. But I didn't mean that you would exactly fade dim, even if Bartley were here."

Mrs. Alexander laughed relentingly. "Oh, I'm not so vain! How terribly discerning you are."

She looked straight at Wilson, and he felt that this quick, frank glance brought about an understanding between them.

He liked everything about her, he told himself, but he particularly liked her eyes; when she looked at one directly for a moment they were like a glimpse of fine windy sky that may bring all sorts of weather.

"Since you noticed something," Mrs. Alexander went on, "it must have been a flash of the distrust I have come to feel whenever I meet any of the people who knew Bartley when he was a boy. It is always as if they were talking of someone I had never met. Really, Professor Wilson, it would seem that he grew up among the strangest people. They usually say that he has turned out very well, or remark that he always was a fine fellow. I never know what reply to make."

Wilson chuckled and leaned back in his chair, shaking his left foot gently. "I expect the fact is that we none of us knew him very well, Mrs. Alexander. Though I will say for myself that I was always confident he'd do something extraordinary."

Mrs. Alexander's shoulders gave a slight movement, suggestive of impatience. "Oh, I should think that might have been a safe prediction. Another cup, please?"

"Yes, thank you. But predicting, in the case of boys, is not so easy as you might imagine, Mrs. Alexander. Some get a bad hurt early and lose their courage; and some never get a fair wind. Bartley"—he dropped his chin on the back of his long hand and looked at her admiringly—"Bartley caught the wind early, and it has sung in his sails ever since."

Mrs. Alexander sat looking into the fire with intent preoccupation, and Wilson studied her half-averted face. He liked the suggestion of stormy possibilities in the proud curve of her lip and nostril. Without that, he reflected, she would be too cold.

"I should like to know what he was really like when he was a boy. I don't believe he remembers," she said suddenly. "Won't you smoke, Mr. Wilson?"

Wilson lit a cigarette. "No, I don't suppose he does. He was never introspective. He was simply the most tremendous response to stimuli I have ever known. We didn't know exactly what to do with him."

A servant came in and noiselessly removed the tea-tray. Mrs. Alexander screened her face from the firelight, which was beginning to throw wavering bright spots on her dress and hair as the dusk deepened.

"Of course," she said, "I now and again hear stories about things that happened when he was in college."

"But that isn't what you want." Wilson wrinkled his brows and looked at her with the smiling familiarity that had come about so quickly. "What you want is a picture of him, standing back there at the other end of twenty years. You want to look down through my memory."

She dropped her hands in her lap. "Yes, yes; that's exactly what I want."

At this moment they heard the front door shut with a jar, and Wilson laughed as Mrs. Alexander rose quickly. "There he is. Away with perspective! No past, no future for Bartley; just the fiery moment. The only moment that ever was or will be in the world!"

The door from the hall opened, a voice called "Winifred?" hurriedly, and a big man came through the drawing-room with a quick, heavy tread, bringing with him a smell of cigar smoke and chill out-of-doors air. When Alexander reached the library door, he switched on the lights and stood six feet and more in the archway, glowing with strength and cordiality and rugged, blond good looks. There were other bridge-builders in the world, certainly, but it was always Alexander's picture that the Sunday Supplement men wanted, because he looked as a tamer of rivers ought to look. Under his tumbled sandy hair his head seemed as hard and powerful as a catapult, and his shoulders looked strong enough in themselves to support a span of any one of his ten great bridges that cut the air above as many rivers.

After dinner Alexander took Wilson up to his study. It was a large room over the library, and looked out upon the black river and the row of white lights along the Cambridge Embankment. The room was not at all what one might expect of an engineer's study. Wilson felt at once the harmony of beautiful things that have lived long together without obtrusions of ugliness or change. It was none of Alexander's doing, of course; those warm consonances of color had been blending and mellowing before he was born. But the wonder was that he was not out of place there,—that it all seemed to glow like the inevitable background for his vigor and vehemence. He sat before the fire, his shoulders deep in the cushions of his chair, his powerful head upright, his hair rumpled above his broad forehead. He sat heavily, a cigar in his large, smooth hand, a flush of after-dinner color in his face, which wind and sun and exposure to all sorts of weather had left fair and clear-skinned.

"You are off for England on Saturday, Bartley, Mrs. Alexander tells me."

"Yes, for a few weeks only. There's a meeting of British engineers, and I'm doing another bridge in Canada, you know."

"Oh, every one knows about that. And it was in Canada that you met your wife, wasn't it?"

"Yes, at Allway. She was visiting her great-aunt there. A most remarkable old lady. I was working with MacKeller then, an old Scotch engineer who had picked me up in London and taken me back to Quebec with him. He had the contract for the Allway Bridge, but before he began work on it he found out that he was going to die, and he advised the committee to turn the job over to me. Otherwise I'd never have got anything good so early. MacKeller was an old friend of Mrs. Pemberton, Winifred's aunt. He had mentioned me to her, so when I went to Allway she asked me to come to see her. She was a wonderful old lady."

"Like her niece?" Wilson queried.

Bartley laughed. "She had been very handsome, but not in Winifred's way. When I knew her she was little and fragile, very pink and white, with a splendid head and a face like fine old lace, somehow,—but perhaps I always think of that because she wore a lace scarf on her hair. She had such a flavor of life about her. She had known Gordon and Livingstone and Beaconsfield when she was young,—every one. She was the first woman of that sort I'd ever known. You know how it is in the West,—old people are poked out of the way. Aunt Eleanor fascinated me as few young women have ever done. I used to go up from the works to have tea with her, and sit talking to her for hours. It was very stimulating, for she couldn't tolerate stupidity."

"It must have been then that your luck began, Bartley," said Wilson, flicking his cigar ash with his long finger. "It's curious, watching boys," he went on reflectively. "I'm sure I did you justice in the matter of ability. Yet I always used to feel that there was a weak spot where some day strain would tell. Even after you began to climb, I stood down in the crowd and watched you with—well, not with confidence. The more dazzling the front you presented, the higher your facade rose, the more I expected to see a big crack zigzagging from top to bottom,"—he indicated its course in the air with his forefinger,—"then a crash and clouds of dust. It was curious. I had such a clear picture of it. And another curious thing, Bartley," Wilson spoke with deliberateness and settled deeper into his chair, "is that I don't feel it any longer. I am sure of you."

Alexander laughed. "Nonsense! It's not I you feel sure of; it's Winifred. People often make that mistake."

"No, I'm serious, Alexander. You've changed. You have decided to leave some birds in the bushes. You used to want them all."

Alexander's chair creaked. "I still want a good many," he said rather gloomily. "After all, life doesn't offer a man much. You work like the devil and think you're getting on, and suddenly you discover that you've only been getting yourself tied up. A million details drink you dry. Your life keeps going for things you don't want, and all the while you are being built alive into a social structure you don't care a rap about. I sometimes wonder what sort of chap

I'd have been if I hadn't been this sort; I want to go and live out his potentialities, too. I haven't forgotten that there are birds in the bushes."

Bartley stopped and sat frowning into the fire, his shoulders thrust forward as if he were about to spring at something. Wilson watched him, wondering. His old pupil always stimulated him at first, and then vastly wearied him. The machinery was always pounding away in this man, and Wilson preferred companions of a more reflective habit of mind. He could not help feeling that there were unreasoning and unreasonable activities going on in Alexander all the while; that even after dinner, when most men achieve a decent impersonality, Bartley had merely closed the door of the engine-room and come up for an airing. The machinery itself was still pounding on.

Bartley's abstraction and Wilson's reflections were cut short by a rustle at the door, and almost before they could rise Mrs. Alexander was standing by the hearth. Alexander brought a chair for her, but she shook her head.

"No, dear, thank you. I only came in to see whether you and Professor Wilson were quite comfortable. I am going down to the music-room."

"Why not practice here? Wilson and I are growing very dull. We are tired of talk."

"Yes, I beg you, Mrs. Alexander," Wilson began, but he got no further.

"Why, certainly, if you won't find me too noisy. I am working on the Schumann `Carnival,' and, though I don't practice a great many hours, I am very methodical," Mrs. Alexander explained, as she crossed to an upright piano that stood at the back of the room, near the windows.

Wilson followed, and, having seen her seated, dropped into a chair behind her. She played brilliantly and with great musical feeling. Wilson could not imagine her permitting herself to do anything badly, but he was surprised at the cleanness of her execution. He wondered how a woman with so many duties had managed to keep herself up to a standard really professional. It must take a great deal of time, certainly, and Bartley must take a great deal of time. Wilson reflected that he had never before known a woman who had been able, for any considerable while, to support both a personal and an intellectual passion. Sitting behind her, he watched her with perplexed admiration, shading his eyes with his hand. In her dinner dress she looked even younger than in street clothes, and, for all her composure and self-sufficiency, she seemed to him strangely alert and vibrating, as if in her, too, there were something never altogether at rest. He felt that he knew pretty much what she demanded in people and what she demanded from life, and he wondered how she squared Bartley. After ten years she must know him; and however one took him, however much one admired him, one had to admit that he simply wouldn't square. He was a natural force, certainly, but beyond that, Wilson felt, he was not anything very really or for very long at a time.

Wilson glanced toward the fire, where Bartley's profile was still wreathed in cigar smoke that curled up more and more slowly. His shoulders were sunk deep in the cushions and one hand hung large and passive over the arm of his chair. He had slipped on a purple velvet smoking-coat. His wife, Wilson surmised, had chosen it. She was clearly very proud of his good looks and his fine color. But, with the glow of an immediate interest gone out of it, the engineer's face looked tired, even a little haggard. The three lines in his forehead, directly above the nose, deepened as he sat thinking, and his powerful head drooped forward heavily. Although Alexander was only forty-three, Wilson thought that beneath his vigorous color he detected the dulling weariness of on-coming middle age.

The next afternoon, at the hour when the river was beginning to redden under the declining sun, Wilson again found himself facing Mrs. Alexander at the tea-table in the library.

"Well," he remarked, when he was bidden to give an account of himself, "there was a long morning with the psychologists, luncheon with Bartley at his club, more psychologists, and here I am. I've looked forward to this hour all day."

Mrs. Alexander smiled at him across the vapor from the kettle. "And do you remember where we stopped yesterday?"

"Perfectly. I was going to show you a picture. But I doubt whether I have color enough in me. Bartley makes me feel a faded monochrome. You can't get at the young Bartley except by means of color." Wilson paused and deliberated. Suddenly he broke out: "He wasn't a remarkable student, you know, though he was always strong in higher mathematics. His work in my own department was quite ordinary. It was as a powerfully equipped nature that I found him interesting. That is the most interesting thing a teacher can find. It has the fascination of a scientific discovery. We come across other pleasing and endearing qualities so much oftener than we find force."

"And, after all," said Mrs. Alexander, "that is the thing we all live upon. It is the thing that takes us forward."

Wilson thought she spoke a little wistfully. "Exactly," he assented warmly. "It builds the bridges into the future, over which the feet of every one of us will go."

"How interested I am to hear you put it in that way. The bridges into the future—I often say that to myself. Bartley's bridges always seem to me like that. Have you ever seen his first suspension bridge in Canada, the one he was doing when I first knew him? I hope you will see it sometime. We were married as soon as it was finished, and you will laugh when I tell you that it always has a rather bridal look to me. It is over the wildest river, with mists and clouds always battling about it, and it is as delicate as a cobweb hanging in the sky. It really was a bridge into the future. You have only to look at it to feel that it meant the beginning of a great career. But I have a photograph of it here." She drew a portfolio from behind a bookcase. "And there, you see, on the hill, is my aunt's house."

Wilson took up the photograph. "Bartley was telling me something about your aunt last night. She must have been a delightful person."

Winifred laughed. "The bridge, you see, was just at the foot of the hill, and the noise of the engines annoyed her very much at first. But after she met Bartley she pretended to like it, and said it was a good thing to be reminded that there were things going on in the world. She loved life, and Bartley brought a great deal of it in to her when he came to the house. Aunt Eleanor was very worldly in a frank, Early-Victorian manner. She liked men of action, and disliked young men who were careful of themselves and who, as she put it, were always trimming their wick as if they were afraid of their oil's giving out. MacKeller, Bartley's first chief, was an old friend of my aunt, and he told her that Bartley was a wild, ill-governed youth, which really pleased her very much. I remember we were sitting alone in the dusk after Bartley had been there for the first time. I knew that Aunt Eleanor had found him much to her taste, but she hadn't said anything. Presently she came out, with a chuckle: `MacKeller found him sowing wild oats in London, I believe. I hope he didn't stop him too soon. Life coquets with dashing fellows. The coming men are always like that. We must have him to dinner, my dear.' And we did. She grew much fonder of Bartley than she was of me. I had been studying in Vienna, and she thought that absurd. She was interested in the army and in politics, and she had a great contempt for music and art and philosophy. She used to declare that the Prince Consort had brought all that stuff over out of Germany. She always sniffed when Bartley asked me to play for him. She considered that a newfangled way of making a match of it."

When Alexander came in a few moments later, he found Wilson and his wife still confronting the photograph. "Oh, let us get that out of the way," he said, laughing. "Winifred, Thomas can bring my trunk down. I've decided to go over to New York tomorrow night and take a fast boat. I shall save two days."

II.

On the night of his arrival in London, Alexander went immediately to the hotel on the Embankment at which he always stopped, and in the lobby he was accosted by an old acquaintance, Maurice Mainhall, who fell upon him with effusive cordiality and indicated a willingness to dine with him. Bartley never dined alone if he could help it, and Mainhall was a good gossip who always knew what had been going on in town; especially, he knew everything that was not printed in the newspapers. The nephew of one of the standard Victorian novelists, Mainhall bobbed about among the various literary cliques of London and its outlying suburbs, careful to lose touch with none of them. He had written a number of books himself; among them a "History of Dancing," a "History of Costume," a "Key to Shakespeare's Sonnets," a study of "The Poetry of Ernest Dowson," etc. Although Mainhall's enthusiasm was often tiresome, and although he was often unable to distinguish between facts and vivid figments of his imagination, his imperturbable good nature overcame even the people whom he bored most, so that they ended by becoming, in a reluctant manner, his friends. In appearance, Mainhall was astonishingly like the conventional stage-Englishman of American drama: tall and thin, with high, hitching shoulders and a small head glistening with closely brushed yellow hair. He spoke with an extreme Oxford accent, and when he was talking well, his face sometimes wore the rapt expression of a very emotional man listening to music. Mainhall liked Alexander because he was an engineer. He had preconceived ideas about everything, and his idea about Americans was that they should be engineers or mechanics. He hated them when they presumed to be anything else.

While they sat at dinner Mainhall acquainted Bartley with the fortunes of his old friends in London, and as they left the table he proposed that they should go to see Hugh MacConnell's new comedy, "Bog Lights."

"It's really quite the best thing MacConnell's done," he explained as they got into a hansom. "It's tremendously well put on, too. Florence Merrill and Cyril Henderson. But Hilda Burgoyne's the hit of the piece. Hugh's written a delightful part for her, and she's quite inexpressible. It's been on only two weeks, and I've been half a dozen times already. I happen to have MacConnell's box for tonight or there'd be no chance of our getting places. There's everything in seeing Hilda while she's fresh in a part. She's apt to grow a bit stale after a time. The ones who have any imagination do."

"Hilda Burgoyne!" Alexander exclaimed mildly. "Why, I haven't heard of her for—years."

Mainhall laughed. "Then you can't have heard much at all, my dear Alexander. It's only lately, since MacConnell and his set have got hold of her, that she's come up. Myself, I always knew she had it in her. If we had one real critic in London—but what can one expect? Do you know, Alexander,"—Mainhall looked with perplexity up into the top of the hansom and rubbed his pink cheek with his gloved finger,—"do you know, I sometimes think of taking to criticism seriously myself. In a way, it would be a sacrifice; but, dear me, we do need some one."

Just then they drove up to the Duke of York's, so Alexander did not commit himself, but followed Mainhall into the theatre. When they entered the stage-box on the left the first act was well under way, the scene being the interior of a cabin in the south of Ireland. As they sat down, a burst of applause drew Alexander's attention to the stage. Miss Burgoyne and her donkey were thrusting their heads in at the half door. "After all," he reflected, "there's small probability of her recognizing me. She doubtless hasn't thought of me for years." He felt the enthusiasm of the house at once, and in a few moments he was caught up by the current of MacConnell's irresistible comedy. The audience had come forewarned, evidently, and whenever the ragged slip of a donkey-girl ran upon the stage there was a deep murmur of approbation, every one smiled and glowed, and Mainhall hitched his heavy chair a little nearer the brass railing.

"You see," he murmured in Alexander's ear, as the curtain fell on the first act, "one almost never sees a part like that done without smartness or mawkishness. Of course, Hilda is Irish, —the Burgoynes have been stage people for generations,—and she has the Irish voice. It's delightful to hear it in a London theatre. That laugh, now, when she doubles over at the hips —who ever heard it out of Galway? She saves her hand, too. She's at her best in the second act. She's really MacConnell's poetic motif, you see; makes the whole thing a fairy tale."

The second act opened before Philly Doyle's underground still, with Peggy and her battered donkey come in to smuggle a load of potheen across the bog, and to bring Philly word of what was doing in the world without, and of what was happening along the roadsides and ditches with the first gleam of fine weather. Alexander, annoyed by Mainhall's sighs and exclamations, watched her with keen, half-skeptical interest. As Mainhall had said, she was the second act; the plot and feeling alike depended upon her lightness of foot, her lightness of touch, upon the shrewdness and deft fancifulness that played alternately, and sometimes together, in her mirthful brown eyes. When she began to dance, by way of showing the gossoons what she had seen in the fairy rings at night, the house broke into a prolonged uproar. After her dance she withdrew from the dialogue and retreated to the ditch wall back of Philly's burrow, where she sat singing "The Rising of the Moon" and making a wreath of primroses for her donkey.

When the act was over Alexander and Mainhall strolled out into the corridor. They met a good many acquaintances; Mainhall, indeed, knew almost every one, and he babbled on incontinently, screwing his small head about over his high collar. Presently he hailed a tall, bearded man, grim-browed and rather battered-looking, who had his opera cloak on his arm and his hat in his hand, and who seemed to be on the point of leaving the theatre.

"MacConnell, let me introduce Mr. Bartley Alexander. I say! It's going famously to-night, Mac. And what an audience! You'll never do anything like this again, mark me. A man writes to the top of his bent only once."

The playwright gave Mainhall a curious look out of his deep-set faded eyes and made a wry face. "And have I done anything so fool as that, now?" he asked.

"That's what I was saying," Mainhall lounged a little nearer and dropped into a tone even more conspicuously confidential. "And you'll never bring Hilda out like this again. Dear me, Mac, the girl couldn't possibly be better, you know."

MacConnell grunted. "She'll do well enough if she keeps her pace and doesn't go off on us in the middle of the season, as she's more than like to do."

He nodded curtly and made for the door, dodging acquaintances as he went.

"Poor old Hugh," Mainhall murmured. "He's hit terribly hard. He's been wanting to marry Hilda these three years and more. She doesn't take up with anybody, you know. Irene Burgoyne, one of her family, told me in confidence that there was a romance somewhere back in the beginning. One of your countrymen, Alexander, by the way; an American student whom she met in Paris, I believe. I dare say it's quite true that there's never been any one else." Mainhall vouched for her constancy with a loftiness that made Alexander smile, even while a kind of rapid excitement was tingling through him. Blinking up at the lights, Mainhall added in his luxurious, worldly way: "She's an elegant little person, and quite capable of an extravagant bit of sentiment like that. Here comes Sir Harry Towne. He's another who's awfully keen about her. Let me introduce you. Sir Harry Towne, Mr. Bartley Alexander, the American engineer."

Sir Harry Towne bowed and said that he had met Mr. Alexander and his wife in Tokyo.

Mainhall cut in impatiently.

"I say, Sir Harry, the little girl's going famously to-night, isn't she?"

Sir Harry wrinkled his brows judiciously. "Do you know, I thought the dance a bit conscious to-night, for the first time. The fact is, she's feeling rather seedy, poor child. Westmere and I were back after the first act, and we thought she seemed quite uncertain of herself. A little attack of nerves, possibly."

He bowed as the warning bell rang, and Mainhall whispered: "You know Lord Westmere, of course,—the stooped man with the long gray mustache, talking to Lady Dowle. Lady Westmere is very fond of Hilda."

When they reached their box the house was darkened and the orchestra was playing "The Cloak of Old Gaul." In a moment Peggy was on the stage again, and Alexander applauded vigorously with the rest. He even leaned forward over the rail a little. For some reason he felt pleased and flattered by the enthusiasm of the audience. In the half-light he looked about at the stalls and boxes and smiled a little consciously, recalling with amusement Sir Harry's judicial frown. He was beginning to feel a keen interest in the slender, barefoot donkey-girl who slipped in and out of the play, singing, like some one winding through a hilly field. He leaned forward and beamed felicitations as warmly as Mainhall himself when, at the end of the play, she came again and again before the curtain, panting a little and flushed, her eyes dancing and her eager, nervous little mouth tremulous with excitement.

When Alexander returned to his hotel—he shook Mainhall at the door of the theatre—he had some supper brought up to his room, and it was late before he went to bed. He had not thought of Hilda Burgoyne for years; indeed, he had almost forgotten her. He had last written to her from Canada, after he first met Winifred, telling her that everything was changed with him—that he had met a woman whom he would marry if he could; if he could not, then all the more was everything changed for him. Hilda had never replied to his letter. He felt guilty and unhappy about her for a time, but after Winifred promised to marry him he really forgot Hilda altogether. When he wrote her that everything was changed for him, he was telling the truth. After he met Winifred Pemberton he seemed to himself like a different man. One night when he and Winifred were sitting together on the bridge, he told her that things had happened while he was studying abroad that he was sorry for,—one thing in particular,—and he asked her whether she thought she ought to know about them. She considered a moment and then said "No, I think not, though I am glad you ask me. You see, one can't be jealous about things in general; but about particular, definite, personal things,"—here she had thrown her hands up to his shoulders with a quick, impulsive gesture—"oh, about those I should be very jealous. I should torture myself—I couldn't help it." After that it was easy to forget, actually to forget. He wondered to-night, as he poured his wine, how many times he had thought of Hilda in the last ten years. He had been in London more or less, but he had never happened to hear of her. "All the same," he lifted his glass, "here's to you, little Hilda. You've made things come your way, and I never thought you'd do it.

"Of course," he reflected, "she always had that combination of something homely and sensible, and something utterly wild and daft. But I never thought she'd do anything. She hadn't much ambition then, and she was too fond of trifles. She must care about the theatre a great deal more than she used to. Perhaps she has me to thank for something, after all. Sometimes a little jolt like that does one good. She was a daft, generous little thing. I'm glad she's held her own since. After all, we were awfully young. It was youth and poverty and proximity, and everything was young and kindly. I shouldn't wonder if she could laugh about it with me now. I shouldn't wonder— But they've probably spoiled her, so that she'd be tiresome if one met her again."

Bartley smiled and yawned and went to bed.

III.

THE NEXT EVENING Alexander dined alone at a club, and at about nine o'clock he dropped in at the Duke of York's. The house was sold out and he stood through the second act. When he returned to his hotel he examined the new directory, and found Miss Burgoyne's address still given as off Bedford Square, though at a new number. He remembered that, in so far as she had been brought up at all, she had been brought up in Bloomsbury. Her father and mother played in the provinces most of the year, and she was left a great deal in the care of an old aunt who was crippled by rheumatism and who had had to leave the stage altogether. In the days when Alexander knew her, Hilda always managed to have a lodging of some sort about Bedford Square, because she clung tenaciously to such scraps and shreds of memories as were connected with it. The mummy room of the British Museum had been one of the chief delights of her childhood. That forbidding pile was the goal of her truant fancy, and she was sometimes taken there for a treat, as other children are taken to the theatre. It was long since Alexander had thought of any of these things, but now they came back to him quite fresh, and had a significance they did not have when they were first told him in his restless twenties. So she was still in the old neighborhood, near Bedford Square. The new number probably meant increased prosperity. He hoped so. He would like to know that she was snugly settled. He looked at his watch. It was a quarter past ten; she would not be home for a good two hours yet, and he might as well walk over and have a look at the place. He remembered the shortest way.

It was a warm, smoky evening, and there was a grimy moon. He went through Covent Garden to Oxford Street, and as he turned into Museum Street he walked more slowly, smiling at his own nervousness as he approached the sullen gray mass at the end. He had not been inside the Museum, actually, since he and Hilda used to meet there; sometimes to set out for gay adventures at Twickenham or Richmond, sometimes to linger about the place for a while and to ponder by Lord Elgin's marbles upon the lastingness of some things, or, in the mummy room, upon the awful brevity of others. Since then Bartley had always thought of the British Museum as the ultimate repository of mortality, where all the dead things in the world were assembled to make one's hour of youth the more precious. One trembled lest before he got out it might somehow escape him, lest he might drop the glass from over-eagerness and see it shivered on the stone floor at his feet. How one hid his youth under his coat and hugged it! And how good it was to turn one's back upon all that vaulted cold, to take Hilda's arm and hurry out of the great door and down the steps into the sunlight among the pigeons—to know that the warm and vital thing within him was still there and had not been snatched away to flush Caesar's lean cheek or to feed the veins of some bearded Assyrian king. They in their day had carried the flaming liquor, but to-day was his! So the song used to run in his head those summer mornings a dozen years ago. Alexander walked by the place very quietly, as if he were afraid of waking some one.

He crossed Bedford Square and found the number he was looking for. The house, a comfortable, well-kept place enough, was dark except for the four front windows on the second floor, where a low, even light was burning behind the white muslin sash curtains. Outside there were window boxes, painted white and full of flowers. Bartley was making a third round of the Square when he heard the far-flung hoof-beats of a hansom-cab horse, driven rapidly. He looked at his watch, and was astonished to find that it was a few minutes after twelve. He turned and walked back along the iron railing as the cab came up to Hilda's number and stopped. The hansom must have been one that she employed regularly, for she did not stop to pay the driver. She stepped out quickly and lightly. He heard her cheerful "Good-night, cabby," as she ran up the steps and opened the door with a latchkey. In a few moments the lights flared up brightly behind the white curtains, and as he walked away he heard a window raised. But he had gone too far to look up without turning round. He went back to his hotel, feeling that he had had a good evening, and he slept well.

For the next few days Alexander was very busy. He took a desk in the office of a Scotch engineering firm on Henrietta Street, and was at work almost constantly. He avoided the clubs and usually dined alone at his hotel. One afternoon, after he had tea, he started for a walk down the Embankment toward Westminster, intending to end his stroll at Bedford Square and to ask whether Miss Burgoyne would let him take her to the theatre. But he did not go so far. When he reached the Abbey, he turned back and crossed Westminster Bridge and sat down to watch the trails of smoke behind the Houses of Parliament catch fire with the sunset. The slender towers were washed by a rain of golden light and licked by little flickering flames; Somerset House and the bleached gray pinnacles about Whitehall were floated in a luminous haze. The yellow light poured through the trees and the leaves seemed to burn with soft fires. There was a smell of acacias in the air everywhere, and the laburnums were dripping gold over the walls of the gardens. It was a sweet, lonely kind of summer evening. Remembering Hilda as she used to be, was doubtless more satisfactory than seeing her as she must be now—and, after all, Alexander asked himself, what was it but his own young years that he was remembering?

He crossed back to Westminster, went up to the Temple, and sat down to smoke in the Middle Temple gardens, listening to the thin voice of the fountain and smelling the spice of the sycamores that came out heavily in the damp evening air. He thought, as he sat there, about a great many things: about his own youth and Hilda's; above all, he thought of how glorious it had been, and how quickly it had passed; and, when it had passed, how little worth while anything was. None of the things he had gained in the least compensated. In the last six years his reputation had become, as the saying is, popular. Four years ago he had been called to Japan to deliver, at the Emperor's request, a course of lectures at the Imperial University, and had instituted reforms throughout the islands, not only in the practice of bridge-building but in drainage and road-making. On his return he had undertaken the bridge at Moorlock, in Canada, the most important piece of bridge-building going on in the world,—a test, indeed, of how far the latest practice in bridge structure could be carried. It was a spectacular undertaking by reason of its very size, and Bartley realized that, whatever else he might do, he would probably always be known as the engineer who designed the great Moorlock Bridge, the longest cantilever in existence. Yet it was to him the least satisfactory thing he had ever done. He was cramped in every way by a niggardly commission, and was using lighter structural material than he thought proper. He had vexations enough, too, with his work at home. He had several bridges under way in the

United States, and they were always being held up by strikes and delays resulting from a general industrial unrest.

Though Alexander often told himself he had never put more into his work than he had done in the last few years, he had to admit that he had never got so little out of it. He was paying for success, too, in the demands made on his time by boards of civic enterprise and committees of public welfare. The obligations imposed by his wife's fortune and position were sometimes distracting to a man who followed his profession, and he was expected to be interested in a great many worthy endeavors on her account as well as on his own. His existence was becoming a network of great and little details. He had expected that success would bring him freedom and power; but it had brought only power that was in itself another kind of restraint. He had always meant to keep his personal liberty at all costs, as old MacKeller, his first chief, had done, and not, like so many American engineers, to become a part of a professional movement, a cautious board member, a Nestor de pontibus. He happened to be engaged in work of public utility, but he was not willing to become what is called a public man. He found himself living exactly the kind of life he had determined to escape. What, he asked himself, did he want with these genial honors and substantial comforts? Hardships and difficulties he had carried lightly; overwork had not exhausted him; but this dead calm of middle life which confronted him,—of that he was afraid. He was not ready for it. It was like being buried alive. In his youth he would not have believed such a thing possible. The one thing he had really wanted all his life was to be free; and there was still something unconquered in him, something besides the strong work-horse that his profession had made of him. He felt rich to-night in the possession of that unstultified survival; in the light of his experience, it was more precious than honors or achievement. In all those busy, successful years there had been nothing so good as this hour of wild light-heartedness. This feeling was the only happiness that was real to him, and such hours were the only ones in which he could feel his own continuous identity—feel the boy he had been in the rough days of the old West, feel the youth who had worked his way across the ocean on a cattle-ship and gone to study in Paris without a dollar in his pocket. The man who sat in his offices in Boston was only a powerful machine. Under the activities of that machine the person who, in such moments as this, he felt to be himself, was fading and dying. He remembered how, when he was a little boy and his father called him in the morning, he used to leap from his bed into the full consciousness of himself. That consciousness was Life itself. Whatever took its place, action, reflection, the power of concentrated thought, were only functions of a mechanism useful to society; things that could be bought in the market. There was only one thing that had an absolute value for each individual, and it was just that original impulse, that internal heat, that feeling of one's self in one's own breast.

When Alexander walked back to his hotel, the red and green lights were blinking along the docks on the farther shore, and the soft white stars were shining in the wide sky above the river.

The next night, and the next, Alexander repeated this same foolish performance. It was always Miss Burgoyne whom he started out to find, and he got no farther than the Temple gardens and the Embankment. It was a pleasant kind of loneliness. To a man who was so little given to reflection, whose dreams always took the form of definite ideas, reaching into the future, there was a seductive excitement in renewing old experiences in imagination. He started out upon these walks half guiltily, with a curious longing and expectancy which were wholly gratified by solitude. Solitude, but not solitariness; for he walked shoulder to shoulder with a shadowy companion—not little Hilda Burgoyne, by any means, but some one vastly dearer to him than she had ever been—his own young self, the youth who had waited for him upon the steps of the British Museum that night, and who, though he had tried to pass so quietly, had known him and come down and linked an arm in his.

It was not until long afterward that Alexander learned that for him this youth was the most dangerous of companions.

One Sunday evening, at Lady Walford's, Alexander did at last meet Hilda Burgoyne. Mainhall had told him that she would probably be there. He looked about for her rather nervously, and finally found her at the farther end of the large drawing-room, the centre of a circle of men, young and old. She was apparently telling them a story. They were all laughing and bending toward her. When she saw Alexander, she rose quickly and put out her hand. The other men drew back a little to let him approach.

"Mr. Alexander! I am delighted. Have you been in London long?"

Bartley bowed, somewhat laboriously, over her hand. "Long enough to have seen you more than once. How fine it all is!"

She laughed as if she were pleased. "I'm glad you think so. I like it. Won't you join us here?"

"Miss Burgoyne was just telling us about a donkey-boy she had in Galway last summer," Sir Harry Towne explained as the circle closed up again. Lord Westmere stroked his long white mustache with his bloodless hand and looked at Alexander blankly. Hilda was a good story-teller. She was sitting on the edge of her chair, as if she had alighted there for a moment only. Her primrose satin gown seemed like a soft sheath for her slender, supple figure, and its delicate color suited her white Irish skin and brown hair. Whatever she wore, people felt the charm of her active, girlish body with its slender hips and quick, eager shoulders. Alexander heard little of the story, but he watched Hilda intently. She must certainly, he reflected, be thirty, and he was honestly delighted to see that the years had treated her so indulgently. If her face had changed at all, it was in a slight hardening of the mouth—still eager enough to be very disconcerting at times, he felt—and in an added air of self-possession and self-reliance. She carried her head, too, a little more resolutely.

When the story was finished, Miss Burgoyne turned pointedly to Alexander, and the other men drifted away.

"I thought I saw you in MacConnell's box with Mainhall one evening, but I supposed you had left town before this."

She looked at him frankly and cordially, as if he were indeed merely an old friend whom she was glad to meet again.

"No, I've been mooning about here."

Hilda laughed gayly. "Mooning! I see you mooning! You must be the busiest man in the world. Time and success have done well by you, you know. You're handsomer than ever and you've gained a grand manner."

Alexander blushed and bowed. "Time and success have been good friends to both of us. Aren't you tremendously pleased with yourself?"

She laughed again and shrugged her shoulders. "Oh, so-so. But I want to hear about you. Several years ago I read such a lot in the papers about the wonderful things you did in Japan, and how the Emperor decorated you. What was it, Commander of the Order of the Rising Sun? That sounds like 'The Mikado.' And what about your new bridge—in Canada, isn't it, and it's to be the longest one in the world and has some queer name I can't remember."

Bartley shook his head and smiled drolly. "Since when have you been interested in bridges? Or have you learned to be interested in everything? And is that a part of success?"

"Why, how absurd! As if I were not always interested!" Hilda exclaimed.

"Well, I think we won't talk about bridges here, at any rate." Bartley looked down at the toe of her yellow slipper which was tapping the rug impatiently under the hem of her gown. "But I wonder whether you'd think me impertinent if I asked you to let me come to see you sometime and tell you about them?"

"Why should I? Ever so many people come on Sunday afternoons."

"I know. Mainhall offered to take me. But you must know that I've been in London several times within the last few years, and you might very well think that just now is a rather inopportune time—"

She cut him short. "Nonsense. One of the pleasantest things about success is that it makes people want to look one up, if that's what you mean. I'm like every one else—more agreeable to meet when things are going well with me. Don't you suppose it gives me any pleasure to do something that people like?"

"Does it? Oh, how fine it all is, your coming on like this! But I didn't want you to think it was because of that I wanted to see you." He spoke very seriously and looked down at the floor.

Hilda studied him in wide-eyed astonishment for a moment, and then broke into a low, amused laugh. "My dear Mr. Alexander, you have strange delicacies. If you please, that is exactly why you wish to see me. We understand that, do we not?"

Bartley looked ruffled and turned the seal ring on his little finger about awkwardly.

Hilda leaned back in her chair, watching him indulgently out of her shrewd eyes. "Come, don't be angry, but don't try to pose for me, or to be anything but what you are. If you care to come, it's yourself I'll be glad to see, and you thinking well of yourself. Don't try to wear a cloak of humility; it doesn't become you. Stalk in as you are and don't make excuses. I'm not accustomed to inquiring into the motives of my guests. That would hardly be safe, even for Lady Walford, in a great house like this."

"Sunday afternoon, then," said Alexander, as she rose to join her hostess. "How early may I come?"

She gave him her hand and flushed and laughed. He bent over it a little stiffly. She went away on Lady Walford's arm, and as he stood watching her yellow train glide down the long floor he looked rather sullen. He felt that he had not come out of it very brilliantly.

IV.

ON SUNDAY AFTERNOON Alexander remembered Miss Burgoyne's invitation and called at her apartment. He found it a delightful little place and he met charming people there. Hilda lived alone, attended by a very pretty and competent French servant who answered the door and brought in the tea. Alexander arrived early, and some twenty-odd people dropped in during the course of the afternoon. Hugh MacConnell came with his sister, and stood about, managing his tea-cup awkwardly and watching every one out of his deep-set, faded eyes. He seemed to have made a resolute effort at tidiness of attire, and his sister, a robust, florid woman with a splendid joviality about her, kept eyeing his freshly creased clothes apprehensively. It was not very long, indeed, before his coat hung with a discouraged sag from his gaunt shoulders and his hair and beard were rumpled as if he had been out in a gale. His dry humor went under a cloud of absent-minded kindliness which, Mainhall explained, always overtook him here. He was never so witty or so sharp here as elsewhere, and Alexander thought he behaved as if he were an elderly relative come in to a young girl's party.

The editor of a monthly review came with his wife, and Lady Kildare, the Irish philanthropist, brought her young nephew, Robert Owen, who had come up from Oxford, and who was visibly excited and gratified by his first introduction to Miss Burgoyne. Hilda was very nice to him, and he sat on the edge of his chair, flushed with his conversational efforts and moving his chin about nervously over his high collar. Sarah Frost, the novelist, came with her husband, a very genial and placid old scholar who had become slightly deranged upon the subject of the fourth dimension. On other matters he was perfectly rational and he was easy and pleasing in conversation. He looked very much like Agassiz, and his wife, in her old-fashioned black silk dress, overskirted and tight-sleeved, reminded Alexander of the early pictures of Mrs. Browning. Hilda seemed particularly fond of this quaint couple, and Bartley himself was so pleased with their mild and thoughtful converse that he took his leave when they did, and walked with them over to Oxford Street, where they waited for their 'bus. They asked him to come to see them in Chelsea, and they spoke very tenderly of Hilda. "She's a dear, unworldly little thing," said the philosopher absently; "more like the stage people of my young days—folk of simple manners. There aren't many such left. American tours have spoiled them, I'm afraid. They have all grown very smart. Lamb wouldn't care a great deal about many of them, I fancy."

Alexander went back to Bedford Square a second Sunday afternoon. He had a long talk with MacConnell, but he got no word with Hilda alone, and he left in a discontented state of mind. For the rest of the week he was nervous and unsettled, and kept rushing his work as if he were preparing for immediate departure. On Thursday afternoon he cut short a committee meeting, jumped into a hansom, and drove to Bedford Square. He sent up his card, but it came back to him with a message scribbled across the front.

So sorry I can't see you. Will you come and dine with me Sunday evening at half-past seven?
H.B.

When Bartley arrived at Bedford Square on Sunday evening, Marie, the pretty little French girl, met him at the door and conducted him upstairs. Hilda was writing in her living-room, under the light of a tall desk lamp. Bartley recognized the primrose satin gown she had worn that first evening at Lady Walford's.

"I'm so pleased that you think me worth that yellow dress, you know," he said, taking her hand and looking her over admiringly from the toes of her canary slippers to her smoothly parted brown hair. "Yes, it's very, very pretty. Every one at Lady Walford's was looking at it."

Hilda curtsied. "Is that why you think it pretty? I've no need for fine clothes in Mac's play this time, so I can afford a few duddies for myself. It's owing to that same chance, by the way, that I am able to ask you to dinner. I don't need Marie to dress me this season, so she keeps house for me, and my little Galway girl has gone home for a visit. I should never have asked you if Molly had been here, for I remember you don't like English cookery."

Alexander walked about the room, looking at everything.

"I haven't had a chance yet to tell you what a jolly little place I think this is. Where did you get those etchings? They're quite unusual, aren't they?"

"Lady Westmere sent them to me from Rome last Christmas. She is very much interested in the American artist who did them. They are all sketches made about the Villa d'Este, you see. He painted that group of cypresses for the Salon, and it was bought for the Luxembourg."

Alexander walked over to the bookcases. "It's the air of the whole place here that I like. You haven't got anything that doesn't belong. Seems to me it looks particularly well to-night. And you have so many flowers. I like these little yellow irises."

"Rooms always look better by lamplight—in London, at least. Though Marie is clean—really clean, as the French are. Why do you look at the flowers so critically? Marie got them all fresh in Covent Garden market yesterday morning."

"I'm glad," said Alexander simply. "I can't tell you how glad I am to have you so pretty and comfortable here, and to hear every one saying such nice things about you. You've got awfully nice friends," he added humbly, picking up a little jade elephant from her desk. "Those fellows are all very loyal, even Mainhall. They don't talk of any one else as they do of you."

Hilda sat down on the couch and said seriously: "I've a neat little sum in the bank, too, now, and I own a mite of a hut in Galway. It's not worth much, but I love it. I've managed to save something every year, and that with helping my three sisters now and then, and tiding poor Cousin Mike over bad seasons. He's that gifted, you know, but he will drink and loses more good engagements than other fellows ever get. And I've traveled a bit, too."

Marie opened the door and smilingly announced that dinner was served.

"My dining-room," Hilda explained, as she led the way, "is the tiniest place you have ever seen."

It was a tiny room, hung all round with French prints, above which ran a shelf full of china. Hilda saw Alexander look up at it.

"It's not particularly rare," she said, "but some of it was my mother's. Heaven knows how she managed to keep it whole, through all our wanderings, or in what baskets and bundles and theatre trunks it hasn't been stowed away. We always had our tea out of those blue cups when I was a little girl, sometimes in the queerest lodgings, and sometimes on a trunk at the theatre—queer theatres, for that matter."

It was a wonderful little dinner. There was watercress soup, and sole, and a delightful omelette stuffed with mushrooms and truffles, and two small rare ducklings, and artichokes, and a dry yellow Rhone wine of which Bartley had always been very fond. He drank it appreciatively and remarked that there was still no other he liked so well.

"I have some champagne for you, too. I don't drink it myself, but I like to see it behave when it's poured. There is nothing else that looks so jolly."

"Thank you. But I don't like it so well as this." Bartley held the yellow wine against the light and squinted into it as he turned the glass slowly about. "You have traveled, you say. Have you been in Paris much these late years?"

Hilda lowered one of the candle-shades carefully. "Oh, yes, I go over to Paris often. There are few changes in the old Quarter. Dear old Madame Anger is dead—but perhaps you don't remember her?"

"Don't I, though! I'm so sorry to hear it. How did her son turn out? I remember how she saved and scraped for him, and how he always lay abed till ten o'clock. He was the laziest fellow at the Beaux Arts; and that's saying a good deal."

"Well, he is still clever and lazy. They say he is a good architect when he will work. He's a big, handsome creature, and he hates Americans as much as ever. But Angel—do you remember Angel?"

"Perfectly. Did she ever get back to Brittany and her bains de mer?"

"Ah, no. Poor Angel! She got tired of cooking and scouring the coppers in Madame Anger's little kitchen, so she ran away with a soldier, and then with another soldier. Too bad! She still lives about the Quarter, and, though there is always a soldat, she has become a blanchisseuse de fin. She did my blouses beautifully the last time I was there, and was so delighted to see me again. I gave her all my old clothes, even my old hats, though she always wears her Breton headdress. Her hair is still like flax, and her blue eyes are just like a baby's, and she has the same three freckles on her little nose, and talks about going back to her bains de mer."

Bartley looked at Hilda across the yellow light of the candles and broke into a low, happy laugh. "How jolly it was being young, Hilda! Do you remember that first walk we took together in Paris? We walked down to the Place Saint-Michel to buy some lilacs. Do you remember how sweet they smelled?"

"Indeed I do. Come, we'll have our coffee in the other room, and you can smoke."

Hilda rose quickly, as if she wished to change the drift of their talk, but Bartley found it pleasant to continue it.

"What a warm, soft spring evening that was," he went on, as they sat down in the study with the coffee on a little table between them; "and the sky, over the bridges, was just the color of the lilacs. We walked on down by the river, didn't we?"

Hilda laughed and looked at him questioningly. He saw a gleam in her eyes that he remembered even better than the episode he was recalling.

"I think we did," she answered demurely. "It was on the Quai we met that woman who was crying so bitterly. I gave her a spray of lilac, I remember, and you gave her a franc. I was frightened at your prodigality."

"I expect it was the last franc I had. What a strong brown face she had, and very tragic. She looked at us with such despair and longing, out from under her black shawl. What she wanted from us was neither our flowers nor our francs, but just our youth. I remember it touched me so. I would have given her some of mine off my back, if I could. I had enough and to spare then," Bartley mused, and looked thoughtfully at his cigar.

They were both remembering what the woman had said when she took the money: "God give you a happy love!" It was not in the ingratiating tone of the habitual beggar: it had come out of the depths of the poor creature's sorrow, vibrating with pity for their youth and despair at the terribleness of human life; it had the anguish of a voice of prophecy. Until she spoke, Bartley had not realized that he was in love. The strange woman, and her passionate sentence that rang out so sharply, had frightened them both. They went home sadly with the lilacs, back to the Rue Saint-Jacques, walking very slowly, arm in arm. When they reached the house where Hilda lodged, Bartley went across the court with her, and up the dark old stairs to the third landing; and there he had kissed her for the first time. He had shut his eyes to give him the courage, he remembered, and she had trembled so—

Bartley started when Hilda rang the little bell beside her. "Dear me, why did you do that? I had quite forgotten—I was back there. It was very jolly," he murmured lazily, as Marie came in to take away the coffee.

Hilda laughed and went over to the piano. "Well, we are neither of us twenty now, you know. Have I told you about my new play? Mac is writing one; really for me this time. You see, I'm coming on."

"I've seen nothing else. What kind of a part is it? Shall you wear yellow gowns? I hope so."

He was looking at her round slender figure, as she stood by the piano, turning over a pile of music, and he felt the energy in every line of it.

"No, it isn't a dress-up part. He doesn't seem to fancy me in fine feathers. He says I ought to be minding the pigs at home, and I suppose I ought. But he's given me some good Irish songs. Listen."

She sat down at the piano and sang. When she finished, Alexander shook himself out of a reverie.

"Sing `The Harp That Once,' Hilda. You used to sing it so well."

"Nonsense. Of course I can't really sing, except the way my mother and grandmother did before me. Most actresses nowadays learn to sing properly, so I tried a master; but he confused me, just!"

Alexander laughed. "All the same, sing it, Hilda."

Hilda started up from the stool and moved restlessly toward the window. "It's really too warm in this room to sing. Don't you feel it?"

Alexander went over and opened the window for her. "Aren't you afraid to let the wind low like that on your neck? Can't I get a scarf or something?"

"Ask a theatre lady if she's afraid of drafts!" Hilda laughed. "But perhaps, as I'm so warm—give me your handkerchief. There, just in front." He slipped the corners carefully under her shoulder-straps. "There, that will do. It looks like a bib." She pushed his hand away quickly and stood looking out into the deserted square. "Isn't London a tomb on Sunday night?"

Alexander caught the agitation in her voice. He stood a little behind her, and tried to steady himself as he said: "It's soft and misty. See how white the stars are."

For a long time neither Hilda nor Bartley spoke. They stood close together, looking out into the wan, watery sky, breathing always more quickly and lightly, and it seemed as if all the clocks in the world had stopped. Suddenly he moved the clenched hand he held behind him and dropped it violently at his side. He felt a tremor run through the slender yellow figure in front of him.

She caught his handkerchief from her throat and thrust it at him without turning round. "Here, take it. You must go now, Bartley. Good-night."

Bartley leaned over her shoulder, without touching her, and whispered in her ear: "You are giving me a chance?"

"Yes. Take it and go. This isn't fair, you know. Good-night."

Alexander unclenched the two hands at his sides. With one he threw down the window and with the other—still standing behind her—he drew her back against him.

She uttered a little cry, threw her arms over her head, and drew his face down to hers. "Are you going to let me love you a little, Bartley?" she whispered.

V.

It was the afternoon of the day before Christmas. Mrs. Alexander had been driving about all the morning, leaving presents at the houses of her friends. She lunched alone, and as she rose from the table she spoke to the butler: "Thomas, I am going down to the kitchen now to see Norah. In half an hour you are to bring the greens up from the cellar and put them in the library. Mr. Alexander will be home at three to hang them himself. Don't forget the stepladder, and plenty of tacks and string. You may bring the azaleas upstairs. Take the white one to Mr. Alexander's study. Put the two pink ones in this room, and the red one in the drawing-room."

A little before three o'clock Mrs. Alexander went into the library to see that everything was ready. She pulled the window shades high, for the weather was dark and stormy, and there was little light, even in the streets. A foot of snow had fallen during the morning, and the wide space over the river was thick with flying flakes that fell and wreathed the masses of floating ice. Winifred was standing by the window when she heard the front door open. She hurried to the hall as Alexander came stamping in, covered with snow. He kissed her joyfully and brushed away the snow that fell on her hair.

"I wish I had asked you to meet me at the office and walk home with me, Winifred. The Common is beautiful. The boys have swept the snow off the pond and are skating furiously. Did the cyclamens come?"

"An hour ago. What splendid ones! But aren't you frightfully extravagant?"

"Not for Christmas-time. I'll go upstairs and change my coat. I shall be down in a moment. Tell Thomas to get everything ready."

When Alexander reappeared, he took his wife's arm and went with her into the library. "When did the azaleas get here? Thomas has got the white one in my room."

"I told him to put it there."

"But, I say, it's much the finest of the lot!"

"That's why I had it put there. There is too much color in that room for a red one, you know."

Bartley began to sort the greens. "It looks very splendid there, but I feel piggish to have it. However, we really spend more time there than anywhere else in the house. Will you hand me the holly?"

He climbed up the stepladder, which creaked under his weight, and began to twist the tough stems of the holly into the frame-work of the chandelier.

"I forgot to tell you that I had a letter from Wilson, this morning, explaining his telegram. He is coming on because an old uncle up in Vermont has conveniently died and left Wilson a little money—something like ten thousand. He's coming on to settle up the estate. Won't it be jolly to have him?"

"And how fine that he's come into a little money. I can see him posting down State Street to the steamship offices. He will get a good many trips out of that ten thousand. What can have detained him? I expected him here for luncheon."

"Those trains from Albany are always late. He'll be along sometime this afternoon. And now, don't you want to go upstairs and lie down for an hour? You've had a busy morning and I don't want you to be tired to-night."

After his wife went upstairs Alexander worked energetically at the greens for a few moments. Then, as he was cutting off a length of string, he sighed suddenly and sat down, staring out of the window at the snow. The animation died out of his face, but in his eyes there was a restless light, a look of apprehension and suspense. He kept clasping and unclasping his big hands as if he were trying to realize something. The clock ticked through the minutes of a half-hour and the afternoon outside began to thicken and darken turbidly. Alexander, since he first sat down, had not changed his position. He leaned forward, his hands between his knees, scarcely breathing, as if he were holding himself away from his surroundings, from the room, and from the very chair in which he sat, from everything except the wild eddies of snow above the river on which his eyes were fixed with feverish intentness, as if he were trying to project himself thither. When at last Lucius Wilson was announced, Alexander sprang eagerly to his feet and hurried to meet his old instructor.

"Hello, Wilson. What luck! Come into the library. We are to have a lot of people to dinner to-night, and Winifred's lying down. You will excuse her, won't you? And now what about yourself? Sit down and tell me everything."

"I think I'd rather move about, if you don't mind. I've been sitting in the train for a week, it seems to me." Wilson stood before the fire with his hands behind him and looked about the room. "You HAVE been busy. Bartley, if I'd had my choice of all possible places in which to spend Christmas, your house would certainly be the place I'd have chosen. Happy people do a great deal for their friends. A house like this throws its warmth out. I felt it distinctly as I was coming through the Berkshires. I could scarcely believe that I was to see Mrs. Bartley again so soon."

"Thank you, Wilson. She'll be as glad to see you. Shall we have tea now? I'll ring for Thomas to clear away this litter. Winifred says I always wreck the house when I try to do anything. Do you know, I am quite tired. Looks as if I were not used to work, doesn't it?" Alexander laughed and dropped into a chair. "You know, I'm sailing the day after New Year's."

"Again? Why, you've been over twice since I was here in the spring, haven't you?"

"Oh, I was in London about ten days in the summer. Went to escape the hot weather more than anything else. I shan't be gone more than a month this time. Winifred and I have been up in Canada for most of the autumn. That Moorlock Bridge is on my back all the time. I never had so much trouble with a job before." Alexander moved about restlessly and fell to poking the fire.

"Haven't I seen in the papers that there is some trouble about a tidewater bridge of yours in New Jersey?"

"Oh, that doesn't amount to anything. It's held up by a steel strike. A bother, of course, but the sort of thing one is always having to put up with. But the Moorlock Bridge is a continual anxiety. You see, the truth is, we are having to build pretty well to the strain limit up there. They've crowded me too much on the cost. It's all very well if everything goes well, but these estimates have never been used for anything of such length before. However, there's nothing to be done. They hold me to the scale I've used in shorter bridges. The last thing a bridge commission cares about is the kind of bridge you build."

When Bartley had finished dressing for dinner he went into his study, where he found his wife arranging flowers on his writing-table.

"These pink roses just came from Mrs. Hastings," she said, smiling, "and I am sure she meant them for you."

Bartley looked about with an air of satisfaction at the greens and the wreaths in the windows. "Have you a moment, Winifred? I have just now been thinking that this is our twelfth Christmas. Can you realize it?" He went up to the table and took her hands away from the flowers, drying them with his pocket handkerchief. "They've been awfully happy ones, all of them, haven't they?" He took her in his arms and bent back, lifting her a little and giving her a long kiss. "You are happy, aren't you Winifred? More than anything else in the world, I want you to be happy. Sometimes, of late, I've thought you looked as if you were troubled."

"No; it's only when you are troubled and harassed that I feel worried, Bartley. I wish you always seemed as you do to-night. But you don't, always." She looked earnestly and inquiringly into his eyes.

Alexander took her two hands from his shoulders and swung them back and forth in his own, laughing his big blond laugh.

"I'm growing older, my dear; that's what you feel. Now, may I show you something? I meant to save them until to-morrow, but I want you to wear them to-night." He took a little leather box out of his pocket and opened it. On the white velvet lay two long pendants of curiously worked gold, set with pearls. Winifred looked from the box to Bartley and exclaimed:—

"Where did you ever find such gold work, Bartley?"

"It's old Flemish. Isn't it fine?"

"They are the most beautiful things, dear. But, you know, I never wear earrings."

"Yes, yes, I know. But I want you to wear them. I have always wanted you to. So few women can. There must be a good ear, to begin with, and a nose"—he waved his hand —"above reproach. Most women look silly in them. They go only with faces like yours—very, very proud, and just a little hard."

Winifred laughed as she went over to the mirror and fitted the delicate springs to the lobes of her ears. "Oh, Bartley, that old foolishness about my being hard. It really hurts my feelings. But I must go down now. People are beginning to come."

Bartley drew her arm about his neck and went to the door with her. "Not hard to me, Winifred," he whispered. "Never, never hard to me."

Left alone, he paced up and down his study. He was at home again, among all the dear familiar things that spoke to him of so many happy years. His house to-night would be full of charming people, who liked and admired him. Yet all the time, underneath his pleasure and hopefulness and satisfaction, he was conscious of the vibration of an unnatural excitement. Amid this light and warmth and friendliness, he sometimes started and shuddered, as if some one had stepped on his grave. Something had broken loose in him of which he knew nothing except that it was sullen and powerful, and that it wrung and tortured him. Sometimes it came upon him softly, in enervating reveries. Sometimes it battered him like the cannon rolling in the hold of the vessel. Always, now, it brought with it a sense of quickened life, of stimulating danger. To-night it came upon him suddenly, as he was walking the floor, after his wife left him. It seemed impossible; he could not believe it. He glanced entreatingly at the door, as if to call her back. He heard voices in the hall below, and knew that he must go down. Going over to the window, he looked out at the lights across the river. How could this happen here, in his own house, among the things he loved? What was it that reached in out of the darkness and thrilled him? As he stood there he had a feeling that he would never escape. He shut his eyes and pressed his forehead against the cold window glass, breathing in the chill that came through it. "That this," he groaned, "that this should have happened to ME!"

On New Year's day a thaw set in, and during the night torrents of rain fell. In the morning, the morning of Alexander's departure for England, the river was streaked with fog and the rain drove hard against the windows of the breakfast-room. Alexander had finished his coffee and was pacing up and down. His wife sat at the table, watching him. She was pale and unnaturally calm. When Thomas brought the letters, Bartley sank into his chair and ran them over rapidly.

"Here's a note from old Wilson. He's safe back at his grind, and says he had a bully time. `The memory of Mrs. Bartley will make my whole winter fragrant.' Just like him. He will go on getting measureless satisfaction out of you by his study fire. What a man he is for looking on at life!" Bartley sighed, pushed the letters back impatiently, and went over to the window. "This is a nasty sort of day to sail. I've a notion to call it off. Next week would be time enough."

"That would only mean starting twice. It wouldn't really help you out at all," Mrs. Alexander spoke soothingly. "And you'd come back late for all your engagements."

Bartley began jingling some loose coins in his pocket. "I wish things would let me rest. I'm tired of work, tired of people, tired of trailing about." He looked out at the storm-beaten river.

Winifred came up behind him and put a hand on his shoulder. "That's what you always say, poor Bartley! At bottom you really like all these things. Can't you remember that?"

He put his arm about her. "All the same, life runs smoothly enough with some people, and with me it's always a messy sort of patchwork. It's like the song; peace is where I am not. How can you face it all with so much fortitude?"

She looked at him with that clear gaze which Wilson had so much admired, which he had felt implied such high confidence and fearless pride. "Oh, I faced that long ago, when you were on your first bridge, up at old Allway. I knew then that your paths were not to be paths of peace, but I decided that I wanted to follow them."

Bartley and his wife stood silent for a long time; the fire crackled in the grate, the rain beat insistently upon the windows, and the sleepy Angora looked up at them curiously.

Presently Thomas made a discreet sound at the door. "Shall Edward bring down your trunks, sir?"

"Yes; they are ready. Tell him not to forget the big portfolio on the study table."

Thomas withdrew, closing the door softly. Bartley turned away from his wife, still holding her hand. "It never gets any easier, Winifred."

They both started at the sound of the carriage on the pavement outside. Alexander sat down and leaned his head on his hand. His wife bent over him. "Courage," she said gayly. Bartley rose and rang the bell. Thomas brought him his hat and stick and ulster. At the sight of these, the supercilious Angora moved restlessly, quitted her red cushion by the fire, and came up, waving her tail in vexation at these ominous indications of change. Alexander stooped to stroke her, and then plunged into his coat and drew on his gloves. His wife held his stick, smiling. Bartley smiled too, and his eyes cleared. "I'll work like the devil, Winifred, and be home again before you realize I've gone." He kissed her quickly several times, hurried out of the front door into the rain, and waved to her from the carriage window as the driver was starting his melancholy, dripping black horses. Alexander sat with his hands clenched on his knees. As the carriage turned up the hill, he lifted one hand and brought it down violently. "This time"—he spoke aloud and through his set teeth—"this time I'm going to end it!"

On the afternoon of the third day out, Alexander was sitting well to the stern, on the windward side where the chairs were few, his rugs over him and the collar of his fur-lined coat turned up about his ears. The weather had so far been dark and raw. For two hours he had been watching the low, dirty sky and the beating of the heavy rain upon the iron-colored sea. There was a long, oily swell that made exercise laborious. The decks smelled of damp woolens, and the air was so humid that drops of moisture kept gathering upon his hair and mustache. He seldom moved except to brush them away. The great open spaces made him passive and the restlessness of the water quieted him. He intended during the voyage to decide upon a course of action, but he held all this away from him for the present and lay in a blessed gray oblivion. Deep down in him somewhere his resolution was weakening and strengthening, ebbing and flowing. The thing that perturbed him went on as steadily as his pulse, but he was almost unconscious of it. He was submerged in the vast impersonal grayness about him, and at intervals the sidelong roll of the boat measured off time like the ticking of a clock. He felt released from everything that troubled and perplexed him. It was as if he had tricked and outwitted torturing memories, had actually managed to get on board without them. He thought of nothing at all. If his mind now and again picked a face out of the grayness, it was Lucius Wilson's, or the face of an old schoolmate, forgotten for years; or it was the slim outline of a favorite greyhound he used to hunt jack-rabbits with when he was a boy.

Toward six o'clock the wind rose and tugged at the tarpaulin and brought the swell higher. After dinner Alexander came back to the wet deck, piled his damp rugs over him again, and sat smoking, losing himself in the obliterating blackness and drowsing in the rush of the gale. Before he went below a few bright stars were pricked off between heavily moving masses of cloud.

The next morning was bright and mild, with a fresh breeze. Alexander felt the need of exercise even before he came out of his cabin. When he went on deck the sky was blue and blinding, with heavy whiffs of white cloud, smoke-colored at the edges, moving rapidly across it. The water was roughish, a cold, clear indigo breaking into whitecaps. Bartley walked for two hours, and then stretched himself in the sun until lunch-time.

In the afternoon he wrote a long letter to Winifred. Later, as he walked the deck through a splendid golden sunset, his spirits rose continually. It was agreeable to come to himself again after several days of numbness and torpor. He stayed out until the last tinge of violet had faded from the water. There was literally a taste of life on his lips as he sat down to dinner and ordered a bottle of champagne. He was late in finishing his dinner, and drank rather more wine than he had meant to. When he went above, the wind had risen and the deck was almost deserted. As he stepped out of the door a gale lifted his heavy fur coat about his shoulders. He fought his way up the deck with keen exhilaration. The moment he stepped, almost out of breath, behind the shelter of the stern, the wind was cut off, and he felt, like a rush of warm air, a sense of close and intimate companionship. He started back and tore his coat open as if something warm were actually clinging to him beneath it. He hurried up the deck and went into the saloon parlor, full of women who had retreated thither from the sharp wind. He threw himself upon them. He talked delightfully to the older ones and played accompaniments for the younger ones until the last sleepy girl had followed her mother below. Then he went into the smoking-room. He played bridge until two o'clock in the morning, and managed to lose a considerable sum of money without really noticing that he was doing so.

After the break of one fine day the weather was pretty consistently dull. When the low sky thinned a trifle, the pale white spot of a sun did no more than throw a bluish lustre on the water, giving it the dark brightness of newly cut lead. Through one after another of those gray days Alexander drowsed and mused, drinking in the grateful moisture. But the complete peace of the first part of the voyage was over. Sometimes he rose suddenly from his chair as if driven out, and paced the deck for hours. People noticed his propensity for walking in rough weather, and watched him curiously as he did his rounds. From his abstraction and the determined set of his jaw, they fancied he must be thinking about his bridge. Every one had heard of the new cantilever bridge in Canada.

But Alexander was not thinking about his work. After the fourth night out, when his will suddenly softened under his hands, he had been continually hammering away at himself. More and more often, when he first wakened in the morning or when he stepped into a warm place after being chilled on the deck, he felt a sudden painful delight at being nearer another shore. Sometimes when he was most despondent, when he thought himself worn out with this struggle, in a flash he was free of it and leaped into an overwhelming consciousness of himself. On the instant he felt that marvelous return of the impetuousness, the intense excitement, the increasing expectancy of youth.

VI.

The last two days of the voyage Bartley found almost intolerable. The stop at Queenstown, the tedious passage up the Mersey, were things that he noted dimly through his growing impatience. He had planned to stop in Liverpool; but, instead, he took the boat train for London.

Emerging at Euston at half-past three o'clock in the afternoon, Alexander had his luggage sent to the Savoy and drove at once to Bedford Square. When Marie met him at the door, even her strong sense of the proprieties could not restrain her surprise and delight. She blushed and smiled and fumbled his card in her confusion before she ran upstairs. Alexander paced up and down the hallway, buttoning and unbuttoning his overcoat, until she returned and took him up to Hilda's living-room. The room was empty when he entered. A coal fire was crackling in the grate and the lamps were lit, for it was already beginning to grow dark outside. Alexander did not sit down. He stood his ground over by the windows until Hilda came in. She called his name on the threshold, but in her swift flight across the room she felt a change in him and caught herself up so deftly that he could not tell just when she did it. She merely brushed his cheek with her lips and put a hand lightly and joyously on either shoulder. "Oh, what a grand thing to happen on a raw day! I felt it in my bones when I woke this morning that something splendid was going to turn up. I thought it might be Sister Kate or Cousin Mike would be happening along. I never dreamed it would be you, Bartley. But why do you let me chatter on like this? Come over to the fire; you're chilled through."

She pushed him toward the big chair by the fire, and sat down on a stool at the opposite side of the hearth, her knees drawn up to her chin, laughing like a happy little girl.

"When did you come, Bartley, and how did it happen? You haven't spoken a word."

"I got in about ten minutes ago. I landed at Liverpool this morning and came down on the boat train."

Alexander leaned forward and warmed his hands before the blaze. Hilda watched him with perplexity.

"There's something troubling you, Bartley. What is it?"

Bartley bent lower over the fire. "It's the whole thing that troubles me, Hilda. You and I."

Hilda took a quick, soft breath. She looked at his heavy shoulders and big, determined head, thrust forward like a catapult in leash.

"What about us, Bartley?" she asked in a thin voice.

He locked and unlocked his hands over the grate and spread his fingers close to the bluish flame, while the coals crackled and the clock ticked and a street vendor began to call under the window. At last Alexander brought out one word:—

"Everything!"

Hilda was pale by this time, and her eyes were wide with fright. She looked about desperately from Bartley to the door, then to the windows, and back again to Bartley. She rose uncertainly, touched his hair with her hand, then sank back upon her stool.

"I'll do anything you wish me to, Bartley," she said tremulously. "I can't stand seeing you miserable."

"I can't live with myself any longer," he answered roughly.

He rose and pushed the chair behind him and began to walk miserably about the room, seeming to find it too small for him. He pulled up a window as if the air were heavy.

Hilda watched him from her corner, trembling and scarcely breathing, dark shadows growing about her eyes.

"It . . . it hasn't always made you miserable, has it?" Her eyelids fell and her lips quivered.

"Always. But it's worse now. It's unbearable. It tortures me every minute."

"But why NOW?" she asked piteously, wringing her hands.

He ignored her question. "I am not a man who can live two lives," he went on feverishly. "Each life spoils the other. I get nothing but misery out of either. The world is all there, just as it used to be, but I can't get at it any more. There is this deception between me and everything."

At that word "deception," spoken with such self-contempt, the color flashed back into Hilda's face as suddenly as if she had been struck by a whiplash. She bit her lip and looked down at her hands, which were clasped tightly in front of her.

"Could you—could you sit down and talk about it quietly, Bartley, as if I were a friend, and not some one who had to be defied?"

He dropped back heavily into his chair by the fire. "It was myself I was defying, Hilda. I have thought about it until I am worn out."

He looked at her and his haggard face softened. He put out his hand toward her as he looked away again into the fire.

She crept across to him, drawing her stool after her. "When did you first begin to feel like this, Bartley?"

"After the very first. The first was—sort of in play, wasn't it?"

Hilda's face quivered, but she whispered: "Yes, I think it must have been. But why didn't you tell me when you were here in the summer?"

Alexander groaned. "I meant to, but somehow I couldn't. We had only a few days, and your new play was just on, and you were so happy."

"Yes, I was happy, wasn't I?" She pressed his hand gently in gratitude. "Weren't you happy then, at all?"

She closed her eyes and took a deep breath, as if to draw in again the fragrance of those days. Something of their troubling sweetness came back to Alexander, too. He moved uneasily and his chair creaked.

"Yes, I was then. You know. But afterward. . ."

"Yes, yes," she hurried, pulling her hand gently away from him. Presently it stole back to his coat sleeve. "Please tell me one thing, Bartley. At least, tell me that you believe I thought I was making you happy."

His hand shut down quickly over the questioning fingers on his sleeves. "Yes, Hilda; I know that," he said simply.

She leaned her head against his arm and spoke softly:—

"You see, my mistake was in wanting you to have everything. I wanted you to eat all the cakes and have them, too. I somehow believed that I could take all the bad consequences for you. I wanted you always to be happy and handsome and successful—to have all the things that a great man ought to have, and, once in a way, the careless holidays that great men are not permitted."

Bartley gave a bitter little laugh, and Hilda looked up and read in the deepening lines of his face that youth and Bartley would not much longer struggle together.

"I understand, Bartley. I was wrong. But I didn't know. You've only to tell me now. What must I do that I've not done, or what must I not do?" She listened intently, but she heard nothing but the creaking of his chair. "You want me to say it?" she whispered. "You want to tell me that you can only see me like this, as old friends do, or out in the world among people? I can do that."

"I can't," he said heavily.

Hilda shivered and sat still. Bartley leaned his head in his hands and spoke through his teeth. "It's got to be a clean break, Hilda. I can't see you at all, anywhere. What I mean is that I want you to promise never to see me again, no matter how often I come, no matter how hard I beg."

Hilda sprang up like a flame. She stood over him with her hands clenched at her side, her body rigid.

"No!" she gasped. "It's too late to ask that. Do you hear me, Bartley? It's too late. I won't promise. It's abominable of you to ask me. Keep away if you wish; when have I ever followed you? But, if you come to me, I'll do as I see fit. The shamefulness of your asking me to do that! If you come to me, I'll do as I see fit. Do you understand? Bartley, you're cowardly!"

Alexander rose and shook himself angrily. "Yes, I know I'm cowardly. I'm afraid of myself. I don't trust myself any more. I carried it all lightly enough at first, but now I don't dare trifle with it. It's getting the better of me. It's different now. I'm growing older, and you've got my young self here with you. It's through him that I've come to wish for you all and all the time." He took her roughly in his arms. "Do you know what I mean?"

Hilda held her face back from him and began to cry bitterly. "Oh, Bartley, what am I to do? Why didn't you let me be angry with you? You ask me to stay away from you because you want me! And I've got nobody but you. I will do anything you say—but that! I will ask the least imaginable, but I must have SOMETHING!"

Bartley turned away and sank down in his chair again. Hilda sat on the arm of it and put her hands lightly on his shoulders.

"Just something Bartley. I must have you to think of through the months and months of loneliness. I must see you. I must know about you. The sight of you, Bartley, to see you living and happy and successful—can I never make you understand what that means to me?" She pressed his shoulders gently. "You see, loving some one as I love you makes the whole world different. If I'd met you later, if I hadn't loved you so well—but that's all over, long ago. Then came all those years without you, lonely and hurt and discouraged; those decent young fellows and poor Mac, and me never heeding—hard as a steel spring. And then you came back, not caring very much, but it made no difference."

She slid to the floor beside him, as if she were too tired to sit up any longer. Bartley bent over and took her in his arms, kissing her mouth and her wet, tired eyes.

"Don't cry, don't cry," he whispered. "We've tortured each other enough for tonight. Forget everything except that I am here."

"I think I have forgotten everything but that already," she murmured. "Ah, your dear arms!"

VII.

DURING THE FORTNIGHT that Alexander was in London he drove himself hard. He got through a great deal of personal business and saw a great many men who were doing interesting things in his own profession. He disliked to think of his visits to London as holidays, and when he was there he worked even harder than he did at home.

The day before his departure for Liverpool was a singularly fine one. The thick air had cleared overnight in a strong wind which brought in a golden dawn and then fell off to a fresh breeze. When Bartley looked out of his windows from the Savoy, the river was flashing silver and the gray stone along the Embankment was bathed in bright, clear sunshine. London had wakened to life after three weeks of cold and sodden rain. Bartley breakfasted hurriedly and went over his mail while the hotel valet packed his trunks. Then he paid his account and walked rapidly down the Strand past Charing Cross Station. His spirits rose with every step, and when he reached Trafalgar Square, blazing in the sun, with its fountains playing and its column reaching up into the bright air, he signaled to a hansom, and, before he knew what he was about, told the driver to go to Bedford Square by way of the British Museum.

When he reached Hilda's apartment she met him, fresh as the morning itself. Her rooms were flooded with sunshine and full of the flowers he had been sending her. She would never let him give her anything else.

"Are you busy this morning, Hilda?" he asked as he sat down, his hat and gloves in his hand.

"Very. I've been up and about three hours, working at my part. We open in February, you know."

"Well, then you've worked enough. And so have I. I've seen all my men, my packing is done, and I go up to Liverpool this evening. But this morning we are going to have a holiday. What do you say to a drive out to Kew and Richmond? You may not get another day like this all winter. It's like a fine April day at home. May I use your telephone? I want to order the carriage."

"Oh, how jolly! There, sit down at the desk. And while you are telephoning I'll change my dress. I shan't be long. All the morning papers are on the table."

Hilda was back in a few moments wearing a long gray squirrel coat and a broad fur hat.

Bartley rose and inspected her. "Why don't you wear some of those pink roses?" he asked.

"But they came only this morning, and they have not even begun to open. I was saving them. I am so unconsciously thrifty!" She laughed as she looked about the room. "You've been sending me far too many flowers, Bartley. New ones every day. That's too often; though I do love to open the boxes, and I take good care of them."

"Why won't you let me send you any of those jade or ivory things you are so fond of? Or pictures? I know a good deal about pictures."

Hilda shook her large hat as she drew the roses out of the tall glass. "No, there are some things you can't do. There's the carriage. Will you button my gloves for me?"

Bartley took her wrist and began to button the long gray suede glove. "How gay your eyes are this morning, Hilda."

"That's because I've been studying. It always stirs me up a little."

He pushed the top of the glove up slowly. "When did you learn to take hold of your parts like that?"

"When I had nothing else to think of. Come, the carriage is waiting. What a shocking while you take."

"I'm in no hurry. We've plenty of time."

They found all London abroad. Piccadilly was a stream of rapidly moving carriages, from which flashed furs and flowers and bright winter costumes. The metal trappings of the harnesses shone dazzlingly, and the wheels were revolving disks that threw off rays of light. The parks were full of children and nursemaids and joyful dogs that leaped and yelped and scratched up the brown earth with their paws.

"I'm not going until to-morrow, you know," Bartley announced suddenly. "I'll cut off a day in Liverpool. I haven't felt so jolly this long while."

Hilda looked up with a smile which she tried not to make too glad. "I think people were meant to be happy, a little," she said.

They had lunch at Richmond and then walked to Twickenham, where they had sent the carriage. They drove back, with a glorious sunset behind them, toward the distant gold-washed city. It was one of those rare afternoons when all the thickness and shadow of London are changed to a kind of shining, pulsing, special atmosphere; when the smoky vapors become fluttering golden clouds, nacreous veils of pink and amber; when all that bleakness of gray stone and dullness of dirty brick trembles in aureate light, and all the roofs and spires, and one great dome, are floated in golden haze. On such rare afternoons the ugliest of cities becomes the most poetic, and months of sodden days are offset by a moment of miracle.

"It's like that with us Londoners, too," Hilda was saying. "Everything is awfully grim and cheerless, our weather and our houses and our ways of amusing ourselves. But we can be happier than anybody. We can go mad with joy, as the people do out in the fields on a fine Whitsunday. We make the most of our moment."

She thrust her little chin out defiantly over her gray fur collar, and Bartley looked down at her and laughed.

"You are a plucky one, you." He patted her glove with his hand. "Yes, you are a plucky one."

Hilda sighed. "No, I'm not. Not about some things, at any rate. It doesn't take pluck to fight for one's moment, but it takes pluck to go without—a lot. More than I have. I can't help it," she added fiercely.

After miles of outlying streets and little gloomy houses, they reached London itself, red and roaring and murky, with a thick dampness coming up from the river, that betokened fog again to-morrow. The streets were full of people who had worked indoors all through the priceless day and had now come hungrily out to drink the muddy lees of it. They stood in long black lines, waiting before the pit entrances of the theatres—short-coated boys, and girls in sailor hats, all shivering and chatting gayly. There was a blurred rhythm in all the dull city noises—in the clatter of the cab horses and the rumbling of the busses, in the street calls, and in the undulating tramp, tramp of the crowd. It was like the deep vibration of some vast underground machinery, and like the muffled pulsations of millions of human hearts.

[See "The Barrel Organ by Alfred Noyes. Ed.] [I have placed it at the end for your convenience]

"Seems good to get back, doesn't it?" Bartley whispered, as they drove from Bayswater Road into Oxford Street. "London always makes me want to live more than any other city in the world. You remember our priestess mummy over in the mummy-room, and how we used to long to go and bring her out on nights like this? Three thousand years! Ugh!"

"All the same, I believe she used to feel it when we stood there and watched her and wished her well. I believe she used to remember," Hilda said thoughtfully.

"I hope so. Now let's go to some awfully jolly place for dinner before we go home. I could eat all the dinners there are in London to-night. Where shall I tell the driver? The Piccadilly Restaurant? The music's good there."

"There are too many people there whom one knows. Why not that little French place in Soho, where we went so often when you were here in the summer? I love it, and I've never been there with any one but you. Sometimes I go by myself, when I am particularly lonely."

"Very well, the sole's good there. How many street pianos there are about to-night! The fine weather must have thawed them out. We've had five miles of `Il Trovatore' now. They always make me feel jaunty. Are you comfy, and not too tired?"

"I'm not tired at all. I was just wondering how people can ever die. Why did you remind me of the mummy? Life seems the strongest and most indestructible thing in the world. Do you really believe that all those people rushing about down there, going to good dinners and clubs and theatres, will be dead some day, and not care about anything? I don't believe it, and I know I shan't die, ever! You see, I feel too—too powerful!"

The carriage stopped. Bartley sprang out and swung her quickly to the pavement. As he lifted her in his two hands he whispered: "You are—powerful!"

VIII.

THE LAST REHEARSAL WAS OVER, a tedious dress rehearsal which had lasted all day and exhausted the patience of every one who had to do with it. When Hilda had dressed for the street and came out of her dressing-room, she found Hugh MacConnell waiting for her in the corridor.

"The fog's thicker than ever, Hilda. There have been a great many accidents to-day. It's positively unsafe for you to be out alone. Will you let me take you home?"

"How good of you, Mac. If you are going with me, I think I'd rather walk. I've had no exercise to-day, and all this has made me nervous."

"I shouldn't wonder," said MacConnell dryly. Hilda pulled down her veil and they stepped out into the thick brown wash that submerged St. Martin's Lane. MacConnell took her hand and tucked it snugly under his arm. "I'm sorry I was such a savage. I hope you didn't think I made an ass of myself."

"Not a bit of it. I don't wonder you were peppery. Those things are awfully trying. How do you think it's going?"

"Magnificently. That's why I got so stirred up. We are going to hear from this, both of us. And that reminds me; I've got news for you. They are going to begin repairs on the theatre about the middle of March, and we are to run over to New York for six weeks. Bennett told me yesterday that it was decided."

Hilda looked up delightedly at the tall gray figure beside her. He was the only thing she could see, for they were moving through a dense opaqueness, as if they were walking at the bottom of the ocean.

"Oh, Mac, how glad I am! And they love your things over there, don't they?"

"Shall you be glad for—any other reason, Hilda?"

MacConnell put his hand in front of her to ward off some dark object. It proved to be only a lamp-post, and they beat in farther from the edge of the pavement.

"What do you mean, Mac?" Hilda asked nervously.

"I was just thinking there might be people over there you'd be glad to see," he brought out awkwardly. Hilda said nothing, and as they walked on MacConnell spoke again, apologetically: "I hope you don't mind my knowing about it, Hilda. Don't stiffen up like that. No one else knows, and I didn't try to find out anything. I felt it, even before I knew who he was. I knew there was somebody, and that it wasn't I."

They crossed Oxford Street in silence, feeling their way. The busses had stopped running and the cab-drivers were leading their horses. When they reached the other side, MacConnell said suddenly, "I hope you are happy."

"Terribly, dangerously happy, Mac,"—Hilda spoke quietly, pressing the rough sleeve of his greatcoat with her gloved hand.

"You've always thought me too old for you, Hilda,—oh, of course you've never said just that,—and here this fellow is not more than eight years younger than I. I've always felt that if I could get out of my old case I might win you yet. It's a fine, brave youth I carry inside me, only he'll never be seen."

"Nonsense, Mac. That has nothing to do with it. It's because you seem too close to me, too much my own kind. It would be like marrying Cousin Mike, almost. I really tried to care as you wanted me to, away back in the beginning."

"Well, here we are, turning out of the Square. You are not angry with me, Hilda? Thank you for this walk, my dear. Go in and get dry things on at once. You'll be having a great night to-morrow."

She put out her hand. "Thank you, Mac, for everything. Good-night."

MacConnell trudged off through the fog, and she went slowly upstairs. Her slippers and dressing gown were waiting for her before the fire. "I shall certainly see him in New York. He will see by the papers that we are coming. Perhaps he knows it already," Hilda kept thinking as she undressed. "Perhaps he will be at the dock. No, scarcely that; but I may meet him in the street even before he comes to see me." Marie placed the tea-table by the fire and brought Hilda her letters. She looked them over, and started as she came to one in a handwriting that she did not often see; Alexander had written to her only twice before, and he did not allow her to write to him at all. "Thank you, Marie. You may go now."

Hilda sat down by the table with the letter in her hand, still unopened. She looked at it intently, turned it over, and felt its thickness with her fingers. She believed that she sometimes had a kind of second-sight about letters, and could tell before she read them whether they brought good or evil tidings. She put this one down on the table in front of her while she poured her tea. At last, with a little shiver of expectancy, she tore open the envelope and read:—

Boston, February —

MY DEAR HILDA:—

It is after twelve o'clock. Every one else is in bed and I am sitting alone in my study. I have been happier in this room than anywhere else in the world. Happiness like that makes one insolent. I used to think these four walls could stand against anything. And now I scarcely know myself here. Now I know that no one can build his security upon the nobleness of another person. Two people, when they love each other, grow alike in their tastes and habits and pride, but their moral natures (whatever we may mean by that canting expression) are never welded. The base one goes on being base, and the noble one noble, to the end.

The last week has been a bad one; I have been realizing how things used to be with me. Sometimes I get used to being dead inside, but lately it has been as if a window beside me had suddenly opened, and as if all the smells of spring blew in to me. There is a garden out there, with stars overhead, where I used to walk at night when I had a single purpose and a single heart. I can remember how I used to feel there, how beautiful everything about me was, and what life and power and freedom I felt in myself. When the window opens I know exactly how it would feel to be out there. But that garden is closed to me. How is it, I ask myself, that everything can be so different with me when nothing here has changed? I am in my own house, in my own study, in the midst of all these quiet streets where my friends live. They are all safe and at peace with themselves. But I am never at peace. I feel always on the edge of danger and change.

I keep remembering locoed horses I used to see on the range when I was a boy. They changed like that. We used to catch them and put them up in the corral, and they developed great cunning. They would pretend to eat their oats like the other horses, but we knew they were always scheming to get back at the loco.

It seems that a man is meant to live only one life in this world. When he tries to live a second, he develops another nature. I feel as if a second man had been grafted into me. At first he seemed only a pleasure-loving simpleton, of whose company I was rather ashamed, and whom I used to hide under my coat when I walked the Embankment, in London. But now he is strong and sullen, and he is fighting for his life at the cost of mine. That is his one activity: to grow strong. No creature ever wanted so much to live. Eventually, I suppose, he will absorb me altogether. Believe me, you will hate me then.

And what have you to do, Hilda, with this ugly story? Nothing at all. The little boy drank of the prettiest brook in the forest and he became a stag. I write all this because I can never tell it to you, and because it seems as if I could not keep silent any longer. And because I suffer, Hilda. If any one I loved suffered like this, I'd want to know it. Help me, Hilda!

B.A.

IX.

On the last Saturday in April, the New York "Times" published an account of the strike complications which were delaying Alexander's New Jersey bridge, and stated that the engineer himself was in town and at his office on West Tenth Street.

On Sunday, the day after this notice appeared, Alexander worked all day at his Tenth Street rooms. His business often called him to New York, and he had kept an apartment there for years, subletting it when he went abroad for any length of time. Besides his sleeping-room and bath, there was a large room, formerly a painter's studio, which he used as a study and office. It was furnished with the cast-off possessions of his bachelor days and with odd things which he sheltered for friends of his who followed itinerant and more or less artistic callings. Over the fireplace there was a large old-fashioned gilt mirror. Alexander's big work-table stood in front of one of the three windows, and above the couch hung the one picture in the room, a big canvas of charming color and spirit, a study of the Luxembourg Gardens in early spring, painted in his youth by a man who had since become a portrait-painter of international renown. He had done it for Alexander when they were students together in Paris.

Sunday was a cold, raw day and a fine rain fell continuously. When Alexander came back from dinner he put more wood on his fire, made himself comfortable, and settled down at his desk, where he began checking over estimate sheets. It was after nine o'clock and he was lighting a second pipe, when he thought he heard a sound at his door. He started and listened, holding the burning match in his hand; again he heard the same sound, like a firm, light tap. He rose and crossed the room quickly. When he threw open the door he recognized the figure that shrank back into the bare, dimly lit hallway. He stood for a moment in awkward constraint, his pipe in his hand.

"Come in," he said to Hilda at last, and closed the door behind her. He pointed to a chair by the fire and went back to his worktable. "Won't you sit down?"

He was standing behind the table, turning over a pile of blueprints nervously. The yellow light from the student's lamp fell on his hands and the purple sleeves of his velvet smoking-jacket, but his flushed face and big, hard head were in the shadow. There was something about him that made Hilda wish herself at her hotel again, in the street below, anywhere but where she was.

"Of course I know, Bartley," she said at last, "that after this you won't owe me the least consideration. But we sail on Tuesday. I saw that interview in the paper yesterday, telling where you were, and I thought I had to see you. That's all. Good-night; I'm going now." She turned and her hand closed on the door-knob.

Alexander hurried toward her and took her gently by the arm. "Sit down, Hilda; you're wet through. Let me take off your coat—and your boots; they're oozing water." He knelt down and began to unlace her shoes, while Hilda shrank into the chair. "Here, put your feet on this stool. You don't mean to say you walked down—and without overshoes!"

Hilda hid her face in her hands. "I was afraid to take a cab. Can't you see, Bartley, that I'm terribly frightened? I've been through this a hundred times to-day. Don't be any more angry than you can help. I was all right until I knew you were in town. If you'd sent me a note, or telephoned me, or anything! But you won't let me write to you, and I had to see you after that letter, that terrible letter you wrote me when you got home."

Alexander faced her, resting his arm on the mantel behind him, and began to brush the sleeve of his jacket. "Is this the way you mean to answer it, Hilda?" he asked unsteadily.

She was afraid to look up at him. "Didn't—didn't you mean even to say goodbye to me, Bartley? Did you mean just to—quit me?" she asked. "I came to tell you that I'm willing to do as you asked me. But it's no use talking about that now. Give me my things, please." She put her hand out toward the fender.

Alexander sat down on the arm of her chair. "Did you think I had forgotten you were in town, Hilda? Do you think I kept away by accident? Did you suppose I didn't know you were sailing on Tuesday? There is a letter for you there, in my desk drawer. It was to have reached you on the steamer. I was all the morning writing it. I told myself that if I were really thinking of you, and not of myself, a letter would be better than nothing. Marks on paper mean something to you." He paused. "They never did to me."

Hilda smiled up at him beautifully and put her hand on his sleeve. "Oh, Bartley! Did you write to me? Why didn't you telephone me to let me know that you had? Then I wouldn't have come."

Alexander slipped his arm about her. "I didn't know it before, Hilda, on my honor I didn't, but I believe it was because, deep down in me somewhere, I was hoping I might drive you to do just this. I've watched that door all day. I've jumped up if the fire crackled. I think I have felt that you were coming." He bent his face over her hair.

"And I," she whispered,—"I felt that you were feeling that. But when I came, I thought I had been mistaken."

Alexander started up and began to walk up and down the room.

"No, you weren't mistaken. I've been up in Canada with my bridge, and I arranged not to come to New York until after you had gone. Then, when your manager added two more weeks, I was already committed." He dropped upon the stool in front of her and sat with his hands hanging between his knees. "What am I to do, Hilda?"

"That's what I wanted to see you about, Bartley. I'm going to do what you asked me to do when you were in London. Only I'll do it more completely. I'm going to marry."

"Who?"

"Oh, it doesn't matter much! One of them. Only not Mac. I'm too fond of him."

Alexander moved restlessly. "Are you joking, Hilda?"

"Indeed I'm not."

"Then you don't know what you're talking about."

"Yes, I know very well. I've thought about it a great deal, and I've quite decided. I never used to understand how women did things like that, but I know now. It's because they can't be at the mercy of the man they love any longer."

Alexander flushed angrily. "So it's better to be at the mercy of a man you don't love?"

"Under such circumstances, infinitely!"

There was a flash in her eyes that made Alexander's fall. He got up and went over to the window, threw it open, and leaned out. He heard Hilda moving about behind him. When he looked over his shoulder she was lacing her boots. He went back and stood over her.

"Hilda you'd better think a while longer before you do that. I don't know what I ought to say, but I don't believe you'd be happy; truly I don't. Aren't you trying to frighten me?"

She tied the knot of the last lacing and put her boot-heel down firmly. "No; I'm telling you what I've made up my mind to do. I suppose I would better do it without telling you. But afterward I shan't have an opportunity to explain, for I shan't be seeing you again."

Alexander started to speak, but caught himself. When Hilda rose he sat down on the arm of her chair and drew her back into it.

"I wouldn't be so much alarmed if I didn't know how utterly reckless you CAN be. Don't do anything like that rashly." His face grew troubled. "You wouldn't be happy. You are not that kind of woman. I'd never have another hour's peace if I helped to make you do a thing like that." He took her face between his hands and looked down into it. "You see, you are different, Hilda. Don't you know you are?" His voice grew softer, his touch more and more tender. "Some women can do that sort of thing, but you—you can love as queens did, in the old time."

Hilda had heard that soft, deep tone in his voice only once before. She closed her eyes; her lips and eyelids trembled. "Only one, Bartley. Only one. And he threw it back at me a second time."

She felt the strength leap in the arms that held her so lightly.

"Try him again, Hilda. Try him once again."

She looked up into his eyes, and hid her face in her hands.

X.

ON TUESDAY AFTERNOON A BOSTON LAWYER, who had been trying a case in Vermont, was standing on the siding at White River Junction when the Canadian Express pulled by on its northward journey. As the day-coaches at the rear end of the long train swept by him, the lawyer noticed at one of the windows a man's head, with thick rumpled hair. "Curious," he thought; "that looked like Alexander, but what would he be doing back there in the daycoaches?"

It was, indeed, Alexander.

That morning a telegram from Moorlock had reached him, telling him that there was serious trouble with the bridge and that he was needed there at once, so he had caught the first train out of New York. He had taken a seat in a day-coach to avoid the risk of meeting any one he knew, and because he did not wish to be comfortable. When the telegram arrived, Alexander was at his rooms on Tenth Street, packing his bag to go to Boston. On Monday night he had written a long letter to his wife, but when morning came he was afraid to send it, and the letter was still in his pocket. Winifred was not a woman who could bear disappointment. She demanded a great deal of herself and of the people she loved; and she never failed herself. If he told her now, he knew, it would be irretrievable. There would be no going back. He would lose the thing he valued most in the world; he would be destroying himself and his own happiness. There would be nothing for him afterward. He seemed to see himself dragging out a restless existence on the Continent—Cannes, Hyeres, Algiers, Cairo—among smartly dressed, disabled men of every nationality; forever going on journeys that led nowhere; hurrying to catch trains that he might just as well miss; getting up in the morning with a great bustle and splashing of water, to begin a day that had no purpose and no meaning; dining late to shorten the night, sleeping late to shorten the day.

And for what? For a mere folly, a masquerade, a little thing that he could not let go. AND HE COULD EVEN LET IT GO, he told himself. But he had promised to be in London at mid-summer, and he knew that he would go. . . . It was impossible to live like this any longer.

And this, then, was to be the disaster that his old professor had foreseen for him: the crack in the wall, the crash, the cloud of dust. And he could not understand how it had come about. He felt that he himself was unchanged, that he was still there, the same man he had been five years ago, and that he was sitting stupidly by and letting some resolute offshoot of himself spoil his life for him. This new force was not he, it was but a part of him. He would not even admit that it was stronger than he; but it was more active. It was by its energy that this new feeling got the better of him. His wife was the woman who had made his life, gratified his pride, given direction to his tastes and habits. The life they led together seemed to him beautiful. Winifred still was, as she had always been, Romance for him, and whenever he was deeply stirred he turned to her. When the grandeur and beauty of the world challenged him—as it challenges even the most self-absorbed people—he always answered with her name. That was his reply to the question put by the mountains and the stars; to all the spiritual aspects of life. In his feeling for his wife there was all the tenderness, all the pride, all the devotion of which he was capable. There was everything but energy; the energy of youth which must register itself and cut its name before it passes. This new feeling was so fresh, so unsatisfied and light of foot. It ran and was not wearied, anticipated him everywhere. It put a girdle round the earth while he was going from New York to Moorlock. At this moment, it was tingling through him, exultant, and live as quicksilver, whispering, "In July you will be in England."

Already he dreaded the long, empty days at sea, the monotonous Irish coast, the sluggish passage up the Mersey, the flash of the boat train through the summer country. He closed his eyes and gave himself up to the feeling of rapid motion and to swift, terrifying thoughts. He was sitting so, his face shaded by his hand, when the Boston lawyer saw him from the siding at White River Junction.

When at last Alexander roused himself, the afternoon had waned to sunset. The train was passing through a gray country and the sky overhead was flushed with a wide flood of clear color. There was a rose-colored light over the gray rocks and hills and meadows. Off to the left, under the approach of a weather-stained wooden bridge, a group of boys were sitting around a little fire. The smell of the wood smoke blew in at the window. Except for an old farmer, jogging along the highroad in his box-wagon, there was not another living creature to be seen. Alexander looked back wistfully at the boys, camped on the edge of a little marsh, crouching under their shelter and looking gravely at their fire. They took his mind back a long way, to a campfire on a sandbar in a Western river, and he wished he could go back and sit down with them. He could remember exactly how the world had looked then.

It was quite dark and Alexander was still thinking of the boys, when it occurred to him that the train must be nearing Allway. In going to his new bridge at Moorlock he had always to pass through Allway. The train stopped at Allway Mills, then wound two miles up the river, and then the hollow sound under his feet told Bartley that he was on his first bridge again. The bridge seemed longer than it had ever seemed before, and he was glad when he felt the beat of the wheels on the solid roadbed again. He did not like coming and going across that bridge, or remembering the man who built it. And was he, indeed, the same man who used to walk that bridge at night, promising such things to himself and to the stars? And yet, he could remember it all so well: the quiet hills sleeping in the moonlight, the slender skeleton of the bridge reaching out into the river, and up yonder, alone on the hill, the big white house; upstairs, in Winifred's window, the light that told him she was still awake and still thinking of him. And after the light went out he walked alone, taking the heavens into his confidence, unable to tear himself away from the white magic of the night, unwilling to sleep because longing was so sweet to him, and because, for the first time since first the hills were hung with moonlight, there was a lover in the world. And always there was the sound of the rushing water underneath, the sound which, more than anything else, meant death; the wearing away of things under the impact of physical forces which men could direct but never circumvent or diminish. Then, in the exaltation of love, more than ever it seemed to him to mean death, the only other thing as strong as love. Under the moon, under the cold, splendid stars, there were only those two things awake and sleepless; death and love, the rushing river and his burning heart.

Alexander sat up and looked about him. The train was tearing on through the darkness. All his companions in the day-coach were either dozing or sleeping heavily, and the murky lamps were turned low. How came he here among all these dirty people? Why was he going to London? What did it mean—what was the answer? How could this happen to a man who had lived through that magical spring and summer, and who had felt that the stars themselves were but flaming particles in the far-away infinitudes of his love?

What had he done to lose it? How could he endure the baseness of life without it? And with every revolution of the wheels beneath him, the unquiet quicksilver in his breast told him that at midsummer he would be in London. He remembered his last night there: the red foggy darkness, the hungry crowds before the theatres, the hand-organs, the feverish rhythm of the blurred, crowded streets, and the feeling of letting himself go with the crowd. He shuddered and looked about him at the poor unconscious companions of his journey, unkempt and travel-stained, now doubled in unlovely attitudes, who had come to stand to him for the ugliness he had brought into the world.

And those boys back there, beginning it all just as he had begun it; he wished he could promise them better luck. Ah, if one could promise any one better luck, if one could assure a single human being of happiness! He had thought he could do so, once; and it was thinking of that that he at last fell asleep. In his sleep, as if it had nothing fresher to work upon, his mind went back and tortured itself with something years and years away, an old, long-forgotten sorrow of his childhood.

When Alexander awoke in the morning, the sun was just rising through pale golden ripples of cloud, and the fresh yellow light was vibrating through the pine woods. The white birches, with their little unfolding leaves, gleamed in the lowlands, and the marsh meadows were already coming to life with their first green, a thin, bright color which had run over them like fire. As the train rushed along the trestles, thousands of wild birds rose screaming into the light. The sky was already a pale blue and of the clearness of crystal. Bartley caught up his bag and hurried through the Pullman coaches until he found the conductor. There was a stateroom unoccupied, and he took it and set about changing his clothes. Last night he would not have believed that anything could be so pleasant as the cold water he dashed over his head and shoulders and the freshness of clean linen on his body.

After he had dressed, Alexander sat down at the window and drew into his lungs deep breaths of the pine-scented air. He had awakened with all his old sense of power. He could not believe that things were as bad with him as they had seemed last night, that there was no way to set them entirely right. Even if he went to London at midsummer, what would that mean except that he was a fool? And he had been a fool before. That was not the reality of his life. Yet he knew that he would go to London.

Half an hour later the train stopped at Moorlock. Alexander sprang to the platform and hurried up the siding, waving to Philip Horton, one of his assistants, who was anxiously looking up at the windows of the coaches. Bartley took his arm and they went together into the station buffet.

"I'll have my coffee first, Philip. Have you had yours? And now, what seems to be the matter up here?"

The young man, in a hurried, nervous way, began his explanation.

But Alexander cut him short. "When did you stop work?" he asked sharply.

The young engineer looked confused. "I haven't stopped work yet, Mr. Alexander. I didn't feel that I could go so far without definite authorization from you."

"Then why didn't you say in your telegram exactly what you thought, and ask for your authorization? You'd have got it quick enough."

"Well, really, Mr. Alexander, I couldn't be absolutely sure, you know, and I didn't like to take the responsibility of making it public."

Alexander pushed back his chair and rose. "Anything I do can be made public, Phil. You say that you believe the lower chords are showing strain, and that even the workmen have been talking about it, and yet you've gone on adding weight."

"I'm sorry, Mr. Alexander, but I had counted on your getting here yesterday. My first telegram missed you somehow. I sent one Sunday evening, to the same address, but it was returned to me."

"Have you a carriage out there? I must stop to send a wire."

Alexander went up to the telegraph-desk and penciled the following message to his wife: —

I may have to be here for some time. Can you come up at once? Urgent.
BARTLEY.

The Moorlock Bridge lay three miles above the town. When they were seated in the carriage, Alexander began to question his assistant further. If it were true that the compression members showed strain, with the bridge only two thirds done, then there was nothing to do but pull the whole structure down and begin over again. Horton kept repeating that he was sure there could be nothing wrong with the estimates.

Alexander grew impatient. "That's all true, Phil, but we never were justified in assuming that a scale that was perfectly safe for an ordinary bridge would work with anything of such length. It's all very well on paper, but it remains to be seen whether it can be done in practice. I should have thrown up the job when they crowded me. It's all nonsense to try to do what other engineers are doing when you know they're not sound."

"But just now, when there is such competition," the younger man demurred. "And certainly that's the new line of development."

Alexander shrugged his shoulders and made no reply.

When they reached the bridge works, Alexander began his examination immediately. An hour later he sent for the superintendent. "I think you had better stop work out there at once, Dan. I should say that the lower chord here might buckle at any moment. I told the Commission that we were using higher unit stresses than any practice has established, and we've put the dead load at a low estimate. Theoretically it worked out well enough, but it had never actually been tried." Alexander put on his overcoat and took the superintendent by the arm. "Don't look so chopfallen, Dan. It's a jolt, but we've got to face it. It isn't the end of the world, you know. Now we'll go out and call the men off quietly. They're already nervous, Horton tells me, and there's no use alarming them. I'll go with you, and we'll send the end riveters in first."

Alexander and the superintendent picked their way out slowly over the long span. They went deliberately, stopping to see what each gang was doing, as if they were on an ordinary round of inspection. When they reached the end of the river span, Alexander nodded to the superintendent, who quietly gave an order to the foreman. The men in the end gang picked up their tools and, glancing curiously at each other, started back across the bridge toward the river-bank. Alexander himself remained standing where they had been working, looking about him. It was hard to believe, as he looked back over it, that the whole great span was incurably disabled, was already as good as condemned, because something was out of line in the lower chord of the cantilever arm.

The end riveters had reached the bank and were dispersing among the tool-houses, and the second gang had picked up their tools and were starting toward the shore. Alexander, still standing at the end of the river span, saw the lower chord of the cantilever arm give a little, like an elbow bending. He shouted and ran after the second gang, but by this time every one knew that the big river span was slowly settling. There was a burst of shouting that was immediately drowned by the scream and cracking of tearing iron, as all the tension work began to pull asunder. Once the chords began to buckle, there were thousands of tons of ironwork, all riveted together and lying in midair without support. It tore itself to pieces with roaring and grinding and noises that were like the shrieks of a steam whistle. There was no shock of any kind; the bridge had no impetus except from its own weight. It lurched neither to right nor left, but sank almost in a vertical line, snapping and breaking and tearing as it went, because no integral part could bear for an instant the enormous strain loosed upon it. Some of the men jumped and some ran, trying to make the shore.

At the first shriek of the tearing iron, Alexander jumped from the downstream side of the bridge. He struck the water without injury and disappeared. He was under the river a long time and had great difficulty in holding his breath. When it seemed impossible, and his chest was about to heave, he thought he heard his wife telling him that he could hold out a little longer. An instant later his face cleared the water. For a moment, in the depths of the river, he had realized what it would mean to die a hypocrite, and to lie dead under the last abandonment of her tenderness. But once in the light and air, he knew he should live to tell her and to recover all he had lost. Now, at last, he felt sure of himself. He was not startled. It seemed to him that he had been through something of this sort before. There was nothing horrible about it. This, too, was life, and life was activity, just as it was in Boston or in London. He was himself, and there was something to be done; everything seemed perfectly natural. Alexander was a strong swimmer, but he had gone scarcely a dozen strokes when the bridge itself, which had been settling faster and faster, crashed into the water behind him. Immediately the river was full of drowning men. A gang of French Canadians fell almost on top of him. He thought he had cleared them, when they began coming up all around him, clutching at him and at each other. Some of them could swim, but they were either hurt or crazed with fright. Alexander tried to beat them off, but there were too many of them. One caught him about the neck, another gripped him about the middle, and they went down together. When he sank, his wife seemed to be there in the water beside him, telling him to keep his head, that if he could hold out the men would drown and release him. There was something he wanted to tell his wife, but he could not think clearly for the roaring in his ears. Suddenly he remembered what it was. He caught his breath, and then she let him go.

The work of recovering the dead went on all day and all the following night. By the next morning forty-eight bodies had been taken out of the river, but there were still twenty missing. Many of the men had fallen with the bridge and were held down under the debris. Early on the morning of the second day a closed carriage was driven slowly along the river-bank and stopped a little below the works, where the river boiled and churned about the great iron carcass which lay in a straight line two thirds across it. The carriage stood there hour after hour, and word soon spread among the crowds on the shore that its occupant was the wife of the Chief Engineer; his body had not yet been found. The widows of the lost workmen, moving up and down the bank with shawls over their heads, some of them carrying babies, looked at the rusty hired hack many times that morning. They drew near it and walked about it, but none of them ventured to peer within. Even half-indifferent sightseers dropped their voices as they told a newcomer: "You see that carriage over there? That's Mrs. Alexander. They haven't found him yet. She got off the train this morning. Horton met her. She heard it in Boston yesterday—heard the newsboys crying it in the street."

At noon Philip Horton made his way through the crowd with a tray and a tin coffee-pot from the camp kitchen. When he reached the carriage he found Mrs. Alexander just as he had left her in the early morning, leaning forward a little, with her hand on the lowered window, looking at the river. Hour after hour she had been watching the water, the lonely, useless stone towers, and the convulsed mass of iron wreckage over which the angry river continually spat up its yellow foam.

"Those poor women out there, do they blame him very much?" she asked, as she handed the coffee-cup back to Horton.

"Nobody blames him, Mrs. Alexander. If any one is to blame, I'm afraid it's I. I should have stopped work before he came. He said so as soon as I met him. I tried to get him here a day earlier, but my telegram missed him, somehow. He didn't have time really to explain to me. If he'd got here Monday, he'd have had all the men off at once. But, you see, Mrs. Alexander, such a thing never happened before. According to all human calculations, it simply couldn't happen."

Horton leaned wearily against the front wheel of the cab. He had not had his clothes off for thirty hours, and the stimulus of violent excitement was beginning to wear off.

"Don't be afraid to tell me the worst, Mr. Horton. Don't leave me to the dread of finding out things that people may be saying. If he is blamed, if he needs any one to speak for him,"—for the first time her voice broke and a flush of life, tearful, painful, and confused, swept over her rigid pallor,—"if he needs any one, tell me, show me what to do." She began to sob, and Horton hurried away.

When he came back at four o'clock in the afternoon he was carrying his hat in his hand, and Winifred knew as soon as she saw him that they had found Bartley. She opened the carriage door before he reached her and stepped to the ground.

Horton put out his hand as if to hold her back and spoke pleadingly: "Won't you drive up to my house, Mrs. Alexander? They will take him up there."

"Take me to him now, please. I shall not make any trouble."

The group of men down under the riverbank fell back when they saw a woman coming, and one of them threw a tarpaulin over the stretcher. They took off their hats and caps as Winifred approached, and although she had pulled her veil down over her face they did not look up at her. She was taller than Horton, and some of the men thought she was the tallest woman they had ever seen. "As tall as himself," some one whispered. Horton motioned to the men, and six of them lifted the stretcher and began to carry it up the embankment. Winifred followed them the half-mile to Horton's house. She walked quietly, without once breaking or stumbling. When the bearers put the stretcher down in Horton's spare bedroom, she thanked them and gave her hand to each in turn. The men went out of the house and through the yard with their caps in their hands. They were too much confused to say anything as they went down the hill.

Horton himself was almost as deeply perplexed. "Mamie," he said to his wife, when he came out of the spare room half an hour later, "will you take Mrs. Alexander the things she needs? She is going to do everything herself. Just stay about where you can hear her and go in if she wants you."

Everything happened as Alexander had foreseen in that moment of prescience under the river. With her own hands she washed him clean of every mark of disaster. All night he was alone with her in the still house, his great head lying deep in the pillow. In the pocket of his coat Winifred found the letter that he had written her the night before he left New York, water-soaked and illegible, but because of its length, she knew it had been meant for her.

For Alexander death was an easy creditor. Fortune, which had smiled upon him consistently all his life, did not desert him in the end. His harshest critics did not doubt that, had he lived, he would have retrieved himself. Even Lucius Wilson did not see in this accident the disaster he had once foretold.

When a great man dies in his prime there is no surgeon who can say whether he did well; whether or not the future was his, as it seemed to be. The mind that society had come to regard as a powerful and reliable machine, dedicated to its service, may for a long time have been sick within itself and bent upon its own destruction.

EPILOGUE

PROFESSOR WILSON HAD BEEN LIVING in London for six years and he was just back from a visit to America. One afternoon, soon after his return, he put on his frock-coat and drove in a hansom to pay a call upon Hilda Burgoyne, who still lived at her old number, off Bedford Square. He and Miss Burgoyne had been fast friends for a long time. He had first noticed her about the corridors of the British Museum, where he read constantly. Her being there so often had made him feel that he would like to know her, and as she was not an inaccessible person, an introduction was not difficult. The preliminaries once over, they came to depend a great deal upon each other, and Wilson, after his day's reading, often went round to Bedford Square for his tea. They had much more in common than their memories of a common friend. Indeed, they seldom spoke of him. They saved that for the deep moments which do not come often, and then their talk of him was mostly silence. Wilson knew that Hilda had loved him; more than this he had not tried to know.

It was late when Wilson reached Hilda's apartment on this particular December afternoon, and he found her alone. She sent for fresh tea and made him comfortable, as she had such a knack of making people comfortable.

"How good you were to come back before Christmas! I quite dreaded the Holidays without you. You've helped me over a good many Christmases." She smiled at him gayly.

"As if you needed me for that! But, at any rate, I needed YOU. How well you are looking, my dear, and how rested."

He peered up at her from his low chair, balancing the tips of his long fingers together in a judicial manner which had grown on him with years.

Hilda laughed as she carefully poured his cream. "That means that I was looking very seedy at the end of the season, doesn't it? Well, we must show wear at last, you know."

Wilson took the cup gratefully. "Ah, no need to remind a man of seventy, who has just been home to find that he has survived all his contemporaries. I was most gently treated—as a sort of precious relic. But, do you know, it made me feel awkward to be hanging about still."

"Seventy? Never mention it to me." Hilda looked appreciatively at the Professor's alert face, with so many kindly lines about the mouth and so many quizzical ones about the eyes. "You've got to hang about for me, you know. I can't even let you go home again. You must stay put, now that I have you back. You're the realest thing I have."

Wilson chuckled. "Dear me, am I? Out of so many conquests and the spoils of conquered cities! You've really missed me? Well, then, I shall hang. Even if you have at last to put ME in the mummy-room with the others. You'll visit me often, won't you?"

"Every day in the calendar. Here, your cigarettes are in this drawer, where you left them." She struck a match and lit one for him. "But you did, after all, enjoy being at home again?"

"Oh, yes. I found the long railway journeys trying. People live a thousand miles apart. But I did it thoroughly; I was all over the place. It was in Boston I lingered longest."

"Ah, you saw Mrs. Alexander?"

"Often. I dined with her, and had tea there a dozen different times, I should think. Indeed, it was to see her that I lingered on and on. I found that I still loved to go to the house. It always seemed as if Bartley were there, somehow, and that at any moment one might hear his heavy tramp on the stairs. Do you know, I kept feeling that he must be up in his study." The Professor looked reflectively into the grate. "I should really have liked to go up there. That was where I had my last long talk with him. But Mrs. Alexander never suggested it."

"Why?"

Wilson was a little startled by her tone, and he turned his head so quickly that his cuff-link caught the string of his nose-glasses and pulled them awry. "Why? Why, dear me, I don't know. She probably never thought of it."

Hilda bit her lip. "I don't know what made me say that. I didn't mean to interrupt. Go on please, and tell me how it was."

"Well, it was like that. Almost as if he were there. In a way, he really is there. She never lets him go. It's the most beautiful and dignified sorrow I've ever known. It's so beautiful that it has its compensations, I should think. Its very completeness is a compensation. It gives her a fixed star to steer by. She doesn't drift. We sat there evening after evening in the quiet of that magically haunted room, and watched the sunset burn on the river, and felt him. Felt him with a difference, of course."

Hilda leaned forward, her elbow on her knee, her chin on her hand. "With a difference? Because of her, you mean?"

Wilson's brow wrinkled. "Something like that, yes. Of course, as time goes on, to her he becomes more and more their simple personal relation."

Hilda studied the droop of the Professor's head intently. "You didn't altogether like that? You felt it wasn't wholly fair to him?"

Wilson shook himself and readjusted his glasses. "Oh, fair enough. More than fair. Of course, I always felt that my image of him was just a little different from hers. No relation is so complete that it can hold absolutely all of a person. And I liked him just as he was; his deviations, too; the places where he didn't square."

Hilda considered vaguely. "Has she grown much older?" she asked at last.

"Yes, and no. In a tragic way she is even handsomer. But colder. Cold for everything but him. `Forget thyself to marble'; I kept thinking of that. Her happiness was a happiness a deux, not apart from the world, but actually against it. And now her grief is like that. She saves herself for it and doesn't even go through the form of seeing people much. I'm sorry. It would be better for her, and might be so good for them, if she could let other people in."

"Perhaps she's afraid of letting him out a little, of sharing him with somebody."

Wilson put down his cup and looked up with vague alarm. "Dear me, it takes a woman to think of that, now! I don't, you know, think we ought to be hard on her. More, even, than the rest of us she didn't choose her destiny. She underwent it. And it has left her chilled. As to her not wishing to take the world into her confidence—well, it is a pretty brutal and stupid world, after all, you know."

Hilda leaned forward. "Yes, I know, I know. Only I can't help being glad that there was something for him even in stupid and vulgar people. My little Marie worshiped him. When she is dusting I always know when she has come to his picture."

Wilson nodded. "Oh, yes! He left an echo. The ripples go on in all of us. He belonged to the people who make the play, and most of us are only onlookers at the best. We shouldn't wonder too much at Mrs. Alexander. She must feel how useless it would be to stir about, that she may as well sit still; that nothing can happen to her after Bartley."

"Yes," said Hilda softly, "nothing can happen to one after Bartley."

They both sat looking into the fire.

O PIONEERS!

I

THE WILD LAND

I.

One January day, thirty years ago, the little town of Hanover, anchored on a windy Nebraska tableland, was trying not to be blown away. A mist of fine snowflakes was curling and eddying about the cluster of low drab buildings huddled on the gray prairie, under a gray sky. The dwelling-houses were set about haphazard on the tough prairie sod; some of them looked as if they had been moved in overnight, and others as if they were straying off by themselves, headed straight for the open plain. None of them had any appearance of permanence, and the howling wind blew under them as well as over them. The main street was a deeply rutted road, now frozen hard, which ran from the squat red railway station and the grain "elevator" at the north end of the town to the lumber yard and the horse pond at the south end. On either side of this road straggled two uneven rows of wooden buildings; the general merchandise stores, the two banks, the drug store, the feed store, the saloon, the post-office. The board sidewalks were gray with trampled snow, but at two o'clock in the afternoon the shopkeepers, having come back from dinner, were keeping well behind their frosty windows. The children were all in school, and there was nobody abroad in the streets but a few rough-looking countrymen in coarse overcoats, with their long caps pulled down to their noses. Some of them had brought their wives to town, and now and then a red or a plaid shawl flashed out of one store into the shelter of another. At the hitch-bars along the street a few heavy work-horses, harnessed to farm wagons, shivered under their blankets. About the station everything was quiet, for there would not be another train in until night.

On the sidewalk in front of one of the stores sat a little Swede boy, crying bitterly. He was about five years old. His black cloth coat was much too big for him and made him look like a little old man. His shrunken brown flannel dress had been washed many times and left a long stretch of stocking between the hem of his skirt and the tops of his clumsy, copper-toed shoes. His cap was pulled down over his ears; his nose and his chubby cheeks were chapped and red with cold. He cried quietly, and the few people who hurried by did not notice him. He was afraid to stop any one, afraid to go into the store and ask for help, so he sat wringing his long sleeves and looking up a telegraph pole beside him, whimpering, "My kitten, oh, my kitten! Her will fweeze!" At the top of the pole crouched a shivering gray kitten, mewing faintly and clinging desperately to the wood with her claws. The boy had been left at the store while his sister went to the doctor's office, and in her absence a dog had chased his kitten up the pole. The little creature had never been so high before, and she was too frightened to move. Her master was sunk in despair. He was a little country boy, and this village was to him a very strange and perplexing place, where people wore fine clothes and had hard hearts. He always felt shy and awkward here, and wanted to hide behind things for fear some one might laugh at him. Just now, he was too unhappy to care who laughed. At last he seemed to see a ray of hope: his sister was coming, and he got up and ran toward her in his heavy shoes.

His sister was a tall, strong girl, and she walked rapidly and resolutely, as if she knew exactly where she was going and what she was going to do next. She wore a man's long ulster (not as if it were an affliction, but as if it were very comfortable and belonged to her; carried it like a young soldier), and a round plush cap, tied down with a thick veil. She had a serious, thoughtful face, and her clear, deep blue eyes were fixed intently on the distance, without seeming to see anything, as if she were in trouble. She did not notice the little boy until he pulled her by the coat. Then she stopped short and stooped down to wipe his wet face.

"Why, Emil! I told you to stay in the store and not to come out. What is the matter with you?"

"My kitten, sister, my kitten! A man put her out, and a dog chased her up there." His forefinger, projecting from the sleeve of his coat, pointed up to the wretched little creature on the pole.

"Oh, Emil! Didn't I tell you she'd get us into trouble of some kind, if you brought her? What made you tease me so? But there, I ought to have known better myself." She went to the foot of the pole and held out her arms, crying, "Kitty, kitty, kitty," but the kitten only mewed and faintly waved its tail. Alexandra turned away decidedly. "No, she won't come down. Somebody will have to go up after her. I saw the Linstrums' wagon in town. I'll go and see if I can find Carl. Maybe he can do something. Only you must stop crying, or I won't go a step. Where's your comforter? Did you leave it in the store? Never mind. Hold still, till I put this on you."

She unwound the brown veil from her head and tied it about his throat. A shabby little traveling man, who was just then coming out of the store on his way to the saloon, stopped and gazed stupidly at the shining mass of hair she bared when she took off her veil; two thick braids, pinned about her head in the German way, with a fringe of reddish-yellow curls blowing out from under her cap. He took his cigar out of his mouth and held the wet end between the fingers of his woolen glove. "My God, girl, what a head of hair!" he exclaimed, quite innocently and foolishly. She stabbed him with a glance of Amazonian fierceness and drew in her lower lip—most unnecessary severity. It gave the little clothing drummer such a start that he actually let his cigar fall to the sidewalk and went off weakly in the teeth of the wind to the saloon. His hand was still unsteady when he took his glass from the bartender. His feeble flirtatious instincts had been crushed before, but never so mercilessly. He felt cheap and ill-used, as if some one had taken advantage of him. When a drummer had been knocking about in little drab towns and crawling across the wintry country in dirty smoking-cars, was he to be blamed if, when he chanced upon a fine human creature, he suddenly wished himself more of a man?

While the little drummer was drinking to recover his nerve, Alexandra hurried to the drug store as the most likely place to find Carl Linstrum. There he was, turning over a portfolio of chromo "studies" which the druggist sold to the Hanover women who did china-painting. Alexandra explained her predicament, and the boy followed her to the corner, where Emil still sat by the pole.

"I'll have to go up after her, Alexandra. I think at the depot they have some spikes I can strap on my feet. Wait a minute." Carl thrust his hands into his pockets, lowered his head, and darted up the street against the north wind. He was a tall boy of fifteen, slight and narrow-chested. When he came back with the spikes, Alexandra asked him what he had done with his overcoat.

"I left it in the drug store. I couldn't climb in it, anyhow. Catch me if I fall, Emil," he called back as he began his ascent. Alexandra watched him anxiously; the cold was bitter enough on the ground. The kitten would not budge an inch. Carl had to go to the very top of the pole, and then had some difficulty in tearing her from her hold. When he reached the ground, he handed the cat to her tearful little master. "Now go into the store with her, Emil, and get warm." He opened the door for the child. "Wait a minute, Alexandra. Why can't I drive for you as far as our place? It's getting colder every minute. Have you seen the doctor?"

"Yes. He is coming over to-morrow. But he says father can't get better; can't get well." The girl's lip trembled. She looked fixedly up the bleak street as if she were gathering her strength to face something, as if she were trying with all her might to grasp a situation which, no matter how painful, must be met and dealt with somehow. The wind flapped the skirts of her heavy coat about her.

Carl did not say anything, but she felt his sympathy. He, too, was lonely. He was a thin, frail boy, with brooding dark eyes, very quiet in all his movements. There was a delicate pallor in his thin face, and his mouth was too sensitive for a boy's. The lips had already a little curl of bitterness and skepticism. The two friends stood for a few moments on the windy street corner, not speaking a word, as two travelers, who have lost their way, sometimes stand and admit their perplexity in silence. When Carl turned away he said, "I'll see to your team." Alexandra went into the store to have her purchases packed in the egg-boxes, and to get warm before she set out on her long cold drive.

When she looked for Emil, she found him sitting on a step of the staircase that led up to the clothing and carpet department. He was playing with a little Bohemian girl, Marie Tovesky, who was tying her handkerchief over the kitten's head for a bonnet. Marie was a stranger in the country, having come from Omaha with her mother to visit her uncle, Joe Tovesky. She was a dark child, with brown curly hair, like a brunette doll's, a coaxing little red mouth, and round, yellow-brown eyes. Every one noticed her eyes; the brown iris had golden glints that made them look like gold-stone, or, in softer lights, like that Colorado mineral called tiger-eye.

The country children thereabouts wore their dresses to their shoe-tops, but this city child was dressed in what was then called the "Kate Greenaway" manner, and her red cashmere frock, gathered full from the yoke, came almost to the floor. This, with her poke bonnet, gave her the look of a quaint little woman. She had a white fur tippet about her neck and made no fussy objections when Emil fingered it admiringly. Alexandra had not the heart to take him away from so pretty a playfellow, and she let them tease the kitten together until Joe Tovesky came in noisily and picked up his little niece, setting her on his shoulder for every one to see. His children were all boys, and he adored this little creature. His cronies formed a circle about him, admiring and teasing the little girl, who took their jokes with great good nature. They were all delighted with her, for they seldom saw so pretty and carefully nurtured a child. They told her that she must choose one of them for a sweetheart, and each began pressing his suit and offering her bribes; candy, and little pigs, and spotted calves. She looked archly into the big, brown, mustached faces, smelling of spirits and tobacco, then she ran her tiny forefinger delicately over Joe's bristly chin and said, "Here is my sweetheart."

The Bohemians roared with laughter, and Marie's uncle hugged her until she cried, "Please don't, Uncle Joe! You hurt me." Each of Joe's friends gave her a bag of candy, and she kissed them all around, though she did not like country candy very well. Perhaps that was why she bethought herself of Emil. "Let me down, Uncle Joe," she said, "I want to give some of my candy to that nice little boy I found." She walked graciously over to Emil, followed by her lusty admirers, who formed a new circle and teased the little boy until he hid his face in his sister's skirts, and she had to scold him for being such a baby.

The farm people were making preparations to start for home. The women were checking over their groceries and pinning their big red shawls about their heads. The men were buying tobacco and candy with what money they had left, were showing each other new boots and gloves and blue flannel shirts. Three big Bohemians were drinking raw alcohol, tinctured with oil of cinnamon. This was said to fortify one effectually against the cold, and they smacked their lips after each pull at the flask. Their volubility drowned every other noise in the place, and the overheated store sounded of their spirited language as it reeked of pipe smoke, damp woolens, and kerosene.

Carl came in, wearing his overcoat and carrying a wooden box with a brass handle. "Come," he said, "I've fed and watered your team, and the wagon is ready." He carried Emil out and tucked him down in the straw in the wagonbox. The heat had made the little boy sleepy, but he still clung to his kitten.

"You were awful good to climb so high and get my kitten, Carl. When I get big I'll climb and get little boys' kittens for them," he murmured drowsily. Before the horses were over the first hill, Emil and his cat were both fast asleep.

Although it was only four o'clock, the winter day was fading. The road led southwest, toward the streak of pale, watery light that glimmered in the leaden sky. The light fell upon the two sad young faces that were turned mutely toward it: upon the eyes of the girl, who seemed to be looking with such anguished perplexity into the future; upon the sombre eyes of the boy, who seemed already to be looking into the past. The little town behind them had vanished as if it had never been, had fallen behind the swell of the prairie, and the stern frozen country received them into its bosom. The homesteads were few and far apart; here and there a windmill gaunt against the sky, a sod house crouching in a hollow. But the great fact was the land itself, which seemed to overwhelm the little beginnings of human society that struggled in its sombre wastes. It was from facing this vast hardness that the boy's mouth had become so bitter; because he felt that men were too weak to make any mark here, that the land wanted to be let alone, to preserve its own fierce strength, its peculiar, savage kind of beauty, its uninterrupted mournfulness.

The wagon jolted along over the frozen road. The two friends had less to say to each other than usual, as if the cold had somehow penetrated to their hearts.

"Did Lou and Oscar go to the Blue to cut wood to-day?" Carl asked.

"Yes. I'm almost sorry I let them go, it's turned so cold. But mother frets if the wood gets low." She stopped and put her hand to her forehead, brushing back her hair. "I don't know what is to become of us, Carl, if father has to die. I don't dare to think about it. I wish we could all go with him and let the grass grow back over everything."

Carl made no reply. Just ahead of them was the Norwegian graveyard, where the grass had, indeed, grown back over everything, shaggy and red, hiding even the wire fence. Carl realized that he was not a very helpful companion, but there was nothing he could say.

"Of course," Alexandra went on, steadying her voice a little, "the boys are strong and work hard, but we've always depended so on father that I don't see how we can go ahead. I almost feel as if there were nothing to go ahead for."

"Does your father know?"

"Yes, I think he does. He lies and counts on his fingers all day. I think he is trying to count up what he is leaving for us. It's a comfort to him that my chickens are laying right on through the cold weather and bringing in a little money. I wish we could keep his mind off such things, but I don't have much time to be with him now."

"I wonder if he'd like to have me bring my magic lantern over some evening?"

Alexandra turned her face toward him. "Oh, Carl! Have you got it?"

"Yes. It's back there in the straw. Didn't you notice the box I was carrying? I tried it all morning in the drug-store cellar, and it worked ever so well, makes fine big pictures."

"What are they about?"

"Oh, hunting pictures in Germany, and Robinson Crusoe and funny pictures about cannibals. I'm going to paint some slides for it on glass, out of the Hans Andersen book."

Alexandra seemed actually cheered. There is often a good deal of the child left in people who have had to grow up too soon. "Do bring it over, Carl. I can hardly wait to see it, and I'm sure it will please father. Are the pictures colored? Then I know he'll like them. He likes the calendars I get him in town. I wish I could get more. You must leave me here, mustn't you? It's been nice to have company."

Carl stopped the horses and looked dubiously up at the black sky. "It's pretty dark. Of course the horses will take you home, but I think I'd better light your lantern, in case you should need it."

He gave her the reins and climbed back into the wagon-box, where he crouched down and made a tent of his overcoat. After a dozen trials he succeeded in lighting the lantern, which he placed in front of Alexandra, half covering it with a blanket so that the light would not shine in her eyes. "Now, wait until I find my box. Yes, here it is. Good-night, Alexandra. Try not to worry." Carl sprang to the ground and ran off across the fields toward the Linstrum homestead. "Hoo, hoo-o-o-o!" he called back as he disappeared over a ridge and dropped into a sand gully. The wind answered him like an echo, "Hoo, hoo-o-o-o-o-o!" Alexandra drove off alone. The rattle of her wagon was lost in the howling of the wind, but her lantern, held firmly between her feet, made a moving point of light along the highway, going deeper and deeper into the dark country.

II.

On one of the ridges of that wintry waste stood the low log house in which John Bergson was dying. The Bergson homestead was easier to find than many another, because it overlooked Norway Creek, a shallow, muddy stream that sometimes flowed, and sometimes stood still, at the bottom of a winding ravine with steep, shelving sides overgrown with brush and cottonwoods and dwarf ash. This creek gave a sort of identity to the farms that bordered upon it. Of all the bewildering things about a new country, the absence of human landmarks is one of the most depressing and disheartening. The houses on the Divide were small and were usually tucked away in low places; you did not see them until you came directly upon them. Most of them were built of the sod itself, and were only the unescapable ground in another form. The roads were but faint tracks in the grass, and the fields were scarcely noticeable. The record of the plow was insignificant, like the feeble scratches on stone left by prehistoric races, so indeterminate that they may, after all, be only the markings of glaciers, and not a record of human strivings.

In eleven long years John Bergson had made but little impression upon the wild land he had come to tame. It was still a wild thing that had its ugly moods; and no one knew when they were likely to come, or why. Mischance hung over it. Its Genius was unfriendly to man. The sick man was feeling this as he lay looking out of the window, after the doctor had left him, on the day following Alexandra's trip to town. There it lay outside his door, the same land, the same lead-colored miles. He knew every ridge and draw and gully between him and the horizon. To the south, his plowed fields; to the east, the sod stables, the cattle corral, the pond,—and then the grass.

Bergson went over in his mind the things that had held him back. One winter his cattle had perished in a blizzard. The next summer one of his plow horses broke its leg in a prairiedog hole and had to be shot. Another summer he lost his hogs from cholera, and a valuable stallion died from a rattlesnake bite. Time and again his crops had failed. He had lost two children, boys, that came between Lou and Emil, and there had been the cost of sickness and death. Now, when he had at last struggled out of debt, he was going to die himself. He was only forty-six, and had, of course, counted upon more time.

Bergson had spent his first five years on the Divide getting into debt, and the last six getting out. He had paid off his mortgages and had ended pretty much where he began, with the land. He owned exactly six hundred and forty acres of what stretched outside his door; his own original homestead and timber claim, making three hundred and twenty acres, and the half-section adjoining, the homestead of a younger brother who had given up the fight, gone back to Chicago to work in a fancy bakery and distinguish himself in a Swedish athletic club. So far John had not attempted to cultivate the second half-section, but used it for pasture land, and one of his sons rode herd there in open weather.

John Bergson had the Old-World belief that land, in itself, is desirable. But this land was an enigma. It was like a horse that no one knows how to break to harness, that runs wild and kicks things to pieces. He had an idea that no one understood how to farm it properly, and this he often discussed with Alexandra. Their neighbors, certainly, knew even less about farming than he did. Many of them had never worked on a farm until they took up their homesteads. They had been HANDWERKERS at home; tailors, locksmiths, joiners, cigar-makers, etc. Bergson himself had worked in a shipyard.

For weeks, John Bergson had been thinking about these things. His bed stood in the sitting-room, next to the kitchen. Through the day, while the baking and washing and ironing were going on, the father lay and looked up at the roof beams that he himself had hewn, or out at the cattle in the corral. He counted the cattle over and over. It diverted him to speculate as to how much weight each of the steers would probably put on by spring. He often called his daughter in to talk to her about this. Before Alexandra was twelve years old she had begun to be a help to him, and as she grew older he had come to depend more and more upon her resourcefulness and good judgment. His boys were willing enough to work, but when he talked with them they usually irritated him. It was Alexandra who read the papers and followed the markets, and who learned by the mistakes of their neighbors. It was Alexandra who could always tell about what it had cost to fatten each steer, and who could guess the weight of a hog before it went on the scales closer than John Bergson himself. Lou and Oscar were industrious, but he could never teach them to use their heads about their work.

Alexandra, her father often said to himself, was like her grandfather; which was his way of saying that she was intelligent. John Bergson's father had been a shipbuilder, a man of considerable force and of some fortune. Late in life he married a second time, a Stockholm woman of questionable character, much younger than he, who goaded him into every sort of extravagance. On the shipbuilder's part, this marriage was an infatuation, the despairing folly of a powerful man who cannot bear to grow old. In a few years his unprincipled wife warped the probity of a lifetime. He speculated, lost his own fortune and funds entrusted to him by poor seafaring men, and died disgraced, leaving his children nothing. But when all was said, he had come up from the sea himself, had built up a proud little business with no capital but his own skill and foresight, and had proved himself a man. In his daughter, John Bergson recognized the strength of will, and the simple direct way of thinking things out, that had characterized his father in his better days. He would much rather, of course, have seen this likeness in one of his sons, but it was not a question of choice. As he lay there day after day he had to accept the situation as it was, and to be thankful that there was one among his children to whom he could entrust the future of his family and the possibilities of his hard-won land.

The winter twilight was fading. The sick man heard his wife strike a match in the kitchen, and the light of a lamp glimmered through the cracks of the door. It seemed like a light shining far away. He turned painfully in his bed and looked at his white hands, with all the work gone out of them. He was ready to give up, he felt. He did not know how it had come about, but he was quite willing to go deep under his fields and rest, where the plow could not find him. He was tired of making mistakes. He was content to leave the tangle to other hands; he thought of his Alexandra's strong ones.

"DOTTER," he called feebly, "DOTTER!" He heard her quick step and saw her tall figure appear in the doorway, with the light of the lamp behind her. He felt her youth and strength, how easily she moved and stooped and lifted. But he would not have had it again if he could, not he! He knew the end too well to wish to begin again. He knew where it all went to, what it all became.

His daughter came and lifted him up on his pillows. She called him by an old Swedish name that she used to call him when she was little and took his dinner to him in the shipyard.

"Tell the boys to come here, daughter. I want to speak to them."

"They are feeding the horses, father. They have just come back from the Blue. Shall I call them?"

He sighed. "No, no. Wait until they come in. Alexandra, you will have to do the best you can for your brothers. Everything will come on you."

"I will do all I can, father."

"Don't let them get discouraged and go off like Uncle Otto. I want them to keep the land."

"We will, father. We will never lose the land."

There was a sound of heavy feet in the kitchen. Alexandra went to the door and beckoned to her brothers, two strapping boys of seventeen and nineteen. They came in and stood at the foot of the bed. Their father looked at them searchingly, though it was too dark to see their faces; they were just the same boys, he told himself, he had not been mistaken in them. The square head and heavy shoulders belonged to Oscar, the elder. The younger boy was quicker, but vacillating.

"Boys," said the father wearily, "I want you to keep the land together and to be guided by your sister. I have talked to her since I have been sick, and she knows all my wishes. I want no quarrels among my children, and so long as there is one house there must be one head.

Alexandra is the oldest, and she knows my wishes. She will do the best she can. If she makes mistakes, she will not make so many as I have made. When you marry, and want a house of your own, the land will be divided fairly, according to the courts. But for the next few years you will have it hard, and you must all keep together. Alexandra will manage the best she can."

Oscar, who was usually the last to speak, replied because he was the older, "Yes, father. It would be so anyway, without your speaking. We will all work the place together."

"And you will be guided by your sister, boys, and be good brothers to her, and good sons to your mother? That is good. And Alexandra must not work in the fields any more. There is no necessity now. Hire a man when you need help. She can make much more with her eggs and butter than the wages of a man. It was one of my mistakes that I did not find that out sooner. Try to break a little more land every year; sod corn is good for fodder. Keep turning the land, and always put up more hay than you need. Don't grudge your mother a little time for plowing her garden and setting out fruit trees, even if it comes in a busy season. She has been a good mother to you, and she has always missed the old country."

When they went back to the kitchen the boys sat down silently at the table. Throughout the meal they looked down at their plates and did not lift their red eyes. They did not eat much, although they had been working in the cold all day, and there was a rabbit stewed in gravy for supper, and prune pies.

John Bergson had married beneath him, but he had married a good housewife. Mrs. Bergson was a fair-skinned, corpulent woman, heavy and placid like her son, Oscar, but there was something comfortable about her; perhaps it was her own love of comfort. For eleven years she had worthily striven to maintain some semblance of household order amid conditions that made order very difficult. Habit was very strong with Mrs. Bergson, and her unremitting efforts to repeat the routine of her old life among new surroundings had done a great deal to keep the family from disintegrating morally and getting careless in their ways. The Bergsons had a log house, for instance, only because Mrs. Bergson would not live in a sod house. She missed the fish diet of her own country, and twice every summer she sent the boys to the river, twenty miles to the southward, to fish for channel cat. When the children were little she used to load them all into the wagon, the baby in its crib, and go fishing herself.

Alexandra often said that if her mother were cast upon a desert island, she would thank God for her deliverance, make a garden, and find something to preserve. Preserving was almost a mania with Mrs. Bergson. Stout as she was, she roamed the scrubby banks of Norway Creek looking for fox grapes and goose plums, like a wild creature in search of prey. She made a yellow jam of the insipid ground-cherries that grew on the prairie, flavoring it with lemon peel; and she made a sticky dark conserve of garden tomatoes. She had experimented even with the rank buffalo-pea, and she could not see a fine bronze cluster of them without shaking her head and murmuring, "What a pity!" When there was nothing more to preserve, she began to pickle. The amount of sugar she used in these processes was sometimes a serious drain upon the family resources. She was a good mother, but she was glad when her children were old enough not to be in her way in the kitchen. She had never quite forgiven John Bergson for bringing her to the end of the earth; but, now that she was there, she wanted to be let alone to reconstruct her old life in so far as that was possible. She could still take some comfort in the world if she had bacon in the cave, glass jars on the shelves, and sheets in the press. She disapproved of all her neighbors because of their slovenly housekeeping, and the women thought her very proud. Once when Mrs. Bergson, on her way to Norway Creek, stopped to see old Mrs. Lee, the old woman hid in the haymow "for fear Mis' Bergson would catch her barefoot."

III.

One Sunday afternoon in July, six months after John Bergson's death, Carl was sitting in the doorway of the Linstrum kitchen, dreaming over an illustrated paper, when he heard the rattle of a wagon along the hill road. Looking up he recognized the Bergsons' team, with two seats in the wagon, which meant they were off for a pleasure excursion. Oscar and Lou, on the front seat, wore their cloth hats and coats, never worn except on Sundays, and Emil, on the second seat with Alexandra, sat proudly in his new trousers, made from a pair of his father's, and a pink-striped shirt, with a wide ruffled collar. Oscar stopped the horses and waved to Carl, who caught up his hat and ran through the melon patch to join them.

"Want to go with us?" Lou called. "We're going to Crazy Ivar's to buy a hammock."

"Sure." Carl ran up panting, and clambering over the wheel sat down beside Emil. "I've always wanted to see Ivar's pond. They say it's the biggest in all the country. Aren't you afraid to go to Ivar's in that new shirt, Emil? He might want it and take it right off your back."

Emil grinned. "I'd be awful scared to go," he admitted, "if you big boys weren't along to take care of me. Did you ever hear him howl, Carl? People say sometimes he runs about the country howling at night because he is afraid the Lord will destroy him. Mother thinks he must have done something awful wicked."

Lou looked back and winked at Carl. "What would you do, Emil, if you was out on the prairie by yourself and seen him coming?"

Emil stared. "Maybe I could hide in a badger-hole," he suggested doubtfully.

"But suppose there wasn't any badger-hole," Lou persisted. "Would you run?"

"No, I'd be too scared to run," Emil admitted mournfully, twisting his fingers. "I guess I'd sit right down on the ground and say my prayers."

The big boys laughed, and Oscar brandished his whip over the broad backs of the horses.

"He wouldn't hurt you, Emil," said Carl persuasively. "He came to doctor our mare when she ate green corn and swelled up most as big as the water-tank. He petted her just like you do your cats. I couldn't understand much he said, for he don't talk any English, but he kept patting her and groaning as if he had the pain himself, and saying, 'There now, sister, that's easier, that's better!'"

Lou and Oscar laughed, and Emil giggled delightedly and looked up at his sister.

"I don't think he knows anything at all about doctoring," said Oscar scornfully. "They say when horses have distemper he takes the medicine himself, and then prays over the horses."

Alexandra spoke up. "That's what the Crows said, but he cured their horses, all the same. Some days his mind is cloudy, like. But if you can get him on a clear day, you can learn a great deal from him. He understands animals. Didn't I see him take the horn off the Berquist's cow when she had torn it loose and went crazy? She was tearing all over the place, knocking herself against things. And at last she ran out on the roof of the old dugout and her legs went through and there she stuck, bellowing. Ivar came running with his white bag, and the moment he got to her she was quiet and let him saw her horn off and daub the place with tar."

Emil had been watching his sister, his face reflecting the sufferings of the cow. "And then didn't it hurt her any more?" he asked.

Alexandra patted him. "No, not any more. And in two days they could use her milk again."

The road to Ivar's homestead was a very poor one. He had settled in the rough country across the county line, where no one lived but some Russians,—half a dozen families who dwelt together in one long house, divided off like barracks. Ivar had explained his choice by saying that the fewer neighbors he had, the fewer temptations. Nevertheless, when one considered that his chief business was horse-doctoring, it seemed rather short-sighted of him to live in the most inaccessible place he could find. The Bergson wagon lurched along over the rough hummocks and grass banks, followed the bottom of winding draws, or skirted the margin of wide lagoons, where the golden coreopsis grew up out of the clear water and the wild ducks rose with a whirr of wings.

Lou looked after them helplessly. "I wish I'd brought my gun, anyway, Alexandra," he said fretfully. "I could have hidden it under the straw in the bottom of the wagon."

"Then we'd have had to lie to Ivar. Besides, they say he can smell dead birds. And if he knew, we wouldn't get anything out of him, not even a hammock. I want to talk to him, and he won't talk sense if he's angry. It makes him foolish."

Lou sniffed. "Whoever heard of him talking sense, anyhow! I'd rather have ducks for supper than Crazy Ivar's tongue."

Emil was alarmed. "Oh, but, Lou, you don't want to make him mad! He might howl!"

They all laughed again, and Oscar urged the horses up the crumbling side of a clay bank. They had left the lagoons and the red grass behind them. In Crazy Ivar's country the grass was short and gray, the draws deeper than they were in the Bergsons' neighborhood, and the land was all broken up into hillocks and clay ridges. The wild flowers disappeared, and only in the bottom of the draws and gullies grew a few of the very toughest and hardiest: shoestring, and ironweed, and snow-on-the-mountain.

"Look, look, Emil, there's Ivar's big pond!" Alexandra pointed to a shining sheet of water that lay at the bottom of a shallow draw. At one end of the pond was an earthen dam, planted with green willow bushes, and above it a door and a single window were set into the hillside. You would not have seen them at all but for the reflection of the sunlight upon the four panes of window-glass. And that was all you saw. Not a shed, not a corral, not a well, not even a path broken in the curly grass. But for the piece of rusty stovepipe sticking up through the sod, you could have walked over the roof of Ivar's dwelling without dreaming that you were near a human habitation. Ivar had lived for three years in the clay bank, without defiling the face of nature any more than the coyote that had lived there before him had done.

When the Bergsons drove over the hill, Ivar was sitting in the doorway of his house, reading the Norwegian Bible. He was a queerly shaped old man, with a thick, powerful body set on short bow-legs. His shaggy white hair, falling in a thick mane about his ruddy cheeks, made him look older than he was. He was barefoot, but he wore a clean shirt of unbleached cotton, open at the neck. He always put on a clean shirt when Sunday morning came round, though he never went to church. He had a peculiar religion of his own and could not get on with any of the denominations. Often he did not see anybody from one week's end to another. He kept a calendar, and every morning he checked off a day, so that he was never in any doubt as to which day of the week it was. Ivar hired himself out in threshing and corn-husking time, and he doctored sick animals when he was sent for. When he was at home, he made hammocks out of twine and committed chapters of the Bible to memory.

Ivar found contentment in the solitude he had sought out for himself. He disliked the litter of human dwellings: the broken food, the bits of broken china, the old wash-boilers and tea-kettles thrown into the sunflower patch. He preferred the cleanness and tidiness of the wild sod. He always said that the badgers had cleaner houses than people, and that when he took a housekeeper her name would be Mrs. Badger. He best expressed his preference for his wild homestead by saying that his Bible seemed truer to him there. If one stood in the doorway of his cave, and looked off at the rough land, the smiling sky, the curly grass white in the hot sunlight; if one listened to the rapturous song of the lark, the drumming of the quail, the burr of the locust against that vast silence, one understood what Ivar meant.

On this Sunday afternoon his face shone with happiness. He closed the book on his knee, keeping the place with his horny finger, and repeated softly:—

He sendeth the springs into the valleys, which run among the hills;
They give drink to every beast of the field; the wild asses quench their thirst.
The trees of the Lord are full of sap; the cedars of Lebanon which he hath planted;
Where the birds make their nests: as for the stork, the fir trees are her house.
The high hills are a refuge for the wild goats; and the rocks for the conies.

Before he opened his Bible again, Ivar heard the Bergsons' wagon approaching, and he sprang up and ran toward it.

"No guns, no guns!" he shouted, waving his arms distractedly.

"No, Ivar, no guns," Alexandra called reassuringly.

He dropped his arms and went up to the wagon, smiling amiably and looking at them out of his pale blue eyes.

"We want to buy a hammock, if you have one," Alexandra explained, "and my little brother, here, wants to see your big pond, where so many birds come."

Ivar smiled foolishly, and began rubbing the horses' noses and feeling about their mouths behind the bits. "Not many birds just now. A few ducks this morning; and some snipe come to drink. But there was a crane last week. She spent one night and came back the next evening. I don't know why. It is not her season, of course. Many of them go over in the fall. Then the pond is full of strange voices every night."

Alexandra translated for Carl, who looked thoughtful. "Ask him, Alexandra, if it is true that a sea gull came here once. I have heard so."

She had some difficulty in making the old man understand.

He looked puzzled at first, then smote his hands together as he remembered. "Oh, yes, yes! A big white bird with long wings and pink feet. My! what a voice she had! She came in the afternoon and kept flying about the pond and screaming until dark. She was in trouble of some sort, but I could not understand her. She was going over to the other ocean, maybe, and did not know how far it was. She was afraid of never getting there. She was more mournful than our birds here; she cried in the night. She saw the light from my window and darted up to it. Maybe she thought my house was a boat, she was such a wild thing. Next morning, when the sun rose, I went out to take her food, but she flew up into the sky and went on her way." Ivar ran his fingers through his thick hair. "I have many strange birds stop with me here. They come from very far away and are great company. I hope you boys never shoot wild birds?"

Lou and Oscar grinned, and Ivar shook his bushy head. "Yes, I know boys are thoughtless. But these wild things are God's birds. He watches over them and counts them, as we do our cattle; Christ says so in the New Testament."

"Now, Ivar," Lou asked, "may we water our horses at your pond and give them some feed? It's a bad road to your place."

"Yes, yes, it is." The old man scrambled about and began to loose the tugs. "A bad road, eh, girls? And the bay with a colt at home!"

Oscar brushed the old man aside. "We'll take care of the horses, Ivar. You'll be finding some disease on them. Alexandra wants to see your hammocks."

Ivar led Alexandra and Emil to his little cave house. He had but one room, neatly plastered and whitewashed, and there was a wooden floor. There was a kitchen stove, a table covered with oilcloth, two chairs, a clock, a calendar, a few books on the window-shelf; nothing more. But the place was as clean as a cupboard.

"But where do you sleep, Ivar?" Emil asked, looking about.

Ivar unslung a hammock from a hook on the wall; in it was rolled a buffalo robe. "There, my son. A hammock is a good bed, and in winter I wrap up in this skin. Where I go to work, the beds are not half so easy as this."

By this time Emil had lost all his timidity. He thought a cave a very superior kind of house. There was something pleasantly unusual about it and about Ivar. "Do the birds know you will be kind to them, Ivar? Is that why so many come?" he asked.

Ivar sat down on the floor and tucked his feet under him. "See, little brother, they have come from a long way, and they are very tired. From up there where they are flying, our country looks dark and flat. They must have water to drink and to bathe in before they can go on with their journey. They look this way and that, and far below them they see something shining, like a piece of glass set in the dark earth. That is my pond. They come to it and are not disturbed. Maybe I sprinkle a little corn. They tell the other birds, and next year more come this way. They have their roads up there, as we have down here."

Emil rubbed his knees thoughtfully. "And is that true, Ivar, about the head ducks falling back when they are tired, and the hind ones taking their place?"

"Yes. The point of the wedge gets the worst of it; they cut the wind. They can only stand it there a little while—half an hour, maybe. Then they fall back and the wedge splits a little, while the rear ones come up the middle to the front. Then it closes up and they fly on, with a new edge. They are always changing like that, up in the air. Never any confusion; just like soldiers who have been drilled."

Alexandra had selected her hammock by the time the boys came up from the pond. They would not come in, but sat in the shade of the bank outside while Alexandra and Ivar talked about the birds and about his housekeeping, and why he never ate meat, fresh or salt.

Alexandra was sitting on one of the wooden chairs, her arms resting on the table. Ivar was sitting on the floor at her feet. "Ivar," she said suddenly, beginning to trace the pattern on the oilcloth with her forefinger, "I came to-day more because I wanted to talk to you than because I wanted to buy a hammock."

"Yes?" The old man scraped his bare feet on the plank floor.

"We have a big bunch of hogs, Ivar. I wouldn't sell in the spring, when everybody advised me to, and now so many people are losing their hogs that I am frightened. What can be done?"

Ivar's little eyes began to shine. They lost their vagueness.

"You feed them swill and such stuff? Of course! And sour milk? Oh, yes! And keep them in a stinking pen? I tell you, sister, the hogs of this country are put upon! They become unclean, like the hogs in the Bible. If you kept your chickens like that, what would happen? You have a little sorghum patch, maybe? Put a fence around it, and turn the hogs in. Build a shed to give them shade, a thatch on poles. Let the boys haul water to them in barrels, clean water, and plenty. Get them off the old stinking ground, and do not let them go back there until winter. Give them only grain and clean feed, such as you would give horses or cattle. Hogs do not like to be filthy."

The boys outside the door had been listening. Lou nudged his brother. "Come, the horses are done eating. Let's hitch up and get out of here. He'll fill her full of notions. She'll be for having the pigs sleep with us, next."

Oscar grunted and got up. Carl, who could not understand what Ivar said, saw that the two boys were displeased. They did not mind hard work, but they hated experiments and could never see the use of taking pains. Even Lou, who was more elastic than his older brother, disliked to do anything different from their neighbors. He felt that it made them conspicuous and gave people a chance to talk about them.

Once they were on the homeward road, the boys forgot their ill-humor and joked about Ivar and his birds. Alexandra did not propose any reforms in the care of the pigs, and they hoped she had forgotten Ivar's talk. They agreed that he was crazier than ever, and would never be able to prove up on his land because he worked it so little. Alexandra privately resolved that she would have a talk with Ivar about this and stir him up. The boys persuaded Carl to stay for supper and go swimming in the pasture pond after dark.

That evening, after she had washed the supper dishes, Alexandra sat down on the kitchen doorstep, while her mother was mixing the bread. It was a still, deep-breathing summer night, full of the smell of the hay fields. Sounds of laughter and splashing came up from the pasture, and when the moon rose rapidly above the bare rim of the prairie, the pond glittered like polished metal, and she could see the flash of white bodies as the boys ran about the edge, or jumped into the water. Alexandra watched the shimmering pool dreamily, but eventually her eyes went back to the sorghum patch south of the barn, where she was planning to make her new pig corral.

IV.

For the first three years after John Bergson's death, the affairs of his family prospered. Then came the hard times that brought every one on the Divide to the brink of despair; three years of drouth and failure, the last struggle of a wild soil against the encroaching plowshare. The first of these fruitless summers the Bergson boys bore courageously. The failure of the corn crop made labor cheap. Lou and Oscar hired two men and put in bigger crops than ever before. They lost everything they spent. The whole country was discouraged. Farmers who were already in debt had to give up their land. A few foreclosures demoralized the county. The settlers sat about on the wooden sidewalks in the little town and told each other that the country was never meant for men to live in; the thing to do was to get back to Iowa, to Illinois, to any place that had been proved habitable. The Bergson boys, certainly, would have been happier with their uncle Otto, in the bakery shop in Chicago. Like most of their neighbors, they were meant to follow in paths already marked out for them, not to break trails in a new country. A steady job, a few holidays, nothing to think about, and they would have been very happy. It was no fault of theirs that they had been dragged into the wilderness when they were little boys. A pioneer should have imagination, should be able to enjoy the idea of things more than the things themselves.

The second of these barren summers was passing. One September afternoon Alexandra had gone over to the garden across the draw to dig sweet potatoes—they had been thriving upon the weather that was fatal to everything else. But when Carl Linstrum came up the garden rows to find her, she was not working. She was standing lost in thought, leaning upon her pitchfork, her sunbonnet lying beside her on the ground. The dry garden patch smelled of drying vines and was strewn with yellow seed-cucumbers and pumpkins and citrons. At one end, next the rhubarb, grew feathery asparagus, with red berries. Down the middle of the garden was a row of gooseberry and currant bushes. A few tough zenias and marigolds and a row of scarlet sage bore witness to the buckets of water that Mrs. Bergson had carried there after sundown, against the prohibition of her sons. Carl came quietly and slowly up the garden path, looking intently at Alexandra. She did not hear him. She was standing perfectly still, with that serious ease so characteristic of her. Her thick, reddish braids, twisted about her head, fairly burned in the sunlight. The air was cool enough to make the warm sun pleasant on one's back and shoulders, and so clear that the eye could follow a hawk up and up, into the blazing blue depths of the sky. Even Carl, never a very cheerful boy, and considerably darkened by these last two bitter years, loved the country on days like this, felt something strong and young and wild come out of it, that laughed at care.

"Alexandra," he said as he approached her, "I want to talk to you. Let's sit down by the gooseberry bushes." He picked up her sack of potatoes and they crossed the garden. "Boys gone to town?" he asked as he sank down on the warm, sun-baked earth. "Well, we have made up our minds at last, Alexandra. We are really going away."

She looked at him as if she were a little frightened. "Really, Carl? Is it settled?"

"Yes, father has heard from St. Louis, and they will give him back his old job in the cigar factory. He must be there by the first of November. They are taking on new men then. We will sell the place for whatever we can get, and auction the stock. We haven't enough to ship. I am going to learn engraving with a German engraver there, and then try to get work in Chicago."

Alexandra's hands dropped in her lap. Her eyes became dreamy and filled with tears.

Carl's sensitive lower lip trembled. He scratched in the soft earth beside him with a stick. "That's all I hate about it, Alexandra," he said slowly. "You've stood by us through so much and helped father out so many times, and now it seems as if we were running off and leaving you to face the worst of it. But it isn't as if we could really ever be of any help to you. We are only one more drag, one more thing you look out for and feel responsible for. Father was never meant for a farmer, you know that. And I hate it. We'd only get in deeper and deeper."

"Yes, yes, Carl, I know. You are wasting your life here. You are able to do much better things. You are nearly nineteen now, and I wouldn't have you stay. I've always hoped you would get away. But I can't help feeling scared when I think how I will miss you—more than you will ever know." She brushed the tears from her cheeks, not trying to hide them.

"But, Alexandra," he said sadly and wistfully, "I've never been any real help to you, beyond sometimes trying to keep the boys in a good humor."

Alexandra smiled and shook her head. "Oh, it's not that. Nothing like that. It's by understanding me, and the boys, and mother, that you've helped me. I expect that is the only way one person ever really can help another. I think you are about the only one that ever helped me. Somehow it will take more courage to bear your going than everything that has happened before."

Carl looked at the ground. "You see, we've all depended so on you," he said, "even father. He makes me laugh. When anything comes up he always says, 'I wonder what the Bergsons are going to do about that? I guess I'll go and ask her.' I'll never forget that time, when we first came here, and our horse had the colic, and I ran over to your place—your father was away, and you came home with me and showed father how to let the wind out of the horse. You were only a little girl then, but you knew ever so much more about farm work than poor father. You remember how homesick I used to get, and what long talks we used to have coming from school? We've someway always felt alike about things."

"Yes, that's it; we've liked the same things and we've liked them together, without anybody else knowing. And we've had good times, hunting for Christmas trees and going for ducks and making our plum wine together every year. We've never either of us had any other close friend. And now—" Alexandra wiped her eyes with the corner of her apron, "and now I must remember that you are going where you will have many friends, and will find the work you were meant to do. But you'll write to me, Carl? That will mean a great deal to me here."

"I'll write as long as I live," cried the boy impetuously. "And I'll be working for you as much as for myself, Alexandra. I want to do something you'll like and be proud of. I'm a fool here, but I know I can do something!" He sat up and frowned at the red grass.

Alexandra sighed. "How discouraged the boys will be when they hear. They always come home from town discouraged, anyway. So many people are trying to leave the country, and they talk to our boys and make them low-spirited. I'm afraid they are beginning to feel hard toward me because I won't listen to any talk about going. Sometimes I feel like I'm getting tired of standing up for this country."

"I won't tell the boys yet, if you'd rather not."

"Oh, I'll tell them myself, to-night, when they come home. They'll be talking wild, anyway, and no good comes of keeping bad news. It's all harder on them than it is on me. Lou wants to get married, poor boy, and he can't until times are better. See, there goes the sun, Carl. I must be getting back. Mother will want her potatoes. It's chilly already, the moment the light goes."

Alexandra rose and looked about. A golden afterglow throbbed in the west, but the country already looked empty and mournful. A dark moving mass came over the western hill, the Lee boy was bringing in the herd from the other half-section. Emil ran from the windmill to open the corral gate. From the log house, on the little rise across the draw, the smoke was curling. The cattle lowed and bellowed. In the sky the pale half-moon was slowly silvering. Alexandra and Carl walked together down the potato rows. "I have to keep telling myself what is going to happen," she said softly. "Since you have been here, ten years now, I have never really been lonely. But I can remember what it was like before. Now I shall have nobody but Emil. But he is my boy, and he is tender-hearted."

That night, when the boys were called to supper, they sat down moodily. They had worn their coats to town, but they ate in their striped shirts and suspenders. They were grown men now, and, as Alexandra said, for the last few years they had been growing more and more like themselves. Lou was still the slighter of the two, the quicker and more intelligent, but apt to go off at half-cock. He had a lively blue eye, a thin, fair skin (always burned red to the neckband of his shirt in summer), stiff, yellow hair that would not lie down on his head, and a bristly little yellow mustache, of which he was very proud. Oscar could not grow a mustache; his pale face was as bare as an egg, and his white eyebrows gave it an empty look. He was a man of powerful body and unusual endurance; the sort of man you could attach to a corn-sheller as you would an engine. He would turn it all day, without hurrying, without slowing down. But he was as indolent of mind as he was unsparing of his body. His love of routine amounted to a vice. He worked like an insect, always doing the same thing over in the same way, regardless of whether it was best or no. He felt that there was a sovereign virtue in mere bodily toil, and he rather liked to do things in the hardest way. If a field had once been in corn, he couldn't bear to put it into wheat. He liked to begin his corn-planting at the same time every year, whether the season were backward or forward. He seemed to feel that by his own irreproachable regularity he would clear himself of blame and reprove the weather. When the wheat crop failed, he threshed the straw at a dead loss to demonstrate how little grain there was, and thus prove his case against Providence.

Lou, on the other hand, was fussy and flighty; always planned to get through two days' work in one, and often got only the least important things done. He liked to keep the place up, but he never got round to doing odd jobs until he had to neglect more pressing work to attend to them. In the middle of the wheat harvest, when the grain was over-ripe and every hand was needed, he would stop to mend fences or to patch the harness; then dash down to the field and overwork and be laid up in bed for a week. The two boys balanced each other, and they pulled well together. They had been good friends since they were children. One seldom went anywhere, even to town, without the other.

To-night, after they sat down to supper, Oscar kept looking at Lou as if he expected him to say something, and Lou blinked his eyes and frowned at his plate. It was Alexandra herself who at last opened the discussion.

"The Linstrums," she said calmly, as she put another plate of hot biscuit on the table, "are going back to St. Louis. The old man is going to work in the cigar factory again."

At this Lou plunged in. "You see, Alexandra, everybody who can crawl out is going away. There's no use of us trying to stick it out, just to be stubborn. There's something in knowing when to quit."

"Where do you want to go, Lou?"

"Any place where things will grow," said Oscar grimly.

Lou reached for a potato. "Chris Arnson has traded his half-section for a place down on the river."

"Who did he trade with?"

"Charley Fuller, in town."

"Fuller the real estate man? You see, Lou, that Fuller has a head on him. He's buying and trading for every bit of land he can get up here. It'll make him a rich man, some day."

"He's rich now, that's why he can take a chance."

"Why can't we? We'll live longer than he will. Some day the land itself will be worth more than all we can ever raise on it."

Lou laughed. "It could be worth that, and still not be worth much. Why, Alexandra, you don't know what you're talking about. Our place wouldn't bring now what it would six years ago. The fellows that settled up here just made a mistake. Now they're beginning to see this high land wasn't never meant to grow nothing on, and everybody who ain't fixed to graze cattle is trying to crawl out. It's too high to farm up here. All the Americans are skinning out. That man Percy Adams, north of town, told me that he was going to let Fuller take his land and stuff for four hundred dollars and a ticket to Chicago."

"There's Fuller again!" Alexandra exclaimed. "I wish that man would take me for a partner. He's feathering his nest! If only poor people could learn a little from rich people! But all these fellows who are running off are bad farmers, like poor Mr. Linstrum. They couldn't get ahead even in good years, and they all got into debt while father was getting out. I think we ought to hold on as long as we can on father's account. He was so set on keeping this land. He must have seen harder times than this, here. How was it in the early days, mother?"

Mrs. Bergson was weeping quietly. These family discussions always depressed her, and made her remember all that she had been torn away from. "I don't see why the boys are always taking on about going away," she said, wiping her eyes. "I don't want to move again; out to some raw place, maybe, where we'd be worse off than we are here, and all to do over again. I won't move! If the rest of you go, I will ask some of the neighbors to take me in, and stay and be buried by father. I'm not going to leave him by himself on the prairie, for cattle to run over." She began to cry more bitterly.

The boys looked angry. Alexandra put a soothing hand on her mother's shoulder. "There's no question of that, mother. You don't have to go if you don't want to. A third of the place belongs to you by American law, and we can't sell without your consent. We only want you to advise us. How did it use to be when you and father first came? Was it really as bad as this, or not?"

"Oh, worse! Much worse," moaned Mrs. Bergson. "Drouth, chince-bugs, hail, everything! My garden all cut to pieces like sauerkraut. No grapes on the creek, no nothing. The people all lived just like coyotes."

Oscar got up and tramped out of the kitchen. Lou followed him. They felt that Alexandra had taken an unfair advantage in turning their mother loose on them. The next morning they were silent and reserved. They did not offer to take the women to church, but went down to the barn immediately after breakfast and stayed there all day. When Carl Linstrum came over in the afternoon, Alexandra winked to him and pointed toward the barn. He understood her and went down to play cards with the boys. They believed that a very wicked thing to do on Sunday, and it relieved their feelings.

Alexandra stayed in the house. On Sunday afternoon Mrs. Bergson always took a nap, and Alexandra read. During the week she read only the newspaper, but on Sunday, and in the long evenings of winter, she read a good deal; read a few things over a great many times. She knew long portions of the "Frithjof Saga" by heart, and, like most Swedes who read at all, she was fond of Longfellow's verse,—the ballads and the "Golden Legend" and "The Spanish Student." To-day she sat in the wooden rocking-chair with the Swedish Bible open on her knees, but she was not reading. She was looking thoughtfully away at the point where the upland road disappeared over the rim of the prairie. Her body was in an attitude of perfect repose, such as it was apt to take when she was thinking earnestly. Her mind was slow, truthful, steadfast. She had not the least spark of cleverness.

All afternoon the sitting-room was full of quiet and sunlight. Emil was making rabbit traps in the kitchen shed. The hens were clucking and scratching brown holes in the flower beds, and the wind was teasing the prince's feather by the door.

That evening Carl came in with the boys to supper.

"Emil," said Alexandra, when they were all seated at the table, "how would you like to go traveling? Because I am going to take a trip, and you can go with me if you want to."

The boys looked up in amazement; they were always afraid of Alexandra's schemes. Carl was interested.

"I've been thinking, boys," she went on, "that maybe I am too set against making a change. I'm going to take Brigham and the buckboard to-morrow and drive down to the river country and spend a few days looking over what they've got down there. If I find anything good, you boys can go down and make a trade."

"Nobody down there will trade for anything up here," said Oscar gloomily.

"That's just what I want to find out. Maybe they are just as discontented down there as we are up here. Things away from home often look better than they are. You know what your Hans Andersen book says, Carl, about the Swedes liking to buy Danish bread and the Danes liking to buy Swedish bread, because people always think the bread of another country is better than their own. Anyway, I've heard so much about the river farms, I won't be satisfied till I've seen for myself."

Lou fidgeted. "Look out! Don't agree to anything. Don't let them fool you."

Lou was apt to be fooled himself. He had not yet learned to keep away from the shell-game wagons that followed the circus.

After supper Lou put on a necktie and went across the fields to court Annie Lee, and Carl and Oscar sat down to a game of checkers, while Alexandra read "The Swiss Family Robinson" aloud to her mother and Emil. It was not long before the two boys at the table neglected their game to listen. They were all big children together, and they found the adventures of the family in the tree house so absorbing that they gave them their undivided attention.

V.

Alexandra and Emil spent five days down among the river farms, driving up and down the valley. Alexandra talked to the men about their crops and to the women about their poultry. She spent a whole day with one young farmer who had been away at school, and who was experimenting with a new kind of clover hay. She learned a great deal. As they drove along, she and Emil talked and planned. At last, on the sixth day, Alexandra turned Brigham's head northward and left the river behind.

"There's nothing in it for us down there, Emil. There are a few fine farms, but they are owned by the rich men in town, and couldn't be bought. Most of the land is rough and hilly. They can always scrape along down there, but they can never do anything big. Down there they have a little certainty, but up with us there is a big chance. We must have faith in the high land, Emil. I want to hold on harder than ever, and when you're a man you'll thank me." She urged Brigham forward.

When the road began to climb the first long swells of the Divide, Alexandra hummed an old Swedish hymn, and Emil wondered why his sister looked so happy. Her face was so radiant that he felt shy about asking her. For the first time, perhaps, since that land emerged from the waters of geologic ages, a human face was set toward it with love and yearning. It seemed beautiful to her, rich and strong and glorious. Her eyes drank in the breadth of it, until her tears blinded her. Then the Genius of the Divide, the great, free spirit which breathes across it, must have bent lower than it ever bent to a human will before. The history of every country begins in the heart of a man or a woman.

Alexandra reached home in the afternoon. That evening she held a family council and told her brothers all that she had seen and heard.

"I want you boys to go down yourselves and look it over. Nothing will convince you like seeing with your own eyes. The river land was settled before this, and so they are a few years ahead of us, and have learned more about farming. The land sells for three times as much as this, but in five years we will double it. The rich men down there own all the best land, and they are buying all they can get. The thing to do is to sell our cattle and what little old corn we have, and buy the Linstrum place. Then the next thing to do is to take out two loans on our half-sections, and buy Peter Crow's place; raise every dollar we can, and buy every acre we can."

"Mortgage the homestead again?" Lou cried. He sprang up and began to wind the clock furiously. "I won't slave to pay off another mortgage. I'll never do it. You'd just as soon kill us all, Alexandra, to carry out some scheme!"

Oscar rubbed his high, pale forehead. "How do you propose to pay off your mortgages?"

Alexandra looked from one to the other and bit her lip. They had never seen her so nervous. "See here," she brought out at last. "We borrow the money for six years. Well, with the money we buy a half-section from Linstrum and a half from Crow, and a quarter from Struble, maybe. That will give us upwards of fourteen hundred acres, won't it? You won't have to pay off your mortgages for six years. By that time, any of this land will be worth thirty dollars an acre—it will be worth fifty, but we'll say thirty; then you can sell a garden patch anywhere, and pay off a debt of sixteen hundred dollars. It's not the principal I'm worried about, it's the interest and taxes. We'll have to strain to meet the payments. But as sure as we are sitting here to-night, we can sit down here ten years from now independent landowners, not struggling farmers any longer. The chance that father was always looking for has come."

Lou was pacing the floor. "But how do you KNOW that land is going to go up enough to pay the mortgages and—"

"And make us rich besides?" Alexandra put in firmly. "I can't explain that, Lou. You'll have to take my word for it. I KNOW, that's all. When you drive about over the country you can feel it coming."

Oscar had been sitting with his head lowered, his hands hanging between his knees. "But we can't work so much land," he said dully, as if he were talking to himself. "We can't even try. It would just lie there and we'd work ourselves to death." He sighed, and laid his calloused fist on the table.

Alexandra's eyes filled with tears. She put her hand on his shoulder. "You poor boy, you won't have to work it. The men in town who are buying up other people's land don't try to farm it. They are the men to watch, in a new country. Let's try to do like the shrewd ones, and not like these stupid fellows. I don't want you boys always to have to work like this. I want you to be independent, and Emil to go to school."

Lou held his head as if it were splitting. "Everybody will say we are crazy. It must be crazy, or everybody would be doing it."

"If they were, we wouldn't have much chance. No, Lou, I was talking about that with the smart young man who is raising the new kind of clover. He says the right thing is usually just what everybody don't do. Why are we better fixed than any of our neighbors? Because father had more brains. Our people were better people than these in the old country. We OUGHT to do more than they do, and see further ahead. Yes, mother, I'm going to clear the table now."

Alexandra rose. The boys went to the stable to see to the stock, and they were gone a long while. When they came back Lou played on his DRAGHARMONIKA and Oscar sat figuring at his father's secretary all evening. They said nothing more about Alexandra's project, but she felt sure now that they would consent to it. Just before bedtime Oscar went out for a pail of water. When he did not come back, Alexandra threw a shawl over her head and ran down the path to the windmill. She found him sitting there with his head in his hands, and she sat down beside him.

"Don't do anything you don't want to do, Oscar," she whispered. She waited a moment, but he did not stir. "I won't say any more about it, if you'd rather not. What makes you so discouraged?"

"I dread signing my name to them pieces of paper," he said slowly. "All the time I was a boy we had a mortgage hanging over us."

"Then don't sign one. I don't want you to, if you feel that way."

Oscar shook his head. "No, I can see there's a chance that way. I've thought a good while there might be. We're in so deep now, we might as well go deeper. But it's hard work pulling out of debt. Like pulling a threshing-machine out of the mud; breaks your back. Me and Lou's worked hard, and I can't see it's got us ahead much."

"Nobody knows about that as well as I do, Oscar. That's why I want to try an easier way. I don't want you to have to grub for every dollar."

"Yes, I know what you mean. Maybe it'll come out right. But signing papers is signing papers. There ain't no maybe about that." He took his pail and trudged up the path to the house.

Alexandra drew her shawl closer about her and stood leaning against the frame of the mill, looking at the stars which glittered so keenly through the frosty autumn air. She always loved to watch them, to think of their vastness and distance, and of their ordered march. It fortified her to reflect upon the great operations of nature, and when she thought of the law that lay behind them, she felt a sense of personal security. That night she had a new consciousness of the country, felt almost a new relation to it. Even her talk with the boys had not taken away the feeling that had overwhelmed her when she drove back to the Divide that afternoon. She had never known before how much the country meant to her. The chirping of the insects down in the long grass had been like the sweetest music. She had felt as if her heart were hiding down there, somewhere, with the quail and the plover and all the little wild things that crooned or buzzed in the sun. Under the long shaggy ridges, she felt the future stirring.

2

NEIGHBORING FIELDS

I.

It is sixteen years since John Bergson died. His wife now lies beside him, and the white shaft that marks their graves gleams across the wheat-fields. Could he rise from beneath it, he would not know the country under which he has been asleep. The shaggy coat of the prairie, which they lifted to make him a bed, has vanished forever. From the Norwegian graveyard one looks out over a vast checker-board, marked off in squares of wheat and corn; light and dark, dark and light. Telephone wires hum along the white roads, which always run at right angles. From the graveyard gate one can count a dozen gayly painted farmhouses; the gilded weather-vanes on the big red barns wink at each other across the green and brown and yellow fields. The light steel windmills tremble throughout their frames and tug at their moorings, as they vibrate in the wind that often blows from one week's end to another across that high, active, resolute stretch of country.

The Divide is now thickly populated. The rich soil yields heavy harvests; the dry, bracing climate and the smoothness of the land make labor easy for men and beasts. There are few scenes more gratifying than a spring plowing in that country, where the furrows of a single field often lie a mile in length, and the brown earth, with such a strong, clean smell, and such a power of growth and fertility in it, yields itself eagerly to the plow; rolls away from the shear, not even dimming the brightness of the metal, with a soft, deep sigh of happiness. The wheat-cutting sometimes goes on all night as well as all day, and in good seasons there are scarcely men and horses enough to do the harvesting. The grain is so heavy that it bends toward the blade and cuts like velvet.

There is something frank and joyous and young in the open face of the country. It gives itself ungrudgingly to the moods of the season, holding nothing back. Like the plains of Lombardy, it seems to rise a little to meet the sun. The air and the earth are curiously mated and intermingled, as if the one were the breath of the other. You feel in the atmosphere the same tonic, puissant quality that is in the tilth, the same strength and resoluteness.

One June morning a young man stood at the gate of the Norwegian graveyard, sharpening his scythe in strokes unconsciously timed to the tune he was whistling. He wore a flannel cap and duck trousers, and the sleeves of his white flannel shirt were rolled back to the elbow. When he was satisfied with the edge of his blade, he slipped the whetstone into his hip pocket and began to swing his scythe, still whistling, but softly, out of respect to the quiet folk about him. Unconscious respect, probably, for he seemed intent upon his own thoughts, and, like the Gladiator's, they were far away. He was a splendid figure of a boy, tall and straight as a young pine tree, with a handsome head, and stormy gray eyes, deeply set under a serious brow. The space between his two front teeth, which were unusually far apart, gave him the proficiency in whistling for which he was distinguished at college. (He also played the cornet in the University band.)

When the grass required his close attention, or when he had to stoop to cut about a headstone, he paused in his lively air,—the "Jewel" song,—taking it up where he had left it when his scythe swung free again. He was not thinking about the tired pioneers over whom his blade glittered. The old wild country, the struggle in which his sister was destined to succeed while so many men broke their hearts and died, he can scarcely remember. That is all among the dim things of childhood and has been forgotten in the brighter pattern life weaves to-day, in the bright facts of being captain of the track team, and holding the interstate record for the high jump, in the all-suffusing brightness of being twenty-one. Yet sometimes, in the pauses of his work, the young man frowned and looked at the ground with an intentness which suggested that even twenty-one might have its problems.

When he had been mowing the better part of an hour, he heard the rattle of a light cart on the road behind him. Supposing that it was his sister coming back from one of her farms, he kept on with his work. The cart stopped at the gate and a merry contralto voice called, "Almost through, Emil?" He dropped his scythe and went toward the fence, wiping his face and neck with his handkerchief. In the cart sat a young woman who wore driving gauntlets and a wide shade hat, trimmed with red poppies. Her face, too, was rather like a poppy, round and brown, with rich color in her cheeks and lips, and her dancing yellow-brown eyes bubbled with gayety. The wind was flapping her big hat and teasing a curl of her chestnut-colored hair. She shook her head at the tall youth.

"What time did you get over here? That's not much of a job for an athlete. Here I've been to town and back. Alexandra lets you sleep late. Oh, I know! Lou's wife was telling me about the way she spoils you. I was going to give you a lift, if you were done." She gathered up her reins.

"But I will be, in a minute. Please wait for me, Marie," Emil coaxed. "Alexandra sent me to mow our lot, but I've done half a dozen others, you see. Just wait till I finish off the Kourdnas'. By the way, they were Bohemians. Why aren't they up in the Catholic graveyard?"

"Free-thinkers," replied the young woman laconically.

"Lots of the Bohemian boys at the University are," said Emil, taking up his scythe again. "What did you ever burn John Huss for, anyway? It's made an awful row. They still jaw about it in history classes."

"We'd do it right over again, most of us," said the young woman hotly. "Don't they ever teach you in your history classes that you'd all be heathen Turks if it hadn't been for the Bohemians?"

Emil had fallen to mowing. "Oh, there's no denying you're a spunky little bunch, you Czechs," he called back over his shoulder.

Marie Shabata settled herself in her seat and watched the rhythmical movement of the young man's long arms, swinging her foot as if in time to some air that was going through her mind. The minutes passed. Emil mowed vigorously and Marie sat sunning herself and watching the long grass fall. She sat with the ease that belongs to persons of an essentially happy nature, who can find a comfortable spot almost anywhere; who are supple, and quick in adapting themselves to circumstances. After a final swish, Emil snapped the gate and sprang into the cart, holding his scythe well out over the wheel. "There," he sighed. "I gave old man Lee a cut or so, too. Lou's wife needn't talk. I never see Lou's scythe over here."

Marie clucked to her horse. "Oh, you know Annie!" She looked at the young man's bare arms. "How brown you've got since you came home. I wish I had an athlete to mow my orchard. I get wet to my knees when I go down to pick cherries."

"You can have one, any time you want him. Better wait until after it rains." Emil squinted off at the horizon as if he were looking for clouds.

"Will you? Oh, there's a good boy!" She turned her head to him with a quick, bright smile. He felt it rather than saw it. Indeed, he had looked away with the purpose of not seeing it. "I've been up looking at Angelique's wedding clothes," Marie went on, "and I'm so excited I can hardly wait until Sunday. Amedee will be a handsome bridegroom. Is anybody but you going to stand up with him? Well, then it will be a handsome wedding party." She made a droll face at Emil, who flushed. "Frank," Marie continued, flicking her horse, "is cranky at me because I loaned his saddle to Jan Smirka, and I'm terribly afraid he won't take me to the dance in the evening. Maybe the supper will tempt him. All Angelique's folks are baking for it, and all Amedee's twenty cousins. There will be barrels of beer. If once I get Frank to the supper, I'll see that I stay for the dance. And by the way, Emil, you mustn't dance with me but once or twice. You must dance with all the French girls. It hurts their feelings if you don't. They think you're proud because you've been away to school or something."

Emil sniffed. "How do you know they think that?"

"Well, you didn't dance with them much at Raoul Marcel's party, and I could tell how they took it by the way they looked at you—and at me."

"All right," said Emil shortly, studying the glittering blade of his scythe.

They drove westward toward Norway Creek, and toward a big white house that stood on a hill, several miles across the fields. There were so many sheds and outbuildings grouped about it that the place looked not unlike a tiny village. A stranger, approaching it, could not help noticing the beauty and fruitfulness of the outlying fields. There was something individual about the great farm, a most unusual trimness and care for detail. On either side of the road, for a mile before you reached the foot of the hill, stood tall osage orange hedges, their glossy green marking off the yellow fields. South of the hill, in a low, sheltered swale, surrounded by a mulberry hedge, was the orchard, its fruit trees knee-deep in timothy grass. Any one thereabouts would have told you that this was one of the richest farms on the Divide, and that the farmer was a woman, Alexandra Bergson.

If you go up the hill and enter Alexandra's big house, you will find that it is curiously unfinished and uneven in comfort. One room is papered, carpeted, over-furnished; the next is almost bare. The pleasantest rooms in the house are the kitchen—where Alexandra's three young Swedish girls chatter and cook and pickle and preserve all summer long—and the sitting-room, in which Alexandra has brought together the old homely furniture that the Bergsons used in their first log house, the family portraits, and the few things her mother brought from Sweden.

When you go out of the house into the flower garden, there you feel again the order and fine arrangement manifest all over the great farm; in the fencing and hedging, in the windbreaks and sheds, in the symmetrical pasture ponds, planted with scrub willows to give shade to the cattle in fly-time. There is even a white row of beehives in the orchard, under the walnut trees. You feel that, properly, Alexandra's house is the big out-of-doors, and that it is in the soil that she expresses herself best.

II.

Emil reached home a little past noon, and when he went into the kitchen Alexandra was already seated at the head of the long table, having dinner with her men, as she always did unless there were visitors. He slipped into his empty place at his sister's right. The three pretty young Swedish girls who did Alexandra's housework were cutting pies, refilling coffeecups, placing platters of bread and meat and potatoes upon the red tablecloth, and continually getting in each other's way between the table and the stove. To be sure they always wasted a good deal of time getting in each other's way and giggling at each other's mistakes. But, as Alexandra had pointedly told her sisters-in-law, it was to hear them giggle that she kept three young things in her kitchen; the work she could do herself, if it were necessary. These girls, with their long letters from home, their finery, and their love-affairs, afforded her a great deal of entertainment, and they were company for her when Emil was away at school.

Of the youngest girl, Signa, who has a pretty figure, mottled pink cheeks, and yellow hair, Alexandra is very fond, though she keeps a sharp eye upon her. Signa is apt to be skittish at mealtime, when the men are about, and to spill the coffee or upset the cream. It is supposed that Nelse Jensen, one of the six men at the dinner-table, is courting Signa, though he has been so careful not to commit himself that no one in the house, least of all Signa, can tell just how far the matter has progressed. Nelse watches her glumly as she waits upon the table, and in the evening he sits on a bench behind the stove with his DRAGHARMONIKA, playing mournful airs and watching her as she goes about her work. When Alexandra asked Signa whether she thought Nelse was in earnest, the poor child hid her hands under her apron and murmured, "I don't know, ma'm. But he scolds me about everything, like as if he wanted to have me!"

At Alexandra's left sat a very old man, barefoot and wearing a long blue blouse, open at the neck. His shaggy head is scarcely whiter than it was sixteen years ago, but his little blue eyes have become pale and watery, and his ruddy face is withered, like an apple that has clung all winter to the tree. When Ivar lost his land through mismanagement a dozen years ago, Alexandra took him in, and he has been a member of her household ever since. He is too old to work in the fields, but he hitches and unhitches the work-teams and looks after the health of the stock. Sometimes of a winter evening Alexandra calls him into the sitting-room to read the Bible aloud to her, for he still reads very well. He dislikes human habitations, so Alexandra has fitted him up a room in the barn, where he is very comfortable, being near the horses and, as he says, further from temptations. No one has ever found out what his temptations are. In cold weather he sits by the kitchen fire and makes hammocks or mends harness until it is time to go to bed. Then he says his prayers at great length behind the stove, puts on his buffalo-skin coat and goes out to his room in the barn.

Alexandra herself has changed very little. Her figure is fuller, and she has more color. She seems sunnier and more vigorous than she did as a young girl. But she still has the same calmness and deliberation of manner, the same clear eyes, and she still wears her hair in two braids wound round her head. It is so curly that fiery ends escape from the braids and make her head look like one of the big double sunflowers that fringe her vegetable garden. Her face is always tanned in summer, for her sunbonnet is oftener on her arm than on her head.

But where her collar falls away from her neck, or where her sleeves are pushed back from her wrist, the skin is of such smoothness and whiteness as none but Swedish women ever possess; skin with the freshness of the snow itself.

Alexandra did not talk much at the table, but she encouraged her men to talk, and she always listened attentively, even when they seemed to be talking foolishly.

To-day Barney Flinn, the big red-headed Irishman who had been with Alexandra for five years and who was actually her foreman, though he had no such title, was grumbling about the new silo she had put up that spring. It happened to be the first silo on the Divide, and Alexandra's neighbors and her men were skeptical about it. "To be sure, if the thing don't work, we'll have plenty of feed without it, indeed," Barney conceded.

Nelse Jensen, Signa's gloomy suitor, had his word. "Lou, he says he wouldn't have no silo on his place if you'd give it to him. He says the feed outen it gives the stock the bloat. He heard of somebody lost four head of horses, feedin' 'em that stuff."

Alexandra looked down the table from one to another. "Well, the only way we can find out is to try. Lou and I have different notions about feeding stock, and that's a good thing. It's bad if all the members of a family think alike. They never get anywhere. Lou can learn by my mistakes and I can learn by his. Isn't that fair, Barney?"

The Irishman laughed. He had no love for Lou, who was always uppish with him and who said that Alexandra paid her hands too much. "I've no thought but to give the thing an honest try, mum. 'T would be only right, after puttin' so much expense into it. Maybe Emil will come out an' have a look at it wid me." He pushed back his chair, took his hat from the nail, and marched out with Emil, who, with his university ideas, was supposed to have instigated the silo. The other hands followed them, all except old Ivar. He had been depressed throughout the meal and had paid no heed to the talk of the men, even when they mentioned cornstalk bloat, upon which he was sure to have opinions.

"Did you want to speak to me, Ivar?" Alexandra asked as she rose from the table. "Come into the sitting-room."

The old man followed Alexandra, but when she motioned him to a chair he shook his head. She took up her workbasket and waited for him to speak. He stood looking at the carpet, his bushy head bowed, his hands clasped in front of him. Ivar's bandy legs seemed to have grown shorter with years, and they were completely misfitted to his broad, thick body and heavy shoulders.

"Well, Ivar, what is it?" Alexandra asked after she had waited longer than usual.

Ivar had never learned to speak English and his Norwegian was quaint and grave, like the speech of the more old-fashioned people. He always addressed Alexandra in terms of the deepest respect, hoping to set a good example to the kitchen girls, whom he thought too familiar in their manners.

"Mistress," he began faintly, without raising his eyes, "the folk have been looking coldly at me of late. You know there has been talk."

"Talk about what, Ivar?"

"About sending me away; to the asylum."

Alexandra put down her sewing-basket. "Nobody has come to me with such talk," she said decidedly. "Why need you listen? You know I would never consent to such a thing."

Ivar lifted his shaggy head and looked at her out of his little eyes. "They say that you cannot prevent it if the folk complain of me, if your brothers complain to the authorities. They say that your brothers are afraid—God forbid!—that I may do you some injury when my spells are on me. Mistress, how can any one think that?—that I could bite the hand that fed me!" The tears trickled down on the old man's beard.

Alexandra frowned. "Ivar, I wonder at you, that you should come bothering me with such nonsense. I am still running my own house, and other people have nothing to do with either you or me. So long as I am suited with you, there is nothing to be said."

Ivar pulled a red handkerchief out of the breast of his blouse and wiped his eyes and beard. "But I should not wish you to keep me if, as they say, it is against your interests, and if it is hard for you to get hands because I am here."

Alexandra made an impatient gesture, but the old man put out his hand and went on earnestly:—

"Listen, mistress, it is right that you should take these things into account. You know that my spells come from God, and that I would not harm any living creature. You believe that every one should worship God in the way revealed to him. But that is not the way of this country. The way here is for all to do alike. I am despised because I do not wear shoes, because I do not cut my hair, and because I have visions. At home, in the old country, there were many like me, who had been touched by God, or who had seen things in the graveyard at night and were different afterward. We thought nothing of it, and let them alone. But here, if a man is different in his feet or in his head, they put him in the asylum. Look at Peter Kralik; when he was a boy, drinking out of a creek, he swallowed a snake, and always after that he could eat only such food as the creature liked, for when he ate anything else, it became enraged and gnawed him. When he felt it whipping about in him, he drank alcohol to stupefy it and get some ease for himself. He could work as good as any man, and his head was clear, but they locked him up for being different in his stomach. That is the way; they have built the asylum for people who are different, and they will not even let us live in the holes with the badgers. Only your great prosperity has protected me so far. If you had had ill-fortune, they would have taken me to Hastings long ago."

As Ivar talked, his gloom lifted. Alexandra had found that she could often break his fasts and long penances by talking to him and letting him pour out the thoughts that troubled him. Sympathy always cleared his mind, and ridicule was poison to him.

"There is a great deal in what you say, Ivar. Like as not they will be wanting to take me to Hastings because I have built a silo; and then I may take you with me. But at present I need you here. Only don't come to me again telling me what people say. Let people go on talking as they like, and we will go on living as we think best. You have been with me now for twelve years, and I have gone to you for advice oftener than I have ever gone to any one. That ought to satisfy you."

Ivar bowed humbly. "Yes, mistress, I shall not trouble you with their talk again. And as for my feet, I have observed your wishes all these years, though you have never questioned me; washing them every night, even in winter."

Alexandra laughed. "Oh, never mind about your feet, Ivar. We can remember when half our neighbors went barefoot in summer. I expect old Mrs. Lee would love to slip her shoes off now sometimes, if she dared. I'm glad I'm not Lou's mother-in-law."

Ivar looked about mysteriously and lowered his voice almost to a whisper. "You know what they have over at Lou's house? A great white tub, like the stone water-troughs in the old country, to wash themselves in. When you sent me over with the strawberries, they were all in town but the old woman Lee and the baby. She took me in and showed me the thing, and she told me it was impossible to wash yourself clean in it, because, in so much water, you could not make a strong suds. So when they fill it up and send her in there, she pretends, and makes a splashing noise. Then, when they are all asleep, she washes herself in a little wooden tub she keeps under her bed."

Alexandra shook with laughter. "Poor old Mrs. Lee! They won't let her wear nightcaps, either. Never mind, when she comes to visit me, she can do all the old things in the old way, and have as much beer as she wants. We'll start an asylum for old-time people, Ivar."

Ivar folded his big handkerchief carefully and thrust it back into his blouse. "This is always the way, mistress. I come to you sorrowing, and you send me away with a light heart. And will you be so good as to tell the Irishman that he is not to work the brown gelding until the sore on its shoulder is healed?"

"That I will. Now go and put Emil's mare to the cart. I am going to drive up to the north quarter to meet the man from town who is to buy my alfalfa hay."

III.

Alexandra was to hear more of Ivar's case, however. On Sunday her married brothers came to dinner. She had asked them for that day because Emil, who hated family parties, would be absent, dancing at Amedee Chevalier's wedding, up in the French country. The table was set for company in the dining-room, where highly varnished wood and colored glass and useless pieces of china were conspicuous enough to satisfy the standards of the new prosperity. Alexandra had put herself into the hands of the Hanover furniture dealer, and he had conscientiously done his best to make her dining-room look like his display window. She said frankly that she knew nothing about such things, and she was willing to be governed by the general conviction that the more useless and utterly unusable objects were, the greater their virtue as ornament. That seemed reasonable enough. Since she liked plain things herself, it was all the more necessary to have jars and punchbowls and candlesticks in the company rooms for people who did appreciate them. Her guests liked to see about them these reassuring emblems of prosperity.

The family party was complete except for Emil, and Oscar's wife who, in the country phrase, "was not going anywhere just now." Oscar sat at the foot of the table and his four tow-headed little boys, aged from twelve to five, were ranged at one side. Neither Oscar nor Lou has changed much; they have simply, as Alexandra said of them long ago, grown to be more and more like themselves. Lou now looks the older of the two; his face is thin and shrewd and wrinkled about the eyes, while Oscar's is thick and dull. For all his dullness, however, Oscar makes more money than his brother, which adds to Lou's sharpness and uneasiness and tempts him to make a show. The trouble with Lou is that he is tricky, and his neighbors have found out that, as Ivar says, he has not a fox's face for nothing. Politics being the natural field for such talents, he neglects his farm to attend conventions and to run for county offices.

Lou's wife, formerly Annie Lee, has grown to look curiously like her husband. Her face has become longer, sharper, more aggressive. She wears her yellow hair in a high pompadour, and is bedecked with rings and chains and "beauty pins." Her tight, high-heeled shoes give her an awkward walk, and she is always more or less preoccupied with her clothes. As she sat at the table, she kept telling her youngest daughter to "be careful now, and not drop anything on mother."

The conversation at the table was all in English. Oscar's wife, from the malaria district of Missouri, was ashamed of marrying a foreigner, and his boys do not understand a word of Swedish. Annie and Lou sometimes speak Swedish at home, but Annie is almost as much afraid of being "caught" at it as ever her mother was of being caught barefoot. Oscar still has a thick accent, but Lou speaks like anybody from Iowa.

"When I was in Hastings to attend the convention," he was saying, "I saw the superintendent of the asylum, and I was telling him about Ivar's symptoms. He says Ivar's case is one of the most dangerous kind, and it's a wonder he hasn't done something violent before this."

Alexandra laughed good-humoredly. "Oh, nonsense, Lou! The doctors would have us all crazy if they could. Ivar's queer, certainly, but he has more sense than half the hands I hire."

Lou flew at his fried chicken. "Oh, I guess the doctor knows his business, Alexandra. He was very much surprised when I told him how you'd put up with Ivar. He says he's likely to set fire to the barn any night, or to take after you and the girls with an axe."

Little Signa, who was waiting on the table, giggled and fled to the kitchen. Alexandra's eyes twinkled. "That was too much for Signa, Lou. We all know that Ivar's perfectly harmless. The girls would as soon expect me to chase them with an axe."

Lou flushed and signaled to his wife. "All the same, the neighbors will be having a say about it before long. He may burn anybody's barn. It's only necessary for one property-owner in the township to make complaint, and he'll be taken up by force. You'd better send him yourself and not have any hard feelings."

Alexandra helped one of her little nephews to gravy. "Well, Lou, if any of the neighbors try that, I'll have myself appointed Ivar's guardian and take the case to court, that's all. I am perfectly satisfied with him."

"Pass the preserves, Lou," said Annie in a warning tone. She had reasons for not wishing her husband to cross Alexandra too openly. "But don't you sort of hate to have people see him around here, Alexandra?" she went on with persuasive smoothness. "He IS a disgraceful object, and you're fixed up so nice now. It sort of makes people distant with you, when they never know when they'll hear him scratching about. My girls are afraid as death of him, aren't you, Milly, dear?"

Milly was fifteen, fat and jolly and pompadoured, with a creamy complexion, square white teeth, and a short upper lip. She looked like her grandmother Bergson, and had her comfortable and comfort-loving nature. She grinned at her aunt, with whom she was a great deal more at ease than she was with her mother. Alexandra winked a reply.

"Milly needn't be afraid of Ivar. She's an especial favorite of his. In my opinion Ivar has just as much right to his own way of dressing and thinking as we have. But I'll see that he doesn't bother other people. I'll keep him at home, so don't trouble any more about him, Lou. I've been wanting to ask you about your new bathtub. How does it work?"

Annie came to the fore to give Lou time to recover himself. "Oh, it works something grand! I can't keep him out of it. He washes himself all over three times a week now, and uses all the hot water. I think it's weakening to stay in as long as he does. You ought to have one, Alexandra."

"I'm thinking of it. I might have one put in the barn for Ivar, if it will ease people's minds. But before I get a bathtub, I'm going to get a piano for Milly."

Oscar, at the end of the table, looked up from his plate. "What does Milly want of a pianny? What's the matter with her organ? She can make some use of that, and play in church."

Annie looked flustered. She had begged Alexandra not to say anything about this plan before Oscar, who was apt to be jealous of what his sister did for Lou's children. Alexandra did not get on with Oscar's wife at all. "Milly can play in church just the same, and she'll still play on the organ. But practising on it so much spoils her touch. Her teacher says so," Annie brought out with spirit.

Oscar rolled his eyes. "Well, Milly must have got on pretty good if she's got past the organ. I know plenty of grown folks that ain't," he said bluntly.

Annie threw up her chin. "She has got on good, and she's going to play for her commencement when she graduates in town next year."

"Yes," said Alexandra firmly, "I think Milly deserves a piano. All the girls around here have been taking lessons for years, but Milly is the only one of them who can ever play anything when you ask her. I'll tell you when I first thought I would like to give you a piano, Milly, and that was when you learned that book of old Swedish songs that your grandfather used to sing. He had a sweet tenor voice, and when he was a young man he loved to sing. I can remember hearing him singing with the sailors down in the shipyard, when I was no bigger than Stella here," pointing to Annie's younger daughter.

Milly and Stella both looked through the door into the sitting-room, where a crayon portrait of John Bergson hung on the wall. Alexandra had had it made from a little photograph, taken for his friends just before he left Sweden; a slender man of thirty-five, with soft hair curling about his high forehead, a drooping mustache, and wondering, sad eyes that looked forward into the distance, as if they already beheld the New World.

After dinner Lou and Oscar went to the orchard to pick cherries—they had neither of them had the patience to grow an orchard of their own—and Annie went down to gossip with Alexandra's kitchen girls while they washed the dishes. She could always find out more about Alexandra's domestic economy from the prattling maids than from Alexandra herself, and what she discovered she used to her own advantage with Lou. On the Divide, farmers' daughters no longer went out into service, so Alexandra got her girls from Sweden, by paying their fare over. They stayed with her until they married, and were replaced by sisters or cousins from the old country.

Alexandra took her three nieces into the flower garden. She was fond of the little girls, especially of Milly, who came to spend a week with her aunt now and then, and read aloud to her from the old books about the house, or listened to stories about the early days on the Divide. While they were walking among the flower beds, a buggy drove up the hill and stopped in front of the gate. A man got out and stood talking to the driver. The little girls were delighted at the advent of a stranger, some one from very far away, they knew by his clothes, his gloves, and the sharp, pointed cut of his dark beard. The girls fell behind their aunt and peeped out at him from among the castor beans. The stranger came up to the gate and stood holding his hat in his hand, smiling, while Alexandra advanced slowly to meet him. As she approached he spoke in a low, pleasant voice.

"Don't you know me, Alexandra? I would have known you, anywhere."

Alexandra shaded her eyes with her hand. Suddenly she took a quick step forward. "Can it be!" she exclaimed with feeling; "can it be that it is Carl Linstrum? Why, Carl, it is!" She threw out both her hands and caught his across the gate. "Sadie, Milly, run tell your father and Uncle Oscar that our old friend Carl Linstrum is here. Be quick! Why, Carl, how did it happen? I can't believe this!" Alexandra shook the tears from her eyes and laughed.

The stranger nodded to his driver, dropped his suitcase inside the fence, and opened the gate. "Then you are glad to see me, and you can put me up overnight? I couldn't go through this country without stopping off to have a look at you. How little you have changed! Do you know, I was sure it would be like that. You simply couldn't be different. How fine you are!" He stepped back and looked at her admiringly.

Alexandra blushed and laughed again. "But you yourself, Carl—with that beard—how could I have known you? You went away a little boy." She reached for his suitcase and when he intercepted her she threw up her hands. "You see, I give myself away. I have only women come to visit me, and I do not know how to behave. Where is your trunk?"

"It's in Hanover. I can stay only a few days. I am on my way to the coast."

They started up the path. "A few days? After all these years!" Alexandra shook her finger at him. "See this, you have walked into a trap. You do not get away so easy." She put her hand affectionately on his shoulder. "You owe me a visit for the sake of old times. Why must you go to the coast at all?"

"Oh, I must! I am a fortune hunter. From Seattle I go on to Alaska."

"Alaska?" She looked at him in astonishment. "Are you going to paint the Indians?"

"Paint?" the young man frowned. "Oh! I'm not a painter, Alexandra. I'm an engraver. I have nothing to do with painting."

"But on my parlor wall I have the paintings—"

He interrupted nervously. "Oh, water-color sketches—done for amusement. I sent them to remind you of me, not because they were good. What a wonderful place you have made of this, Alexandra." He turned and looked back at the wide, map-like prospect of field and hedge and pasture. "I would never have believed it could be done. I'm disappointed in my own eye, in my imagination."

At this moment Lou and Oscar came up the hill from the orchard. They did not quicken their pace when they saw Carl; indeed, they did not openly look in his direction. They advanced distrustfully, and as if they wished the distance were longer.

Alexandra beckoned to them. "They think I am trying to fool them. Come, boys, it's Carl Linstrum, our old Carl!"

Lou gave the visitor a quick, sidelong glance and thrust out his hand. "Glad to see you."

Oscar followed with "How d' do." Carl could not tell whether their offishness came from unfriendliness or from embarrassment. He and Alexandra led the way to the porch.

"Carl," Alexandra explained, "is on his way to Seattle. He is going to Alaska."

Oscar studied the visitor's yellow shoes. "Got business there?" he asked.

Carl laughed. "Yes, very pressing business. I'm going there to get rich. Engraving's a very interesting profession, but a man never makes any money at it. So I'm going to try the goldfields."

Alexandra felt that this was a tactful speech, and Lou looked up with some interest. "Ever done anything in that line before?"

"No, but I'm going to join a friend of mine who went out from New York and has done well. He has offered to break me in."

"Turrible cold winters, there, I hear," remarked Oscar. "I thought people went up there in the spring."

"They do. But my friend is going to spend the winter in Seattle and I am to stay with him there and learn something about prospecting before we start north next year."

Lou looked skeptical. "Let's see, how long have you been away from here?"

"Sixteen years. You ought to remember that, Lou, for you were married just after we went away."

"Going to stay with us some time?" Oscar asked.

"A few days, if Alexandra can keep me."

"I expect you'll be wanting to see your old place," Lou observed more cordially. "You won't hardly know it. But there's a few chunks of your old sod house left. Alexandra wouldn't never let Frank Shabata plough over it."

Annie Lee, who, ever since the visitor was announced, had been touching up her hair and settling her lace and wishing she had worn another dress, now emerged with her three daughters and introduced them. She was greatly impressed by Carl's urban appearance, and in her excitement talked very loud and threw her head about. "And you ain't married yet? At your age, now! Think of that! You'll have to wait for Milly. Yes, we've got a boy, too. The youngest. He's at home with his grandma. You must come over to see mother and hear Milly play. She's the musician of the family. She does pyrography, too. That's burnt wood, you know. You wouldn't believe what she can do with her poker. Yes, she goes to school in town, and she is the youngest in her class by two years."

Milly looked uncomfortable and Carl took her hand again. He liked her creamy skin and happy, innocent eyes, and he could see that her mother's way of talking distressed her. "I'm sure she's a clever little girl," he murmured, looking at her thoughtfully. "Let me see—Ah, it's your mother that she looks like, Alexandra. Mrs. Bergson must have looked just like this when she was a little girl. Does Milly run about over the country as you and Alexandra used to, Annie?"

Milly's mother protested. "Oh, my, no! Things has changed since we was girls. Milly has it very different. We are going to rent the place and move into town as soon as the girls are old enough to go out into company. A good many are doing that here now. Lou is going into business."

Lou grinned. "That's what she says. You better go get your things on. Ivar's hitching up," he added, turning to Annie.

Young farmers seldom address their wives by name. It is always "you," or "she."

Having got his wife out of the way, Lou sat down on the step and began to whittle. "Well, what do folks in New York think of William Jennings Bryan?" Lou began to bluster, as he always did when he talked politics. "We gave Wall Street a scare in ninety-six, all right, and we're fixing another to hand them. Silver wasn't the only issue," he nodded mysteriously. "There's a good many things got to be changed. The West is going to make itself heard."

Carl laughed. "But, surely, it did do that, if nothing else."

Lou's thin face reddened up to the roots of his bristly hair. "Oh, we've only begun. We're waking up to a sense of our responsibilities, out here, and we ain't afraid, neither. You fellows back there must be a tame lot. If you had any nerve you'd get together and march down to Wall Street and blow it up. Dynamite it, I mean," with a threatening nod.

He was so much in earnest that Carl scarcely knew how to answer him. "That would be a waste of powder. The same business would go on in another street. The street doesn't matter. But what have you fellows out here got to kick about? You have the only safe place there is. Morgan himself couldn't touch you. One only has to drive through this country to see that you're all as rich as barons."

"We have a good deal more to say than we had when we were poor," said Lou threateningly. "We're getting on to a whole lot of things."

As Ivar drove a double carriage up to the gate, Annie came out in a hat that looked like the model of a battleship. Carl rose and took her down to the carriage, while Lou lingered for a word with his sister.

"What do you suppose he's come for?" he asked, jerking his head toward the gate.

"Why, to pay us a visit. I've been begging him to for years."

Oscar looked at Alexandra. "He didn't let you know he was coming?"

"No. Why should he? I told him to come at any time."

Lou shrugged his shoulders. "He doesn't seem to have done much for himself. Wandering around this way!"

Oscar spoke solemnly, as from the depths of a cavern. "He never was much account."

Alexandra left them and hurried down to the gate where Annie was rattling on to Carl about her new dining-room furniture. "You must bring Mr. Linstrum over real soon, only be sure to telephone me first," she called back, as Carl helped her into the carriage. Old Ivar, his white head bare, stood holding the horses. Lou came down the path and climbed into the front seat, took up the reins, and drove off without saying anything further to any one. Oscar picked up his youngest boy and trudged off down the road, the other three trotting after him. Carl, holding the gate open for Alexandra, began to laugh. "Up and coming on the Divide, eh, Alexandra?" he cried gayly.

IV.

Carl had changed, Alexandra felt, much less than one might have expected. He had not become a trim, self-satisfied city man. There was still something homely and wayward and definitely personal about him. Even his clothes, his Norfolk coat and his very high collars, were a little unconventional. He seemed to shrink into himself as he used to do; to hold himself away from things, as if he were afraid of being hurt. In short, he was more self-conscious than a man of thirty-five is expected to be. He looked older than his years and not very strong. His black hair, which still hung in a triangle over his pale forehead, was thin at the crown, and there were fine, relentless lines about his eyes. His back, with its high, sharp shoulders, looked like the back of an over-worked German professor off on his holiday. His face was intelligent, sensitive, unhappy.

That evening after supper, Carl and Alexandra were sitting by the clump of castor beans in the middle of the flower garden. The gravel paths glittered in the moonlight, and below them the fields lay white and still.

"Do you know, Alexandra," he was saying, "I've been thinking how strangely things work out. I've been away engraving other men's pictures, and you've stayed at home and made your own." He pointed with his cigar toward the sleeping landscape. "How in the world have you done it? How have your neighbors done it?"

"We hadn't any of us much to do with it, Carl. The land did it. It had its little joke. It pretended to be poor because nobody knew how to work it right; and then, all at once, it worked itself. It woke up out of its sleep and stretched itself, and it was so big, so rich, that we suddenly found we were rich, just from sitting still. As for me, you remember when I began to buy land. For years after that I was always squeezing and borrowing until I was ashamed to show my face in the banks. And then, all at once, men began to come to me offering to lend me money—and I didn't need it! Then I went ahead and built this house. I really built it for Emil. I want you to see Emil, Carl. He is so different from the rest of us!"

"How different?"

"Oh, you'll see! I'm sure it was to have sons like Emil, and to give them a chance, that father left the old country. It's curious, too; on the outside Emil is just like an American boy, —he graduated from the State University in June, you know,—but underneath he is more Swedish than any of us. Sometimes he is so like father that he frightens me; he is so violent in his feelings like that."

"Is he going to farm here with you?"

"He shall do whatever he wants to," Alexandra declared warmly. "He is going to have a chance, a whole chance; that's what I've worked for. Sometimes he talks about studying law, and sometimes, just lately, he's been talking about going out into the sand hills and taking up more land. He has his sad times, like father. But I hope he won't do that. We have land enough, at last!" Alexandra laughed.

"How about Lou and Oscar? They've done well, haven't they?"

"Yes, very well; but they are different, and now that they have farms of their own I do not see so much of them. We divided the land equally when Lou married. They have their own way of doing things, and they do not altogether like my way, I am afraid. Perhaps they think me too independent. But I have had to think for myself a good many years and am not likely to change. On the whole, though, we take as much comfort in each other as most brothers and sisters do. And I am very fond of Lou's oldest daughter."

"I think I liked the old Lou and Oscar better, and they probably feel the same about me. I even, if you can keep a secret,"—Carl leaned forward and touched her arm, smiling, —"I even think I liked the old country better. This is all very splendid in its way, but there was something about this country when it was a wild old beast that has haunted me all these years. Now, when I come back to all this milk and honey, I feel like the old German song, 'Wo bist du, wo bist du, mein geliebtest Land?'—Do you ever feel like that, I wonder?"

"Yes, sometimes, when I think about father and mother and those who are gone; so many of our old neighbors." Alexandra paused and looked up thoughtfully at the stars. "We can remember the graveyard when it was wild prairie, Carl, and now—"

"And now the old story has begun to write itself over there," said Carl softly. "Isn't it queer: there are only two or three human stories, and they go on repeating themselves as fiercely as if they had never happened before; like the larks in this country, that have been singing the same five notes over for thousands of years."

"Oh, yes! The young people, they live so hard. And yet I sometimes envy them. There is my little neighbor, now; the people who bought your old place. I wouldn't have sold it to any one else, but I was always fond of that girl. You must remember her, little Marie Tovesky, from Omaha, who used to visit here? When she was eighteen she ran away from the convent school and got married, crazy child! She came out here a bride, with her father and husband. He had nothing, and the old man was willing to buy them a place and set them up. Your farm took her fancy, and I was glad to have her so near me. I've never been sorry, either. I even try to get along with Frank on her account."

"Is Frank her husband?"

"Yes. He's one of these wild fellows. Most Bohemians are good-natured, but Frank thinks we don't appreciate him here, I guess. He's jealous about everything, his farm and his horses and his pretty wife. Everybody likes her, just the same as when she was little. Sometimes I go up to the Catholic church with Emil, and it's funny to see Marie standing there laughing and shaking hands with people, looking so excited and gay, with Frank sulking behind her as if he could eat everybody alive. Frank's not a bad neighbor, but to get on with him you've got to make a fuss over him and act as if you thought he was a very important person all the time, and different from other people. I find it hard to keep that up from one year's end to another."

"I shouldn't think you'd be very successful at that kind of thing, Alexandra." Carl seemed to find the idea amusing.

"Well," said Alexandra firmly, "I do the best I can, on Marie's account. She has it hard enough, anyway. She's too young and pretty for this sort of life. We're all ever so much older and slower. But she's the kind that won't be downed easily. She'll work all day and go to a Bohemian wedding and dance all night, and drive the hay wagon for a cross man next morning. I could stay by a job, but I never had the go in me that she has, when I was going my best. I'll have to take you over to see her to-morrow."

Carl dropped the end of his cigar softly among the castor beans and sighed. "Yes, I suppose I must see the old place. I'm cowardly about things that remind me of myself. It took courage to come at all, Alexandra. I wouldn't have, if I hadn't wanted to see you very, very much."

Alexandra looked at him with her calm, deliberate eyes. "Why do you dread things like that, Carl?" she asked earnestly. "Why are you dissatisfied with yourself?"

Her visitor winced. "How direct you are, Alexandra! Just like you used to be. Do I give myself away so quickly? Well, you see, for one thing, there's nothing to look forward to in my profession. Wood-engraving is the only thing I care about, and that had gone out before I began. Everything's cheap metal work nowadays, touching up miserable photographs, forcing up poor drawings, and spoiling good ones. I'm absolutely sick of it all." Carl frowned. "Alexandra, all the way out from New York I've been planning how I could deceive you and make you think me a very enviable fellow, and here I am telling you the truth the first night. I waste a lot of time pretending to people, and the joke of it is, I don't think I ever deceive any one. There are too many of my kind; people know us on sight."

Carl paused. Alexandra pushed her hair back from her brow with a puzzled, thoughtful gesture. "You see," he went on calmly, "measured by your standards here, I'm a failure. I couldn't buy even one of your cornfields. I've enjoyed a great many things, but I've got nothing to show for it all."

"But you show for it yourself, Carl. I'd rather have had your freedom than my land."

Carl shook his head mournfully. "Freedom so often means that one isn't needed anywhere. Here you are an individual, you have a background of your own, you would be missed. But off there in the cities there are thousands of rolling stones like me. We are all alike; we have no ties, we know nobody, we own nothing. When one of us dies, they scarcely know where to bury him. Our landlady and the delicatessen man are our mourners, and we leave nothing behind us but a frock-coat and a fiddle, or an easel, or a typewriter, or whatever tool we got our living by. All we have ever managed to do is to pay our rent, the exorbitant rent that one has to pay for a few square feet of space near the heart of things. We have no house, no place, no people of our own. We live in the streets, in the parks, in the theatres. We sit in restaurants and concert halls and look about at the hundreds of our own kind and shudder."

Alexandra was silent. She sat looking at the silver spot the moon made on the surface of the pond down in the pasture. He knew that she understood what he meant. At last she said slowly, "And yet I would rather have Emil grow up like that than like his two brothers. We pay a high rent, too, though we pay differently. We grow hard and heavy here. We don't move lightly and easily as you do, and our minds get stiff. If the world were no wider than my cornfields, if there were not something beside this, I wouldn't feel that it was much worth while to work. No, I would rather have Emil like you than like them. I felt that as soon as you came."

"I wonder why you feel like that?" Carl mused.

"I don't know. Perhaps I am like Carrie Jensen, the sister of one of my hired men. She had never been out of the cornfields, and a few years ago she got despondent and said life was just the same thing over and over, and she didn't see the use of it. After she had tried to kill herself once or twice, her folks got worried and sent her over to Iowa to visit some relations. Ever since she's come back she's been perfectly cheerful, and she says she's contented to live and work in a world that's so big and interesting. She said that anything as big as the bridges over the Platte and the Missouri reconciled her. And it's what goes on in the world that reconciles me."

V.

Alexandra did not find time to go to her neighbor's the next day, nor the next. It was a busy season on the farm, with the corn-plowing going on, and even Emil was in the field with a team and cultivator. Carl went about over the farms with Alexandra in the morning, and in the afternoon and evening they found a great deal to talk about. Emil, for all his track practice, did not stand up under farmwork very well, and by night he was too tired to talk or even to practise on his cornet.

On Wednesday morning Carl got up before it was light, and stole downstairs and out of the kitchen door just as old Ivar was making his morning ablutions at the pump. Carl nodded to him and hurried up the draw, past the garden, and into the pasture where the milking cows used to be kept.

The dawn in the east looked like the light from some great fire that was burning under the edge of the world. The color was reflected in the globules of dew that sheathed the short gray pasture grass. Carl walked rapidly until he came to the crest of the second hill, where the Bergson pasture joined the one that had belonged to his father. There he sat down and waited for the sun to rise. It was just there that he and Alexandra used to do their milking together, he on his side of the fence, she on hers. He could remember exactly how she looked when she came over the close-cropped grass, her skirts pinned up, her head bare, a bright tin pail in either hand, and the milky light of the early morning all about her. Even as a boy he used to feel, when he saw her coming with her free step, her upright head and calm shoulders, that she looked as if she had walked straight out of the morning itself. Since then, when he had happened to see the sun come up in the country or on the water, he had often remembered the young Swedish girl and her milking pails.

Carl sat musing until the sun leaped above the prairie, and in the grass about him all the small creatures of day began to tune their tiny instruments. Birds and insects without number began to chirp, to twitter, to snap and whistle, to make all manner of fresh shrill noises. The pasture was flooded with light; every clump of ironweed and snow-on-the-mountain threw a long shadow, and the golden light seemed to be rippling through the curly grass like the tide racing in.

He crossed the fence into the pasture that was now the Shabatas' and continued his walk toward the pond. He had not gone far, however, when he discovered that he was not the only person abroad. In the draw below, his gun in his hands, was Emil, advancing cautiously, with a young woman beside him. They were moving softly, keeping close together, and Carl knew that they expected to find ducks on the pond. At the moment when they came in sight of the bright spot of water, he heard a whirr of wings and the ducks shot up into the air. There was a sharp crack from the gun, and five of the birds fell to the ground. Emil and his companion laughed delightedly, and Emil ran to pick them up. When he came back, dangling the ducks by their feet, Marie held her apron and he dropped them into it. As she stood looking down at them, her face changed. She took up one of the birds, a rumpled ball of feathers with the blood dripping slowly from its mouth, and looked at the live color that still burned on its plumage.

As she let it fall, she cried in distress, "Oh, Emil, why did you?"

"I like that!" the boy exclaimed indignantly. "Why, Marie, you asked me to come yourself."

"Yes, yes, I know," she said tearfully, "but I didn't think. I hate to see them when they are first shot. They were having such a good time, and we've spoiled it all for them."

Emil gave a rather sore laugh. "I should say we had! I'm not going hunting with you any more. You're as bad as Ivar. Here, let me take them." He snatched the ducks out of her apron.

"Don't be cross, Emil. Only—Ivar's right about wild things. They're too happy to kill. You can tell just how they felt when they flew up. They were scared, but they didn't really think anything could hurt them. No, we won't do that any more."

"All right," Emil assented. "I'm sorry I made you feel bad." As he looked down into her tearful eyes, there was a curious, sharp young bitterness in his own.

Carl watched them as they moved slowly down the draw. They had not seen him at all. He had not overheard much of their dialogue, but he felt the import of it. It made him, somehow, unreasonably mournful to find two young things abroad in the pasture in the early morning. He decided that he needed his breakfast.

VI.

At dinner that day Alexandra said she thought they must really manage to go over to the Shabatas' that afternoon. "It's not often I let three days go by without seeing Marie. She will think I have forsaken her, now that my old friend has come back."

After the men had gone back to work, Alexandra put on a white dress and her sun-hat, and she and Carl set forth across the fields. "You see we have kept up the old path, Carl. It has been so nice for me to feel that there was a friend at the other end of it again."

Carl smiled a little ruefully. "All the same, I hope it hasn't been QUITE the same."

Alexandra looked at him with surprise. "Why, no, of course not. Not the same. She could not very well take your place, if that's what you mean. I'm friendly with all my neighbors, I hope. But Marie is really a companion, some one I can talk to quite frankly. You wouldn't want me to be more lonely than I have been, would you?"

Carl laughed and pushed back the triangular lock of hair with the edge of his hat. "Of course I don't. I ought to be thankful that this path hasn't been worn by—well, by friends with more pressing errands than your little Bohemian is likely to have." He paused to give Alexandra his hand as she stepped over the stile. "Are you the least bit disappointed in our coming together again?" he asked abruptly. "Is it the way you hoped it would be?"

Alexandra smiled at this. "Only better. When I've thought about your coming, I've sometimes been a little afraid of it. You have lived where things move so fast, and everything is slow here; the people slowest of all. Our lives are like the years, all made up of weather and crops and cows. How you hated cows!" She shook her head and laughed to herself.

"I didn't when we milked together. I walked up to the pasture corners this morning. I wonder whether I shall ever be able to tell you all that I was thinking about up there. It's a strange thing, Alexandra; I find it easy to be frank with you about everything under the sun except—yourself!"

"You are afraid of hurting my feelings, perhaps." Alexandra looked at him thoughtfully.

"No, I'm afraid of giving you a shock. You've seen yourself for so long in the dull minds of the people about you, that if I were to tell you how you seem to me, it would startle you. But you must see that you astonish me. You must feel when people admire you."

Alexandra blushed and laughed with some confusion. "I felt that you were pleased with me, if you mean that."

"And you've felt when other people were pleased with you?" he insisted.

"Well, sometimes. The men in town, at the banks and the county offices, seem glad to see me. I think, myself, it is more pleasant to do business with people who are clean and healthy-looking," she admitted blandly.

Carl gave a little chuckle as he opened the Shabatas' gate for her. "Oh, do you?" he asked dryly.

There was no sign of life about the Shabatas' house except a big yellow cat, sunning itself on the kitchen doorstep.

Alexandra took the path that led to the orchard. "She often sits there and sews. I didn't telephone her we were coming, because I didn't want her to go to work and bake cake and freeze ice-cream. She'll always make a party if you give her the least excuse. Do you recognize the apple trees, Carl?"

Linstrum looked about him. "I wish I had a dollar for every bucket of water I've carried for those trees. Poor father, he was an easy man, but he was perfectly merciless when it came to watering the orchard."

"That's one thing I like about Germans; they make an orchard grow if they can't make anything else. I'm so glad these trees belong to some one who takes comfort in them. When I rented this place, the tenants never kept the orchard up, and Emil and I used to come over and take care of it ourselves. It needs mowing now. There she is, down in the corner. Maria-a-a!" she called.

A recumbent figure started up from the grass and came running toward them through the flickering screen of light and shade.

"Look at her! Isn't she like a little brown rabbit?" Alexandra laughed.

Maria ran up panting and threw her arms about Alexandra. "Oh, I had begun to think you were not coming at all, maybe. I knew you were so busy. Yes, Emil told me about Mr. Linstrum being here. Won't you come up to the house?"

"Why not sit down there in your corner? Carl wants to see the orchard. He kept all these trees alive for years, watering them with his own back."

Marie turned to Carl. "Then I'm thankful to you, Mr. Linstrum. We'd never have bought the place if it hadn't been for this orchard, and then I wouldn't have had Alexandra, either." She gave Alexandra's arm a little squeeze as she walked beside her. "How nice your dress smells, Alexandra; you put rosemary leaves in your chest, like I told you."

She led them to the northwest corner of the orchard, sheltered on one side by a thick mulberry hedge and bordered on the other by a wheatfield, just beginning to yellow. In this corner the ground dipped a little, and the blue-grass, which the weeds had driven out in the upper part of the orchard, grew thick and luxuriant. Wild roses were flaming in the tufts of bunchgrass along the fence. Under a white mulberry tree there was an old wagon-seat. Beside it lay a book and a workbasket.

"You must have the seat, Alexandra. The grass would stain your dress," the hostess insisted. She dropped down on the ground at Alexandra's side and tucked her feet under her. Carl sat at a little distance from the two women, his back to the wheatfield, and watched them. Alexandra took off her shade-hat and threw it on the ground. Marie picked it up and played with the white ribbons, twisting them about her brown fingers as she talked. They made a pretty picture in the strong sunlight, the leafy pattern surrounding them like a net; the Swedish woman so white and gold, kindly and amused, but armored in calm, and the alert brown one, her full lips parted, points of yellow light dancing in her eyes as she laughed and chattered. Carl had never forgotten little Marie Tovesky's eyes, and he was glad to have an opportunity to study them. The brown iris, he found, was curiously slashed with yellow, the color of sunflower honey, or of old amber. In each eye one of these streaks must have been larger than the others, for the effect was that of two dancing points of light, two little yellow bubbles, such as rise in a glass of champagne. Sometimes they seemed like the sparks from a forge. She seemed so easily excited, to kindle with a fierce little flame if one but breathed upon her. "What a waste," Carl reflected. "She ought to be doing all that for a sweetheart. How awkwardly things come about!"

It was not very long before Marie sprang up out of the grass again. "Wait a moment. I want to show you something." She ran away and disappeared behind the low-growing apple trees.

"What a charming creature," Carl murmured. "I don't wonder that her husband is jealous. But can't she walk? does she always run?"

Alexandra nodded. "Always. I don't see many people, but I don't believe there are many like her, anywhere."

Marie came back with a branch she had broken from an apricot tree, laden with pale yellow, pink-cheeked fruit. She dropped it beside Carl. "Did you plant those, too? They are such beautiful little trees."

Carl fingered the blue-green leaves, porous like blotting-paper and shaped like birch leaves, hung on waxen red stems. "Yes, I think I did. Are these the circus trees, Alexandra?"

"Shall I tell her about them?" Alexandra asked. "Sit down like a good girl, Marie, and don't ruin my poor hat, and I'll tell you a story. A long time ago, when Carl and I were, say, sixteen and twelve, a circus came to Hanover and we went to town in our wagon, with Lou and Oscar, to see the parade. We hadn't money enough to go to the circus. We followed the parade out to the circus grounds and hung around until the show began and the crowd went inside the tent. Then Lou was afraid we looked foolish standing outside in the pasture, so we went back to Hanover feeling very sad. There was a man in the streets selling apricots, and we had never seen any before. He had driven down from somewhere up in the French country, and he was selling them twenty-five cents a peck. We had a little money our fathers had given us for candy, and I bought two pecks and Carl bought one. They cheered us a good deal, and we saved all the seeds and planted them. Up to the time Carl went away, they hadn't borne at all."

"And now he's come back to eat them," cried Marie, nodding at Carl. "That IS a good story. I can remember you a little, Mr. Linstrum. I used to see you in Hanover sometimes, when Uncle Joe took me to town. I remember you because you were always buying pencils and tubes of paint at the drug store. Once, when my uncle left me at the store, you drew a lot of little birds and flowers for me on a piece of wrapping-paper. I kept them for a long while. I thought you were very romantic because you could draw and had such black eyes."

Carl smiled. "Yes, I remember that time. Your uncle bought you some kind of a mechanical toy, a Turkish lady sitting on an ottoman and smoking a hookah, wasn't it? And she turned her head backwards and forwards."

"Oh, yes! Wasn't she splendid! I knew well enough I ought not to tell Uncle Joe I wanted it, for he had just come back from the saloon and was feeling good. You remember how he laughed? She tickled him, too. But when we got home, my aunt scolded him for buying toys when she needed so many things. We wound our lady up every night, and when she began to move her head my aunt used to laugh as hard as any of us. It was a music-box, you know, and the Turkish lady played a tune while she smoked. That was how she made you feel so jolly. As I remember her, she was lovely, and had a gold crescent on her turban."

Half an hour later, as they were leaving the house, Carl and Alexandra were met in the path by a strapping fellow in overalls and a blue shirt. He was breathing hard, as if he had been running, and was muttering to himself.

Marie ran forward, and, taking him by the arm, gave him a little push toward her guests. "Frank, this is Mr. Linstrum."

Frank took off his broad straw hat and nodded to Alexandra. When he spoke to Carl, he showed a fine set of white teeth. He was burned a dull red down to his neckband, and there was a heavy three-days' stubble on his face. Even in his agitation he was handsome, but he looked a rash and violent man.

Barely saluting the callers, he turned at once to his wife and began, in an outraged tone, "I have to leave my team to drive the old woman Hiller's hogs out-a my wheat. I go to take dat old woman to de court if she ain't careful, I tell you!"

His wife spoke soothingly. "But, Frank, she has only her lame boy to help her. She does the best she can."

Alexandra looked at the excited man and offered a suggestion. "Why don't you go over there some afternoon and hog-tight her fences? You'd save time for yourself in the end."

Frank's neck stiffened. "Not-a-much, I won't. I keep my hogs home. Other peoples can do like me. See? If that Louis can mend shoes, he can mend fence."

"Maybe," said Alexandra placidly; "but I've found it sometimes pays to mend other people's fences. Good-bye, Marie. Come to see me soon."

Alexandra walked firmly down the path and Carl followed her.

Frank went into the house and threw himself on the sofa, his face to the wall, his clenched fist on his hip. Marie, having seen her guests off, came in and put her hand coaxingly on his shoulder.

"Poor Frank! You've run until you've made your head ache, now haven't you? Let me make you some coffee."

"What else am I to do?" he cried hotly in Bohemian. "Am I to let any old woman's hogs root up my wheat? Is that what I work myself to death for?"

"Don't worry about it, Frank. I'll speak to Mrs. Hiller again. But, really, she almost cried last time they got out, she was so sorry."

Frank bounced over on his other side. "That's it; you always side with them against me. They all know it. Anybody here feels free to borrow the mower and break it, or turn their hogs in on me. They know you won't care!"

Marie hurried away to make his coffee. When she came back, he was fast asleep. She sat down and looked at him for a long while, very thoughtfully. When the kitchen clock struck six she went out to get supper, closing the door gently behind her. She was always sorry for Frank when he worked himself into one of these rages, and she was sorry to have him rough and quarrelsome with his neighbors. She was perfectly aware that the neighbors had a good deal to put up with, and that they bore with Frank for her sake.

VII.

Marie's father, Albert Tovesky, was one of the more intelligent Bohemians who came West in the early seventies. He settled in Omaha and became a leader and adviser among his people there. Marie was his youngest child, by a second wife, and was the apple of his eye. She was barely sixteen, and was in the graduating class of the Omaha High School, when Frank Shabata arrived from the old country and set all the Bohemian girls in a flutter. He was easily the buck of the beer-gardens, and on Sunday he was a sight to see, with his silk hat and tucked shirt and blue frock-coat, wearing gloves and carrying a little wisp of a yellow cane. He was tall and fair, with splendid teeth and close-cropped yellow curls, and he wore a slightly disdainful expression, proper for a young man with high connections, whose mother had a big farm in the Elbe valley. There was often an interesting discontent in his blue eyes, and every Bohemian girl he met imagined herself the cause of that unsatisfied expression. He had a way of drawing out his cambric handkerchief slowly, by one corner, from his breast-pocket, that was melancholy and romantic in the extreme. He took a little flight with each of the more eligible Bohemian girls, but it was when he was with little Marie Tovesky that he drew his handkerchief out most slowly, and, after he had lit a fresh cigar, dropped the match most despairingly. Any one could see, with half an eye, that his proud heart was bleeding for somebody.

One Sunday, late in the summer after Marie's graduation, she met Frank at a Bohemian picnic down the river and went rowing with him all the afternoon. When she got home that evening she went straight to her father's room and told him that she was engaged to Shabata. Old Tovesky was having a comfortable pipe before he went to bed. When he heard his daughter's announcement, he first prudently corked his beer bottle and then leaped to his feet and had a turn of temper. He characterized Frank Shabata by a Bohemian expression which is the equivalent of stuffed shirt.

"Why don't he go to work like the rest of us did? His farm in the Elbe valley, indeed! Ain't he got plenty brothers and sisters? It's his mother's farm, and why don't he stay at home and help her? Haven't I seen his mother out in the morning at five o'clock with her ladle and her big bucket on wheels, putting liquid manure on the cabbages? Don't I know the look of old Eva Shabata's hands? Like an old horse's hoofs they are—and this fellow wearing gloves and rings! Engaged, indeed! You aren't fit to be out of school, and that's what's the matter with you. I will send you off to the Sisters of the Sacred Heart in St. Louis, and they will teach you some sense, *I* guess!"

Accordingly, the very next week, Albert Tovesky took his daughter, pale and tearful, down the river to the convent. But the way to make Frank want anything was to tell him he couldn't have it. He managed to have an interview with Marie before she went away, and whereas he had been only half in love with her before, he now persuaded himself that he would not stop at anything. Marie took with her to the convent, under the canvas lining of her trunk, the results of a laborious and satisfying morning on Frank's part; no less than a dozen photographs of himself, taken in a dozen different love-lorn attitudes. There was a little round photograph for her watch-case, photographs for her wall and dresser, and even long narrow ones to be used as bookmarks. More than once the handsome gentleman was torn to pieces before the French class by an indignant nun.

Marie pined in the convent for a year, until her eighteenth birthday was passed. Then she met Frank Shabata in the Union Station in St. Louis and ran away with him. Old Tovesky forgave his daughter because there was nothing else to do, and bought her a farm in the country that she had loved so well as a child. Since then her story had been a part of the history of the Divide. She and Frank had been living there for five years when Carl Linstrum came back to pay his long deferred visit to Alexandra. Frank had, on the whole, done better than one might have expected. He had flung himself at the soil with savage energy. Once a year he went to Hastings or to Omaha, on a spree. He stayed away for a week or two, and then came home and worked like a demon. He did work; if he felt sorry for himself, that was his own affair.

VIII.

On the evening of the day of Alexandra's call at the Shabatas', a heavy rain set in. Frank sat up until a late hour reading the Sunday newspapers. One of the Goulds was getting a divorce, and Frank took it as a personal affront. In printing the story of the young man's marital troubles, the knowing editor gave a sufficiently colored account of his career, stating the amount of his income and the manner in which he was supposed to spend it. Frank read English slowly, and the more he read about this divorce case, the angrier he grew. At last he threw down the page with a snort. He turned to his farm-hand who was reading the other half of the paper.

"By God! if I have that young feller in de hayfield once, I show him someting. Listen here what he do wit his money." And Frank began the catalogue of the young man's reputed extravagances.

Marie sighed. She thought it hard that the Goulds, for whom she had nothing but good will, should make her so much trouble. She hated to see the Sunday newspapers come into the house. Frank was always reading about the doings of rich people and feeling outraged. He had an inexhaustible stock of stories about their crimes and follies, how they bribed the courts and shot down their butlers with impunity whenever they chose. Frank and Lou Bergson had very similar ideas, and they were two of the political agitators of the county.

The next morning broke clear and brilliant, but Frank said the ground was too wet to plough, so he took the cart and drove over to Sainte-Agnes to spend the day at Moses Marcel's saloon. After he was gone, Marie went out to the back porch to begin her butter-making. A brisk wind had come up and was driving puffy white clouds across the sky. The orchard was sparkling and rippling in the sun. Marie stood looking toward it wistfully, her hand on the lid of the churn, when she heard a sharp ring in the air, the merry sound of the whetstone on the scythe. That invitation decided her. She ran into the house, put on a short skirt and a pair of her husband's boots, caught up a tin pail and started for the orchard. Emil had already begun work and was mowing vigorously. When he saw her coming, he stopped and wiped his brow. His yellow canvas leggings and khaki trousers were splashed to the knees.

"Don't let me disturb you, Emil. I'm going to pick cherries. Isn't everything beautiful after the rain? Oh, but I'm glad to get this place mowed! When I heard it raining in the night, I thought maybe you would come and do it for me to-day. The wind wakened me. Didn't it blow dreadfully? Just smell the wild roses! They are always so spicy after a rain. We never had so many of them in here before. I suppose it's the wet season. Will you have to cut them, too?"

"If I cut the grass, I will," Emil said teasingly. "What's the matter with you? What makes you so flighty?"

"Am I flighty? I suppose that's the wet season, too, then. It's exciting to see everything growing so fast,—and to get the grass cut! Please leave the roses till last, if you must cut them. Oh, I don't mean all of them, I mean that low place down by my tree, where there are so many. Aren't you splashed! Look at the spider-webs all over the grass. Good-bye. I'll call you if I see a snake."

She tripped away and Emil stood looking after her. In a few moments he heard the cherries dropping smartly into the pail, and he began to swing his scythe with that long, even stroke that few American boys ever learn. Marie picked cherries and sang softly to herself, stripping one glittering branch after another, shivering when she caught a shower of raindrops on her neck and hair. And Emil mowed his way slowly down toward the cherry trees.

That summer the rains had been so many and opportune that it was almost more than Shabata and his man could do to keep up with the corn; the orchard was a neglected wilderness. All sorts of weeds and herbs and flowers had grown up there; splotches of wild larkspur, pale green-and-white spikes of hoarhound, plantations of wild cotton, tangles of foxtail and wild wheat. South of the apricot trees, cornering on the wheatfield, was Frank's alfalfa, where myriads of white and yellow butterflies were always fluttering above the purple blossoms. When Emil reached the lower corner by the hedge, Marie was sitting under her white mulberry tree, the pailful of cherries beside her, looking off at the gentle, tireless swelling of the wheat.

"Emil," she said suddenly—he was mowing quietly about under the tree so as not to disturb her—"what religion did the Swedes have away back, before they were Christians?"

Emil paused and straightened his back. "I don't know. About like the Germans', wasn't it?"

Marie went on as if she had not heard him. "The Bohemians, you know, were tree worshipers before the missionaries came. Father says the people in the mountains still do queer things, sometimes,—they believe that trees bring good or bad luck."

Emil looked superior. "Do they? Well, which are the lucky trees? I'd like to know."

"I don't know all of them, but I know lindens are. The old people in the mountains plant lindens to purify the forest, and to do away with the spells that come from the old trees they say have lasted from heathen times. I'm a good Catholic, but I think I could get along with caring for trees, if I hadn't anything else."

"That's a poor saying," said Emil, stooping over to wipe his hands in the wet grass.

"Why is it? If I feel that way, I feel that way. I like trees because they seem more resigned to the way they have to live than other things do. I feel as if this tree knows everything I ever think of when I sit here. When I come back to it, I never have to remind it of anything; I begin just where I left off."

Emil had nothing to say to this. He reached up among the branches and began to pick the sweet, insipid fruit,—long ivory-colored berries, tipped with faint pink, like white coral, that fall to the ground unheeded all summer through. He dropped a handful into her lap.

"Do you like Mr. Linstrum?" Marie asked suddenly.

"Yes. Don't you?"

"Oh, ever so much; only he seems kind of staid and school-teachery. But, of course, he is older than Frank, even. I'm sure I don't want to live to be more than thirty, do you? Do you think Alexandra likes him very much?"

"I suppose so. They were old friends."

"Oh, Emil, you know what I mean!" Marie tossed her head impatiently. "Does she really care about him? When she used to tell me about him, I always wondered whether she wasn't a little in love with him."

"Who, Alexandra?" Emil laughed and thrust his hands into his trousers pockets. "Alexandra's never been in love, you crazy!" He laughed again. "She wouldn't know how to go about it. The idea!"

Marie shrugged her shoulders. "Oh, you don't know Alexandra as well as you think you do! If you had any eyes, you would see that she is very fond of him. It would serve you all right if she walked off with Carl. I like him because he appreciates her more than you do."

Emil frowned. "What are you talking about, Marie? Alexandra's all right. She and I have always been good friends. What more do you want? I like to talk to Carl about New York and what a fellow can do there."

"Oh, Emil! Surely you are not thinking of going off there?"

"Why not? I must go somewhere, mustn't I?" The young man took up his scythe and leaned on it. "Would you rather I went off in the sand hills and lived like Ivar?"

Marie's face fell under his brooding gaze. She looked down at his wet leggings. "I'm sure Alexandra hopes you will stay on here," she murmured.

"Then Alexandra will be disappointed," the young man said roughly. "What do I want to hang around here for? Alexandra can run the farm all right, without me. I don't want to stand around and look on. I want to be doing something on my own account."

"That's so," Marie sighed. "There are so many, many things you can do. Almost anything you choose."

"And there are so many, many things I can't do." Emil echoed her tone sarcastically. "Sometimes I don't want to do anything at all, and sometimes I want to pull the four corners of the Divide together,"—he threw out his arm and brought it back with a jerk,—"so, like a table-cloth. I get tired of seeing men and horses going up and down, up and down."

Marie looked up at his defiant figure and her face clouded. "I wish you weren't so restless, and didn't get so worked up over things," she said sadly.

"Thank you," he returned shortly.

She sighed despondently. "Everything I say makes you cross, don't it? And you never used to be cross to me."

Emil took a step nearer and stood frowning down at her bent head. He stood in an attitude of self-defense, his feet well apart, his hands clenched and drawn up at his sides, so that the cords stood out on his bare arms. "I can't play with you like a little boy any more," he said slowly. "That's what you miss, Marie. You'll have to get some other little boy to play with." He stopped and took a deep breath. Then he went on in a low tone, so intense that it was almost threatening: "Sometimes you seem to understand perfectly, and then sometimes you pretend you don't. You don't help things any by pretending. It's then that I want to pull the corners of the Divide together. If you WON'T understand, you know, I could make you!"

Marie clasped her hands and started up from her seat. She had grown very pale and her eyes were shining with excitement and distress. "But, Emil, if I understand, then all our good times are over, we can never do nice things together any more. We shall have to behave like Mr. Linstrum. And, anyhow, there's nothing to understand!" She struck the ground with her little foot fiercely. "That won't last. It will go away, and things will be just as they used to. I wish you were a Catholic. The Church helps people, indeed it does. I pray for you, but that's not the same as if you prayed yourself."

She spoke rapidly and pleadingly, looked entreatingly into his face. Emil stood defiant, gazing down at her.

"I can't pray to have the things I want," he said slowly, "and I won't pray not to have them, not if I'm damned for it."

Marie turned away, wringing her hands. "Oh, Emil, you won't try! Then all our good times are over."

"Yes; over. I never expect to have any more."

Emil gripped the hand-holds of his scythe and began to mow. Marie took up her cherries and went slowly toward the house, crying bitterly.

IX.

On Sunday afternoon, a month after Carl Linstrum's arrival, he rode with Emil up into the French country to attend a Catholic fair. He sat for most of the afternoon in the basement of the church, where the fair was held, talking to Marie Shabata, or strolled about the gravel terrace, thrown up on the hillside in front of the basement doors, where the French boys were jumping and wrestling and throwing the discus. Some of the boys were in their white baseball suits; they had just come up from a Sunday practice game down in the ballgrounds. Amedee, the newly married, Emil's best friend, was their pitcher, renowned among the country towns for his dash and skill. Amedee was a little fellow, a year younger than Emil and much more boyish in appearance; very lithe and active and neatly made, with a clear brown and white skin, and flashing white teeth. The Sainte-Agnes boys were to play the

Hastings nine in a fortnight, and Amedee's lightning balls were the hope of his team. The little Frenchman seemed to get every ounce there was in him behind the ball as it left his hand.

"You'd have made the battery at the University for sure, 'Medee," Emil said as they were walking from the ball-grounds back to the church on the hill. "You're pitching better than you did in the spring."

Amedee grinned. "Sure! A married man don't lose his head no more." He slapped Emil on the back as he caught step with him. "Oh, Emil, you wanna get married right off quick! It's the greatest thing ever!"

Emil laughed. "How am I going to get married without any girl?"

Amedee took his arm. "Pooh! There are plenty girls will have you. You wanna get some nice French girl, now. She treat you well; always be jolly. See,"—he began checking off on his fingers,—"there is Severine, and Alphosen, and Josephine, and Hectorine, and Louise, and Malvina—why, I could love any of them girls! Why don't you get after them? Are you stuck up, Emil, or is anything the matter with you? I never did know a boy twenty-two years old before that didn't have no girl. You wanna be a priest, maybe? Not-a for me!" Amedee swaggered. "I bring many good Catholics into this world, I hope, and that's a way I help the Church."

Emil looked down and patted him on the shoulder. "Now you're windy, 'Medee. You Frenchies like to brag."

But Amedee had the zeal of the newly married, and he was not to be lightly shaken off. "Honest and true, Emil, don't you want ANY girl? Maybe there's some young lady in Lincoln, now, very grand,"—Amedee waved his hand languidly before his face to denote the fan of heartless beauty,—"and you lost your heart up there. Is that it?"

"Maybe," said Emil.

But Amedee saw no appropriate glow in his friend's face. "Bah!" he exclaimed in disgust. "I tell all the French girls to keep 'way from you. You gotta rock in there," thumping Emil on the ribs.

When they reached the terrace at the side of the church, Amedee, who was excited by his success on the ball-grounds, challenged Emil to a jumping-match, though he knew he would be beaten. They belted themselves up, and Raoul Marcel, the choir tenor and Father Duchesne's pet, and Jean Bordelau, held the string over which they vaulted. All the French boys stood round, cheering and humping themselves up when Emil or Amedee went over the wire, as if they were helping in the lift. Emil stopped at five-feet-five, declaring that he would spoil his appetite for supper if he jumped any more.

Angelique, Amedee's pretty bride, as blonde and fair as her name, who had come out to watch the match, tossed her head at Emil and said:—

"'Medee could jump much higher than you if he were as tall. And anyhow, he is much more graceful. He goes over like a bird, and you have to hump yourself all up."

"Oh, I do, do I?" Emil caught her and kissed her saucy mouth squarely, while she laughed and struggled and called, "'Medee! 'Medee!"

"There, you see your 'Medee isn't even big enough to get you away from me. I could run away with you right now and he could only sit down and cry about it. I'll show you whether I have to hump myself!" Laughing and panting, he picked Angelique up in his arms and began running about the rectangle with her. Not until he saw Marie Shabata's tiger eyes flashing from the gloom of the basement doorway did he hand the disheveled bride over to her husband. "There, go to your graceful; I haven't the heart to take you away from him."

Angelique clung to her husband and made faces at Emil over the white shoulder of

Amedee's ball-shirt. Emil was greatly amused at her air of proprietorship and at Amedee's shameless submission to it. He was delighted with his friend's good fortune. He liked to see and to think about Amedee's sunny, natural, happy love.

He and Amedee had ridden and wrestled and larked together since they were lads of twelve. On Sundays and holidays they were always arm in arm. It seemed strange that now he should have to hide the thing that Amedee was so proud of, that the feeling which gave one of them such happiness should bring the other such despair. It was like that when Alexandra tested her seed-corn in the spring, he mused. From two ears that had grown side by side, the grains of one shot up joyfully into the light, projecting themselves into the future, and the grains from the other lay still in the earth and rotted; and nobody knew why.

X.

While Emil and Carl were amusing themselves at the fair, Alexandra was at home, busy with her account-books, which had been neglected of late. She was almost through with her figures when she heard a cart drive up to the gate, and looking out of the window she saw her two older brothers. They had seemed to avoid her ever since Carl Linstrum's arrival, four weeks ago that day, and she hurried to the door to welcome them. She saw at once that they had come with some very definite purpose. They followed her stiffly into the sitting-room. Oscar sat down, but Lou walked over to the window and remained standing, his hands behind him.

"You are by yourself?" he asked, looking toward the doorway into the parlor.

"Yes. Carl and Emil went up to the Catholic fair."

For a few moments neither of the men spoke.

Then Lou came out sharply. "How soon does he intend to go away from here?"

"I don't know, Lou. Not for some time, I hope." Alexandra spoke in an even, quiet tone that often exasperated her brothers. They felt that she was trying to be superior with them.

Oscar spoke up grimly. "We thought we ought to tell you that people have begun to talk," he said meaningly.

Alexandra looked at him. "What about?"

Oscar met her eyes blankly. "About you, keeping him here so long. It looks bad for him to be hanging on to a woman this way. People think you're getting taken in."

Alexandra shut her account-book firmly. "Boys," she said seriously, "don't let's go on with this. We won't come out anywhere. I can't take advice on such a matter. I know you mean well, but you must not feel responsible for me in things of this sort. If we go on with this talk it will only make hard feeling."

Lou whipped about from the window. "You ought to think a little about your family. You're making us all ridiculous."

"How am I?"

"People are beginning to say you want to marry the fellow."

"Well, and what is ridiculous about that?"

Lou and Oscar exchanged outraged looks. "Alexandra! Can't you see he's just a tramp and he's after your money? He wants to be taken care of, he does!"

"Well, suppose I want to take care of him? Whose business is it but my own?"

"Don't you know he'd get hold of your property?"

"He'd get hold of what I wished to give him, certainly."

Oscar sat up suddenly and Lou clutched at his bristly hair.

"Give him?" Lou shouted. "Our property, our homestead?"

"I don't know about the homestead," said Alexandra quietly. "I know you and Oscar have always expected that it would be left to your children, and I'm not sure but what you're right. But I'll do exactly as I please with the rest of my land, boys."

"The rest of your land!" cried Lou, growing more excited every minute. "Didn't all the land come out of the homestead? It was bought with money borrowed on the homestead, and Oscar and me worked ourselves to the bone paying interest on it."

"Yes, you paid the interest. But when you married we made a division of the land, and you were satisfied. I've made more on my farms since I've been alone than when we all worked together."

"Everything you've made has come out of the original land that us boys worked for, hasn't it? The farms and all that comes out of them belongs to us as a family."

Alexandra waved her hand impatiently. "Come now, Lou. Stick to the facts. You are talking nonsense. Go to the county clerk and ask him who owns my land, and whether my titles are good."

Lou turned to his brother. "This is what comes of letting a woman meddle in business," he said bitterly. "We ought to have taken things in our own hands years ago. But she liked to run things, and we humored her. We thought you had good sense, Alexandra. We never thought you'd do anything foolish."

Alexandra rapped impatiently on her desk with her knuckles. "Listen, Lou. Don't talk wild. You say you ought to have taken things into your own hands years ago. I suppose you mean before you left home. But how could you take hold of what wasn't there? I've got most of what I have now since we divided the property; I've built it up myself, and it has nothing to do with you."

Oscar spoke up solemnly. "The property of a family really belongs to the men of the family, no matter about the title. If anything goes wrong, it's the men that are held responsible."

"Yes, of course," Lou broke in. "Everybody knows that. Oscar and me have always been easy-going and we've never made any fuss. We were willing you should hold the land and have the good of it, but you got no right to part with any of it. We worked in the fields to pay for the first land you bought, and whatever's come out of it has got to be kept in the family."

Oscar reinforced his brother, his mind fixed on the one point he could see. "The property of a family belongs to the men of the family, because they are held responsible, and because they do the work."

Alexandra looked from one to the other, her eyes full of indignation. She had been impatient before, but now she was beginning to feel angry. "And what about my work?" she asked in an unsteady voice.

Lou looked at the carpet. "Oh, now, Alexandra, you always took it pretty easy! Of course we wanted you to. You liked to manage round, and we always humored you. We realize you were a great deal of help to us. There's no woman anywhere around that knows as much about business as you do, and we've always been proud of that, and thought you were pretty smart. But, of course, the real work always fell on us. Good advice is all right, but it don't get the weeds out of the corn."

"Maybe not, but it sometimes puts in the crop, and it sometimes keeps the fields for corn to grow in," said Alexandra dryly. "Why, Lou, I can remember when you and Oscar wanted to sell this homestead and all the improvements to old preacher Ericson for two thousand dollars. If I'd consented, you'd have gone down to the river and scraped along on poor farms for the rest of your lives. When I put in our first field of alfalfa you both opposed me, just because I first heard about it from a young man who had been to the University. You said I was being taken in then, and all the neighbors said so. You know as well as I do that alfalfa has been the salvation of this country. You all laughed at me when I said our land here was about ready for wheat, and I had to raise three big wheat crops before the neighbors quit putting all their land in corn. Why, I remember you cried, Lou, when we put in the first big wheat-planting, and said everybody was laughing at us."

Lou turned to Oscar. "That's the woman of it; if she tells you to put in a crop, she thinks she's put it in. It makes women conceited to meddle in business. I shouldn't think you'd want to remind us how hard you were on us, Alexandra, after the way you baby Emil."

"Hard on you? I never meant to be hard. Conditions were hard. Maybe I would never have been very soft, anyhow; but I certainly didn't choose to be the kind of girl I was. If you take even a vine and cut it back again and again, it grows hard, like a tree."

Lou felt that they were wandering from the point, and that in digression Alexandra might unnerve him. He wiped his forehead with a jerk of his handkerchief. "We never doubted you, Alexandra. We never questioned anything you did. You've always had your own way. But you can't expect us to sit like stumps and see you done out of the property by any loafer who happens along, and making yourself ridiculous into the bargain."

Oscar rose. "Yes," he broke in, "everybody's laughing to see you get took in; at your age, too. Everybody knows he's nearly five years younger than you, and is after your money. Why, Alexandra, you are forty years old!"

"All that doesn't concern anybody but Carl and me. Go to town and ask your lawyers what you can do to restrain me from disposing of my own property. And I advise you to do what they tell you; for the authority you can exert by law is the only influence you will ever have over me again." Alexandra rose. "I think I would rather not have lived to find out what I have to-day," she said quietly, closing her desk.

Lou and Oscar looked at each other questioningly. There seemed to be nothing to do but to go, and they walked out.

"You can't do business with women," Oscar said heavily as he clambered into the cart. "But anyhow, we've had our say, at last."

Lou scratched his head. "Talk of that kind might come too high, you know; but she's apt to be sensible. You hadn't ought to said that about her age, though, Oscar. I'm afraid that hurt her feelings; and the worst thing we can do is to make her sore at us. She'd marry him out of contrariness."

"I only meant," said Oscar, "that she is old enough to know better, and she is. If she was going to marry, she ought to done it long ago, and not go making a fool of herself now."

Lou looked anxious, nevertheless. "Of course," he reflected hopefully and inconsistently, "Alexandra ain't much like other women-folks. Maybe it won't make her sore. Maybe she'd as soon be forty as not!"

XI.

Emil came home at about half-past seven o'clock that evening. Old Ivar met him at the windmill and took his horse, and the young man went directly into the house. He called to his sister and she answered from her bedroom, behind the sitting-room, saying that she was lying down.

Emil went to her door.

"Can I see you for a minute?" he asked. "I want to talk to you about something before Carl comes."

Alexandra rose quickly and came to the door. "Where is Carl?"

"Lou and Oscar met us and said they wanted to talk to him, so he rode over to Oscar's with them. Are you coming out?" Emil asked impatiently.

"Yes, sit down. I'll be dressed in a moment."

Alexandra closed her door, and Emil sank down on the old slat lounge and sat with his head in his hands. When his sister came out, he looked up, not knowing whether the interval had been short or long, and he was surprised to see that the room had grown quite dark. That was just as well; it would be easier to talk if he were not under the gaze of those clear, deliberate eyes, that saw so far in some directions and were so blind in others. Alexandra, too, was glad of the dusk. Her face was swollen from crying.

Emil started up and then sat down again. "Alexandra," he said slowly, in his deep young baritone, "I don't want to go away to law school this fall. Let me put it off another year. I want to take a year off and look around. It's awfully easy to rush into a profession you don't really like, and awfully hard to get out of it. Linstrum and I have been talking about that."

"Very well, Emil. Only don't go off looking for land." She came up and put her hand on his shoulder. "I've been wishing you could stay with me this winter."

"That's just what I don't want to do, Alexandra. I'm restless. I want to go to a new place. I want to go down to the City of Mexico to join one of the University fellows who's at the head of an electrical plant. He wrote me he could give me a little job, enough to pay my way, and I could look around and see what I want to do. I want to go as soon as harvest is over. I guess Lou and Oscar will be sore about it."

"I suppose they will." Alexandra sat down on the lounge beside him. "They are very angry with me, Emil. We have had a quarrel. They will not come here again."

Emil scarcely heard what she was saying; he did not notice the sadness of her tone. He was thinking about the reckless life he meant to live in Mexico.

"What about?" he asked absently.

"About Carl Linstrum. They are afraid I am going to marry him, and that some of my property will get away from them."

Emil shrugged his shoulders. "What nonsense!" he murmured. "Just like them."

Alexandra drew back. "Why nonsense, Emil?"

"Why, you've never thought of such a thing, have you? They always have to have something to fuss about."

"Emil," said his sister slowly, "you ought not to take things for granted. Do you agree with them that I have no right to change my way of living?"

Emil looked at the outline of his sister's head in the dim light. They were sitting close together and he somehow felt that she could hear his thoughts. He was silent for a moment, and then said in an embarrassed tone, "Why, no, certainly not. You ought to do whatever you want to. I'll always back you."

"But it would seem a little bit ridiculous to you if I married Carl?"

Emil fidgeted. The issue seemed to him too far-fetched to warrant discussion. "Why, no. I should be surprised if you wanted to. I can't see exactly why. But that's none of my business. You ought to do as you please. Certainly you ought not to pay any attention to what the boys say."

Alexandra sighed. "I had hoped you might understand, a little, why I do want to. But I suppose that's too much to expect. I've had a pretty lonely life, Emil. Besides Marie, Carl is the only friend I have ever had."

Emil was awake now; a name in her last sentence roused him. He put out his hand and took his sister's awkwardly. "You ought to do just as you wish, and I think Carl's a fine fellow. He and I would always get on. I don't believe any of the things the boys say about him, honest I don't. They are suspicious of him because he's intelligent. You know their way. They've been sore at me ever since you let me go away to college. They're always trying to catch me up. If I were you, I wouldn't pay any attention to them. There's nothing to get upset about. Carl's a sensible fellow. He won't mind them."

"I don't know. If they talk to him the way they did to me, I think he'll go away."

Emil grew more and more uneasy. "Think so? Well, Marie said it would serve us all right if you walked off with him."

"Did she? Bless her little heart! SHE would." Alexandra's voice broke.

Emil began unlacing his leggings. "Why don't you talk to her about it? There's Carl, I hear his horse. I guess I'll go upstairs and get my boots off. No, I don't want any supper. We had supper at five o'clock, at the fair."

Emil was glad to escape and get to his own room. He was a little ashamed for his sister, though he had tried not to show it. He felt that there was something indecorous in her proposal, and she did seem to him somewhat ridiculous. There was trouble enough in the world, he reflected, as he threw himself upon his bed, without people who were forty years old imagining they wanted to get married. In the darkness and silence Emil was not likely to think long about Alexandra. Every image slipped away but one. He had seen Marie in the crowd that afternoon. She sold candy at the fair. WHY had she ever run away with Frank Shabata, and how could she go on laughing and working and taking an interest in things? Why did she like so many people, and why had she seemed pleased when all the French and Bohemian boys, and the priest himself, crowded round her candy stand? Why did she care about any one but him? Why could he never, never find the thing he looked for in her playful, affectionate eyes?

Then he fell to imagining that he looked once more and found it there, and what it would be like if she loved him,—she who, as Alexandra said, could give her whole heart. In that dream he could lie for hours, as if in a trance. His spirit went out of his body and crossed the fields to Marie Shabata.

At the University dances the girls had often looked wonderingly at the tall young Swede with the fine head, leaning against the wall and frowning, his arms folded, his eyes fixed on the ceiling or the floor. All the girls were a little afraid of him. He was distinguished-looking, and not the jollying kind. They felt that he was too intense and preoccupied. There was something queer about him. Emil's fraternity rather prided itself upon its dances, and sometimes he did his duty and danced every dance. But whether he was on the floor or brooding in a corner, he was always thinking about Marie Shabata. For two years the storm had been gathering in him.

XII.

Carl came into the sitting-room while Alexandra was lighting the lamp. She looked up at him as she adjusted the shade. His sharp shoulders stooped as if he were very tired, his face was pale, and there were bluish shadows under his dark eyes. His anger had burned itself out and left him sick and disgusted.

"You have seen Lou and Oscar?" Alexandra asked.

"Yes." His eyes avoided hers.

Alexandra took a deep breath. "And now you are going away. I thought so."

Carl threw himself into a chair and pushed the dark lock back from his forehead with his white, nervous hand. "What a hopeless position you are in, Alexandra!" he exclaimed feverishly. "It is your fate to be always surrounded by little men. And I am no better than the rest. I am too little to face the criticism of even such men as Lou and Oscar. Yes, I am going away; to-morrow. I cannot even ask you to give me a promise until I have something to offer you. I thought, perhaps, I could do that; but I find I can't."

"What good comes of offering people things they don't need?" Alexandra asked sadly. "I don't need money. But I have needed you for a great many years. I wonder why I have been permitted to prosper, if it is only to take my friends away from me."

"I don't deceive myself," Carl said frankly. "I know that I am going away on my own account. I must make the usual effort. I must have something to show for myself. To take what you would give me, I should have to be either a very large man or a very small one, and I am only in the middle class."

Alexandra sighed. "I have a feeling that if you go away, you will not come back. Something will happen to one of us, or to both. People have to snatch at happiness when they can, in this world. It is always easier to lose than to find. What I have is yours, if you care enough about me to take it."

Carl rose and looked up at the picture of John Bergson. "But I can't, my dear, I can't! I will go North at once. Instead of idling about in California all winter, I shall be getting my bearings up there. I won't waste another week. Be patient with me, Alexandra. Give me a year!"

"As you will," said Alexandra wearily. "All at once, in a single day, I lose everything; and I do not know why. Emil, too, is going away." Carl was still studying John Bergson's face and Alexandra's eyes followed his. "Yes," she said, "if he could have seen all that would come of the task he gave me, he would have been sorry. I hope he does not see me now. I hope that he is among the old people of his blood and country, and that tidings do not reach him from the New World."

3

WINTER MEMORIES

I.

WINTER HAS SETTLED down over the Divide again; the season in which Nature recuperates, in which she sinks to sleep between the fruitfulness of autumn and the passion of spring. The birds have gone. The teeming life that goes on down in the long grass is exterminated. The prairie-dog keeps his hole. The rabbits run shivering from one frozen garden patch to another and are hard put to it to find frost-bitten cabbage-stalks. At night the coyotes roam the wintry waste, howling for food. The variegated fields are all one color now; the pastures, the stubble, the roads, the sky are the same leaden gray. The hedgerows and trees are scarcely perceptible against the bare earth, whose slaty hue they have taken on. The ground is frozen so hard that it bruises the foot to walk in the roads or in the ploughed fields. It is like an iron country, and the spirit is oppressed by its rigor and melancholy. One could easily believe that in that dead landscape the germs of life and fruitfulness were extinct forever.

Alexandra has settled back into her old routine. There are weekly letters from Emil. Lou and Oscar she has not seen since Carl went away. To avoid awkward encounters in the presence of curious spectators, she has stopped going to the Norwegian Church and drives up to the Reform Church at Hanover, or goes with Marie Shabata to the Catholic Church, locally known as "the French Church." She has not told Marie about Carl, or her differences with her brothers. She was never very communicative about her own affairs, and when she came to the point, an instinct told her that about such things she and Marie would not understand one another.

Old Mrs. Lee had been afraid that family misunderstandings might deprive her of her yearly visit to Alexandra. But on the first day of December Alexandra telephoned Annie that to-morrow she would send Ivar over for her mother, and the next day the old lady arrived with her bundles. For twelve years Mrs. Lee had always entered Alexandra's sitting-room with the same exclamation, "Now we be yust-a like old times!" She enjoyed the liberty Alexandra gave her, and hearing her own language about her all day long. Here she could wear her nightcap and sleep with all her windows shut, listen to Ivar reading the Bible, and here she could run about among the stables in a pair of Emil's old boots. Though she was bent almost double, she was as spry as a gopher. Her face was as brown as if it had been varnished, and as full of wrinkles as a washerwoman's hands. She had three jolly old teeth left in the front of her mouth, and when she grinned she looked very knowing, as if when you found out how to take it, life wasn't half bad. While she and Alexandra patched and pieced and quilted, she talked incessantly about stories she read in a Swedish family paper, telling the plots in great detail; or about her life on a dairy farm in Gottland when she was a girl. Sometimes she forgot which were the printed stories and which were the real stories, it all seemed so far away. She loved to take a little brandy, with hot water and sugar, before she went to bed, and Alexandra always had it ready for her. "It sends good dreams," she would say with a twinkle in her eye.

When Mrs. Lee had been with Alexandra for a week, Marie Shabata telephoned one morning to say that Frank had gone to town for the day, and she would like them to come over for coffee in the afternoon. Mrs. Lee hurried to wash out and iron her new cross-stitched apron, which she had finished only the night before; a checked gingham apron worked with a design ten inches broad across the bottom; a hunting scene, with fir trees and a stag and dogs and huntsmen. Mrs. Lee was firm with herself at dinner, and refused a second helping of apple dumplings. "I ta-ank I save up," she said with a giggle.

At two o'clock in the afternoon Alexandra's cart drove up to the Shabatas' gate, and Marie saw Mrs. Lee's red shawl come bobbing up the path. She ran to the door and pulled the old woman into the house with a hug, helping her to take off her wraps while Alexandra blanketed the horse outside. Mrs. Lee had put on her best black satine dress—she abominated woolen stuffs, even in winter—and a crocheted collar, fastened with a big pale gold pin, containing faded daguerreotypes of her father and mother. She had not worn her apron for fear of rumpling it, and now she shook it out and tied it round her waist with a conscious air. Marie drew back and threw up her hands, exclaiming, "Oh, what a beauty! I've never seen this one before, have I, Mrs. Lee?"

The old woman giggled and ducked her head. "No, yust las' night I ma-ake. See dis tread; verra strong, no wa-ash out, no fade. My sister send from Sveden. I yust-a ta-ank you like dis."

Marie ran to the door again. "Come in, Alexandra. I have been looking at Mrs. Lee's apron. Do stop on your way home and show it to Mrs. Hiller. She's crazy about cross-stitch."

While Alexandra removed her hat and veil, Mrs. Lee went out to the kitchen and settled herself in a wooden rocking-chair by the stove, looking with great interest at the table, set for three, with a white cloth, and a pot of pink geraniums in the middle. "My, a-an't you gotta fine plants; such-a much flower. How you keep from freeze?"

She pointed to the window-shelves, full of blooming fuchsias and geraniums.

"I keep the fire all night, Mrs. Lee, and when it's very cold I put them all on the table, in the middle of the room. Other nights I only put newspapers behind them. Frank laughs at me for fussing, but when they don't bloom he says, 'What's the matter with the darned things?'—What do you hear from Carl, Alexandra?"

"He got to Dawson before the river froze, and now I suppose I won't hear any more until spring. Before he left California he sent me a box of orange flowers, but they didn't keep very well. I have brought a bunch of Emil's letters for you." Alexandra came out from the sitting-room and pinched Marie's cheek playfully. "You don't look as if the weather ever froze you up. Never have colds, do you? That's a good girl. She had dark red cheeks like this when she was a little girl, Mrs. Lee. She looked like some queer foreign kind of a doll. I've never forgot the first time I saw you in Mieklejohn's store, Marie, the time father was lying sick. Carl and I were talking about that before he went away."

"I remember, and Emil had his kitten along. When are you going to send Emil's Christmas box?"

"It ought to have gone before this. I'll have to send it by mail now, to get it there in time."

Marie pulled a dark purple silk necktie from her workbasket. "I knit this for him. It's a good color, don't you think? Will you please put it in with your things and tell him it's from me, to wear when he goes serenading."

Alexandra laughed. "I don't believe he goes serenading much. He says in one letter that the Mexican ladies are said to be very beautiful, but that don't seem to me very warm praise."

Marie tossed her head. "Emil can't fool me. If he's bought a guitar, he goes serenading. Who wouldn't, with all those Spanish girls dropping flowers down from their windows! I'd sing to them every night, wouldn't you, Mrs. Lee?"

The old lady chuckled. Her eyes lit up as Marie bent down and opened the oven door. A delicious hot fragrance blew out into the tidy kitchen. "My, somet'ing smell good!" She turned to Alexandra with a wink, her three yellow teeth making a brave show, "I ta-ank dat stop my yaw from ache no more!" she said contentedly.

Marie took out a pan of delicate little rolls, stuffed with stewed apricots, and began to dust them over with powdered sugar. "I hope you'll like these, Mrs. Lee; Alexandra does. The Bohemians always like them with their coffee. But if you don't, I have a coffee-cake with nuts and poppy seeds. Alexandra, will you get the cream jug? I put it in the window to keep cool."

"The Bohemians," said Alexandra, as they drew up to the table, "certainly know how to make more kinds of bread than any other people in the world. Old Mrs. Hiller told me once at the church supper that she could make seven kinds of fancy bread, but Marie could make a dozen."

Mrs. Lee held up one of the apricot rolls between her brown thumb and forefinger and weighed it critically. "Yust like-a fedders," she pronounced with satisfaction. "My, a-an't dis nice!" she exclaimed as she stirred her coffee. "I yust ta-ake a liddle yelly now, too, I ta-ank."

Alexandra and Marie laughed at her forehandedness, and fell to talking of their own affairs. "I was afraid you had a cold when I talked to you over the telephone the other night, Marie. What was the matter, had you been crying?"

"Maybe I had," Marie smiled guiltily. "Frank was out late that night. Don't you get lonely sometimes in the winter, when everybody has gone away?"

"I thought it was something like that. If I hadn't had company, I'd have run over to see for myself. If you get down-hearted, what will become of the rest of us?" Alexandra asked.

"I don't, very often. There's Mrs. Lee without any coffee!"

Later, when Mrs. Lee declared that her powers were spent, Marie and Alexandra went upstairs to look for some crochet patterns the old lady wanted to borrow. "Better put on your coat, Alexandra. It's cold up there, and I have no idea where those patterns are. I may have to look through my old trunks." Marie caught up a shawl and opened the stair door, running up the steps ahead of her guest. "While I go through the bureau drawers, you might look in those hat-boxes on the closet-shelf, over where Frank's clothes hang. There are a lot of odds and ends in them."

She began tossing over the contents of the drawers, and Alexandra went into the clothes-closet. Presently she came back, holding a slender elastic yellow stick in her hand.

"What in the world is this, Marie? You don't mean to tell me Frank ever carried such a thing?"

Marie blinked at it with astonishment and sat down on the floor. "Where did you find it? I didn't know he had kept it. I haven't seen it for years."

"It really is a cane, then?"

"Yes. One he brought from the old country. He used to carry it when I first knew him. Isn't it foolish? Poor Frank!"

Alexandra twirled the stick in her fingers and laughed. "He must have looked funny!"

Marie was thoughtful. "No, he didn't, really. It didn't seem out of place. He used to be awfully gay like that when he was a young man. I guess people always get what's hardest for them, Alexandra." Marie gathered the shawl closer about her and still looked hard at the cane. "Frank would be all right in the right place," she said reflectively. "He ought to have a different kind of wife, for one thing. Do you know, Alexandra, I could pick out exactly the right sort of woman for Frank—now. The trouble is you almost have to marry a man before you can find out the sort of wife he needs; and usually it's exactly the sort you are not. Then what are you going to do about it?" she asked candidly.

Alexandra confessed she didn't know. "However," she added, "it seems to me that you get along with Frank about as well as any woman I've ever seen or heard of could."

Marie shook her head, pursing her lips and blowing her warm breath softly out into the frosty air. "No; I was spoiled at home. I like my own way, and I have a quick tongue. When Frank brags, I say sharp things, and he never forgets. He goes over and over it in his mind; I can feel him. Then I'm too giddy. Frank's wife ought to be timid, and she ought not to care about another living thing in the world but just Frank! I didn't, when I married him, but I suppose I was too young to stay like that." Marie sighed.

Alexandra had never heard Marie speak so frankly about her husband before, and she felt that it was wiser not to encourage her. No good, she reasoned, ever came from talking about such things, and while Marie was thinking aloud, Alexandra had been steadily searching the hat-boxes. "Aren't these the patterns, Maria?"

Maria sprang up from the floor. "Sure enough, we were looking for patterns, weren't we? I'd forgot about everything but Frank's other wife. I'll put that away."

She poked the cane behind Frank's Sunday clothes, and though she laughed, Alexandra saw there were tears in her eyes.

When they went back to the kitchen, the snow had begun to fall, and Marie's visitors thought they must be getting home. She went out to the cart with them, and tucked the robes about old Mrs. Lee while Alexandra took the blanket off her horse. As they drove away, Marie turned and went slowly back to the house. She took up the package of letters Alexandra had brought, but she did not read them. She turned them over and looked at the foreign stamps, and then sat watching the flying snow while the dusk deepened in the kitchen and the stove sent out a red glow.

Marie knew perfectly well that Emil's letters were written more for her than for Alexandra. They were not the sort of letters that a young man writes to his sister. They were both more personal and more painstaking; full of descriptions of the gay life in the old Mexican capital in the days when the strong hand of Porfirio Diaz was still strong. He told about bull-fights and cock-fights, churches and FIESTAS, the flower-markets and the fountains, the music and dancing, the people of all nations he met in the Italian restaurants on San Francisco Street. In short, they were the kind of letters a young man writes to a woman when he wishes himself and his life to seem interesting to her, when he wishes to enlist her imagination in his behalf.

Marie, when she was alone or when she sat sewing in the evening, often thought about what it must be like down there where Emil was; where there were flowers and street bands everywhere, and carriages rattling up and down, and where there was a little blind bootblack in front of the cathedral who could play any tune you asked for by dropping the lids of blacking-boxes on the stone steps. When everything is done and over for one at twenty-three, it is pleasant to let the mind wander forth and follow a young adventurer who has life before him. "And if it had not been for me," she thought, "Frank might still be free like that, and having a good time making people admire him. Poor Frank, getting married wasn't very good for him either. I'm afraid I do set people against him, as he says. I seem, somehow, to give him away all the time. Perhaps he would try to be agreeable to people again, if I were not around. It seems as if I always make him just as bad as he can be."

Later in the winter, Alexandra looked back upon that afternoon as the last satisfactory visit she had had with Marie. After that day the younger woman seemed to shrink more and more into herself. When she was with Alexandra she was not spontaneous and frank as she used to be. She seemed to be brooding over something, and holding something back. The weather had a good deal to do with their seeing less of each other than usual. There had not been such snowstorms in twenty years, and the path across the fields was drifted deep from Christmas until March. When the two neighbors went to see each other, they had to go round by the wagon-road, which was twice as far. They telephoned each other almost every night, though in January there was a stretch of three weeks when the wires were down, and when the postman did not come at all.

Marie often ran in to see her nearest neighbor, old Mrs. Hiller, who was crippled with rheumatism and had only her son, the lame shoemaker, to take care of her; and she went to the French Church, whatever the weather. She was a sincerely devout girl. She prayed for herself and for Frank, and for Emil, among the temptations of that gay, corrupt old city. She found more comfort in the Church that winter than ever before. It seemed to come closer to her, and to fill an emptiness that ached in her heart. She tried to be patient with her husband. He and his hired man usually played California Jack in the evening. Marie sat sewing or crocheting and tried to take a friendly interest in the game, but she was always thinking about the wide fields outside, where the snow was drifting over the fences; and about the orchard, where the snow was falling and packing, crust over crust. When she went out into the dark kitchen to fix her plants for the night, she used to stand by the window and look out at the white fields, or watch the currents of snow whirling over the orchard. She seemed to feel the weight of all the snow that lay down there. The branches had become so hard that they wounded your hand if you but tried to break a twig. And yet, down under the frozen crusts, at the roots of the trees, the secret of life was still safe, warm as the blood in one's heart; and the spring would come again! Oh, it would come again!

II.

If Alexandra had had much imagination she might have guessed what was going on in Marie's mind, and she would have seen long before what was going on in Emil's. But that, as Emil himself had more than once reflected, was Alexandra's blind side, and her life had not been of the kind to sharpen her vision. Her training had all been toward the end of making her proficient in what she had undertaken to do. Her personal life, her own realization of herself, was almost a subconscious existence; like an underground river that came to the surface only here and there, at intervals months apart, and then sank again to flow on under her own fields. Nevertheless, the underground stream was there, and it was because she had so much personality to put into her enterprises and succeeded in putting it into them so completely, that her affairs prospered better than those of her neighbors.

There were certain days in her life, outwardly uneventful, which Alexandra remembered as peculiarly happy; days when she was close to the flat, fallow world about her, and felt, as it were, in her own body the joyous germination in the soil. There were days, too, which she and Emil had spent together, upon which she loved to look back. There had been such a day when they were down on the river in the dry year, looking over the land. They had made an early start one morning and had driven a long way before noon. When Emil said he was hungry, they drew back from the road, gave Brigham his oats among the bushes, and climbed up to the top of a grassy bluff to eat their lunch under the shade of some little elm trees. The river was clear there, and shallow, since there had been no rain, and it ran in ripples over the sparkling sand. Under the overhanging willows of the opposite bank there was an inlet where the water was deeper and flowed so slowly that it seemed to sleep in the sun. In this little bay a single wild duck was swimming and diving and preening her feathers, disporting herself very happily in the flickering light and shade. They sat for a long time, watching the solitary bird take its pleasure. No living thing had ever seemed to Alexandra as beautiful as that wild duck. Emil must have felt about it as she did, for afterward, when they were at home, he used sometimes to say, "Sister, you know our duck down there—" Alexandra remembered that day as one of the happiest in her life. Years afterward she thought of the duck as still there, swimming and diving all by herself in the sunlight, a kind of enchanted bird that did not know age or change.

Most of Alexandra's happy memories were as impersonal as this one; yet to her they were very personal. Her mind was a white book, with clear writing about weather and beasts and growing things. Not many people would have cared to read it; only a happy few. She had never been in love, she had never indulged in sentimental reveries. Even as a girl she had looked upon men as work-fellows. She had grown up in serious times.

There was one fancy indeed, which persisted through her girlhood. It most often came to her on Sunday mornings, the one day in the week when she lay late abed listening to the familiar morning sounds; the windmill singing in the brisk breeze, Emil whistling as he blacked his boots down by the kitchen door. Sometimes, as she lay thus luxuriously idle, her eyes closed, she used to have an illusion of being lifted up bodily and carried lightly by some one very strong. It was a man, certainly, who carried her, but he was like no man she knew; he was much larger and stronger and swifter, and he carried her as easily as if she were a sheaf of wheat. She never saw him, but, with eyes closed, she could feel that he was yellow like the sunlight, and there was the smell of ripe cornfields about him. She could feel him approach, bend over her and lift her, and then she could feel herself being carried swiftly off across the fields. After such a reverie she would rise hastily, angry with herself, and go down to the bath-house that was partitioned off the kitchen shed. There she would stand in a tin tub and prosecute her bath with vigor, finishing it by pouring buckets of cold well-water over her gleaming white body which no man on the Divide could have carried very far.

As she grew older, this fancy more often came to her when she was tired than when she was fresh and strong. Sometimes, after she had been in the open all day, overseeing the branding of the cattle or the loading of the pigs, she would come in chilled, take a concoction of spices and warm home-made wine, and go to bed with her body actually aching with fatigue. Then, just before she went to sleep, she had the old sensation of being lifted and carried by a strong being who took from her all her bodily weariness.

4

THE WHITE MULBERRY TREE

I.

THE FRENCH CHURCH, properly the Church of Sainte-Agnes, stood upon a hill. The high, narrow, red-brick building, with its tall steeple and steep roof, could be seen for miles across the wheatfields, though the little town of Sainte-Agnes was completely hidden away at the foot of the hill. The church looked powerful and triumphant there on its eminence, so high above the rest of the landscape, with miles of warm color lying at its feet, and by its position and setting it reminded one of some of the churches built long ago in the wheat-lands of middle France.

Late one June afternoon Alexandra Bergson was driving along one of the many roads that led through the rich French farming country to the big church. The sunlight was shining directly in her face, and there was a blaze of light all about the red church on the hill. Beside Alexandra lounged a strikingly exotic figure in a tall Mexican hat, a silk sash, and a black velvet jacket sewn with silver buttons. Emil had returned only the night before, and his sister was so proud of him that she decided at once to take him up to the church supper, and to make him wear the Mexican costume he had brought home in his trunk. "All the girls who have stands are going to wear fancy costumes," she argued, "and some of the boys. Marie is going to tell fortunes, and she sent to Omaha for a Bohemian dress her father brought back from a visit to the old country. If you wear those clothes, they will all be pleased. And you must take your guitar. Everybody ought to do what they can to help along, and we have never done much. We are not a talented family."

The supper was to be at six o'clock, in the basement of the church, and afterward there would be a fair, with charades and an auction. Alexandra had set out from home early, leaving the house to Signa and Nelse Jensen, who were to be married next week. Signa had shyly asked to have the wedding put off until Emil came home.

Alexandra was well satisfied with her brother. As they drove through the rolling French country toward the westering sun and the stalwart church, she was thinking of that time long ago when she and Emil drove back from the river valley to the still unconquered Divide. Yes, she told herself, it had been worth while; both Emil and the country had become what she had hoped. Out of her father's children there was one who was fit to cope with the world, who had not been tied to the plow, and who had a personality apart from the soil. And that, she reflected, was what she had worked for. She felt well satisfied with her life.

When they reached the church, a score of teams were hitched in front of the basement doors that opened from the hillside upon the sanded terrace, where the boys wrestled and had jumping-matches. Amedee Chevalier, a proud father of one week, rushed out and embraced Emil. Amedee was an only son,—hence he was a very rich young man,—but he meant to have twenty children himself, like his uncle Xavier. "Oh, Emil," he cried, hugging his old friend rapturously, "why ain't you been up to see my boy? You come to-morrow, sure? Emil, you wanna get a boy right off! It's the greatest thing ever! No, no, no! Angel not sick at all. Everything just fine. That boy he come into this world laughin', and he been laughin' ever since. You come an' see!" He pounded Emil's ribs to emphasize each announcement.

Emil caught his arms. "Stop, Amedee. You're knocking the wind out of me. I brought him cups and spoons and blankets and moccasins enough for an orphan asylum. I'm awful glad it's a boy, sure enough!"

The young men crowded round Emil to admire his costume and to tell him in a breath everything that had happened since he went away. Emil had more friends up here in the French country than down on Norway Creek. The French and Bohemian boys were spirited and jolly, liked variety, and were as much predisposed to favor anything new as the Scandinavian boys were to reject it. The Norwegian and Swedish lads were much more self-centred, apt to be egotistical and jealous. They were cautious and reserved with Emil because he had been away to college, and were prepared to take him down if he should try to put on airs with them. The French boys liked a bit of swagger, and they were always delighted to hear about anything new: new clothes, new games, new songs, new dances. Now they carried Emil off to show him the club room they had just fitted up over the post-office, down in the village. They ran down the hill in a drove, all laughing and chattering at once, some in French, some in English.

Alexandra went into the cool, whitewashed basement where the women were setting the tables. Marie was standing on a chair, building a little tent of shawls where she was to tell fortunes. She sprang down and ran toward Alexandra, stopping short and looking at her in disappointment. Alexandra nodded to her encouragingly.

"Oh, he will be here, Marie. The boys have taken him off to show him something. You won't know him. He is a man now, sure enough. I have no boy left. He smokes terrible-smelling Mexican cigarettes and talks Spanish. How pretty you look, child. Where did you get those beautiful earrings?"

"They belonged to father's mother. He always promised them to me. He sent them with the dress and said I could keep them."

Marie wore a short red skirt of stoutly woven cloth, a white bodice and kirtle, a yellow silk turban wound low over her brown curls, and long coral pendants in her ears. Her ears had been pierced against a piece of cork by her great-aunt when she was seven years old. In those germless days she had worn bits of broom-straw, plucked from the common sweeping-broom, in the lobes until the holes were healed and ready for little gold rings.

When Emil came back from the village, he lingered outside on the terrace with the boys. Marie could hear him talking and strumming on his guitar while Raoul Marcel sang falsetto. She was vexed with him for staying out there. It made her very nervous to hear him and not to see him; for, certainly, she told herself, she was not going out to look for him. When the supper bell rang and the boys came trooping in to get seats at the first table, she forgot all about her annoyance and ran to greet the tallest of the crowd, in his conspicuous attire. She didn't mind showing her embarrassment at all. She blushed and laughed excitedly as she gave Emil her hand, and looked delightedly at the black velvet coat that brought out his fair skin and fine blond head. Marie was incapable of being lukewarm about anything that pleased her. She simply did not know how to give a half-hearted response. When she was delighted, she was as likely as not to stand on her tip-toes and clap her hands. If people laughed at her, she laughed with them.

"Do the men wear clothes like that every day, in the street?" She caught Emil by his sleeve and turned him about. "Oh, I wish I lived where people wore things like that! Are the buttons real silver? Put on the hat, please. What a heavy thing! How do you ever wear it? Why don't you tell us about the bull-fights?"

She wanted to wring all his experiences from him at once, without waiting a moment. Emil smiled tolerantly and stood looking down at her with his old, brooding gaze, while the French girls fluttered about him in their white dresses and ribbons, and Alexandra watched the scene with pride. Several of the French girls, Marie knew, were hoping that Emil would take them to supper, and she was relieved when he took only his sister. Marie caught Frank's arm and dragged him to the same table, managing to get seats opposite the Bergsons, so that she could hear what they were talking about. Alexandra made Emil tell Mrs. Xavier Chevalier, the mother of the twenty, about how he had seen a famous matador killed in the bull-ring. Marie listened to every word, only taking her eyes from Emil to watch Frank's plate and keep it filled. When Emil finished his account,—bloody enough to satisfy Mrs. Xavier and to make her feel thankful that she was not a matador,—Marie broke out with a volley of questions. How did the women dress when they went to bull-fights? Did they wear mantillas? Did they never wear hats?

After supper the young people played charades for the amusement of their elders, who sat gossiping between their guesses. All the shops in Sainte-Agnes were closed at eight o'clock that night, so that the merchants and their clerks could attend the fair. The auction was the liveliest part of the entertainment, for the French boys always lost their heads when they began to bid, satisfied that their extravagance was in a good cause. After all the pincushions and sofa pillows and embroidered slippers were sold, Emil precipitated a panic by taking out one of his turquoise shirt studs, which every one had been admiring, and handing it to the auctioneer. All the French girls clamored for it, and their sweethearts bid against each other recklessly. Marie wanted it, too, and she kept making signals to Frank, which he took a sour pleasure in disregarding. He didn't see the use of making a fuss over a fellow just because he was dressed like a clown. When the turquoise went to Malvina Sauvage, the French banker's daughter, Marie shrugged her shoulders and betook herself to her little tent of shawls, where she began to shuffle her cards by the light of a tallow candle, calling out, "Fortunes, fortunes!"

The young priest, Father Duchesne, went first to have his fortune read. Marie took his long white hand, looked at it, and then began to run off her cards. "I see a long journey across water for you, Father. You will go to a town all cut up by water; built on islands, it seems to be, with rivers and green fields all about. And you will visit an old lady with a white cap and gold hoops in her ears, and you will be very happy there."

"Mais, oui," said the priest, with a melancholy smile. "C'est L'Isle-Adam, chez ma mere. Vous etes tres savante, ma fille." He patted her yellow turban, calling, "Venez donc, mes garcons! Il y a ici une veritable clairvoyante!"

Marie was clever at fortune-telling, indulging in a light irony that amused the crowd. She told old Brunot, the miser, that he would lose all his money, marry a girl of sixteen, and live happily on a crust. Sholte, the fat Russian boy, who lived for his stomach, was to be disappointed in love, grow thin, and shoot himself from despondency. Amedee was to have twenty children, and nineteen of them were to be girls. Amedee slapped Frank on the back and asked him why he didn't see what the fortune-teller would promise him. But Frank shook off his friendly hand and grunted, "She tell my fortune long ago; bad enough!" Then he withdrew to a corner and sat glowering at his wife.

Frank's case was all the more painful because he had no one in particular to fix his jealousy upon. Sometimes he could have thanked the man who would bring him evidence against his wife. He had discharged a good farm-boy, Jan Smirka, because he thought Marie was fond of him; but she had not seemed to miss Jan when he was gone, and she had been just as kind to the next boy. The farm-hands would always do anything for Marie; Frank couldn't find one so surly that he would not make an effort to please her. At the bottom of his heart Frank knew well enough that if he could once give up his grudge, his wife would come back to him. But he could never in the world do that. The grudge was fundamental. Perhaps he could not have given it up if he had tried. Perhaps he got more satisfaction out of feeling himself abused than he would have got out of being loved. If he could once have made Marie thoroughly unhappy, he might have relented and raised her from the dust. But she had never humbled herself. In the first days of their love she had been his slave; she had admired him abandonedly. But the moment he began to bully her and to be unjust, she began to draw away; at first in tearful amazement, then in quiet, unspoken disgust. The distance between them had widened and hardened. It no longer contracted and brought them suddenly together. The spark of her life went somewhere else, and he was always watching to surprise it. He knew that somewhere she must get a feeling to live upon, for she was not a woman who could live without loving. He wanted to prove to himself the wrong he felt. What did she hide in her heart? Where did it go? Even Frank had his churlish delicacies; he never reminded her of how much she had once loved him. For that Marie was grateful to him.

While Marie was chattering to the French boys, Amedee called Emil to the back of the room and whispered to him that they were going to play a joke on the girls. At eleven o'clock, Amedee was to go up to the switchboard in the vestibule and turn off the electric lights, and every boy would have a chance to kiss his sweetheart before Father Duchesne could find his way up the stairs to turn the current on again. The only difficulty was the candle in Marie's tent; perhaps, as Emil had no sweetheart, he would oblige the boys by blowing out the candle. Emil said he would undertake to do that.

At five minutes to eleven he sauntered up to Marie's booth, and the French boys dispersed to find their girls. He leaned over the card-table and gave himself up to looking at her. "Do you think you could tell my fortune?" he murmured. It was the first word he had had alone with her for almost a year. "My luck hasn't changed any. It's just the same."

Marie had often wondered whether there was anyone else who could look his thoughts to you as Emil could. To-night, when she met his steady, powerful eyes, it was impossible not to feel the sweetness of the dream he was dreaming; it reached her before she could shut it out, and hid itself in her heart. She began to shuffle her cards furiously. "I'm angry with you, Emil," she broke out with petulance. "Why did you give them that lovely blue stone to sell? You might have known Frank wouldn't buy it for me, and I wanted it awfully!"

Emil laughed shortly. "People who want such little things surely ought to have them," he said dryly. He thrust his hand into the pocket of his velvet trousers and brought out a handful of uncut turquoises, as big as marbles. Leaning over the table he dropped them into her lap. "There, will those do? Be careful, don't let any one see them. Now, I suppose you want me to go away and let you play with them?"

Marie was gazing in rapture at the soft blue color of the stones. "Oh, Emil! Is everything down there beautiful like these? How could you ever come away?"

At that instant Amedee laid hands on the switchboard. There was a shiver and a giggle, and every one looked toward the red blur that Marie's candle made in the dark. Immediately that, too, was gone. Little shrieks and currents of soft laughter ran up and down the dark hall. Marie started up,—directly into Emil's arms. In the same instant she felt his lips. The veil that had hung uncertainly between them for so long was dissolved. Before she knew what she was doing, she had committed herself to that kiss that was at once a boy's and a man's, as timid as it was tender; so like Emil and so unlike any one else in the world. Not until it was over did she realize what it meant. And Emil, who had so often imagined the shock of this first kiss, was surprised at its gentleness and naturalness. It was like a sigh which they had breathed together; almost sorrowful, as if each were afraid of wakening something in the other.

When the lights came on again, everybody was laughing and shouting, and all the French girls were rosy and shining with mirth. Only Marie, in her little tent of shawls, was pale and quiet. Under her yellow turban the red coral pendants swung against white cheeks. Frank was still staring at her, but he seemed to see nothing. Years ago, he himself had had the power to take the blood from her cheeks like that. Perhaps he did not remember—perhaps he had never noticed! Emil was already at the other end of the hall, walking about with the shoulder-motion he had acquired among the Mexicans, studying the floor with his intent, deep-set eyes. Marie began to take down and fold her shawls. She did not glance up again. The young people drifted to the other end of the hall where the guitar was sounding. In a moment she heard Emil and Raoul singing:—

"Across the Rio Grand-e There lies a sunny land-e, My bright-eyed Mexico!"

Alexandra Bergson came up to the card booth. "Let me help you, Marie. You look tired."

She placed her hand on Marie's arm and felt her shiver. Marie stiffened under that kind, calm hand. Alexandra drew back, perplexed and hurt.

There was about Alexandra something of the impervious calm of the fatalist, always disconcerting to very young people, who cannot feel that the heart lives at all unless it is still at the mercy of storms; unless its strings can scream to the touch of pain.

II.

Signa's wedding supper was over. The guests, and the tiresome little Norwegian preacher who had performed the marriage ceremony, were saying good-night. Old Ivar was hitching the horses to the wagon to take the wedding presents and the bride and groom up to their new home, on Alexandra's north quarter. When Ivar drove up to the gate, Emil and Marie Shabata began to carry out the presents, and Alexandra went into her bedroom to bid Signa good-bye and to give her a few words of good counsel. She was surprised to find that the bride had changed her slippers for heavy shoes and was pinning up her skirts. At that moment Nelse appeared at the gate with the two milk cows that Alexandra had given Signa for a wedding present.

Alexandra began to laugh. "Why, Signa, you and Nelse are to ride home. I'll send Ivar over with the cows in the morning."

Signa hesitated and looked perplexed. When her husband called her, she pinned her hat on resolutely. "I ta-ank I better do yust like he say," she murmured in confusion.

Alexandra and Marie accompanied Signa to the gate and saw the party set off, old Ivar driving ahead in the wagon and the bride and groom following on foot, each leading a cow. Emil burst into a laugh before they were out of hearing.

"Those two will get on," said Alexandra as they turned back to the house. "They are not going to take any chances. They will feel safer with those cows in their own stable. Marie, I am going to send for an old woman next. As soon as I get the girls broken in, I marry them off."

"I've no patience with Signa, marrying that grumpy fellow!" Marie declared. "I wanted her to marry that nice Smirka boy who worked for us last winter. I think she liked him, too."

"Yes, I think she did," Alexandra assented, "but I suppose she was too much afraid of Nelse to marry any one else. Now that I think of it, most of my girls have married men they were afraid of. I believe there is a good deal of the cow in most Swedish girls. You high-strung Bohemian can't understand us. We're a terribly practical people, and I guess we think a cross man makes a good manager."

Marie shrugged her shoulders and turned to pin up a lock of hair that had fallen on her neck. Somehow Alexandra had irritated her of late. Everybody irritated her. She was tired of everybody. "I'm going home alone, Emil, so you needn't get your hat," she said as she wound her scarf quickly about her head. "Good-night, Alexandra," she called back in a strained voice, running down the gravel walk.

Emil followed with long strides until he overtook her. Then she began to walk slowly. It was a night of warm wind and faint starlight, and the fireflies were glimmering over the wheat.

"Marie," said Emil after they had walked for a while, "I wonder if you know how unhappy I am?"

Marie did not answer him. Her head, in its white scarf, drooped forward a little.

Emil kicked a clod from the path and went on:—

"I wonder whether you are really shallow-hearted, like you seem? Sometimes I think one boy does just as well as another for you. It never seems to make much difference whether it is me or Raoul Marcel or Jan Smirka. Are you really like that?"

"Perhaps I am. What do you want me to do? Sit round and cry all day? When I've cried until I can't cry any more, then—then I must do something else."

"Are you sorry for me?" he persisted.

"No, I'm not. If I were big and free like you, I wouldn't let anything make me unhappy. As old Napoleon Brunot said at the fair, I wouldn't go lovering after no woman. I'd take the first train and go off and have all the fun there is."

"I tried that, but it didn't do any good. Everything reminded me. The nicer the place was, the more I wanted you." They had come to the stile and Emil pointed to it persuasively. "Sit down a moment, I want to ask you something." Marie sat down on the top step and Emil drew nearer. "Would you tell me something that's none of my business if you thought it would help me out? Well, then, tell me, PLEASE tell me, why you ran away with Frank Shabata!"

Marie drew back. "Because I was in love with him," she said firmly.

"Really?" he asked incredulously.

"Yes, indeed. Very much in love with him. I think I was the one who suggested our running away. From the first it was more my fault than his."

Emil turned away his face.

"And now," Marie went on, "I've got to remember that. Frank is just the same now as he was then, only then I would see him as I wanted him to be. I would have my own way. And now I pay for it."

"You don't do all the paying."

"That's it. When one makes a mistake, there's no telling where it will stop. But you can go away; you can leave all this behind you."

"Not everything. I can't leave you behind. Will you go away with me, Marie?"

Marie started up and stepped across the stile. "Emil! How wickedly you talk! I am not that kind of a girl, and you know it. But what am I going to do if you keep tormenting me like this!" she added plaintively.

"Marie, I won't bother you any more if you will tell me just one thing. Stop a minute and look at me. No, nobody can see us. Everybody's asleep. That was only a firefly. Marie, STOP and tell me!"

Emil overtook her and catching her by the shoulders shook her gently, as if he were trying to awaken a sleepwalker.

Marie hid her face on his arm. "Don't ask me anything more. I don't know anything except how miserable I am. And I thought it would be all right when you came back. Oh, Emil," she clutched his sleeve and began to cry, "what am I to do if you don't go away? I can't go, and one of us must. Can't you see?"

Emil stood looking down at her, holding his shoulders stiff and stiffening the arm to which she clung. Her white dress looked gray in the darkness. She seemed like a troubled spirit, like some shadow out of the earth, clinging to him and entreating him to give her peace. Behind her the fireflies were weaving in and out over the wheat. He put his hand on her bent head. "On my honor, Marie, if you will say you love me, I will go away."

She lifted her face to his. "How could I help it? Didn't you know?"

Emil was the one who trembled, through all his frame. After he left Marie at her gate, he wandered about the fields all night, till morning put out the fireflies and the stars.

III.

One evening, a week after Signa's wedding, Emil was kneeling before a box in the sitting-room, packing his books. From time to time he rose and wandered about the house, picking up stray volumes and bringing them listlessly back to his box. He was packing without enthusiasm. He was not very sanguine about his future. Alexandra sat sewing by the table. She had helped him pack his trunk in the afternoon. As Emil came and went by her chair with his books, he thought to himself that it had not been so hard to leave his sister since he first went away to school. He was going directly to Omaha, to read law in the office of a Swedish lawyer until October, when he would enter the law school at Ann Arbor. They had planned that Alexandra was to come to Michigan—a long journey for her—at Christmas time, and spend several weeks with him. Nevertheless, he felt that this leave-taking would be more final than his earlier ones had been; that it meant a definite break with his old home and the beginning of something new—he did not know what. His ideas about the future would not crystallize; the more he tried to think about it, the vaguer his conception of it became. But one thing was clear, he told himself; it was high time that he made good to Alexandra, and that ought to be incentive enough to begin with.

As he went about gathering up his books he felt as if he were uprooting things. At last he threw himself down on the old slat lounge where he had slept when he was little, and lay looking up at the familiar cracks in the ceiling.

"Tired, Emil?" his sister asked.

"Lazy," he murmured, turning on his side and looking at her. He studied Alexandra's face for a long time in the lamplight. It had never occurred to him that his sister was a handsome woman until Marie Shabata had told him so. Indeed, he had never thought of her as being a woman at all, only a sister. As he studied her bent head, he looked up at the picture of John Bergson above the lamp. "No," he thought to himself, "she didn't get it there. I suppose I am more like that."

"Alexandra," he said suddenly, "that old walnut secretary you use for a desk was father's, wasn't it?"

Alexandra went on stitching. "Yes. It was one of the first things he bought for the old log house. It was a great extravagance in those days. But he wrote a great many letters back to the old country. He had many friends there, and they wrote to him up to the time he died. No one ever blamed him for grandfather's disgrace. I can see him now, sitting there on Sundays, in his white shirt, writing pages and pages, so carefully. He wrote a fine, regular hand, almost like engraving. Yours is something like his, when you take pains."

"Grandfather was really crooked, was he?"

"He married an unscrupulous woman, and then—then I'm afraid he was really crooked. When we first came here father used to have dreams about making a great fortune and going back to Sweden to pay back to the poor sailors the money grandfather had lost."

Emil stirred on the lounge. "I say, that would have been worth while, wouldn't it? Father wasn't a bit like Lou or Oscar, was he? I can't remember much about him before he got sick."

"Oh, not at all!" Alexandra dropped her sewing on her knee. "He had better opportunities; not to make money, but to make something of himself. He was a quiet man, but he was very intelligent. You would have been proud of him, Emil."

Alexandra felt that he would like to know there had been a man of his kin whom he could admire. She knew that Emil was ashamed of Lou and Oscar, because they were bigoted and self-satisfied. He never said much about them, but she could feel his disgust. His brothers had shown their disapproval of him ever since he first went away to school. The only thing that would have satisfied them would have been his failure at the University. As it was, they resented every change in his speech, in his dress, in his point of view; though the latter they had to conjecture, for Emil avoided talking to them about any but family matters. All his interests they treated as affectations.

Alexandra took up her sewing again. "I can remember father when he was quite a young man. He belonged to some kind of a musical society, a male chorus, in Stockholm. I can remember going with mother to hear them sing. There must have been a hundred of them, and they all wore long black coats and white neckties. I was used to seeing father in a blue coat, a sort of jacket, and when I recognized him on the platform, I was very proud. Do you remember that Swedish song he taught you, about the ship boy?"

"Yes. I used to sing it to the Mexicans. They like anything different." Emil paused. "Father had a hard fight here, didn't he?" he added thoughtfully.

"Yes, and he died in a dark time. Still, he had hope. He believed in the land."

"And in you, I guess," Emil said to himself. There was another period of silence; that warm, friendly silence, full of perfect understanding, in which Emil and Alexandra had spent many of their happiest half-hours.

At last Emil said abruptly, "Lou and Oscar would be better off if they were poor, wouldn't they?"

Alexandra smiled. "Maybe. But their children wouldn't. I have great hopes of Milly."

Emil shivered. "I don't know. Seems to me it gets worse as it goes on. The worst of the Swedes is that they're never willing to find out how much they don't know. It was like that at the University. Always so pleased with themselves! There's no getting behind that conceited Swedish grin. The Bohemians and Germans were so different."

"Come, Emil, don't go back on your own people. Father wasn't conceited, Uncle Otto wasn't. Even Lou and Oscar weren't when they were boys."

Emil looked incredulous, but he did not dispute the point. He turned on his back and lay still for a long time, his hands locked under his head, looking up at the ceiling. Alexandra knew that he was thinking of many things. She felt no anxiety about Emil. She had always believed in him, as she had believed in the land. He had been more like himself since he got back from Mexico; seemed glad to be at home, and talked to her as he used to do. She had no doubt that his wandering fit was over, and that he would soon be settled in life.

"Alexandra," said Emil suddenly, "do you remember the wild duck we saw down on the river that time?"

His sister looked up. "I often think of her. It always seems to me she's there still, just like we saw her."

"I know. It's queer what things one remembers and what things one forgets." Emil yawned and sat up. "Well, it's time to turn in." He rose, and going over to Alexandra stooped down and kissed her lightly on the cheek. "Good-night, sister. I think you did pretty well by us."

Emil took up his lamp and went upstairs. Alexandra sat finishing his new nightshirt, that must go in the top tray of his trunk.

IV.

The next morning Angelique, Amedee's wife, was in the kitchen baking pies, assisted by old Mrs. Chevalier. Between the mixing-board and the stove stood the old cradle that had been Amedee's, and in it was his black-eyed son. As Angelique, flushed and excited, with flour on her hands, stopped to smile at the baby, Emil Bergson rode up to the kitchen door on his mare and dismounted.

"'Medee is out in the field, Emil," Angelique called as she ran across the kitchen to the oven. "He begins to cut his wheat to-day; the first wheat ready to cut anywhere about here. He bought a new header, you know, because all the wheat's so short this year. I hope he can rent it to the neighbors, it cost so much. He and his cousins bought a steam thresher on shares. You ought to go out and see that header work. I watched it an hour this morning, busy as I am with all the men to feed. He has a lot of hands, but he's the only one that knows how to drive the header or how to run the engine, so he has to be everywhere at once. He's sick, too, and ought to be in his bed."

Emil bent over Hector Baptiste, trying to make him blink his round, bead-like black eyes. "Sick? What's the matter with your daddy, kid? Been making him walk the floor with you?"

Angelique sniffed. "Not much! We don't have that kind of babies. It was his father that kept Baptiste awake. All night I had to be getting up and making mustard plasters to put on his stomach. He had an awful colic. He said he felt better this morning, but I don't think he ought to be out in the field, overheating himself."

Angelique did not speak with much anxiety, not because she was indifferent, but because she felt so secure in their good fortune. Only good things could happen to a rich, energetic, handsome young man like Amedee, with a new baby in the cradle and a new header in the field.

Emil stroked the black fuzz on Baptiste's head. "I say, Angelique, one of 'Medee's grandmothers, 'way back, must have been a squaw. This kid looks exactly like the Indian babies."

Angelique made a face at him, but old Mrs. Chevalier had been touched on a sore point, and she let out such a stream of fiery PATOIS that Emil fled from the kitchen and mounted his mare.

Opening the pasture gate from the saddle, Emil rode across the field to the clearing where the thresher stood, driven by a stationary engine and fed from the header boxes. As Amedee was not on the engine, Emil rode on to the wheatfield, where he recognized, on the header, the slight, wiry figure of his friend, coatless, his white shirt puffed out by the wind, his straw hat stuck jauntily on the side of his head. The six big work-horses that drew, or rather pushed, the header, went abreast at a rapid walk, and as they were still green at the work they required a good deal of management on Amedee's part; especially when they turned the corners, where they divided, three and three, and then swung round into line again with a movement that looked as complicated as a wheel of artillery. Emil felt a new thrill of admiration for his friend, and with it the old pang of envy at the way in which Amedee could do with his might what his hand found to do, and feel that, whatever it was, it was the most important thing in the world. "I'll have to bring Alexandra up to see this thing work," Emil thought; "it's splendid!"

When he saw Emil, Amedee waved to him and called to one of his twenty cousins to take the reins. Stepping off the header without stopping it, he ran up to Emil who had dismounted. "Come along," he called. "I have to go over to the engine for a minute. I gotta green man running it, and I gotta to keep an eye on him."

Emil thought the lad was unnaturally flushed and more excited than even the cares of managing a big farm at a critical time warranted. As they passed behind a last year's stack, Amedee clutched at his right side and sank down for a moment on the straw.

"Ouch! I got an awful pain in me, Emil. Something's the matter with my insides, for sure."

Emil felt his fiery cheek. "You ought to go straight to bed, 'Medee, and telephone for the doctor; that's what you ought to do."

Amedee staggered up with a gesture of despair. "How can I? I got no time to be sick. Three thousand dollars' worth of new machinery to manage, and the wheat so ripe it will begin to shatter next week. My wheat's short, but it's gotta grand full berries. What's he slowing down for? We haven't got header boxes enough to feed the thresher, I guess."

Amedee started hot-foot across the stubble, leaning a little to the right as he ran, and waved to the engineer not to stop the engine.

Emil saw that this was no time to talk about his own affairs. He mounted his mare and rode on to Sainte-Agnes, to bid his friends there good-bye. He went first to see Raoul Marcel, and found him innocently practising the "Gloria" for the big confirmation service on Sunday while he polished the mirrors of his father's saloon.

As Emil rode homewards at three o'clock in the afternoon, he saw Amedee staggering out of the wheatfield, supported by two of his cousins. Emil stopped and helped them put the boy to bed.

V.

When Frank Shabata came in from work at five o'clock that evening, old Moses Marcel, Raoul's father, telephoned him that Amedee had had a seizure in the wheatfield, and that Doctor Paradis was going to operate on him as soon as the Hanover doctor got there to help.

Frank dropped a word of this at the table, bolted his supper, and rode off to Sainte-Agnes, where there would be sympathetic discussion of Amedee's case at Marcel's saloon.

As soon as Frank was gone, Marie telephoned Alexandra. It was a comfort to hear her friend's voice. Yes, Alexandra knew what there was to be known about Amedee. Emil had been there when they carried him out of the field, and had stayed with him until the doctors operated for appendicitis at five o'clock. They were afraid it was too late to do much good; it should have been done three days ago. Amedee was in a very bad way. Emil had just come home, worn out and sick himself. She had given him some brandy and put him to bed.

Marie hung up the receiver. Poor Amedee's illness had taken on a new meaning to her, now that she knew Emil had been with him. And it might so easily have been the other way—Emil who was ill and Amedee who was sad! Marie looked about the dusky sitting-room. She had seldom felt so utterly lonely. If Emil was asleep, there was not even a chance of his coming; and she could not go to Alexandra for sympathy. She meant to tell Alexandra everything, as soon as Emil went away. Then whatever was left between them would be honest.

But she could not stay in the house this evening. Where should she go? She walked slowly down through the orchard, where the evening air was heavy with the smell of wild cotton. The fresh, salty scent of the wild roses had given way before this more powerful perfume of midsummer. Wherever those ashes-of-rose balls hung on their milky stalks, the air about them was saturated with their breath. The sky was still red in the west and the evening star hung directly over the Bergsons' wind-mill. Marie crossed the fence at the wheatfield corner, and walked slowly along the path that led to Alexandra's. She could not help feeling hurt that Emil had not come to tell her about Amedee. It seemed to her most unnatural that he should not have come. If she were in trouble, certainly he was the one person in the world she would want to see. Perhaps he wished her to understand that for her he was as good as gone already.

Marie stole slowly, flutteringly, along the path, like a white night-moth out of the fields. The years seemed to stretch before her like the land; spring, summer, autumn, winter, spring; always the same patient fields, the patient little trees, the patient lives; always the same yearning, the same pulling at the chain—until the instinct to live had torn itself and bled and weakened for the last time, until the chain secured a dead woman, who might cautiously be released. Marie walked on, her face lifted toward the remote, inaccessible evening star.

When she reached the stile she sat down and waited. How terrible it was to love people when you could not really share their lives!

Yes, in so far as she was concerned, Emil was already gone. They couldn't meet any more. There was nothing for them to say. They had spent the last penny of their small change; there was nothing left but gold. The day of love-tokens was past. They had now only their hearts to give each other. And Emil being gone, what was her life to be like? In some ways, it would be easier. She would not, at least, live in perpetual fear. If Emil were once away and settled at work, she would not have the feeling that she was spoiling his life. With the memory he left her, she could be as rash as she chose. Nobody could be the worse for it but herself; and that, surely, did not matter. Her own case was clear. When a girl had loved one man, and then loved another while that man was still alive, everybody knew what to think of her. What happened to her was of little consequence, so long as she did not drag other people down with her. Emil once away, she could let everything else go and live a new life of perfect love.

Marie left the stile reluctantly. She had, after all, thought he might come. And how glad she ought to be, she told herself, that he was asleep. She left the path and went across the pasture. The moon was almost full. An owl was hooting somewhere in the fields. She had scarcely thought about where she was going when the pond glittered before her, where Emil had shot the ducks. She stopped and looked at it. Yes, there would be a dirty way out of life, if one chose to take it. But she did not want to die. She wanted to live and dream—a hundred years, forever! As long as this sweetness welled up in her heart, as long as her breast could hold this treasure of pain! She felt as the pond must feel when it held the moon like that; when it encircled and swelled with that image of gold.

In the morning, when Emil came down-stairs, Alexandra met him in the sitting-room and put her hands on his shoulders. "Emil, I went to your room as soon as it was light, but you were sleeping so sound I hated to wake you. There was nothing you could do, so I let you sleep. They telephoned from Sainte-Agnes that Amedee died at three o'clock this morning."

VI.

The Church has always held that life is for the living. On Saturday, while half the village of Sainte-Agnes was mourning for Amedee and preparing the funeral black for his burial on Monday, the other half was busy with white dresses and white veils for the great confirmation service to-morrow, when the bishop was to confirm a class of one hundred boys and girls. Father Duchesne divided his time between the living and the dead. All day Saturday the church was a scene of bustling activity, a little hushed by the thought of Amedee. The choir were busy rehearsing a mass of Rossini, which they had studied and practised for this occasion. The women were trimming the altar, the boys and girls were bringing flowers.

On Sunday morning the bishop was to drive overland to Sainte-Agnes from Hanover, and Emil Bergson had been asked to take the place of one of Amedee's cousins in the cavalcade of forty French boys who were to ride across country to meet the bishop's carriage. At six o'clock on Sunday morning the boys met at the church. As they stood holding their horses by the bridle, they talked in low tones of their dead comrade. They kept repeating that Amedee had always been a good boy, glancing toward the red brick church which had played so large a part in Amedee's life, had been the scene of his most serious moments and of his happiest hours. He had played and wrestled and sung and courted under its shadow. Only three weeks ago he had proudly carried his baby there to be christened. They could not doubt that that invisible arm was still about Amedee; that through the church on earth he had passed to the church triumphant, the goal of the hopes and faith of so many hundred years.

When the word was given to mount, the young men rode at a walk out of the village; but once out among the wheatfields in the morning sun, their horses and their own youth got the better of them. A wave of zeal and fiery enthusiasm swept over them. They longed for a Jerusalem to deliver. The thud of their galloping hoofs interrupted many a country breakfast and brought many a woman and child to the door of the farmhouses as they passed. Five miles east of Sainte-Agnes they met the bishop in his open carriage, attended by two priests. Like one man the boys swung off their hats in a broad salute, and bowed their heads as the handsome old man lifted his two fingers in the episcopal blessing. The horsemen closed about the carriage like a guard, and whenever a restless horse broke from control and shot down the road ahead of the body, the bishop laughed and rubbed his plump hands together. "What fine boys!" he said to his priests. "The Church still has her cavalry."

As the troop swept past the graveyard half a mile east of the town,—the first frame church of the parish had stood there,—old Pierre Seguin was already out with his pick and spade, digging Amedee's grave. He knelt and uncovered as the bishop passed. The boys with one accord looked away from old Pierre to the red church on the hill, with the gold cross flaming on its steeple.

Mass was at eleven. While the church was filling, Emil Bergson waited outside, watching the wagons and buggies drive up the hill. After the bell began to ring, he saw Frank Shabata ride up on horseback and tie his horse to the hitch-bar. Marie, then, was not coming. Emil turned and went into the church. Amedee's was the only empty pew, and he sat down in it. Some of Amedee's cousins were there, dressed in black and weeping. When all the pews were full, the old men and boys packed the open space at the back of the church, kneeling on the floor. There was scarcely a family in town that was not represented in the confirmation class, by a cousin, at least. The new communicants, with their clear, reverent faces, were beautiful to look upon as they entered in a body and took the front benches reserved for them. Even before the Mass began, the air was charged with feeling. The choir had never sung so well and Raoul Marcel, in the "Gloria," drew even the bishop's eyes to the organ loft. For the offertory he sang Gounod's "Ave Maria,"—always spoken of in Sainte-Agnes as "the Ave Maria."

Emil began to torture himself with questions about Marie. Was she ill? Had she quarreled with her husband? Was she too unhappy to find comfort even here? Had she, perhaps, thought that he would come to her? Was she waiting for him? Overtaxed by excitement and sorrow as he was, the rapture of the service took hold upon his body and mind. As he listened to Raoul, he seemed to emerge from the conflicting emotions which had been whirling him about and sucking him under. He felt as if a clear light broke upon his mind, and with it a conviction that good was, after all, stronger than evil, and that good was possible to men. He seemed to discover that there was a kind of rapture in which he could love forever without faltering and without sin. He looked across the heads of the people at Frank Shabata with calmness. That rapture was for those who could feel it; for people who could not, it was non-existent. He coveted nothing that was Frank Shabata's. The spirit he had met in music was his own. Frank Shabata had never found it; would never find it if he lived beside it a thousand years; would have destroyed it if he had found it, as Herod slew the innocents, as Rome slew the martyrs.

SAN—CTA MARI-I-I-A,

wailed Raoul from the organ loft;

O—RA PRO NO-O-BIS!

And it did not occur to Emil that any one had ever reasoned thus before, that music had ever before given a man this equivocal revelation.

The confirmation service followed the Mass. When it was over, the congregation thronged about the newly confirmed. The girls, and even the boys, were kissed and embraced and wept over. All the aunts and grandmothers wept with joy. The housewives had much ado to tear themselves away from the general rejoicing and hurry back to their kitchens. The country parishioners were staying in town for dinner, and nearly every house in Sainte-Agnes entertained visitors that day. Father Duchesne, the bishop, and the visiting priests dined with Fabien Sauvage, the banker. Emil and Frank Shabata were both guests of old Moise Marcel. After dinner Frank and old Moise retired to the rear room of the saloon to play California Jack and drink their cognac, and Emil went over to the banker's with Raoul, who had been asked to sing for the bishop.

At three o'clock, Emil felt that he could stand it no longer. He slipped out under cover of "The Holy City," followed by Malvina's wistful eye, and went to the stable for his mare. He was at that height of excitement from which everything is foreshortened, from which life seems short and simple, death very near, and the soul seems to soar like an eagle. As he rode past the graveyard he looked at the brown hole in the earth where Amedee was to lie, and felt no horror. That, too, was beautiful, that simple doorway into forgetfulness. The heart, when it is too much alive, aches for that brown earth, and ecstasy has no fear of death. It is the old and the poor and the maimed who shrink from that brown hole; its wooers are found among the young, the passionate, the gallant-hearted. It was not until he had passed the graveyard that Emil realized where he was going. It was the hour for saying good-bye. It might be the last time that he would see her alone, and today he could leave her without rancor, without bitterness.

Everywhere the grain stood ripe and the hot afternoon was full of the smell of the ripe wheat, like the smell of bread baking in an oven. The breath of the wheat and the sweet clover passed him like pleasant things in a dream. He could feel nothing but the sense of diminishing distance. It seemed to him that his mare was flying, or running on wheels, like a railway train. The sunlight, flashing on the window-glass of the big red barns, drove him wild with joy. He was like an arrow shot from the bow. His life poured itself out along the road before him as he rode to the Shabata farm.

When Emil alighted at the Shabatas' gate, his horse was in a lather. He tied her in the stable and hurried to the house. It was empty. She might be at Mrs. Hiller's or with Alexandra. But anything that reminded him of her would be enough, the orchard, the mulberry tree... When he reached the orchard the sun was hanging low over the wheatfield. Long fingers of light reached through the apple branches as through a net; the orchard was riddled and shot with gold; light was the reality, the trees were merely interferences that reflected and refracted light. Emil went softly down between the cherry trees toward the wheatfield. When he came to the corner, he stopped short and put his hand over his mouth. Marie was lying on her side under the white mulberry tree, her face half hidden in the grass, her eyes closed, her hands lying limply where they had happened to fall. She had lived a day of her new life of perfect love, and it had left her like this. Her breast rose and fell faintly, as if she were asleep. Emil threw himself down beside her and took her in his arms. The blood came back to her cheeks, her amber eyes opened slowly, and in them Emil saw his own face and the orchard and the sun. "I was dreaming this," she whispered, hiding her face against him, "don't take my dream away!"

VII.

When Frank Shabata got home that night, he found Emil's mare in his stable. Such an impertinence amazed him. Like everybody else, Frank had had an exciting day. Since noon he had been drinking too much, and he was in a bad temper. He talked bitterly to himself while he put his own horse away, and as he went up the path and saw that the house was dark he felt an added sense of injury. He approached quietly and listened on the doorstep. Hearing nothing, he opened the kitchen door and went softly from one room to another. Then he went through the house again, upstairs and down, with no better result. He sat down on the bottom step of the box stairway and tried to get his wits together. In that unnatural quiet there was no sound but his own heavy breathing. Suddenly an owl began to hoot out in the fields. Frank lifted his head. An idea flashed into his mind, and his sense of injury and outrage grew. He went into his bedroom and took his murderous 405 Winchester from the closet.

When Frank took up his gun and walked out of the house, he had not the faintest purpose of doing anything with it. He did not believe that he had any real grievance. But it gratified him to feel like a desperate man. He had got into the habit of seeing himself always in desperate straits. His unhappy temperament was like a cage; he could never get out of it; and he felt that other people, his wife in particular, must have put him there. It had never more than dimly occurred to Frank that he made his own unhappiness. Though he took up his gun with dark projects in his mind, he would have been paralyzed with fright had he known that there was the slightest probability of his ever carrying any of them out.

Frank went slowly down to the orchard gate, stopped and stood for a moment lost in thought. He retraced his steps and looked through the barn and the hayloft. Then he went out to the road, where he took the foot-path along the outside of the orchard hedge. The hedge was twice as tall as Frank himself, and so dense that one could see through it only by peering closely between the leaves. He could see the empty path a long way in the moonlight. His mind traveled ahead to the stile, which he always thought of as haunted by Emil Bergson. But why had he left his horse?

At the wheatfield corner, where the orchard hedge ended and the path led across the pasture to the Bergsons', Frank stopped. In the warm, breathless night air he heard a murmuring sound, perfectly inarticulate, as low as the sound of water coming from a spring, where there is no fall, and where there are no stones to fret it. Frank strained his ears. It ceased. He held his breath and began to tremble. Resting the butt of his gun on the ground, he parted the mulberry leaves softly with his fingers and peered through the hedge at the dark figures on the grass, in the shadow of the mulberry tree. It seemed to him that they must feel his eyes, that they must hear him breathing. But they did not. Frank, who had always wanted to see things blacker than they were, for once wanted to believe less than he saw. The woman lying in the shadow might so easily be one of the Bergsons' farm-girls.... Again the murmur, like water welling out of the ground. This time he heard it more distinctly, and his blood was quicker than his brain. He began to act, just as a man who falls into the fire begins to act. The gun sprang to his shoulder, he sighted mechanically and fired three times without stopping, stopped without knowing why. Either he shut his eyes or he had vertigo. He did not see anything while he was firing. He thought he heard a cry simultaneous with the second report, but he was not sure. He peered again through the hedge, at the two dark figures under the tree. They had fallen a little apart from each other, and were perfectly still—No, not quite; in a white patch of light, where the moon shone through the branches, a man's hand was plucking spasmodically at the grass.

Suddenly the woman stirred and uttered a cry, then another, and another. She was living! She was dragging herself toward the hedge! Frank dropped his gun and ran back along the path, shaking, stumbling, gasping. He had never imagined such horror. The cries followed him. They grew fainter and thicker, as if she were choking. He dropped on his knees beside the hedge and crouched like a rabbit, listening; fainter, fainter; a sound like a whine; again—a moan—another—silence. Frank scrambled to his feet and ran on, groaning and praying. From habit he went toward the house, where he was used to being soothed when he had worked himself into a frenzy, but at the sight of the black, open door, he started back. He knew that he had murdered somebody, that a woman was bleeding and moaning in the orchard, but he had not realized before that it was his wife. The gate stared him in the face. He threw his hands over his head. Which way to turn? He lifted his tormented face and looked at the sky. "Holy Mother of God, not to suffer! She was a good girl—not to suffer!"

Frank had been wont to see himself in dramatic situations; but now, when he stood by the windmill, in the bright space between the barn and the house, facing his own black doorway, he did not see himself at all. He stood like the hare when the dogs are approaching from all sides. And he ran like a hare, back and forth about that moonlit space, before he could make up his mind to go into the dark stable for a horse. The thought of going into a doorway was terrible to him. He caught Emil's horse by the bit and led it out. He could not have buckled a bridle on his own. After two or three attempts, he lifted himself into the saddle and started for Hanover. If he could catch the one o'clock train, he had money enough to get as far as Omaha.

While he was thinking dully of this in some less sensitized part of his brain, his acuter faculties were going over and over the cries he had heard in the orchard. Terror was the only thing that kept him from going back to her, terror that she might still be she, that she might still be suffering. A woman, mutilated and bleeding in his orchard—it was because it was a woman that he was so afraid. It was inconceivable that he should have hurt a woman. He would rather be eaten by wild beasts than see her move on the ground as she had moved in the orchard. Why had she been so careless? She knew he was like a crazy man when he was angry. She had more than once taken that gun away from him and held it, when he was angry with other people. Once it had gone off while they were struggling over it. She was never afraid. But, when she knew him, why hadn't she been more careful? Didn't she have all summer before her to love Emil Bergson in, without taking such chances? Probably she had met the Smirka boy, too, down there in the orchard. He didn't care. She could have met all the men on the Divide there, and welcome, if only she hadn't brought this horror on him.

There was a wrench in Frank's mind. He did not honestly believe that of her. He knew that he was doing her wrong. He stopped his horse to admit this to himself the more directly, to think it out the more clearly. He knew that he was to blame. For three years he had been trying to break her spirit. She had a way of making the best of things that seemed to him a sentimental affectation. He wanted his wife to resent that he was wasting his best years among these stupid and unappreciative people; but she had seemed to find the people quite good enough. If he ever got rich he meant to buy her pretty clothes and take her to California in a Pullman car, and treat her like a lady; but in the mean time he wanted her to feel that life was as ugly and as unjust as he felt it. He had tried to make her life ugly. He had refused to share any of the little pleasures she was so plucky about making for herself. She could be gay about the least thing in the world; but she must be gay! When she first came to him, her faith in him, her adoration—Frank struck the mare with his fist. Why had Marie made him do this thing; why had she brought this upon him? He was overwhelmed by sickening misfortune. All at once he heard her cries again—he had forgotten for a moment. "Maria," he sobbed aloud, "Maria!"

When Frank was halfway to Hanover, the motion of his horse brought on a violent attack of nausea. After it had passed, he rode on again, but he could think of nothing except his physical weakness and his desire to be comforted by his wife. He wanted to get into his own bed. Had his wife been at home, he would have turned and gone back to her meekly enough.

VIII.

When old Ivar climbed down from his loft at four o'clock the next morning, he came upon Emil's mare, jaded and lather-stained, her bridle broken, chewing the scattered tufts of hay outside the stable door. The old man was thrown into a fright at once. He put the mare in her stall, threw her a measure of oats, and then set out as fast as his bow-legs could carry him on the path to the nearest neighbor.

"Something is wrong with that boy. Some misfortune has come upon us. He would never have used her so, in his right senses. It is not his way to abuse his mare," the old man kept muttering, as he scuttled through the short, wet pasture grass on his bare feet.

While Ivar was hurrying across the fields, the first long rays of the sun were reaching down between the orchard boughs to those two dew-drenched figures. The story of what had happened was written plainly on the orchard grass, and on the white mulberries that had fallen in the night and were covered with dark stain. For Emil the chapter had been short. He was shot in the heart, and had rolled over on his back and died. His face was turned up to the sky and his brows were drawn in a frown, as if he had realized that something had befallen him. But for Marie Shabata it had not been so easy. One ball had torn through her right lung, another had shattered the carotid artery. She must have started up and gone toward the hedge, leaving a trail of blood. There she had fallen and bled. From that spot there was another trail, heavier than the first, where she must have dragged herself back to Emil's body. Once there, she seemed not to have struggled any more. She had lifted her head to her lover's breast, taken his hand in both her own, and bled quietly to death. She was lying on her right side in an easy and natural position, her cheek on Emil's shoulder. On her face there was a look of ineffable content. Her lips were parted a little; her eyes were lightly closed, as if in a day-dream or a light slumber. After she lay down there, she seemed not to have moved an eyelash. The hand she held was covered with dark stains, where she had kissed it.

But the stained, slippery grass, the darkened mulberries, told only half the story. Above Marie and Emil, two white butterflies from Frank's alfalfa-field were fluttering in and out among the interlacing shadows; diving and soaring, now close together, now far apart; and in the long grass by the fence the last wild roses of the year opened their pink hearts to die.

When Ivar reached the path by the hedge, he saw Shabata's rifle lying in the way. He turned and peered through the branches, falling upon his knees as if his legs had been mowed from under him. "Merciful God!" he groaned.

Alexandra, too, had risen early that morning, because of her anxiety about Emil. She was in Emil's room upstairs when, from the window, she saw Ivar coming along the path that led from the Shabatas'. He was running like a spent man, tottering and lurching from side to side. Ivar never drank, and Alexandra thought at once that one of his spells had come upon him, and that he must be in a very bad way indeed. She ran downstairs and hurried out to meet him, to hide his infirmity from the eyes of her household. The old man fell in the road at her feet and caught her hand, over which he bowed his shaggy head. "Mistress, mistress," he sobbed, "it has fallen! Sin and death for the young ones! God have mercy upon us!"

5
ALEXANDRA

I.

Ivar was sitting at a cobbler's bench in the barn, mending harness by the light of a lantern and repeating to himself the 101st Psalm. It was only five o'clock of a mid-October day, but a storm had come up in the afternoon, bringing black clouds, a cold wind and torrents of rain. The old man wore his buffalo-skin coat, and occasionally stopped to warm his fingers at the lantern. Suddenly a woman burst into the shed, as if she had been blown in, accompanied by a shower of rain-drops. It was Signa, wrapped in a man's overcoat and wearing a pair of boots over her shoes. In time of trouble Signa had come back to stay with her mistress, for she was the only one of the maids from whom Alexandra would accept much personal service. It was three months now since the news of the terrible thing that had happened in Frank Shabata's orchard had first run like a fire over the Divide. Signa and Nelse were staying on with Alexandra until winter.

"Ivar," Signa exclaimed as she wiped the rain from her face, "do you know where she is?"

The old man put down his cobbler's knife. "Who, the mistress?"

"Yes. She went away about three o'clock. I happened to look out of the window and saw her going across the fields in her thin dress and sun-hat. And now this storm has come on. I thought she was going to Mrs. Hiller's, and I telephoned as soon as the thunder stopped, but she had not been there. I'm afraid she is out somewhere and will get her death of cold."

Ivar put on his cap and took up the lantern. "JA, JA, we will see. I will hitch the boy's mare to the cart and go."

Signa followed him across the wagon-shed to the horses' stable. She was shivering with cold and excitement. "Where do you suppose she can be, Ivar?"

The old man lifted a set of single harness carefully from its peg. "How should I know?"

"But you think she is at the graveyard, don't you?" Signa persisted. "So do I. Oh, I wish she would be more like herself! I can't believe it's Alexandra Bergson come to this, with no head about anything. I have to tell her when to eat and when to go to bed."

"Patience, patience, sister," muttered Ivar as he settled the bit in the horse's mouth.

"When the eyes of the flesh are shut, the eyes of the spirit are open. She will have a message from those who are gone, and that will bring her peace. Until then we must bear with her. You and I are the only ones who have weight with her. She trusts us."

"How awful it's been these last three months." Signa held the lantern so that he could see to buckle the straps. "It don't seem right that we must all be so miserable. Why do we all have to be punished? Seems to me like good times would never come again."

Ivar expressed himself in a deep sigh, but said nothing. He stooped and took a sandburr from his toe.

"Ivar," Signa asked suddenly, "will you tell me why you go barefoot? All the time I lived here in the house I wanted to ask you. Is it for a penance, or what?"

"No, sister. It is for the indulgence of the body. From my youth up I have had a strong, rebellious body, and have been subject to every kind of temptation. Even in age my temptations are prolonged. It was necessary to make some allowances; and the feet, as I understand it, are free members. There is no divine prohibition for them in the Ten Commandments. The hands, the tongue, the eyes, the heart, all the bodily desires we are commanded to subdue; but the feet are free members. I indulge them without harm to any one, even to trampling in filth when my desires are low. They are quickly cleaned again."

Signa did not laugh. She looked thoughtful as she followed Ivar out to the wagon-shed and held the shafts up for him, while he backed in the mare and buckled the hold-backs. "You have been a good friend to the mistress, Ivar," she murmured.

"And you, God be with you," replied Ivar as he clambered into the cart and put the lantern under the oilcloth lap-cover. "Now for a ducking, my girl," he said to the mare, gathering up the reins.

As they emerged from the shed, a stream of water, running off the thatch, struck the mare on the neck. She tossed her head indignantly, then struck out bravely on the soft ground, slipping back again and again as she climbed the hill to the main road. Between the rain and the darkness Ivar could see very little, so he let Emil's mare have the rein, keeping her head in the right direction. When the ground was level, he turned her out of the dirt road upon the sod, where she was able to trot without slipping.

Before Ivar reached the graveyard, three miles from the house, the storm had spent itself, and the downpour had died into a soft, dripping rain. The sky and the land were a dark smoke color, and seemed to be coming together, like two waves. When Ivar stopped at the gate and swung out his lantern, a white figure rose from beside John Bergson's white stone.

The old man sprang to the ground and shuffled toward the gate calling, "Mistress, mistress!"

Alexandra hurried to meet him and put her hand on his shoulder. "TYST! Ivar. There's nothing to be worried about. I'm sorry if I've scared you all. I didn't notice the storm till it was on me, and I couldn't walk against it. I'm glad you've come. I am so tired I didn't know how I'd ever get home."

Ivar swung the lantern up so that it shone in her face. "GUD! You are enough to frighten us, mistress. You look like a drowned woman. How could you do such a thing!"

Groaning and mumbling he led her out of the gate and helped her into the cart, wrapping her in the dry blankets on which he had been sitting.

Alexandra smiled at his solicitude. "Not much use in that, Ivar. You will only shut the wet in. I don't feel so cold now; but I'm heavy and numb. I'm glad you came."

Ivar turned the mare and urged her into a sliding trot. Her feet sent back a continual spatter of mud.

Alexandra spoke to the old man as they jogged along through the sullen gray twilight of the storm. "Ivar, I think it has done me good to get cold clear through like this, once. I don't believe I shall suffer so much any more. When you get so near the dead, they seem more real than the living. Worldly thoughts leave one. Ever since Emil died, I've suffered so when it rained. Now that I've been out in it with him, I shan't dread it. After you once get cold clear through, the feeling of the rain on you is sweet. It seems to bring back feelings you had when you were a baby. It carries you back into the dark, before you were born; you can't see things, but they come to you, somehow, and you know them and aren't afraid of them. Maybe it's like that with the dead. If they feel anything at all, it's the old things, before they were born, that comfort people like the feeling of their own bed does when they are little."

"Mistress," said Ivar reproachfully, "those are bad thoughts. The dead are in Paradise."

Then he hung his head, for he did not believe that Emil was in Paradise.

When they got home, Signa had a fire burning in the sitting-room stove. She undressed Alexandra and gave her a hot footbath, while Ivar made ginger tea in the kitchen. When Alexandra was in bed, wrapped in hot blankets, Ivar came in with his tea and saw that she drank it. Signa asked permission to sleep on the slat lounge outside her door. Alexandra endured their attentions patiently, but she was glad when they put out the lamp and left her. As she lay alone in the dark, it occurred to her for the first time that perhaps she was actually tired of life. All the physical operations of life seemed difficult and painful. She longed to be free from her own body, which ached and was so heavy. And longing itself was heavy: she yearned to be free of that.

As she lay with her eyes closed, she had again, more vividly than for many years, the old illusion of her girlhood, of being lifted and carried lightly by some one very strong. He was with her a long while this time, and carried her very far, and in his arms she felt free from pain. When he laid her down on her bed again, she opened her eyes, and, for the first time in her life, she saw him, saw him clearly, though the room was dark, and his face was covered. He was standing in the doorway of her room. His white cloak was thrown over his face, and his head was bent a little forward. His shoulders seemed as strong as the foundations of the world. His right arm, bared from the elbow, was dark and gleaming, like bronze, and she knew at once that it was the arm of the mightiest of all lovers. She knew at last for whom it was she had waited, and where he would carry her. That, she told herself, was very well. Then she went to sleep.

Alexandra wakened in the morning with nothing worse than a hard cold and a stiff shoulder. She kept her bed for several days, and it was during that time that she formed a resolution to go to Lincoln to see Frank Shabata. Ever since she last saw him in the courtroom, Frank's haggard face and wild eyes had haunted her. The trial had lasted only three days. Frank had given himself up to the police in Omaha and pleaded guilty of killing without malice and without premeditation. The gun was, of course, against him, and the judge had given him the full sentence,—ten years. He had now been in the State Penitentiary for a month.

Frank was the only one, Alexandra told herself, for whom anything could be done. He had been less in the wrong than any of them, and he was paying the heaviest penalty. She often felt that she herself had been more to blame than poor Frank. From the time the Shabatas had first moved to the neighboring farm, she had omitted no opportunity of throwing Marie and Emil together. Because she knew Frank was surly about doing little things to help his wife, she was always sending Emil over to spade or plant or carpenter for Marie. She was glad to have Emil see as much as possible of an intelligent, city-bred girl like their neighbor; she noticed that it improved his manners. She knew that Emil was fond of Marie, but it had never occurred to her that Emil's feeling might be different from her own.

She wondered at herself now, but she had never thought of danger in that direction. If Marie had been unmarried,—oh, yes! Then she would have kept her eyes open. But the mere fact that she was Shabata's wife, for Alexandra, settled everything. That she was beautiful, impulsive, barely two years older than Emil, these facts had had no weight with Alexandra. Emil was a good boy, and only bad boys ran after married women.

Now, Alexandra could in a measure realize that Marie was, after all, Marie; not merely a "married woman." Sometimes, when Alexandra thought of her, it was with an aching tenderness. The moment she had reached them in the orchard that morning, everything was clear to her. There was something about those two lying in the grass, something in the way Marie had settled her cheek on Emil's shoulder, that told her everything. She wondered then how they could have helped loving each other; how she could have helped knowing that they must. Emil's cold, frowning face, the girl's content—Alexandra had felt awe of them, even in the first shock of her grief.

The idleness of those days in bed, the relaxation of body which attended them, enabled Alexandra to think more calmly than she had done since Emil's death. She and Frank, she told herself, were left out of that group of friends who had been overwhelmed by disaster. She must certainly see Frank Shabata. Even in the courtroom her heart had grieved for him. He was in a strange country, he had no kinsmen or friends, and in a moment he had ruined his life. Being what he was, she felt, Frank could not have acted otherwise. She could understand his behavior more easily than she could understand Marie's. Yes, she must go to Lincoln to see Frank Shabata.

The day after Emil's funeral, Alexandra had written to Carl Linstrum; a single page of notepaper, a bare statement of what had happened. She was not a woman who could write much about such a thing, and about her own feelings she could never write very freely. She knew that Carl was away from post-offices, prospecting somewhere in the interior. Before he started he had written her where he expected to go, but her ideas about Alaska were vague. As the weeks went by and she heard nothing from him, it seemed to Alexandra that her heart grew hard against Carl. She began to wonder whether she would not do better to finish her life alone. What was left of life seemed unimportant.

II.

Late in the afternoon of a brilliant October day, Alexandra Bergson, dressed in a black suit and traveling-hat, alighted at the Burlington depot in Lincoln. She drove to the Lindell Hotel, where she had stayed two years ago when she came up for Emil's Commencement. In spite of her usual air of sureness and self-possession, Alexandra felt ill at ease in hotels, and she was glad, when she went to the clerk's desk to register, that there were not many people in the lobby. She had her supper early, wearing her hat and black jacket down to the dining-room and carrying her handbag. After supper she went out for a walk.

It was growing dark when she reached the university campus. She did not go into the grounds, but walked slowly up and down the stone walk outside the long iron fence, looking through at the young men who were running from one building to another, at the lights shining from the armory and the library. A squad of cadets were going through their drill behind the armory, and the commands of their young officer rang out at regular intervals, so sharp and quick that Alexandra could not understand them. Two stalwart girls came down the library steps and out through one of the iron gates. As they passed her, Alexandra was pleased to hear them speaking Bohemian to each other. Every few moments a boy would come running down the flagged walk and dash out into the street as if he were rushing to announce some wonder to the world. Alexandra felt a great tenderness for them all. She wished one of them would stop and speak to her. She wished she could ask them whether they had known Emil.

As she lingered by the south gate she actually did encounter one of the boys. He had on his drill cap and was swinging his books at the end of a long strap. It was dark by this time; he did not see her and ran against her. He snatched off his cap and stood bareheaded and panting. "I'm awfully sorry," he said in a bright, clear voice, with a rising inflection, as if he expected her to say something.

"Oh, it was my fault!" said Alexandra eagerly. "Are you an old student here, may I ask?"

"No, ma'am. I'm a Freshie, just off the farm. Cherry County. Were you hunting somebody?"

"No, thank you. That is—" Alexandra wanted to detain him. "That is, I would like to find some of my brother's friends. He graduated two years ago."

"Then you'd have to try the Seniors, wouldn't you? Let's see; I don't know any of them yet, but there'll be sure to be some of them around the library. That red building, right there," he pointed.

"Thank you, I'll try there," said Alexandra lingeringly.

"Oh, that's all right! Good-night." The lad clapped his cap on his head and ran straight down Eleventh Street. Alexandra looked after him wistfully.

She walked back to her hotel unreasonably comforted. "What a nice voice that boy had, and how polite he was. I know Emil was always like that to women." And again, after she had undressed and was standing in her nightgown, brushing her long, heavy hair by the electric light, she remembered him and said to herself, "I don't think I ever heard a nicer voice than that boy had. I hope he will get on well here. Cherry County; that's where the hay is so fine, and the coyotes can scratch down to water."

At nine o'clock the next morning Alexandra presented herself at the warden's office in the State Penitentiary. The warden was a German, a ruddy, cheerful-looking man who had formerly been a harness-maker. Alexandra had a letter to him from the German banker in Hanover. As he glanced at the letter, Mr. Schwartz put away his pipe.

"That big Bohemian, is it? Sure, he's gettin' along fine," said Mr. Schwartz cheerfully.

"I am glad to hear that. I was afraid he might be quarrelsome and get himself into more trouble. Mr. Schwartz, if you have time, I would like to tell you a little about Frank Shabata, and why I am interested in him."

The warden listened genially while she told him briefly something of Frank's history and character, but he did not seem to find anything unusual in her account.

"Sure, I'll keep an eye on him. We'll take care of him all right," he said, rising. "You can talk to him here, while I go to see to things in the kitchen. I'll have him sent in. He ought to be done washing out his cell by this time. We have to keep 'em clean, you know."

The warden paused at the door, speaking back over his shoulder to a pale young man in convicts' clothes who was seated at a desk in the corner, writing in a big ledger.

"Bertie, when 1037 is brought in, you just step out and give this lady a chance to talk."

The young man bowed his head and bent over his ledger again.

When Mr. Schwartz disappeared, Alexandra thrust her black-edged handkerchief nervously into her handbag. Coming out on the streetcar she had not had the least dread of meeting Frank. But since she had been here the sounds and smells in the corridor, the look of the men in convicts' clothes who passed the glass door of the warden's office, affected her unpleasantly.

The warden's clock ticked, the young convict's pen scratched busily in the big book, and his sharp shoulders were shaken every few seconds by a loose cough which he tried to smother. It was easy to see that he was a sick man. Alexandra looked at him timidly, but he did not once raise his eyes. He wore a white shirt under his striped jacket, a high collar, and a necktie, very carefully tied. His hands were thin and white and well cared for, and he had a seal ring on his little finger. When he heard steps approaching in the corridor, he rose, blotted his book, put his pen in the rack, and left the room without raising his eyes. Through the door he opened a guard came in, bringing Frank Shabata.

"You the lady that wanted to talk to 1037? Here he is. Be on your good behavior, now. He can set down, lady," seeing that Alexandra remained standing. "Push that white button when you're through with him, and I'll come."

The guard went out and Alexandra and Frank were left alone.

Alexandra tried not to see his hideous clothes. She tried to look straight into his face, which she could scarcely believe was his. It was already bleached to a chalky gray. His lips were colorless, his fine teeth looked yellowish. He glanced at Alexandra sullenly, blinked as if he had come from a dark place, and one eyebrow twitched continually. She felt at once that this interview was a terrible ordeal to him. His shaved head, showing the conformation of his skull, gave him a criminal look which he had not had during the trial.

Alexandra held out her hand. "Frank," she said, her eyes filling suddenly, "I hope you'll let me be friendly with you. I understand how you did it. I don't feel hard toward you. They were more to blame than you."

Frank jerked a dirty blue handkerchief from his trousers pocket. He had begun to cry. He turned away from Alexandra. "I never did mean to do not'ing to dat woman," he muttered. "I never mean to do not'ing to dat boy. I ain't had not'ing ag'in' dat boy. I always like dat boy fine. An' then I find him—" He stopped. The feeling went out of his face and eyes. He dropped into a chair and sat looking stolidly at the floor, his hands hanging loosely between his knees, the handkerchief lying across his striped leg. He seemed to have stirred up in his mind a disgust that had paralyzed his faculties.

"I haven't come up here to blame you, Frank. I think they were more to blame than you." Alexandra, too, felt benumbed.

Frank looked up suddenly and stared out of the office window. "I guess dat place all go to hell what I work so hard on," he said with a slow, bitter smile. "I not care a damn." He stopped and rubbed the palm of his hand over the light bristles on his head with annoyance. "I no can t'ink without my hair," he complained. "I forget English. We not talk here, except swear."

Alexandra was bewildered. Frank seemed to have undergone a change of personality. There was scarcely anything by which she could recognize her handsome Bohemian neighbor. He seemed, somehow, not altogether human. She did not know what to say to him.

"You do not feel hard to me, Frank?" she asked at last.

Frank clenched his fist and broke out in excitement. "I not feel hard at no woman. I tell you I not that kind-a man. I never hit my wife. No, never I hurt her when she devil me something awful!" He struck his fist down on the warden's desk so hard that he afterward stroked it absently. A pale pink crept over his neck and face. "Two, t'ree years I know dat woman don' care no more 'bout me, Alexandra Bergson. I know she after some other man. I know her, oo-oo! An' I ain't never hurt her. I never would-a done dat, if I ain't had dat gun along. I don' know what in hell make me take dat gun. She always say I ain't no man to carry gun. If she been in dat house, where she ought-a been—But das a foolish talk."

Frank rubbed his head and stopped suddenly, as he had stopped before. Alexandra felt that there was something strange in the way he chilled off, as if something came up in him that extinguished his power of feeling or thinking.

"Yes, Frank," she said kindly. "I know you never meant to hurt Marie."

Frank smiled at her queerly. His eyes filled slowly with tears. "You know, I most forgit dat woman's name. She ain't got no name for me no more. I never hate my wife, but dat woman what make me do dat—Honest to God, but I hate her! I no man to fight. I don' want to kill no boy and no woman. I not care how many men she take under dat tree. I no care for not'ing but dat fine boy I kill, Alexandra Bergson. I guess I go crazy sure 'nough."

Alexandra remembered the little yellow cane she had found in Frank's clothes-closet. She thought of how he had come to this country a gay young fellow, so attractive that the prettiest Bohemian girl in Omaha had run away with him. It seemed unreasonable that life should have landed him in such a place as this. She blamed Marie bitterly. And why, with her happy, affectionate nature, should she have brought destruction and sorrow to all who had loved her, even to poor old Joe Tovesky, the uncle who used to carry her about so proudly when she was a little girl? That was the strangest thing of all. Was there, then, something wrong in being warm-hearted and impulsive like that? Alexandra hated to think so. But there was Emil, in the Norwegian graveyard at home, and here was Frank Shabata. Alexandra rose and took him by the hand.

"Frank Shabata, I am never going to stop trying until I get you pardoned. I'll never give the Governor any peace. I know I can get you out of this place."

Frank looked at her distrustfully, but he gathered confidence from her face. "Alexandra," he said earnestly, "if I git out-a here, I not trouble dis country no more. I go back where I come from; see my mother."

Alexandra tried to withdraw her hand, but Frank held on to it nervously. He put out his finger and absently touched a button on her black jacket. "Alexandra," he said in a low tone, looking steadily at the button, "you ain' t'ink I use dat girl awful bad before—"

"No, Frank. We won't talk about that," Alexandra said, pressing his hand. "I can't help Emil now, so I'm going to do what I can for you. You know I don't go away from home often, and I came up here on purpose to tell you this."

The warden at the glass door looked in inquiringly. Alexandra nodded, and he came in and touched the white button on his desk. The guard appeared, and with a sinking heart Alexandra saw Frank led away down the corridor. After a few words with Mr. Schwartz, she left the prison and made her way to the street-car. She had refused with horror the warden's cordial invitation to "go through the institution." As the car lurched over its uneven roadbed, back toward Lincoln, Alexandra thought of how she and Frank had been wrecked by the same storm and of how, although she could come out into the sunlight, she had not much more left in her life than he. She remembered some lines from a poem she had liked in her schooldays:—

Henceforth the world will only be
A wider prison-house to me,—

and sighed. A disgust of life weighed upon her heart; some such feeling as had twice frozen Frank Shabata's features while they talked together. She wished she were back on the Divide.

When Alexandra entered her hotel, the clerk held up one finger and beckoned to her. As she approached his desk, he handed her a telegram. Alexandra took the yellow envelope and looked at it in perplexity, then stepped into the elevator without opening it. As she walked down the corridor toward her room, she reflected that she was, in a manner, immune from evil tidings. On reaching her room she locked the door, and sitting down on a chair by the dresser, opened the telegram. It was from Hanover, and it read:—

Arrived Hanover last night. Shall wait here until you come.
Please hurry. CARL LINSTRUM.

Alexandra put her head down on the dresser and burst into tears.

III.

The next afternoon Carl and Alexandra were walking across the fields from Mrs. Hiller's. Alexandra had left Lincoln after midnight, and Carl had met her at the Hanover station early in the morning. After they reached home, Alexandra had gone over to Mrs. Hiller's to leave a little present she had bought for her in the city. They stayed at the old lady's door but a moment, and then came out to spend the rest of the afternoon in the sunny fields.

Alexandra had taken off her black traveling suit and put on a white dress; partly because she saw that her black clothes made Carl uncomfortable and partly because she felt oppressed by them herself. They seemed a little like the prison where she had worn them yesterday, and to be out of place in the open fields. Carl had changed very little. His cheeks were browner and fuller. He looked less like a tired scholar than when he went away a year ago, but no one, even now, would have taken him for a man of business. His soft, lustrous black eyes, his whimsical smile, would be less against him in the Klondike than on the Divide. There are always dreamers on the frontier.

Carl and Alexandra had been talking since morning. Her letter had never reached him. He had first learned of her misfortune from a San Francisco paper, four weeks old, which he had picked up in a saloon, and which contained a brief account of Frank Shabata's trial. When he put down the paper, he had already made up his mind that he could reach Alexandra as quickly as a letter could; and ever since he had been on the way; day and night, by the fastest boats and trains he could catch. His steamer had been held back two days by rough weather.

As they came out of Mrs. Hiller's garden they took up their talk again where they had left it.

"But could you come away like that, Carl, without arranging things? Could you just walk off and leave your business?" Alexandra asked.

Carl laughed. "Prudent Alexandra! You see, my dear, I happen to have an honest partner. I trust him with everything. In fact, it's been his enterprise from the beginning, you know. I'm in it only because he took me in. I'll have to go back in the spring. Perhaps you will want to go with me then. We haven't turned up millions yet, but we've got a start that's worth following. But this winter I'd like to spend with you. You won't feel that we ought to wait longer, on Emil's account, will you, Alexandra?"

Alexandra shook her head. "No, Carl; I don't feel that way about it. And surely you needn't mind anything Lou and Oscar say now. They are much angrier with me about Emil, now, than about you. They say it was all my fault. That I ruined him by sending him to college."

"No, I don't care a button for Lou or Oscar. The moment I knew you were in trouble, the moment I thought you might need me, it all looked different. You've always been a triumphant kind of person." Carl hesitated, looking sidewise at her strong, full figure. "But you do need me now, Alexandra?"

She put her hand on his arm. "I needed you terribly when it happened, Carl. I cried for you at night. Then everything seemed to get hard inside of me, and I thought perhaps I should never care for you again. But when I got your telegram yesterday, then—then it was just as it used to be. You are all I have in the world, you know."

Carl pressed her hand in silence. They were passing the Shabatas' empty house now, but they avoided the orchard path and took one that led over by the pasture pond.

"Can you understand it, Carl?" Alexandra murmured. "I have had nobody but Ivar and Signa to talk to. Do talk to me. Can you understand it? Could you have believed that of Marie Tovesky? I would have been cut to pieces, little by little, before I would have betrayed her trust in me!"

Carl looked at the shining spot of water before them. "Maybe she was cut to pieces, too, Alexandra. I am sure she tried hard; they both did. That was why Emil went to Mexico, of course. And he was going away again, you tell me, though he had only been home three weeks. You remember that Sunday when I went with Emil up to the French Church fair? I thought that day there was some kind of feeling, something unusual, between them. I meant to talk to you about it. But on my way back I met Lou and Oscar and got so angry that I forgot everything else. You mustn't be hard on them, Alexandra. Sit down here by the pond a minute. I want to tell you something."

They sat down on the grass-tufted bank and Carl told her how he had seen Emil and Marie out by the pond that morning, more than a year ago, and how young and charming and full of grace they had seemed to him. "It happens like that in the world sometimes, Alexandra," he added earnestly. "I've seen it before. There are women who spread ruin around them through no fault of theirs, just by being too beautiful, too full of life and love. They can't help it. People come to them as people go to a warm fire in winter. I used to feel that in her when she was a little girl. Do you remember how all the Bohemians crowded round her in the store that day, when she gave Emil her candy? You remember those yellow sparks in her eyes?"

Alexandra sighed. "Yes. People couldn't help loving her. Poor Frank does, even now, I think; though he's got himself in such a tangle that for a long time his love has been bitterer than his hate. But if you saw there was anything wrong, you ought to have told me, Carl."

Carl took her hand and smiled patiently. "My dear, it was something one felt in the air, as you feel the spring coming, or a storm in summer. I didn't SEE anything. Simply, when I was with those two young things, I felt my blood go quicker, I felt—how shall I say it?—an acceleration of life. After I got away, it was all too delicate, too intangible, to write about."

Alexandra looked at him mournfully. "I try to be more liberal about such things than I used to be. I try to realize that we are not all made alike. Only, why couldn't it have been Raoul Marcel, or Jan Smirka? Why did it have to be my boy?"

"Because he was the best there was, I suppose. They were both the best you had here."

The sun was dropping low in the west when the two friends rose and took the path again. The straw-stacks were throwing long shadows, the owls were flying home to the prairie-dog town. When they came to the corner where the pastures joined, Alexandra's twelve young colts were galloping in a drove over the brow of the hill.

"Carl," said Alexandra, "I should like to go up there with you in the spring. I haven't been on the water since we crossed the ocean, when I was a little girl. After we first came out here I used to dream sometimes about the shipyard where father worked, and a little sort of inlet, full of masts." Alexandra paused. After a moment's thought she said, "But you would never ask me to go away for good, would you?"

"Of course not, my dearest. I think I know how you feel about this country as well as you do yourself." Carl took her hand in both his own and pressed it tenderly.

"Yes, I still feel that way, though Emil is gone. When I was on the train this morning, and we got near Hanover, I felt something like I did when I drove back with Emil from the river that time, in the dry year. I was glad to come back to it. I've lived here a long time. There is great peace here, Carl, and freedom.... I thought when I came out of that prison, where poor Frank is, that I should never feel free again. But I do, here." Alexandra took a deep breath and looked off into the red west.

"You belong to the land," Carl murmured, "as you have always said. Now more than ever."

"Yes, now more than ever. You remember what you once said about the graveyard, and the old story writing itself over? Only it is we who write it, with the best we have."

They paused on the last ridge of the pasture, overlooking the house and the windmill and the stables that marked the site of John Bergson's homestead. On every side the brown waves of the earth rolled away to meet the sky.

"Lou and Oscar can't see those things," said Alexandra suddenly. "Suppose I do will my land to their children, what difference will that make? The land belongs to the future, Carl; that's the way it seems to me. How many of the names on the county clerk's plat will be there in fifty years? I might as well try to will the sunset over there to my brother's children. We come and go, but the land is always here. And the people who love it and understand it are the people who own it—for a little while."

Carl looked at her wonderingly. She was still gazing into the west, and in her face there was that exalted serenity that sometimes came to her at moments of deep feeling. The level rays of the sinking sun shone in her clear eyes.

"Why are you thinking of such things now, Alexandra?"

"I had a dream before I went to Lincoln—But I will tell you about that afterward, after we are married. It will never come true, now, in the way I thought it might." She took Carl's arm and they walked toward the gate. "How many times we have walked this path together, Carl. How many times we will walk it again! Does it seem to you like coming back to your own place? Do you feel at peace with the world here? I think we shall be very happy. I haven't any fears. I think when friends marry, they are safe. We don't suffer like—those young ones." Alexandra ended with a sigh.

They had reached the gate. Before Carl opened it, he drew Alexandra to him and kissed her softly, on her lips and on her eyes.

She leaned heavily on his shoulder. "I am tired," she murmured. "I have been very lonely, Carl."

They went into the house together, leaving the Divide behind them, under the evening star. Fortunate country, that is one day to receive hearts like Alexandra's into its bosom, to give them out again in the yellow wheat, in the rustling corn, in the shining eyes of youth!

THE SONG OF THE LARK

I

FRIENDS OF CHILDHOOD

I.

DR. HOWARD ARCHIE had just come up from a game of pool with the Jewish clothier and two traveling men who happened to be staying overnight in Moonstone. His offices were in the Duke Block, over the drug store. Larry, the doctor's man, had lit the overhead light in the waiting-room and the double student's lamp on the desk in the study. The isinglass sides of the hard-coal burner were aglow, and the air in the study was so hot that as he came in the doctor opened the door into his little operating-room, where there was no stove. The waiting room was carpeted and stiffly furnished, something like a country parlor. The study had worn, unpainted floors, but there was a look of winter comfort about it. The doctor's flat-top desk was large and well made; the papers were in orderly piles, under glass weights. Behind the stove a wide bookcase, with double glass doors, reached from the floor to the ceiling. It was filled with medical books of every thickness and color. On the top shelf stood a long row of thirty or forty volumes, bound all alike in dark mottled board covers, with imitation leather backs.

As the doctor in New England villages is proverbially old, so the doctor in small Colorado towns twenty-five years ago was generally young. Dr. Archie was barely thirty. He was tall, with massive shoulders which he held stiffly, and a large, well-shaped head. He was a distinguished-looking man, for that part of the world, at least.

There was something individual in the way in which his reddish-brown hair, parted cleanly at the side, bushed over his high forehead. His nose was straight and thick, and his eyes were intelligent. He wore a curly, reddish mustache and an imperial, cut trimly, which made him look a little like the pictures of Napoleon III. His hands were large and well kept, but ruggedly formed, and the backs were shaded with crinkly reddish hair. He wore a blue suit of woolly, wide-waled serge; the traveling men had known at a glance that it was made by a Denver tailor. The doctor was always well dressed.

Dr. Archie turned up the student's lamp and sat down in the swivel chair before his desk. He sat uneasily, beating a tattoo on his knees with his fingers, and looked about him as if he were bored. He glanced at his watch, then absently took from his pocket a bunch of small keys, selected one and looked at it. A contemptuous smile, barely perceptible, played on his lips, but his eyes remained meditative. Behind the door that led into the hall, under his buffalo-skin driving-coat, was a locked cupboard. This the doctor opened mechanically, kicking aside a pile of muddy overshoes. Inside, on the shelves, were whiskey glasses and decanters, lemons, sugar, and bitters. Hearing a step in the empty, echoing hall without, the doctor closed the cupboard again, snapping the Yale lock. The door of the waiting-room opened, a man entered and came on into the consulting-room.

"Good-evening, Mr. Kronborg," said the doctor carelessly. "Sit down."

His visitor was a tall, loosely built man, with a thin brown beard, streaked with gray. He wore a frock coat, a broad-brimmed black hat, a white lawn necktie, and steel rimmed spectacles. Altogether there was a pretentious and important air about him, as he lifted the skirts of his coat and sat down.

"Good-evening, doctor. Can you step around to the house with me? I think Mrs. Kronborg will need you this evening." This was said with profound gravity and, curiously enough, with a slight embarrassment.

"Any hurry?" the doctor asked over his shoulder as he went into his operating-room.

Mr. Kronborg coughed behind his hand, and contracted his brows. His face threatened at every moment to break into a smile of foolish excitement. He controlled it only by calling upon his habitual pulpit manner. "Well, I think it would be as well to go immediately. Mrs. Kronborg will be more comfortable if you are there. She has been suffering for some time."

The doctor came back and threw a black bag upon his desk. He wrote some instructions for his man on a prescription pad and then drew on his overcoat. "All ready," he announced, putting out his lamp. Mr. Kronborg rose and they tramped through the empty hall and down the stairway to the street. The drug store below was dark, and the saloon next door was just closing. Every other light on Main Street was out.

On either side of the road and at the outer edge of the board sidewalk, the snow had been shoveled into breastworks. The town looked small and black, flattened down in the snow, muffled and all but extinguished. Overhead the stars shone gloriously. It was impossible not to notice them. The air was so clear that the white sand hills to the east of Moonstone gleamed softly. Following the Reverend Mr. Kronborg along the narrow walk, past the little dark, sleeping houses, the doctor looked up at the flashing night and whistled softly. It did seem that people were stupider than they need be; as if on a night like this there ought to be something better to do than to sleep nine hours, or to assist Mrs. Kronborg in functions which she could have performed so admirably unaided. He wished he had gone down to Denver to hear Fay Templeton sing "See-Saw." Then he remembered that he had a personal interest in this family, after all. They turned into another street and saw before them lighted windows; a low story-and-a-half house, with a wing built on at the right and a kitchen addition at the back, everything a little on the slant—roofs, windows, and doors. As they approached the gate, Peter Kronborg's pace grew brisker. His nervous, ministerial cough annoyed the doctor. "Exactly as if he were going to give out a text," he thought. He drew off his glove and felt in his vest pocket. "Have a troche, Kronborg," he said, producing some. "Sent me for samples. Very good for a rough throat."

"Ah, thank you, thank you. I was in something of a hurry. I neglected to put on my overshoes. Here we are, doctor." Kronborg opened his front door—seemed delighted to be at home again.

The front hall was dark and cold; the hatrack was hung with an astonishing number of children's hats and caps and cloaks. They were even piled on the table beneath the hatrack.

Under the table was a heap of rubbers and overshoes. While the doctor hung up his coat and hat, Peter Kronborg opened the door into the living-room. A glare of light greeted them, and a rush of hot, stale air, smelling of warming flannels.

At three o'clock in the morning Dr. Archie was in the parlor putting on his cuffs and coat—there was no spare bedroom in that house. Peter Kronborg's seventh child, a boy, was being soothed and cosseted by his aunt, Mrs. Kronborg was asleep, and the doctor was going home. But he wanted first to speak to Kronborg, who, coatless and fluttery, was pouring coal into the kitchen stove. As the doctor crossed the dining-room he paused and listened. From one of the wing rooms, off to the left, he heard rapid, distressed breathing. He went to the kitchen door.

"One of the children sick in there?" he asked, nodding toward the partition.

Kronborg hung up the stove-lifter and dusted his fingers. "It must be Thea. I meant to ask you to look at her. She has a croupy cold. But in my excitement—Mrs. Kronborg is doing finely, eh, doctor? Not many of your patients with such a constitution, I expect."

"Oh, yes. She's a fine mother." The doctor took up the lamp from the kitchen table and unceremoniously went into the wing room. Two chubby little boys were asleep in a double bed, with the coverlids over their noses and their feet drawn up. In a single bed, next to theirs, lay a little girl of eleven, wide awake, two yellow braids sticking up on the pillow behind her. Her face was scarlet and her eyes were blazing.

The doctor shut the door behind him. "Feel pretty sick, Thea?" he asked as he took out his thermometer. "Why didn't you call somebody?"

She looked at him with greedy affection. "I thought you were here," she spoke between quick breaths. "There is a new baby, isn't there? Which?"

"Which?" repeated the doctor.

"Brother or sister?"

He smiled and sat down on the edge of the bed. "Brother," he said, taking her hand. "Open."

"Good. Brothers are better," she murmured as he put the glass tube under her tongue.

"Now, be still, I want to count." Dr. Archie reached for her hand and took out his watch. When he put her hand back under the quilt he went over to one of the windows—they were both tight shut—and lifted it a little way. He reached up and ran his hand along the cold, unpapered wall. "Keep under the covers; I'll come back to you in a moment," he said, bending over the glass lamp with his thermometer. He winked at her from the door before he shut it.

Peter Kronborg was sitting in his wife's room, holding the bundle which contained his son. His air of cheerful importance, his beard and glasses, even his shirt-sleeves, annoyed the doctor. He beckoned Kronborg into the living-room and said sternly:—

"You've got a very sick child in there. Why didn't you call me before? It's pneumonia, and she must have been sick for several days. Put the baby down somewhere, please, and help me make up the bed-lounge here in the parlor. She's got to be in a warm room, and she's got to be quiet. You must keep the other children out. Here, this thing opens up, I see," swinging back the top of the carpet lounge. "We can lift her mattress and carry her in just as she is. I don't want to disturb her more than is necessary."

Kronborg was all concern immediately. The two men took up the mattress and carried the sick child into the parlor. "I'll have to go down to my office to get some medicine, Kronborg. The drug store won't be open. Keep the covers on her. I won't be gone long. Shake down the stove and put on a little coal, but not too much; so it'll catch quickly, I mean. Find an old sheet for me, and put it there to warm."

The doctor caught his coat and hurried out into the dark street. Nobody was stirring yet, and the cold was bitter. He was tired and hungry and in no mild humor. "The idea!" he muttered; "to be such an ass at his age, about the seventh! And to feel no responsibility about the little girl. Silly old goat! The baby would have got into the world somehow; they always do. But a nice little girl like that—she's worth the whole litter. Where she ever got it from—" He turned into the Duke Block and ran up the stairs to his office.

Thea Kronborg, meanwhile, was wondering why she happened to be in the parlor, where nobody but company—usually visiting preachers—ever slept. She had moments of stupor when she did not see anything, and moments of excitement when she felt that something unusual and pleasant was about to happen, when she saw everything clearly in the red light from the isinglass sides of the hard-coal burner—the nickel trimmings on the stove itself, the pictures on the wall, which she thought very beautiful, the flowers on the Brussels carpet, Czerny's "Daily Studies" which stood open on the upright piano. She forgot, for the time being, all about the new baby.

When she heard the front door open, it occurred to her that the pleasant thing which was going to happen was Dr. Archie himself. He came in and warmed his hands at the stove. As he turned to her, she threw herself wearily toward him, half out of her bed. She would have tumbled to the floor had he not caught her. He gave her some medicine and went to the kitchen for something he needed. She drowsed and lost the sense of his being there. When she opened her eyes again, he was kneeling before the stove, spreading something dark and sticky on a white cloth, with a big spoon; batter, perhaps. Presently she felt him taking off her nightgown. He wrapped the hot plaster about her chest. There seemed to be straps which he pinned over her shoulders. Then he took out a thread and needle and began to sew her up in it. That, she felt, was too strange; she must be dreaming anyhow, so she succumbed to her drowsiness.

Thea had been moaning with every breath since the doctor came back, but she did not know it. She did not realize that she was suffering pain. When she was conscious at all, she seemed to be separated from her body; to be perched on top of the piano, or on the hanging lamp, watching the doctor sew her up. It was perplexing and unsatisfactory, like dreaming. She wished she could waken up and see what was going on.

The doctor thanked God that he had persuaded Peter Kronborg to keep out of the way. He could do better by the child if he had her to himself. He had no children of his own. His marriage was a very unhappy one. As he lifted and undressed Thea, he thought to himself what a beautiful thing a little girl's body was,—like a flower. It was so neatly and delicately fashioned, so soft, and so milky white. Thea must have got her hair and her silky skin from her mother. She was a little Swede, through and through. Dr. Archie could not help thinking how he would cherish a little creature like this if she were his. Her hands, so little and hot, so clever, too,—he glanced at the open exercise book on the piano. When he had stitched up the flaxseed jacket, he wiped it neatly about the edges, where the paste had worked out on the skin. He put on her the clean nightgown he had warmed before the fire, and tucked the blankets about her. As he pushed back the hair that had fuzzed down over her eyebrows, he felt her head thoughtfully with the tips of his fingers. No, he couldn't say that it was different from any other child's head, though he believed that there was something very different about her. He looked intently at her wide, flushed face, freckled nose, fierce little mouth, and her delicate, tender chin—the one soft touch in her hard little Scandinavian face, as if some fairy godmother had caressed her there and left a cryptic promise. Her brows were usually drawn together defiantly, but never when she was with Dr. Archie. Her affection for him was prettier than most of the things that went to make up the doctor's life in Moonstone.

The windows grew gray. He heard a tramping on the attic floor, on the back stairs, then cries: "Give me my shirt!" "Where's my other stocking?"

"I'll have to stay till they get off to school," he reflected, "or they'll be in here tormenting her, the whole lot of them."

II.

For the next four days it seemed to Dr. Archie that his patient might slip through his hands, do what he might. But she did not. On the contrary, after that she recovered very rapidly. As her father remarked, she must have inherited the "constitution" which he was never tired of admiring in her mother.

One afternoon, when her new brother was a week old, the doctor found Thea very comfortable and happy in her bed in the parlor. The sunlight was pouring in over her shoulders, the baby was asleep on a pillow in a big rocking-chair beside her. Whenever he stirred, she put out her hand and rocked him. Nothing of him was visible but a flushed, puffy forehead and an uncompromisingly big, bald cranium. The door into her mother's room stood open, and Mrs. Kronborg was sitting up in bed darning stockings. She was a short, stalwart woman, with a short neck and a determined-looking head. Her skin was very fair, her face calm and unwrinkled, and her yellow hair, braided down her back as she lay in bed, still looked like a girl's. She was a woman whom Dr. Archie respected; active, practical, unruffled; goodhumored, but determined. Exactly the sort of woman to take care of a flighty preacher. She had brought her husband some property, too,—one fourth of her father's broad acres in Nebraska,—but this she kept in her own name. She had profound respect for her husband's erudition and eloquence. She sat under his preaching with deep humility, and was as much taken in by his stiff shirt and white neckties as if she had not ironed them herself by lamplight the night before they appeared correct and spotless in the pulpit. But for all this, she had no confidence in his administration of worldly affairs. She looked to him for morning prayers and grace at table; she expected him to name the babies and to supply whatever parental sentiment there was in the house, to remember birthdays and anniversaries, to point the children to moral and patriotic ideals. It was her work to keep their bodies, their clothes, and their conduct in some sort of order, and this she accomplished with a success that was a source of wonder to her neighbors. As she used to remark, and her husband admiringly to echo, she "had never lost one." With all his flightiness, Peter Kronborg appreciated the matter-of-fact, punctual way in which his wife got her children into the world and along in it. He believed, and he was right in believing, that the sovereign State of Colorado was much indebted to Mrs. Kronborg and women like her.

Mrs. Kronborg believed that the size of every family was decided in heaven. More modern views would not have startled her; they would simply have seemed foolish—thin chatter, like the boasts of the men who built the tower of Babel, or like Axel's plan to breed ostriches in the chicken yard. From what evidence Mrs. Kronborg formed her opinions on this and other matters, it would have been difficult to say, but once formed, they were unchangeable. She would no more have questioned her convictions than she would have questioned revelation. Calm and even tempered, naturally kind, she was capable of strong prejudices, and she never forgave.

When the doctor came in to see Thea, Mrs. Kronborg was reflecting that the washing was a week behind, and deciding what she had better do about it. The arrival of a new baby meant a revision of her entire domestic schedule, and as she drove her needle along she had been working out new sleeping arrangements and cleaning days. The doctor had entered the house without knocking, after making noise enough in the hall to prepare his patients. Thea was reading, her book propped up before her in the sunlight.

"Mustn't do that; bad for your eyes," he said, as Thea shut the book quickly and slipped it under the covers.

Mrs. Kronborg called from her bed: "Bring the baby here, doctor, and have that chair. She wanted him in there for company."

Before the doctor picked up the baby, he put a yellow paper bag down on Thea's coverlid and winked at her. They had a code of winks and grimaces. When he went in to chat with her mother, Thea opened the bag cautiously, trying to keep it from crackling. She drew out a long bunch of white grapes, with a little of the sawdust in which they had been packed still clinging to them. They were called Malaga grapes in Moonstone, and once or twice during the winter the leading grocer got a keg of them. They were used mainly for table decoration, about Christmas-time. Thea had never had more than one grape at a time before. When the doctor came back she was holding the almost transparent fruit up in the sunlight, feeling the pale-green skins softly with the tips of her fingers. She did not thank him; she only snapped her eyes at him in a special way which he understood, and, when he gave her his hand, put it quickly and shyly under her cheek, as if she were trying to do so without knowing it—and without his knowing it.

Dr. Archie sat down in the rocking-chair. "And how's Thea feeling to-day?"

He was quite as shy as his patient, especially when a third person overheard his conversation. Big and handsome and superior to his fellow townsmen as Dr. Archie was, he was seldom at his ease, and like Peter Kronborg he often dodged behind a professional manner. There was sometimes a contraction of embarrassment and self consciousness all over his big body, which made him awkward—likely to stumble, to kick up rugs, or to knock over chairs. If any one was very sick, he forgot himself, but he had a clumsy touch in convalescent gossip.

Thea curled up on her side and looked at him with pleasure. "All right. I like to be sick. I have more fun then than other times."

"How's that?"

"I don't have to go to school, and I don't have to practice. I can read all I want to, and have good things,"—she patted the grapes. "I had lots of fun that time I mashed my finger and you wouldn't let Professor Wunsch make me practice. Only I had to do left hand, even then. I think that was mean."

The doctor took her hand and examined the forefinger, where the nail had grown back a little crooked. "You mustn't trim it down close at the corner there, and then it will grow straight. You won't want it crooked when you're a big girl and wear rings and have sweethearts."

She made a mocking little face at him and looked at his new scarf-pin. "That's the prettiest one you ev-ER had. I wish you'd stay a long while and let me look at it. What is it?"

Dr. Archie laughed. "It's an opal. Spanish Johnny brought it up for me from Chihuahua in his shoe. I had it set in Denver, and I wore it to-day for your benefit."

Thea had a curious passion for jewelry. She wanted every shining stone she saw, and in summer she was always going off into the sand hills to hunt for crystals and agates and bits of pink chalcedony. She had two cigar boxes full of stones that she had found or traded for, and she imagined that they were of enormous value. She was always planning how she would have them set.

"What are you reading?" The doctor reached under the covers and pulled out a book of Byron's poems. "Do you like this?"

She looked confused, turned over a few pages rapidly, and pointed to "My native land, good-night." "That," she said sheepishly.

"How about 'Maid of Athens'?"

She blushed and looked at him suspiciously. "I like 'There was a sound of revelry,'" she muttered.

The doctor laughed and closed the book. It was clumsily bound in padded leather and had been presented to the Reverend Peter Kronborg by his Sunday-School class as an ornament for his parlor table.

"Come into the office some day, and I'll lend you a nice book. You can skip the parts you don't understand. You can read it in vacation. Perhaps you'll be able to understand all of it by then."

Thea frowned and looked fretfully toward the piano. "In vacation I have to practice four hours every day, and then there'll be Thor to take care of." She pronounced it "Tor."

"Thor? Oh, you've named the baby Thor?" exclaimed the doctor.

Thea frowned again, still more fiercely, and said quickly, "That's a nice name, only maybe it's a little—old fashioned." She was very sensitive about being thought a foreigner, and was proud of the fact that, in town, her father always preached in English; very bookish English, at that, one might add.

Born in an old Scandinavian colony in Minnesota, Peter Kronborg had been sent to a small divinity school in Indiana by the women of a Swedish evangelical mission, who were convinced of his gifts and who skimped and begged and gave church suppers to get the long, lazy youth through the seminary. He could still speak enough Swedish to exhort and to bury the members of his country church out at Copper Hole, and he wielded in his Moonstone pulpit a somewhat pompous English vocabulary he had learned out of books at college. He always spoke of "the infant Saviour," "our Heavenly Father," etc. The poor man had no natural, spontaneous human speech. If he had his sincere moments, they were perforce inarticulate. Probably a good deal of his pretentiousness was due to the fact that he habitually expressed himself in a book learned language, wholly remote from anything personal, native, or homely. Mrs. Kronborg spoke Swedish to her own sisters and to her sister-in-law Tillie, and colloquial English to her neighbors. Thea, who had a rather sensitive ear, until she went to school never spoke at all, except in monosyllables, and her mother was convinced that she was tongue-tied. She was still inept in speech for a child so intelligent. Her ideas were usually clear, but she seldom attempted to explain them, even at school, where she excelled in "written work" and never did more than mutter a reply.

"Your music professor stopped me on the street to-day and asked me how you were," said the doctor, rising. "He'll be sick himself, trotting around in this slush with no overcoat or overshoes."

"He's poor," said Thea simply.

The doctor sighed. "I'm afraid he's worse than that. Is he always all right when you take your lessons? Never acts as if he'd been drinking?"

Thea looked angry and spoke excitedly. "He knows a lot. More than anybody. I don't care if he does drink; he's old and poor." Her voice shook a little.

Mrs. Kronborg spoke up from the next room. "He's a good teacher, doctor. It's good for us he does drink. He'd never be in a little place like this if he didn't have some weakness. These women that teach music around here don't know nothing. I wouldn't have my child wasting time with them. If Professor Wunsch goes away, Thea'll have nobody to take from. He's careful with his scholars; he don't use bad language. Mrs. Kohler is always present when

Thea takes her lesson. It's all right." Mrs. Kronborg spoke calmly and judicially. One could see that she had thought the matter out before.

"I'm glad to hear that, Mrs. Kronborg. I wish we could get the old man off his bottle and keep him tidy. Do you suppose if I gave you an old overcoat you could get him to wear it?" The doctor went to the bedroom door and Mrs. Kronborg looked up from her darning.

"Why, yes, I guess he'd be glad of it. He'll take most anything from me. He won't buy clothes, but I guess he'd wear 'em if he had 'em. I've never had any clothes to give him, having so many to make over for."

"I'll have Larry bring the coat around to-night. You aren't cross with me, Thea?" taking her hand.

Thea grinned warmly. "Not if you give Professor Wunsch a coat—and things," she tapped the grapes significantly. The doctor bent over and kissed her.

III.

Being sick was all very well, but Thea knew from experience that starting back to school again was attended by depressing difficulties. One Monday morning she got up early with Axel and Gunner, who shared her wing room, and hurried into the back living-room, between the dining-room and the kitchen. There, beside a soft-coal stove, the younger children of the family undressed at night and dressed in the morning. The older daughter, Anna, and the two big boys slept upstairs, where the rooms were theoretically warmed by stovepipes from below. The first (and the worst!) thing that confronted Thea was a suit of clean, prickly red flannel, fresh from the wash. Usually the torment of breaking in a clean suit of flannel came on Sunday, but yesterday, as she was staying in the house, she had begged off. Their winter underwear was a trial to all the children, but it was bitterest to Thea because she happened to have the most sensitive skin. While she was tugging it on, her Aunt Tillie brought in warm water from the boiler and filled the tin pitcher. Thea washed her face, brushed and braided her hair, and got into her blue cashmere dress. Over this she buttoned a long apron, with sleeves, which would not be removed until she put on her cloak to go to school. Gunner and Axel, on the soap box behind the stove, had their usual quarrel about which should wear the tightest stockings, but they exchanged reproaches in low tones, for they were wholesomely afraid of Mrs. Kronborg's rawhide whip. She did not chastise her children often, but she did it thoroughly. Only a somewhat stern system of discipline could have kept any degree of order and quiet in that overcrowded house.

Mrs. Kronborg's children were all trained to dress themselves at the earliest possible age, to make their own beds,—the boys as well as the girls,—to take care of their clothes, to eat what was given them, and to keep out of the way. Mrs. Kronborg would have made a good chess player; she had a head for moves and positions.

Anna, the elder daughter, was her mother's lieutenant. All the children knew that they must obey Anna, who was an obstinate contender for proprieties and not always fair minded. To see the young Kronborgs headed for Sunday School was like watching a military drill. Mrs. Kronborg let her children's minds alone. She did not pry into their thoughts or nag them. She respected them as individuals, and outside of the house they had a great deal of liberty. But their communal life was definitely ordered.

In the winter the children breakfasted in the kitchen; Gus and Charley and Anna first, while the younger children were dressing. Gus was nineteen and was a clerk in a dry-goods store. Charley, eighteen months younger, worked in a feed store. They left the house by the kitchen door at seven o'clock, and then Anna helped her Aunt Tillie get the breakfast for the younger ones. Without the help of this sister-in-law, Tillie Kronborg, Mrs. Kronborg's life would have been a hard one. Mrs. Kronborg often reminded Anna that "no hired help would ever have taken the same interest."

Mr. Kronborg came of a poorer stock than his wife; from a lowly, ignorant family that had lived in a poor part of Sweden. His great-grandfather had gone to Norway to work as a farm laborer and had married a Norwegian girl. This strain of Norwegian blood came out somewhere in each generation of the Kronborgs. The intemperance of one of Peter Kronborg's uncles, and the religious mania of another, had been alike charged to the Norwegian grandmother. Both Peter Kronborg and his sister Tillie were more like the Norwegian root of the family than like the Swedish, and this same Norwegian strain was strong in Thea, though in her it took a very different character.

Tillie was a queer, addle-pated thing, as flighty as a girl at thirty-five, and overweeningly fond of gay clothes—which taste, as Mrs. Kronborg philosophically said, did nobody any harm. Tillie was always cheerful, and her tongue was still for scarcely a minute during the day. She had been cruelly overworked on her father's Minnesota farm when she was a young girl, and she had never been so happy as she was now; had never before, as she said, had such social advantages. She thought her brother the most important man in Moonstone. She never missed a church service, and, much to the embarrassment of the children, she always "spoke a piece" at the Sunday-School concerts. She had a complete set of "Standard Recitations," which she conned on Sundays. This morning, when Thea and her two younger brothers sat down to breakfast, Tillie was remonstrating with Gunner because he had not learned a recitation assigned to him for George Washington Day at school. The unmemorized text lay heavily on Gunner's conscience as he attacked his buckwheat cakes and sausage. He knew that Tillie was in the right, and that "when the day came he would be ashamed of himself."

"I don't care," he muttered, stirring his coffee; "they oughtn't to make boys speak. It's all right for girls. They like to show off."

"No showing off about it. Boys ought to like to speak up for their country. And what was the use of your father buying you a new suit, if you're not going to take part in anything?"

"That was for Sunday-School. I'd rather wear my old one, anyhow. Why didn't they give the piece to Thea?" Gunner grumbled.

Tillie was turning buckwheat cakes at the griddle. "Thea can play and sing, she don't need to speak. But you've got to know how to do something, Gunner, that you have. What are you going to do when you git big and want to git into society, if you can't do nothing? Everybody'll say, 'Can you sing? Can you play? Can you speak? Then git right out of society.' An' that's what they'll say to you, Mr. Gunner."

Gunner and Alex grinned at Anna, who was preparing her mother's breakfast. They never made fun of Tillie, but they understood well enough that there were subjects upon which her ideas were rather foolish. When Tillie struck the shallows, Thea was usually prompt in turning the conversation.

"Will you and Axel let me have your sled at recess?" she asked.

"All the time?" asked Gunner dubiously.

"I'll work your examples for you to-night, if you do."

"Oh, all right. There'll be a lot of 'em."

"I don't mind, I can work 'em fast. How about yours, Axel?"

Axel was a fat little boy of seven, with pretty, lazy blue eyes. "I don't care," he murmured, buttering his last buckwheat cake without ambition; "too much trouble to copy 'em down. Jenny Smiley'll let me have hers."

The boys were to pull Thea to school on their sled, as the snow was deep. The three set off together. Anna was now in the high school, and she no longer went with the family party, but walked to school with some of the older girls who were her friends, and wore a hat, not a hood like Thea.

IV.

"And it was Summer, beautiful Summer!" Those were the closing words of Thea's favorite fairy tale, and she thought of them as she ran out into the world one Saturday morning in May, her music book under her arm. She was going to the Kohlers' to take her lesson, but she was in no hurry.

It was in the summer that one really lived. Then all the little overcrowded houses were opened wide, and the wind blew through them with sweet, earthy smells of garden-planting. The town looked as if it had just been washed. People were out painting their fences. The cottonwood trees were a-flicker with sticky, yellow little leaves, and the feathery tamarisks were in pink bud. With the warm weather came freedom for everybody. People were dug up, as it were. The very old people, whom one had not seen all winter, came out and sunned themselves in the yard. The double windows were taken off the houses, the tormenting flannels in which children had been encased all winter were put away in boxes, and the youngsters felt a pleasure in the cool cotton things next their skin.

Thea had to walk more than a mile to reach the Kohlers' house, a very pleasant mile out of town toward the glittering sand hills,—yellow this morning, with lines of deep violet where the clefts and valleys were. She followed the sidewalk to the depot at the south end of the town; then took the road east to the little group of adobe houses where the Mexicans lived, then dropped into a deep ravine; a dry sand creek, across which the railroad track ran on a trestle. Beyond that gulch, on a little rise of ground that faced the open sandy plain, was the Kohlers' house, where Professor Wunsch lived. Fritz Kohler was the town tailor, one of the first settlers. He had moved there, built a little house and made a garden, when Moonstone was first marked down on the map. He had three sons, but they now worked on the railroad and were stationed in distant cities. One of them had gone to work for the Santa Fe, and lived in New Mexico.

Mrs. Kohler seldom crossed the ravine and went into the town except at Christmas-time, when she had to buy presents and Christmas cards to send to her old friends in Freeport, Illinois. As she did not go to church, she did not possess such a thing as a hat. Year after year she wore the same red hood in winter and a black sunbonnet in summer. She made her own dresses; the skirts came barely to her shoe-tops, and were gathered as full as they could possibly be to the waistband. She preferred men's shoes, and usually wore the cast-offs of one of her sons. She had never learned much English, and her plants and shrubs were her companions. She lived for her men and her garden. Beside that sand gulch, she had tried to reproduce a bit of her own village in the Rhine Valley. She hid herself behind the growth she had fostered, lived under the shade of what she had planted and watered and pruned. In the blaze of the open plain she was stupid and blind like an owl. Shade, shade; that was what she was always planning and making. Behind the high tamarisk hedge, her garden was a jungle of verdure in summer. Above the cherry trees and peach trees and golden plums stood the windmill, with its tank on stilts, which kept all this verdure alive. Outside, the sage-brush grew up to the very edge of the garden, and the sand was always drifting up to the tamarisks.

Every one in Moonstone was astonished when the Kohlers took the wandering music-teacher to live with them. In seventeen years old Fritz had never had a crony, except the harness-maker and Spanish Johnny. This Wunsch came from God knew where,—followed Spanish Johnny into town when that wanderer came back from one of his tramps. Wunsch played in the dance orchestra, tuned pianos, and gave lessons. When Mrs. Kohler rescued him, he was sleeping in a dirty, unfurnished room over one of the saloons, and he had only two shirts in the world. Once he was under her roof, the old woman went at him as she did at her garden. She sewed and washed and mended for him, and made him so clean and respectable that he was able to get a large class of pupils and to rent a piano. As soon as he had money ahead, he sent to the Narrow Gauge lodging-house, in Denver, for a trunkful of music which had been held there for unpaid board. With tears in his eyes the old man—he was not over fifty, but sadly battered—told Mrs. Kohler that he asked nothing better of God than to end his days with her, and to be buried in the garden, under her linden trees. They were not American basswood, but the European linden, which has honey-colored blooms in summer, with a fragrance that surpasses all trees and flowers and drives young people wild with joy.

Thea was reflecting as she walked along that had it not been for Professor Wunsch she might have lived on for years in Moonstone without ever knowing the Kohlers, without ever seeing their garden or the inside of their house. Besides the cuckoo clock,—which was wonderful enough, and which Mrs. Kohler said she kept for "company when she was lonesome,"—the Kohlers had in their house the most wonderful thing Thea had ever seen—but of that later.

Professor Wunsch went to the houses of his other pupils to give them their lessons, but one morning he told Mrs. Kronborg that Thea had talent, and that if she came to him he could teach her in his slippers, and that would be better. Mrs. Kronborg was a strange woman. That word "talent," which no one else in Moonstone, not even Dr. Archie, would have understood, she comprehended perfectly. To any other woman there, it would have meant that a child must have her hair curled every day and must play in public. Mrs. Kronborg knew it meant that Thea must practice four hours a day. A child with talent must be kept at the piano, just as a child with measles must be kept under the blankets. Mrs. Kronborg and her three sisters had all studied piano, and all sang well, but none of them had talent. Their father had played the oboe in an orchestra in Sweden, before he came to America to better his fortunes. He had even known Jenny Lind. A child with talent had to be kept at the piano; so twice a week in summer and once a week in winter Thea went over the gulch to the Kohlers', though the Ladies' Aid Society thought it was not proper for their preacher's daughter to go "where there was so much drinking." Not that the Kohler sons ever so much as looked at a glass of beer. They were ashamed of their old folks and got out into the world as fast as possible; had their clothes made by a Denver tailor and their necks shaved up under their hair and forgot the past. Old Fritz and Wunsch, however, indulged in a friendly bottle pretty often. The two men were like comrades; perhaps the bond between them was the glass wherein lost hopes are found; perhaps it was common memories of another country; perhaps it was the grapevine in the garden—knotty, fibrous shrub, full of homesickness and sentiment, which the Germans have carried around the world with them.

As Thea approached the house she peeped between the pink sprays of the tamarisk hedge and saw the Professor and Mrs. Kohler in the garden, spading and raking. The garden looked like a relief-map now, and gave no indication of what it would be in August; such a jungle! Pole beans and potatoes and corn and leeks and kale and red cabbage—there would even be vegetables for which there is no American name. Mrs. Kohler was always getting by mail packages of seeds from Freeport and from the old country. Then the flowers! There were big sunflowers for the canary bird, tiger lilies and phlox and zinnias and lady's-slippers and portulaca and hollyhocks,—giant hollyhocks. Beside the fruit trees there was a great umbrella-shaped catalpa, and a balm-of-Gilead, two lindens, and even a ginka,—a rigid, pointed tree with leaves shaped like butterflies, which shivered, but never bent to the wind.

This morning Thea saw to her delight that the two oleander trees, one white and one red, had been brought up from their winter quarters in the cellar. There is hardly a German family in the most arid parts of Utah, New Mexico, Arizona, but has its oleander trees. However loutish the American-born sons of the family may be, there was never one who refused to give his muscle to the back-breaking task of getting those tubbed trees down into the cellar in the fall and up into the sunlight in the spring. They may strive to avert the day, but they grapple with the tub at last.

When Thea entered the gate, her professor leaned his spade against the white post that supported the turreted dove-house, and wiped his face with his shirt-sleeve; someway he never managed to have a handkerchief about him. Wunsch was short and stocky, with something rough and bear-like about his shoulders. His face was a dark, bricky red, deeply creased rather than wrinkled, and the skin was like loose leather over his neck band—he wore a brass collar button but no collar. His hair was cropped close; iron-gray bristles on a bullet-like head. His eyes were always suffused and bloodshot. He had a coarse, scornful mouth, and irregular, yellow teeth, much worn at the edges. His hands were square and red, seldom clean, but always alive, impatient, even sympathetic.

"MORGEN," he greeted his pupil in a businesslike way, put on a black alpaca coat, and conducted her at once to the piano in Mrs. Kohler's sitting-room. He twirled the stool to the proper height, pointed to it, and sat down in a wooden chair beside Thea.

"The scale of B flat major," he directed, and then fell into an attitude of deep attention. Without a word his pupil set to work.

To Mrs. Kohler, in the garden, came the cheerful sound of effort, of vigorous striving. Unconsciously she wielded her rake more lightly. Occasionally she heard the teacher's voice. "Scale of E minor...WEITER, WEITER!...IMMER I hear the thumb, like a lame foot. WEITER...WEITER, once...SCHON! The chords, quick!"

The pupil did not open her mouth until they began the second movement of the Clementi sonata, when she remonstrated in low tones about the way he had marked the fingering of a passage.

"It makes no matter what you think," replied her teacher coldly. "There is only one right way. The thumb there. EIN, ZWEI, DREI, VIER," etc. Then for an hour there was no further interruption.

At the end of the lesson Thea turned on her stool and leaned her arm on the keyboard. They usually had a little talk after the lesson.

Herr Wunsch grinned. "How soon is it you are free from school? Then we make ahead faster, eh?"

"First week in June. Then will you give me the 'Invitation to the Dance'?"

He shrugged his shoulders. "It makes no matter. If you want him, you play him out of lesson hours."

"All right." Thea fumbled in her pocket and brought out a crumpled slip of paper. "What does this mean, please? I guess it's Latin."

Wunsch blinked at the line penciled on the paper. "Wherefrom you get this?" he asked gruffly.

"Out of a book Dr. Archie gave me to read. It's all English but that. Did you ever see it before?" she asked, watching his face.

"Yes. A long time ago," he muttered, scowling. "Ovidius!" He took a stub of lead pencil from his vest pocket, steadied his hand by a visible effort, and under the words:

"LENTE CURRITE, LENTE CURRITE, NOCTIS EQUI," he wrote in a clear, elegant Gothic hand,—

"GO SLOWLY, GO SLOWLY, YE STEEDS OF THE NIGHT."

He put the pencil back in his pocket and continued to stare at the Latin. It recalled the poem, which he had read as a student, and thought very fine. There were treasures of memory which no lodging-house keeper could attach. One carried things about in one's head, long after one's linen could be smuggled out in a tuning-bag. He handed the paper back to Thea. "There is the English, quite elegant," he said, rising.

Mrs. Kohler stuck her head in at the door, and Thea slid off the stool. "Come in, Mrs. Kohler," she called, "and show me the piece-picture."

The old woman laughed, pulled off her big gardening gloves, and pushed Thea to the lounge before the object of her delight. The "piece-picture," which hung on the wall and nearly covered one whole end of the room, was the handiwork of Fritz Kohler. He had learned his trade under an old-fashioned tailor in Magdeburg who required from each of his apprentices a thesis: that is, before they left his shop, each apprentice had to copy in cloth some well known German painting, stitching bits of colored stuff together on a linen background; a kind of mosaic. The pupil was allowed to select his subject, and Fritz Kohler had chosen a popular painting of Napoleon's retreat from Moscow. The gloomy Emperor and his staff were represented as crossing a stone bridge, and behind them was the blazing city, the walls and fortresses done in gray cloth with orange tongues of flame darting about the domes and minarets. Napoleon rode his white horse; Murat, in Oriental dress, a bay charger. Thea was never tired of examining this work, of hearing how long it had taken Fritz to make it, how much it had been admired, and what narrow escapes it had had from moths and fire. Silk, Mrs. Kohler explained, would have been much easier to manage than woolen cloth, in which it was often hard to get the right shades. The reins of the horses, the wheels of the spurs, the brooding eyebrows of the Emperor, Murat's fierce mustaches, the great shakos of the Guard, were all worked out with the minutest fidelity. Thea's admiration for this picture had endeared her to Mrs. Kohler. It was now many years since she used to point out its wonders to her own little boys. As Mrs. Kohler did not go to church, she never heard any singing, except the songs that floated over from Mexican Town, and Thea often sang for her after the lesson was over. This morning Wunsch pointed to the piano.

"On Sunday, when I go by the church, I hear you sing something."

Thea obediently sat down on the stool again and began, "COME, YE DISCONSOLATE." Wunsch listened thoughtfully, his hands on his knees. Such a beautiful child's voice! Old Mrs. Kohler's face relaxed in a smile of happiness; she half closed her eyes. A big fly was darting in and out of the window; the sunlight made a golden pool on the rag carpet and bathed the faded cretonne pillows on the lounge, under the piece-picture. "EARTH HAS NO SORROW THAT HEAVEN CANNOT HEAL," the song died away.

"That is a good thing to remember," Wunsch shook himself. "You believe that?" looking quizzically at Thea.

She became confused and pecked nervously at a black key with her middle finger. "I don't know. I guess so," she murmured.

Her teacher rose abruptly. "Remember, for next time, thirds. You ought to get up earlier."

That night the air was so warm that Fritz and Herr Wunsch had their after-supper pipe in the grape arbor, smoking in silence while the sound of fiddles and guitars came across the ravine from Mexican Town. Long after Fritz and his old Paulina had gone to bed, Wunsch sat motionless in the arbor, looking up through the woolly vine leaves at the glittering machinery of heaven.

"LENTE CURRITE, NOCTIS EQUI."

That line awoke many memories. He was thinking of youth; of his own, so long gone by, and of his pupil's, just beginning. He would even have cherished hopes for her, except that he had become superstitious. He believed that whatever he hoped for was destined not to be; that his affection brought ill-fortune, especially to the young; that if he held anything in his thoughts, he harmed it. He had taught in music schools in St. Louis and Kansas City, where the shallowness and complacency of the young misses had maddened him. He had encountered bad manners and bad faith, had been the victim of sharpers of all kinds, was dogged by bad luck. He had played in orchestras that were never paid and wandering opera troupes which disbanded penniless. And there was always the old enemy, more relentless than the others. It was long since he had wished anything or desired anything beyond the necessities of the body. Now that he was tempted to hope for another, he felt alarmed and shook his head.

It was his pupil's power of application, her rugged will, that interested him. He had lived for so long among people whose sole ambition was to get something for nothing that he had learned not to look for seriousness in anything. Now that he by chance encountered it, it recalled standards, ambitions, a society long forgot. What was it she reminded him of? A yellow flower, full of sunlight, perhaps. No; a thin glass full of sweet-smelling, sparkling Moselle wine. He seemed to see such a glass before him in the arbor, to watch the bubbles rising and breaking, like the silent discharge of energy in the nerves and brain, the rapid florescence in young blood—Wunsch felt ashamed and dragged his slippers along the path to the kitchen, his eyes on the ground.

V.

The children in the primary grades were sometimes required to make relief maps of Moonstone in sand. Had they used colored sands, as the Navajo medicine men do in their sand mosaics, they could easily have indicated the social classifications of Moonstone, since these conformed to certain topographical boundaries, and every child understood them perfectly.

The main business street ran, of course, through the center of the town. To the west of this street lived all the people who were, as Tillie Kronborg said, "in society." Sylvester Street, the third parallel with Main Street on the west, was the longest in town, and the best dwellings were built along it. Far out at the north end, nearly a mile from the court-house and its cottonwood grove, was Dr. Archie's house, its big yard and garden surrounded by a white paling fence. The Methodist Church was in the center of the town, facing the court-house square. The Kronborgs lived half a mile south of the church, on the long street that stretched out like an arm to the depot settlement. This was the first street west of Main, and was built up only on one side. The preacher's house faced the backs of the brick and frame store buildings and a draw full of sunflowers and scraps of old iron. The sidewalk which ran in front of the Kronborgs' house was the one continuous sidewalk to the depot, and all the train men and roundhouse employees passed the front gate every time they came uptown. Thea and Mrs. Kronborg had many friends among the railroad men, who often paused to chat across the fence, and of one of these we shall have more to say.

In the part of Moonstone that lay east of Main Street, toward the deep ravine which, farther south, wound by Mexican Town, lived all the humbler citizens, the people who voted but did not run for office. The houses were little story-and-a-half cottages, with none of the fussy architectural efforts that marked those on Sylvester Street. They nestled modestly behind their cottonwoods and Virginia creeper; their occupants had no social pretensions to keep up. There were no half-glass front doors with doorbells, or formidable parlors behind closed shutters. Here the old women washed in the back yard, and the men sat in the front doorway and smoked their pipes. The people on Sylvester Street scarcely knew that this part of the town existed. Thea liked to take Thor and her express wagon and explore these quiet, shady streets, where the people never tried to have lawns or to grow elms and pine trees, but let the native timber have its way and spread in luxuriance. She had many friends there, old women who gave her a yellow rose or a spray of trumpet vine and appeased Thor with a cooky or a doughnut. They called Thea "that preacher's girl," but the demonstrative was misplaced, for when they spoke of Mr. Kronborg they called him "the Methodist preacher."

Dr. Archie was very proud of his yard and garden, which he worked himself. He was the only man in Moonstone who was successful at growing rambler roses, and his strawberries were famous. One morning when Thea was downtown on an errand, the doctor stopped her, took her hand and went over her with a quizzical eye, as he nearly always did when they met.

"You haven't been up to my place to get any strawberries yet, Thea. They're at their best just now. Mrs. Archie doesn't know what to do with them all. Come up this afternoon. Just tell Mrs. Archie I sent you. Bring a big basket and pick till you are tired."

When she got home Thea told her mother that she didn't want to go, because she didn't like Mrs. Archie.

"She is certainly one queer woman," Mrs. Kronborg assented, "but he's asked you so often, I guess you'll have to go this time. She won't bite you."

After dinner Thea took a basket, put Thor in his baby buggy, and set out for Dr. Archie's house at the other end of town. As soon as she came within sight of the house, she slackened her pace. She approached it very slowly, stopping often to pick dandelions and sand-peas for Thor to crush up in his fist.

It was his wife's custom, as soon as Dr. Archie left the house in the morning, to shut all the doors and windows to keep the dust out, and to pull down the shades to keep the sun from fading the carpets. She thought, too, that neighbors were less likely to drop in if the house was closed up. She was one of those people who are stingy without motive or reason, even when they can gain nothing by it. She must have known that skimping the doctor in heat and food made him more extravagant than he would have been had she made him comfortable. He never came home for lunch, because she gave him such miserable scraps and shreds of food. No matter how much milk he bought, he could never get thick cream for his strawberries. Even when he watched his wife lift it from the milk in smooth, ivory-colored blankets, she managed, by some sleight-of-hand, to dilute it before it got to the breakfast table. The butcher's favorite joke was about the kind of meat he sold Mrs. Archie. She felt no interest in food herself, and she hated to prepare it. She liked nothing better than to have Dr. Archie go to Denver for a few days—he often went chiefly because he was hungry—and to be left alone to eat canned salmon and to keep the house shut up from morning until night.

Mrs. Archie would not have a servant because, she said, "they ate too much and broke too much"; she even said they knew too much. She used what mind she had in devising shifts to minimize her housework. She used to tell her neighbors that if there were no men, there would be no housework. When Mrs. Archie was first married, she had been always in a panic for fear she would have children. Now that her apprehensions on that score had grown paler, she was almost as much afraid of having dust in the house as she had once been of having children in it. If dust did not get in, it did not have to be got out, she said. She would take any amount of trouble to avoid trouble. Why, nobody knew. Certainly her husband had never been able to make her out. Such little, mean natures are among the darkest and most baffling of created things. There is no law by which they can be explained. The ordinary incentives of pain and pleasure do not account for their behavior. They live like insects, absorbed in petty activities that seem to have nothing to do with any genial aspect of human life.

Mrs. Archie, as Mrs. Kronborg said, "liked to gad." She liked to have her house clean, empty, dark, locked, and to be out of it—anywhere. A church social, a prayer meeting, a ten-cent show; she seemed to have no preference. When there was nowhere else to go, she used to sit for hours in Mrs. Smiley's millinery and notion store, listening to the talk of the women who came in, watching them while they tried on hats, blinking at them from her corner with her sharp, restless little eyes. She never talked much herself, but she knew all the gossip of the town and she had a sharp ear for racy anecdotes—"traveling men's stories," they used to be called in Moonstone. Her clicking laugh sounded like a typewriting machine in action, and, for very pointed stories, she had a little screech.

Mrs. Archie had been Mrs. Archie for only six years, and when she was Belle White she was one of the "pretty" girls in Lansing, Michigan. She had then a train of suitors. She could truly remind Archie that "the boys hung around her." They did. They thought her very spirited and were always saying, "Oh, that Belle White, she's a case!" She used to play heavy practical jokes which the young men thought very clever. Archie was considered the most promising young man in "the young crowd," so Belle selected him. She let him see, made him fully aware, that she had selected him, and Archie was the sort of boy who could not withstand such enlightenment. Belle's family were sorry for him. On his wedding day her sisters looked at the big, handsome boy—he was twenty-four—as he walked down the aisle with his bride, and then they looked at each other. His besotted confidence, his sober, radiant face, his gentle, protecting arm, made them uncomfortable. Well, they were glad that he was going West at once, to fulfill his doom where they would not be onlookers. Anyhow, they consoled themselves, they had got Belle off their hands.

More than that, Belle seemed to have got herself off her hands. Her reputed prettiness must have been entirely the result of determination, of a fierce little ambition. Once she had married, fastened herself on some one, come to port,—it vanished like the ornamental plumage which drops away from some birds after the mating season. The one aggressive action of her life was over. She began to shrink in face and stature. Of her harum-scarum spirit there was nothing left but the little screech. Within a few years she looked as small and mean as she was.

Thor's chariot crept along. Thea approached the house unwillingly. She didn't care about the strawberries, anyhow. She had come only because she did not want to hurt Dr. Archie's feelings. She not only disliked Mrs. Archie, she was a little afraid of her. While Thea was getting the heavy baby-buggy through the iron gate she heard some one call, "Wait a minute!" and Mrs. Archie came running around the house from the back door, her apron over her head. She came to help with the buggy, because she was afraid the wheels might scratch the paint off the gateposts. She was a skinny little woman with a great pile of frizzy light hair on a small head.

"Dr. Archie told me to come up and pick some strawberries," Thea muttered, wishing she had stayed at home.

Mrs. Archie led the way to the back door, squinting and shading her eyes with her hand. "Wait a minute," she said again, when Thea explained why she had come.

She went into her kitchen and Thea sat down on the porch step. When Mrs. Archie reappeared she carried in her hand a little wooden butter-basket trimmed with fringed tissue paper, which she must have brought home from some church supper. "You'll have to have something to put them in," she said, ignoring the yawning willow basket which stood empty on Thor's feet. "You can have this, and you needn't mind about returning it. You know about not trampling the vines, don't you?"

Mrs. Archie went back into the house and Thea leaned over in the sand and picked a few strawberries. As soon as she was sure that she was not going to cry, she tossed the little basket into the big one and ran Thor's buggy along the gravel walk and out of the gate as fast as she could push it. She was angry, and she was ashamed for Dr. Archie. She could not help thinking how uncomfortable he would be if he ever found out about it. Little things like that were the ones that cut him most. She slunk home by the back way, and again almost cried when she told her mother about it.

Mrs. Kronborg was frying doughnuts for her husband's supper. She laughed as she dropped a new lot into the hot grease. "It's wonderful, the way some people are made," she declared. "But I wouldn't let that upset me if I was you. Think what it would be to live with it all the time. You look in the black pocketbook inside my handbag and take a dime and go downtown and get an ice-cream soda. That'll make you feel better. Thor can have a little of the ice-cream if you feed it to him with a spoon. He likes it, don't you, son?" She stooped to wipe his chin. Thor was only six months old and inarticulate, but it was quite true that he liked ice-cream.

VI.

Seen from a balloon, Moonstone would have looked like a Noah's ark town set out in the sand and lightly shaded by gray-green tamarisks and cottonwoods. A few people were trying to make soft maples grow in their turfed lawns, but the fashion of planting incongruous trees from the North Atlantic States had not become general then, and the frail, brightly painted desert town was shaded by the light-reflecting, wind-loving trees of the desert, whose roots are always seeking water and whose leaves are always talking about it, making the sound of rain. The long porous roots of the cottonwood are irrepressible. They break into the wells as rats do into granaries, and thieve the water.

The long street which connected Moonstone with the depot settlement traversed in its course a considerable stretch of rough open country, staked out in lots but not built up at all, a weedy hiatus between the town and the railroad. When you set out along this street to go to the station, you noticed that the houses became smaller and farther apart, until they ceased altogether, and the board sidewalk continued its uneven course through sunflower patches, until you reached the solitary, new brick Catholic Church. The church stood there because the land was given to the parish by the man who owned the adjoining waste lots, in the hope of making them more salable—"Farrier's Addition," this patch of prairie was called in the clerk's office. An eighth of a mile beyond the church was a washout, a deep sand-gully, where the board sidewalk became a bridge for perhaps fifty feet. Just beyond the gully was old Uncle Billy Beemer's grove,—twelve town lots set out in fine, well-grown cottonwood trees, delightful to look upon, or to listen to, as they swayed and rippled in the wind. Uncle Billy had been one of the most worthless old drunkards who ever sat on a store box and told filthy stories. One night he played hide-and-seek with a switch engine and got his sodden brains knocked out. But his grove, the one creditable thing he had ever done in his life, rustled on. Beyond this grove the houses of the depot settlement began, and the naked board walk, that had run in out of the sunflowers, again became a link between human dwellings.

One afternoon, late in the summer, Dr. Howard Archie was fighting his way back to town along this walk through a blinding sandstorm, a silk handkerchief tied over his mouth. He had been to see a sick woman down in the depot settlement, and he was walking because his ponies had been out for a hard drive that morning.

As he passed the Catholic Church he came upon Thea and Thor. Thea was sitting in a child's express wagon, her feet out behind, kicking the wagon along and steering by the tongue. Thor was on her lap and she held him with one arm. He had grown to be a big cub of a baby, with a constitutional grievance, and he had to be continually amused. Thea took him philosophically, and tugged and pulled him about, getting as much fun as she could under her encumbrance. Her hair was blowing about her face, and her eyes were squinting so intently at the uneven board sidewalk in front of her that she did not see the doctor until he spoke to her.

"Look out, Thea. You'll steer that youngster into the ditch."

The wagon stopped. Thea released the tongue, wiped her hot, sandy face, and pushed back her hair. "Oh, no, I won't! I never ran off but once, and then he didn't get anything but a bump. He likes this better than a baby buggy, and so do I."

"Are you going to kick that cart all the way home?"

"Of course. We take long trips; wherever there is a sidewalk. It's no good on the road."

"Looks to me like working pretty hard for your fun. Are you going to be busy to-night? Want to make a call with me? Spanish Johnny's come home again, all used up. His wife sent me word this morning, and I said I'd go over to see him to-night. He's an old chum of yours, isn't he?"

"Oh, I'm glad. She's been crying her eyes out. When did he come?"

"Last night, on Number Six. Paid his fare, they tell me. Too sick to beat it. There'll come a time when that boy won't get back, I'm afraid. Come around to my office about eight o'clock, —and you needn't bring that!"

Thor seemed to understand that he had been insulted, for he scowled and began to kick the side of the wagon, shouting, "Go-go, go-go!" Thea leaned forward and grabbed the wagon tongue. Dr. Archie stepped in front of her and blocked the way. "Why don't you make him wait? What do you let him boss you like that for?"

"If he gets mad he throws himself, and then I can't do anything with him. When he's mad he's lots stronger than me, aren't you, Thor?" Thea spoke with pride, and the idol was appeased. He grunted approvingly as his sister began to kick rapidly behind her, and the wagon rattled off and soon disappeared in the flying currents of sand.

That evening Dr. Archie was seated in his office, his desk chair tilted back, reading by the light of a hot coal-oil lamp. All the windows were open, but the night was breathless after the sandstorm, and his hair was moist where it hung over his forehead. He was deeply engrossed in his book and sometimes smiled thoughtfully as he read. When Thea Kronborg entered quietly and slipped into a seat, he nodded, finished his paragraph, inserted a bookmark, and rose to put the book back into the case. It was one out of the long row of uniform volumes on the top shelf.

"Nearly every time I come in, when you're alone, you're reading one of those books," Thea remarked thoughtfully. "They must be very nice."

The doctor dropped back into his swivel chair, the mottled volume still in his hand. "They aren't exactly books, Thea," he said seriously. "They're a city."

"A history, you mean?"

"Yes, and no. They're a history of a live city, not a dead one. A Frenchman undertook to write about a whole cityful of people, all the kinds he knew. And he got them nearly all in, I guess. Yes, it's very interesting. You'll like to read it some day, when you're grown up."

Thea leaned forward and made out the title on the back, "A Distinguished Provincial in Paris."

"It doesn't sound very interesting."

"Perhaps not, but it is." The doctor scrutinized her broad face, low enough to be in the direct light from under the green lamp shade. "Yes," he went on with some satisfaction, "I think you'll like them some day. You're always curious about people, and I expect this man knew more about people than anybody that ever lived."

"City people or country people?"

"Both. People are pretty much the same everywhere."

"Oh, no, they're not. The people who go through in the dining-car aren't like us."

"What makes you think they aren't, my girl? Their clothes?"

Thea shook her head. "No, it's something else. I don't know." Her eyes shifted under the doctor's searching gaze and she glanced up at the row of books. "How soon will I be old enough to read them?"

"Soon enough, soon enough, little girl." The doctor patted her hand and looked at her index finger. "The nail's coming all right, isn't it? But I think that man makes you practice too much. You have it on your mind all the time." He had noticed that when she talked to him she was always opening and shutting her hands. "It makes you nervous."

"No, he don't," Thea replied stubbornly, watching Dr. Archie return the book to its niche.

He took up a black leather case, put on his hat, and they went down the dark stairs into the street. The summer moon hung full in the sky. For the time being, it was the great fact in the world. Beyond the edge of the town the plain was so white that every clump of sage stood out distinct from the sand, and the dunes looked like a shining lake. The doctor took off his straw hat and carried it in his hand as they walked toward Mexican Town, across the sand.

North of Pueblo, Mexican settlements were rare in Colorado then. This one had come about accidentally. Spanish Johnny was the first Mexican who came to Moonstone. He was a painter and decorator, and had been working in Trinidad, when Ray Kennedy told him there was a "boom" on in Moonstone, and a good many new buildings were going up. A year after Johnny settled in Moonstone, his cousin, Famos Serrenos, came to work in the brickyard; then Serrenos' cousins came to help him. During the strike, the master mechanic put a gang of Mexicans to work in the roundhouse. The Mexicans had arrived so quietly, with their blankets and musical instruments, that before Moonstone was awake to the fact, there was a Mexican quarter; a dozen families or more.

As Thea and the doctor approached the 'dobe houses, they heard a guitar, and a rich barytone voice—that of Famos Serrenos—singing "La Golandrina." All the Mexican houses had neat little yards, with tamarisk hedges and flowers, and walks bordered with shells or whitewashed stones. Johnny's house was dark. His wife, Mrs. Tellamantez, was sitting on the doorstep, combing her long, blue-black hair. (Mexican women are like the Spartans; when they are in trouble, in love, under stress of any kind, they comb and comb their hair.) She rose without embarrassment or apology, comb in hand, and greeted the doctor.

"Good-evening; will you go in?" she asked in a low, musical voice. "He is in the back room. I will make a light." She followed them indoors, lit a candle and handed it to the doctor, pointing toward the bedroom. Then she went back and sat down on her doorstep.

Dr. Archie and Thea went into the bedroom, which was dark and quiet. There was a bed in the corner, and a man was lying on the clean sheets. On the table beside him was a glass pitcher, half-full of water. Spanish Johnny looked younger than his wife, and when he was in health he was very handsome: slender, gold-colored, with wavy black hair, a round, smooth throat, white teeth, and burning black eyes. His profile was strong and severe, like an Indian's. What was termed his "wildness" showed itself only in his feverish eyes and in the color that burned on his tawny cheeks. That night he was a coppery green, and his eyes were like black holes. He opened them when the doctor held the candle before his face.

"MI TESTA!" he muttered, "MI TESTA," doctor. "LA FIEBRE!" Seeing the doctor's companion at the foot of the bed, he attempted a smile. "MUCHACHA!" he exclaimed deprecatingly.

Dr. Archie stuck a thermometer into his mouth. "Now, Thea, you can run outside and wait for me."

Thea slipped noiselessly through the dark house and joined Mrs. Tellamantez. The somber Mexican woman did not seem inclined to talk, but her nod was friendly. Thea sat down on the warm sand, her back to the moon, facing Mrs. Tellamantez on her doorstep, and began to count the moon flowers on the vine that ran over the house. Mrs. Tellamantez was always considered a very homely woman. Her face was of a strongly marked type not sympathetic to Americans. Such long, oval faces, with a full chin, a large, mobile mouth, a high nose, are not uncommon in Spain. Mrs. Tellamantez could not write her name, and could read but little. Her strong nature lived upon itself. She was chiefly known in Moonstone for her forbearance with her incorrigible husband.

Nobody knew exactly what was the matter with Johnny, and everybody liked him. His popularity would have been unusual for a white man, for a Mexican it was unprecedented. His talents were his undoing. He had a high, uncertain tenor voice, and he played the mandolin with exceptional skill. Periodically he went crazy. There was no other way to explain his behavior. He was a clever workman, and, when he worked, as regular and faithful as a burro. Then some night he would fall in with a crowd at the saloon and begin to sing. He would go on until he had no voice left, until he wheezed and rasped. Then he would play his mandolin furiously, and drink until his eyes sank back into his head. At last, when he was put out of the saloon at closing time, and could get nobody to listen to him, he would run away—along the railroad track, straight across the desert. He always managed to get aboard a freight somewhere. Once beyond Denver, he played his way southward from saloon to saloon until he got across the border. He never wrote to his wife; but she would soon begin to get newspapers from La Junta, Albuquerque, Chihuahua, with marked paragraphs announcing that Juan Tellamantez and his wonderful mandolin could be heard at the Jack Rabbit Grill, or the Pearl of Cadiz Saloon. Mrs. Tellamantez waited and wept and combed her hair. When he was completely wrung out and burned up,—all but destroyed,—her Juan always came back to her to be taken care of,—once with an ugly knife wound in the neck, once with a finger missing from his right hand,—but he played just as well with three fingers as he had with four.

Public sentiment was lenient toward Johnny, but everybody was disgusted with Mrs. Tellamantez for putting up with him. She ought to discipline him, people said; she ought to leave him; she had no self-respect. In short, Mrs. Tellamantez got all the blame. Even Thea thought she was much too humble. To-night, as she sat with her back to the moon, looking at the moon flowers and Mrs. Tellamantez's somber face, she was thinking that there is nothing so sad in the world as that kind of patience and resignation. It was much worse than Johnny's craziness. She even wondered whether it did not help to make Johnny crazy. People had no right to be so passive and resigned. She would like to roll over and over in the sand and screech at Mrs. Tellamantez. She was glad when the doctor came out.

The Mexican woman rose and stood respectful and expectant. The doctor held his hat in his hand and looked kindly at her.

"Same old thing, Mrs. Tellamantez. He's no worse than he's been before. I've left some medicine. Don't give him anything but toast water until I see him again. You're a good nurse; you'll get him out." Dr. Archie smiled encouragingly. He glanced about the little garden and wrinkled his brows. "I can't see what makes him behave so. He's killing himself, and he's not a rowdy sort of fellow. Can't you tie him up someway? Can't you tell when these fits are coming on?"

Mrs. Tellamantez put her hand to her forehead. "The saloon, doctor, the excitement; that is what makes him. People listen to him, and it excites him."

The doctor shook his head. "Maybe. He's too much for my calculations. I don't see what he gets out of it."

"He is always fooled,"—the Mexican woman spoke rapidly and tremulously, her long under lip quivering.

"He is good at heart, but he has no head. He fools himself. You do not understand in this country, you are progressive. But he has no judgment, and he is fooled." She stooped quickly, took up one of the white conch-shells that bordered the walk, and, with an apologetic inclination of her head, held it to Dr. Archie's ear. "Listen, doctor. You hear something in there? You hear the sea; and yet the sea is very far from here. You have judgment, and you know that. But he is fooled. To him, it is the sea itself. A little thing is big to him." She bent and placed the shell in the white row, with its fellows. Thea took it up softly and pressed it to her own ear. The sound in it startled her; it was like something calling one. So that was why Johnny ran away. There was something awe-inspiring about Mrs. Tellamantez and her shell.

Thea caught Dr. Archie's hand and squeezed it hard as she skipped along beside him back toward Moonstone. She went home, and the doctor went back to his lamp and his book. He never left his office until after midnight. If he did not play whist or pool in the evening, he read. It had become a habit with him to lose himself.

VII.

Thea's twelfth birthday had passed a few weeks before her memorable call upon Mrs. Tellamantez. There was a worthy man in Moonstone who was already planning to marry Thea as soon as she should be old enough. His name was Ray Kennedy, his age was thirty, and he was conductor on a freight train, his run being from Moonstone to Denver. Ray was a big fellow, with a square, open American face, a rock chin, and features that one would never happen to remember. He was an aggressive idealist, a freethinker, and, like most railroad men, deeply sentimental. Thea liked him for reasons that had to do with the adventurous life he had led in Mexico and the Southwest, rather than for anything very personal. She liked him, too, because he was the only one of her friends who ever took her to the sand hills. The sand hills were a constant tantalization; she loved them better than anything near Moonstone, and yet she could so seldom get to them. The first dunes were accessible enough;

they were only a few miles beyond the Kohlers', and she could run out there any day when she could do her practicing in the morning and get Thor off her hands for an afternoon. But the real hills—the Turquoise Hills, the Mexicans called them—were ten good miles away, and one reached them by a heavy, sandy road. Dr. Archie sometimes took Thea on his long drives, but as nobody lived in the sand hills, he never had calls to make in that direction. Ray Kennedy was her only hope of getting there.

This summer Thea had not been to the hills once, though Ray had planned several Sunday expeditions. Once Thor was sick, and once the organist in her father's church was away and Thea had to play the organ for the three Sunday services. But on the first Sunday in September, Ray drove up to the Kronborgs' front gate at nine o'clock in the morning and the party actually set off. Gunner and Axel went with Thea, and Ray had asked Spanish Johnny to come and to bring Mrs. Tellamantez and his mandolin. Ray was artlessly fond of music, especially of Mexican music. He and Mrs. Tellamantez had got up the lunch between them, and they were to make coffee in the desert.

When they left Mexican Town, Thea was on the front seat with Ray and Johnny, and Gunner and Axel sat behind with Mrs. Tellamantez. They objected to this, of course, but there were some things about which Thea would have her own way. "As stubborn as a Finn," Mrs. Kronborg sometimes said of her, quoting an old Swedish saying. When they passed the Kohlers', old Fritz and Wunsch were cutting grapes at the arbor. Thea gave them a businesslike nod. Wunsch came to the gate and looked after them. He divined Ray Kennedy's hopes, and he distrusted every expedition that led away from the piano. Unconsciously he made Thea pay for frivolousness of this sort.

As Ray Kennedy's party followed the faint road across the sagebrush, they heard behind them the sound of church bells, which gave them a sense of escape and boundless freedom. Every rabbit that shot across the path, every sage hen that flew up by the trail, was like a runaway thought, a message that one sent into the desert. As they went farther, the illusion of the mirage became more instead of less convincing; a shallow silver lake that spread for many miles, a little misty in the sunlight. Here and there one saw reflected the image of a heifer, turned loose to live upon the sparse sand-grass. They were magnified to a preposterous height and looked like mammoths, prehistoric beasts standing solitary in the waters that for many thousands of years actually washed over that desert;—the mirage itself may be the ghost of that long-vanished sea. Beyond the phantom lake lay the line of many-colored hills; rich, sun-baked yellow, glowing turquoise, lavender, purple; all the open, pastel colors of the desert.

After the first five miles the road grew heavier. The horses had to slow down to a walk and the wheels sank deep into the sand, which now lay in long ridges, like waves, where the last high wind had drifted it. Two hours brought the party to Pedro's Cup, named for a Mexican desperado who had once held the sheriff at bay there. The Cup was a great amphitheater, cut out in the hills, its floor smooth and packed hard, dotted with sagebrush and greasewood.

On either side of the Cup the yellow hills ran north and south, with winding ravines between them, full of soft sand which drained down from the crumbling banks. On the surface of this fluid sand, one could find bits of brilliant stone, crystals and agates and onyx, and petrified wood as red as blood. Dried toads and lizards were to be found there, too. Birds, decomposing more rapidly, left only feathered skeletons.

After a little reconnoitering, Mrs. Tellamantez declared that it was time for lunch, and Ray took his hatchet and began to cut greasewood, which burns fiercely in its green state. The little boys dragged the bushes to the spot that Mrs. Tellamantez had chosen for her fire. Mexican women like to cook out of doors.

After lunch Thea sent Gunner and Axel to hunt for agates. "If you see a rattlesnake, run. Don't try to kill it," she enjoined.

Gunner hesitated. "If Ray would let me take the hatchet, I could kill one all right."

Mrs. Tellamantez smiled and said something to Johnny in Spanish.

"Yes," her husband replied, translating, "they say in Mexico, kill a snake but never hurt his feelings. Down in the hot country, MUCHACHA," turning to Thea, "people keep a pet snake in the house to kill rats and mice. They call him the house snake. They keep a little mat for him by the fire, and at night he curl up there and sit with the family, just as friendly!"

Gunner sniffed with disgust. "Well, I think that's a dirty Mexican way to keep house; so there!"

Johnny shrugged his shoulders. "Perhaps," he muttered. A Mexican learns to dive below insults or soar above them, after he crosses the border.

By this time the south wall of the amphitheater cast a narrow shelf of shadow, and the party withdrew to this refuge. Ray and Johnny began to talk about the Grand Canyon and Death Valley, two places much shrouded in mystery in those days, and Thea listened intently. Mrs. Tellamantez took out her drawn-work and pinned it to her knee. Ray could talk well about the large part of the continent over which he had been knocked about, and Johnny was appreciative.

"You been all over, pretty near. Like a Spanish boy," he commented respectfully.

Ray, who had taken off his coat, whetted his pocketknife thoughtfully on the sole of his shoe. "I began to browse around early. I had a mind to see something of this world, and I ran away from home before I was twelve. Rustled for myself ever since."

"Ran away?" Johnny looked hopeful. "What for?"

"Couldn't make it go with my old man, and didn't take to farming. There were plenty of boys at home. I wasn't missed."

Thea wriggled down in the hot sand and rested her chin on her arm. "Tell Johnny about the melons, Ray, please do!"

Ray's solid, sunburned cheeks grew a shade redder, and he looked reproachfully at Thea. "You're stuck on that story, kid. You like to get the laugh on me, don't you? That was the finishing split I had with my old man, John. He had a claim along the creek, not far from Denver, and raised a little garden stuff for market. One day he had a load of melons and he decided to take 'em to town and sell 'em along the street, and he made me go along and drive for him. Denver wasn't the queen city it is now, by any means, but it seemed a terrible big place to me; and when we got there, if he didn't make me drive right up Capitol Hill! Pap got out and stopped at folkses houses to ask if they didn't want to buy any melons, and I was to drive along slow. The farther I went the madder I got, but I was trying to look unconscious, when the end-gate came loose and one of the melons fell out and squashed. Just then a swell girl, all dressed up, comes out of one of the big houses and calls out, 'Hello, boy, you're losing your melons!' Some dudes on the other side of the street took their hats off to her and began to laugh. I couldn't stand it any longer. I grabbed the whip and lit into that team, and they tore up the hill like jack-rabbits, them damned melons bouncing out the back every jump, the old man cussin' an' yellin' behind and everybody laughin'. I never looked behind, but the whole of Capitol Hill must have been a mess with them squashed melons. I didn't stop the team till I got out of sight of town. Then I pulled up an' left 'em with a rancher I was acquainted with, and I never went home to get the lickin' that was waitin' for me. I expect it's waitin' for me yet."

Thea rolled over in the sand. "Oh, I wish I could have seen those melons fly, Ray! I'll never see anything as funny as that. Now, tell Johnny about your first job."

Ray had a collection of good stories. He was observant, truthful, and kindly—perhaps the chief requisites in a good story-teller. Occasionally he used newspaper phrases, conscientiously learned in his efforts at self-instruction, but when he talked naturally he was always worth listening to. Never having had any schooling to speak of, he had, almost from the time he first ran away, tried to make good his loss. As a sheep-herder he had worried an old grammar to tatters, and read instructive books with the help of a pocket dictionary. By the light of many camp-fires he had pondered upon Prescott's histories, and the works of Washington Irving, which he bought at a high price from a book-agent. Mathematics and physics were easy for him, but general culture came hard, and he was determined to get it. Ray was a freethinker, and inconsistently believed himself damned for being one. When he was braking, down on the Santa Fe, at the end of his run he used to climb into the upper bunk of the caboose, while a noisy gang played poker about the stove below him, and by the roof-lamp read Robert Ingersoll's speeches and "The Age of Reason."

Ray was a loyal-hearted fellow, and it had cost him a great deal to give up his God. He was one of the stepchildren of Fortune, and he had very little to show for all his hard work; the other fellow always got the best of it. He had come in too late, or too early, on several schemes that had made money. He brought with him from all his wanderings a good deal of information (more or less correct in itself, but unrelated, and therefore misleading), a high standard of personal honor, a sentimental veneration for all women, bad as well as good, and a bitter hatred of Englishmen. Thea often thought that the nicest thing about Ray was his love for Mexico and the Mexicans, who had been kind to him when he drifted, a homeless boy, over the border. In Mexico, Ray was Senor Ken-ay-dy, and when he answered to that name he was somehow a different fellow. He spoke Spanish fluently, and the sunny warmth of that tongue kept him from being quite as hard as his chin, or as narrow as his popular science.

While Ray was smoking his cigar, he and Johnny fell to talking about the great fortunes that had been made in the Southwest, and about fellows they knew who had "struck it rich."

"I guess you been in on some big deals down there?" Johnny asked trustfully.

Ray smiled and shook his head. "I've been out on some, John. I've never been exactly in on any. So far, I've either held on too long or let go too soon. But mine's coming to me, all right." Ray looked reflective. He leaned back in the shadow and dug out a rest for his elbow in the sand. "The narrowest escape I ever had, was in the Bridal Chamber. If I hadn't let go there, it would have made me rich. That was a close call."

Johnny looked delighted. "You don' say! She was silver mine, I guess?"

"I guess she was! Down at Lake Valley. I put up a few hundred for the prospector, and he gave me a bunch of stock. Before we'd got anything out of it, my brother-in-law died of the fever in Cuba. My sister was beside herself to get his body back to Colorado to bury him. Seemed foolish to me, but she's the only sister I got. It's expensive for dead folks to travel, and I had to sell my stock in the mine to raise the money to get Elmer on the move. Two months afterward, the boys struck that big pocket in the rock, full of virgin silver. They named her the Bridal Chamber. It wasn't ore, you remember. It was pure, soft metal you could have melted right down into dollars. The boys cut it out with chisels. If old Elmer hadn't played that trick on me, I'd have been in for about fifty thousand. That was a close call, Spanish."

"I recollec'. When the pocket gone, the town go bust."

"You bet. Higher'n a kite. There was no vein, just a pocket in the rock that had sometime or another got filled up with molten silver. You'd think there would be more somewhere about, but NADA. There's fools digging holes in that mountain yet."

When Ray had finished his cigar, Johnny took his mandolin and began Kennedy's favorite, "Ultimo Amor." It was now three o'clock in the afternoon, the hottest hour in the day. The narrow shelf of shadow had widened until the floor of the amphitheater was marked off in two halves, one glittering yellow, and one purple. The little boys had come back and were making a robbers' cave to enact the bold deeds of Pedro the bandit. Johnny, stretched gracefully on the sand, passed from "Ultimo Amor" to "Fluvia de Oro," and then to "Noches de Algeria," playing languidly.

Every one was busy with his own thoughts. Mrs. Tellamantez was thinking of the square in the little town in which she was born; of the white church steps, with people genuflecting as they passed, and the round-topped acacia trees, and the band playing in the plaza. Ray Kennedy was thinking of the future, dreaming the large Western dream of easy money, of a fortune kicked up somewhere in the hills,—an oil well, a gold mine, a ledge of copper. He always told himself, when he accepted a cigar from a newly married railroad man, that he knew enough not to marry until he had found his ideal, and could keep her like a queen. He believed that in the yellow head over there in the sand he had found his ideal, and that by the time she was old enough to marry, he would be able to keep her like a queen. He would kick it up from somewhere, when he got loose from the railroad.

Thea, stirred by tales of adventure, of the Grand Canyon and Death Valley, was recalling a great adventure of her own. Early in the summer her father had been invited to conduct a reunion of old frontiersmen, up in Wyoming, near Laramie, and he took Thea along with him to play the organ and sing patriotic songs. There they stayed at the house of an old ranchman who told them about a ridge up in the hills called Laramie Plain, where the wagon-trails of the Forty-niners and the Mormons were still visible. The old man even volunteered to take Mr. Kronborg up into the hills to see this place, though it was a very long drive to make in one day. Thea had begged frantically to go along, and the old rancher, flattered by her rapt attention to his stories, had interceded for her.

They set out from Laramie before daylight, behind a strong team of mules. All the way there was much talk of the Forty-niners. The old rancher had been a teamster in a freight train that used to crawl back and forth across the plains between Omaha and Cherry Creek, as Denver was then called, and he had met many a wagon train bound for California. He told of Indians and buffalo, thirst and slaughter, wanderings in snowstorms, and lonely graves in the desert.

The road they followed was a wild and beautiful one. It led up and up, by granite rocks and stunted pines, around deep ravines and echoing gorges. The top of the ridge, when they reached it, was a great flat plain, strewn with white boulders, with the wind howling over it. There was not one trail, as Thea had expected; there were a score; deep furrows, cut in the earth by heavy wagon wheels, and now grown over with dry, whitish grass. The furrows ran side by side; when one trail had been worn too deep, the next party had abandoned it and made a new trail to the right or left. They were, indeed, only old wagon ruts, running east and west, and grown over with grass. But as Thea ran about among the white stones, her skirts blowing this way and that, the wind brought to her eyes tears that might have come anyway. The old rancher picked up an iron ox-shoe from one of the furrows and gave it to her for a keepsake. To the west one could see range after range of blue mountains, and at last the snowy range, with its white, windy peaks, the clouds caught here and there on their spurs. Again and again Thea had to hide her face from the cold for a moment. The wind never slept on this plain, the old man said. Every little while eagles flew over.

Coming up from Laramie, the old man had told them that he was in Brownsville, Nebraska, when the first telegraph wires were put across the Missouri River, and that the first message that ever crossed the river was "Westward the course of Empire takes its way." He had been in the room when the instrument began to click, and all the men there had, without thinking what they were doing, taken off their hats, waiting bareheaded to hear the message translated. Thea remembered that message when she sighted down the wagon tracks toward the blue mountains. She told herself she would never, never forget it. The spirit of human courage seemed to live up there with the eagles. For long after, when she was moved by a Fourth-of-July oration, or a band, or a circus parade, she was apt to remember that windy ridge.

To-day she went to sleep while she was thinking about it. When Ray wakened her, the horses were hitched to the wagon and Gunner and Axel were begging for a place on the front seat. The air had cooled, the sun was setting, and the desert was on fire. Thea contentedly took the back seat with Mrs. Tellamantez. As they drove homeward the stars began to come out, pale yellow in a yellow sky, and Ray and Johnny began to sing one of those railroad ditties that are usually born on the Southern Pacific and run the length of the Santa Fe and the "Q" system before they die to give place to a new one. This was a song about a Greaser dance, the refrain being something like this:—

"Pedro, Pedro, swing high, swing low,
And it's allamand left again;
For there's boys that's bold and there's some that's cold,
But the gold boys come from Spain,
Oh, the gold boys come from Spain!"

VIII.

Winter was long in coming that year. Throughout October the days were bathed in sunlight and the air was clear as crystal. The town kept its cheerful summer aspect, the desert glistened with light, the sand hills every day went through magical changes of color. The scarlet sage bloomed late in the front yards, the cottonwood leaves were bright gold long before they fell, and it was not until November that the green on the tamarisks began to cloud and fade. There was a flurry of snow about Thanksgiving, and then December came on warm and clear.

Thea had three music pupils now, little girls whose mothers declared that Professor Wunsch was "much too severe." They took their lessons on Saturday, and this, of course, cut down her time for play. She did not really mind this because she was allowed to use the money—her pupils paid her twenty-five cents a lesson—to fit up a little room for herself upstairs in the half-story. It was the end room of the wing, and was not plastered, but was snugly lined with soft pine. The ceiling was so low that a grown person could reach it with the palm of the hand, and it sloped down on either side. There was only one window, but it was a double one and went to the floor. In October, while the days were still warm, Thea and Tillie papered the room, walls and ceiling in the same paper, small red and brown roses on a yellowish ground. Thea bought a brown cotton carpet, and her big brother, Gus, put it down for her one Sunday. She made white cheesecloth curtains and hung them on a tape. Her mother gave her an old walnut dresser with a broken mirror, and she had her own dumpy walnut single bed, and a blue washbowl and pitcher which she had drawn at a church fair lottery. At the head of her bed she had a tall round wooden hat-crate, from the clothing store.

This, standing on end and draped with cretonne, made a fairly steady table for her lantern. She was not allowed to take a lamp upstairs, so Ray Kennedy gave her a railroad lantern by which she could read at night.

In winter this loft room of Thea's was bitterly cold, but against her mother's advice—and Tillie's—she always left her window open a little way. Mrs. Kronborg declared that she "had no patience with American physiology," though the lessons about the injurious effects of alcohol and tobacco were well enough for the boys. Thea asked Dr. Archie about the window, and he told her that a girl who sang must always have plenty of fresh air, or her voice would get husky, and that the cold would harden her throat. The important thing, he said, was to keep your feet warm. On very cold nights Thea always put a brick in the oven after supper, and when she went upstairs she wrapped it in an old flannel petticoat and put it in her bed. The boys, who would never heat bricks for themselves, sometimes carried off Thea's, and thought it a good joke to get ahead of her.

When Thea first plunged in between her red blankets, the cold sometimes kept her awake for a good while, and she comforted herself by remembering all she could of "Polar Explorations," a fat, calf-bound volume her father had bought from a book-agent, and by thinking about the members of Greely's party: how they lay in their frozen sleeping-bags, each man hoarding the warmth of his own body and trying to make it last as long as possible against the on-coming cold that would be everlasting. After half an hour or so, a warm wave crept over her body and round, sturdy legs; she glowed like a little stove with the warmth of her own blood, and the heavy quilts and red blankets grew warm wherever they touched her, though her breath sometimes froze on the coverlid. Before daylight, her internal fires went down a little, and she often wakened to find herself drawn up into a tight ball, somewhat stiff in the legs. But that made it all the easier to get up.

The acquisition of this room was the beginning of a new era in Thea's life. It was one of the most important things that ever happened to her. Hitherto, except in summer, when she could be out of doors, she had lived in constant turmoil; the family, the day school, the Sunday-School. The clamor about her drowned the voice within herself. In the end of the wing, separated from the other upstairs sleeping-rooms by a long, cold, unfinished lumber room, her mind worked better. She thought things out more clearly. Pleasant plans and ideas occurred to her which had never come before. She had certain thoughts which were like companions, ideas which were like older and wiser friends. She left them there in the morning, when she finished dressing in the cold, and at night, when she came up with her lantern and shut the door after a busy day, she found them awaiting her. There was no possible way of heating the room, but that was fortunate, for otherwise it would have been occupied by one of her older brothers.

From the time when she moved up into the wing, Thea began to live a double life. During the day, when the hours were full of tasks, she was one of the Kronborg children, but at night she was a different person. On Friday and Saturday nights she always read for a long while after she was in bed. She had no clock, and there was no one to nag her.

Ray Kennedy, on his way from the depot to his boardinghouse, often looked up and saw Thea's light burning when the rest of the house was dark, and felt cheered as by a friendly greeting. He was a faithful soul, and many disappointments had not changed his nature. He was still, at heart, the same boy who, when he was sixteen, had settled down to freeze with his sheep in a Wyoming blizzard, and had been rescued only to play the losing game of fidelity to other charges.

Ray had no very clear idea of what might be going on in Thea's head, but he knew that something was. He used to remark to Spanish Johnny, "That girl is developing something fine." Thea was patient with Ray, even in regard to the liberties he took with her name. Outside the family, every one in Moonstone, except Wunsch and Dr. Archie, called her "Thee-a," but this seemed cold and distant to Ray, so he called her "Thee." Once, in a moment of exasperation, Thea asked him why he did this, and he explained that he once had a chum, Theodore, whose name was always abbreviated thus, and that since he was killed down on the Santa Fe, it seemed natural to call somebody "Thee." Thea sighed and submitted. She was always helpless before homely sentiment and usually changed the subject.

It was the custom for each of the different Sunday Schools in Moonstone to give a concert on Christmas Eve. But this year all the churches were to unite and give, as was announced from the pulpits, "a semi-sacred concert of picked talent" at the opera house. The Moonstone Orchestra, under the direction of Professor Wunsch, was to play, and the most talented members of each Sunday School were to take part in the programme. Thea was put down by the committee "for instrumental." This made her indignant, for the vocal numbers were always more popular. Thea went to the president of the committee and demanded hotly if her rival, Lily Fisher, were going to sing. The president was a big, florid, powdered woman, a fierce W.C.T.U. worker, one of Thea's natural enemies. Her name was Johnson; her husband kept the livery stable, and she was called Mrs. Livery Johnson, to distinguish her from other families of the same surname. Mrs. Johnson was a prominent Baptist, and Lily Fisher was the Baptist prodigy. There was a not very Christian rivalry between the Baptist Church and Mr. Kronborg's church.

When Thea asked Mrs. Johnson whether her rival was to be allowed to sing, Mrs. Johnson, with an eagerness which told how she had waited for this moment, replied that "Lily was going to recite to be obliging, and to give other children a chance to sing." As she delivered this thrust, her eyes glittered more than the Ancient Mariner's, Thea thought. Mrs. Johnson disapproved of the way in which Thea was being brought up, of a child whose chosen associates were Mexicans and sinners, and who was, as she pointedly put it, "bold with men." She so enjoyed an opportunity to rebuke Thea, that, tightly corseted as she was, she could scarcely control her breathing, and her lace and her gold watch chain rose and fell "with short, uneasy motion." Frowning, Thea turned away and walked slowly homeward. She suspected guile. Lily Fisher was the most stuck-up doll in the world, and it was certainly not like her to recite to be obliging. Nobody who could sing ever recited, because the warmest applause always went to the singers.

However, when the programme was printed in the Moonstone GLEAM, there it was: "Instrumental solo, Thea Kronborg. Recitation, Lily Fisher."

Because his orchestra was to play for the concert, Mr. Wunsch imagined that he had been put in charge of the music, and he became arrogant. He insisted that Thea should play a "Ballade" by Reinecke. When Thea consulted her mother, Mrs. Kronborg agreed with her that the "Ballade" would "never take" with a Moonstone audience. She advised Thea to play "something with variations," or, at least, "The Invitation to the Dance."

"It makes no matter what they like," Wunsch replied to Thea's entreaties. "It is time already that they learn something."

Thea's fighting powers had been impaired by an ulcerated tooth and consequent loss of sleep, so she gave in. She finally had the molar pulled, though it was a second tooth and should have been saved. The dentist was a clumsy, ignorant country boy, and Mr. Kronborg would not hear of Dr. Archie's taking Thea to a dentist in Denver, though Ray Kennedy said he could get a pass for her. What with the pain of the tooth, and family discussions about it, with trying to make Christmas presents and to keep up her school work and practicing, and giving lessons on Saturdays, Thea was fairly worn out.

On Christmas Eve she was nervous and excited. It was the first time she had ever played in the opera house, and she had never before had to face so many people. Wunsch would not let her play with her notes, and she was afraid of forgetting. Before the concert began, all the participants had to assemble on the stage and sit there to be looked at. Thea wore her white summer dress and a blue sash, but Lily Fisher had a new pink silk, trimmed with white swansdown.

The hall was packed. It seemed as if every one in Moonstone was there, even Mrs. Kohler, in her hood, and old Fritz. The seats were wooden kitchen chairs, numbered, and nailed to long planks which held them together in rows. As the floor was not raised, the chairs were all on the same level. The more interested persons in the audience peered over the heads of the people in front of them to get a good view of the stage. From the platform Thea picked out many friendly faces. There was Dr. Archie, who never went to church entertainments; there was the friendly jeweler who ordered her music for her,—he sold accordions and guitars as well as watches,—and the druggist who often lent her books, and her favorite teacher from the school. There was Ray Kennedy, with a party of freshly barbered railroad men he had brought along with him. There was Mrs. Kronborg with all the children, even Thor, who had been brought out in a new white plush coat. At the back of the hall sat a little group of Mexicans, and among them Thea caught the gleam of Spanish Johnny's white teeth, and of Mrs. Tellamantez's lustrous, smoothly coiled black hair.

After the orchestra played "Selections from Erminie," and the Baptist preacher made a long prayer, Tillie Kronborg came on with a highly colored recitation, "The Polish Boy." When it was over every one breathed more freely. No committee had the courage to leave Tillie off a programme. She was accepted as a trying feature of every entertainment. The Progressive Euchre Club was the only social organization in the town that entirely escaped Tillie. After Tillie sat down, the Ladies' Quartette sang, "Beloved, it is Night," and then it was Thea's turn.

The "Ballade" took ten minutes, which was five minutes too long. The audience grew restive and fell to whispering. Thea could hear Mrs. Livery Johnson's bracelets jangling as she fanned herself, and she could hear her father's nervous, ministerial cough. Thor behaved better than any one else. When Thea bowed and returned to her seat at the back of the stage there was the usual applause, but it was vigorous only from the back of the house where the Mexicans sat, and from Ray Kennedy's CLAQUEURS. Any one could see that a good-natured audience had been bored.

Because Mr. Kronborg's sister was on the programme, it had also been necessary to ask the Baptist preacher's wife's cousin to sing. She was a "deep alto" from McCook, and she sang, "Thy Sentinel Am I." After her came Lily Fisher. Thea's rival was also a blonde, but her hair was much heavier than Thea's, and fell in long round curls over her shoulders. She was the angel-child of the Baptists, and looked exactly like the beautiful children on soap calendars. Her pink-and-white face, her set smile of innocence, were surely born of a color-press. She had long, drooping eyelashes, a little pursed-up mouth, and narrow, pointed teeth, like a squirrel's.

Lily began:—

"ROCK OF AGES, CLEFT FOR ME, carelessly the maiden sang."

Thea drew a long breath. That was the game; it was a recitation and a song in one. Lily trailed the hymn through half a dozen verses with great effect. The Baptist preacher had announced at the beginning of the concert that "owing to the length of the programme, there would be no encores." But the applause which followed Lily to her seat was such an unmistakable expression of enthusiasm that Thea had to admit Lily was justified in going back. She was attended this time by Mrs. Livery Johnson herself, crimson with triumph and gleaming-eyed, nervously rolling and unrolling a sheet of music. She took off her bracelets and played Lily's accompaniment. Lily had the effrontery to come out with, "She sang the song of Home, Sweet Home, the song that touched my heart." But this did not surprise Thea; as Ray said later in the evening, "the cards had been stacked against her from the beginning." The next issue of the GLEAM correctly stated that "unquestionably the honors of the evening must be accorded to Miss Lily Fisher." The Baptists had everything their own way.

After the concert Ray Kennedy joined the Kronborgs' party and walked home with them. Thea was grateful for his silent sympathy, even while it irritated her. She inwardly vowed that she would never take another lesson from old Wunsch. She wished that her father would not keep cheerfully singing, "When Shepherds Watched," as he marched ahead, carrying Thor. She felt that silence would become the Kronborgs for a while. As a family, they somehow seemed a little ridiculous, trooping along in the starlight. There were so many of them, for one thing. Then Tillie was so absurd. She was giggling and talking to Anna just as if she had not made, as even Mrs. Kronborg admitted, an exhibition of herself.

When they got home, Ray took a box from his overcoat pocket and slipped it into Thea's hand as he said goodnight. They all hurried in to the glowing stove in the parlor. The sleepy children were sent to bed. Mrs. Kronborg and Anna stayed up to fill the stockings.

"I guess you're tired, Thea. You needn't stay up." Mrs. Kronborg's clear and seemingly indifferent eye usually measured Thea pretty accurately.

Thea hesitated. She glanced at the presents laid out on the dining-room table, but they looked unattractive. Even the brown plush monkey she had bought for Thor with such enthusiasm seemed to have lost his wise and humorous expression. She murmured, "All right," to her mother, lit her lantern, and went upstairs.

Ray's box contained a hand-painted white satin fan, with pond lilies—an unfortunate reminder. Thea smiled grimly and tossed it into her upper drawer. She was not to be consoled by toys. She undressed quickly and stood for some time in the cold, frowning in the broken looking glass at her flaxen pig-tails, at her white neck and arms. Her own broad, resolute face set its chin at her, her eyes flashed into her own defiantly. Lily Fisher was pretty, and she was willing to be just as big a fool as people wanted her to be. Very well; Thea Kronborg wasn't. She would rather be hated than be stupid, any day. She popped into bed and read stubbornly at a queer paper book the drug-store man had given her because he couldn't sell it. She had trained herself to put her mind on what she was doing, otherwise she would have come to grief with her complicated daily schedule. She read, as intently as if she had not been flushed with anger, the strange "Musical Memories" of the Reverend H. R. Haweis. At last she blew out the lantern and went to sleep. She had many curious dreams that night. In one of them Mrs. Tellamantez held her shell to Thea's ear, and she heard the roaring, as before, and distant voices calling, "Lily Fisher! Lily Fisher!"

IX.

Mr. Kronborg considered Thea a remarkable child; but so were all his children remarkable. If one of the business men downtown remarked to him that he "had a mighty bright little girl, there," he admitted it, and at once began to explain what a "long head for business" his son Gus had, or that Charley was "a natural electrician," and had put in a telephone from the house to the preacher's study behind the church.

Mrs. Kronborg watched her daughter thoughtfully. She found her more interesting than her other children, and she took her more seriously, without thinking much about why she did so. The other children had to be guided, directed, kept from conflicting with one another. Charley and Gus were likely to want the same thing, and to quarrel about it. Anna often demanded unreasonable service from her older brothers; that they should sit up until after midnight to bring her home from parties when she did not like the youth who had offered himself as her escort; or that they should drive twelve miles into the country, on a winter night, to take her to a ranch dance, after they had been working hard all day. Gunner often got bored with his own clothes or stilts or sled, and wanted Axel's. But Thea, from the time she was a little thing, had her own routine. She kept out of every one's way, and was hard to manage only when the other children interfered with her. Then there was trouble indeed: bursts of temper which used to alarm Mrs. Kronborg. "You ought to know enough to let Thea alone. She lets you alone," she often said to the other children.

One may have staunch friends in one's own family, but one seldom has admirers. Thea, however, had one in the person of her addle-pated aunt, Tillie Kronborg. In older countries, where dress and opinions and manners are not so thoroughly standardized as in our own West, there is a belief that people who are foolish about the more obvious things of life are apt to have peculiar insight into what lies beyond the obvious. The old woman who can never learn not to put the kerosene can on the stove, may yet be able to tell fortunes, to persuade a backward child to grow, to cure warts, or to tell people what to do with a young girl who has gone melancholy. Tillie's mind was a curious machine; when she was awake it went round like a wheel when the belt has slipped off, and when she was asleep she dreamed follies. But she had intuitions. She knew, for instance, that Thea was different from the other Kronborgs, worthy though they all were. Her romantic imagination found possibilities in her niece. When she was sweeping or ironing, or turning the ice-cream freezer at a furious rate, she often built up brilliant futures for Thea, adapting freely the latest novel she had read.

Tillie made enemies for her niece among the church people because, at sewing societies and church suppers, she sometimes spoke vauntingly, with a toss of her head, just as if Thea's "wonderfulness" were an accepted fact in Moonstone, like Mrs. Archie's stinginess, or Mrs. Livery Johnson's duplicity. People declared that, on this subject, Tillie made them tired.

Tillie belonged to a dramatic club that once a year performed in the Moonstone Opera House such plays as "Among the Breakers," and "The Veteran of 1812." Tillie played character parts, the flirtatious old maid or the spiteful INTRIGANTE. She used to study her parts up in the attic at home. While she was committing the lines, she got Gunner or Anna to hold the book for her, but when she began "to bring out the expression," as she said, she used, very timorously, to ask Thea to hold the book. Thea was usually—not always—agreeable about it. Her mother had told her that, since she had some influence with Tillie, it would be a good thing for them all if she could tone her down a shade and "keep her from taking on any worse than need be." Thea would sit on the foot of Tillie's bed, her feet tucked under her, and stare at the silly text. "I wouldn't make so much fuss, there, Tillie," she would remark occasionally; "I don't see the point in it"; or, "What do you pitch your voice so high for? It don't carry half as well."

"I don't see how it comes Thea is so patient with Tillie," Mrs. Kronborg more than once remarked to her husband. "She ain't patient with most people, but it seems like she's got a peculiar patience for Tillie."

Tillie always coaxed Thea to go "behind the scenes" with her when the club presented a play, and help her with her make-up. Thea hated it, but she always went. She felt as if she had to do it. There was something in Tillie's adoration of her that compelled her. There was no family impropriety that Thea was so much ashamed of as Tillie's "acting" and yet she was always being dragged in to assist her. Tillie simply had her, there. She didn't know why, but it was so. There was a string in her somewhere that Tillie could pull; a sense of obligation to Tillie's misguided aspirations. The saloon-keepers had some such feeling of responsibility toward Spanish Johnny.

The dramatic club was the pride of Tillie's heart, and her enthusiasm was the principal factor in keeping it together. Sick or well, Tillie always attended rehearsals, and was always urging the young people, who took rehearsals lightly, to "stop fooling and begin now." The young men—bank clerks, grocery clerks, insurance agents—played tricks, laughed at Tillie, and "put it up on each other" about seeing her home; but they often went to tiresome rehearsals just to oblige her. They were good-natured young fellows. Their trainer and stage-manager was young Upping, the jeweler who ordered Thea's music for her.

Though barely thirty, he had followed half a dozen professions, and had once been a violinist in the orchestra of the Andrews Opera Company, then well known in little towns throughout Colorado and Nebraska.

By one amazing indiscretion Tillie very nearly lost her hold upon the Moonstone Drama Club. The club had decided to put on "The Drummer Boy of Shiloh," a very ambitious undertaking because of the many supers needed and the scenic difficulties of the act which took place in Andersonville Prison. The members of the club consulted together in Tillie's absence as to who should play the part of the drummer boy. It must be taken by a very young person, and village boys of that age are self-conscious and are not apt at memorizing. The part was a long one, and clearly it must be given to a girl. Some members of the club suggested Thea Kronborg, others advocated Lily Fisher. Lily's partisans urged that she was much prettier than Thea, and had a much "sweeter disposition." Nobody denied these facts. But there was nothing in the least boyish about Lily, and she sang all songs and played all parts alike. Lily's simper was popular, but it seemed not quite the right thing for the heroic drummer boy.

Upping, the trainer, talked to one and another: "Lily's all right for girl parts," he insisted, "but you've got to get a girl with some ginger in her for this. Thea's got the voice, too. When she sings, 'Just Before the Battle, Mother,' she'll bring down the house."

When all the members of the club had been privately consulted, they announced their decision to Tillie at the first regular meeting that was called to cast the parts. They expected Tillie to be overcome with joy, but, on the contrary, she seemed embarrassed. "I'm afraid Thea hasn't got time for that," she said jerkily. "She is always so busy with her music. Guess you'll have to get somebody else."

The club lifted its eyebrows. Several of Lily Fisher's friends coughed. Mr. Upping flushed. The stout woman who always played the injured wife called Tillie's attention to the fact that this would be a fine opportunity for her niece to show what she could do. Her tone was condescending.

Tillie threw up her head and laughed; there was something sharp and wild about Tillie's laugh—when it was not a giggle. "Oh, I guess Thea hasn't got time to do any showing off. Her time to show off ain't come yet. I expect she'll make us all sit up when it does. No use asking her to take the part. She'd turn her nose up at it. I guess they'd be glad to get her in the Denver Dramatics, if they could."

The company broke up into groups and expressed their amazement. Of course all Swedes were conceited, but they would never have believed that all the conceit of all the Swedes put together would reach such a pitch as this. They confided to each other that Tillie was "just a little off, on the subject of her niece," and agreed that it would be as well not to excite her further. Tillie got a cold reception at rehearsals for a long while afterward, and Thea had a crop of new enemies without even knowing it.

X.

Wunsch and old Fritz and Spanish Johnny celebrated Christmas together, so riotously that Wunsch was unable to give Thea her lesson the next day. In the middle of the vacation week Thea went to the Kohlers' through a soft, beautiful snowstorm. The air was a tender blue-gray, like the color on the doves that flew in and out of the white dove-house on the post in the Kohlers' garden. The sand hills looked dim and sleepy. The tamarisk hedge was full of snow, like a foam of blossoms drifted over it. When Thea opened the gate, old Mrs. Kohler was just coming in from the chicken yard, with five fresh eggs in her apron and a pair of old top-boots on her feet. She called Thea to come and look at a bantam egg, which she held up proudly. Her bantam hens were remiss in zeal, and she was always delighted when they accomplished anything. She took Thea into the sitting-room, very warm and smelling of food, and brought her a plateful of little Christmas cakes, made according to old and hallowed formulae, and put them before her while she warmed her feet. Then she went to the door of the kitchen stairs and called: "Herr Wunsch, Herr Wunsch!"

Wunsch came down wearing an old wadded jacket, with a velvet collar. The brown silk was so worn that the wadding stuck out almost everywhere. He avoided Thea's eyes when he came in, nodded without speaking, and pointed directly to the piano stool. He was not so insistent upon the scales as usual, and throughout the little sonata of Mozart's she was studying, he remained languid and absent-minded. His eyes looked very heavy, and he kept wiping them with one of the new silk handkerchiefs Mrs. Kohler had given him for Christmas. When the lesson was over he did not seem inclined to talk. Thea, loitering on the stool, reached for a tattered book she had taken off the music-rest when she sat down. It was a very old Leipsic edition of the piano score of Gluck's "Orpheus." She turned over the pages curiously.

"Is it nice?" she asked.

"It is the most beautiful opera ever made," Wunsch declared solemnly. "You know the story, eh? How, when she die, Orpheus went down below for his wife?"

"Oh, yes, I know. I didn't know there was an opera about it, though. Do people sing this now?"

"ABER JA! What else? You like to try? See." He drew her from the stool and sat down at the piano. Turning over the leaves to the third act, he handed the score to Thea. "Listen, I play it through and you get the RHYTHMUS. EINS, ZWEI, DREI, VIER." He played through Orpheus' lament, then pushed back his cuffs with awakening interest and nodded at Thea. "Now, VOM BLATT, MIT MIR."

"ACH, ICH HABE SIE VERLOREN, ALL' MEIN GLUCK IST NUN DAHIN."

Wunsch sang the aria with much feeling. It was evidently one that was very dear to him.

"NOCH EINMAL, alone, yourself." He played the introductory measures, then nodded at her vehemently, and she began:—

"ACH, ICH HABE SIE VERLOREN."

When she finished, Wunsch nodded again. "SCHON," he muttered as he finished the accompaniment softly. He dropped his hands on his knees and looked up at Thea. "That is very fine, eh? There is no such beautiful melody in the world. You can take the book for one week and learn something, to pass the time. It is good to know—always. EURIDICE, EU—RI

—DI—CE, WEH DASS ICH AUF ERDEN BIN!" he sang softly, playing the melody with his right hand.

Thea, who was turning over the pages of the third act, stopped and scowled at a passage. The old German's blurred eyes watched her curiously.

"For what do you look so, IMMER?" puckering up his own face. "You see something a little difficult, may-be, and you make such a face like it was an enemy."

Thea laughed, disconcerted. "Well, difficult things are enemies, aren't they? When you have to get them?"

Wunsch lowered his head and threw it up as if he were butting something. "Not at all! By no means." He took the book from her and looked at it. "Yes, that is not so easy, there. This is an old book. They do not print it so now any more, I think. They leave it out, may-be. Only one woman could sing that good."

Thea looked at him in perplexity.

Wunsch went on. "It is written for alto, you see. A woman sings the part, and there was only one to sing that good in there. You understand? Only one!" He glanced at her quickly and lifted his red forefinger upright before her eyes.

Thea looked at the finger as if she were hypnotized. "Only one?" she asked breathlessly; her hands, hanging at her sides, were opening and shutting rapidly.

Wunsch nodded and still held up that compelling finger. When he dropped his hands, there was a look of satisfaction in his face.

"Was she very great?"

Wunsch nodded.

"Was she beautiful?"

"ABER GAR NICHT! Not at all. She was ugly; big mouth, big teeth, no figure, nothing at all," indicating a luxuriant bosom by sweeping his hands over his chest. "A pole, a post! But for the voice—ACH! She have something in there, behind the eyes," tapping his temples.

Thea followed all his gesticulations intently. "Was she German?"

"No, SPANISCH." He looked down and frowned for a moment. "ACH, I tell you, she look like the Frau Tellamantez, some-thing. Long face, long chin, and ugly al-so."

"Did she die a long while ago?"

"Die? I think not. I never hear, anyhow. I guess she is alive somewhere in the world; Paris, may-be. But old, of course. I hear her when I was a youth. She is too old to sing now any more."

"Was she the greatest singer you ever heard?"

Wunsch nodded gravely. "Quite so. She was the most—" he hunted for an English word, lifted his hand over his head and snapped his fingers noiselessly in the air, enunciating fiercely, "KUNST-LER-ISCH!" The word seemed to glitter in his uplifted hand, his voice was so full of emotion.

Wunsch rose from the stool and began to button his wadded jacket, preparing to return to his half-heated room in the loft. Thea regretfully put on her cloak and hood and set out for home.

When Wunsch looked for his score late that afternoon, he found that Thea had not forgotten to take it with her. He smiled his loose, sarcastic smile, and thoughtfully rubbed his stubbly chin with his red fingers. When Fritz came home in the early blue twilight the snow was flying faster, Mrs. Kohler was cooking HASENPFEFFER in the kitchen, and the professor was seated at the piano, playing the Gluck, which he knew by heart. Old Fritz took off his shoes quietly behind the stove and lay down on the lounge before his masterpiece, where the firelight was playing over the walls of Moscow. He listened, while the room grew darker and the windows duller. Wunsch always came back to the same thing:—

"ACH, ICH HABE SIE VERLOREN,...EURIDICE, EURIDICE!"

From time to time Fritz sighed softly. He, too, had lost a Euridice.

XI.

One Saturday, late in June, Thea arrived early for her lesson. As she perched herself upon the piano stool,—a wobbly, old-fashioned thing that worked on a creaky screw,—she gave Wunsch a side glance, smiling. "You must not be cross to me to-day. This is my birthday."

"So?" he pointed to the keyboard.

After the lesson they went out to join Mrs. Kohler, who had asked Thea to come early, so that she could stay and smell the linden bloom. It was one of those still days of intense light, when every particle of mica in the soil flashed like a little mirror, and the glare from the plain below seemed more intense than the rays from above. The sand ridges ran glittering gold out to where the mirage licked them up, shining and steaming like a lake in the tropics. The sky looked like blue lava, forever incapable of clouds,—a turquoise bowl that was the lid of the desert. And yet within Mrs. Kohler's green patch the water dripped, the beds had all been hosed, and the air was fresh with rapidly evaporating moisture.

The two symmetrical linden trees were the proudest things in the garden. Their sweetness embalmed all the air. At every turn of the paths,—whether one went to see the hollyhocks or the bleeding heart, or to look at the purple morning-glories that ran over the bean-poles,—wherever one went, the sweetness of the lindens struck one afresh and one always came back to them. Under the round leaves, where the waxen yellow blossoms hung, bevies of wild bees were buzzing. The tamarisks were still pink, and the flower-beds were doing their best in honor of the linden festival. The white dove-house was shining with a fresh coat of paint, and the pigeons were crooning contentedly, flying down often to drink at the drip from the water tank. Mrs. Kohler, who was transplanting pansies, came up with her trowel and told Thea it was lucky to have your birthday when the lindens were in bloom, and that she must go and look at the sweet peas. Wunsch accompanied her, and as they walked between the flower-beds he took Thea's hand.

"ES FLUSTERN UND SPRECHEN DIE BLUMEN,"—he muttered. "You know that von Heine? IM LEUCHTENDEN SOMMERMORGEN?" He looked down at Thea and softly pressed her hand.

"No, I don't know it. What does FLUSTERN mean?"

"FLUSTERN?—to whisper. You must begin now to know such things. That is necessary. How many birthdays?"

"Thirteen. I'm in my 'teens now. But how can I know words like that? I only know what you say at my lessons. They don't teach German at school. How can I learn?"

"It is always possible to learn when one likes," said Wunsch. His words were peremptory, as usual, but his tone was mild, even confidential. "There is always a way. And if some day you are going to sing, it is necessary to know well the German language."

Thea stooped over to pick a leaf of rosemary. How did Wunsch know that, when the very roses on her wall-paper had never heard it? "But am I going to?" she asked, still stooping.

"That is for you to say," returned Wunsch coldly. "You would better marry some JACOB here and keep the house for him, may-be? That is as one desires."

Thea flashed up at him a clear, laughing look. "No, I don't want to do that. You know," she brushed his coat sleeve quickly with her yellow head. "Only how can I learn anything here? It's so far from Denver."

Wunsch's loose lower lip curled in amusement. Then, as if he suddenly remembered something, he spoke seriously. "Nothing is far and nothing is near, if one desires. The world is little, people are little, human life is little. There is only one big thing—desire. And before it, when it is big, all is little. It brought Columbus across the sea in a little boat, UND SO WEITER." Wunsch made a grimace, took his pupil's hand and drew her toward the grape arbor. "Hereafter I will more speak to you in German. Now, sit down and I will teach you for your birthday that little song. Ask me the words you do not know already. Now: IM LEUCHTENDEN SOMMERMORGEN."

Thea memorized quickly because she had the power of listening intently. In a few moments she could repeat the eight lines for him. Wunsch nodded encouragingly and they went out of the arbor into the sunlight again. As they went up and down the gravel paths between the flowerbeds, the white and yellow butterflies kept darting before them, and the pigeons were washing their pink feet at the drip and crooning in their husky bass. Over and over again Wunsch made her say the lines to him. "You see it is nothing. If you learn a great many of the LIEDER, you will know the German language already. WEITER, NUN." He would incline his head gravely and listen.

"IM LEUCHTENDEN SOMMERMORGEN
GEH' ICH IM GARTEN HERUM;
ES FLUSTERN UND SPRECHEN DIE BLUMEN,
ICH ABER, ICH WANDTE STUMM.

"ES FLUSTERN UND SPRECHEN DIE BLUMEN
UND SCHAU'N MITLEIDIG MICH AN:
'SEI UNSERER SCHWESTER NICHT BOSE,
DU TRAURIGER, BLASSER MANN!'"

(In the soft-shining summer morning
I wandered the garden within.
The flowers they whispered and murmured,
But I, I wandered dumb.

The flowers they whisper and murmur,
And me with compassion they scan:
"Oh, be not harsh to our sister,
Thou sorrowful, death-pale man!")

Wunsch had noticed before that when his pupil read anything in verse the character of her voice changed altogether; it was no longer the voice which spoke the speech of Moonstone. It was a soft, rich contralto, and she read quietly; the feeling was in the voice itself, not indicated by emphasis or change of pitch. She repeated the little verses musically, like a song, and the entreaty of the flowers was even softer than the rest, as the shy speech of flowers might be, and she ended with the voice suspended, almost with a rising inflection. It was a nature-voice, Wunsch told himself, breathed from the creature and apart from language, like the sound of the wind in the trees, or the murmur of water.

"What is it the flowers mean when they ask him not to be harsh to their sister, eh?" he asked, looking down at her curiously and wrinkling his dull red forehead.

Thea glanced at him in surprise. "I suppose he thinks they are asking him not to be harsh to his sweetheart—or some girl they remind him of."

"And why TRAURIGER, BLASSER MANN?"

They had come back to the grape arbor, and Thea picked out a sunny place on the bench, where a tortoise-shell cat was stretched at full length. She sat down, bending over the cat and teasing his whiskers. "Because he had been awake all night, thinking about her, wasn't it? Maybe that was why he was up so early."

Wunsch shrugged his shoulders. "If he think about her all night already, why do you say the flowers remind him?"

Thea looked up at him in perplexity. A flash of comprehension lit her face and she smiled eagerly. "Oh, I didn't mean 'remind' in that way! I didn't mean they brought her to his mind! I meant it was only when he came out in the morning, that she seemed to him like that,—like one of the flowers."

"And before he came out, how did she seem?"

This time it was Thea who shrugged her shoulders. The warm smile left her face. She lifted her eyebrows in annoyance and looked off at the sand hills.

Wunsch persisted. "Why you not answer me?"

"Because it would be silly. You are just trying to make me say things. It spoils things to ask questions."

Wunsch bowed mockingly; his smile was disagreeable. Suddenly his face grew grave, grew fierce, indeed. He pulled himself up from his clumsy stoop and folded his arms. "But it is necessary to know if you know some things. Some things cannot be taught. If you not know in the beginning, you not know in the end. For a singer there must be something in the inside from the beginning. I shall not be long in this place, may-be, and I like to know. Yes,"—he ground his heel in the gravel,—"yes, when you are barely six, you must know that already. That is the beginning of all things; DER GEIST, DIE PHANTASIE. It must be in the baby, when it makes its first cry, like DER RHYTHMUS, or it is not to be. You have some voice already, and if in the beginning, when you are with things-to-play, you know that what you will not tell me, then you can learn to sing, may-be."

Wunsch began to pace the arbor, rubbing his hands together. The dark flush of his face had spread up under the iron-gray bristles on his head. He was talking to himself, not to Thea. Insidious power of the linden bloom! "Oh, much you can learn! ABER NICHT DIE AMERICANISCHEN FRAULEIN. They have nothing inside them," striking his chest with both fists. "They are like the ones in the MARCHEN, a grinning face and hollow in the insides. Something they can learn, oh, yes, may-be! But the secret—what make the rose to red, the sky to blue, the man to love—IN DER BRUST, IN DER BRUST it is, UND OHNE DIESES GIEBT ES KEINE KUNST, GIEBT ES KEINE KUNST!" He threw up his square hand and shook it, all the fingers apart and wagging. Purple and breathless he went out of the arbor and into the house, without saying good-bye. These outbursts frightened Wunsch. They were always harbingers of ill.

Thea got her music-book and stole quietly out of the garden. She did not go home, but wandered off into the sand dunes, where the prickly pear was in blossom and the green lizards were racing each other in the glittering light. She was shaken by a passionate excitement. She did not altogether understand what Wunsch was talking about; and yet, in a way she knew. She knew, of course, that there was something about her that was different.

But it was more like a friendly spirit than like anything that was a part of herself. She thought everything to it, and it answered her; happiness consisted of that backward and forward movement of herself. The something came and went, she never knew how. Sometimes she hunted for it and could not find it; again, she lifted her eyes from a book, or stepped out of doors, or wakened in the morning, and it was there,—under her cheek, it usually seemed to be, or over her breast,—a kind of warm sureness. And when it was there, everything was more interesting and beautiful, even people. When this companion was with her, she could get the most wonderful things out of Spanish Johnny, or Wunsch, or Dr. Archie.

On her thirteenth birthday she wandered for a long while about the sand ridges, picking up crystals and looking into the yellow prickly-pear blossoms with their thousand stamens. She looked at the sand hills until she wished she WERE a sand hill. And yet she knew that she was going to leave them all behind some day. They would be changing all day long, yellow and purple and lavender, and she would not be there. From that day on, she felt there was a secret between her and Wunsch. Together they had lifted a lid, pulled out a drawer, and looked at something. They hid it away and never spoke of what they had seen; but neither of them forgot it.

XII.

One July night, when the moon was full, Dr. Archie was coming up from the depot, restless and discontented, wishing there were something to do. He carried his straw hat in his hand, and kept brushing his hair back from his forehead with a purposeless, unsatisfied gesture. After he passed Uncle Billy Beemer's cottonwood grove, the sidewalk ran out of the shadow into the white moonlight and crossed the sand gully on high posts, like a bridge. As the doctor approached this trestle, he saw a white figure, and recognized Thea Kronborg. He quickened his pace and she came to meet him.

"What are you doing out so late, my girl?" he asked as he took her hand.

"Oh, I don't know. What do people go to bed so early for? I'd like to run along before the houses and screech at them. Isn't it glorious out here?"

The young doctor gave a melancholy laugh and pressed her hand.

"Think of it," Thea snorted impatiently. "Nobody up but us and the rabbits! I've started up half a dozen of 'em. Look at that little one down there now,"—she stooped and pointed. In the gully below them there was, indeed, a little rabbit with a white spot of a tail, crouching down on the sand, quite motionless. It seemed to be lapping up the moonlight like cream. On the other side of the walk, down in the ditch, there was a patch of tall, rank sunflowers, their shaggy leaves white with dust. The moon stood over the cottonwood grove. There was no wind, and no sound but the wheezing of an engine down on the tracks.

"Well, we may as well watch the rabbits." Dr. Archie sat down on the sidewalk and let his feet hang over the edge. He pulled out a smooth linen handkerchief that smelled of German cologne water. "Well, how goes it? Working hard? You must know about all Wunsch can teach you by this time."

Thea shook her head. "Oh, no, I don't, Dr. Archie. He's hard to get at, but he's been a real musician in his time. Mother says she believes he's forgotten more than the music-teachers down in Denver ever knew."

"I'm afraid he won't be around here much longer," said Dr. Archie. "He's been making a tank of himself lately. He'll be pulling his freight one of these days. That's the way they do, you know. I'll be sorry on your account." He paused and ran his fresh handkerchief over his face. "What the deuce are we all here for anyway, Thea?" he said abruptly.

"On earth, you mean?" Thea asked in a low voice.

"Well, primarily, yes. But secondarily, why are we in Moonstone? It isn't as if we'd been born here. You were, but Wunsch wasn't, and I wasn't. I suppose I'm here because I married as soon as I got out of medical school and had to get a practice quick. If you hurry things, you always get left in the end. I don't learn anything here, and as for the people—In my own town in Michigan, now, there were people who liked me on my father's account, who had even known my grandfather. That meant something. But here it's all like the sand: blows north one day and south the next. We're all a lot of gamblers without much nerve, playing for small stakes. The railroad is the one real fact in this country. That has to be; the world has to be got back and forth. But the rest of us are here just because it's the end of a run and the engine has to have a drink. Some day I'll get up and find my hair turning gray, and I'll have nothing to show for it."

Thea slid closer to him and caught his arm. "No, no. I won't let you get gray. You've got to stay young for me. I'm getting young now, too."

Archie laughed. "Getting?"

"Yes. People aren't young when they're children. Look at Thor, now; he's just a little old man. But Gus has a sweetheart, and he's young!"

"Something in that!" Dr. Archie patted her head, and then felt the shape of her skull gently, with the tips of his fingers. "When you were little, Thea, I used always to be curious about the shape of your head. You seemed to have more inside it than most youngsters. I haven't examined it for a long time. Seems to be the usual shape, but uncommonly hard, some how. What are you going to do with yourself, anyway?"

"I don't know."

"Honest, now?" He lifted her chin and looked into her eyes.

Thea laughed and edged away from him.

"You've got something up your sleeve, haven't you? Anything you like; only don't marry and settle down here without giving yourself a chance, will you?"

"Not much. See, there's another rabbit!"

"That's all right about the rabbits, but I don't want you to get tied up. Remember that."

Thea nodded. "Be nice to Wunsch, then. I don't know what I'd do if he went away."

"You've got older friends than Wunsch here, Thea."

"I know." Thea spoke seriously and looked up at the moon, propping her chin on her hand. "But Wunsch is the only one that can teach me what I want to know. I've got to learn to do something well, and that's the thing I can do best."

"Do you want to be a music-teacher?"

"Maybe, but I want to be a good one. I'd like to go to Germany to study, some day. Wunsch says that's the best place,—the only place you can really learn." Thea hesitated and then went on nervously, "I've got a book that says so, too. It's called 'My Musical Memories.' It made me want to go to Germany even before Wunsch said anything. Of course it's a secret. You're the first one I've told."

Dr. Archie smiled indulgently. "That's a long way off. Is that what you've got in your hard noddle?" He put his hand on her hair, but this time she shook him off.

"No, I don't think much about it. But you talk about going, and a body has to have something to go TO!"

"That's so." Dr. Archie sighed. "You're lucky if you have. Poor Wunsch, now, he hasn't. What do such fellows come out here for? He's been asking me about my mining stock, and about mining towns. What would he do in a mining town? He wouldn't know a piece of ore if he saw one. He's got nothing to sell that a mining town wants to buy. Why don't those old fellows stay at home? We won't need them for another hundred years. An engine wiper can get a job, but a piano player! Such people can't make good."

"My grandfather Alstrom was a musician, and he made good."

Dr. Archie chuckled. "Oh, a Swede can make good anywhere, at anything! You've got that in your favor, miss. Come, you must be getting home."

Thea rose. "Yes, I used to be ashamed of being a Swede, but I'm not any more. Swedes are kind of common, but I think it's better to be SOMETHING."

"It surely is! How tall you are getting. You come above my shoulder now."

"I'll keep on growing, don't you think? I particularly want to be tall. Yes, I guess I must go home. I wish there'd be a fire."

"A fire?"

"Yes, so the fire-bell would ring and the roundhouse whistle would blow, and everybody would come running out. Sometime I'm going to ring the fire-bell myself and stir them all up."

"You'd be arrested."

"Well, that would be better than going to bed."

"I'll have to lend you some more books."

Thea shook herself impatiently. "I can't read every night."

Dr. Archie gave one of his low, sympathetic chuckles as he opened the gate for her. "You're beginning to grow up, that's what's the matter with you. I'll have to keep an eye on you. Now you'll have to say good-night to the moon."

"No, I won't. I sleep on the floor now, right in the moonlight. My window comes down to the floor, and I can look at the sky all night."

She shot round the house to the kitchen door, and Dr. Archie watched her disappear with a sigh. He thought of the hard, mean, frizzy little woman who kept his house for him; once the belle of a Michigan town, now dry and withered up at thirty. "If I had a daughter like Thea to watch," he reflected, "I wouldn't mind anything. I wonder if all of my life's going to be a mistake just because I made a big one then? Hardly seems fair."

Howard Archie was "respected" rather than popular in Moonstone. Everyone recognized that he was a good physician, and a progressive Western town likes to be able to point to a handsome, well-set-up, well-dressed man among its citizens. But a great many people thought Archie "distant," and they were right. He had the uneasy manner of a man who is not among his own kind, and who has not seen enough of the world to feel that all people are in some sense his own kind. He knew that every one was curious about his wife, that she played a sort of character part in Moonstone, and that people made fun of her, not very delicately. Her own friends—most of them women who were distasteful to Archie—liked to ask her to contribute to church charities, just to see how mean she could be. The little, lop-sided cake at the church supper, the cheapest pincushion, the skimpiest apron at the bazaar, were always Mrs. Archie's contribution.

All this hurt the doctor's pride. But if there was one thing he had learned, it was that there was no changing Belle's nature. He had married a mean woman; and he must accept the consequences. Even in Colorado he would have had no pretext for divorce, and, to do him justice, he had never thought of such a thing. The tenets of the Presbyterian Church in which he had grown up, though he had long ceased to believe in them, still influenced his conduct and his conception of propriety. To him there was something vulgar about divorce. A divorced man was a disgraced man; at least, he had exhibited his hurt, and made it a matter for common gossip. Respectability was so necessary to Archie that he was willing to pay a high price for it. As long as he could keep up a decent exterior, he could manage to get on; and if he could have concealed his wife's littleness from all his friends, he would scarcely have complained. He was more afraid of pity than he was of any unhappiness. Had there been another woman for whom he cared greatly, he might have had plenty of courage; but he was not likely to meet such a woman in Moonstone.

There was a puzzling timidity in Archie's make-up. The thing that held his shoulders stiff, that made him resort to a mirthless little laugh when he was talking to dull people, that made him sometimes stumble over rugs and carpets, had its counterpart in his mind. He had not the courage to be an honest thinker. He could comfort himself by evasions and compromises. He consoled himself for his own marriage by telling himself that other people's were not much better. In his work he saw pretty deeply into marital relations in Moonstone, and he could honestly say that there were not many of his friends whom he envied. Their wives seemed to suit them well enough, but they would never have suited him.

Although Dr. Archie could not bring himself to regard marriage merely as a social contract, but looked upon it as somehow made sacred by a church in which he did not believe,—as a physician he knew that a young man whose marriage is merely nominal must yet go on living his life. When he went to Denver or to Chicago, he drifted about in careless company where gayety and good-humor can be bought, not because he had any taste for such society, but because he honestly believed that anything was better than divorce. He often told himself that "hanging and wiving go by destiny." If wiving went badly with a man,—and it did oftener than not,—then he must do the best he could to keep up appearances and help the tradition of domestic happiness along. The Moonstone gossips, assembled in Mrs. Smiley's millinery and notion store, often discussed Dr. Archie's politeness to his wife, and his pleasant manner of speaking about her. "Nobody has ever got a thing out of him yet," they agreed. And it was certainly not because no one had ever tried.

When he was down in Denver, feeling a little jolly, Archie could forget how unhappy he was at home, and could even make himself believe that he missed his wife. He always bought her presents, and would have liked to send her flowers if she had not repeatedly told him never to send her anything but bulbs,—which did not appeal to him in his expansive moments. At the Denver Athletic Club banquets, or at dinner with his colleagues at the Brown Palace Hotel, he sometimes spoke sentimentally about "little Mrs. Archie," and he always drank the toast "to our wives, God bless them!" with gusto.

The determining factor about Dr. Archie was that he was romantic. He had married Belle White because he was romantic—too romantic to know anything about women, except what he wished them to be, or to repulse a pretty girl who had set her cap for him. At medical school, though he was a rather wild boy in behavior, he had always disliked coarse jokes and vulgar stories. In his old Flint's Physiology there was still a poem he had pasted there when he was a student; some verses by Dr. Oliver Wendell Holmes about the ideals of the medical profession. After so much and such disillusioning experience with it, he still had a romantic feeling about the human body; a sense that finer things dwelt in it than could be explained by anatomy. He never jested about birth or death or marriage, and did not like to hear other doctors do it. He was a good nurse, and had a reverence for the bodies of women and children. When he was tending them, one saw him at his best. Then his constraint and self-consciousness fell away from him. He was easy, gentle, competent, master of himself and of other people. Then the idealist in him was not afraid of being discovered and ridiculed.

In his tastes, too, the doctor was romantic. Though he read Balzac all the year through, he still enjoyed the Waverley Novels as much as when he had first come upon them, in thick leather-bound volumes, in his grandfather's library. He nearly always read Scott on Christmas and holidays, because it brought back the pleasures of his boyhood so vividly. He liked Scott's women. Constance de Beverley and the minstrel girl in "The Fair Maid of Perth," not the Duchesse de Langeais, were his heroines. But better than anything that ever got from the heart of a man into printer's ink, he loved the poetry of Robert Burns. "Death and Dr. Hornbook" and "The Jolly Beggars," Burns's "Reply to his Tailor," he often read aloud to himself in his office, late at night, after a glass of hot toddy. He used to read "Tam o'Shanter" to Thea Kronborg, and he got her some of the songs, set to the old airs for which they were written. He loved to hear her sing them. Sometimes when she sang, "Oh, wert thou in the cauld blast," the doctor and even Mr. Kronborg joined in. Thea never minded if people could not sing; she directed them with her head and somehow carried them along. When her father got off the pitch she let her own voice out and covered him.

XIII.

At the beginning of June, when school closed, Thea had told Wunsch that she didn't know how much practicing she could get in this summer because Thor had his worst teeth still to cut.

"My God! all last summer he was doing that!" Wunsch exclaimed furiously.

"I know, but it takes them two years, and Thor is slow," Thea answered reprovingly.

The summer went well beyond her hopes, however. She told herself that it was the best summer of her life, so far. Nobody was sick at home, and her lessons were uninterrupted. Now that she had four pupils of her own and made a dollar a week, her practicing was regarded more seriously by the household. Her mother had always arranged things so that she could have the parlor four hours a day in summer. Thor proved a friendly ally. He behaved handsomely about his molars, and never objected to being pulled off into remote places in his cart. When Thea dragged him over the hill and made a camp under the shade of a bush or a bank, he would waddle about and play with his blocks, or bury his monkey in the sand and dig him up again. Sometimes he got into the cactus and set up a howl, but usually he let his sister read peacefully, while he coated his hands and face, first with an all-day sucker and then with gravel.

Life was pleasant and uneventful until the first of September, when Wunsch began to drink so hard that he was unable to appear when Thea went to take her mid-week lesson, and Mrs. Kohler had to send her home after a tearful apology. On Saturday morning she set out for the Kohlers' again, but on her way, when she was crossing the ravine, she noticed a woman sitting at the bottom of the gulch, under the railroad trestle. She turned from her path and saw that it was Mrs. Tellamantez, and she seemed to be doing drawn-work. Then Thea noticed that there was something beside her, covered up with a purple and yellow Mexican blanket. She ran up the gulch and called to Mrs. Tellamantez. The Mexican woman held up a warning finger. Thea glanced at the blanket and recognized a square red hand which protruded. The middle finger twitched slightly.

"Is he hurt?" she gasped.

Mrs. Tellamantez shook her head. "No; very sick. He knows nothing," she said quietly, folding her hands over her drawn-work.

Thea learned that Wunsch had been out all night, that this morning Mrs. Kohler had gone to look for him and found him under the trestle covered with dirt and cinders. Probably he had been trying to get home and had lost his way. Mrs. Tellamantez was watching beside the unconscious man while Mrs. Kohler and Johnny went to get help.

"You better go home now, I think," said Mrs. Tellamantez, in closing her narration.

Thea hung her head and looked wistfully toward the blanket.

"Couldn't I just stay till they come?" she asked. "I'd like to know if he's very bad."

"Bad enough," sighed Mrs. Tellamantez, taking up her work again.

Thea sat down under the narrow shade of one of the trestle posts and listened to the locusts rasping in the hot sand while she watched Mrs. Tellamantez evenly draw her threads. The blanket looked as if it were over a heap of bricks.

"I don't see him breathing any," she said anxiously.

"Yes, he breathes," said Mrs. Tellamantez, not lifting her eyes.

It seemed to Thea that they waited for hours. At last they heard voices, and a party of men came down the hill and up the gulch. Dr. Archie and Fritz Kohler came first; behind were Johnny and Ray, and several men from the roundhouse. Ray had the canvas litter that was kept at the depot for accidents on the road. Behind them trailed half a dozen boys who had been hanging round the depot.

When Ray saw Thea, he dropped his canvas roll and hurried forward. "Better run along home, Thee. This is ugly business." Ray was indignant that anybody who gave Thea music lessons should behave in such a manner.

Thea resented both his proprietary tone and his superior virtue. "I won't. I want to know how bad he is. I'm not a baby!" she exclaimed indignantly, stamping her foot into the sand.

Dr. Archie, who had been kneeling by the blanket, got up and came toward Thea, dusting his knees. He smiled and nodded confidentially. "He'll be all right when we get him home. But he wouldn't want you to see him like this, poor old chap! Understand? Now, skip!"

Thea ran down the gulch and looked back only once, to see them lifting the canvas litter with Wunsch upon it, still covered with the blanket.

The men carried Wunsch up the hill and down the road to the Kohlers'. Mrs. Kohler had gone home and made up a bed in the sitting-room, as she knew the litter could not be got round the turn in the narrow stairway. Wunsch was like a dead man. He lay unconscious all day. Ray Kennedy stayed with him till two o'clock in the afternoon, when he had to go out on his run. It was the first time he had ever been inside the Kohlers' house, and he was so much impressed by Napoleon that the piece-picture formed a new bond between him and Thea.

Dr. Archie went back at six o'clock, and found Mrs. Kohler and Spanish Johnny with Wunsch, who was in a high fever, muttering and groaning.

"There ought to be some one here to look after him to-night, Mrs. Kohler," he said. "I'm on a confinement case, and I can't be here, but there ought to be somebody. He may get violent."

Mrs. Kohler insisted that she could always do anything with Wunsch, but the doctor shook his head and Spanish Johnny grinned. He said he would stay. The doctor laughed at him. "Ten fellows like you couldn't hold him, Spanish, if he got obstreperous; an Irishman would have his hands full. Guess I'd better put the soft pedal on him." He pulled out his hypodermic.

Spanish Johnny stayed, however, and the Kohlers went to bed. At about two o'clock in the morning Wunsch rose from his ignominious cot. Johnny, who was dozing on the lounge, awoke to find the German standing in the middle of the room in his undershirt and drawers, his arms bare, his heavy body seeming twice its natural girth. His face was snarling and savage, and his eyes were crazy. He had risen to avenge himself, to wipe out his shame, to destroy his enemy. One look was enough for Johnny. Wunsch raised a chair threateningly, and Johnny, with the lightness of a PICADOR, darted under the missile and out of the open window. He shot across the gully to get help, meanwhile leaving the Kohlers to their fate.

Fritz, upstairs, heard the chair crash upon the stove. Then he heard doors opening and shutting, and some one stumbling about in the shrubbery of the garden. He and Paulina sat up in bed and held a consultation. Fritz slipped from under the covers, and going cautiously over to the window, poked out his head. Then he rushed to the door and bolted it.

"MEIN GOTT, Paulina," he gasped, "he has the axe, he will kill us!"

"The dresser," cried Mrs. Kohler; "push the dresser before the door. ACH, if you had your rabbit gun, now!"

"It is in the barn," said Fritz sadly. "It would do no good; he would not be afraid of anything now. Stay you in the bed, Paulina." The dresser had lost its casters years ago, but he managed to drag it in front of the door. "He is in the garden. He makes nothing. He will get sick again, may-be."

Fritz went back to bed and his wife pulled the quilt over him and made him lie down. They heard stumbling in the garden again, then a smash of glass.

"ACH, DAS MISTBEET!" gasped Paulina, hearing her hotbed shivered. "The poor soul, Fritz, he will cut himself. ACH! what is that?" They both sat up in bed. "WIEDER! ACH, What is he doing?"

The noise came steadily, a sound of chopping. Paulina tore off her night-cap. "DIE BAUME, DIE BAUME! He is cutting our trees, Fritz!" Before her husband could prevent her, she had sprung from the bed and rushed to the window. "DER TAUBENSCHLAG! GERECHTER HIMMEL, he is chopping the dove-house down!"

Fritz reached her side before she had got her breath again, and poked his head out beside hers. There, in the faint starlight, they saw a bulky man, barefoot, half dressed, chopping away at the white post that formed the pedestal of the dove-house. The startled pigeons were croaking and flying about his head, even beating their wings in his face, so that he struck at them furiously with the axe. In a few seconds there was a crash, and Wunsch had actually felled the dove-house.

"Oh, if only it is not the trees next!" prayed Paulina. "The dove-house you can make new again, but not DIE BAUME."

They watched breathlessly. In the garden below Wunsch stood in the attitude of a woodman, contemplating the fallen cote. Suddenly he threw the axe over his shoulder and went out of the front gate toward the town.

"The poor soul, he will meet his death!" Mrs. Kohler wailed. She ran back to her feather bed and hid her face in the pillow.

Fritz kept watch at the window. "No, no, Paulina," he called presently; "I see lanterns coming. Johnny must have gone for somebody. Yes, four lanterns, coming along the gulch. They stop; they must have seen him already. Now they are under the hill and I cannot see them, but I think they have him. They will bring him back. I must dress and go down." He caught his trousers and began pulling them on by the window. "Yes, here they come, half a dozen men. And they have tied him with a rope, Paulina!"

"ACH, the poor man! To be led like a cow," groaned Mrs. Kohler. "Oh, it is good that he has no wife!" She was reproaching herself for nagging Fritz when he drank himself into foolish pleasantry or mild sulks, and felt that she had never before appreciated her blessings.

Wunsch was in bed for ten days, during which time he was gossiped about and even preached about in Moonstone. The Baptist preacher took a shot at the fallen man from his pulpit, Mrs. Livery Johnson nodding approvingly from her pew. The mothers of Wunsch's pupils sent him notes informing him that their daughters would discontinue their music-lessons. The old maid who had rented him her piano sent the town dray for her contaminated instrument, and ever afterward declared that Wunsch had ruined its tone and scarred its glossy finish. The Kohlers were unremitting in their kindness to their friend. Mrs.

Kohler made him soups and broths without stint, and Fritz repaired the dove-house and mounted it on a new post, lest it might be a sad reminder.

As soon as Wunsch was strong enough to sit about in his slippers and wadded jacket, he told Fritz to bring him some stout thread from the shop. When Fritz asked what he was going to sew, he produced the tattered score of "Orpheus" and said he would like to fix it up for a little present. Fritz carried it over to the shop and stitched it into pasteboards, covered with dark suiting-cloth. Over the stitches he glued a strip of thin red leather which he got from his friend, the harness-maker. After Paulina had cleaned the pages with fresh bread, Wunsch was amazed to see what a fine book he had. It opened stiffly, but that was no matter.

Sitting in the arbor one morning, under the ripe grapes and the brown, curling leaves, with a pen and ink on the bench beside him and the Gluck score on his knee, Wunsch pondered for a long while. Several times he dipped the pen in the ink, and then put it back again in the cigar box in which Mrs. Kohler kept her writing utensils. His thoughts wandered over a wide territory; over many countries and many years. There was no order or logical sequence in his ideas. Pictures came and went without reason. Faces, mountains, rivers, autumn days in other vineyards far away. He thought of a FUSZREISE he had made through the Hartz Mountains in his student days; of the innkeeper's pretty daughter who had lighted his pipe for him in the garden one summer evening, of the woods above Wiesbaden, haymakers on an island in the river. The roundhouse whistle woke him from his reveries. Ah, yes, he was in Moonstone, Colorado. He frowned for a moment and looked at the book on his knee. He had thought of a great many appropriate things to write in it, but suddenly he rejected all of them, opened the book, and at the top of the much-engraved title page he wrote rapidly in purple ink:—

EINST, O WUNDER!—
A. WUNSCH.
MOONSTONE, COLO.
SEPTEMBER 30, 18—

Nobody in Moonstone ever found what Wunsch's first name was. That "A" may have stood for Adam, or August, or even Amadeus; he got very angry if any one asked him.

He remained A. Wunsch to the end of his chapter there. When he presented this score to Thea, he told her that in ten years she would either know what the inscription meant, or she would not have the least idea, in which case it would not matter.

When Wunsch began to pack his trunk, both the Kohlers were very unhappy. He said he was coming back some day, but that for the present, since he had lost all his pupils, it would be better for him to try some "new town." Mrs. Kohler darned and mended all his clothes, and gave him two new shirts she had made for Fritz. Fritz made him a new pair of trousers and would have made him an overcoat but for the fact that overcoats were so easy to pawn.

Wunsch would not go across the ravine to the town until he went to take the morning train for Denver. He said that after he got to Denver he would "look around." He left Moonstone one bright October morning, without telling any one good-bye. He bought his ticket and went directly into the smoking-car. When the train was beginning to pull out, he heard his name called frantically, and looking out of the window he saw Thea Kronborg standing on the siding, bareheaded and panting. Some boys had brought word to school that they saw Wunsch's trunk going over to the station, and Thea had run away from school. She was at the end of the station platform, her hair in two braids, her blue gingham dress wet to the knees because she had run across lots through the weeds. It had rained during the night, and the tall sunflowers behind her were fresh and shining.

"Good-bye, Herr Wunsch, good-bye!" she called waving to him.

He thrust his head out at the car window and called back, "LEBEN SIE WOHL, LEBEN SIE WOHL, MEIN KIND!" He watched her until the train swept around the curve beyond the roundhouse, and then sank back into his seat, muttering, "She had been running. Ah, she will run a long way; they cannot stop her!"

What was it about the child that one believed in? Was it her dogged industry, so unusual in this free-and-easy country? Was it her imagination? More likely it was because she had both imagination and a stubborn will, curiously balancing and interpenetrating each other. There was something unconscious and unawakened about her, that tempted curiosity. She had a kind of seriousness that he had not met with in a pupil before. She hated difficult things, and yet she could never pass one by. They seemed to challenge her; she had no peace until she mastered them. She had the power to make a great effort, to lift a weight heavier than herself. Wunsch hoped he would always remember her as she stood by the track, looking up at him; her broad eager face, so fair in color, with its high cheek-bones, yellow eyebrows and greenishhazel eyes. It was a face full of light and energy, of the unquestioning hopefulness of first youth. Yes, she was like a flower full of sun, but not the soft German flowers of his childhood. He had it now, the comparison he had absently reached for before: she was like the yellow prickly pear blossoms that open there in the desert; thornier and sturdier than the maiden flowers he remembered; not so sweet, but wonderful.

That night Mrs. Kohler brushed away many a tear as she got supper and set the table for two. When they sat down, Fritz was more silent than usual. People who have lived long together need a third at table: they know each other's thoughts so well that they have nothing left to say. Mrs. Kohler stirred and stirred her coffee and clattered the spoon, but she had no heart for her supper. She felt, for the first time in years, that she was tired of her own cooking. She looked across the glass lamp at her husband and asked him if the butcher liked his new overcoat, and whether he had got the shoulders right in a ready-made suit he was patching over for Ray Kennedy. After supper Fritz offered to wipe the dishes for her, but she told him to go about his business, and not to act as if she were sick or getting helpless.

When her work in the kitchen was all done, she went out to cover the oleanders against frost, and to take a last look at her chickens. As she came back from the hen-house she stopped by one of the linden trees and stood resting her hand on the trunk. He would never come back, the poor man; she knew that. He would drift on from new town to new town, from catastrophe to catastrophe. He would hardly find a good home for himself again. He would die at last in some rough place, and be buried in the desert or on the wild prairie, far enough from any linden tree!

Fritz, smoking his pipe on the kitchen doorstep, watched his Paulina and guessed her thoughts. He, too, was sorry to lose his friend. But Fritz was getting old; he had lived a long while and had learned to lose without struggle.

XIV.

"Mother," said Peter Kronborg to his wife one morning about two weeks after Wunsch's departure, "how would you like to drive out to Copper Hole with me to-day?"

Mrs. Kronborg said she thought she would enjoy the drive. She put on her gray cashmere dress and gold watch and chain, as befitted a minister's wife, and while her husband was dressing she packed a black oilcloth satchel with such clothing as she and Thor would need overnight.

Copper Hole was a settlement fifteen miles northwest of Moonstone where Mr. Kronborg preached every Friday evening. There was a big spring there and a creek and a few irrigating ditches. It was a community of discouraged agriculturists who had disastrously experimented with dry farming. Mr. Kronborg always drove out one day and back the next, spending the night with one of his parishioners. Often, when the weather was fine, his wife accompanied him. To-day they set out from home after the midday meal, leaving Tillie in charge of the house. Mrs. Kronborg's maternal feeling was always garnered up in the baby, whoever the baby happened to be. If she had the baby with her, the others could look out for themselves. Thor, of course, was not, accurately speaking, a baby any longer. In the matter of nourishment he was quite independent of his mother, though this independence had not been won without a struggle. Thor was conservative in all things, and the whole family had anguished with him when he was being weaned. Being the youngest, he was still the baby for Mrs. Kronborg, though he was nearly four years old and sat up boldly on her lap this afternoon, holding on to the ends of the lines and shouting "'mup, 'mup, horsey." His father watched him affectionately and hummed hymn tunes in the jovial way that was sometimes such a trial to Thea.

Mrs. Kronborg was enjoying the sunshine and the brilliant sky and all the faintly marked features of the dazzling, monotonous landscape. She had a rather unusual capacity for getting the flavor of places and of people. Although she was so enmeshed in family cares most of the time, she could emerge serene when she was away from them. For a mother of seven, she had a singularly unprejudiced point of view. She was, moreover, a fatalist, and as she did not attempt to direct things beyond her control, she found a good deal of time to enjoy the ways of man and nature.

When they were well upon their road, out where the first lean pasture lands began and the sand grass made a faint showing between the sagebrushes, Mr. Kronborg dropped his tune and turned to his wife. "Mother, I've been thinking about something."

"I guessed you had. What is it?" She shifted Thor to her left knee, where he would be more out of the way.

"Well, it's about Thea. Mr. Follansbee came to my study at the church the other day and said they would like to have their two girls take lessons of Thea. Then I sounded Miss Meyers" (Miss Meyers was the organist in Mr. Kronborg's church) "and she said there was a good deal of talk about whether Thea wouldn't take over Wunsch's pupils. She said if Thea stopped school she wouldn't wonder if she could get pretty much all Wunsch's class. People think Thea knows about all Wunsch could teach."

Mrs. Kronborg looked thoughtful. "Do you think we ought to take her out of school so young?"

"She is young, but next year would be her last year anyway. She's far along for her age. And she can't learn much under the principal we've got now, can she?"

"No, I'm afraid she can't," his wife admitted. "She frets a good deal and says that man always has to look in the back of the book for the answers. She hates all that diagramming they have to do, and I think myself it's a waste of time."

Mr. Kronborg settled himself back into the seat and slowed the mare to a walk. "You see, it occurs to me that we might raise Thea's prices, so it would be worth her while. Seventy-five cents for hour lessons, fifty cents for half-hour lessons. If she got, say two thirds of Wunsch's class, that would bring her in upwards of ten dollars a week. Better pay than teaching a country school, and there would be more work in vacation than in winter. Steady work twelve months in the year; that's an advantage. And she'd be living at home, with no expenses."

"There'd be talk if you raised her prices," said Mrs. Kronborg dubiously.

"At first there would. But Thea is so much the best musician in town that they'd all come into line after a while. A good many people in Moonstone have been making money lately, and have bought new pianos. There were ten new pianos shipped in here from Denver in the last year. People ain't going to let them stand idle; too much money invested. I believe Thea can have as many scholars as she can handle, if we set her up a little."

"How set her up, do you mean?" Mrs. Kronborg felt a certain reluctance about accepting this plan, though she had not yet had time to think out her reasons.

"Well, I've been thinking for some time we could make good use of another room. We couldn't give up the parlor to her all the time. If we built another room on the ell and put the piano in there, she could give lessons all day long and it wouldn't bother us. We could build a clothes-press in it, and put in a bed-lounge and a dresser and let Anna have it for her sleeping-room. She needs a place of her own, now that she's beginning to be dressy."

"Seems like Thea ought to have the choice of the room, herself," said Mrs. Kronborg.

"But, my dear, she don't want it. Won't have it. I sounded her coming home from church on Sunday; asked her if she would like to sleep in a new room, if we built on. She fired up like a little wild-cat and said she'd made her own room all herself, and she didn't think anybody ought to take it away from her."

"She don't mean to be impertinent, father. She's made decided that way, like my father." Mrs. Kronborg spoke warmly. "I never have any trouble with the child. I remember my father's ways and go at her carefully. Thea's all right."

Mr. Kronborg laughed indulgently and pinched Thor's full cheek. "Oh, I didn't mean anything against your girl, mother! She's all right, but she's a little wild-cat, just the same. I think Ray Kennedy's planning to spoil a born old maid."

"Huh! She'll get something a good sight better than Ray Kennedy, you see! Thea's an awful smart girl. I've seen a good many girls take music lessons in my time, but I ain't seen one that took to it so. Wunsch said so, too. She's got the making of something in her."

"I don't deny that, and the sooner she gets at it in a businesslike way, the better. She's the kind that takes responsibility, and it'll be good for her."

Mrs. Kronborg was thoughtful. "In some ways it will, maybe. But there's a good deal of strain about teaching youngsters, and she's always worked so hard with the scholars she has. I've often listened to her pounding it into 'em. I don't want to work her too hard. She's so serious that she's never had what you might call any real childhood. Seems like she ought to have the next few years sort of free and easy. She'll be tied down with responsibilities soon enough."

Mr. Kronborg patted his wife's arm. "Don't you believe it, mother. Thea is not the marrying kind. I've watched 'em. Anna will marry before long and make a good wife, but I don't see Thea bringing up a family. She's got a good deal of her mother in her, but she hasn't got all. She's too peppery and too fond of having her own way. Then she's always got to be ahead in everything. That kind make good church-workers and missionaries and school teachers, but they don't make good wives. They fret all their energy away, like colts, and get cut on the wire."

Mrs. Kronborg laughed. "Give me the graham crackers I put in your pocket for Thor. He's hungry. You're a funny man, Peter. A body wouldn't think, to hear you, you was talking about your own daughters. I guess you see through 'em. Still, even if Thea ain't apt to have children of her own, I don't know as that's a good reason why she should wear herself out on other people's."

"That's just the point, mother. A girl with all that energy has got to do something, same as a boy, to keep her out of mischief. If you don't want her to marry Ray, let her do something to make herself independent."

"Well, I'm not against it. It might be the best thing for her. I wish I felt sure she wouldn't worry. She takes things hard. She nearly cried herself sick about Wunsch's going away. She's the smartest child of 'em all, Peter, by a long ways."

Peter Kronborg smiled. "There you go, Anna. That's you all over again. Now, I have no favorites; they all have their good points. But you," with a twinkle, "always did go in for brains."

Mrs. Kronborg chuckled as she wiped the cracker crumbs from Thor's chin and fists. "Well, you're mighty conceited, Peter! But I don't know as I ever regretted it. I prefer having a family of my own to fussing with other folks' children, that's the truth."

Before the Kronborgs reached Copper Hole, Thea's destiny was pretty well mapped out for her. Mr. Kronborg was always delighted to have an excuse for enlarging the house.

Mrs. Kronborg was quite right in her conjecture that there would be unfriendly comment in Moonstone when Thea raised her prices for music-lessons. People said she was getting too conceited for anything. Mrs. Livery Johnson put on a new bonnet and paid up all her back calls to have the pleasure of announcing in each parlor she entered that her daughters, at least, would "never pay professional prices to Thea Kronborg."

Thea raised no objection to quitting school. She was now in the "high room," as it was called, in next to the highest class, and was studying geometry and beginning Caesar. She no longer recited her lessons to the teacher she liked, but to the Principal, a man who belonged, like Mrs. Livery Johnson, to the camp of Thea's natural enemies. He taught school because he was too lazy to work among grown-up people, and he made an easy job of it. He got out of real work by inventing useless activities for his pupils, such as the "tree-diagramming system." Thea had spent hours making trees out of "Thanatopsis," Hamlet's soliloquy, Cato on "Immortality." She agonized under this waste of time, and was only too glad to accept her father's offer of liberty.

So Thea left school the first of November. By the first of January she had eight one-hour pupils and ten half-hour pupils, and there would be more in the summer. She spent her earnings generously. She bought a new Brussels carpet for the parlor, and a rifle for Gunner and Axel, and an imitation tiger-skin coat and cap for Thor. She enjoyed being able to add to the family possessions, and thought Thor looked quite as handsome in his spots as the rich children she had seen in Denver. Thor was most complacent in his conspicuous apparel. He could walk anywhere by this time—though he always preferred to sit, or to be pulled in his cart. He was a blissfully lazy child, and had a number of long, dull plays, such as making nests for his china duck and waiting for her to lay him an egg. Thea thought him very intelligent, and she was proud that he was so big and burly. She found him restful, loved to hear him call her "sitter," and really liked his companionship, especially when she was tired. On Saturday, for instance, when she taught from nine in the morning until five in the afternoon, she liked to get off in a corner with Thor after supper, away from all the bathing and dressing and joking and talking that went on in the house, and ask him about his duck, or hear him tell one of his rambling stories.

XV.

By the time Thea's fifteenth birthday came round, she was established as a music teacher in Moonstone. The new room had been added to the house early in the spring, and Thea had been giving her lessons there since the middle of May. She liked the personal independence which was accorded her as a wage-earner. The family questioned her comings and goings very little. She could go buggy-riding with Ray Kennedy, for instance, without taking

Gunner or Axel. She could go to Spanish Johnny's and sing part songs with the Mexicans, and nobody objected.

Thea was still under the first excitement of teaching, and was terribly in earnest about it. If a pupil did not get on well, she fumed and fretted. She counted until she was hoarse. She listened to scales in her sleep. Wunsch had taught only one pupil seriously, but Thea taught twenty. The duller they were, the more furiously she poked and prodded them. With the little girls she was nearly always patient, but with pupils older than herself, she sometimes lost her temper. One of her mistakes was to let herself in for a calling-down from Mrs. Livery Johnson. That lady appeared at the Kronborgs' one morning and announced that she would allow no girl to stamp her foot at her daughter Grace. She added that Thea's bad manners with the older girls were being talked about all over town, and that if her temper did not speedily improve she would lose all her advanced pupils. Thea was frightened. She felt she could never bear the disgrace, if such a thing happened. Besides, what would her father say, after he had gone to the expense of building an addition to the house? Mrs. Johnson demanded an apology to Grace. Thea said she was willing to make it. Mrs. Johnson said that hereafter, since she had taken lessons of the best piano teacher in Grinnell, Iowa, she herself would decide what pieces Grace should study. Thea readily consented to that, and Mrs. Johnson rustled away to tell a neighbor woman that Thea Kronborg could be meek enough when you went at her right.

Thea was telling Ray about this unpleasant encounter as they were driving out to the sand hills the next Sunday.

"She was stuffing you, all right, Thee," Ray reassured her. "There's no general dissatisfaction among your scholars. She just wanted to get in a knock. I talked to the piano tuner the last time he was here, and he said all the people he tuned for expressed themselves very favorably about your teaching. I wish you didn't take so much pains with them, myself."

"But I have to, Ray. They're all so dumb. They've got no ambition," Thea exclaimed irritably. "Jenny Smiley is the only one who isn't stupid. She can read pretty well, and she has such good hands. But she don't care a rap about it. She has no pride."

Ray's face was full of complacent satisfaction as he glanced sidewise at Thea, but she was looking off intently into the mirage, at one of those mammoth cattle that are nearly always reflected there. "Do you find it easier to teach in your new room?" he asked.

"Yes; I'm not interrupted so much. Of course, if I ever happen to want to practice at night, that's always the night Anna chooses to go to bed early."

"It's a darned shame, Thee, you didn't cop that room for yourself. I'm sore at the PADRE about that. He ought to give you that room. You could fix it up so pretty."

"I didn't want it, honest I didn't. Father would have let me have it. I like my own room better. Somehow I can think better in a little room. Besides, up there I am away from everybody, and I can read as late as I please and nobody nags me."

"A growing girl needs lots of sleep," Ray providently remarked.

Thea moved restlessly on the buggy cushions. "They need other things more," she muttered. "Oh, I forgot. I brought something to show you. Look here, it came on my birthday. Wasn't it nice of him to remember?" She took from her pocket a postcard, bent in the middle and folded, and handed it to Ray. On it was a white dove, perched on a wreath of very blue forget-me-nots, and "Birthday Greetings" in gold letters. Under this was written, "From A. Wunsch."

Ray turned the card over, examined the postmark, and then began to laugh.

"Concord, Kansas. He has my sympathy!"

"Why, is that a poor town?"

"It's the jumping-off place, no town at all. Some houses dumped down in the middle of a cornfield. You get lost in the corn. Not even a saloon to keep things going; sell whiskey without a license at the butcher shop, beer on ice with the liver and beefsteak. I wouldn't stay there over Sunday for a ten-dollar bill."

"Oh, dear! What do you suppose he's doing there? Maybe he just stopped off there a few days to tune pianos," Thea suggested hopefully.

Ray gave her back the card. "He's headed in the wrong direction. What does he want to get back into a grass country for? Now, there are lots of good live towns down on the Santa Fe, and everybody down there is musical. He could always get a job playing in saloons if he was dead broke. I've figured out that I've got no years of my life to waste in a Methodist country where they raise pork."

"We must stop on our way back and show this card to Mrs. Kohler. She misses him so."

"By the way, Thee, I hear the old woman goes to church every Sunday to hear you sing. Fritz tells me he has to wait till two o'clock for his Sunday dinner these days. The church people ought to give you credit for that, when they go for you."

Thea shook her head and spoke in a tone of resignation. "They'll always go for me, just as they did for Wunsch. It wasn't because he drank they went for him; not really. It was something else."

"You want to salt your money down, Thee, and go to Chicago and take some lessons. Then you come back, and wear a long feather and high heels and put on a few airs, and that'll fix 'em. That's what they like."

"I'll never have money enough to go to Chicago. Mother meant to lend me some, I think, but now they've got hard times back in Nebraska, and her farm don't bring her in anything. Takes all the tenant can raise to pay the taxes. Don't let's talk about that. You promised to tell me about the play you went to see in Denver."

Any one would have liked to hear Ray's simple and clear account of the performance he had seen at the Tabor Grand Opera House—Maggie Mitchell in LITTLE BAREFOOT—and any one would have liked to watch his kind face. Ray looked his best out of doors, when his thick red hands were covered by gloves, and the dull red of his sunburned face somehow seemed right in the light and wind. He looked better, too, with his hat on; his hair was thin and dry, with no particular color or character, "regular Willy-boy hair," as he himself described it. His eyes were pale beside the reddish bronze of his skin. They had the faded look often seen in the eyes of men who have lived much in the sun and wind and who have been accustomed to train their vision upon distant objects.

Ray realized that Thea's life was dull and exacting, and that she missed Wunsch. He knew she worked hard, that she put up with a great many little annoyances, and that her duties as a teacher separated her more than ever from the boys and girls of her own age. He did everything he could to provide recreation for her. He brought her candy and magazines and pineapples—of which she was very fond—from Denver, and kept his eyes and ears open for anything that might interest her. He was, of course, living for Thea. He had thought it all out carefully and had made up his mind just when he would speak to her. When she was seventeen, then he would tell her his plan and ask her to marry him. He would be willing to wait two, or even three years, until she was twenty, if she thought best. By that time he would surely have got in on something: copper, oil, gold, silver, sheep,—something.

Meanwhile, it was pleasure enough to feel that she depended on him more and more, that she leaned upon his steady kindness. He never broke faith with himself about her; he never hinted to her of his hopes for the future, never suggested that she might be more intimately confidential with him, or talked to her of the thing he thought about so constantly. He had the chivalry which is perhaps the proudest possession of his race. He had never embarrassed her by so much as a glance. Sometimes, when they drove out to the sand hills, he let his left arm lie along the back of the buggy seat, but it never came any nearer to Thea than that, never touched her. He often turned to her a face full of pride, and frank admiration, but his glance was never so intimate or so penetrating as Dr. Archie's. His blue eyes were clear and shallow, friendly, uninquiring. He rested Thea because he was so different; because, though he often told her interesting things, he never set lively fancies going in her head; because he never misunderstood her, and because he never, by any chance, for a single instant, understood her! Yes, with Ray she was safe; by him she would never be discovered!

XVI.

The pleasantest experience Thea had that summer was a trip that she and her mother made to Denver in Ray Kennedy's caboose. Mrs. Kronborg had been looking forward to this excursion for a long while, but as Ray never knew at what hour his freight would leave Moonstone, it was difficult to arrange. The call-boy was as likely to summon him to start on his run at twelve o'clock midnight as at twelve o'clock noon. The first week in June started out with all the scheduled trains running on time, and a light freight business. Tuesday evening Ray, after consulting with the dispatcher, stopped at the Kronborgs' front gate to tell Mrs. Kronborg—who was helping Tillie water the flowers—that if she and Thea could be at the depot at eight o'clock the next morning, he thought he could promise them a pleasant ride and get them into Denver before nine o'clock in the evening. Mrs. Kronborg told him cheerfully, across the fence, that she would "take him up on it," and Ray hurried back to the yards to scrub out his car.

The one complaint Ray's brakemen had to make of him was that he was too fussy about his caboose. His former brakeman had asked to be transferred because, he said, "Kennedy was as fussy about his car as an old maid about her bird-cage." Joe Giddy, who was braking with Ray now, called him "the bride," because he kept the caboose and bunks so clean.

It was properly the brakeman's business to keep the car clean, but when Ray got back to the depot, Giddy was nowhere to be found. Muttering that all his brakemen seemed to consider him "easy," Ray went down to his car alone. He built a fire in the stove and put water on to heat while he got into his overalls and jumper. Then he set to work with a scrubbing-brush and plenty of soap and "cleaner." He scrubbed the floor and seats, blacked the stove, put clean sheets on the bunks, and then began to demolish Giddy's picture gallery. Ray found that his brakemen were likely to have what he termed "a taste for the nude in art," and Giddy was no exception. Ray took down half a dozen girls in tights and ballet skirts,—premiums for cigarette coupons,—and some racy calendars advertising saloons and sporting clubs, which had cost Giddy both time and trouble; he even removed Giddy's particular pet, a naked girl lying on a couch with her knee carelessly poised in the air. Underneath the picture was printed the title, "The Odalisque." Giddy was under the happy delusion that this title meant something wicked,—there was a wicked look about the consonants,—but Ray, of course, had looked it up, and Giddy was indebted to the dictionary for the privilege of keeping his lady. If "odalisque" had been what Ray called an objectionable word, he would have thrown the picture out in the first place. Ray even took down a picture of Mrs. Langtry in evening dress, because it was entitled the "Jersey Lily," and because there was a small head of Edward VII, then Prince of Wales, in one corner. Albert Edward's conduct was a popular subject of discussion among railroad men in those days, and as Ray pulled the tacks out of this lithograph he felt more indignant with the English than ever. He deposited all these pictures under the mattress of Giddy's bunk, and stood admiring his clean car in the lamplight; the walls now exhibited only a wheatfield, advertising agricultural implements, a map of Colorado, and some pictures of race-horses and hunting-dogs. At this moment Giddy, freshly shaved and shampooed, his shirt shining with the highest polish known to Chinese laundrymen, his straw hat tipped over his right eye, thrust his head in at the door.

"What in hell—" he brought out furiously. His good humored, sunburned face seemed fairly to swell with amazement and anger.

"That's all right, Giddy," Ray called in a conciliatory tone. "Nothing injured. I'll put 'em all up again as I found 'em. Going to take some ladies down in the car to-morrow."

Giddy scowled. He did not dispute the propriety of Ray's measures, if there were to be ladies on board, but he felt injured. "I suppose you'll expect me to behave like a Y.M.C.A. secretary," he growled. "I can't do my work and serve tea at the same time."

"No need to have a tea-party," said Ray with determined cheerfulness. "Mrs. Kronborg will bring the lunch, and it will be a darned good one."

Giddy lounged against the car, holding his cigar between two thick fingers. "Then I guess she'll get it," he observed knowingly. "I don't think your musical friend is much on the grub-box. Has to keep her hands white to tickle the ivories." Giddy had nothing against Thea, but he felt cantankerous and wanted to get a rise out of Kennedy.

"Every man to his own job," Ray replied agreeably, pulling his white shirt on over his head.

Giddy emitted smoke disdainfully. "I suppose so. The man that gets her will have to wear an apron and bake the pancakes. Well, some men like to mess about the kitchen." He paused, but Ray was intent on getting into his clothes as quickly as possible. Giddy thought he could go a little further. "Of course, I don't dispute your right to haul women in this car if you want to; but personally, so far as I'm concerned, I'd a good deal rather drink a can of tomatoes and do without the women AND their lunch. I was never much enslaved to hard-boiled eggs, anyhow."

"You'll eat 'em to-morrow, all the same." Ray's tone had a steely glitter as he jumped out of the car, and Giddy stood aside to let him pass. He knew that Kennedy's next reply would be delivered by hand. He had once seen Ray beat up a nasty fellow for insulting a Mexican woman who helped about the grub-car in the work train, and his fists had worked like two steel hammers. Giddy wasn't looking for trouble.

At eight o'clock the next morning Ray greeted his ladies and helped them into the car. Giddy had put on a clean shirt and yellow pig-skin gloves and was whistling his best. He considered Kennedy a fluke as a ladies' man, and if there was to be a party, the honors had to be done by some one who wasn't a blacksmith at small-talk. Giddy had, as Ray sarcastically admitted, "a local reputation as a jollier," and he was fluent in gallant speeches of a not too-veiled nature. He insisted that Thea should take his seat in the cupola, opposite Ray's, where she could look out over the country. Thea told him, as she clambered up, that she cared a good deal more about riding in that seat than about going to Denver. Ray was never so companionable and easy as when he sat chatting in the lookout of his little house on wheels. Good stories came to him, and interesting recollections. Thea had a great respect for the reports he had to write out, and for the telegrams that were handed to him at stations; for all the knowledge and experience it must take to run a freight train.

Giddy, down in the car, in the pauses of his work, made himself agreeable to Mrs. Kronborg.

"It's a great rest to be where my family can't get at me, Mr. Giddy," she told him. "I thought you and Ray might have some housework here for me to look after, but I couldn't improve any on this car."

"Oh, we like to keep her neat," returned Giddy glibly, winking up at Ray's expressive back. "If you want to see a clean ice-box, look at this one. Yes, Kennedy always carries fresh cream to eat on his oatmeal. I'm not particular. The tin cow's good enough for me."

"Most of you boys smoke so much that all victuals taste alike to you," said Mrs. Kronborg. "I've got no religious scruples against smoking, but I couldn't take as much interest cooking for a man that used tobacco. I guess it's all right for bachelors who have to eat round."

Mrs. Kronborg took off her hat and veil and made herself comfortable. She seldom had an opportunity to be idle, and she enjoyed it. She could sit for hours and watch the sage-hens fly up and the jack-rabbits dart away from the track, without being bored. She wore a tan bombazine dress, made very plainly, and carried a roomy, worn, mother-of-the-family handbag.

Ray Kennedy always insisted that Mrs. Kronborg was "a fine-looking lady," but this was not the common opinion in Moonstone. Ray had lived long enough among the Mexicans to dislike fussiness, to feel that there was something more attractive in ease of manner than in absentminded concern about hairpins and dabs of lace. He had learned to think that the way a woman stood, moved, sat in her chair, looked at you, was more important than the absence of wrinkles from her skirt. Ray had, indeed, such unusual perceptions in some directions, that one could not help wondering what he would have been if he had ever, as he said, had "half a chance."

He was right; Mrs. Kronborg was a fine-looking woman. She was short and square, but her head was a real head, not a mere jerky termination of the body. It had some individuality apart from hats and hairpins. Her hair, Moonstone women admitted, would have been very pretty "on anybody else." Frizzy bangs were worn then, but Mrs. Kronborg always dressed her hair in the same way, parted in the middle, brushed smoothly back from her low, white forehead, pinned loosely on the back of her head in two thick braids. It was growing gray about the temples, but after the manner of yellow hair it seemed only to have grown paler there, and had taken on a color like that of English primroses. Her eyes were clear and untroubled; her face smooth and calm, and, as Ray said, "strong."

Thea and Ray, up in the sunny cupola, were laughing and talking. Ray got great pleasure out of seeing her face there in the little box where he so often imagined it. They were crossing a plateau where great red sandstone boulders lay about, most of them much wider at the top than at the base, so that they looked like great toadstools.

"The sand has been blowing against them for a good many hundred years," Ray explained, directing Thea's eyes with his gloved hand. "You see the sand blows low, being so heavy, and cuts them out underneath. Wind and sand are pretty high-class architects. That's the principle of most of the Cliff-Dweller remains down at Canyon de Chelly. The sandstorms had dug out big depressions in the face of a cliff, and the Indians built their houses back in that depression."

"You told me that before, Ray, and of course you know. But the geography says their houses were cut out of the face of the living rock, and I like that better."

Ray sniffed. "What nonsense does get printed! It's enough to give a man disrespect for learning. How could them Indians cut houses out of the living rock, when they knew nothing about the art of forging metals?" Ray leaned back in his chair, swung his foot, and looked thoughtful and happy. He was in one of his favorite fields of speculation, and nothing gave him more pleasure than talking these things over with Thea Kronborg. "I'll tell you, Thee, if those old fellows had learned to work metals once, your ancient Egyptians and Assyrians wouldn't have beat them very much. Whatever they did do, they did well. Their masonry's standing there to-day, the corners as true as the Denver Capitol. They were clever at most everything but metals; and that one failure kept them from getting across. It was the quicksand that swallowed 'em up, as a race. I guess civilization proper began when men mastered metals."

Ray was not vain about his bookish phrases. He did not use them to show off, but because they seemed to him more adequate than colloquial speech. He felt strongly about these things, and groped for words, as he said, "to express himself." He had the lamentable American belief that "expression" is obligatory. He still carried in his trunk, among the unrelated possessions of a railroad man, a notebook on the title-page of which was written "Impressions on First Viewing the Grand Canyon, Ray H. Kennedy." The pages of that book were like a battlefield; the laboring author had fallen back from metaphor after metaphor, abandoned position after position. He would have admitted that the art of forging metals was nothing to this treacherous business of recording impressions, in which the material you were so full of vanished mysteriously under your striving hand. "Escaping steam!" he had said to himself, the last time he tried to read that notebook.

Thea didn't mind Ray's travel-lecture expressions. She dodged them, unconsciously, as she did her father's professional palaver. The light in Ray's pale-blue eyes and the feeling in his voice more than made up for the stiffness of his language.

"Were the Cliff-Dwellers really clever with their hands, Ray, or do you always have to make allowance and say, 'That was pretty good for an Indian'?" she asked.

Ray went down into the car to give some instructions to Giddy. "Well," he said when he returned, "about the aborigines: once or twice I've been with some fellows who were cracking burial mounds. Always felt a little ashamed of it, but we did pull out some remarkable things. We got some pottery out whole; seemed pretty fine to me. I guess their women were their artists. We found lots of old shoes and sandals made out of yucca fiber, neat and strong; and feather blankets, too."

"Feather blankets? You never told me about them."

"Didn't I? The old fellows—or the squaws—wove a close netting of yucca fiber, and then tied on little bunches of down feathers, overlapping, just the way feathers grow on a bird. Some of them were feathered on both sides. You can't get anything warmer than that, now, can you?—or prettier. What I like about those old aborigines is, that they got all their ideas from nature."

Thea laughed. "That means you're going to say something about girls' wearing corsets. But some of your Indians flattened their babies' heads, and that's worse than wearing corsets."

"Give me an Indian girl's figure for beauty," Ray insisted. "And a girl with a voice like yours ought to have plenty of lung-action. But you know my sentiments on that subject. I was going to tell you about the handsomest thing we ever looted out of those burial mounds. It was on a woman, too, I regret to say. She was preserved as perfect as any mummy that ever came out of the pyramids. She had a big string of turquoises around her neck, and she was wrapped in a fox-fur cloak, lined with little yellow feathers that must have come off wild canaries. Can you beat that, now? The fellow that claimed it sold it to a Boston man for a hundred and fifty dollars."

Thea looked at him admiringly. "Oh, Ray, and didn't you get anything off her, to remember her by, even? She must have been a princess."

Ray took a wallet from the pocket of the coat that was hanging beside him, and drew from it a little lump wrapped in worn tissue paper. In a moment a stone, soft and blue as a robin's egg, lay in the hard palm of his hand. It was a turquoise, rubbed smooth in the Indian finish, which is so much more beautiful than the incongruous high polish the white man gives that tender stone. "I got this from her necklace. See the hole where the string went through? You know how the Indians drill them? Work the drill with their teeth. You like it, don't you? They're just right for you. Blue and yellow are the Swedish colors." Ray looked intently at her head, bent over his hand, and then gave his whole attention to the track.

"I'll tell you, Thee," he began after a pause, "I'm going to form a camping party one of these days and persuade your PADRE to take you and your mother down to that country, and we'll live in the rock houses—they're as comfortable as can be—and start the cook fires up in 'em once again. I'll go into the burial mounds and get you more keepsakes than any girl ever had before." Ray had planned such an expedition for his wedding journey, and it made his heart thump to see how Thea's eyes kindled when he talked about it. "I've learned more down there about what makes history," he went on, "than in all the books I've ever read. When you sit in the sun and let your heels hang out of a doorway that drops a thousand feet, ideas come to you. You begin to feel what the human race has been up against from the beginning. There's something mighty elevating about those old habitations. You feel like it's up to you to do your best, on account of those fellows having it so hard. You feel like you owed them something."

At Wassiwappa, Ray got instructions to sidetrack until Thirty-six went by. After reading the message, he turned to his guests. "I'm afraid this will hold us up about two hours, Mrs. Kronborg, and we won't get into Denver till near midnight."

"That won't trouble me," said Mrs. Kronborg contentedly. "They know me at the Y.W.C.A., and they'll let me in any time of night. I came to see the country, not to make time. I've always wanted to get out at this white place and look around, and now I'll have a chance. What makes it so white?"

"Some kind of chalky rock." Ray sprang to the ground and gave Mrs. Kronborg his hand. "You can get soil of any color in Colorado; match most any ribbon."

While Ray was getting his train on to a side track, Mrs. Kronborg strolled off to examine the post-office and station house; these, with the water tank, made up the town. The station agent "batched" and raised chickens. He ran out to meet Mrs. Kronborg, clutched at her feverishly, and began telling her at once how lonely he was and what bad luck he was having with his poultry. She went to his chicken yard with him, and prescribed for gapes.

Wassiwappa seemed a dreary place enough to people who looked for verdure, a brilliant place to people who liked color. Beside the station house there was a blue-grass plot, protected by a red plank fence, and six fly-bitten box-elder trees, not much larger than bushes, were kept alive by frequent hosings from the water plug. Over the windows some dusty morning-glory vines were trained on strings. All the country about was broken up into low chalky hills, which were so intensely white, and spotted so evenly with sage, that they looked like white leopards crouching. White dust powdered everything, and the light was so intense that the station agent usually wore blue glasses. Behind the station there was a water course, which roared in flood time, and a basin in the soft white rock where a pool of alkali water flashed in the sun like a mirror. The agent looked almost as sick as his chickens, and Mrs. Kronborg at once invited him to lunch with her party. He had, he confessed, a distaste for his own cooking, and lived mainly on soda crackers and canned beef. He laughed apologetically when Mrs. Kronborg said she guessed she'd look about for a shady place to eat lunch.

She walked up the track to the water tank, and there, in the narrow shadows cast by the uprights on which the tank stood, she found two tramps. They sat up and stared at her, heavy with sleep. When she asked them where they were going, they told her "to the coast." They rested by day and traveled by night; walked the ties unless they could steal a ride, they said; adding that "these Western roads were getting strict." Their faces were blistered, their eyes blood-shot, and their shoes looked fit only for the trash pile.

"I suppose you're hungry?" Mrs. Kronborg asked. "I suppose you both drink?" she went on thoughtfully, not censoriously.

The huskier of the two hoboes, a bushy, bearded fellow, rolled his eyes and said, "I wonder?" But the other, who was old and spare, with a sharp nose and watery eyes, sighed. "Some has one affliction, some another," he said.

Mrs. Kronborg reflected. "Well," she said at last, "you can't get liquor here, anyway. I am going to ask you to vacate, because I want to have a little picnic under this tank for the freight crew that brought me along. I wish I had lunch enough to provide you, but I ain't. The station agent says he gets his provisions over there at the post office store, and if you are hungry you can get some canned stuff there." She opened her handbag and gave each of the tramps a half-dollar.

The old man wiped his eyes with his forefinger. "Thank 'ee, ma'am. A can of tomatters will taste pretty good to me. I wasn't always walkin' ties; I had a good job in Cleveland before—"

The hairy tramp turned on him fiercely. "Aw, shut up on that, grandpaw! Ain't you got no gratitude? What do you want to hand the lady that fur?"

The old man hung his head and turned away. As he went off, his comrade looked after him and said to Mrs. Kronborg: "It's true, what he says. He had a job in the car shops; but he had bad luck." They both limped away toward the store, and Mrs. Kronborg sighed. She was not afraid of tramps. She always talked to them, and never turned one away. She hated to think how many of them there were, crawling along the tracks over that vast country.

Her reflections were cut short by Ray and Giddy and Thea, who came bringing the lunch box and water bottles. Although there was not shadow enough to accommodate all the party at once, the air under the tank was distinctly cooler than the surrounding air, and the drip made a pleasant sound in that breathless noon. The station agent ate as if he had never been fed before, apologizing every time he took another piece of fried chicken. Giddy was unabashed before the devilled eggs of which he had spoken so scornfully last night. After lunch the men lit their pipes and lay back against the uprights that supported the tank.

"This is the sunny side of railroading, all right," Giddy drawled luxuriously.

"You fellows grumble too much," said Mrs. Kronborg as she corked the pickle jar. "Your job has its drawbacks, but it don't tie you down. Of course there's the risk; but I believe a man's watched over, and he can't be hurt on the railroad or anywhere else if it's intended he shouldn't be."

Giddy laughed. "Then the trains must be operated by fellows the Lord has it in for, Mrs. Kronborg. They figure it out that a railroad man's only due to last eleven years; then it's his turn to be smashed."

"That's a dark Providence, I don't deny," Mrs. Kronborg admitted. "But there's lots of things in life that's hard to understand."

"I guess!" murmured Giddy, looking off at the spotted white hills.

Ray smoked in silence, watching Thea and her mother clear away the lunch. He was thinking that Mrs. Kronborg had in her face the same serious look that Thea had; only hers was calm and satisfied, and Thea's was intense and questioning. But in both it was a large kind of look, that was not all the time being broken up and convulsed by trivial things. They both carried their heads like Indian women, with a kind of noble unconsciousness. He got so tired of women who were always nodding and jerking; apologizing, deprecating, coaxing, insinuating with their heads.

When Ray's party set off again that afternoon the sun beat fiercely into the cupola, and Thea curled up in one of the seats at the back of the car and had a nap.

As the short twilight came on, Giddy took a turn in the cupola, and Ray came down and sat with Thea on the rear platform of the caboose and watched the darkness come in soft waves over the plain. They were now about thirty miles from Denver, and the mountains looked very near. The great toothed wall behind which the sun had gone down now separated into four distinct ranges, one behind the other. They were a very pale blue, a color scarcely stronger than wood smoke, and the sunset had left bright streaks in the snow-filled gorges. In the clear, yellow-streaked sky the stars were coming out, flickering like newly lighted lamps, growing steadier and more golden as the sky darkened and the land beneath them fell into complete shadow. It was a cool, restful darkness that was not black or forbidding, but somehow open and free; the night of high plains where there is no moistness or mistiness in the atmosphere.

Ray lit his pipe. "I never get tired of them old stars, Thee. I miss 'em up in Washington and Oregon where it's misty. Like 'em best down in Mother Mexico, where they have everything their own way. I'm not for any country where the stars are dim." Ray paused and drew on his pipe. "I don't know as I ever really noticed 'em much till that first year I herded sheep up in Wyoming. That was the year the blizzard caught me."

"And you lost all your sheep, didn't you, Ray?" Thea spoke sympathetically. "Was the man who owned them nice about it?"

"Yes, he was a good loser. But I didn't get over it for a long while. Sheep are so damned resigned. Sometimes, to this day, when I'm dog-tired, I try to save them sheep all night long. It comes kind of hard on a boy when he first finds out how little he is, and how big everything else is."

Thea moved restlessly toward him and dropped her chin on her hand, looking at a low star that seemed to rest just on the rim of the earth. "I don't see how you stood it. I don't believe I could. I don't see how people can stand it to get knocked out, anyhow!" She spoke with such fierceness that Ray glanced at her in surprise. She was sitting on the floor of the car, crouching like a little animal about to spring.

"No occasion for you to see," he said warmly. "There'll always be plenty of other people to take the knocks for you."

"That's nonsense, Ray." Thea spoke impatiently and leaned lower still, frowning at the red star. "Everybody's up against it for himself, succeeds or fails—himself."

"In one way, yes," Ray admitted, knocking the sparks from his pipe out into the soft darkness that seemed to flow like a river beside the car. "But when you look at it another way, there are a lot of halfway people in this world who help the winners win, and the failers fail. If a man stumbles, there's plenty of people to push him down. But if he's like 'the youth who bore,' those same people are foreordained to help him along. They may hate to, worse than blazes, and they may do a lot of cussin' about it, but they have to help the winners and they can't dodge it. It's a natural law, like what keeps the big clock up there going, little wheels and big, and no mix-up." Ray's hand and his pipe were suddenly outlined against the sky. "Ever occur to you, Thee, that they have to be on time close enough to MAKE TIME? The Dispatcher up there must have a long head." Pleased with his similitude, Ray went back to the lookout. Going into Denver, he had to keep a sharp watch.

Giddy came down, cheerful at the prospect of getting into port, and singing a new topical ditty that had come up from the Santa Fe by way of La Junta. Nobody knows who makes these songs; they seem to follow events automatically. Mrs. Kronborg made Giddy sing the whole twelve verses of this one, and laughed until she wiped her eyes. The story was that of Katie Casey, head diningroom girl at Winslow, Arizona, who was unjustly discharged by the Harvey House manager. Her suitor, the yardmaster, took the switchmen out on a strike until she was reinstated. Freight trains from the east and the west piled up at Winslow until the yards looked like a log-jam. The division superintendent, who was in California, had to wire instructions for Katie Casey's restoration before he could get his trains running. Giddy's song told all this with much detail, both tender and technical, and after each of the dozen verses came the refrain:—

"Oh, who would think that Katie Casey owned the Santa Fe?
But it really looks that way,
The dispatcher's turnin' gray,
All the crews is off their pay;
She can hold the freight from Albuquerq' to Needles any day;
The division superintendent, he come home from Monterey,
Just to see if things was pleasin' Katie Ca—a—a—sey."

Thea laughed with her mother and applauded Giddy. Everything was so kindly and comfortable; Giddy and Ray, and their hospitable little house, and the easy-going country, and the stars. She curled up on the seat again with that warm, sleepy feeling of the friendliness of the world—which nobody keeps very long, and which she was to lose early and irrevocably.

XVII.

The summer flew by. Thea was glad when Ray Kennedy had a Sunday in town and could take her driving. Out among the sand hills she could forget the "new room" which was the scene of wearing and fruitless labor. Dr. Archie was away from home a good deal that year. He had put all his money into mines above Colorado Springs, and he hoped for great returns from them.

In the fall of that year, Mr. Kronborg decided that Thea ought to show more interest in church work. He put it to her frankly, one night at supper, before the whole family. "How can I insist on the other girls in the congregation being active in the work, when one of my own daughters manifests so little interest?"

"But I sing every Sunday morning, and I have to give up one night a week to choir practice," Thea declared rebelliously, pushing back her plate with an angry determination to eat nothing more.

"One night a week is not enough for the pastor's daughter," her father replied. "You won't do anything in the sewing society, and you won't take part in the Christian Endeavor or the Band of Hope. Very well, you must make it up in other ways. I want some one to play the organ and lead the singing at prayer-meeting this winter. Deacon Potter told me some time ago that he thought there would be more interest in our prayer-meetings if we had the organ. Miss Meyers don't feel that she can play on Wednesday nights. And there ought to be somebody to start the hymns. Mrs. Potter is getting old, and she always starts them too high. It won't take much of your time, and it will keep people from talking."

This argument conquered Thea, though she left the table sullenly. The fear of the tongue, that terror of little towns, is usually felt more keenly by the minister's family than by other households. Whenever the Kronborgs wanted to do anything, even to buy a new carpet, they had to take counsel together as to whether people would talk. Mrs. Kronborg had her own conviction that people talked when they felt like it, and said what they chose, no matter how the minister's family conducted themselves. But she did not impart these dangerous ideas to her children. Thea was still under the belief that public opinion could be placated; that if you clucked often enough, the hens would mistake you for one of themselves.

Mrs. Kronborg did not have any particular zest for prayer-meetings, and she stayed at home whenever she had a valid excuse. Thor was too old to furnish such an excuse now, so every Wednesday night, unless one of the children was sick, she trudged off with Thea, behind Mr. Kronborg. At first Thea was terribly bored. But she got used to prayer-meeting, got even to feel a mournful interest in it.

The exercises were always pretty much the same. After the first hymn her father read a passage from the Bible, usually a Psalm. Then there was another hymn, and then her father commented upon the passage he had read and, as he said, "applied the Word to our necessities." After a third hymn, the meeting was declared open, and the old men and women took turns at praying and talking. Mrs. Kronborg never spoke in meeting. She told people firmly that she had been brought up to keep silent and let the men talk, but she gave respectful attention to the others, sitting with her hands folded in her lap.

The prayer-meeting audience was always small. The young and energetic members of the congregation came only once or twice a year, "to keep people from talking." The usual Wednesday night gathering was made up of old women, with perhaps six or eight old men, and a few sickly girls who had not much interest in life; two of them, indeed, were already preparing to die. Thea accepted the mournfulness of the prayer-meetings as a kind of spiritual discipline, like funerals. She always read late after she went home and felt a stronger wish than usual to live and to be happy.

The meetings were conducted in the Sunday-School room, where there were wooden chairs instead of pews; an old map of Palestine hung on the wall, and the bracket lamps gave out only a dim light. The old women sat motionless as Indians in their shawls and bonnets; some of them wore long black mourning veils. The old men drooped in their chairs. Every back, every face, every head said "resignation." Often there were long silences, when you could hear nothing but the crackling of the soft coal in the stove and the muffled cough of one of the sick girls.

There was one nice old lady,—tall, erect, self-respecting, with a delicate white face and a soft voice. She never whined, and what she said was always cheerful, though she spoke so nervously that Thea knew she dreaded getting up, and that she made a real sacrifice to, as she said, "testify to the goodness of her Saviour." She was the mother of the girl who coughed, and Thea used to wonder how she explained things to herself. There was, indeed, only one woman who talked because she was, as Mr. Kronborg said, "tonguey." The others were somehow impressive. They told about the sweet thoughts that came to them while they were at their work; how, amid their household tasks, they were suddenly lifted by the sense of a divine Presence. Sometimes they told of their first conversion, of how in their youth that higher Power had made itself known to them. Old Mr. Carsen, the carpenter, who gave his services as janitor to the church, used often to tell how, when he was a young man and a scoffer, bent on the destruction of both body and soul, his Saviour had come to him in the Michigan woods and had stood, it seemed to him, beside the tree he was felling; and how he dropped his axe and knelt in prayer "to Him who died for us upon the tree." Thea always wanted to ask him more about it; about his mysterious wickedness, and about the vision.

Sometimes the old people would ask for prayers for their absent children. Sometimes they asked their brothers and sisters in Christ to pray that they might be stronger against temptations. One of the sick girls used to ask them to pray that she might have more faith in the times of depression that came to her, "when all the way before seemed dark." She repeated that husky phrase so often, that Thea always remembered it.

One old woman, who never missed a Wednesday night, and who nearly always took part in the meeting, came all the way up from the depot settlement. She always wore a black crocheted "fascinator" over her thin white hair, and she made long, tremulous prayers, full of railroad terminology. She had six sons in the service of different railroads, and she always prayed "for the boys on the road, who know not at what moment they may be cut off. When, in Thy divine wisdom, their hour is upon them, may they, O our Heavenly Father, see only white lights along the road to Eternity." She used to speak, too, of "the engines that race with death"; and though she looked so old and little when she was on her knees, and her voice was so shaky, her prayers had a thrill of speed and danger in them; they made one think of the deep black canyons, the slender trestles, the pounding trains. Thea liked to look at her sunken eyes that seemed full of wisdom, at her black thread gloves, much too long in the fingers and so meekly folded one over the other. Her face was brown, and worn away as rocks are worn by water. There are many ways of describing that color of age, but in reality it is not like parchment, or like any of the things it is said to be like. That brownness and that texture of skin are found only in the faces of old human creatures, who have worked hard and who have always been poor.

One bitterly cold night in December the prayer-meeting seemed to Thea longer than usual. The prayers and the talks went on and on. It was as if the old people were afraid to go out into the cold, or were stupefied by the hot air of the room. She had left a book at home that she was impatient to get back to. At last the Doxology was sung, but the old people lingered about the stove to greet each other, and Thea took her mother's arm and hurried out to the frozen sidewalk, before her father could get away. The wind was whistling up the street and whipping the naked cottonwood trees against the telegraph poles and the sides of the houses. Thin snow clouds were flying overhead, so that the sky looked gray, with a dull phosphorescence. The icy streets and the shingle roofs of the houses were gray, too. All along the street, shutters banged or windows rattled, or gates wobbled, held by their latch but shaking on loose hinges. There was not a cat or a dog in Moonstone that night that was not given a warm shelter; the cats under the kitchen stove, the dogs in barns or coal-sheds. When Thea and her mother reached home, their mufflers were covered with ice, where their breath had frozen. They hurried into the house and made a dash for the parlor and the hard-coal burner, behind which Gunner was sitting on a stool, reading his Jules Verne book. The door stood open into the dining-room, which was heated from the parlor. Mr. Kronborg always had a lunch when he came home from prayer-meeting, and his pumpkin pie and milk were set out on the dining-table. Mrs. Kronborg said she thought she felt hungry, too, and asked Thea if she didn't want something to eat.

"No, I'm not hungry, mother. I guess I'll go upstairs."

"I expect you've got some book up there," said Mrs. Kronborg, bringing out another pie. "You'd better bring it down here and read. Nobody'll disturb you, and it's terrible cold up in that loft."

Thea was always assured that no one would disturb her if she read downstairs, but the boys talked when they came in, and her father fairly delivered discourses after he had been renewed by half a pie and a pitcher of milk.

"I don't mind the cold. I'll take a hot brick up for my feet. I put one in the stove before I left, if one of the boys hasn't stolen it. Good-night, mother." Thea got her brick and lantern, and dashed upstairs through the windy loft. She undressed at top speed and got into bed with her brick. She put a pair of white knitted gloves on her hands, and pinned over her head a piece of soft flannel that had been one of Thor's long petticoats when he was a baby. Thus equipped, she was ready for business. She took from her table a thick paper-backed volume, one of the "line" of paper novels the druggist kept to sell to traveling men. She had bought it, only yesterday, because the first sentence interested her very much, and because she saw, as she glanced over the pages, the magical names of two Russian cities. The book was a poor translation of "Anna Karenina." Thea opened it at a mark, and fixed her eyes intently upon the small print. The hymns, the sick girl, the resigned black figures were forgotten. It was the night of the ball in Moscow.

Thea would have been astonished if she could have known how, years afterward, when she had need of them, those old faces were to come back to her, long after they were hidden away under the earth; that they would seem to her then as full of meaning, as mysteriously marked by Destiny, as the people who danced the mazurka under the elegant Korsunsky.

XVIII.

Mr. Kronborg was too fond of his ease and too sensible to worry his children much about religion. He was more sincere than many preachers, but when he spoke to his family about matters of conduct it was usually with a regard for keeping up appearances. The church and church work were discussed in the family like the routine of any other business. Sunday was the hard day of the week with them, just as Saturday was the busy day with the merchants on Main Street. Revivals were seasons of extra work and pressure, just as threshing-time was on the farms. Visiting elders had to be lodged and cooked for, the folding-bed in the parlor was let down, and Mrs. Kronborg had to work in the kitchen all day long and attend the night meetings.

During one of these revivals Thea's sister Anna professed religion with, as Mrs. Kronborg said, "a good deal of fluster." While Anna was going up to the mourners' bench nightly and asking for the prayers of the congregation, she disseminated general gloom throughout the household, and after she joined the church she took on an air of "set-apartness" that was extremely trying to her brothers and her sister, though they realized that Anna's sanctimoniousness was perhaps a good thing for their father. A preacher ought to have one child who did more than merely acquiesce in religious observances, and Thea and the boys were glad enough that it was Anna and not one of themselves who assumed this obligation.

"Anna, she's American," Mrs. Kronborg used to say. The Scandinavian mould of countenance, more or less marked in each of the other children, was scarcely discernible in her, and she looked enough like other Moonstone girls to be thought pretty. Anna's nature was conventional, like her face. Her position as the minister's eldest daughter was important to her, and she tried to live up to it. She read sentimental religious story-books and emulated the spiritual struggles and magnanimous behavior of their persecuted heroines. Everything had to be interpreted for Anna. Her opinions about the smallest and most commonplace things were gleaned from the Denver papers, the church weeklies, from sermons and Sunday-School addresses. Scarcely anything was attractive to her in its natural state—indeed, scarcely anything was decent until it was clothed by the opinion of some authority. Her ideas about habit, character, duty, love, marriage, were grouped under heads, like a book of popular quotations, and were totally unrelated to the emergencies of human living. She discussed all these subjects with other Methodist girls of her age. They would spend hours, for instance, in deciding what they would or would not tolerate in a suitor or a husband, and the frailties of masculine nature were too often a subject of discussion among them. In her behavior Anna was a harmless girl, mild except where her prejudices were concerned, neat and industrious, with no graver fault than priggishness; but her mind had really shocking habits of classification. The wickedness of Denver and of Chicago, and even of Moonstone, occupied her thoughts too much. She had none of the delicacy that goes with a nature of warm impulses, but the kind of fishy curiosity which justifies itself by an expression of horror.

Thea, and all Thea's ways and friends, seemed indecorous to Anna. She not only felt a grave social discrimination against the Mexicans; she could not forget that Spanish Johnny was a drunkard and that "nobody knew what he did when he ran away from home." Thea pretended, of course, that she liked the Mexicans because they were fond of music; but every one knew that music was nothing very real, and that it did not matter in a girl's relations with people. What was real, then, and what did matter? Poor Anna!

Anna approved of Ray Kennedy as a young man of steady habits and blameless life, but she regretted that he was an atheist, and that he was not a passenger conductor with brass buttons on his coat. On the whole, she wondered what such an exemplary young man found to like in Thea. Dr. Archie she treated respectfully because of his position in Moonstone, but she KNEW he had kissed the Mexican barytone's pretty daughter, and she had a whole DOSSIER of evidence about his behavior in his hours of relaxation in Denver. He was "fast," and it was because he was "fast" that Thea liked him. Thea always liked that kind of people. Dr. Archie's whole manner with Thea, Anna often told her mother, was too free. He was always putting his hand on Thea's head, or holding her hand while he laughed and looked down at her. The kindlier manifestation of human nature (about which Anna sang and talked, in the interests of which she went to conventions and wore white ribbons) were never realities to her after all. She did not believe in them. It was only in attitudes of protest or reproof, clinging to the cross, that human beings could be even temporarily decent.

Preacher Kronborg's secret convictions were very much like Anna's. He believed that his wife was absolutely good, but there was not a man or woman in his congregation whom he trusted all the way.

Mrs. Kronborg, on the other hand, was likely to find something to admire in almost any human conduct that was positive and energetic. She could always be taken in by the stories of tramps and runaway boys. She went to the circus and admired the bareback riders, who were "likely good enough women in their way." She admired Dr. Archie's fine physique and well-cut clothes as much as Thea did, and said she "felt it was a privilege to be handled by such a gentleman when she was sick."

Soon after Anna became a church member she began to remonstrate with Thea about practicing—playing "secular music"—on Sunday. One Sunday the dispute in the parlor grew warm and was carried to Mrs. Kronborg in the kitchen. She listened judicially and told Anna to read the chapter about how Naaman the leper was permitted to bow down in the house of Rimmon. Thea went back to the piano, and Anna lingered to say that, since she was in the right, her mother should have supported her.

"No," said Mrs. Kronborg, rather indifferently, "I can't see it that way, Anna. I never forced you to practice, and I don't see as I should keep Thea from it. I like to hear her, and I guess your father does. You and Thea will likely follow different lines, and I don't see as I'm called upon to bring you up alike."

Anna looked meek and abused. "Of course all the church people must hear her. Ours is the only noisy house on this street. You hear what she's playing now, don't you?"

Mrs. Kronborg rose from browning her coffee. "Yes; it's the Blue Danube waltzes. I'm familiar with 'em. If any of the church people come at you, you just send 'em to me. I ain't afraid to speak out on occasion, and I wouldn't mind one bit telling the Ladies' Aid a few things about standard composers." Mrs. Kronborg smiled, and added thoughtfully, "No, I wouldn't mind that one bit."

Anna went about with a reserved and distant air for a week, and Mrs. Kronborg suspected that she held a larger place than usual in her daughter's prayers; but that was another thing she didn't mind.

Although revivals were merely a part of the year's work, like examination week at school, and although Anna's piety impressed her very little, a time came when Thea was perplexed about religion. A scourge of typhoid broke out in Moonstone and several of Thea's schoolmates died of it. She went to their funerals, saw them put into the ground, and wondered a good deal about them. But a certain grim incident, which caused the epidemic, troubled her even more than the death of her friends.

Early in July, soon after Thea's fifteenth birthday, a particularly disgusting sort of tramp came into Moonstone in an empty box car. Thea was sitting in the hammock in the front yard when he first crawled up to the town from the depot, carrying a bundle wrapped in dirty ticking under one arm, and under the other a wooden box with rusty screening nailed over one end. He had a thin, hungry face covered with black hair. It was just before suppertime when he came along, and the street smelled of fried potatoes and fried onions and coffee. Thea saw him sniffing the air greedily and walking slower and slower. He looked over the fence. She hoped he would not stop at their gate, for her mother never turned any one away, and this was the dirtiest and most utterly wretched-looking tramp she had ever seen. There was a terrible odor about him, too. She caught it even at that distance, and put her handkerchief to her nose. A moment later she was sorry, for she knew that he had noticed it. He looked away and shuffled a little faster.

A few days later Thea heard that the tramp had camped in an empty shack over on the east edge of town, beside the ravine, and was trying to give a miserable sort of show there. He told the boys who went to see what he was doing, that he had traveled with a circus. His bundle contained a filthy clown's suit, and his box held half a dozen rattlesnakes.

Saturday night, when Thea went to the butcher shop to get the chickens for Sunday, she heard the whine of an accordion and saw a crowd before one of the saloons. There she found the tramp, his bony body grotesquely attired in the clown's suit, his face shaved and painted white,—the sweat trickling through the paint and washing it away,—and his eyes wild and feverish. Pulling the accordion in and out seemed to be almost too great an effort for him, and he panted to the tune of "Marching through Georgia." After a considerable crowd had gathered, the tramp exhibited his box of snakes, announced that he would now pass the hat, and that when the onlookers had contributed the sum of one dollar, he would eat "one of these living reptiles." The crowd began to cough and murmur, and the saloon keeper rushed off for the marshal, who arrested the wretch for giving a show without a license and hurried him away to the calaboose.

The calaboose stood in a sunflower patch,—an old hut with a barred window and a padlock on the door. The tramp was utterly filthy and there was no way to give him a bath. The law made no provision to grub-stake vagrants, so after the constable had detained the tramp for twentyfour hours, he released him and told him to "get out of town, and get quick." The fellow's rattlesnakes had been killed by the saloon keeper. He hid in a box car in the freight yard, probably hoping to get a ride to the next station, but he was found and put out. After that he was seen no more. He had disappeared and left no trace except an ugly, stupid word, chalked on the black paint of the seventy-five-foot standpipe which was the reservoir for the Moonstone water-supply; the same word, in another tongue, that the French soldier shouted at Waterloo to the English officer who bade the Old Guard surrender; a comment on life which the defeated, along the hard roads of the world, sometimes bawl at the victorious.

A week after the tramp excitement had passed over, the city water began to smell and to taste. The Kronborgs had a well in their back yard and did not use city water, but they heard the complaints of their neighbors. At first people said that the town well was full of rotting cottonwood roots, but the engineer at the pumping-station convinced the mayor that the water left the well untainted. Mayors reason slowly, but, the well being eliminated, the official mind had to travel toward the standpipe—there was no other track for it to go in. The standpipe amply rewarded investigation. The tramp had got even with Moonstone. He had climbed the standpipe by the handholds and let himself down into seventy-five feet of cold water, with his shoes and hat and roll of ticking. The city council had a mild panic and passed a new ordinance about tramps. But the fever had already broken out, and several adults and half a dozen children died of it.

Thea had always found everything that happened in Moonstone exciting, disasters particularly so. It was gratifying to read sensational Moonstone items in the Denver paper. But she wished she had not chanced to see the tramp as he came into town that evening, sniffing the supper-laden air. His face remained unpleasantly clear in her memory, and her mind struggled with the problem of his behavior as if it were a hard page in arithmetic. Even when she was practicing, the drama of the tramp kept going on in the back of her head, and she was constantly trying to make herself realize what pitch of hatred or despair could drive a man to do such a hideous thing. She kept seeing him in his bedraggled clown suit, the white paint on his roughly shaven face, playing his accordion before the saloon. She had noticed his lean body, his high, bald forehead that sloped back like a curved metal lid. How could people fall so far out of fortune? She tried to talk to Ray Kennedy about her perplexity, but Ray would not discuss things of that sort with her. It was in his sentimental conception of women that they should be deeply religious, though men were at liberty to doubt and finally to deny. A picture called "The Soul Awakened," popular in Moonstone parlors, pretty well interpreted Ray's idea of woman's spiritual nature.

One evening when she was haunted by the figure of the tramp, Thea went up to Dr. Archie's office. She found him sewing up two bad gashes in the face of a little boy who had been kicked by a mule. After the boy had been bandaged and sent away with his father, Thea helped the doctor wash and put away the surgical instruments. Then she dropped into her accustomed seat beside his desk and began to talk about the tramp. Her eyes were hard and green with excitement, the doctor noticed.

"It seems to me, Dr. Archie, that the whole town's to blame. I'm to blame, myself. I know he saw me hold my nose when he went by. Father's to blame. If he believes the Bible, he ought to have gone to the calaboose and cleaned that man up and taken care of him. That's what I can't understand; do people believe the Bible, or don't they? If the next life is all that matters, and we're put here to get ready for it, then why do we try to make money, or learn things, or have a good time? There's not one person in Moonstone that really lives the way the New Testament says. Does it matter, or don't it?"

Dr. Archie swung round in his chair and looked at her, honestly and leniently. "Well, Thea, it seems to me like this. Every people has had its religion. All religions are good, and all are pretty much alike. But I don't see how we could live up to them in the sense you mean. I've thought about it a good deal, and I can't help feeling that while we are in this world we have to live for the best things of this world, and those things are material and positive. Now, most religions are passive, and they tell us chiefly what we should not do." The doctor moved restlessly, and his eyes hunted for something along the opposite wall: "See here, my girl, take out the years of early childhood and the time we spend in sleep and dull old age, and we only have about twenty able, waking years. That's not long enough to get acquainted with half the fine things that have been done in the world, much less to do anything ourselves. I think we ought to keep the Commandments and help other people all we can; but the main thing is to live those twenty splendid years; to do all we can and enjoy all we can."

Dr. Archie met his little friend's searching gaze, the look of acute inquiry which always touched him.

"But poor fellows like that tramp—" she hesitated and wrinkled her forehead.

The doctor leaned forward and put his hand protectingly over hers, which lay clenched on the green felt desktop. "Ugly accidents happen, Thea; always have and always will. But the failures are swept back into the pile and forgotten. They don't leave any lasting scar in the world, and they don't affect the future. The things that last are the good things. The people who forge ahead and do something, they really count." He saw tears on her cheeks, and he remembered that he had never seen her cry before, not even when she crushed her finger when she was little. He rose and walked to the window, came back and sat down on the edge of his chair.

"Forget the tramp, Thea. This is a great big world, and I want you to get about and see it all. You're going to Chicago some day, and do something with that fine voice of yours. You're going to be a number one musician and make us proud of you. Take Mary Anderson, now; even the tramps are proud of her. There isn't a tramp along the 'Q' system who hasn't heard of her. We all like people who do things, even if we only see their faces on a cigar-box lid."

They had a long talk. Thea felt that Dr. Archie had never let himself out to her so much before. It was the most grown-up conversation she had ever had with him. She left his office happy, flattered and stimulated. She ran for a long while about the white, moonlit streets, looking up at the stars and the bluish night, at the quiet houses sunk in black shade, the glittering sand hills. She loved the familiar trees, and the people in those little houses, and she loved the unknown world beyond Denver. She felt as if she were being pulled in two, between the desire to go away forever and the desire to stay forever. She had only twenty years—no time to lose.

Many a night that summer she left Dr. Archie's office with a desire to run and run about those quiet streets until she wore out her shoes, or wore out the streets themselves; when her chest ached and it seemed as if her heart were spreading all over the desert. When she went home, it was not to go to sleep. She used to drag her mattress beside her low window and lie awake for a long while, vibrating with excitement, as a machine vibrates from speed. Life rushed in upon her through that window—or so it seemed. In reality, of course, life rushes from within, not from without. There is no work of art so big or so beautiful that it was not once all contained in some youthful body, like this one which lay on the floor in the moonlight, pulsing with ardor and anticipation. It was on such nights that Thea Kronborg learned the thing that old Dumas meant when he told the Romanticists that to make a drama he needed but one passion and four walls.

XIX.

It is well for its peace of mind that the traveling public takes railroads so much for granted. The only men who are incurably nervous about railway travel are the railroad operatives. A railroad man never forgets that the next run may be his turn.

On a single-track road, like that upon which Ray Kennedy worked, the freight trains make their way as best they can between passenger trains. Even when there is such a thing as a freight time-schedule, it is merely a form. Along the one track dozens of fast and slow trains dash in both directions, kept from collision only by the brains in the dispatcher's office. If one passenger train is late, the whole schedule must be revised in an instant; the trains following must be warned, and those moving toward the belated train must be assigned new meeting-places.

Between the shifts and modifications of the passenger schedule, the freight trains play a game of their own. They have no right to the track at any given time, but are supposed to be on it when it is free, and to make the best time they can between passenger trains. A freight train, on a single-track road, gets anywhere at all only by stealing bases.

Ray Kennedy had stuck to the freight service, although he had had opportunities to go into the passenger service at higher pay. He always regarded railroading as a temporary makeshift, until he "got into something," and he disliked the passenger service. No brass buttons for him, he said; too much like a livery. While he was railroading he would wear a jumper, thank you!

The wreck that "caught" Ray was a very commonplace one; nothing thrilling about it, and it got only six lines in the Denver papers. It happened about daybreak one morning, only thirty-two miles from home.

At four o'clock in the morning Ray's train had stopped to take water at Saxony, having just rounded the long curve which lies south of that station. It was Joe Giddy's business to walk back along the curve about three hundred yards and put out torpedoes to warn any train which might be coming up from behind—a freight crew is not notified of trains following, and the brakeman is supposed to protect his train. Ray was so fussy about the punctilious observance of orders that almost any brakeman would take a chance once in a while, from natural perversity.

When the train stopped for water that morning, Ray was at the desk in his caboose, making out his report. Giddy took his torpedoes, swung off the rear platform, and glanced back at the curve. He decided that he would not go back to flag this time. If anything was coming up behind, he could hear it in plenty of time. So he ran forward to look after a hot journal that had been bothering him. In a general way, Giddy's reasoning was sound. If a freight train, or even a passenger train, had been coming up behind them, he could have heard it in time. But as it happened, a light engine, which made no noise at all, was coming, —ordered out to help with the freight that was piling up at the other end of the division. This engine got no warning, came round the curve, struck the caboose, went straight through it, and crashed into the heavy lumber car ahead.

The Kronborgs were just sitting down to breakfast, when the night telegraph operator dashed into the yard at a run and hammered on the front door. Gunner answered the knock, and the telegraph operator told him he wanted to see his father a minute, quick. Mr. Kronborg appeared at the door, napkin in hand. The operator was pale and panting.

"Fourteen was wrecked down at Saxony this morning," he shouted, "and Kennedy's all broke up. We're sending an engine down with the doctor, and the operator at Saxony says Kennedy wants you to come along with us and bring your girl." He stopped for breath.

Mr. Kronborg took off his glasses and began rubbing them with his napkin.

"Bring—I don't understand," he muttered. "How did this happen?"

"No time for that, sir. Getting the engine out now. Your girl, Thea. You'll surely do that for the poor chap. Everybody knows he thinks the world of her." Seeing that Mr. Kronborg showed no indication of having made up his mind, the operator turned to Gunner. "Call your sister, kid. I'm going to ask the girl herself," he blurted out.

"Yes, yes, certainly. Daughter," Mr. Kronborg called. He had somewhat recovered himself and reached to the hall hatrack for his hat.

Just as Thea came out on the front porch, before the operator had had time to explain to her, Dr. Archie's ponies came up to the gate at a brisk trot. Archie jumped out the moment his driver stopped the team and came up to the bewildered girl without so much as saying good-morning to any one. He took her hand with the sympathetic, reassuring graveness which had helped her at more than one hard time in her life. "Get your hat, my girl. Kennedy's hurt down the road, and he wants you to run down with me. They'll have a car for us. Get into my buggy, Mr. Kronborg. I'll drive you down, and Larry can come for the team."

The driver jumped out of the buggy and Mr. Kronborg and the doctor got in. Thea, still bewildered, sat on her father's knee. Dr. Archie gave his ponies a smart cut with the whip.

When they reached the depot, the engine, with one car attached, was standing on the main track. The engineer had got his steam up, and was leaning out of the cab impatiently. In a moment they were off. The run to Saxony took forty minutes. Thea sat still in her seat while Dr. Archie and her father talked about the wreck. She took no part in the conversation and asked no questions, but occasionally she looked at Dr. Archie with a frightened, inquiring glance, which he answered by an encouraging nod. Neither he nor her father said anything about how badly Ray was hurt. When the engine stopped near Saxony, the main track was already cleared. As they got out of the car, Dr. Archie pointed to a pile of ties.

"Thea, you'd better sit down here and watch the wreck crew while your father and I go up and look Kennedy over. I'll come back for you when I get him fixed up."

The two men went off up the sand gulch, and Thea sat down and looked at the pile of splintered wood and twisted iron that had lately been Ray's caboose. She was frightened and absent-minded. She felt that she ought to be thinking about Ray, but her mind kept racing off to all sorts of trivial and irrelevant things. She wondered whether Grace Johnson would be furious when she came to take her music lesson and found nobody there to give it to her; whether she had forgotten to close the piano last night and whether Thor would get into the new room and mess the keys all up with his sticky fingers; whether Tillie would go upstairs and make her bed for her. Her mind worked fast, but she could fix it upon nothing. The grasshoppers, the lizards, distracted her attention and seemed more real to her than poor Ray.

On their way to the sand bank where Ray had been carried, Dr. Archie and Mr. Kronborg met the Saxony doctor. He shook hands with them.

"Nothing you can do, doctor. I couldn't count the fractures. His back's broken, too. He wouldn't be alive now if he weren't so confoundedly strong, poor chap. No use bothering him. I've given him morphia, one and a half, in eighths."

Dr. Archie hurried on. Ray was lying on a flat canvas litter, under the shelter of a shelving bank, lightly shaded by a slender cottonwood tree. When the doctor and the preacher approached, he looked at them intently.

"Didn't—" he closed his eyes to hide his bitter disappointment.

Dr. Archie knew what was the matter. "Thea's back there, Ray. I'll bring her as soon as I've had a look at you."

Ray looked up. "You might clean me up a trifle, doc. Won't need you for anything else, thank you all the same."

However little there was left of him, that little was certainly Ray Kennedy. His personality was as positive as ever, and the blood and dirt on his face seemed merely accidental, to have nothing to do with the man himself. Dr. Archie told Mr. Kronborg to bring a pail of water, and he began to sponge Ray's face and neck. Mr. Kronborg stood by, nervously rubbing his hands together and trying to think of something to say. Serious situations always embarrassed him and made him formal, even when he felt real sympathy.

"In times like this, Ray," he brought out at last, crumpling up his handkerchief in his long fingers,—"in times like this, we don't want to forget the Friend that sticketh closer than a brother."

Ray looked up at him; a lonely, disconsolate smile played over his mouth and his square cheeks. "Never mind about all that, PADRE," he said quietly. "Christ and me fell out long ago."

There was a moment of silence. Then Ray took pity on Mr. Kronborg's embarrassment. "You go back for the little girl, PADRE. I want a word with the doc in private."

Ray talked to Dr. Archie for a few moments, then stopped suddenly, with a broad smile. Over the doctor's shoulder he saw Thea coming up the gulch, in her pink chambray dress, carrying her sun-hat by the strings. Such a yellow head! He often told himself that he "was perfectly foolish about her hair." The sight of her, coming, went through him softly, like the morphia. "There she is," he whispered. "Get the old preacher out of the way, doc. I want to have a little talk with her."

Dr. Archie looked up. Thea was hurrying and yet hanging back. She was more frightened than he had thought she would be. She had gone with him to see very sick people and had always been steady and calm. As she came up, she looked at the ground, and he could see that she had been crying.

Ray Kennedy made an unsuccessful effort to put out his hand. "Hello, little kid, nothing to be afraid of. Darned if I don't believe they've gone and scared you! Nothing to cry about. I'm the same old goods, only a little dented. Sit down on my coat there, and keep me company. I've got to lay still a bit."

Dr. Archie and Mr. Kronborg disappeared. Thea cast a timid glance after them, but she sat down resolutely and took Ray's hand.

"You ain't scared now, are you?" he asked affectionately. "You were a regular brick to come, Thee. Did you get any breakfast?"

"No, Ray, I'm not scared. Only I'm dreadful sorry you're hurt, and I can't help crying."

His broad, earnest face, languid from the opium and smiling with such simple happiness, reassured her. She drew nearer to him and lifted his hand to her knee. He looked at her with his clear, shallow blue eyes. How he loved everything about that face and head! How many nights in his cupola, looking up the track, he had seen that face in the darkness; through the sleet and snow, or in the soft blue air when the moonlight slept on the desert.

"You needn't bother to talk, Thee. The doctor's medicine makes me sort of dopey. But it's nice to have company. Kind of cozy, don't you think? Pull my coat under you more. It's a darned shame I can't wait on you."

"No, no, Ray. I'm all right. Yes, I like it here. And I guess you ought not to talk much, ought you? If you can sleep, I'll stay right here, and be awful quiet. I feel just as much at home with you as ever, now."

That simple, humble, faithful something in Ray's eyes went straight to Thea's heart. She did feel comfortable with him, and happy to give him so much happiness. It was the first time she had ever been conscious of that power to bestow intense happiness by simply being near any one. She always remembered this day as the beginning of that knowledge. She bent over him and put her lips softly to his cheek.

Ray's eyes filled with light. "Oh, do that again, kid!" he said impulsively. Thea kissed him on the forehead, blushing faintly. Ray held her hand fast and closed his eyes with a deep sigh of happiness. The morphia and the sense of her nearness filled him with content. The gold mine, the oil well, the copper ledge—all pipe dreams, he mused, and this was a dream, too. He might have known it before. It had always been like that; the things he admired had always been away out of his reach: a college education, a gentleman's manner, an Englishman's accent—things over his head. And Thea was farther out of his reach than all the rest put together. He had been a fool to imagine it, but he was glad he had been a fool. She had given him one grand dream. Every mile of his run, from Moonstone to Denver, was painted with the colors of that hope. Every cactus knew about it. But now that it was not to be, he knew the truth. Thea was never meant for any rough fellow like him—hadn't he really known that all along, he asked himself? She wasn't meant for common men. She was like wedding cake, a thing to dream on. He raised his eyelids a little. She was stroking his hand and looking off into the distance. He felt in her face that look of unconscious power that Wunsch had seen there. Yes, she was bound for the big terminals of the world; no way stations for her. His lids drooped. In the dark he could see her as she would be after a while; in a box at the Tabor Grand in Denver, with diamonds on her neck and a tiara in her yellow hair, with all the people looking at her through their opera-glasses, and a United States Senator, maybe, talking to her. "Then you'll remember me!" He opened his eyes, and they were full of tears.

Thea leaned closer. "What did you say, Ray? I couldn't hear."

"Then you'll remember me," he whispered.

The spark in his eye, which is one's very self, caught the spark in hers that was herself, and for a moment they looked into each other's natures. Thea realized how good and how great-hearted he was, and he realized about her many things. When that elusive spark of personality retreated in each of them, Thea still saw in his wet eyes her own face, very small, but much prettier than the cracked glass at home had ever shown it. It was the first time she had seen her face in that kindest mirror a woman can ever find.

Ray had felt things in that moment when he seemed to be looking into the very soul of Thea Kronborg. Yes, the gold mine, the oil well, the copper ledge, they'd all got away from him, as things will; but he'd backed a winner once in his life! With all his might he gave his faith to the broad little hand he held. He wished he could leave her the rugged strength of his body to help her through with it all. He would have liked to tell her a little about his old dream,—there seemed long years between him and it already,—but to tell her now would somehow be unfair; wouldn't be quite the straightest thing in the world. Probably she knew, anyway. He looked up quickly. "You know, don't you, Thee, that I think you are just the finest thing I've struck in this world?"

The tears ran down Thea's cheeks. "You're too good to me, Ray. You're a lot too good to me," she faltered.

"Why, kid," he murmured, "everybody in this world's going to be good to you!"

Dr. Archie came to the gulch and stood over his patient. "How's it going?"

"Can't you give me another punch with your pacifier, doc? The little girl had better run along now." Ray released Thea's hand. "See you later, Thee."

She got up and moved away aimlessly, carrying her hat by the strings. Ray looked after her with the exaltation born of bodily pain and said between his teeth, "Always look after that girl, doc. She's a queen!"

Thea and her father went back to Moonstone on the one-o'clock passenger. Dr. Archie stayed with Ray Kennedy until he died, late in the afternoon.

XX.

On Monday morning, the day after Ray Kennedy's funeral, Dr. Archie called at Mr. Kronborg's study, a little room behind the church. Mr. Kronborg did not write out his sermons, but spoke from notes jotted upon small pieces of cardboard in a kind of shorthand of his own. As sermons go, they were not worse than most. His conventional rhetoric pleased the majority of his congregation, and Mr. Kronborg was generally regarded as a model preacher. He did not smoke, he never touched spirits. His indulgence in the pleasures of the table was an endearing bond between him and the women of his congregation. He ate enormously, with a zest which seemed incongruous with his spare frame.

This morning the doctor found him opening his mail and reading a pile of advertising circulars with deep attention.

"Good-morning, Mr. Kronborg," said Dr. Archie, sitting down. "I came to see you on business. Poor Kennedy asked me to look after his affairs for him. Like most railroad men he spent his wages, except for a few investments in mines which don't look to me very promising. But his life was insured for six hundred dollars in Thea's favor."

Mr. Kronborg wound his feet about the standard of his desk-chair. "I assure you, doctor, this is a complete surprise to me."

"Well, it's not very surprising to me," Dr. Archie went on. "He talked to me about it the day he was hurt. He said he wanted the money to be used in a particular way, and in no other." Dr. Archie paused meaningly.

Mr. Kronborg fidgeted. "I am sure Thea would observe his wishes in every respect."

"No doubt; but he wanted me to see that you agreed to his plan. It seems that for some time Thea has wanted to go away to study music. It was Kennedy's wish that she should take this money and go to Chicago this winter. He felt that it would be an advantage to her in a business way: that even if she came back here to teach, it would give her more authority and make her position here more comfortable."

Mr. Kronborg looked a little startled. "She is very young," he hesitated; "she is barely seventeen. Chicago is a long way from home. We would have to consider. I think, Dr. Archie, we had better consult Mrs. Kronborg."

"I think I can bring Mrs. Kronborg around, if I have your consent. I've always found her pretty level-headed. I have several old classmates practicing in Chicago. One is a throat specialist. He has a good deal to do with singers. He probably knows the best piano teachers and could recommend a boarding-house where music students stay. I think Thea needs to get among a lot of young people who are clever like herself. Here she has no companions but old fellows like me. It's not a natural life for a young girl. She'll either get warped, or wither up before her time. If it will make you and Mrs. Kronborg feel any easier, I'll be glad to take Thea to Chicago and see that she gets started right. This throat man I speak of is a big fellow in his line, and if I can get him interested, he may be able to put her in the way of a good many things. At any rate, he'll know the right teachers. Of course, six hundred dollars won't take her very far, but even half the winter there would be a great advantage. I think Kennedy sized the situation up exactly."

"Perhaps; I don't doubt it. You are very kind, Dr. Archie." Mr. Kronborg was ornamenting his desk-blotter with hieroglyphics. "I should think Denver might be better. There we could watch over her. She is very young."

Dr. Archie rose. "Kennedy didn't mention Denver. He said Chicago, repeatedly. Under the circumstances, it seems to me we ought to try to carry out his wishes exactly, if Thea is willing."

"Certainly, certainly. Thea is conscientious. She would not waste her opportunities." Mr. Kronborg paused. "If Thea were your own daughter, doctor, would you consent to such a plan, at her present age?"

"I most certainly should. In fact, if she were my daughter, I'd have sent her away before this. She's a most unusual child, and she's only wasting herself here. At her age she ought to be learning, not teaching. She'll never learn so quickly and easily as she will right now."

"Well, doctor, you had better talk it over with Mrs. Kronborg. I make it a point to defer to her wishes in such matters. She understands all her children perfectly. I may say that she has all a mother's insight, and more."

Dr. Archie smiled. "Yes, and then some. I feel quite confident about Mrs. Kronborg. We usually agree. Good-morning."

Dr. Archie stepped out into the hot sunshine and walked rapidly toward his office, with a determined look on his face. He found his waiting-room full of patients, and it was one o'clock before he had dismissed the last one. Then he shut his door and took a drink before going over to the hotel for his lunch. He smiled as he locked his cupboard. "I feel almost as gay as if I were going to get away for a winter myself," he thought.

Afterward Thea could never remember much about that summer, or how she lived through her impatience. She was to set off with Dr. Archie on the fifteenth of October, and she gave lessons until the first of September. Then she began to get her clothes ready, and spent whole afternoons in the village dressmaker's stuffy, littered little sewing-room. Thea and her mother made a trip to Denver to buy the materials for her dresses. Ready-made clothes for girls were not to be had in those days. Miss Spencer, the dressmaker, declared that she could do handsomely by Thea if they would only let her carry out her own ideas. But Mrs. Kronborg and Thea felt that Miss Spencer's most daring productions might seem out of place in Chicago, so they restrained her with a firm hand. Tillie, who always helped Mrs. Kronborg with the family sewing, was for letting Miss Spencer challenge Chicago on Thea's person. Since Ray Kennedy's death, Thea had become more than ever one of Tillie's heroines. Tillie swore each of her friends to secrecy, and, coming home from church or leaning over the fence, told them the most touching stories about Ray's devotion, and how Thea would "never get over it."

Tillie's confidences stimulated the general discussion of Thea's venture. This discussion went on, upon front porches and in back yards, pretty much all summer. Some people approved of Thea's going to Chicago, but most people did not. There were others who changed their minds about it every day.

Tillie said she wanted Thea to have a ball dress "above all things." She bought a fashion book especially devoted to evening clothes and looked hungrily over the colored plates, picking out costumes that would be becoming to "a blonde." She wanted Thea to have all the gay clothes she herself had always longed for; clothes she often told herself she needed "to recite in."

"Tillie," Thea used to cry impatiently, "can't you see that if Miss Spencer tried to make one of those things, she'd make me look like a circus girl? Anyhow, I don't know anybody in Chicago. I won't be going to parties."

Tillie always replied with a knowing toss of her head, "You see! You'll be in society before you know it. There ain't many girls as accomplished as you."

On the morning of the fifteenth of October the Kronborg family, all of them but Gus, who couldn't leave the store, started for the station an hour before train time. Charley had taken Thea's trunk and telescope to the depot in his delivery wagon early that morning. Thea wore her new blue serge traveling-dress, chosen for its serviceable qualities. She had done her hair up carefully, and had put a pale-blue ribbon around her throat, under a little lace collar that Mrs. Kohler had crocheted for her. As they went out of the gate, Mrs. Kronborg looked her over thoughtfully. Yes, that blue ribbon went very well with the dress, and with Thea's eyes. Thea had a rather unusual touch about such things, she reflected comfortably. Tillie always said that Thea was "so indifferent to dress," but her mother noticed that she usually put her clothes on well. She felt the more at ease about letting Thea go away from home, because she had good sense about her clothes and never tried to dress up too much. Her coloring was so individual, she was so unusually fair, that in the wrong clothes she might easily have been "conspicuous."

It was a fine morning, and the family set out from the house in good spirits. Thea was quiet and calm. She had forgotten nothing, and she clung tightly to her handbag, which held her trunk-key and all of her money that was not in an envelope pinned to her chemise. Thea walked behind the others, holding Thor by the hand, and this time she did not feel that the procession was too long. Thor was uncommunicative that morning, and would only talk about how he would rather get a sand bur in his toe every day than wear shoes and stockings. As they passed the cottonwood grove where Thea often used to bring him in his cart, she asked him who would take him for nice long walks after sister went away.

"Oh, I can walk in our yard," he replied unappreciatively. "I guess I can make a pond for my duck."

Thea leaned down and looked into his face. "But you won't forget about sister, will you?" Thor shook his head. "And won't you be glad when sister comes back and can take you over to Mrs. Kohler's to see the pigeons?"

"Yes, I'll be glad. But I'm going to have a pigeon my own self."

"But you haven't got any little house for one. Maybe Axel would make you a little house."

"Oh, her can live in the barn, her can," Thor drawled indifferently.

Thea laughed and squeezed his hand. She always liked his sturdy matter-of-factness. Boys ought to be like that, she thought.

When they reached the depot, Mr. Kronborg paced the platform somewhat ceremoniously with his daughter. Any member of his flock would have gathered that he was giving her good counsel about meeting the temptations of the world. He did, indeed, begin to admonish her not to forget that talents come from our Heavenly Father and are to be used for his glory, but he cut his remarks short and looked at his watch. He believed that Thea was a religious girl, but when she looked at him with that intent, that passionately inquiring gaze which used to move even Wunsch, Mr. Kronborg suddenly felt his eloquence fail. Thea was like her mother, he reflected; you couldn't put much sentiment across with her. As a usual thing, he liked girls to be a little more responsive. He liked them to blush at his compliments; as Mrs. Kronborg candidly said, "Father could be very soft with the girls." But this morning he was thinking that hard-headedness was a reassuring quality in a daughter who was going to Chicago alone.

Mr. Kronborg believed that big cities were places where people went to lose their identity and to be wicked. He himself, when he was a student at the Seminary—he coughed and opened his watch again. He knew, of course, that a great deal of business went on in Chicago, that there was an active Board of Trade, and that hogs and cattle were slaughtered there. But when, as a young man, he had stopped over in Chicago, he had not interested himself in the commercial activities of the city. He remembered it as a place full of cheap shows and dance halls and boys from the country who were behaving disgustingly.

Dr. Archie drove up to the station about ten minutes before the train was due. His man tied the ponies and stood holding the doctor's alligator-skin bag—very elegant, Thea thought it. Mrs. Kronborg did not burden the doctor with warnings and cautions. She said again that she hoped he could get Thea a comfortable place to stay, where they had good beds, and she hoped the landlady would be a woman who'd had children of her own. "I don't go much on old maids looking after girls," she remarked as she took a pin out of her own hat and thrust it into Thea's blue turban. "You'll be sure to lose your hatpins on the train, Thea. It's better to have an extra one in case." She tucked in a little curl that had escaped from Thea's careful twist. "Don't forget to brush your dress often, and pin it up to the curtains of your berth to-night, so it won't wrinkle. If you get it wet, have a tailor press it before it draws."

She turned Thea about by the shoulders and looked her over a last time. Yes, she looked very well. She wasn't pretty, exactly,—her face was too broad and her nose was too big. But she had that lovely skin, and she looked fresh and sweet. She had always been a sweet-smelling child. Her mother had always liked to kiss her, when she happened to think of it.

The train whistled in, and Mr. Kronborg carried the canvas "telescope" into the car. Thea kissed them all good-bye. Tillie cried, but she was the only one who did. They all shouted things up at the closed window of the Pullman car, from which Thea looked down at them as from a frame, her face glowing with excitement, her turban a little tilted in spite of three hatpins. She had already taken off her new gloves to save them. Mrs. Kronborg reflected that she would never see just that same picture again, and as Thea's car slid off along the rails, she wiped a tear from her eye. "She won't come back a little girl," Mrs. Kronborg said to her husband as they turned to go home. "Anyhow, she's been a sweet one."

While the Kronborg family were trooping slowly homeward, Thea was sitting in the Pullman, her telescope in the seat beside her, her handbag tightly gripped in her fingers. Dr. Archie had gone into the smoker. He thought she might be a little tearful, and that it would be kinder to leave her alone for a while. Her eyes did fill once, when she saw the last of the sand hills and realized that she was going to leave them behind for a long while. They always made her think of Ray, too. She had had such good times with him out there.

But, of course, it was herself and her own adventure that mattered to her. If youth did not matter so much to itself, it would never have the heart to go on. Thea was surprised that she did not feel a deeper sense of loss at leaving her old life behind her. It seemed, on the contrary, as she looked out at the yellow desert speeding by, that she had left very little. Everything that was essential seemed to be right there in the car with her. She lacked nothing. She even felt more compact and confident than usual. She was all there, and something else was there, too,—in her heart, was it, or under her cheek? Anyhow, it was about her somewhere, that warm sureness, that sturdy little companion with whom she shared a secret.

When Dr. Archie came in from the smoker, she was sitting still, looking intently out of the window and smiling, her lips a little parted, her hair in a blaze of sunshine. The doctor thought she was the prettiest thing he had ever seen, and very funny, with her telescope and big handbag. She made him feel jolly, and a little mournful, too. He knew that the splendid things of life are few, after all, and so very easy to miss.

2

THE SONG OF THE LARK

I.

THEA AND DR. ARCHIE had been gone from Moonstone four days. On the afternoon of the nineteenth of October they were in a street-car, riding through the depressing, unkept wastes of North Chicago, on their way to call upon the Reverend Lars Larsen, a friend to whom Mr. Kronborg had written. Thea was still staying at the rooms of the Young Women's Christian Association, and was miserable and homesick there. The housekeeper watched her in a way that made her uncomfortable. Things had not gone very well, so far. The noise and confusion of a big city tired and disheartened her. She had not had her trunk sent to the Christian Association rooms because she did not want to double cartage charges, and now she was running up a bill for storage on it. The contents of her gray telescope were becoming untidy, and it seemed impossible to keep one's face and hands clean in Chicago. She felt as if she were still on the train, traveling without enough clothes to keep clean. She wanted another nightgown, and it did not occur to her that she could buy one. There were other clothes in her trunk that she needed very much, and she seemed no nearer a place to stay than when she arrived in the rain, on that first disillusioning morning.

Dr. Archie had gone at once to his friend Hartley Evans, the throat specialist, and had asked him to tell him of a good piano teacher and direct him to a good boarding-house. Dr. Evans said he could easily tell him who was the best piano teacher in Chicago, but that most students' boarding-houses were "abominable places, where girls got poor food for body and mind." He gave Dr. Archie several addresses, however, and the doctor went to look the places over. He left Thea in her room, for she seemed tired and was not at all like herself. His inspection of boardinghouses was not encouraging. The only place that seemed to him at all desirable was full, and the mistress of the house could not give Thea a room in which she could have a piano. She said Thea might use the piano in her parlor; but when Dr. Archie went to look at the parlor he found a girl talking to a young man on one of the corner sofas. Learning that the boarders received all their callers there, he gave up that house, too, as hopeless.

So when they set out to make the acquaintance of Mr. Larsen on the afternoon he had appointed, the question of a lodging was still undecided. The Swedish Reform Church was in a sloughy, weedy district, near a group of factories. The church itself was a very neat little building. The parsonage, next door, looked clean and comfortable, and there was a well-kept yard about it, with a picket fence. Thea saw several little children playing under a swing, and wondered why ministers always had so many. When they rang at the parsonage door, a capable-looking Swedish servant girl answered the bell and told them that Mr. Larsen's study was in the church, and that he was waiting for them there.

Mr. Larsen received them very cordially. The furniture in his study was so new and the pictures were so heavily framed, that Thea thought it looked more like the waiting-room of the fashionable Denver dentist to whom Dr. Archie had taken her that summer, than like a preacher's study. There were even flowers in a glass vase on the desk. Mr. Larsen was a small, plump man, with a short, yellow beard, very white teeth, and a little turned-up nose on which he wore gold-rimmed eye-glasses. He looked about thirty-five, but he was growing bald, and his thin, hair was parted above his left ear and brought up over the bare spot on the top of his head. He looked cheerful and agreeable. He wore a blue coat and no cuffs.

After Dr. Archie and Thea sat down on a slippery leather couch, the minister asked for an outline of Thea's plans. Dr. Archie explained that she meant to study piano with Andor Harsanyi; that they had already seen him, that Thea had played for him and he said he would be glad to teach her.

Mr. Larsen lifted his pale eyebrows and rubbed his plump white hands together. "But he is a concert pianist already. He will be very expensive."

"That's why Miss Kronborg wants to get a church position if possible. She has not money enough to see her through the winter. There's no use her coming all the way from Colorado and studying with a second-rate teacher. My friends here tell me Harsanyi is the best."

"Oh, very likely! I have heard him play with Thomas. You Western people do things on a big scale. There are half a dozen teachers that I should think—However, you know what you want." Mr. Larsen showed his contempt for such extravagant standards by a shrug. He felt that Dr. Archie was trying to impress him. He had succeeded, indeed, in bringing out the doctor's stiffest manner. Mr. Larsen went on to explain that he managed the music in his church himself, and drilled his choir, though the tenor was the official choirmaster. Unfortunately there were no vacancies in his choir just now. He had his four voices, very good ones. He looked away from Dr. Archie and glanced at Thea. She looked troubled, even a little frightened when he said this, and drew in her lower lip. She, certainly, was not pretentious, if her protector was. He continued to study her. She was sitting on the lounge, her knees far apart, her gloved hands lying stiffly in her lap, like a country girl. Her turban, which seemed a little too big for her, had got tilted in the wind,—it was always windy in that part of Chicago,—and she looked tired. She wore no veil, and her hair, too, was the worse for the wind and dust. When he said he had all the voices he required, he noticed that her gloved hands shut tightly. Mr. Larsen reflected that she was not, after all, responsible for the lofty manner of her father's physician; that she was not even responsible for her father, whom he remembered as a tiresome fellow. As he watched her tired, worried face, he felt sorry for her.

"All the same, I would like to try your voice," he said, turning pointedly away from her companion. "I am interested in voices. Can you sing to the violin?"

"I guess so," Thea replied dully. "I don't know. I never tried."

Mr. Larsen took his violin out of the case and began to tighten the keys. "We might go into the lecture-room and see how it goes. I can't tell much about a voice by the organ. The violin is really the proper instrument to try a voice." He opened a door at the back of his study, pushed Thea gently through it, and looking over his shoulder to Dr. Archie said, "Excuse us, sir. We will be back soon."

Dr. Archie chuckled. All preachers were alike, officious and on their dignity; liked to deal with women and girls, but not with men. He took up a thin volume from the minister's desk. To his amusement it proved to be a book of "Devotional and Kindred Poems; by Mrs. Aurelia S. Larsen." He looked them over, thinking that the world changed very little. He could remember when the wife of his father's minister had published a volume of verses, which all the church members had to buy and all the children were encouraged to read. His grandfather had made a face at the book and said, "Puir body!" Both ladies seemed to have chosen the same subjects, too: Jephthah's Daughter, Rizpah, David's Lament for Absalom, etc. The doctor found the book very amusing.

The Reverend Lars Larsen was a reactionary Swede. His father came to Iowa in the sixties, married a Swedish girl who was ambitious, like himself, and they moved to Kansas and took up land under the Homestead Act. After that, they bought land and leased it from the Government, acquired land in every possible way. They worked like horses, both of them; indeed, they would never have used any horse-flesh they owned as they used themselves. They reared a large family and worked their sons and daughters as mercilessly as they worked themselves; all of them but Lars. Lars was the fourth son, and he was born lazy. He seemed to bear the mark of overstrain on the part of his parents. Even in his cradle he was an example of physical inertia; anything to lie still. When he was a growing boy his mother had to drag him out of bed every morning, and he had to be driven to his chores. At school he had a model "attendance record," because he found getting his lessons easier than farm work. He was the only one of the family who went through the high school, and by the time he graduated he had already made up his mind to study for the ministry, because it seemed to him the least laborious of all callings. In so far as he could see, it was the only business in which there was practically no competition, in which a man was not all the time pitted against other men who were willing to work themselves to death. His father stubbornly opposed Lars's plan, but after keeping the boy at home for a year and finding how useless he was on the farm, he sent him to a theological seminary—as much to conceal his laziness from the neighbors as because he did not know what else to do with him.

Larsen, like Peter Kronborg, got on well in the ministry, because he got on well with the women. His English was no worse than that of most young preachers of American parentage, and he made the most of his skill with the violin. He was supposed to exert a very desirable influence over young people and to stimulate their interest in church work. He married an American girl, and when his father died he got his share of the property—which was very considerable. He invested his money carefully and was that rare thing, a preacher of independent means. His white, well-kept hands were his result,—the evidence that he had worked out his life successfully in the way that pleased him. His Kansas brothers hated the sight of his hands.

Larsen liked all the softer things of life,—in so far as he knew about them. He slept late in the morning, was fussy about his food, and read a great many novels, preferring sentimental ones. He did not smoke, but he ate a great deal of candy "for his throat," and always kept a box of chocolate drops in the upper right-hand drawer of his desk. He always bought season tickets for the symphony concerts, and he played his violin for women's culture clubs. He did not wear cuffs, except on Sunday, because he believed that a free wrist facilitated his violin practice. When he drilled his choir he always held his hand with the little and index fingers curved higher than the other two, like a noted German conductor he had seen. On the whole, the Reverend Larsen was not an insincere man; he merely spent his life resting and playing, to make up for the time his forebears had wasted grubbing in the earth. He was simple-hearted and kind; he enjoyed his candy and his children and his sacred cantatas. He could work energetically at almost any form of play.

Dr. Archie was deep in "The Lament of Mary Magdalen," when Mr. Larsen and Thea came back to the study. From the minister's expression he judged that Thea had succeeded in interesting him.

Mr. Larsen seemed to have forgotten his hostility toward him, and addressed him frankly as soon as he entered. He stood holding his violin, and as Thea sat down he pointed to her with his bow:—

"I have just been telling Miss Kronborg that though I cannot promise her anything permanent, I might give her something for the next few months. My soprano is a young married woman and is temporarily indisposed. She would be glad to be excused from her duties for a while. I like Miss Kronborg's singing very much, and I think she would benefit by the instruction in my choir. Singing here might very well lead to something else. We pay our soprano only eight dollars a Sunday, but she always gets ten dollars for singing at funerals. Miss Kronborg has a sympathetic voice, and I think there would be a good deal of demand for her at funerals. Several American churches apply to me for a soloist on such occasions, and I could help her to pick up quite a little money that way."

This sounded lugubrious to Dr. Archie, who had a physician's dislike of funerals, but he tried to accept the suggestion cordially.

"Miss Kronborg tells me she is having some trouble getting located," Mr. Larsen went on with animation, still holding his violin. "I would advise her to keep away from boarding-houses altogether. Among my parishioners there are two German women, a mother and daughter. The daughter is a Swede by marriage, and clings to the Swedish Church. They live near here, and they rent some of their rooms. They have now a large room vacant, and have asked me to recommend some one. They have never taken boarders, but Mrs. Lorch, the mother, is a good cook,—at least, I am always glad to take supper with her,—and I think I could persuade her to let this young woman partake of the family table. The daughter, Mrs. Andersen, is musical, too, and sings in the Mozart Society. I think they might like to have a music student in the house. You speak German, I suppose?" he turned to Thea.

"Oh, no; a few words. I don't know the grammar," she murmured.

Dr. Archie noticed that her eyes looked alive again, not frozen as they had looked all morning. "If this fellow can help her, it's not for me to be stand-offish," he said to himself.

"Do you think you would like to stay in such a quiet place, with old-fashioned people?" Mr. Larsen asked. "I shouldn't think you could find a better place to work, if that's what you want."

"I think mother would like to have me with people like that," Thea replied. "And I'd be glad to settle down most anywhere. I'm losing time."

"Very well, there's no time like the present. Let us go to see Mrs. Lorch and Mrs. Andersen."

The minister put his violin in its case and caught up a black-and-white checked traveling-cap that he wore when he rode his high Columbia wheel. The three left the church together.

II.

So Thea did not go to a boarding-house after all. When Dr. Archie left Chicago she was comfortably settled with Mrs. Lorch, and her happy reunion with her trunk somewhat consoled her for his departure.

Mrs. Lorch and her daughter lived half a mile from the Swedish Reform Church, in an old square frame house, with a porch supported by frail pillars, set in a damp yard full of big lilac bushes. The house, which had been left over from country times, needed paint badly, and looked gloomy and despondent among its smart Queen Anne neighbors. There was a big back yard with two rows of apple trees and a grape arbor, and a warped walk, two planks wide, which led to the coal bins at the back of the lot. Thea's room was on the second floor, overlooking this back yard, and she understood that in the winter she must carry up her own coal and kindling from the bin. There was no furnace in the house, no running water except in the kitchen, and that was why the room rent was small. All the rooms were heated by stoves, and the lodgers pumped the water they needed from the cistern under the porch, or from the well at the entrance of the grape arbor. Old Mrs. Lorch could never bring herself to have costly improvements made in her house; indeed she had very little money. She preferred to keep the house just as her husband built it, and she thought her way of living good enough for plain people.

Thea's room was large enough to admit a rented upright piano without crowding. It was, the widowed daughter said, "a double room that had always before been occupied by two gentlemen"; the piano now took the place of a second occupant. There was an ingrain carpet on the floor, green ivy leaves on a red ground, and clumsy, old-fashioned walnut furniture. The bed was very wide, and the mattress thin and hard. Over the fat pillows were "shams" embroidered in Turkey red, each with a flowering scroll—one with "Gute' Nacht," the other with "Guten Morgen." The dresser was so big that Thea wondered how it had ever been got into the house and up the narrow stairs. Besides an old horsehair armchair, there were two low plush "spring-rockers," against the massive pedestals of which one was always stumbling in the dark. Thea sat in the dark a good deal those first weeks, and sometimes a painful bump against one of those brutally immovable pedestals roused her temper and pulled her out of a heavy hour. The wall-paper was brownish yellow, with blue flowers. When it was put on, the carpet, certainly, had not been consulted. There was only one picture on the wall when Thea moved in: a large colored print of a brightly lighted church in a snow-storm, on Christmas Eve, with greens hanging about the stone doorway and arched windows. There was something warm and home, like about this picture, and Thea grew fond of it. One day, on her way into town to take her lesson, she stopped at a bookstore and bought a photograph of the Naples bust of Julius Caesar. This she had framed, and hung it on the big bare wall behind her stove. It was a curious choice, but she was at the age when people do inexplicable things. She had been interested in Caesar's "Commentaries" when she left school to begin teaching, and she loved to read about great generals; but these facts would scarcely explain her wanting that grim bald head to share her daily existence. It seemed a strange freak, when she bought so few things, and when she had, as Mrs. Andersen said to Mrs. Lorch, "no pictures of the composers at all."

Both the widows were kind to her, but Thea liked the mother better. Old Mrs. Lorch was fat and jolly, with a red face, always shining as if she had just come from the stove, bright little eyes, and hair of several colors. Her own hair was one cast of iron-gray, her switch another, and her false front still another. Her clothes always smelled of savory cooking, except when she was dressed for church or KAFFEEKLATSCH, and then she smelled of bay rum or of the lemon-verbena sprig which she tucked inside her puffy black kid glove. Her cooking justified all that Mr. Larsen had said of it, and Thea had never been so well nourished before.

The daughter, Mrs. Andersen,—Irene, her mother called her,—was a different sort of woman altogether. She was perhaps forty years old, angular, big-boned, with large, thin features, light-blue eyes, and dry, yellow hair, the bang tightly frizzed. She was pale, anaemic, and sentimental. She had married the youngest son of a rich, arrogant Swedish family who were lumber merchants in St. Paul. There she dwelt during her married life. Oscar Andersen was a strong, full-blooded fellow who had counted on a long life and had been rather careless about his business affairs. He was killed by the explosion of a steam boiler in the mills, and his brothers managed to prove that he had very little stock in the big business. They had strongly disapproved of his marriage and they agreed among themselves that they were entirely justified in defrauding his widow, who, they said, "would only marry again and give some fellow a good thing of it." Mrs. Andersen would not go to law with the family that had always snubbed and wounded her—she felt the humiliation of being thrust out more than she felt her impoverishment; so she went back to Chicago to live with her widowed mother on an income of five hundred a year. This experience had given her sentimental nature an incurable hurt. Something withered away in her. Her head had a downward droop; her step was soft and apologetic, even in her mother's house, and her smile had the sickly, uncertain flicker that so often comes from a secret humiliation. She was affable and yet shrinking, like one who has come down in the world, who has known better clothes, better carpets, better people, brighter hopes. Her husband was buried in the Andersen lot in St. Paul, with a locked iron fence around it. She had to go to his eldest brother for the key when she went to say good-bye to his grave. She clung to the Swedish Church because it had been her husband's church.

As her mother had no room for her household belongings, Mrs. Andersen had brought home with her only her bedroom set, which now furnished her own room at Mrs. Lorch's. There she spent most of her time, doing fancywork or writing letters to sympathizing German friends in St. Paul, surrounded by keepsakes and photographs of the burly Oscar Andersen. Thea, when she was admitted to this room, and shown these photographs, found herself wondering, like the Andersen family, why such a lusty, gay-looking fellow ever thought he wanted this pallid, long-cheeked woman, whose manner was always that of withdrawing, and who must have been rather thin-blooded even as a girl.

Mrs. Andersen was certainly a depressing person. It sometimes annoyed Thea very much to hear her insinuating knock on the door, her flurried explanation of why she had come, as she backed toward the stairs. Mrs. Andersen admired Thea greatly. She thought it a distinction to be even a "temporary soprano"—Thea called herself so quite seriously—in the Swedish Church. She also thought it distinguished to be a pupil of Harsanyi's. She considered Thea very handsome, very Swedish, very talented. She fluttered about the upper floor when Thea was practicing. In short, she tried to make a heroine of her, just as Tillie Kronborg had always done, and Thea was conscious of something of the sort. When she was working and heard Mrs. Andersen tip-toeing past her door, she used to shrug her shoulders and wonder whether she was always to have a Tillie diving furtively about her in some disguise or other.

At the dressmaker's Mrs. Andersen recalled Tillie even more painfully. After her first Sunday in Mr. Larsen's choir, Thea saw that she must have a proper dress for morning service. Her Moonstone party dress might do to wear in the evening, but she must have one frock that could stand the light of day. She, of course, knew nothing about Chicago dressmakers, so she let Mrs. Andersen take her to a German woman whom she recommended warmly. The German dressmaker was excitable and dramatic. Concert dresses, she said, were her specialty. In her fitting-room there were photographs of singers in the dresses she had made them for this or that SANGERFEST. She and Mrs. Andersen together achieved a costume which would have warmed Tillie Kronborg's heart. It was clearly intended for a woman of forty, with violent tastes. There seemed to be a piece of every known fabric in it somewhere. When it came home, and was spread out on her huge bed, Thea looked it over and told herself candidly that it was "a horror." However, her money was gone, and there was nothing to do but make the best of the dress. She never wore it except, as she said, "to sing in," as if it were an unbecoming uniform. When Mrs. Lorch and Irene told her that she "looked like a little bird-of-Paradise in it," Thea shut her teeth and repeated to herself words she had learned from Joe Giddy and Spanish Johnny.

In these two good women Thea found faithful friends, and in their house she found the quiet and peace which helped her to support the great experiences of that winter.

III.

Andor Harsanyi had never had a pupil in the least like Thea Kronborg. He had never had one more intelligent, and he had never had one so ignorant. When Thea sat down to take her first lesson from him, she had never heard a work by Beethoven or a composition by Chopin. She knew their names vaguely. Wunsch had been a musician once, long before he wandered into Moonstone, but when Thea awoke his interest there was not much left of him. From him Thea had learned something about the works of Gluck and Bach, and he used to play her some of the compositions of Schumann. In his trunk he had a mutilated score of the F sharp minor sonata, which he had heard Clara Schumann play at a festival in Leipsic. Though his powers of execution were at such a low ebb, he used to play at this sonata for his pupil and managed to give her some idea of its beauty. When Wunsch was a young man, it was still daring to like Schumann; enthusiasm for his work was considered an expression of youthful waywardness. Perhaps that was why Wunsch remembered him best. Thea studied some of the KINDERSZENEN with him, as well as some little sonatas by Mozart and Clementi. But for the most part Wunsch stuck to Czerny and Hummel.

Harsanyi found in Thea a pupil with sure, strong hands, one who read rapidly and intelligently, who had, he felt, a richly gifted nature. But she had been given no direction, and her ardor was unawakened. She had never heard a symphony orchestra. The literature of the piano was an undiscovered world to her. He wondered how she had been able to work so hard when she knew so little of what she was working toward. She had been taught according to the old Stuttgart method; stiff back, stiff elbows, a very formal position of the hands. The best thing about her preparation was that she had developed an unusual power of work. He noticed at once her way of charging at difficulties. She ran to meet them as if they were foes she had long been seeking, seized them as if they were destined for her and she for them. Whatever she did well, she took for granted. Her eagerness aroused all the young Hungarian's chivalry. Instinctively one went to the rescue of a creature who had so much to overcome and who struggled so hard. He used to tell his wife that Miss Kronborg's hour took more out of him than half a dozen other lessons. He usually kept her long over time; he changed her lessons about so that he could do so, and often gave her time at the end of the day, when he could talk to her afterward and play for her a little from what he happened to be studying. It was always interesting to play for her. Sometimes she was so silent that he wondered, when she left him, whether she had got anything out of it. But a week later, two weeks later, she would give back his idea again in a way that set him vibrating.

All this was very well for Harsanyi; an interesting variation in the routine of teaching. But for Thea Kronborg, that winter was almost beyond enduring. She always remembered it as the happiest and wildest and saddest of her life. Things came too fast for her; she had not had enough preparation. There were times when she came home from her lesson and lay upon her bed hating Wunsch and her family, hating a world that had let her grow up so ignorant; when she wished that she could die then and there, and be born over again to begin anew. She said something of this kind once to her teacher, in the midst of a bitter struggle. Harsanyi turned the light of his wonderful eye upon her—poor fellow, he had but one, though that was set in such a handsome head—and said slowly: "Every artist makes himself born. It is very much harder than the other time, and longer. Your mother did not bring anything into the world to play piano. That you must bring into the world yourself."

This comforted Thea temporarily, for it seemed to give her a chance. But a great deal of the time she was comfortless. Her letters to Dr. Archie were brief and businesslike. She was not apt to chatter much, even in the stimulating company of people she liked, and to chatter on paper was simply impossible for her. If she tried to write him anything definite about her work, she immediately scratched it out as being only partially true, or not true at all. Nothing that she could say about her studies seemed unqualifiedly true, once she put it down on paper.

Late one afternoon, when she was thoroughly tired and wanted to struggle on into the dusk, Harsanyi, tired too, threw up his hands and laughed at her. "Not to-day, Miss Kronborg. That sonata will keep; it won't run away. Even if you and I should not waken up to-morrow, it will be there."

Thea turned to him fiercely. "No, it isn't here unless I have it—not for me," she cried passionately. "Only what I hold in my two hands is there for me!"

Harsanyi made no reply. He took a deep breath and sat down again. "The second movement now, quietly, with the shoulders relaxed."

There were hours, too, of great exaltation; when she was at her best and became a part of what she was doing and ceased to exist in any other sense. There were other times when she was so shattered by ideas that she could do nothing worth while; when they trampled over her like an army and she felt as if she were bleeding to death under them. She sometimes came home from a late lesson so exhausted that she could eat no supper. If she tried to eat, she was ill afterward. She used to throw herself upon the bed and lie there in the dark, not thinking, not feeling, but evaporating. That same night, perhaps, she would waken up rested and calm, and as she went over her work in her mind, the passages seemed to become something of themselves, to take a sort of pattern in the darkness. She had never learned to work away from the piano until she came to Harsanyi, and it helped her more than anything had ever helped her before.

She almost never worked now with the sunny, happy contentment that had filled the hours when she worked with Wunsch—"like a fat horse turning a sorgum mill," she said bitterly to herself. Then, by sticking to it, she could always do what she set out to do. Now, everything that she really wanted was impossible; a CANTABILE like Harsanyi's, for instance, instead of her own cloudy tone. No use telling her she might have it in ten years. She wanted it now. She wondered how she had ever found other things interesting: books, "Anna Karenina"—all that seemed so unreal and on the outside of things. She was not born a musician, she decided; there was no other way of explaining it.

Sometimes she got so nervous at the piano that she left it, and snatching up her hat and cape went out and walked, hurrying through the streets like Christian fleeing from the City of Destruction. And while she walked she cried. There was scarcely a street in the neighborhood that she had not cried up and down before that winter was over. The thing that used to lie under her cheek, that sat so warmly over her heart when she glided away from the sand hills that autumn morning, was far from her. She had come to Chicago to be with it, and it had deserted her, leaving in its place a painful longing, an unresigned despair.

Harsanyi knew that his interesting pupil—"the savage blonde," one of his male students called her—was sometimes very unhappy. He saw in her discontent a curious definition of character. He would have said that a girl with so much musical feeling, so intelligent, with good training of eye and hand, would, when thus suddenly introduced to the great literature of the piano, have found boundless happiness. But he soon learned that she was not able to forget her own poverty in the richness of the world he opened to her. Often when he played to her, her face was the picture of restless misery. She would sit crouching forward, her elbows on her knees, her brows drawn together and her gray-green eyes smaller than ever, reduced to mere pin-points of cold, piercing light. Sometimes, while she listened, she would swallow hard, two or three times, and look nervously from left to right, drawing her shoulders together. "Exactly," he thought, "as if she were being watched, or as if she were naked and heard some one coming."

On the other hand, when she came several times to see Mrs. Harsanyi and the two babies, she was like a little girl, jolly and gay and eager to play with the children, who loved her. The little daughter, Tanya, liked to touch Miss Kronborg's yellow hair and pat it, saying, "Dolly, dolly," because it was of a color much oftener seen on dolls than on people. But if Harsanyi opened the piano and sat down to play, Miss Kronborg gradually drew away from the children, retreated to a corner and became sullen or troubled. Mrs. Harsanyi noticed this, also, and thought it very strange behavior.

Another thing that puzzled Harsanyi was Thea's apparent lack of curiosity. Several times he offered to give her tickets to concerts, but she said she was too tired or that it "knocked her out to be up late." Harsanyi did not know that she was singing in a choir, and had often to sing at funerals, neither did he realize how much her work with him stirred her and exhausted her. Once, just as she was leaving his studio, he called her back and told her he could give her some tickets that had been sent him for Emma Juch that evening. Thea fingered the black wool on the edge of her plush cape and replied, "Oh, thank you, Mr. Harsanyi, but I have to wash my hair to-night."

Mrs. Harsanyi liked Miss Kronborg thoroughly. She saw in her the making of a pupil who would reflect credit upon Harsanyi. She felt that the girl could be made to look strikingly handsome, and that she had the kind of personality which takes hold of audiences. Moreover, Miss Kronborg was not in the least sentimental about her husband. Sometimes from the show pupils one had to endure a good deal. "I like that girl," she used to say, when Harsanyi told her of one of Thea's GAUCHERIES. "She doesn't sigh every time the wind blows. With her one swallow doesn't make a summer."

Thea told them very little about herself. She was not naturally communicative, and she found it hard to feel confidence in new people. She did not know why, but she could not talk to Harsanyi as she could to Dr. Archie, or to Johnny and Mrs. Tellamantez. With Mr. Larsen she felt more at home, and when she was walking she sometimes stopped at his study to eat candy with him or to hear the plot of the novel he happened to be reading.

One evening toward the middle of December Thea was to dine with the Harsanyis. She arrived early, to have time to play with the children before they went to bed. Mrs. Harsanyi took her into her own room and helped her take off her country "fascinator" and her clumsy plush cape. Thea had bought this cape at a big department store and had paid $16.50 for it. As she had never paid more than ten dollars for a coat before, that seemed to her a large price. It was very heavy and not very warm, ornamented with a showy pattern in black disks, and trimmed around the collar and the edges with some kind of black wool that "crocked" badly in snow or rain. It was lined with a cotton stuff called "farmer's satin." Mrs. Harsanyi was one woman in a thousand. As she lifted this cape from Thea's shoulders and laid it on her white bed, she wished that her husband did not have to charge pupils like this one for their lessons. Thea wore her Moonstone party dress, white organdie, made with a "V" neck and elbow sleeves, and a blue sash. She looked very pretty in it, and around her throat she had a string of pink coral and tiny white shells that Ray once brought her from Los Angeles. Mrs. Harsanyi noticed that she wore high heavy shoes which needed blacking. The choir in Mr. Larsen's church stood behind a railing, so Thea did not pay much attention to her shoes.

"You have nothing to do to your hair," Mrs. Harsanyi said kindly, as Thea turned to the mirror. "However it happens to lie, it's always pretty. I admire it as much as Tanya does."

Thea glanced awkwardly away from her and looked stern, but Mrs. Harsanyi knew that she was pleased. They went into the living-room, behind the studio, where the two children were playing on the big rug before the coal grate. Andor, the boy, was six, a sturdy, handsome child, and the little girl was four. She came tripping to meet Thea, looking like a little doll in her white net dress—her mother made all her clothes. Thea picked her up and hugged her. Mrs. Harsanyi excused herself and went to the dining-room. She kept only one maid and did a good deal of the housework herself, besides cooking her husband's favorite dishes for him. She was still under thirty, a slender, graceful woman, gracious, intelligent, and capable. She adapted herself to circumstances with a well-bred ease which solved many of her husband's difficulties, and kept him, as he said, from feeling cheap and down at the heel. No musician ever had a better wife. Unfortunately her beauty was of a very frail and impressionable kind, and she was beginning to lose it. Her face was too thin now, and there were often dark circles under her eyes.

Left alone with the children, Thea sat down on Tanya's little chair—she would rather have sat on the floor, but was afraid of rumpling her dress—and helped them play "cars" with Andor's iron railway set. She showed him new ways to lay his tracks and how to make switches, set up his Noah's ark village for stations and packed the animals in the open coal cars to send them to the stockyards. They worked out their shipment so realistically that when Andor put the two little reindeer into the stock car, Tanya snatched them out and began to cry, saying she wasn't going to have all their animals killed.

Harsanyi came in, jaded and tired, and asked Thea to go on with her game, as he was not equal to talking much before dinner. He sat down and made pretense of glancing at the evening paper, but he soon dropped it. After the railroad began to grow tiresome, Thea went with the children to the lounge in the corner, and played for them the game with which she used to amuse Thor for hours together behind the parlor stove at home, making shadow pictures against the wall with her hands. Her fingers were very supple, and she could make a duck and a cow and a sheep and a fox and a rabbit and even an elephant. Harsanyi, from his low chair, watched them, smiling. The boy was on his knees, jumping up and down with the excitement of guessing the beasts, and Tanya sat with her feet tucked under her and clapped her frail little hands. Thea's profile, in the lamplight, teased his fancy. Where had he seen a head like it before?

When dinner was announced, little Andor took Thea's hand and walked to the dining-room with her. The children always had dinner with their parents and behaved very nicely at table. "Mamma," said Andor seriously as he climbed into his chair and tucked his napkin into the collar of his blouse, "Miss Kronborg's hands are every kind of animal there is."

His father laughed. "I wish somebody would say that about my hands, Andor."

When Thea dined at the Harsanyis before, she noticed that there was an intense suspense from the moment they took their places at the table until the master of the house had tasted the soup. He had a theory that if the soup went well, the dinner would go well; but if the soup was poor, all was lost. To-night he tasted his soup and smiled, and Mrs. Harsanyi sat more easily in her chair and turned her attention to Thea. Thea loved their dinner table, because it was lighted by candles in silver candle-sticks, and she had never seen a table so lighted anywhere else. There were always flowers, too. To-night there was a little orange tree, with oranges on it, that one of Harsanyi's pupils had sent him at Thanksgiving time. After Harsanyi had finished his soup and a glass of red Hungarian wine, he lost his fagged look and became cordial and witty. He persuaded Thea to drink a little wine to-night. The first time she dined with them, when he urged her to taste the glass of sherry beside her plate, she astonished them by telling them that she "never drank."

Harsanyi was then a man of thirty-two. He was to have a very brilliant career, but he did not know it then. Theodore Thomas was perhaps the only man in Chicago who felt that Harsanyi might have a great future. Harsanyi belonged to the softer Slavic type, and was more like a Pole than a Hungarian. He was tall, slender, active, with sloping, graceful shoulders and long arms. His head was very fine, strongly and delicately modelled, and, as Thea put it, "so independent." A lock of his thick brown hair usually hung over his forehead. His eye was wonderful; full of light and fire when he was interested, soft and thoughtful when he was tired or melancholy. The meaning and power of two very fine eyes must all have gone into this one—the right one, fortunately, the one next his audience when he played. He believed that the glass eye which gave one side of his face such a dull, blind look, had ruined his career, or rather had made a career impossible for him. Harsanyi lost his eye when he was twelve years old, in a Pennsylvania mining town where explosives happened to be kept too near the frame shanties in which the company packed newly arrived Hungarian families.

His father was a musician and a good one, but he had cruelly over-worked the boy; keeping him at the piano for six hours a day and making him play in cafes and dance halls for half the night. Andor ran away and crossed the ocean with an uncle, who smuggled him through the port as one of his own many children. The explosion in which Andor was hurt killed a score of people, and he was thought lucky to get off with an eye. He still had a clipping from a Pittsburg paper, giving a list of the dead and injured. He appeared as "Harsanyi, Andor, left eye and slight injuries about the head." That was his first American "notice"; and he kept it. He held no grudge against the coal company; he understood that the accident was merely one of the things that are bound to happen in the general scramble of American life, where every one comes to grab and takes his chance.

While they were eating dessert, Thea asked Harsanyi if she could change her Tuesday lesson from afternoon to morning. "I have to be at a choir rehearsal in the afternoon, to get ready for the Christmas music, and I expect it will last until late."

Harsanyi put down his fork and looked up. "A choir rehearsal? You sing in a church?"

"Yes. A little Swedish church, over on the North side."

"Why did you not tell us?"

"Oh, I'm only a temporary. The regular soprano is not well."

"How long have you been singing there?"

"Ever since I came. I had to get a position of some kind," Thea explained, flushing, "and the preacher took me on. He runs the choir himself. He knew my father, and I guess he took me to oblige."

Harsanyi tapped the tablecloth with the ends of his fingers. "But why did you never tell us? Why are you so reticent with us?"

Thea looked shyly at him from under her brows. "Well, it's certainly not very interesting. It's only a little church. I only do it for business reasons."

"What do you mean? Don't you like to sing? Don't you sing well?"

"I like it well enough, but, of course, I don't know anything about singing. I guess that's why I never said anything about it. Anybody that's got a voice can sing in a little church like that."

Harsanyi laughed softly—a little scornfully, Thea thought. "So you have a voice, have you?"

Thea hesitated, looked intently at the candles and then at Harsanyi. "Yes," she said firmly; "I have got some, anyway."

"Good girl," said Mrs. Harsanyi, nodding and smiling at Thea. "You must let us hear you sing after dinner."

This remark seemingly closed the subject, and when the coffee was brought they began to talk of other things. Harsanyi asked Thea how she happened to know so much about the way in which freight trains are operated, and she tried to give him some idea of how the people in little desert towns live by the railway and order their lives by the coming and going of the trains. When they left the diningroom the children were sent to bed and Mrs. Harsanyi took Thea into the studio. She and her husband usually sat there in the evening.

Although their apartment seemed so elegant to Thea, it was small and cramped. The studio was the only spacious room. The Harsanyis were poor, and it was due to Mrs. Harsanyi's good management that their lives, even in hard times, moved along with dignity and order. She had long ago found out that bills or debts of any kind frightened her husband and crippled his working power. He said they were like bars on the windows, and shut out the future; they meant that just so many hundred dollars' worth of his life was debilitated and exhausted before he got to it. So Mrs. Harsanyi saw to it that they never owed anything. Harsanyi was not extravagant, though he was sometimes careless about money. Quiet and order and his wife's good taste were the things that meant most to him. After these, good food, good cigars, a little good wine. He wore his clothes until they were shabby, until his wife had to ask the tailor to come to the house and measure him for new ones. His neckties she usually made herself, and when she was in shops she always kept her eye open for silks in very dull or pale shades, grays and olives, warm blacks and browns.

When they went into the studio Mrs. Harsanyi took up her embroidery and Thea sat down beside her on a low stool, her hands clasped about her knees. While his wife and his pupil talked, Harsanyi sank into a CHAISE LONGUE in which he sometimes snatched a few moments' rest between his lessons, and smoked. He sat well out of the circle of the lamplight, his feet to the fire. His feet were slender and well shaped, always elegantly shod. Much of the grace of his movements was due to the fact that his feet were almost as sure and flexible as his hands. He listened to the conversation with amusement. He admired his wife's tact and kindness with crude young people; she taught them so much without seeming to be instructing. When the clock struck nine, Thea said she must be going home.

Harsanyi rose and flung away his cigarette. "Not yet. We have just begun the evening. Now you are going to sing for us. I have been waiting for you to recover from dinner. Come, what shall it be?" he crossed to the piano.

Thea laughed and shook her head, locking her elbows still tighter about her knees. "Thank you, Mr. Harsanyi, but if you really make me sing, I'll accompany myself. You couldn't stand it to play the sort of things I have to sing."

As Harsanyi still pointed to the chair at the piano, she left her stool and went to it, while he returned to his CHAISE LONGUE. Thea looked at the keyboard uneasily for a moment, then she began "Come, ye Disconsolate," the hymn Wunsch had always liked to hear her sing. Mrs. Harsanyi glanced questioningly at her husband, but he was looking intently at the toes of his boots, shading his forehead with his long white hand. When Thea finished the hymn she did not turn around, but immediately began "The Ninety and Nine." Mrs. Harsanyi kept trying to catch her husband's eye; but his chin only sank lower on his collar.

"There were ninety and nine that safely lay In the shelter of the fold, But one was out on the hills away, Far off from the gates of gold."

Harsanyi looked at her, then back at the fire.

"Rejoice, for the Shepherd has found his sheep."

Thea turned on the chair and grinned. "That's about enough, isn't it? That song got me my job. The preacher said it was sympathetic," she minced the word, remembering Mr. Larsen's manner.

Harsanyi drew himself up in his chair, resting his elbows on the low arms. "Yes? That is better suited to your voice. Your upper tones are good, above G. I must teach you some songs. Don't you know anything—pleasant?"

Thea shook her head ruefully. "I'm afraid I don't. Let me see—Perhaps," she turned to the piano and put her hands on the keys. "I used to sing this for Mr. Wunsch a long while ago. It's for contralto, but I'll try it." She frowned at the keyboard a moment, played the few introductory measures, and began:

"ACH, ICH HABE SIE VERLOREN,"

She had not sung it for a long time, and it came back like an old friendship. When she finished, Harsanyi sprang from his chair and dropped lightly upon his toes, a kind of ENTRE-CHAT that he sometimes executed when he formed a sudden resolution, or when he was about to follow a pure intuition, against reason. His wife said that when he gave that spring he was shot from the bow of his ancestors, and now when he left his chair in that manner she knew he was intensely interested. He went quickly to the piano.

"Sing that again. There is nothing the matter with your low voice, my girl. I will play for you. Let your voice out." Without looking at her he began the accompaniment. Thea drew back her shoulders, relaxed them instinctively, and sang.

When she finished the aria, Harsanyi beckoned her nearer. "Sing AH—AH for me, as I indicate." He kept his right hand on the keyboard and put his left to her throat, placing the tips of his delicate fingers over her larynx. "Again,—until your breath is gone.—Trill between the two tones, always; good! Again; excellent!—Now up,—stay there. E and F. Not so good, is it? F is always a hard one.—Now, try the half-tone.—That's right, nothing difficult about it. —Now, pianissimo, AH—AH. Now, swell it, AH—AH.—Again, follow my hand.—Now, carry it down.—Anybody ever tell you anything about your breathing?"

"Mr. Larsen says I have an unusually long breath," Thea replied with spirit.

Harsanyi smiled. "So you have, so you have. That was what I meant. Now, once more; carry it up and then down, AH—AH." He put his hand back to her throat and sat with his head bent, his one eye closed. He loved to hear a big voice throb in a relaxed, natural throat, and he was thinking that no one had ever felt this voice vibrate before. It was like a wild bird that had flown into his studio on Middleton Street from goodness knew how far! No one knew that it had come, or even that it existed; least of all the strange, crude girl in whose throat it beat its passionate wings. What a simple thing it was, he reflected; why had he never guessed it before? Everything about her indicated it,—the big mouth, the wide jaw and chin, the strong white teeth, the deep laugh. The machine was so simple and strong, seemed to be so easily operated. She sang from the bottom of herself. Her breath came from down where her laugh came from, the deep laugh which Mrs. Harsanyi had once called "the laugh of the people." A relaxed throat, a voice that lay on the breath, that had never been forced off the breath; it rose and fell in the air-column like the little balls which are put to shine in the jet of a fountain. The voice did not thin as it went up; the upper tones were as full and rich as the lower, produced in the same way and as unconsciously, only with deeper breath.

At last Harsanyi threw back his head and rose. "You must be tired, Miss Kronborg."

When she replied, she startled him; he had forgotten how hard and full of burs her speaking voice was. "No," she said, "singing never tires me."

Harsanyi pushed back his hair with a nervous hand. "I don't know much about the voice, but I shall take liberties and teach you some good songs. I think you have a very interesting voice."

"I'm glad if you like it. Good-night, Mr. Harsanyi." Thea went with Mrs. Harsanyi to get her wraps.

When Mrs. Harsanyi came back to her husband, she found him walking restlessly up and down the room.

"Don't you think her voice wonderful, dear?" she asked.

"I scarcely know what to think. All I really know about that girl is that she tires me to death. We must not have her often. If I did not have my living to make, then—" he dropped into a chair and closed his eyes. "How tired I am. What a voice!"

IV.

After that evening Thea's work with Harsanyi changed somewhat. He insisted that she should study some songs with him, and after almost every lesson he gave up half an hour of his own time to practicing them with her. He did not pretend to know much about voice production, but so far, he thought, she had acquired no really injurious habits. A healthy and powerful organ had found its own method, which was not a bad one. He wished to find out a good deal before he recommended a vocal teacher. He never told Thea what he thought about her voice, and made her general ignorance of anything worth singing his pretext for the trouble he took. That was in the beginning. After the first few lessons his own pleasure and hers were pretext enough. The singing came at the end of the lesson hour, and they both treated it as a form of relaxation.

Harsanyi did not say much even to his wife about his discovery. He brooded upon it in a curious way. He found that these unscientific singing lessons stimulated him in his own study. After Miss Kronborg left him he often lay down in his studio for an hour before dinner, with his head full of musical ideas, with an effervescence in his brain which he had sometimes lost for weeks together under the grind of teaching. He had never got so much back for himself from any pupil as he did from Miss Kronborg. From the first she had stimulated him; something in her personality invariably affected him. Now that he was feeling his way toward her voice, he found her more interesting than ever before. She lifted the tedium of the winter for him, gave him curious fancies and reveries. Musically, she was sympathetic to him. Why all this was true, he never asked himself. He had learned that one must take where and when one can the mysterious mental irritant that rouses one's imagination; that it is not to be had by order. She often wearied him, but she never bored him. Under her crudeness and brusque hardness, he felt there was a nature quite different, of which he never got so much as a hint except when she was at the piano, or when she sang. It was toward this hidden creature that he was trying, for his own pleasure, to find his way. In short, Harsanyi looked forward to his hour with Thea for the same reason that poor Wunsch had sometimes dreaded his; because she stirred him more than anything she did could adequately explain.

One afternoon Harsanyi, after the lesson, was standing by the window putting some collodion on a cracked finger, and Thea was at the piano trying over "Die Lorelei" which he had given her last week to practice. It was scarcely a song which a singing master would have given her, but he had his own reasons. How she sang it mattered only to him and to her. He was playing his own game now, without interference; he suspected that he could not do so always.

When she finished the song, she looked back over her shoulder at him and spoke thoughtfully. "That wasn't right, at the end, was it?"

"No, that should be an open, flowing tone, something like this,"—he waved his fingers rapidly in the air. "You get the idea?"

"No, I don't. Seems a queer ending, after the rest."

Harsanyi corked his little bottle and dropped it into the pocket of his velvet coat. "Why so? Shipwrecks come and go, MARCHEN come and go, but the river keeps right on. There you have your open, flowing tone."

Thea looked intently at the music. "I see," she said dully. "Oh, I see!" she repeated quickly and turned to him a glowing countenance. "It is the river.—Oh, yes, I get it now!" She looked at him but long enough to catch his glance, then turned to the piano again. Harsanyi was never quite sure where the light came from when her face suddenly flashed out at him in that way. Her eyes were too small to account for it, though they glittered like green ice in the sun. At such moments her hair was yellower, her skin whiter, her cheeks pinker, as if a lamp had suddenly been turned up inside of her. She went at the song again:

"ICH WEISS NICHT, WAS SOLL ES BEDEUTEN, DAS ICH SO TRAURIG BIN."

A kind of happiness vibrated in her voice. Harsanyi noticed how much and how unhesitatingly she changed her delivery of the whole song, the first part as well as the last. He had often noticed that she could not think a thing out in passages. Until she saw it as a whole, she wandered like a blind man surrounded by torments. After she once had her "revelation," after she got the idea that to her—not always to him—explained everything, then she went forward rapidly. But she was not always easy to help. She was sometimes impervious to suggestion; she would stare at him as if she were deaf and ignore everything he told her to do. Then, all at once, something would happen in her brain and she would begin to do all that he had been for weeks telling her to do, without realizing that he had ever told her.

To-night Thea forgot Harsanyi and his finger. She finished the song only to begin it with fresh enthusiasm.

"UND DAS HAT MIT IHREM SINGEN DIE LORELEI GETHAN."

She sat there singing it until the darkening room was so flooded with it that Harsanyi threw open a window.

"You really must stop it, Miss Kronborg. I shan't be able to get it out of my head to-night."

Thea laughed tolerantly as she began to gather up her music. "Why, I thought you had gone, Mr. Harsanyi. I like that song."

That evening at dinner Harsanyi sat looking intently into a glass of heavy yellow wine; boring into it, indeed, with his one eye, when his face suddenly broke into a smile.

"What is it, Andor?" his wife asked.

He smiled again, this time at her, and took up the nutcrackers and a Brazil nut. "Do you know," he said in a tone so intimate and confidential that he might have been speaking to himself,—"do you know, I like to see Miss Kronborg get hold of an idea. In spite of being so talented, she's not quick. But when she does get an idea, it fills her up to the eyes. She had my room so reeking of a song this afternoon that I couldn't stay there."

Mrs. Harsanyi looked up quickly, "'Die Lorelei,' you mean? One couldn't think of anything else anywhere in the house. I thought she was possessed. But don't you think her voice is wonderful sometimes?"

Harsanyi tasted his wine slowly. "My dear, I've told you before that I don't know what I think about Miss Kronborg, except that I'm glad there are not two of her. I sometimes wonder whether she is not glad. Fresh as she is at it all, I've occasionally fancied that, if she knew how, she would like to—diminish." He moved his left hand out into the air as if he were suggesting a DIMINUENDO to an orchestra.

V.

By the first of February Thea had been in Chicago almost four months, and she did not know much more about the city than if she had never quitted Moonstone. She was, as Harsanyi said, incurious. Her work took most of her time, and she found that she had to sleep a good deal. It had never before been so hard to get up in the morning. She had the bother of caring for her room, and she had to build her fire and bring up her coal. Her routine was frequently interrupted by a message from Mr. Larsen summoning her to sing at a funeral. Every funeral took half a day, and the time had to be made up. When Mrs. Harsanyi asked her if it did not depress her to sing at funerals, she replied that she "had been brought up to go to funerals and didn't mind."

Thea never went into shops unless she had to, and she felt no interest in them. Indeed, she shunned them, as places where one was sure to be parted from one's money in some way. She was nervous about counting her change, and she could not accustom herself to having her purchases sent to her address. She felt much safer with her bundles under her arm.

During this first winter Thea got no city consciousness. Chicago was simply a wilderness through which one had to find one's way. She felt no interest in the general briskness and zest of the crowds. The crash and scramble of that big, rich, appetent Western city she did not take in at all, except to notice that the noise of the drays and street-cars tired her. The brilliant window displays, the splendid furs and stuffs, the gorgeous flower-shops, the gay candy-shops, she scarcely noticed. At Christmas-time she did feel some curiosity about the toy-stores, and she wished she held Thor's little mittened fist in her hand as she stood before the windows. The jewelers' windows, too, had a strong attraction for her—she had always liked bright stones. When she went into the city she used to brave the biting lake winds and stand gazing in at the displays of diamonds and pearls and emeralds; the tiaras and necklaces and earrings, on white velvet. These seemed very well worth while to her, things worth coveting.

Mrs. Lorch and Mrs. Andersen often told each other it was strange that Miss Kronborg had so little initiative about "visiting points of interest." When Thea came to live with them she had expressed a wish to see two places: Montgomery Ward and Company's big mail-order store, and the packing-houses, to which all the hogs and cattle that went through Moonstone were bound. One of Mrs. Lorch's lodgers worked in a packing-house, and Mrs. Andersen brought Thea word that she had spoken to Mr. Eckman and he would gladly take her to Packingtown. Eckman was a toughish young Swede, and he thought it would be something of a lark to take a pretty girl through the slaughter-houses. But he was disappointed. Thea neither grew faint nor clung to the arm he kept offering her. She asked innumerable questions and was impatient because he knew so little of what was going on outside of his own department. When they got off the street-car and walked back to Mrs. Lorch's house in the dusk, Eckman put her hand in his overcoat pocket—she had no muff—and kept squeezing it ardently until she said, "Don't do that; my ring cuts me." That night he told his roommate that he "could have kissed her as easy as rolling off a log, but she wasn't worth the trouble." As for Thea, she had enjoyed the afternoon very much, and wrote her father a brief but clear account of what she had seen.

One night at supper Mrs. Andersen was talking about the exhibit of students' work she had seen at the Art Institute that afternoon. Several of her friends had sketches in the exhibit. Thea, who always felt that she was behindhand in courtesy to Mrs. Andersen, thought that here was an opportunity to show interest without committing herself to anything. "Where is that, the Institute?" she asked absently.

Mrs. Andersen clasped her napkin in both hands. "The Art Institute? Our beautiful Art Institute on Michigan Avenue? Do you mean to say you have never visited it?"

"Oh, is it the place with the big lions out in front? I remember; I saw it when I went to Montgomery Ward's. Yes, I thought the lions were beautiful."

"But the pictures! Didn't you visit the galleries?"

"No. The sign outside said it was a pay-day. I've always meant to go back, but I haven't happened to be down that way since."

Mrs. Lorch and Mrs. Andersen looked at each other. The old mother spoke, fixing her shining little eyes upon Thea across the table. "Ah, but Miss Kronborg, there are old masters! Oh, many of them, such as you could not see anywhere out of Europe."

"And Corots," breathed Mrs. Andersen, tilting her head feelingly. "Such examples of the Barbizon school!" This was meaningless to Thea, who did not read the art columns of the Sunday INTER-OCEAN as Mrs. Andersen did.

"Oh, I'm going there some day," she reassured them. "I like to look at oil paintings."

One bleak day in February, when the wind was blowing clouds of dirt like a Moonstone sandstorm, dirt that filled your eyes and ears and mouth, Thea fought her way across the unprotected space in front of the Art Institute and into the doors of the building. She did not come out again until the closing hour. In the street-car, on the long cold ride home, while she sat staring at the waistcoat buttons of a fat strap-hanger, she had a serious reckoning with herself. She seldom thought about her way of life, about what she ought or ought not to do; usually there was but one obvious and important thing to be done. But that afternoon she remonstrated with herself severely. She told herself that she was missing a great deal; that she ought to be more willing to take advice and to go to see things. She was sorry that she had let months pass without going to the Art Institute. After this she would go once a week.

The Institute proved, indeed, a place of retreat, as the sand hills or the Kohlers' garden used to be; a place where she could forget Mrs. Andersen's tiresome overtures of friendship, the stout contralto in the choir whom she so unreasonably hated, and even, for a little while, the torment of her work. That building was a place in which she could relax and play, and she could hardly ever play now. On the whole, she spent more time with the casts than with the pictures. They were at once more simple and more perplexing; and some way they seemed more important, harder to overlook. It never occurred to her to buy a catalogue, so she called most of the casts by names she made up for them. Some of them she knew; the Dying Gladiator she had read about in "Childe Harold" almost as long ago as she could remember; he was strongly associated with Dr. Archie and childish illnesses. The Venus di Milo puzzled her; she could not see why people thought her so beautiful. She told herself over and over that she did not think the Apollo Belvedere "at all handsome." Better than anything else she liked a great equestrian statue of an evil, cruel-looking general with an unpronounceable name. She used to walk round and round this terrible man and his terrible horse, frowning at him, brooding upon him, as if she had to make some momentous decision about him.

The casts, when she lingered long among them, always made her gloomy. It was with a lightening of the heart, a feeling of throwing off the old miseries and old sorrows of the world, that she ran up the wide staircase to the pictures. There she liked best the ones that told stories. There was a painting by Gerome called "The Pasha's Grief" which always made her wish for Gunner and Axel. The Pasha was seated on a rug, beside a green candle almost as big as a telegraph pole, and before him was stretched his dead tiger, a splendid beast, and there were pink roses scattered about him. She loved, too, a picture of some boys bringing in a newborn calf on a litter, the cow walking beside it and licking it. The Corot which hung next to this painting she did not like or dislike; she never saw it.

But in that same room there was a picture—oh, that was the thing she ran upstairs so fast to see! That was her picture. She imagined that nobody cared for it but herself, and that it waited for her. That was a picture indeed. She liked even the name of it, "The Song of the Lark." The flat country, the early morning light, the wet fields, the look in the girl's heavy face—well, they were all hers, anyhow, whatever was there. She told herself that that picture was "right." Just what she meant by this, it would take a clever person to explain. But to her the word covered the almost boundless satisfaction she felt when she looked at the picture.

Before Thea had any idea how fast the weeks were flying, before Mr. Larsen's "permanent" soprano had returned to her duties, spring came; windy, dusty, strident, shrill; a season almost more violent in Chicago than the winter from which it releases one, or the heat to which it eventually delivers one. One sunny morning the apple trees in Mrs. Lorch's back yard burst into bloom, and for the first time in months Thea dressed without building a fire. The morning shone like a holiday, and for her it was to be a holiday. There was in the air that sudden, treacherous softness which makes the Poles who work in the packing-houses get drunk. At such times beauty is necessary, and in Packingtown there is no place to get it except at the saloons, where one can buy for a few hours the illusion of comfort, hope, love, —whatever one most longs for.

Harsanyi had given Thea a ticket for the symphony concert that afternoon, and when she looked out at the white apple trees her doubts as to whether she ought to go vanished at once. She would make her work light that morning, she told herself. She would go to the concert full of energy. When she set off, after dinner, Mrs. Lorch, who knew Chicago weather, prevailed upon her to take her cape. The old lady said that such sudden mildness, so early in April, presaged a sharp return of winter, and she was anxious about her apple trees.

The concert began at two-thirty, and Thea was in her seat in the Auditorium at ten minutes after two—a fine seat in the first row of the balcony, on the side, where she could see the house as well as the orchestra. She had been to so few concerts that the great house, the crowd of people, and the lights, all had a stimulating effect. She was surprised to see so many men in the audience, and wondered how they could leave their business in the afternoon. During the first number Thea was so much interested in the orchestra itself, in the men, the instruments, the volume of sound, that she paid little attention to what they were playing. Her excitement impaired her power of listening. She kept saying to herself, "Now I must stop this foolishness and listen; I may never hear this again"; but her mind was like a glass that is hard to focus. She was not ready to listen until the second number, Dvorak's Symphony in E minor, called on the programme, "From the New World." The first theme had scarcely been given out when her mind became clear; instant composure fell upon her, and with it came the power of concentration. This was music she could understand, music from the New World indeed! Strange how, as the first movement went on, it brought back to her that high tableland above Laramie; the grass-grown wagon trails, the far-away peaks of the snowy range, the wind and the eagles, that old man and the first telegraph message.

When the first movement ended, Thea's hands and feet were cold as ice. She was too much excited to know anything except that she wanted something desperately, and when the English horns gave out the theme of the Largo, she knew that what she wanted was exactly that. Here were the sand hills, the grasshoppers and locusts, all the things that wakened and chirped in the early morning; the reaching and reaching of high plains, the immeasurable yearning of all flat lands. There was home in it, too; first memories, first mornings long ago; the amazement of a new soul in a new world; a soul new and yet old, that had dreamed something despairing, something glorious, in the dark before it was born; a soul obsessed by what it did not know, under the cloud of a past it could not recall.

If Thea had had much experience in concert-going, and had known her own capacity, she would have left the hall when the symphony was over. But she sat still, scarcely knowing where she was, because her mind had been far away and had not yet come back to her. She was startled when the orchestra began to play again—the entry of the gods into Walhalla. She heard it as people hear things in their sleep. She knew scarcely anything about the Wagner operas. She had a vague idea that "Rhinegold" was about the strife between gods and men; she had read something about it in Mr. Haweis's book long ago. Too tired to follow the orchestra with much understanding, she crouched down in her seat and closed her eyes. The cold, stately measures of the Walhalla music rang out, far away; the rainbow bridge throbbed out into the air, under it the wailing of the Rhine daughters and the singing of the Rhine. But Thea was sunk in twilight; it was all going on in another world. So it happened that with a dull, almost listless ear she heard for the first time that troubled music, ever-darkening, ever-brightening, which was to flow through so many years of her life.

When Thea emerged from the concert hall, Mrs. Lorch's predictions had been fulfilled. A furious gale was beating over the city from Lake Michigan. The streets were full of cold, hurrying, angry people, running for street-cars and barking at each other. The sun was setting in a clear, windy sky, that flamed with red as if there were a great fire somewhere on the edge of the city. For almost the first time Thea was conscious of the city itself, of the congestion of life all about her, of the brutality and power of those streams that flowed in the streets, threatening to drive one under. People jostled her, ran into her, poked her aside with their elbows, uttering angry exclamations. She got on the wrong car and was roughly ejected by the conductor at a windy corner, in front of a saloon. She stood there dazed and shivering. The cars passed, screaming as they rounded curves, but either they were full to the doors, or were bound for places where she did not want to go. Her hands were so cold that she took off her tight kid gloves. The street lights began to gleam in the dusk. A young man came out of the saloon and stood eyeing her questioningly while he lit a cigarette. "Looking for a friend to-night?" he asked. Thea drew up the collar of her cape and walked on a few paces. The young man shrugged his shoulders and drifted away.

Thea came back to the corner and stood there irresolutely. An old man approached her. He, too, seemed to be waiting for a car. He wore an overcoat with a black fur collar, his gray mustache was waxed into little points, and his eyes were watery. He kept thrusting his face up near hers. Her hat blew off and he ran after it—a stiff, pitiful skip he had—and brought it back to her. Then, while she was pinning her hat on, her cape blew up, and he held it down for her, looking at her intently. His face worked as if he were going to cry or were frightened. He leaned over and whispered something to her. It struck her as curious that he was really quite timid, like an old beggar. "Oh, let me ALONE!" she cried miserably between her teeth. He vanished, disappeared like the Devil in a play. But in the mean time something had got away from her; she could not remember how the violins came in after the horns, just there. When her cape blew up, perhaps—Why did these men torment her? A cloud of dust blew in her face and blinded her. There was some power abroad in the world bent upon taking away from her that feeling with which she had come out of the concert hall. Everything seemed to sweep down on her to tear it out from under her cape. If one had that, the world became one's enemy; people, buildings, wagons, cars, rushed at one to crush it under, to make one let go of it. Thea glared round her at the crowds, the ugly, sprawling streets, the long lines of lights, and she was not crying now. Her eyes were brighter than even Harsanyi had ever seen them. All these things and people were no longer remote and negligible; they had to be met, they were lined up against her, they were there to take something from her. Very well; they should never have it. They might trample her to death, but they should never have it. As long as she lived that ecstasy was going to be hers. She would live for it, work for it, die for it; but she was going to have it, time after time, height after height. She could hear the crash of the orchestra again, and she rose on the brasses. She would have it, what the trumpets were singing! She would have it, have it,—it! Under the old cape she pressed her hands upon her heaving bosom, that was a little girl's no longer.

VI.

One afternoon in April, Theodore Thomas, the conductor of the Chicago Symphony Orchestra, had turned out his desk light and was about to leave his office in the Auditorium Building, when Harsanyi appeared in the doorway. The conductor welcomed him with a hearty hand-grip and threw off the overcoat he had just put on. He pushed Harsanyi into a chair and sat down at his burdened desk, pointing to the piles of papers and railway folders upon it.

"Another tour, clear to the coast. This traveling is the part of my work that grinds me, Andor. You know what it means: bad food, dirt, noise, exhaustion for the men and for me. I'm not so young as I once was. It's time I quit the highway. This is the last tour, I swear!"

"Then I'm sorry for the 'highway.' I remember when I first heard you in Pittsburg, long ago. It was a life-line you threw me. It's about one of the people along your highway that I've come to see you. Whom do you consider the best teacher for voice in Chicago?"

Mr. Thomas frowned and pulled his heavy mustache. "Let me see; I suppose on the whole Madison Bowers is the best. He's intelligent, and he had good training. I don't like him."

Harsanyi nodded. "I thought there was no one else. I don't like him, either, so I hesitated. But I suppose he must do, for the present."

"Have you found anything promising? One of your own students?"

"Yes, sir. A young Swedish girl from somewhere in Colorado. She is very talented, and she seems to me to have a remarkable voice."

"High voice?"

"I think it will be; though her low voice has a beautiful quality, very individual. She has had no instruction in voice at all, and I shrink from handing her over to anybody; her own instinct about it has been so good. It is one of those voices that manages itself easily, without thinning as it goes up; good breathing and perfect relaxation. But she must have a teacher, of course. There is a break in the middle voice, so that the voice does not all work together; an unevenness."

Thomas looked up. "So? Curious; that cleft often happens with the Swedes. Some of their best singers have had it. It always reminds me of the space you so often see between their front teeth. Is she strong physically?"

Harsanyi's eye flashed. He lifted his hand before him and clenched it. "Like a horse, like a tree! Every time I give her a lesson, I lose a pound. She goes after what she wants."

"Intelligent, you say? Musically intelligent?"

"Yes; but no cultivation whatever. She came to me like a fine young savage, a book with nothing written in it. That is why I feel the responsibility of directing her." Harsanyi paused and crushed his soft gray hat over his knee. "She would interest you, Mr. Thomas," he added slowly. "She has a quality—very individual."

"Yes; the Scandinavians are apt to have that, too. She can't go to Germany, I suppose?"

"Not now, at any rate. She is poor."

Thomas frowned again "I don't think Bowers a really first-rate man. He's too petty to be really first-rate; in his nature, I mean. But I dare say he's the best you can do, if you can't give her time enough yourself."

Harsanyi waved his hand. "Oh, the time is nothing—she may have all she wants. But I cannot teach her to sing."

"Might not come amiss if you made a musician of her, however," said Mr. Thomas dryly.

"I have done my best. But I can only play with a voice, and this is not a voice to be played with. I think she will be a musician, whatever happens. She is not quick, but she is solid, real; not like these others. My wife says that with that girl one swallow does not make a summer."

Mr. Thomas laughed. "Tell Mrs. Harsanyi that her remark conveys something to me. Don't let yourself get too much interested. Voices are so often disappointing; especially women's voices. So much chance about it, so many factors."

"Perhaps that is why they interest one. All the intelligence and talent in the world can't make a singer. The voice is a wild thing. It can't be bred in captivity. It is a sport, like the silver fox. It happens."

Mr. Thomas smiled into Harsanyi's gleaming eye. "Why haven't you brought her to sing for me?"

"I've been tempted to, but I knew you were driven to death, with this tour confronting you."

"Oh, I can always find time to listen to a girl who has a voice, if she means business. I'm sorry I'm leaving so soon. I could advise you better if I had heard her. I can sometimes give a singer suggestions. I've worked so much with them."

"You're the only conductor I know who is not snobbish about singers." Harsanyi spoke warmly.

"Dear me, why should I be? They've learned from me, and I've learned from them." As they rose, Thomas took the younger man affectionately by the arm. "Tell me about that wife of yours. Is she well, and as lovely as ever? And such fine children! Come to see me oftener, when I get back. I miss it when you don't."

The two men left the Auditorium Building together. Harsanyi walked home. Even a short talk with Thomas always stimulated him. As he walked he was recalling an evening they once spent together in Cincinnati.

Harsanyi was the soloist at one of Thomas's concerts there, and after the performance the conductor had taken him off to a RATHSKELLER where there was excellent German cooking, and where the proprietor saw to it that Thomas had the best wines procurable. Thomas had been working with the great chorus of the Festival Association and was speaking of it with enthusiasm when Harsanyi asked him how it was that he was able to feel such an interest in choral directing and in voices generally. Thomas seldom spoke of his youth or his early struggles, but that night he turned back the pages and told Harsanyi a long story.

He said he had spent the summer of his fifteenth year wandering about alone in the South, giving violin concerts in little towns. He traveled on horseback. When he came into a town, he went about all day tacking up posters announcing his concert in the evening. Before the concert, he stood at the door taking in the admission money until his audience had arrived, and then he went on the platform and played. It was a lazy, hand-to-mouth existence, and Thomas said he must have got to like that easy way of living and the relaxing Southern atmosphere. At any rate, when he got back to New York in the fall, he was rather torpid; perhaps he had been growing too fast. From this adolescent drowsiness the lad was awakened by two voices, by two women who sang in New York in 1851,—Jenny Lind and Henrietta Sontag. They were the first great artists he had ever heard, and he never forgot his debt to them.

As he said, "It was not voice and execution alone. There was a greatness about them. They were great women, great artists. They opened a new world to me." Night after night he went to hear them, striving to reproduce the quality of their tone upon his violin. From that time his idea about strings was completely changed, and on his violin he tried always for the singing, vibrating tone, instead of the loud and somewhat harsh tone then prevalent among even the best German violinists. In later years he often advised violinists to study singing, and singers to study violin. He told Harsanyi that he got his first conception of tone quality from Jenny Lind.

"But, of course," he added, "the great thing I got from Lind and Sontag was the indefinite, not the definite, thing. For an impressionable boy, their inspiration was incalculable. They gave me my first feeling for the Italian style—but I could never say how much they gave me. At that age, such influences are actually creative. I always think of my artistic consciousness as beginning then."

All his life Thomas did his best to repay what he felt he owed to the singer's art. No man could get such singing from choruses, and no man worked harder to raise the standard of singing in schools and churches and choral societies.

VII.

All through the lesson Thea had felt that Harsanyi was restless and abstracted. Before the hour was over, he pushed back his chair and said resolutely, "I am not in the mood, Miss Kronborg. I have something on my mind, and I must talk to you. When do you intend to go home?"

Thea turned to him in surprise. "The first of June, about. Mr. Larsen will not need me after that, and I have not much money ahead. I shall work hard this summer, though."

"And to-day is the first of May; May-day." Harsanyi leaned forward, his elbows on his knees, his hands locked between them. "Yes, I must talk to you about something. I have asked Madison Bowers to let me bring you to him on Thursday, at your usual lesson-time. He is the best vocal teacher in Chicago, and it is time you began to work seriously with your voice."

Thea's brow wrinkled. "You mean take lessons of Bowers?"

Harsanyi nodded, without lifting his head.

"But I can't, Mr. Harsanyi. I haven't got the time, and, besides—" she blushed and drew her shoulders up stiffly—"besides, I can't afford to pay two teachers." Thea felt that she had blurted this out in the worst possible way, and she turned back to the keyboard to hide her chagrin.

"I know that. I don't mean that you shall pay two teachers. After you go to Bowers you will not need me. I need scarcely tell you that I shan't be happy at losing you."

Thea turned to him, hurt and angry. "But I don't want to go to Bowers. I don't want to leave you. What's the matter? Don't I work hard enough? I'm sure you teach people that don't try half as hard."

Harsanyi rose to his feet. "Don't misunderstand me, Miss Kronborg. You interest me more than any pupil I have. I have been thinking for months about what you ought to do, since that night when you first sang for me." He walked over to the window, turned, and came toward her again. "I believe that your voice is worth all that you can put into it. I have not come to this decision rashly. I have studied you, and I have become more and more convinced, against my own desires. I cannot make a singer of you, so it was my business to find a man who could. I have even consulted Theodore Thomas about it."

"But suppose I don't want to be a singer? I want to study with you. What's the matter? Do you really think I've no talent? Can't I be a pianist?"

Harsanyi paced up and down the long rug in front of her. "My girl, you are very talented. You could be a pianist, a good one. But the early training of a pianist, such a pianist as you would want to be, must be something tremendous. He must have had no other life than music. At your age he must be the master of his instrument. Nothing can ever take the place of that first training. You know very well that your technique is good, but it is not remarkable. It will never overtake your intelligence. You have a fine power of work, but you are not by nature a student. You are not by nature, I think, a pianist. You would never find yourself. In the effort to do so, I'm afraid your playing would become warped, eccentric." He threw back his head and looked at his pupil intently with that one eye which sometimes seemed to see deeper than any two eyes, as if its singleness gave it privileges. "Oh, I have watched you very carefully, Miss Kronborg. Because you had had so little and had yet done so much for yourself, I had a great wish to help you. I believe that the strongest need of your nature is to find yourself, to emerge AS yourself. Until I heard you sing I wondered how you were to do this, but it has grown clearer to me every day."

Thea looked away toward the window with hard, narrow eyes. "You mean I can be a singer because I haven't brains enough to be a pianist."

"You have brains enough and talent enough. But to do what you will want to do, it takes more than these—it takes vocation. Now, I think you have vocation, but for the voice, not for the piano. If you knew,"—he stopped and sighed,—"if you knew how fortunate I sometimes think you. With the voice the way is so much shorter, the rewards are more easily won. In your voice I think Nature herself did for you what it would take you many years to do at the piano. Perhaps you were not born in the wrong place after all. Let us talk frankly now. We have never done so before, and I have respected your reticence. What you want more than anything else in the world is to be an artist; is that true?"

She turned her face away from him and looked down at the keyboard. Her answer came in a thickened voice. "Yes, I suppose so."

"When did you first feel that you wanted to be an artist?"

"I don't know. There was always—something."

"Did you never think that you were going to sing?"

"Yes."

"How long ago was that?"

"Always, until I came to you. It was you who made me want to play piano." Her voice trembled. "Before, I tried to think I did, but I was pretending."

Harsanyi reached out and caught the hand that was hanging at her side. He pressed it as if to give her something. "Can't you see, my dear girl, that was only because I happened to be the first artist you have ever known? If I had been a trombone player, it would have been the same; you would have wanted to play trombone. But all the while you have been working with such good-will, something has been struggling against me. See, here we were, you and I and this instrument,"—he tapped the piano,—"three good friends, working so hard. But all the while there was something fighting us: your gift, and the woman you were meant to be. When you find your way to that gift and to that woman, you will be at peace. In the beginning it was an artist that you wanted to be; well, you may be an artist, always."

Thea drew a long breath. Her hands fell in her lap. "So I'm just where I began. No teacher, nothing done. No money."

Harsanyi turned away. "Feel no apprehension about the money, Miss Kronborg. Come back in the fall and we shall manage that. I shall even go to Mr. Thomas if necessary. This year will not be lost. If you but knew what an advantage this winter's study, all your study of the piano, will give you over most singers. Perhaps things have come out better for you than if we had planned them knowingly."

"You mean they have IF I can sing."

Thea spoke with a heavy irony, so heavy, indeed, that it was coarse. It grated upon Harsanyi because he felt that it was not sincere, an awkward affectation.

He wheeled toward her. "Miss Kronborg, answer me this. YOU KNOW THAT YOU CAN SING, do you not? You have always known it. While we worked here together you sometimes said to yourself, 'I have something you know nothing about; I could surprise you.' Is that also true?"

Thea nodded and hung her head.

"Why were you not frank with me? Did I not deserve it?"

She shuddered. Her bent shoulders trembled. "I don't know," she muttered. "I didn't mean to be like that. I couldn't. I can't. It's different."

"You mean it is very personal?" he asked kindly.

She nodded. "Not at church or funerals, or with people like Mr. Larsen. But with you it was—personal. I'm not like you and Mrs. Harsanyi. I come of rough people. I'm rough. But I'm independent, too. It was—all I had. There is no use my talking, Mr. Harsanyi. I can't tell you."

"You needn't tell me. I know. Every artist knows." Harsanyi stood looking at his pupil's back, bent as if she were pushing something, at her lowered head. "You can sing for those people because with them you do not commit yourself. But the reality, one cannot uncover THAT until one is sure. One can fail one's self, but one must not live to see that fail; better never reveal it. Let me help you to make yourself sure of it. That I can do better than Bowers."

Thea lifted her face and threw out her hands.

Harsanyi shook his head and smiled. "Oh, promise nothing! You will have much to do. There will not be voice only, but French, German, Italian. You will have work enough. But sometimes you will need to be understood; what you never show to any one will need companionship. And then you must come to me." He peered into her face with that searching, intimate glance. "You know what I mean, the thing in you that has no business with what is little, that will have to do only with beauty and power."

Thea threw out her hands fiercely, as if to push him away. She made a sound in her throat, but it was not articulate. Harsanyi took one of her hands and kissed it lightly upon the back. His salute was one of greeting, not of farewell, and it was for some one he had never seen.

When Mrs. Harsanyi came in at six o'clock, she found her husband sitting listlessly by the window. "Tired?" she asked.

"A little. I've just got through a difficulty. I've sent Miss Kronborg away; turned her over to Bowers, for voice."

"Sent Miss Kronborg away? Andor, what is the matter with you?"

"It's nothing rash. I've known for a long while I ought to do it. She is made for a singer, not a pianist."

Mrs. Harsanyi sat down on the piano chair. She spoke a little bitterly: "How can you be sure of that? She was, at least, the best you had. I thought you meant to have her play at your students' recital next fall. I am sure she would have made an impression. I could have dressed her so that she would have been very striking. She had so much individuality."

Harsanyi bent forward, looking at the floor. "Yes, I know. I shall miss her, of course."

Mrs. Harsanyi looked at her husband's fine head against the gray window. She had never felt deeper tenderness for him than she did at that moment. Her heart ached for him. "You will never get on, Andor," she said mournfully.

Harsanyi sat motionless. "No, I shall never get on," he repeated quietly. Suddenly he sprang up with that light movement she knew so well, and stood in the window, with folded arms. "But some day I shall be able to look her in the face and laugh because I did what I could for her. I believe in her. She will do nothing common. She is uncommon, in a common, common world. That is what I get out of it. It means more to me than if she played at my concert and brought me a dozen pupils. All this drudgery will kill me if once in a while I cannot hope something, for somebody! If I cannot sometimes see a bird fly and wave my hand to it."

His tone was angry and injured. Mrs. Harsanyi understood that this was one of the times when his wife was a part of the drudgery, of the "common, common world."

He had let something he cared for go, and he felt bitterly about whatever was left. The mood would pass, and he would be sorry. She knew him. It wounded her, of course, but that hurt was not new. It was as old as her love for him. She went out and left him alone.

VIII.

One warm damp June night the Denver Express was speeding westward across the earthy-smelling plains of Iowa. The lights in the day-coach were turned low and the ventilators were open, admitting showers of soot and dust upon the occupants of the narrow green plush chairs which were tilted at various angles of discomfort. In each of these chairs some uncomfortable human being lay drawn up, or stretched out, or writhing from one position to another. There were tired men in rumpled shirts, their necks bare and their suspenders down; old women with their heads tied up in black handkerchiefs; bedraggled young women who went to sleep while they were nursing their babies and forgot to button up their dresses; dirty boys who added to the general discomfort by taking off their boots. The brakeman, when he came through at midnight, sniffed the heavy air disdainfully and looked up at the ventilators. As he glanced down the double rows of contorted figures, he saw one pair of eyes that were wide open and bright, a yellow head that was not overcome by the stupefying heat and smell in the car. "There's a girl for you," he thought as he stopped by Thea's chair.

"Like to have the window up a little?" he asked.

Thea smiled up at him, not misunderstanding his friendliness. "The girl behind me is sick; she can't stand a draft. What time is it, please?"

He took out his open-faced watch and held it before her eyes with a knowing look. "In a hurry?" he asked. "I'll leave the end door open and air you out. Catch a wink; the time'll go faster."

Thea nodded good-night to him and settled her head back on her pillow, looking up at the oil lamps. She was going back to Moonstone for her summer vacation, and she was sitting up all night in a day-coach because that seemed such an easy way to save money. At her age discomfort was a small matter, when one made five dollars a day by it. She had confidently expected to sleep after the car got quiet, but in the two chairs behind her were a sick girl and her mother, and the girl had been coughing steadily since ten o'clock. They had come from somewhere in Pennsylvania, and this was their second night on the road. The mother said they were going to Colorado "for her daughter's lungs." The daughter was a little older than Thea, perhaps nineteen, with patient dark eyes and curly brown hair. She was pretty in spite of being so sooty and travel-stained. She had put on an ugly figured satine kimono over her loosened clothes. Thea, when she boarded the train in Chicago, happened to stop and plant her heavy telescope on this seat. She had not intended to remain there, but the sick girl had looked up at her with an eager smile and said, "Do sit there, miss. I'd so much rather not have a gentleman in front of me."

After the girl began to cough there were no empty seats left, and if there had been Thea could scarcely have changed without hurting her feelings. The mother turned on her side and went to sleep; she was used to the cough. But the girl lay wide awake, her eyes fixed on the roof of the car, as Thea's were. The two girls must have seen very different things there.

Thea fell to going over her winter in Chicago. It was only under unusual or uncomfortable conditions like these that she could keep her mind fixed upon herself or her own affairs for any length of time. The rapid motion and the vibration of the wheels under her seemed to give her thoughts rapidity and clearness. She had taken twenty very expensive lessons from Madison Bowers, but she did not yet know what he thought of her or of her ability. He was different from any man with whom she had ever had to do. With her other teachers she had felt a personal relation; but with him she did not. Bowers was a cold, bitter, avaricious man, but he knew a great deal about voices. He worked with a voice as if he were in a laboratory, conducting a series of experiments. He was conscientious and industrious, even capable of a certain cold fury when he was working with an interesting voice, but Harsanyi declared that he had the soul of a shrimp, and could no more make an artist than a throat specialist could. Thea realized that he had taught her a great deal in twenty lessons.

Although she cared so much less for Bowers than for Harsanyi, Thea was, on the whole, happier since she had been studying with him than she had been before. She had always told herself that she studied piano to fit herself to be a music teacher. But she never asked herself why she was studying voice. Her voice, more than any other part of her, had to do with that confidence, that sense of wholeness and inner well-being that she had felt at moments ever since she could remember.

Of this feeling Thea had never spoken to any human being until that day when she told Harsanyi that "there had always been—something." Hitherto she had felt but one obligation toward it—secrecy; to protect it even from herself. She had always believed that by doing all that was required of her by her family, her teachers, her pupils, she kept that part of herself from being caught up in the meshes of common things. She took it for granted that some day, when she was older, she would know a great deal more about it. It was as if she had an appointment to meet the rest of herself sometime, somewhere. It was moving to meet her and she was moving to meet it. That meeting awaited her, just as surely as, for the poor girl in the seat behind her, there awaited a hole in the earth, already dug.

For Thea, so much had begun with a hole in the earth. Yes, she reflected, this new part of her life had all begun that morning when she sat on the clay bank beside Ray Kennedy, under the flickering shade of the cottonwood tree. She remembered the way Ray had looked at her that morning. Why had he cared so much? And Wunsch, and Dr. Archie, and Spanish Johnny, why had they? It was something that had to do with her that made them care, but it was not she. It was something they believed in, but it was not she. Perhaps each of them concealed another person in himself, just as she did. Why was it that they seemed to feel and to hunt for a second person in her and not in each other? Thea frowned up at the dull lamp in the roof of the car. What if one's second self could somehow speak to all these second selves? What if one could bring them out, as whiskey did Spanish Johnny's? How deep they lay, these second persons, and how little one knew about them, except to guard them fiercely. It was to music, more than to anything else, that these hidden things in people responded. Her mother—even her mother had something of that sort which replied to music.

Thea found herself listening for the coughing behind her and not hearing it. She turned cautiously and looked back over the head-rest of her chair. The poor girl had fallen asleep. Thea looked at her intently. Why was she so afraid of men? Why did she shrink into herself and avert her face whenever a man passed her chair? Thea thought she knew; of course, she knew. How horrible to waste away like that, in the time when one ought to be growing fuller and stronger and rounder every day. Suppose there were such a dark hole open for her, between to-night and that place where she was to meet herself? Her eyes narrowed. She put her hand on her breast and felt how warm it was; and within it there was a full, powerful pulsation. She smiled—though she was ashamed of it—with the natural contempt of strength for weakness, with the sense of physical security which makes the savage merciless. Nobody could die while they felt like that inside. The springs there were wound so tight that it would be a long while before there was any slack in them. The life in there was rooted deep. She was going to have a few things before she died. She realized that there were a great many trains dashing east and west on the face of the continent that night, and that they all carried young people who meant to have things. But the difference was that SHE WAS GOING TO GET THEM! That was all. Let people try to stop her! She glowered at the rows of feckless bodies that lay sprawled in the chairs. Let them try it once! Along with the yearning that came from some deep part of her, that was selfless and exalted, Thea had a hard kind of cockiness, a determination to get ahead. Well, there are passages in life when that fierce, stubborn self-assertion will stand its ground after the nobler feeling is overwhelmed and beaten under.

Having told herself once more that she meant to grab a few things, Thea went to sleep.

She was wakened in the morning by the sunlight, which beat fiercely through the glass of the car window upon her face. She made herself as clean as she could, and while the people all about her were getting cold food out of their lunch-baskets she escaped into the dining-car. Her thrift did not go to the point of enabling her to carry a lunchbasket. At that early hour there were few people in the dining-car. The linen was white and fresh, the darkies were trim and smiling, and the sunlight gleamed pleasantly upon the silver and the glass water-bottles. On each table there was a slender vase with a single pink rose in it. When Thea sat down she looked into her rose and thought it the most beautiful thing in the world; it was wide open, recklessly offering its yellow heart, and there were drops of water on the petals. All the future was in that rose, all that one would like to be. The flower put her in an absolutely regal mood. She had a whole pot of coffee, and scrambled eggs with chopped ham, utterly disregarding the astonishing price they cost. She had faith enough in what she could do, she told herself, to have eggs if she wanted them. At the table opposite her sat a man and his wife and little boy—Thea classified them as being "from the East." They spoke in that quick, sure staccato, which Thea, like Ray Kennedy, pretended to scorn and secretly admired. People who could use words in that confident way, and who spoke them elegantly, had a great advantage in life, she reflected. There were so many words which she could not pronounce in speech as she had to do in singing. Language was like clothes; it could be a help to one, or it could give one away. But the most important thing was that one should not pretend to be what one was not.

When she paid her check she consulted the waiter. "Waiter, do you suppose I could buy one of those roses? I'm out of the day-coach, and there is a sick girl in there. I'd like to take her a cup of coffee and one of those flowers."

The waiter liked nothing better than advising travelers less sophisticated than himself. He told Thea there were a few roses left in the icebox and he would get one. He took the flower and the coffee into the day-coach. Thea pointed out the girl, but she did not accompany him. She hated thanks and never received them gracefully. She stood outside on the platform to get some fresh air into her lungs. The train was crossing the Platte River now, and the sunlight was so intense that it seemed to quiver in little flames on the glittering sandbars, the scrub willows, and the curling, fretted shallows.

Thea felt that she was coming back to her own land. She had often heard Mrs. Kronborg say that she "believed in immigration," and so did Thea believe in it. This earth seemed to her young and fresh and kindly, a place where refugees from old, sad countries were given another chance. The mere absence of rocks gave the soil a kind of amiability and generosity, and the absence of natural boundaries gave the spirit a wider range. Wire fences might mark the end of a man's pasture, but they could not shut in his thoughts as mountains and forests can. It was over flat lands like this, stretching out to drink the sun, that the larks sang—and one's heart sang there, too. Thea was glad that this was her country, even if one did not learn to speak elegantly there. It was, somehow, an honest country, and there was a new song in that blue air which had never been sung in the world before. It was hard to tell about it, for it had nothing to do with words; it was like the light of the desert at noon, or the smell of the sagebrush after rain; intangible but powerful. She had the sense of going back to a friendly soil, whose friendship was somehow going to strengthen her; a naive, generous country that gave one its joyous force, its large-hearted, childlike power to love, just as it gave one its coarse, brilliant flowers.

As she drew in that glorious air Thea's mind went back to Ray Kennedy. He, too, had that feeling of empire; as if all the Southwest really belonged to him because he had knocked about over it so much, and knew it, as he said, "like the blisters on his own hands." That feeling, she reflected, was the real element of companionship between her and Ray. Now that she was going back to Colorado, she realized this as she had not done before.

IX.

Thea reached Moonstone in the late afternoon, and all the Kronborgs were there to meet her except her two older brothers. Gus and Charley were young men now, and they had declared at noon that it would "look silly if the whole bunch went down to the train." "There's no use making a fuss over Thea just because she's been to Chicago," Charley warned his mother. "She's inclined to think pretty well of herself, anyhow, and if you go treating her like company, there'll be no living in the house with her." Mrs. Kronborg simply leveled her eyes at Charley, and he faded away, muttering. She had, as Mr. Kronborg always said with an inclination of his head, good control over her children. Anna, too, wished to absent herself from the party, but in the end her curiosity got the better of her. So when Thea stepped down from the porter's stool, a very creditable Kronborg representation was grouped on the platform to greet her. After they had all kissed her (Gunner and Axel shyly), Mr. Kronborg hurried his flock into the hotel omnibus, in which they were to be driven ceremoniously home, with the neighbors looking out of their windows to see them go by.

All the family talked to her at once, except Thor,—impressive in new trousers,—who was gravely silent and who refused to sit on Thea's lap. One of the first things Anna told her was that Maggie Evans, the girl who used to cough in prayer meeting, died yesterday, and had made a request that Thea sing at her funeral.

Thea's smile froze. "I'm not going to sing at all this summer, except my exercises. Bowers says I taxed my voice last winter, singing at funerals so much. If I begin the first day after I get home, there'll be no end to it. You can tell them I caught cold on the train, or something."

Thea saw Anna glance at their mother. Thea remembered having seen that look on Anna's face often before, but she had never thought anything about it because she was used to it. Now she realized that the look was distinctly spiteful, even vindictive. She suddenly realized that Anna had always disliked her.

Mrs. Kronborg seemed to notice nothing, and changed the trend of the conversation, telling Thea that Dr. Archie and Mr. Upping, the jeweler, were both coming in to see her that evening, and that she had asked Spanish Johnny to come, because he had behaved well all winter and ought to be encouraged.

The next morning Thea wakened early in her own room up under the eaves and lay watching the sunlight shine on the roses of her wall-paper. She wondered whether she would ever like a plastered room as well as this one lined with scantlings. It was snug and tight, like the cabin of a little boat. Her bed faced the window and stood against the wall, under the slant of the ceiling. When she went away she could just touch the ceiling with the tips of her fingers; now she could touch it with the palm of her hand. It was so little that it was like a sunny cave, with roses running all over the roof. Through the low window, as she lay there, she could watch people going by on the farther side of the street; men, going downtown to open their stores. Thor was over there, rattling his express wagon along the sidewalk. Tillie had put a bunch of French pinks in a tumbler of water on her dresser, and they gave out a pleasant perfume. The blue jays were fighting and screeching in the cottonwood tree outside her window, as they always did, and she could hear the old Baptist deacon across the street calling his chickens, as she had heard him do every summer morning since she could remember. It was pleasant to waken up in that bed, in that room, and to feel the brightness of the morning, while light quivered about the low, papered ceiling in golden spots, refracted by the broken mirror and the glass of water that held the pinks. "IM LEUCHTENDEN SOMMERMORGEN"; those lines, and the face of her old teacher, came back to Thea, floated to her out of sleep, perhaps. She had been dreaming something pleasant, but she could not remember what. She would go to call upon Mrs. Kohler to-day, and see the pigeons washing their pink feet in the drip under the water tank, and flying about their house that was sure to have a fresh coat of white paint on it for summer. On the way home she would stop to see Mrs. Tellamantez. On Sunday she would coax Gunner to take her out to the sand hills. She had missed them in Chicago; had been homesick for their brilliant morning gold and for their soft colors at evening. The Lake, somehow, had never taken their place.

While she lay planning, relaxed in warm drowsiness, she heard a knock at her door. She supposed it was Tillie, who sometimes fluttered in on her before she was out of bed to offer some service which the family would have ridiculed. But instead, Mrs. Kronborg herself came in, carrying a tray with Thea's breakfast set out on one of the best white napkins. Thea sat up with some embarrassment and pulled her nightgown together across her chest. Mrs. Kronborg was always busy downstairs in the morning, and Thea could not remember when her mother had come to her room before.

"I thought you'd be tired, after traveling, and might like to take it easy for once." Mrs. Kronborg put the tray on the edge of the bed. "I took some thick cream for you before the boys got at it. They raised a howl." She chuckled and sat down in the big wooden rocking chair. Her visit made Thea feel grown-up, and, somehow, important.

Mrs. Kronborg asked her about Bowers and the Harsanyis. She felt a great change in Thea, in her face and in her manner. Mr. Kronborg had noticed it, too, and had spoken of it to his wife with great satisfaction while they were undressing last night. Mrs. Kronborg sat looking at her daughter, who lay on her side, supporting herself on her elbow and lazily drinking her coffee from the tray before her. Her short-sleeved nightgown had come open at the throat again, and Mrs. Kronborg noticed how white her arms and shoulders were, as if they had been dipped in new milk. Her chest was fuller than when she went away, her breasts rounder and firmer, and though she was so white where she was uncovered, they looked rosy through the thin muslin. Her body had the elasticity that comes of being highly charged with the desire to live. Her hair, hanging in two loose braids, one by either cheek, was just enough disordered to catch the light in all its curly ends.

Thea always woke with a pink flush on her cheeks, and this morning her mother thought she had never seen her eyes so wide-open and bright; like clear green springs in the wood, when the early sunlight sparkles in them. She would make a very handsome woman, Mrs. Kronborg said to herself, if she would only get rid of that fierce look she had sometimes. Mrs. Kronborg took great pleasure in good looks, wherever she found them. She still remembered that, as a baby, Thea had been the "best-formed" of any of her children.

"I'll have to get you a longer bed," she remarked, as she put the tray on the table. "You're getting too long for that one."

Thea looked up at her mother and laughed, dropping back on her pillow with a magnificent stretch of her whole body. Mrs. Kronborg sat down again.

"I don't like to press you, Thea, but I think you'd better sing at that funeral to-morrow. I'm afraid you'll always be sorry if you don't. Sometimes a little thing like that, that seems nothing at the time, comes back on one afterward and troubles one a good deal. I don't mean the church shall run you to death this summer, like they used to. I've spoken my mind to your father about that, and he's very reasonable. But Maggie talked a good deal about you to people this winter; always asked what word we'd had, and said how she missed your singing and all. I guess you ought to do that much for her."

"All right, mother, if you think so." Thea lay looking at her mother with intensely bright eyes.

"That's right, daughter." Mrs. Kronborg rose and went over to get the tray, stopping to put her hand on Thea's chest. "You're filling out nice," she said, feeling about. "No, I wouldn't bother about the buttons. Leave 'em stay off. This is a good time to harden your chest."

Thea lay still and heard her mother's firm step receding along the bare floor of the trunk loft. There was no sham about her mother, she reflected. Her mother knew a great many things of which she never talked, and all the church people were forever chattering about things of which they knew nothing. She liked her mother.

Now for Mexican Town and the Kohlers! She meant to run in on the old woman without warning, and hug her.

X.

Spanish Johnny had no shop of his own, but he kept a table and an order-book in one corner of the drug store where paints and wall-paper were sold, and he was sometimes to be found there for an hour or so about noon. Thea had gone into the drug store to have a friendly chat with the proprietor, who used to lend her books from his shelves. She found Johnny there, trimming rolls of wall-paper for the parlor of Banker Smith's new house. She sat down on the top of his table and watched him.

"Johnny," she said suddenly, "I want you to write down the words of that Mexican serenade you used to sing; you know, 'ROSA DE NOCHE.' It's an unusual song. I'm going to study it. I know enough Spanish for that."

Johnny looked up from his roller with his bright, affable smile. "SI, but it is low for you, I think; VOZ CONTRALTO. It is low for me."

"Nonsense. I can do more with my low voice than I used to. I'll show you. Sit down and write it out for me, please." Thea beckoned him with the short yellow pencil tied to his order-book.

Johnny ran his fingers through his curly black hair. "If you wish. I do not know if that SERENATA all right for young ladies. Down there it is more for married ladies. They sing it for husbands—or somebody else, may-bee." Johnny's eyes twinkled and he apologized gracefully with his shoulders. He sat down at the table, and while Thea looked over his arm, began to write the song down in a long, slanting script, with highly ornamental capitals. Presently he looked up. "This-a song not exactly Mexican," he said thoughtfully. "It come from farther down; Brazil, Venezuela, may-bee. I learn it from some fellow down there, and he learn it from another fellow. It is-a most like Mexican, but not quite." Thea did not release him, but pointed to the paper. There were three verses of the song in all, and when Johnny had written them down, he sat looking at them meditatively, his head on one side. "I don' think for a high voice, SENORITA," he objected with polite persistence. "How you accompany with piano?"

"Oh, that will be easy enough."

"For you, may-bee!" Johnny smiled and drummed on the table with the tips of his agile brown fingers. "You know something? Listen, I tell you." He rose and sat down on the table beside her, putting his foot on the chair. He loved to talk at the hour of noon. "When you was a little girl, no bigger than that, you come to my house one day 'bout noon, like this, and I was in the door, playing guitar. You was barehead, barefoot; you run away from home. You stand there and make a frown at me an' listen. By 'n by you say for me to sing. I sing some lil' ting, and then I say for you to sing with me. You don' know no words, of course, but you take the air and you sing it justa beauti-ful! I never see a child do that, outside Mexico. You was, oh, I do' know—seven year, may-bee. By 'n by the preacher come look for you and begin for scold. I say, 'Don' scold, Meester Kronborg. She come for hear guitar. She gotta some music in her, that child. Where she get?' Then he tell me 'bout your gran'papa play oboe in the old country. I never forgetta that time." Johnny chuckled softly.

Thea nodded. "I remember that day, too. I liked your music better than the church music. When are you going to have a dance over there, Johnny?"

Johnny tilted his head. "Well, Saturday night the Spanish boys have a lil' party, some DANZA. You know Miguel Ramas? He have some young cousins, two boys, very nice-a, come from Torreon. They going to Salt Lake for some job-a, and stay off with him two-three days, and he mus' have a party. You like to come?"

That was how Thea came to go to the Mexican ball. Mexican Town had been increased by half a dozen new families during the last few years, and the Mexicans had put up an adobe dance-hall, that looked exactly like one of their own dwellings, except that it was a little longer, and was so unpretentious that nobody in Moonstone knew of its existence. The "Spanish boys" are reticent about their own affairs. Ray Kennedy used to know about all their little doings, but since his death there was no one whom the Mexicans considered SIMPATICO.

On Saturday evening after supper Thea told her mother that she was going over to Mrs. Tellamantez's to watch the Mexicans dance for a while, and that Johnny would bring her home.

Mrs. Kronborg smiled. She noticed that Thea had put on a white dress and had done her hair up with unusual care, and that she carried her best blue scarf. "Maybe you'll take a turn yourself, eh? I wouldn't mind watching them Mexicans. They're lovely dancers."

Thea made a feeble suggestion that her mother might go with her, but Mrs. Kronborg was too wise for that. She knew that Thea would have a better time if she went alone, and she watched her daughter go out of the gate and down the sidewalk that led to the depot.

Thea walked slowly. It was a soft, rosy evening. The sand hills were lavender. The sun had gone down a glowing copper disk, and the fleecy clouds in the east were a burning rose-color, flecked with gold. Thea passed the cottonwood grove and then the depot, where she left the sidewalk and took the sandy path toward Mexican Town. She could hear the scraping of violins being tuned, the tinkle of mandolins, and the growl of a double bass. Where had they got a double bass? She did not know there was one in Moonstone. She found later that it was the property of one of Ramas's young cousins, who was taking it to Utah with him to cheer him at his "job-a."

The Mexicans never wait until it is dark to begin to dance, and Thea had no difficulty in finding the new hall, because every other house in the town was deserted. Even the babies had gone to the ball; a neighbor was always willing to hold the baby while the mother danced. Mrs. Tellamantez came out to meet Thea and led her in. Johnny bowed to her from the platform at the end of the room, where he was playing the mandolin along with two fiddles and the bass. The hall was a long low room, with whitewashed walls, a fairly tight plank floor, wooden benches along the sides, and a few bracket lamps screwed to the frame timbers. There must have been fifty people there, counting the children. The Mexican dances were very much family affairs. The fathers always danced again and again with their little daughters, as well as with their wives. One of the girls came up to greet Thea, her dark cheeks glowing with pleasure and cordiality, and introduced her brother, with whom she had just been dancing. "You better take him every time he asks you," she whispered. "He's the best dancer here, except Johnny."

Thea soon decided that the poorest dancer was herself. Even Mrs. Tellamantez, who always held her shoulders so stiffly, danced better than she did. The musicians did not remain long at their post. When one of them felt like dancing, he called some other boy to take his instrument, put on his coat, and went down on the floor. Johnny, who wore a blousy white silk shirt, did not even put on his coat.

The dances the railroad men gave in Firemen's Hall were the only dances Thea had ever been allowed to go to, and they were very different from this. The boys played rough jokes and thought it smart to be clumsy and to run into each other on the floor. For the square dances there was always the bawling voice of the caller, who was also the county auctioneer.

This Mexican dance was soft and quiet. There was no calling, the conversation was very low, the rhythm of the music was smooth and engaging, the men were graceful and courteous. Some of them Thea had never before seen out of their working clothes, smeared with grease from the round-house or clay from the brickyard. Sometimes, when the music happened to be a popular Mexican waltz song, the dancers sang it softly as they moved. There were three little girls under twelve, in their first communion dresses, and one of them had an orange marigold in her black hair, just over her ear. They danced with the men and with each other. There was an atmosphere of ease and friendly pleasure in the low, dimly lit room, and Thea could not help wondering whether the Mexicans had no jealousies or neighborly grudges as the people in Moonstone had. There was no constraint of any kind there to-night, but a kind of natural harmony about their movements, their greetings, their low conversation, their smiles.

Ramas brought up his two young cousins, Silvo and Felipe, and presented them. They were handsome, smiling youths, of eighteen and twenty, with pale-gold skins, smooth cheeks, aquiline features, and wavy black hair, like Johnny's. They were dressed alike, in black velvet jackets and soft silk shirts, with opal shirt-buttons and flowing black ties looped through gold rings. They had charming manners, and low, guitar-like voices. They knew almost no English, but a Mexican boy can pay a great many compliments with a very limited vocabulary. The Ramas boys thought Thea dazzlingly beautiful. They had never seen a Scandinavian girl before, and her hair and fair skin bewitched them. "BLANCO Y ORO, SEMEJANTE LA PASCUA!" (White and gold, like Easter!) they exclaimed to each other. Silvo, the younger, declared that he could never go on to Utah; that he and his double bass had reached their ultimate destination. The elder was more crafty; he asked Miguel Ramas whether there would be "plenty more girls like that *A* Salt Lake, maybee?"

Silvo, overhearing, gave his brother a contemptuous glance. "Plenty more A PARAISO may-bee!" he retorted. When they were not dancing with her, their eyes followed her, over the coiffures of their other partners. That was not difficult; one blonde head moving among so many dark ones.

Thea had not meant to dance much, but the Ramas boys danced so well and were so handsome and adoring that she yielded to their entreaties. When she sat out a dance with them, they talked to her about their family at home, and told her how their mother had once punned upon their name. RAMA, in Spanish, meant a branch, they explained. Once when they were little lads their mother took them along when she went to help the women decorate the church for Easter. Some one asked her whether she had brought any flowers, and she replied that she had brought her "ramas." This was evidently a cherished family story.

When it was nearly midnight, Johnny announced that every one was going to his house to have "some lil' icecream and some lil' MUSICA." He began to put out the lights and Mrs. Tellamantez led the way across the square to her CASA. The Ramas brothers escorted Thea, and as they stepped out of the door, Silvo exclaimed, "HACE FRIO!" and threw his velvet coat about her shoulders.

Most of the company followed Mrs. Tellamantez, and they sat about on the gravel in her little yard while she and Johnny and Mrs. Miguel Ramas served the ice-cream. Thea sat on Felipe's coat, since Silvo's was already about her shoulders. The youths lay down on the shining gravel beside her, one on her right and one on her left. Johnny already called them "LOS ACOLITOS," the altar-boys. The talk all about them was low, and indolent. One of the girls was playing on Johnny's guitar, another was picking lightly at a mandolin. The moonlight was so bright that one could see every glance and smile, and the flash of their teeth. The moonflowers over Mrs. Tellamantez's door were wide open and of an unearthly white. The moon itself looked like a great pale flower in the sky.

After all the ice-cream was gone, Johnny approached Thea, his guitar under his arm, and the elder Ramas boy politely gave up his place. Johnny sat down, took a long breath, struck a fierce chord, and then hushed it with his other hand. "Now we have some lil' SERENATA, eh? You wan' a try?"

When Thea began to sing, instant silence fell upon the company. She felt all those dark eyes fix themselves upon her intently. She could see them shine. The faces came out of the shadow like the white flowers over the door. Felipe leaned his head upon his hand. Silvo dropped on his back and lay looking at the moon, under the impression that he was still looking at Thea. When she finished the first verse, Thea whispered to Johnny, "Again, I can do it better than that."

She had sung for churches and funerals and teachers, but she had never before sung for a really musical people, and this was the first time she had ever felt the response that such a people can give. They turned themselves and all they had over to her. For the moment they cared about nothing in the world but what she was doing. Their faces confronted her, open, eager, unprotected. She felt as if all these warm-blooded people debouched into her. Mrs. Tellamantez's fateful resignation, Johnny's madness, the adoration of the boy who lay still in the sand; in an instant these things seemed to be within her instead of without, as if they had come from her in the first place.

When she finished, her listeners broke into excited murmur. The men began hunting feverishly for cigarettes. Famos Serranos the barytone bricklayer, touched Johnny's arm, gave him a questioning look, then heaved a deep sigh. Johnny dropped on his elbow, wiping his face and neck and hands with his handkerchief. "SENORITA," he panted, "if you sing like that once in the City of Mexico, they just-a go crazy. In the City of Mexico they ain't-a sit like stumps when they hear that, not-a much! When they like, they just-a give you the town."

Thea laughed. She, too, was excited. "Think so, Johnny? Come, sing something with me. EL PARRENO; I haven't sung that for a long time."

Johnny laughed and hugged his guitar. "You not-a forget him?" He began teasing his strings. "Come!" He threw back his head, "ANOCHE-E-E—"

"ANOCHE ME CONFESSE CON UN PADRE CARMELITE, Y ME DIO PENITENCIA QUE BESARAS TU BOQUITA."

(Last night I made confession With a Carmelite father, And he gave me absolution For the kisses you imprinted.)

Johnny had almost every fault that a tenor can have. His voice was thin, unsteady, husky in the middle tones. But it was distinctly a voice, and sometimes he managed to get something very sweet out of it. Certainly it made him happy to sing. Thea kept glancing down at him as he lay there on his elbow. His eyes seemed twice as large as usual and had lights in them like those the moonlight makes on black, running water. Thea remembered the old stories about his "spells." She had never seen him when his madness was on him, but she felt something tonight at her elbow that gave her an idea of what it might be like. For the first time she fully understood the cryptic explanation that Mrs. Tellamantez had made to Dr. Archie, long ago. There were the same shells along the walk; she believed she could pick out the very one. There was the same moon up yonder, and panting at her elbow was the same Johnny—fooled by the same old things!

When they had finished, Famos, the barytone, murmured something to Johnny; who replied, "Sure we can sing 'Trovatore.' We have no alto, but all the girls can sing alto and make some noise."

The women laughed. Mexican women of the poorer class do not sing like the men. Perhaps they are too indolent. In the evening, when the men are singing their throats dry on the doorstep, or around the camp-fire beside the work-train, the women usually sit and comb their hair.

While Johnny was gesticulating and telling everybody what to sing and how to sing it, Thea put out her foot and touched the corpse of Silvo with the toe of her slipper. "Aren't you going to sing, Silvo?" she asked teasingly.

The boy turned on his side and raised himself on his elbow for a moment. "Not this night, SENORITA," he pleaded softly, "not this night!" He dropped back again, and lay with his cheek on his right arm, the hand lying passive on the sand above his head.

"How does he flatten himself into the ground like that?" Thea asked herself. "I wish I knew. It's very effective, somehow."

Across the gulch the Kohlers' little house slept among its trees, a dark spot on the white face of the desert. The windows of their upstairs bedroom were open, and Paulina had listened to the dance music for a long while before she drowsed off. She was a light sleeper, and when she woke again, after midnight, Johnny's concert was at its height. She lay still until she could bear it no longer. Then she wakened Fritz and they went over to the window and leaned out. They could hear clearly there.

"DIE THEA," whispered Mrs. Kohler; "it must be. ACH, WUNDERSCHON!"

Fritz was not so wide awake as his wife. He grunted and scratched on the floor with his bare foot. They were listening to a Mexican part-song; the tenor, then the soprano, then both together; the barytone joins them, rages, is extinguished; the tenor expires in sobs, and the soprano finishes alone. When the soprano's last note died away, Fritz nodded to his wife. "JA," he said; "SCHON."

There was silence for a few moments. Then the guitar sounded fiercely, and several male voices began the sextette from "Lucia." Johnny's reedy tenor they knew well, and the bricklayer's big, opaque barytone; the others might be anybody over there—just Mexican voices. Then at the appointed, at the acute, moment, the soprano voice, like a fountain jet, shot up into the light. "HORCH! HORCH!" the old people whispered, both at once. How it leaped from among those dusky male voices! How it played in and about and around and over them, like a goldfish darting among creek minnows, like a yellow butterfly soaring above a swarm of dark ones. "Ah," said Mrs. Kohler softly, "the dear man; if he could hear her now!"

XI.

Mrs. Kronborg had said that Thea was not to be disturbed on Sunday morning, and she slept until noon. When she came downstairs the family were just sitting down to dinner, Mr. Kronborg at one end of the long table, Mrs. Kronborg at the other. Anna, stiff and ceremonious, in her summer silk, sat at her father's right, and the boys were strung along on either side of the table. There was a place left for Thea between her mother and Thor. During the silence which preceded the blessing, Thea felt something uncomfortable in the air. Anna and her older brothers had lowered their eyes when she came in. Mrs. Kronborg nodded cheerfully, and after the blessing, as she began to pour the coffee, turned to her.

"I expect you had a good time at that dance, Thea. I hope you got your sleep out."

"High society, that," remarked Charley, giving the mashed potatoes a vicious swat. Anna's mouth and eyebrows became half-moons.

Thea looked across the table at the uncompromising countenances of her older brothers.

"Why, what's the matter with the Mexicans?" she asked, flushing. "They don't trouble anybody, and they are kind to their families and have good manners."

"Nice clean people; got some style about them. Do you really like that kind, Thea, or do you just pretend to? That's what I'd like to know." Gus looked at her with pained inquiry. But he at least looked at her.

"They're just as clean as white people, and they have a perfect right to their own ways. Of course I like 'em. I don't pretend things."

"Everybody according to their own taste," remarked Charley bitterly. "Quit crumbing your bread up, Thor. Ain't you learned how to eat yet?"

"Children, children!" said Mr. Kronborg nervously, looking up from the chicken he was dismembering. He glanced at his wife, whom he expected to maintain harmony in the family.

"That's all right, Charley. Drop it there," said Mrs. Kronborg. "No use spoiling your Sunday dinner with race prejudices. The Mexicans suit me and Thea very well. They are a useful people. Now you can just talk about something else."

Conversation, however, did not flourish at that dinner. Everybody ate as fast as possible. Charley and Gus said they had engagements and left the table as soon as they finished their apple pie. Anna sat primly and ate with great elegance. When she spoke at all she spoke to her father, about church matters, and always in a commiserating tone, as if he had met with some misfortune. Mr. Kronborg, quite innocent of her intentions, replied kindly and absent-mindedly. After the dessert he went to take his usual Sunday afternoon nap, and Mrs. Kronborg carried some dinner to a sick neighbor. Thea and Anna began to clear the table.

"I should think you would show more consideration for father's position, Thea," Anna began as soon as she and her sister were alone.

Thea gave her a sidelong glance. "Why, what have I done to father?"

"Everybody at Sunday-School was talking about you going over there and singing with the Mexicans all night, when you won't sing for the church. Somebody heard you, and told it all over town. Of course, we all get the blame for it."

"Anything disgraceful about singing?" Thea asked with a provoking yawn.

"I must say you choose your company! You always had that streak in you, Thea. We all hoped that going away would improve you. Of course, it reflects on father when you are scarcely polite to the nice people here and make up to the rowdies."

"Oh, it's my singing with the Mexicans you object to?" Thea put down a tray full of dishes. "Well, I like to sing over there, and I don't like to over here. I'll sing for them any time they ask me to. They know something about what I'm doing. They're a talented people."

"Talented!" Anna made the word sound like escaping steam. "I suppose you think it's smart to come home and throw that at your family!"

Thea picked up the tray. By this time she was as white as the Sunday tablecloth. "Well," she replied in a cold, even tone, "I'll have to throw it at them sooner or later. It's just a question of when, and it might as well be now as any time." She carried the tray blindly into the kitchen.

Tillie, who was always listening and looking out for her, took the dishes from her with a furtive, frightened glance at her stony face. Thea went slowly up the back stairs to her loft. Her legs seemed as heavy as lead as she climbed the stairs, and she felt as if everything inside her had solidified and grown hard.

After shutting her door and locking it, she sat down on the edge of her bed. This place had always been her refuge, but there was a hostility in the house now which this door could not shut out. This would be her last summer in that room. Its services were over; its time was done. She rose and put her hand on the low ceiling. Two tears ran down her cheeks, as if they came from ice that melted slowly. She was not ready to leave her little shell. She was being pulled out too soon. She would never be able to think anywhere else as well as here. She would never sleep so well or have such dreams in any other bed; even last night, such sweet, breathless dreams—Thea hid her face in the pillow. Wherever she went she would like to take that little bed with her. When she went away from it for good, she would leave something that she could never recover; memories of pleasant excitement, of happy adventures in her mind; of warm sleep on howling winter nights, and joyous awakenings on summer mornings. There were certain dreams that might refuse to come to her at all except in a little morning cave, facing the sun—where they came to her so powerfully, where they beat a triumph in her!

The room was hot as an oven. The sun was beating fiercely on the shingles behind the board ceiling. She undressed, and before she threw herself upon her bed in her chemise, she frowned at herself for a long while in her looking-glass. Yes, she and It must fight it out together. The thing that looked at her out of her own eyes was the only friend she could count on. Oh, she would make these people sorry enough! There would come a time when they would want to make it up with her. But, never again! She had no little vanities, only one big one, and she would never forgive.

Her mother was all right, but her mother was a part of the family, and she was not. In the nature of things, her mother had to be on both sides. Thea felt that she had been betrayed. A truce had been broken behind her back. She had never had much individual affection for any of her brothers except Thor, but she had never been disloyal, never felt scorn or held grudges. As a little girl she had always been good friends with Gunner and Axel, whenever she had time to play. Even before she got her own room, when they were all sleeping and dressing together, like little cubs, and breakfasting in the kitchen, she had led an absorbing personal life of her own. But she had a cub loyalty to the other cubs. She thought them nice boys and tried to make them get their lessons. She once fought a bully who "picked on" Axel at school. She never made fun of Anna's crimpings and curlings and beauty-rites.

Thea had always taken it for granted that her sister and brothers recognized that she had special abilities, and that they were proud of it. She had done them the honor, she told herself bitterly, to believe that though they had no particular endowments, THEY WERE OF HER KIND, and not of the Moonstone kind. Now they had all grown up and become persons. They faced each other as individuals, and she saw that Anna and Gus and Charley were among the people whom she had always recognized as her natural enemies. Their ambitions and sacred proprieties were meaningless to her. She had neglected to congratulate Charley upon having been promoted from the grocery department of Commings's store to the drygoods department. Her mother had reproved her for this omission. And how was she to know, Thea asked herself, that Anna expected to be teased because Bert Rice now came and sat in the hammock with her every night? No, it was all clear enough. Nothing that she would ever do in the world would seem important to them, and nothing they would ever do would seem important to her.

Thea lay thinking intently all through the stifling afternoon. Tillie whispered something outside her door once, but she did not answer. She lay on her bed until the second church bell rang, and she saw the family go trooping up the sidewalk on the opposite side of the street, Anna and her father in the lead. Anna seemed to have taken on a very story-book attitude toward her father; patronizing and condescending, it seemed to Thea. The older boys were not in the family band. They now took their girls to church. Tillie had stayed at home to get supper. Thea got up, washed her hot face and arms, and put on the white organdie dress she had worn last night; it was getting too small for her, and she might as well wear it out. After she was dressed she unlocked her door and went cautiously downstairs. She felt as if chilling hostilities might be awaiting her in the trunk loft, on the stairway, almost anywhere. In the dining-room she found Tillie, sitting by the open window, reading the dramatic news in a Denver Sunday paper. Tillie kept a scrapbook in which she pasted clippings about actors and actresses.

"Come look at this picture of Pauline Hall in tights, Thea," she called. "Ain't she cute? It's too bad you didn't go to the theater more when you was in Chicago; such a good chance! Didn't you even get to see Clara Morris or Modjeska?"

"No; I didn't have time. Besides, it costs money, Tillie," Thea replied wearily, glancing at the paper Tillie held out to her.

Tillie looked up at her niece. "Don't you go and be upset about any of Anna's notions. She's one of these narrow kind. Your father and mother don't pay any attention to what she says. Anna's fussy; she is with me, but I don't mind her."

"Oh, I don't mind her. That's all right, Tillie. I guess I'll take a walk."

Thea knew that Tillie hoped she would stay and talk to her for a while, and she would have liked to please her. But in a house as small as that one, everything was too intimate and mixed up together. The family was the family, an integral thing. One couldn't discuss Anna there. She felt differently toward the house and everything in it, as if the battered old furniture that seemed so kindly, and the old carpets on which she had played, had been nourishing a secret grudge against her and were not to be trusted any more.

She went aimlessly out of the front gate, not knowing what to do with herself. Mexican Town, somehow, was spoiled for her just then, and she felt that she would hide if she saw Silvo or Felipe coming toward her. She walked down through the empty main street. All the stores were closed, their blinds down. On the steps of the bank some idle boys were sitting, telling disgusting stories because there was nothing else to do. Several of them had gone to school with Thea, but when she nodded to them they hung their heads and did not speak. Thea's body was often curiously expressive of what was going on in her mind, and to-night there was something in her walk and carriage that made these boys feel that she was "stuck up." If she had stopped and talked to them, they would have thawed out on the instant and would have been friendly and grateful. But Thea was hurt afresh, and walked on, holding her chin higher than ever. As she passed the Duke Block, she saw a light in Dr. Archie's office, and she went up the stairs and opened the door into his study. She found him with a pile of papers and accountbooks before him. He pointed her to her old chair at the end of his desk and leaned back in his own, looking at her with satisfaction. How handsome she was growing!

"I'm still chasing the elusive metal, Thea,"—he pointed to the papers before him,—"I'm up to my neck in mines, and I'm going to be a rich man some day."

"I hope you will; awfully rich. That's the only thing that counts." She looked restlessly about the consulting-room. "To do any of the things one wants to do, one has to have lots and lots of money."

Dr. Archie was direct. "What's the matter? Do you need some?"

Thea shrugged. "Oh, I can get along, in a little way." She looked intently out of the window at the arc streetlamp that was just beginning to sputter. "But it's silly to live at all for little things," she added quietly. "Living's too much trouble unless one can get something big out of it."

Dr. Archie rested his elbows on the arms of his chair, dropped his chin on his clasped hands and looked at her. "Living is no trouble for little people, believe me!" he exclaimed. "What do you want to get out of it?"

"Oh—so many things!" Thea shivered.

"But what? Money? You mentioned that. Well, you can make money, if you care about that more than anything else." He nodded prophetically above his interlacing fingers.

"But I don't. That's only one thing. Anyhow, I couldn't if I did." She pulled her dress lower at the neck as if she were suffocating. "I only want impossible things," she said roughly. "The others don't interest me."

Dr. Archie watched her contemplatively, as if she were a beaker full of chemicals working. A few years ago, when she used to sit there, the light from under his green lampshade used to fall full upon her broad face and yellow pigtails. Now her face was in the shadow and the line of light fell below her bare throat, directly across her bosom. The shrunken white organdie rose and fell as if she were struggling to be free and to break out of it altogether. He felt that her heart must be laboring heavily in there, but he was afraid to touch her; he was, indeed. He had never seen her like this before. Her hair, piled high on her head, gave her a commanding look, and her eyes, that used to be so inquisitive, were stormy.

"Thea," he said slowly, "I won't say that you can have everything you want—that means having nothing, in reality. But if you decide what it is you want most, YOU CAN GET IT." His eye caught hers for a moment. "Not everybody can, but you can. Only, if you want a big thing, you've got to have nerve enough to cut out all that's easy, everything that's to be had cheap." Dr. Archie paused. He picked up a paper-cutter and, feeling the edge of it softly with his fingers, he added slowly, as if to himself:—

"He either fears his fate too much, Or his deserts are small, Who dares not put it to the touch To win...or lose it all."

Thea's lips parted; she looked at him from under a frown, searching his face. "Do you mean to break loose, too, and—do something?" she asked in a low voice.

"I mean to get rich, if you call that doing anything. I've found what I can do without. You make such bargains in your mind, first."

Thea sprang up and took the paper-cutter he had put down, twisting it in her hands. "A long while first, sometimes," she said with a short laugh. "But suppose one can never get out what they've got in them? Suppose they make a mess of it in the end; then what?" She threw the paper-cutter on the desk and took a step toward the doctor, until her dress touched him. She stood looking down at him. "Oh, it's easy to fail!" She was breathing through her mouth and her throat was throbbing with excitement.

As he looked up at her, Dr. Archie's hands tightened on the arms of his chair. He had thought he knew Thea Kronborg pretty well, but he did not know the girl who was standing there. She was beautiful, as his little Swede had never been, but she frightened him. Her pale cheeks, her parted lips, her flashing eyes, seemed suddenly to mean one thing—he did not know what. A light seemed to break upon her from far away—or perhaps from far within. She seemed to grow taller, like a scarf drawn out long; looked as if she were pursued and fleeing, and—yes, she looked tormented. "It's easy to fail," he heard her say again, "and if I fail, you'd better forget about me, for I'll be one of the worst women that ever lived. I'll be an awful woman!"

In the shadowy light above the lampshade he caught her glance again and held it for a moment. Wild as her eyes were, that yellow gleam at the back of them was as hard as a diamond drill-point. He rose with a nervous laugh and dropped his hand lightly on her shoulder. "No, you won't. You'll be a splendid one!"

She shook him off before he could say anything more, and went out of his door with a kind of bound. She left so quickly and so lightly that he could not even hear her footstep in the hallway outside. Archie dropped back into his chair and sat motionless for a long while.

So it went; one loved a quaint little girl, cheerful, industrious, always on the run and hustling through her tasks; and suddenly one lost her. He had thought he knew that child like the glove on his hand. But about this tall girl who threw up her head and glittered like that all over, he knew nothing. She was goaded by desires, ambitions, revulsions that were dark to him. One thing he knew: the old highroad of life, worn safe and easy, hugging the sunny slopes, would scarcely hold her again.

After that night Thea could have asked pretty much anything of him. He could have refused her nothing. Years ago a crafty little bunch of hair and smiles had shown him what she wanted, and he had promptly married her. To-night a very different sort of girl—driven wild by doubts and youth, by poverty and riches—had let him see the fierceness of her nature. She went out still distraught, not knowing or caring what she had shown him. But to Archie knowledge of that sort was obligation. Oh, he was the same old Howard Archie!

That Sunday in July was the turning-point; Thea's peace of mind did not come back. She found it hard even to practice at home. There was something in the air there that froze her throat. In the morning, she walked as far as she could walk. In the hot afternoons she lay on her bed in her nightgown, planning fiercely. She haunted the post-office. She must have worn a path in the sidewalk that led to the post-office, that summer. She was there the moment the mail-sacks came up from the depot, morning and evening, and while the letters were being sorted and distributed she paced up and down outside, under the cottonwood trees, listening to the thump, thump, thump of Mr. Thompson's stamp. She hung upon any sort of word from Chicago; a card from Bowers, a letter from Mrs. Harsanyi, from Mr. Larsen, from her landlady,—anything to reassure her that Chicago was still there. She began to feel the same restlessness that had tortured her the last spring when she was teaching in Moonstone. Suppose she never got away again, after all? Suppose one broke a leg and had to lie in bed at home for weeks, or had pneumonia and died there. The desert was so big and thirsty; if one's foot slipped, it could drink one up like a drop of water.

This time, when Thea left Moonstone to go back to Chicago, she went alone. As the train pulled out, she looked back at her mother and father and Thor. They were calm and cheerful; they did not know, they did not understand. Something pulled in her—and broke. She cried all the way to Denver, and that night, in her berth, she kept sobbing and waking herself. But when the sun rose in the morning, she was far away. It was all behind her, and she knew that she would never cry like that again. People live through such pain only once; pain comes again, but it finds a tougher surface. Thea remembered how she had gone away the first time, with what confidence in everything, and what pitiful ignorance. Such a silly! She felt resentful toward that stupid, good-natured child. How much older she was now, and how much harder! She was going away to fight, and she was going away forever.

3
STUPID FACES

I.

SO MANY GRINNING, stupid faces! Thea was sitting by the window in Bowers's studio, waiting for him to come back from lunch. On her knee was the latest number of an illustrated musical journal in which musicians great and little stridently advertised their wares. Every afternoon she played accompaniments for people who looked and smiled like these. She was getting tired of the human countenance.

Thea had been in Chicago for two months. She had a small church position which partly paid her living expenses, and she paid for her singing lessons by playing Bowers's accompaniments every afternoon from two until six. She had been compelled to leave her old friends Mrs. Lorch and Mrs. Andersen, because the long ride from North Chicago to Bowers's studio on Michigan Avenue took too much time—an hour in the morning, and at night, when the cars were crowded, an hour and a half. For the first month she had clung to her old room, but the bad air in the cars, at the end of a long day's work, fatigued her greatly and was bad for her voice. Since she left Mrs. Lorch, she had been staying at a students' club to which she was introduced by Miss Adler, Bowers's morning accompanist, an intelligent Jewish girl from Evanston.

Thea took her lesson from Bowers every day from eleven-thirty until twelve. Then she went out to lunch with an Italian grammar under her arm, and came back to the studio to begin her work at two. In the afternoon Bowers coached professionals and taught his advanced pupils. It was his theory that Thea ought to be able to learn a great deal by keeping her ears open while she played for him.

The concert-going public of Chicago still remembers the long, sallow, discontented face of Madison Bowers. He seldom missed an evening concert, and was usually to be seen lounging somewhere at the back of the concert hall, reading a newspaper or review, and conspicuously ignoring the efforts of the performers. At the end of a number he looked up from his paper long enough to sweep the applauding audience with a contemptuous eye. His face was intelligent, with a narrow lower jaw, a thin nose, faded gray eyes, and a close-cut brown mustache. His hair was iron-gray, thin and dead-looking. He went to concerts chiefly to satisfy himself as to how badly things were done and how gullible the public was. He hated the whole race of artists; the work they did, the wages they got, and the way they spent their money. His father, old Hiram Bowers, was still alive and at work, a genial old choirmaster in Boston, full of enthusiasm at seventy. But Madison was of the colder stuff of his grandfathers, a long line of New Hampshire farmers; hard workers, close traders, with good minds, mean natures, and flinty eyes. As a boy Madison had a fine barytone voice, and his father made great sacrifices for him, sending him to Germany at an early age and keeping him abroad at his studies for years. Madison worked under the best teachers, and afterward sang in England in oratorio. His cold nature and academic methods were against him. His audiences were always aware of the contempt he felt for them. A dozen poorer singers succeeded, but Bowers did not.

Bowers had all the qualities which go to make a good teacher—except generosity and warmth. His intelligence was of a high order, his taste never at fault. He seldom worked with a voice without improving it, and in teaching the delivery of oratorio he was without a rival. Singers came from far and near to study Bach and Handel with him. Even the fashionable sopranos and contraltos of Chicago, St. Paul, and St. Louis (they were usually ladies with very rich husbands, and Bowers called them the "pampered jades of Asia") humbly endured his sardonic humor for the sake of what he could do for them. He was not at all above helping a very lame singer across, if her husband's check-book warranted it. He had a whole bag of tricks for stupid people, "life-preservers," he called them. "Cheap repairs for a cheap 'un," he used to say, but the husbands never found the repairs very cheap. Those were the days when lumbermen's daughters and brewers' wives contended in song; studied in Germany and then floated from SANGERFEST to SANGERFEST. Choral societies flourished in all the rich lake cities and river cities. The soloists came to Chicago to coach with Bowers, and he often took long journeys to hear and instruct a chorus. He was intensely avaricious, and from these semi-professionals he reaped a golden harvest. They fed his pockets and they fed his ever-hungry contempt, his scorn of himself and his accomplices. The more money he made, the more parsimonious he became. His wife was so shabby that she never went anywhere with him, which suited him exactly. Because his clients were luxurious and extravagant, he took a revengeful pleasure in having his shoes halfsoled a second time, and in getting the last wear out of a broken collar. He had first been interested in Thea Kronborg because of her bluntness, her country roughness, and her manifest carefulness about money. The mention of Harsanyi's name always made him pull a wry face. For the first time Thea had a friend who, in his own cool and guarded way, liked her for whatever was least admirable in her.

Thea was still looking at the musical paper, her grammar unopened on the window-sill, when Bowers sauntered in a little before two o'clock. He was smoking a cheap cigarette and wore the same soft felt hat he had worn all last winter. He never carried a cane or wore gloves.

Thea followed him from the reception-room into the studio. "I may cut my lesson out to-morrow, Mr. Bowers. I have to hunt a new boarding-place."

Bowers looked up languidly from his desk where he had begun to go over a pile of letters. "What's the matter with the Studio Club? Been fighting with them again?"

"The Club's all right for people who like to live that way. I don't."

Bowers lifted his eyebrows. "Why so tempery?" he asked as he drew a check from an envelope postmarked "Minneapolis."

"I can't work with a lot of girls around. They're too familiar. I never could get along with girls of my own age. It's all too chummy. Gets on my nerves. I didn't come here to play kindergarten games." Thea began energetically to arrange the scattered music on the piano.

Bowers grimaced good-humoredly at her over the three checks he was pinning together. He liked to play at a rough game of banter with her. He flattered himself that he had made her harsher than she was when she first came to him; that he had got off a little of the sugar-coating Harsanyi always put on his pupils.

"The art of making yourself agreeable never comes amiss, Miss Kronborg. I should say you rather need a little practice along that line. When you come to marketing your wares in the world, a little smoothness goes farther than a great deal of talent sometimes. If you happen to be cursed with a real talent, then you've got to be very smooth indeed, or you'll never get your money back." Bowers snapped the elastic band around his bank-book.

Thea gave him a sharp, recognizing glance. "Well, that's the money I'll have to go without," she replied.

"Just what do you mean?"

"I mean the money people have to grin for. I used to know a railroad man who said there was money in every profession that you couldn't take. He'd tried a good many jobs," Thea added musingly; "perhaps he was too particular about the kind he could take, for he never picked up much. He was proud, but I liked him for that."

Bowers rose and closed his desk. "Mrs. Priest is late again. By the way, Miss Kronborg, remember not to frown when you are playing for Mrs. Priest. You did not remember yesterday."

"You mean when she hits a tone with her breath like that? Why do you let her? You wouldn't let me."

"I certainly would not. But that is a mannerism of Mrs. Priest's. The public like it, and they pay a great deal of money for the pleasure of hearing her do it. There she is. Remember!"

Bowers opened the door of the reception-room and a tall, imposing woman rustled in, bringing with her a glow of animation which pervaded the room as if half a dozen persons, all talking gayly, had come in instead of one. She was large, handsome, expansive, uncontrolled; one felt this the moment she crossed the threshold. She shone with care and cleanliness, mature vigor, unchallenged authority, gracious good-humor, and absolute confidence in her person, her powers, her position, and her way of life; a glowing, overwhelming self-satisfaction, only to be found where human society is young and strong and without yesterdays. Her face had a kind of heavy, thoughtless beauty, like a pink peony just at the point of beginning to fade. Her brown hair was waved in front and done up behind in a great twist, held by a tortoiseshell comb with gold filigree. She wore a beautiful little green hat with three long green feathers sticking straight up in front, a little cape made of velvet and fur with a yellow satin rose on it. Her gloves, her shoes, her veil, somehow made themselves felt. She gave the impression of wearing a cargo of splendid merchandise.

Mrs. Priest nodded graciously to Thea, coquettishly to Bowers, and asked him to untie her veil for her. She threw her splendid wrap on a chair, the yellow lining out. Thea was already at the piano. Mrs. Priest stood behind her.

"'Rejoice Greatly' first, please. And please don't hurry it in there," she put her arm over Thea's shoulder, and indicated the passage by a sweep of her white glove. She threw out her chest, clasped her hands over her abdomen, lifted her chin, worked the muscles of her cheeks back and forth for a moment, and then began with conviction, "Re-jo-oice! Re-jo-oice!"

Bowers paced the room with his catlike tread. When he checked Mrs. Priest's vehemence at all, he handled her roughly; poked and hammered her massive person with cold satisfaction, almost as if he were taking out a grudge on this splendid creation. Such treatment the imposing lady did not at all resent. She tried harder and harder, her eyes growing all the while more lustrous and her lips redder. Thea played on as she was told, ignoring the singer's struggles.

When she first heard Mrs. Priest sing in church, Thea admired her. Since she had found out how dull the goodnatured soprano really was, she felt a deep contempt for her. She felt that Mrs. Priest ought to be reproved and even punished for her shortcomings; that she ought to be exposed,—at least to herself,—and not be permitted to live and shine in happy ignorance of what a poor thing it was she brought across so radiantly. Thea's cold looks of reproof were lost upon Mrs. Priest; although the lady did murmur one day when she took Bowers home in her carriage, "How handsome your afternoon girl would be if she did not have that unfortunate squint; it gives her that vacant Swede look, like an animal." That amused Bowers. He liked to watch the germination and growth of antipathies.

One of the first disappointments Thea had to face when she returned to Chicago that fall, was the news that the Harsanyis were not coming back. They had spent the summer in a camp in the Adirondacks and were moving to New York. An old teacher and friend of Harsanyi's, one of the best-known piano teachers in New York, was about to retire because of failing health and had arranged to turn his pupils over to Harsanyi. Andor was to give two recitals in New York in November, to devote himself to his new students until spring, and then to go on a short concert tour. The Harsanyis had taken a furnished apartment in New York, as they would not attempt to settle a place of their own until Andor's recitals were over. The first of December, however, Thea received a note from Mrs. Harsanyi, asking her to call at the old studio, where she was packing their goods for shipment.

The morning after this invitation reached her, Thea climbed the stairs and knocked at the familiar door. Mrs. Harsanyi herself opened it, and embraced her visitor warmly. Taking Thea into the studio, which was littered with excelsior and packing-cases, she stood holding her hand and looking at her in the strong light from the big window before she allowed her to sit down. Her quick eye saw many changes. The girl was taller, her figure had become definite, her carriage positive. She had got used to living in the body of a young woman, and she no longer tried to ignore it and behave as if she were a little girl. With that increased independence of body there had come a change in her face; an indifference, something hard and skeptical. Her clothes, too, were different, like the attire of a shopgirl who tries to follow the fashions; a purple suit, a piece of cheap fur, a three-cornered purple hat with a pompon sticking up in front. The queer country clothes she used to wear suited her much better, Mrs. Harsanyi thought. But such trifles, after all, were accidental and remediable. She put her hand on the girl's strong shoulder.

"How much the summer has done for you! Yes, you are a young lady at last. Andor will be so glad to hear about you."

Thea looked about at the disorder of the familiar room. The pictures were piled in a corner, the piano and the CHAISE LONGUE were gone. "I suppose I ought to be glad you have gone away," she said, "but I'm not. It's a fine thing for Mr. Harsanyi, I suppose."

Mrs. Harsanyi gave her a quick glance that said more than words. "If you knew how long I have wanted to get him away from here, Miss Kronborg! He is never tired, never discouraged, now."

Thea sighed. "I'm glad for that, then." Her eyes traveled over the faint discolorations on the walls where the pictures had hung. "I may run away myself. I don't know whether I can stand it here without you."

"We hope that you can come to New York to study before very long. We have thought of that. And you must tell me how you are getting on with Bowers. Andor will want to know all about it."

"I guess I get on more or less. But I don't like my work very well. It never seems serious as my work with Mr. Harsanyi did. I play Bowers's accompaniments in the afternoons, you know. I thought I would learn a good deal from the people who work with him, but I don't think I get much."

Mrs. Harsanyi looked at her inquiringly. Thea took out a carefully folded handkerchief from the bosom of her dress and began to draw the corners apart. "Singing doesn't seem to be a very brainy profession, Mrs. Harsanyi," she said slowly. "The people I see now are not a bit like the ones I used to meet here. Mr. Harsanyi's pupils, even the dumb ones, had more—well, more of everything, it seems to me. The people I have to play accompaniments for are discouraging. The professionals, like Katharine Priest and Miles Murdstone, are worst of all. If I have to play 'The Messiah' much longer for Mrs. Priest, I'll go out of my mind!" Thea brought her foot down sharply on the bare floor.

Mrs. Harsanyi looked down at the foot in perplexity. "You mustn't wear such high heels, my dear. They will spoil your walk and make you mince along. Can't you at least learn to avoid what you dislike in these singers? I was never able to care for Mrs. Priest's singing."

Thea was sitting with her chin lowered. Without moving her head she looked up at Mrs. Harsanyi and smiled; a smile much too cold and desperate to be seen on a young face, Mrs. Harsanyi felt. "Mrs. Harsanyi, it seems to me that what I learn is just TO DISLIKE. I dislike so much and so hard that it tires me out. I've got no heart for anything." She threw up her head suddenly and sat in defiance, her hand clenched on the arm of the chair. "Mr. Harsanyi couldn't stand these people an hour, I know he couldn't. He'd put them right out of the window there, frizzes and feathers and all. Now, take that new soprano they're all making such a fuss about, Jessie Darcey. She's going on tour with a symphony orchestra and she's working up her repertory with Bowers. She's singing some Schumann songs Mr. Harsanyi used to go over with me. Well, I don't know what he WOULD do if he heard her."

"But if your own work goes well, and you know these people are wrong, why do you let them discourage you?"

Thea shook her head. "That's just what I don't understand myself. Only, after I've heard them all afternoon, I come out frozen up. Somehow it takes the shine off of everything. People want Jessie Darcey and the kind of thing she does; so what's the use?"

Mrs. Harsanyi smiled. "That stile you must simply vault over. You must not begin to fret about the successes of cheap people. After all, what have they to do with you?"

"Well, if I had somebody like Mr. Harsanyi, perhaps I wouldn't fret about them. He was the teacher for me. Please tell him so."

Thea rose and Mrs. Harsanyi took her hand again. "I am sorry you have to go through this time of discouragement. I wish Andor could talk to you, he would understand it so well. But I feel like urging you to keep clear of Mrs. Priest and Jessie Darcey and all their works."

Thea laughed discordantly. "No use urging me. I don't get on with them AT ALL. My spine gets like a steel rail when they come near me. I liked them at first, you know. Their clothes and their manners were so fine, and Mrs. Priest IS handsome. But now I keep wanting to tell them how stupid they are. Seems like they ought to be informed, don't you think so?" There was a flash of the shrewd grin that Mrs. Harsanyi remembered. Thea pressed her hand. "I must go now. I had to give my lesson hour this morning to a Duluth woman who has come on to coach, and I must go and play 'On Mighty Pens' for her. Please tell Mr. Harsanyi that I think oratorio is a great chance for bluffers."

Mrs. Harsanyi detained her. "But he will want to know much more than that about you.

You are free at seven? Come back this evening, then, and we will go to dinner somewhere, to some cheerful place. I think you need a party."

Thea brightened. "Oh, I do! I'll love to come; that will be like old times. You see," she lingered a moment, softening, "I wouldn't mind if there were only ONE of them I could really admire."

"How about Bowers?" Mrs. Harsanyi asked as they were approaching the stairway.

"Well, there's nothing he loves like a good fakir, and nothing he hates like a good artist. I always remember something Mr. Harsanyi said about him. He said Bowers was the cold muffin that had been left on the plate."

Mrs. Harsanyi stopped short at the head of the stairs and said decidedly: "I think Andor made a mistake. I can't believe that is the right atmosphere for you. It would hurt you more than most people. It's all wrong."

"Something's wrong," Thea called back as she clattered down the stairs in her high heels.

II.

During that winter Thea lived in so many places that sometimes at night when she left Bowers's studio and emerged into the street she had to stop and think for a moment to remember where she was living now and what was the best way to get there.

When she moved into a new place her eyes challenged the beds, the carpets, the food, the mistress of the house. The boarding-houses were wretchedly conducted and Thea's complaints sometimes took an insulting form. She quarreled with one landlady after another and moved on. When she moved into a new room, she was almost sure to hate it on sight and to begin planning to hunt another place before she unpacked her trunk. She was moody and contemptuous toward her fellow boarders, except toward the young men, whom she treated with a careless familiarity which they usually misunderstood. They liked her, however, and when she left the house after a storm, they helped her to move her things and came to see her after she got settled in a new place. But she moved so often that they soon ceased to follow her. They could see no reason for keeping up with a girl who, under her jocularity, was cold, self-centered, and unimpressionable. They soon felt that she did not admire them.

Thea used to waken up in the night and wonder why she was so unhappy. She would have been amazed if she had known how much the people whom she met in Bowers's studio had to do with her low spirits. She had never been conscious of those instinctive standards which are called ideals, and she did not know that she was suffering for them. She often found herself sneering when she was on a street-car, or when she was brushing out her hair before her mirror, as some inane remark or too familiar mannerism flitted across her mind.

She felt no creature kindness, no tolerant good-will for Mrs. Priest or Jessie Darcey. After one of Jessie Darcey's concerts the glowing press notices, and the admiring comments that floated about Bowers's studio, caused Thea bitter unhappiness. It was not the torment of personal jealousy. She had never thought of herself as even a possible rival of Miss Darcey. She was a poor music student, and Jessie Darcey was a popular and petted professional. Mrs. Priest, whatever one held against her, had a fine, big, showy voice and an impressive presence. She read indifferently, was inaccurate, and was always putting other people wrong, but she at least had the material out of which singers can be made. But people seemed to like Jessie Darcey exactly because she could not sing; because, as they put it, she was "so natural and unprofessional." Her singing was pronounced "artless," her voice "birdlike." Miss Darcey was thin and awkward in person, with a sharp, sallow face. Thea noticed that her plainness was accounted to her credit, and that people spoke of it affectionately. Miss Darcey was singing everywhere just then; one could not help hearing about her. She was backed by some of the packing-house people and by the Chicago Northwestern Railroad. Only one critic raised his voice against her. Thea went to several of Jessie Darcey's concerts. It was the first time she had had an opportunity to observe the whims of the public which singers live by interesting. She saw that people liked in Miss Darcey every quality a singer ought not to have, and especially the nervous complacency that stamped her as a commonplace young woman. They seemed to have a warmer feeling for Jessie than for Mrs. Priest, an affectionate and cherishing regard. Chicago was not so very different from Moonstone, after all, and Jessie Darcey was only Lily Fisher under another name.

Thea particularly hated to accompany for Miss Darcey because she sang off pitch and didn't mind it in the least. It was excruciating to sit there day after day and hear her; there was something shameless and indecent about not singing true.

One morning Miss Darcey came by appointment to go over the programme for her Peoria concert. She was such a frail-looking girl that Thea ought to have felt sorry for her. True, she had an arch, sprightly little manner, and a flash of salmon-pink on either brown cheek. But a narrow upper jaw gave her face a pinched look, and her eyelids were heavy and relaxed. By the morning light, the purplish brown circles under her eyes were pathetic enough, and foretold no long or brilliant future. A singer with a poor digestion and low vitality; she needed no seer to cast her horoscope. If Thea had ever taken the pains to study her, she would have seen that, under all her smiles and archness, poor Miss Darcey was really frightened to death. She could not understand her success any more than Thea could; she kept catching her breath and lifting her eyebrows and trying to believe that it was true. Her loquacity was not natural, she forced herself to it, and when she confided to you how many defects she could overcome by her unusual command of head resonance, she was not so much trying to persuade you as to persuade herself.

When she took a note that was high for her, Miss Darcey always put her right hand out into the air, as if she were indicating height, or giving an exact measurement. Some early teacher had told her that she could "place" a tone more surely by the help of such a gesture, and she firmly believed that it was of great assistance to her. (Even when she was singing in public, she kept her right hand down with difficulty, nervously clasping her white kid fingers together when she took a high note. Thea could always see her elbows stiffen.) She unvaryingly executed this gesture with a smile of gracious confidence, as if she were actually putting her finger on the tone: "There it is, friends!"

This morning, in Gounod's "Ave Maria," as Miss Darcey approached her B natural:—

DANS—NOS—A—LAR—MES!

Out went the hand, with the sure airy gesture, though it was little above A she got with her voice, whatever she touched with her finger. Often Bowers let such things pass—with the right people—but this morning he snapped his jaws together and muttered, "God!" Miss Darcey tried again, with the same gesture as of putting the crowning touch, tilting her head and smiling radiantly at Bowers, as if to say, "It is for you I do all this!"

DANS—NOS A—LAR———MES!

This time she made B flat, and went on in the happy belief that she had done well enough, when she suddenly found that her accompanist was not going on with her, and this put her out completely.

She turned to Thea, whose hands had fallen in her lap. "Oh why did you stop just there! It IS too trying! Now we'd better go back to that other CRESCENDO and try it from there."

"I beg your pardon," Thea muttered. "I thought you wanted to get that B natural." She began again, as Miss Darcey indicated.

After the singer was gone, Bowers walked up to Thea and asked languidly, "Why do you hate Jessie so? Her little variations from pitch are between her and her public; they don't hurt you. Has she ever done anything to you except be very agreeable?"

"Yes, she has done things to me," Thea retorted hotly.

Bowers looked interested. "What, for example?"

"I can't explain, but I've got it in for her."

Bowers laughed. "No doubt about that. I'll have to suggest that you conceal it a little more effectually. That is—necessary, Miss Kronborg," he added, looking back over the shoulder of the overcoat he was putting on.

He went out to lunch and Thea thought the subject closed. But late in the afternoon, when he was taking his dyspepsia tablet and a glass of water between lessons, he looked up and said in a voice ironically coaxing:—

"Miss Kronborg, I wish you would tell me why you hate Jessie."

Taken by surprise Thea put down the score she was reading and answered before she knew what she was saying, "I hate her for the sake of what I used to think a singer might be."

Bowers balanced the tablet on the end of his long forefinger and whistled softly. "And how did you form your conception of what a singer ought to be?" he asked.

"I don't know." Thea flushed and spoke under her breath; "but I suppose I got most of it from Harsanyi."

Bowers made no comment upon this reply, but opened the door for the next pupil, who was waiting in the reception-room.

It was dark when Thea left the studio that night. She knew she had offended Bowers. Somehow she had hurt herself, too. She felt unequal to the boarding-house table, the sneaking divinity student who sat next her and had tried to kiss her on the stairs last night. She went over to the waterside of Michigan Avenue and walked along beside the lake. It was a clear, frosty winter night. The great empty space over the water was restful and spoke of freedom. If she had any money at all, she would go away. The stars glittered over the wide black water. She looked up at them wearily and shook her head. She believed that what she felt was despair, but it was only one of the forms of hope. She felt, indeed, as if she were bidding the stars good-bye; but she was renewing a promise. Though their challenge is universal and eternal, the stars get no answer but that,—the brief light flashed back to them from the eyes of the young who unaccountably aspire.

The rich, noisy, city, fat with food and drink, is a spent thing; its chief concern is its digestion and its little game of hide-and-seek with the undertaker. Money and office and success are the consolations of impotence. Fortune turns kind to such solid people and lets them suck their bone in peace. She flecks her whip upon flesh that is more alive, upon that stream of hungry boys and girls who tramp the streets of every city, recognizable by their pride and discontent, who are the Future, and who possess the treasure of creative power.

III.

While her living arrangements were so casual and fortuitous, Bowers's studio was the one fixed thing in Thea's life. She went out from it to uncertainties, and hastened to it from nebulous confusion. She was more influenced by Bowers than she knew. Unconsciously she began to take on something of his dry contempt, and to share his grudge without understanding exactly what it was about. His cynicism seemed to her honest, and the amiability of his pupils artificial. She admired his drastic treatment of his dull pupils. The stupid deserved all they got, and more. Bowers knew that she thought him a very clever man.

One afternoon when Bowers came in from lunch Thea handed him a card on which he read the name, "Mr. Philip Frederick Ottenburg."

"He said he would be in again to-morrow and that he wanted some time. Who is he? I like him better than the others."

Bowers nodded. "So do I. He's not a singer. He's a beer prince: son of the big brewer in St. Louis. He's been in Germany with his mother. I didn't know he was back."

"Does he take lessons?"

"Now and again. He sings rather well. He's at the head of the Chicago branch of the Ottenburg business, but he can't stick to work and is always running away. He has great ideas in beer, people tell me. He's what they call an imaginative business man; goes over to Bayreuth and seems to do nothing but give parties and spend money, and brings back more good notions for the brewery than the fellows who sit tight dig out in five years. I was born too long ago to be much taken in by these chesty boys with flowered vests, but I like Fred, all the same."

"So do I," said Thea positively.

Bowers made a sound between a cough and a laugh. "Oh, he's a lady-killer, all right! The girls in here are always making eyes at him. You won't be the first." He threw some sheets of music on the piano. "Better look that over; accompaniment's a little tricky. It's for that new woman from Detroit. And Mrs. Priest will be in this afternoon."

Thea sighed. "'I Know that my Redeemer Liveth'?"

"The same. She starts on her concert tour next week, and we'll have a rest. Until then, I suppose we'll have to be going over her programme."

The next day Thea hurried through her luncheon at a German bakery and got back to the studio at ten minutes past one. She felt sure that the young brewer would come early, before it was time for Bowers to arrive. He had not said he would, but yesterday, when he opened the door to go, he had glanced about the room and at her, and something in his eye had conveyed that suggestion.

Sure enough, at twenty minutes past one the door of the reception-room opened, and a tall, robust young man with a cane and an English hat and ulster looked in expectantly. "Ah—ha!" he exclaimed, "I thought if I came early I might have good luck. And how are you to-day, Miss Kronborg?"

Thea was sitting in the window chair. At her left elbow there was a table, and upon this table the young man sat down, holding his hat and cane in his hand, loosening his long coat so that it fell back from his shoulders. He was a gleaming, florid young fellow. His hair, thick and yellow, was cut very short, and he wore a closely trimmed beard, long enough on the chin to curl a little. Even his eyebrows were thick and yellow, like fleece. He had lively blue eyes—Thea looked up at them with great interest as he sat chatting and swinging his foot rhythmically. He was easily familiar, and frankly so. Wherever people met young Ottenburg, in his office, on shipboard, in a foreign hotel or railway compartment, they always felt (and usually liked) that artless presumption which seemed to say, "In this case we may waive formalities. We really haven't time. This is to-day, but it will soon be to-morrow, and then we may be very different people, and in some other country." He had a way of floating people out of dull or awkward situations, out of their own torpor or constraint or discouragement. It was a marked personal talent, of almost incalculable value in the representative of a great business founded on social amenities. Thea had liked him yesterday for the way in which he had picked her up out of herself and her German grammar for a few exciting moments.

"By the way, will you tell me your first name, please? Thea? Oh, then you ARE a Swede, sure enough! I thought so. Let me call you Miss Thea, after the German fashion. You won't mind? Of course not!" He usually made his assumption of a special understanding seem a tribute to the other person and not to himself.

"How long have you been with Bowers here? Do you like the old grouch? So do I. I've come to tell him about a new soprano I heard at Bayreuth. He'll pretend not to care, but he does. Do you warble with him? Have you anything of a voice? Honest? You look it, you know. What are you going in for, something big? Opera?"

Thea blushed crimson. "Oh, I'm not going in for anything. I'm trying to learn to sing at funerals."

Ottenburg leaned forward. His eyes twinkled. "I'll engage you to sing at mine. You can't fool me, Miss Thea. May I hear you take your lesson this afternoon?"

"No, you may not. I took it this morning."

He picked up a roll of music that lay behind him on the table. "Is this yours? Let me see what you are doing."

He snapped back the clasp and began turning over the songs. "All very fine, but tame. What's he got you at this Mozart stuff for? I shouldn't think it would suit your voice. Oh, I can make a pretty good guess at what will suit you! This from 'Gioconda' is more in your line. What's this Grieg? It looks interesting. TAK FOR DITT ROD. What does that mean?"

"'Thanks for your Advice.' Don't you know it?"

"No; not at all. Let's try it." He rose, pushed open the door into the music-room, and motioned Thea to enter before him. She hung back.

"I couldn't give you much of an idea of it. It's a big song."

Ottenburg took her gently by the elbow and pushed her into the other room. He sat down carelessly at the piano and looked over the music for a moment. "I think I can get you through it. But how stupid not to have the German words. Can you really sing the Norwegian? What an infernal language to sing. Translate the text for me." He handed her the music.

Thea looked at it, then at him, and shook her head. "I can't. The truth is I don't know either English or Swedish very well, and Norwegian's still worse," she said confidentially. She not infrequently refused to do what she was asked to do, but it was not like her to explain her refusal, even when she had a good reason.

"I understand. We immigrants never speak any language well. But you know what it means, don't you?"

"Of course I do!"

"Then don't frown at me like that, but tell me."

Thea continued to frown, but she also smiled. She was confused, but not embarrassed. She was not afraid of Ottenburg. He was not one of those people who made her spine like a steel rail. On the contrary, he made one venturesome.

"Well, it goes something like this: Thanks for your advice! But I prefer to steer my boat into the din of roaring breakers. Even if the journey is my last, I may find what I have never found before. Onward must I go, for I yearn for the wild sea. I long to fight my way through the angry waves, and to see how far, and how long I can make them carry me."

Ottenburg took the music and began: "Wait a moment. Is that too fast? How do you take it? That right?" He pulled up his cuffs and began the accompaniment again. He had become entirely serious, and he played with fine enthusiasm and with understanding.

Fred's talent was worth almost as much to old Otto Ottenburg as the steady industry of his older sons. When Fred sang the Prize Song at an interstate meet of the TURNVEREIN, ten thousand TURNERS went forth pledged to Ottenburg beer.

As Thea finished the song Fred turned back to the first page, without looking up from the music. "Now, once more," he called. They began again, and did not hear Bowers when he came in and stood in the doorway. He stood still, blinking like an owl at their two heads shining in the sun. He could not see their faces, but there was something about his girl's back that he had not noticed before: a very slight and yet very free motion, from the toes up. Her whole back seemed plastic, seemed to be moulding itself to the galloping rhythm of the song. Bowers perceived such things sometimes—unwillingly. He had known to-day that there was something afoot. The river of sound which had its source in his pupil had caught him two flights down. He had stopped and listened with a kind of sneering admiration. From the door he watched her with a half-incredulous, half-malicious smile.

When he had struck the keys for the last time, Ottenburg dropped his hands on his knees and looked up with a quick breath. "I got you through. What a stunning song! Did I play it right?"

Thea studied his excited face. There was a good deal of meaning in it, and there was a good deal in her own as she answered him. "You suited me," she said ungrudgingly.

After Ottenburg was gone, Thea noticed that Bowers was more agreeable than usual. She had heard the young brewer ask Bowers to dine with him at his club that evening, and she saw that he looked forward to the dinner with pleasure. He dropped a remark to the effect that Fred knew as much about food and wines as any man in Chicago. He said this boastfully.

"If he's such a grand business man, how does he have time to run around listening to singing-lessons?" Thea asked suspiciously.

As she went home to her boarding-house through the February slush, she wished she were going to dine with them. At nine o'clock she looked up from her grammar to wonder what Bowers and Ottenburg were having to eat. At that moment they were talking of her.

IV.

Thea noticed that Bowers took rather more pains with her now that Fred Ottenburg often dropped in at eleven-thirty to hear her lesson. After the lesson the young man took Bowers off to lunch with him, and Bowers liked good food when another man paid for it. He encouraged Fred's visits, and Thea soon saw that Fred knew exactly why.

One morning, after her lesson, Ottenburg turned to Bowers. "If you'll lend me Miss Thea, I think I have an engagement for her. Mrs. Henry Nathanmeyer is going to give three musical evenings in April, first three Saturdays, and she has consulted me about soloists. For the first evening she has a young violinist, and she would be charmed to have Miss Kronborg. She will pay fifty dollars. Not much, but Miss Thea would meet some people there who might be useful. What do you say?"

Bowers passed the question on to Thea. "I guess you could use the fifty, couldn't you, Miss Kronborg? You can easily work up some songs."

Thea was perplexed. "I need the money awfully," she said frankly; "but I haven't got the right clothes for that sort of thing. I suppose I'd better try to get some."

Ottenburg spoke up quickly, "Oh, you'd make nothing out of it if you went to buying evening clothes. I've thought of that. Mrs. Nathanmeyer has a troop of daughters, a perfect seraglio, all ages and sizes. She'll be glad to fit you out, if you aren't sensitive about wearing kosher clothes. Let me take you to see her, and you'll find that she'll arrange that easily enough. I told her she must produce something nice, blue or yellow, and properly cut. I brought half a dozen Worth gowns through the customs for her two weeks ago, and she's not ungrateful. When can we go to see her?"

"I haven't any time free, except at night," Thea replied in some confusion.

"To-morrow evening, then? I shall call for you at eight. Bring all your songs along; she will want us to give her a little rehearsal, perhaps. I'll play your accompaniments, if you've no objection. That will save money for you and for Mrs. Nathanmeyer. She needs it." Ottenburg chuckled as he took down the number of Thea's boarding-house.

The Nathanmeyers were so rich and great that even Thea had heard of them, and this seemed a very remarkable opportunity. Ottenburg had brought it about by merely lifting a finger, apparently. He was a beer prince sure enough, as Bowers had said.

The next evening at a quarter to eight Thea was dressed and waiting in the boarding-house parlor. She was nervous and fidgety and found it difficult to sit still on the hard, convex upholstery of the chairs. She tried them one after another, moving about the dimly lighted, musty room, where the gas always leaked gently and sang in the burners. There was no one in the parlor but the medical student, who was playing one of Sousa's marches so vigorously that the china ornaments on the top of the piano rattled. In a few moments some of the pension-office girls would come in and begin to two-step. Thea wished that Ottenburg would come and let her escape. She glanced at herself in the long, somber mirror. She was wearing her pale-blue broadcloth church dress, which was not unbecoming but was certainly too heavy to wear to anybody's house in the evening. Her slippers were run over at the heel and she had not had time to have them mended, and her white gloves were not so clean as they should be. However, she knew that she would forget these annoying things as soon as Ottenburg came.

Mary, the Hungarian chambermaid, came to the door, stood between the plush portieres, beckoned to Thea, and made an inarticulate sound in her throat. Thea jumped up and ran into the hall, where Ottenburg stood smiling, his caped cloak open, his silk hat in his white-kid hand. The Hungarian girl stood like a monument on her flat heels, staring at the pink carnation in Ottenburg's coat. Her broad, pockmarked face wore the only expression of which it was capable, a kind of animal wonder. As the young man followed Thea out, he glanced back over his shoulder through the crack of the door; the Hun clapped her hands over her stomach, opened her mouth, and made another raucous sound in her throat.

"Isn't she awful?" Thea exclaimed. "I think she's half-witted. Can you understand her?"

Ottenburg laughed as he helped her into the carriage. "Oh, yes; I can understand her!" He settled himself on the front seat opposite Thea. "Now, I want to tell you about the people we are going to see. We may have a musical public in this country some day, but as yet there are only the Germans and the Jews. All the other people go to hear Jessie Darcey sing, 'O, Promise Me!' The Nathanmeyers are the finest kind of Jews. If you do anything for Mrs. Henry Nathanmeyer, you must put yourself into her hands. Whatever she says about music, about clothes, about life, will be correct. And you may feel at ease with her. She expects nothing of people; she has lived in Chicago twenty years. If you were to behave like the Magyar who was so interested in my buttonhole, she would not be surprised. If you were to sing like Jessie Darcey, she would not be surprised; but she would manage not to hear you again."

"Would she? Well, that's the kind of people I want to find." Thea felt herself growing bolder.

"You will be all right with her so long as you do not try to be anything that you are not.

Her standards have nothing to do with Chicago. Her perceptions—or her grandmother's, which is the same thing—were keen when all this was an Indian village. So merely be yourself, and you will like her. She will like you because the Jews always sense talent, and," he added ironically, "they admire certain qualities of feeling that are found only in the white-skinned races."

Thea looked into the young man's face as the light of a street lamp flashed into the carriage. His somewhat academic manner amused her.

"What makes you take such an interest in singers?" she asked curiously. "You seem to have a perfect passion for hearing music-lessons. I wish I could trade jobs with you!"

"I'm not interested in singers." His tone was offended. "I am interested in talent. There are only two interesting things in the world, anyhow; and talent is one of them."

"What's the other?" The question came meekly from the figure opposite him. Another arc-light flashed in at the window.

Fred saw her face and broke into a laugh. "Why, you're guying me, you little wretch! You won't let me behave properly." He dropped his gloved hand lightly on her knee, took it away and let it hang between his own. "Do you know," he said confidentially, "I believe I'm more in earnest about all this than you are."

"About all what?"

"All you've got in your throat there."

"Oh! I'm in earnest all right; only I never was much good at talking. Jessie Darcey is the smooth talker. 'You notice the effect I get there—' If she only got 'em, she'd be a wonder, you know!"

Mr. and Mrs. Nathanmeyer were alone in their great library. Their three unmarried daughters had departed in successive carriages, one to a dinner, one to a Nietszche club, one to a ball given for the girls employed in the big department stores. When Ottenburg and Thea entered, Henry Nathanmeyer and his wife were sitting at a table at the farther end of the long room, with a reading-lamp and a tray of cigarettes and cordial-glasses between them. The overhead lights were too soft to bring out the colors of the big rugs, and none of the picture lights were on. One could merely see that there were pictures there. Fred whispered that they were Rousseaus and Corots, very fine ones which the old banker had bought long ago for next to nothing. In the hall Ottenburg had stopped Thea before a painting of a woman eating grapes out of a paper bag, and had told her gravely that there was the most beautiful Manet in the world. He made her take off her hat and gloves in the hall, and looked her over a little before he took her in. But once they were in the library he seemed perfectly satisfied with her and led her down the long room to their hostess.

Mrs. Nathanmeyer was a heavy, powerful old Jewess, with a great pompadour of white hair, a swarthy complexion, an eagle nose, and sharp, glittering eyes. She wore a black velvet dress with a long train, and a diamond necklace and earrings. She took Thea to the other side of the table and presented her to Mr. Nathanmeyer, who apologized for not rising, pointing to a slippered foot on a cushion; he said that he suffered from gout. He had a very soft voice and spoke with an accent which would have been heavy if it had not been so caressing. He kept Thea standing beside him for some time. He noticed that she stood easily, looked straight down into his face, and was not embarrassed. Even when Mrs. Nathanmeyer told Ottenburg to bring a chair for Thea, the old man did not release her hand, and she did not sit down. He admired her just as she was, as she happened to be standing, and she felt it. He was much handsomer than his wife, Thea thought. His forehead was high, his hair soft and white, his skin pink, a little puffy under his clear blue eyes. She noticed how warm and delicate his hands were, pleasant to touch and beautiful to look at. Ottenburg had told her that Mr. Nathanmeyer had a very fine collection of medals and cameos, and his fingers looked as if they had never touched anything but delicately cut surfaces.

He asked Thea where Moonstone was; how many inhabitants it had; what her father's business was; from what part of Sweden her grandfather came; and whether she spoke Swedish as a child. He was interested to hear that her mother's mother was still living, and that her grandfather had played the oboe. Thea felt at home standing there beside him; she felt that he was very wise, and that he some way took one's life up and looked it over kindly, as if it were a story. She was sorry when they left him to go into the music-room.

As they reached the door of the music-room, Mrs. Nathanmeyer turned a switch that threw on many lights. The room was even larger than the library, all glittering surfaces, with two Steinway pianos.

Mrs. Nathanmeyer rang for her own maid. "Selma will take you upstairs, Miss Kronborg, and you will find some dresses on the bed. Try several of them, and take the one you like best. Selma will help you. She has a great deal of taste. When you are dressed, come down and let us go over some of your songs with Mr. Ottenburg."

After Thea went away with the maid, Ottenburg came up to Mrs. Nathanmeyer and stood beside her, resting his hand on the high back of her chair.

"Well, GNADIGE FRAU, do you like her?"

"I think so. I liked her when she talked to father. She will always get on better with men."

Ottenburg leaned over her chair. "Prophetess! Do you see what I meant?"

"About her beauty? She has great possibilities, but you can never tell about those Northern women. They look so strong, but they are easily battered. The face falls so early under those wide cheek-bones. A single idea—hate or greed, or even love—can tear them to shreds. She is nineteen? Well, in ten years she may have quite a regal beauty, or she may have a heavy, discontented face, all dug out in channels. That will depend upon the kind of ideas she lives with."

"Or the kind of people?" Ottenburg suggested.

The old Jewess folded her arms over her massive chest, drew back her shoulders, and looked up at the young man. "With that hard glint in her eye? The people won't matter much, I fancy. They will come and go. She is very much interested in herself—as she should be."

Ottenburg frowned. "Wait until you hear her sing. Her eyes are different then. That gleam that comes in them is curious, isn't it? As you say, it's impersonal."

The object of this discussion came in, smiling. She had chosen neither the blue nor the yellow gown, but a pale rose-color, with silver butterflies. Mrs. Nathanmeyer lifted her lorgnette and studied her as she approached. She caught the characteristic things at once: the free, strong walk, the calm carriage of the head, the milky whiteness of the girl's arms and shoulders.

"Yes, that color is good for you," she said approvingly. "The yellow one probably killed your hair? Yes; this does very well indeed, so we need think no more about it."

Thea glanced questioningly at Ottenburg. He smiled and bowed, seemed perfectly satisfied. He asked her to stand in the elbow of the piano, in front of him, instead of behind him as she had been taught to do.

"Yes," said the hostess with feeling. "That other position is barbarous."

Thea sang an aria from 'Gioconda,' some songs by Schumann which she had studied with Harsanyi, and the "TAK FOR DIT ROD," which Ottenburg liked.

"That you must do again," he declared when they finished this song. "You did it much better the other day. You accented it more, like a dance or a galop. How did you do it?"

Thea laughed, glancing sidewise at Mrs. Nathanmeyer. "You want it rough-house, do you? Bowers likes me to sing it more seriously, but it always makes me think about a story my grandmother used to tell."

Fred pointed to the chair behind her. "Won't you rest a moment and tell us about it? I thought you had some notion about it when you first sang it for me."

Thea sat down. "In Norway my grandmother knew a girl who was awfully in love with a young fellow. She went into service on a big dairy farm to make enough money for her outfit. They were married at Christmastime, and everybody was glad, because they'd been sighing around about each other for so long. That very summer, the day before St. John's Day, her husband caught her carrying on with another farm-hand. The next night all the farm people had a bonfire and a big dance up on the mountain, and everybody was dancing and singing. I guess they were all a little drunk, for they got to seeing how near they could make the girls dance to the edge of the cliff. Ole—he was the girl's husband—seemed the jolliest and the drunkest of anybody. He danced his wife nearer and nearer the edge of the rock, and his wife began to scream so that the others stopped dancing and the music stopped; but Ole went right on singing, and he danced her over the edge of the cliff and they fell hundreds of feet and were all smashed to pieces."

Ottenburg turned back to the piano. "That's the idea! Now, come Miss Thea. Let it go!"

Thea took her place. She laughed and drew herself up out of her corsets, threw her shoulders high and let them drop again. She had never sung in a low dress before, and she found it comfortable. Ottenburg jerked his head and they began the song. The accompaniment sounded more than ever like the thumping and scraping of heavy feet.

When they stopped, they heard a sympathetic tapping at the end of the room. Old Mr. Nathanmeyer had come to the door and was sitting back in the shadow, just inside the library, applauding with his cane. Thea threw him a bright smile. He continued to sit there, his slippered foot on a low chair, his cane between his fingers, and she glanced at him from time to time. The doorway made a frame for him, and he looked like a man in a picture, with the long, shadowy room behind him.

Mrs. Nathanmeyer summoned the maid again. "Selma will pack that gown in a box for you, and you can take it home in Mr. Ottenburg's carriage."

Thea turned to follow the maid, but hesitated. "Shall I wear gloves?" she asked, turning again to Mrs. Nathanmeyer.

"No, I think not. Your arms are good, and you will feel freer without. You will need light slippers, pink—or white, if you have them, will do quite as well."

Thea went upstairs with the maid and Mrs. Nathanmeyer rose, took Ottenburg's arm, and walked toward her husband. "That's the first real voice I have heard in Chicago," she said decidedly. "I don't count that stupid Priest woman. What do you say, father?"

Mr. Nathanmeyer shook his white head and smiled softly, as if he were thinking about something very agreeable. "SVENSK SOMMAR," he murmured. "She is like a Swedish summer. I spent nearly a year there when I was a young man," he explained to Ottenburg.

When Ottenburg got Thea and her big box into the carriage, it occurred to him that she must be hungry, after singing so much. When he asked her, she admitted that she was very hungry, indeed.

He took out his watch. "Would you mind stopping somewhere with me? It's only eleven."

"Mind? Of course, I wouldn't mind. I wasn't brought up like that. I can take care of myself."

Ottenburg laughed. "And I can take care of myself, so we can do lots of jolly things together." He opened the carriage door and spoke to the driver. "I'm stuck on the way you sing that Grieg song," he declared.

When Thea got into bed that night she told herself that this was the happiest evening she had had in Chicago. She had enjoyed the Nathanmeyers and their grand house, her new dress, and Ottenburg, her first real carriage ride, and the good supper when she was so hungry. And Ottenburg WAS jolly! He made you want to come back at him. You weren't always being caught up and mystified. When you started in with him, you went; you cut the breeze, as Ray used to say. He had some go in him.

Philip Frederick Ottenburg was the third son of the great brewer. His mother was Katarina Furst, the daughter and heiress of a brewing business older and richer than Otto Ottenburg's. As a young woman she had been a conspicuous figure in German-American society in New York, and not untouched by scandal. She was a handsome, headstrong girl, a rebellious and violent force in a provincial society. She was brutally sentimental and heavily romantic. Her free speech, her Continental ideas, and her proclivity for championing new causes, even when she did not know much about them, made her an object of suspicion. She was always going abroad to seek out intellectual affinities, and was one of the group of young women who followed Wagner about in his old age, keeping at a respectful distance, but receiving now and then a gracious acknowledgment that he appreciated their homage. When the composer died, Katarina, then a matron with a family, took to her bed and saw no one for a week.

After having been engaged to an American actor, a Welsh socialist agitator, and a German army officer, Fraulein Furst at last placed herself and her great brewery interests into the trustworthy hands of Otto Ottenburg, who had been her suitor ever since he was a clerk, learning his business in her father's office.

Her first two sons were exactly like their father. Even as children they were industrious, earnest little tradesmen. As Frau Ottenburg said, "she had to wait for her Fred, but she got him at last," the first man who had altogether pleased her. Frederick entered Harvard when he was eighteen. When his mother went to Boston to visit him, she not only got him everything he wished for, but she made handsome and often embarrassing presents to all his friends. She gave dinners and supper parties for the Glee Club, made the crew break training, and was a generally disturbing influence. In his third year Fred left the university because of a serious escapade which had somewhat hampered his life ever since. He went at once into his father's business, where, in his own way, he had made himself very useful.

Fred Ottenburg was now twenty-eight, and people could only say of him that he had been less hurt by his mother's indulgence than most boys would have been. He had never wanted anything that he could not have it, and he might have had a great many things that he had never wanted. He was extravagant, but not prodigal. He turned most of the money his mother gave him into the business, and lived on his generous salary.

Fred had never been bored for a whole day in his life. When he was in Chicago or St. Louis, he went to ballgames, prize-fights, and horse-races. When he was in Germany, he went to concerts and to the opera. He belonged to a long list of sporting-clubs and hunting-clubs, and was a good boxer. He had so many natural interests that he had no affectations. At Harvard he kept away from the aesthetic circle that had already discovered Francis Thompson. He liked no poetry but German poetry. Physical energy was the thing he was full to the brim of, and music was one of its natural forms of expression. He had a healthy love of sport and art, of eating and drinking. When he was in Germany, he scarcely knew where the soup ended and the symphony began.

V.

March began badly for Thea. She had a cold during the first week, and after she got through her church duties on Sunday she had to go to bed with tonsilitis. She was still in the boarding-house at which young Ottenburg had called when he took her to see Mrs. Nathanmeyer. She had stayed on there because her room, although it was inconvenient and very small, was at the corner of the house and got the sunlight.

Since she left Mrs. Lorch, this was the first place where she had got away from a north light. Her rooms had all been as damp and mouldy as they were dark, with deep foundations of dirt under the carpets, and dirty walls. In her present room there was no running water and no clothes closet, and she had to have the dresser moved out to make room for her piano. But there were two windows, one on the south and one on the west, a light wall-paper with morning-glory vines, and on the floor a clean matting. The landlady had tried to make the room look cheerful, because it was hard to let. It was so small that Thea could keep it clean herself, after the Hun had done her worst. She hung her dresses on the door under a sheet, used the washstand for a dresser, slept on a cot, and opened both the windows when she practiced. She felt less walled in than she had in the other houses.

Wednesday was her third day in bed. The medical student who lived in the house had been in to see her, had left some tablets and a foamy gargle, and told her that she could probably go back to work on Monday. The landlady stuck her head in once a day, but Thea did not encourage her visits. The Hungarian chambermaid brought her soup and toast. She made a sloppy pretense of putting the room in order, but she was such a dirty creature that Thea would not let her touch her cot; she got up every morning and turned the mattress and made the bed herself. The exertion made her feel miserably ill, but at least she could lie still contentedly for a long while afterward. She hated the poisoned feeling in her throat, and no matter how often she gargled she felt unclean and disgusting. Still, if she had to be ill, she was almost glad that she had a contagious illness. Otherwise she would have been at the mercy of the people in the house. She knew that they disliked her, yet now that she was ill, they took it upon themselves to tap at her door, send her messages, books, even a miserable flower or two. Thea knew that their sympathy was an expression of self-righteousness, and she hated them for it. The divinity student, who was always whispering soft things to her, sent her "The Kreutzer Sonata."

The medical student had been kind to her: he knew that she did not want to pay a doctor. His gargle had helped her, and he gave her things to make her sleep at night. But he had been a cheat, too. He had exceeded his rights. She had no soreness in her chest, and had told him so clearly. All this thumping of her back, and listening to her breathing, was done to satisfy personal curiosity. She had watched him with a contemptuous smile. She was too sick to care; if it amused him—She made him wash his hands before he touched her; he was never very clean. All the same, it wounded her and made her feel that the world was a pretty disgusting place. "The Kreutzer Sonata" did not make her feel any more cheerful. She threw it aside with hatred. She could not believe it was written by the same man who wrote the novel that had thrilled her.

Her cot was beside the south window, and on Wednesday afternoon she lay thinking about the Harsanyis, about old Mr. Nathanmeyer, and about how she was missing Fred Ottenburg's visits to the studio. That was much the worst thing about being sick. If she were going to the studio every day, she might be having pleasant encounters with Fred. He was always running away, Bowers said, and he might be planning to go away as soon as Mrs. Nathanmeyer's evenings were over. And here she was losing all this time!

After a while she heard the Hun's clumsy trot in the hall, and then a pound on the door. Mary came in, making her usual uncouth sounds, carrying a long box and a big basket. Thea sat up in bed and tore off the strings and paper. The basket was full of fruit, with a big Hawaiian pineapple in the middle, and in the box there were layers of pink roses with long, woody stems and dark-green leaves. They filled the room with a cool smell that made another air to breathe. Mary stood with her apron full of paper and cardboard. When she saw Thea take an envelope out from under the flowers, she uttered an exclamation, pointed to the roses, and then to the bosom of her own dress, on the left side. Thea laughed and nodded. She understood that Mary associated the color with Ottenburg's BOUTONNIERE. She pointed to the water pitcher,—she had nothing else big enough to hold the flowers,—and made Mary put it on the window sill beside her.

After Mary was gone Thea locked the door. When the landlady knocked, she pretended that she was asleep. She lay still all afternoon and with drowsy eyes watched the roses open. They were the first hothouse flowers she had ever had. The cool fragrance they released was soothing, and as the pink petals curled back, they were the only things between her and the gray sky. She lay on her side, putting the room and the boarding-house behind her. Fred knew where all the pleasant things in the world were, she reflected, and knew the road to them. He had keys to all the nice places in his pocket, and seemed to jingle them from time to time. And then, he was young; and her friends had always been old. Her mind went back over them. They had all been teachers; wonderfully kind, but still teachers. Ray Kennedy, she knew, had wanted to marry her, but he was the most protecting and teacher-like of them all. She moved impatiently in her cot and threw her braids away from her hot neck, over her pillow. "I don't want him for a teacher," she thought, frowning petulantly out of the window. "I've had such a string of them. I want him for a sweetheart."

VI.

"Thea," said Fred Ottenburg one drizzly afternoon in April, while they sat waiting for their tea at a restaurant in the Pullman Building, overlooking the lake, "what are you going to do this summer?"

"I don't know. Work, I suppose."

"With Bowers, you mean? Even Bowers goes fishing for a month. Chicago's no place to work, in the summer. Haven't you made any plans?"

Thea shrugged her shoulders. "No use having any plans when you haven't any money. They are unbecoming."

"Aren't you going home?"

She shook her head. "No. It won't be comfortable there till I've got something to show for myself. I'm not getting on at all, you know. This year has been mostly wasted."

"You're stale; that's what's the matter with you. And just now you're dead tired. You'll talk more rationally after you've had some tea. Rest your throat until it comes." They were sitting by a window. As Ottenburg looked at her in the gray light, he remembered what Mrs. Nathanmeyer had said about the Swedish face "breaking early." Thea was as gray as the weather. Her skin looked sick. Her hair, too, though on a damp day it curled charmingly about her face, looked pale.

Fred beckoned the waiter and increased his order for food. Thea did not hear him. She was staring out of the window, down at the roof of the Art Institute and the green lions, dripping in the rain. The lake was all rolling mist, with a soft shimmer of robin's-egg blue in the gray. A lumber boat, with two very tall masts, was emerging gaunt and black out of the fog. When the tea came Thea ate hungrily, and Fred watched her. He thought her eyes became a little less bleak. The kettle sang cheerfully over the spirit lamp, and she seemed to concentrate her attention upon that pleasant sound. She kept looking toward it listlessly and indulgently, in a way that gave him a realization of her loneliness. Fred lit a cigarette and smoked thoughtfully. He and Thea were alone in the quiet, dusky room full of white tables. In those days Chicago people never stopped for tea. "Come," he said at last, "what would you do this summer, if you could do whatever you wished?"

"I'd go a long way from here! West, I think. Maybe I could get some of my spring back. All this cold, cloudy weather,"—she looked out at the lake and shivered,—"I don't know, it does things to me," she ended abruptly.

Fred nodded. "I know. You've been going down ever since you had tonsilitis. I've seen it. What you need is to sit in the sun and bake for three months. You've got the right idea. I remember once when we were having dinner somewhere you kept asking me about the Cliff-Dweller ruins. Do they still interest you?"

"Of course they do. I've always wanted to go down there—long before I ever got in for this."

"I don't think I told you, but my father owns a whole canyon full of Cliff-Dweller ruins. He has a big worthless ranch down in Arizona, near a Navajo reservation, and there's a canyon on the place they call Panther Canyon, chock full of that sort of thing. I often go down there to hunt. Henry Biltmer and his wife live there and keep a tidy place. He's an old German who worked in the brewery until he lost his health. Now he runs a few cattle. Henry likes to do me a favor. I've done a few for him." Fred drowned his cigarette in his saucer and studied Thea's expression, which was wistful and intent, envious and admiring. He continued with satisfaction: "If you went down there and stayed with them for two or three months, they wouldn't let you pay anything. I might send Henry a new gun, but even I couldn't offer him money for putting up a friend of mine. I'll get you transportation. It would make a new girl of you. Let me write to Henry, and you pack your trunk. That's all that's necessary. No red tape about it. What do you say, Thea?"

She bit her lip, and sighed as if she were waking up.

Fred crumpled his napkin impatiently. "Well, isn't it easy enough?"

"That's the trouble; it's TOO easy. Doesn't sound probable. I'm not used to getting things for nothing."

Ottenburg laughed. "Oh, if that's all, I'll show you how to begin. You won't get this for nothing, quite. I'll ask you to let me stop off and see you on my way to California. Perhaps by that time you will be glad to see me. Better let me break the news to Bowers. I can manage him. He needs a little transportation himself now and then. You must get corduroy riding-things and leather leggings. There are a few snakes about. Why do you keep frowning?"

"Well, I don't exactly see why you take the trouble. What do you get out of it? You haven't liked me so well the last two or three weeks."

Fred dropped his third cigarette and looked at his watch. "If you don't see that, it's because you need a tonic. I'll show you what I'll get out of it. Now I'm going to get a cab and take you home. You are too tired to walk a step. You'd better get to bed as soon as you get there. Of course, I don't like you so well when you're half anaesthetized all the time. What have you been doing to yourself?"

Thea rose. "I don't know. Being bored eats the heart out of me, I guess." She walked meekly in front of him to the elevator. Fred noticed for the hundredth time how vehemently her body proclaimed her state of feeling. He remembered how remarkably brilliant and beautiful she had been when she sang at Mrs. Nathanmeyer's: flushed and gleaming, round and supple, something that couldn't be dimmed or downed. And now she seemed a moving figure of discouragement. The very waiters glanced at her apprehensively. It was not that she made a fuss, but her back was most extraordinarily vocal. One never needed to see her face to know what she was full of that day. Yet she was certainly not mercurial. Her flesh seemed to take a mood and to "set," like plaster. As he put her into the cab, Fred reflected once more that he "gave her up." He would attack her when his lance was brighter.

❧ 4 ❧

THE ANCIENT PEOPLE

I.

THE SAN FRANCISCO MOUNTAIN lies in Northern Arizona, above Flagstaff, and its blue slopes and snowy summit entice the eye for a hundred miles across the desert. About its base lie the pine forests of the Navajos, where the great red-trunked trees live out their peaceful centuries in that sparkling air. The PINONS and scrub begin only where the forest ends, where the country breaks into open, stony clearings and the surface of the earth cracks into deep canyons. The great pines stand at a considerable distance from each other. Each tree grows alone, murmurs alone, thinks alone. They do not intrude upon each other. The Navajos are not much in the habit of giving or of asking help. Their language is not a communicative one, and they never attempt an interchange of personality in speech. Over their forests there is the same inexorable reserve. Each tree has its exalted power to bear.

That was the first thing Thea Kronborg felt about the forest, as she drove through it one May morning in Henry Biltmer's democrat wagon—and it was the first great forest she had ever seen. She had got off the train at Flagstaff that morning, rolled off into the high, chill air when all the pines on the mountain were fired by sunrise, so that she seemed to fall from sleep directly into the forest.

Old Biltmer followed a faint wagon trail which ran southeast, and which, as they traveled, continually dipped lower, falling away from the high plateau on the slope of which Flagstaff sits. The white peak of the mountain, the snow gorges above the timber, now disappeared from time to time as the road dropped and dropped, and the forest closed behind the wagon. More than the mountain disappeared as the forest closed thus. Thea seemed to be taking very little through the wood with her. The personality of which she was so tired seemed to let go of her. The high, sparkling air drank it up like blotting-paper. It was lost in the thrilling blue of the new sky and the song of the thin wind in the PINONS. The old, fretted lines which marked one off, which defined her,—made her Thea Kronborg, Bowers's accompanist, a soprano with a faulty middle voice,—were all erased.

So far she had failed. Her two years in Chicago had not resulted in anything. She had failed with Harsanyi, and she had made no great progress with her voice. She had come to believe that whatever Bowers had taught her was of secondary importance, and that in the essential things she had made no advance. Her student life closed behind her, like the forest, and she doubted whether she could go back to it if she tried. Probably she would teach music in little country towns all her life. Failure was not so tragic as she would have supposed; she was tired enough not to care.

She was getting back to the earliest sources of gladness that she could remember. She had loved the sun, and the brilliant solitudes of sand and sun, long before these other things had come along to fasten themselves upon her and torment her. That night, when she clambered into her big German feather bed, she felt completely released from the enslaving desire to get on in the world. Darkness had once again the sweet wonder that it had in childhood.

II.

Thea's life at the Ottenburg ranch was simple and full of light, like the days themselves. She awoke every morning when the first fierce shafts of sunlight darted through the curtainless windows of her room at the ranch house. After breakfast she took her lunch-basket and went down to the canyon. Usually she did not return until sunset.

Panther Canyon was like a thousand others—one of those abrupt fissures with which the earth in the Southwest is riddled; so abrupt that you might walk over the edge of any one of them on a dark night and never know what had happened to you. This canyon headed on the Ottenburg ranch, about a mile from the ranch house, and it was accessible only at its head. The canyon walls, for the first two hundred feet below the surface, were perpendicular cliffs, striped with even-running strata of rock. From there on to the bottom the sides were less abrupt, were shelving, and lightly fringed with PINONS and dwarf cedars. The effect was that of a gentler canyon within a wilder one. The dead city lay at the point where the perpendicular outer wall ceased and the V-shaped inner gorge began. There a stratum of rock, softer than those above, had been hollowed out by the action of time until it was like a deep groove running along the sides of the canyon. In this hollow (like a great fold in the rock) the Ancient People had built their houses of yellowish stone and mortar. The over-hanging cliff above made a roof two hundred feet thick. The hard stratum below was an everlasting floor. The houses stood along in a row, like the buildings in a city block, or like a barracks.

In both walls of the canyon the same streak of soft rock had been washed out, and the long horizontal groove had been built up with houses. The dead city had thus two streets, one set in either cliff, facing each other across the ravine, with a river of blue air between them.

The canyon twisted and wound like a snake, and these two streets went on for four miles or more, interrupted by the abrupt turnings of the gorge, but beginning again within each turn. The canyon had a dozen of these false endings near its head. Beyond, the windings were larger and less perceptible, and it went on for a hundred miles, too narrow, precipitous, and terrible for man to follow it. The Cliff Dwellers liked wide canyons, where the great cliffs caught the sun. Panther Canyon had been deserted for hundreds of years when the first Spanish missionaries came into Arizona, but the masonry of the houses was still wonderfully firm; had crumbled only where a landslide or a rolling boulder had torn it.

All the houses in the canyon were clean with the cleanness of sun-baked, wind-swept places, and they all smelled of the tough little cedars that twisted themselves into the very doorways. One of these rock-rooms Thea took for her own. Fred had told her how to make it comfortable. The day after she came old Henry brought over on one of the pack-ponies a roll of Navajo blankets that belonged to Fred, and Thea lined her cave with them. The room was not more than eight by ten feet, and she could touch the stone roof with her finger-tips. This was her old idea: a nest in a high cliff, full of sun. All morning long the sun beat upon her cliff, while the ruins on the opposite side of the canyon were in shadow. In the afternoon, when she had the shade of two hundred feet of rock wall, the ruins on the other side of the gulf stood out in the blazing sunlight. Before her door ran the narrow, winding path that had been the street of the Ancient People. The yucca and niggerhead cactus grew everywhere. From her doorstep she looked out on the ocher-colored slope that ran down several hundred feet to the stream, and this hot rock was sparsely grown with dwarf trees. Their colors were so pale that the shadows of the little trees on the rock stood out sharper than the trees themselves. When Thea first came, the chokecherry bushes were in blossom, and the scent of them was almost sickeningly sweet after a shower. At the very bottom of the canyon, along the stream, there was a thread of bright, flickering, golden-green,—cottonwood seedlings. They made a living, chattering screen behind which she took her bath every morning.

Thea went down to the stream by the Indian water trail. She had found a bathing-pool with a sand bottom, where the creek was damned by fallen trees. The climb back was long and steep, and when she reached her little house in the cliff she always felt fresh delight in its comfort and inaccessibility. By the time she got there, the woolly red-and-gray blankets were saturated with sunlight, and she sometimes fell asleep as soon as she stretched her body on their warm surfaces. She used to wonder at her own inactivity. She could lie there hour after hour in the sun and listen to the strident whir of the big locusts, and to the light, ironical laughter of the quaking asps. All her life she had been hurrying and sputtering, as if she had been born behind time and had been trying to catch up. Now, she reflected, as she drew herself out long upon the rugs, it was as if she were waiting for something to catch up with her. She had got to a place where she was out of the stream of meaningless activity and undirected effort.

Here she could lie for half a day undistracted, holding pleasant and incomplete conceptions in her mind—almost in her hands. They were scarcely clear enough to be called ideas. They had something to do with fragrance and color and sound, but almost nothing to do with words. She was singing very little now, but a song would go through her head all morning, as a spring keeps welling up, and it was like a pleasant sensation indefinitely prolonged. It was much more like a sensation than like an idea, or an act of remembering. Music had never come to her in that sensuous form before. It had always been a thing to be struggled with, had always brought anxiety and exaltation and chagrin—never content and indolence. Thea began to wonder whether people could not utterly lose the power to work, as they can lose their voice or their memory. She had always been a little drudge, hurrying from one task to another—as if it mattered! And now her power to think seemed converted into a power of sustained sensation. She could become a mere receptacle for heat, or become a color, like the bright lizards that darted about on the hot stones outside her door; or she could become a continuous repetition of sound, like the cicadas.

III.

The faculty of observation was never highly developed in Thea Kronborg. A great deal escaped her eye as she passed through the world. But the things which were for her, she saw; she experienced them physically and remembered them as if they had once been a part of herself. The roses she used to see in the florists' shops in Chicago were merely roses. But when she thought of the moonflowers that grew over Mrs. Tellamantez's door, it was as if she had been that vine and had opened up in white flowers every night. There were memories of light on the sand hills, of masses of prickly-pear blossoms she had found in the desert in early childhood, of the late afternoon sun pouring through the grape leaves and the mint bed in Mrs. Kohler's garden, which she would never lose. These recollections were a part of her mind and personality. In Chicago she had got almost nothing that went into her subconscious self and took root there. But here, in Panther Canyon, there were again things which seemed destined for her.

Panther Canyon was the home of innumerable swallows. They built nests in the wall far above the hollow groove in which Thea's own rock chamber lay. They seldom ventured above the rim of the canyon, to the flat, wind-swept tableland. Their world was the blue air-river between the canyon walls. In that blue gulf the arrow-shaped birds swam all day long, with only an occasional movement of the wings. The only sad thing about them was their timidity; the way in which they lived their lives between the echoing cliffs and never dared to rise out of the shadow of the canyon walls. As they swam past her door, Thea often felt how easy it would be to dream one's life out in some cleft in the world.

From the ancient dwelling there came always a dignified, unobtrusive sadness; now stronger, now fainter,—like the aromatic smell which the dwarf cedars gave out in the sun,—but always present, a part of the air one breathed. At night, when Thea dreamed about the canyon,—or in the early morning when she hurried toward it, anticipating it,—her conception of it was of yellow rocks baking in sunlight, the swallows, the cedar smell, and that peculiar sadness—a voice out of the past, not very loud, that went on saying a few simple things to the solitude eternally.

Standing up in her lodge, Thea could with her thumb nail dislodge flakes of carbon from the rock roof—the cooking-smoke of the Ancient People. They were that near! A timid, nest-building folk, like the swallows. How often Thea remembered Ray Kennedy's moralizing about the cliff cities. He used to say that he never felt the hardness of the human struggle or the sadness of history as he felt it among those ruins. He used to say, too, that it made one feel an obligation to do one's best. On the first day that Thea climbed the water trail she began to have intuitions about the women who had worn the path, and who had spent so great a part of their lives going up and down it. She found herself trying to walk as they must have walked, with a feeling in her feet and knees and loins which she had never known before,—which must have come up to her out of the accustomed dust of that rocky trail. She could feel the weight of an Indian baby hanging to her back as she climbed.

The empty houses, among which she wandered in the afternoon, the blanketed one in which she lay all morning, were haunted by certain fears and desires; feelings about warmth and cold and water and physical strength. It seemed to Thea that a certain understanding of those old people came up to her out of the rock shelf on which she lay; that certain feelings were transmitted to her, suggestions that were simple, insistent, and monotonous, like the beating of Indian drums. They were not expressible in words, but seemed rather to translate themselves into attitudes of body, into degrees of muscular tension or relaxation; the naked strength of youth, sharp as the sunshafts; the crouching timorousness of age, the sullenness of women who waited for their captors. At the first turning of the canyon there was a half-ruined tower of yellow masonry, a watch-tower upon which the young men used to entice eagles and snare them with nets. Sometimes for a whole morning Thea could see the coppery breast and shoulders of an Indian youth there against the sky; see him throw the net, and watch the struggle with the eagle.

Old Henry Biltmer, at the ranch, had been a great deal among the Pueblo Indians who are the descendants of the Cliff-Dwellers. After supper he used to sit and smoke his pipe by the kitchen stove and talk to Thea about them. He had never found any one before who was interested in his ruins. Every Sunday the old man prowled about in the canyon, and he had come to know a good deal more about it than he could account for. He had gathered up a whole chestful of Cliff-Dweller relics which he meant to take back to Germany with him some day. He taught Thea how to find things among the ruins: grinding-stones, and drills and needles made of turkey-bones. There were fragments of pottery everywhere. Old Henry explained to her that the Ancient People had developed masonry and pottery far beyond any other crafts. After they had made houses for themselves, the next thing was to house the precious water. He explained to her how all their customs and ceremonies and their religion went back to water. The men provided the food, but water was the care of the women. The stupid women carried water for most of their lives; the cleverer ones made the vessels to hold it. Their pottery was their most direct appeal to water, the envelope and sheath of the precious element itself. The strongest Indian need was expressed in those graceful jars, fashioned slowly by hand, without the aid of a wheel.

When Thea took her bath at the bottom of the canyon, in the sunny pool behind the screen of cottonwoods, she sometimes felt as if the water must have sovereign qualities, from having been the object of so much service and desire. That stream was the only living thing left of the drama that had been played out in the canyon centuries ago. In the rapid, restless heart of it, flowing swifter than the rest, there was a continuity of life that reached back into the old time. The glittering thread of current had a kind of lightly worn, loosely knit personality, graceful and laughing. Thea's bath came to have a ceremonial gravity. The atmosphere of the canyon was ritualistic.

One morning, as she was standing upright in the pool, splashing water between her shoulder-blades with a big sponge, something flashed through her mind that made her draw herself up and stand still until the water had quite dried upon her flushed skin. The stream and the broken pottery: what was any art but an effort to make a sheath, a mould in which to imprison for a moment the shining, elusive element which is life itself,—life hurrying past us and running away, too strong to stop, too sweet to lose? The Indian women had held it in their jars. In the sculpture she had seen in the Art Institute, it had been caught in a flash of arrested motion. In singing, one made a vessel of one's throat and nostrils and held it on one's breath, caught the stream in a scale of natural intervals.

IV.

Thea had a superstitious feeling about the potsherds, and liked better to leave them in the dwellings where she found them. If she took a few bits back to her own lodge and hid them under the blankets, she did it guiltily, as if she were being watched. She was a guest in these houses, and ought to behave as such. Nearly every afternoon she went to the chambers which contained the most interesting fragments of pottery, sat and looked at them for a while. Some of them were beautifully decorated. This care, expended upon vessels that could not hold food or water any better for the additional labor put upon them, made her heart go out to those ancient potters. They had not only expressed their desire, but they had expressed it as beautifully as they could. Food, fire, water, and something else—even here, in this crack in the world, so far back in the night of the past! Down here at the beginning that painful thing was already stirring; the seed of sorrow, and of so much delight.

There were jars done in a delicate overlay, like pine cones; and there were many patterns in a low relief, like basket-work. Some of the pottery was decorated in color, red and brown, black and white, in graceful geometrical patterns. One day, on a fragment of a shallow bowl, she found a crested serpent's head, painted in red on terra-cotta. Again she found half a bowl with a broad band of white cliff-houses painted on a black ground. They were scarcely conventionalized at all; there they were in the black border, just as they stood in the rock before her. It brought her centuries nearer to these people to find that they saw their houses exactly as she saw them.

Yes, Ray Kennedy was right. All these things made one feel that one ought to do one's best, and help to fulfill some desire of the dust that slept there. A dream had been dreamed there long ago, in the night of ages, and the wind had whispered some promise to the sadness of the savage. In their own way, those people had felt the beginnings of what was to come. These potsherds were like fetters that bound one to a long chain of human endeavor.

Not only did the world seem older and richer to Thea now, but she herself seemed older. She had never been alone for so long before, or thought so much. Nothing had ever engrossed her so deeply as the daily contemplation of that line of pale-yellow houses tucked into the wrinkle of the cliff. Moonstone and Chicago had become vague. Here everything was simple and definite, as things had been in childhood. Her mind was like a ragbag into which she had been frantically thrusting whatever she could grab. And here she must throw this lumber away. The things that were really hers separated themselves from the rest. Her ideas were simplified, became sharper and clearer. She felt united and strong.

When Thea had been at the Ottenburg ranch for two months, she got a letter from Fred announcing that he "might be along at almost any time now." The letter came at night, and the next morning she took it down into the canyon with her. She was delighted that he was coming soon. She had never felt so grateful to any one, and she wanted to tell him everything that had happened to her since she had been there—more than had happened in all her life before. Certainly she liked Fred better than any one else in the world. There was Harsanyi, of course—but Harsanyi was always tired. Just now, and here, she wanted some one who had never been tired, who could catch an idea and run with it.

She was ashamed to think what an apprehensive drudge she must always have seemed to Fred, and she wondered why he had concerned himself about her at all. Perhaps she would never be so happy or so good-looking again, and she would like Fred to see her, for once, at her best. She had not been singing much, but she knew that her voice was more interesting than it had ever been before. She had begun to understand that—with her, at least—voice was, first of all, vitality; a lightness in the body and a driving power in the blood. If she had that, she could sing. When she felt so keenly alive, lying on that insensible shelf of stone, when her body bounded like a rubber ball away from its hardness, then she could sing. This, too, she could explain to Fred. He would know what she meant.

Another week passed. Thea did the same things as before, felt the same influences, went over the same ideas; but there was a livelier movement in her thoughts, and a freshening of sensation, like the brightness which came over the underbrush after a shower. A persistent affirmation—or denial—was going on in her, like the tapping of the woodpecker in the one tall pine tree across the chasm. Musical phrases drove each other rapidly through her mind, and the song of the cicada was now too long and too sharp. Everything seemed suddenly to take the form of a desire for action.

It was while she was in this abstracted state, waiting for the clock to strike, that Thea at last made up her mind what she was going to try to do in the world, and that she was going to Germany to study without further loss of time. Only by the merest chance had she ever got to Panther Canyon. There was certainly no kindly Providence that directed one's life; and one's parents did not in the least care what became of one, so long as one did not misbehave and endanger their comfort. One's life was at the mercy of blind chance. She had better take it in her own hands and lose everything than meekly draw the plough under the rod of parental guidance. She had seen it when she was at home last summer,—the hostility of comfortable, self-satisfied people toward any serious effort. Even to her father it seemed indecorous. Whenever she spoke seriously, he looked apologetic. Yet she had clung fast to whatever was left of Moonstone in her mind. No more of that! The Cliff-Dwellers had lengthened her past. She had older and higher obligations.

V.

One Sunday afternoon late in July old Henry Biltmer was rheumatically descending into the head of the canyon. The Sunday before had been one of those cloudy days—fortunately rare—when the life goes out of that country and it becomes a gray ghost, an empty, shivering uncertainty. Henry had spent the day in the barn; his canyon was a reality only when it was flooded with the light of its great lamp, when the yellow rocks cast purple shadows, and the resin was fairly cooking in the corkscrew cedars. The yuccas were in blossom now. Out of each clump of sharp bayonet leaves rose a tall stalk hung with greenish-white bells with thick, fleshy petals. The niggerhead cactus was thrusting its crimson blooms up out of every crevice in the rocks.

Henry had come out on the pretext of hunting a spade and pick-axe that young Ottenburg had borrowed, but he was keeping his eyes open. He was really very curious about the new occupants of the canyon, and what they found to do there all day long. He let his eye travel along the gulf for a mile or so to the first turning, where the fissure zigzagged out and then receded behind a stone promontory on which stood the yellowish, crumbling ruin of the old watch-tower.

From the base of this tower, which now threw its shadow forward, bits of rock kept flying out into the open gulf—skating upon the air until they lost their momentum, then falling like chips until they rang upon the ledges at the bottom of the gorge or splashed into the stream. Biltmer shaded his eyes with his hand. There on the promontory, against the cream-colored cliff, were two figures nimbly moving in the light, both slender and agile, entirely absorbed in their game. They looked like two boys. Both were hatless and both wore white shirts.

Henry forgot his pick-axe and followed the trail before the cliff-houses toward the tower. Behind the tower, as he well knew, were heaps of stones, large and small, piled against the face of the cliff. He had always believed that the Indian watchmen piled them there for ammunition. Thea and Fred had come upon these missiles and were throwing them for distance. As Biltmer approached he could hear them laughing, and he caught Thea's voice, high and excited, with a ring of vexation in it. Fred was teaching her to throw a heavy stone like a discus. When it was Fred's turn, he sent a triangular-shaped stone out into the air with considerable skill. Thea watched it enviously, standing in a half-defiant posture, her sleeves rolled above her elbows and her face flushed with heat and excitement. After Fred's third missile had rung upon the rocks below, she snatched up a stone and stepped impatiently out on the ledge in front of him. He caught her by the elbows and pulled her back.

"Not so close, you silly! You'll spin yourself off in a minute."

"You went that close. There's your heel-mark," she retorted.

"Well, I know how. That makes a difference." He drew a mark in the dust with his toe. "There, that's right. Don't step over that. Pivot yourself on your spine, and make a half turn. When you've swung your length, let it go."

Thea settled the flat piece of rock between her wrist and fingers, faced the cliff wall, stretched her arm in position, whirled round on her left foot to the full stretch of her body, and let the missile spin out over the gulf. She hung expectantly in the air, forgetting to draw back her arm, her eyes following the stone as if it carried her fortunes with it. Her comrade watched her; there weren't many girls who could show a line like that from the toe to the thigh, from the shoulder to the tip of the outstretched hand. The stone spent itself and began to fall. Thea drew back and struck her knee furiously with her palm.

"There it goes again! Not nearly so far as yours. What IS the matter with me? Give me another." She faced the cliff and whirled again. The stone spun out, not quite so far as before.

Ottenburg laughed. "Why do you keep on working AFTER you've thrown it? You can't help it along then."

Without replying, Thea stooped and selected another stone, took a deep breath and made another turn. Fred watched the disk, exclaiming, "Good girl! You got past the pine that time. That's a good throw."

She took out her handkerchief and wiped her glowing face and throat, pausing to feel her right shoulder with her left hand.

"Ah—ha, you've made yourself sore, haven't you? What did I tell you? You go at things too hard. I'll tell you what I'm going to do, Thea," Fred dusted his hands and began tucking in the blouse of his shirt, "I'm going to make some single-sticks and teach you to fence. You'd be all right there. You're light and quick and you've got lots of drive in you. I'd like to have you come at me with foils; you'd look so fierce," he chuckled.

She turned away from him and stubbornly sent out another stone, hanging in the air after its flight. Her fury amused Fred, who took all games lightly and played them well. She was breathing hard, and little beads of moisture had gathered on her upper lip. He slipped his arm about her. "If you will look as pretty as that—" he bent his head and kissed her. Thea was startled, gave him an angry push, drove at him with her free hand in a manner quite hostile. Fred was on his mettle in an instant. He pinned both her arms down and kissed her resolutely.

When he released her, she turned away and spoke over her shoulder. "That was mean of you, but I suppose I deserved what I got."

"I should say you did deserve it," Fred panted, "turning savage on me like that! I should say you did deserve it!"

He saw her shoulders harden. "Well, I just said I deserved it, didn't I? What more do you want?"

"I want you to tell me why you flew at me like that! You weren't playing; you looked as if you'd like to murder me."

She brushed back her hair impatiently. "I didn't mean anything, really. You interrupted me when I was watching the stone. I can't jump from one thing to another. I pushed you without thinking."

Fred thought her back expressed contrition. He went up to her, stood behind her with his chin above her shoulder, and said something in her ear. Thea laughed and turned toward him. They left the stone-pile carelessly, as if they had never been interested in it, rounded the yellow tower, and disappeared into the second turn of the canyon, where the dead city, interrupted by the jutting promontory, began again.

Old Biltmer had been somewhat embarrassed by the turn the game had taken. He had not heard their conversation, but the pantomime against the rocks was clear enough. When the two young people disappeared, their host retreated rapidly toward the head of the canyon.

"I guess that young lady can take care of herself," he chuckled. "Young Fred, though, he has quite a way with them."

VI.

Day was breaking over Panther Canyon. The gulf was cold and full of heavy, purplish twilight. The wood smoke which drifted from one of the cliff-houses hung in a blue scarf across the chasm, until the draft caught it and whirled it away. Thea was crouching in the doorway of her rock house, while Ottenburg looked after the crackling fire in the next cave. He was waiting for it to burn down to coals before he put the coffee on to boil.

They had left the ranch house that morning a little after three o'clock, having packed their camp equipment the day before, and had crossed the open pasture land with their lantern while the stars were still bright. During the descent into the canyon by lantern-light, they were chilled through their coats and sweaters. The lantern crept slowly along the rock trail, where the heavy air seemed to offer resistance. The voice of the stream at the bottom of the gorge was hollow and threatening, much louder and deeper than it ever was by day—another voice altogether. The sullenness of the place seemed to say that the world could get on very well without people, red or white; that under the human world there was a geological world, conducting its silent, immense operations which were indifferent to man. Thea had often seen the desert sunrise,—a lighthearted affair, where the sun springs out of bed and the world is golden in an instant. But this canyon seemed to waken like an old man, with rheum and stiffness of the joints, with heaviness, and a dull, malignant mind. She crouched against the wall while the stars faded, and thought what courage the early races must have had to endure so much for the little they got out of life.

At last a kind of hopefulness broke in the air. In a moment the pine trees up on the edge of the rim were flashing with coppery fire. The thin red clouds which hung above their pointed tops began to boil and move rapidly, weaving in and out like smoke. The swallows darted out of their rock houses as at a signal, and flew upward, toward the rim. Little brown birds began to chirp in the bushes along the watercourse down at the bottom of the ravine, where everything was still dusky and pale. At first the golden light seemed to hang like a wave upon the rim of the canyon; the trees and bushes up there, which one scarcely noticed at noon, stood out magnified by the slanting rays. Long, thin streaks of light began to reach quiveringly down into the canyon. The red sun rose rapidly above the tops of the blazing pines, and its glow burst into the gulf, about the very doorstep on which Thea sat. It bored into the wet, dark underbrush. The dripping cherry bushes, the pale aspens, and the frosty PINONS were glittering and trembling, swimming in the liquid gold. All the pale, dusty little herbs of the bean family, never seen by any one but a botanist, became for a moment individual and important, their silky leaves quite beautiful with dew and light. The arch of sky overhead, heavy as lead a little while before, lifted, became more and more transparent, and one could look up into depths of pearly blue.

The savor of coffee and bacon mingled with the smell of wet cedars drying, and Fred called to Thea that he was ready for her. They sat down in the doorway of his kitchen, with the warmth of the live coals behind them and the sunlight on their faces, and began their breakfast, Mrs. Biltmer's thick coffee cups and the cream bottle between them, the coffee-pot and frying-pan conveniently keeping hot among the embers.

"I thought you were going back on the whole proposition, Thea, when you were crawling along with that lantern. I couldn't get a word out of you."

"I know. I was cold and hungry, and I didn't believe there was going to be any morning, anyway. Didn't you feel queer, at all?"

Fred squinted above his smoking cup. "Well, I am never strong for getting up before the sun. The world looks unfurnished. When I first lit the fire and had a square look at you, I thought I'd got the wrong girl. Pale, grim—you were a sight!"

Thea leaned back into the shadow of the rock room and warmed her hands over the coals. "It was dismal enough. How warm these walls are, all the way round; and your breakfast is so good. I'm all right now, Fred."

"Yes, you're all right now." Fred lit a cigarette and looked at her critically as her head emerged into the sun again. "You get up every morning just a little bit handsomer than you were the day before. I'd love you just as much if you were not turning into one of the loveliest women I've ever seen; but you are, and that's a fact to be reckoned with." He watched her across the thin line of smoke he blew from his lips. "What are you going to do with all that beauty and all that talent, Miss Kronborg?"

She turned away to the fire again. "I don't know what you're talking about," she muttered with an awkwardness which did not conceal her pleasure.

Ottenburg laughed softly. "Oh, yes, you do! Nobody better! You're a close one, but you give yourself away sometimes, like everybody else. Do you know, I've decided that you never do a single thing without an ulterior motive." He threw away his cigarette, took out his tobacco-pouch and began to fill his pipe. "You ride and fence and walk and climb, but I know that all the while you're getting somewhere in your mind. All these things are instruments; and I, too, am an instrument." He looked up in time to intercept a quick, startled glance from Thea. "Oh, I don't mind," he chuckled; "not a bit. Every woman, every interesting woman, has ulterior motives, many of 'em less creditable than yours. It's your constancy that amuses me. You must have been doing it ever since you were two feet high."

Thea looked slowly up at her companion's good-humored face. His eyes, sometimes too restless and sympathetic in town, had grown steadier and clearer in the open air. His short curly beard and yellow hair had reddened in the sun and wind. The pleasant vigor of his person was always delightful to her, something to signal to and laugh with in a world of negative people. With Fred she was never becalmed. There was always life in the air, always something coming and going, a rhythm of feeling and action,—stronger than the natural accord of youth. As she looked at him, leaning against the sunny wall, she felt a desire to be frank with him. She was not willfully holding anything back. But, on the other hand, she could not force things that held themselves back. "Yes, it was like that when I was little," she said at last. "I had to be close, as you call it, or go under. But I didn't know I had been like that since you came. I've had nothing to be close about. I haven't thought about anything but having a good time with you. I've just drifted."

Fred blew a trail of smoke out into the breeze and looked knowing. "Yes, you drift like a rifle ball, my dear. It's your—your direction that I like best of all. Most fellows wouldn't, you know. I'm unusual."

They both laughed, but Thea frowned questioningly. "Why wouldn't most fellows? Other fellows have liked me."

"Yes, serious fellows. You told me yourself they were all old, or solemn. But jolly fellows want to be the whole target. They would say you were all brain and muscle; that you have no feeling."

She glanced at him sidewise. "Oh, they would, would they?"

"Of course they would," Fred continued blandly. "Jolly fellows have no imagination. They want to be the animating force. When they are not around, they want a girl to be—extinct," he waved his hand. "Old fellows like Mr. Nathanmeyer understand your kind; but among the young ones, you are rather lucky to have found me. Even I wasn't always so wise. I've had my time of thinking it would not bore me to be the Apollo of a homey flat, and I've paid out a trifle to learn better. All those things get very tedious unless they are hooked up with an idea of some sort. It's because we DON'T come out here only to look at each other and drink coffee that it's so pleasant to—look at each other." Fred drew on his pipe for a while, studying Thea's abstraction. She was staring up at the far wall of the canyon with a troubled expression that drew her eyes narrow and her mouth hard. Her hands lay in her lap, one over the other, the fingers interlacing. "Suppose," Fred came out at length, —"suppose I were to offer you what most of the young men I know would offer a girl they'd been sitting up nights about: a comfortable flat in Chicago, a summer camp up in the woods, musical evenings, and a family to bring up. Would it look attractive to you?"

Thea sat up straight and stared at him in alarm, glared into his eyes. "Perfectly hideous!" she exclaimed.

Fred dropped back against the old stonework and laughed deep in his chest. "Well, don't be frightened. I won't offer them. You're not a nest-building bird. You know I always liked your song, 'Me for the jolt of the breakers!' I understand."

She rose impatiently and walked to the edge of the cliff. "It's not that so much. It's waking up every morning with the feeling that your life is your own, and your strength is your own, and your talent is your own; that you're all there, and there's no sag in you." She stood for a moment as if she were tortured by uncertainty, then turned suddenly back to him. "Don't talk about these things any more now," she entreated. "It isn't that I want to keep anything from you. The trouble is that I've got nothing to keep—except (you know as well as I) that feeling. I told you about it in Chicago once. But it always makes me unhappy to talk about it. It will spoil the day. Will you go for a climb with me?" She held out her hands with a smile so eager that it made Ottenburg feel how much she needed to get away from herself.

He sprang up and caught the hands she put out so cordially, and stood swinging them back and forth. "I won't tease you. A word's enough to me. But I love it, all the same. Understand?" He pressed her hands and dropped them. "Now, where are you going to drag me?"

"I want you to drag me. Over there, to the other houses. They are more interesting than these." She pointed across the gorge to the row of white houses in the other cliff. "The trail is broken away, but I got up there once. It's possible. You have to go to the bottom of the canyon, cross the creek, and then go up hand-over-hand."

Ottenburg, lounging against the sunny wall, his hands in the pockets of his jacket, looked across at the distant dwellings. "It's an awful climb," he sighed, "when I could be perfectly happy here with my pipe. However—" He took up his stick and hat and followed Thea down the water trail. "Do you climb this path every day? You surely earn your bath. I went down and had a look at your pool the other afternoon. Neat place, with all those little cottonwoods. Must be very becoming."

"Think so?" Thea said over her shoulder, as she swung round a turn.

"Yes, and so do you, evidently. I'm becoming expert at reading your meaning in your back. I'm behind you so much on these single-foot trails. You don't wear stays, do you?"

"Not here."

"I wouldn't, anywhere, if I were you. They will make you less elastic. The side muscles get flabby. If you go in for opera, there's a fortune in a flexible body. Most of the German singers are clumsy, even when they're well set up."

Thea switched a PINON branch back at him. "Oh, I'll never get fat! That I can promise you."

Fred smiled, looking after her. "Keep that promise, no matter how many others you break," he drawled.

The upward climb, after they had crossed the stream, was at first a breathless scramble through underbrush. When they reached the big boulders, Ottenburg went first because he had the longer leg-reach, and gave Thea a hand when the step was quite beyond her, swinging her up until she could get a foothold. At last they reached a little platform among the rocks, with only a hundred feet of jagged, sloping wall between them and the cliff-houses.

Ottenburg lay down under a pine tree and declared that he was going to have a pipe before he went any farther. "It's a good thing to know when to stop, Thea," he said meaningly.

"I'm not going to stop now until I get there," Thea insisted. "I'll go on alone."

Fred settled his shoulder against the tree-trunk. "Go on if you like, but I'm here to enjoy myself. If you meet a rattler on the way, have it out with him."

She hesitated, fanning herself with her felt hat. "I never have met one."

"There's reasoning for you," Fred murmured languidly.

Thea turned away resolutely and began to go up the wall, using an irregular cleft in the rock for a path. The cliff, which looked almost perpendicular from the bottom, was really made up of ledges and boulders, and behind these she soon disappeared. For a long while Fred smoked with half-closed eyes, smiling to himself now and again. Occasionally he lifted an eyebrow as he heard the rattle of small stones among the rocks above. "In a temper," he concluded; "do her good." Then he subsided into warm drowsiness and listened to the locusts in the yuccas, and the tap-tap of the old woodpecker that was never weary of assaulting the big pine.

Fred had finished his pipe and was wondering whether he wanted another, when he heard a call from the cliff far above him. Looking up, he saw Thea standing on the edge of a projecting crag. She waved to him and threw her arm over her head, as if she were snapping her fingers in the air.

As he saw her there between the sky and the gulf, with that great wash of air and the morning light about her, Fred recalled the brilliant figure at Mrs. Nathanmeyer's. Thea was one of those people who emerge, unexpectedly, larger than we are accustomed to see them. Even at this distance one got the impression of muscular energy and audacity,—a kind of brilliancy of motion,—of a personality that carried across big spaces and expanded among big things. Lying still, with his hands under his head, Ottenburg rhetorically addressed the figure in the air. "You are the sort that used to run wild in Germany, dressed in their hair and a piece of skin. Soldiers caught 'em in nets. Old Nathanmeyer," he mused, "would like a peep at her now. Knowing old fellow. Always buying those Zorn etchings of peasant girls bathing. No sag in them either. Must be the cold climate." He sat up. "She'll begin to pitch rocks on me if I don't move." In response to another impatient gesture from the crag, he rose and began swinging slowly up the trail.

It was the afternoon of that long day. Thea was lying on a blanket in the door of her rock house. She and Ottenburg had come back from their climb and had lunch, and he had gone off for a nap in one of the cliff-houses farther down the path. He was sleeping peacefully, his coat under his head and his face turned toward the wall.

Thea, too, was drowsy, and lay looking through halfclosed eyes up at the blazing blue arch over the rim of the canyon. She was thinking of nothing at all. Her mind, like her body, was full of warmth, lassitude, physical content. Suddenly an eagle, tawny and of great size, sailed over the cleft in which she lay, across the arch of sky. He dropped for a moment into the gulf between the walls, then wheeled, and mounted until his plumage was so steeped in light that he looked like a golden bird. He swept on, following the course of the canyon a little way and then disappearing beyond the rim. Thea sprang to her feet as if she had been thrown up from the rock by volcanic action. She stood rigid on the edge of the stone shelf, straining her eyes after that strong, tawny flight. O eagle of eagles! Endeavor, achievement, desire, glorious striving of human art! From a cleft in the heart of the world she saluted it...It had come all the way; when men lived in caves, it was there. A vanished race; but along the trails, in the stream, under the spreading cactus, there still glittered in the sun the bits of their frail clay vessels, fragments of their desire.

VII.

From the day of Fred's arrival, he and Thea were unceasingly active. They took long rides into the Navajo pine forests, bought turquoises and silver bracelets from the wandering Indian herdsmen, and rode twenty miles to Flagstaff upon the slightest pretext. Thea had never felt this pleasant excitement about any man before, and she found herself trying very hard to please young Ottenburg. She was never tired, never dull. There was a zest about waking up in the morning and dressing, about walking, riding, even about sleep.

One morning when Thea came out from her room at seven o'clock, she found Henry and Fred on the porch, looking up at the sky. The day was already hot and there was no breeze. The sun was shining, but heavy brown clouds were hanging in the west, like the smoke of a forest fire. She and Fred had meant to ride to Flagstaff that morning, but Biltmer advised against it, foretelling a storm. After breakfast they lingered about the house, waiting for the weather to make up its mind. Fred had brought his guitar, and as they had the dining-room to themselves, he made Thea go over some songs with him. They got interested and kept it up until Mrs. Biltmer came to set the table for dinner. Ottenburg knew some of the Mexican things Spanish Johnny used to sing. Thea had never before happened to tell him about Spanish Johnny, and he seemed more interested in Johnny than in Dr. Archie or Wunsch.

After dinner they were too restless to endure the ranch house any longer, and ran away to the canyon to practice with single-sticks. Fred carried a slicker and a sweater, and he made Thea wear one of the rubber hats that hung in Biltmer's gun-room. As they crossed the pasture land the clumsy slicker kept catching in the lacings of his leggings.

"Why don't you drop that thing?" Thea asked. "I won't mind a shower. I've been wet before."

"No use taking chances."

From the canyon they were unable to watch the sky, since only a strip of the zenith was visible. The flat ledge about the watch-tower was the only level spot large enough for single-stick exercise, and they were still practicing there when, at about four o'clock, a tremendous roll of thunder echoed between the cliffs and the atmosphere suddenly became thick.

Fred thrust the sticks in a cleft in the rock. "We're in for it, Thea. Better make for your cave where there are blankets." He caught her elbow and hurried her along the path before the cliff-houses. They made the half-mile at a quick trot, and as they ran the rocks and the sky and the air between the cliffs turned a turbid green, like the color in a moss agate. When they reached the blanketed rock room, they looked at each other and laughed. Their faces had taken on a greenish pallor. Thea's hair, even, was green.

"Dark as pitch in here," Fred exclaimed as they hurried over the old rock doorstep. "But it's warm. The rocks hold the heat. It's going to be terribly cold outside, all right." He was interrupted by a deafening peal of thunder. "Lord, what an echo! Lucky you don't mind. It's worth watching out there. We needn't come in yet."

The green light grew murkier and murkier. The smaller vegetation was blotted out. The yuccas, the cedars, and PINONS stood dark and rigid, like bronze. The swallows flew up with sharp, terrified twitterings. Even the quaking asps were still. While Fred and Thea watched from the doorway, the light changed to purple. Clouds of dark vapor, like chlorine gas, began to float down from the head of the canyon and hung between them and the cliff-houses in the opposite wall. Before they knew it, the wall itself had disappeared. The air was positively venomous-looking, and grew colder every minute. The thunder seemed to crash against one cliff, then against the other, and to go shrieking off into the inner canyon.

The moment the rain broke, it beat the vapors down. In the gulf before them the water fell in spouts, and dashed from the high cliffs overhead. It tore aspens and chokecherry bushes out of the ground and left the yuccas hanging by their tough roots. Only the little cedars stood black and unmoved in the torrents that fell from so far above. The rock chamber was full of fine spray from the streams of water that shot over the doorway. Thea crept to the back wall and rolled herself in a blanket, and Fred threw the heavier blankets over her. The wool of the Navajo sheep was soon kindled by the warmth of her body, and was impenetrable to dampness. Her hair, where it hung below the rubber hat, gathered the moisture like a sponge. Fred put on the slicker, tied the sweater about his neck, and settled himself cross-legged beside her. The chamber was so dark that, although he could see the outline of her head and shoulders, he could not see her face. He struck a wax match to light his pipe. As he sheltered it between his hands, it sizzled and sputtered, throwing a yellow flicker over Thea and her blankets.

"You look like a gypsy," he said as he dropped the match. "Any one you'd rather be shut up with than me? No? Sure about that?"

"I think I am. Aren't you cold?"

"Not especially." Fred smoked in silence, listening to the roar of the water outside. "We may not get away from here right away," he remarked.

"I shan't mind. Shall you?"

He laughed grimly and pulled on his pipe. "Do you know where you're at, Miss Thea Kronborg?" he said at last. "You've got me going pretty hard, I suppose you know. I've had a lot of sweethearts, but I've never been so much—engrossed before. What are you going to do about it?" He heard nothing from the blankets. "Are you going to play fair, or is it about my cue to cut away?"

"I'll play fair. I don't see why you want to go."

"What do you want me around for?—to play with?"

Thea struggled up among the blankets. "I want you for everything. I don't know whether I'm what people call in love with you or not. In Moonstone that meant sitting in a hammock with somebody. I don't want to sit in a hammock with you, but I want to do almost everything else. Oh, hundreds of things!"

"If I run away, will you go with me?"

"I don't know. I'll have to think about that. Maybe I would." She freed herself from her wrappings and stood up. "It's not raining so hard now. Hadn't we better start this minute? It will be night before we get to Biltmer's."

Fred struck another match. "It's seven. I don't know how much of the path may be washed away. I don't even know whether I ought to let you try it without a lantern."

Thea went to the doorway and looked out. "There's nothing else to do. The sweater and the slicker will keep me dry, and this will be my chance to find out whether these shoes are really water-tight. They cost a week's salary." She retreated to the back of the cave. "It's getting blacker every minute."

Ottenburg took a brandy flask from his coat pocket. "Better have some of this before we start. Can you take it without water?"

Thea lifted it obediently to her lips. She put on the sweater and Fred helped her to get the clumsy slicker on over it. He buttoned it and fastened the high collar. She could feel that his hands were hurried and clumsy. The coat was too big, and he took off his necktie and belted it in at the waist. While she tucked her hair more securely under the rubber hat he stood in front of her, between her and the gray doorway, without moving.

"Are you ready to go?" she asked carelessly.

"If you are," he spoke quietly, without moving, except to bend his head forward a little.

Thea laughed and put her hands on his shoulders. "You know how to handle me, don't you?" she whispered. For the first time, she kissed him without constraint or embarrassment.

"Thea, Thea, Thea!" Fred whispered her name three times, shaking her a little as if to waken her. It was too dark to see, but he could feel that she was smiling.

When she kissed him she had not hidden her face on his shoulder,—she had risen a little on her toes, and stood straight and free. In that moment when he came close to her actual personality, he felt in her the same expansion that he had noticed at Mrs. Nathanmeyer's. She became freer and stronger under impulses. When she rose to meet him like that, he felt her flash into everything that she had ever suggested to him, as if she filled out her own shadow.

She pushed him away and shot past him out into the rain. "Now for it, Fred," she called back exultantly. The rain was pouring steadily down through the dying gray twilight, and muddy streams were spouting and foaming over the cliff.

Fred caught her and held her back. "Keep behind me, Thea. I don't know about the path. It may be gone altogether. Can't tell what there is under this water."

But the path was older than the white man's Arizona. The rush of water had washed away the dust and stones that lay on the surface, but the rock skeleton of the Indian trail was there, ready for the foot. Where the streams poured down through gullies, there was always a cedar or a PINON to cling to. By wading and slipping and climbing, they got along. As they neared the head of the canyon, where the path lifted and rose in steep loops to the surface of the plateau, the climb was more difficult. The earth above had broken away and washed down over the trail, bringing rocks and bushes and even young trees with it. The last ghost of daylight was dying and there was no time to lose. The canyon behind them was already black.

"We've got to go right through the top of this pine tree, Thea. No time to hunt a way around. Give me your hand." After they had crashed through the mass of branches, Fred stopped abruptly. "Gosh, what a hole! Can you jump it? Wait a minute."

He cleared the washout, slipped on the wet rock at the farther side, and caught himself just in time to escape a tumble. "If I could only find something to hold to, I could give you a hand. It's so cursed dark, and there are no trees here where they're needed. Here's something; it's a root. It will hold all right." He braced himself on the rock, gripped the crooked root with one hand and swung himself across toward Thea, holding out his arm. "Good jump! I must say you don't lose your nerve in a tight place. Can you keep at it a little longer? We're almost out. Have to make that next ledge. Put your foot on my knee and catch something to pull by."

Thea went up over his shoulder. "It's hard ground up here," she panted. "Did I wrench your arm when I slipped then? It was a cactus I grabbed, and it startled me."

"Now, one more pull and we're on the level."

They emerged gasping upon the black plateau. In the last five minutes the darkness had solidified and it seemed as if the skies were pouring black water. They could not see where the sky ended or the plain began. The light at the ranch house burned a steady spark through the rain. Fred drew Thea's arm through his and they struck off toward the light. They could not see each other, and the rain at their backs seemed to drive them along. They kept laughing as they stumbled over tufts of grass or stepped into slippery pools. They were delighted with each other and with the adventure which lay behind them.

"I can't even see the whites of your eyes, Thea. But I'd know who was here stepping out with me, anywhere. Part coyote you are, by the feel of you. When you make up your mind to jump, you jump! My gracious, what's the matter with your hand?"

"Cactus spines. Didn't I tell you when I grabbed the cactus? I thought it was a root. Are we going straight?"

"I don't know. Somewhere near it, I think. I'm very comfortable, aren't you? You're warm, except your cheeks. How funny they are when they're wet. Still, you always feel like you. I like this. I could walk to Flagstaff. It's fun, not being able to see anything. I feel surer of you when I can't see you. Will you run away with me?"

Thea laughed. "I won't run far to-night. I'll think about it. Look, Fred, there's somebody coming."

"Henry, with his lantern. Good enough! Halloo! Hallo—o—o!" Fred shouted.

The moving light bobbed toward them. In half an hour Thea was in her big feather bed, drinking hot lentil soup, and almost before the soup was swallowed she was asleep.

VIII.

On the first day of September Fred Ottenburg and Thea Kronborg left Flagstaff by the east-bound express. As the bright morning advanced, they sat alone on the rear platform of the observation car, watching the yellow miles unfold and disappear. With complete content they saw the brilliant, empty country flash by. They were tired of the desert and the dead races, of a world without change or ideas. Fred said he was glad to sit back and let the Santa Fe do the work for a while.

"And where are we going, anyhow?" he added.

"To Chicago, I suppose. Where else would we be going?" Thea hunted for a handkerchief in her handbag.

"I wasn't sure, so I had the trunks checked to Albuquerque. We can recheck there to Chicago, if you like. Why Chicago? You'll never go back to Bowers. Why wouldn't this be a good time to make a run for it? We could take the southern branch at Albuquerque, down to El Paso, and then over into Mexico. We are exceptionally free. Nobody waiting for us anywhere."

Thea sighted along the steel rails that quivered in the light behind them. "I don't see why I couldn't marry you in Chicago, as well as any place," she brought out with some embarrassment.

Fred took the handbag out of her nervous clasp and swung it about on his finger. "You've no particular love for that spot, have you? Besides, as I've told you, my family would make a row. They are an excitable lot. They discuss and argue everlastingly. The only way I can ever put anything through is to go ahead, and convince them afterward."

"Yes; I understand. I don't mind that. I don't want to marry your family. I'm sure you wouldn't want to marry mine. But I don't see why we have to go so far."

"When we get to Winslow, you look about the freight yards and you'll probably see several yellow cars with my name on them. That's why, my dear. When your visiting-card is on every beer bottle, you can't do things quietly. Things get into the papers." As he watched her troubled expression, he grew anxious. He leaned forward on his camp-chair, and kept twirling the handbag between his knees. "Here's a suggestion, Thea," he said presently. "Dismiss it if you don't like it: suppose we go down to Mexico on the chance. You've never seen anything like Mexico City; it will be a lark for you, anyhow. If you change your mind, and don't want to marry me, you can go back to Chicago, and I'll take a steamer from Vera Cruz and go up to New York. When I get to Chicago, you'll be at work, and nobody will ever be the wiser. No reason why we shouldn't both travel in Mexico, is there? You'll be traveling alone. I'll merely tell you the right places to stop, and come to take you driving. I won't put any pressure on you. Have I ever?" He swung the bag toward her and looked up under her hat.

"No, you haven't," she murmured. She was thinking that her own position might be less difficult if he had used what he called pressure. He clearly wished her to take the responsibility.

"You have your own future in the back of your mind all the time," Fred began, "and I have it in mine. I'm not going to try to carry you off, as I might another girl. If you wanted to quit me, I couldn't hold you, no matter how many times you had married me. I don't want to overpersuade you. But I'd like mighty well to get you down to that jolly old city, where everything would please you, and give myself a chance. Then, if you thought you could have a better time with me than without me, I'd try to grab you before you changed your mind. You are not a sentimental person."

Thea drew her veil down over her face. "I think I am, a little; about you," she said quietly. Fred's irony somehow hurt her.

"What's at the bottom of your mind, Thea?" he asked hurriedly. "I can't tell. Why do you consider it at all, if you're not sure? Why are you here with me now?"

Her face was half-averted. He was thinking that it looked older and more firm—almost hard—under a veil.

"Isn't it possible to do things without having any very clear reason?" she asked slowly. "I have no plan in the back of my mind. Now that I'm with you, I want to be with you; that's all. I can't settle down to being alone again. I am here to-day because I want to be with you to-day." She paused. "One thing, though; if I gave you my word, I'd keep it. And you could hold me, though you don't seem to think so. Maybe I'm not sentimental, but I'm not very light, either. If I went off with you like this, it wouldn't be to amuse myself."

Ottenburg's eyes fell. His lips worked nervously for a moment. "Do you mean that you really care for me, Thea Kronborg?" he asked unsteadily.

"I guess so. It's like anything else. It takes hold of you and you've got to go through with it, even if you're afraid. I was afraid to leave Moonstone, and afraid to leave Harsanyi. But I had to go through with it."

"And are you afraid now?" Fred asked slowly.

"Yes; more than I've ever been. But I don't think I could go back. The past closes up behind one, somehow. One would rather have a new kind of misery. The old kind seems like death or unconsciousness. You can't force your life back into that mould again. No, one can't go back." She rose and stood by the back grating of the platform, her hand on the brass rail.

Fred went to her side. She pushed up her veil and turned her most glowing face to him. Her eyes were wet and there were tears on her lashes, but she was smiling the rare, whole-hearted smile he had seen once or twice before. He looked at her shining eyes, her parted lips, her chin a little lifted. It was as if they were colored by a sunrise he could not see. He put his hand over hers and clasped it with a strength she felt. Her eyelashes trembled, her mouth softened, but her eyes were still brilliant.

"Will you always be like you were down there, if I go with you?" she asked under her breath.

His fingers tightened on hers. "By God, I will!" he muttered.

"That's the only promise I'll ask you for. Now go away for a while and let me think about it. Come back at lunchtime and I'll tell you. Will that do?"

"Anything will do, Thea, if you'll only let me keep an eye on you. The rest of the world doesn't interest me much. You've got me in deep."

Fred dropped her hand and turned away. As he glanced back from the front end of the observation car, he saw that she was still standing there, and any one would have known that she was brooding over something. The earnestness of her head and shoulders had a certain nobility. He stood looking at her for a moment.

When he reached the forward smoking-car, Fred took a seat at the end, where he could shut the other passengers from his sight. He put on his traveling-cap and sat down wearily, keeping his head near the window. "In any case, I shall help her more than I shall hurt her," he kept saying to himself. He admitted that this was not the only motive which impelled him, but it was one of them. "I'll make it my business in life to get her on. There's nothing else I care about so much as seeing her have her chance. She hasn't touched her real force yet. She isn't even aware of it. Lord, don't I know something about them? There isn't one of them that has such a depth to draw from. She'll be one of the great artists of our time. Playing accompaniments for that cheese-faced sneak! I'll get her off to Germany this winter, or take her. She hasn't got any time to waste now. I'll make it up to her, all right."

Ottenburg certainly meant to make it up to her, in so far as he could. His feeling was as generous as strong human feelings are likely to be. The only trouble was, that he was married already, and had been since he was twenty.

His older friends in Chicago, people who had been friends of his family, knew of the unfortunate state of his personal affairs; but they were people whom in the natural course of things Thea Kronborg would scarcely meet. Mrs. Frederick Ottenburg lived in California, at Santa Barbara, where her health was supposed to be better than elsewhere, and her husband lived in Chicago. He visited his wife every winter to reinforce her position, and his devoted mother, although her hatred for her daughter-in-law was scarcely approachable in words, went to Santa Barbara every year to make things look better and to relieve her son.

When Frederick Ottenburg was beginning his junior year at Harvard, he got a letter from Dick Brisbane, a Kansas City boy he knew, telling him that his FIANCEE, Miss Edith Beers, was going to New York to buy her trousseau. She would be at the Holland House, with her aunt and a girl from Kansas City who was to be a bridesmaid, for two weeks or more. If Ottenburg happened to be going down to New York, would he call upon Miss Beers and "show her a good time"?

Fred did happen to be going to New York. He was going down from New Haven, after the Thanksgiving game. He called on Miss Beers and found her, as he that night telegraphed Brisbane, a "ripping beauty, no mistake." He took her and her aunt and her uninteresting friend to the theater and to the opera, and he asked them to lunch with him at the Waldorf. He took no little pains in arranging the luncheon with the head waiter. Miss Beers was the sort of girl with whom a young man liked to seem experienced. She was dark and slender and fiery. She was witty and slangy; said daring things and carried them off with NONCHALANCE. Her childish extravagance and contempt for all the serious facts of life could be charged to her father's generosity and his long packing-house purse. Freaks that would have been vulgar and ostentatious in a more simpleminded girl, in Miss Beers seemed whimsical and picturesque. She darted about in magnificent furs and pumps and close-clinging gowns, though that was the day of full skirts. Her hats were large and floppy. When she wriggled out of her moleskin coat at luncheon, she looked like a slim black weasel. Her satin dress was a mere sheath, so conspicuous by its severity and scantness that every one in the dining-room stared. She ate nothing but alligator-pear salad and hothouse grapes, drank a little champagne, and took cognac in her coffee. She ridiculed, in the raciest slang, the singers they had heard at the opera the night before, and when her aunt pretended to reprove her, she murmured indifferently, "What's the matter with you, old sport?" She rattled on with a subdued loquaciousness, always keeping her voice low and monotonous, always looking out of the corner of her eye and speaking, as it were, in asides, out of the corner of her mouth. She was scornful of everything,—which became her eyebrows. Her face was mobile and discontented, her eyes quick and black. There was a sort of smouldering fire about her, young Ottenburg thought. She entertained him prodigiously.

After luncheon Miss Beers said she was going uptown to be fitted, and that she would go alone because her aunt made her nervous. When Fred held her coat for her, she murmured, "Thank you, Alphonse," as if she were addressing the waiter. As she stepped into a hansom, with a long stretch of thin silk stocking, she said negligently, over her fur collar, "Better let me take you along and drop you somewhere." He sprang in after her, and she told the driver to go to the Park.

It was a bright winter day, and bitterly cold. Miss Beers asked Fred to tell her about the game at New Haven, and when he did so paid no attention to what he said. She sank back into the hansom and held her muff before her face, lowering it occasionally to utter laconic remarks about the people in the carriages they passed, interrupting Fred's narrative in a disconcerting manner. As they entered the Park he happened to glance under her wide black hat at her black eyes and hair—the muff hid everything else—and discovered that she was crying. To his solicitous inquiry she replied that it "was enough to make you damp, to go and try on dresses to marry a man you weren't keen about."

Further explanations followed. She had thought she was "perfectly cracked" about Brisbane, until she met Fred at the Holland House three days ago. Then she knew she would scratch Brisbane's eyes out if she married him. What was she going to do?

Fred told the driver to keep going. What did she want to do? Well, she didn't know. One had to marry somebody, after all the machinery had been put in motion. Perhaps she might as well scratch Brisbane as anybody else; for scratch she would, if she didn't get what she wanted.

Of course, Fred agreed, one had to marry somebody. And certainly this girl beat anything he had ever been up against before. Again he told the driver to go ahead. Did she mean that she would think of marrying him, by any chance? Of course she did, Alphonse. Hadn't he seen that all over her face three days ago? If he hadn't, he was a snowball.

By this time Fred was beginning to feel sorry for the driver. Miss Beers, however, was compassionless. After a few more turns, Fred suggested tea at the Casino. He was very cold himself, and remembering the shining silk hose and pumps, he wondered that the girl was not frozen. As they got out of the hansom, he slipped the driver a bill and told him to have something hot while he waited.

At the tea-table, in a snug glass enclosure, with the steam sputtering in the pipes beside them and a brilliant winter sunset without, they developed their plan. Miss Beers had with her plenty of money, destined for tradesmen, which she was quite willing to divert into other channels—the first excitement of buying a trousseau had worn off, anyway. It was very much like any other shopping. Fred had his allowance and a few hundred he had won on the game. She would meet him to-morrow morning at the Jersey ferry. They could take one of the west-bound Pennsylvania trains and go—anywhere, some place where the laws weren't too fussy.—Fred had not even thought about the laws!—It would be all right with her father; he knew Fred's family.

Now that they were engaged, she thought she would like to drive a little more. They were jerked about in the cab for another hour through the deserted Park. Miss Beers, having removed her hat, reclined upon Fred's shoulder.

The next morning they left Jersey City by the latest fast train out. They had some misadventures, crossed several States before they found a justice obliging enough to marry two persons whose names automatically instigated inquiry. The bride's family were rather pleased with her originality; besides, any one of the Ottenburg boys was clearly a better match than young Brisbane. With Otto Ottenburg, however, the affair went down hard, and to his wife, the once proud Katarina Furst, such a disappointment was almost unbearable. Her sons had always been clay in her hands, and now the GELIEBTER SOHN had escaped her.

Beers, the packer, gave his daughter a house in St. Louis, and Fred went into his father's business. At the end of a year, he was mutely appealing to his mother for sympathy. At the end of two, he was drinking and in open rebellion. He had learned to detest his wife. Her wastefulness and cruelty revolted him. The ignorance and the fatuous conceit which lay behind her grimacing mask of slang and ridicule humiliated him so deeply that he became absolutely reckless. Her grace was only an uneasy wriggle, her audacity was the result of insolence and envy, and her wit was restless spite. As her personal mannerisms grew more and more odious to him, he began to dull his perceptions with champagne. He had it for tea, he drank it with dinner, and during the evening he took enough to insure that he would be well insulated when he got home. This behavior spread alarm among his friends. It was scandalous, and it did not occur among brewers. He was violating the NOBLESSE OBLIGE of his guild. His father and his father's partners looked alarmed.

When Fred's mother went to him and with clasped hands entreated an explanation, he told her that the only trouble was that he couldn't hold enough wine to make life endurable, so he was going to get out from under and enlist in the navy. He didn't want anything but the shirt on his back and clean salt air. His mother could look out; he was going to make a scandal.

Mrs. Otto Ottenburg went to Kansas City to see Mr. Beers, and had the satisfaction of telling him that he had brought up his daughter like a savage, EINE UNGEBILDETE. All the Ottenburgs and all the Beers, and many of their friends, were drawn into the quarrel. It was to public opinion, however and not to his mother's activities, that Fred owed his partial escape from bondage. The cosmopolitan brewing world of St. Louis had conservative standards. The Ottenburgs' friends were not predisposed in favor of the plunging Kansas City set, and they disliked young Fred's wife from the day that she was brought among them. They found her ignorant and ill-bred and insufferably impertinent. When they became aware of how matters were going between her and Fred, they omitted no opportunity to snub her. Young Fred had always been popular, and St. Louis people took up his cause with warmth. Even the younger men, among whom Mrs. Fred tried to draft a following, at first avoided and then ignored her. Her defeat was so conspicuous, her life became such a desert, that she at last consented to accept the house in Santa Barbara which Mrs. Otto Ottenburg had long owned and cherished. This villa, with its luxuriant gardens, was the price of Fred's furlough. His mother was only too glad to offer it in his behalf. As soon as his wife was established in California, Fred was transferred from St. Louis to Chicago.

A divorce was the one thing Edith would never, never, give him. She told him so, and she told his family so, and her father stood behind her. She would enter into no arrangement that might eventually lead to divorce. She had insulted her husband before guests and servants, had scratched his face, thrown hand-mirrors and hairbrushes and nail-scissors at him often enough, but she knew that Fred was hardly the fellow who would go into court and offer that sort of evidence. In her behavior with other men she was discreet.

After Fred went to Chicago, his mother visited him often, and dropped a word to her old friends there, who were already kindly disposed toward the young man. They gossiped as little as was compatible with the interest they felt, undertook to make life agreeable for Fred, and told his story only where they felt it would do good: to girls who seemed to find the young brewer attractive. So far, he had behaved well, and had kept out of entanglements.

Since he was transferred to Chicago, Fred had been abroad several times, and had fallen more and more into the way of going about among young artists,—people with whom personal relations were incidental. With women, and even girls, who had careers to follow, a young man might have pleasant friendships without being regarded as a prospective suitor or lover. Among artists his position was not irregular, because with them his marriageableness was not an issue. His tastes, his enthusiasm, and his agreeable personality made him welcome.

With Thea Kronborg he had allowed himself more liberty than he usually did in his friendships or gallantries with young artists, because she seemed to him distinctly not the marrying kind. She impressed him as equipped to be an artist, and to be nothing else; already directed, concentrated, formed as to mental habit. He was generous and sympathetic, and she was lonely and needed friendship; needed cheerfulness. She had not much power of reaching out toward useful people or useful experiences, did not see opportunities. She had no tact about going after good positions or enlisting the interest of influential persons. She antagonized people rather than conciliated them. He discovered at once that she had a merry side, a robust humor that was deep and hearty, like her laugh, but it slept most of the time under her own doubts and the dullness of her life. She had not what is called a "sense of humor." That is, she had no intellectual humor; no power to enjoy the absurdities of people, no relish of their pretentiousness and inconsistencies—which only depressed her. But her joviality, Fred felt, was an asset, and ought to be developed. He discovered that she was more receptive and more effective under a pleasant stimulus than she was under the gray grind which she considered her salvation. She was still Methodist enough to believe that if a thing were hard and irksome, it must be good for her. And yet, whatever she did well was spontaneous. Under the least glow of excitement, as at Mrs. Nathanmeyer's, he had seen the apprehensive, frowning drudge of Bowers's studio flash into a resourceful and consciously beautiful woman.

His interest in Thea was serious, almost from the first, and so sincere that he felt no distrust of himself. He believed that he knew a great deal more about her possibilities than Bowers knew, and he liked to think that he had given her a stronger hold on life. She had never seen herself or known herself as she did at Mrs. Nathanmeyer's musical evenings. She had been a different girl ever since. He had not anticipated that she would grow more fond of him than his immediate usefulness warranted. He thought he knew the ways of artists, and, as he said, she must have been "at it from her cradle." He had imagined, perhaps, but never really believed, that he would find her waiting for him sometime as he found her waiting on the day he reached the Biltmer ranch. Once he found her so—well, he did not pretend to be anything more or less than a reasonably well-intentioned young man. A lovesick girl or a flirtatious woman he could have handled easily enough. But a personality like that, unconsciously revealing itself for the first time under the exaltation of a personal feeling,—what could one do but watch it? As he used to say to himself, in reckless moments back there in the canyon, "You can't put out a sunrise." He had to watch it, and then he had to share it.

Besides, was he really going to do her any harm? The Lord knew he would marry her if he could! Marriage would be an incident, not an end with her; he was sure of that. If it were not he, it would be some one else; some one who would be a weight about her neck, probably; who would hold her back and beat her down and divert her from the first plunge for which he felt she was gathering all her energies. He meant to help her, and he could not think of another man who would. He went over his unmarried friends, East and West, and he could not think of one who would know what she was driving at—or care. The clever ones were selfish, the kindly ones were stupid.

"Damn it, if she's going to fall in love with somebody, it had better be me than any of the others—of the sort she'd find. Get her tied up with some conceited ass who'd try to make her over, train her like a puppy! Give one of 'em a big nature like that, and he'd be horrified. He wouldn't show his face in the clubs until he'd gone after her and combed her down to conform to some fool idea in his own head—put there by some other woman, too, his first sweetheart or his grandmother or a maiden aunt. At least, I understand her. I know what she needs and where she's bound, and I mean to see that she has a fighting chance."

His own conduct looked crooked, he admitted; but he asked himself whether, between men and women, all ways were not more or less crooked. He believed those which are called straight were the most dangerous of all. They seemed to him, for the most part, to lie between windowless stone walls, and their rectitude had been achieved at the expense of light and air. In their unquestioned regularity lurked every sort of human cruelty and meanness, and every kind of humiliation and suffering. He would rather have any woman he cared for wounded than crushed. He would deceive her not once, he told himself fiercely, but a hundred times, to keep her free.

When Fred went back to the observation car at one o'clock, after the luncheon call, it was empty, and he found Thea alone on the platform. She put out her hand, and met his eyes.

"It's as I said. Things have closed behind me. I can't go back, so I am going on—to Mexico?" She lifted her face with an eager, questioning smile.

Fred met it with a sinking heart. Had he really hoped she would give him another answer? He would have given pretty much anything—But there, that did no good. He could give only what he had. Things were never complete in this world; you had to snatch at them as they came or go without. Nobody could look into her face and draw back, nobody who had any courage. She had courage enough for anything—look at her mouth and chin and eyes! Where did it come from, that light? How could a face, a familiar face, become so the picture of hope, be painted with the very colors of youth's exaltation? She was right; she was not one of those who draw back. Some people get on by avoiding dangers, others by riding through them.

They stood by the railing looking back at the sand levels, both feeling that the train was steaming ahead very fast. Fred's mind was a confusion of images and ideas. Only two things were clear to him: the force of her determination, and the belief that, handicapped as he was, he could do better by her than another man would do. He knew he would always remember her, standing there with that expectant, forward-looking smile, enough to turn the future into summer.

5

DR. ARCHIE'S VENTURE

I.

Dr. Howard Archie had come down to Denver for a meeting of the stockholders in the San Felipe silver mine. It was not absolutely necessary for him to come, but he had no very pressing cases at home. Winter was closing down in Moonstone, and he dreaded the dullness of it. On the 10th day of January, therefore, he was registered at the Brown Palace Hotel. On the morning of the 11th he came down to breakfast to find the streets white and the air thick with snow. A wild northwester was blowing down from the mountains, one of those beautiful storms that wrap Denver in dry, furry snow, and make the city a loadstone to thousands of men in the mountains and on the plains. The brakemen out on their box-cars, the miners up in their diggings, the lonely homesteaders in the sand hills of Yucca and Kit Carson Counties, begin to think of Denver, muffled in snow, full of food and drink and good cheer, and to yearn for her with that admiration which makes her, more than other American cities, an object of sentiment.

Howard Archie was glad he had got in before the storm came. He felt as cheerful as if he had received a legacy that morning, and he greeted the clerk with even greater friendliness than usual when he stopped at the desk for his mail. In the dining-room he found several old friends seated here and there before substantial breakfasts: cattlemen and mining engineers from odd corners of the State, all looking fresh and well pleased with themselves. He had a word with one and another before he sat down at the little table by a window, where the Austrian head waiter stood attentively behind a chair. After his breakfast was put before him, the doctor began to run over his letters. There was one directed in Thea Kronborg's handwriting, forwarded from Moonstone. He saw with astonishment, as he put another lump of sugar into his cup, that this letter bore a New York postmark. He had known that Thea was in Mexico, traveling with some Chicago people, but New York, to a Denver man, seems much farther away than Mexico City. He put the letter behind his plate, upright against the stem of his water goblet, and looked at it thoughtfully while he drank his second cup of coffee. He had been a little anxious about Thea; she had not written to him for a long while.

As he never got good coffee at home, the doctor always drank three cups for breakfast when he was in Denver. Oscar knew just when to bring him a second pot, fresh and smoking. "And more cream, Oscar, please. You know I like lots of cream," the doctor murmured, as he opened the square envelope, marked in the upper right-hand corner, "Everett House, Union Square." The text of the letter was as follows:—

DEAR DOCTOR ARCHIE:—

I have not written to you for a long time, but it has not been unintentional. I could not write you frankly, and so I would not write at all. I can be frank with you now, but not by letter. It is a great deal to ask, but I wonder if you could come to New York to help me out? I have got into difficulties, and I need your advice. I need your friendship. I am afraid I must even ask you to lend me money, if you can without serious inconvenience. I have to go to Germany to study, and it can't be put off any longer. My voice is ready. Needless to say, I don't want any word of this to reach my family. They are the last people I would turn to, though I love my mother dearly. If you can come, please telegraph me at this hotel. Don't despair of me. I'll make it up to you yet.

Your old friend,

THEA KRONBORG.

This in a bold, jagged handwriting with a Gothic turn to the letters,—something between a highly sophisticated hand and a very unsophisticated one,—not in the least smooth or flowing.

The doctor bit off the end of a cigar nervously and read the letter through again, fumbling distractedly in his pockets for matches, while the waiter kept trying to call his attention to the box he had just placed before him. At last Oscar came out, as if the idea had just struck him, "Matches, sir?"

"Yes, thank you." The doctor slipped a coin into his palm and rose, crumpling Thea's letter in his hand and thrusting the others into his pocket unopened. He went back to the desk in the lobby and beckoned to the clerk, upon whose kindness he threw himself apologetically.

"Harry, I've got to pull out unexpectedly. Call up the Burlington, will you, and ask them to route me to New York the quickest way, and to let us know. Ask for the hour I'll get in. I have to wire."

"Certainly, Dr. Archie. Have it for you in a minute." The young man's pallid, clean-scraped face was all sympathetic interest as he reached for the telephone. Dr. Archie put out his hand and stopped him.

"Wait a minute. Tell me, first, is Captain Harris down yet?"

"No, sir. The Captain hasn't come down yet this morning."

"I'll wait here for him. If I don't happen to catch him, nail him and get me. Thank you, Harry."

The doctor spoke gratefully and turned away. He began to pace the lobby, his hands behind him, watching the bronze elevator doors like a hawk. At last Captain Harris issued from one of them, tall and imposing, wearing a Stetson and fierce mustaches, a fur coat on his arm, a solitaire glittering upon his little finger and another in his black satin ascot. He was one of the grand old bluffers of those good old days. As gullible as a schoolboy, he had managed, with his sharp eye and knowing air and twisted blond mustaches, to pass himself off for an astute financier, and the Denver papers respectfully referred to him as the Rothschild of Cripple Creek.

Dr. Archie stopped the Captain on his way to breakfast. "Must see you a minute, Captain. Can't wait. Want to sell you some shares in the San Felipe. Got to raise money."

The Captain grandly bestowed his hat upon an eager porter who had already lifted his fur coat tenderly from his arm and stood nursing it. In removing his hat, the Captain exposed a bald, flushed dome, thatched about the ears with yellowish gray hair. "Bad time to sell, doctor. You want to hold on to San Felipe, and buy more. What have you got to raise?"

"Oh, not a great sum. Five or six thousand. I've been buying up close and have run short."

"I see, I see. Well, doctor, you'll have to let me get through that door. I was out last night, and I'm going to get my bacon, if you lose your mine." He clapped Archie on the shoulder and pushed him along in front of him. "Come ahead with me, and we'll talk business."

Dr. Archie attended the Captain and waited while he gave his order, taking the seat the old promoter indicated.

"Now, sir," the Captain turned to him, "you don't want to sell anything. You must be under the impression that I'm one of these damned New England sharks that get their pound of flesh off the widow and orphan. If you're a little short, sign a note and I'll write a check. That's the way gentlemen do business. If you want to put up some San Felipe as collateral, let her go, but I shan't touch a share of it. Pens and ink, please, Oscar,"—he lifted a large forefinger to the Austrian.

The Captain took out his checkbook and a book of blank notes, and adjusted his nose-nippers. He wrote a few words in one book and Archie wrote a few in the other. Then they each tore across perforations and exchanged slips of paper.

"That's the way. Saves office rent," the Captain commented with satisfaction, returning the books to his pocket. "And now, Archie, where are you off to?"

"Got to go East to-night. A deal waiting for me in New York." Dr. Archie rose.

The Captain's face brightened as he saw Oscar approaching with a tray, and he began tucking the corner of his napkin inside his collar, over his ascot. "Don't let them unload anything on you back there, doctor," he said genially, "and don't let them relieve you of anything, either. Don't let them get any Cripple stuff off you. We can manage our own silver out here, and we're going to take it out by the ton, sir!"

The doctor left the dining-room, and after another consultation with the clerk, he wrote his first telegram to Thea:—

Miss Thea Kronborg, Everett House, New York.

Will call at your hotel eleven o'clock Friday morning. Glad to come. Thank you.

ARCHIE

He stood and heard the message actually clicked off on the wire, with the feeling that she was hearing the click at the other end. Then he sat down in the lobby and wrote a note to his wife and one to the other doctor in Moonstone. When he at last issued out into the storm, it was with a feeling of elation rather than of anxiety. Whatever was wrong, he could make it right. Her letter had practically said so.

He tramped about the snowy streets, from the bank to the Union Station, where he shoved his money under the grating of the ticket window as if he could not get rid of it fast enough. He had never been in New York, never been farther east than Buffalo. "That's rather a shame," he reflected boyishly as he put the long tickets in his pocket, "for a man nearly forty years old." However, he thought as he walked up toward the club, he was on the whole glad that his first trip had a human interest, that he was going for something, and because he was wanted. He loved holidays. He felt as if he were going to Germany himself. "Queer,"—he went over it with the snow blowing in his face,—"but that sort of thing is more interesting than mines and making your daily bread. It's worth paying out to be in on it,—for a fellow like me. And when it's Thea—Oh, I back her!" he laughed aloud as he burst in at the door of the Athletic Club, powdered with snow.

Archie sat down before the New York papers and ran over the advertisements of hotels, but he was too restless to read. Probably he had better get a new overcoat, and he was not sure about the shape of his collars. "I don't want to look different to her from everybody else there," he mused. "I guess I'll go down and have Van look me over. He'll put me right."

So he plunged out into the snow again and started for his tailor's. When he passed a florist's shop he stopped and looked in at the window, smiling; how naturally pleasant things recalled one another. At the tailor's he kept whistling, "Flow gently, Sweet Afton," while Van Dusen advised him, until that resourceful tailor and haberdasher exclaimed, "You must have a date back there, doctor; you behave like a bridegroom," and made him remember that he wasn't one.

Before he let him go, Van put his finger on the Masonic pin in his client's lapel. "Mustn't wear that, doctor. Very bad form back there."

II.

Fred Ottenburg, smartly dressed for the afternoon, with a long black coat and gaiters was sitting in the dusty parlor of the Everett House. His manner was not in accord with his personal freshness, the good lines of his clothes, and the shining smoothness of his hair. His attitude was one of deep dejection, and his face, though it had the cool, unimpeachable fairness possible only to a very blond young man, was by no means happy. A page shuffled into the room and looked about. When he made out the dark figure in a shadowy corner, tracing over the carpet pattern with a cane, he droned, "The lady says you can come up, sir."

Fred picked up his hat and gloves and followed the creature, who seemed an aged boy in uniform, through dark corridors that smelled of old carpets. The page knocked at the door of Thea's sitting-room, and then wandered away. Thea came to the door with a telegram in her hand. She asked Ottenburg to come in and pointed to one of the clumsy, sullen-looking chairs that were as thick as they were high. The room was brown with time, dark in spite of two windows that opened on Union Square, with dull curtains and carpet, and heavy, respectable-looking furniture in somber colors. The place was saved from utter dismalness by a coal fire under the black marble mantelpiece,—brilliantly reflected in a long mirror that hung between the two windows. This was the first time Fred had seen the room, and he took it in quickly, as he put down his hat and gloves.

Thea seated herself at the walnut writing-desk, still holding the slip of yellow paper. "Dr. Archie is coming," she said. "He will be here Friday morning."

"Well, that's good, at any rate," her visitor replied with a determined effort at cheerfulness. Then, turning to the fire, he added blankly, "If you want him."

"Of course I want him. I would never have asked such a thing of him if I hadn't wanted him a great deal. It's a very expensive trip." Thea spoke severely. Then she went on, in a milder tone. "He doesn't say anything about the money, but I think his coming means that he can let me have it."

Fred was standing before the mantel, rubbing his hands together nervously. "Probably. You are still determined to call on him?" He sat down tentatively in the chair Thea had indicated. "I don't see why you won't borrow from me, and let him sign with you, for instance. That would constitute a perfectly regular business transaction. I could bring suit against either of you for my money."

Thea turned toward him from the desk. "We won't take that up again, Fred. I should have a different feeling about it if I went on your money. In a way I shall feel freer on Dr. Archie's, and in another way I shall feel more bound. I shall try even harder." She paused. "He is almost like my father," she added irrelevantly.

"Still, he isn't, you know," Fred persisted. "It wouldn't be anything new. I've loaned money to students before, and got it back, too."

"Yes; I know you're generous," Thea hurried over it, "but this will be the best way. He will be here on Friday did I tell you?"

"I think you mentioned it. That's rather soon. May I smoke?" he took out a small cigarette case. "I suppose you'll be off next week?" he asked as he struck a match.

"Just as soon as I can," she replied with a restless movement of her arms, as if her dark-blue dress were too tight for her. "It seems as if I'd been here forever."

"And yet," the young man mused, "we got in only four days ago. Facts really don't count for much, do they? It's all in the way people feel: even in little things."

Thea winced, but she did not answer him. She put the telegram back in its envelope and placed it carefully in one of the pigeonholes of the desk.

"I suppose," Fred brought out with effort, "that your friend is in your confidence?"

"He always has been. I shall have to tell him about myself. I wish I could without dragging you in."

Fred shook himself. "Don't bother about where you drag me, please," he put in, flushing. "I don't give—" he subsided suddenly.

"I'm afraid," Thea went on gravely, "that he won't understand. He'll be hard on you."

Fred studied the white ash of his cigarette before he flicked it off. "You mean he'll see me as even worse than I am. Yes, I suppose I shall look very low to him: a fifthrate scoundrel. But that only matters in so far as it hurts his feelings."

Thea sighed. "We'll both look pretty low. And after all, we must really be just about as we shall look to him."

Ottenburg started up and threw his cigarette into the grate. "That I deny. Have you ever been really frank with this preceptor of your childhood, even when you WERE a child? Think a minute, have you? Of course not! From your cradle, as I once told you, you've been 'doing it' on the side, living your own life, admitting to yourself things that would horrify him. You've always deceived him to the extent of letting him think you different from what you are. He couldn't understand then, he can't understand now. So why not spare yourself and him?"

She shook her head. "Of course, I've had my own thoughts. Maybe he has had his, too. But I've never done anything before that he would much mind. I must put myself right with him,—as right as I can,—to begin over. He'll make allowances for me. He always has. But I'm afraid he won't for you."

"Leave that to him and me. I take it you want me to see him?" Fred sat down again and began absently to trace the carpet pattern with his cane. "At the worst," he spoke wanderingly, "I thought you'd perhaps let me go in on the business end of it and invest along with you. You'd put in your talent and ambition and hard work, and I'd put in the money and—well, nobody's good wishes are to be scorned, not even mine. Then, when the thing panned out big, we could share together. Your doctor friend hasn't cared half so much about your future as I have."

"He's cared a good deal. He doesn't know as much about such things as you do. Of course you've been a great deal more help to me than any one else ever has," Thea said quietly. The black clock on the mantel began to strike. She listened to the five strokes and then said, "I'd have liked your helping me eight months ago. But now, you'd simply be keeping me."

"You weren't ready for it eight months ago." Fred leaned back at last in his chair. "You simply weren't ready for it. You were too tired. You were too timid. Your whole tone was too low. You couldn't rise from a chair like that,"—she had started up apprehensively and gone toward the window.—"You were fumbling and awkward. Since then you've come into your personality. You were always locking horns with it before. You were a sullen little drudge eight months ago, afraid of being caught at either looking or moving like yourself. Nobody could tell anything about you. A voice is not an instrument that's found ready-made. A voice is personality. It can be as big as a circus and as common as dirt.—There's good money in that kind, too, but I don't happen to be interested in them.—Nobody could tell much about what you might be able to do, last winter. I divined more than anybody else."

"Yes, I know you did." Thea walked over to the old-fashioned mantel and held her hands down to the glow of the fire. "I owe so much to you, and that's what makes things hard. That's why I have to get away from you altogether. I depend on you for so many things. Oh, I did even last winter, in Chicago!" She knelt down by the grate and held her hands closer to the coals. "And one thing leads to another."

Ottenburg watched her as she bent toward the fire. His glance brightened a little. "Anyhow, you couldn't look as you do now, before you knew me. You WERE clumsy. And whatever you do now, you do splendidly. And you can't cry enough to spoil your face for more than ten minutes. It comes right back, in spite of you. It's only since you've known me that you've let yourself be beautiful."

Without rising she turned her face away. Fred went on impetuously. "Oh, you can turn it away from me, Thea; you can take it away from me! All the same—" his spurt died and he fell back. "How can you turn on me so, after all!" he sighed.

"I haven't. But when you arranged with yourself to take me in like that, you couldn't have been thinking very kindly of me. I can't understand how you carried it through, when I was so easy, and all the circumstances were so easy."

Her crouching position by the fire became threatening. Fred got up, and Thea also rose.

"No," he said, "I can't make you see that now. Some time later, perhaps, you will understand better. For one thing, I honestly could not imagine that words, names, meant so much to you." Fred was talking with the desperation of a man who has put himself in the wrong and who yet feels that there was an idea of truth in his conduct. "Suppose that you had married your brakeman and lived with him year after year, caring for him even less than you do for your doctor, or for Harsanyi. I suppose you would have felt quite all right about it, because that relation has a name in good standing. To me, that seems—sickening!" He took a rapid turn about the room and then as Thea remained standing, he rolled one of the elephantine chairs up to the hearth for her.

"Sit down and listen to me for a moment, Thea." He began pacing from the hearthrug to the window and back again, while she sat down compliantly. "Don't you know most of the people in the world are not individuals at all? They never have an individual idea or experience. A lot of girls go to boarding-school together, come out the same season, dance at the same parties, are married off in groups, have their babies at about the same time, send their children to school together, and so the human crop renews itself. Such women know as much about the reality of the forms they go through as they know about the wars they learn the dates of. They get their most personal experiences out of novels and plays. Everything is second-hand with them. Why, you COULDN'T live like that."

Thea sat looking toward the mantel, her eyes half closed, her chin level, her head set as if she were enduring something. Her hands, very white, lay passive on her dark gown. From the window corner Fred looked at them and at her. He shook his head and flashed an angry, tormented look out into the blue twilight over the Square, through which muffled cries and calls and the clang of car bells came up from the street. He turned again and began to pace the floor, his hands in his pockets.

"Say what you will, Thea Kronborg, you are not that sort of person. You will never sit alone with a pacifier and a novel. You won't subsist on what the old ladies have put into the bottle for you. You will always break through into the realities. That was the first thing Harsanyi found out about you; that you couldn't be kept on the outside. If you'd lived in Moonstone all your life and got on with the discreet brakeman, you'd have had just the same nature. Your children would have been the realities then, probably. If they'd been commonplace, you'd have killed them with driving. You'd have managed some way to live twenty times as much as the people around you."

Fred paused. He sought along the shadowy ceiling and heavy mouldings for words. When he began again, his voice was lower, and at first he spoke with less conviction, though again it grew on him. "Now I knew all this—oh, knew it better than I can ever make you understand! You've been running a handicap. You had no time to lose. I wanted you to have what you need and to get on fast—get through with me, if need be; I counted on that. You've no time to sit round and analyze your conduct or your feelings. Other women give their whole lives to it. They've nothing else to do. Helping a man to get his divorce is a career for them; just the sort of intellectual exercise they like."

Fred dived fiercely into his pockets as if he would rip them out and scatter their contents to the winds. Stopping before her, he took a deep breath and went on again, this time slowly. "All that sort of thing is foreign to you. You'd be nowhere at it. You haven't that kind of mind. The grammatical niceties of conduct are dark to you. You're simple—and poetic." Fred's voice seemed to be wandering about in the thickening dusk. "You won't play much. You won't, perhaps, love many times." He paused. "And you did love me, you know. Your railroad friend would have understood me. I COULD have thrown you back. The reverse was there,—it stared me in the face,—but I couldn't pull it. I let you drive ahead." He threw out his hands. What Thea noticed, oddly enough, was the flash of the firelight on his cuff link. He turned again. "And you'll always drive ahead," he muttered. "It's your way."

There was a long silence. Fred had dropped into a chair. He seemed, after such an explosion, not to have a word left in him. Thea put her hand to the back of her neck and pressed it, as if the muscles there were aching.

"Well," she said at last, "I at least overlook more in you than I do in myself. I am always excusing you to myself. I don't do much else."

"Then why, in Heaven's name, won't you let me be your friend? You make a scoundrel of me, borrowing money from another man to get out of my clutches."

"If I borrow from him, it's to study. Anything I took from you would be different. As I said before, you'd be keeping me."

"Keeping! I like your language. It's pure Moonstone, Thea,—like your point of view. I wonder how long you'll be a Methodist." He turned away bitterly.

"Well, I've never said I wasn't Moonstone, have I? I am, and that's why I want Dr. Archie. I can't see anything so funny about Moonstone, you know." She pushed her chair back a little from the hearth and clasped her hands over her knee, still looking thoughtfully into the red coals. "We always come back to the same thing, Fred. The name, as you call it, makes a difference to me how I feel about myself. You would have acted very differently with a girl of your own kind, and that's why I can't take anything from you now. You've made everything impossible. Being married is one thing and not being married is the other thing, and that's all there is to it. I can't see how you reasoned with yourself, if you took the trouble to reason. You say I was too much alone, and yet what you did was to cut me off more than I ever had been. Now I'm going to try to make good to my friends out there. That's all there is left for me."

"Make good to your friends!" Fred burst out. "What one of them cares as I care, or believes as I believe? I've told you I'll never ask a gracious word from you until I can ask it with all the churches in Christendom at my back."

Thea looked up, and when she saw Fred's face, she thought sadly that he, too, looked as if things were spoiled for him. "If you know me as well as you say you do, Fred," she said slowly, "then you are not being honest with yourself. You know that I can't do things halfway. If you kept me at all—you'd keep me." She dropped her head wearily on her hand and sat with her forehead resting on her fingers.

Fred leaned over her and said just above his breath, "Then, when I get that divorce, you'll take it up with me again? You'll at least let me know, warn me, before there is a serious question of anybody else?"

Without lifting her head, Thea answered him. "Oh, I don't think there will ever be a question of anybody else. Not if I can help it. I suppose I've given you every reason to think there will be,—at once, on shipboard, any time."

Ottenburg drew himself up like a shot. "Stop it, Thea!" he said sharply. "That's one thing you've never done. That's like any common woman." He saw her shoulders lift a little and grow calm. Then he went to the other side of the room and took up his hat and gloves from the sofa. He came back cheerfully. "I didn't drop in to bully you this afternoon. I came to coax you to go out for tea with me somewhere." He waited, but she did not look up or lift her head, still sunk on her hand.

Her handkerchief had fallen. Fred picked it up and put it on her knee, pressing her fingers over it. "Good-night, dear and wonderful," he whispered,—"wonderful and dear! How can you ever get away from me when I will always follow you, through every wall, through every door, wherever you go." He looked down at her bent head, and the curve of her neck that was so sad. He stooped, and with his lips just touched her hair where the firelight made it ruddiest. "I didn't know I had it in me, Thea. I thought it was all a fairy tale. I don't know myself any more." He closed his eyes and breathed deeply. "The salt's all gone out of your hair. It's full of sun and wind again. I believe it has memories." Again she heard him take a deep breath. "I could do without you for a lifetime, if that would give you to yourself. A woman like you doesn't find herself, alone."

She thrust her free hand up to him. He kissed it softly, as if she were asleep and he were afraid of waking her.

From the door he turned back irrelevantly. "As to your old friend, Thea, if he's to be here on Friday, why,"—he snatched out his watch and held it down to catch the light from the grate,—"he's on the train now! That ought to cheer you. Good-night." She heard the door close.

III.

On Friday afternoon Thea Kronborg was walking excitedly up and down her sitting-room, which at that hour was flooded by thin, clear sunshine. Both windows were open, and the fire in the grate was low, for the day was one of those false springs that sometimes blow into New York from the sea in the middle of winter, soft, warm, with a persuasive salty moisture in the air and a relaxing thaw under foot. Thea was flushed and animated, and she seemed as restless as the sooty sparrows that chirped and cheeped distractingly about the windows. She kept looking at the black clock, and then down into the Square. The room was full of flowers, and she stopped now and then to arrange them or to move them into the sunlight. After the bellboy came to announce a visitor, she took some Roman hyacinths from a glass and stuck them in the front of her dark-blue dress.

When at last Fred Ottenburg appeared in the doorway, she met him with an exclamation of pleasure. "I am glad you've come, Fred. I was afraid you might not get my note, and I wanted to see you before you see Dr. Archie. He's so nice!" She brought her hands together to emphasize her statement.

"Is he? I'm glad. You see I'm quite out of breath. I didn't wait for the elevator, but ran upstairs. I was so pleased at being sent for." He dropped his hat and overcoat. "Yes, I should say he is nice! I don't seem to recognize all of these," waving his handkerchief about at the flowers.

"Yes, he brought them himself, in a big box. He brought lots with him besides flowers. Oh, lots of things! The old Moonstone feeling,"—Thea moved her hand back and forth in the air, fluttering her fingers,—"the feeling of starting out, early in the morning, to take my lesson."

"And you've had everything out with him?"

"No, I haven't."

"Haven't?" He looked up in consternation.

"No, I haven't!" Thea spoke excitedly, moving about over the sunny patches on the grimy carpet. "I've lied to him, just as you said I had always lied to him, and that's why I'm so happy. I've let him think what he likes to think. Oh, I couldn't do anything else, Fred,"—she shook her head emphatically. "If you'd seen him when he came in, so pleased and excited! You see this is a great adventure for him. From the moment I began to talk to him, he entreated me not to say too much, not to spoil his notion of me. Not in so many words, of course. But if you'd seen his eyes, his face, his kind hands! Oh, no! I couldn't." She took a deep breath, as if with a renewed sense of her narrow escape.

"Then, what did you tell him?" Fred demanded.

Thea sat down on the edge of the sofa and began shutting and opening her hands nervously. "Well, I told him enough, and not too much. I told him all about how good you were to me last winter, getting me engagements and things, and how you had helped me with my work more than anybody. Then I told him about how you sent me down to the ranch when I had no money or anything." She paused and wrinkled her forehead. "And I told him that I wanted to marry you and ran away to Mexico with you, and that I was awfully happy until you told me that you couldn't marry me because—well, I told him why."

Thea dropped her eyes and moved the toe of her shoe about restlessly on the carpet.

"And he took it from you, like that?" Fred asked, almost with awe.

"Yes, just like that, and asked no questions. He was hurt; he had some wretched moments. I could see him squirming and squirming and trying to get past it. He kept shutting his eyes and rubbing his forehead. But when I told him that I absolutely knew you wanted to marry me, that you would whenever you could, that seemed to help him a good deal."

"And that satisfied him?" Fred asked wonderingly. He could not quite imagine what kind of person Dr. Archie might be.

"He took me by the shoulders once and asked, oh, in such a frightened way, 'Thea, was he GOOD to you, this young man?' When I told him you were, he looked at me again: 'And you care for him a great deal, you believe in him?' Then he seemed satisfied." Thea paused. "You see, he's just tremendously good, and tremendously afraid of things—of some things. Otherwise he would have got rid of Mrs. Archie." She looked up suddenly: "You were right, though; one can't tell people about things they don't know already."

Fred stood in the window, his back to the sunlight, fingering the jonquils. "Yes, you can, my dear. But you must tell it in such a way that they don't know you're telling it, and that they don't know they're hearing it."

Thea smiled past him, out into the air. "I see. It's a secret. Like the sound in the shell."

"What's that?" Fred was watching her and thinking how moving that faraway expression, in her, happened to be. "What did you say?"

She came back. "Oh, something old and Moonstony! I have almost forgotten it myself. But I feel better than I thought I ever could again. I can't wait to be off. Oh, Fred," she sprang up, "I want to get at it!"

As she broke out with this, she threw up her head and lifted herself a little on her toes. Fred colored and looked at her fearfully, hesitatingly. Her eyes, which looked out through the window, were bright—they had no memories. No, she did not remember. That momentary elevation had no associations for her. It was unconscious.

He looked her up and down and laughed and shook his head. "You are just all I want you to be—and that is,—not for me! Don't worry, you'll get at it. You are at it. My God! have you ever, for one moment, been at anything else?"

Thea did not answer him, and clearly she had not heard him. She was watching something out in the thin light of the false spring and its treacherously soft air.

Fred waited a moment. "Are you going to dine with your friend to-night?"

"Yes. He has never been in New York before. He wants to go about. Where shall I tell him to go?"

"Wouldn't it be a better plan, since you wish me to meet him, for you both to dine with me? It would seem only natural and friendly. You'll have to live up a little to his notion of us." Thea seemed to consider the suggestion favorably. "If you wish him to be easy in his mind," Fred went on, "that would help. I think, myself, that we are rather nice together. Put on one of the new dresses you got down there, and let him see how lovely you can be. You owe him some pleasure, after all the trouble he has taken."

Thea laughed, and seemed to find the idea exciting and pleasant. "Oh, very well! I'll do my best. Only don't wear a dress coat, please. He hasn't one, and he's nervous about it."

Fred looked at his watch. "Your monument up there is fast. I'll be here with a cab at eight. I'm anxious to meet him. You've given me the strangest idea of his callow innocence and aged indifference."

She shook her head. "No, he's none of that. He's very good, and he won't admit things. I love him for it. Now, as I look back on it, I see that I've always, even when I was little, shielded him."

As she laughed, Fred caught the bright spark in her eye that he knew so well, and held it for a happy instant. Then he blew her a kiss with his finger-tips and fled.

IV.

At nine o'clock that evening our three friends were seated in the balcony of a French restaurant, much gayer and more intimate than any that exists in New York to-day. This old restaurant was built by a lover of pleasure, who knew that to dine gayly human beings must have the reassurance of certain limitations of space and of a certain definite style; that the walls must be near enough to suggest shelter, the ceiling high enough to give the chandeliers a setting. The place was crowded with the kind of people who dine late and well, and Dr. Archie, as he watched the animated groups in the long room below the balcony, found this much the most festive scene he had ever looked out upon. He said to himself, in a jovial mood somewhat sustained by the cheer of the board, that this evening alone was worth his long journey. He followed attentively the orchestra, ensconced at the farther end of the balcony, and told Thea it made him feel "quite musical" to recognize "The Invitation to the Dance" or "The Blue Danube," and that he could remember just what kind of day it was when he heard her practicing them at home, and lingered at the gate to listen.

For the first few moments, when he was introduced to young Ottenburg in the parlor of the Everett House, the doctor had been awkward and unbending. But Fred, as his father had often observed, "was not a good mixer for nothing." He had brought Dr. Archie around during the short cab ride, and in an hour they had become old friends.

From the moment when the doctor lifted his glass and, looking consciously at Thea, said, "To your success," Fred liked him. He felt his quality; understood his courage in some directions and what Thea called his timidity in others, his unspent and miraculously preserved youthfulness. Men could never impose upon the doctor, he guessed, but women always could. Fred liked, too, the doctor's manner with Thea, his bashful admiration and the little hesitancy by which he betrayed his consciousness of the change in her. It was just this change that, at present, interested Fred more than anything else. That, he felt, was his "created value," and it was his best chance for any peace of mind. If that were not real, obvious to an old friend like Archie, then he cut a very poor figure, indeed.

Fred got a good deal, too, out of their talk about Moonstone. From her questions and the doctor's answers he was able to form some conception of the little world that was almost the measure of Thea's experience, the one bit of the human drama that she had followed with sympathy and understanding. As the two ran over the list of their friends, the mere sound of a name seemed to recall volumes to each of them, to indicate mines of knowledge and observation they had in common. At some names they laughed delightedly, at some indulgently and even tenderly.

"You two young people must come out to Moonstone when Thea gets back," the doctor said hospitably.

"Oh, we shall!" Fred caught it up. "I'm keen to know all these people. It is very tantalizing to hear only their names."

"Would they interest an outsider very much, do you think, Dr. Archie?" Thea leaned toward him. "Isn't it only because we've known them since I was little?"

The doctor glanced at her deferentially. Fred had noticed that he seemed a little afraid to look at her squarely—perhaps a trifle embarrassed by a mode of dress to which he was unaccustomed. "Well, you are practically an outsider yourself, Thea, now," he observed smiling. "Oh, I know," he went on quickly in response to her gesture of protest,—"I know you don't change toward your old friends, but you can see us all from a distance now. It's all to your advantage that you can still take your old interest, isn't it, Mr. Ottenburg?"

"That's exactly one of her advantages, Dr. Archie. Nobody can ever take that away from her, and none of us who came later can ever hope to rival Moonstone in the impression we make. Her scale of values will always be the Moonstone scale. And, with an artist, that IS an advantage." Fred nodded.

Dr. Archie looked at him seriously. "You mean it keeps them from getting affected?"

"Yes; keeps them from getting off the track generally."

While the waiter filled the glasses, Fred pointed out to Thea a big black French barytone who was eating anchovies by their tails at one of the tables below, and the doctor looked about and studied his fellow diners.

"Do you know, Mr. Ottenburg," he said deeply, "these people all look happier to me than our Western people do. Is it simply good manners on their part, or do they get more out of life?"

Fred laughed to Thea above the glass he had just lifted. "Some of them are getting a good deal out of it now, doctor. This is the hour when bench-joy brightens."

Thea chuckled and darted him a quick glance. "Benchjoy! Where did you get that slang?"

"That happens to be very old slang, my dear. Older than Moonstone or the sovereign State of Colorado. Our old friend Mr. Nathanmeyer could tell us why it happens to hit you." He leaned forward and touched Thea's wrist, "See that fur coat just coming in, Thea. It's D'Albert. He's just back from his Western tour. Fine head, hasn't he?"

"To go back," said Dr. Archie; "I insist that people do look happier here. I've noticed it even on the street, and especially in the hotels."

Fred turned to him cheerfully. "New York people live a good deal in the fourth dimension, Dr. Archie. It's that you notice in their faces."

The doctor was interested. "The fourth dimension," he repeated slowly; "and is that slang, too?"

"No,"—Fred shook his head,—"that's merely a figure. I mean that life is not quite so personal here as it is in your part of the world. People are more taken up by hobbies, interests that are less subject to reverses than their personal affairs. If you're interested in Thea's voice, for instance, or in voices in general, that interest is just the same, even if your mining stocks go down."

The doctor looked at him narrowly. "You think that's about the principal difference between country people and city people, don't you?"

Fred was a little disconcerted at being followed up so resolutely, and he attempted to dismiss it with a pleasantry. "I've never thought much about it, doctor. But I should say, on the spur of the moment, that that is one of the principal differences between people anywhere. It's the consolation of fellows like me who don't accomplish much. The fourth dimension is not good for business, but we think we have a better time."

Dr. Archie leaned back in his chair. His heavy shoulders were contemplative. "And she," he said slowly; "should you say that she is one of the kind you refer to?" He inclined his head toward the shimmer of the pale-green dress beside him. Thea was leaning, just then, over the balcony rail, her head in the light from the chandeliers below.

"Never, never!" Fred protested. "She's as hard-headed as the worst of you—with a difference."

The doctor sighed. "Yes, with a difference; something that makes a good many revolutions to the second. When she was little I used to feel her head to try to locate it."

Fred laughed. "Did you, though? So you were on the track of it? Oh, it's there! We can't get round it, miss," as Thea looked back inquiringly. "Dr. Archie, there's a fellow townsman of yours I feel a real kinship for." He pressed a cigar upon Dr. Archie and struck a match for him. "Tell me about Spanish Johnny."

The doctor smiled benignantly through the first waves of smoke. "Well, Johnny's an old patient of mine, and he's an old admirer of Thea's. She was born a cosmopolitan, and I expect she learned a good deal from Johnny when she used to run away and go to Mexican Town. We thought it a queer freak then."

The doctor launched into a long story, in which he was often eagerly interrupted or joyously confirmed by Thea, who was drinking her coffee and forcing open the petals of the roses with an ardent and rather rude hand. Fred settled down into enjoying his comprehension of his guests. Thea, watching Dr. Archie and interested in his presentation, was unconsciously impersonating her suave, gold-tinted friend. It was delightful to see her so radiant and responsive again. She had kept her promise about looking her best; when one could so easily get together the colors of an apple branch in early spring, that was not hard to do. Even Dr. Archie felt, each time he looked at her, a fresh consciousness. He recognized the fine texture of her mother's skin, with the difference that, when she reached across the table to give him a bunch of grapes, her arm was not only white, but somehow a little dazzling. She seemed to him taller, and freer in all her movements. She had now a way of taking a deep breath when she was interested, that made her seem very strong, somehow, and brought her at one quite overpoweringly. If he seemed shy, it was not that he was intimidated by her worldly clothes, but that her greater positiveness, her whole augmented self, made him feel that his accustomed manner toward her was inadequate.

Fred, on his part, was reflecting that the awkward position in which he had placed her would not confine or chafe her long. She looked about at other people, at other women, curiously. She was not quite sure of herself, but she was not in the least afraid or apologetic. She seemed to sit there on the edge, emerging from one world into another, taking her bearings, getting an idea of the concerted movement about her, but with absolute self-confidence. So far from shrinking, she expanded. The mere kindly effort to please Dr. Archie was enough to bring her out.

There was much talk of aurae at that time, and Fred mused that every beautiful, every compellingly beautiful woman, had an aura, whether other people did or no. There was, certainly, about the woman he had brought up from Mexico, such an emanation. She existed in more space than she occupied by measurement. The enveloping air about her head and shoulders was subsidized—was more moving than she herself, for in it lived the awakenings, all the first sweetness that life kills in people. One felt in her such a wealth of JUGENDZEIT, all those flowers of the mind and the blood that bloom and perish by the myriad in the few exhaustless years when the imagination first kindles. It was in watching her as she emerged like this, in being near and not too near, that one got, for a moment, so much that one had lost; among other legendary things the legendary theme of the absolutely magical power of a beautiful woman.

After they had left Thea at her hotel, Dr. Archie admitted to Fred, as they walked up Broadway through the rapidly chilling air, that once before he had seen their young friend flash up into a more potent self, but in a darker mood. It was in his office one night, when she was at home the summer before last. "And then I got the idea," he added simply, "that she would not live like other people: that, for better or worse, she had uncommon gifts."

"Oh, we'll see that it's for better, you and I," Fred reassured him. "Won't you come up to my hotel with me? I think we ought to have a long talk."

"Yes, indeed," said Dr. Archie gratefully; "I think we ought."

V.

Thea was to sail on Tuesday, at noon, and on Saturday Fred Ottenburg arranged for her passage, while she and Dr. Archie went shopping. With rugs and sea-clothes she was already provided; Fred had got everything of that sort she needed for the voyage up from Vera Cruz. On Sunday afternoon Thea went to see the Harsanyis. When she returned to her hotel, she found a note from Ottenburg, saying that he had called and would come again to-morrow.

On Monday morning, while she was at breakfast, Fred came in. She knew by his hurried, distracted air as he entered the dining-room that something had gone wrong. He had just got a telegram from home. His mother had been thrown from her carriage and hurt; a concussion of some sort, and she was unconscious. He was leaving for St. Louis that night on the eleven o'clock train. He had a great deal to attend to during the day. He would come that evening, if he might, and stay with her until train time, while she was doing her packing. Scarcely waiting for her consent, he hurried away.

All day Thea was somewhat cast down. She was sorry for Fred, and she missed the feeling that she was the one person in his mind. He had scarcely looked at her when they exchanged words at the breakfast-table. She felt as if she were set aside, and she did not seem so important even to herself as she had yesterday. Certainly, she reflected, it was high time that she began to take care of herself again. Dr. Archie came for dinner, but she sent him away early, telling him that she would be ready to go to the boat with him at half-past ten the next morning. When she went upstairs, she looked gloomily at the open trunk in her sitting-room, and at the trays piled on the sofa. She stood at the window and watched a quiet snowstorm spending itself over the city. More than anything else, falling snow always made her think of Moonstone; of the Kohlers' garden, of Thor's sled, of dressing by lamplight and starting off to school before the paths were broken.

When Fred came, he looked tired, and he took her hand almost without seeing her.

"I'm so sorry, Fred. Have you had any more word?"

"She was still unconscious at four this afternoon. It doesn't look very encouraging." He approached the fire and warmed his hands. He seemed to have contracted, and he had not at all his habitual ease of manner. "Poor mother!" he exclaimed; "nothing like this should have happened to her. She has so much pride of person. She's not at all an old woman, you know. She's never got beyond vigorous and rather dashing middle age." He turned abruptly to Thea and for the first time really looked at her. "How badly things come out! She'd have liked you for a daughter-in-law. Oh, you'd have fought like the devil, but you'd have respected each other." He sank into a chair and thrust his feet out to the fire. "Still," he went on thoughtfully, seeming to address the ceiling, "it might have been bad for you. Our big German houses, our good German cooking—you might have got lost in the upholstery. That substantial comfort might take the temper out of you, dull your edge. Yes," he sighed, "I guess you were meant for the jolt of the breakers."

"I guess I'll get plenty of jolt," Thea murmured, turning to her trunk.

"I'm rather glad I'm not staying over until to-morrow," Fred reflected. "I think it's easier for me to glide out like this. I feel now as if everything were rather casual, anyhow. A thing like that dulls one's feelings."

Thea, standing by her trunk, made no reply. Presently he shook himself and rose. "Want me to put those trays in for you?"

"No, thank you. I'm not ready for them yet."

Fred strolled over to the sofa, lifted a scarf from one of the trays and stood abstractedly drawing it through his fingers. "You've been so kind these last few days, Thea, that I began to hope you might soften a little; that you might ask me to come over and see you this summer."

"If you thought that, you were mistaken," she said slowly. "I've hardened, if anything. But I shan't carry any grudge away with me, if you mean that."

He dropped the scarf. "And there's nothing—nothing at all you'll let me do?"

"Yes, there is one thing, and it's a good deal to ask. If I get knocked out, or never get on, I'd like you to see that Dr. Archie gets his money back. I'm taking three thousand dollars of his."

"Why, of course I shall. You may dismiss that from your mind. How fussy you are about money, Thea. You make such a point of it." He turned sharply and walked to the windows.

Thea sat down in the chair he had quitted. "It's only poor people who feel that way about money, and who are really honest," she said gravely. "Sometimes I think that to be really honest, you must have been so poor that you've been tempted to steal."

"To what?"

"To steal. I used to be, when I first went to Chicago and saw all the things in the big stores there. Never anything big, but little things, the kind I'd never seen before and could never afford. I did take something once, before I knew it."

Fred came toward her. For the first time she had his whole attention, in the degree to which she was accustomed to having it. "Did you? What was it?" he asked with interest.

"A sachet. A little blue silk bag of orris-root powder. There was a whole counterful of them, marked down to fifty cents. I'd never seen any before, and they seemed irresistible. I took one up and wandered about the store with it. Nobody seemed to notice, so I carried it off."

Fred laughed. "Crazy child! Why, your things always smell of orris; is it a penance?"

"No, I love it. But I saw that the firm didn't lose anything by me. I went back and bought it there whenever I had a quarter to spend. I got a lot to take to Arizona. I made it up to them."

"I'll bet you did!" Fred took her hand. "Why didn't I find you that first winter? I'd have loved you just as you came!"

Thea shook her head. "No, you wouldn't, but you might have found me amusing. The Harsanyis said yesterday afternoon that I wore such a funny cape and that my shoes always squeaked. They think I've improved. I told them it was your doing if I had, and then they looked scared."

"Did you sing for Harsanyi?"

"Yes. He thinks I've improved there, too. He said nice things to me. Oh, he was very nice! He agrees with you about my going to Lehmann, if she'll take me. He came out to the elevator with me, after we had said good-bye. He said something nice out there, too, but he seemed sad."

"What was it that he said?"

"He said, 'When people, serious people, believe in you, they give you some of their best, so—take care of it, Miss Kronborg.' Then he waved his hands and went back."

"If you sang, I wish you had taken me along. Did you sing well?" Fred turned from her and went back to the window. "I wonder when I shall hear you sing again." He picked up a bunch of violets and smelled them. "You know, your leaving me like this—well, it's almost inhuman to be able to do it so kindly and unconditionally."

"I suppose it is. It was almost inhuman to be able to leave home, too,—the last time, when I knew it was for good. But all the same, I cared a great deal more than anybody else did. I lived through it. I have no choice now. No matter how much it breaks me up, I have to go. Do I seem to enjoy it?"

Fred bent over her trunk and picked up something which proved to be a score, clumsily bound. "What's this? Did you ever try to sing this?" He opened it and on the engraved title-page read Wunsch's inscription, "EINST, O WUNDER!" He looked up sharply at Thea.

"Wunsch gave me that when he went away. I've told you about him, my old teacher in Moonstone. He loved that opera."

Fred went toward the fireplace, the book under his arm, singing softly:—

"EINST, O WUNDER, ENTBLUHT AUF MEINEM GRABE, EINE BLUME DER ASCHE MEINES HERZENS;"

"You have no idea at all where he is, Thea?" He leaned against the mantel and looked down at her.

"No, I wish I had. He may be dead by this time. That was five years ago, and he used himself hard. Mrs. Kohler was always afraid he would die off alone somewhere and be stuck under the prairie. When we last heard of him, he was in Kansas."

"If he were to be found, I'd like to do something for him. I seem to get a good deal of him from this." He opened the book again, where he kept the place with his finger, and scrutinized the purple ink. "How like a German! Had he ever sung the song for you?"

"No. I didn't know where the words were from until once, when Harsanyi sang it for me, I recognized them."

Fred closed the book. "Let me see, what was your noble brakeman's name?"

Thea looked up with surprise. "Ray, Ray Kennedy."

"Ray Kennedy!" he laughed. "It couldn't well have been better! Wunsch and Dr. Archie, and Ray, and I,"—he told them off on his fingers,—"your whistling-posts! You haven't done so badly. We've backed you as we could, some in our weakness and some in our might. In your dark hours—and you'll have them—you may like to remember us." He smiled whimsically and dropped the score into the trunk. "You are taking that with you?"

"Surely I am. I haven't so many keepsakes that I can afford to leave that. I haven't got many that I value so highly."

"That you value so highly?" Fred echoed her gravity playfully. "You are delicious when you fall into your vernacular." He laughed half to himself.

"What's the matter with that? Isn't it perfectly good English?"

"Perfectly good Moonstone, my dear. Like the readymade clothes that hang in the windows, made to fit everybody and fit nobody, a phrase that can be used on all occasions. Oh,"—he started across the room again,—"that's one of the fine things about your going! You'll be with the right sort of people and you'll learn a good, live, warm German, that will be like yourself. You'll get a new speech full of shades and color like your voice; alive, like your mind. It will be almost like being born again, Thea."

She was not offended. Fred had said such things to her before, and she wanted to learn. In the natural course of things she would never have loved a man from whom she could not learn a great deal.

"Harsanyi said once," she remarked thoughtfully, "that if one became an artist one had to be born again, and that one owed nothing to anybody."

"Exactly. And when I see you again I shall not see you, but your daughter. May I?" He held up his cigarette case questioningly and then began to smoke, taking up again the song which ran in his head:—

"DEUTLICH SCHIMMERT AUF JEDEM, PURPURBLATTCHEN, ADELAIDE!"

"I have half an hour with you yet, and then, exit Fred." He walked about the room, smoking and singing the words under his breath. "You'll like the voyage," he said abruptly. "That first approach to a foreign shore, stealing up on it and finding it—there's nothing like it. It wakes up everything that's asleep in you. You won't mind my writing to some people in Berlin? They'll be nice to you."

"I wish you would." Thea gave a deep sigh. "I wish one could look ahead and see what is coming to one."

"Oh, no!" Fred was smoking nervously; "that would never do. It's the uncertainty that makes one try. You've never had any sort of chance, and now I fancy you'll make it up to yourself. You'll find the way to let yourself out in one long flight."

Thea put her hand on her heart. "And then drop like the rocks we used to throw—anywhere." She left the chair and went over to the sofa, hunting for something in the trunk trays. When she came back she found Fred sitting in her place. "Here are some handkerchiefs of yours. I've kept one or two. They're larger than mine and useful if one has a headache."

"Thank you. How nicely they smell of your things!" He looked at the white squares for a moment and then put them in his pocket. He kept the low chair, and as she stood beside him he took her hands and sat looking intently at them, as if he were examining them for some special purpose, tracing the long round fingers with the tips of his own. "Ordinarily, you know, there are reefs that a man catches to and keeps his nose above water. But this is a case by itself. There seems to be no limit as to how much I can be in love with you. I keep going." He did not lift his eyes from her fingers, which he continued to study with the same fervor. "Every kind of stringed instrument there is plays in your hands, Thea," he whispered, pressing them to his face.

She dropped beside him and slipped into his arms, shutting her eyes and lifting her cheek to his. "Tell me one thing," Fred whispered. "You said that night on the boat, when I first told you, that if you could you would crush it all up in your hands and throw it into the sea. Would you, all those weeks?"

She shook her head.

"Answer me, would you?"

"No, I was angry then. I'm not now. I'd never give them up. Don't make me pay too much." In that embrace they lived over again all the others. When Thea drew away from him, she dropped her face in her hands. "You are good to me," she breathed, "you are!"

Rising to his feet, he put his hands under her elbows and lifted her gently. He drew her toward the door with him. "Get all you can. Be generous with yourself. Don't stop short of splendid things. I want them for you more than I want anything else, more than I want one splendid thing for myself. I can't help feeling that you'll gain, somehow, by my losing so much. That you'll gain the very thing I lose. Take care of her, as Harsanyi said. She's wonderful!" He kissed her and went out of the door without looking back, just as if he were coming again to-morrow.

Thea went quickly into her bedroom. She brought out an armful of muslin things, knelt down, and began to lay them in the trays. Suddenly she stopped, dropped forward and leaned against the open trunk, her head on her arms. The tears fell down on the dark old carpet. It came over her how many people must have said good-bye and been unhappy in that room. Other people, before her time, had hired this room to cry in. Strange rooms and strange streets and faces, how sick at heart they made one! Why was she going so far, when what she wanted was some familiar place to hide in?—the rock house, her little room in Moonstone, her own bed. Oh, how good it would be to lie down in that little bed, to cut the nerve that kept one struggling, that pulled one on and on, to sink into peace there, with all the family safe and happy downstairs. After all, she was a Moonstone girl, one of the preacher's children. Everything else was in Fred's imagination. Why was she called upon to take such chances? Any safe, humdrum work that did not compromise her would be better. But if she failed now, she would lose her soul. There was nowhere to fall, after one took that step, except into abysses of wretchedness. She knew what abysses, for she could still hear the old man playing in the snowstorm, it was released in her like a passion of longing. Every nerve in her body thrilled to it. It brought her to her feet, carried her somehow to bed and into troubled sleep.

That night she taught in Moonstone again: she beat her pupils in hideous rages, she kept on beating them. She sang at funerals, and struggled at the piano with Harsanyi. In one dream she was looking into a hand-glass and thinking that she was getting better-looking, when the glass began to grow smaller and smaller and her own reflection to shrink, until she realized that she was looking into Ray Kennedy's eyes, seeing her face in that look of his which she could never forget. All at once the eyes were Fred Ottenburg's, and not Ray's. All night she heard the shrieking of trains, whistling in and out of Moonstone, as she used to hear them in her sleep when they blew shrill in the winter air. But to-night they were terrifying,—the spectral, fated trains that "raced with death," about which the old woman from the depot used to pray.

In the morning she wakened breathless after a struggle with Mrs. Livery Johnson's daughter. She started up with a bound, threw the blankets back and sat on the edge of the bed, her night-dress open, her long braids hanging over her bosom, blinking at the daylight. After all, it was not too late. She was only twenty years old, and the boat sailed at noon. There was still time!

6

KRONBORG

I.

It is a glorious winter day. Denver, standing on her high plateau under a thrilling green-blue sky, is masked in snow and glittering with sunlight. The Capitol building is actually in armor, and throws off the shafts of the sun until the beholder is dazzled and the outlines of the building are lost in a blaze of reflected light. The stone terrace is a white field over which fiery reflections dance, and the trees and bushes are faithfully repeated in snow—on every black twig a soft, blurred line of white. From the terrace one looks directly over to where the mountains break in their sharp, familiar lines against the sky. Snow fills the gorges, hangs in scarfs on the great slopes, and on the peaks the fiery sunshine is gathered up as by a burning-glass.

Howard Archie is standing at the window of his private room in the offices of the San Felipe Mining Company, on the sixth floor of the Raton Building, looking off at the mountain glories of his State while he gives dictation to his secretary. He is ten years older than when we saw him last, and emphatically ten years more prosperous. A decade of coming into things has not so much aged him as it has fortified, smoothed, and assured him. His sandy hair and imperial conceal whatever gray they harbor. He has not grown heavier, but more flexible, and his massive shoulders carry fifty years and the control of his great mining interests more lightly than they carried forty years and a country practice. In short, he is one of the friends to whom we feel grateful for having got on in the world, for helping to keep up the general temperature and our own confidence in life. He is an acquaintance that one would hurry to overtake and greet among a hundred. In his warm handshake and generous smile there is the stimulating cordiality of good fellows come into good fortune and eager to pass it on; something that makes one think better of the lottery of life and resolve to try again.

When Archie had finished his morning mail, he turned away from the window and faced his secretary. "Did anything come up yesterday afternoon while I was away, T. B.?"

Thomas Burk turned over the leaf of his calendar. "Governor Alden sent down to say that he wanted to see you before he sends his letter to the Board of Pardons. Asked if you could go over to the State House this morning."

Archie shrugged his shoulders. "I'll think about it."

The young man grinned.

"Anything else?" his chief continued.

T. B. swung round in his chair with a look of interest on his shrewd, clean-shaven face. "Old Jasper Flight was in, Dr. Archie. I never expected to see him alive again. Seems he's tucked away for the winter with a sister who's a housekeeper at the Oxford. He's all crippled up with rheumatism, but as fierce after it as ever. Wants to know if you or the company won't grub-stake him again. Says he's sure of it this time; had located something when the snow shut down on him in December. He wants to crawl out at the first break in the weather, with that same old burro with the split ear. He got somebody to winter the beast for him. He's superstitious about that burro, too; thinks it's divinely guided. You ought to hear the line of talk he put up here yesterday; said when he rode in his carriage, that burro was a-going to ride along with him."

Archie laughed. "Did he leave you his address?"

"He didn't neglect anything," replied the clerk cynically.

"Well, send him a line and tell him to come in again. I like to hear him. Of all the crazy prospectors I've ever known, he's the most interesting, because he's really crazy. It's a religious conviction with him, and with most of 'em it's a gambling fever or pure vagrancy. But Jasper Flight believes that the Almighty keeps the secret of the silver deposits in these hills, and gives it away to the deserving. He's a downright noble figure. Of course I'll stake him! As long as he can crawl out in the spring. He and that burro are a sight together. The beast is nearly as white as Jasper; must be twenty years old."

"If you stake him this time, you won't have to again," said T. B. knowingly. "He'll croak up there, mark my word. Says he never ties the burro at night now, for fear he might be called sudden, and the beast would starve. I guess that animal could eat a lariat rope, all right, and enjoy it."

"I guess if we knew the things those two have eaten, and haven't eaten, in their time, T. B., it would make us vegetarians." The doctor sat down and looked thoughtful. "That's the way for the old man to go. It would be pretty hard luck if he had to die in a hospital. I wish he could turn up something before he cashes in. But his kind seldom do; they're bewitched. Still, there was Stratton. I've been meeting Jasper Flight, and his side meat and tin pans, up in the mountains for years, and I'd miss him. I always halfway believe the fairy tales he spins me. Old Jasper Flight," Archie murmured, as if he liked the name or the picture it called up.

A clerk came in from the outer office and handed Archie a card. He sprang up and exclaimed, "Mr. Ottenburg? Bring him in."

Fred Ottenburg entered, clad in a long, fur-lined coat, holding a checked-cloth hat in his hand, his cheeks and eyes bright with the outdoor cold. The two men met before Archie's desk and their handclasp was longer than friendship prompts except in regions where the blood warms and quickens to meet the dry cold. Under the general keyingup of the altitude, manners take on a heartiness, a vivacity, that is one expression of the half-unconscious excitement which Colorado people miss when they drop into lower strata of air. The heart, we are told, wears out early in that high atmosphere, but while it pumps it sends out no sluggish stream. Our two friends stood gripping each other by the hand and smiling.

"When did you get in, Fred? And what have you come for?" Archie gave him a quizzical glance.

"I've come to find out what you think you're doing out here," the younger man declared emphatically. "I want to get next, I do. When can you see me?"

"Anything on to-night? Then suppose you dine with me. Where can I pick you up at five-thirty?"

"Bixby's office, general freight agent of the Burlington." Ottenburg began to button his overcoat and drew on his gloves. "I've got to have one shot at you before I go, Archie. Didn't I tell you Pinky Alden was a cheap squirt?"

Alden's backer laughed and shook his head. "Oh, he's worse than that, Fred. It isn't polite to mention what he is, outside of the Arabian Nights. I guessed you'd come to rub it into me."

Ottenburg paused, his hand on the doorknob, his high color challenging the doctor's calm. "I'm disgusted with you, Archie, for training with such a pup. A man of your experience!"

"Well, he's been an experience," Archie muttered. "I'm not coy about admitting it, am I?"

Ottenburg flung open the door. "Small credit to you. Even the women are out for capital and corruption, I hear. Your Governor's done more for the United Breweries in six months than I've been able to do in six years. He's the lily-livered sort we're looking for. Good-morning."

That afternoon at five o'clock Dr. Archie emerged from the State House after his talk with Governor Alden, and crossed the terrace under a saffron sky. The snow, beaten hard, was blue in the dusk; a day of blinding sunlight had not even started a thaw. The lights of the city twinkled pale below him in the quivering violet air, and the dome of the State House behind him was still red with the light from the west. Before he got into his car, the doctor paused to look about him at the scene of which he never tired. Archie lived in his own house on Colfax Avenue, where he had roomy grounds and a rose garden and a conservatory. His housekeeping was done by three Japanese boys, devoted and resourceful, who were able to manage Archie's dinner parties, to see that he kept his engagements, and to make visitors who stayed at the house so comfortable that they were always loath to go away.

Archie had never known what comfort was until he became a widower, though with characteristic delicacy, or dishonesty, he insisted upon accrediting his peace of mind to the San Felipe, to Time, to anything but his release from Mrs. Archie.

Mrs. Archie died just before her husband left Moonstone and came to Denver to live, six years ago. The poor woman's fight against dust was her undoing at last. One summer day when she was rubbing the parlor upholstery with gasoline,—the doctor had often forbidden her to use it on any account, so that was one of the pleasures she seized upon in his absence,—an explosion occurred. Nobody ever knew exactly how it happened, for Mrs. Archie was dead when the neighbors rushed in to save her from the burning house. She must have inhaled the burning gas and died instantly.

Moonstone severity relented toward her somewhat after her death. But even while her old cronies at Mrs. Smiley's millinery store said that it was a terrible thing, they added that nothing but a powerful explosive COULD have killed Mrs. Archie, and that it was only right the doctor should have a chance.

Archie's past was literally destroyed when his wife died. The house burned to the ground, and all those material reminders which have such power over people disappeared in an hour. His mining interests now took him to Denver so often that it seemed better to make his headquarters there. He gave up his practice and left Moonstone for good. Six months afterward, while Dr. Archie was living at the Brown Palace Hotel, the San Felipe mine began to give up that silver hoard which old Captain Harris had always accused it of concealing, and San Felipe headed the list of mining quotations in every daily paper, East and West. In a few years Dr. Archie was a very rich man. His mine was such an important item in the mineral output of the State, and Archie had a hand in so many of the new industries of Colorado and New Mexico, that his political influence was considerable. He had thrown it all, two years ago, to the new reform party, and had brought about the election of a governor of whose conduct he was now heartily ashamed. His friends believed that Archie himself had ambitious political plans.

II.

When Ottenburg and his host reached the house on Colfax Avenue, they went directly to the library, a long double room on the second floor which Archie had arranged exactly to his own taste. It was full of books and mounted specimens of wild game, with a big writing-table at either end, stiff, old-fashioned engravings, heavy hangings and deep upholstery.

When one of the Japanese boys brought the cocktails, Fred turned from the fine specimen of peccoray he had been examining and said, "A man is an owl to live in such a place alone, Archie. Why don't you marry? As for me, just because I can't marry, I find the world full of charming, unattached women, any one of whom I could fit up a house for with alacrity."

"You're more knowing than I." Archie spoke politely. "I'm not very wide awake about women. I'd be likely to pick out one of the uncomfortable ones—and there are a few of them, you know." He drank his cocktail and rubbed his hands together in a friendly way. "My friends here have charming wives, and they don't give me a chance to get lonely. They are very kind to me, and I have a great many pleasant friendships."

Fred put down his glass. "Yes, I've always noticed that women have confidence in you. You have the doctor's way of getting next. And you enjoy that kind of thing?"

"The friendship of attractive women? Oh, dear, yes! I depend upon it a great deal."

The butler announced dinner, and the two men went downstairs to the dining-room. Dr. Archie's dinners were always good and well served, and his wines were excellent.

"I saw the Fuel and Iron people to-day," Ottenburg said, looking up from his soup. "Their heart is in the right place. I can't see why in the mischief you ever got mixed up with that reform gang, Archie. You've got nothing to reform out here. The situation has always been as simple as two and two in Colorado; mostly a matter of a friendly understanding."

"Well,"—Archie spoke tolerantly,—"some of the young fellows seemed to have red-hot convictions, and I thought it was better to let them try their ideas out."

Ottenburg shrugged his shoulders. "A few dull young men who haven't ability enough to play the old game the old way, so they want to put on a new game which doesn't take so much brains and gives away more advertising that's what your anti-saloon league and vice commission amounts to. They provide notoriety for the fellows who can't distinguish themselves at running a business or practicing law or developing an industry. Here you have a mediocre lawyer with no brains and no practice, trying to get a look-in on something. He comes up with the novel proposition that the prostitute has a hard time of it, puts his picture in the paper, and the first thing you know, he's a celebrity. He gets the rake-off and she's just where she was before. How could you fall for a mouse-trap like Pink Alden, Archie?"

Dr. Archie laughed as he began to carve. "Pink seems to get under your skin. He's not worth talking about. He's gone his limit. People won't read about his blameless life any more. I knew those interviews he gave out would cook him. They were a last resort. I could have stopped him, but by that time I'd come to the conclusion that I'd let the reformers down. I'm not against a general shaking-up, but the trouble with Pinky's crowd is they never get beyond a general writing-up. We gave them a chance to do something, and they just kept on writing about each other and what temptations they had overcome."

While Archie and his friend were busy with Colorado politics, the impeccable Japanese attended swiftly and intelligently to his duties, and the dinner, as Ottenburg at last remarked, was worthy of more profitable conversation.

"So it is," the doctor admitted. "Well, we'll go upstairs for our coffee and cut this out. Bring up some cognac and arak, Tai," he added as he rose from the table.

They stopped to examine a moose's head on the stairway, and when they reached the library the pine logs in the fireplace had been lighted, and the coffee was bubbling before the hearth. Tai placed two chairs before the fire and brought a tray of cigarettes.

"Bring the cigars in my lower desk drawer, boy," the doctor directed. "Too much light in here, isn't there, Fred? Light the lamp there on my desk, Tai." He turned off the electric glare and settled himself deep into the chair opposite Ottenburg's.

"To go back to our conversation, doctor," Fred began while he waited for the first steam to blow off his coffee; "why don't you make up your mind to go to Washington? There'd be no fight made against you. I needn't say the United Breweries would back you. There'd be some KUDOS coming to us, too; backing a reform candidate."

Dr. Archie measured his length in his chair and thrust his large boots toward the crackling pitch-pine. He drank his coffee and lit a big black cigar while his guest looked over the assortment of cigarettes on the tray. "You say why don't I," the doctor spoke with the deliberation of a man in the position of having several courses to choose from, "but, on the other hand, why should I?" He puffed away and seemed, through his half-closed eyes, to look down several long roads with the intention of luxuriously rejecting all of them and remaining where he was. "I'm sick of politics. I'm disillusioned about serving my crowd, and I don't particularly want to serve yours. Nothing in it that I particularly want; and a man's not effective in politics unless he wants something for himself, and wants it hard. I can reach my ends by straighter roads. There are plenty of things to keep me busy. We haven't begun to develop our resources in this State; we haven't had a look in on them yet. That's the only thing that isn't fake—making men and machines go, and actually turning out a product."

The doctor poured himself some white cordial and looked over the little glass into the fire with an expression which led Ottenburg to believe that he was getting at something in his own mind. Fred lit a cigarette and let his friend grope for his idea.

"My boys, here," Archie went on, "have got me rather interested in Japan. Think I'll go out there in the spring, and come back the other way, through Siberia. I've always wanted to go to Russia." His eyes still hunted for something in his big fireplace. With a slow turn of his head he brought them back to his guest and fixed them upon him. "Just now, I'm thinking of running on to New York for a few weeks," he ended abruptly.

Ottenburg lifted his chin. "Ah!" he exclaimed, as if he began to see Archie's drift. "Shall you see Thea?"

"Yes." The doctor replenished his cordial glass. "In fact, I suspect I am going exactly TO see her. I'm getting stale on things here, Fred. Best people in the world and always doing things for me. I'm fond of them, too, but I've been with them too much. I'm getting ill-tempered, and the first thing I know I'll be hurting people's feelings. I snapped Mrs. Dandridge up over the telephone this afternoon when she asked me to go out to Colorado Springs on Sunday to meet some English people who are staying at the Antlers. Very nice of her to want me, and I was as sour as if she'd been trying to work me for something. I've got to get out for a while, to save my reputation."

To this explanation Ottenburg had not paid much attention. He seemed to be looking at a fixed point: the yellow glass eyes of a fine wildcat over one of the bookcases. "You've never heard her at all, have you?" he asked reflectively. "Curious, when this is her second season in New York."

"I was going on last March. Had everything arranged. And then old Cap Harris thought he could drive his car and me through a lamp-post and I was laid up with a compound fracture for two months. So I didn't get to see Thea."

Ottenburg studied the red end of his cigarette attentively. "She might have come out to see you. I remember you covered the distance like a streak when she wanted you."

Archie moved uneasily. "Oh, she couldn't do that. She had to get back to Vienna to work on some new parts for this year. She sailed two days after the New York season closed."

"Well, then she couldn't, of course." Fred smoked his cigarette close and tossed the end into the fire. "I'm tremendously glad you're going now. If you're stale, she'll jack you up. That's one of her specialties. She got a rise out of me last December that lasted me all winter."

"Of course," the doctor apologized, "you know so much more about such things. I'm afraid it will be rather wasted on me. I'm no judge of music."

"Never mind that." The younger man pulled himself up in his chair. "She gets it across to people who aren't judges. That's just what she does." He relapsed into his former lassitude. "If you were stone deaf, it wouldn't all be wasted. It's a great deal to watch her. Incidentally, you know, she is very beautiful. Photographs give you no idea."

Dr. Archie clasped his large hands under his chin. "Oh, I'm counting on that. I don't suppose her voice will sound natural to me. Probably I wouldn't know it."

Ottenburg smiled. "You'll know it, if you ever knew it. It's the same voice, only more so. You'll know it."

"Did you, in Germany that time, when you wrote me? Seven years ago, now. That must have been at the very beginning."

"Yes, somewhere near the beginning. She sang one of the Rhine daughters." Fred paused and drew himself up again. "Sure, I knew it from the first note. I'd heard a good many young voices come up out of the Rhine, but, by gracious, I hadn't heard one like that!" He fumbled for another cigarette. "Mahler was conducting that night. I met him as he was leaving the house and had a word with him. 'Interesting voice you tried out this evening,' I said. He stopped and smiled. 'Miss Kronborg, you mean? Yes, very. She seems to sing for the idea. Unusual in a young singer.' I'd never heard him admit before that a singer could have an idea. She not only had it, but she got it across. The Rhine music, that I'd known since I was a boy, was fresh to me, vocalized for the first time. You realized that she was beginning that long story, adequately, with the end in view. Every phrase she sang was basic. She simply WAS the idea of the Rhine music." Ottenburg rose and stood with his back to the fire. "And at the end, where you don't see the maidens at all, the same thing again: two pretty voices AND the Rhine voice." Fred snapped his fingers and dropped his hand.

The doctor looked up at him enviously. "You see, all that would be lost on me," he said modestly. "I don't know the dream nor the interpretation thereof. I'm out of it. It's too bad that so few of her old friends can appreciate her."

"Take a try at it," Fred encouraged him. "You'll get in deeper than you can explain to yourself. People with no personal interest do that."

"I suppose," said Archie diffidently, "that college German, gone to seed, wouldn't help me out much. I used to be able to make my German patients understand me."

"Sure it would!" cried Ottenburg heartily. "Don't be above knowing your libretto. That's all very well for musicians, but common mortals like you and me have got to know what she's singing about. Get out your dictionary and go at it as you would at any other proposition. Her diction is beautiful, and if you know the text you'll get a great deal. So long as you're going to hear her, get all that's coming to you. You bet in Germany people know their librettos by heart! You Americans are so afraid of stooping to learn anything."

"I AM a little ashamed," Archie admitted. "I guess that's the way we mask our general ignorance. However, I'll stoop this time; I'm more ashamed not to be able to follow her. The papers always say she's such a fine actress." He took up the tongs and began to rearrange the logs that had burned through and fallen apart. "I suppose she has changed a great deal?" he asked absently.

"We've all changed, my dear Archie,—she more than most of us. Yes, and no. She's all there, only there's a great deal more of her. I've had only a few words with her in several years. It's better not, when I'm tied up this way. The laws are barbarous, Archie."

"Your wife is—still the same?" the doctor asked sympathetically.

"Absolutely. Hasn't been out of a sanitarium for seven years now. No prospect of her ever being out, and as long as she's there I'm tied hand and foot. What does society get out of such a state of things, I'd like to know, except a tangle of irregularities? If you want to reform, there's an opening for you!"

"It's bad, oh, very bad; I agree with you!" Dr. Archie shook his head. "But there would be complications under another system, too. The whole question of a young man's marrying has looked pretty grave to me for a long while. How have they the courage to keep on doing it? It depresses me now to buy wedding presents." For some time the doctor watched his guest, who was sunk in bitter reflections. "Such things used to go better than they do now, I believe. Seems to me all the married people I knew when I was a boy were happy enough." He paused again and bit the end off a fresh cigar. "You never saw Thea's mother, did you, Ottenburg? That's a pity. Mrs. Kronborg was a fine woman. I've always been afraid Thea made a mistake, not coming home when Mrs. Kronborg was ill, no matter what it cost her."

Ottenburg moved about restlessly. "She couldn't, Archie, she positively couldn't. I felt you never understood that, but I was in Dresden at the time, and though I wasn't seeing much of her, I could size up the situation for myself. It was by just a lucky chance that she got to sing ELIZABETH that time at the Dresden Opera, a complication of circumstances. If she'd run away, for any reason, she might have waited years for such a chance to come again. She gave a wonderful performance and made a great impression. They offered her certain terms; she had to take them and follow it up then and there. In that game you can't lose a single trick. She was ill herself, but she sang. Her mother was ill, and she sang. No, you mustn't hold that against her, Archie. She did the right thing there." Ottenburg drew out his watch. "Hello! I must be traveling. You hear from her regularly?"

"More or less regularly. She was never much of a letter-writer. She tells me about her engagements and contracts, but I know so little about that business that it doesn't mean much to me beyond the figures, which seem very impressive. We've had a good deal of business correspondence, about putting up a stone to her father and mother, and, lately, about her youngest brother, Thor. He is with me now; he drives my car. To-day he's up at the mine."

Ottenburg, who had picked up his overcoat, dropped it. "Drives your car?" he asked incredulously.

"Yes. Thea and I have had a good deal of bother about Thor. We tried a business college, and an engineering school, but it was no good. Thor was born a chauffeur before there were cars to drive. He was never good for anything else; lay around home and collected postage stamps and took bicycles to pieces, waiting for the automobile to be invented. He's just as much a part of a car as the steering-gear. I can't find out whether he likes his job with me or not, or whether he feels any curiosity about his sister. You can't find anything out from a Kronborg nowadays. The mother was different."

Fred plunged into his coat. "Well, it's a queer world, Archie. But you'll think better of it, if you go to New York. Wish I were going with you. I'll drop in on you in the morning at about eleven. I want a word with you about this Interstate Commerce Bill. Good-night."

Dr. Archie saw his guest to the motor which was waiting below, and then went back to his library, where he replenished the fire and sat down for a long smoke. A man of Archie's modest and rather credulous nature develops late, and makes his largest gain between forty and fifty. At thirty, indeed, as we have seen, Archie was a soft-hearted boy under a manly exterior, still whistling to keep up his courage. Prosperity and large responsibilities—above all, getting free of poor Mrs. Archie—had brought out a good deal more than he knew was in him. He was thinking tonight as he sat before the fire, in the comfort he liked so well, that but for lucky chances, and lucky holes in the ground, he would still be a country practitioner, reading his old books by his office lamp. And yet, he was not so fresh and energetic as he ought to be. He was tired of business and of politics. Worse than that, he was tired of the men with whom he had to do and of the women who, as he said, had been kind to him. He felt as if he were still hunting for something, like old Jasper Flight. He knew that this was an unbecoming and ungrateful state of mind, and he reproached himself for it. But he could not help wondering why it was that life, even when it gave so much, after all gave so little. What was it that he had expected and missed? Why was he, more than he was anything else, disappointed?

He fell to looking back over his life and asking himself which years of it he would like to live over again,—just as they had been,—and they were not many. His college years he would live again, gladly. After them there was nothing he would care to repeat until he came to Thea Kronborg. There had been something stirring about those years in Moonstone, when he was a restless young man on the verge of breaking into larger enterprises, and when she was a restless child on the verge of growing up into something unknown. He realized now that she had counted for a great deal more to him than he knew at the time. It was a continuous sort of relationship. He was always on the lookout for her as he went about the town, always vaguely expecting her as he sat in his office at night. He had never asked himself then if it was strange that he should find a child of twelve the most interesting and companionable person in Moonstone. It had seemed a pleasant, natural kind of solicitude. He explained it then by the fact that he had no children of his own. But now, as he looked back at those years, the other interests were faded and inanimate. The thought of them was heavy. But wherever his life had touched Thea Kronborg's, there was still a little warmth left, a little sparkle. Their friendship seemed to run over those discontented years like a leafy pattern, still bright and fresh when the other patterns had faded into the dull background. Their walks and drives and confidences, the night they watched the rabbit in the moonlight, —why were these things stirring to remember? Whenever he thought of them, they were distinctly different from the other memories of his life; always seemed humorous, gay, with a little thrill of anticipation and mystery about them. They came nearer to being tender secrets than any others he possessed. Nearer than anything else they corresponded to what he had hoped to find in the world, and had not found. It came over him now that the unexpected favors of fortune, no matter how dazzling, do not mean very much to us. They may excite or divert us for a time, but when we look back, the only things we cherish are those which in some way met our original want; the desire which formed in us in early youth, undirected, and of its own accord.

III.

For the first four years after Thea went to Germany things went on as usual with the Kronborg family. Mrs. Kronborg's land in Nebraska increased in value and brought her in a good rental. The family drifted into an easier way of living, half without realizing it, as families will. Then Mr. Kronborg, who had never been ill, died suddenly of cancer of the liver, and after his death Mrs. Kronborg went, as her neighbors said, into a decline. Hearing discouraging reports of her from the physician who had taken over his practice, Dr. Archie went up from Denver to see her. He found her in bed, in the room where he had more than once attended her, a handsome woman of sixty with a body still firm and white, her hair, faded now to a very pale primrose, in two thick braids down her back, her eyes clear and calm. When the doctor arrived, she was sitting up in her bed, knitting. He felt at once how glad she was to see him, but he soon gathered that she had made no determination to get well. She told him, indeed, that she could not very well get along without Mr. Kronborg. The doctor looked at her with astonishment. Was it possible that she could miss the foolish old man so much? He reminded her of her children.

"Yes," she replied; "the children are all very well, but they are not father. We were married young."

The doctor watched her wonderingly as she went on knitting, thinking how much she looked like Thea. The difference was one of degree rather than of kind. The daughter had a compelling enthusiasm, the mother had none. But their framework, their foundation, was very much the same.

In a moment Mrs. Kronborg spoke again. "Have you heard anything from Thea lately?"

During his talk with her, the doctor gathered that what Mrs. Kronborg really wanted was to see her daughter Thea. Lying there day after day, she wanted it calmly and continuously. He told her that, since she felt so, he thought they might ask Thea to come home.

"I've thought a good deal about it," said Mrs. Kronborg slowly. "I hate to interrupt her, now that she's begun to get advancement. I expect she's seen some pretty hard times, though she was never one to complain. Perhaps she'd feel that she would like to come. It would be hard, losing both of us while she's off there."

When Dr. Archie got back to Denver he wrote a long letter to Thea, explaining her mother's condition and how much she wished to see her, and asking Thea to come, if only for a few weeks. Thea had repaid the money she had borrowed from him, and he assured her that if she happened to be short of funds for the journey, she had only to cable him.

A month later he got a frantic sort of reply from Thea. Complications in the opera at Dresden had given her an unhoped-for opportunity to go on in a big part. Before this letter reached the doctor, she would have made her debut as ELIZABETH, in "Tannhauser." She wanted to go to her mother more than she wanted anything else in the world, but, unless she failed,—which she would not,—she absolutely could not leave Dresden for six months. It was not that she chose to stay; she had to stay—or lose everything. The next few months would put her five years ahead, or would put her back so far that it would be of no use to struggle further. As soon as she was free, she would go to Moonstone and take her mother back to Germany with her. Her mother, she was sure, could live for years yet, and she would like German people and German ways, and could be hearing music all the time. Thea said she was writing her mother and begging her to help her one last time; to get strength and to wait for her six months, and then she (Thea) would do everything. Her mother would never have to make an effort again.

Dr. Archie went up to Moonstone at once. He had great confidence in Mrs. Kronborg's power of will, and if Thea's appeal took hold of her enough, he believed she might get better. But when he was shown into the familiar room off the parlor, his heart sank. Mrs. Kronborg was lying serene and fateful on her pillows. On the dresser at the foot of her bed there was a large photograph of Thea in the character in which she was to make her debut. Mrs. Kronborg pointed to it.

"Isn't she lovely, doctor? It's nice that she hasn't changed much. I've seen her look like that many a time."

They talked for a while about Thea's good fortune. Mrs. Kronborg had had a cablegram saying, "First performance well received. Great relief." In her letter Thea said; "If you'll only get better, dear mother, there's nothing I can't do. I will make a really great success, if you'll try with me. You shall have everything you want, and we will always be together. I have a little house all picked out where we are to live."

"Bringing up a family is not all it's cracked up to be," said Mrs. Kronborg with a flicker of irony, as she tucked the letter back under her pillow. "The children you don't especially need, you have always with you, like the poor. But the bright ones get away from you. They have their own way to make in the world. Seems like the brighter they are, the farther they go. I used to feel sorry that you had no family, doctor, but maybe you're as well off."

"Thea's plan seems sound to me, Mrs. Kronborg. There's no reason I can see why you shouldn't pull up and live for years yet, under proper care. You'd have the best doctors in the world over there, and it would be wonderful to live with anybody who looks like that." He nodded at the photograph of the young woman who must have been singing "DICH, THEURE HALLE, GRUSS' ICH WIEDER," her eyes looking up, her beautiful hands outspread with pleasure.

Mrs. Kronborg laughed quite cheerfully. "Yes, wouldn't it? If father were here, I might rouse myself. But sometimes it's hard to come back. Or if she were in trouble, maybe I could rouse myself."

"But, dear Mrs. Kronborg, she is in trouble," her old friend expostulated. "As she says, she's never needed you as she needs you now. I make my guess that she's never begged anybody to help her before."

Mrs. Kronborg smiled. "Yes, it's pretty of her. But that will pass. When these things happen far away they don't make such a mark; especially if your hands are full and you've duties of your own to think about. My own father died in Nebraska when Gunner was born,—we were living in Iowa then,—and I was sorry, but the baby made it up to me. I was father's favorite, too. That's the way it goes, you see."

The doctor took out Thea's letter to him, and read it over to Mrs. Kronborg. She seemed to listen, and not to listen.

When he finished, she said thoughtfully: "I'd counted on hearing her sing again. But I always took my pleasures as they come. I always enjoyed her singing when she was here about the house. While she was practicing I often used to leave my work and sit down in a rocker and give myself up to it, the same as if I'd been at an entertainment. I was never one of these housekeepers that let their work drive them to death. And when she had the Mexicans over here, I always took it in. First and last,"—she glanced judicially at the photograph,—"I guess I got about as much out of Thea's voice as anybody will ever get."

"I guess you did!" the doctor assented heartily; "and I got a good deal myself. You remember how she used to sing those Scotch songs for me, and lead us with her head, her hair bobbing?"

"'Flow Gently, Sweet Afton,'—I can hear it now," said Mrs. Kronborg; "and poor father never knew when he sang sharp! He used to say, 'Mother, how do you always know when they make mistakes practicing?'" Mrs. Kronborg chuckled.

Dr. Archie took her hand, still firm like the hand of a young woman. "It was lucky for her that you did know. I always thought she got more from you than from any of her teachers."

"Except Wunsch; he was a real musician," said Mrs. Kronborg respectfully. "I gave her what chance I could, in a crowded house. I kept the other children out of the parlor for her. That was about all I could do. If she wasn't disturbed, she needed no watching. She went after it like a terrier after rats from the first, poor child. She was downright afraid of it. That's why I always encouraged her taking Thor off to outlandish places. When she was out of the house, then she was rid of it."

After they had recalled many pleasant memories together, Mrs. Kronborg said suddenly: "I always understood about her going off without coming to see us that time. Oh, I know! You had to keep your own counsel. You were a good friend to her. I've never forgot that." She patted the doctor's sleeve and went on absently. "There was something she didn't want to tell me, and that's why she didn't come. Something happened when she was with those people in Mexico. I worried for a good while, but I guess she's come out of it all right. She'd had a pretty hard time, scratching along alone like that when she was so young, and my farms in Nebraska were down so low that I couldn't help her none. That's no way to send a girl out. But I guess, whatever there was, she wouldn't be afraid to tell me now." Mrs. Kronborg looked up at the photograph with a smile. "She doesn't look like she was beholding to anybody, does she?"

"She isn't, Mrs. Kronborg. She never has been. That was why she borrowed the money from me."

"Oh, I knew she'd never have sent for you if she'd done anything to shame us. She was always proud." Mrs. Kronborg paused and turned a little on her side. "It's been quite a satisfaction to you and me, doctor, having her voice turn out so fine. The things you hope for don't always turn out like that, by a long sight. As long as old Mrs. Kohler lived, she used always to translate what it said about Thea in the German papers she sent. I could make some of it out myself,—it's not very different from Swedish,—but it pleased the old lady. She left Thea her piece-picture of the burning of Moscow. I've got it put away in moth-balls for her, along with the oboe her grandfather brought from Sweden. I want her to take father's oboe back there some day." Mrs. Kronborg paused a moment and compressed her lips. "But I guess she'll take a finer instrument than that with her, back to Sweden!" she added.

Her tone fairly startled the doctor, it was so vibrating with a fierce, defiant kind of pride he had heard often in Thea's voice. He looked down wonderingly at his old friend and patient. After all, one never knew people to the core. Did she, within her, hide some of that still passion of which her daughter was all-compact?

"That last summer at home wasn't very nice for her," Mrs. Kronborg began as placidly as if the fire had never leaped up in her. "The other children were acting-up because they thought I might make a fuss over her and give her the big-head. We gave her the dare, somehow, the lot of us, because we couldn't understand her changing teachers and all that. That's the trouble about giving the dare to them quiet, unboastful children; you never know how far it'll take 'em. Well, we ought not to complain, doctor; she's given us a good deal to think about."

The next time Dr. Archie came to Moonstone, he came to be a pall-bearer at Mrs. Kronborg's funeral. When he last looked at her, she was so serene and queenly that he went back to Denver feeling almost as if he had helped to bury Thea Kronborg herself. The handsome head in the coffin seemed to him much more really Thea than did the radiant young woman in the picture, looking about at the Gothic vaultings and greeting the Hall of Song.

IV.

One bright morning late in February Dr. Archie was breakfasting comfortably at the Waldorf. He had got into Jersey City on an early train, and a red, windy sunrise over the North River had given him a good appetite. He consulted the morning paper while he drank his coffee and saw that "Lohengrin" was to be sung at the opera that evening. In the list of the artists who would appear was the name "Kronborg." Such abruptness rather startled him. "Kronborg": it was impressive and yet, somehow, disrespectful; somewhat rude and brazen, on the back page of the morning paper. After breakfast he went to the hotel ticket office and asked the girl if she could give him something for "Lohengrin," "near the front." His manner was a trifle awkward and he wondered whether the girl noticed it. Even if she did, of course, she could scarcely suspect. Before the ticket stand he saw a bunch of blue posters announcing the opera casts for the week. There was "Lohengrin," and under it he saw:—

ELSA VON BRABANT...Thea Kronborg.

That looked better. The girl gave him a ticket for a seat which she said was excellent. He paid for it and went out to the cabstand. He mentioned to the driver a number on Riverside Drive and got into a taxi. It would not, of course, be the right thing to call upon Thea when she was going to sing in the evening. He knew that much, thank goodness! Fred Ottenburg had hinted to him that, more than almost anything else, that would put one in wrong.

When he reached the number to which he directed his letters, he dismissed the cab and got out for a walk. The house in which Thea lived was as impersonal as the Waldorf, and quite as large. It was above 116th Street, where the Drive narrows, and in front of it the shelving bank dropped to the North River. As Archie strolled about the paths which traversed this slope, below the street level, the fourteen stories of the apartment hotel rose above him like a perpendicular cliff. He had no idea on which floor Thea lived, but he reflected, as his eye ran over the many windows, that the outlook would be fine from any floor. The forbidding hugeness of the house made him feel as if he had expected to meet Thea in a crowd and had missed her. He did not really believe that she was hidden away behind any of those glittering windows, or that he was to hear her this evening. His walk was curiously uninspiring and unsuggestive. Presently remembering that Ottenburg had encouraged him to study his lesson, he went down to the opera house and bought a libretto. He had even brought his old "Adler's German and English" in his trunk, and after luncheon he settled down in his gilded suite at the Waldorf with a big cigar and the text of "Lohengrin."

The opera was announced for seven-forty-five, but at half-past seven Archie took his seat in the right front of the orchestra circle. He had never been inside the Metropolitan Opera House before, and the height of the audience room, the rich color, and the sweep of the balconies were not without their effect upon him. He watched the house fill with a growing feeling of expectation. When the steel curtain rose and the men of the orchestra took their places, he felt distinctly nervous. The burst of applause which greeted the conductor keyed him still higher. He found that he had taken off his gloves and twisted them to a string. When the lights went down and the violins began the overture, the place looked larger than ever; a great pit, shadowy and solemn. The whole atmosphere, he reflected, was somehow more serious than he had anticipated.

After the curtains were drawn back upon the scene beside the Scheldt, he got readily into the swing of the story. He was so much interested in the bass who sang KING HENRY that he had almost forgotten for what he was waiting so nervously, when the HERALD began in stentorian tones to summon ELSA VON BRABANT. Then he began to realize that he was rather frightened. There was a flutter of white at the back of the stage, and women began to come in: two, four, six, eight, but not the right one. It flashed across him that this was something like buck-fever, the paralyzing moment that comes upon a man when his first elk looks at him through the bushes, under its great antlers; the moment when a man's mind is so full of shooting that he forgets the gun in his hand until the buck nods adieu to him from a distant hill.

All at once, before the buck had left him, she was there. Yes, unquestionably it was she. Her eyes were downcast, but the head, the cheeks, the chin—there could be no mistake; she advanced slowly, as if she were walking in her sleep. Some one spoke to her; she only inclined her head. He spoke again, and she bowed her head still lower. Archie had forgotten his libretto, and he had not counted upon these long pauses. He had expected her to appear and sing and reassure him. They seemed to be waiting for her. Did she ever forget? Why in thunder didn't she—She made a sound, a faint one. The people on the stage whispered together and seemed confounded. His nervousness was absurd. She must have done this often before; she knew her bearings. She made another sound, but he could make nothing of it. Then the King sang to her, and Archie began to remember where they were in the story. She came to the front of the stage, lifted her eyes for the first time, clasped her hands and began, "EINSAM IN TRUBEN TAGEN."

Yes, it was exactly like buck-fever. Her face was there, toward the house now, before his eyes, and he positively could not see it. She was singing, at last, and he positively could not hear her. He was conscious of nothing but an uncomfortable dread and a sense of crushing disappointment. He had, after all, missed her. Whatever was there, she was not there —for him.

The King interrupted her. She began again, "IN LICHTER WAFFEN SCHEINE." Archie did not know when his buckfever passed, but presently he found that he was sitting quietly in a darkened house, not listening to but dreaming upon a river of silver sound. He felt apart from the others, drifting alone on the melody, as if he had been alone with it for a long while and had known it all before. His power of attention was not great just then, but in so far as it went he seemed to be looking through an exalted calmness at a beautiful woman from far away, from another sort of life and feeling and understanding than his own, who had in her face something he had known long ago, much brightened and beautified. As a lad he used to believe that the faces of people who died were like that in the next world; the same faces, but shining with the light of a new understanding. No, Ottenburg had not prepared him!

What he felt was admiration and estrangement. The homely reunion, that he had somehow expected, now seemed foolish. Instead of feeling proud that he knew her better than all these people about him, he felt chagrined at his own ingenuousness. For he did not know her better. This woman he had never known; she had somehow devoured his little friend, as the wolf ate up Red Ridinghood. Beautiful, radiant, tender as she was, she chilled his old affection; that sort of feeling was not appropriate. She seemed much, much farther away from him than she had seemed all those years when she was in Germany. The ocean he could cross, but there was something here he could not cross. There was a moment, when she turned to the King and smiled that rare, sunrise smile of her childhood, when he thought she was coming back to him. After the HERALD'S second call for her champion, when she knelt in her impassioned prayer, there was again something familiar, a kind of wild wonder that she had had the power to call up long ago. But she merely reminded him of Thea; this was not the girl herself.

After the tenor came on, the doctor ceased trying to make the woman before him fit into any of his cherished recollections. He took her, in so far as he could, for what she was then and there. When the knight raised the kneeling girl and put his mailed hand on her hair, when she lifted to him a face full of worship and passionate humility, Archie gave up his last reservation. He knew no more about her than did the hundreds around him, who sat in the shadow and looked on, as he looked, some with more understanding, some with less. He knew as much about ORTRUDE or LOHENGRIN as he knew about ELSA—more, because she went further than they, she sustained the legendary beauty of her conception more consistently. Even he could see that. Attitudes, movements, her face, her white arms and fingers, everything was suffused with a rosy tenderness, a warm humility, a gracious and yet —to him—wholly estranging beauty.

During the balcony singing in the second act the doctor's thoughts were as far away from Moonstone as the singer's doubtless were. He had begun, indeed, to feel the exhilaration of getting free from personalities, of being released from his own past as well as from Thea Kronborg's. It was very much, he told himself, like a military funeral, exalting and impersonal. Something old died in one, and out of it something new was born. During the duet with ORTRUDE, and the splendors of the wedding processional, this new feeling grew and grew. At the end of the act there were many curtain calls and ELSA acknowledged them, brilliant, gracious, spirited, with her far-breaking smile; but on the whole she was harder and more self-contained before the curtain than she was in the scene behind it. Archie did his part in the applause that greeted her, but it was the new and wonderful he applauded, not the old and dear. His personal, proprietary pride in her was frozen out.

He walked about the house during the ENTR'ACTE, and here and there among the people in the foyer he caught the name "Kronborg." On the staircase, in front of the coffeeroom, a long-haired youth with a fat face was discoursing to a group of old women about "die Kronborg." Dr. Archie gathered that he had crossed on the boat with her.

After the performance was over, Archie took a taxi and started for Riverside Drive. He meant to see it through to-night. When he entered the reception hall of the hotel before which he had strolled that morning, the hall porter challenged him. He said he was waiting for Miss Kronborg. The porter looked at him suspiciously and asked whether he had an appointment. He answered brazenly that he had. He was not used to being questioned by hall boys. Archie sat first in one tapestry chair and then in another, keeping a sharp eye on the people who came in and went up in the elevators. He walked about and looked at his watch. An hour dragged by. No one had come in from the street now for about twenty minutes, when two women entered, carrying a great many flowers and followed by a tall young man in chauffeur's uniform. Archie advanced toward the taller of the two women, who was veiled and carried her head very firmly. He confronted her just as she reached the elevator. Although he did not stand directly in her way, something in his attitude compelled her to stop. She gave him a piercing, defiant glance through the white scarf that covered her face. Then she lifted her hand and brushed the scarf back from her head. There was still black on her brows and lashes. She was very pale and her face was drawn and deeply lined. She looked, the doctor told himself with a sinking heart, forty years old. Her suspicious, mystified stare cleared slowly.

"Pardon me," the doctor murmured, not knowing just how to address her here before the porters, "I came up from the opera. I merely wanted to say good-night to you."

Without speaking, still looking incredulous, she pushed him into the elevator. She kept her hand on his arm while the cage shot up, and she looked away from him, frowning, as if she were trying to remember or realize something. When the cage stopped, she pushed him out of the elevator through another door, which a maid opened, into a square hall. There she sank down on a chair and looked up at him.

"Why didn't you let me know?" she asked in a hoarse voice.

Archie heard himself laughing the old, embarrassed laugh that seldom happened to him now. "Oh, I wanted to take my chance with you, like anybody else. It's been so long, now!"

She took his hand through her thick glove and her head dropped forward. "Yes, it has been long," she said in the same husky voice, "and so much has happened."

"And you are so tired, and I am a clumsy old fellow to break in on you to-night," the doctor added sympathetically. "Forgive me, this time." He bent over and put his hand soothingly on her shoulder. He felt a strong shudder run through her from head to foot.

Still bundled in her fur coat as she was, she threw both arms about him and hugged him. "Oh, Dr. Archie, DR. ARCHIE,"—she shook him,—"don't let me go. Hold on, now you're here," she laughed, breaking away from him at the same moment and sliding out of her fur coat. She left it for the maid to pick up and pushed the doctor into the sitting-room, where she turned on the lights. "Let me LOOK at you. Yes; hands, feet, head, shoulders—just the same. You've grown no older. You can't say as much for me, can you?"

She was standing in the middle of the room, in a white silk shirtwaist and a short black velvet skirt, which somehow suggested that they had 'cut off her petticoats all round about.' She looked distinctly clipped and plucked. Her hair was parted in the middle and done very close to her head, as she had worn it under the wig. She looked like a fugitive, who had escaped from something in clothes caught up at hazard. It flashed across Dr. Archie that she was running away from the other woman down at the opera house, who had used her hardly.

He took a step toward her. "I can't tell a thing in the world about you, Thea—if I may still call you that."

She took hold of the collar of his overcoat. "Yes, call me that. Do: I like to hear it. You frighten me a little, but I expect I frighten you more. I'm always a scarecrow after I sing a long part like that—so high, too." She absently pulled out the handkerchief that protruded from his breast pocket and began to wipe the black paint off her eyebrows and lashes. "I can't take you in much to-night, but I must see you for a little while." She pushed him to a chair. "I shall be more recognizable to-morrow. You mustn't think of me as you see me to-night. Come at four to-morrow afternoon and have tea with me. Can you? That's good."

She sat down in a low chair beside him and leaned forward, drawing her shoulders together. She seemed to him inappropriately young and inappropriately old, shorn of her long tresses at one end and of her long robes at the other.

"How do you happen to be here?" she asked abruptly. "How can you leave a silver mine? I couldn't! Sure nobody'll cheat you? But you can explain everything tomorrow." She paused. "You remember how you sewed me up in a poultice, once? I wish you could to-night. I need a poultice, from top to toe. Something very disagreeable happened down there. You said you were out front? Oh, don't say anything about it. I always know exactly how it goes, unfortunately. I was rotten in the balcony. I never get that. You didn't notice it? Probably not, but I did."

Here the maid appeared at the door and her mistress rose. "My supper? Very well, I'll come. I'd ask you to stay, doctor, but there wouldn't be enough for two. They seldom send up enough for one,"—she spoke bitterly. "I haven't got a sense of you yet,"—turning directly to Archie again. "You haven't been here. You've only announced yourself, and told me you are coming to-morrow. You haven't seen me, either. This is not I. But I'll be here waiting for you to-morrow, my whole works! Goodnight, till then." She patted him absently on the sleeve and gave him a little shove toward the door.

V.

When Archie got back to his hotel at two o'clock in the morning, he found Fred Ottenburg's card under his door, with a message scribbled across the top: "When you come in, please call up room 811, this hotel." A moment later Fred's voice reached him over the telephone.

"That you, Archie? Won't you come up? I'm having some supper and I'd like company. Late? What does that matter? I won't keep you long."

Archie dropped his overcoat and set out for room 811. He found Ottenburg in the act of touching a match to a chafing-dish, at a table laid for two in his sitting-room. "I'm catering here," he announced cheerfully. "I let the waiter off at midnight, after he'd set me up. You'll have to account for yourself, Archie."

The doctor laughed, pointing to three wine-coolers under the table. "Are you expecting guests?"

"Yes, two." Ottenburg held up two fingers,—"you, and my higher self. He's a thirsty boy, and I don't invite him often. He has been known to give me a headache. Now, where have you been, Archie, until this shocking hour?"

"Bah, you've been banting!" the doctor exclaimed, pulling out his white gloves as he searched for his handkerchief and throwing them into a chair. Ottenburg was in evening clothes and very pointed dress shoes. His white waistcoat, upon which the doctor had fixed a challenging eye, went down straight from the top button, and he wore a camelia. He was conspicuously brushed and trimmed and polished. His smoothly controlled excitement was wholly different from his usual easy cordiality, though he had his face, as well as his figure, well in hand. On the serving-table there was an empty champagne pint and a glass. He had been having a little starter, the doctor told himself, and would probably be running on high gear before he got through. There was even now an air of speed about him.

"Been, Freddy?"—the doctor at last took up his question. "I expect I've been exactly where you have. Why didn't you tell me you were coming on?"

"I wasn't, Archie." Fred lifted the cover of the chafingdish and stirred the contents. He stood behind the table, holding the lid with his handkerchief. "I had never thought of such a thing. But Landry, a young chap who plays her accompaniments and who keeps an eye out for me, telegraphed me that Madame Rheinecker had gone to Atlantic City with a bad throat, and Thea might have a chance to sing ELSA. She has sung it only twice here before, and I missed it in Dresden. So I came on. I got in at four this afternoon and saw you registered, but I thought I wouldn't butt in. How lucky you got here just when she was coming on for this. You couldn't have hit a better time." Ottenburg stirred the contents of the dish faster and put in more sherry. "And where have you been since twelve o'clock, may I ask?"

Archie looked rather self-conscious, as he sat down on a fragile gilt chair that rocked under him, and stretched out his long legs. "Well, if you'll believe me, I had the brutality to go to see her. I wanted to identify her. Couldn't wait."

Ottenburg placed the cover quickly on the chafing-dish and took a step backward. "You did, old sport? My word! None but the brave deserve the fair. Well,"—he stooped to turn the wine,—"and how was she?"

"She seemed rather dazed, and pretty well used up. She seemed disappointed in herself, and said she hadn't done herself justice in the balcony scene."

"Well, if she didn't, she's not the first. Beastly stuff to sing right in there; lies just on the 'break' in the voice." Fred pulled a bottle out of the ice and drew the cork. Lifting his glass he looked meaningly at Archie. "You know who, doctor. Here goes!" He drank off his glass with a sigh of satisfaction. After he had turned the lamp low under the chafing-dish, he remained standing, looking pensively down at the food on the table. "Well, she rather pulled it off! As a backer, you're a winner, Archie. I congratulate you." Fred poured himself another glass. "Now you must eat something, and so must I. Here, get off that bird cage and find a steady chair. This stuff ought to be rather good; head waiter's suggestion. Smells all right." He bent over the chafing-dish and began to serve the contents. "Perfectly innocuous: mushrooms and truffles and a little crab-meat. And now, on the level, Archie, how did it hit you?"

Archie turned a frank smile to his friend and shook his head. "It was all miles beyond me, of course, but it gave me a pulse. The general excitement got hold of me, I suppose. I like your wine, Freddy." He put down his glass. "It goes to the spot to-night. She WAS all right, then? You weren't disappointed?"

"Disappointed? My dear Archie, that's the high voice we dream of; so pure and yet so virile and human. That combination hardly ever happens with sopranos." Ottenburg sat down and turned to the doctor, speaking calmly and trying to dispel his friend's manifest bewilderment. "You see, Archie, there's the voice itself, so beautiful and individual, and then there's something else; the thing in it which responds to every shade of thought and feeling, spontaneously, almost unconsciously. That color has to be born in a singer, it can't be acquired; lots of beautiful voices haven't a vestige of it. It's almost like another gift—the rarest of all. The voice simply is the mind and is the heart. It can't go wrong in interpretation, because it has in it the thing that makes all interpretation. That's why you feel so sure of her. After you've listened to her for an hour or so, you aren't afraid of anything. All the little dreads you have with other artists vanish. You lean back and you say to yourself, 'No, THAT voice will never betray.' TREULICH GEFUHRT, TREULICH BEWACHT."

Archie looked envyingly at Fred's excited, triumphant face. How satisfactory it must be, he thought, to really know what she was doing and not to have to take it on hearsay. He took up his glass with a sigh. "I seem to need a good deal of cooling off to-night. I'd just as lief forget the Reform Party for once.

"Yes, Fred," he went on seriously; "I thought it sounded very beautiful, and I thought she was very beautiful, too. I never imagined she could be as beautiful as that."

"Wasn't she? Every attitude a picture, and always the right kind of picture, full of that legendary, supernatural thing she gets into it. I never heard the prayer sung like that before. That look that came in her eyes; it went right out through the back of the roof. Of course, you get an ELSA who can look through walls like that, and visions and Grail-knights happen naturally. She becomes an abbess, that girl, after LOHENGRIN leaves her. She's made to live with ideas and enthusiasms, not with a husband." Fred folded his arms, leaned back in his chair, and began to sing softly:—

"Ein Ritter nahte da."

"Doesn't she die, then, at the end?" the doctor asked guardedly.

Fred smiled, reaching under the table. "Some ELSAS do; she didn't. She left me with the distinct impression that she was just beginning. Now, doctor, here's a cold one." He twirled a napkin smoothly about the green glass, the cork gave and slipped out with a soft explosion. "And now we must have another toast. It's up to you, this time."

The doctor watched the agitation in his glass. "The same," he said without lifting his eyes. "That's good enough. I can't raise you."

Fred leaned forward, and looked sharply into his face. "That's the point; how COULD you raise me? Once again!"

"Once again, and always the same!" The doctor put down his glass. "This doesn't seem to produce any symptoms in me to-night." He lit a cigar. "Seriously, Freddy, I wish I knew more about what she's driving at. It makes me jealous, when you are so in it and I'm not."

"In it?" Fred started up. "My God, haven't you seen her this blessed night?—when she'd have kicked any other man down the elevator shaft, if I know her. Leave me something; at least what I can pay my five bucks for."

"Seems to me you get a good deal for your five bucks," said Archie ruefully. "And that, after all, is what she cares about,—what people get."

Fred lit a cigarette, took a puff or two, and then threw it away. He was lounging back in his chair, and his face was pale and drawn hard by that mood of intense concentration which lurks under the sunny shallows of the vineyard. In his voice there was a longer perspective than usual, a slight remoteness. "You see, Archie, it's all very simple, a natural development. It's exactly what Mahler said back there in the beginning, when she sang WOGLINDE. It's the idea, the basic idea, pulsing behind every bar she sings. She simplifies a character down to the musical idea it's built on, and makes everything conform to that. The people who chatter about her being a great actress don't seem to get the notion of where SHE gets the notion. It all goes back to her original endowment, her tremendous musical talent. Instead of inventing a lot of business and expedients to suggest character, she knows the thing at the root, and lets the musical pattern take care of her. The score pours her into all those lovely postures, makes the light and shadow go over her face, lifts her and drops her. She lies on it, the way she used to lie on the Rhine music. Talk about rhythm!"

The doctor frowned dubiously as a third bottle made its appearance above the cloth. "Aren't you going in rather strong?"

Fred laughed. "No, I'm becoming too sober. You see this is breakfast now; kind of wedding breakfast. I feel rather weddingish. I don't mind. You know," he went on as the wine gurgled out, "I was thinking to-night when they sprung the wedding music, how any fool can have that stuff played over him when he walks up the aisle with some dough-faced little hussy who's hooked him. But it isn't every fellow who can see—well, what we saw tonight. There are compensations in life, Dr. Howard Archie, though they come in disguise. Did you notice her when she came down the stairs? Wonder where she gets that bright-and-morning star look? Carries to the last row of the family circle. I moved about all over the house. I'll tell you a secret, Archie: that carrying power was one of the first things that put me wise. Noticed it down there in Arizona, in the open. That, I said, belongs only to the big ones." Fred got up and began to move rhythmically about the room, his hands in his pockets. The doctor was astonished at his ease and steadiness, for there were slight lapses in his speech. "You see, Archie, ELSA isn't a part that's particularly suited to Thea's voice at all, as I see her voice. It's over-lyrical for her. She makes it, but there's nothing in it that fits her like a glove, except, maybe, that long duet in the third act. There, of course,"—he held out his hands as if he were measuring something,—"we know exactly where we are. But wait until they give her a chance at something that lies properly in her voice, and you'll see me rosier than I am to-night."

Archie smoothed the tablecloth with his hand. "I am sure I don't want to see you any rosier, Fred."

Ottenburg threw back his head and laughed. "It's enthusiasm, doctor. It's not the wine.

I've got as much inflated as this for a dozen trashy things: brewers' dinners and political orgies. You, too, have your extravagances, Archie. And what I like best in you is this particular enthusiasm, which is not at all practical or sensible, which is downright Quixotic. You are not altogether what you seem, and you have your reservations. Living among the wolves, you have not become one. LUPIBUS VIVENDI NON LUPUS SUM."

The doctor seemed embarrassed. "I was just thinking how tired she looked, plucked of all her fine feathers, while we get all the fun. Instead of sitting here carousing, we ought to go solemnly to bed."

"I get your idea." Ottenburg crossed to the window and threw it open. "Fine night outside; a hag of a moon just setting. It begins to smell like morning. After all, Archie, think of the lonely and rather solemn hours we've spent waiting for all this, while she's been —reveling."

Archie lifted his brows. "I somehow didn't get the idea to-night that she revels much."

"I don't mean this sort of thing." Fred turned toward the light and stood with his back to the window. "That," with a nod toward the wine-cooler, "is only a cheap imitation, that any poor stiff-fingered fool can buy and feel his shell grow thinner. But take it from me, no matter what she pays, or how much she may see fit to lie about it, the real, the master revel is hers." He leaned back against the window sill and crossed his arms. "Anybody with all that voice and all that talent and all that beauty, has her hour. Her hour," he went on deliberately, "when she can say, 'there it is, at last, WIE IM TRAUM ICH. As in my dream I dreamed it, as in my will it was.'"

He stood silent a moment, twisting the flower from his coat by the stem and staring at the blank wall with haggard abstraction. "Even I can say to-night, Archie," he brought out slowly, "'As in my dream I dreamed it, as in my will it was.' Now, doctor, you may leave me. I'm beautifully drunk, but not with anything that ever grew in France."

The doctor rose. Fred tossed his flower out of the window behind him and came toward the door. "I say," he called, "have you a date with anybody?"

The doctor paused, his hand on the knob. "With Thea, you mean? Yes. I'm to go to her at four this afternoon—if you haven't paralyzed me."

"Well, you won't eat me, will you, if I break in and send up my card? She'll probably turn me down cold, but that won't hurt my feelings. If she ducks me, you tell her for me, that to spite me now she'd have to cut off more than she can spare. Good-night, Archie."

VI.

It was late on the morning after the night she sang ELSA, when Thea Kronborg stirred uneasily in her bed. The room was darkened by two sets of window shades, and the day outside was thick and cloudy. She turned and tried to recapture unconsciousness, knowing that she would not be able to do so. She dreaded waking stale and disappointed after a great effort. The first thing that came was always the sense of the futility of such endeavor, and of the absurdity of trying too hard. Up to a certain point, say eighty degrees, artistic endeavor could be fat and comfortable, methodical and prudent. But if you went further than that, if you drew yourself up toward ninety degrees, you parted with your defenses and left yourself exposed to mischance. The legend was that in those upper reaches you might be divine; but you were much likelier to be ridiculous. Your public wanted just about eighty degrees; if you gave it more it blew its nose and put a crimp in you. In the morning, especially, it seemed to her very probable that whatever struggled above the good average was not quite sound. Certainly very little of that superfluous ardor, which cost so dear, ever got across the footlights. These misgivings waited to pounce upon her when she wakened. They hovered about her bed like vultures.

She reached under her pillow for her handkerchief, without opening her eyes. She had a shadowy memory that there was to be something unusual, that this day held more disquieting possibilities than days commonly held. There was something she dreaded; what was it? Oh, yes, Dr. Archie was to come at four.

A reality like Dr. Archie, poking up out of the past, reminded one of disappointments and losses, of a freedom that was no more: reminded her of blue, golden mornings long ago, when she used to waken with a burst of joy at recovering her precious self and her precious world; when she never lay on her pillows at eleven o'clock like something the waves had washed up. After all, why had he come? It had been so long, and so much had happened. The things she had lost, he would miss readily enough. What she had gained, he would scarcely perceive. He, and all that he recalled, lived for her as memories. In sleep, and in hours of illness or exhaustion, she went back to them and held them to her heart. But they were better as memories. They had nothing to do with the struggle that made up her actual life. She felt drearily that she was not flexible enough to be the person her old friend expected her to be, the person she herself wished to be with him.

Thea reached for the bell and rang twice,—a signal to her maid to order her breakfast. She rose and ran up the window shades and turned on the water in her bathroom, glancing into the mirror apprehensively as she passed it. Her bath usually cheered her, even on low mornings like this. Her white bathroom, almost as large as her sleeping-room, she regarded as a refuge. When she turned the key behind her, she left care and vexation on the other side of the door. Neither her maid nor the management nor her letters nor her accompanist could get at her now.

When she pinned her braids about her head, dropped her nightgown and stepped out to begin her Swedish movements, she was a natural creature again, and it was so that she liked herself best. She slid into the tub with anticipation and splashed and tumbled about a good deal. Whatever else she hurried, she never hurried her bath. She used her brushes and sponges and soaps like toys, fairly playing in the water. Her own body was always a cheering sight to her. When she was careworn, when her mind felt old and tired, the freshness of her physical self, her long, firm lines, the smoothness of her skin, reassured her. This morning, because of awakened memories, she looked at herself more carefully than usual, and was not discouraged. While she was in the tub she began to whistle softly the tenor aria, "AH! FUYEZ, DOUCE IMAGE," somehow appropriate to the bath. After a noisy moment under the cold shower, she stepped out on the rug flushed and glowing, threw her arms above her head, and rose on her toes, keeping the elevation as long as she could. When she dropped back on her heels and began to rub herself with the towels, she took up the aria again, and felt quite in the humor for seeing Dr. Archie. After she had returned to her bed, the maid brought her letters and the morning papers with her breakfast.

"Telephone Mr. Landry and ask him if he can come at half-past three, Theresa, and order tea to be brought up at five."

When Howard Archie was admitted to Thea's apartment that afternoon, he was shown into the music-room back of the little reception room. Thea was sitting in a davenport behind the piano, talking to a young man whom she later introduced as her friend Mr. Landry. As she rose, and came to meet him, Archie felt a deep relief, a sudden thankfulness. She no longer looked clipped and plucked, or dazed and fleeing.

Dr. Archie neglected to take account of the young man to whom he was presented. He kept Thea's hands and held her where he met her, taking in the light, lively sweep of her hair, her clear green eyes and her throat that came up strong and dazzlingly white from her green velvet gown. The chin was as lovely as ever, the cheeks as smooth. All the lines of last night had disappeared. Only at the outer corners of her eyes, between the eye and the temple, were the faintest indications of a future attack—mere kitten scratches that playfully hinted where one day the cat would claw her. He studied her without any embarrassment. Last night everything had been awkward; but now, as he held her hands, a kind of harmony came between them, a reestablishment of confidence.

"After all, Thea,—in spite of all, I still know you," he murmured.

She took his arm and led him up to the young man who was standing beside the piano. "Mr. Landry knows all about you, Dr. Archie. He has known about you for many years." While the two men shook hands she stood between them, drawing them together by her presence and her glances. "When I first went to Germany, Landry was studying there. He used to be good enough to work with me when I could not afford to have an accompanist for more than two hours a day. We got into the way of working together. He is a singer, too, and has his own career to look after, but he still manages to give me some time. I want you to be friends." She smiled from one to the other.

The rooms, Archie noticed, full of last night's flowers, were furnished in light colors, the hotel bleakness of them a little softened by a magnificent Steinway piano, white bookshelves full of books and scores, some drawings of ballet dancers, and the very deep sofa behind the piano.

"Of course," Archie asked apologetically, "you have seen the papers?"

"Very cordial, aren't they? They evidently did not expect as much as I did. ELSA is not really in my voice. I can sing the music, but I have to go after it."

"That is exactly," the doctor came out boldly, "what Fred Ottenburg said this morning."

They had remained standing, the three of them, by the piano, where the gray afternoon light was strongest. Thea turned to the doctor with interest. "Is Fred in town? They were from him, then—some flowers that came last night without a card." She indicated the white lilacs on the window sill. "Yes, he would know, certainly," she said thoughtfully. "Why don't we sit down? There will be some tea for you in a minute, Landry. He's very dependent upon it," disapprovingly to Archie. "Now tell me, Doctor, did you really have a good time last night, or were you uncomfortable? Did you feel as if I were trying to hold my hat on by my eyebrows?"

He smiled. "I had all kinds of a time. But I had no feeling of that sort. I couldn't be quite sure that it was you at all. That was why I came up here last night. I felt as if I'd lost you."

She leaned toward him and brushed his sleeve reassuringly. "Then I didn't give you an impression of painful struggle? Landry was singing at Weber and Fields' last night. He didn't get in until the performance was half over. But I see the TRIBUNE man felt that I was working pretty hard. Did you see that notice, Oliver?"

Dr. Archie looked closely at the red-headed young man for the first time, and met his lively brown eyes, full of a droll, confiding sort of humor. Mr. Landry was not prepossessing. He was undersized and clumsily made, with a red, shiny face and a sharp little nose that looked as if it had been whittled out of wood and was always in the air, on the scent of something. Yet it was this queer little beak, with his eyes, that made his countenance anything of a face at all. From a distance he looked like the groceryman's delivery boy in a small town. His dress seemed an acknowledgment of his grotesqueness: a short coat, like a little boys' roundabout, and a vest fantastically sprigged and dotted, over a lavender shirt.

At the sound of a muffled buzz, Mr. Landry sprang up.

"May I answer the telephone for you?" He went to the writing-table and took up the receiver. "Mr. Ottenburg is downstairs," he said, turning to Thea and holding the mouthpiece against his coat.

"Tell him to come up," she replied without hesitation. "How long are you going to be in town, Dr. Archie?"

"Oh, several weeks, if you'll let me stay. I won't hang around and be a burden to you, but I want to try to get educated up to you, though I expect it's late to begin."

Thea rose and touched him lightly on the shoulder. "Well, you'll never be any younger, will you?"

"I'm not so sure about that," the doctor replied gallantly.

The maid appeared at the door and announced Mr. Frederick Ottenburg. Fred came in, very much got up, the doctor reflected, as he watched him bending over Thea's hand. He was still pale and looked somewhat chastened, and the lock of hair that hung down over his forehead was distinctly moist. But his black afternoon coat, his gray tie and gaiters were of a correctness that Dr. Archie could never attain for all the efforts of his faithful slave, Van Deusen, the Denver haberdasher. To be properly up to those tricks, the doctor supposed, you had to learn them young. If he were to buy a silk hat that was the twin of Ottenburg's, it would be shaggy in a week, and he could never carry it as Fred held his.

Ottenburg had greeted Thea in German, and as she replied in the same language, Archie joined Mr. Landry at the window. "You know Mr. Ottenburg, he tells me?"

Mr. Landry's eyes twinkled. "Yes, I regularly follow him about, when he's in town. I would, even if he didn't send me such wonderful Christmas presents: Russian vodka by the half-dozen!"

Thea called to them, "Come, Mr. Ottenburg is calling on all of us. Here's the tea."

The maid opened the door and two waiters from downstairs appeared with covered trays. The tea-table was in the parlor. Thea drew Ottenburg with her and went to inspect it. "Where's the rum? Oh, yes, in that thing! Everything seems to be here, but send up some currant preserves and cream cheese for Mr. Ottenburg. And in about fifteen minutes, bring some fresh toast. That's all, thank you."

For the next few minutes there was a clatter of teacups and responses about sugar. "Landry always takes rum. I'm glad the rest of you don't. I'm sure it's bad." Thea poured the tea standing and got through with it as quickly as possible, as if it were a refreshment snatched between trains. The tea-table and the little room in which it stood seemed to be out of scale with her long step, her long reach, and the energy of her movements. Dr. Archie, standing near her, was pleasantly aware of the animation of her figure. Under the clinging velvet, her body seemed independent and unsubdued.

They drifted, with their plates and cups, back to the music-room. When Thea followed them, Ottenburg put down his tea suddenly. "Aren't you taking anything? Please let me." He started back to the table.

"No, thank you, nothing. I'm going to run over that aria for you presently, to convince you that I can do it. How did the duet go, with Schlag?"

She was standing in the doorway and Fred came up to her: "That you'll never do any better. You've worked your voice into it perfectly. Every NUANCE—wonderful!"

"Think so?" She gave him a sidelong glance and spoke with a certain gruff shyness which did not deceive anybody, and was not meant to deceive. The tone was equivalent to "Keep it up. I like it, but I'm awkward with it."

Fred held her by the door and did keep it up, furiously, for full five minutes. She took it with some confusion, seeming all the while to be hesitating, to be arrested in her course and trying to pass him. But she did not really try to pass, and her color deepened. Fred spoke in German, and Archie caught from her an occasional JA? SO? muttered rather than spoken.

When they rejoined Landry and Dr. Archie, Fred took up his tea again. "I see you're singing VENUS Saturday night. Will they never let you have a chance at ELIZABETH?"

She shrugged her shoulders. "Not here. There are so many singers here, and they try us out in such a stingy way. Think of it, last year I came over in October, and it was the first of December before I went on at all! I'm often sorry I left Dresden."

"Still," Fred argued, "Dresden is limited."

"Just so, and I've begun to sigh for those very limitations. In New York everything is impersonal. Your audience never knows its own mind, and its mind is never twice the same. I'd rather sing where the people are pig-headed and throw carrots at you if you don't do it the way they like it. The house here is splendid, and the night audiences are exciting. I hate the matinees; like singing at a KAFFEKLATSCH." She rose and turned on the lights.

"Ah!" Fred exclaimed, "why do you do that? That is a signal that tea is over." He got up and drew out his gloves.

"Not at all. Shall you be here Saturday night?" She sat down on the piano bench and leaned her elbow back on the keyboard. "Necker sings ELIZABETH. Make Dr. Archie go. Everything she sings is worth hearing."

"But she's failing so. The last time I heard her she had no voice at all. She IS a poor vocalist!"

Thea cut him off. "She's a great artist, whether she's in voice or not, and she's the only one here. If you want a big voice, you can take my ORTRUDE of last night; that's big enough, and vulgar enough."

Fred laughed and turned away, this time with decision. "I don't want her!" he protested energetically. "I only wanted to get a rise out of you. I like Necker's ELIZABETH well enough. I like your VENUS well enough, too."

"It's a beautiful part, and it's often dreadfully sung. It's very hard to sing, of course."

Ottenburg bent over the hand she held out to him. "For an uninvited guest, I've fared very well. You were nice to let me come up. I'd have been terribly cut up if you'd sent me away. May I?" He kissed her hand lightly and backed toward the door, still smiling, and promising to keep an eye on Archie. "He can't be trusted at all, Thea. One of the waiters at Martin's worked a Tourainian hare off on him at luncheon yesterday, for seven twenty-five."

Thea broke into a laugh, the deep one he recognized. "Did he have a ribbon on, this hare? Did they bring him in a gilt cage?"

"No,"—Archie spoke up for himself,—"they brought him in a brown sauce, which was very good. He didn't taste very different from any rabbit."

"Probably came from a push-cart on the East Side." Thea looked at her old friend commiseratingly. "Yes, DO keep an eye on him, Fred. I had no idea," shaking her head. "Yes, I'll be obliged to you."

"Count on me!" Their eyes met in a gay smile, and Fred bowed himself out.

VII.

On Saturday night Dr. Archie went with Fred Ottenburg to hear "Tannhauser." Thea had a rehearsal on Sunday afternoon, but as she was not on the bill again until Wednesday, she promised to dine with Archie and Ottenburg on Monday, if they could make the dinner early.

At a little after eight on Monday evening, the three friends returned to Thea's apartment and seated themselves for an hour of quiet talk.

"I'm sorry we couldn't have had Landry with us tonight," Thea said, "but he's on at Weber and Fields' every night now. You ought to hear him, Dr. Archie. He often sings the old Scotch airs you used to love."

"Why not go down this evening?" Fred suggested hopefully, glancing at his watch. "That is, if you'd like to go. I can telephone and find what time he comes on."

Thea hesitated. "No, I think not. I took a long walk this afternoon and I'm rather tired. I think I can get to sleep early and be so much ahead. I don't mean at once, however," seeing Dr. Archie's disappointed look. "I always like to hear Landry," she added. "He never had much voice, and it's worn, but there's a sweetness about it, and he sings with such taste."

"Yes, doesn't he? May I?" Fred took out his cigarette case. "It really doesn't bother your throat?"

"A little doesn't. But cigar smoke does. Poor Dr. Archie! Can you do with one of those?"

"I'm learning to like them," the doctor declared, taking one from the case Fred proffered him.

"Landry's the only fellow I know in this country who can do that sort of thing," Fred went on. "Like the best English ballad singers. He can sing even popular stuff by higher lights, as it were."

Thea nodded. "Yes; sometimes I make him sing his most foolish things for me. It's restful, as he does it. That's when I'm homesick, Dr. Archie."

"You knew him in Germany, Thea?" Dr. Archie had quietly abandoned his cigarette as a comfortless article. "When you first went over?"

"Yes. He was a good friend to a green girl. He helped me with my German and my music and my general discouragement. Seemed to care more about my getting on than about himself. He had no money, either. An old aunt had loaned him a little to study on.—Will you answer that, Fred?"

Fred caught up the telephone and stopped the buzz while Thea went on talking to Dr. Archie about Landry. Telling some one to hold the wire, he presently put down the instrument and approached Thea with a startled expression on his face.

"It's the management," he said quietly. "Gloeckler has broken down: fainting fits. Madame Rheinecker is in Atlantic City and Schramm is singing in Philadelphia tonight. They want to know whether you can come down and finish SIEGLINDE."

"What time is it?"

"Eight fifty-five. The first act is just over. They can hold the curtain twenty-five minutes."

Thea did not move. "Twenty-five and thirty-five makes sixty," she muttered. "Tell them I'll come if they hold the curtain till I am in the dressing-room. Say I'll have to wear her costumes, and the dresser must have everything ready. Then call a taxi, please."

Thea had not changed her position since he first interrupted her, but she had grown pale and was opening and shutting her hands rapidly. She looked, Fred thought, terrified. He half turned toward the telephone, but hung on one foot.

"Have you ever sung the part?" he asked.

"No, but I've rehearsed it. That's all right. Get the cab." Still she made no move. She merely turned perfectly blank eyes to Dr. Archie and said absently, "It's curious, but just at this minute I can't remember a bar of 'Walkure' after the first act. And I let my maid go out." She sprang up and beckoned Archie without so much, he felt sure, as knowing who he was. "Come with me." She went quickly into her sleeping-chamber and threw open a door into a trunk-room. "See that white trunk? It's not locked. It's full of wigs, in boxes. Look until you find one marked 'Ring 2.' Bring it quick!" While she directed him, she threw open a square trunk and began tossing out shoes of every shape and color.

Ottenburg appeared at the door. "Can I help you?"

She threw him some white sandals with long laces and silk stockings pinned to them. "Put those in something, and then go to the piano and give me a few measures in there—you know." She was behaving somewhat like a cyclone now, and while she wrenched open drawers and closet doors, Ottenburg got to the piano as quickly as possible and began to herald the reappearance of the Volsung pair, trusting to memory.

In a few moments Thea came out enveloped in her long fur coat with a scarf over her head and knitted woolen gloves on her hands. Her glassy eye took in the fact that Fred was playing from memory, and even in her distracted state, a faint smile flickered over her colorless lips. She stretched out a woolly hand, "The score, please. Behind you, there."

Dr. Archie followed with a canvas box and a satchel. As they went through the hall, the men caught up their hats and coats. They left the music-room, Fred noticed, just seven minutes after he got the telephone message. In the elevator Thea said in that husky whisper which had so perplexed Dr. Archie when he first heard it, "Tell the driver he must do it in twenty minutes, less if he can. He must leave the light on in the cab. I can do a good deal in twenty minutes. If only you hadn't made me eat—Damn that duck!" she broke out bitterly; "why did you?"

"Wish I had it back! But it won't bother you, to-night. You need strength," he pleaded consolingly.

But she only muttered angrily under her breath, "Idiot, idiot!"

Ottenburg shot ahead and instructed the driver, while the doctor put Thea into the cab and shut the door. She did not speak to either of them again. As the driver scrambled into his seat she opened the score and fixed her eyes upon it. Her face, in the white light, looked as bleak as a stone quarry.

As her cab slid away, Ottenburg shoved Archie into a second taxi that waited by the curb. "We'd better trail her," he explained. "There might be a hold-up of some kind." As the cab whizzed off he broke into an eruption of profanity.

"What's the matter, Fred?" the doctor asked. He was a good deal dazed by the rapid evolutions of the last ten minutes.

"Matter enough!" Fred growled, buttoning his overcoat with a shiver. "What a way to sing a part for the first time! That duck really is on my conscience. It will be a wonder if she can do anything but quack! Scrambling on in the middle of a performance like this, with no rehearsal! The stuff she has to sing in there is a fright—rhythm, pitch,—and terribly difficult intervals."

"She looked frightened," Dr. Archie said thoughtfully, "but I thought she looked —determined."

Fred sniffed. "Oh, determined! That's the kind of rough deal that makes savages of singers. Here's a part she's worked on and got ready for for years, and now they give her a chance to go on and butcher it. Goodness knows when she's looked at the score last, or whether she can use the business she's studied with this cast. Necker's singing BRUNNHILDE; she may help her, if it's not one of her sore nights."

"Is she sore at Thea?" Dr. Archie asked wonderingly.

"My dear man, Necker's sore at everything. She's breaking up; too early; just when she ought to be at her best. There's one story that she is struggling under some serious malady, another that she learned a bad method at the Prague Conservatory and has ruined her organ. She's the sorest thing in the world. If she weathers this winter through, it'll be her last. She's paying for it with the last rags of her voice. And then—" Fred whistled softly.

"Well, what then?"

"Then our girl may come in for some of it. It's dog eat dog, in this game as in every other."

The cab stopped and Fred and Dr. Archie hurried to the box office. The Monday-night house was sold out. They bought standing room and entered the auditorium just as the press representative of the house was thanking the audience for their patience and telling them that although Madame Gloeckler was too ill to sing, Miss Kronborg had kindly consented to finish her part. This announcement was met with vehement applause from the upper circles of the house.

"She has her—constituents," Dr. Archie murmured.

"Yes, up there, where they're young and hungry. These people down here have dined too well. They won't mind, however. They like fires and accidents and DIVERTISSEMENTS. Two SIEGLINDES are more unusual than one, so they'll be satisfied."

After the final disappearance of the mother of Siegfried, Ottenburg and the doctor slipped out through the crowd and left the house. Near the stage entrance Fred found the driver who had brought Thea down. He dismissed him and got a larger car. He and Archie waited on the sidewalk, and when Kronborg came out alone they gathered her into the cab and sprang in after her.

Thea sank back into a corner of the back seat and yawned. "Well, I got through, eh?" Her tone was reassuring. "On the whole, I think I've given you gentlemen a pretty lively evening, for one who has no social accomplishments."

"Rather! There was something like a popular uprising at the end of the second act. Archie and I couldn't keep it up as long as the rest of them did. A howl like that ought to show the management which way the wind is blowing. You probably know you were magnificent."

"I thought it went pretty well," she spoke impartially. "I was rather smart to catch his tempo there, at the beginning of the first recitative, when he came in too soon, don't you think? It's tricky in there, without a rehearsal. Oh, I was all right! He took that syncopation too fast in the beginning. Some singers take it fast there—think it sounds more impassioned. That's one way!" She sniffed, and Fred shot a mirthful glance at Archie. Her boastfulness would have been childish in a schoolboy. In the light of what she had done, of the strain they had lived through during the last two hours, it made one laugh,—almost cry. She went on, robustly: "And I didn't feel my dinner, really, Fred. I am hungry again, I'm ashamed to say,—and I forgot to order anything at my hotel."

Fred put his hand on the door. "Where to? You must have food."

"Do you know any quiet place, where I won't be stared at? I've still got make-up on."

"I do. Nice English chop-house on Forty-fourth Street. Nobody there at night but theater people after the show, and a few bachelors." He opened the door and spoke to the driver.

As the car turned, Thea reached across to the front seat and drew Dr. Archie's handkerchief out of his breast pocket.

"This comes to me naturally," she said, rubbing her cheeks and eyebrows. "When I was little I always loved your handkerchiefs because they were silk and smelled of Cologne water. I think they must have been the only really clean handkerchiefs in Moonstone. You were always wiping my face with them, when you met me out in the dust, I remember. Did I never have any?"

"I think you'd nearly always used yours up on your baby brother."

Thea sighed. "Yes, Thor had such a way of getting messy. You say he's a good chauffeur?"

She closed her eyes for a moment as if they were tired. Suddenly she looked up. "Isn't it funny, how we travel in circles? Here you are, still getting me clean, and Fred is still feeding me. I would have died of starvation at that boarding-house on Indiana Avenue if he hadn't taken me out to the Buckingham and filled me up once in a while. What a cavern I was to fill, too. The waiters used to look astonished. I'm still singing on that food."

Fred alighted and gave Thea his arm as they crossed the icy sidewalk. They were taken upstairs in an antiquated lift and found the cheerful chop-room half full of supper parties. An English company playing at the Empire had just come in. The waiters, in red waistcoats, were hurrying about. Fred got a table at the back of the room, in a corner, and urged his waiter to get the oysters on at once.

"Takes a few minutes to open them, sir," the man expostulated.

"Yes, but make it as few as possible, and bring the lady's first. Then grilled chops with kidneys, and salad."

Thea began eating celery stalks at once, from the base to the foliage. "Necker said something nice to me tonight. You might have thought the management would say something, but not they." She looked at Fred from under her blackened lashes. "It WAS a stunt, to jump in and sing that second act without rehearsal. It doesn't sing itself."

Ottenburg was watching her brilliant eyes and her face. She was much handsomer than she had been early in the evening. Excitement of this sort enriched her. It was only under such excitement, he reflected, that she was entirely illuminated, or wholly present. At other times there was something a little cold and empty, like a big room with no people in it. Even in her most genial moods there was a shadow of restlessness, as if she were waiting for something and were exercising the virtue of patience. During dinner she had been as kind as she knew how to be, to him and to Archie, and had given them as much of herself as she could. But, clearly, she knew only one way of being really kind, from the core of her heart out; and there was but one way in which she could give herself to people largely and gladly, spontaneously. Even as a girl she had been at her best in vigorous effort, he remembered; physical effort, when there was no other kind at hand. She could be expansive only in explosions. Old Nathanmeyer had seen it. In the very first song Fred had ever heard her sing, she had unconsciously declared it.

Thea Kronborg turned suddenly from her talk with Archie and peered suspiciously into the corner where Ottenburg sat with folded arms, observing her. "What's the matter with you, Fred? I'm afraid of you when you're quiet,—fortunately you almost never are. What are you thinking about?"

"I was wondering how you got right with the orchestra so quickly, there at first. I had a flash of terror," he replied easily.

She bolted her last oyster and ducked her head. "So had I! I don't know how I did catch it. Desperation, I suppose; same way the Indian babies swim when they're thrown into the river. I HAD to. Now it's over, I'm glad I had to. I learned a whole lot to-night."

Archie, who usually felt that it behooved him to be silent during such discussions, was encouraged by her geniality to venture, "I don't see how you can learn anything in such a turmoil; or how you can keep your mind on it, for that matter."

Thea glanced about the room and suddenly put her hand up to her hair. "Mercy, I've no hat on! Why didn't you tell me? And I seem to be wearing a rumpled dinner dress, with all this paint on my face! I must look like something you picked up on Second Avenue. I hope there are no Colorado reformers about, Dr. Archie. What a dreadful old pair these people must be thinking you! Well, I had to eat." She sniffed the savor of the grill as the waiter uncovered it. "Yes, draught beer, please. No, thank you, Fred, NO champagne.—To go back to your question, Dr. Archie, you can believe I keep my mind on it. That's the whole trick, in so far as stage experience goes; keeping right there every second. If I think of anything else for a flash, I'm gone, done for. But at the same time, one can take things in—with another part of your brain, maybe. It's different from what you get in study, more practical and conclusive. There are some things you learn best in calm, and some in storm. You learn the delivery of a part only before an audience."

"Heaven help us," gasped Ottenburg. "Weren't you hungry, though! It's beautiful to see you eat."

"Glad you like it. Of course I'm hungry. Are you staying over for 'Rheingold' Friday afternoon?"

"My dear Thea,"—Fred lit a cigarette,—"I'm a serious business man now. I have to sell beer. I'm due in Chicago on Wednesday. I'd come back to hear you, but FRICKA is not an alluring part."

"Then you've never heard it well done." She spoke up hotly. "Fat German woman scolding her husband, eh? That's not my idea. Wait till you hear my FRICKA. It's a beautiful part." Thea leaned forward on the table and touched Archie's arm. "You remember, Dr. Archie, how my mother always wore her hair, parted in the middle and done low on her neck behind, so you got the shape of her head and such a calm, white forehead? I wear mine like that for FRICKA. A little more coronet effect, built up a little higher at the sides, but the idea's the same. I think you'll notice it." She turned to Ottenburg reproachfully: "It's noble music, Fred, from the first measure. There's nothing lovelier than the WONNIGER HAUSRATH. It's all such comprehensive sort of music—fateful. Of course, FRICKA KNOWS," Thea ended quietly.

Fred sighed. "There, you've spoiled my itinerary. Now I'll have to come back, of course. Archie, you'd better get busy about seats to-morrow."

"I can get you box seats, somewhere. I know nobody here, and I never ask for any." Thea began hunting among her wraps. "Oh, how funny! I've only these short woolen gloves, and no sleeves. Put on my coat first. Those English people can't make out where you got your lady, she's so made up of contradictions." She rose laughing and plunged her arms into the coat Dr. Archie held for her. As she settled herself into it and buttoned it under her chin, she gave him an old signal with her eyelid. "I'd like to sing another part to-night. This is the sort of evening I fancy, when there's something to do. Let me see: I have to sing in 'Trovatore' Wednesday night, and there are rehearsals for the 'Ring' every day this week. Consider me dead until Saturday, Dr. Archie. I invite you both to dine with me on Saturday night, the day after 'Rheingold.' And Fred must leave early, for I want to talk to you alone. You've been here nearly a week, and I haven't had a serious word with you. TAK FOR MAD, Fred, as the Norwegians say."

VIII.

The "Ring of the Niebelungs" was to be given at the Metropolitan on four successive Friday afternoons. After the first of these performances, Fred Ottenburg went home with Landry for tea. Landry was one of the few public entertainers who own real estate in New York. He lived in a little three-story brick house on Jane Street, in Greenwich Village, which had been left to him by the same aunt who paid for his musical education.

Landry was born, and spent the first fifteen years of his life, on a rocky Connecticut farm not far from Cos Cob. His father was an ignorant, violent man, a bungling farmer and a brutal husband. The farmhouse, dilapidated and damp, stood in a hollow beside a marshy pond. Oliver had worked hard while he lived at home, although he was never clean or warm in winter and had wretched food all the year round. His spare, dry figure, his prominent larynx, and the peculiar red of his face and hands belonged to the choreboy he had never outgrown. It was as if the farm, knowing he would escape from it as early as he could, had ground its mark on him deep. When he was fifteen Oliver ran away and went to live with his Catholic aunt, on Jane Street, whom his mother was never allowed to visit. The priest of St. Joseph's Parish discovered that he had a voice.

Landry had an affection for the house on Jane Street, where he had first learned what cleanliness and order and courtesy were. When his aunt died he had the place done over, got an Irish housekeeper, and lived there with a great many beautiful things he had collected. His living expenses were never large, but he could not restrain himself from buying graceful and useless objects. He was a collector for much the same reason that he was a Catholic, and he was a Catholic chiefly because his father used to sit in the kitchen and read aloud to his hired men disgusting "exposures" of the Roman Church, enjoying equally the hideous stories and the outrage to his wife's feelings.

At first Landry bought books; then rugs, drawings, china. He had a beautiful collection of old French and Spanish fans. He kept them in an escritoire he had brought from Spain, but there were always a few of them lying about in his sitting-room.

While Landry and his guest were waiting for the tea to be brought, Ottenburg took up one of these fans from the low marble mantel-shelf and opened it in the firelight. One side was painted with a pearly sky and floating clouds. On the other was a formal garden where an elegant shepherdess with a mask and crook was fleeing on high heels from a satin-coated shepherd.

"You ought not to keep these things about, like this, Oliver. The dust from your grate must get at them."

"It does, but I get them to enjoy them, not to have them. They're pleasant to glance at and to play with at odd times like this, when one is waiting for tea or something."

Fred smiled. The idea of Landry stretched out before his fire playing with his fans, amused him. Mrs. McGinnis brought the tea and put it before the hearth: old teacups that were velvety to the touch and a pot-bellied silver cream pitcher of an Early Georgian pattern, which was always brought, though Landry took rum.

Fred drank his tea walking about, examining Landry's sumptuous writing-table in the alcove and the Boucher drawing in red chalk over the mantel. "I don't see how you can stand this place without a heroine. It would give me a raging thirst for gallantries."

Landry was helping himself to a second cup of tea. "Works quite the other way with me. It consoles me for the lack of her. It's just feminine enough to be pleasant to return to. Not any more tea? Then sit down and play for me. I'm always playing for other people, and I never have a chance to sit here quietly and listen."

Ottenburg opened the piano and began softly to boom forth the shadowy introduction to the opera they had just heard. "Will that do?" he asked jokingly. "I can't seem to get it out of my head."

"Oh, excellently! Thea told me it was quite wonderful, the way you can do Wagner scores on the piano. So few people can give one any idea of the music. Go ahead, as long as you like. I can smoke, too." Landry flattened himself out on his cushions and abandoned himself to ease with the circumstance of one who has never grown quite accustomed to ease.

Ottenburg played on, as he happened to remember. He understood now why Thea wished him to hear her in "Rheingold." It had been clear to him as soon as FRICKA rose from sleep and looked out over the young world, stretching one white arm toward the new

Gotterburg shining on the heights. "WOTAN! GEMAHL! ERWACHE!" She was pure Scandinavian, this FRICKA: "Swedish summer"! he remembered old Mr. Nathanmeyer's phrase. She had wished him to see her because she had a distinct kind of loveliness for this part, a shining beauty like the light of sunset on distant sails. She seemed to take on the look of immortal loveliness, the youth of the golden apples, the shining body and the shining mind. FRICKA had been a jealous spouse to him for so long that he had forgot she meant wisdom before she meant domestic order, and that, in any event, she was always a goddess. The FRICKA of that afternoon was so clear and sunny, so nobly conceived, that she made a whole atmosphere about herself and quite redeemed from shabbiness the helplessness and unscrupulousness of the gods. Her reproaches to WOTAN were the pleadings of a tempered mind, a consistent sense of beauty. In the long silences of her part, her shining presence was a visible complement to the discussion of the orchestra. As the themes which were to help in weaving the drama to its end first came vaguely upon the ear, one saw their import and tendency in the face of this clearest-visioned of the gods.

In the scene between FRICKA and WOTAN, Ottenburg stopped. "I can't seem to get the voices, in there."

Landry chuckled. "Don't try. I know it well enough. I expect I've been over that with her a thousand times. I was playing for her almost every day when she was first working on it. When she begins with a part she's hard to work with: so slow you'd think she was stupid if you didn't know her. Of course she blames it all on her accompanist. It goes on like that for weeks sometimes. This did. She kept shaking her head and staring and looking gloomy. All at once, she got her line—it usually comes suddenly, after stretches of not getting anywhere at all—and after that it kept changing and clearing. As she worked her voice into it, it got more and more of that 'gold' quality that makes her FRICKA so different."

Fred began FRICKA'S first aria again. "It's certainly different. Curious how she does it. Such a beautiful idea, out of a part that's always been so ungrateful. She's a lovely thing, but she was never so beautiful as that, really. Nobody is." He repeated the loveliest phrase. "How does she manage it, Landry? You've worked with her."

Landry drew cherishingly on the last cigarette he meant to permit himself before singing. "Oh, it's a question of a big personality—and all that goes with it. Brains, of course. Imagination, of course. But the important thing is that she was born full of color, with a rich personality. That's a gift of the gods, like a fine nose. You have it, or you haven't. Against it, intelligence and musicianship and habits of industry don't count at all. Singers are a conventional race. When Thea was studying in Berlin the other girls were mortally afraid of her. She has a pretty rough hand with women, dull ones, and she could be rude, too! The girls used to call her DIE WOLFIN."

Fred thrust his hands into his pockets and leaned back against the piano. "Of course, even a stupid woman could get effects with such machinery: such a voice and body and face. But they couldn't possibly belong to a stupid woman, could they?"

Landry shook his head. "It's personality; that's as near as you can come to it. That's what constitutes real equipment. What she does is interesting because she does it. Even the things she discards are suggestive. I regret some of them. Her conceptions are colored in so many different ways. You've heard her ELIZABETH? Wonderful, isn't it? She was working on that part years ago when her mother was ill. I could see her anxiety and grief getting more and more into the part. The last act is heart-breaking. It's as homely as a country prayer meeting: might be any lonely woman getting ready to die. It's full of the thing every plain creature finds out for himself, but that never gets written down. It's unconscious memory, maybe; inherited memory, like folk-music. I call it personality."

Fred laughed, and turning to the piano began coaxing the FRICKA music again. "Call it anything you like, my boy. I have a name for it myself, but I shan't tell you." He looked over his shoulder at Landry, stretched out by the fire. "You have a great time watching her, don't you?"

"Oh, yes!" replied Landry simply. "I'm not interested in much that goes on in New York. Now, if you'll excuse me, I'll have to dress." He rose with a reluctant sigh. "Can I get you anything? Some whiskey?"

"Thank you, no. I'll amuse myself here. I don't often get a chance at a good piano when I'm away from home. You haven't had this one long, have you? Action's a bit stiff. I say," he stopped Landry in the doorway, "has Thea ever been down here?"

Landry turned back. "Yes. She came several times when I had erysipelas. I was a nice mess, with two nurses. She brought down some inside window-boxes, planted with crocuses and things. Very cheering, only I couldn't see them or her."

"Didn't she like your place?"

"She thought she did, but I fancy it was a good deal cluttered up for her taste. I could hear her pacing about like something in a cage. She pushed the piano back against the wall and the chairs into corners, and she broke my amber elephant." Landry took a yellow object some four inches high from one of his low bookcases. "You can see where his leg is glued on,—a souvenir. Yes, he's lemon amber, very fine."

Landry disappeared behind the curtains and in a moment Fred heard the wheeze of an atomizer. He put the amber elephant on the piano beside him and seemed to get a great deal of amusement out of the beast.

IX.

When Archie and Ottenburg dined with Thea on Saturday evening, they were served downstairs in the hotel dining-room, but they were to have their coffee in her own apartment. As they were going up in the elevator after dinner, Fred turned suddenly to Thea. "And why, please, did you break Landry's amber elephant?"

She looked guilty and began to laugh. "Hasn't he got over that yet? I didn't really mean to break it. I was perhaps careless. His things are so over-petted that I was tempted to be careless with a lot of them."

"How can you be so heartless, when they're all he has in the world?"

"He has me. I'm a great deal of diversion for him; all he needs. There," she said as she opened the door into her own hall, "I shouldn't have said that before the elevator boy."

"Even an elevator boy couldn't make a scandal about Oliver. He's such a catnip man."

Dr. Archie laughed, but Thea, who seemed suddenly to have thought of something annoying, repeated blankly, "Catnip man?"

"Yes, he lives on catnip, and rum tea. But he's not the only one. You are like an eccentric old woman I know in Boston, who goes about in the spring feeding catnip to street cats. You dispense it to a lot of fellows. Your pull seems to be more with men than with women, you know; with seasoned men, about my age, or older. Even on Friday afternoon I kept running into them, old boys I hadn't seen for years, thin at the part and thick at the girth, until I stood still in the draft and held my hair on. They're always there; I hear them talking about you in the smoking room. Probably we don't get to the point of apprehending anything good until we're about forty. Then, in the light of what is going, and of what, God help us! is coming, we arrive at understanding."

"I don't see why people go to the opera, anyway,—serious people." She spoke discontentedly. "I suppose they get something, or think they do. Here's the coffee. There, please," she directed the waiter. Going to the table she began to pour the coffee, standing. She wore a white dress trimmed with crystals which had rattled a good deal during dinner, as all her movements had been impatient and nervous, and she had twisted the dark velvet rose at her girdle until it looked rumpled and weary. She poured the coffee as if it were a ceremony in which she did not believe. "Can you make anything of Fred's nonsense, Dr. Archie?" she asked, as he came to take his cup.

Fred approached her. "My nonsense is all right. The same brand has gone with you before. It's you who won't be jollied. What's the matter? You have something on your mind."

"I've a good deal. Too much to be an agreeable hostess." She turned quickly away from the coffee and sat down on the piano bench, facing the two men. "For one thing, there's a change in the cast for Friday afternoon. They're going to let me sing SIEGLINDE." Her frown did not conceal the pleasure with which she made this announcement.

"Are you going to keep us dangling about here forever, Thea? Archie and I are supposed to have other things to do." Fred looked at her with an excitement quite as apparent as her own.

"Here I've been ready to sing SIEGLINDE for two years, kept in torment, and now it comes off within two weeks, just when I want to be seeing something of Dr. Archie. I don't know what their plans are down there. After Friday they may let me cool for several weeks, and they may rush me. I suppose it depends somewhat on how things go Friday afternoon."

"Oh, they'll go fast enough! That's better suited to your voice than anything you've sung here. That gives you every opportunity I've waited for." Ottenburg crossed the room and standing beside her began to play "DU BIST DER LENZ."

With a violent movement Thea caught his wrists and pushed his hands away from the keys.

"Fred, can't you be serious? A thousand things may happen between this and Friday to put me out. Something will happen. If that part were sung well, as well as it ought to be, it would be one of the most beautiful things in the world. That's why it never is sung right, and never will be." She clenched her hands and opened them despairingly, looking out of the open window. "It's inaccessibly beautiful!" she brought out sharply.

Fred and Dr. Archie watched her. In a moment she turned back to them. "It's impossible to sing a part like that well for the first time, except for the sort who will never sing it any better. Everything hangs on that first night, and that's bound to be bad. There you are," she shrugged impatiently. "For one thing, they change the cast at the eleventh hour and then rehearse the life out of me."

Ottenburg put down his cup with exaggerated care. "Still, you really want to do it, you know."

"Want to?" she repeated indignantly; "of course I want to! If this were only next Thursday night—But between now and Friday I'll do nothing but fret away my strength. Oh, I'm not saying I don't need the rehearsals! But I don't need them strung out through a week. That system's well enough for phlegmatic singers; it only drains me. Every single feature of operatic routine is detrimental to me. I usually go on like a horse that's been fixed to lose a race. I have to work hard to do my worst, let alone my best. I wish you could hear me sing well, once," she turned to Fred defiantly; "I have, a few times in my life, when there was nothing to gain by it."

Fred approached her again and held out his hand. "I recall my instructions, and now I'll leave you to fight it out with Archie. He can't possibly represent managerial stupidity to you as I seem to have a gift for doing."

As he smiled down at her, his good humor, his good wishes, his understanding, embarrassed her and recalled her to herself. She kept her seat, still holding his hand. "All the same, Fred, isn't it too bad, that there are so many things—" She broke off with a shake of the head.

"My dear girl, if I could bridge over the agony between now and Friday for you—But you know the rules of the game; why torment yourself? You saw the other night that you had the part under your thumb. Now walk, sleep, play with Archie, keep your tiger hungry, and she'll spring all right on Friday. I'll be there to see her, and there'll be more than I, I suspect. Harsanyi's on the Wilhelm der Grosse; gets in on Thursday."

"Harsanyi?" Thea's eye lighted. "I haven't seen him for years. We always miss each other." She paused, hesitating. "Yes, I should like that. But he'll be busy, maybe?"

"He gives his first concert at Carnegie Hall, week after next. Better send him a box if you can."

"Yes, I'll manage it." Thea took his hand again. "Oh, I should like that, Fred!" she added impulsively. "Even if I were put out, he'd get the idea,"—she threw back her head,—"for there is an idea!"

"Which won't penetrate here," he tapped his brow and began to laugh. "You are an ungrateful huzzy, COMME LES AUTRES!"

Thea detained him as he turned away. She pulled a flower out of a bouquet on the piano and absently drew the stem through the lapel of his coat. "I shall be walking in the Park to-morrow afternoon, on the reservoir path, between four and five, if you care to join me. You know that after Harsanyi I'd rather please you than anyone else. You know a lot, but he knows even more than you."

"Thank you. Don't try to analyze it. SCHLAFEN SIE WOHL!" he kissed her fingers and waved from the door, closing it behind him.

"He's the right sort, Thea." Dr. Archie looked warmly after his disappearing friend. "I've always hoped you'd make it up with Fred."

"Well, haven't I? Oh, marry him, you mean! Perhaps it may come about, some day. Just at present he's not in the marriage market any more than I am, is he?"

"No, I suppose not. It's a damned shame that a man like Ottenburg should be tied up as he is, wasting all the best years of his life. A woman with general paresis ought to be legally dead."

"Don't let us talk about Fred's wife, please. He had no business to get into such a mess, and he had no business to stay in it. He's always been a softy where women were concerned."

"Most of us are, I'm afraid," Dr. Archie admitted meekly.

"Too much light in here, isn't there? Tires one's eyes. The stage lights are hard on mine." Thea began turning them out. "We'll leave the little one, over the piano." She sank down by Archie on the deep sofa. "We two have so much to talk about that we keep away from it altogether; have you noticed? We don't even nibble the edges. I wish we had Landry here to-night to play for us. He's very comforting."

"I'm afraid you don't have enough personal life, outside your work, Thea." The doctor looked at her anxiously.

She smiled at him with her eyes half closed. "My dear doctor, I don't have any. Your work becomes your personal life. You are not much good until it does. It's like being woven into a big web. You can't pull away, because all your little tendrils are woven into the picture. It takes you up, and uses you, and spins you out; and that is your life. Not much else can happen to you."

"Didn't you think of marrying, several years ago?"

"You mean Nordquist? Yes; but I changed my mind. We had been singing a good deal together. He's a splendid creature."

"Were you much in love with him, Thea?" the doctor asked hopefully.

She smiled again. "I don't think I know just what that expression means. I've never been able to find out. I think I was in love with you when I was little, but not with any one since then. There are a great many ways of caring for people. It's not, after all, a simple state, like measles or tonsilitis. Nordquist is a taking sort of man. He and I were out in a rowboat once in a terrible storm. The lake was fed by glaciers,—ice water,—and we couldn't have swum a stroke if the boat had filled. If we hadn't both been strong and kept our heads, we'd have gone down. We pulled for every ounce there was in us, and we just got off with our lives. We were always being thrown together like that, under some kind of pressure. Yes, for a while I thought he would make everything right." She paused and sank back, resting her head on a cushion, pressing her eyelids down with her fingers. "You see," she went on abruptly, "he had a wife and two children. He hadn't lived with her for several years, but when she heard that he wanted to marry again, she began to make trouble. He earned a good deal of money, but he was careless and always wretchedly in debt. He came to me one day and told me he thought his wife would settle for a hundred thousand marks and consent to a divorce. I got very angry and sent him away. Next day he came back and said he thought she'd take fifty thousand."

Dr. Archie drew away from her, to the end of the sofa.

"Good God, Thea,"—He ran his handkerchief over his forehead. "What sort of people—" He stopped and shook his head.

Thea rose and stood beside him, her hand on his shoulder. "That's exactly how it struck me," she said quietly. "Oh, we have things in common, things that go away back, under everything. You understand, of course. Nordquist didn't. He thought I wasn't willing to part with the money. I couldn't let myself buy him from Fru Nordquist, and he couldn't see why. He had always thought I was close about money, so he attributed it to that. I am careful,"—she ran her arm through Archie's and when he rose began to walk about the room with him. "I can't be careless with money. I began the world on six hundred dollars, and it was the price of a man's life. Ray Kennedy had worked hard and been sober and denied himself, and when he died he had six hundred dollars to show for it. I always measure things by that six hundred dollars, just as I measure high buildings by the Moonstone standpipe. There are standards we can't get away from."

Dr. Archie took her hand. "I don't believe we should be any happier if we did get away from them. I think it gives you some of your poise, having that anchor. You look," glancing down at her head and shoulders, "sometimes so like your mother."

"Thank you. You couldn't say anything nicer to me than that. On Friday afternoon, didn't you think?"

"Yes, but at other times, too. I love to see it. Do you know what I thought about that first night when I heard you sing? I kept remembering the night I took care of you when you had pneumonia, when you were ten years old. You were a terribly sick child, and I was a country doctor without much experience. There were no oxygen tanks about then. You pretty nearly slipped away from me. If you had—"

Thea dropped her head on his shoulder. "I'd have saved myself and you a lot of trouble, wouldn't I? Dear Dr. Archie!" she murmured.

"As for me, life would have been a pretty bleak stretch, with you left out." The doctor took one of the crystal pendants that hung from her shoulder and looked into it thoughtfully.

"I guess I'm a romantic old fellow, underneath. And you've always been my romance. Those years when you were growing up were my happiest. When I dream about you, I always see you as a little girl."

They paused by the open window. "Do you? Nearly all my dreams, except those about breaking down on the stage or missing trains, are about Moonstone. You tell me the old house has been pulled down, but it stands in my mind, every stick and timber. In my sleep I go all about it, and look in the right drawers and cupboards for everything. I often dream that I'm hunting for my rubbers in that pile of overshoes that was always under the hatrack in the hall. I pick up every overshoe and know whose it is, but I can't find my own. Then the school bell begins to ring and I begin to cry. That's the house I rest in when I'm tired. All the old furniture and the worn spots in the carpet—it rests my mind to go over them."

They were looking out of the window. Thea kept his arm. Down on the river four battleships were anchored in line, brilliantly lighted, and launches were coming and going, bringing the men ashore. A searchlight from one of the ironclads was playing on the great headland up the river, where it makes its first resolute turn. Overhead the night-blue sky was intense and clear.

"There's so much that I want to tell you," she said at last, "and it's hard to explain. My life is full of jealousies and disappointments, you know. You get to hating people who do contemptible work and who get on just as well as you do. There are many disappointments in my profession, and bitter, bitter contempts!" Her face hardened, and looked much older. "If you love the good thing vitally, enough to give up for it all that one must give up for it, then you must hate the cheap thing just as hard. I tell you, there is such a thing as creative hate! A contempt that drives you through fire, makes you risk everything and lose everything, makes you a long sight better than you ever knew you could be." As she glanced at Dr. Archie's face, Thea stopped short and turned her own face away. Her eyes followed the path of the searchlight up the river and rested upon the illumined headland.

"You see," she went on more calmly, "voices are accidental things. You find plenty of good voices in common women, with common minds and common hearts. Look at that woman who sang ORTRUDE with me last week. She's new here and the people are wild about her. 'Such a beautiful volume of tone!' they say. I give you my word she's as stupid as an owl and as coarse as a pig, and any one who knows anything about singing would see that in an instant. Yet she's quite as popular as Necker, who's a great artist. How can I get much satisfaction out of the enthusiasm of a house that likes her atrociously bad performance at the same time that it pretends to like mine? If they like her, then they ought to hiss me off the stage. We stand for things that are irreconcilable, absolutely. You can't try to do things right and not despise the people who do them wrong. How can I be indifferent? If that doesn't matter, then nothing matters. Well, sometimes I've come home as I did the other night when you first saw me, so full of bitterness that it was as if my mind were full of daggers. And I've gone to sleep and wakened up in the Kohlers' garden, with the pigeons and the white rabbits, so happy! And that saves me." She sat down on the piano bench. Archie thought she had forgotten all about him, until she called his name. Her voice was soft now, and wonderfully sweet. It seemed to come from somewhere deep within her, there were such strong vibrations in it. "You see, Dr. Archie, what one really strives for in art is not the sort of thing you are likely to find when you drop in for a performance at the opera. What one strives for is so far away, so deep, so beautiful"—she lifted her shoulders with a long breath, folded her hands in her lap and sat looking at him with a resignation that made her face noble,—"that there's nothing one can say about it, Dr. Archie."

Without knowing very well what it was all about, Archie was passionately stirred for her. "I've always believed in you, Thea; always believed," he muttered.

She smiled and closed her eyes. "They save me: the old things, things like the Kohlers' garden. They are in everything I do."

"In what you sing, you mean?"

"Yes. Not in any direct way,"—she spoke hurriedly,—"the light, the color, the feeling. Most of all the feeling. It comes in when I'm working on a part, like the smell of a garden coming in at the window. I try all the new things, and then go back to the old. Perhaps my feelings were stronger then. A child's attitude toward everything is an artist's attitude. I am more or less of an artist now, but then I was nothing else. When I went with you to Chicago that first time, I carried with me the essentials, the foundation of all I do now. The point to which I could go was scratched in me then. I haven't reached it yet, by a long way."

Archie had a swift flash of memory. Pictures passed before him. "You mean," he asked wonderingly, "that you knew then that you were so gifted?"

Thea looked up at him and smiled. "Oh, I didn't know anything! Not enough to ask you for my trunk when I needed it. But you see, when I set out from Moonstone with you, I had had a rich, romantic past. I had lived a long, eventful life, and an artist's life, every hour of it. Wagner says, in his most beautiful opera, that art is only a way of remembering youth. And the older we grow the more precious it seems to us, and the more richly we can present that memory. When we've got it all out,—the last, the finest thrill of it, the brightest hope of it,"—she lifted her hand above her head and dropped it,—"then we stop. We do nothing but repeat after that. The stream has reached the level of its source. That's our measure."

There was a long, warm silence. Thea was looking hard at the floor, as if she were seeing down through years and years, and her old friend stood watching her bent head. His look was one with which he used to watch her long ago, and which, even in thinking about her, had become a habit of his face. It was full of solicitude, and a kind of secret gratitude, as if to thank her for some inexpressible pleasure of the heart. Thea turned presently toward the piano and began softly to waken an old air:—

"Ca' the yowes to the knowes,
Ca' them where the heather grows,
Ca' them where the burnie rowes,
My bonnie dear-ie."

Archie sat down and shaded his eyes with his hand. She turned her head and spoke to him over her shoulder. "Come on, you know the words better than I. That's right."

"We'll gae down by Clouden's side, Through the hazels spreading wide, O'er the waves that sweetly glide, To the moon sae clearly. Ghaist nor bogle shalt thou fear, Thou'rt to love and Heav'n sae dear, Nocht of ill may come thee near, My bonnie dear-ie!"

"We can get on without Landry. Let's try it again, I have all the words now. Then we'll have 'Sweet Afton.' Come: 'CA' THE YOWES TO THE KNOWES'—"

X.

Ottenburg dismissed his taxicab at the 91st Street entrance of the Park and floundered across the drive through a wild spring snowstorm. When he reached the reservoir path he saw Thea ahead of him, walking rapidly against the wind. Except for that one figure, the path was deserted. A flock of gulls were hovering over the reservoir, seeming bewildered by the driving currents of snow that whirled above the black water and then disappeared within it. When he had almost overtaken Thea, Fred called to her, and she turned and waited for him with her back to the wind. Her hair and furs were powdered with snowflakes, and she looked like some rich-pelted animal, with warm blood, that had run in out of the woods. Fred laughed as he took her hand.

"No use asking how you do. You surely needn't feel much anxiety about Friday, when you can look like this."

She moved close to the iron fence to make room for him beside her, and faced the wind again. "Oh, I'm WELL enough, in so far as that goes. But I'm not lucky about stage appearances. I'm easily upset, and the most perverse things happen."

"What's the matter? Do you still get nervous?"

"Of course I do. I don't mind nerves so much as getting numbed," Thea muttered, sheltering her face for a moment with her muff. "I'm under a spell, you know, hoodooed. It's the thing I WANT to do that I can never do. Any other effects I can get easily enough."

"Yes, you get effects, and not only with your voice. That's where you have it over all the rest of them; you're as much at home on the stage as you were down in Panther Canyon—as if you'd just been let out of a cage. Didn't you get some of your ideas down there?"

Thea nodded. "Oh, yes! For heroic parts, at least. Out of the rocks, out of the dead people. You mean the idea of standing up under things, don't you, meeting catastrophe? No fussiness. Seems to me they must have been a reserved, somber people, with only a muscular language, all their movements for a purpose; simple, strong, as if they were dealing with fate bare-handed." She put her gloved fingers on Fred's arm. "I don't know how I can ever thank you enough. I don't know if I'd ever have got anywhere without Panther Canyon. How did you know that was the one thing to do for me? It's the sort of thing nobody ever helps one to, in this world. One can learn how to sing, but no singing teacher can give anybody what I got down there. How did you know?"

"I didn't know. Anything else would have done as well. It was your creative hour. I knew you were getting a lot, but I didn't realize how much."

Thea walked on in silence. She seemed to be thinking.

"Do you know what they really taught me?" she came out suddenly. "They taught me the inevitable hardness of human life. No artist gets far who doesn't know that. And you can't know it with your mind. You have to realize it in your body, somehow; deep. It's an animal sort of feeling. I sometimes think it's the strongest of all. Do you know what I'm driving at?"

"I think so. Even your audiences feel it, vaguely: that you've sometime or other faced things that make you different."

Thea turned her back to the wind, wiping away the snow that clung to her brows and lashes. "Ugh!" she exclaimed; "no matter how long a breath you have, the storm has a longer. I haven't signed for next season, yet, Fred. I'm holding out for a big contract: forty performances. Necker won't be able to do much next winter. It's going to be one of those between seasons; the old singers are too old, and the new ones are too new. They might as well risk me as anybody. So I want good terms. The next five or six years are going to be my best."

"You'll get what you demand, if you are uncompromising. I'm safe in congratulating you now."

Thea laughed. "It's a little early. I may not get it at all. They don't seem to be breaking their necks to meet me. I can go back to Dresden."

As they turned the curve and walked westward they got the wind from the side, and talking was easier.

Fred lowered his collar and shook the snow from his shoulders. "Oh, I don't mean on the contract particularly. I congratulate you on what you can do, Thea, and on all that lies behind what you do. On the life that's led up to it, and on being able to care so much. That, after all, is the unusual thing."

She looked at him sharply, with a certain apprehension. "Care? Why shouldn't I care? If I didn't, I'd be in a bad way. What else have I got?" She stopped with a challenging interrogation, but Ottenburg did not reply. "You mean," she persisted, "that you don't care as much as you used to?"

"I care about your success, of course." Fred fell into a slower pace. Thea felt at once that he was talking seriously and had dropped the tone of half-ironical exaggeration he had used with her of late years. "And I'm grateful to you for what you demand from yourself, when you might get off so easily. You demand more and more all the time, and you'll do more and more. One is grateful to anybody for that; it makes life in general a little less sordid. But as a matter of fact, I'm not much interested in how anybody sings anything."

"That's too bad of you, when I'm just beginning to see what is worth doing, and how I want to do it!" Thea spoke in an injured tone.

"That's what I congratulate you on. That's the great difference between your kind and the rest of us. It's how long you're able to keep it up that tells the story. When you needed enthusiasm from the outside, I was able to give it to you. Now you must let me withdraw."

"I'm not tying you, am I?" she flashed out. "But withdraw to what? What do you want?"

Fred shrugged. "I might ask you, What have I got? I want things that wouldn't interest you; that you probably wouldn't understand. For one thing, I want a son to bring up."

"I can understand that. It seems to me reasonable. Have you also found somebody you want to marry?"

"Not particularly." They turned another curve, which brought the wind to their backs, and they walked on in comparative calm, with the snow blowing past them. "It's not your fault, Thea, but I've had you too much in my mind. I've not given myself a fair chance in other directions. I was in Rome when you and Nordquist were there. If that had kept up, it might have cured me."

"It might have cured a good many things," remarked Thea grimly.

Fred nodded sympathetically and went on. "In my library in St. Louis, over the fireplace, I have a property spear I had copied from one in Venice,—oh, years ago, after you first went abroad, while you were studying. You'll probably be singing BRUNNHILDE pretty soon now, and I'll send it on to you, if I may. You can take it and its history for what they're worth. But I'm nearly forty years old, and I've served my turn. You've done what I hoped for you, what I was honestly willing to lose you for—then. I'm older now, and I think I was an ass. I wouldn't do it again if I had the chance, not much! But I'm not sorry. It takes a great many people to make one—BRUNNHILDE."

Thea stopped by the fence and looked over into the black choppiness on which the snowflakes fell and disappeared with magical rapidity. Her face was both angry and troubled. "So you really feel I've been ungrateful. I thought you sent me out to get something. I didn't know you wanted me to bring in something easy. I thought you wanted something—" She took a deep breath and shrugged her shoulders. "But there! nobody on God's earth wants it, REALLY! If one other person wanted it,"—she thrust her hand out before him and clenched it,—"my God, what I could do!"

Fred laughed dismally. "Even in my ashes I feel myself pushing you! How can anybody help it? My dear girl, can't you see that anybody else who wanted it as you do would be your rival, your deadliest danger? Can't you see that it's your great good fortune that other people can't care about it so much?"

But Thea seemed not to take in his protest at all. She went on vindicating herself. "It's taken me a long while to do anything, of course, and I've only begun to see daylight. But anything good is—expensive. It hasn't seemed long. I've always felt responsible to you."

Fred looked at her face intently, through the veil of snowflakes, and shook his head. "To me? You are a truthful woman, and you don't mean to lie to me. But after the one responsibility you do feel, I doubt if you've enough left to feel responsible to God! Still, if you've ever in an idle hour fooled yourself with thinking I had anything to do with it, Heaven knows I'm grateful."

"Even if I'd married Nordquist," Thea went on, turning down the path again, "there would have been something left out. There always is. In a way, I've always been married to you. I'm not very flexible; never was and never shall be. You caught me young. I could never have that over again. One can't, after one begins to know anything. But I look back on it. My life hasn't been a gay one, any more than yours. If I shut things out from you, you shut them out from me. We've been a help and a hindrance to each other. I guess it's always that way, the good and the bad all mixed up. There's only one thing that's all beautiful—and always beautiful! That's why my interest keeps up."

"Yes, I know." Fred looked sidewise at the outline of her head against the thickening atmosphere. "And you give one the impression that that is enough. I've gradually, gradually given you up."

"See, the lights are coming out." Thea pointed to where they flickered, flashes of violet through the gray tree-tops. Lower down the globes along the drives were becoming a pale lemon color. "Yes, I don't see why anybody wants to marry an artist, anyhow. I remember Ray Kennedy used to say he didn't see how any woman could marry a gambler, for she would only be marrying what the game left." She shook her shoulders impatiently. "Who marries who is a small matter, after all. But I hope I can bring back your interest in my work. You've cared longer and more than anybody else, and I'd like to have somebody human to make a report to once in a while. You can send me your spear. I'll do my best. If you're not interested, I'll do my best anyhow. I've only a few friends, but I can lose every one of them, if it has to be. I learned how to lose when my mother died.—We must hurry now. My taxi must be waiting."

The blue light about them was growing deeper and darker, and the falling snow and the faint trees had become violet. To the south, over Broadway, there was an orange reflection in the clouds. Motors and carriage lights flashed by on the drive below the reservoir path, and the air was strident with horns and shrieks from the whistles of the mounted policemen.

Fred gave Thea his arm as they descended from the embankment. "I guess you'll never manage to lose me or Archie, Thea. You do pick up queer ones. But loving you is a heroic discipline. It wears a man out. Tell me one thing: could I have kept you, once, if I'd put on every screw?"

Thea hurried him along, talking rapidly, as if to get it over. "You might have kept me in misery for a while, perhaps. I don't know. I have to think well of myself, to work. You could have made it hard. I'm not ungrateful. I was a difficult proposition to deal with. I understand now, of course. Since you didn't tell me the truth in the beginning, you couldn't very well turn back after I'd set my head. At least, if you'd been the sort who could, you wouldn't have had to,—for I'd not have cared a button for that sort, even then." She stopped beside a car that waited at the curb and gave him her hand. "There. We part friends?"

Fred looked at her. "You know. Ten years."

"I'm not ungrateful," Thea repeated as she got into her cab.

"Yes," she reflected, as the taxi cut into the Park carriage road, "we don't get fairy tales in this world, and he has, after all, cared more and longer than anybody else." It was dark outside now, and the light from the lamps along the drive flashed into the cab. The snowflakes hovered like swarms of white bees about the globes.

Thea sat motionless in one corner staring out of the window at the cab lights that wove in and out among the trees, all seeming to be bent upon joyous courses. Taxicabs were still new in New York, and the theme of popular minstrelsy. Landry had sung her a ditty he heard in some theater on Third Avenue, about:

"But there passed him a bright-eyed taxi With the girl of his heart inside."

Almost inaudibly Thea began to hum the air, though she was thinking of something serious, something that had touched her deeply. At the beginning of the season, when she was not singing often, she had gone one afternoon to hear Paderewski's recital. In front of her sat an old German couple, evidently poor people who had made sacrifices to pay for their excellent seats. Their intelligent enjoyment of the music, and their friendliness with each other, had interested her more than anything on the programme. When the pianist began a lovely melody in the first movement of the Beethoven D minor sonata, the old lady put out her plump hand and touched her husband's sleeve and they looked at each other in recognition. They both wore glasses, but such a look! Like forget-menots, and so full of happy recollections. Thea wanted to put her arms around them and ask them how they had been able to keep a feeling like that, like a nosegay in a glass of water.

XI.

Dr. Archie saw nothing of Thea during the following week. After several fruitless efforts, he succeeded in getting a word with her over the telephone, but she sounded so distracted and driven that he was glad to say good-night and hang up the instrument. There were, she told him, rehearsals not only for "Walkure," but also for "Gotterdammerung," in which she was to sing WALTRAUTE two weeks later.

On Thursday afternoon Thea got home late, after an exhausting rehearsal. She was in no happy frame of mind. Madame Necker, who had been very gracious to her that night when she went on to complete Gloeckler's performance of SIEGLINDE, had, since Thea was cast to sing the part instead of Gloeckler in the production of the "Ring," been chilly and disapproving, distinctly hostile. Thea had always felt that she and Necker stood for the same sort of endeavor, and that Necker recognized it and had a cordial feeling for her. In Germany she had several times sung BRANGAENA to Necker's ISOLDE, and the older artist had let her know that she thought she sang it beautifully. It was a bitter disappointment to find that the approval of so honest an artist as Necker could not stand the test of any significant recognition by the management. Madame Necker was forty, and her voice was failing just when her powers were at their height. Every fresh young voice was an enemy, and this one was accompanied by gifts which she could not fail to recognize.

Thea had her dinner sent up to her apartment, and it was a very poor one. She tasted the soup and then indignantly put on her wraps to go out and hunt a dinner. As she was going to the elevator, she had to admit that she was behaving foolishly. She took off her hat and coat and ordered another dinner. When it arrived, it was no better than the first. There was even a burnt match under the milk toast. She had a sore throat, which made swallowing painful and boded ill for the morrow. Although she had been speaking in whispers all day to save her throat, she now perversely summoned the housekeeper and demanded an account of some laundry that had been lost. The housekeeper was indifferent and impertinent, and Thea got angry and scolded violently. She knew it was very bad for her to get into a rage just before bedtime, and after the housekeeper left she realized that for ten dollars' worth of underclothing she had been unfitting herself for a performance which might eventually mean many thousands. The best thing now was to stop reproaching herself for her lack of sense, but she was too tired to control her thoughts.

While she was undressing—Therese was brushing out her SIEGLINDE wig in the trunk-room—she went on chiding herself bitterly. "And how am I ever going to get to sleep in this state?" she kept asking herself. "If I don't sleep, I'll be perfectly worthless to-morrow. I'll go down there to-morrow and make a fool of myself. If I'd let that laundry alone with whatever nigger has stolen it—WHY did I undertake to reform the management of this hotel to-night? After to-morrow I could pack up and leave the place. There's the Phillamon—I liked the rooms there better, anyhow—and the Umberto—" She began going over the advantages and disadvantages of different apartment hotels. Suddenly she checked herself. "What AM I doing this for? I can't move into another hotel to-night. I'll keep this up till morning. I shan't sleep a wink."

Should she take a hot bath, or shouldn't she? Sometimes it relaxed her, and sometimes it roused her and fairly put her beside herself. Between the conviction that she must sleep and the fear that she couldn't, she hung paralyzed. When she looked at her bed, she shrank from it in every nerve. She was much more afraid of it than she had ever been of the stage of any opera house. It yawned before her like the sunken road at Waterloo.

She rushed into her bathroom and locked the door. She would risk the bath, and defer the encounter with the bed a little longer. She lay in the bath half an hour. The warmth of the water penetrated to her bones, induced pleasant reflections and a feeling of well-being. It was very nice to have Dr. Archie in New York, after all, and to see him get so much satisfaction out of the little companionship she was able to give him. She liked people who got on, and who became more interesting as they grew older. There was Fred; he was much more interesting now than he had been at thirty. He was intelligent about music, and he must be very intelligent in his business, or he would not be at the head of the Brewers' Trust. She respected that kind of intelligence and success. Any success was good. She herself had made a good start, at any rate, and now, if she could get to sleep—Yes, they were all more interesting than they used to be. Look at Harsanyi, who had been so long retarded; what a place he had made for himself in Vienna. If she could get to sleep, she would show him something to-morrow that he would understand.

She got quickly into bed and moved about freely between the sheets. Yes, she was warm all over. A cold, dry breeze was coming in from the river, thank goodness! She tried to think about her little rock house and the Arizona sun and the blue sky. But that led to memories which were still too disturbing. She turned on her side, closed her eyes, and tried an old device.

She entered her father's front door, hung her hat and coat on the rack, and stopped in the parlor to warm her hands at the stove. Then she went out through the diningroom, where the boys were getting their lessons at the long table; through the sitting-room, where Thor was asleep in his cot bed, his dress and stocking hanging on a chair. In the kitchen she stopped for her lantern and her hot brick. She hurried up the back stairs and through the windy loft to her own glacial room. The illusion was marred only by the consciousness that she ought to brush her teeth before she went to bed, and that she never used to do it. Why—? The water was frozen solid in the pitcher, so she got over that. Once between the red blankets there was a short, fierce battle with the cold; then, warmer—warmer. She could hear her father shaking down the hard-coal burner for the night, and the wind rushing and banging down the village street. The boughs of the cottonwood, hard as bone, rattled against her gable. The bed grew softer and warmer. Everybody was warm and well downstairs. The sprawling old house had gathered them all in, like a hen, and had settled down over its brood. They were all warm in her father's house. Softer and softer. She was asleep. She slept ten hours without turning over. From sleep like that, one awakes in shining armor.

On Friday afternoon there was an inspiring audience; there was not an empty chair in the house. Ottenburg and Dr. Archie had seats in the orchestra circle, got from a ticket broker. Landry had not been able to get a seat, so he roamed about in the back of the house, where he usually stood when he dropped in after his own turn in vaudeville was over. He was there so often and at such irregular hours that the ushers thought he was a singer's husband, or had something to do with the electrical plant.

Harsanyi and his wife were in a box, near the stage, in the second circle. Mrs. Harsanyi's hair was noticeably gray, but her face was fuller and handsomer than in those early years of struggle, and she was beautifully dressed. Harsanyi himself had changed very little. He had put on his best afternoon coat in honor of his pupil, and wore a pearl in his black ascot. His hair was longer and more bushy than he used to wear it, and there was now one gray lock on the right side. He had always been an elegant figure, even when he went about in shabby clothes and was crushed with work. Before the curtain rose he was restless and nervous, and kept looking at his watch and wishing he had got a few more letters off before he left his hotel. He had not been in New York since the advent of the taxicab, and had allowed himself too much time. His wife knew that he was afraid of being disappointed this afternoon. He did not often go to the opera because the stupid things that singers did vexed him so, and it always put him in a rage if the conductor held the tempo or in any way accommodated the score to the singer.

When the lights went out and the violins began to quaver their long D against the rude figure of the basses, Mrs. Harsanyi saw her husband's fingers fluttering on his knee in a rapid tattoo. At the moment when SIEGLINDE entered from the side door, she leaned toward him and whispered in his ear, "Oh, the lovely creature!" But he made no response, either by voice or gesture. Throughout the first scene he sat sunk in his chair, his head forward and his one yellow eye rolling restlessly and shining like a tiger's in the dark. His eye followed SIEGLINDE about the stage like a satellite, and as she sat at the table listening to SIEGMUND'S long narrative, it never left her. When she prepared the sleeping draught and disappeared after HUNDING, Harsanyi bowed his head still lower and put his hand over his eye to rest it. The tenor,—a young man who sang with great vigor, went on:—

"WALSE! WALSE! WO IST DEIN SCHWERT?"

Harsanyi smiled, but he did not look forth again until SIEGLINDE reappeared. She went through the story of her shameful bridal feast and into the Walhall' music, which she always sang so nobly, and the entrance of the one-eyed stranger:—

"MIR ALLEIN WECKTE DAS AUGE."

Mrs. Harsanyi glanced at her husband, wondering whether the singer on the stage could not feel his commanding glance. On came the CRESCENDO:—

"WAS JE ICH VERLOR, WAS JE ICH BEWEINT WAR' MIR GEWONNEN."

(All that I have lost, All that I have mourned, Would I then have won.)

Harsanyi touched his wife's arm softly.

Seated in the moonlight, the VOLSUNG pair began their loving inspection of each other's beauties, and the music born of murmuring sound passed into her face, as the old poet said,—and into her body as well. Into one lovely attitude after another the music swept her, love impelled her. And the voice gave out all that was best in it. Like the spring, indeed, it blossomed into memories and prophecies, it recounted and it foretold, as she sang the story of her friendless life, and of how the thing which was truly herself, "bright as the day, rose to the surface" when in the hostile world she for the first time beheld her Friend. Fervently she rose into the hardier feeling of action and daring, the pride in hero-strength and hero-blood, until in a splendid burst, tall and shining like a Victory, she christened him: —

"SIEGMUND—SO NENN ICH DICH!"

Her impatience for the sword swelled with her anticipation of his act, and throwing her arms above her head, she fairly tore a sword out of the empty air for him, before NOTHUNG had left the tree. IN HOCHSTER TRUNKENHEIT, indeed, she burst out with the flaming cry of their kinship: "If you are SIEGMUND, I am SIEGLINDE!" Laughing, singing, bounding, exulting,—with their passion and their sword,—the VOLSUNGS ran out into the spring night.

As the curtain fell, Harsanyi turned to his wife. "At last," he sighed, "somebody with ENOUGH! Enough voice and talent and beauty, enough physical power. And such a noble, noble style!"

"I can scarcely believe it, Andor. I can see her now, that clumsy girl, hunched up over your piano. I can see her shoulders. She always seemed to labor so with her back. And I shall never forget that night when you found her voice."

The audience kept up its clamor until, after many reappearances with the tenor, Kronborg came before the curtain alone. The house met her with a roar, a greeting that was almost savage in its fierceness. The singer's eyes, sweeping the house, rested for a moment on Harsanyi, and she waved her long sleeve toward his box.

"She OUGHT to be pleased that you are here," said Mrs. Harsanyi. "I wonder if she knows how much she owes to you."

"She owes me nothing," replied her husband quickly. "She paid her way. She always gave something back, even then."

"I remember you said once that she would do nothing common," said Mrs. Harsanyi thoughtfully.

"Just so. She might fail, die, get lost in the pack. But if she achieved, it would be nothing common. There are people whom one can trust for that. There is one way in which they will never fail." Harsanyi retired into his own reflections.

After the second act Fred Ottenburg brought Archie to the Harsanyis' box and introduced him as an old friend of Miss Kronborg. The head of a musical publishing house joined them, bringing with him a journalist and the president of a German singing society. The conversation was chiefly about the new SIEGLINDE. Mrs. Harsanyi was gracious and enthusiastic, her husband nervous and uncommunicative. He smiled mechanically, and politely answered questions addressed to him. "Yes, quite so." "Oh, certainly." Every one, of course, said very usual things with great conviction. Mrs. Harsanyi was used to hearing and uttering the commonplaces which such occasions demanded. When her husband withdrew into the shadow, she covered his retreat by her sympathy and cordiality. In reply to a direct question from Ottenburg, Harsanyi said, flinching, "ISOLDE? Yes, why not? She will sing all the great roles, I should think."

The chorus director said something about "dramatic temperament." The journalist insisted that it was "explosive force," "projecting power."

Ottenburg turned to Harsanyi. "What is it, Mr. Harsanyi? Miss Kronborg says if there is anything in her, you are the man who can say what it is."

The journalist scented copy and was eager. "Yes, Harsanyi. You know all about her. What's her secret?"

Harsanyi rumpled his hair irritably and shrugged his shoulders. "Her secret? It is every artist's secret,"—he waved his hand,—"passion. That is all. It is an open secret, and perfectly safe. Like heroism, it is inimitable in cheap materials."

The lights went out. Fred and Archie left the box as the second act came on.

Artistic growth is, more than it is anything else, a refining of the sense of truthfulness. The stupid believe that to be truthful is easy; only the artist, the great artist, knows how difficult it is. That afternoon nothing new came to Thea Kronborg, no enlightenment, no inspiration. She merely came into full possession of things she had been refining and perfecting for so long. Her inhibitions chanced to be fewer than usual, and, within herself, she entered into the inheritance that she herself had laid up, into the fullness of the faith she had kept before she knew its name or its meaning.

Often when she sang, the best she had was unavailable; she could not break through to it, and every sort of distraction and mischance came between it and her. But this afternoon the closed roads opened, the gates dropped. What she had so often tried to reach, lay under her hand. She had only to touch an idea to make it live.

While she was on the stage she was conscious that every movement was the right movement, that her body was absolutely the instrument of her idea. Not for nothing had she kept it so severely, kept it filled with such energy and fire. All that deep-rooted vitality flowered in her voice, her face, in her very finger-tips. She felt like a tree bursting into bloom. And her voice was as flexible as her body; equal to any demand, capable of every NUANCE. With the sense of its perfect companionship, its entire trustworthiness, she had been able to throw herself into the dramatic exigencies of the part, everything in her at its best and everything working together.

The third act came on, and the afternoon slipped by. Thea Kronborg's friends, old and new, seated about the house on different floors and levels, enjoyed her triumph according to their natures. There was one there, whom nobody knew, who perhaps got greater pleasure out of that afternoon than Harsanyi himself. Up in the top gallery a gray-haired little Mexican, withered and bright as a string of peppers beside a'dobe door, kept praying and cursing under his breath, beating on the brass railing and shouting "Bravo! Bravo!" until he was repressed by his neighbors.

He happened to be there because a Mexican band was to be a feature of Barnum and Bailey's circus that year. One of the managers of the show had traveled about the Southwest, signing up a lot of Mexican musicians at low wages, and had brought them to New York. Among them was Spanish Johnny. After Mrs. Tellamantez died, Johnny abandoned his trade and went out with his mandolin to pick up a living for one. His irregularities had become his regular mode of life.

When Thea Kronborg came out of the stage entrance on Fortieth Street, the sky was still flaming with the last rays of the sun that was sinking off behind the North River. A little crowd of people was lingering about the door—musicians from the orchestra who were waiting for their comrades, curious young men, and some poorly dressed girls who were hoping to get a glimpse of the singer. She bowed graciously to the group, through her veil, but she did not look to the right or left as she crossed the sidewalk to her cab. Had she lifted her eyes an instant and glanced out through her white scarf, she must have seen the only man in the crowd who had removed his hat when she emerged, and who stood with it crushed up in his hand. And she would have known him, changed as he was. His lustrous black hair was full of gray, and his face was a good deal worn by the EXTASI, so that it seemed to have shrunk away from his shining eyes and teeth and left them too prominent. But she would have known him. She passed so near that he could have touched her, and he did not put on his hat until her taxi had snorted away. Then he walked down Broadway with his hands in his overcoat pockets, wearing a smile which embraced all the stream of life that passed him and the lighted towers that rose into the limpid blue of the evening sky. If the singer, going home exhausted in her cab, was wondering what was the good of it all, that smile, could she have seen it, would have answered her. It is the only commensurate answer.

Here we must leave Thea Kronborg. From this time on the story of her life is the story of her achievement. The growth of an artist is an intellectual and spiritual development which can scarcely be followed in a personal narrative. This story attempts to deal only with the simple and concrete beginnings which color and accent an artist's work, and to give some account of how a Moonstone girl found her way out of a vague, easy-going world into a life of disciplined endeavor. Any account of the loyalty of young hearts to some exalted ideal, and the passion with which they strive, will always, in some of us, rekindle generous emotions.

EPILOGUE

MOONSTONE AGAIN, in the year 1909. The Methodists are giving an ice-cream sociable in the grove about the new court-house. It is a warm summer night of full moon. The paper lanterns which hang among the trees are foolish toys, only dimming, in little lurid circles, the great softness of the lunar light that floods the blue heavens and the high plateau. To the east the sand hills shine white as of old, but the empire of the sand is gradually diminishing. The grass grows thicker over the dunes than it used to, and the streets of the town are harder and firmer than they were twenty-five years ago. The old inhabitants will tell you that sandstorms are infrequent now, that the wind blows less persistently in the spring and plays a milder tune. Cultivation has modified the soil and the climate, as it modifies human life.

The people seated about under the cottonwoods are much smarter than the Methodists we used to know. The interior of the new Methodist Church looks like a theater, with a sloping floor, and as the congregation proudly say, "opera chairs." The matrons who attend to serving the refreshments to-night look younger for their years than did the women of Mrs. Kronborg's time, and the children all look like city children. The little boys wear "Buster Browns" and the little girls Russian blouses. The country child, in made-overs and cut-downs, seems to have vanished from the face of the earth.

At one of the tables, with her Dutch-cut twin boys, sits a fair-haired, dimpled matron who was once Lily Fisher. Her husband is president of the new bank, and she "goes East for her summers," a practice which causes envy and discontent among her neighbors. The twins are well-behaved children, biddable, meek, neat about their clothes, and always mindful of the proprieties they have learned at summer hotels. While they are eating their icecream and trying not to twist the spoon in their mouths, a little shriek of laughter breaks from an adjacent table. The twins look up. There sits a spry little old spinster whom they know well. She has a long chin, a long nose, and she is dressed like a young girl, with a pink sash and a lace garden hat with pink rosebuds. She is surrounded by a crowd of boys,—loose and lanky, short and thick,—who are joking with her roughly, but not unkindly.

"Mamma," one of the twins comes out in a shrill treble, "why is Tillie Kronborg always talking about a thousand dollars?"

The boys, hearing this question, break into a roar of laughter, the women titter behind their paper napkins, and even from Tillie there is a little shriek of appreciation. The observing child's remark had made every one suddenly realize that Tillie never stopped talking about that particular sum of money. In the spring, when she went to buy early strawberries, and was told that they were thirty cents a box, she was sure to remind the grocer that though her name was Kronborg she didn't get a thousand dollars a night. In the autumn, when she went to buy her coal for the winter, she expressed amazement at the price quoted her, and told the dealer he must have got her mixed up with her niece to think she could pay such a sum. When she was making her Christmas presents, she never failed to ask the women who came into her shop what you COULD make for anybody who got a thousand dollars a night. When the Denver papers announced that Thea Kronborg had married Frederick Ottenburg, the head of the Brewers' Trust, Moonstone people expected that Tillie's vain-gloriousness would take another form. But Tillie had hoped that Thea would marry a title, and she did not boast much about Ottenburg,—at least not until after her memorable trip to Kansas City to hear Thea sing.

Tillie is the last Kronborg left in Moonstone. She lives alone in a little house with a green yard, and keeps a fancywork and millinery store. Her business methods are informal, and she would never come out even at the end of the year, if she did not receive a draft for a good round sum from her niece at Christmas time. The arrival of this draft always renews the discussion as to what Thea would do for her aunt if she really did the right thing. Most of the Moonstone people think Thea ought to take Tillie to New York and keep her as a companion. While they are feeling sorry for Tillie because she does not live at the Plaza, Tillie is trying not to hurt their feelings by showing too plainly how much she realizes the superiority of her position. She tries to be modest when she complains to the postmaster that her New York paper is more than three days late. It means enough, surely, on the face of it, that she is the only person in Moonstone who takes a New York paper or who has any reason for taking one. A foolish young girl, Tillie lived in the splendid sorrows of "Wanda" and "Strathmore"; a foolish old girl, she lives in her niece's triumphs. As she often says, she just missed going on the stage herself.

That night after the sociable, as Tillie tripped home with a crowd of noisy boys and girls, she was perhaps a shade troubled. The twin's question rather lingered in her ears. Did she, perhaps, insist too much on that thousand dollars? Surely, people didn't for a minute think it was the money she cared about? As for that, Tillie tossed her head, she didn't care a rap. They must understand that this money was different.

When the laughing little group that brought her home had gone weaving down the sidewalk through the leafy shadows and had disappeared, Tillie brought out a rocking chair and sat down on her porch. On glorious, soft summer nights like this, when the moon is opulent and full, the day submerged and forgotten, she loves to sit there behind her rose-vine and let her fancy wander where it will. If you chanced to be passing down that Moonstone street and saw that alert white figure rocking there behind the screen of roses and lingering late into the night, you might feel sorry for her, and how mistaken you would be! Tillie lives in a little magic world, full of secret satisfactions. Thea Kronborg has given much noble pleasure to a world that needs all it can get, but to no individual has she given more than to her queer old aunt in Moonstone. The legend of Kronborg, the artist, fills Tillie's life; she feels rich and exalted in it. What delightful things happen in her mind as she sits there rocking! She goes back to those early days of sand and sun, when Thea was a child and Tillie was herself, so it seems to her, "young." When she used to hurry to church to hear Mr. Kronborg's wonderful sermons, and when Thea used to stand up by the organ of a bright Sunday morning and sing "Come, Ye Disconsolate." Or she thinks about that wonderful time when the Metropolitan Opera Company sang a week's engagement in Kansas City, and Thea sent for her and had her stay with her at the Coates House and go to every performance at Convention Hall. Thea let Tillie go through her costume trunks and try on her wigs and jewels. And the kindness of Mr. Ottenburg! When Thea dined in her own room, he went down to dinner with Tillie, and never looked bored or absent-minded when she chattered. He took her to the hall the first time Thea sang there, and sat in the box with her and helped her through "Lohengrin." After the first act, when Tillie turned tearful eyes to him and burst out, "I don't care, she always seemed grand like that, even when she was a girl. I expect I'm crazy, but she just seems to me full of all them old times!"—Ottenburg was so sympathetic and patted her hand and said, "But that's just what she is, full of the old times, and you are a wise woman to see it." Yes, he said that to her. Tillie often wondered how she had been able to bear it when Thea came down the stairs in the wedding robe embroidered in silver, with a train so long it took six women to carry it.

Tillie had lived fifty-odd years for that week, but she got it, and no miracle was ever more miraculous than that. When she used to be working in the fields on her father's Minnesota farm, she couldn't help believing that she would some day have to do with the "wonderful," though her chances for it had then looked so slender.

The morning after the sociable, Tillie, curled up in bed, was roused by the rattle of the milk cart down the street. Then a neighbor boy came down the sidewalk outside her window, singing "Casey Jones" as if he hadn't a care in the world. By this time Tillie was wide awake. The twin's question, and the subsequent laughter, came back with a faint twinge. Tillie knew she was short-sighted about facts, but this time—Why, there were her scrapbooks, full of newspaper and magazine articles about Thea, and half-tone cuts, snap-shots of her on land and sea, and photographs of her in all her parts. There, in her parlor, was the phonograph that had come from Mr. Ottenburg last June, on Thea's birthday; she had only to go in there and turn it on, and let Thea speak for herself. Tillie finished brushing her white hair and laughed as she gave it a smart turn and brought it into her usual French twist. If Moonstone doubted, she had evidence enough: in black and white, in figures and photographs, evidence in hair lines on metal disks. For one who had so often seen two and two as making six, who had so often stretched a point, added a touch, in the good game of trying to make the world brighter than it is, there was positive bliss in having such deep foundations of support. She need never tremble in secret lest she might sometime stretch a point in Thea's favor.—Oh, the comfort, to a soul too zealous, of having at last a rose so red it could not be further painted, a lily so truly auriferous that no amount of gilding could exceed the fact!

Tillie hurried from her bedroom, threw open the doors and windows, and let the morning breeze blow through her little house.

In two minutes a cob fire was roaring in her kitchen stove, in five she had set the table. At her household work Tillie was always bursting out with shrill snatches of song, and as suddenly stopping, right in the middle of a phrase, as if she had been struck dumb. She emerged upon the back porch with one of these bursts, and bent down to get her butter and cream out of the ice-box. The cat was purring on the bench and the morning-glories were thrusting their purple trumpets in through the lattice-work in a friendly way. They reminded Tillie that while she was waiting for the coffee to boil she could get some flowers for her breakfast table. She looked out uncertainly at a bush of sweet-briar that grew at the edge of her yard, off across the long grass and the tomato vines. The front porch, to be sure, was dripping with crimson ramblers that ought to be cut for the good of the vines; but never the rose in the hand for Tillie! She caught up the kitchen shears and off she dashed through grass and drenching dew. Snip, snip; the short-stemmed sweet-briars, salmon-pink and golden-hearted, with their unique and inimitable woody perfume, fell into her apron.

After she put the eggs and toast on the table, Tillie took last Sunday's New York paper from the rack beside the cupboard and sat down, with it for company. In the Sunday paper there was always a page about singers, even in summer, and that week the musical page began with a sympathetic account of Madame Kronborg's first performance of ISOLDE in London. At the end of the notice, there was a short paragraph about her having sung for the King at Buckingham Palace and having been presented with a jewel by His Majesty.

Singing for the King; but Goodness! she was always doing things like that! Tillie tossed her head. All through breakfast she kept sticking her sharp nose down into the glass of sweet-briar, with the old incredible lightness of heart, like a child's balloon tugging at its string. She had always insisted, against all evidence, that life was full of fairy tales, and it was! She had been feeling a little down, perhaps, and Thea had answered her, from so far. From a common person, now, if you were troubled, you might get a letter. But Thea almost never wrote letters. She answered every one, friends and foes alike, in one way, her own way, her only way. Once more Tillie has to remind herself that it is all true, and is not something she has "made up." Like all romancers, she is a little terrified at seeing one of her wildest conceits admitted by the hardheaded world. If our dream comes true, we are almost afraid to believe it; for that is the best of all good fortune, and nothing better can happen to any of us.

When the people on Sylvester Street tire of Tillie's stories, she goes over to the east part of town, where her legends are always welcome. The humbler people of Moonstone still live there. The same little houses sit under the cottonwoods; the men smoke their pipes in the front doorways, and the women do their washing in the back yard. The older women remember Thea, and how she used to come kicking her express wagon along the sidewalk, steering by the tongue and holding Thor in her lap. Not much happens in that part of town, and the people have long memories. A boy grew up on one of those streets who went to Omaha and built up a great business, and is now very rich. Moonstone people always speak of him and Thea together, as examples of Moonstone enterprise. They do, however, talk oftener of Thea. A voice has even a wider appeal than a fortune. It is the one gift that all creatures would possess if they could. Dreary Maggie Evans, dead nearly twenty years, is still remembered because Thea sang at her funeral "after she had studied in Chicago."

However much they may smile at her, the old inhabitants would miss Tillie. Her stories give them something to talk about and to conjecture about, cut off as they are from the restless currents of the world. The many naked little sandbars which lie between Venice and the mainland, in the seemingly stagnant water of the lagoons, are made habitable and wholesome only because, every night, a foot and a half of tide creeps in from the sea and winds its fresh brine up through all that network of shining waterways. So, into all the little settlements of quiet people, tidings of what their boys and girls are doing in the world bring real refreshment; bring to the old, memories, and to the young, dreams.

MY ANTONIA

INTRODUCTION

Last summer I happened to be crossing the plains of Iowa in a season of intense heat, and it was my good fortune to have for a traveling companion James Quayle Burden—Jim Burden, as we still call him in the West. He and I are old friends—we grew up together in the same Nebraska town—and we had much to say to each other. While the train flashed through never-ending miles of ripe wheat, by country towns and bright-flowered pastures and oak groves wilting in the sun, we sat in the observation car, where the woodwork was hot to the touch and red dust lay deep over everything. The dust and heat, the burning wind, reminded us of many things. We were talking about what it is like to spend one's childhood in little towns like these, buried in wheat and corn, under stimulating extremes of climate: burning summers when the world lies green and billowy beneath a brilliant sky, when one is fairly stifled in vegetation, in the color and smell of strong weeds and heavy harvests; blustery winters with little snow, when the whole country is stripped bare and gray as sheet-iron. We agreed that no one who had not grown up in a little prairie town could know anything about it. It was a kind of freemasonry, we said.

Although Jim Burden and I both live in New York, and are old friends, I do not see much of him there. He is legal counsel for one of the great Western railways, and is sometimes away from his New York office for weeks together. That is one reason why we do not often meet. Another is that I do not like his wife

When Jim was still an obscure young lawyer, struggling to make his way in New York, his career was suddenly advanced by a brilliant marriage. Genevieve Whitney was the only daughter of a distinguished man. Her marriage with young Burden was the subject of sharp comment at the time. It was said she had been brutally jilted by her cousin, Rutland Whitney, and that she married this unknown man from the West out of bravado. She was a restless, headstrong girl, even then, who liked to astonish her friends. Later, when I knew her, she was always doing something unexpected. She gave one of her town houses for a Suffrage headquarters, produced one of her own plays at the Princess Theater, was arrested for picketing during a garment-makers' strike, etc. I am never able to believe that she has much feeling for the causes to which she lends her name and her fleeting interest. She is handsome, energetic, executive, but to me she seems unimpressionable and temperamentally incapable of enthusiasm. Her husband's quiet tastes irritate her, I think, and she finds it worth while to play the patroness to a group of young poets and painters of advanced ideas and mediocre ability. She has her own fortune and lives her own life. For some reason, she wishes to remain Mrs. James Burden.

As for Jim, no disappointments have been severe enough to chill his naturally romantic and ardent disposition. This disposition, though it often made him seem very funny when he was a boy, has been one of the strongest elements in his success. He loves with a personal passion the great country through which his railway runs and branches. His faith in it and his knowledge of it have played an important part in its development. He is always able to raise capital for new enterprises in Wyoming or Montana, and has helped young men out there to do remarkable things in mines and timber and oil. If a young man with an idea can once get Jim Burden's attention, can manage to accompany him when he goes off into the wilds hunting for lost parks or exploring new canyons, then the money which means action is usually forthcoming. Jim is still able to lose himself in those big Western dreams. Though he is over forty now, he meets new people and new enterprises with the impulsiveness by which his boyhood friends remember him. He never seems to me to grow older. His fresh color and sandy hair and quick-changing blue eyes are those of a young man, and his sympathetic, solicitous interest in women is as youthful as it is Western and American.

During that burning day when we were crossing Iowa, our talk kept returning to a central figure, a Bohemian girl whom we had known long ago and whom both of us admired. More than any other person we remembered, this girl seemed to mean to us the country, the conditions, the whole adventure of our childhood. To speak her name was to call up pictures of people and places, to set a quiet drama going in one's brain. I had lost sight of her altogether, but Jim had found her again after long years, had renewed a friendship that meant a great deal to him, and out of his busy life had set apart time enough to enjoy that friendship. His mind was full of her that day. He made me see her again, feel her presence, revived all my old affection for her.

"I can't see," he said impetuously, "why you have never written anything about Antonia."[1]

I told him I had always felt that other people—he himself, for one knew her much better than I. I was ready, however, to make an agreement with him; I would set down on paper all that I remembered of Antonia if he would do the same. We might, in this way, get a picture of her.

He rumpled his hair with a quick, excited gesture, which with him often announces a new determination, and I could see that my suggestion took hold of him. "Maybe I will, maybe I will!" he declared. He stared out of the window for a few moments, and when he turned to me again his eyes had the sudden clearness that comes from something the mind itself sees. "Of course," he said, "I should have to do it in a direct way, and say a great deal about myself. It's through myself that I knew and felt her, and I've had no practice in any other form of presentation."

I told him that how he knew her and felt her was exactly what I most wanted to know about Antonia. He had had opportunities that I, as a little girl who watched her come and go, had not.

Months afterward Jim Burden arrived at my apartment one stormy winter afternoon, with a bulging legal portfolio sheltered under his fur overcoat. He brought it into the sitting-room with him and tapped it with some pride as he stood warming his hands.

"I finished it last night—the thing about Antonia," he said. "Now, what about yours?"

I had to confess that mine had not gone beyond a few straggling notes.

"Notes? I didn't make any." He drank his tea all at once and put down the cup. "I didn't arrange or rearrange. I simply wrote down what of herself and myself and other people Antonia's name recalls to me. I suppose it hasn't any form. It hasn't any title, either." He went into the next room, sat down at my desk and wrote on the pinkish face of the portfolio the word, "Antonia." He frowned at this a moment, then prefixed another word, making it "My Antonia." That seemed to satisfy him.

"Read it as soon as you can," he said, rising, "but don't let it influence your own story."

My own story was never written, but the following narrative is Jim's manuscript, substantially as he brought it to me.

---

1. The Bohemian name Antonia is strongly accented on the first syllable, like the English name Anthony, and the 'i' is, of course, given the sound of long 'e'. The name is pronounced An'-ton-ee-ah.

I
THE SHIMERDAS

I.

I FIRST HEARD of Antonia on what seemed to me an interminable journey across the great midland plain of North America. I was ten years old then; I had lost both my father and mother within a year, and my Virginia relatives were sending me out to my grandparents, who lived in Nebraska. I travelled in the care of a mountain boy, Jake Marpole, one of the 'hands' on my father's old farm under the Blue Ridge, who was now going West to work for my grandfather. Jake's experience of the world was not much wider than mine. He had never been in a railway train until the morning when we set out together to try our fortunes in a new world.

We went all the way in day-coaches, becoming more sticky and grimy with each stage of the journey. Jake bought everything the newsboys offered him: candy, oranges, brass collar buttons, a watch-charm, and for me a 'Life of Jesse James,' which I remember as one of the most satisfactory books I have ever read. Beyond Chicago we were under the protection of a friendly passenger conductor, who knew all about the country to which we were going and gave us a great deal of advice in exchange for our confidence. He seemed to us an experienced and worldly man who had been almost everywhere; in his conversation he threw out lightly the names of distant states and cities. He wore the rings and pins and badges of different fraternal orders to which he belonged. Even his cuff-buttons were engraved with hieroglyphics, and he was more inscribed than an Egyptian obelisk.

Once when he sat down to chat, he told us that in the immigrant car ahead there was a family from 'across the water' whose destination was the same as ours.

'They can't any of them speak English, except one little girl, and all she can say is "We go Black Hawk, Nebraska." She's not much older than you, twelve or thirteen, maybe, and she's as bright as a new dollar. Don't you want to go ahead and see her, Jimmy? She's got the pretty brown eyes, too!'

This last remark made me bashful, and I shook my head and settled down to 'Jesse

James.' Jake nodded at me approvingly and said you were likely to get diseases from foreigners.

I do not remember crossing the Missouri River, or anything about the long day's journey through Nebraska. Probably by that time I had crossed so many rivers that I was dull to them. The only thing very noticeable about Nebraska was that it was still, all day long, Nebraska.

I had been sleeping, curled up in a red plush seat, for a long while when we reached Black Hawk. Jake roused me and took me by the hand. We stumbled down from the train to a wooden siding, where men were running about with lanterns. I couldn't see any town, or even distant lights; we were surrounded by utter darkness. The engine was panting heavily after its long run. In the red glow from the fire-box, a group of people stood huddled together on the platform, encumbered by bundles and boxes. I knew this must be the immigrant family the conductor had told us about. The woman wore a fringed shawl tied over her head, and she carried a little tin trunk in her arms, hugging it as if it were a baby. There was an old man, tall and stooped. Two half-grown boys and a girl stood holding oilcloth bundles, and a little girl clung to her mother's skirts. Presently a man with a lantern approached them and began to talk, shouting and exclaiming. I pricked up my ears, for it was positively the first time I had ever heard a foreign tongue.

Another lantern came along. A bantering voice called out: 'Hello, are you Mr. Burden's folks? If you are, it's me you're looking for. I'm Otto Fuchs. I'm Mr. Burden's hired man, and I'm to drive you out. Hello, Jimmy, ain't you scared to come so far west?'

I looked up with interest at the new face in the lantern-light. He might have stepped out of the pages of 'Jesse James.' He wore a sombrero hat, with a wide leather band and a bright buckle, and the ends of his moustache were twisted up stiffly, like little horns. He looked lively and ferocious, I thought, and as if he had a history. A long scar ran across one cheek and drew the corner of his mouth up in a sinister curl. The top of his left ear was gone, and his skin was brown as an Indian's. Surely this was the face of a desperado. As he walked about the platform in his high-heeled boots, looking for our trunks, I saw that he was a rather slight man, quick and wiry, and light on his feet. He told us we had a long night drive ahead of us, and had better be on the hike. He led us to a hitching-bar where two farm-wagons were tied, and I saw the foreign family crowding into one of them. The other was for us. Jake got on the front seat with Otto Fuchs, and I rode on the straw in the bottom of the wagon-box, covered up with a buffalo hide. The immigrants rumbled off into the empty darkness, and we followed them.

I tried to go to sleep, but the jolting made me bite my tongue, and I soon began to ache all over. When the straw settled down, I had a hard bed. Cautiously I slipped from under the buffalo hide, got up on my knees and peered over the side of the wagon. There seemed to be nothing to see; no fences, no creeks or trees, no hills or fields. If there was a road, I could not make it out in the faint starlight. There was nothing but land: not a country at all, but the material out of which countries are made. No, there was nothing but land—slightly undulating, I knew, because often our wheels ground against the brake as we went down into a hollow and lurched up again on the other side. I had the feeling that the world was left behind, that we had got over the edge of it, and were outside man's jurisdiction. I had never before looked up at the sky when there was not a familiar mountain ridge against it. But this was the complete dome of heaven, all there was of it. I did not believe that my dead father and mother were watching me from up there; they would still be looking for me at the sheep-fold down by the creek, or along the white road that led to the mountain pastures. I had left even their spirits behind me. The wagon jolted on, carrying me I knew not whither. I don't think I was homesick. If we never arrived anywhere, it did not matter. Between that earth and that sky I felt erased, blotted out. I did not say my prayers that night: here, I felt, what would be would be.

II.

I do not remember our arrival at my grandfather's farm sometime before daybreak, after a drive of nearly twenty miles with heavy work-horses. When I awoke, it was afternoon. I was lying in a little room, scarcely larger than the bed that held me, and the window-shade at my head was flapping softly in a warm wind. A tall woman, with wrinkled brown skin and black hair, stood looking down at me; I knew that she must be my grandmother. She had been crying, I could see, but when I opened my eyes she smiled, peered at me anxiously, and sat down on the foot of my bed.

'Had a good sleep, Jimmy?' she asked briskly. Then in a very different tone she said, as if to herself, 'My, how you do look like your father!' I remembered that my father had been her little boy; she must often have come to wake him like this when he overslept. 'Here are your clean clothes,' she went on, stroking my coverlid with her brown hand as she talked. 'But first you come down to the kitchen with me, and have a nice warm bath behind the stove. Bring your things; there's nobody about.'

'Down to the kitchen' struck me as curious; it was always 'out in the kitchen' at home. I picked up my shoes and stockings and followed her through the living-room and down a flight of stairs into a basement. This basement was divided into a dining-room at the right of the stairs and a kitchen at the left. Both rooms were plastered and whitewashed—the plaster laid directly upon the earth walls, as it used to be in dugouts. The floor was of hard cement. Up under the wooden ceiling there were little half-windows with white curtains, and pots of geraniums and wandering Jew in the deep sills. As I entered the kitchen, I sniffed a pleasant smell of gingerbread baking. The stove was very large, with bright nickel trimmings, and behind it there was a long wooden bench against the wall, and a tin washtub, into which grandmother poured hot and cold water. When she brought the soap and towels, I told her that I was used to taking my bath without help. 'Can you do your ears, Jimmy? Are you sure? Well, now, I call you a right smart little boy.'

It was pleasant there in the kitchen. The sun shone into my bath-water through the west half-window, and a big Maltese cat came up and rubbed himself against the tub, watching me curiously. While I scrubbed, my grandmother busied herself in the dining-room until I called anxiously, 'Grandmother, I'm afraid the cakes are burning!' Then she came laughing, waving her apron before her as if she were shooing chickens.

She was a spare, tall woman, a little stooped, and she was apt to carry her head thrust forward in an attitude of attention, as if she were looking at something, or listening to something, far away. As I grew older, I came to believe that it was only because she was so often thinking of things that were far away. She was quick-footed and energetic in all her movements. Her voice was high and rather shrill, and she often spoke with an anxious inflection, for she was exceedingly desirous that everything should go with due order and decorum. Her laugh, too, was high, and perhaps a little strident, but there was a lively intelligence in it. She was then fifty-five years old, a strong woman, of unusual endurance.

After I was dressed, I explored the long cellar next the kitchen. It was dug out under the wing of the house, was plastered and cemented, with a stairway and an outside door by which the men came and went. Under one of the windows there was a place for them to wash when they came in from work.

While my grandmother was busy about supper, I settled myself on the wooden bench behind the stove and got acquainted with the cat—he caught not only rats and mice, but gophers, I was told. The patch of yellow sunlight on the floor travelled back toward the stairway, and grandmother and I talked about my journey, and about the arrival of the new Bohemian family; she said they were to be our nearest neighbours. We did not talk about the farm in Virginia, which had been her home for so many years. But after the men came in from the fields, and we were all seated at the supper table, then she asked Jake about the old place and about our friends and neighbours there.

My grandfather said little. When he first came in he kissed me and spoke kindly to me, but he was not demonstrative. I felt at once his deliberateness and personal dignity, and was a little in awe of him. The thing one immediately noticed about him was his beautiful, crinkly, snow-white beard. I once heard a missionary say it was like the beard of an Arabian sheik. His bald crown only made it more impressive.

Grandfather's eyes were not at all like those of an old man; they were bright blue, and had a fresh, frosty sparkle. His teeth were white and regular—so sound that he had never been to a dentist in his life. He had a delicate skin, easily roughened by sun and wind. When he was a young man his hair and beard were red; his eyebrows were still coppery.

As we sat at the table, Otto Fuchs and I kept stealing covert glances at each other. Grandmother had told me while she was getting supper that he was an Austrian who came to this country a young boy and had led an adventurous life in the Far West among mining-camps and cow outfits. His iron constitution was somewhat broken by mountain pneumonia, and he had drifted back to live in a milder country for a while. He had relatives in Bismarck, a German settlement to the north of us, but for a year now he had been working for grandfather.

The minute supper was over, Otto took me into the kitchen to whisper to me about a pony down in the barn that had been bought for me at a sale; he had been riding him to find out whether he had any bad tricks, but he was a 'perfect gentleman,' and his name was Dude. Fuchs told me everything I wanted to know: how he had lost his ear in a Wyoming blizzard when he was a stage-driver, and how to throw a lasso. He promised to rope a steer for me before sundown next day. He got out his 'chaps' and silver spurs to show them to Jake and me, and his best cowboy boots, with tops stitched in bold design—roses, and true-lover's knots, and undraped female figures. These, he solemnly explained, were angels.

Before we went to bed, Jake and Otto were called up to the living-room for prayers. Grandfather put on silver-rimmed spectacles and read several Psalms. His voice was so sympathetic and he read so interestingly that I wished he had chosen one of my favourite chapters in the Book of Kings. I was awed by his intonation of the word 'Selah.' 'He shall choose our inheritance for us, the excellency of Jacob whom He loved. Selah.' I had no idea what the word meant; perhaps he had not. But, as he uttered it, it became oracular, the most sacred of words.

Early the next morning I ran out-of-doors to look about me. I had been told that ours was the only wooden house west of Black Hawk—until you came to the Norwegian settlement, where there were several. Our neighbours lived in sod houses and dugouts—comfortable, but not very roomy. Our white frame house, with a storey and half-storey above the basement, stood at the east end of what I might call the farmyard, with the windmill close by the kitchen door. From the windmill the ground sloped westward, down to the barns and granaries and pig-yards. This slope was trampled hard and bare, and washed out in winding gullies by the rain. Beyond the corncribs, at the bottom of the shallow draw, was a muddy little pond, with rusty willow bushes growing about it. The road from the post-office came directly by our door, crossed the farmyard, and curved round this little pond, beyond which it began to climb the gentle swell of unbroken prairie to the west. There, along the western sky-line it skirted a great cornfield, much larger than any field I had ever seen. This cornfield, and the sorghum patch behind the barn, were the only broken land in sight. Everywhere, as far as the eye could reach, there was nothing but rough, shaggy, red grass, most of it as tall as I.

North of the house, inside the ploughed fire-breaks, grew a thick-set strip of box-elder trees, low and bushy, their leaves already turning yellow. This hedge was nearly a quarter of a mile long, but I had to look very hard to see it at all. The little trees were insignificant against the grass. It seemed as if the grass were about to run over them, and over the plum-patch behind the sod chicken-house.

As I looked about me I felt that the grass was the country, as the water is the sea. The red of the grass made all the great prairie the colour of winestains, or of certain seaweeds when they are first washed up. And there was so much motion in it; the whole country seemed, somehow, to be running.

I had almost forgotten that I had a grandmother, when she came out, her sunbonnet on her head, a grain-sack in her hand, and asked me if I did not want to go to the garden with her to dig potatoes for dinner.

The garden, curiously enough, was a quarter of a mile from the house, and the way to it led up a shallow draw past the cattle corral. Grandmother called my attention to a stout hickory cane, tipped with copper, which hung by a leather thong from her belt. This, she said, was her rattlesnake cane. I must never go to the garden without a heavy stick or a corn-knife; she had killed a good many rattlers on her way back and forth. A little girl who lived on the Black Hawk road was bitten on the ankle and had been sick all summer.

I can remember exactly how the country looked to me as I walked beside my grandmother along the faint wagon-tracks on that early September morning. Perhaps the glide of long railway travel was still with me, for more than anything else I felt motion in the landscape; in the fresh, easy-blowing morning wind, and in the earth itself, as if the shaggy grass were a sort of loose hide, and underneath it herds of wild buffalo were galloping, galloping...

Alone, I should never have found the garden—except, perhaps, for the big yellow pumpkins that lay about unprotected by their withering vines—and I felt very little interest in it when I got there. I wanted to walk straight on through the red grass and over the edge of the world, which could not be very far away. The light air about me told me that the world ended here: only the ground and sun and sky were left, and if one went a little farther there would be only sun and sky, and one would float off into them, like the tawny hawks which sailed over our heads making slow shadows on the grass. While grandmother took the pitchfork we found standing in one of the rows and dug potatoes, while I picked them up out of the soft brown earth and put them into the bag, I kept looking up at the hawks that were doing what I might so easily do.

When grandmother was ready to go, I said I would like to stay up there in the garden awhile.

She peered down at me from under her sunbonnet. 'Aren't you afraid of snakes?'

'A little,' I admitted, 'but I'd like to stay, anyhow.'

'Well, if you see one, don't have anything to do with him. The big yellow and brown ones won't hurt you; they're bull-snakes and help to keep the gophers down. Don't be scared if you see anything look out of that hole in the bank over there. That's a badger hole. He's about as big as a big 'possum, and his face is striped, black and white. He takes a chicken once in a while, but I won't let the men harm him. In a new country a body feels friendly to the animals. I like to have him come out and watch me when I'm at work.'

Grandmother swung the bag of potatoes over her shoulder and went down the path, leaning forward a little. The road followed the windings of the draw; when she came to the first bend, she waved at me and disappeared. I was left alone with this new feeling of lightness and content.

I sat down in the middle of the garden, where snakes could scarcely approach unseen, and leaned my back against a warm yellow pumpkin. There were some ground-cherry bushes growing along the furrows, full of fruit. I turned back the papery triangular sheaths that protected the berries and ate a few. All about me giant grasshoppers, twice as big as any I had ever seen, were doing acrobatic feats among the dried vines. The gophers scurried up and down the ploughed ground. There in the sheltered draw-bottom the wind did not blow very hard, but I could hear it singing its humming tune up on the level, and I could see the tall grasses wave. The earth was warm under me, and warm as I crumbled it through my fingers. Queer little red bugs came out and moved in slow squadrons around me. Their backs were polished vermilion, with black spots. I kept as still as I could. Nothing happened. I did not expect anything to happen. I was something that lay under the sun and felt it, like the pumpkins, and I did not want to be anything more. I was entirely happy. Perhaps we feel like that when we die and become a part of something entire, whether it is sun and air, or goodness and knowledge. At any rate, that is happiness; to be dissolved into something complete and great. When it comes to one, it comes as naturally as sleep.

III.

On Sunday morning Otto Fuchs was to drive us over to make the acquaintance of our new Bohemian neighbours. We were taking them some provisions, as they had come to live on a wild place where there was no garden or chicken-house, and very little broken land. Fuchs brought up a sack of potatoes and a piece of cured pork from the cellar, and grandmother packed some loaves of Saturday's bread, a jar of butter, and several pumpkin pies in the straw of the wagon-box. We clambered up to the front seat and jolted off past the little pond and along the road that climbed to the big cornfield.

I could hardly wait to see what lay beyond that cornfield; but there was only red grass like ours, and nothing else, though from the high wagon-seat one could look off a long way. The road ran about like a wild thing, avoiding the deep draws, crossing them where they were wide and shallow. And all along it, wherever it looped or ran, the sunflowers grew; some of them were as big as little trees, with great rough leaves and many branches which bore dozens of blossoms. They made a gold ribbon across the prairie. Occasionally one of the horses would tear off with his teeth a plant full of blossoms, and walk along munching it, the flowers nodding in time to his bites as he ate down toward them.

The Bohemian family, grandmother told me as we drove along, had bought the homestead of a fellow countryman, Peter Krajiek, and had paid him more than it was worth. Their agreement with him was made before they left the old country, through a cousin of his, who was also a relative of Mrs. Shimerda. The Shimerdas were the first Bohemian family to come to this part of the county. Krajiek was their only interpreter, and could tell them anything he chose. They could not speak enough English to ask for advice, or even to make their most pressing wants known. One son, Fuchs said, was well-grown, and strong enough to work the land; but the father was old and frail and knew nothing about farming. He was a weaver by trade; had been a skilled workman on tapestries and upholstery materials. He had brought his fiddle with him, which wouldn't be of much use here, though he used to pick up money by it at home.

'If they're nice people, I hate to think of them spending the winter in that cave of Krajiek's,' said grandmother. 'It's no better than a badger hole; no proper dugout at all. And I hear he's made them pay twenty dollars for his old cookstove that ain't worth ten.'

'Yes'm,' said Otto; 'and he's sold 'em his oxen and his two bony old horses for the price of good workteams. I'd have interfered about the horses—the old man can understand some German—if I'd I a' thought it would do any good. But Bohemians has a natural distrust of Austrians.'

Grandmother looked interested. 'Now, why is that, Otto?'

Fuchs wrinkled his brow and nose. 'Well, ma'm, it's politics. It would take me a long while to explain.'

The land was growing rougher; I was told that we were approaching Squaw Creek, which cut up the west half of the Shimerdas' place and made the land of little value for farming. Soon we could see the broken, grassy clay cliffs which indicated the windings of the stream, and the glittering tops of the cottonwoods and ash trees that grew down in the ravine. Some of the cottonwoods had already turned, and the yellow leaves and shining white bark made them look like the gold and silver trees in fairy tales.

As we approached the Shimerdas' dwelling, I could still see nothing but rough red hillocks, and draws with shelving banks and long roots hanging out where the earth had crumbled away. Presently, against one of those banks, I saw a sort of shed, thatched with the same wine-coloured grass that grew everywhere. Near it tilted a shattered windmill frame, that had no wheel. We drove up to this skeleton to tie our horses, and then I saw a door and window sunk deep in the drawbank. The door stood open, and a woman and a girl of fourteen ran out and looked up at us hopefully. A little girl trailed along behind them. The woman had on her head the same embroidered shawl with silk fringes that she wore when she had alighted from the train at Black Hawk. She was not old, but she was certainly not young. Her face was alert and lively, with a sharp chin and shrewd little eyes. She shook grandmother's hand energetically.

'Very glad, very glad!' she ejaculated. Immediately she pointed to the bank out of which she had emerged and said, 'House no good, house no good!'

Grandmother nodded consolingly. 'You'll get fixed up comfortable after while, Mrs. Shimerda; make good house.'

My grandmother always spoke in a very loud tone to foreigners, as if they were deaf. She made Mrs. Shimerda understand the friendly intention of our visit, and the Bohemian woman handled the loaves of bread and even smelled them, and examined the pies with lively curiosity, exclaiming, 'Much good, much thank!'—and again she wrung grandmother's hand.

The oldest son, Ambroz—they called it Ambrosch—came out of the cave and stood beside his mother. He was nineteen years old, short and broad-backed, with a close-cropped, flat head, and a wide, flat face. His hazel eyes were little and shrewd, like his mother's, but more sly and suspicious; they fairly snapped at the food. The family had been living on corncakes and sorghum molasses for three days.

The little girl was pretty, but Antonia—they accented the name thus, strongly, when they spoke to her—was still prettier. I remembered what the conductor had said about her eyes. They were big and warm and full of light, like the sun shining on brown pools in the wood. Her skin was brown, too, and in her cheeks she had a glow of rich, dark colour. Her brown hair was curly and wild-looking. The little sister, whom they called Yulka (Julka), was fair, and seemed mild and obedient. While I stood awkwardly confronting the two girls, Krajiek came up from the barn to see what was going on. With him was another Shimerda son. Even from a distance one could see that there was something strange about this boy. As he approached us, he began to make uncouth noises, and held up his hands to show us his fingers, which were webbed to the first knuckle, like a duck's foot. When he saw me draw back, he began to crow delightedly, 'Hoo, hoo-hoo, hoo-hoo!' like a rooster. His mother scowled and said sternly, 'Marek!' then spoke rapidly to Krajiek in Bohemian.

'She wants me to tell you he won't hurt nobody, Mrs. Burden. He was born like that. The others are smart. Ambrosch, he make good farmer.' He struck Ambrosch on the back, and the boy smiled knowingly.

At that moment the father came out of the hole in the bank. He wore no hat, and his thick, iron-grey hair was brushed straight back from his forehead. It was so long that it bushed out behind his ears, and made him look like the old portraits I remembered in Virginia. He was tall and slender, and his thin shoulders stooped. He looked at us understandingly, then took grandmother's hand and bent over it. I noticed how white and well-shaped his own hands were. They looked calm, somehow, and skilled. His eyes were melancholy, and were set back deep under his brow. His face was ruggedly formed, but it looked like ashes—like something from which all the warmth and light had died out. Everything about this old man was in keeping with his dignified manner. He was neatly dressed. Under his coat he wore a knitted grey vest, and, instead of a collar, a silk scarf of a dark bronze-green, carefully crossed and held together by a red coral pin. While Krajiek was translating for Mr. Shimerda, Antonia came up to me and held out her hand coaxingly. In a moment we were running up the steep drawside together, Yulka trotting after us.

When we reached the level and could see the gold tree-tops, I pointed toward them, and Antonia laughed and squeezed my hand as if to tell me how glad she was I had come. We raced off toward Squaw Creek and did not stop until the ground itself stopped—fell away before us so abruptly that the next step would have been out into the tree-tops. We stood panting on the edge of the ravine, looking down at the trees and bushes that grew below us. The wind was so strong that I had to hold my hat on, and the girls' skirts were blown out before them. Antonia seemed to like it; she held her little sister by the hand and chattered away in that language which seemed to me spoken so much more rapidly than mine. She looked at me, her eyes fairly blazing with things she could not say.

'Name? What name?' she asked, touching me on the shoulder. I told her my name, and she repeated it after me and made Yulka say it. She pointed into the gold cottonwood tree behind whose top we stood and said again, 'What name?'

We sat down and made a nest in the long red grass. Yulka curled up like a baby rabbit and played with a grasshopper. Antonia pointed up to the sky and questioned me with her glance. I gave her the word, but she was not satisfied and pointed to my eyes. I told her, and she repeated the word, making it sound like 'ice.' She pointed up to the sky, then to my eyes, then back to the sky, with movements so quick and impulsive that she distracted me, and I had no idea what she wanted. She got up on her knees and wrung her hands. She pointed to her own eyes and shook her head, then to mine and to the sky, nodding violently.

'Oh,' I exclaimed, 'blue; blue sky.'

She clapped her hands and murmured, 'Blue sky, blue eyes,' as if it amused her. While we snuggled down there out of the wind, she learned a score of words. She was alive, and very eager. We were so deep in the grass that we could see nothing but the blue sky over us and the gold tree in front of us. It was wonderfully pleasant. After Antonia had said the new words over and over, she wanted to give me a little chased silver ring she wore on her middle finger. When she coaxed and insisted, I repulsed her quite sternly. I didn't want her ring, and I felt there was something reckless and extravagant about her wishing to give it away to a boy she had never seen before. No wonder Krajiek got the better of these people, if this was how they behaved.

While we were disputing 'about the ring, I heard a mournful voice calling, 'Antonia, Antonia!' She sprang up like a hare. 'Tatinek! Tatinek!' she shouted, and we ran to meet the old man who was coming toward us. Antonia reached him first, took his hand and kissed it. When I came up, he touched my shoulder and looked searchingly down into my face for several seconds. I became somewhat embarrassed, for I was used to being taken for granted by my elders.

We went with Mr. Shimerda back to the dugout, where grandmother was waiting for me. Before I got into the wagon, he took a book out of his pocket, opened it, and showed me a page with two alphabets, one English and the other Bohemian. He placed this book in my grandmother's hands, looked at her entreatingly, and said, with an earnestness which I shall never forget, 'Te-e-ach, te-e-ach my Antonia!'

IV.

On the afternoon of that same Sunday I took my first long ride on my pony, under Otto's direction. After that Dude and I went twice a week to the post-office, six miles east of us, and I saved the men a good deal of time by riding on errands to our neighbours. When we had to borrow anything, or to send about word that there would be preaching at the sod schoolhouse, I was always the messenger. Formerly Fuchs attended to such things after working hours.

All the years that have passed have not dimmed my memory of that first glorious autumn. The new country lay open before me: there were no fences in those days, and I could choose my own way over the grass uplands, trusting the pony to get me home again. Sometimes I followed the sunflower-bordered roads. Fuchs told me that the sunflowers were introduced into that country by the Mormons; that at the time of the persecution, when they left Missouri and struck out into the wilderness to find a place where they could worship God in their own way, the members of the first exploring party, crossing the plains to Utah, scattered sunflower seed as they went. The next summer, when the long trains of wagons came through with all the women and children, they had the sunflower trail to follow. I believe that botanists do not confirm Fuchs's story, but insist that the sunflower was native to those plains. Nevertheless, that legend has stuck in my mind, and sunflower-bordered roads always seem to me the roads to freedom.

I used to love to drift along the pale-yellow cornfields, looking for the damp spots one sometimes found at their edges, where the smartweed soon turned a rich copper colour and the narrow brown leaves hung curled like cocoons about the swollen joints of the stem. Sometimes I went south to visit our German neighbours and to admire their catalpa grove, or to see the big elm tree that grew up out of a deep crack in the earth and had a hawk's nest in its branches. Trees were so rare in that country, and they had to make such a hard fight to grow, that we used to feel anxious about them, and visit them as if they were persons. It must have been the scarcity of detail in that tawny landscape that made detail so precious.

Sometimes I rode north to the big prairie-dog town to watch the brown earth-owls fly home in the late afternoon and go down to their nests underground with the dogs. Antonia Shimerda liked to go with me, and we used to wonder a great deal about these birds of subterranean habit. We had to be on our guard there, for rattlesnakes were always lurking about. They came to pick up an easy living among the dogs and owls, which were quite defenceless against them; took possession of their comfortable houses and ate the eggs and puppies. We felt sorry for the owls. It was always mournful to see them come flying home at sunset and disappear under the earth. But, after all, we felt, winged things who would live like that must be rather degraded creatures. The dog-town was a long way from any pond or creek. Otto Fuchs said he had seen populous dog-towns in the desert where there was no surface water for fifty miles; he insisted that some of the holes must go down to water—nearly two hundred feet, hereabouts. Antonia said she didn't believe it; that the dogs probably lapped up the dew in the early morning, like the rabbits.

Antonia had opinions about everything, and she was soon able to make them known. Almost every day she came running across the prairie to have her reading lesson with me. Mrs. Shimerda grumbled, but realized it was important that one member of the family should learn English. When the lesson was over, we used to go up to the watermelon patch behind the garden. I split the melons with an old corn-knife, and we lifted out the hearts and ate them with the juice trickling through our fingers. The white Christmas melons we did not touch, but we watched them with curiosity. They were to be picked late, when the hard frosts had set in, and put away for winter use. After weeks on the ocean, the Shimerdas were famished for fruit. The two girls would wander for miles along the edge of the cornfields, hunting for ground-cherries.

Antonia loved to help grandmother in the kitchen and to learn about cooking and housekeeping. She would stand beside her, watching her every movement. We were willing to believe that Mrs. Shimerda was a good housewife in her own country, but she managed poorly under new conditions: the conditions were bad enough, certainly!

I remember how horrified we were at the sour, ashy-grey bread she gave her family to eat. She mixed her dough, we discovered, in an old tin peck-measure that Krajiek had used about the barn. When she took the paste out to bake it, she left smears of dough sticking to the sides of the measure, put the measure on the shelf behind the stove, and let this residue ferment. The next time she made bread, she scraped this sour stuff down into the fresh dough to serve as yeast.

During those first months the Shimerdas never went to town. Krajiek encouraged them in the belief that in Black Hawk they would somehow be mysteriously separated from their money. They hated Krajiek, but they clung to him because he was the only human being with whom they could talk or from whom they could get information. He slept with the old man and the two boys in the dugout barn, along with the oxen. They kept him in their hole and fed him for the same reason that the prairie-dogs and the brown owls house the rattlesnakes—because they did not know how to get rid of him.

V.

We knew that things were hard for our Bohemian neighbours, but the two girls were lighthearted and never complained. They were always ready to forget their troubles at home, and to run away with me over the prairie, scaring rabbits or starting up flocks of quail.

I remember Antonia's excitement when she came into our kitchen one afternoon and announced: 'My papa find friends up north, with Russian mans. Last night he take me for see, and I can understand very much talk. Nice mans, Mrs. Burden. One is fat and all the time laugh. Everybody laugh. The first time I see my papa laugh in this kawntree. Oh, very nice!'

I asked her if she meant the two Russians who lived up by the big dog-town. I had often been tempted to go to see them when I was riding in that direction, but one of them was a wild-looking fellow and I was a little afraid of him. Russia seemed to me more remote than any other country—farther away than China, almost as far as the North Pole. Of all the strange, uprooted people among the first settlers, those two men were the strangest and the most aloof. Their last names were unpronounceable, so they were called Pavel and Peter. They went about making signs to people, and until the Shimerdas came they had no friends. Krajiek could understand them a little, but he had cheated them in a trade, so they avoided him. Pavel, the tall one, was said to be an anarchist; since he had no means of imparting his opinions, probably his wild gesticulations and his generally excited and rebellious manner gave rise to this supposition. He must once have been a very strong man, but now his great frame, with big, knotty joints, had a wasted look, and the skin was drawn tight over his high cheekbones. His breathing was hoarse, and he always had a cough.

Peter, his companion, was a very different sort of fellow; short, bow-legged, and as fat as butter. He always seemed pleased when he met people on the road, smiled and took off his cap to everyone, men as well as women. At a distance, on his wagon, he looked like an old man; his hair and beard were of such a pale flaxen colour that they seemed white in the sun. They were as thick and curly as carded wool. His rosy face, with its snub nose, set in this fleece, was like a melon among its leaves. He was usually called 'Curly Peter,' or 'Rooshian Peter.'

The two Russians made good farm-hands, and in summer they worked out together. I had heard our neighbours laughing when they told how Peter always had to go home at night to milk his cow. Other bachelor homesteaders used canned milk, to save trouble. Sometimes Peter came to church at the sod schoolhouse. It was there I first saw him, sitting on a low bench by the door, his plush cap in his hands, his bare feet tucked apologetically under the seat.

After Mr. Shimerda discovered the Russians, he went to see them almost every evening, and sometimes took Antonia with him. She said they came from a part of Russia where the language was not very different from Bohemian, and if I wanted to go to their place, she could talk to them for me. One afternoon, before the heavy frosts began, we rode up there together on my pony.

The Russians had a neat log house built on a grassy slope, with a windlass well beside the door. As we rode up the draw, we skirted a big melon patch, and a garden where squashes and yellow cucumbers lay about on the sod. We found Peter out behind his kitchen, bending over a washtub. He was working so hard that he did not hear us coming. His whole body moved up and down as he rubbed, and he was a funny sight from the rear, with his shaggy head and bandy legs. When he straightened himself up to greet us, drops of perspiration were rolling from his thick nose down onto his curly beard. Peter dried his hands and seemed glad to leave his washing. He took us down to see his chickens, and his cow that was grazing on the hillside. He told Antonia that in his country only rich people had cows, but here any man could have one who would take care of her. The milk was good for Pavel, who was often sick, and he could make butter by beating sour cream with a wooden spoon. Peter was very fond of his cow. He patted her flanks and talked to her in Russian while he pulled up her lariat pin and set it in a new place.

After he had shown us his garden, Peter trundled a load of watermelons up the hill in his wheelbarrow. Pavel was not at home. He was off somewhere helping to dig a well. The house I thought very comfortable for two men who were 'batching.' Besides the kitchen, there was a living-room, with a wide double bed built against the wall, properly made up with blue gingham sheets and pillows. There was a little storeroom, too, with a window, where they kept guns and saddles and tools, and old coats and boots. That day the floor was covered with garden things, drying for winter; corn and beans and fat yellow cucumbers. There were no screens or window-blinds in the house, and all the doors and windows stood wide open, letting in flies and sunshine alike.

Peter put the melons in a row on the oilcloth-covered table and stood over them, brandishing a butcher knife. Before the blade got fairly into them, they split of their own ripeness, with a delicious sound. He gave us knives, but no plates, and the top of the table was soon swimming with juice and seeds. I had never seen anyone eat so many melons as Peter ate. He assured us that they were good for one—better than medicine; in his country people lived on them at this time of year. He was very hospitable and jolly. Once, while he was looking at Antonia, he sighed and told us that if he had stayed at home in Russia perhaps by this time he would have had a pretty daughter of his own to cook and keep house for him. He said he had left his country because of a 'great trouble.'

When we got up to go, Peter looked about in perplexity for something that would entertain us. He ran into the storeroom and brought out a gaudily painted harmonica, sat down on a bench, and spreading his fat legs apart began to play like a whole band. The tunes were either very lively or very doleful, and he sang words to some of them.

Before we left, Peter put ripe cucumbers into a sack for Mrs. Shimerda and gave us a lard-pail full of milk to cook them in. I had never heard of cooking cucumbers, but Antonia assured me they were very good. We had to walk the pony all the way home to keep from spilling the milk.

VI.

One afternoon we were having our reading lesson on the warm, grassy bank where the badger lived. It was a day of amber sunlight, but there was a shiver of coming winter in the air. I had seen ice on the little horsepond that morning, and as we went through the garden we found the tall asparagus, with its red berries, lying on the ground, a mass of slimy green.

Tony was barefooted, and she shivered in her cotton dress and was comfortable only when we were tucked down on the baked earth, in the full blaze of the sun. She could talk to me about almost anything by this time. That afternoon she was telling me how highly esteemed our friend the badger was in her part of the world, and how men kept a special kind of dog, with very short legs, to hunt him. Those dogs, she said, went down into the hole after the badger and killed him there in a terrific struggle underground; you could hear the barks and yelps outside. Then the dog dragged himself back, covered with bites and scratches, to be rewarded and petted by his master. She knew a dog who had a star on his collar for every badger he had killed.

The rabbits were unusually spry that afternoon. They kept starting up all about us, and dashing off down the draw as if they were playing a game of some kind. But the little buzzing things that lived in the grass were all dead—all but one. While we were lying there against the warm bank, a little insect of the palest, frailest green hopped painfully out of the buffalo grass and tried to leap into a bunch of bluestem. He missed it, fell back, and sat with his head sunk between his long legs, his antennae quivering, as if he were waiting for something to come and finish him. Tony made a warm nest for him in her hands; talked to him gaily and indulgently in Bohemian. Presently he began to sing for us—a thin, rusty little chirp. She held him close to her ear and laughed, but a moment afterward I saw there were tears in her eyes. She told me that in her village at home there was an old beggar woman who went about selling herbs and roots she had dug up in the forest. If you took her in and gave her a warm place by the fire, she sang old songs to the children in a cracked voice, like this. Old Hata, she was called, and the children loved to see her coming and saved their cakes and sweets for her.

When the bank on the other side of the draw began to throw a narrow shelf of shadow, we knew we ought to be starting homeward; the chill came on quickly when the sun got low, and Antonia's dress was thin. What were we to do with the frail little creature we had lured back to life by false pretences? I offered my pockets, but Tony shook her head and carefully put the green insect in her hair, tying her big handkerchief down loosely over her curls. I said I would go with her until we could see Squaw Creek, and then turn and run home. We drifted along lazily, very happy, through the magical light of the late afternoon.

All those fall afternoons were the same, but I never got used to them. As far as we could see, the miles of copper-red grass were drenched in sunlight that was stronger and fiercer than at any other time of the day. The blond cornfields were red gold, the haystacks turned rosy and threw long shadows. The whole prairie was like the bush that burned with fire and was not consumed. That hour always had the exultation of victory, of triumphant ending, like a hero's death—heroes who died young and gloriously. It was a sudden transfiguration, a lifting-up of day.

How many an afternoon Antonia and I have trailed along the prairie under that magnificence! And always two long black shadows flitted before us or followed after, dark spots on the ruddy grass.

We had been silent a long time, and the edge of the sun sank nearer and nearer the prairie floor, when we saw a figure moving on the edge of the upland, a gun over his shoulder. He was walking slowly, dragging his feet along as if he had no purpose. We broke into a run to overtake him.

'My papa sick all the time,' Tony panted as we flew. 'He not look good, Jim.'

As we neared Mr. Shimerda she shouted, and he lifted his head and peered about. Tony ran up to him, caught his hand and pressed it against her cheek. She was the only one of his family who could rouse the old man from the torpor in which he seemed to live. He took the bag from his belt and showed us three rabbits he had shot, looked at Antonia with a wintry flicker of a smile and began to tell her something. She turned to me.

'My tatinek make me little hat with the skins, little hat for winter!' she exclaimed joyfully. 'Meat for eat, skin for hat'—she told off these benefits on her fingers.

Her father put his hand on her hair, but she caught his wrist and lifted it carefully away, talking to him rapidly. I heard the name of old Hata. He untied the handkerchief, separated her hair with his fingers, and stood looking down at the green insect. When it began to chirp faintly, he listened as if it were a beautiful sound.

I picked up the gun he had dropped; a queer piece from the old country, short and heavy, with a stag's head on the cock. When he saw me examining it, he turned to me with his far-away look that always made me feel as if I were down at the bottom of a well. He spoke kindly and gravely, and Antonia translated:

'My tatinek say when you are big boy, he give you his gun. Very fine, from Bohemie. It was belong to a great man, very rich, like what you not got here; many fields, many forests, many big house. My papa play for his wedding, and he give my papa fine gun, and my papa give you.'

I was glad that this project was one of futurity. There never were such people as the Shimerdas for wanting to give away everything they had. Even the mother was always offering me things, though I knew she expected substantial presents in return. We stood there in friendly silence, while the feeble minstrel sheltered in Antonia's hair went on with its scratchy chirp. The old man's smile, as he listened, was so full of sadness, of pity for things, that I never afterward forgot it. As the sun sank there came a sudden coolness and the strong smell of earth and drying grass. Antonia and her father went off hand in hand, and I buttoned up my jacket and raced my shadow home.

VII.

Much as I liked Antonia, I hated a superior tone that she sometimes took with me. She was four years older than I, to be sure, and had seen more of the world; but I was a boy and she was a girl, and I resented her protecting manner. Before the autumn was over, she began to treat me more like an equal and to defer to me in other things than reading lessons. This change came about from an adventure we had together.

One day when I rode over to the Shimerdas' I found Antonia starting off on foot for Russian Peter's house, to borrow a spade Ambrosch needed. I offered to take her on the pony, and she got up behind me. There had been another black frost the night before, and the air was clear and heady as wine. Within a week all the blooming roads had been despoiled, hundreds of miles of yellow sunflowers had been transformed into brown, rattling, burry stalks.

We found Russian Peter digging his potatoes. We were glad to go in and get warm by his kitchen stove and to see his squashes and Christmas melons, heaped in the storeroom for winter. As we rode away with the spade, Antonia suggested that we stop at the prairie-dog-town and dig into one of the holes. We could find out whether they ran straight down, or were horizontal, like mole-holes; whether they had underground connections; whether the owls had nests down there, lined with feathers. We might get some puppies, or owl eggs, or snakeskins.

The dog-town was spread out over perhaps ten acres. The grass had been nibbled short and even, so this stretch was not shaggy and red like the surrounding country, but grey and velvety. The holes were several yards apart, and were disposed with a good deal of regularity, almost as if the town had been laid out in streets and avenues. One always felt that an orderly and very sociable kind of life was going on there. I picketed Dude down in a draw, and we went wandering about, looking for a hole that would be easy to dig. The dogs were out, as usual, dozens of them, sitting up on their hind legs over the doors of their houses. As we approached, they barked, shook their tails at us, and scurried underground. Before the mouths of the holes were little patches of sand and gravel, scratched up, we supposed, from a long way below the surface. Here and there, in the town, we came on larger gravel patches, several yards away from any hole. If the dogs had scratched the sand up in excavating, how had they carried it so far? It was on one of these gravel beds that I met my adventure.

We were examining a big hole with two entrances. The burrow sloped into the ground at a gentle angle, so that we could see where the two corridors united, and the floor was dusty from use, like a little highway over which much travel went. I was walking backward, in a crouching position, when I heard Antonia scream. She was standing opposite me, pointing behind me and shouting something in Bohemian. I whirled round, and there, on one of those dry gravel beds, was the biggest snake I had ever seen. He was sunning himself, after the cold night, and he must have been asleep when Antonia screamed. When I turned, he was lying in long loose waves, like a letter 'W.' He twitched and began to coil slowly. He was not merely a big snake, I thought—he was a circus monstrosity. His abominable muscularity, his loathsome, fluid motion, somehow made me sick. He was as thick as my leg, and looked as if millstones couldn't crush the disgusting vitality out of him. He lifted his hideous little head, and rattled. I didn't run because I didn't think of it—if my back had been against a stone wall I couldn't have felt more cornered. I saw his coils tighten—now he would spring, spring his length, I remembered. I ran up and drove at his head with my spade, struck him fairly across the neck, and in a minute he was all about my feet in wavy loops. I struck now from hate. Antonia, barefooted as she was, ran up behind me. Even after I had pounded his ugly head flat, his body kept on coiling and winding, doubling and falling back on itself. I walked away and turned my back. I felt seasick.

Antonia came after me, crying, 'O Jimmy, he not bite you? You sure? Why you not run when I say?'

'What did you jabber Bohunk for? You might have told me there was a snake behind me!' I said petulantly.

'I know I am just awful, Jim, I was so scared.' She took my handkerchief from my pocket and tried to wipe my face with it, but I snatched it away from her. I suppose I looked as sick as I felt.

'I never know you was so brave, Jim,' she went on comfortingly. 'You is just like big mans; you wait for him lift his head and then you go for him. Ain't you feel scared a bit? Now we take that snake home and show everybody. Nobody ain't seen in this kawntree so big snake like you kill.'

She went on in this strain until I began to think that I had longed for this opportunity, and had hailed it with joy. Cautiously we went back to the snake; he was still groping with his tail, turning up his ugly belly in the light. A faint, fetid smell came from him, and a thread of green liquid oozed from his crushed head.

'Look, Tony, that's his poison,' I said.

I took a long piece of string from my pocket, and she lifted his head with the spade while I tied a noose around it. We pulled him out straight and measured him by my riding-quirt; he was about five and a half feet long. He had twelve rattles, but they were broken off before they began to taper, so I insisted that he must once have had twenty-four. I explained to Antonia how this meant that he was twenty-four years old, that he must have been there when white men first came, left on from buffalo and Indian times. As I turned him over, I began to feel proud of him, to have a kind of respect for his age and size. He seemed like the ancient, eldest Evil. Certainly his kind have left horrible unconscious memories in all warm-blooded life. When we dragged him down into the draw, Dude sprang off to the end of his tether and shivered all over—wouldn't let us come near him.

We decided that Antonia should ride Dude home, and I would walk. As she rode along slowly, her bare legs swinging against the pony's sides, she kept shouting back to me about how astonished everybody would be. I followed with the spade over my shoulder, dragging my snake. Her exultation was contagious. The great land had never looked to me so big and free. If the red grass were full of rattlers, I was equal to them all. Nevertheless, I stole furtive glances behind me now and then to see that no avenging mate, older and bigger than my quarry, was racing up from the rear.

The sun had set when we reached our garden and went down the draw toward the house. Otto Fuchs was the first one we met. He was sitting on the edge of the cattle-pond, having a quiet pipe before supper. Antonia called him to come quick and look. He did not say anything for a minute, but scratched his head and turned the snake over with his boot.

'Where did you run onto that beauty, Jim?'

'Up at the dog-town,' I answered laconically.

'Kill him yourself? How come you to have a weepon?'

'We'd been up to Russian Peter's, to borrow a spade for Ambrosch.'

Otto shook the ashes out of his pipe and squatted down to count the rattles. 'It was just luck you had a tool,' he said cautiously. 'Gosh! I wouldn't want to do any business with that fellow myself, unless I had a fence-post along. Your grandmother's snake-cane wouldn't more than tickle him. He could stand right up and talk to you, he could. Did he fight hard?'

Antonia broke in: 'He fight something awful! He is all over Jimmy's boots. I scream for him to run, but he just hit and hit that snake like he was crazy.'

Otto winked at me. After Antonia rode on he said: 'Got him in the head first crack, didn't you? That was just as well.'

We hung him up to the windmill, and when I went down to the kitchen, I found Antonia standing in the middle of the floor, telling the story with a great deal of colour.

Subsequent experiences with rattlesnakes taught me that my first encounter was fortunate in circumstance. My big rattler was old, and had led too easy a life; there was not much fight in him. He had probably lived there for years, with a fat prairie-dog for breakfast whenever he felt like it, a sheltered home, even an owl-feather bed, perhaps, and he had forgot that the world doesn't owe rattlers a living. A snake of his size, in fighting trim, would be more than any boy could handle. So in reality it was a mock adventure; the game was fixed for me by chance, as it probably was for many a dragon-slayer. I had been adequately armed by Russian Peter; the snake was old and lazy; and I had Antonia beside me, to appreciate and admire.

That snake hung on our corral fence for several days; some of the neighbours came to see it and agreed that it was the biggest rattler ever killed in those parts. This was enough for Antonia. She liked me better from that time on, and she never took a supercilious air with me again. I had killed a big snake—I was now a big fellow.

VIII.

While the autumn color was growing pale on the grass and cornfields, things went badly with our friends the Russians. Peter told his troubles to Mr. Shimerda: he was unable to meet a note which fell due on the first of November; had to pay an exorbitant bonus on renewing it, and to give a mortgage on his pigs and horses and even his milk cow. His creditor was Wick Cutter, the merciless Black Hawk money-lender, a man of evil name throughout the county, of whom I shall have more to say later. Peter could give no very clear account of his transactions with Cutter. He only knew that he had first borrowed two hundred dollars, then another hundred, then fifty—that each time a bonus was added to the principal, and the debt grew faster than any crop he planted. Now everything was plastered with mortgages.

Soon after Peter renewed his note, Pavel strained himself lifting timbers for a new barn, and fell over among the shavings with such a gush of blood from the lungs that his fellow workmen thought he would die on the spot. They hauled him home and put him into his bed, and there he lay, very ill indeed. Misfortune seemed to settle like an evil bird on the roof of the log house, and to flap its wings there, warning human beings away. The Russians had such bad luck that people were afraid of them and liked to put them out of mind.

One afternoon Antonia and her father came over to our house to get buttermilk, and lingered, as they usually did, until the sun was low. Just as they were leaving, Russian Peter drove up. Pavel was very bad, he said, and wanted to talk to Mr. Shimerda and his daughter; he had come to fetch them. When Antonia and her father got into the wagon, I entreated grandmother to let me go with them: I would gladly go without my supper, I would sleep in the Shimerdas' barn and run home in the morning. My plan must have seemed very foolish to her, but she was often large-minded about humouring the desires of other people. She asked Peter to wait a moment, and when she came back from the kitchen she brought a bag of sandwiches and doughnuts for us.

Mr. Shimerda and Peter were on the front seat; Antonia and I sat in the straw behind and ate our lunch as we bumped along. After the sun sank, a cold wind sprang up and moaned over the prairie. If this turn in the weather had come sooner, I should not have got away. We burrowed down in the straw and curled up close together, watching the angry red die out of the west and the stars begin to shine in the clear, windy sky. Peter kept sighing and groaning. Tony whispered to me that he was afraid Pavel would never get well. We lay still and did not talk. Up there the stars grew magnificently bright. Though we had come from such different parts of the world, in both of us there was some dusky superstition that those shining groups have their influence upon what is and what is not to be. Perhaps Russian Peter, come from farther away than any of us, had brought from his land, too, some such belief.

The little house on the hillside was so much the colour of the night that we could not see it as we came up the draw. The ruddy windows guided us—the light from the kitchen stove, for there was no lamp burning.

We entered softly. The man in the wide bed seemed to be asleep. Tony and I sat down on the bench by the wall and leaned our arms on the table in front of us. The firelight flickered on the hewn logs that supported the thatch overhead. Pavel made a rasping sound when he breathed, and he kept moaning. We waited. The wind shook the doors and windows impatiently, then swept on again, singing through the big spaces. Each gust, as it bore down, rattled the panes, and swelled off like the others. They made me think of defeated armies, retreating; or of ghosts who were trying desperately to get in for shelter, and then went moaning on. Presently, in one of those sobbing intervals between the blasts, the coyotes tuned up with their whining howl; one, two, three, then all together—to tell us that winter was coming. This sound brought an answer from the bed—a long complaining cry—as if Pavel were having bad dreams or were waking to some old misery. Peter listened, but did not stir. He was sitting on the floor by the kitchen stove. The coyotes broke out again; yap, yap, yap—then the high whine. Pavel called for something and struggled up on his elbow.

'He is scared of the wolves,' Antonia whispered to me. 'In his country there are very many, and they eat men and women.' We slid closer together along the bench.

I could not take my eyes off the man in the bed. His shirt was hanging open, and his emaciated chest, covered with yellow bristle, rose and fell horribly. He began to cough. Peter shuffled to his feet, caught up the teakettle and mixed him some hot water and whiskey. The sharp smell of spirits went through the room.

Pavel snatched the cup and drank, then made Peter give him the bottle and slipped it under his pillow, grinning disagreeably, as if he had outwitted someone. His eyes followed Peter about the room with a contemptuous, unfriendly expression. It seemed to me that he despised him for being so simple and docile.

Presently Pavel began to talk to Mr. Shimerda, scarcely above a whisper. He was telling a long story, and as he went on, Antonia took my hand under the table and held it tight. She leaned forward and strained her ears to hear him. He grew more and more excited, and kept pointing all around his bed, as if there were things there and he wanted Mr. Shimerda to see them.

'It's wolves, Jimmy,' Antonia whispered. 'It's awful, what he says!'

The sick man raged and shook his fist. He seemed to be cursing people who had wronged him. Mr. Shimerda caught him by the shoulders, but could hardly hold him in bed. At last he was shut off by a coughing fit which fairly choked him. He pulled a cloth from under his pillow and held it to his mouth. Quickly it was covered with bright red spots—I thought I had never seen any blood so bright. When he lay down and turned his face to the wall, all the rage had gone out of him. He lay patiently fighting for breath, like a child with croup. Antonia's father uncovered one of his long bony legs and rubbed it rhythmically. From our bench we could see what a hollow case his body was. His spine and shoulder-blades stood out like the bones under the hide of a dead steer left in the fields. That sharp backbone must have hurt him when he lay on it.

Gradually, relief came to all of us. Whatever it was, the worst was over. Mr. Shimerda signed to us that Pavel was asleep. Without a word Peter got up and lit his lantern. He was going out to get his team to drive us home. Mr. Shimerda went with him. We sat and watched the long bowed back under the blue sheet, scarcely daring to breathe.

On the way home, when we were lying in the straw, under the jolting and rattling Antonia told me as much of the story as she could. What she did not tell me then, she told later; we talked of nothing else for days afterward.

When Pavel and Peter were young men, living at home in Russia, they were asked to be groomsmen for a friend who was to marry the belle of another village. It was in the dead of winter and the groom's party went over to the wedding in sledges. Peter and Pavel drove in the groom's sledge, and six sledges followed with all his relatives and friends.

After the ceremony at the church, the party went to a dinner given by the parents of the bride. The dinner lasted all afternoon; then it became a supper and continued far into the night. There was much dancing and drinking. At midnight the parents of the bride said good-bye to her and blessed her. The groom took her up in his arms and carried her out to his sledge and tucked her under the blankets. He sprang in beside her, and Pavel and Peter (our Pavel and Peter!) took the front seat. Pavel drove. The party set out with singing and the jingle of sleigh-bells, the groom's sledge going first. All the drivers were more or less the worse for merry-making, and the groom was absorbed in his bride.

The wolves were bad that winter, and everyone knew it, yet when they heard the first wolf-cry, the drivers were not much alarmed. They had too much good food and drink inside them. The first howls were taken up and echoed and with quickening repetitions. The wolves were coming together. There was no moon, but the starlight was clear on the snow. A black drove came up over the hill behind the wedding party. The wolves ran like streaks of shadow; they looked no bigger than dogs, but there were hundreds of them.

Something happened to the hindmost sledge: the driver lost control—he was probably very drunk—the horses left the road, the sledge was caught in a clump of trees, and overturned. The occupants rolled out over the snow, and the fleetest of the wolves sprang upon them. The shrieks that followed made everybody sober. The drivers stood up and lashed their horses. The groom had the best team and his sledge was lightest—all the others carried from six to a dozen people.

Another driver lost control. The screams of the horses were more terrible to hear than the cries of the men and women. Nothing seemed to check the wolves. It was hard to tell what was happening in the rear; the people who were falling behind shrieked as piteously as those who were already lost. The little bride hid her face on the groom's shoulder and sobbed. Pavel sat still and watched his horses. The road was clear and white, and the groom's three blacks went like the wind. It was only necessary to be calm and to guide them carefully.

At length, as they breasted a long hill, Peter rose cautiously and looked back. 'There are only three sledges left,' he whispered.

'And the wolves?' Pavel asked.

'Enough! Enough for all of us.'

Pavel reached the brow of the hill, but only two sledges followed him down the other side. In that moment on the hilltop, they saw behind them a whirling black group on the snow. Presently the groom screamed. He saw his father's sledge overturned, with his mother and sisters. He sprang up as if he meant to jump, but the girl shrieked and held him back. It was even then too late. The black ground-shadows were already crowding over the heap in the road, and one horse ran out across the fields, his harness hanging to him, wolves at his heels. But the groom's movement had given Pavel an idea.

They were within a few miles of their village now. The only sledge left out of six was not very far behind them, and Pavel's middle horse was failing. Beside a frozen pond something happened to the other sledge; Peter saw it plainly. Three big wolves got abreast of the horses, and the horses went crazy. They tried to jump over each other, got tangled up in the harness, and overturned the sledge.

When the shrieking behind them died away, Pavel realized that he was alone upon the familiar road. 'They still come?' he asked Peter.

'Yes.'

'How many?'

'Twenty, thirty—enough.'

Now his middle horse was being almost dragged by the other two. Pavel gave Peter the reins and stepped carefully into the back of the sledge. He called to the groom that they must lighten—and pointed to the bride. The young man cursed him and held her tighter. Pavel tried to drag her away. In the struggle, the groom rose. Pavel knocked him over the side of the sledge and threw the girl after him. He said he never remembered exactly how he did it, or what happened afterward. Peter, crouching in the front seat, saw nothing. The first thing either of them noticed was a new sound that broke into the clear air, louder than they had ever heard it before—the bell of the monastery of their own village, ringing for early prayers.

Pavel and Peter drove into the village alone, and they had been alone ever since. They were run out of their village. Pavel's own mother would not look at him. They went away to strange towns, but when people learned where they came from, they were always asked if they knew the two men who had fed the bride to the wolves. Wherever they went, the story followed them. It took them five years to save money enough to come to America. They worked in Chicago, Des Moines, Fort Wayne, but they were always unfortunate. When Pavel's health grew so bad, they decided to try farming.

Pavel died a few days after he unburdened his mind to Mr. Shimerda, and was buried in the Norwegian graveyard. Peter sold off everything, and left the country—went to be cook in a railway construction camp where gangs of Russians were employed.

At his sale we bought Peter's wheelbarrow and some of his harness. During the auction he went about with his head down, and never lifted his eyes. He seemed not to care about anything. The Black Hawk money-lender who held mortgages on Peter's livestock was there, and he bought in the sale notes at about fifty cents on the dollar. Everyone said Peter kissed the cow before she was led away by her new owner. I did not see him do it, but this I know:

after all his furniture and his cookstove and pots and pans had been hauled off by the purchasers, when his house was stripped and bare, he sat down on the floor with his clasp-knife and ate all the melons that he had put away for winter. When Mr. Shimerda and Krajiek drove up in their wagon to take Peter to the train, they found him with a dripping beard, surrounded by heaps of melon rinds.

The loss of his two friends had a depressing effect upon old Mr. Shimerda. When he was out hunting, he used to go into the empty log house and sit there, brooding. This cabin was his hermitage until the winter snows penned him in his cave. For Antonia and me, the story of the wedding party was never at an end. We did not tell Pavel's secret to anyone, but guarded it jealously—as if the wolves of the Ukraine had gathered that night long ago, and the wedding party been sacrificed, to give us a painful and peculiar pleasure. At night, before I went to sleep, I often found myself in a sledge drawn by three horses, dashing through a country that looked something like Nebraska and something like Virginia.

IX.

The first snowfall came early in December. I remember how the world looked from our sitting-room window as I dressed behind the stove that morning: the low sky was like a sheet of metal; the blond cornfields had faded out into ghostliness at last; the little pond was frozen under its stiff willow bushes. Big white flakes were whirling over everything and disappearing in the red grass.

Beyond the pond, on the slope that climbed to the cornfield, there was, faintly marked in the grass, a great circle where the Indians used to ride. Jake and Otto were sure that when they galloped round that ring the Indians tortured prisoners, bound to a stake in the centre; but grandfather thought they merely ran races or trained horses there. Whenever one looked at this slope against the setting sun, the circle showed like a pattern in the grass; and this morning, when the first light spray of snow lay over it, it came out with wonderful distinctness, like strokes of Chinese white on canvas. The old figure stirred me as it had never done before and seemed a good omen for the winter.

As soon as the snow had packed hard, I began to drive about the country in a clumsy sleigh that Otto Fuchs made for me by fastening a wooden goods-box on bobs. Fuchs had been apprenticed to a cabinetmaker in the old country and was very handy with tools. He would have done a better job if I hadn't hurried him. My first trip was to the post-office, and the next day I went over to take Yulka and Antonia for a sleigh-ride.

It was a bright, cold day. I piled straw and buffalo robes into the box, and took two hot bricks wrapped in old blankets. When I got to the Shimerdas', I did not go up to the house, but sat in my sleigh at the bottom of the draw and called. Antonia and Yulka came running out, wearing little rabbit-skin hats their father had made for them. They had heard about my sledge from Ambrosch and knew why I had come. They tumbled in beside me and we set off toward the north, along a road that happened to be broken.

The sky was brilliantly blue, and the sunlight on the glittering white stretches of prairie was almost blinding. As Antonia said, the whole world was changed by the snow; we kept looking in vain for familiar landmarks. The deep arroyo through which Squaw Creek wound was now only a cleft between snowdrifts—very blue when one looked down into it. The tree-tops that had been gold all the autumn were dwarfed and twisted, as if they would never have any life in them again. The few little cedars, which were so dull and dingy before, now stood out a strong, dusky green. The wind had the burning taste of fresh snow; my throat and nostrils smarted as if someone had opened a hartshorn bottle. The cold stung, and at the same time delighted one. My horse's breath rose like steam, and whenever we stopped he smoked all over. The cornfields got back a little of their colour under the dazzling light, and stood the palest possible gold in the sun and snow. All about us the snow was crusted in shallow terraces, with tracings like ripple-marks at the edges, curly waves that were the actual impression of the stinging lash in the wind.

The girls had on cotton dresses under their shawls; they kept shivering beneath the buffalo robes and hugging each other for warmth. But they were so glad to get away from their ugly cave and their mother's scolding that they begged me to go on and on, as far as Russian Peter's house. The great fresh open, after the stupefying warmth indoors, made them behave like wild things. They laughed and shouted, and said they never wanted to go home again. Couldn't we settle down and live in Russian Peter's house, Yulka asked, and couldn't I go to town and buy things for us to keep house with?

All the way to Russian Peter's we were extravagantly happy, but when we turned back—it must have been about four o'clock—the east wind grew stronger and began to howl; the sun lost its heartening power and the sky became grey and sombre. I took off my long woollen comforter and wound it around Yulka's throat. She got so cold that we made her hide her head under the buffalo robe. Antonia and I sat erect, but I held the reins clumsily, and my eyes were blinded by the wind a good deal of the time. It was growing dark when we got to their house, but I refused to go in with them and get warm. I knew my hands would ache terribly if I went near a fire. Yulka forgot to give me back my comforter, and I had to drive home directly against the wind. The next day I came down with an attack of quinsy, which kept me in the house for nearly two weeks.

The basement kitchen seemed heavenly safe and warm in those days—like a tight little boat in a winter sea. The men were out in the fields all day, husking corn, and when they came in at noon, with long caps pulled down over their ears and their feet in red-lined overshoes, I used to think they were like Arctic explorers. In the afternoons, when grandmother sat upstairs darning, or making husking-gloves, I read 'The Swiss Family Robinson' aloud to her, and I felt that the Swiss family had no advantages over us in the way of an adventurous life. I was convinced that man's strongest antagonist is the cold. I admired the cheerful zest with which grandmother went about keeping us warm and comfortable and well-fed. She often reminded me, when she was preparing for the return of the hungry men, that this country was not like Virginia; and that here a cook had, as she said, 'very little to do with.' On Sundays she gave us as much chicken as we could eat, and on other days we had ham or bacon or sausage meat. She baked either pies or cake for us every day, unless, for a change, she made my favourite pudding, striped with currants and boiled in a bag.

Next to getting warm and keeping warm, dinner and supper were the most interesting things we had to think about. Our lives centred around warmth and food and the return of the men at nightfall. I used to wonder, when they came in tired from the fields, their feet numb and their hands cracked and sore, how they could do all the chores so conscientiously: feed and water and bed the horses, milk the cows, and look after the pigs. When supper was over, it took them a long while to get the cold out of their bones. While grandmother and I washed the dishes and grandfather read his paper upstairs, Jake and Otto sat on the long bench behind the stove, 'easing' their inside boots, or rubbing mutton tallow into their cracked hands.

Every Saturday night we popped corn or made taffy, and Otto Fuchs used to sing, 'For I Am a Cowboy and Know I've Done Wrong,' or, 'Bury Me Not on the Lone Prairee.' He had a good baritone voice and always led the singing when we went to church services at the sod schoolhouse.

I can still see those two men sitting on the bench; Otto's close-clipped head and Jake's shaggy hair slicked flat in front by a wet comb. I can see the sag of their tired shoulders against the whitewashed wall. What good fellows they were, how much they knew, and how many things they had kept faith with!

Fuchs had been a cowboy, a stage-driver, a bartender, a miner; had wandered all over that great Western country and done hard work everywhere, though, as grandmother said, he had nothing to show for it. Jake was duller than Otto. He could scarcely read, wrote even his name with difficulty, and he had a violent temper which sometimes made him behave like a crazy man—tore him all to pieces and actually made him ill. But he was so soft-hearted that anyone could impose upon him. If he, as he said, 'forgot himself' and swore before grandmother, he went about depressed and shamefaced all day. They were both of them jovial about the cold in winter and the heat in summer, always ready to work overtime and to meet emergencies. It was a matter of pride with them not to spare themselves. Yet they were the sort of men who never get on, somehow, or do anything but work hard for a dollar or two a day.

On those bitter, starlit nights, as we sat around the old stove that fed us and warmed us and kept us cheerful, we could hear the coyotes howling down by the corrals, and their hungry, wintry cry used to remind the boys of wonderful animal stories; about grey wolves and bears in the Rockies, wildcats and panthers in the Virginia mountains. Sometimes Fuchs could be persuaded to talk about the outlaws and desperate characters he had known. I remember one funny story about himself that made grandmother, who was working her bread on the bread-board, laugh until she wiped her eyes with her bare arm, her hands being floury. It was like this:

When Otto left Austria to come to America, he was asked by one of his relatives to look after a woman who was crossing on the same boat, to join her husband in Chicago. The woman started off with two children, but it was clear that her family might grow larger on the journey. Fuchs said he 'got on fine with the kids,' and liked the mother, though she played a sorry trick on him. In mid-ocean she proceeded to have not one baby, but three! This event made Fuchs the object of undeserved notoriety, since he was travelling with her. The steerage stewardess was indignant with him, the doctor regarded him with suspicion. The first-cabin passengers, who made up a purse for the woman, took an embarrassing interest in Otto, and often enquired of him about his charge. When the triplets were taken ashore at New York, he had, as he said, 'to carry some of them.' The trip to Chicago was even worse than the ocean voyage. On the train it was very difficult to get milk for the babies and to keep their bottles clean. The mother did her best, but no woman, out of her natural resources, could feed three babies. The husband, in Chicago, was working in a furniture factory for modest wages, and when he met his family at the station he was rather crushed by the size of it. He, too, seemed to consider Fuchs in some fashion to blame. 'I was sure glad,' Otto concluded, 'that he didn't take his hard feeling out on that poor woman; but he had a sullen eye for me, all right! Now, did you ever hear of a young feller's having such hard luck, Mrs. Burden?'

Grandmother told him she was sure the Lord had remembered these things to his credit, and had helped him out of many a scrape when he didn't realize that he was being protected by Providence.

X.

For several weeks after my sleigh-ride, we heard nothing from the Shimerdas. My sore throat kept me indoors, and grandmother had a cold which made the housework heavy for her. When Sunday came she was glad to have a day of rest. One night at supper Fuchs told us he had seen Mr. Shimerda out hunting.

'He's made himself a rabbit-skin cap, Jim, and a rabbit-skin collar that he buttons on outside his coat. They ain't got but one overcoat among 'em over there, and they take turns wearing it. They seem awful scared of cold, and stick in that hole in the bank like badgers.'

'All but the crazy boy,' Jake put in. 'He never wears the coat. Krajiek says he's turrible strong and can stand anything. I guess rabbits must be getting scarce in this locality. Ambrosch come along by the cornfield yesterday where I was at work and showed me three prairie dogs he'd shot. He asked me if they was good to eat. I spit and made a face and took on, to scare him, but he just looked like he was smarter'n me and put 'em back in his sack and walked off.'

Grandmother looked up in alarm and spoke to grandfather. 'Josiah, you don't suppose Krajiek would let them poor creatures eat prairie dogs, do you?'

'You had better go over and see our neighbours tomorrow, Emmaline,' he replied gravely.

Fuchs put in a cheerful word and said prairie dogs were clean beasts and ought to be good for food, but their family connections were against them. I asked what he meant, and he grinned and said they belonged to the rat family.

When I went downstairs in the morning, I found grandmother and Jake packing a hamper basket in the kitchen.

'Now, Jake,' grandmother was saying, 'if you can find that old rooster that got his comb froze, just give his neck a twist, and we'll take him along. There's no good reason why Mrs. Shimerda couldn't have got hens from her neighbours last fall and had a hen-house going by now. I reckon she was confused and didn't know where to begin. I've come strange to a new country myself, but I never forgot hens are a good thing to have, no matter what you don't have.

'Just as you say, ma'm,' said Jake, 'but I hate to think of Krajiek getting a leg of that old rooster.' He tramped out through the long cellar and dropped the heavy door behind him.

After breakfast grandmother and Jake and I bundled ourselves up and climbed into the cold front wagon-seat. As we approached the Shimerdas', we heard the frosty whine of the pump and saw Antonia, her head tied up and her cotton dress blown about her, throwing all her weight on the pump-handle as it went up and down. She heard our wagon, looked back over her shoulder, and, catching up her pail of water, started at a run for the hole in the bank.

Jake helped grandmother to the ground, saying he would bring the provisions after he had blanketed his horses. We went slowly up the icy path toward the door sunk in the drawside. Blue puffs of smoke came from the stovepipe that stuck out through the grass and snow, but the wind whisked them roughly away.

Mrs. Shimerda opened the door before we knocked and seized grandmother's hand. She did not say 'How do!' as usual, but at once began to cry, talking very fast in her own language, pointing to her feet which were tied up in rags, and looking about accusingly at everyone.

The old man was sitting on a stump behind the stove, crouching over as if he were trying to hide from us. Yulka was on the floor at his feet, her kitten in her lap. She peeped out at me and smiled, but, glancing up at her mother, hid again. Antonia was washing pans and dishes in a dark corner. The crazy boy lay under the only window, stretched on a gunny-sack stuffed with straw. As soon as we entered, he threw a grain-sack over the crack at the bottom of the door. The air in the cave was stifling, and it was very dark, too. A lighted lantern, hung over the stove, threw out a feeble yellow glimmer.

Mrs. Shimerda snatched off the covers of two barrels behind the door, and made us look into them. In one there were some potatoes that had been frozen and were rotting, in the other was a little pile of flour. Grandmother murmured something in embarrassment, but the Bohemian woman laughed scornfully, a kind of whinny-laugh, and, catching up an empty coffee-pot from the shelf, shook it at us with a look positively vindictive.

Grandmother went on talking in her polite Virginia way, not admitting their stark need or her own remissness, until Jake arrived with the hamper, as if in direct answer to Mrs. Shimerda's reproaches. Then the poor woman broke down. She dropped on the floor beside her crazy son, hid her face on her knees, and sat crying bitterly. Grandmother paid no heed to her, but called Antonia to come and help empty the basket. Tony left her corner reluctantly. I had never seen her crushed like this before.

'You not mind my poor mamenka, Mrs. Burden. She is so sad,' she whispered, as she wiped her wet hands on her skirt and took the things grandmother handed her.

The crazy boy, seeing the food, began to make soft, gurgling noises and stroked his stomach. Jake came in again, this time with a sack of potatoes. Grandmother looked about in perplexity.

'Haven't you got any sort of cave or cellar outside, Antonia? This is no place to keep vegetables. How did your potatoes get frozen?'

'We get from Mr. Bushy, at the post-office what he throw out. We got no potatoes, Mrs. Burden,' Tony admitted mournfully.

When Jake went out, Marek crawled along the floor and stuffed up the door-crack again. Then, quietly as a shadow, Mr. Shimerda came out from behind the stove. He stood brushing his hand over his smooth grey hair, as if he were trying to clear away a fog about his head. He was clean and neat as usual, with his green neckcloth and his coral pin. He took grandmother's arm and led her behind the stove, to the back of the room. In the rear wall was another little cave; a round hole, not much bigger than an oil barrel, scooped out in the black earth. When I got up on one of the stools and peered into it, I saw some quilts and a pile of straw. The old man held the lantern. 'Yulka,' he said in a low, despairing voice, 'Yulka; my Antonia!'

Grandmother drew back. 'You mean they sleep in there—your girls?' He bowed his head.

Tony slipped under his arm. 'It is very cold on the floor, and this is warm like the badger hole. I like for sleep there,' she insisted eagerly. 'My mamenka have nice bed, with pillows from our own geese in Bohemie. See, Jim?' She pointed to the narrow bunk which Krajiek had built against the wall for himself before the Shimerdas came.

Grandmother sighed. 'Sure enough, where WOULD you sleep, dear! I don't doubt you're warm there. You'll have a better house after while, Antonia, and then you will forget these hard times.'

Mr. Shimerda made grandmother sit down on the only chair and pointed his wife to a stool beside her. Standing before them with his hand on Antonia's shoulder, he talked in a low tone, and his daughter translated. He wanted us to know that they were not beggars in the old country; he made good wages, and his family were respected there. He left Bohemia with more than a thousand dollars in savings, after their passage money was paid. He had in some way lost on exchange in New York, and the railway fare to Nebraska was more than they had expected. By the time they paid Krajiek for the land, and bought his horses and oxen and some old farm machinery, they had very little money left. He wished grandmother to know, however, that he still had some money. If they could get through until spring came, they would buy a cow and chickens and plant a garden, and would then do very well.

Ambrosch and Antonia were both old enough to work in the fields, and they were willing to work. But the snow and the bitter weather had disheartened them all.

Antonia explained that her father meant to build a new house for them in the spring; he and Ambrosch had already split the logs for it, but the logs were all buried in the snow, along the creek where they had been felled.

While grandmother encouraged and gave them advice, I sat down on the floor with Yulka and let her show me her kitten. Marek slid cautiously toward us and began to exhibit his webbed fingers. I knew he wanted to make his queer noises for me—to bark like a dog or whinny like a horse—but he did not dare in the presence of his elders. Marek was always trying to be agreeable, poor fellow, as if he had it on his mind that he must make up for his deficiencies.

Mrs. Shimerda grew more calm and reasonable before our visit was over, and, while Antonia translated, put in a word now and then on her own account. The woman had a quick ear, and caught up phrases whenever she heard English spoken. As we rose to go, she opened her wooden chest and brought out a bag made of bed-ticking, about as long as a flour sack and half as wide, stuffed full of something. At sight of it, the crazy boy began to smack his lips. When Mrs. Shimerda opened the bag and stirred the contents with her hand, it gave out a salty, earthy smell, very pungent, even among the other odours of that cave. She measured a teacup full, tied it up in a bit of sacking, and presented it ceremoniously to grandmother.

'For cook,' she announced. 'Little now; be very much when cook,' spreading out her hands as if to indicate that the pint would swell to a gallon. 'Very good. You no have in this country. All things for eat better in my country.'

'Maybe so, Mrs. Shimerda,' grandmother said dryly. 'I can't say but I prefer our bread to yours, myself.'

Antonia undertook to explain. 'This very good, Mrs. Burden'—she clasped her hands as if she could not express how good—'it make very much when you cook, like what my mama say. Cook with rabbit, cook with chicken, in the gravy—oh, so good!'

All the way home grandmother and Jake talked about how easily good Christian people could forget they were their brothers' keepers.

'I will say, Jake, some of our brothers and sisters are hard to keep. Where's a body to begin, with these people? They're wanting in everything, and most of all in horse-sense. Nobody can give 'em that, I guess. Jimmy, here, is about as able to take over a homestead as they are. Do you reckon that boy Ambrosch has any real push in him?'

'He's a worker, all right, ma'm, and he's got some ketch-on about him; but he's a mean one. Folks can be mean enough to get on in this world; and then, ag'in, they can be too mean.'

That night, while grandmother was getting supper, we opened the package Mrs. Shimerda had given her. It was full of little brown chips that looked like the shavings of some root. They were as light as feathers, and the most noticeable thing about them was their penetrating, earthy odour. We could not determine whether they were animal or vegetable.

'They might be dried meat from some queer beast, Jim. They ain't dried fish, and they never grew on stalk or vine. I'm afraid of 'em. Anyhow, I shouldn't want to eat anything that had been shut up for months with old clothes and goose pillows.'

She threw the package into the stove, but I bit off a corner of one of the chips I held in my hand, and chewed it tentatively. I never forgot the strange taste; though it was many years before I knew that those little brown shavings, which the Shimerdas had brought so far and treasured so jealously, were dried mushrooms. They had been gathered, probably, in some deep Bohemian forest....

XI.

During the week before Christmas, Jake was the most important person of our household, for he was to go to town and do all our Christmas shopping. But on the twenty-first of December, the snow began to fall. The flakes came down so thickly that from the sitting-room windows I could not see beyond the windmill—its frame looked dim and grey, unsubstantial like a shadow. The snow did not stop falling all day, or during the night that followed. The cold was not severe, but the storm was quiet and resistless. The men could not go farther than the barns and corral. They sat about the house most of the day as if it were Sunday; greasing their boots, mending their suspenders, plaiting whiplashes.

On the morning of the twenty-second, grandfather announced at breakfast that it would be impossible to go to Black Hawk for Christmas purchases. Jake was sure he could get through on horseback, and bring home our things in saddle-bags; but grandfather told him the roads would be obliterated, and a newcomer in the country would be lost ten times over. Anyway, he would never allow one of his horses to be put to such a strain.

We decided to have a country Christmas, without any help from town. I had wanted to get some picture books for Yulka and Antonia; even Yulka was able to read a little now. Grandmother took me into the ice-cold storeroom, where she had some bolts of gingham and sheeting. She cut squares of cotton cloth and we sewed them together into a book. We bound it between pasteboards, which I covered with brilliant calico, representing scenes from a circus. For two days I sat at the dining-room table, pasting this book full of pictures for Yulka. We had files of those good old family magazines which used to publish coloured lithographs of popular paintings, and I was allowed to use some of these. I took 'Napoleon Announcing the Divorce to Josephine' for my frontispiece. On the white pages I grouped Sunday-School cards and advertising cards which I had brought from my 'old country.' Fuchs got out the old candle-moulds and made tallow candles. Grandmother hunted up her fancy cake-cutters and baked gingerbread men and roosters, which we decorated with burnt sugar and red cinnamon drops.

On the day before Christmas, Jake packed the things we were sending to the Shimerdas in his saddle-bags and set off on grandfather's grey gelding. When he mounted his horse at the door, I saw that he had a hatchet slung to his belt, and he gave grandmother a meaning look which told me he was planning a surprise for me. That afternoon I watched long and eagerly from the sitting-room window. At last I saw a dark spot moving on the west hill, beside the half-buried cornfield, where the sky was taking on a coppery flush from the sun that did not quite break through. I put on my cap and ran out to meet Jake. When I got to the pond, I could see that he was bringing in a little cedar tree across his pommel. He used to help my father cut Christmas trees for me in Virginia, and he had not forgotten how much I liked them.

By the time we had placed the cold, fresh-smelling little tree in a corner of the sitting-room, it was already Christmas Eve. After supper we all gathered there, and even grandfather, reading his paper by the table, looked up with friendly interest now and then. The cedar was about five feet high and very shapely. We hung it with the gingerbread animals, strings of popcorn, and bits of candle which Fuchs had fitted into pasteboard sockets. Its real splendours, however, came from the most unlikely place in the world—from Otto's cowboy trunk. I had never seen anything in that trunk but old boots and spurs and pistols, and a fascinating mixture of yellow leather thongs, cartridges, and shoemaker's wax. From under the lining he now produced a collection of brilliantly coloured paper figures, several inches high and stiff enough to stand alone. They had been sent to him year after year, by his old mother in Austria. There was a bleeding heart, in tufts of paper lace; there were the three kings, gorgeously apparelled, and the ox and the ass and the shepherds; there was the Baby in the manger, and a group of angels, singing; there were camels and leopards, held by the black slaves of the three kings. Our tree became the talking tree of the fairy tale; legends and stories nestled like birds in its branches. Grandmother said it reminded her of the Tree of Knowledge. We put sheets of cotton wool under it for a snow-field, and Jake's pocket-mirror for a frozen lake.

I can see them now, exactly as they looked, working about the table in the lamplight: Jake with his heavy features, so rudely moulded that his face seemed, somehow, unfinished; Otto with his half-ear and the savage scar that made his upper lip curl so ferociously under his twisted moustache. As I remember them, what unprotected faces they were; their very roughness and violence made them defenceless. These boys had no practised manner behind which they could retreat and hold people at a distance. They had only their hard fists to batter at the world with. Otto was already one of those drifting, case-hardened labourers who never marry or have children of their own. Yet he was so fond of children!

XII.

ON CHRISTMAS MORNING, when I got down to the kitchen, the men were just coming in from their morning chores—the horses and pigs always had their breakfast before we did. Jake and Otto shouted 'Merry Christmas!' to me, and winked at each other when they saw the waffle-irons on the stove. Grandfather came down, wearing a white shirt and his Sunday coat. Morning prayers were longer than usual. He read the chapters from Saint Matthew about the birth of Christ, and as we listened, it all seemed like something that had happened lately, and near at hand. In his prayer he thanked the Lord for the first Christmas, and for all that it had meant to the world ever since. He gave thanks for our food and comfort, and prayed for the poor and destitute in great cities, where the struggle for life was harder than it was here with us. Grandfather's prayers were often very interesting. He had the gift of simple and moving expression. Because he talked so little, his words had a peculiar force; they were not worn dull from constant use. His prayers reflected what he was thinking about at the time, and it was chiefly through them that we got to know his feelings and his views about things.

After we sat down to our waffles and sausage, Jake told us how pleased the Shimerdas had been with their presents; even Ambrosch was friendly and went to the creek with him to cut the Christmas tree. It was a soft grey day outside, with heavy clouds working across the sky, and occasional squalls of snow. There were always odd jobs to be done about the barn on holidays, and the men were busy until afternoon. Then Jake and I played dominoes, while Otto wrote a long letter home to his mother. He always wrote to her on Christmas Day, he said, no matter where he was, and no matter how long it had been since his last letter. All afternoon he sat in the dining-room. He would write for a while, then sit idle, his clenched fist lying on the table, his eyes following the pattern of the oilcloth. He spoke and wrote his own language so seldom that it came to him awkwardly. His effort to remember entirely absorbed him.

At about four o'clock a visitor appeared: Mr. Shimerda, wearing his rabbit-skin cap and collar, and new mittens his wife had knitted. He had come to thank us for the presents, and for all grandmother's kindness to his family. Jake and Otto joined us from the basement and we sat about the stove, enjoying the deepening grey of the winter afternoon and the atmosphere of comfort and security in my grandfather's house. This feeling seemed completely to take possession of Mr. Shimerda. I suppose, in the crowded clutter of their cave, the old man had come to believe that peace and order had vanished from the earth, or existed only in the old world he had left so far behind. He sat still and passive, his head resting against the back of the wooden rocking-chair, his hands relaxed upon the arms. His face had a look of weariness and pleasure, like that of sick people when they feel relief from pain. Grandmother insisted on his drinking a glass of Virginia apple-brandy after his long walk in the cold, and when a faint flush came up in his cheeks, his features might have been cut out of a shell, they were so transparent. He said almost nothing, and smiled rarely; but as he rested there we all had a sense of his utter content.

As it grew dark, I asked whether I might light the Christmas tree before the lamp was brought. When the candle-ends sent up their conical yellow flames, all the coloured figures from Austria stood out clear and full of meaning against the green boughs. Mr. Shimerda rose, crossed himself, and quietly knelt down before the tree, his head sunk forward. His long body formed a letter 'S.' I saw grandmother look apprehensively at grandfather. He was rather narrow in religious matters, and sometimes spoke out and hurt people's feelings. There had been nothing strange about the tree before, but now, with some one kneeling before it—images, candles... Grandfather merely put his finger-tips to his brow and bowed his venerable head, thus Protestantizing the atmosphere.

We persuaded our guest to stay for supper with us. He needed little urging. As we sat down to the table, it occurred to me that he liked to look at us, and that our faces were open books to him. When his deep-seeing eyes rested on me, I felt as if he were looking far ahead into the future for me, down the road I would have to travel.

At nine o'clock Mr. Shimerda lighted one of our lanterns and put on his overcoat and fur collar. He stood in the little entry hall, the lantern and his fur cap under his arm, shaking hands with us. When he took grandmother's hand, he bent over it as he always did, and said slowly, 'Good woman!' He made the sign of the cross over me, put on his cap and went off in the dark. As we turned back to the sitting-room, grandfather looked at me searchingly. 'The prayers of all good people are good,' he said quietly.

XIII.

The week following Christmas brought in a thaw, and by New Year's Day all the world about us was a broth of grey slush, and the guttered slope between the windmill and the barn was running black water. The soft black earth stood out in patches along the roadsides. I resumed all my chores, carried in the cobs and wood and water, and spent the afternoons at the barn, watching Jake shell corn with a hand-sheller.

One morning, during this interval of fine weather, Antonia and her mother rode over on one of their shaggy old horses to pay us a visit. It was the first time Mrs. Shimerda had been to our house, and she ran about examining our carpets and curtains and furniture, all the while commenting upon them to her daughter in an envious, complaining tone. In the kitchen she caught up an iron pot that stood on the back of the stove and said: 'You got many, Shimerdas no got.' I thought it weak-minded of grandmother to give the pot to her.

After dinner, when she was helping to wash the dishes, she said, tossing her head: 'You got many things for cook. If I got all things like you, I make much better.'

She was a conceited, boastful old thing, and even misfortune could not humble her. I was so annoyed that I felt coldly even toward Antonia and listened unsympathetically when she told me her father was not well.

'My papa sad for the old country. He not look good. He never make music any more. At home he play violin all the time; for weddings and for dance. Here never. When I beg him for play, he shake his head no. Some days he take his violin out of his box and make with his fingers on the strings, like this, but never he make the music. He don't like this kawntree.'

'People who don't like this country ought to stay at home,' I said severely. 'We don't make them come here.'

'He not want to come, never!' she burst out. 'My mamenka make him come. All the time she say: "America big country; much money, much land for my boys, much husband for my girls." My papa, he cry for leave his old friends what make music with him. He love very much the man what play the long horn like this'—she indicated a slide trombone. "They go to school together and are friends from boys. But my mama, she want Ambrosch for be rich, with many cattle."'

'Your mama,' I said angrily, 'wants other people's things.'

"Your grandfather is rich," she retorted fiercely. 'Why he not help my papa? Ambrosch be rich, too, after while, and he pay back. He is very smart boy. For Ambrosch my mama come here.'

Ambrosch was considered the important person in the family. Mrs. Shimerda and Antonia always deferred to him, though he was often surly with them and contemptuous toward his father. Ambrosch and his mother had everything their own way. Though Antonia loved her father more than she did anyone else, she stood in awe of her elder brother.

After I watched Antonia and her mother go over the hill on their miserable horse, carrying our iron pot with them, I turned to grandmother, who had taken up her darning, and said I hoped that snooping old woman wouldn't come to see us any more.

Grandmother chuckled and drove her bright needle across a hole in Otto's sock. 'She's not old, Jim, though I expect she seems old to you. No, I wouldn't mourn if she never came again. But, you see, a body never knows what traits poverty might bring out in 'em. It makes a woman grasping to see her children want for things. Now read me a chapter in "The Prince of the House of David." Let's forget the Bohemians.'

We had three weeks of this mild, open weather. The cattle in the corral ate corn almost as fast as the men could shell it for them, and we hoped they would be ready for an early market. One morning the two big bulls, Gladstone and Brigham Young, thought spring had come, and they began to tease and butt at each other across the barbed wire that separated them. Soon they got angry. They bellowed and pawed up the soft earth with their hoofs, rolling their eyes and tossing their heads. Each withdrew to a far corner of his own corral, and then they made for each other at a gallop. Thud, thud, we could hear the impact of their great heads, and their bellowing shook the pans on the kitchen shelves. Had they not been dehorned, they would have torn each other to pieces. Pretty soon the fat steers took it up and began butting and horning each other. Clearly, the affair had to be stopped. We all stood by and watched admiringly while Fuchs rode into the corral with a pitchfork and prodded the bulls again and again, finally driving them apart.

The big storm of the winter began on my eleventh birthday, the twentieth of January. When I went down to breakfast that morning, Jake and Otto came in white as snow-men, beating their hands and stamping their feet. They began to laugh boisterously when they saw me, calling:

'You've got a birthday present this time, Jim, and no mistake. They was a full-grown blizzard ordered for you.'

All day the storm went on. The snow did not fall this time, it simply spilled out of heaven, like thousands of featherbeds being emptied. That afternoon the kitchen was a carpenter-shop; the men brought in their tools and made two great wooden shovels with long handles. Neither grandmother nor I could go out in the storm, so Jake fed the chickens and brought in a pitiful contribution of eggs.

Next day our men had to shovel until noon to reach the barn—and the snow was still falling! There had not been such a storm in the ten years my grandfather had lived in Nebraska. He said at dinner that we would not try to reach the cattle—they were fat enough to go without their corn for a day or two; but tomorrow we must feed them and thaw out their water-tap so that they could drink. We could not so much as see the corrals, but we knew the steers were over there, huddled together under the north bank. Our ferocious bulls, subdued enough by this time, were probably warming each other's backs. 'This'll take the bile out of 'em!' Fuchs remarked gleefully.

At noon that day the hens had not been heard from. After dinner Jake and Otto, their damp clothes now dried on them, stretched their stiff arms and plunged again into the drifts. They made a tunnel through the snow to the hen-house, with walls so solid that grandmother and I could walk back and forth in it. We found the chickens asleep; perhaps they thought night had come to stay. One old rooster was stirring about, pecking at the solid lump of ice in their water-tin. When we flashed the lantern in their eyes, the hens set up a great cackling and flew about clumsily, scattering down-feathers. The mottled, pin-headed guinea-hens, always resentful of captivity, ran screeching out into the tunnel and tried to poke their ugly, painted faces through the snow walls. By five o'clock the chores were done just when it was time to begin them all over again! That was a strange, unnatural sort of day.

XIV.

On the morning of the twenty-second I wakened with a start. Before I opened my eyes, I seemed to know that something had happened. I heard excited voices in the kitchen—grandmother's was so shrill that I knew she must be almost beside herself. I looked forward to any new crisis with delight. What could it be, I wondered, as I hurried into my clothes. Perhaps the barn had burned; perhaps the cattle had frozen to death; perhaps a neighbour was lost in the storm.

Down in the kitchen grandfather was standing before the stove with his hands behind him. Jake and Otto had taken off their boots and were rubbing their woollen socks. Their clothes and boots were steaming, and they both looked exhausted. On the bench behind the stove lay a man, covered up with a blanket. Grandmother motioned me to the dining-room. I obeyed reluctantly. I watched her as she came and went, carrying dishes. Her lips were tightly compressed and she kept whispering to herself: 'Oh, dear Saviour!' 'Lord, Thou knowest!'

Presently grandfather came in and spoke to me: 'Jimmy, we will not have prayers this morning, because we have a great deal to do. Old Mr. Shimerda is dead, and his family are in great distress. Ambrosch came over here in the middle of the night, and Jake and Otto went back with him. The boys have had a hard night, and you must not bother them with questions. That is Ambrosch, asleep on the bench. Come in to breakfast, boys.'

After Jake and Otto had swallowed their first cup of coffee, they began to talk excitedly, disregarding grandmother's warning glances. I held my tongue, but I listened with all my ears.

'No, sir,' Fuchs said in answer to a question from grandfather, 'nobody heard the gun go off. Ambrosch was out with the ox-team, trying to break a road, and the women-folks was shut up tight in their cave. When Ambrosch come in, it was dark and he didn't see nothing, but the oxen acted kind of queer. One of 'em ripped around and got away from him—bolted clean out of the stable. His hands is blistered where the rope run through. He got a lantern and went back and found the old man, just as we seen him.'

'Poor soul, poor soul!' grandmother groaned. 'I'd like to think he never done it. He was always considerate and un-wishful to give trouble. How could he forget himself and bring this on us!'

'I don't think he was out of his head for a minute, Mrs. Burden,' Fuchs declared. 'He done everything natural. You know he was always sort of fixy, and fixy he was to the last. He shaved after dinner, and washed hisself all over after the girls had done the dishes. Antonia heated the water for him. Then he put on a clean shirt and clean socks, and after he was dressed he kissed her and the little one and took his gun and said he was going out to hunt rabbits. He must have gone right down to the barn and done it then. He layed down on that bunk-bed, close to the ox stalls, where he always slept. When we found him, everything was decent except'—Fuchs wrinkled his brow and hesitated—'except what he couldn't nowise foresee. His coat was hung on a peg, and his boots was under the bed. He'd took off that silk neckcloth he always wore, and folded it smooth and stuck his pin through it. He turned back his shirt at the neck and rolled up his sleeves.'

'I don't see how he could do it!' grandmother kept saying.

Otto misunderstood her. 'Why, ma'am, it was simple enough; he pulled the trigger with his big toe. He layed over on his side and put the end of the barrel in his mouth, then he drew up one foot and felt for the trigger. He found it all right!'

'Maybe he did,' said Jake grimly. 'There's something mighty queer about it.'

'Now what do you mean, Jake?' grandmother asked sharply.

'Well, ma'm, I found Krajiek's axe under the manger, and I picks it up and carries it over to the corpse, and I take my oath it just fit the gash in the front of the old man's face. That there Krajiek had been sneakin' round, pale and quiet, and when he seen me examinin' the axe, he begun whimperin', "My God, man, don't do that!" "I reckon I'm a-goin' to look into this," says I. Then he begun to squeal like a rat and run about wringin' his hands. "They'll hang me!" says he. "My God, they'll hang me sure!"'

Fuchs spoke up impatiently. 'Krajiek's gone silly, Jake, and so have you. The old man wouldn't have made all them preparations for Krajiek to murder him, would he? It don't hang together. The gun was right beside him when Ambrosch found him.'

'Krajiek could 'a' put it there, couldn't he?' Jake demanded.

Grandmother broke in excitedly: 'See here, Jake Marpole, don't you go trying to add murder to suicide. We're deep enough in trouble. Otto reads you too many of them detective stories.'

'It will be easy to decide all that, Emmaline,' said grandfather quietly. 'If he shot himself in the way they think, the gash will be torn from the inside outward.'

'Just so it is, Mr. Burden,' Otto affirmed. 'I seen bunches of hair and stuff sticking to the poles and straw along the roof. They was blown up there by gunshot, no question.'

Grandmother told grandfather she meant to go over to the Shimerdas' with him.

'There is nothing you can do,' he said doubtfully. 'The body can't be touched until we get the coroner here from Black Hawk, and that will be a matter of several days, this weather.'

'Well, I can take them some victuals, anyway, and say a word of comfort to them poor little girls. The oldest one was his darling, and was like a right hand to him. He might have thought of her. He's left her alone in a hard world.' She glanced distrustfully at Ambrosch, who was now eating his breakfast at the kitchen table.

Fuchs, although he had been up in the cold nearly all night, was going to make the long ride to Black Hawk to fetch the priest and the coroner. On the grey gelding, our best horse, he would try to pick his way across the country with no roads to guide him.

'Don't you worry about me, Mrs. Burden,' he said cheerfully, as he put on a second pair of socks. 'I've got a good nose for directions, and I never did need much sleep. It's the grey I'm worried about. I'll save him what I can, but it'll strain him, as sure as I'm telling you!'

'This is no time to be over-considerate of animals, Otto; do the best you can for yourself. Stop at the Widow Steavens's for dinner. She's a good woman, and she'll do well by you.'

After Fuchs rode away, I was left with Ambrosch. I saw a side of him I had not seen before. He was deeply, even slavishly, devout. He did not say a word all morning, but sat with his rosary in his hands, praying, now silently, now aloud. He never looked away from his beads, nor lifted his hands except to cross himself. Several times the poor boy fell asleep where he sat, wakened with a start, and began to pray again.

No wagon could be got to the Shimerdas' until a road was broken, and that would be a day's job. Grandfather came from the barn on one of our big black horses, and Jake lifted grandmother up behind him. She wore her black hood and was bundled up in shawls. Grandfather tucked his bushy white beard inside his overcoat. They looked very Biblical as they set off, I thought. Jake and Ambrosch followed them, riding the other black and my pony, carrying bundles of clothes that we had got together for Mrs. Shimerda. I watched them go past the pond and over the hill by the drifted cornfield. Then, for the first time, I realized that I was alone in the house.

I felt a considerable extension of power and authority, and was anxious to acquit myself creditably. I carried in cobs and wood from the long cellar, and filled both the stoves. I remembered that in the hurry and excitement of the morning nobody had thought of the chickens, and the eggs had not been gathered. Going out through the tunnel, I gave the hens their corn, emptied the ice from their drinking-pan, and filled it with water. After the cat had had his milk, I could think of nothing else to do, and I sat down to get warm. The quiet was delightful, and the ticking clock was the most pleasant of companions. I got 'Robinson Crusoe' and tried to read, but his life on the island seemed dull compared with ours. Presently, as I looked with satisfaction about our comfortable sitting-room, it flashed upon me that if Mr. Shimerda's soul were lingering about in this world at all, it would be here, in our house, which had been more to his liking than any other in the neighbourhood. I remembered his contented face when he was with us on Christmas Day. If he could have lived with us, this terrible thing would never have happened.

I knew it was homesickness that had killed Mr. Shimerda, and I wondered whether his released spirit would not eventually find its way back to his own country. I thought of how far it was to Chicago, and then to Virginia, to Baltimore—and then the great wintry ocean. No, he would not at once set out upon that long journey. Surely, his exhausted spirit, so tired of cold and crowding and the struggle with the ever-falling snow, was resting now in this quiet house.

I was not frightened, but I made no noise. I did not wish to disturb him. I went softly down to the kitchen which, tucked away so snugly underground, always seemed to me the heart and centre of the house. There, on the bench behind the stove, I thought and thought about Mr. Shimerda. Outside I could hear the wind singing over hundreds of miles of snow.

It was as if I had let the old man in out of the tormenting winter, and were sitting there with him. I went over all that Antonia had ever told me about his life before he came to this country; how he used to play the fiddle at weddings and dances. I thought about the friends he had mourned to leave, the trombone-player, the great forest full of game—belonging, as Antonia said, to the 'nobles'—from which she and her mother used to steal wood on moonlight nights. There was a white hart that lived in that forest, and if anyone killed it, he would be hanged, she said. Such vivid pictures came to me that they might have been Mr. Shimerda's memories, not yet faded out from the air in which they had haunted him.

It had begun to grow dark when my household returned, and grandmother was so tired that she went at once to bed. Jake and I got supper, and while we were washing the dishes he told me in loud whispers about the state of things over at the Shimerdas'. Nobody could touch the body until the coroner came. If anyone did, something terrible would happen, apparently. The dead man was frozen through, 'just as stiff as a dressed turkey you hang out to freeze,' Jake said. The horses and oxen would not go into the barn until he was frozen so hard that there was no longer any smell of blood. They were stabled there now, with the dead man, because there was no other place to keep them. A lighted lantern was kept hanging over Mr. Shimerda's head. Antonia and Ambrosch and the mother took turns going down to pray beside him. The crazy boy went with them, because he did not feel the cold. I believed he felt cold as much as anyone else, but he liked to be thought insensible to it. He was always coveting distinction, poor Marek!

Ambrosch, Jake said, showed more human feeling than he would have supposed him capable of, but he was chiefly concerned about getting a priest, and about his father's soul, which he believed was in a place of torment and would remain there until his family and the priest had prayed a great deal for him. 'As I understand it,' Jake concluded, 'it will be a matter of years to pray his soul out of Purgatory, and right now he's in torment.'

'I don't believe it,' I said stoutly. 'I almost know it isn't true.' I did not, of course, say that I believed he had been in that very kitchen all afternoon, on his way back to his own country. Nevertheless, after I went to bed, this idea of punishment and Purgatory came back on me crushingly. I remembered the account of Dives in torment, and shuddered. But Mr. Shimerda had not been rich and selfish: he had only been so unhappy that he could not live any longer.

XV.

Otto Fuchs got back from Black Hawk at noon the next day. He reported that the coroner would reach the Shimerdas' sometime that afternoon, but the missionary priest was at the other end of his parish, a hundred miles away, and the trains were not running. Fuchs had got a few hours' sleep at the livery barn in town, but he was afraid the grey gelding had strained himself. Indeed, he was never the same horse afterward. That long trip through the deep snow had taken all the endurance out of him.

Fuchs brought home with him a stranger, a young Bohemian who had taken a homestead near Black Hawk, and who came on his only horse to help his fellow countrymen in their trouble. That was the first time I ever saw Anton Jelinek. He was a strapping young fellow in the early twenties then, handsome, warm-hearted, and full of life, and he came to us like a miracle in the midst of that grim business. I remember exactly how he strode into our kitchen in his felt boots and long wolfskin coat, his eyes and cheeks bright with the cold. At sight of grandmother, he snatched off his fur cap, greeting her in a deep, rolling voice which seemed older than he.

'I want to thank you very much, Mrs. Burden, for that you are so kind to poor strangers from my kawntree.'

He did not hesitate like a farmer boy, but looked one eagerly in the eye when he spoke. Everything about him was warm and spontaneous. He said he would have come to see the Shimerdas before, but he had hired out to husk corn all the fall, and since winter began he had been going to the school by the mill, to learn English, along with the little children. He told me he had a nice 'lady-teacher' and that he liked to go to school.

At dinner grandfather talked to Jelinek more than he usually did to strangers.

'Will they be much disappointed because we cannot get a priest?' he asked.

Jelinek looked serious.

'Yes, sir, that is very bad for them. Their father has done a great sin'—he looked straight at grandfather. 'Our Lord has said that.'

Grandfather seemed to like his frankness.

'We believe that, too, Jelinek. But we believe that Mr. Shimerda's soul will come to its Creator as well off without a priest. We believe that Christ is our only intercessor.'

The young man shook his head. 'I know how you think. My teacher at the school has explain. But I have seen too much. I believe in prayer for the dead. I have seen too much.'

We asked him what he meant.

He glanced around the table. 'You want I shall tell you? When I was a little boy like this one, I begin to help the priest at the altar. I make my first communion very young; what the Church teach seem plain to me. By 'n' by war-times come, when the Prussians fight us. We have very many soldiers in camp near my village, and the cholera break out in that camp, and the men die like flies. All day long our priest go about there to give the Sacrament to dying men, and I go with him to carry the vessels with the Holy Sacrament. Everybody that go near that camp catch the sickness but me and the priest. But we have no sickness, we have no fear, because we carry that blood and that body of Christ, and it preserve us.' He paused, looking at grandfather. 'That I know, Mr. Burden, for it happened to myself. All the soldiers know, too. When we walk along the road, the old priest and me, we meet all the time soldiers marching and officers on horse. All those officers, when they see what I carry under the cloth, pull up their horses and kneel down on the ground in the road until we pass. So I feel very bad for my kawntree-man to die without the Sacrament, and to die in a bad way for his soul, and I feel sad for his family.'

We had listened attentively. It was impossible not to admire his frank, manly faith.

'I am always glad to meet a young man who thinks seriously about these things,' said grandfather, 'and I would never be the one to say you were not in God's care when you were among the soldiers.' After dinner it was decided that young Jelinek should hook our two strong black farm-horses to the scraper and break a road through to the Shimerdas', so that a wagon could go when it was necessary. Fuchs, who was the only cabinetmaker in the neighbourhood was set to work on a coffin.

Jelinek put on his long wolfskin coat, and when we admired it, he told us that he had shot and skinned the coyotes, and the young man who 'batched' with him, Jan Bouska, who had been a fur-worker in Vienna, made the coat. From the windmill I watched Jelinek come out of the barn with the blacks, and work his way up the hillside toward the cornfield. Sometimes he was completely hidden by the clouds of snow that rose about him; then he and the horses would emerge black and shining.

Our heavy carpenter's bench had to be brought from the barn and carried down into the kitchen. Fuchs selected boards from a pile of planks grandfather had hauled out from town in the fall to make a new floor for the oats-bin. When at last the lumber and tools were assembled, and the doors were closed again and the cold draughts shut out, grandfather rode away to meet the coroner at the Shimerdas', and Fuchs took off his coat and settled down to work. I sat on his worktable and watched him. He did not touch his tools at first, but figured for a long while on a piece of paper, and measured the planks and made marks on them. While he was thus engaged, he whistled softly to himself, or teasingly pulled at his half-ear. Grandmother moved about quietly, so as not to disturb him. At last he folded his ruler and turned a cheerful face to us.

'The hardest part of my job's done,' he announced. 'It's the head end of it that comes hard with me, especially when I'm out of practice. The last time I made one of these, Mrs. Burden,' he continued, as he sorted and tried his chisels, 'was for a fellow in the Black Tiger Mine, up above Silverton, Colorado. The mouth of that mine goes right into the face of the cliff, and they used to put us in a bucket and run us over on a trolley and shoot us into the shaft. The bucket travelled across a box canon three hundred feet deep, and about a third full of water. Two Swedes had fell out of that bucket once, and hit the water, feet down. If you'll believe it, they went to work the next day. You can't kill a Swede. But in my time a little Eyetalian tried the high dive, and it turned out different with him. We was snowed in then, like we are now, and I happened to be the only man in camp that could make a coffin for him. It's a handy thing to know, when you knock about like I've done.'

'We'd be hard put to it now, if you didn't know, Otto,' grandmother said.

'Yes, 'm,' Fuchs admitted with modest pride. 'So few folks does know how to make a good tight box that'll turn water. I sometimes wonder if there'll be anybody about to do it for me. However, I'm not at all particular that way.'

All afternoon, wherever one went in the house, one could hear the panting wheeze of the saw or the pleasant purring of the plane. They were such cheerful noises, seeming to promise new things for living people: it was a pity that those freshly planed pine boards were to be put underground so soon. The lumber was hard to work because it was full of frost, and the boards gave off a sweet smell of pine woods, as the heap of yellow shavings grew higher and higher. I wondered why Fuchs had not stuck to cabinet-work, he settled down to it with such ease and content. He handled the tools as if he liked the feel of them; and when he planed, his hands went back and forth over the boards in an eager, beneficent way as if he were blessing them. He broke out now and then into German hymns, as if this occupation brought back old times to him.

At four o'clock Mr. Bushy, the postmaster, with another neighbour who lived east of us, stopped in to get warm. They were on their way to the Shimerdas'. The news of what had happened over there had somehow got abroad through the snow-blocked country. Grandmother gave the visitors sugar-cakes and hot coffee. Before these callers were gone, the brother of the Widow Steavens, who lived on the Black Hawk road, drew up at our door, and after him came the father of the German family, our nearest neighbours on the south. They dismounted and joined us in the dining-room. They were all eager for any details about the suicide, and they were greatly concerned as to where Mr. Shimerda would be buried. The nearest Catholic cemetery was at Black Hawk, and it might be weeks before a wagon could get so far. Besides, Mr. Bushy and grandmother were sure that a man who had killed himself could not be buried in a Catholic graveyard. There was a burying-ground over by the Norwegian church, west of Squaw Creek; perhaps the Norwegians would take Mr. Shimerda in.

After our visitors rode away in single file over the hill, we returned to the kitchen. Grandmother began to make the icing for a chocolate cake, and Otto again filled the house with the exciting, expectant song of the plane. One pleasant thing about this time was that everybody talked more than usual. I had never heard the postmaster say anything but 'Only papers, to-day,' or, 'I've got a sackful of mail for ye,' until this afternoon. Grandmother always talked, dear woman: to herself or to the Lord, if there was no one else to listen; but grandfather was naturally taciturn, and Jake and Otto were often so tired after supper that I used to feel as if I were surrounded by a wall of silence. Now everyone seemed eager to talk. That afternoon Fuchs told me story after story: about the Black Tiger Mine, and about violent deaths and casual buryings, and the queer fancies of dying men. You never really knew a man, he said, until you saw him die. Most men were game, and went without a grudge.

The postmaster, going home, stopped to say that grandfather would bring the coroner back with him to spend the night. The officers of the Norwegian church, he told us, had held a meeting and decided that the Norwegian graveyard could not extend its hospitality to Mr. Shimerda.

Grandmother was indignant. 'If these foreigners are so clannish, Mr. Bushy, we'll have to have an American graveyard that will be more liberal-minded. I'll get right after Josiah to start one in the spring. If anything was to happen to me, I don't want the Norwegians holding inquisitions over me to see whether I'm good enough to be laid amongst 'em.'

Soon grandfather returned, bringing with him Anton Jelinek, and that important person, the coroner. He was a mild, flurried old man, a Civil War veteran, with one sleeve hanging empty. He seemed to find this case very perplexing, and said if it had not been for grandfather he would have sworn out a warrant against Krajiek. 'The way he acted, and the way his axe fit the wound, was enough to convict any man.'

Although it was perfectly clear that Mr. Shimerda had killed himself, Jake and the coroner thought something ought to be done to Krajiek because he behaved like a guilty man. He was badly frightened, certainly, and perhaps he even felt some stirrings of remorse for his indifference to the old man's misery and loneliness.

At supper the men ate like vikings, and the chocolate cake, which I had hoped would linger on until tomorrow in a mutilated condition, disappeared on the second round. They talked excitedly about where they should bury Mr. Shimerda; I gathered that the neighbours were all disturbed and shocked about something. It developed that Mrs. Shimerda and Ambrosch wanted the old man buried on the southwest corner of their own land; indeed, under the very stake that marked the corner. Grandfather had explained to Ambrosch that some day, when the country was put under fence and the roads were confined to section lines, two roads would cross exactly on that corner. But Ambrosch only said, 'It makes no matter.'

Grandfather asked Jelinek whether in the old country there was some superstition to the effect that a suicide must be buried at the cross-roads.

Jelinek said he didn't know; he seemed to remember hearing there had once been such a custom in Bohemia. 'Mrs. Shimerda is made up her mind,' he added. 'I try to persuade her, and say it looks bad for her to all the neighbours; but she say so it must be. "There I will bury him, if I dig the grave myself," she say. I have to promise her I help Ambrosch make the grave tomorrow.'

Grandfather smoothed his beard and looked judicial. 'I don't know whose wish should decide the matter, if not hers. But if she thinks she will live to see the people of this country ride over that old man's head, she is mistaken.'

XVI.

Mr. Shimerda lay dead in the barn four days, and on the fifth they buried him. All day

Friday Jelinek was off with Ambrosch digging the grave, chopping out the frozen earth with old axes. On Saturday we breakfasted before daylight and got into the wagon with the coffin. Jake and Jelinek went ahead on horseback to cut the body loose from the pool of blood in which it was frozen fast to the ground.

When grandmother and I went into the Shimerdas' house, we found the womenfolk alone; Ambrosch and Marek were at the barn. Mrs. Shimerda sat crouching by the stove, Antonia was washing dishes. When she saw me, she ran out of her dark corner and threw her arms around me. 'Oh, Jimmy,' she sobbed, 'what you tink for my lovely papa!' It seemed to me that I could feel her heart breaking as she clung to me.

Mrs. Shimerda, sitting on the stump by the stove, kept looking over her shoulder toward the door while the neighbours were arriving. They came on horseback, all except the postmaster, who brought his family in a wagon over the only broken wagon-trail. The Widow Steavens rode up from her farm eight miles down the Black Hawk road. The cold drove the women into the cave-house, and it was soon crowded. A fine, sleety snow was beginning to fall, and everyone was afraid of another storm and anxious to have the burial over with.

Grandfather and Jelinek came to tell Mrs. Shimerda that it was time to start. After bundling her mother up in clothes the neighbours had brought, Antonia put on an old cape from our house and the rabbit-skin hat her father had made for her. Four men carried Mr. Shimerda's box up the hill; Krajiek slunk along behind them. The coffin was too wide for the door, so it was put down on the slope outside. I slipped out from the cave and looked at Mr. Shimerda. He was lying on his side, with his knees drawn up. His body was draped in a black shawl, and his head was bandaged in white muslin, like a mummy's; one of his long, shapely hands lay out on the black cloth; that was all one could see of him.

Mrs. Shimerda came out and placed an open prayer-book against the body, making the sign of the cross on the bandaged head with her fingers. Ambrosch knelt down and made the same gesture, and after him Antonia and Marek. Yulka hung back. Her mother pushed her forward, and kept saying something to her over and over. Yulka knelt down, shut her eyes, and put out her hand a little way, but she drew it back and began to cry wildly. She was afraid to touch the bandage. Mrs. Shimerda caught her by the shoulders and pushed her toward the coffin, but grandmother interfered.

'No, Mrs. Shimerda,' she said firmly, 'I won't stand by and see that child frightened into spasms. She is too little to understand what you want of her. Let her alone.'

At a look from grandfather, Fuchs and Jelinek placed the lid on the box, and began to nail it down over Mr. Shimerda. I was afraid to look at Antonia. She put her arms round Yulka and held the little girl close to her.

The coffin was put into the wagon. We drove slowly away, against the fine, icy snow which cut our faces like a sand-blast. When we reached the grave, it looked a very little spot in that snow-covered waste. The men took the coffin to the edge of the hole and lowered it with ropes. We stood about watching them, and the powdery snow lay without melting on the caps and shoulders of the men and the shawls of the women. Jelinek spoke in a persuasive tone to Mrs. Shimerda, and then turned to grandfather.

'She says, Mr. Burden, she is very glad if you can make some prayer for him here in English, for the neighbours to understand.'

Grandmother looked anxiously at grandfather. He took off his hat, and the other men did likewise. I thought his prayer remarkable. I still remember it. He began, 'Oh, great and just God, no man among us knows what the sleeper knows, nor is it for us to judge what lies between him and Thee.' He prayed that if any man there had been remiss toward the stranger come to a far country, God would forgive him and soften his heart. He recalled the promises to the widow and the fatherless, and asked God to smooth the way before this widow and her children, and to 'incline the hearts of men to deal justly with her.' In closing, he said we were leaving Mr. Shimerda at 'Thy judgment seat, which is also Thy mercy seat.'

All the time he was praying, grandmother watched him through the black fingers of her glove, and when he said 'Amen,' I thought she looked satisfied with him. She turned to Otto and whispered, 'Can't you start a hymn, Fuchs? It would seem less heathenish.'

Fuchs glanced about to see if there was general approval of her suggestion, then began, 'Jesus, Lover of my Soul,' and all the men and women took it up after him. Whenever I have heard the hymn since, it has made me remember that white waste and the little group of people; and the bluish air, full of fine, eddying snow, like long veils flying:

'While the nearer waters roll, While the tempest still is high.'

Years afterward, when the open-grazing days were over, and the red grass had been ploughed under and under until it had almost disappeared from the prairie; when all the fields were under fence, and the roads no longer ran about like wild things, but followed the surveyed section-lines, Mr. Shimerda's grave was still there, with a sagging wire fence around it, and an unpainted wooden cross. As grandfather had predicted, Mrs. Shimerda never saw the roads going over his head. The road from the north curved a little to the east just there, and the road from the west swung out a little to the south; so that the grave, with its tall red grass that was never mowed, was like a little island; and at twilight, under a new moon or the clear evening star, the dusty roads used to look like soft grey rivers flowing past it. I never came upon the place without emotion, and in all that country it was the spot most dear to me. I loved the dim superstition, the propitiatory intent, that had put the grave there; and still more I loved the spirit that could not carry out the sentence—the error from the surveyed lines, the clemency of the soft earth roads along which the home-coming wagons rattled after sunset. Never a tired driver passed the wooden cross, I am sure, without wishing well to the sleeper.

XVII.

When spring came, after that hard winter, one could not get enough of the nimble air. Every morning I wakened with a fresh consciousness that winter was over. There were none of the signs of spring for which I used to watch in Virginia, no budding woods or blooming gardens. There was only—spring itself; the throb of it, the light restlessness, the vital essence of it everywhere: in the sky, in the swift clouds, in the pale sunshine, and in the warm, high wind—rising suddenly, sinking suddenly, impulsive and playful like a big puppy that pawed you and then lay down to be petted. If I had been tossed down blindfold on that red prairie, I should have known that it was spring.

Everywhere now there was the smell of burning grass. Our neighbours burned off their pasture before the new grass made a start, so that the fresh growth would not be mixed with the dead stand of last year. Those light, swift fires, running about the country, seemed a part of the same kindling that was in the air.

The Shimerdas were in their new log house by then. The neighbours had helped them to build it in March. It stood directly in front of their old cave, which they used as a cellar. The family were now fairly equipped to begin their struggle with the soil. They had four comfortable rooms to live in, a new windmill—bought on credit—a chicken-house and poultry. Mrs. Shimerda had paid grandfather ten dollars for a milk cow, and was to give him fifteen more as soon as they harvested their first crop.

When I rode up to the Shimerdas' one bright windy afternoon in April, Yulka ran out to meet me. It was to her, now, that I gave reading lessons; Antonia was busy with other things. I tied my pony and went into the kitchen where Mrs. Shimerda was baking bread, chewing poppy seeds as she worked. By this time she could speak enough English to ask me a great many questions about what our men were doing in the fields. She seemed to think that my elders withheld helpful information, and that from me she might get valuable secrets. On this occasion she asked me very craftily when grandfather expected to begin planting corn. I told her, adding that he thought we should have a dry spring and that the corn would not be held back by too much rain, as it had been last year.

She gave me a shrewd glance. 'He not Jesus,' she blustered; 'he not know about the wet and the dry.

I did not answer her; what was the use? As I sat waiting for the hour when Ambrosch and Antonia would return from the fields, I watched Mrs. Shimerda at her work. She took from the oven a coffee-cake which she wanted to keep warm for supper, and wrapped it in a quilt stuffed with feathers. I have seen her put even a roast goose in this quilt to keep it hot. When the neighbours were there building the new house, they saw her do this, and the story got abroad that the Shimerdas kept their food in their featherbeds.

When the sun was dropping low, Antonia came up the big south draw with her team. How much older she had grown in eight months! She had come to us a child, and now she was a tall, strong young girl, although her fifteenth birthday had just slipped by. I ran out and met her as she brought her horses up to the windmill to water them. She wore the boots her father had so thoughtfully taken off before he shot himself, and his old fur cap. Her outgrown cotton dress switched about her calves, over the boot-tops. She kept her sleeves rolled up all day, and her arms and throat were burned as brown as a sailor's. Her neck came up strongly out of her shoulders, like the bole of a tree out of the turf. One sees that draught-horse neck among the peasant women in all old countries.

She greeted me gaily, and began at once to tell me how much ploughing she had done that day. Ambrosch, she said, was on the north quarter, breaking sod with the oxen.

'Jim, you ask Jake how much he ploughed to-day. I don't want that Jake get more done in one day than me. I want we have very much corn this fall.'

While the horses drew in the water, and nosed each other, and then drank again, Antonia sat down on the windmill step and rested her head on her hand.

'You see the big prairie fire from your place last night? I hope your grandpa ain't lose no stacks?'

'No, we didn't. I came to ask you something, Tony. Grandmother wants to know if you can't go to the term of school that begins next week over at the sod schoolhouse. She says there's a good teacher, and you'd learn a lot.'

Antonia stood up, lifting and dropping her shoulders as if they were stiff. 'I ain't got time to learn. I can work like mans now. My mother can't say no more how Ambrosch do all and nobody to help him. I can work as much as him. School is all right for little boys. I help make this land one good farm.'

She clucked to her team and started for the barn. I walked beside her, feeling vexed. Was she going to grow up boastful like her mother, I wondered? Before we reached the stable, I felt something tense in her silence, and glancing up I saw that she was crying. She turned her face from me and looked off at the red streak of dying light, over the dark prairie.

I climbed up into the loft and threw down the hay for her, while she unharnessed her team. We walked slowly back toward the house. Ambrosch had come in from the north quarter, and was watering his oxen at the tank.

Antonia took my hand. 'Sometime you will tell me all those nice things you learn at the school, won't you, Jimmy?' she asked with a sudden rush of feeling in her voice. 'My father, he went much to school. He know a great deal; how to make the fine cloth like what you not got here. He play horn and violin, and he read so many books that the priests in Bohemie come to talk to him. You won't forget my father, Jim?' 'No,' I said, 'I will never forget him.'

Mrs. Shimerda asked me to stay for supper. After Ambrosch and Antonia had washed the field dust from their hands and faces at the wash-basin by the kitchen door, we sat down at the oilcloth-covered table. Mrs. Shimerda ladled meal mush out of an iron pot and poured milk on it. After the mush we had fresh bread and sorghum molasses, and coffee with the cake that had been kept warm in the feathers. Antonia and Ambrosch were talking in Bohemian; disputing about which of them had done more ploughing that day. Mrs. Shimerda egged them on, chuckling while she gobbled her food.

Presently Ambrosch said sullenly in English: 'You take them ox tomorrow and try the sod plough. Then you not be so smart.'

His sister laughed. 'Don't be mad. I know it's awful hard work for break sod. I milk the cow for you tomorrow, if you want.'

Mrs. Shimerda turned quickly to me. 'That cow not give so much milk like what your grandpa say. If he make talk about fifteen dollars, I send him back the cow.'

'He doesn't talk about the fifteen dollars,' I exclaimed indignantly. 'He doesn't find fault with people.'

'He say I break his saw when we build, and I never,' grumbled Ambrosch.

I knew he had broken the saw, and then hid it and lied about it. I began to wish I had not stayed for supper. Everything was disagreeable to me. Antonia ate so noisily now, like a man, and she yawned often at the table and kept stretching her arms over her head, as if they ached. Grandmother had said, 'Heavy field work'll spoil that girl. She'll lose all her nice ways and get rough ones.' She had lost them already.

After supper I rode home through the sad, soft spring twilight. Since winter I had seen very little of Antonia. She was out in the fields from sunup until sundown. If I rode over to see her where she was ploughing, she stopped at the end of a row to chat for a moment, then gripped her plough-handles, clucked to her team, and waded on down the furrow, making me feel that she was now grown up and had no time for me. On Sundays she helped her mother make garden or sewed all day. Grandfather was pleased with Antonia. When we complained of her, he only smiled and said, 'She will help some fellow get ahead in the world.'

Nowadays Tony could talk of nothing but the prices of things, or how much she could lift and endure. She was too proud of her strength. I knew, too, that Ambrosch put upon her some chores a girl ought not to do, and that the farm-hands around the country joked in a nasty way about it. Whenever I saw her come up the furrow, shouting to her beasts, sunburned, sweaty, her dress open at the neck, and her throat and chest dust-plastered, I used to think of the tone in which poor Mr. Shimerda, who could say so little, yet managed to say so much when he exclaimed, 'My Antonia!'

XVIII.

After I began to go to the country school, I saw less of the Bohemians. We were sixteen pupils at the sod schoolhouse, and we all came on horseback and brought our dinner. My schoolmates were none of them very interesting, but I somehow felt that, by making comrades of them, I was getting even with Antonia for her indifference. Since the father's death, Ambrosch was more than ever the head of the house, and he seemed to direct the feelings as well as the fortunes of his womenfolk. Antonia often quoted his opinions to me, and she let me see that she admired him, while she thought of me only as a little boy. Before the spring was over, there was a distinct coldness between us and the Shimerdas. It came about in this way.

One Sunday I rode over there with Jake to get a horse-collar which Ambrosch had borrowed from him and had not returned. It was a beautiful blue morning. The buffalo-peas were blooming in pink and purple masses along the roadside, and the larks, perched on last year's dried sunflower stalks, were singing straight at the sun, their heads thrown back and their yellow breasts a-quiver. The wind blew about us in warm, sweet gusts. We rode slowly, with a pleasant sense of Sunday indolence.

We found the Shimerdas working just as if it were a week-day. Marek was cleaning out the stable, and Antonia and her mother were making garden, off across the pond in the draw-head. Ambrosch was up on the windmill tower, oiling the wheel. He came down, not very cordially. When Jake asked for the collar, he grunted and scratched his head. The collar belonged to grandfather, of course, and Jake, feeling responsible for it, flared up. 'Now, don't you say you haven't got it, Ambrosch, because I know you have, and if you ain't a-going to look for it, I will.'

Ambrosch shrugged his shoulders and sauntered down the hill toward the stable. I could see that it was one of his mean days. Presently he returned, carrying a collar that had been badly used—trampled in the dirt and gnawed by rats until the hair was sticking out of it.

'This what you want?' he asked surlily.

Jake jumped off his horse. I saw a wave of red come up under the rough stubble on his face. 'That ain't the piece of harness I loaned you, Ambrosch; or, if it is, you've used it shameful. I ain't a-going to carry such a looking thing back to Mr. Burden.'

Ambrosch dropped the collar on the ground. 'All right,' he said coolly, took up his oil-can, and began to climb the mill. Jake caught him by the belt of his trousers and yanked him back. Ambrosch's feet had scarcely touched the ground when he lunged out with a vicious kick at Jake's stomach. Fortunately, Jake was in such a position that he could dodge it. This was not the sort of thing country boys did when they played at fisticuffs, and Jake was furious. He landed Ambrosch a blow on the head—it sounded like the crack of an axe on a cow-pumpkin. Ambrosch dropped over, stunned.

We heard squeals, and looking up saw Antonia and her mother coming on the run. They did not take the path around the pond, but plunged through the muddy water, without even lifting their skirts. They came on, screaming and clawing the air. By this time Ambrosch had come to his senses and was sputtering with nosebleed.

Jake sprang into his saddle. 'Let's get out of this, Jim,' he called.

Mrs. Shimerda threw her hands over her head and clutched as if she were going to pull down lightning. 'Law, law!' she shrieked after us. 'Law for knock my Ambrosch down!'

'I never like you no more, Jake and Jim Burden,' Antonia panted. 'No friends any more!'

Jake stopped and turned his horse for a second. 'Well, you're a damned ungrateful lot, the whole pack of you,' he shouted back. 'I guess the Burdens can get along without you. You've been a sight of trouble to them, anyhow!'

We rode away, feeling so outraged that the fine morning was spoiled for us. I hadn't a word to say, and poor Jake was white as paper and trembling all over. It made him sick to get so angry.

'They ain't the same, Jimmy,' he kept saying in a hurt tone. 'These foreigners ain't the same. You can't trust 'em to be fair. It's dirty to kick a feller. You heard how the women turned on you—and after all we went through on account of 'em last winter! They ain't to be trusted. I don't want to see you get too thick with any of 'em.'

'I'll never be friends with them again, Jake,' I declared hotly. 'I believe they are all like Krajiek and Ambrosch underneath.'

Grandfather heard our story with a twinkle in his eye. He advised Jake to ride to town tomorrow, go to a justice of the peace, tell him he had knocked young Shimerda down, and pay his fine. Then if Mrs. Shimerda was inclined to make trouble—her son was still under age—she would be forestalled. Jake said he might as well take the wagon and haul to market the pig he had been fattening. On Monday, about an hour after Jake had started, we saw Mrs. Shimerda and her Ambrosch proudly driving by, looking neither to the right nor left. As they rattled out of sight down the Black Hawk road, grandfather chuckled, saying he had rather expected she would follow the matter up.

Jake paid his fine with a ten-dollar bill grandfather had given him for that purpose. But when the Shimerdas found that Jake sold his pig in town that day, Ambrosch worked it out in his shrewd head that Jake had to sell his pig to pay his fine. This theory afforded the Shimerdas great satisfaction, apparently. For weeks afterward, whenever Jake and I met Antonia on her way to the post-office, or going along the road with her work-team, she would clap her hands and call to us in a spiteful, crowing voice:

'Jake-y, Jake-y, sell the pig and pay the slap!'

Otto pretended not to be surprised at Antonia's behaviour. He only lifted his brows and said, 'You can't tell me anything new about a Czech; I'm an Austrian.'

Grandfather was never a party to what Jake called our feud with the Shimerdas. Ambrosch and Antonia always greeted him respectfully, and he asked them about their affairs and gave them advice as usual. He thought the future looked hopeful for them. Ambrosch was a far-seeing fellow; he soon realized that his oxen were too heavy for any work except breaking sod, and he succeeded in selling them to a newly arrived German. With the money he bought another team of horses, which grandfather selected for him. Marek was strong, and Ambrosch worked him hard; but he could never teach him to cultivate corn, I remember. The one idea that had ever got through poor Marek's thick head was that all exertion was meritorious. He always bore down on the handles of the cultivator and drove the blades so deep into the earth that the horses were soon exhausted.

In June, Ambrosch went to work at Mr. Bushy's for a week, and took Marek with him at full wages. Mrs. Shimerda then drove the second cultivator; she and Antonia worked in the fields all day and did the chores at night. While the two women were running the place alone, one of the new horses got colic and gave them a terrible fright.

Antonia had gone down to the barn one night to see that all was well before she went to bed, and she noticed that one of the roans was swollen about the middle and stood with its head hanging. She mounted another horse, without waiting to saddle him, and hammered on our door just as we were going to bed. Grandfather answered her knock. He did not send one of his men, but rode back with her himself, taking a syringe and an old piece of carpet he kept for hot applications when our horses were sick. He found Mrs. Shimerda sitting by the horse with her lantern, groaning and wringing her hands. It took but a few moments to release the gases pent up in the poor beast, and the two women heard the rush of wind and saw the roan visibly diminish in girth.

'If I lose that horse, Mr. Burden,' Antonia exclaimed, 'I never stay here till Ambrosch come home! I go drown myself in the pond before morning.'

When Ambrosch came back from Mr. Bushy's, we learned that he had given Marek's wages to the priest at Black Hawk, for Masses for their father's soul. Grandmother thought

Antonia needed shoes more than Mr. Shimerda needed prayers, but grandfather said tolerantly, 'If he can spare six dollars, pinched as he is, it shows he believes what he professes.'

It was grandfather who brought about a reconciliation with the Shimerdas. One morning he told us that the small grain was coming on so well, he thought he would begin to cut his wheat on the first of July. He would need more men, and if it were agreeable to everyone he would engage Ambrosch for the reaping and threshing, as the Shimerdas had no small grain of their own.

'I think, Emmaline,' he concluded, 'I will ask Antonia to come over and help you in the kitchen. She will be glad to earn something, and it will be a good time to end misunderstandings. I may as well ride over this morning and make arrangements. Do you want to go with me, Jim?' His tone told me that he had already decided for me.

After breakfast we set off together. When Mrs. Shimerda saw us coming, she ran from her door down into the draw behind the stable, as if she did not want to meet us. Grandfather smiled to himself while he tied his horse, and we followed her.

Behind the barn we came upon a funny sight. The cow had evidently been grazing somewhere in the draw. Mrs. Shimerda had run to the animal, pulled up the lariat pin, and, when we came upon her, she was trying to hide the cow in an old cave in the bank. As the hole was narrow and dark, the cow held back, and the old woman was slapping and pushing at her hind quarters, trying to spank her into the drawside.

Grandfather ignored her singular occupation and greeted her politely. 'Good morning, Mrs. Shimerda. Can you tell me where I will find Ambrosch? Which field?'

'He with the sod corn.' She pointed toward the north, still standing in front of the cow as if she hoped to conceal it.

'His sod corn will be good for fodder this winter,' said grandfather encouragingly. 'And where is Antonia?'

'She go with.' Mrs. Shimerda kept wiggling her bare feet about nervously in the dust.

'Very well. I will ride up there. I want them to come over and help me cut my oats and wheat next month. I will pay them wages. Good morning. By the way, Mrs. Shimerda,' he said as he turned up the path, 'I think we may as well call it square about the cow.'

She started and clutched the rope tighter. Seeing that she did not understand, grandfather turned back. 'You need not pay me anything more; no more money. The cow is yours.'

'Pay no more, keep cow?' she asked in a bewildered tone, her narrow eyes snapping at us in the sunlight.

'Exactly. Pay no more, keep cow.' He nodded.

Mrs. Shimerda dropped the rope, ran after us, and, crouching down beside grandfather, she took his hand and kissed it. I doubt if he had ever been so much embarrassed before. I was a little startled, too. Somehow, that seemed to bring the Old World very close.

We rode away laughing, and grandfather said: 'I expect she thought we had come to take the cow away for certain, Jim. I wonder if she wouldn't have scratched a little if we'd laid hold of that lariat rope!'

Our neighbours seemed glad to make peace with us. The next Sunday Mrs. Shimerda came over and brought Jake a pair of socks she had knitted. She presented them with an air of great magnanimity, saying, 'Now you not come any more for knock my Ambrosch down?'

Jake laughed sheepishly. 'I don't want to have no trouble with Ambrosch. If he'll let me alone, I'll let him alone.'

'If he slap you, we ain't got no pig for pay the fine,' she said insinuatingly.

Jake was not at all disconcerted. 'Have the last word ma'm,' he said cheerfully. 'It's a lady's privilege.'

XIX.

July came on with that breathless, brilliant heat which makes the plains of Kansas and Nebraska the best corn country in the world. It seemed as if we could hear the corn growing in the night; under the stars one caught a faint crackling in the dewy, heavy-odoured cornfields where the feathered stalks stood so juicy and green. If all the great plain from the Missouri to the Rocky Mountains had been under glass, and the heat regulated by a thermometer, it could not have been better for the yellow tassels that were ripening and fertilizing the silk day by day. The cornfields were far apart in those times, with miles of wild grazing land between. It took a clear, meditative eye like my grandfather's to foresee that they would enlarge and multiply until they would be, not the Shimerdas' cornfields, or Mr. Bushy's, but the world's cornfields; that their yield would be one of the great economic facts, like the wheat crop of Russia, which underlie all the activities of men, in peace or war.

The burning sun of those few weeks, with occasional rains at night, secured the corn. After the milky ears were once formed, we had little to fear from dry weather. The men were working so hard in the wheatfields that they did not notice the heat—though I was kept busy carrying water for them—and grandmother and Antonia had so much to do in the kitchen that they could not have told whether one day was hotter than another. Each morning, while the dew was still on the grass, Antonia went with me up to the garden to get early vegetables for dinner. Grandmother made her wear a sunbonnet, but as soon as we reached the garden she threw it on the grass and let her hair fly in the breeze. I remember how, as we bent over the pea-vines, beads of perspiration used to gather on her upper lip like a little moustache.

'Oh, better I like to work out-of-doors than in a house!' she used to sing joyfully. 'I not care that your grandmother say it makes me like a man. I like to be like a man.' She would toss her head and ask me to feel the muscles swell in her brown arm.

We were glad to have her in the house. She was so gay and responsive that one did not mind her heavy, running step, or her clattery way with pans. Grandmother was in high spirits during the weeks that Antonia worked for us.

All the nights were close and hot during that harvest season. The harvesters slept in the hayloft because it was cooler there than in the house. I used to lie in my bed by the open window, watching the heat lightning play softly along the horizon, or looking up at the gaunt frame of the windmill against the blue night sky. One night there was a beautiful electric storm, though not enough rain fell to damage the cut grain. The men went down to the barn immediately after supper, and when the dishes were washed, Antonia and I climbed up on the slanting roof of the chicken-house to watch the clouds. The thunder was loud and metallic, like the rattle of sheet iron, and the lightning broke in great zigzags across the heavens, making everything stand out and come close to us for a moment. Half the sky was chequered with black thunderheads, but all the west was luminous and clear: in the lightning flashes it looked like deep blue water, with the sheen of moonlight on it; and the mottled part of the sky was like marble pavement, like the quay of some splendid seacoast city, doomed to destruction. Great warm splashes of rain fell on our upturned faces. One black cloud, no bigger than a little boat, drifted out into the clear space unattended, and kept moving westward. All about us we could hear the felty beat of the raindrops on the soft dust of the farmyard. Grandmother came to the door and said it was late, and we would get wet out there.

'In a minute we come,' Antonia called back to her. 'I like your grandmother, and all things here,' she sighed. 'I wish my papa live to see this summer. I wish no winter ever come again.'

'It will be summer a long while yet,' I reassured her. 'Why aren't you always nice like this, Tony?'

'How nice?'

'Why, just like this; like yourself. Why do you all the time try to be like Ambrosch?'

She put her arms under her head and lay back, looking up at the sky. 'If I live here, like you, that is different. Things will be easy for you. But they will be hard for us.'

2

THE HIRED GIRLS

I.

I HAD BEEN LIVING with my grandfather for nearly three years when he decided to move to Black Hawk. He and grandmother were getting old for the heavy work of a farm, and as I was now thirteen they thought I ought to be going to school. Accordingly our homestead was rented to 'that good woman, the Widow Steavens,' and her bachelor brother, and we bought Preacher White's house, at the north end of Black Hawk. This was the first town house one passed driving in from the farm, a landmark which told country people their long ride was over.

We were to move to Black Hawk in March, and as soon as grandfather had fixed the date he let Jake and Otto know of his intention. Otto said he would not be likely to find another place that suited him so well; that he was tired of farming and thought he would go back to what he called the 'wild West.' Jake Marpole, lured by Otto's stories of adventure, decided to go with him. We did our best to dissuade Jake. He was so handicapped by illiteracy and by his trusting disposition that he would be an easy prey to sharpers. Grandmother begged him to stay among kindly, Christian people, where he was known; but there was no reasoning with him. He wanted to be a prospector. He thought a silver mine was waiting for him in Colorado.

Jake and Otto served us to the last. They moved us into town, put down the carpets in our new house, made shelves and cupboards for grandmother's kitchen, and seemed loath to leave us. But at last they went, without warning. Those two fellows had been faithful to us through sun and storm, had given us things that cannot be bought in any market in the world. With me they had been like older brothers; had restrained their speech and manners out of care for me, and given me so much good comradeship. Now they got on the westbound train one morning, in their Sunday clothes, with their oilcloth valises—and I never saw them again. Months afterward we got a card from Otto, saying that Jake had been down with mountain fever, but now they were both working in the Yankee Girl Mine, and were doing well. I wrote to them at that address, but my letter was returned to me, 'Unclaimed.' After that we never heard from them.

Black Hawk, the new world in which we had come to live, was a clean, well-planted little prairie town, with white fences and good green yards about the dwellings, wide, dusty streets, and shapely little trees growing along the wooden sidewalks. In the centre of the town there were two rows of new brick 'store' buildings, a brick schoolhouse, the court-house, and four white churches. Our own house looked down over the town, and from our upstairs windows we could see the winding line of the river bluffs, two miles south of us. That river was to be my compensation for the lost freedom of the farming country.

We came to Black Hawk in March, and by the end of April we felt like town people. Grandfather was a deacon in the new Baptist Church, grandmother was busy with church suppers and missionary societies, and I was quite another boy, or thought I was. Suddenly put down among boys of my own age, I found I had a great deal to learn. Before the spring term of school was over, I could fight, play 'keeps,' tease the little girls, and use forbidden words as well as any boy in my class. I was restrained from utter savagery only by the fact that Mrs. Harling, our nearest neighbour, kept an eye on me, and if my behaviour went beyond certain bounds I was not permitted to come into her yard or to play with her jolly children.

We saw more of our country neighbours now than when we lived on the farm. Our house was a convenient stopping-place for them. We had a big barn where the farmers could put up their teams, and their womenfolk more often accompanied them, now that they could stay with us for dinner, and rest and set their bonnets right before they went shopping. The more our house was like a country hotel, the better I liked it. I was glad, when I came home from school at noon, to see a farm-wagon standing in the back yard, and I was always ready to run downtown to get beefsteak or baker's bread for unexpected company. All through that first spring and summer I kept hoping that Ambrosch would bring Antonia and Yulka to see our new house. I wanted to show them our red plush furniture, and the trumpet-blowing cherubs the German paperhanger had put on our parlour ceiling.

When Ambrosch came to town, however, he came alone, and though he put his horses in our barn, he would never stay for dinner, or tell us anything about his mother and sisters. If we ran out and questioned him as he was slipping through the yard, he would merely work his shoulders about in his coat and say, 'They all right, I guess.'

Mrs. Steavens, who now lived on our farm, grew as fond of Antonia as we had been, and always brought us news of her. All through the wheat season, she told us, Ambrosch hired his sister out like a man, and she went from farm to farm, binding sheaves or working with the threshers. The farmers liked her and were kind to her; said they would rather have her for a hand than Ambrosch. When fall came she was to husk corn for the neighbours until Christmas, as she had done the year before; but grandmother saved her from this by getting her a place to work with our neighbours, the Harlings.

II.

Grandmother often said that if she had to live in town, she thanked God she lived next the Harlings. They had been farming people, like ourselves, and their place was like a little farm, with a big barn and a garden, and an orchard and grazing lots—even a windmill. The Harlings were Norwegians, and Mrs. Harling had lived in Christiania until she was ten years old. Her husband was born in Minnesota. He was a grain merchant and cattle-buyer, and was generally considered the most enterprising business man in our county. He controlled a line of grain elevators in the little towns along the railroad to the west of us, and was away from home a great deal. In his absence his wife was the head of the household.

Mrs. Harling was short and square and sturdy-looking, like her house. Every inch of her was charged with an energy that made itself felt the moment she entered a room. Her face was rosy and solid, with bright, twinkling eyes and a stubborn little chin. She was quick to anger, quick to laughter, and jolly from the depths of her soul. How well I remember her laugh; it had in it the same sudden recognition that flashed into her eyes, was a burst of humour, short and intelligent. Her rapid footsteps shook her own floors, and she routed lassitude and indifference wherever she came. She could not be negative or perfunctory about anything. Her enthusiasm, and her violent likes and dislikes, asserted themselves in all the everyday occupations of life. Wash-day was interesting, never dreary, at the Harlings'. Preserving-time was a prolonged festival, and house-cleaning was like a revolution. When Mrs. Harling made garden that spring, we could feel the stir of her undertaking through the willow hedge that separated our place from hers.

Three of the Harling children were near me in age. Charley, the only son—they had lost an older boy—was sixteen; Julia, who was known as the musical one, was fourteen when I was; and Sally, the tomboy with short hair, was a year younger. She was nearly as strong as I, and uncannily clever at all boys' sports. Sally was a wild thing, with sunburned yellow hair, bobbed about her ears, and a brown skin, for she never wore a hat. She raced all over town on one roller skate, often cheated at 'keeps,' but was such a quick shot one couldn't catch her at it.

The grown-up daughter, Frances, was a very important person in our world. She was her father's chief clerk, and virtually managed his Black Hawk office during his frequent absences. Because of her unusual business ability, he was stern and exacting with her. He paid her a good salary, but she had few holidays and never got away from her responsibilities. Even on Sundays she went to the office to open the mail and read the markets. With Charley, who was not interested in business, but was already preparing for Annapolis, Mr. Harling was very indulgent; bought him guns and tools and electric batteries, and never asked what he did with them.

Frances was dark, like her father, and quite as tall. In winter she wore a sealskin coat and cap, and she and Mr. Harling used to walk home together in the evening, talking about grain-cars and cattle, like two men. Sometimes she came over to see grandfather after supper, and her visits flattered him. More than once they put their wits together to rescue some unfortunate farmer from the clutches of Wick Cutter, the Black Hawk money-lender. Grandfather said Frances Harling was as good a judge of credits as any banker in the county. The two or three men who had tried to take advantage of her in a deal acquired celebrity by their defeat. She knew every farmer for miles about: how much land he had under cultivation, how many cattle he was feeding, what his liabilities were. Her interest in these people was more than a business interest. She carried them all in her mind as if they were characters in a book or a play.

When Frances drove out into the country on business, she would go miles out of her way to call on some of the old people, or to see the women who seldom got to town. She was quick at understanding the grandmothers who spoke no English, and the most reticent and distrustful of them would tell her their story without realizing they were doing so. She went to country funerals and weddings in all weathers. A farmer's daughter who was to be married could count on a wedding present from Frances Harling.

In August the Harlings' Danish cook had to leave them. Grandmother entreated them to try Antonia. She cornered Ambrosch the next time he came to town, and pointed out to him that any connection with Christian Harling would strengthen his credit and be of advantage to him. One Sunday Mrs. Harling took the long ride out to the Shimerdas' with Frances. She said she wanted to see 'what the girl came from' and to have a clear understanding with her mother. I was in our yard when they came driving home, just before sunset. They laughed and waved to me as they passed, and I could see they were in great good humour. After supper, when grandfather set off to church, grandmother and I took my short cut through the willow hedge and went over to hear about the visit to the Shimerdas'.

We found Mrs. Harling with Charley and Sally on the front porch, resting after her hard drive. Julia was in the hammock—she was fond of repose—and Frances was at the piano, playing without a light and talking to her mother through the open window.

Mrs. Harling laughed when she saw us coming. 'I expect you left your dishes on the table tonight, Mrs. Burden,' she called. Frances shut the piano and came out to join us.

They had liked Antonia from their first glimpse of her; felt they knew exactly what kind of girl she was. As for Mrs. Shimerda, they found her very amusing. Mrs. Harling chuckled whenever she spoke of her. 'I expect I am more at home with that sort of bird than you are, Mrs. Burden. They're a pair, Ambrosch and that old woman!'

They had had a long argument with Ambrosch about Antonia's allowance for clothes and pocket-money. It was his plan that every cent of his sister's wages should be paid over to him each month, and he would provide her with such clothing as he thought necessary. When Mrs. Harling told him firmly that she would keep fifty dollars a year for Antonia's own use, he declared they wanted to take his sister to town and dress her up and make a fool of her. Mrs. Harling gave us a lively account of Ambrosch's behaviour throughout the interview; how he kept jumping up and putting on his cap as if he were through with the whole business, and how his mother tweaked his coat-tail and prompted him in Bohemian. Mrs. Harling finally agreed to pay three dollars a week for Antonia's services—good wages in those days—and to keep her in shoes. There had been hot dispute about the shoes, Mrs. Shimerda finally saying persuasively that she would send Mrs. Harling three fat geese every year to 'make even.' Ambrosch was to bring his sister to town next Saturday.

'She'll be awkward and rough at first, like enough,' grandmother said anxiously, 'but unless she's been spoiled by the hard life she's led, she has it in her to be a real helpful girl.'

Mrs. Harling laughed her quick, decided laugh. 'Oh, I'm not worrying, Mrs. Burden! I can bring something out of that girl. She's barely seventeen, not too old to learn new ways. She's good-looking, too!' she added warmly.

Frances turned to grandmother. 'Oh, yes, Mrs. Burden, you didn't tell us that! She was working in the garden when we got there, barefoot and ragged. But she has such fine brown legs and arms, and splendid colour in her cheeks—like those big dark red plums.'

We were pleased at this praise. Grandmother spoke feelingly. 'When she first came to this country, Frances, and had that genteel old man to watch over her, she was as pretty a girl as ever I saw. But, dear me, what a life she's led, out in the fields with those rough threshers! Things would have been very different with poor Antonia if her father had lived.'

The Harlings begged us to tell them about Mr. Shimerda's death and the big snowstorm. By the time we saw grandfather coming home from church, we had told them pretty much all we knew of the Shimerdas.

'The girl will be happy here, and she'll forget those things,' said Mrs. Harling confidently, as we rose to take our leave.

III.

On Saturday Ambrosch drove up to the back gate, and Antonia jumped down from the wagon and ran into our kitchen just as she used to do. She was wearing shoes and stockings, and was breathless and excited. She gave me a playful shake by the shoulders. 'You ain't forget about me, Jim?'

Grandmother kissed her. 'God bless you, child! Now you've come, you must try to do right and be a credit to us.'

Antonia looked eagerly about the house and admired everything. 'Maybe I be the kind of girl you like better; now I come to town,' she suggested hopefully.

How good it was to have Antonia near us again; to see her every day and almost every night! Her greatest fault, Mrs. Harling found, was that she so often stopped her work and fell to playing with the children. She would race about the orchard with us, or take sides in our hay-fights in the barn, or be the old bear that came down from the mountain and carried off Nina. Tony learned English so quickly that by the time school began she could speak as well as any of us.

I was jealous of Tony's admiration for Charley Harling. Because he was always first in his classes at school, and could mend the water-pipes or the doorbell and take the clock to pieces, she seemed to think him a sort of prince. Nothing that Charley wanted was too much trouble for her. She loved to put up lunches for him when he went hunting, to mend his ball-gloves and sew buttons on his shooting-coat, baked the kind of nut-cake he liked, and fed his setter dog when he was away on trips with his father. Antonia had made herself cloth working-slippers out of Mr. Harling's old coats, and in these she went padding about after Charley, fairly panting with eagerness to please him.

Next to Charley, I think she loved Nina best. Nina was only six, and she was rather more complex than the other children. She was fanciful, had all sorts of unspoken preferences, and was easily offended. At the slightest disappointment or displeasure, her velvety brown eyes filled with tears, and she would lift her chin and walk silently away. If we ran after her and tried to appease her, it did no good. She walked on unmollified. I used to think that no eyes in the world could grow so large or hold so many tears as Nina's. Mrs. Harling and Antonia invariably took her part. We were never given a chance to explain. The charge was simply: 'You have made Nina cry. Now, Jimmy can go home, and Sally must get her arithmetic.' I liked Nina, too; she was so quaint and unexpected, and her eyes were lovely; but I often wanted to shake her.

We had jolly evenings at the Harlings' when the father was away. If he was at home, the children had to go to bed early, or they came over to my house to play. Mr. Harling not only demanded a quiet house, he demanded all his wife's attention. He used to take her away to their room in the west ell, and talk over his business with her all evening. Though we did not realize it then, Mrs. Harling was our audience when we played, and we always looked to her for suggestions. Nothing flattered one like her quick laugh.

Mr. Harling had a desk in his bedroom, and his own easy-chair by the window, in which no one else ever sat. On the nights when he was at home, I could see his shadow on the blind, and it seemed to me an arrogant shadow. Mrs. Harling paid no heed to anyone else if he was there. Before he went to bed she always got him a lunch of smoked salmon or anchovies and beer. He kept an alcohol lamp in his room, and a French coffee-pot, and his wife made coffee for him at any hour of the night he happened to want it.

Most Black Hawk fathers had no personal habits outside their domestic ones; they paid the bills, pushed the baby-carriage after office hours, moved the sprinkler about over the lawn, and took the family driving on Sunday. Mr. Harling, therefore, seemed to me autocratic and imperial in his ways. He walked, talked, put on his gloves, shook hands, like a man who felt that he had power. He was not tall, but he carried his head so haughtily that he looked a commanding figure, and there was something daring and challenging in his eyes. I used to imagine that the 'nobles' of whom Antonia was always talking probably looked very much like Christian Harling, wore caped overcoats like his, and just such a glittering diamond upon the little finger.

Except when the father was at home, the Harling house was never quiet. Mrs. Harling and Nina and Antonia made as much noise as a houseful of children, and there was usually somebody at the piano. Julia was the only one who was held down to regular hours of practising, but they all played. When Frances came home at noon, she played until dinner was ready. When Sally got back from school, she sat down in her hat and coat and drummed the plantation melodies that Negro minstrel troupes brought to town. Even Nina played the Swedish Wedding March.

Mrs. Harling had studied the piano under a good teacher, and somehow she managed to practise every day. I soon learned that if I were sent over on an errand and found Mrs. Harling at the piano, I must sit down and wait quietly until she turned to me. I can see her at this moment: her short, square person planted firmly on the stool, her little fat hands moving quickly and neatly over the keys, her eyes fixed on the music with intelligent concentration.

IV.

'I won't have none of your weevily wheat,
and I won't have none of your barley,
But I'll take a measure of fine white
flour, to make a cake for Charley.'

We were singing rhymes to tease Antonia while she was beating up one of Charley's favourite cakes in her big mixing-bowl.

It was a crisp autumn evening, just cold enough to make one glad to quit playing tag in the yard, and retreat into the kitchen. We had begun to roll popcorn balls with syrup when we heard a knock at the back door, and Tony dropped her spoon and went to open it.

A plump, fair-skinned girl was standing in the doorway. She looked demure and pretty, and made a graceful picture in her blue cashmere dress and little blue hat, with a plaid shawl drawn neatly about her shoulders and a clumsy pocket-book in her hand.

'Hello, Tony. Don't you know me?' she asked in a smooth, low voice, looking in at us archly.

Antonia gasped and stepped back.

'Why, it's Lena! Of course I didn't know you, so dressed up!'

Lena Lingard laughed, as if this pleased her. I had not recognized her for a moment, either. I had never seen her before with a hat on her head—or with shoes and stockings on her feet, for that matter. And here she was, brushed and smoothed and dressed like a town girl, smiling at us with perfect composure.

'Hello, Jim,' she said carelessly as she walked into the kitchen and looked about her. 'I've come to town to work, too, Tony.'

'Have you, now? Well, ain't that funny!' Antonia stood ill at ease, and didn't seem to know just what to do with her visitor.

The door was open into the dining-room, where Mrs. Harling sat crocheting and Frances was reading. Frances asked Lena to come in and join them.

'You are Lena Lingard, aren't you? I've been to see your mother, but you were off herding cattle that day. Mama, this is Chris Lingard's oldest girl.'

Mrs. Harling dropped her worsted and examined the visitor with quick, keen eyes. Lena was not at all disconcerted. She sat down in the chair Frances pointed out, carefully arranging her pocket-book and grey cotton gloves on her lap. We followed with our popcorn, but Antonia hung back—said she had to get her cake into the oven.

'So you have come to town,' said Mrs. Harling, her eyes still fixed on Lena. 'Where are you working?'

'For Mrs. Thomas, the dressmaker. She is going to teach me to sew. She says I have quite a knack. I'm through with the farm. There ain't any end to the work on a farm, and always so much trouble happens. I'm going to be a dressmaker.'

'Well, there have to be dressmakers. It's a good trade. But I wouldn't run down the farm, if I were you,' said Mrs. Harling rather severely. 'How is your mother?'

'Oh, mother's never very well; she has too much to do. She'd get away from the farm, too, if she could. She was willing for me to come. After I learn to do sewing, I can make money and help her.'

'See that you don't forget to,' said Mrs. Harling sceptically, as she took up her crocheting again and sent the hook in and out with nimble fingers.

'No, 'm, I won't,' said Lena blandly. She took a few grains of the popcorn we pressed upon her, eating them discreetly and taking care not to get her fingers sticky.

Frances drew her chair up nearer to the visitor. 'I thought you were going to be married, Lena,' she said teasingly. 'Didn't I hear that Nick Svendsen was rushing you pretty hard?'

Lena looked up with her curiously innocent smile. 'He did go with me quite a while. But his father made a fuss about it and said he wouldn't give Nick any land if he married me, so he's going to marry Annie Iverson. I wouldn't like to be her; Nick's awful sullen, and he'll take it out on her. He ain't spoke to his father since he promised.'

Frances laughed. 'And how do you feel about it?'

'I don't want to marry Nick, or any other man,' Lena murmured. 'I've seen a good deal of married life, and I don't care for it. I want to be so I can help my mother and the children at home, and not have to ask lief of anybody.'

'That's right,' said Frances. 'And Mrs. Thomas thinks you can learn dressmaking?'

'Yes, 'm. I've always liked to sew, but I never had much to do with. Mrs. Thomas makes lovely things for all the town ladies. Did you know Mrs. Gardener is having a purple velvet made? The velvet came from Omaha. My, but it's lovely!' Lena sighed softly and stroked her cashmere folds. 'Tony knows I never did like out-of-door work,' she added.

Mrs. Harling glanced at her. 'I expect you'll learn to sew all right, Lena, if you'll only keep your head and not go gadding about to dances all the time and neglect your work, the way some country girls do.'

'Yes, 'm. Tiny Soderball is coming to town, too. She's going to work at the Boys' Home Hotel. She'll see lots of strangers,' Lena added wistfully.

'Too many, like enough,' said Mrs. Harling. 'I don't think a hotel is a good place for a girl; though I guess Mrs. Gardener keeps an eye on her waitresses.'

Lena's candid eyes, that always looked a little sleepy under their long lashes, kept straying about the cheerful rooms with naive admiration. Presently she drew on her cotton gloves. 'I guess I must be leaving,' she said irresolutely.

Frances told her to come again, whenever she was lonesome or wanted advice about anything. Lena replied that she didn't believe she would ever get lonesome in Black Hawk.

She lingered at the kitchen door and begged Antonia to come and see her often. 'I've got a room of my own at Mrs. Thomas's, with a carpet.'

Tony shuffled uneasily in her cloth slippers. 'I'll come sometime, but Mrs. Harling don't like to have me run much,' she said evasively.

'You can do what you please when you go out, can't you?' Lena asked in a guarded whisper. 'Ain't you crazy about town, Tony? I don't care what anybody says, I'm done with the farm!' She glanced back over her shoulder toward the dining-room, where Mrs. Harling sat.

When Lena was gone, Frances asked Antonia why she hadn't been a little more cordial to her.

'I didn't know if your mother would like her coming here,' said Antonia, looking troubled. 'She was kind of talked about, out there.'

'Yes, I know. But mother won't hold it against her if she behaves well here. You needn't say anything about that to the children. I guess Jim has heard all that gossip?'

When I nodded, she pulled my hair and told me I knew too much, anyhow. We were good friends, Frances and I.

I ran home to tell grandmother that Lena Lingard had come to town. We were glad of it, for she had a hard life on the farm.

Lena lived in the Norwegian settlement west of Squaw Creek, and she used to herd her father's cattle in the open country between his place and the Shimerdas'. Whenever we rode over in that direction we saw her out among her cattle, bareheaded and barefooted, scantily dressed in tattered clothing, always knitting as she watched her herd. Before I knew Lena, I thought of her as something wild, that always lived on the prairie, because I had never seen her under a roof. Her yellow hair was burned to a ruddy thatch on her head; but her legs and arms, curiously enough, in spite of constant exposure to the sun, kept a miraculous whiteness which somehow made her seem more undressed than other girls who went scantily clad. The first time I stopped to talk to her, I was astonished at her soft voice and easy, gentle ways. The girls out there usually got rough and mannish after they went to herding. But Lena asked Jake and me to get off our horses and stay awhile, and behaved exactly as if she were in a house and were accustomed to having visitors. She was not embarrassed by her ragged clothes, and treated us as if we were old acquaintances. Even then I noticed the unusual colour of her eyes—a shade of deep violet—and their soft, confiding expression.

Chris Lingard was not a very successful farmer, and he had a large family. Lena was always knitting stockings for little brothers and sisters, and even the Norwegian women, who disapproved of her, admitted that she was a good daughter to her mother. As Tony said, she had been talked about. She was accused of making Ole Benson lose the little sense he had —and that at an age when she should still have been in pinafores.

Ole lived in a leaky dugout somewhere at the edge of the settlement. He was fat and lazy and discouraged, and bad luck had become a habit with him. After he had had every other kind of misfortune, his wife, 'Crazy Mary,' tried to set a neighbour's barn on fire, and was sent to the asylum at Lincoln. She was kept there for a few months, then escaped and walked all the way home, nearly two hundred miles, travelling by night and hiding in barns and haystacks by day. When she got back to the Norwegian settlement, her poor feet were as hard as hoofs. She promised to be good, and was allowed to stay at home—though everyone realized she was as crazy as ever, and she still ran about barefooted through the snow, telling her domestic troubles to her neighbours.

Not long after Mary came back from the asylum, I heard a young Dane, who was helping us to thresh, tell Jake and Otto that Chris Lingard's oldest girl had put Ole Benson out of his head, until he had no more sense than his crazy wife. When Ole was cultivating his corn that summer, he used to get discouraged in the field, tie up his team, and wander off to wherever Lena Lingard was herding. There he would sit down on the drawside and help her watch her cattle. All the settlement was talking about it. The Norwegian preacher's wife went to Lena and told her she ought not to allow this; she begged Lena to come to church on Sundays. Lena said she hadn't a dress in the world any less ragged than the one on her back. Then the minister's wife went through her old trunks and found some things she had worn before her marriage.

The next Sunday Lena appeared at church, a little late, with her hair done up neatly on her head, like a young woman, wearing shoes and stockings, and the new dress, which she had made over for herself very becomingly. The congregation stared at her. Until that morning no one—unless it were Ole—had realized how pretty she was, or that she was growing up. The swelling lines of her figure had been hidden under the shapeless rags she wore in the fields. After the last hymn had been sung, and the congregation was dismissed, Ole slipped out to the hitch-bar and lifted Lena on her horse. That, in itself, was shocking; a married man was not expected to do such things. But it was nothing to the scene that followed. Crazy Mary darted out from the group of women at the church door, and ran down the road after Lena, shouting horrible threats.

'Look out, you Lena Lingard, look out! I'll come over with a corn-knife one day and trim some of that shape off you. Then you won't sail round so fine, making eyes at the men!...'

The Norwegian women didn't know where to look. They were formal housewives, most of them, with a severe sense of decorum. But Lena Lingard only laughed her lazy, good-natured laugh and rode on, gazing back over her shoulder at Ole's infuriated wife.

The time came, however, when Lena didn't laugh. More than once Crazy Mary chased her across the prairie and round and round the Shimerdas' cornfield. Lena never told her father; perhaps she was ashamed; perhaps she was more afraid of his anger than of the corn-knife. I was at the Shimerdas' one afternoon when Lena came bounding through the red grass as fast as her white legs could carry her. She ran straight into the house and hid in Antonia's feather-bed. Mary was not far behind: she came right up to the door and made us feel how sharp her blade was, showing us very graphically just what she meant to do to Lena. Mrs. Shimerda, leaning out of the window, enjoyed the situation keenly, and was sorry when Antonia sent Mary away, mollified by an apronful of bottle-tomatoes. Lena came out from Tony's room behind the kitchen, very pink from the heat of the feathers, but otherwise calm. She begged Antonia and me to go with her, and help get her cattle together; they were scattered and might be gorging themselves in somebody's cornfield.

'Maybe you lose a steer and learn not to make somethings with your eyes at married men,' Mrs. Shimerda told her hectoringly.

Lena only smiled her sleepy smile. 'I never made anything to him with my eyes. I can't help it if he hangs around, and I can't order him off. It ain't my prairie.'

V.

After Lena came to Black Hawk, I often met her downtown, where she would be matching sewing silk or buying 'findings' for Mrs. Thomas. If I happened to walk home with her, she told me all about the dresses she was helping to make, or about what she saw and heard when she was with Tiny Soderball at the hotel on Saturday nights.

The Boys' Home was the best hotel on our branch of the Burlington, and all the commercial travellers in that territory tried to get into Black Hawk for Sunday. They used to assemble in the parlour after supper on Saturday nights. Marshall Field's man, Anson Kirkpatrick, played the piano and sang all the latest sentimental songs. After Tiny had helped the cook wash the dishes, she and Lena sat on the other side of the double doors between the parlour and the dining-room, listening to the music and giggling at the jokes and stories. Lena often said she hoped I would be a travelling man when I grew up. They had a gay life of it; nothing to do but ride about on trains all day and go to theatres when they were in big cities. Behind the hotel there was an old store building, where the salesmen opened their big trunks and spread out their samples on the counters. The Black Hawk merchants went to look at these things and order goods, and Mrs. Thomas, though she was I retail trade,' was permitted to see them and to 'get ideas.' They were all generous, these travelling men; they gave Tiny Soderball handkerchiefs and gloves and ribbons and striped stockings, and so many bottles of perfume and cakes of scented soap that she bestowed some of them on Lena.

One afternoon in the week before Christmas, I came upon Lena and her funny, square-headed little brother Chris, standing before the drugstore, gazing in at the wax dolls and blocks and Noah's Arks arranged in the frosty show window. The boy had come to town with a neighbour to do his Christmas shopping, for he had money of his own this year. He was only twelve, but that winter he had got the job of sweeping out the Norwegian church and making the fire in it every Sunday morning. A cold job it must have been, too!

We went into Duckford's dry-goods store, and Chris unwrapped all his presents and showed them to me something for each of the six younger than himself, even a rubber pig for the baby. Lena had given him one of Tiny Soderball's bottles of perfume for his mother, and he thought he would get some handkerchiefs to go with it. They were cheap, and he hadn't much money left. We found a tableful of handkerchiefs spread out for view at Duckford's. Chris wanted those with initial letters in the corner, because he had never seen any before. He studied them seriously, while Lena looked over his shoulder, telling him she thought the red letters would hold their colour best. He seemed so perplexed that I thought perhaps he hadn't enough money, after all. Presently he said gravely:

'Sister, you know mother's name is Berthe. I don't know if I ought to get B for Berthe, or M for Mother.'

Lena patted his bristly head. 'I'd get the B, Chrissy. It will please her for you to think about her name. Nobody ever calls her by it now.'

That satisfied him. His face cleared at once, and he took three reds and three blues. When the neighbour came in to say that it was time to start, Lena wound Chris's comforter about his neck and turned up his jacket collar—he had no overcoat—and we watched him climb into the wagon and start on his long, cold drive. As we walked together up the windy street, Lena wiped her eyes with the back of her woollen glove. 'I get awful homesick for them, all the same,' she murmured, as if she were answering some remembered reproach.

VI.

Winter comes down savagely over a little town on the prairie. The wind that sweeps in from the open country strips away all the leafy screens that hide one yard from another in summer, and the houses seem to draw closer together. The roofs, that looked so far away across the green tree-tops, now stare you in the face, and they are so much uglier than when their angles were softened by vines and shrubs.

In the morning, when I was fighting my way to school against the wind, I couldn't see anything but the road in front of me; but in the late afternoon, when I was coming home, the town looked bleak and desolate to me. The pale, cold light of the winter sunset did not beautify—it was like the light of truth itself. When the smoky clouds hung low in the west and the red sun went down behind them, leaving a pink flush on the snowy roofs and the blue drifts, then the wind sprang up afresh, with a kind of bitter song, as if it said: 'This is reality, whether you like it or not. All those frivolities of summer, the light and shadow, the living mask of green that trembled over everything, they were lies, and this is what was underneath. This is the truth.' It was as if we were being punished for loving the loveliness of summer.

If I loitered on the playground after school, or went to the post-office for the mail and lingered to hear the gossip about the cigar-stand, it would be growing dark by the time I came home. The sun was gone; the frozen streets stretched long and blue before me; the lights were shining pale in kitchen windows, and I could smell the suppers cooking as I passed. Few people were abroad, and each one of them was hurrying toward a fire. The glowing stoves in the houses were like magnets. When one passed an old man, one could see nothing of his face but a red nose sticking out between a frosted beard and a long plush cap. The young men capered along with their hands in their pockets, and sometimes tried a slide on the icy sidewalk. The children, in their bright hoods and comforters, never walked, but always ran from the moment they left their door, beating their mittens against their sides. When I got as far as the Methodist Church, I was about halfway home. I can remember how glad I was when there happened to be a light in the church, and the painted glass window shone out at us as we came along the frozen street. In the winter bleakness a hunger for colour came over people, like the Laplander's craving for fats and sugar. Without knowing why, we used to linger on the sidewalk outside the church when the lamps were lighted early for choir practice or prayer-meeting, shivering and talking until our feet were like lumps of ice. The crude reds and greens and blues of that coloured glass held us there.

On winter nights, the lights in the Harlings' windows drew me like the painted glass. Inside that warm, roomy house there was colour, too. After supper I used to catch up my cap, stick my hands in my pockets, and dive through the willow hedge as if witches were after me. Of course, if Mr. Harling was at home, if his shadow stood out on the blind of the west room, I did not go in, but turned and walked home by the long way, through the street, wondering what book I should read as I sat down with the two old people.

Such disappointments only gave greater zest to the nights when we acted charades, or had a costume ball in the back parlour, with Sally always dressed like a boy. Frances taught us to dance that winter, and she said, from the first lesson, that Antonia would make the best dancer among us. On Saturday nights, Mrs. Harling used to play the old operas for us —'Martha,' 'Norma,' 'Rigoletto'—telling us the story while she played. Every Saturday night was like a party. The parlour, the back parlour, and the dining-room were warm and brightly lighted, with comfortable chairs and sofas, and gay pictures on the walls. One always felt at ease there. Antonia brought her sewing and sat with us—she was already beginning to make pretty clothes for herself. After the long winter evenings on the prairie, with Ambrosch's sullen silences and her mother's complaints, the Harlings' house seemed, as she said, 'like Heaven' to her. She was never too tired to make taffy or chocolate cookies for us. If Sally whispered in her ear, or Charley gave her three winks, Tony would rush into the kitchen and build a fire in the range on which she had already cooked three meals that day.

While we sat in the kitchen waiting for the cookies to bake or the taffy to cool, Nina used to coax Antonia to tell her stories—about the calf that broke its leg, or how Yulka saved her little turkeys from drowning in the freshet, or about old Christmases and weddings in

Bohemia. Nina interpreted the stories about the creche fancifully, and in spite of our derision she cherished a belief that Christ was born in Bohemia a short time before the Shimerdas left that country. We all liked Tony's stories. Her voice had a peculiarly engaging quality; it was deep, a little husky, and one always heard the breath vibrating behind it. Everything she said seemed to come right out of her heart.

One evening when we were picking out kernels for walnut taffy, Tony told us a new story.

'Mrs. Harling, did you ever hear about what happened up in the Norwegian settlement last summer, when I was threshing there? We were at Iversons', and I was driving one of the grain-wagons.'

Mrs. Harling came out and sat down among us. 'Could you throw the wheat into the bin yourself, Tony?' She knew what heavy work it was.

'Yes, ma'm, I did. I could shovel just as fast as that fat Andern boy that drove the other wagon. One day it was just awful hot. When we got back to the field from dinner, we took things kind of easy. The men put in the horses and got the machine going, and Ole Iverson was up on the deck, cutting bands. I was sitting against a straw-stack, trying to get some shade. My wagon wasn't going out first, and somehow I felt the heat awful that day. The sun was so hot like it was going to burn the world up. After a while I see a man coming across the stubble, and when he got close I see it was a tramp. His toes stuck out of his shoes, and he hadn't shaved for a long while, and his eyes was awful red and wild, like he had some sickness. He comes right up and begins to talk like he knows me already. He says: 'The ponds in this country is done got so low a man couldn't drownd himself in one of 'em.'

'I told him nobody wanted to drownd themselves, but if we didn't have rain soon we'd have to pump water for the cattle.

'"Oh, cattle," he says, "you'll all take care of your cattle! Ain't you got no beer here?" I told him he'd have to go to the Bohemians for beer; the Norwegians didn't have none when they threshed. "My God!" he says, "so it's Norwegians now, is it? I thought this was Americy."

'Then he goes up to the machine and yells out to Ole Iverson, "Hello, partner, let me up there. I can cut bands, and I'm tired of trampin'. I won't go no farther."

'I tried to make signs to Ole, 'cause I thought that man was crazy and might get the machine stopped up. But Ole, he was glad to get down out of the sun and chaff—it gets down your neck and sticks to you something awful when it's hot like that. So Ole jumped down and crawled under one of the wagons for shade, and the tramp got on the machine. He cut bands all right for a few minutes, and then, Mrs. Harling, he waved his hand to me and jumped head-first right into the threshing machine after the wheat.

'I begun to scream, and the men run to stop the horses, but the belt had sucked him down, and by the time they got her stopped, he was all beat and cut to pieces. He was wedged in so tight it was a hard job to get him out, and the machine ain't never worked right since.'

'Was he clear dead, Tony?' we cried.

'Was he dead? Well, I guess so! There, now, Nina's all upset. We won't talk about it. Don't you cry, Nina. No old tramp won't get you while Tony's here.'

Mrs. Harling spoke up sternly. 'Stop crying, Nina, or I'll always send you upstairs when Antonia tells us about the country. Did they never find out where he came from, Antonia?'

'Never, ma'm. He hadn't been seen nowhere except in a little town they call Conway. He tried to get beer there, but there wasn't any saloon. Maybe he came in on a freight, but the brakeman hadn't seen him. They couldn't find no letters nor nothing on him; nothing but an old penknife in his pocket and the wishbone of a chicken wrapped up in a piece of paper, and some poetry.'

'Some poetry?' we exclaimed.

'I remember,' said Frances. 'It was "The Old Oaken Bucket," cut out of a newspaper and nearly worn out. Ole Iverson brought it into the office and showed it to me.'

'Now, wasn't that strange, Miss Frances?' Tony asked thoughtfully. 'What would anybody want to kill themselves in summer for? In threshing time, too! It's nice everywhere then.'

'So it is, Antonia,' said Mrs. Harling heartily. 'Maybe I'll go home and help you thresh next summer. Isn't that taffy nearly ready to eat? I've been smelling it a long while.'

There was a basic harmony between Antonia and her mistress. They had strong, independent natures, both of them. They knew what they liked, and were not always trying to imitate other people. They loved children and animals and music, and rough play and digging in the earth. They liked to prepare rich, hearty food and to see people eat it; to make up soft white beds and to see youngsters asleep in them. They ridiculed conceited people and were quick to help unfortunate ones. Deep down in each of them there was a kind of hearty joviality, a relish of life, not over-delicate, but very invigorating. I never tried to define it, but I was distinctly conscious of it. I could not imagine Antonia's living for a week in any other house in Black Hawk than the Harlings'.

VII.

Winter lies too long in country towns; hangs on until it is stale and shabby, old and sullen. On the farm the weather was the great fact, and men's affairs went on underneath it, as the streams creep under the ice. But in Black Hawk the scene of human life was spread out shrunken and pinched, frozen down to the bare stalk.

Through January and February I went to the river with the Harlings on clear nights, and we skated up to the big island and made bonfires on the frozen sand. But by March the ice was rough and choppy, and the snow on the river bluffs was grey and mournful-looking. I was tired of school, tired of winter clothes, of the rutted streets, of the dirty drifts and the piles of cinders that had lain in the yards so long. There was only one break in the dreary monotony of that month: when Blind d'Arnault, the Negro pianist, came to town. He gave a concert at the Opera House on Monday night, and he and his manager spent Saturday and Sunday at our comfortable hotel. Mrs. Harling had known d'Arnault for years. She told Antonia she had better go to see Tiny that Saturday evening, as there would certainly be music at the Boys' Home.

Saturday night after supper I ran downtown to the hotel and slipped quietly into the parlour. The chairs and sofas were already occupied, and the air smelled pleasantly of cigar smoke. The parlour had once been two rooms, and the floor was swaybacked where the partition had been cut away. The wind from without made waves in the long carpet. A coal stove glowed at either end of the room, and the grand piano in the middle stood open.

There was an atmosphere of unusual freedom about the house that night, for Mrs. Gardener had gone to Omaha for a week. Johnnie had been having drinks with the guests until he was rather absent-minded. It was Mrs. Gardener who ran the business and looked after everything. Her husband stood at the desk and welcomed incoming travellers. He was a popular fellow, but no manager.

Mrs. Gardener was admittedly the best-dressed woman in Black Hawk, drove the best horse, and had a smart trap and a little white-and-gold sleigh. She seemed indifferent to her possessions, was not half so solicitous about them as her friends were. She was tall, dark, severe, with something Indian-like in the rigid immobility of her face. Her manner was cold, and she talked little. Guests felt that they were receiving, not conferring, a favour when they stayed at her house. Even the smartest travelling men were flattered when Mrs. Gardener stopped to chat with them for a moment. The patrons of the hotel were divided into two classes: those who had seen Mrs. Gardener's diamonds, and those who had not.

When I stole into the parlour, Anson Kirkpatrick, Marshall Field's man, was at the piano, playing airs from a musical comedy then running in Chicago. He was a dapper little Irishman, very vain, homely as a monkey, with friends everywhere, and a sweetheart in every port, like a sailor. I did not know all the men who were sitting about, but I recognized a furniture salesman from Kansas City, a drug man, and Willy O'Reilly, who travelled for a jewellery house and sold musical instruments. The talk was all about good and bad hotels, actors and actresses and musical prodigies. I learned that Mrs. Gardener had gone to Omaha to hear Booth and Barrett, who were to play there next week, and that Mary Anderson was having a great success in 'A Winter's Tale,' in London.

The door from the office opened, and Johnnie Gardener came in, directing Blind d'Arnault—he would never consent to be led. He was a heavy, bulky mulatto, on short legs, and he came tapping the floor in front of him with his gold-headed cane. His yellow face was lifted in the light, with a show of white teeth, all grinning, and his shrunken, papery eyelids lay motionless over his blind eyes.

'Good evening, gentlemen. No ladies here? Good evening, gentlemen. We going to have a little music? Some of you gentlemen going to play for me this evening?' It was the soft, amiable Negro voice, like those I remembered from early childhood, with the note of docile subservience in it. He had the Negro head, too; almost no head at all; nothing behind the ears but folds of neck under close-clipped wool. He would have been repulsive if his face had not been so kindly and happy. It was the happiest face I had seen since I left Virginia.

He felt his way directly to the piano. The moment he sat down, I noticed the nervous infirmity of which Mrs. Harling had told me. When he was sitting, or standing still, he swayed back and forth incessantly, like a rocking toy. At the piano, he swayed in time to the music, and when he was not playing, his body kept up this motion, like an empty mill grinding on. He found the pedals and tried them, ran his yellow hands up and down the keys a few times, tinkling off scales, then turned to the company.

'She seems all right, gentlemen. Nothing happened to her since the last time I was here. Mrs. Gardener, she always has this piano tuned up before I come. Now gentlemen, I expect you've all got grand voices. Seems like we might have some good old plantation songs tonight.'

The men gathered round him, as he began to play 'My Old Kentucky Home.' They sang one Negro melody after another, while the mulatto sat rocking himself, his head thrown back, his yellow face lifted, his shrivelled eyelids never fluttering.

He was born in the Far South, on the d'Arnault plantation, where the spirit if not the fact of slavery persisted. When he was three weeks old, he had an illness which left him totally blind. As soon as he was old enough to sit up alone and toddle about, another affliction, the nervous motion of his body, became apparent. His mother, a buxom young Negro wench who was laundress for the d'Arnaults, concluded that her blind baby was 'not right' in his head, and she was ashamed of him. She loved him devotedly, but he was so ugly, with his sunken eyes and his 'fidgets,' that she hid him away from people. All the dainties she brought down from the Big House were for the blind child, and she beat and cuffed her other children whenever she found them teasing him or trying to get his chicken-bone away from him. He began to talk early, remembered everything he heard, and his mammy said he 'wasn't all wrong.' She named him Samson, because he was blind, but on the plantation he was known as 'yellow Martha's simple child.' He was docile and obedient, but when he was six years old he began to run away from home, always taking the same direction. He felt his way through the lilacs, along the boxwood hedge, up to the south wing of the Big House, where Miss Nellie d'Arnault practised the piano every morning. This angered his mother more than anything else he could have done; she was so ashamed of his ugliness that she couldn't bear to have white folks see him. Whenever she caught him slipping away from the cabin, she whipped him unmercifully, and told him what dreadful things old Mr. d'Arnault would do to him if he ever found him near the Big House. But the next time Samson had a chance, he ran away again. If Miss d'Arnault stopped practising for a moment and went toward the window, she saw this hideous little pickaninny, dressed in an old piece of sacking, standing in the open space between the hollyhock rows, his body rocking automatically, his blind face lifted to the sun and wearing an expression of idiotic rapture. Often she was tempted to tell Martha that the child must be kept at home, but somehow the memory of his foolish, happy face deterred her. She remembered that his sense of hearing was nearly all he had—though it did not occur to her that he might have more of it than other children.

One day Samson was standing thus while Miss Nellie was playing her lesson to her music-teacher. The windows were open. He heard them get up from the piano, talk a little while, and then leave the room. He heard the door close after them. He crept up to the front windows and stuck his head in: there was no one there. He could always detect the presence of anyone in a room. He put one foot over the window-sill and straddled it.

His mother had told him over and over how his master would give him to the big mastiff if he ever found him 'meddling.' Samson had got too near the mastiff's kennel once, and had felt his terrible breath in his face. He thought about that, but he pulled in his other foot.

Through the dark he found his way to the Thing, to its mouth. He touched it softly, and it answered softly, kindly. He shivered and stood still. Then he began to feel it all over, ran his finger-tips along the slippery sides, embraced the carved legs, tried to get some conception of its shape and size, of the space it occupied in primeval night. It was cold and hard, and like nothing else in his black universe. He went back to its mouth, began at one end of the keyboard and felt his way down into the mellow thunder, as far as he could go. He seemed to know that it must be done with the fingers, not with the fists or the feet. He approached this highly artificial instrument through a mere instinct, and coupled himself to it, as if he knew it was to piece him out and make a whole creature of him. After he had tried over all the sounds, he began to finger out passages from things Miss Nellie had been practising, passages that were already his, that lay under the bone of his pinched, conical little skull, definite as animal desires.

The door opened; Miss Nellie and her music-master stood behind it, but blind Samson, who was so sensitive to presences, did not know they were there. He was feeling out the pattern that lay all ready-made on the big and little keys. When he paused for a moment, because the sound was wrong and he wanted another, Miss Nellie spoke softly. He whirled about in a spasm of terror, leaped forward in the dark, struck his head on the open window, and fell screaming and bleeding to the floor. He had what his mother called a fit. The doctor came and gave him opium.

When Samson was well again, his young mistress led him back to the piano. Several teachers experimented with him. They found he had absolute pitch, and a remarkable memory. As a very young child he could repeat, after a fashion, any composition that was played for him. No matter how many wrong notes he struck, he never lost the intention of a passage, he brought the substance of it across by irregular and astonishing means. He wore his teachers out. He could never learn like other people, never acquired any finish. He was always a Negro prodigy who played barbarously and wonderfully. As piano-playing, it was perhaps abominable, but as music it was something real, vitalized by a sense of rhythm that was stronger than his other physical senses—that not only filled his dark mind, but worried his body incessantly. To hear him, to watch him, was to see a Negro enjoying himself as only a Negro can. It was as if all the agreeable sensations possible to creatures of flesh and blood were heaped up on those black-and-white keys, and he were gloating over them and trickling them through his yellow fingers.

In the middle of a crashing waltz, d'Arnault suddenly began to play softly, and, turning to one of the men who stood behind him, whispered, 'Somebody dancing in there.' He jerked his bullet-head toward the dining-room. 'I hear little feet—girls, I spect.'

Anson Kirkpatrick mounted a chair and peeped over the transom. Springing down, he wrenched open the doors and ran out into the dining-room. Tiny and Lena, Antonia and Mary Dusak, were waltzing in the middle of the floor. They separated and fled toward the kitchen, giggling.

Kirkpatrick caught Tiny by the elbows. 'What's the matter with you girls? Dancing out here by yourselves, when there's a roomful of lonesome men on the other side of the partition! Introduce me to your friends, Tiny.'

The girls, still laughing, were trying to escape. Tiny looked alarmed. 'Mrs. Gardener wouldn't like it,' she protested. 'She'd be awful mad if you was to come out here and dance with us.'

'Mrs. Gardener's in Omaha, girl. Now, you're Lena, are you?—and you're Tony and you're Mary. Have I got you all straight?'

O'Reilly and the others began to pile the chairs on the tables. Johnnie Gardener ran in from the office.

'Easy, boys, easy!' he entreated them. 'You'll wake the cook, and there'll be the devil to pay for me. She won't hear the music, but she'll be down the minute anything's moved in the dining-room.'

'Oh, what do you care, Johnnie? Fire the cook and wire Molly to bring another. Come along, nobody'll tell tales.'

Johnnie shook his head. ''S a fact, boys,' he said confidentially. 'If I take a drink in Black Hawk, Molly knows it in Omaha!'

His guests laughed and slapped him on the shoulder. 'Oh, we'll make it all right with Molly. Get your back up, Johnnie.'

Molly was Mrs. Gardener's name, of course. 'Molly Bawn' was painted in large blue letters on the glossy white sides of the hotel bus, and 'Molly' was engraved inside Johnnie's ring and on his watch-case—doubtless on his heart, too. He was an affectionate little man, and he thought his wife a wonderful woman; he knew that without her he would hardly be more than a clerk in some other man's hotel.

At a word from Kirkpatrick, d'Arnault spread himself out over the piano, and began to draw the dance music out of it, while the perspiration shone on his short wool and on his uplifted face. He looked like some glistening African god of pleasure, full of strong, savage blood. Whenever the dancers paused to change partners or to catch breath, he would boom out softly, 'Who's that goin' back on me? One of these city gentlemen, I bet! Now, you girls, you ain't goin' to let that floor get cold?'

Antonia seemed frightened at first, and kept looking questioningly at Lena and Tiny over Willy O'Reilly's shoulder. Tiny Soderball was trim and slender, with lively little feet and pretty ankles—she wore her dresses very short. She was quicker in speech, lighter in movement and manner than the other girls. Mary Dusak was broad and brown of countenance, slightly marked by smallpox, but handsome for all that. She had beautiful chestnut hair, coils of it; her forehead was low and smooth, and her commanding dark eyes regarded the world indifferently and fearlessly. She looked bold and resourceful and unscrupulous, and she was all of these. They were handsome girls, had the fresh colour of their country upbringing, and in their eyes that brilliancy which is called—by no metaphor, alas!—'the light of youth.'

D'Arnault played until his manager came and shut the piano. Before he left us, he showed us his gold watch which struck the hours, and a topaz ring, given him by some Russian nobleman who delighted in Negro melodies, and had heard d'Arnault play in New Orleans. At last he tapped his way upstairs, after bowing to everybody, docile and happy. I walked home with Antonia. We were so excited that we dreaded to go to bed. We lingered a long while at the Harlings' gate, whispering in the cold until the restlessness was slowly chilled out of us.

VIII.

The Harling children and I were never happier, never felt more contented and secure, than in the weeks of spring which broke that long winter. We were out all day in the thin sunshine, helping Mrs. Harling and Tony break the ground and plant the garden, dig around the orchard trees, tie up vines and clip the hedges. Every morning, before I was up, I could hear Tony singing in the garden rows. After the apple and cherry trees broke into bloom, we ran about under them, hunting for the new nests the birds were building, throwing clods at each other, and playing hide-and-seek with Nina. Yet the summer which was to change everything was coming nearer every day. When boys and girls are growing up, life can't stand still, not even in the quietest of country towns; and they have to grow up, whether they will or no. That is what their elders are always forgetting.

It must have been in June, for Mrs. Harling and Antonia were preserving cherries, when I stopped one morning to tell them that a dancing pavilion had come to town. I had seen two drays hauling the canvas and painted poles up from the depot.

That afternoon three cheerful-looking Italians strolled about Black Hawk, looking at everything, and with them was a dark, stout woman who wore a long gold watch-chain about her neck and carried a black lace parasol. They seemed especially interested in children and vacant lots. When I overtook them and stopped to say a word, I found them affable and confiding. They told me they worked in Kansas City in the winter, and in summer they went out among the farming towns with their tent and taught dancing. When business fell off in one place, they moved on to another.

The dancing pavilion was put up near the Danish laundry, on a vacant lot surrounded by tall, arched cottonwood trees. It was very much like a merry-go-round tent, with open sides and gay flags flying from the poles. Before the week was over, all the ambitious mothers were sending their children to the afternoon dancing class. At three o'clock one met little girls in white dresses and little boys in the round-collared shirts of the time, hurrying along the sidewalk on their way to the tent. Mrs. Vanni received them at the entrance, always dressed in lavender with a great deal of black lace, her important watch-chain lying on her bosom. She wore her hair on the top of her head, built up in a black tower, with red coral combs. When she smiled, she showed two rows of strong, crooked yellow teeth. She taught the little children herself, and her husband, the harpist, taught the older ones.

Often the mothers brought their fancywork and sat on the shady side of the tent during the lesson. The popcorn man wheeled his glass wagon under the big cottonwood by the door, and lounged in the sun, sure of a good trade when the dancing was over. Mr. Jensen, the Danish laundryman, used to bring a chair from his porch and sit out in the grass plot. Some ragged little boys from the depot sold pop and iced lemonade under a white umbrella at the corner, and made faces at the spruce youngsters who came to dance. That vacant lot soon became the most cheerful place in town. Even on the hottest afternoons the cottonwoods made a rustling shade, and the air smelled of popcorn and melted butter, and Bouncing Bets wilting in the sun. Those hardy flowers had run away from the laundryman's garden, and the grass in the middle of the lot was pink with them.

The Vannis kept exemplary order, and closed every evening at the hour suggested by the city council. When Mrs. Vanni gave the signal, and the harp struck up 'Home, Sweet Home,' all Black Hawk knew it was ten o'clock. You could set your watch by that tune as confidently as by the roundhouse whistle.

At last there was something to do in those long, empty summer evenings, when the married people sat like images on their front porches, and the boys and girls tramped and tramped the board sidewalks—northward to the edge of the open prairie, south to the depot, then back again to the post-office, the ice-cream parlour, the butcher shop. Now there was a place where the girls could wear their new dresses, and where one could laugh aloud without being reproved by the ensuing silence. That silence seemed to ooze out of the ground, to hang under the foliage of the black maple trees with the bats and shadows. Now it was broken by lighthearted sounds. First the deep purring of Mr. Vanni's harp came in silvery ripples through the blackness of the dusty-smelling night; then the violins fell in—one of them was almost like a flute. They called so archly, so seductively, that our feet hurried toward the tent of themselves. Why hadn't we had a tent before?

Dancing became popular now, just as roller skating had been the summer before. The Progressive Euchre Club arranged with the Vannis for the exclusive use of the floor on Tuesday and Friday nights. At other times anyone could dance who paid his money and was orderly; the railroad men, the roundhouse mechanics, the delivery boys, the iceman, the farm-hands who lived near enough to ride into town after their day's work was over.

I never missed a Saturday night dance. The tent was open until midnight then. The country boys came in from farms eight and ten miles away, and all the country girls were on the floor—Antonia and Lena and Tiny, and the Danish laundry girls and their friends. I was not the only boy who found these dances gayer than the others. The young men who belonged to the Progressive Euchre Club used to drop in late and risk a tiff with their sweethearts and general condemnation for a waltz with 'the hired girls.'

IX.

There was a curious social situation in Black Hawk. All the young men felt the attraction of the fine, well-set-up country girls who had come to town to earn a living, and, in nearly every case, to help the father struggle out of debt, or to make it possible for the younger children of the family to go to school.

Those girls had grown up in the first bitter-hard times, and had got little schooling themselves. But the younger brothers and sisters, for whom they made such sacrifices and who have had 'advantages,' never seem to me, when I meet them now, half as interesting or as well educated. The older girls, who helped to break up the wild sod, learned so much from life, from poverty, from their mothers and grandmothers; they had all, like Antonia, been early awakened and made observant by coming at a tender age from an old country to a new.

I can remember a score of these country girls who were in service in Black Hawk during the few years I lived there, and I can remember something unusual and engaging about each of them. Physically they were almost a race apart, and out-of-door work had given them a vigour which, when they got over their first shyness on coming to town, developed into a positive carriage and freedom of movement, and made them conspicuous among Black Hawk women.

That was before the day of high-school athletics. Girls who had to walk more than half a mile to school were pitied. There was not a tennis-court in the town; physical exercise was thought rather inelegant for the daughters of well-to-do families. Some of the high-school girls were jolly and pretty, but they stayed indoors in winter because of the cold, and in summer because of the heat. When one danced with them, their bodies never moved inside their clothes; their muscles seemed to ask but one thing—not to be disturbed. I remember those girls merely as faces in the schoolroom, gay and rosy, or listless and dull, cut off below the shoulders, like cherubs, by the ink-smeared tops of the high desks that were surely put there to make us round-shouldered and hollow-chested.

The daughters of Black Hawk merchants had a confident, unenquiring belief that they were 'refined,' and that the country girls, who 'worked out,' were not. The American farmers in our county were quite as hard-pressed as their neighbours from other countries. All alike had come to Nebraska with little capital and no knowledge of the soil they must subdue. All had borrowed money on their land. But no matter in what straits the Pennsylvanian or Virginian found himself, he would not let his daughters go out into service. Unless his girls could teach a country school, they sat at home in poverty.

The Bohemian and Scandinavian girls could not get positions as teachers, because they had had no opportunity to learn the language. Determined to help in the struggle to clear the homestead from debt, they had no alternative but to go into service. Some of them, after they came to town, remained as serious and as discreet in behaviour as they had been when they ploughed and herded on their father's farm. Others, like the three Bohemian Marys, tried to make up for the years of youth they had lost. But every one of them did what she had set out to do, and sent home those hard-earned dollars. The girls I knew were always helping to pay for ploughs and reapers, brood-sows, or steers to fatten.

One result of this family solidarity was that the foreign farmers in our county were the first to become prosperous. After the fathers were out of debt, the daughters married the sons of neighbours—usually of like nationality—and the girls who once worked in Black Hawk kitchens are to-day managing big farms and fine families of their own; their children are better off than the children of the town women they used to serve.

I thought the attitude of the town people toward these girls very stupid. If I told my schoolmates that Lena Lingard's grandfather was a clergyman, and much respected in Norway, they looked at me blankly. What did it matter? All foreigners were ignorant people who couldn't speak English. There was not a man in Black Hawk who had the intelligence or cultivation, much less the personal distinction, of Antonia's father. Yet people saw no difference between her and the three Marys; they were all Bohemians, all 'hired girls.'

I always knew I should live long enough to see my country girls come into their own, and I have. To-day the best that a harassed Black Hawk merchant can hope for is to sell provisions and farm machinery and automobiles to the rich farms where that first crop of stalwart Bohemian and Scandinavian girls are now the mistresses.

The Black Hawk boys looked forward to marrying Black Hawk girls, and living in a brand new little house with best chairs that must not be sat upon, and hand-painted china that must not be used. But sometimes a young fellow would look up from his ledger, or out through the grating of his father's bank, and let his eyes follow Lena Lingard, as she passed the window with her slow, undulating walk, or Tiny Soderball, tripping by in her short skirt and striped stockings.

The country girls were considered a menace to the social order. Their beauty shone out too boldly against a conventional background. But anxious mothers need have felt no alarm. They mistook the mettle of their sons. The respect for respectability was stronger than any desire in Black Hawk youth.

Our young man of position was like the son of a royal house; the boy who swept out his office or drove his delivery wagon might frolic with the jolly country girls, but he himself must sit all evening in a plush parlour where conversation dragged so perceptibly that the father often came in and made blundering efforts to warm up the atmosphere. On his way home from his dull call, he would perhaps meet Tony and Lena, coming along the sidewalk whispering to each other, or the three Bohemian Marys in their long plush coats and caps, comporting themselves with a dignity that only made their eventful histories the more piquant. If he went to the hotel to see a travelling man on business, there was Tiny, arching her shoulders at him like a kitten. If he went into the laundry to get his collars, there were the four Danish girls, smiling up from their ironing-boards, with their white throats and their pink cheeks.

The three Marys were the heroines of a cycle of scandalous stories, which the old men were fond of relating as they sat about the cigar-stand in the drugstore. Mary Dusak had been housekeeper for a bachelor rancher from Boston, and after several years in his service she was forced to retire from the world for a short time. Later she came back to town to take the place of her friend, Mary Svoboda, who was similarly embarrassed. The three Marys were considered as dangerous as high explosives to have about the kitchen, yet they were such good cooks and such admirable housekeepers that they never had to look for a place.

The Vannis' tent brought the town boys and the country girls together on neutral ground. Sylvester Lovett, who was cashier in his father's bank, always found his way to the tent on Saturday night. He took all the dances Lena Lingard would give him, and even grew bold enough to walk home with her. If his sisters or their friends happened to be among the onlookers on 'popular nights,' Sylvester stood back in the shadow under the cottonwood trees, smoking and watching Lena with a harassed expression. Several times I stumbled upon him there in the dark, and I felt rather sorry for him. He reminded me of Ole Benson, who used to sit on the drawside and watch Lena herd her cattle. Later in the summer, when Lena went home for a week to visit her mother, I heard from Antonia that young Lovett drove all the way out there to see her, and took her buggy-riding. In my ingenuousness I hoped that Sylvester would marry Lena, and thus give all the country girls a better position in the town.

Sylvester dallied about Lena until he began to make mistakes in his work; had to stay at the bank until after dark to make his books balance. He was daft about her, and everyone knew it. To escape from his predicament he ran away with a widow six years older than himself, who owned a half-section. This remedy worked, apparently. He never looked at Lena again, nor lifted his eyes as he ceremoniously tipped his hat when he happened to meet her on the sidewalk.

So that was what they were like, I thought, these white-handed, high-collared clerks and bookkeepers! I used to glare at young Lovett from a distance and only wished I had some way of showing my contempt for him.

X.

It was at the Vannis' tent that Antonia was discovered. Hitherto she had been looked upon more as a ward of the Harlings than as one of the 'hired girls.' She had lived in their house and yard and garden; her thoughts never seemed to stray outside that little kingdom. But after the tent came to town she began to go about with Tiny and Lena and their friends. The Vannis often said that Antonia was the best dancer of them all. I sometimes heard murmurs in the crowd outside the pavilion that Mrs. Harling would soon have her hands full with that girl. The young men began to joke with each other about 'the Harlings' Tony' as they did about 'the Marshalls' Anna' or 'the Gardeners' Tiny.'

Antonia talked and thought of nothing but the tent. She hummed the dance tunes all day. When supper was late, she hurried with her dishes, dropped and smashed them in her excitement. At the first call of the music, she became irresponsible. If she hadn't time to dress, she merely flung off her apron and shot out of the kitchen door. Sometimes I went with her; the moment the lighted tent came into view she would break into a run, like a boy. There were always partners waiting for her; she began to dance before she got her breath.

Antonia's success at the tent had its consequences. The iceman lingered too long now, when he came into the covered porch to fill the refrigerator. The delivery boys hung about the kitchen when they brought the groceries. Young farmers who were in town for Saturday came tramping through the yard to the back door to engage dances, or to invite Tony to parties and picnics. Lena and Norwegian Anna dropped in to help her with her work, so that she could get away early. The boys who brought her home after the dances sometimes laughed at the back gate and wakened Mr. Harling from his first sleep. A crisis was inevitable.

One Saturday night Mr. Harling had gone down to the cellar for beer. As he came up the stairs in the dark, he heard scuffling on the back porch, and then the sound of a vigorous slap. He looked out through the side door in time to see a pair of long legs vaulting over the picket fence. Antonia was standing there, angry and excited. Young Harry Paine, who was to marry his employer's daughter on Monday, had come to the tent with a crowd of friends and danced all evening. Afterward, he begged Antonia to let him walk home with her. She said she supposed he was a nice young man, as he was one of Miss Frances's friends, and she didn't mind. On the back porch he tried to kiss her, and when she protested—because he was going to be married on Monday—he caught her and kissed her until she got one hand free and slapped him.

Mr. Harling put his beer-bottles down on the table. 'This is what I've been expecting, Antonia. You've been going with girls who have a reputation for being free and easy, and now you've got the same reputation. I won't have this and that fellow tramping about my back yard all the time. This is the end of it, tonight. It stops, short. You can quit going to these dances, or you can hunt another place. Think it over.'

The next morning when Mrs. Harling and Frances tried to reason with Antonia, they found her agitated but determined. 'Stop going to the tent?' she panted. 'I wouldn't think of it for a minute! My own father couldn't make me stop! Mr. Harling ain't my boss outside my work. I won't give up my friends, either. The boys I go with are nice fellows. I thought Mr. Paine was all right, too, because he used to come here. I guess I gave him a red face for his wedding, all right!' she blazed out indignantly.

'You'll have to do one thing or the other, Antonia,' Mrs. Harling told her decidedly. 'I can't go back on what Mr. Harling has said. This is his house.'

'Then I'll just leave, Mrs. Harling. Lena's been wanting me to get a place closer to her for a long while. Mary Svoboda's going away from the Cutters' to work at the hotel, and I can have her place.'

Mrs. Harling rose from her chair. 'Antonia, if you go to the Cutters' to work, you cannot come back to this house again. You know what that man is. It will be the ruin of you.'

Tony snatched up the teakettle and began to pour boiling water over the glasses, laughing excitedly. 'Oh, I can take care of myself! I'm a lot stronger than Cutter is. They pay four dollars there, and there's no children. The work's nothing; I can have every evening, and be out a lot in the afternoons.'

'I thought you liked children. Tony, what's come over you?'

'I don't know, something has.' Antonia tossed her head and set her jaw. 'A girl like me has got to take her good times when she can. Maybe there won't be any tent next year. I guess I want to have my fling, like the other girls.'

Mrs. Harling gave a short, harsh laugh. 'If you go to work for the Cutters, you're likely to have a fling that you won't get up from in a hurry.'

Frances said, when she told grandmother and me about this scene, that every pan and plate and cup on the shelves trembled when her mother walked out of the kitchen. Mrs. Harling declared bitterly that she wished she had never let herself get fond of Antonia.

XI.

Wick Cutter was the money-lender who had fleeced poor Russian Peter. When a farmer once got into the habit of going to Cutter, it was like gambling or the lottery; in an hour of discouragement he went back.

Cutter's first name was Wycliffe, and he liked to talk about his pious bringing-up. He contributed regularly to the Protestant churches, 'for sentiment's sake,' as he said with a flourish of the hand. He came from a town in Iowa where there were a great many Swedes, and could speak a little Swedish, which gave him a great advantage with the early Scandinavian settlers.

In every frontier settlement there are men who have come there to escape restraint. Cutter was one of the 'fast set' of Black Hawk business men. He was an inveterate gambler, though a poor loser. When we saw a light burning in his office late at night, we knew that a game of poker was going on. Cutter boasted that he never drank anything stronger than sherry, and he said he got his start in life by saving the money that other young men spent for cigars. He was full of moral maxims for boys. When he came to our house on business, he quoted 'Poor Richard's Almanack' to me, and told me he was delighted to find a town boy who could milk a cow. He was particularly affable to grandmother, and whenever they met he would begin at once to talk about 'the good old times' and simple living. I detested his pink, bald head, and his yellow whiskers, always soft and glistening. It was said he brushed them every night, as a woman does her hair. His white teeth looked factory-made. His skin was red and rough, as if from perpetual sunburn; he often went away to hot springs to take mud baths. He was notoriously dissolute with women. Two Swedish girls who had lived in his house were the worse for the experience. One of them he had taken to Omaha and established in the business for which he had fitted her. He still visited her.

Cutter lived in a state of perpetual warfare with his wife, and yet, apparently, they never thought of separating. They dwelt in a fussy, scroll-work house, painted white and buried in thick evergreens, with a fussy white fence and barn. Cutter thought he knew a great deal about horses, and usually had a colt which he was training for the track. On Sunday mornings one could see him out at the fair grounds, speeding around the race-course in his trotting-buggy, wearing yellow gloves and a black-and-white-check travelling cap, his whiskers blowing back in the breeze. If there were any boys about, Cutter would offer one of them a quarter to hold the stop-watch, and then drive off, saying he had no change and would 'fix it up next time.' No one could cut his lawn or wash his buggy to suit him. He was so fastidious and prim about his place that a boy would go to a good deal of trouble to throw a dead cat into his back yard, or to dump a sackful of tin cans in his alley. It was a peculiar combination of old-maidishness and licentiousness that made Cutter seem so despicable.

He had certainly met his match when he married Mrs. Cutter. She was a terrifying-looking person; almost a giantess in height, raw-boned, with iron-grey hair, a face always flushed, and prominent, hysterical eyes. When she meant to be entertaining and agreeable, she nodded her head incessantly and snapped her eyes at one. Her teeth were long and curved, like a horse's; people said babies always cried if she smiled at them. Her face had a kind of fascination for me: it was the very colour and shape of anger. There was a gleam of something akin to insanity in her full, intense eyes. She was formal in manner, and made calls in rustling, steel-grey brocades and a tall bonnet with bristling aigrettes.

Mrs. Cutter painted china so assiduously that even her wash-bowls and pitchers, and her husband's shaving-mug, were covered with violets and lilies. Once, when Cutter was exhibiting some of his wife's china to a caller, he dropped a piece. Mrs. Cutter put her handkerchief to her lips as if she were going to faint and said grandly: 'Mr. Cutter, you have broken all the Commandments—spare the finger-bowls!'

They quarrelled from the moment Cutter came into the house until they went to bed at night, and their hired girls reported these scenes to the town at large. Mrs. Cutter had several times cut paragraphs about unfaithful husbands out of the newspapers and mailed them to Cutter in a disguised handwriting. Cutter would come home at noon, find the mutilated journal in the paper-rack, and triumphantly fit the clipping into the space from which it had been cut. Those two could quarrel all morning about whether he ought to put on his heavy or his light underwear, and all evening about whether he had taken cold or not.

The Cutters had major as well as minor subjects for dispute. The chief of these was the question of inheritance: Mrs. Cutter told her husband it was plainly his fault they had no children. He insisted that Mrs. Cutter had purposely remained childless, with the determination to outlive him and to share his property with her 'people,' whom he detested. To this she would reply that unless he changed his mode of life, she would certainly outlive him. After listening to her insinuations about his physical soundness, Cutter would resume his dumb-bell practice for a month, or rise daily at the hour when his wife most liked to sleep, dress noisily, and drive out to the track with his trotting-horse.

Once when they had quarrelled about household expenses, Mrs. Cutter put on her brocade and went among their friends soliciting orders for painted china, saying that Mr. Cutter had compelled her 'to live by her brush.' Cutter wasn't shamed as she had expected; he was delighted!

Cutter often threatened to chop down the cedar trees which half-buried the house. His wife declared she would leave him if she were stripped of the I privacy' which she felt these trees afforded her. That was his opportunity, surely; but he never cut down the trees. The Cutters seemed to find their relations to each other interesting and stimulating, and certainly the rest of us found them so. Wick Cutter was different from any other rascal I have ever known, but I have found Mrs. Cutters all over the world; sometimes founding new religions, sometimes being forcibly fed—easily recognizable, even when superficially tamed.

XII.

After Antonia went to live with the Cutters, she seemed to care about nothing but picnics and parties and having a good time. When she was not going to a dance, she sewed until midnight. Her new clothes were the subject of caustic comment. Under Lena's direction she copied Mrs. Gardener's new party dress and Mrs. Smith's street costume so ingeniously in cheap materials that those ladies were greatly annoyed, and Mrs. Cutter, who was jealous of them, was secretly pleased.

Tony wore gloves now, and high-heeled shoes and feathered bonnets, and she went downtown nearly every afternoon with Tiny and Lena and the Marshalls' Norwegian Anna. We high-school boys used to linger on the playground at the afternoon recess to watch them as they came tripping down the hill along the board sidewalk, two and two. They were growing prettier every day, but as they passed us, I used to think with pride that Antonia, like Snow-White in the fairy tale, was still 'fairest of them all.'

Being a senior now, I got away from school early. Sometimes I overtook the girls downtown and coaxed them into the ice-cream parlour, where they would sit chattering and laughing, telling me all the news from the country.

I remember how angry Tiny Soderball made me one afternoon. She declared she had heard grandmother was going to make a Baptist preacher of me. 'I guess you'll have to stop dancing and wear a white necktie then. Won't he look funny, girls?'

Lena laughed. 'You'll have to hurry up, Jim. If you're going to be a preacher, I want you to marry me. You must promise to marry us all, and then baptize the babies.'

Norwegian Anna, always dignified, looked at her reprovingly.

'Baptists don't believe in christening babies, do they, Jim?'

I told her I didn't know what they believed, and didn't care, and that I certainly wasn't going to be a preacher.

'That's too bad,' Tiny simpered. She was in a teasing mood. 'You'd make such a good one. You're so studious. Maybe you'd like to be a professor. You used to teach Tony, didn't you?'

Antonia broke in. 'I've set my heart on Jim being a doctor. You'd be good with sick people, Jim. Your grandmother's trained you up so nice. My papa always said you were an awful smart boy.'

I said I was going to be whatever I pleased. 'Won't you be surprised, Miss Tiny, if I turn out to be a regular devil of a fellow?'

They laughed until a glance from Norwegian Anna checked them; the high-school principal had just come into the front part of the shop to buy bread for supper. Anna knew the whisper was going about that I was a sly one. People said there must be something queer about a boy who showed no interest in girls of his own age, but who could be lively enough when he was with Tony and Lena or the three Marys.

The enthusiasm for the dance, which the Vannis had kindled, did not at once die out. After the tent left town, the Euchre Club became the Owl Club, and gave dances in the Masonic Hall once a week. I was invited to join, but declined. I was moody and restless that winter, and tired of the people I saw every day. Charley Harling was already at Annapolis, while I was still sitting in Black Hawk, answering to my name at roll-call every morning, rising from my desk at the sound of a bell and marching out like the grammar-school children. Mrs. Harling was a little cool toward me, because I continued to champion Antonia. What was there for me to do after supper? Usually I had learned next day's lessons by the time I left the school building, and I couldn't sit still and read forever.

In the evening I used to prowl about, hunting for diversion. There lay the familiar streets, frozen with snow or liquid with mud. They led to the houses of good people who were putting the babies to bed, or simply sitting still before the parlour stove, digesting their supper. Black Hawk had two saloons. One of them was admitted, even by the church people, to be as respectable as a saloon could be. Handsome Anton Jelinek, who had rented his homestead and come to town, was the proprietor. In his saloon there were long tables where the Bohemian and German farmers could eat the lunches they brought from home while they drank their beer. Jelinek kept rye bread on hand and smoked fish and strong imported cheeses to please the foreign palate. I liked to drop into his bar-room and listen to the talk. But one day he overtook me on the street and clapped me on the shoulder.

'Jim,' he said, 'I am good friends with you and I always like to see you. But you know how the church people think about saloons. Your grandpa has always treated me fine, and I don't like to have you come into my place, because I know he don't like it, and it puts me in bad with him.'

So I was shut out of that.

One could hang about the drugstore; and listen to the old men who sat there every evening, talking politics and telling raw stories. One could go to the cigar factory and chat with the old German who raised canaries for sale, and look at his stuffed birds. But whatever you began with him, the talk went back to taxidermy. There was the depot, of course; I often went down to see the night train come in, and afterward sat awhile with the disconsolate telegrapher who was always hoping to be transferred to Omaha or Denver, 'where there was some life.' He was sure to bring out his pictures of actresses and dancers. He got them with cigarette coupons, and nearly smoked himself to death to possess these desired forms and faces. For a change, one could talk to the station agent; but he was another malcontent; spent all his spare time writing letters to officials requesting a transfer. He wanted to get back to Wyoming where he could go trout-fishing on Sundays. He used to say 'there was nothing in life for him but trout streams, ever since he'd lost his twins.'

These were the distractions I had to choose from. There were no other lights burning downtown after nine o'clock. On starlight nights I used to pace up and down those long, cold streets, scowling at the little, sleeping houses on either side, with their storm-windows and covered back porches. They were flimsy shelters, most of them poorly built of light wood, with spindle porch-posts horribly mutilated by the turning-lathe. Yet for all their frailness, how much jealousy and envy and unhappiness some of them managed to contain! The life that went on in them seemed to me made up of evasions and negations; shifts to save cooking, to save washing and cleaning, devices to propitiate the tongue of gossip. This guarded mode of existence was like living under a tyranny. People's speech, their voices, their very glances, became furtive and repressed. Every individual taste, every natural appetite, was bridled by caution. The people asleep in those houses, I thought, tried to live like the mice in their own kitchens; to make no noise, to leave no trace, to slip over the surface of things in the dark. The growing piles of ashes and cinders in the back yards were the only evidence that the wasteful, consuming process of life went on at all. On Tuesday nights the Owl Club danced; then there was a little stir in the streets, and here and there one could see a lighted window until midnight. But the next night all was dark again.

After I refused to join 'the Owls,' as they were called, I made a bold resolve to go to the Saturday night dances at Firemen's Hall. I knew it would be useless to acquaint my elders with any such plan. Grandfather didn't approve of dancing, anyway; he would only say that if I wanted to dance I could go to the Masonic Hall, among 'the people we knew.' It was just my point that I saw altogether too much of the people we knew.

My bedroom was on the ground floor, and as I studied there, I had a stove in it. I used to retire to my room early on Saturday night, change my shirt and collar and put on my Sunday coat. I waited until all was quiet and the old people were asleep, then raised my window, climbed out, and went softly through the yard. The first time I deceived my grandparents I felt rather shabby, perhaps even the second time, but I soon ceased to think about it.

The dance at the Firemen's Hall was the one thing I looked forward to all the week. There I met the same people I used to see at the Vannis' tent. Sometimes there were Bohemians from Wilber, or German boys who came down on the afternoon freight from Bismarck. Tony and Lena and Tiny were always there, and the three Bohemian Marys, and the Danish laundry girls.

The four Danish girls lived with the laundryman and his wife in their house behind the laundry, with a big garden where the clothes were hung out to dry. The laundryman was a kind, wise old fellow, who paid his girls well, looked out for them, and gave them a good home. He told me once that his own daughter died just as she was getting old enough to help her mother, and that he had been 'trying to make up for it ever since.' On summer afternoons he used to sit for hours on the sidewalk in front of his laundry, his newspaper lying on his knee, watching his girls through the big open window while they ironed and talked in Danish. The clouds of white dust that blew up the street, the gusts of hot wind that withered his vegetable garden, never disturbed his calm. His droll expression seemed to say that he had found the secret of contentment. Morning and evening he drove about in his spring wagon, distributing freshly ironed clothes, and collecting bags of linen that cried out for his suds and sunny drying-lines. His girls never looked so pretty at the dances as they did standing by the ironing-board, or over the tubs, washing the fine pieces, their white arms and throats bare, their cheeks bright as the brightest wild roses, their gold hair moist with the steam or the heat and curling in little damp spirals about their ears. They had not learned much English, and were not so ambitious as Tony or Lena; but they were kind, simple girls and they were always happy. When one danced with them, one smelled their clean, freshly ironed clothes that had been put away with rosemary leaves from Mr. Jensen's garden.

There were never girls enough to go round at those dances, but everyone wanted a turn with Tony and Lena.

Lena moved without exertion, rather indolently, and her hand often accented the rhythm softly on her partner's shoulder. She smiled if one spoke to her, but seldom answered. The music seemed to put her into a soft, waking dream, and her violet-coloured eyes looked sleepily and confidingly at one from under her long lashes. When she sighed she exhaled a heavy perfume of sachet powder. To dance 'Home, Sweet Home,' with Lena was like coming in with the tide. She danced every dance like a waltz, and it was always the same waltz—the waltz of coming home to something, of inevitable, fated return. After a while one got restless under it, as one does under the heat of a soft, sultry summer day.

When you spun out into the floor with Tony, you didn't return to anything. You set out every time upon a new adventure. I liked to schottische with her; she had so much spring and variety, and was always putting in new steps and slides. She taught me to dance against and around the hard-and-fast beat of the music. If, instead of going to the end of the railroad, old Mr. Shimerda had stayed in New York and picked up a living with his fiddle, how different Antonia's life might have been!

Antonia often went to the dances with Larry Donovan, a passenger conductor who was a kind of professional ladies' man, as we said. I remember how admiringly all the boys looked at her the night she first wore her velveteen dress, made like Mrs. Gardener's black velvet. She was lovely to see, with her eyes shining, and her lips always a little parted when she danced. That constant, dark colour in her cheeks never changed.

One evening when Donovan was out on his run, Antonia came to the hall with

Norwegian Anna and her young man, and that night I took her home. When we were in the Cutters' yard, sheltered by the evergreens, I told her she must kiss me good night.

'Why, sure, Jim.' A moment later she drew her face away and whispered indignantly, 'Why, Jim! You know you ain't right to kiss me like that. I'll tell your grandmother on you!'

'Lena Lingard lets me kiss her,' I retorted, 'and I'm not half as fond of her as I am of you.'

'Lena does?' Tony gasped. 'If she's up to any of her nonsense with you, I'll scratch her eyes out!' She took my arm again and we walked out of the gate and up and down the sidewalk. 'Now, don't you go and be a fool like some of these town boys. You're not going to sit around here and whittle store-boxes and tell stories all your life. You are going away to school and make something of yourself. I'm just awful proud of you. You won't go and get mixed up with the Swedes, will you?'

'I don't care anything about any of them but you,' I said. 'And you'll always treat me like a kid, suppose.'

She laughed and threw her arms around me. 'I expect I will, but you're a kid I'm awful fond of, anyhow! You can like me all you want to, but if I see you hanging round with Lena much, I'll go to your grandmother, as sure as your name's Jim Burden! Lena's all right, only —well, you know yourself she's soft that way. She can't help it. It's natural to her.'

If she was proud of me, I was so proud of her that I carried my head high as I emerged from the dark cedars and shut the Cutters' gate softly behind me. Her warm, sweet face, her kind arms, and the true heart in her; she was, oh, she was still my Antonia! I looked with contempt at the dark, silent little houses about me as I walked home, and thought of the stupid young men who were asleep in some of them. I knew where the real women were, though I was only a boy; and I would not be afraid of them, either!

I hated to enter the still house when I went home from the dances, and it was long before I could get to sleep. Toward morning I used to have pleasant dreams: sometimes Tony and I were out in the country, sliding down straw-stacks as we used to do; climbing up the yellow mountains over and over, and slipping down the smooth sides into soft piles of chaff.

One dream I dreamed a great many times, and it was always the same. I was in a harvest-field full of shocks, and I was lying against one of them. Lena Lingard came across the stubble barefoot, in a short skirt, with a curved reaping-hook in her hand, and she was flushed like the dawn, with a kind of luminous rosiness all about her. She sat down beside me, turned to me with a soft sigh and said, 'Now they are all gone, and I can kiss you as much as I like.'

I used to wish I could have this flattering dream about Antonia, but I never did.

XIII.

I noticed one afternoon that grandmother had been crying. Her feet seemed to drag as she moved about the house, and I got up from the table where I was studying and went to her, asking if she didn't feel well, and if I couldn't help her with her work.

'No, thank you, Jim. I'm troubled, but I guess I'm well enough. Getting a little rusty in the bones, maybe,' she added bitterly.

I stood hesitating. 'What are you fretting about, grandmother? Has grandfather lost any money?'

'No, it ain't money. I wish it was. But I've heard things. You must 'a' known it would come back to me sometime.' She dropped into a chair, and, covering her face with her apron, began to cry. 'Jim,' she said, 'I was never one that claimed old folks could bring up their grandchildren. But it came about so; there wasn't any other way for you, it seemed like.'

I put my arms around her. I couldn't bear to see her cry.

'What is it, grandmother? Is it the Firemen's dances?'

She nodded.

'I'm sorry I sneaked off like that. But there's nothing wrong about the dances, and I haven't done anything wrong. I like all those country girls, and I like to dance with them. That's all there is to it.'

'But it ain't right to deceive us, son, and it brings blame on us. People say you are growing up to be a bad boy, and that ain't just to us.'

'I don't care what they say about me, but if it hurts you, that settles it. I won't go to the Firemen's Hall again.'

I kept my promise, of course, but I found the spring months dull enough. I sat at home with the old people in the evenings now, reading Latin that was not in our high-school course. I had made up my mind to do a lot of college requirement work in the summer, and to enter the freshman class at the university without conditions in the fall. I wanted to get away as soon as possible.

Disapprobation hurt me, I found—even that of people whom I did not admire. As the spring came on, I grew more and more lonely, and fell back on the telegrapher and the cigar-maker and his canaries for companionship. I remember I took a melancholy pleasure in hanging a May-basket for Nina Harling that spring. I bought the flowers from an old German woman who always had more window plants than anyone else, and spent an afternoon trimming a little workbasket. When dusk came on, and the new moon hung in the sky, I went quietly to the Harlings' front door with my offering, rang the bell, and then ran away as was the custom. Through the willow hedge I could hear Nina's cries of delight, and I felt comforted.

On those warm, soft spring evenings I often lingered downtown to walk home with Frances, and talked to her about my plans and about the reading I was doing. One evening she said she thought Mrs. Harling was not seriously offended with me.

'Mama is as broad-minded as mothers ever are, I guess. But you know she was hurt about Antonia, and she can't understand why you like to be with Tiny and Lena better than with the girls of your own set.'

'Can you?' I asked bluntly.

Frances laughed. 'Yes, I think I can. You knew them in the country, and you like to take sides. In some ways you're older than boys of your age. It will be all right with mama after you pass your college examinations and she sees you're in earnest.'

'If you were a boy,' I persisted, 'you wouldn't belong to the Owl Club, either. You'd be just like me.'

She shook her head. 'I would and I wouldn't. I expect I know the country girls better than you do. You always put a kind of glamour over them. The trouble with you, Jim, is that you're romantic. Mama's going to your Commencement. She asked me the other day if I knew what your oration is to be about. She wants you to do well.'

I thought my oration very good. It stated with fervour a great many things I had lately discovered. Mrs. Harling came to the Opera House to hear the Commencement exercises, and I looked at her most of the time while I made my speech. Her keen, intelligent eyes never left my face. Afterward she came back to the dressing-room where we stood, with our diplomas in our hands, walked up to me, and said heartily: 'You surprised me, Jim. I didn't believe you could do as well as that. You didn't get that speech out of books.' Among my graduation presents there was a silk umbrella from Mrs. Harling, with my name on the handle.

I walked home from the Opera House alone. As I passed the Methodist Church, I saw three white figures ahead of me, pacing up and down under the arching maple trees, where the moonlight filtered through the lush June foliage. They hurried toward me; they were waiting for me—Lena and Tony and Anna Hansen.

'Oh, Jim, it was splendid!' Tony was breathing hard, as she always did when her feelings outran her language. 'There ain't a lawyer in Black Hawk could make a speech like that. I just stopped your grandpa and said so to him. He won't tell you, but he told us he was awful surprised himself, didn't he, girls?'

Lena sidled up to me and said teasingly, 'What made you so solemn? I thought you were scared. I was sure you'd forget.'

Anna spoke wistfully.

'It must make you very happy, Jim, to have fine thoughts like that in your mind all the time, and to have words to put them in. I always wanted to go to school, you know.'

'Oh, I just sat there and wished my papa could hear you! Jim'—Antonia took hold of my coat lapels—'there was something in your speech that made me think so about my papa!'

'I thought about your papa when I wrote my speech, Tony,' I said. 'I dedicated it to him.'

She threw her arms around me, and her dear face was all wet with tears.

I stood watching their white dresses glimmer smaller and smaller down the sidewalk as they went away. I have had no other success that pulled at my heartstrings like that one.

XIV.

The day after commencement I moved my books and desk upstairs, to an empty room where I should be undisturbed, and I fell to studying in earnest. I worked off a year's trigonometry that summer, and began Virgil alone. Morning after morning I used to pace up and down my sunny little room, looking off at the distant river bluffs and the roll of the blond pastures between, scanning the 'Aeneid' aloud and committing long passages to memory. Sometimes in the evening Mrs. Harling called to me as I passed her gate, and asked me to come in and let her play for me. She was lonely for Charley, she said, and liked to have a boy about. Whenever my grandparents had misgivings, and began to wonder whether I was not too young to go off to college alone, Mrs. Harling took up my cause vigorously. Grandfather had such respect for her judgment that I knew he would not go against her.

I had only one holiday that summer. It was in July. I met Antonia downtown on Saturday afternoon, and learned that she and Tiny and Lena were going to the river next day with Anna Hansen—the elder was all in bloom now, and Anna wanted to make elderblow wine.

'Anna's to drive us down in the Marshalls' delivery wagon, and we'll take a nice lunch and have a picnic. Just us; nobody else. Couldn't you happen along, Jim? It would be like old times.'

I considered a moment. 'Maybe I can, if I won't be in the way.'

On Sunday morning I rose early and got out of Black Hawk while the dew was still heavy on the long meadow grasses. It was the high season for summer flowers. The pink bee-bush stood tall along the sandy roadsides, and the cone-flowers and rose mallow grew everywhere. Across the wire fence, in the long grass, I saw a clump of flaming orange-coloured milkweed, rare in that part of the state. I left the road and went around through a stretch of pasture that was always cropped short in summer, where the gaillardia came up year after year and matted over the ground with the deep, velvety red that is in Bokhara carpets. The country was empty and solitary except for the larks that Sunday morning, and it seemed to lift itself up to me and to come very close.

The river was running strong for midsummer; heavy rains to the west of us had kept it full. I crossed the bridge and went upstream along the wooded shore to a pleasant dressing-room I knew among the dogwood bushes, all overgrown with wild grapevines. I began to undress for a swim. The girls would not be along yet. For the first time it occurred to me that I should be homesick for that river after I left it. The sandbars, with their clean white beaches and their little groves of willows and cottonwood seedlings, were a sort of No Man's Land, little newly created worlds that belonged to the Black Hawk boys. Charley Harling and I had hunted through these woods, fished from the fallen logs, until I knew every inch of the river shores and had a friendly feeling for every bar and shallow.

After my swim, while I was playing about indolently in the water, I heard the sound of hoofs and wheels on the bridge. I struck downstream and shouted, as the open spring wagon came into view on the middle span. They stopped the horse, and the two girls in the bottom of the cart stood up, steadying themselves by the shoulders of the two in front, so that they could see me better. They were charming up there, huddled together in the cart and peering down at me like curious deer when they come out of the thicket to drink. I found bottom near the bridge and stood up, waving to them.

'How pretty you look!' I called.

'So do you!' they shouted altogether, and broke into peals of laughter. Anna Hansen shook the reins and they drove on, while I zigzagged back to my inlet and clambered up behind an overhanging elm. I dried myself in the sun, and dressed slowly, reluctant to leave that green enclosure where the sunlight flickered so bright through the grapevine leaves and the woodpecker hammered away in the crooked elm that trailed out over the water. As I went along the road back to the bridge, I kept picking off little pieces of scaly chalk from the dried water gullies, and breaking them up in my hands.

When I came upon the Marshalls' delivery horse, tied in the shade, the girls had already taken their baskets and gone down the east road which wound through the sand and scrub. I could hear them calling to each other. The elder bushes did not grow back in the shady ravines between the bluffs, but in the hot, sandy bottoms along the stream, where their roots were always in moisture and their tops in the sun. The blossoms were unusually luxuriant and beautiful that summer.

I followed a cattle path through the thick under-brush until I came to a slope that fell away abruptly to the water's edge. A great chunk of the shore had been bitten out by some spring freshet, and the scar was masked by elder bushes, growing down to the water in flowery terraces. I did not touch them. I was overcome by content and drowsiness and by the warm silence about me. There was no sound but the high, singsong buzz of wild bees and the sunny gurgle of the water underneath. I peeped over the edge of the bank to see the little stream that made the noise; it flowed along perfectly clear over the sand and gravel, cut off from the muddy main current by a long sandbar. Down there, on the lower shelf of the bank, I saw Antonia, seated alone under the pagoda-like elders. She looked up when she heard me, and smiled, but I saw that she had been crying. I slid down into the soft sand beside her and asked her what was the matter.

'It makes me homesick, Jimmy, this flower, this smell,' she said softly. 'We have this flower very much at home, in the old country. It always grew in our yard and my papa had a green bench and a table under the bushes. In summer, when they were in bloom, he used to sit there with his friend that played the trombone. When I was little I used to go down there to hear them talk—beautiful talk, like what I never hear in this country.'

'What did they talk about?' I asked her.

She sighed and shook her head. 'Oh, I don't know! About music, and the woods, and about God, and when they were young.' She turned to me suddenly and looked into my eyes. 'You think, Jimmy, that maybe my father's spirit can go back to those old places?'

I told her about the feeling of her father's presence I had on that winter day when my grandparents had gone over to see his dead body and I was left alone in the house. I said I felt sure then that he was on his way back to his own country, and that even now, when I passed his grave, I always thought of him as being among the woods and fields that were so dear to him.

Antonia had the most trusting, responsive eyes in the world; love and credulousness seemed to look out of them with open faces.

'Why didn't you ever tell me that before? It makes me feel more sure for him.' After a while she said: 'You know, Jim, my father was different from my mother. He did not have to marry my mother, and all his brothers quarrelled with him because he did. I used to hear the old people at home whisper about it. They said he could have paid my mother money, and not married her. But he was older than she was, and he was too kind to treat her like that. He lived in his mother's house, and she was a poor girl come in to do the work. After my father married her, my grandmother never let my mother come into her house again. When I went to my grandmother's funeral was the only time I was ever in my grandmother's house. Don't that seem strange?'

While she talked, I lay back in the hot sand and looked up at the blue sky between the flat bouquets of elder. I could hear the bees humming and singing, but they stayed up in the sun above the flowers and did not come down into the shadow of the leaves. Antonia seemed to me that day exactly like the little girl who used to come to our house with Mr. Shimerda.

'Some day, Tony, I am going over to your country, and I am going to the little town where you lived. Do you remember all about it?'

'Jim,' she said earnestly, 'if I was put down there in the middle of the night, I could find my way all over that little town; and along the river to the next town, where my grandmother lived. My feet remember all the little paths through the woods, and where the big roots stick out to trip you. I ain't never forgot my own country.'

There was a crackling in the branches above us, and Lena Lingard peered down over the edge of the bank.

'You lazy things!' she cried. 'All this elder, and you two lying there! Didn't you hear us calling you?' Almost as flushed as she had been in my dream, she leaned over the edge of the bank and began to demolish our flowery pagoda. I had never seen her so energetic; she was panting with zeal, and the perspiration stood in drops on her short, yielding upper lip. I sprang to my feet and ran up the bank.

It was noon now, and so hot that the dogwoods and scrub-oaks began to turn up the silvery underside of their leaves, and all the foliage looked soft and wilted. I carried the lunch-basket to the top of one of the chalk bluffs, where even on the calmest days there was always a breeze. The flat-topped, twisted little oaks threw light shadows on the grass. Below us we could see the windings of the river, and Black Hawk, grouped among its trees, and, beyond, the rolling country, swelling gently until it met the sky. We could recognize familiar farm-houses and windmills. Each of the girls pointed out to me the direction in which her father's farm lay, and told me how many acres were in wheat that year and how many in corn.

'My old folks,' said Tiny Soderball, 'have put in twenty acres of rye. They get it ground at the mill, and it makes nice bread. It seems like my mother ain't been so homesick, ever since father's raised rye flour for her.'

'It must have been a trial for our mothers,' said Lena, 'coming out here and having to do everything different. My mother had always lived in town. She says she started behind in farm-work, and never has caught up.'

'Yes, a new country's hard on the old ones, sometimes,' said Anna thoughtfully. 'My grandmother's getting feeble now, and her mind wanders. She's forgot about this country, and thinks she's at home in Norway. She keeps asking mother to take her down to the waterside and the fish market. She craves fish all the time. Whenever I go home I take her canned salmon and mackerel.'

'Mercy, it's hot!' Lena yawned. She was supine under a little oak, resting after the fury of her elder-hunting, and had taken off the high-heeled slippers she had been silly enough to wear. 'Come here, Jim. You never got the sand out of your hair.' She began to draw her fingers slowly through my hair.

Antonia pushed her away. 'You'll never get it out like that,' she said sharply. She gave my head a rough touzling and finished me off with something like a box on the ear. 'Lena, you oughtn't to try to wear those slippers any more. They're too small for your feet. You'd better give them to me for Yulka.'

'All right,' said Lena good-naturedly, tucking her white stockings under her skirt. 'You get all Yulka's things, don't you? I wish father didn't have such bad luck with his farm machinery; then I could buy more things for my sisters. I'm going to get Mary a new coat this fall, if the sulky plough's never paid for!'

Tiny asked her why she didn't wait until after Christmas, when coats would be cheaper. 'What do you think of poor me?' she added; 'with six at home, younger than I am? And they all think I'm rich, because when I go back to the country I'm dressed so fine!' She shrugged her shoulders. 'But, you know, my weakness is playthings. I like to buy them playthings better than what they need.'

'I know how that is,' said Anna. 'When we first came here, and I was little, we were too poor to buy toys. I never got over the loss of a doll somebody gave me before we left Norway. A boy on the boat broke her and I still hate him for it.'

'I guess after you got here you had plenty of live dolls to nurse, like me!' Lena remarked cynically.

'Yes, the babies came along pretty fast, to be sure. But I never minded. I was fond of them all. The youngest one, that we didn't any of us want, is the one we love best now.'

Lena sighed. 'Oh, the babies are all right; if only they don't come in winter. Ours nearly always did. I don't see how mother stood it. I tell you what, girls'—she sat up with sudden energy—'I'm going to get my mother out of that old sod house where she's lived so many years. The men will never do it. Johnnie, that's my oldest brother, he's wanting to get married now, and build a house for his girl instead of his mother. Mrs. Thomas says she thinks I can move to some other town pretty soon, and go into business for myself. If I don't get into business, I'll maybe marry a rich gambler.'

'That would be a poor way to get on,' said Anna sarcastically. 'I wish I could teach school, like Selma Kronn. Just think! She'll be the first Scandinavian girl to get a position in the high school. We ought to be proud of her.'

Selma was a studious girl, who had not much tolerance for giddy things like Tiny and Lena; but they always spoke of her with admiration.

Tiny moved about restlessly, fanning herself with her straw hat. 'If I was smart like her, I'd be at my books day and night. But she was born smart—and look how her father's trained her! He was something high up in the old country.'

'So was my mother's father,' murmured Lena, 'but that's all the good it does us! My father's father was smart, too, but he was wild. He married a Lapp. I guess that's what's the matter with me; they say Lapp blood will out.'

'A real Lapp, Lena?' I exclaimed. 'The kind that wear skins?'

'I don't know if she wore skins, but she was a Lapps all right, and his folks felt dreadful about it. He was sent up North on some government job he had, and fell in with her. He would marry her.'

'But I thought Lapland women were fat and ugly, and had squint eyes, like Chinese?' I objected.

'I don't know, maybe. There must be something mighty taking about the Lapp girls, though; mother says the Norwegians up North are always afraid their boys will run after them.'

In the afternoon, when the heat was less oppressive, we had a lively game of 'Pussy Wants a Corner,' on the flat bluff-top, with the little trees for bases. Lena was Pussy so often that she finally said she wouldn't play any more. We threw ourselves down on the grass, out of breath.

'Jim,' Antonia said dreamily, 'I want you to tell the girls about how the Spanish first came here, like you and Charley Harling used to talk about. I've tried to tell them, but I leave out so much.'

They sat under a little oak, Tony resting against the trunk and the other girls leaning against her and each other, and listened to the little I was able to tell them about Coronado and his search for the Seven Golden Cities. At school we were taught that he had not got so far north as Nebraska, but had given up his quest and turned back somewhere in Kansas. But Charley Harling and I had a strong belief that he had been along this very river. A farmer in the county north of ours, when he was breaking sod, had turned up a metal stirrup of fine workmanship, and a sword with a Spanish inscription on the blade. He lent these relics to Mr. Harling, who brought them home with him. Charley and I scoured them, and they were on exhibition in the Harling office all summer. Father Kelly, the priest, had found the name of the Spanish maker on the sword and an abbreviation that stood for the city of Cordova.

'And that I saw with my own eyes,' Antonia put in triumphantly. 'So Jim and Charley were right, and the teachers were wrong!'

The girls began to wonder among themselves. Why had the Spaniards come so far? What must this country have been like, then? Why had Coronado never gone back to Spain, to his riches and his castles and his king? I couldn't tell them. I only knew the schoolbooks said he 'died in the wilderness, of a broken heart.'

'More than him has done that,' said Antonia sadly, and the girls murmured assent.

We sat looking off across the country, watching the sun go down. The curly grass about us was on fire now. The bark of the oaks turned red as copper. There was a shimmer of gold on the brown river. Out in the stream the sandbars glittered like glass, and the light trembled in the willow thickets as if little flames were leaping among them. The breeze sank to stillness. In the ravine a ringdove mourned plaintively, and somewhere off in the bushes an owl hooted. The girls sat listless, leaning against each other. The long fingers of the sun touched their foreheads.

Presently we saw a curious thing: There were no clouds, the sun was going down in a limpid, gold-washed sky. Just as the lower edge of the red disk rested on the high fields against the horizon, a great black figure suddenly appeared on the face of the sun. We sprang to our feet, straining our eyes toward it. In a moment we realized what it was. On some upland farm, a plough had been left standing in the field. The sun was sinking just behind it. Magnified across the distance by the horizontal light, it stood out against the sun, was exactly contained within the circle of the disk; the handles, the tongue, the share—black against the molten red. There it was, heroic in size, a picture writing on the sun.

Even while we whispered about it, our vision disappeared; the ball dropped and dropped until the red tip went beneath the earth. The fields below us were dark, the sky was growing pale, and that forgotten plough had sunk back to its own littleness somewhere on the prairie.

XV.

Late in August the Cutters went to Omaha for a few days, leaving Antonia in charge of the house. Since the scandal about the Swedish girl, Wick Cutter could never get his wife to stir out of Black Hawk without him.

The day after the Cutters left, Antonia came over to see us. Grandmother noticed that she seemed troubled and distracted. 'You've got something on your mind, Antonia,' she said anxiously.

'Yes, Mrs. Burden. I couldn't sleep much last night.' She hesitated, and then told us how strangely Mr. Cutter had behaved before he went away. He put all the silver in a basket and placed it under her bed, and with it a box of papers which he told her were valuable. He made her promise that she would not sleep away from the house, or be out late in the evening, while he was gone. He strictly forbade her to ask any of the girls she knew to stay with her at night. She would be perfectly safe, he said, as he had just put a new Yale lock on the front door.

Cutter had been so insistent in regard to these details that now she felt uncomfortable about staying there alone. She hadn't liked the way he kept coming into the kitchen to instruct her, or the way he looked at her. 'I feel as if he is up to some of his tricks again, and is going to try to scare me, somehow.'

Grandmother was apprehensive at once. 'I don't think it's right for you to stay there, feeling that way. I suppose it wouldn't be right for you to leave the place alone, either, after giving your word. Maybe Jim would be willing to go over there and sleep, and you could come here nights. I'd feel safer, knowing you were under my own roof. I guess Jim could take care of their silver and old usury notes as well as you could.'

Antonia turned to me eagerly. 'Oh, would you, Jim? I'd make up my bed nice and fresh for you. It's a real cool room, and the bed's right next the window. I was afraid to leave the window open last night.'

I liked my own room, and I didn't like the Cutters' house under any circumstances; but Tony looked so troubled that I consented to try this arrangement. I found that I slept there as well as anywhere, and when I got home in the morning, Tony had a good breakfast waiting for me. After prayers she sat down at the table with us, and it was like old times in the country.

The third night I spent at the Cutters', I awoke suddenly with the impression that I had heard a door open and shut. Everything was still, however, and I must have gone to sleep again immediately.

The next thing I knew, I felt someone sit down on the edge of the bed. I was only half awake, but I decided that he might take the Cutters' silver, whoever he was. Perhaps if I did not move, he would find it and get out without troubling me. I held my breath and lay absolutely still. A hand closed softly on my shoulder, and at the same moment I felt something hairy and cologne-scented brushing my face. If the room had suddenly been flooded with electric light, I couldn't have seen more clearly the detestable bearded countenance that I knew was bending over me. I caught a handful of whiskers and pulled, shouting something. The hand that held my shoulder was instantly at my throat. The man became insane; he stood over me, choking me with one fist and beating me in the face with the other, hissing and chuckling and letting out a flood of abuse.

'So this is what she's up to when I'm away, is it? Where is she, you nasty whelp, where is she? Under the bed, are you, hussy? I know your tricks! Wait till I get at you! I'll fix this rat you've got in here. He's caught, all right!'

So long as Cutter had me by the throat, there was no chance for me at all. I got hold of his thumb and bent it back, until he let go with a yell. In a bound, I was on my feet, and easily sent him sprawling to the floor. Then I made a dive for the open window, struck the wire screen, knocked it out, and tumbled after it into the yard.

Suddenly I found myself running across the north end of Black Hawk in my night-shirt, just as one sometimes finds one's self behaving in bad dreams. When I got home, I climbed in at the kitchen window. I was covered with blood from my nose and lip, but I was too sick to do anything about it. I found a shawl and an overcoat on the hat-rack, lay down on the parlour sofa, and in spite of my hurts, went to sleep.

Grandmother found me there in the morning. Her cry of fright awakened me. Truly, I was a battered object. As she helped me to my room, I caught a glimpse of myself in the mirror. My lip was cut and stood out like a snout. My nose looked like a big blue plum, and one eye was swollen shut and hideously discoloured. Grandmother said we must have the doctor at once, but I implored her, as I had never begged for anything before, not to send for him. I could stand anything, I told her, so long as nobody saw me or knew what had happened to me. I entreated her not to let grandfather, even, come into my room. She seemed to understand, though I was too faint and miserable to go into explanations. When she took off my night-shirt, she found such bruises on my chest and shoulders that she began to cry. She spent the whole morning bathing and poulticing me, and rubbing me with arnica. I heard Antonia sobbing outside my door, but I asked grandmother to send her away. I felt that I never wanted to see her again. I hated her almost as much as I hated Cutter. She had let me in for all this disgustingness. Grandmother kept saying how thankful we ought to be that I had been there instead of Antonia. But I lay with my disfigured face to the wall and felt no particular gratitude. My one concern was that grandmother should keep everyone away from me. If the story once got abroad, I would never hear the last of it. I could well imagine what the old men down at the drugstore would do with such a theme.

While grandmother was trying to make me comfortable, grandfather went to the depot and learned that Wick Cutter had come home on the night express from the east, and had left again on the six o'clock train for Denver that morning. The agent said his face was striped with court-plaster, and he carried his left hand in a sling. He looked so used up, that the agent asked him what had happened to him since ten o'clock the night before; whereat Cutter began to swear at him and said he would have him discharged for incivility.

That afternoon, while I was asleep, Antonia took grandmother with her, and went over to the Cutters' to pack her trunk. They found the place locked up, and they had to break the window to get into Antonia's bedroom. There everything was in shocking disorder. Her clothes had been taken out of her closet, thrown into the middle of the room, and trampled and torn. My own garments had been treated so badly that I never saw them again; grandmother burned them in the Cutters' kitchen range.

While Antonia was packing her trunk and putting her room in order, to leave it, the front doorbell rang violently. There stood Mrs. Cutter—locked out, for she had no key to the new lock—her head trembling with rage. 'I advised her to control herself, or she would have a stroke,' grandmother said afterward.

Grandmother would not let her see Antonia at all, but made her sit down in the parlour while she related to her just what had occurred the night before. Antonia was frightened, and was going home to stay for a while, she told Mrs. Cutter; it would be useless to interrogate the girl, for she knew nothing of what had happened.

Then Mrs. Cutter told her story. She and her husband had started home from Omaha together the morning before. They had to stop over several hours at Waymore Junction to catch the Black Hawk train. During the wait, Cutter left her at the depot and went to the Waymore bank to attend to some business. When he returned, he told her that he would have to stay overnight there, but she could go on home. He bought her ticket and put her on the train. She saw him slip a twenty-dollar bill into her handbag with her ticket. That bill, she said, should have aroused her suspicions at once—but did not.

The trains are never called at little junction towns; everybody knows when they come in. Mr. Cutter showed his wife's ticket to the conductor, and settled her in her seat before the train moved off. It was not until nearly nightfall that she discovered she was on the express bound for Kansas City, that her ticket was made out to that point, and that Cutter must have planned it so. The conductor told her the Black Hawk train was due at Waymore twelve minutes after the Kansas City train left. She saw at once that her husband had played this trick in order to get back to Black Hawk without her. She had no choice but to go on to Kansas City and take the first fast train for home.

Cutter could have got home a day earlier than his wife by any one of a dozen simpler devices; he could have left her in the Omaha hotel, and said he was going on to Chicago for a few days. But apparently it was part of his fun to outrage her feelings as much as possible.

'Mr. Cutter will pay for this, Mrs. Burden. He will pay!' Mrs. Cutter avouched, nodding her horse-like head and rolling her eyes.

Grandmother said she hadn't a doubt of it.

Certainly Cutter liked to have his wife think him a devil. In some way he depended upon the excitement He could arouse in her hysterical nature. Perhaps he got the feeling of being a rake more from his wife's rage and amazement than from any experiences of his own. His zest in debauchery might wane, but never Mrs. Cutter's belief in it. The reckoning with his wife at the end of an escapade was something he counted on—like the last powerful liqueur after a long dinner. The one excitement he really couldn't do without was quarrelling with Mrs. Cutter!

❧ 3 ❧

LENA LINGARD

I.

AT THE UNIVERSITY I had the good fortune to come immediately under the influence of a brilliant and inspiring young scholar. Gaston Cleric had arrived in Lincoln only a few weeks earlier than I, to begin his work as head of the Latin Department. He came West at the suggestion of his physicians, his health having been enfeebled by a long illness in Italy. When I took my entrance examinations, he was my examiner, and my course was arranged under his supervision.

I did not go home for my first summer vacation, but stayed in Lincoln, working off a year's Greek, which had been my only condition on entering the freshman class. Cleric's doctor advised against his going back to New England, and, except for a few weeks in Colorado, he, too, was in Lincoln all that summer. We played tennis, read, and took long walks together. I shall always look back on that time of mental awakening as one of the happiest in my life. Gaston Cleric introduced me to the world of ideas; when one first enters that world everything else fades for a time, and all that went before is as if it had not been. Yet I found curious survivals; some of the figures of my old life seemed to be waiting for me in the new.

In those days there were many serious young men among the students who had come up to the university from the farms and the little towns scattered over the thinly settled state. Some of those boys came straight from the cornfields with only a summer's wages in their pockets, hung on through the four years, shabby and underfed, and completed the course by really heroic self-sacrifice. Our instructors were oddly assorted; wandering pioneer school-teachers, stranded ministers of the Gospel, a few enthusiastic young men just out of graduate schools. There was an atmosphere of endeavour, of expectancy and bright hopefulness about the young college that had lifted its head from the prairie only a few years before.

Our personal life was as free as that of our instructors. There were no college dormitories; we lived where we could and as we could. I took rooms with an old couple, early settlers in Lincoln, who had married off their children and now lived quietly in their house at the edge of town, near the open country. The house was inconveniently situated for students, and on that account I got two rooms for the price of one. My bedroom, originally a linen-closet, was unheated and was barely large enough to contain my cot-bed, but it enabled me to call the other room my study. The dresser, and the great walnut wardrobe which held all my clothes, even my hats and shoes, I had pushed out of the way, and I considered them non-existent, as children eliminate incongruous objects when they are playing house. I worked at a commodious green-topped table placed directly in front of the west window which looked out over the prairie. In the corner at my right were all my books, in shelves I had made and painted myself. On the blank wall at my left the dark, old-fashioned wall-paper was covered by a large map of ancient Rome, the work of some German scholar. Cleric had ordered it for me when he was sending for books from abroad. Over the bookcase hung a photograph of the Tragic Theatre at Pompeii, which he had given me from his collection.

When I sat at work I half-faced a deep, upholstered chair which stood at the end of my table, its high back against the wall. I had bought it with great care. My instructor sometimes looked in upon me when he was out for an evening tramp, and I noticed that he was more likely to linger and become talkative if I had a comfortable chair for him to sit in, and if he found a bottle of Benedictine and plenty of the kind of cigarettes he liked, at his elbow. He was, I had discovered, parsimonious about small expenditures—a trait absolutely inconsistent with his general character. Sometimes when he came he was silent and moody, and after a few sarcastic remarks went away again, to tramp the streets of Lincoln, which were almost as quiet and oppressively domestic as those of Black Hawk. Again, he would sit until nearly midnight, talking about Latin and English poetry, or telling me about his long stay in Italy.

I can give no idea of the peculiar charm and vividness of his talk. In a crowd he was nearly always silent. Even for his classroom he had no platitudes, no stock of professorial anecdotes. When he was tired, his lectures were clouded, obscure, elliptical; but when he was interested they were wonderful. I believe that Gaston Cleric narrowly missed being a great poet, and I have sometimes thought that his bursts of imaginative talk were fatal to his poetic gift. He squandered too much in the heat of personal communication. How often I have seen him draw his dark brows together, fix his eyes upon some object on the wall or a figure in the carpet, and then flash into the lamplight the very image that was in his brain. He could bring the drama of antique life before one out of the shadows—white figures against blue backgrounds. I shall never forget his face as it looked one night when he told me about the solitary day he spent among the sea temples at Paestum: the soft wind blowing through the roofless columns, the birds flying low over the flowering marsh grasses, the changing lights on the silver, cloud-hung mountains. He had wilfully stayed the short summer night there, wrapped in his coat and rug, watching the constellations on their path down the sky until 'the bride of old Tithonus' rose out of the sea, and the mountains stood sharp in the dawn. It was there he caught the fever which held him back on the eve of his departure for Greece and of which he lay ill so long in Naples. He was still, indeed, doing penance for it.

I remember vividly another evening, when something led us to talk of Dante's veneration for Virgil. Cleric went through canto after canto of the 'Commedia,' repeating the discourse between Dante and his 'sweet teacher,' while his cigarette burned itself out unheeded between his long fingers. I can hear him now, speaking the lines of the poet Statius, who spoke for Dante: 'I was famous on earth with the name which endures longest and honours most. The seeds of my ardour were the sparks from that divine flame whereby more than a thousand have kindled; I speak of the "Aeneid," mother to me and nurse to me in poetry.'

Although I admired scholarship so much in Cleric, I was not deceived about myself; I knew that I should never be a scholar. I could never lose myself for long among impersonal things. Mental excitement was apt to send me with a rush back to my own naked land and the figures scattered upon it. While I was in the very act of yearning toward the new forms that Cleric brought up before me, my mind plunged away from me, and I suddenly found myself thinking of the places and people of my own infinitesimal past. They stood out strengthened and simplified now, like the image of the plough against the sun. They were all I had for an answer to the new appeal. I begrudged the room that Jake and Otto and Russian Peter took up in my memory, which I wanted to crowd with other things. But whenever my consciousness was quickened, all those early friends were quickened within it, and in some strange way they accompanied me through all my new experiences. They were so much alive in me that I scarcely stopped to wonder whether they were alive anywhere else, or how.

II.

One March evening in my sophomore year I was sitting alone in my room after supper. There had been a warm thaw all day, with mushy yards and little streams of dark water gurgling cheerfully into the streets out of old snow-banks. My window was open, and the earthy wind blowing through made me indolent. On the edge of the prairie, where the sun had gone down, the sky was turquoise blue, like a lake, with gold light throbbing in it. Higher up, in the utter clarity of the western slope, the evening star hung like a lamp suspended by silver chains—like the lamp engraved upon the title-page of old Latin texts, which is always appearing in new heavens, and waking new desires in men. It reminded me, at any rate, to shut my window and light my wick in answer. I did so regretfully, and the dim objects in the room emerged from the shadows and took their place about me with the helpfulness which custom breeds.

I propped my book open and stared listlessly at the page of the 'Georgics' where tomorrow's lesson began. It opened with the melancholy reflection that, in the lives of mortals the best days are the first to flee. 'Optima dies... prima fugit.' I turned back to the beginning of the third book, which we had read in class that morning. '*Primus ego in patriam mecum... deducam Musas*'; 'for I shall be the first, if I live, to bring the Muse into my country.' Cleric had explained to us that '*patria*' here meant, not a nation or even a province, but the little rural neighbourhood on the Mincio where the poet was born. This was not a boast, but a hope, at once bold and devoutly humble, that he might bring the Muse (but lately come to Italy from her cloudy Grecian mountains), not to the capital, the palatia Romana, but to his own little I country'; to his father's fields, 'sloping down to the river and to the old beech trees with broken tops.'

Cleric said he thought Virgil, when he was dying at Brindisi, must have remembered that passage. After he had faced the bitter fact that he was to leave the 'Aeneid' unfinished, and had decreed that the great canvas, crowded with figures of gods and men, should be burned rather than survive him unperfected, then his mind must have gone back to the perfect utterance of the 'Georgics,' where the pen was fitted to the matter as the plough is to the furrow; and he must have said to himself, with the thankfulness of a good man, 'I was the first to bring the Muse into my country.'

We left the classroom quietly, conscious that we had been brushed by the wing of a great feeling, though perhaps I alone knew Cleric intimately enough to guess what that feeling was. In the evening, as I sat staring at my book, the fervour of his voice stirred through the quantities on the page before me. I was wondering whether that particular rocky strip of New England coast about which he had so often told me was Cleric's patria. Before I had got far with my reading, I was disturbed by a knock. I hurried to the door and when I opened it saw a woman standing in the dark hall.

'I expect you hardly know me, Jim.'

The voice seemed familiar, but I did not recognize her until she stepped into the light of my doorway and I beheld—Lena Lingard! She was so quietly conventionalized by city clothes that I might have passed her on the street without seeing her. Her black suit fitted her figure smoothly, and a black lace hat, with pale-blue forget-me-nots, sat demurely on her yellow hair.

I led her toward Cleric's chair, the only comfortable one I had, questioning her confusedly.

She was not disconcerted by my embarrassment. She looked about her with the naive curiosity I remembered so well. 'You are quite comfortable here, aren't you? I live in Lincoln now, too, Jim. I'm in business for myself. I have a dressmaking shop in the Raleigh Block, out on O Street. I've made a real good start.'

'But, Lena, when did you come?'

'Oh, I've been here all winter. Didn't your grandmother ever write you? I've thought about looking you up lots of times. But we've all heard what a studious young man you've got to be, and I felt bashful. I didn't know whether you'd be glad to see me.' She laughed her mellow, easy laugh, that was either very artless or very comprehending, one never quite knew which. 'You seem the same, though—except you're a young man, now, of course. Do you think I've changed?'

'Maybe you're prettier—though you were always pretty enough. Perhaps it's your clothes that make a difference.'

'You like my new suit? I have to dress pretty well in my business.'

She took off her jacket and sat more at ease in her blouse, of some soft, flimsy silk. She was already at home in my place, had slipped quietly into it, as she did into everything. She told me her business was going well, and she had saved a little money.

'This summer I'm going to build the house for mother I've talked about so long. I won't be able to pay up on it at first, but I want her to have it before she is too old to enjoy it. Next summer I'll take her down new furniture and carpets, so she'll have something to look forward to all winter.'

I watched Lena sitting there so smooth and sunny and well-cared-for, and thought of how she used to run barefoot over the prairie until after the snow began to fly, and how Crazy Mary chased her round and round the cornfields. It seemed to me wonderful that she should have got on so well in the world. Certainly she had no one but herself to thank for it.

'You must feel proud of yourself, Lena,' I said heartily. 'Look at me; I've never earned a dollar, and I don't know that I'll ever be able to.'

'Tony says you're going to be richer than Mr. Harling some day. She's always bragging about you, you know.'

'Tell me, how IS Tony?'

'She's fine. She works for Mrs. Gardener at the hotel now. She's housekeeper. Mrs. Gardener's health isn't what it was, and she can't see after everything like she used to. She has great confidence in Tony. Tony's made it up with the Harlings, too. Little Nina is so fond of her that Mrs. Harling kind of overlooked things.'

'Is she still going with Larry Donovan?'

'Oh, that's on, worse than ever! I guess they're engaged. Tony talks about him like he was president of the railroad. Everybody laughs about it, because she was never a girl to be soft. She won't hear a word against him. She's so sort of innocent.'

I said I didn't like Larry, and never would.

Lena's face dimpled. 'Some of us could tell her things, but it wouldn't do any good. She'd always believe him. That's Antonia's failing, you know; if she once likes people, she won't hear anything against them.'

'I think I'd better go home and look after Antonia,' I said.

'I think you had.' Lena looked up at me in frank amusement. 'It's a good thing the Harlings are friendly with her again. Larry's afraid of them. They ship so much grain, they have influence with the railroad people. What are you studying?' She leaned her elbows on the table and drew my book toward her. I caught a faint odour of violet sachet. 'So that's Latin, is it? It looks hard. You do go to the theatre sometimes, though, for I've seen you there. Don't you just love a good play, Jim? I can't stay at home in the evening if there's one in town. I'd be willing to work like a slave, it seems to me, to live in a place where there are theatres.'

'Let's go to a show together sometime. You are going to let me come to see you, aren't you?'

'Would you like to? I'd be ever so pleased. I'm never busy after six o'clock, and I let my sewing girls go at half-past five. I board, to save time, but sometimes I cook a chop for myself, and I'd be glad to cook one for you. Well'—she began to put on her white gloves —'it's been awful good to see you, Jim.'

'You needn't hurry, need you? You've hardly told me anything yet.'

'We can talk when you come to see me. I expect you don't often have lady visitors. The old woman downstairs didn't want to let me come up very much. I told her I was from your home town, and had promised your grandmother to come and see you. How surprised Mrs. Burden would be!' Lena laughed softly as she rose.

When I caught up my hat, she shook her head. 'No, I don't want you to go with me. I'm to meet some Swedes at the drugstore. You wouldn't care for them. I wanted to see your room so I could write Tony all about it, but I must tell her how I left you right here with your books. She's always so afraid someone will run off with you!' Lena slipped her silk sleeves into the jacket I held for her, smoothed it over her person, and buttoned it slowly. I walked with her to the door. 'Come and see me sometimes when you're lonesome. But maybe you have all the friends you want. Have you?' She turned her soft cheek to me. 'Have you?' she whispered teasingly in my ear. In a moment I watched her fade down the dusky stairway.

When I turned back to my room the place seemed much pleasanter than before. Lena had left something warm and friendly in the lamplight. How I loved to hear her laugh again! It was so soft and unexcited and appreciative gave a favourable interpretation to everything. When I closed my eyes I could hear them all laughing—the Danish laundry girls and the three Bohemian Marys. Lena had brought them all back to me. It came over me, as it had never done before, the relation between girls like those and the poetry of Virgil. If there were no girls like them in the world, there would be no poetry. I understood that clearly, for the first time. This revelation seemed to me inestimably precious. I clung to it as if it might suddenly vanish.

As I sat down to my book at last, my old dream about Lena coming across the harvest-field in her short skirt seemed to me like the memory of an actual experience. It floated before me on the page like a picture, and underneath it stood the mournful line: 'Optima dies... prima fugit.'

III.

In Lincoln the best part of the theatrical season came late, when the good companies stopped off there for one-night stands, after their long runs in New York and Chicago. That spring Lena went with me to see Joseph Jefferson in 'Rip Van Winkle,' and to a war play called 'Shenandoah.' She was inflexible about paying for her own seat; said she was in business now, and she wouldn't have a schoolboy spending his money on her. I liked to watch a play with Lena; everything was wonderful to her, and everything was true. It was like going to revival meetings with someone who was always being converted. She handed her feelings over to the actors with a kind of fatalistic resignation. Accessories of costume and scene meant much more to her than to me. She sat entranced through 'Robin Hood' and hung upon the lips of the contralto who sang, 'Oh, Promise Me!'

Toward the end of April, the billboards, which I watched anxiously in those days, bloomed out one morning with gleaming white posters on which two names were impressively printed in blue Gothic letters: the name of an actress of whom I had often heard, and the name 'Camille.'

I called at the Raleigh Block for Lena on Saturday evening, and we walked down to the theatre. The weather was warm and sultry and put us both in a holiday humour. We arrived early, because Lena liked to watch the people come in. There was a note on the programme, saying that the 'incidental music' would be from the opera 'Traviata,' which was made from the same story as the play. We had neither of us read the play, and we did not know what it was about—though I seemed to remember having heard it was a piece in which great actresses shone. 'The Count of Monte Cristo,' which I had seen James O'Neill play that winter, was by the only Alexandre Dumas I knew. This play, I saw, was by his son, and I expected a family resemblance. A couple of jack-rabbits, run in off the prairie, could not have been more innocent of what awaited them than were Lena and I.

Our excitement began with the rise of the curtain, when the moody Varville, seated before the fire, interrogated Nanine. Decidedly, there was a new tang about this dialogue. I had never heard in the theatre lines that were alive, that presupposed and took for granted, like those which passed between Varville and Marguerite in the brief encounter before her friends entered. This introduced the most brilliant, worldly, the most enchantingly gay scene I had ever looked upon. I had never seen champagne bottles opened on the stage before—indeed, I had never seen them opened anywhere. The memory of that supper makes me hungry now; the sight of it then, when I had only a students' boarding-house dinner behind me, was delicate torment. I seem to remember gilded chairs and tables (arranged hurriedly by footmen in white gloves and stockings), linen of dazzling whiteness, glittering glass, silver dishes, a great bowl of fruit, and the reddest of roses. The room was invaded by beautiful women and dashing young men, laughing and talking together. The men were dressed more or less after the period in which the play was written; the women were not. I saw no inconsistency. Their talk seemed to open to one the brilliant world in which they lived; every sentence made one older and wiser, every pleasantry enlarged one's horizon. One could experience excess and satiety without the inconvenience of learning what to do with one's hands in a drawing-room! When the characters all spoke at once and I missed some of the phrases they flashed at each other, I was in misery. I strained my ears and eyes to catch every exclamation.

The actress who played Marguerite was even then old-fashioned, though historic. She had been a member of Daly's famous New York company, and afterward a 'star' under his direction. She was a woman who could not be taught, it is said, though she had a crude natural force which carried with people whose feelings were accessible and whose taste was not squeamish. She was already old, with a ravaged countenance and a physique curiously hard and stiff. She moved with difficulty—I think she was lame—I seem to remember some story about a malady of the spine. Her Armand was disproportionately young and slight, a handsome youth, perplexed in the extreme. But what did it matter? I believed devoutly in her power to fascinate him, in her dazzling loveliness. I believed her young, ardent, reckless, disillusioned, under sentence, feverish, avid of pleasure. I wanted to cross the footlights and help the slim-waisted Armand in the frilled shirt to convince her that there was still loyalty and devotion in the world. Her sudden illness, when the gaiety was at its height, her pallor, the handkerchief she crushed against her lips, the cough she smothered under the laughter while Gaston kept playing the piano lightly—it all wrung my heart. But not so much as her cynicism in the long dialogue with her lover which followed. How far was I from questioning her unbelief! While the charmingly sincere young man pleaded with her—accompanied by the orchestra in the old 'Traviata' duet, *'misterioso, misterios' altero!'*—she maintained her bitter scepticism, and the curtain fell on her dancing recklessly with the others, after Armand had been sent away with his flower.

Between the acts we had no time to forget. The orchestra kept sawing away at the 'Traviata' music, so joyous and sad, so thin and far-away, so clap-trap and yet so heart-breaking. After the second act I left Lena in tearful contemplation of the ceiling, and went out into the lobby to smoke. As I walked about there I congratulated myself that I had not brought some Lincoln girl who would talk during the waits about the junior dances, or whether the cadets would camp at Plattsmouth. Lena was at least a woman, and I was a man.

Through the scene between Marguerite and the elder Duval, Lena wept unceasingly, and I sat helpless to prevent the closing of that chapter of idyllic love, dreading the return of the young man whose ineffable happiness was only to be the measure of his fall.

I suppose no woman could have been further in person, voice, and temperament from Dumas' appealing heroine than the veteran actress who first acquainted me with her. Her conception of the character was as heavy and uncompromising as her diction; she bore hard on the idea and on the consonants. At all times she was highly tragic, devoured by remorse. Lightness of stress or behaviour was far from her. Her voice was heavy and deep: 'Ar-r-r-mond!' she would begin, as if she were summoning him to the bar of Judgment. But the lines were enough. She had only to utter them. They created the character in spite of her.

The heartless world which Marguerite re-entered with Varville had never been so glittering and reckless as on the night when it gathered in Olympe's salon for the fourth act. There were chandeliers hung from the ceiling, I remember, many servants in livery, gaming-tables where the men played with piles of gold, and a staircase down which the guests made their entrance. After all the others had gathered round the card-tables and young Duval had been warned by Prudence, Marguerite descended the staircase with Varville; such a cloak, such a fan, such jewels—and her face! One knew at a glance how it was with her. When Armand, with the terrible words, 'Look, all of you, I owe this woman nothing!' flung the gold and bank-notes at the half-swooning Marguerite, Lena cowered beside me and covered her face with her hands.

The curtain rose on the bedroom scene. By this time there wasn't a nerve in me that hadn't been twisted. Nanine alone could have made me cry. I loved Nanine tenderly; and Gaston, how one clung to that good fellow! The New Year's presents were not too much; nothing could be too much now. I wept unrestrainedly. Even the handkerchief in my breast-pocket, worn for elegance and not at all for use, was wet through by the time that moribund woman sank for the last time into the arms of her lover.

When we reached the door of the theatre, the streets were shining with rain. I had prudently brought along Mrs. Harling's useful Commencement present, and I took Lena home under its shelter. After leaving her, I walked slowly out into the country part of the town where I lived. The lilacs were all blooming in the yards, and the smell of them after the rain, of the new leaves and the blossoms together, blew into my face with a sort of bitter sweetness. I tramped through the puddles and under the showery trees, mourning for Marguerite Gauthier as if she had died only yesterday, sighing with the spirit of 1840, which had sighed so much, and which had reached me only that night, across long years and several languages, through the person of an infirm old actress. The idea is one that no circumstances can frustrate. Wherever and whenever that piece is put on, it is April.

IV.

How well I remember the stiff little parlour where I used to wait for Lena: the hard horsehair furniture, bought at some auction sale, the long mirror, the fashion-plates on the wall. If I sat down even for a moment, I was sure to find threads and bits of coloured silk clinging to my clothes after I went away. Lena's success puzzled me. She was so easygoing; had none of the push and self-assertiveness that get people ahead in business. She had come to Lincoln, a country girl, with no introductions except to some cousins of Mrs. Thomas who lived there, and she was already making clothes for the women of 'the young married set.' Evidently she had great natural aptitude for her work. She knew, as she said, 'what people looked well in.' She never tired of poring over fashion-books. Sometimes in the evening I would find her alone in her work-room, draping folds of satin on a wire figure, with a quite blissful expression of countenance. I couldn't help thinking that the years when Lena literally hadn't enough clothes to cover herself might have something to do with her untiring interest in dressing the human figure. Her clients said that Lena 'had style,' and overlooked her habitual inaccuracies. She never, I discovered, finished anything by the time she had promised, and she frequently spent more money on materials than her customer had authorized. Once, when I arrived at six o'clock, Lena was ushering out a fidgety mother and her awkward, overgrown daughter. The woman detained Lena at the door to say apologetically:

'You'll try to keep it under fifty for me, won't you, Miss Lingard? You see, she's really too young to come to an expensive dressmaker, but I knew you could do more with her than anybody else.'

'Oh, that will be all right, Mrs. Herron. I think we'll manage to get a good effect,' Lena replied blandly.

I thought her manner with her customers very good, and wondered where she had learned such self-possession.

Sometimes after my morning classes were over, I used to encounter Lena downtown, in her velvet suit and a little black hat, with a veil tied smoothly over her face, looking as fresh as the spring morning. Maybe she would be carrying home a bunch of jonquils or a hyacinth plant. When we passed a candy store her footsteps would hesitate and linger. 'Don't let me go in,' she would murmur. 'Get me by if you can.' She was very fond of sweets, and was afraid of growing too plump.

We had delightful Sunday breakfasts together at Lena's. At the back of her long work-room was a bay-window, large enough to hold a box-couch and a reading-table. We breakfasted in this recess, after drawing the curtains that shut out the long room, with cutting-tables and wire women and sheet-draped garments on the walls. The sunlight poured in, making everything on the table shine and glitter and the flame of the alcohol lamp disappear altogether. Lena's curly black water-spaniel, Prince, breakfasted with us. He sat beside her on the couch and behaved very well until the Polish violin-teacher across the hall began to practise, when Prince would growl and sniff the air with disgust. Lena's landlord, old Colonel Raleigh, had given her the dog, and at first she was not at all pleased. She had spent too much of her life taking care of animals to have much sentiment about them. But Prince was a knowing little beast, and she grew fond of him. After breakfast I made him do his lessons; play dead dog, shake hands, stand up like a soldier. We used to put my cadet cap on his head—I had to take military drill at the university—and give him a yard-measure to hold with his front leg. His gravity made us laugh immoderately.

Lena's talk always amused me. Antonia had never talked like the people about her. Even after she learned to speak English readily, there was always something impulsive and foreign in her speech. But Lena had picked up all the conventional expressions she heard at Mrs. Thomas's dressmaking shop. Those formal phrases, the very flower of small-town proprieties, and the flat commonplaces, nearly all hypocritical in their origin, became very funny, very engaging, when they were uttered in Lena's soft voice, with her caressing intonation and arch naivete. Nothing could be more diverting than to hear Lena, who was almost as candid as Nature, call a leg a 'limb' or a house a 'home.'

We used to linger a long while over our coffee in that sunny corner. Lena was never so pretty as in the morning; she wakened fresh with the world every day, and her eyes had a deeper colour then, like the blue flowers that are never so blue as when they first open. I could sit idle all through a Sunday morning and look at her. Ole Benson's behaviour was now no mystery to me.

'There was never any harm in Ole,' she said once. 'People needn't have troubled themselves. He just liked to come over and sit on the drawside and forget about his bad luck. I liked to have him. Any company's welcome when you're off with cattle all the time.'

'But wasn't he always glum?' I asked. 'People said he never talked at all.'

'Sure he talked, in Norwegian. He'd been a sailor on an English boat and had seen lots of queer places. He had wonderful tattoos. We used to sit and look at them for hours; there wasn't much to look at out there. He was like a picture book. He had a ship and a strawberry girl on one arm, and on the other a girl standing before a little house, with a fence and gate and all, waiting for her sweetheart. Farther up his arm, her sailor had come back and was kissing her. "The Sailor's Return," he called it.'

I admitted it was no wonder Ole liked to look at a pretty girl once in a while, with such a fright at home.

'You know,' Lena said confidentially, 'he married Mary because he thought she was strong-minded and would keep him straight. He never could keep straight on shore. The last time he landed in Liverpool he'd been out on a two years' voyage. He was paid off one morning, and by the next he hadn't a cent left, and his watch and compass were gone. He'd got with some women, and they'd taken everything. He worked his way to this country on a little passenger boat. Mary was a stewardess, and she tried to convert him on the way over. He thought she was just the one to keep him steady. Poor Ole! He used to bring me candy from town, hidden in his feed-bag. He couldn't refuse anything to a girl. He'd have given away his tattoos long ago, if he could. He's one of the people I'm sorriest for.'

If I happened to spend an evening with Lena and stayed late, the Polish violin-teacher across the hall used to come out and watch me descend the stairs, muttering so threateningly that it would have been easy to fall into a quarrel with him. Lena had told him once that she liked to hear him practise, so he always left his door open, and watched who came and went.

There was a coolness between the Pole and Lena's landlord on her account. Old Colonel

Raleigh had come to Lincoln from Kentucky and invested an inherited fortune in real estate, at the time of inflated prices. Now he sat day after day in his office in the Raleigh Block, trying to discover where his money had gone and how he could get some of it back. He was a widower, and found very little congenial companionship in this casual Western city. Lena's good looks and gentle manners appealed to him. He said her voice reminded him of Southern voices, and he found as many opportunities of hearing it as possible. He painted and papered her rooms for her that spring, and put in a porcelain bathtub in place of the tin one that had satisfied the former tenant. While these repairs were being made, the old gentleman often dropped in to consult Lena's preferences. She told me with amusement how Ordinsky, the Pole, had presented himself at her door one evening, and said that if the landlord was annoying her by his attentions, he would promptly put a stop to it.

'I don't exactly know what to do about him,' she said, shaking her head, 'he's so sort of wild all the time. I wouldn't like to have him say anything rough to that nice old man. The colonel is long-winded, but then I expect he's lonesome. I don't think he cares much for Ordinsky, either. He said once that if I had any complaints to make of my neighbours, I mustn't hesitate.'

One Saturday evening when I was having supper with Lena, we heard a knock at her parlour door, and there stood the Pole, coatless, in a dress shirt and collar. Prince dropped on his paws and began to growl like a mastiff, while the visitor apologized, saying that he could not possibly come in thus attired, but he begged Lena to lend him some safety pins.

'Oh, you'll have to come in, Mr. Ordinsky, and let me see what's the matter.' She closed the door behind him. 'Jim, won't you make Prince behave?'

I rapped Prince on the nose, while Ordinsky explained that he had not had his dress clothes on for a long time, and tonight, when he was going to play for a concert, his waistcoat had split down the back. He thought he could pin it together until he got it to a tailor.

Lena took him by the elbow and turned him round. She laughed when she saw the long gap in the satin. 'You could never pin that, Mr. Ordinsky. You've kept it folded too long, and the goods is all gone along the crease. Take it off. I can put a new piece of lining-silk in there for you in ten minutes.' She disappeared into her work-room with the vest, leaving me to confront the Pole, who stood against the door like a wooden figure. He folded his arms and glared at me with his excitable, slanting brown eyes. His head was the shape of a chocolate drop, and was covered with dry, straw-coloured hair that fuzzed up about his pointed crown. He had never done more than mutter at me as I passed him, and I was surprised when he now addressed me. 'Miss Lingard,' he said haughtily, 'is a young woman for whom I have the utmost, the utmost respect.'

'So have I,' I said coldly.

He paid no heed to my remark, but began to do rapid finger-exercises on his shirt-sleeves, as he stood with tightly folded arms.

'Kindness of heart,' he went on, staring at the ceiling, 'sentiment, are not understood in a place like this. The noblest qualities are ridiculed. Grinning college boys, ignorant and conceited, what do they know of delicacy!'

I controlled my features and tried to speak seriously.

'If you mean me, Mr. Ordinsky, I have known Miss Lingard a long time, and I think I appreciate her kindness. We come from the same town, and we grew up together.'

His gaze travelled slowly down from the ceiling and rested on me. 'Am I to understand that you have this young woman's interests at heart? That you do not wish to compromise her?'

'That's a word we don't use much here, Mr. Ordinsky. A girl who makes her own living can ask a college boy to supper without being talked about. We take some things for granted.'

'Then I have misjudged you, and I ask your pardon'—he bowed gravely. 'Miss Lingard,' he went on, 'is an absolutely trustful heart. She has not learned the hard lessons of life. As for you and me, noblesse oblige'—he watched me narrowly.

Lena returned with the vest. 'Come in and let us look at you as you go out, Mr. Ordinsky. I've never seen you in your dress suit,' she said as she opened the door for him.

A few moments later he reappeared with his violin-case a heavy muffler about his neck and thick woollen gloves on his bony hands. Lena spoke encouragingly to him, and he went off with such an important professional air that we fell to laughing as soon as we had shut the door. 'Poor fellow,' Lena said indulgently, 'he takes everything so hard.'

After that Ordinsky was friendly to me, and behaved as if there were some deep understanding between us. He wrote a furious article, attacking the musical taste of the town, and asked me to do him a great service by taking it to the editor of the morning paper. If the editor refused to print it, I was to tell him that he would be answerable to Ordinsky 'in person.' He declared that he would never retract one word, and that he was quite prepared to lose all his pupils. In spite of the fact that nobody ever mentioned his article to him after it appeared—full of typographical errors which he thought intentional—he got a certain satisfaction from believing that the citizens of Lincoln had meekly accepted the epithet 'coarse barbarians.' 'You see how it is,' he said to me, 'where there is no chivalry, there is no amour-propre.' When I met him on his rounds now, I thought he carried his head more disdainfully than ever, and strode up the steps of front porches and rang doorbells with more assurance. He told Lena he would never forget how I had stood by him when he was 'under fire.'

All this time, of course, I was drifting. Lena had broken up my serious mood. I wasn't interested in my classes. I played with Lena and Prince, I played with the Pole, I went buggy-riding with the old colonel, who had taken a fancy to me and used to talk to me about Lena and the 'great beauties' he had known in his youth. We were all three in love with Lena.

Before the first of June, Gaston Cleric was offered an instructorship at Harvard College, and accepted it. He suggested that I should follow him in the fall, and complete my course at Harvard. He had found out about Lena—not from me—and he talked to me seriously.

'You won't do anything here now. You should either quit school and go to work, or change your college and begin again in earnest. You won't recover yourself while you are playing about with this handsome Norwegian. Yes, I've seen her with you at the theatre. She's very pretty, and perfectly irresponsible, I should judge.'

Cleric wrote my grandfather that he would like to take me East with him. To my astonishment, grandfather replied that I might go if I wished. I was both glad and sorry on the day when the letter came. I stayed in my room all evening and thought things over. I even tried to persuade myself that I was standing in Lena's way—it is so necessary to be a little noble!—and that if she had not me to play with, she would probably marry and secure her future.

The next evening I went to call on Lena. I found her propped up on the couch in her bay-window, with her foot in a big slipper. An awkward little Russian girl whom she had taken into her work-room had dropped a flat-iron on Lena's toe. On the table beside her there was a basket of early summer flowers which the Pole had left after he heard of the accident. He always managed to know what went on in Lena's apartment.

Lena was telling me some amusing piece of gossip about one of her clients, when I interrupted her and picked up the flower basket.

'This old chap will be proposing to you some day, Lena.'

'Oh, he has—often!' she murmured.

'What! After you've refused him?'

'He doesn't mind that. It seems to cheer him to mention the subject. Old men are like that, you know. It makes them feel important to think they're in love with somebody.'

'The colonel would marry you in a minute. I hope you won't marry some old fellow; not even a rich one.' Lena shifted her pillows and looked up at me in surprise.

'Why, I'm not going to marry anybody. Didn't you know that?'

'Nonsense, Lena. That's what girls say, but you know better. Every handsome girl like you marries, of course.'

She shook her head. 'Not me.'

'But why not? What makes you say that?' I persisted.

Lena laughed.

'Well, it's mainly because I don't want a husband. Men are all right for friends, but as soon as you marry them they turn into cranky old fathers, even the wild ones. They begin to tell you what's sensible and what's foolish, and want you to stick at home all the time. I prefer to be foolish when I feel like it, and be accountable to nobody.'

'But you'll be lonesome. You'll get tired of this sort of life, and you'll want a family.'

'Not me. I like to be lonesome. When I went to work for Mrs. Thomas I was nineteen years old, and I had never slept a night in my life when there weren't three in the bed. I never had a minute to myself except when I was off with the cattle.'

Usually, when Lena referred to her life in the country at all, she dismissed it with a single remark, humorous or mildly cynical. But tonight her mind seemed to dwell on those early years. She told me she couldn't remember a time when she was so little that she wasn't lugging a heavy baby about, helping to wash for babies, trying to keep their little chapped hands and faces clean. She remembered home as a place where there were always too many children, a cross man and work piling up around a sick woman.

'It wasn't mother's fault. She would have made us comfortable if she could. But that was no life for a girl! After I began to herd and milk, I could never get the smell of the cattle off me. The few underclothes I had I kept in a cracker-box. On Saturday nights, after everybody was in bed, then I could take a bath if I wasn't too tired. I could make two trips to the windmill to carry water, and heat it in the wash-boiler on the stove. While the water was heating, I could bring in a washtub out of the cave, and take my bath in the kitchen. Then I could put on a clean night-gown and get into bed with two others, who likely hadn't had a bath unless I'd given it to them. You can't tell me anything about family life. I've had plenty to last me.'

'But it's not all like that,' I objected.

'Near enough. It's all being under somebody's thumb. What's on your mind, Jim? Are you afraid I'll want you to marry me some day?'

Then I told her I was going away.

'What makes you want to go away, Jim? Haven't I been nice to you?'

'You've been just awfully good to me, Lena,' I blurted. 'I don't think about much else. I never shall think about much else while I'm with you. I'll never settle down and grind if I stay here. You know that.'

I dropped down beside her and sat looking at the floor. I seemed to have forgotten all my reasonable explanations.

Lena drew close to me, and the little hesitation in her voice that had hurt me was not there when she spoke again.

'I oughtn't to have begun it, ought I?' she murmured. 'I oughtn't to have gone to see you that first time. But I did want to. I guess I've always been a little foolish about you. I don't know what first put it into my head, unless it was Antonia, always telling me I mustn't be up to any of my nonsense with you. I let you alone for a long while, though, didn't I?'

She was a sweet creature to those she loved, that Lena Lingard!

At last she sent me away with her soft, slow, renunciatory kiss.

'You aren't sorry I came to see you that time?' she whispered. 'It seemed so natural. I used to think I'd like to be your first sweetheart. You were such a funny kid!'

She always kissed one as if she were sadly and wisely sending one away forever.

We said many good-byes before I left Lincoln, but she never tried to hinder me or hold me back. 'You are going, but you haven't gone yet, have you?' she used to say.

My Lincoln chapter closed abruptly. I went home to my grandparents for a few weeks, and afterward visited my relatives in Virginia until I joined Cleric in Boston. I was then nineteen years old.

4

THE PIONEER WOMAN'S STORY

I.

Two years after I left Lincoln, I completed my academic course at Harvard. Before I entered the Law School I went home for the summer vacation. On the night of my arrival, Mrs. Harling and Frances and Sally came over to greet me. Everything seemed just as it used to be. My grandparents looked very little older. Frances Harling was married now, and she and her husband managed the Harling interests in Black Hawk. When we gathered in grandmother's parlour, I could hardly believe that I had been away at all. One subject, however, we avoided all evening.

When I was walking home with Frances, after we had left Mrs. Harling at her gate, she said simply, 'You know, of course, about poor Antonia.'

Poor Antonia! Everyone would be saying that now, I thought bitterly. I replied that grandmother had written me how Antonia went away to marry Larry Donovan at some place where he was working; that he had deserted her, and that there was now a baby. This was all I knew.

'He never married her,' Frances said. 'I haven't seen her since she came back. She lives at home, on the farm, and almost never comes to town. She brought the baby in to show it to mama once. I'm afraid she's settled down to be Ambrosch's drudge for good.'

I tried to shut Antonia out of my mind. I was bitterly disappointed in her. I could not forgive her for becoming an object of pity, while Lena Lingard, for whom people had always foretold trouble, was now the leading dressmaker of Lincoln, much respected in Black Hawk. Lena gave her heart away when she felt like it, but she kept her head for her business and had got on in the world.

Just then it was the fashion to speak indulgently of Lena and severely of Tiny Soderball, who had quietly gone West to try her fortune the year before. A Black Hawk boy, just back from Seattle, brought the news that Tiny had not gone to the coast on a venture, as she had allowed people to think, but with very definite plans. One of the roving promoters that used to stop at Mrs. Gardener's hotel owned idle property along the waterfront in Seattle, and he had offered to set Tiny up in business in one of his empty buildings. She was now conducting a sailors' lodging-house. This, everyone said, would be the end of Tiny. Even if she had begun by running a decent place, she couldn't keep it up; all sailors' boarding-houses were alike.

When I thought about it, I discovered that I had never known Tiny as well as I knew the other girls. I remembered her tripping briskly about the dining-room on her high heels, carrying a big trayful of dishes, glancing rather pertly at the spruce travelling men, and contemptuously at the scrubby ones—who were so afraid of her that they didn't dare to ask for two kinds of pie. Now it occurred to me that perhaps the sailors, too, might be afraid of Tiny. How astonished we should have been, as we sat talking about her on Frances Harling's front porch, if we could have known what her future was really to be! Of all the girls and boys who grew up together in Black Hawk, Tiny Soderball was to lead the most adventurous life and to achieve the most solid worldly success.

This is what actually happened to Tiny: While she was running her lodging-house in Seattle, gold was discovered in Alaska. Miners and sailors came back from the North with wonderful stories and pouches of gold. Tiny saw it and weighed it in her hands. That daring, which nobody had ever suspected in her, awoke. She sold her business and set out for Circle City, in company with a carpenter and his wife whom she had persuaded to go along with her. They reached Skaguay in a snowstorm, went in dog-sledges over the Chilkoot Pass, and shot the Yukon in flatboats. They reached Circle City on the very day when some Siwash Indians came into the settlement with the report that there had been a rich gold strike farther up the river, on a certain Klondike Creek. Two days later Tiny and her friends, and nearly everyone else in Circle City, started for the Klondike fields on the last steamer that went up the Yukon before it froze for the winter. That boatload of people founded Dawson City. Within a few weeks there were fifteen hundred homeless men in camp. Tiny and the carpenter's wife began to cook for them, in a tent. The miners gave her a building lot, and the carpenter put up a log hotel for her. There she sometimes fed a hundred and fifty men a day. Miners came in on snowshoes from their placer claims twenty miles away to buy fresh bread from her, and paid for it in gold.

That winter Tiny kept in her hotel a Swede whose legs had been frozen one night in a storm when he was trying to find his way back to his cabin. The poor fellow thought it great good fortune to be cared for by a woman, and a woman who spoke his own tongue. When he was told that his feet must be amputated, he said he hoped he would not get well; what could a working-man do in this hard world without feet? He did, in fact, die from the operation, but not before he had deeded Tiny Soderball his claim on Hunker Creek. Tiny sold her hotel, invested half her money in Dawson building lots, and with the rest she developed her claim. She went off into the wilds and lived on the claim. She bought other claims from discouraged miners, traded or sold them on percentages.

After nearly ten years in the Klondike, Tiny returned, with a considerable fortune, to live in San Francisco. I met her in Salt Lake City in 1908. She was a thin, hard-faced woman, very well-dressed, very reserved in manner. Curiously enough, she reminded me of Mrs. Gardener, for whom she had worked in Black Hawk so long ago. She told me about some of the desperate chances she had taken in the gold country, but the thrill of them was quite gone. She said frankly that nothing interested her much now but making money. The only two human beings of whom she spoke with any feeling were the Swede, Johnson, who had given her his claim, and Lena Lingard. She had persuaded Lena to come to San Francisco and go into business there.

'Lincoln was never any place for her,' Tiny remarked. 'In a town of that size Lena would always be gossiped about. Frisco's the right field for her. She has a fine class of trade. Oh, she's just the same as she always was! She's careless, but she's level-headed. She's the only person I know who never gets any older. It's fine for me to have her there; somebody who enjoys things like that. She keeps an eye on me and won't let me be shabby. When she thinks I need a new dress, she makes it and sends it home with a bill that's long enough, I can tell you!'

Tiny limped slightly when she walked. The claim on Hunker Creek took toll from its possessors. Tiny had been caught in a sudden turn of weather, like poor Johnson. She lost three toes from one of those pretty little feet that used to trip about Black Hawk in pointed slippers and striped stockings. Tiny mentioned this mutilation quite casually—didn't seem sensitive about it. She was satisfied with her success, but not elated. She was like someone in whom the faculty of becoming interested is worn out.

II.

Soon after I got home that summer, I persuaded my grandparents to have their photographs taken, and one morning I went into the photographer's shop to arrange for sittings. While I was waiting for him to come out of his developing-room, I walked about trying to recognize the likenesses on his walls: girls in Commencement dresses, country brides and grooms holding hands, family groups of three generations. I noticed, in a heavy frame, one of those depressing 'crayon enlargements' often seen in farm-house parlours, the subject being a round-eyed baby in short dresses. The photographer came out and gave a constrained, apologetic laugh.

'That's Tony Shimerda's baby. You remember her; she used to be the Harlings' Tony. Too bad! She seems proud of the baby, though; wouldn't hear to a cheap frame for the picture. I expect her brother will be in for it Saturday.'

I went away feeling that I must see Antonia again. Another girl would have kept her baby out of sight, but Tony, of course, must have its picture on exhibition at the town photographer's, in a great gilt frame. How like her! I could forgive her, I told myself, if she hadn't thrown herself away on such a cheap sort of fellow.

Larry Donovan was a passenger conductor, one of those train-crew aristocrats who are always afraid that someone may ask them to put up a car-window, and who, if requested to perform such a menial service, silently point to the button that calls the porter. Larry wore this air of official aloofness even on the street, where there were no car-windows to compromise his dignity. At the end of his run he stepped indifferently from the train along with the passengers, his street hat on his head and his conductor's cap in an alligator-skin bag, went directly into the station and changed his clothes. It was a matter of the utmost importance to him never to be seen in his blue trousers away from his train. He was usually cold and distant with men, but with all women he had a silent, grave familiarity, a special handshake, accompanied by a significant, deliberate look. He took women, married or single, into his confidence; walked them up and down in the moonlight, telling them what a mistake he had made by not entering the office branch of the service, and how much better fitted he was to fill the post of General Passenger Agent in Denver than the rough-shod man who then bore that title. His unappreciated worth was the tender secret Larry shared with his sweethearts, and he was always able to make some foolish heart ache over it.

As I drew near home that morning, I saw Mrs. Harling out in her yard, digging round her mountain-ash tree. It was a dry summer, and she had now no boy to help her. Charley was off in his battleship, cruising somewhere on the Caribbean sea. I turned in at the gate it was with a feeling of pleasure that I opened and shut that gate in those days; I liked the feel of it under my hand. I took the spade away from Mrs. Harling, and while I loosened the earth around the tree, she sat down on the steps and talked about the oriole family that had a nest in its branches.

'Mrs. Harling,' I said presently, 'I wish I could find out exactly how Antonia's marriage fell through.'

'Why don't you go out and see your grandfather's tenant, the Widow Steavens? She knows more about it than anybody else. She helped Antonia get ready to be married, and she was there when Antonia came back. She took care of her when the baby was born. She could tell you everything. Besides, the Widow Steavens is a good talker, and she has a remarkable memory.'

III.

On the first or second day of August I got a horse and cart and set out for the high country, to visit the Widow Steavens. The wheat harvest was over, and here and there along the horizon I could see black puffs of smoke from the steam threshing-machines. The old pasture land was now being broken up into wheatfields and cornfields, the red grass was disappearing, and the whole face of the country was changing. There were wooden houses where the old sod dwellings used to be, and little orchards, and big red barns; all this meant happy children, contented women, and men who saw their lives coming to a fortunate issue. The windy springs and the blazing summers, one after another, had enriched and mellowed that flat tableland; all the human effort that had gone into it was coming back in long, sweeping lines of fertility. The changes seemed beautiful and harmonious to me; it was like watching the growth of a great man or of a great idea. I recognized every tree and sandbank and rugged draw. I found that I remembered the conformation of the land as one remembers the modelling of human faces.

When I drew up to our old windmill, the Widow Steavens came out to meet me. She was brown as an Indian woman, tall, and very strong. When I was little, her massive head had always seemed to me like a Roman senator's. I told her at once why I had come.

'You'll stay the night with us, Jimmy? I'll talk to you after supper. I can take more interest when my work is off my mind. You've no prejudice against hot biscuit for supper? Some have, these days.'

While I was putting my horse away, I heard a rooster squawking. I looked at my watch and sighed; it was three o'clock, and I knew that I must eat him at six.

After supper Mrs. Steavens and I went upstairs to the old sitting-room, while her grave, silent brother remained in the basement to read his farm papers. All the windows were open. The white summer moon was shining outside, the windmill was pumping lazily in the light breeze. My hostess put the lamp on a stand in the corner, and turned it low because of the heat. She sat down in her favourite rocking-chair and settled a little stool comfortably under her tired feet. 'I'm troubled with calluses, Jim; getting old,' she sighed cheerfully. She crossed her hands in her lap and sat as if she were at a meeting of some kind.

'Now, it's about that dear Antonia you want to know? Well, you've come to the right person. I've watched her like she'd been my own daughter.

'When she came home to do her sewing that summer before she was to be married, she was over here about every day. They've never had a sewing-machine at the Shimerdas', and she made all her things here. I taught her hemstitching, and I helped her to cut and fit. She used to sit there at that machine by the window, pedalling the life out of it—she was so strong—and always singing them queer Bohemian songs, like she was the happiest thing in the world.

'"Antonia," I used to say, "don't run that machine so fast. You won't hasten the day none that way."

'Then she'd laugh and slow down for a little, but she'd soon forget and begin to pedal and sing again. I never saw a girl work harder to go to housekeeping right and well-prepared. Lovely table-linen the Harlings had given her, and Lena Lingard had sent her nice things from Lincoln. We hemstitched all the tablecloths and pillow-cases, and some of the sheets. Old Mrs. Shimerda knit yards and yards of lace for her underclothes. Tony told me just how she meant to have everything in her house. She'd even bought silver spoons and forks, and kept them in her trunk. She was always coaxing brother to go to the post-office. Her young man did write her real often, from the different towns along his run.

'The first thing that troubled her was when he wrote that his run had been changed, and they would likely have to live in Denver. "I'm a country girl," she said, "and I doubt if I'll be able to manage so well for him in a city. I was counting on keeping chickens, and maybe a cow." She soon cheered up, though.

'At last she got the letter telling her when to come. She was shaken by it; she broke the seal and read it in this room. I suspected then that she'd begun to get faint-hearted, waiting; though she'd never let me see it.

'Then there was a great time of packing. It was in March, if I remember rightly, and a terrible muddy, raw spell, with the roads bad for hauling her things to town. And here let me say, Ambrosch did the right thing. He went to Black Hawk and bought her a set of plated silver in a purple velvet box, good enough for her station. He gave her three hundred dollars in money; I saw the cheque. He'd collected her wages all those first years she worked out, and it was but right. I shook him by the hand in this room. "You're behaving like a man, Ambrosch," I said, "and I'm glad to see it, son."

"Twas a cold, raw day he drove her and her three trunks into Black Hawk to take the night train for Denver—the boxes had been shipped before. He stopped the wagon here, and she ran in to tell me good-bye. She threw her arms around me and kissed me, and thanked me for all I'd done for her. She was so happy she was crying and laughing at the same time, and her red cheeks was all wet with rain.

'"You're surely handsome enough for any man," I said, looking her over.

'She laughed kind of flighty like, and whispered, "Good-bye, dear house!" and then ran out to the wagon. I expect she meant that for you and your grandmother, as much as for me, so I'm particular to tell you. This house had always been a refuge to her.

'Well, in a few days we had a letter saying she got to Denver safe, and he was there to meet her. They were to be married in a few days. He was trying to get his promotion before he married, she said. I didn't like that, but I said nothing. The next week Yulka got a postal card, saying she was "well and happy." After that we heard nothing. A month went by, and old Mrs. Shimerda began to get fretful. Ambrosch was as sulky with me as if I'd picked out the man and arranged the match.

'One night brother William came in and said that on his way back from the fields he had passed a livery team from town, driving fast out the west road. There was a trunk on the front seat with the driver, and another behind. In the back seat there was a woman all bundled up; but for all her veils, he thought 'twas Antonia Shimerda, or Antonia Donovan, as her name ought now to be.

'The next morning I got brother to drive me over. I can walk still, but my feet ain't what they used to be, and I try to save myself. The lines outside the Shimerdas' house was full of washing, though it was the middle of the week. As we got nearer, I saw a sight that made my heart sink—all those underclothes we'd put so much work on, out there swinging in the wind. Yulka came bringing a dishpanful of wrung clothes, but she darted back into the house like she was loath to see us. When I went in, Antonia was standing over the tubs, just finishing up a big washing. Mrs. Shimerda was going about her work, talking and scolding to herself. She didn't so much as raise her eyes. Tony wiped her hand on her apron and held it out to me, looking at me steady but mournful. When I took her in my arms she drew away. "Don't, Mrs. Steavens," she says, "you'll make me cry, and I don't want to."

'I whispered and asked her to come out-of-doors with me. I knew she couldn't talk free before her mother. She went out with me, bareheaded, and we walked up toward the garden.

'"I'm not married, Mrs. Steavens," she says to me very quiet and natural-like, "and I ought to be."

'"Oh, my child," says I, "what's happened to you? Don't be afraid to tell me!"

'She sat down on the drawside, out of sight of the house. "He's run away from me," she said. "I don't know if he ever meant to marry me."

'"You mean he's thrown up his job and quit the country?" says I.

'"He didn't have any job. He'd been fired; blacklisted for knocking down fares. I didn't know. I thought he hadn't been treated right. He was sick when I got there. He'd just come out of the hospital. He lived with me till my money gave out, and afterward I found he hadn't really been hunting work at all. Then he just didn't come back. One nice fellow at the station told me, when I kept going to look for him, to give it up. He said he was afraid Larry'd gone bad and wouldn't come back any more. I guess he's gone to Old Mexico. The conductors get rich down there, collecting half-fares off the natives and robbing the company. He was always talking about fellows who had got ahead that way."

'I asked her, of course, why she didn't insist on a civil marriage at once—that would have given her some hold on him. She leaned her head on her hands, poor child, and said, "I just don't know, Mrs. Steavens. I guess my patience was wore out, waiting so long. I thought if he saw how well I could do for him, he'd want to stay with me."

'Jimmy, I sat right down on that bank beside her and made lament. I cried like a young thing. I couldn't help it. I was just about heart-broke. It was one of them lovely warm May days, and the wind was blowing and the colts jumping around in the pastures; but I felt bowed with despair. My Antonia, that had so much good in her, had come home disgraced. And that Lena Lingard, that was always a bad one, say what you will, had turned out so well, and was coming home here every summer in her silks and her satins, and doing so much for her mother. I give credit where credit is due, but you know well enough, Jim Burden, there is a great difference in the principles of those two girls. And here it was the good one that had come to grief! I was poor comfort to her. I marvelled at her calm. As we went back to the house, she stopped to feel of her clothes to see if they was drying well, and seemed to take pride in their whiteness—she said she'd been living in a brick block, where she didn't have proper conveniences to wash them.

'The next time I saw Antonia, she was out in the fields ploughing corn. All that spring and summer she did the work of a man on the farm; it seemed to be an understood thing. Ambrosch didn't get any other hand to help him. Poor Marek had got violent and been sent away to an institution a good while back. We never even saw any of Tony's pretty dresses. She didn't take them out of her trunks. She was quiet and steady. Folks respected her industry and tried to treat her as if nothing had happened. They talked, to be sure; but not like they would if she'd put on airs. She was so crushed and quiet that nobody seemed to want to humble her. She never went anywhere. All that summer she never once came to see me. At first I was hurt, but I got to feel that it was because this house reminded her of too much. I went over there when I could, but the times when she was in from the fields were the times when I was busiest here. She talked about the grain and the weather as if she'd never had another interest, and if I went over at night she always looked dead weary. She was afflicted with toothache; one tooth after another ulcerated, and she went about with her face swollen half the time. She wouldn't go to Black Hawk to a dentist for fear of meeting people she knew. Ambrosch had got over his good spell long ago, and was always surly. Once I told him he ought not to let Antonia work so hard and pull herself down. He said, "If you put that in her head, you better stay home." And after that I did.

'Antonia worked on through harvest and threshing, though she was too modest to go out threshing for the neighbours, like when she was young and free. I didn't see much of her until late that fall when she begun to herd Ambrosch's cattle in the open ground north of here, up toward the big dog-town. Sometimes she used to bring them over the west hill, there, and I would run to meet her and walk north a piece with her. She had thirty cattle in her bunch; it had been dry, and the pasture was short, or she wouldn't have brought them so far.

'It was a fine open fall, and she liked to be alone. While the steers grazed, she used to sit on them grassy banks along the draws and sun herself for hours. Sometimes I slipped up to visit with her, when she hadn't gone too far.

'"It does seem like I ought to make lace, or knit like Lena used to," she said one day, "but if I start to work, I look around and forget to go on. It seems such a little while ago when Jim Burden and I was playing all over this country. Up here I can pick out the very places where my father used to stand. Sometimes I feel like I'm not going to live very long, so I'm just enjoying every day of this fall."

'After the winter begun she wore a man's long overcoat and boots, and a man's felt hat with a wide brim. I used to watch her coming and going, and I could see that her steps were getting heavier. One day in December, the snow began to fall. Late in the afternoon I saw Antonia driving her cattle homeward across the hill. The snow was flying round her and she bent to face it, looking more lonesome-like to me than usual. "Deary me," I says to myself, "the girl's stayed out too late. It'll be dark before she gets them cattle put into the corral." I seemed to sense she'd been feeling too miserable to get up and drive them.

'That very night, it happened. She got her cattle home, turned them into the corral, and went into the house, into her room behind the kitchen, and shut the door. There, without calling to anybody, without a groan, she lay down on the bed and bore her child.

'I was lifting supper when old Mrs. Shimerda came running down the basement stairs, out of breath and screeching:

'"Baby come, baby come!" she says. "Ambrosch much like devil!"

'Brother William is surely a patient man. He was just ready to sit down to a hot supper after a long day in the fields. Without a word he rose and went down to the barn and hooked up his team. He got us over there as quick as it was humanly possible. I went right in, and began to do for Antonia; but she laid there with her eyes shut and took no account of me. The old woman got a tubful of warm water to wash the baby. I overlooked what she was doing and I said out loud: "Mrs. Shimerda, don't you put that strong yellow soap near that baby. You'll blister its little skin." I was indignant.

'"Mrs. Steavens," Antonia said from the bed, "if you'll look in the top tray of my trunk, you'll see some fine soap." That was the first word she spoke.

'After I'd dressed the baby, I took it out to show it to Ambrosch. He was muttering behind the stove and wouldn't look at it.

'"You'd better put it out in the rain-barrel," he says.

'"Now, see here, Ambrosch," says I, "there's a law in this land, don't forget that. I stand here a witness that this baby has come into the world sound and strong, and I intend to keep an eye on what befalls it." I pride myself I cowed him.

'Well I expect you're not much interested in babies, but Antonia's got on fine. She loved it from the first as dearly as if she'd had a ring on her finger, and was never ashamed of it. It's a year and eight months old now, and no baby was ever better cared-for. Antonia is a natural-born mother. I wish she could marry and raise a family, but I don't know as there's much chance now.'

I slept that night in the room I used to have when I was a little boy, with the summer wind blowing in at the windows, bringing the smell of the ripe fields. I lay awake and watched the moonlight shining over the barn and the stacks and the pond, and the windmill making its old dark shadow against the blue sky.

IV.

The next afternoon I walked over to the Shimerdas'. Yulka showed me the baby and told me that Antonia was shocking wheat on the southwest quarter. I went down across the fields, and Tony saw me from a long way off. She stood still by her shocks, leaning on her pitchfork, watching me as I came. We met like the people in the old song, in silence, if not in tears. Her warm hand clasped mine.

'I thought you'd come, Jim. I heard you were at Mrs. Steavens's last night. I've been looking for you all day.'

She was thinner than I had ever seen her, and looked as Mrs. Steavens said, 'worked down,' but there was a new kind of strength in the gravity of her face, and her colour still gave her that look of deep-seated health and ardour. Still? Why, it flashed across me that though so much had happened in her life and in mine, she was barely twenty-four years old.

Antonia stuck her fork in the ground, and instinctively we walked toward that unploughed patch at the crossing of the roads as the fittest place to talk to each other. We sat down outside the sagging wire fence that shut Mr. Shimerda's plot off from the rest of the world. The tall red grass had never been cut there. It had died down in winter and come up again in the spring until it was as thick and shrubby as some tropical garden-grass. I found myself telling her everything: why I had decided to study law and to go into the law office of one of my mother's relatives in New York City; about Gaston Cleric's death from pneumonia last winter, and the difference it had made in my life. She wanted to know about my friends, and my way of living, and my dearest hopes.

'Of course it means you are going away from us for good,' she said with a sigh. 'But that don't mean I'll lose you. Look at my papa here; he's been dead all these years, and yet he is more real to me than almost anybody else. He never goes out of my life. I talk to him and consult him all the time. The older I grow, the better I know him and the more I understand him.'

She asked me whether I had learned to like big cities. 'I'd always be miserable in a city. I'd die of lonesomeness. I like to be where I know every stack and tree, and where all the ground is friendly. I want to live and die here. Father Kelly says everybody's put into this world for something, and I know what I've got to do. I'm going to see that my little girl has a better chance than ever I had. I'm going to take care of that girl, Jim.'

I told her I knew she would. 'Do you know, Antonia, since I've been away, I think of you more often than of anyone else in this part of the world. I'd have liked to have you for a sweetheart, or a wife, or my mother or my sister—anything that a woman can be to a man. The idea of you is a part of my mind; you influence my likes and dislikes, all my tastes, hundreds of times when I don't realize it. You really are a part of me.'

She turned her bright, believing eyes to me, and the tears came up in them slowly, 'How can it be like that, when you know so many people, and when I've disappointed you so? Ain't it wonderful, Jim, how much people can mean to each other? I'm so glad we had each other when we were little. I can't wait till my little girl's old enough to tell her about all the things we used to do. You'll always remember me when you think about old times, won't you? And I guess everybody thinks about old times, even the happiest people.'

As we walked homeward across the fields, the sun dropped and lay like a great golden globe in the low west. While it hung there, the moon rose in the east, as big as a cart-wheel, pale silver and streaked with rose colour, thin as a bubble or a ghost-moon. For five, perhaps ten minutes, the two luminaries confronted each other across the level land, resting on opposite edges of the world.

In that singular light every little tree and shock of wheat, every sunflower stalk and clump of snow-on-the-mountain, drew itself up high and pointed; the very clods and furrows in the fields seemed to stand up sharply. I felt the old pull of the earth, the solemn magic that comes out of those fields at nightfall. I wished I could be a little boy again, and that my way could end there.

We reached the edge of the field, where our ways parted. I took her hands and held them against my breast, feeling once more how strong and warm and good they were, those brown hands, and remembering how many kind things they had done for me. I held them now a long while, over my heart. About us it was growing darker and darker, and I had to look hard to see her face, which I meant always to carry with me; the closest, realest face, under all the shadows of women's faces, at the very bottom of my memory.

'I'll come back,' I said earnestly, through the soft, intrusive darkness.

'Perhaps you will'—I felt rather than saw her smile. 'But even if you don't, you're here, like my father. So I won't be lonesome.'

As I went back alone over that familiar road, I could almost believe that a boy and girl ran along beside me, as our shadows used to do, laughing and whispering to each other in the grass.

❧ 5 ❧

CUZAK'S BOYS

I.

I TOLD Antonia I would come back, but life intervened, and it was twenty years before I kept my promise. I heard of her from time to time; that she married, very soon after I last saw her, a young Bohemian, a cousin of Anton Jelinek; that they were poor, and had a large family. Once when I was abroad I went into Bohemia, and from Prague I sent Antonia some photographs of her native village. Months afterward came a letter from her, telling me the names and ages of her many children, but little else; signed, 'Your old friend, Antonia Cuzak.' When I met Tiny Soderball in Salt Lake, she told me that Antonia had not 'done very well'; that her husband was not a man of much force, and she had had a hard life. Perhaps it was cowardice that kept me away so long. My business took me West several times every year, and it was always in the back of my mind that I would stop in Nebraska some day and go to see Antonia. But I kept putting it off until the next trip. I did not want to find her aged and broken; I really dreaded it. In the course of twenty crowded years one parts with many illusions. I did not wish to lose the early ones. Some memories are realities, and are better than anything that can ever happen to one again.

I owe it to Lena Lingard that I went to see Antonia at last. I was in San Francisco two summers ago when both Lena and Tiny Soderball were in town. Tiny lives in a house of her own, and Lena's shop is in an apartment house just around the corner. It interested me, after so many years, to see the two women together. Tiny audits Lena's accounts occasionally, and invests her money for her; and Lena, apparently, takes care that Tiny doesn't grow too miserly. 'If there's anything I can't stand,' she said to me in Tiny's presence, 'it's a shabby rich woman.' Tiny smiled grimly and assured me that Lena would never be either shabby or rich. 'And I don't want to be,' the other agreed complacently.

Lena gave me a cheerful account of Antonia and urged me to make her a visit.

'You really ought to go, Jim. It would be such a satisfaction to her. Never mind what Tiny says. There's nothing the matter with Cuzak. You'd like him. He isn't a hustler, but a rough man would never have suited Tony. Tony has nice children—ten or eleven of them by this time, I guess. I shouldn't care for a family of that size myself, but somehow it's just right for Tony. She'd love to show them to you.'

On my way East I broke my journey at Hastings, in Nebraska, and set off with an open buggy and a fairly good livery team to find the Cuzak farm. At a little past midday, I knew I must be nearing my destination. Set back on a swell of land at my right, I saw a wide farm-house, with a red barn and an ash grove, and cattle-yards in front that sloped down to the highroad. I drew up my horses and was wondering whether I should drive in here, when I heard low voices. Ahead of me, in a plum thicket beside the road, I saw two boys bending over a dead dog. The little one, not more than four or five, was on his knees, his hands folded, and his close-clipped, bare head drooping forward in deep dejection. The other stood beside him, a hand on his shoulder, and was comforting him in a language I had not heard for a long while. When I stopped my horses opposite them, the older boy took his brother by the hand and came toward me. He, too, looked grave. This was evidently a sad afternoon for them.

'Are you Mrs. Cuzak's boys?' I asked.

The younger one did not look up; he was submerged in his own feelings, but his brother met me with intelligent grey eyes. 'Yes, sir.'

'Does she live up there on the hill? I am going to see her. Get in and ride up with me.'

He glanced at his reluctant little brother. 'I guess we'd better walk. But we'll open the gate for you.'

I drove along the side-road and they followed slowly behind. When I pulled up at the windmill, another boy, barefooted and curly-headed, ran out of the barn to tie my team for me. He was a handsome one, this chap, fair-skinned and freckled, with red cheeks and a ruddy pelt as thick as a lamb's wool, growing down on his neck in little tufts. He tied my team with two flourishes of his hands, and nodded when I asked him if his mother was at home. As he glanced at me, his face dimpled with a seizure of irrelevant merriment, and he shot up the windmill tower with a lightness that struck me as disdainful. I knew he was peering down at me as I walked toward the house.

Ducks and geese ran quacking across my path. White cats were sunning themselves among yellow pumpkins on the porch steps. I looked through the wire screen into a big, light kitchen with a white floor. I saw a long table, rows of wooden chairs against the wall, and a shining range in one corner. Two girls were washing dishes at the sink, laughing and chattering, and a little one, in a short pinafore, sat on a stool playing with a rag baby. When I asked for their mother, one of the girls dropped her towel, ran across the floor with noiseless bare feet, and disappeared. The older one, who wore shoes and stockings, came to the door to admit me. She was a buxom girl with dark hair and eyes, calm and self-possessed.

'Won't you come in? Mother will be here in a minute.'

Before I could sit down in the chair she offered me, the miracle happened; one of those quiet moments that clutch the heart, and take more courage than the noisy, excited passages in life. Antonia came in and stood before me; a stalwart, brown woman, flat-chested, her curly brown hair a little grizzled. It was a shock, of course. It always is, to meet people after long years, especially if they have lived as much and as hard as this woman had. We stood looking at each other. The eyes that peered anxiously at me were—simply Antonia's eyes. I had seen no others like them since I looked into them last, though I had looked at so many thousands of human faces. As I confronted her, the changes grew less apparent to me, her identity stronger. She was there, in the full vigour of her personality, battered but not diminished, looking at me, speaking to me in the husky, breathy voice I remembered so well.

'My husband's not at home, sir. Can I do anything?'

'Don't you remember me, Antonia? Have I changed so much?'

She frowned into the slanting sunlight that made her brown hair look redder than it was. Suddenly her eyes widened, her whole face seemed to grow broader. She caught her breath and put out two hard-worked hands.

'Why, it's Jim! Anna, Yulka, it's Jim Burden!' She had no sooner caught my hands than she looked alarmed. 'What's happened? Is anybody dead?'

I patted her arm.

'No. I didn't come to a funeral this time. I got off the train at Hastings and drove down to see you and your family.'

She dropped my hand and began rushing about. 'Anton, Yulka, Nina, where are you all? Run, Anna, and hunt for the boys. They're off looking for that dog, somewhere. And call Leo. Where is that Leo!' She pulled them out of corners and came bringing them like a mother cat bringing in her kittens. 'You don't have to go right off, Jim? My oldest boy's not here. He's gone with papa to the street fair at Wilber. I won't let you go! You've got to stay and see Rudolph and our papa.' She looked at me imploringly, panting with excitement.

While I reassured her and told her there would be plenty of time, the barefooted boys from outside were slipping into the kitchen and gathering about her.

'Now, tell me their names, and how old they are.'

As she told them off in turn, she made several mistakes about ages, and they roared with laughter. When she came to my light-footed friend of the windmill, she said, 'This is Leo, and he's old enough to be better than he is.'

He ran up to her and butted her playfully with his curly head, like a little ram, but his voice was quite desperate. 'You've forgot! You always forget mine. It's mean! Please tell him, mother!' He clenched his fists in vexation and looked up at her impetuously.

She wound her forefinger in his yellow fleece and pulled it, watching him. 'Well, how old are you?'

'I'm twelve,' he panted, looking not at me but at her; 'I'm twelve years old, and I was born on Easter Day!'

She nodded to me. 'It's true. He was an Easter baby.'

The children all looked at me, as if they expected me to exhibit astonishment or delight at this information. Clearly, they were proud of each other, and of being so many. When they had all been introduced, Anna, the eldest daughter, who had met me at the door, scattered them gently, and came bringing a white apron which she tied round her mother's waist.

'Now, mother, sit down and talk to Mr. Burden. We'll finish the dishes quietly and not disturb you.'

Antonia looked about, quite distracted. 'Yes, child, but why don't we take him into the parlour, now that we've got a nice parlour for company?'

The daughter laughed indulgently, and took my hat from me. 'Well, you're here, now, mother, and if you talk here, Yulka and I can listen, too. You can show him the parlour after while.' She smiled at me, and went back to the dishes, with her sister. The little girl with the rag doll found a place on the bottom step of an enclosed back stairway, and sat with her toes curled up, looking out at us expectantly.

'She's Nina, after Nina Harling,' Antonia explained. 'Ain't her eyes like Nina's? I declare, Jim, I loved you children almost as much as I love my own. These children know all about you and Charley and Sally, like as if they'd grown up with you. I can't think of what I want to say, you've got me so stirred up. And then, I've forgot my English so. I don't often talk it any more. I tell the children I used to speak real well.' She said they always spoke Bohemian at home. The little ones could not speak English at all—didn't learn it until they went to school.

'I can't believe it's you, sitting here, in my own kitchen. You wouldn't have known me, would you, Jim? You've kept so young, yourself. But it's easier for a man. I can't see how my Anton looks any older than the day I married him. His teeth have kept so nice. I haven't got many left. But I feel just as young as I used to, and I can do as much work. Oh, we don't have to work so hard now! We've got plenty to help us, papa and me. And how many have you got, Jim?'

When I told her I had no children, she seemed embarrassed. 'Oh, ain't that too bad! Maybe you could take one of my bad ones, now? That Leo; he's the worst of all.' She leaned toward me with a smile. 'And I love him the best,' she whispered.

'Mother!' the two girls murmured reproachfully from the dishes.

Antonia threw up her head and laughed. 'I can't help it. You know I do. Maybe it's because he came on Easter Day, I don't know. And he's never out of mischief one minute!'

I was thinking, as I watched her, how little it mattered—about her teeth, for instance. I know so many women who have kept all the things that she had lost, but whose inner glow has faded. Whatever else was gone, Antonia had not lost the fire of life. Her skin, so brown and hardened, had not that look of flabbiness, as if the sap beneath it had been secretly drawn away.

While we were talking, the little boy whom they called Jan came in and sat down on the step beside Nina, under the hood of the stairway. He wore a funny long gingham apron, like a smock, over his trousers, and his hair was clipped so short that his head looked white and naked. He watched us out of his big, sorrowful grey eyes.

'He wants to tell you about the dog, mother. They found it dead,' Anna said, as she passed us on her way to the cupboard.

Antonia beckoned the boy to her. He stood by her chair, leaning his elbows on her knees and twisting her apron strings in his slender fingers, while he told her his story softly in Bohemian, and the tears brimmed over and hung on his long lashes. His mother listened, spoke soothingly to him and in a whisper promised him something that made him give her a quick, teary smile. He slipped away and whispered his secret to Nina, sitting close to her and talking behind his hand.

When Anna finished her work and had washed her hands, she came and stood behind her mother's chair. 'Why don't we show Mr. Burden our new fruit cave?' she asked.

We started off across the yard with the children at our heels. The boys were standing by the windmill, talking about the dog; some of them ran ahead to open the cellar door. When we descended, they all came down after us, and seemed quite as proud of the cave as the girls were.

Ambrosch, the thoughtful-looking one who had directed me down by the plum bushes, called my attention to the stout brick walls and the cement floor. 'Yes, it is a good way from the house,' he admitted. 'But, you see, in winter there are nearly always some of us around to come out and get things.'

Anna and Yulka showed me three small barrels; one full of dill pickles, one full of chopped pickles, and one full of pickled watermelon rinds.

'You wouldn't believe, Jim, what it takes to feed them all!' their mother exclaimed. 'You ought to see the bread we bake on Wednesdays and Saturdays! It's no wonder their poor papa can't get rich, he has to buy so much sugar for us to preserve with. We have our own wheat ground for flour—but then there's that much less to sell.'

Nina and Jan, and a little girl named Lucie, kept shyly pointing out to me the shelves of glass jars. They said nothing, but, glancing at me, traced on the glass with their finger-tips the outline of the cherries and strawberries and crabapples within, trying by a blissful expression of countenance to give me some idea of their deliciousness.

'Show him the spiced plums, mother. Americans don't have those,' said one of the older boys. 'Mother uses them to make kolaches,' he added.

Leo, in a low voice, tossed off some scornful remark in Bohemian.

I turned to him. 'You think I don't know what kolaches are, eh? You're mistaken, young man. I've eaten your mother's kolaches long before that Easter Day when you were born.'

'Always too fresh, Leo,' Ambrosch remarked with a shrug.

Leo dived behind his mother and grinned out at me.

We turned to leave the cave; Antonia and I went up the stairs first, and the children waited. We were standing outside talking, when they all came running up the steps together, big and little, tow heads and gold heads and brown, and flashing little naked legs; a veritable explosion of life out of the dark cave into the sunlight. It made me dizzy for a moment.

The boys escorted us to the front of the house, which I hadn't yet seen; in farm-houses, somehow, life comes and goes by the back door. The roof was so steep that the eaves were not much above the forest of tall hollyhocks, now brown and in seed. Through July, Antonia said, the house was buried in them; the Bohemians, I remembered, always planted hollyhocks. The front yard was enclosed by a thorny locust hedge, and at the gate grew two silvery, moth-like trees of the mimosa family. From here one looked down over the cattle-yards, with their two long ponds, and over a wide stretch of stubble which they told me was a rye field in summer.

At some distance behind the house were an ash grove and two orchards: a cherry orchard, with gooseberry and currant bushes between the rows, and an apple orchard, sheltered by a high hedge from the hot winds. The older children turned back when we reached the hedge, but Jan and Nina and Lucie crept through it by a hole known only to themselves and hid under the low-branching mulberry bushes.

As we walked through the apple orchard, grown up in tall bluegrass, Antonia kept stopping to tell me about one tree and another. 'I love them as if they were people,' she said, rubbing her hand over the bark. 'There wasn't a tree here when we first came. We planted every one, and used to carry water for them, too—after we'd been working in the fields all day. Anton, he was a city man, and he used to get discouraged. But I couldn't feel so tired that I wouldn't fret about these trees when there was a dry time. They were on my mind like children. Many a night after he was asleep I've got up and come out and carried water to the poor things. And now, you see, we have the good of them. My man worked in the orange groves in Florida, and he knows all about grafting. There ain't one of our neighbours has an orchard that bears like ours.'

In the middle of the orchard we came upon a grape arbour, with seats built along the sides and a warped plank table. The three children were waiting for us there. They looked up at me bashfully and made some request of their mother.

'They want me to tell you how the teacher has the school picnic here every year. These don't go to school yet, so they think it's all like the picnic.'

After I had admired the arbour sufficiently, the youngsters ran away to an open place where there was a rough jungle of French pinks, and squatted down among them, crawling about and measuring with a string.

'Jan wants to bury his dog there,' Antonia explained. 'I had to tell him he could. He's kind of like Nina Harling; you remember how hard she used to take little things? He has funny notions, like her.'

We sat down and watched them. Antonia leaned her elbows on the table. There was the deepest peace in that orchard. It was surrounded by a triple enclosure; the wire fence, then the hedge of thorny locusts, then the mulberry hedge which kept out the hot winds of summer and held fast to the protecting snows of winter. The hedges were so tall that we could see nothing but the blue sky above them, neither the barn roof nor the windmill. The afternoon sun poured down on us through the drying grape leaves. The orchard seemed full of sun, like a cup, and we could smell the ripe apples on the trees. The crabs hung on the branches as thick as beads on a string, purple-red, with a thin silvery glaze over them. Some hens and ducks had crept through the hedge and were pecking at the fallen apples. The drakes were handsome fellows, with pinkish grey bodies, their heads and necks covered with iridescent green feathers which grew close and full, changing to blue like a peacock's neck. Antonia said they always reminded her of soldiers—some uniform she had seen in the old country, when she was a child.

'Are there any quail left now?' I asked. I reminded her how she used to go hunting with me the last summer before we moved to town. 'You weren't a bad shot, Tony. Do you remember how you used to want to run away and go for ducks with Charley Harling and me?'

'I know, but I'm afraid to look at a gun now.' She picked up one of the drakes and ruffled his green capote with her fingers. 'Ever since I've had children, I don't like to kill anything. It makes me kind of faint to wring an old goose's neck. Ain't that strange, Jim?'

'I don't know. The young Queen of Italy said the same thing once, to a friend of mine. She used to be a great huntswoman, but now she feels as you do, and only shoots clay pigeons.'

'Then I'm sure she's a good mother,' Antonia said warmly.

She told me how she and her husband had come out to this new country when the farm-land was cheap and could be had on easy payments. The first ten years were a hard struggle. Her husband knew very little about farming and often grew discouraged. 'We'd never have got through if I hadn't been so strong. I've always had good health, thank God, and I was able to help him in the fields until right up to the time before my babies came. Our children were good about taking care of each other. Martha, the one you saw when she was a baby, was such a help to me, and she trained Anna to be just like her. My Martha's married now, and has a baby of her own. Think of that, Jim!

'No, I never got down-hearted. Anton's a good man, and I loved my children and always believed they would turn out well. I belong on a farm. I'm never lonesome here like I used to be in town. You remember what sad spells I used to have, when I didn't know what was the matter with me? I've never had them out here. And I don't mind work a bit, if I don't have to put up with sadness.' She leaned her chin on her hand and looked down through the orchard, where the sunlight was growing more and more golden.

'You ought never to have gone to town, Tony,' I said, wondering at her.

She turned to me eagerly.

'Oh, I'm glad I went! I'd never have known anything about cooking or housekeeping if I hadn't. I learned nice ways at the Harlings', and I've been able to bring my children up so much better. Don't you think they are pretty well-behaved for country children? If it hadn't been for what Mrs. Harling taught me, I expect I'd have brought them up like wild rabbits. No, I'm glad I had a chance to learn; but I'm thankful none of my daughters will ever have to work out. The trouble with me was, Jim, I never could believe harm of anybody I loved.'

While we were talking, Antonia assured me that she could keep me for the night. 'We've plenty of room. Two of the boys sleep in the haymow till cold weather comes, but there's no need for it. Leo always begs to sleep there, and Ambrosch goes along to look after him.'

I told her I would like to sleep in the haymow, with the boys.

'You can do just as you want to. The chest is full of clean blankets, put away for winter. Now I must go, or my girls will be doing all the work, and I want to cook your supper myself.'

As we went toward the house, we met Ambrosch and Anton, starting off with their milking-pails to hunt the cows. I joined them, and Leo accompanied us at some distance, running ahead and starting up at us out of clumps of ironweed, calling, 'I'm a jack rabbit,' or, 'I'm a big bull-snake.'

I walked between the two older boys—straight, well-made fellows, with good heads and clear eyes. They talked about their school and the new teacher, told me about the crops and the harvest, and how many steers they would feed that winter. They were easy and confidential with me, as if I were an old friend of the family—and not too old. I felt like a boy in their company, and all manner of forgotten interests revived in me. It seemed, after all, so natural to be walking along a barbed-wire fence beside the sunset, toward a red pond, and to see my shadow moving along at my right, over the close-cropped grass.

'Has mother shown you the pictures you sent her from the old country?' Ambrosch asked. 'We've had them framed and they're hung up in the parlour. She was so glad to get them. I don't believe I ever saw her so pleased about anything.' There was a note of simple gratitude in his voice that made me wish I had given more occasion for it.

I put my hand on his shoulder. 'Your mother, you know, was very much loved by all of us. She was a beautiful girl.'

'Oh, we know!' They both spoke together; seemed a little surprised that I should think it necessary to mention this. 'Everybody liked her, didn't they? The Harlings and your grandmother, and all the town people.'

'Sometimes,' I ventured, 'it doesn't occur to boys that their mother was ever young and pretty.'

'Oh, we know!' they said again, warmly. 'She's not very old now,' Ambrosch added. 'Not much older than you.'

'Well,' I said, 'if you weren't nice to her, I think I'd take a club and go for the whole lot of you. I couldn't stand it if you boys were inconsiderate, or thought of her as if she were just somebody who looked after you. You see I was very much in love with your mother once, and I know there's nobody like her.'

The boys laughed and seemed pleased and embarrassed.

'She never told us that,' said Anton. 'But she's always talked lots about you, and about what good times you used to have. She has a picture of you that she cut out of the Chicago paper once, and Leo says he recognized you when you drove up to the windmill. You can't tell about Leo, though; sometimes he likes to be smart.'

We brought the cows home to the corner nearest the barn, and the boys milked them while night came on. Everything was as it should be: the strong smell of sunflowers and ironweed in the dew, the clear blue and gold of the sky, the evening star, the purr of the milk into the pails, the grunts and squeals of the pigs fighting over their supper. I began to feel the loneliness of the farm-boy at evening, when the chores seem everlastingly the same, and the world so far away.

What a tableful we were at supper: two long rows of restless heads in the lamplight, and so many eyes fastened excitedly upon Antonia as she sat at the head of the table, filling the plates and starting the dishes on their way. The children were seated according to a system; a little one next an older one, who was to watch over his behaviour and to see that he got his food. Anna and Yulka left their chairs from time to time to bring fresh plates of kolaches and pitchers of milk.

After supper we went into the parlour, so that Yulka and Leo could play for me. Antonia went first, carrying the lamp. There were not nearly chairs enough to go round, so the younger children sat down on the bare floor. Little Lucie whispered to me that they were going to have a parlour carpet if they got ninety cents for their wheat. Leo, with a good deal of fussing, got out his violin. It was old Mr. Shimerda's instrument, which Antonia had always kept, and it was too big for him. But he played very well for a self-taught boy. Poor Yulka's efforts were not so successful. While they were playing, little Nina got up from her corner, came out into the middle of the floor, and began to do a pretty little dance on the boards with her bare feet. No one paid the least attention to her, and when she was through she stole back and sat down by her brother.

Antonia spoke to Leo in Bohemian. He frowned and wrinkled up his face. He seemed to be trying to pout, but his attempt only brought out dimples in unusual places. After twisting and screwing the keys, he played some Bohemian airs, without the organ to hold him back, and that went better. The boy was so restless that I had not had a chance to look at his face before. My first impression was right; he really was faun-like. He hadn't much head behind his ears, and his tawny fleece grew down thick to the back of his neck. His eyes were not frank and wide apart like those of the other boys, but were deep-set, gold-green in colour, and seemed sensitive to the light. His mother said he got hurt oftener than all the others put together. He was always trying to ride the colts before they were broken, teasing the turkey gobbler, seeing just how much red the bull would stand for, or how sharp the new axe was.

After the concert was over, Antonia brought out a big boxful of photographs: she and Anton in their wedding clothes, holding hands; her brother Ambrosch and his very fat wife, who had a farm of her own, and who bossed her husband, I was delighted to hear; the three Bohemian Marys and their large families.

'You wouldn't believe how steady those girls have turned out,' Antonia remarked. 'Mary Svoboda's the best butter-maker in all this country, and a fine manager. Her children will have a grand chance.'

As Antonia turned over the pictures the young Cuzaks stood behind her chair, looking over her shoulder with interested faces. Nina and Jan, after trying to see round the taller ones, quietly brought a chair, climbed up on it, and stood close together, looking. The little boy forgot his shyness and grinned delightedly when familiar faces came into view. In the group about Antonia I was conscious of a kind of physical harmony. They leaned this way and that, and were not afraid to touch each other. They contemplated the photographs with pleased recognition; looked at some admiringly, as if these characters in their mother's girlhood had been remarkable people. The little children, who could not speak English, murmured comments to each other in their rich old language.

Antonia held out a photograph of Lena that had come from San Francisco last Christmas. 'Does she still look like that? She hasn't been home for six years now.' Yes, it was exactly like Lena, I told her; a comely woman, a trifle too plump, in a hat a trifle too large, but with the old lazy eyes, and the old dimpled ingenuousness still lurking at the corners of her mouth.

There was a picture of Frances Harling in a befrogged riding costume that I remembered well. 'Isn't she fine!' the girls murmured. They all assented. One could see that Frances had come down as a heroine in the family legend. Only Leo was unmoved.

'And there's Mr. Harling, in his grand fur coat. He was awfully rich, wasn't he, mother?'

'He wasn't any Rockefeller,' put in Master Leo, in a very low tone, which reminded me of the way in which Mrs. Shimerda had once said that my grandfather 'wasn't Jesus.' His habitual scepticism was like a direct inheritance from that old woman.

'None of your smart speeches,' said Ambrosch severely.

Leo poked out a supple red tongue at him, but a moment later broke into a giggle at a tintype of two men, uncomfortably seated, with an awkward-looking boy in baggy clothes standing between them: Jake and Otto and I! We had it taken, I remembered, when we went to Black Hawk on the first Fourth of July I spent in Nebraska. I was glad to see Jake's grin again, and Otto's ferocious moustaches. The young Cuzaks knew all about them. 'He made grandfather's coffin, didn't he?' Anton asked.

'Wasn't they good fellows, Jim?' Antonia's eyes filled. 'To this day I'm ashamed because I quarrelled with Jake that way. I was saucy and impertinent to him, Leo, like you are with people sometimes, and I wish somebody had made me behave.'

'We aren't through with you, yet,' they warned me. They produced a photograph taken just before I went away to college: a tall youth in striped trousers and a straw hat, trying to look easy and jaunty.

'Tell us, Mr. Burden,' said Charley, 'about the rattler you killed at the dog-town. How long was he? Sometimes mother says six feet and sometimes she says five.'

These children seemed to be upon very much the same terms with Antonia as the Harling children had been so many years before. They seemed to feel the same pride in her, and to look to her for stories and entertainment as we used to do.

It was eleven o'clock when I at last took my bag and some blankets and started for the barn with the boys. Their mother came to the door with us, and we tarried for a moment to look out at the white slope of the corral and the two ponds asleep in the moonlight, and the long sweep of the pasture under the star-sprinkled sky.

The boys told me to choose my own place in the haymow, and I lay down before a big window, left open in warm weather, that looked out into the stars. Ambrosch and Leo cuddled up in a hay-cave, back under the eaves, and lay giggling and whispering. They tickled each other and tossed and tumbled in the hay; and then, all at once, as if they had been shot, they were still. There was hardly a minute between giggles and bland slumber.

I lay awake for a long while, until the slow-moving moon passed my window on its way up the heavens. I was thinking about Antonia and her children; about Anna's solicitude for her, Ambrosch's grave affection, Leo's jealous, animal little love. That moment, when they all came tumbling out of the cave into the light, was a sight any man might have come far to see. Antonia had always been one to leave images in the mind that did not fade—that grew stronger with time. In my memory there was a succession of such pictures, fixed there like the old woodcuts of one's first primer: Antonia kicking her bare legs against the sides of my pony when we came home in triumph with our snake; Antonia in her black shawl and fur cap, as she stood by her father's grave in the snowstorm; Antonia coming in with her work-team along the evening sky-line. She lent herself to immemorial human attitudes which we recognize by instinct as universal and true. I had not been mistaken. She was a battered woman now, not a lovely girl; but she still had that something which fires the imagination, could still stop one's breath for a moment by a look or gesture that somehow revealed the meaning in common things. She had only to stand in the orchard, to put her hand on a little crab tree and look up at the apples, to make you feel the goodness of planting and tending and harvesting at last. All the strong things of her heart came out in her body, that had been so tireless in serving generous emotions.

It was no wonder that her sons stood tall and straight. She was a rich mine of life, like the founders of early races.

II.

When I awoke in the morning, long bands of sunshine were coming in at the window and reaching back under the eaves where the two boys lay. Leo was wide awake and was tickling his brother's leg with a dried cone-flower he had pulled out of the hay. Ambrosch kicked at him and turned over. I closed my eyes and pretended to be asleep. Leo lay on his back, elevated one foot, and began exercising his toes. He picked up dried flowers with his toes and brandished them in the belt of sunlight. After he had amused himself thus for some time, he rose on one elbow and began to look at me, cautiously, then critically, blinking his eyes in the light. His expression was droll; it dismissed me lightly. 'This old fellow is no different from other people. He doesn't know my secret.' He seemed conscious of possessing a keener power of enjoyment than other people; his quick recognitions made him frantically impatient of deliberate judgments. He always knew what he wanted without thinking.

After dressing in the hay, I washed my face in cold water at the windmill. Breakfast was ready when I entered the kitchen, and Yulka was baking griddle-cakes. The three older boys set off for the fields early. Leo and Yulka were to drive to town to meet their father, who would return from Wilber on the noon train.

'We'll only have a lunch at noon,' Antonia said, and cook the geese for supper, when our papa will be here. I wish my Martha could come down to see you. They have a Ford car now, and she don't seem so far away from me as she used to. But her husband's crazy about his farm and about having everything just right, and they almost never get away except on Sundays. He's a handsome boy, and he'll be rich some day. Everything he takes hold of turns out well. When they bring that baby in here, and unwrap him, he looks like a little prince; Martha takes care of him so beautiful. I'm reconciled to her being away from me now, but at first I cried like I was putting her into her coffin.'

We were alone in the kitchen, except for Anna, who was pouring cream into the churn. She looked up at me. 'Yes, she did. We were just ashamed of mother. She went round crying, when Martha was so happy, and the rest of us were all glad. Joe certainly was patient with you, mother.'

Antonia nodded and smiled at herself. 'I know it was silly, but I couldn't help it. I wanted her right here. She'd never been away from me a night since she was born. If Anton had made trouble about her when she was a baby, or wanted me to leave her with my mother, I wouldn't have married him. I couldn't. But he always loved her like she was his own.'

'I didn't even know Martha wasn't my full sister until after she was engaged to Joe,' Anna told me.

Toward the middle of the afternoon, the wagon drove in, with the father and the eldest son. I was smoking in the orchard, and as I went out to meet them, Antonia came running down from the house and hugged the two men as if they had been away for months.

'Papa,' interested me, from my first glimpse of him. He was shorter than his older sons; a crumpled little man, with run-over boot-heels, and he carried one shoulder higher than the other. But he moved very quickly, and there was an air of jaunty liveliness about him. He had a strong, ruddy colour, thick black hair, a little grizzled, a curly moustache, and red lips. His smile showed the strong teeth of which his wife was so proud, and as he saw me his lively, quizzical eyes told me that he knew all about me. He looked like a humorous philosopher who had hitched up one shoulder under the burdens of life, and gone on his way having a good time when he could. He advanced to meet me and gave me a hard hand, burned red on the back and heavily coated with hair. He wore his Sunday clothes, very thick and hot for the weather, an unstarched white shirt, and a blue necktie with big white dots, like a little boy's, tied in a flowing bow. Cuzak began at once to talk about his holiday—from politeness he spoke in English.

'Mama, I wish you had see the lady dance on the slack-wire in the street at night. They throw a bright light on her and she float through the air something beautiful, like a bird! They have a dancing bear, like in the old country, and two-three merry-go-around, and people in balloons, and what you call the big wheel, Rudolph?'

'A Ferris wheel,' Rudolph entered the conversation in a deep baritone voice. He was six foot two, and had a chest like a young blacksmith. 'We went to the big dance in the hall behind the saloon last night, mother, and I danced with all the girls, and so did father. I never saw so many pretty girls. It was a Bohunk crowd, for sure. We didn't hear a word of English on the street, except from the show people, did we, papa?'

Cuzak nodded. 'And very many send word to you, Antonia. You will excuse'—turning to me—'if I tell her.' While we walked toward the house he related incidents and delivered messages in the tongue he spoke fluently, and I dropped a little behind, curious to know what their relations had become—or remained. The two seemed to be on terms of easy friendliness, touched with humour. Clearly, she was the impulse, and he the corrective. As they went up the hill he kept glancing at her sidewise, to see whether she got his point, or how she received it. I noticed later that he always looked at people sidewise, as a work-horse does at its yokemate. Even when he sat opposite me in the kitchen, talking, he would turn his head a little toward the clock or the stove and look at me from the side, but with frankness and good nature. This trick did not suggest duplicity or secretiveness, but merely long habit, as with the horse.

He had brought a tintype of himself and Rudolph for Antonia's collection, and several paper bags of candy for the children. He looked a little disappointed when his wife showed him a big box of candy I had got in Denver—she hadn't let the children touch it the night before. He put his candy away in the cupboard, 'for when she rains,' and glanced at the box, chuckling. 'I guess you must have hear about how my family ain't so small,' he said.

Cuzak sat down behind the stove and watched his womenfolk and the little children with equal amusement. He thought they were nice, and he thought they were funny, evidently. He had been off dancing with the girls and forgetting that he was an old fellow, and now his family rather surprised him; he seemed to think it a joke that all these children should belong to him. As the younger ones slipped up to him in his retreat, he kept taking things out of his pockets; penny dolls, a wooden clown, a balloon pig that was inflated by a whistle. He beckoned to the little boy they called Jan, whispered to him, and presented him with a paper snake, gently, so as not to startle him. Looking over the boy's head he said to me, 'This one is bashful. He gets left.'

Cuzak had brought home with him a roll of illustrated Bohemian papers. He opened them and began to tell his wife the news, much of which seemed to relate to one person. I heard the name Vasakova, Vasakova, repeated several times with lively interest, and presently I asked him whether he were talking about the singer, Maria Vasak.

'You know? You have heard, maybe?' he asked incredulously. When I assured him that I had heard her, he pointed out her picture and told me that Vasak had broken her leg, climbing in the Austrian Alps, and would not be able to fill her engagements. He seemed delighted to find that I had heard her sing in London and in Vienna; got out his pipe and lit it to enjoy our talk the better. She came from his part of Prague. His father used to mend her shoes for her when she was a student. Cuzak questioned me about her looks, her popularity, her voice; but he particularly wanted to know whether I had noticed her tiny feet, and whether I thought she had saved much money. She was extravagant, of course, but he hoped she wouldn't squander everything, and have nothing left when she was old. As a young man, working in Wienn, he had seen a good many artists who were old and poor, making one glass of beer last all evening, and 'it was not very nice, that.'

When the boys came in from milking and feeding, the long table was laid, and two brown geese, stuffed with apples, were put down sizzling before Antonia. She began to carve, and Rudolph, who sat next his mother, started the plates on their way. When everybody was served, he looked across the table at me.

'Have you been to Black Hawk lately, Mr. Burden? Then I wonder if you've heard about the Cutters?'

No, I had heard nothing at all about them.

'Then you must tell him, son, though it's a terrible thing to talk about at supper. Now, all you children be quiet, Rudolph is going to tell about the murder.'

'Hurrah! The murder!' the children murmured, looking pleased and interested.

Rudolph told his story in great detail, with occasional promptings from his mother or father.

Wick Cutter and his wife had gone on living in the house that Antonia and I knew so well, and in the way we knew so well. They grew to be very old people. He shrivelled up, Antonia said, until he looked like a little old yellow monkey, for his beard and his fringe of hair never changed colour. Mrs. Cutter remained flushed and wild-eyed as we had known her, but as the years passed she became afflicted with a shaking palsy which made her nervous nod continuous instead of occasional. Her hands were so uncertain that she could no longer disfigure china, poor woman! As the couple grew older, they quarrelled more and more often about the ultimate disposition of their 'property.' A new law was passed in the state, securing the surviving wife a third of her husband's estate under all conditions. Cutter was tormented by the fear that Mrs. Cutter would live longer than he, and that eventually her 'people,' whom he had always hated so violently, would inherit. Their quarrels on this subject passed the boundary of the close-growing cedars, and were heard in the street by whoever wished to loiter and listen.

One morning, two years ago, Cutter went into the hardware store and bought a pistol, saying he was going to shoot a dog, and adding that he 'thought he would take a shot at an old cat while he was about it.' (Here the children interrupted Rudolph's narrative by smothered giggles.)

Cutter went out behind the hardware store, put up a target, practised for an hour or so, and then went home. At six o'clock that evening, when several men were passing the Cutter house on their way home to supper, they heard a pistol shot. They paused and were looking doubtfully at one another, when another shot came crashing through an upstairs window. They ran into the house and found Wick Cutter lying on a sofa in his upstairs bedroom, with his throat torn open, bleeding on a roll of sheets he had placed beside his head.

'Walk in, gentlemen,' he said weakly. 'I am alive, you see, and competent. You are witnesses that I have survived my wife. You will find her in her own room. Please make your examination at once, so that there will be no mistake.'

One of the neighbours telephoned for a doctor, while the others went into Mrs. Cutter's room. She was lying on her bed, in her night-gown and wrapper, shot through the heart. Her husband must have come in while she was taking her afternoon nap and shot her, holding the revolver near her breast. Her night-gown was burned from the powder.

The horrified neighbours rushed back to Cutter. He opened his eyes and said distinctly, 'Mrs. Cutter is quite dead, gentlemen, and I am conscious. My affairs are in order.' Then, Rudolph said, 'he let go and died.'

On his desk the coroner found a letter, dated at five o'clock that afternoon. It stated that he had just shot his wife; that any will she might secretly have made would be invalid, as he survived her. He meant to shoot himself at six o'clock and would, if he had strength, fire a shot through the window in the hope that passersby might come in and see him 'before life was extinct,' as he wrote.

'Now, would you have thought that man had such a cruel heart?' Antonia turned to me after the story was told. 'To go and do that poor woman out of any comfort she might have from his money after he was gone!'

'Did you ever hear of anybody else that killed himself for spite, Mr. Burden?' asked Rudolph.

I admitted that I hadn't. Every lawyer learns over and over how strong a motive hate can be, but in my collection of legal anecdotes I had nothing to match this one. When I asked how much the estate amounted to, Rudolph said it was a little over a hundred thousand dollars.

Cuzak gave me a twinkling, sidelong glance. 'The lawyers, they got a good deal of it, sure,' he said merrily.

A hundred thousand dollars; so that was the fortune that had been scraped together by such hard dealing, and that Cutter himself had died for in the end!

After supper Cuzak and I took a stroll in the orchard and sat down by the windmill to smoke. He told me his story as if it were my business to know it.

His father was a shoemaker, his uncle a furrier, and he, being a younger son, was apprenticed to the latter's trade. You never got anywhere working for your relatives, he said, so when he was a journeyman he went to Vienna and worked in a big fur shop, earning good money. But a young fellow who liked a good time didn't save anything in Vienna; there were too many pleasant ways of spending every night what he'd made in the day. After three years there, he came to New York. He was badly advised and went to work on furs during a strike, when the factories were offering big wages. The strikers won, and Cuzak was blacklisted. As he had a few hundred dollars ahead, he decided to go to Florida and raise oranges. He had always thought he would like to raise oranges! The second year a hard frost killed his young grove, and he fell ill with malaria. He came to Nebraska to visit his cousin, Anton Jelinek, and to look about. When he began to look about, he saw Antonia, and she was exactly the kind of girl he had always been hunting for. They were married at once, though he had to borrow money from his cousin to buy the wedding ring.

'It was a pretty hard job, breaking up this place and making the first crops grow,' he said, pushing back his hat and scratching his grizzled hair. 'Sometimes I git awful sore on this place and want to quit, but my wife she always say we better stick it out. The babies come along pretty fast, so it look like it be hard to move, anyhow. I guess she was right, all right. We got this place clear now. We pay only twenty dollars an acre then, and I been offered a hundred. We bought another quarter ten years ago, and we got it most paid for. We got plenty boys; we can work a lot of land. Yes, she is a good wife for a poor man. She ain't always so strict with me, neither. Sometimes maybe I drink a little too much beer in town, and when I come home she don't say nothing. She don't ask me no questions. We always get along fine, her and me, like at first. The children don't make trouble between us, like sometimes happens.' He lit another pipe and pulled on it contentedly.

I found Cuzak a most companionable fellow. He asked me a great many questions about my trip through Bohemia, about Vienna and the Ringstrasse and the theatres.

'Gee! I like to go back there once, when the boys is big enough to farm the place.

Sometimes when I read the papers from the old country, I pretty near run away,' he confessed with a little laugh. 'I never did think how I would be a settled man like this.'

He was still, as Antonia said, a city man. He liked theatres and lighted streets and music and a game of dominoes after the day's work was over. His sociability was stronger than his acquisitive instinct. He liked to live day by day and night by night, sharing in the excitement of the crowd.—Yet his wife had managed to hold him here on a farm, in one of the loneliest countries in the world.

I could see the little chap, sitting here every evening by the windmill, nursing his pipe and listening to the silence; the wheeze of the pump, the grunting of the pigs, an occasional squawking when the hens were disturbed by a rat. It did rather seem to me that Cuzak had been made the instrument of Antonia's special mission. This was a fine life, certainly, but it wasn't the kind of life he had wanted to live. I wondered whether the life that was right for one was ever right for two!

I asked Cuzak if he didn't find it hard to do without the gay company he had always been used to. He knocked out his pipe against an upright, sighed, and dropped it into his pocket.

'At first I near go crazy with lonesomeness,' he said frankly, 'but my woman is got such a warm heart. She always make it as good for me as she could. Now it ain't so bad; I can begin to have some fun with my boys, already!'

As we walked toward the house, Cuzak cocked his hat jauntily over one ear and looked up at the moon. 'Gee!' he said in a hushed voice, as if he had just wakened up, 'it don't seem like I am away from there twenty-six year!'

III.

After dinner the next day I said good-bye and drove back to Hastings to take the train for Black Hawk. Antonia and her children gathered round my buggy before I started, and even the little ones looked up at me with friendly faces. Leo and Ambrosch ran ahead to open the lane gate. When I reached the bottom of the hill, I glanced back. The group was still there by the windmill. Antonia was waving her apron.

At the gate Ambrosch lingered beside my buggy, resting his arm on the wheel-rim. Leo slipped through the fence and ran off into the pasture.

'That's like him,' his brother said with a shrug. 'He's a crazy kid. Maybe he's sorry to have you go, and maybe he's jealous. He's jealous of anybody mother makes a fuss over, even the priest.'

I found I hated to leave this boy, with his pleasant voice and his fine head and eyes. He looked very manly as he stood there without a hat, the wind rippling his shirt about his brown neck and shoulders.

'Don't forget that you and Rudolph are going hunting with me up on the Niobrara next summer,' I said. 'Your father's agreed to let you off after harvest.'

He smiled. 'I won't likely forget. I've never had such a nice thing offered to me before. I don't know what makes you so nice to us boys,' he added, blushing.

'Oh, yes, you do!' I said, gathering up my reins.

He made no answer to this, except to smile at me with unabashed pleasure and affection as I drove away.

My day in Black Hawk was disappointing. Most of my old friends were dead or had moved away. Strange children, who meant nothing to me, were playing in the Harlings' big yard when I passed; the mountain ash had been cut down, and only a sprouting stump was left of the tall Lombardy poplar that used to guard the gate. I hurried on. The rest of the morning I spent with Anton Jelinek, under a shady cottonwood tree in the yard behind his saloon. While I was having my midday dinner at the hotel, I met one of the old lawyers who was still in practice, and he took me up to his office and talked over the Cutter case with me. After that, I scarcely knew how to put in the time until the night express was due.

I took a long walk north of the town, out into the pastures where the land was so rough that it had never been ploughed up, and the long red grass of early times still grew shaggy over the draws and hillocks. Out there I felt at home again. Overhead the sky was that indescribable blue of autumn; bright and shadowless, hard as enamel. To the south I could see the dun-shaded river bluffs that used to look so big to me, and all about stretched drying cornfields, of the pale-gold colour, I remembered so well. Russian thistles were blowing across the uplands and piling against the wire fences like barricades. Along the cattle-paths the plumes of goldenrod were already fading into sun-warmed velvet, grey with gold threads in it. I had escaped from the curious depression that hangs over little towns, and my mind was full of pleasant things; trips I meant to take with the Cuzak boys, in the Bad Lands and up on the Stinking Water. There were enough Cuzaks to play with for a long while yet. Even after the boys grew up, there would always be Cuzak himself! I meant to tramp along a few miles of lighted streets with Cuzak.

As I wandered over those rough pastures, I had the good luck to stumble upon a bit of the first road that went from Black Hawk out to the north country; to my grandfather's farm, then on to the Shimerdas' and to the Norwegian settlement. Everywhere else it had been ploughed under when the highways were surveyed; this half-mile or so within the pasture fence was all that was left of that old road which used to run like a wild thing across the open prairie, clinging to the high places and circling and doubling like a rabbit before the hounds.

On the level land the tracks had almost disappeared—were mere shadings in the grass, and a stranger would not have noticed them. But wherever the road had crossed a draw, it was easy to find. The rains had made channels of the wheel-ruts and washed them so deeply that the sod had never healed over them. They looked like gashes torn by a grizzly's claws, on the slopes where the farm-wagons used to lurch up out of the hollows with a pull that brought curling muscles on the smooth hips of the horses. I sat down and watched the haystacks turn rosy in the slanting sunlight.

This was the road over which Antonia and I came on that night when we got off the train at Black Hawk and were bedded down in the straw, wondering children, being taken we knew not whither. I had only to close my eyes to hear the rumbling of the wagons in the dark, and to be again overcome by that obliterating strangeness. The feelings of that night were so near that I could reach out and touch them with my hand. I had the sense of coming home to myself, and of having found out what a little circle man's experience is. For Antonia and for me, this had been the road of Destiny; had taken us to those early accidents of fortune which predetermined for us all that we can ever be. Now I understood that the same road was to bring us together again. Whatever we had missed, we possessed together the precious, the incommunicable past.

ONE OF OURS

I
ON LOVELY CREEK

I.

CLAUDE WHEELER OPENED his eyes before the sun was up and vigorously shook his younger brother, who lay in the other half of the same bed.

"Ralph, Ralph, get awake! Come down and help me wash the car."

"What for?"

"Why, aren't we going to the circus today?"

"Car's all right. Let me alone." The boy turned over and pulled the sheet up to his face, to shut out the light which was beginning to come through the curtainless windows.

Claude rose and dressed,—a simple operation which took very little time. He crept down two flights of stairs, feeling his way in the dusk, his red hair standing up in peaks, like a cock's comb. He went through the kitchen into the adjoining washroom, which held two porcelain stands with running water. Everybody had washed before going to bed, apparently, and the bowls were ringed with a dark sediment which the hard, alkaline water had not dissolved. Shutting the door on this disorder, he turned back to the kitchen, took Mahailey's tin basin, doused his face and head in cold water, and began to plaster down his wet hair.

Old Mahailey herself came in from the yard, with her apron full of corn-cobs to start a fire in the kitchen stove. She smiled at him in the foolish fond way she often had with him when they were alone.

"What air you gittin' up for a-ready, boy? You goin' to the circus before breakfast? Don't you make no noise, else you'll have 'em all down here before I git my fire a-goin'."

"All right, Mahailey." Claude caught up his cap and ran out of doors, down the hillside toward the barn. The sun popped up over the edge of the prairie like a broad, smiling face; the light poured across the close-cropped August pastures and the hilly, timbered windings of Lovely Creek, a clear little stream with a sand bottom, that curled and twisted playfully about through the south section of the big Wheeler ranch. It was a fine day to go to the circus at Frankfort, a fine day to do anything; the sort of day that must, somehow, turn out well.

Claude backed the little Ford car out of its shed, ran it up to the horse-tank, and began to throw water on the mud-crusted wheels and windshield. While he was at work the two hired men, Dan and Jerry, came shambling down the hill to feed the stock. Jerry was grumbling and swearing about something, but Claude wrung out his wet rags and, beyond a nod, paid no attention to them. Somehow his father always managed to have the roughest and dirtiest hired men in the country working for him. Claude had a grievance against Jerry just now, because of his treatment of one of the horses.

Molly was a faithful old mare, the mother of many colts; Claude and his younger brother had learned to ride on her. This man Jerry, taking her out to work one morning, let her step on a board with a nail sticking up in it. He pulled the nail out of her foot, said nothing to anybody, and drove her to the cultivator all day. Now she had been standing in her stall for weeks, patiently suffering, her body wretchedly thin, and her leg swollen until it looked like an elephant's. She would have to stand there, the veterinary said, until her hoof came off and she grew a new one, and she would always be stiff. Jerry had not been discharged, and he exhibited the poor animal as if she were a credit to him.

Mahailey came out on the hilltop and rang the breakfast bell. After the hired men went up to the house, Claude slipped into the barn to see that Molly had got her share of oats. She was eating quietly, her head hanging, and her scaly, dead-looking foot lifted just a little from the ground. When he stroked her neck and talked to her she stopped grinding and gazed at him mournfully. She knew him, and wrinkled her nose and drew her upper lip back from her worn teeth, to show that she liked being petted. She let him touch her foot and examine her leg.

When Claude reached the kitchen, his mother was sitting at one end of the breakfast table, pouring weak coffee, his brother and Dan and Jerry were in their chairs, and Mahailey was baking griddle cakes at the stove. A moment later Mr. Wheeler came down the enclosed stairway and walked the length of the table to his own place. He was a very large man, taller and broader than any of his neighbours. He seldom wore a coat in summer, and his rumpled shirt bulged out carelessly over the belt of his trousers. His florid face was clean shaven, likely to be a trifle tobacco-stained about the mouth, and it was conspicuous both for good-nature and coarse humour, and for an imperturbable physical composure. Nobody in the county had ever seen Nat Wheeler flustered about anything, and nobody had ever heard him speak with complete seriousness. He kept up his easy-going, jocular affability even with his own family.

As soon as he was seated, Mr. Wheeler reached for the two-pint sugar bowl and began to pour sugar into his coffee. Ralph asked him if he were going to the circus. Mr. Wheeler winked.

"I shouldn't wonder if I happened in town sometime before the elephants get away." He spoke very deliberately, with a State-of-Maine drawl, and his voice was smooth and agreeable. "You boys better start in early, though. You can take the wagon and the mules, and load in the cowhides. The butcher has agreed to take them."

Claude put down his knife. "Can't we have the car? I've washed it on purpose."

"And what about Dan and Jerry? They want to see the circus just as much as you do, and I want the hides should go in; they're bringing a good price now. I don't mind about your washing the car; mud preserves the paint, they say, but it'll be all right this time, Claude."

The hired men haw-hawed and Ralph giggled. Claude's freckled face got very red. The pancake grew stiff and heavy in his mouth and was hard to swallow. His father knew he hated to drive the mules to town, and knew how he hated to go anywhere with Dan and Jerry. As for the hides, they were the skins of four steers that had perished in the blizzard last winter through the wanton carelessness of these same hired men, and the price they would bring would not half pay for the time his father had spent in stripping and curing them. They had lain in a shed loft all summer, and the wagon had been to town a dozen times. But today, when he wanted to go to Frankfort clean and care-free, he must take these stinking hides and two coarse-mouthed men, and drive a pair of mules that always brayed and balked and behaved ridiculously in a crowd. Probably his father had looked out of the window and seen him washing the car, and had put this up on him while he dressed. It was like his father's idea of a joke.

Mrs. Wheeler looked at Claude sympathetically, feeling that he was disappointed. Perhaps she, too, suspected a joke. She had learned that humour might wear almost any guise.

When Claude started for the barn after breakfast, she came running down the path, calling to him faintly,—hurrying always made her short of breath. Overtaking him, she looked up with solicitude, shading her eyes with her delicately formed hand. "If you want I should do up your linen coat, Claude, I can iron it while you're hitching," she said wistfully.

Claude stood kicking at a bunch of mottled feathers that had once been a young chicken. His shoulders were drawn high, his mother saw, and his figure suggested energy and determined self-control.

"You needn't mind, mother." He spoke rapidly, muttering his words. "I'd better wear my old clothes if I have to take the hides. They're greasy, and in the sun they'll smell worse than fertilizer."

"The men can handle the hides, I should think. Wouldn't you feel better in town to be dressed?" She was still blinking up at him.

"Don't bother about it. Put me out a clean coloured shirt, if you want to. That's all right."

He turned toward the barn, and his mother went slowly back the path up to the house. She was so plucky and so stooped, his dear mother! He guessed if she could stand having these men about, could cook and wash for them, he could drive them to town!

Half an hour after the wagon left, Nat Wheeler put on an alpaca coat and went off in the rattling buckboard in which, though he kept two automobiles, he still drove about the country. He said nothing to his wife; it was her business to guess whether or not he would be home for dinner. She and Mahailey could have a good time scrubbing and sweeping all day, with no men around to bother them.

There were few days in the year when Wheeler did not drive off somewhere; to an auction sale, or a political convention, or a meeting of the Farmers' Telephone directors;—to see how his neighbours were getting on with their work, if there was nothing else to look after. He preferred his buckboard to a car because it was light, went easily over heavy or rough roads, and was so rickety that he never felt he must suggest his wife's accompanying him. Besides he could see the country better when he didn't have to keep his mind on the road. He had come to this part of Nebraska when the Indians and the buffalo were still about, remembered the grasshopper year and the big cyclone, had watched the farms emerge one by one from the great rolling page where once only the wind wrote its story. He had encouraged new settlers to take up homesteads, urged on courtships, lent young fellows the money to marry on, seen families grow and prosper; until he felt a little as if all this were his own enterprise. The changes, not only those the years made, but those the seasons made, were interesting to him.

People recognized Nat Wheeler and his cart a mile away. He sat massive and comfortable, weighing down one end of the slanting seat, his driving hand lying on his knee. Even his German neighbours, the Yoeders, who hated to stop work for a quarter of an hour on any account, were glad to see him coming. The merchants in the little towns about the county missed him if he didn't drop in once a week or so. He was active in politics; never ran for an office himself, but often took up the cause of a friend and conducted his campaign for him.

The French saying, "Joy of the street, sorrow of the home," was exemplified in Mr. Wheeler, though not at all in the French way. His own affairs were of secondary importance to him. In the early days he had homesteaded and bought and leased enough land to make him rich. Now he had only to rent it out to good farmers who liked to work—he didn't, and of that he made no secret. When he was at home, he usually sat upstairs in the living room, reading newspapers. He subscribed for a dozen or more—the list included a weekly devoted to scandal—and he was well informed about what was going on in the world. He had magnificent health, and illness in himself or in other people struck him as humorous. To be sure, he never suffered from anything more perplexing than toothache or boils, or an occasional bilious attack.

Wheeler gave liberally to churches and charities, was always ready to lend money or machinery to a neighbour who was short of anything. He liked to tease and shock diffident people, and had an inexhaustible supply of funny stories. Everybody marveled that he got on so well with his oldest son, Bayliss Wheeler. Not that Bayliss was exactly diffident, but he was a narrow gauge fellow, the sort of prudent young man one wouldn't expect Nat Wheeler to like.

Bayliss had a farm implement business in Frankfort, and though he was still under thirty he had made a very considerable financial success. Perhaps Wheeler was proud of his son's business acumen. At any rate, he drove to town to see Bayliss several times a week, went to sales and stock exhibits with him, and sat about his store for hours at a stretch, joking with the farmers who came in. Wheeler had been a heavy drinker in his day, and was still a heavy feeder. Bayliss was thin and dyspeptic, and a virulent Prohibitionist; he would have liked to regulate everybody's diet by his own feeble constitution. Even Mrs. Wheeler, who took the men God had apportioned her for granted, wondered how Bayliss and his father could go off to conventions together and have a good time, since their ideas of what made a good time were so different.

Once every few years, Mr. Wheeler bought a new suit and a dozen stiff shirts and went back to Maine to visit his brothers and sisters, who were very quiet, conventional people. But he was always glad to get home to his old clothes, his big farm, his buckboard, and Bayliss.

Mrs. Wheeler had come out from Vermont to be Principal of the High School, when Frankfort was a frontier town and Nat Wheeler was a prosperous bachelor. He must have fancied her for the same reason he liked his son Bayliss, because she was so different. There was this to be said for Nat Wheeler, that he liked every sort of human creature; he liked good people and honest people, and he liked rascals and hypocrites almost to the point of loving them. If he heard that a neighbour had played a sharp trick or done something particularly mean, he was sure to drive over to see the man at once, as if he hadn't hitherto appreciated him.

There was a large, loafing dignity about Claude's father. He liked to provoke others to uncouth laughter, but he never laughed immoderately himself. In telling stories about him, people often tried to imitate his smooth, senatorial voice, robust but never loud. Even when he was hilariously delighted by anything,—as when poor Mahailey, undressing in the dark on a summer night, sat down on the sticky fly-paper,—he was not boisterous. He was a jolly, easy-going father, indeed, for a boy who was not thin-skinned.

II.

Claude and his mules rattled into Frankfort just as the calliope went screaming down Main street at the head of the circus parade. Getting rid of his disagreeable freight and his uncongenial companions as soon as possible, he elbowed his way along the crowded sidewalk, looking for some of the neighbour boys. Mr. Wheeler was standing on the Farmer's Bank corner, towering a head above the throng, chaffing with a little hunchback who was setting up a shell-game. To avoid his father, Claude turned and went in to his brother's store. The two big show windows were full of country children, their mothers standing behind them to watch the parade. Bayliss was seated in the little glass cage where he did his writing and bookkeeping. He nodded at Claude from his desk.

"Hello," said Claude, bustling in as if he were in a great hurry. "Have you seen Ernest Havel? I thought I might find him in here."

Bayliss swung round in his swivel chair to return a plough catalogue to the shelf. "What would he be in here for? Better look for him in the saloon." Nobody could put meaner insinuations into a slow, dry remark than Bayliss.

Claude's cheeks flamed with anger. As he turned away, he noticed something unusual about his brother's face, but he wasn't going to give him the satisfaction of asking him how he had got a black eye. Ernest Havel was a Bohemian, and he usually drank a glass of beer when he came to town; but he was sober and thoughtful beyond the wont of young men. From Bayliss' drawl one might have supposed that the boy was a drunken loafer.

At that very moment Claude saw his friend on the other side of the street, following the wagon of trained dogs that brought up the rear of the procession. He ran across, through a crowd of shouting youngsters, and caught Ernest by the arm.

"Hello, where are you off to?"

"I'm going to eat my lunch before show-time. I left my wagon out by the pumping station, on the creek. What about you?"

"I've got no program. Can I go along?"

Ernest smiled. "I expect. I've got enough lunch for two."

"Yes, I know. You always have. I'll join you later."

Claude would have liked to take Ernest to the hotel for dinner. He had more than enough money in his pockets; and his father was a rich farmer. In the Wheeler family a new thrasher or a new automobile was ordered without a question, but it was considered extravagant to go to a hotel for dinner. If his father or Bayliss heard that he had been there-and Bayliss heard everything they would say he was putting on airs, and would get back at him. He tried to excuse his cowardice to himself by saying that he was dirty and smelled of the hides; but in his heart he knew that he did not ask Ernest to go to the hotel with him because he had been so brought up that it would be difficult for him to do this simple thing. He made some purchases at the fruit stand and the cigar counter, and then hurried out along the dusty road toward the pumping station. Ernest's wagon was standing under the shade of some willow trees, on a little sandy bottom half enclosed by a loop of the creek which curved like a horseshoe. Claude threw himself on the sand beside the stream and wiped the dust from his hot face. He felt he had now closed the door on his disagreeable morning.

Ernest produced his lunch basket.

"I got a couple bottles of beer cooling in the creek," he said. "I knew you wouldn't want to go in a saloon."

"Oh, forget it!" Claude muttered, ripping the cover off a jar of pickles. He was nineteen years old, and he was afraid to go into a saloon, and his friend knew he was afraid.

After lunch, Claude took out a handful of good cigars he had bought at the drugstore. Ernest, who couldn't afford cigars, was pleased. He lit one, and as he smoked he kept looking at it with an air of pride and turning it around between his fingers.

The horses stood with their heads over the wagon-box, munching their oats. The stream trickled by under the willow roots with a cool, persuasive sound. Claude and Ernest lay in the shade, their coats under their heads, talking very little. Occasionally a motor dashed along the road toward town, and a cloud of dust and a smell of gasoline blew in over the creek bottom; but for the most part the silence of the warm, lazy summer noon was undisturbed. Claude could usually forget his own vexations and chagrins when he was with Ernest. The Bohemian boy was never uncertain, was not pulled in two or three ways at once. He was simple and direct. He had a number of impersonal preoccupations; was interested in politics and history and in new inventions. Claude felt that his friend lived in an atmosphere of mental liberty to which he himself could never hope to attain. After he had talked with Ernest for awhile, the things that did not go right on the farm seemed less important. Claude's mother was almost as fond of Ernest as he was himself. When the two boys were going to high school, Ernest often came over in the evening to study with Claude, and while they worked at the long kitchen table Mrs. Wheeler brought her darning and sat near them, helping them with their Latin and algebra. Even old Mahailey was enlightened by their words of wisdom.

Mrs. Wheeler said she would never forget the night Ernest arrived from the Old Country. His brother, Joe Havel, had gone to Frankfort to meet him, and was to stop on the way home and leave some groceries for the Wheelers. The train from the east was late; it was ten o'clock that night when Mrs. Wheeler, waiting in the kitchen, heard Havel's wagon rumble across the little bridge over Lovely Creek. She opened the outside door, and presently Joe came in with a bucket of salt fish in one hand and a sack of flour on his shoulder. While he took the fish down to the cellar for her, another figure appeared in the doorway; a young boy, short, stooped, with a flat cap on his head and a great oilcloth valise, such as pedlars carry, strapped to his back. He had fallen asleep in the wagon, and on waking and finding his brother gone, he had supposed they were at home and scrambled for his pack. He stood in the doorway, blinking his eyes at the light, looking astonished but eager to do whatever was required of him. What if one of her own boys, Mrs. Wheeler thought.... She went up to him and put her arm around him, laughing a little and saying in her quiet voice, just as if he could understand her, "Why, you're only a little boy after all, aren't you?"

Ernest said afterwards that it was his first welcome to this country, though he had travelled so far, and had been pushed and hauled and shouted at for so many days, he had lost count of them. That night he and Claude only shook hands and looked at each other suspiciously, but ever since they had been good friends.

After their picnic the two boys went to the circus in a happy frame of mind. In the animal tent they met big Leonard Dawson, the oldest son of one of the Wheelers' near neighbours, and the three sat together for the performance. Leonard said he had come to town alone in his car; wouldn't Claude ride out with him? Claude was glad enough to turn the mules over to Ralph, who didn't mind the hired men as much as he did.

Leonard was a strapping brown fellow of twenty-five, with big hands and big feet, white teeth, and flashing eyes full of energy. He and his father and two brothers not only worked their own big farm, but rented a quarter section from Nat Wheeler. They were master farmers. If there was a dry summer and a failure, Leonard only laughed and stretched his long arms, and put in a bigger crop next year. Claude was always a little reserved with Leonard; he felt that the young man was rather contemptuous of the hap-hazard way in which things were done on the Wheeler place, and thought his going to college a waste of money. Leonard had not even gone through the Frankfort High School, and he was already a more successful man than Claude was ever likely to be. Leonard did think these things, but he was fond of Claude, all the same.

At sunset the car was speeding over a fine stretch of smooth road across the level country that lay between Frankfort and the rougher land along Lovely Creek. Leonard's attention was largely given up to admiring the faultless behaviour of his engine. Presently he chuckled to himself and turned to Claude.

"I wonder if you'd take it all right if I told you a joke on Bayliss?"

"I expect I would." Claude's tone was not at all eager.

"You saw Bayliss today? Notice anything queer about him, one eye a little off colour? Did he tell you how he got it?"

"No. I didn't ask him."

"Just as well. A lot of people did ask him, though, and he said he was hunting around his place for something in the dark and ran into a reaper. Well, I'm the reaper!"

Claude looked interested. "You mean to say Bayliss was in a fight?"

Leonard laughed. "Lord, no! Don't you know Bayliss? I went in there to pay a bill yesterday, and Susie Gray and another girl came in to sell tickets for the firemen's dinner. An advance man for this circus was hanging around, and he began talking a little smart,—nothing rough, but the way such fellows will. The girls handed it back to him, and sold him three tickets and shut him up. I couldn't see how Susie thought so quick what to say. The minute the girls went out Bayliss started knocking them; said all the country girls were getting too fresh and knew more than they ought to about managing sporty men and right there I reached out and handed him one. I hit harder than I meant to. I meant to slap him, not to give him a black eye. But you can't always regulate things, and I was hot all over. I waited for him to come back at me. I'm bigger than he is, and I wanted to give him satisfaction. Well, sir, he never moved a muscle! He stood there getting redder and redder, and his eyes watered. I don't say he cried, but his eyes watered. 'All right, Bayliss,' said I. 'Slow with your fists, if that's your principle; but slow with your tongue, too,—especially when the parties mentioned aren't present.'"

"Bayliss will never get over that," was Claude's only comment.

"He don't have to!" Leonard threw up his head. "I'm a good customer; he can like it or lump it, till the price of binding twine goes down!"

For the next few minutes the driver was occupied with trying to get up a long, rough hill on high gear. Sometimes he could make that hill, and sometimes he couldn't, and he was not able to account for the difference. After he pulled the second lever with some disgust and let the car amble on as she would, he noticed that his companion was disconcerted.

"I'll tell you what, Leonard," Claude spoke in a strained voice, "I think the fair thing for you to do is to get out here by the road and give me a chance."

Leonard swung his steering wheel savagely to pass a wagon on the down side of the hill. "What the devil are you talking about, boy?"

"You think you've got our measure all right, but you ought to give me a chance first."

Leonard looked down in amazement at his own big brown hands, lying on the wheel. "You mortal fool kid, what would I be telling you all this for, if I didn't know you were another breed of cats? I never thought you got on too well with Bayliss yourself."

"I don't, but I won't have you thinking you can slap the men in my family whenever you feel like it." Claude knew that his explanation sounded foolish, and his voice, in spite of all he could do, was weak and angry.

Young Leonard Dawson saw he had hurt the boy's feelings. "Lord, Claude, I know you're a fighter. Bayliss never was. I went to school with him."

The ride ended amicably, but Claude wouldn't let Leonard take him home. He jumped out of the car with a curt goodnight, and ran across the dusky fields toward the light that shone from the house on the hill. At the little bridge over the creek, he stopped to get his breath and to be sure that he was outwardly composed before he went in to see his mother.

"Ran against a reaper in the dark!" he muttered aloud, clenching his fist.

Listening to the deep singing of the frogs, and to the distant barking of the dogs up at the house, he grew calmer. Nevertheless, he wondered why it was that one had sometimes to feel responsible for the behaviour of people whose natures were wholly antipathetic to one's own.

III.

THE CIRCUS WAS ON SATURDAY. The next morning Claude was standing at his dresser, shaving. His beard was already strong, a shade darker than his hair and not so red as his skin. His eyebrows and long lashes were a pale corn-colour—made his blue eyes seem lighter than they were, and, he thought, gave a look of shyness and weakness to the upper part of his face. He was exactly the sort of looking boy he didn't want to be. He especially hated his head,—so big that he had trouble in buying his hats, and uncompromisingly square in shape; a perfect block-head. His name was another source of humiliation. Claude: it was a "chump" name, like Elmer and Roy; a hayseed name trying to be fine. In country schools there was always a red-headed, warty-handed, runny-nosed little boy who was called Claude. His good physique he took for granted; smooth, muscular arms and legs, and strong shoulders, a farmer boy might be supposed to have. Unfortunately he had none of his father's physical repose, and his strength often asserted itself inharmoniously. The storms that went on in his mind sometimes made him rise, or sit down, or lift something, more violently than there was any apparent reason for his doing.

The household slept late on Sunday morning; even Mahailey did not get up until seven. The general signal for breakfast was the smell of doughnuts frying. This morning Ralph rolled out of bed at the last minute and callously put on his clean underwear without taking a bath. This cost him not one regret, though he took time to polish his new ox-blood shoes tenderly with a pocket handkerchief. He reached the table when all the others were half through breakfast, and made his peace by genially asking his mother if she didn't want him to drive her to church in the car.

"I'd like to go if I can get the work done in time," she said, doubtfully glancing at the clock.

"Can't Mahailey tend to things for you this morning?"

Mrs. Wheeler hesitated. "Everything but the separator, she can. But she can't fit all the parts together. It's a good deal of work, you know."

"Now, Mother," said Ralph good-humouredly, as he emptied the syrup pitcher over his cakes, "you're prejudiced. Nobody ever thinks of skimming milk now-a-days. Every up-to-date farmer uses a separator."

Mrs. Wheeler's pale eyes twinkled. "Mahailey and I will never be quite up-to-date, Ralph. We're old-fashioned, and I don't know but you'd better let us be. I could see the advantage of a separator if we milked half-a-dozen cows. It's a very ingenious machine. But it's a great deal more work to scald it and fit it together than it was to take care of the milk in the old way."

"It won't be when you get used to it," Ralph assured her. He was the chief mechanic of the Wheeler farm, and when the farm implements and the automobiles did not give him enough to do, he went to town and bought machines for the house. As soon as Mahailey got used to a washing-machine or a churn, Ralph, to keep up with the bristling march of invention, brought home a still newer one. The mechanical dish-washer she had never been able to use, and patent flat-irons and oil-stoves drove her wild.

Claude told his mother to go upstairs and dress; he would scald the separator while Ralph got the car ready. He was still working at it when his brother came in from the garage to wash his hands.

"You really oughtn't to load mother up with things like this, Ralph," he exclaimed fretfully. "Did you ever try washing this damned thing yourself?"

"Of course I have. If Mrs. Dawson can manage it, I should think mother could."

"Mrs. Dawson is a younger woman. Anyhow, there's no point in trying to make machinists of Mahailey and mother."

Ralph lifted his eyebrows to excuse Claude's bluntness. "See here," he said persuasively, "don't you go encouraging her into thinking she can't change her ways. Mother's entitled to all the labour-saving devices we can get her."

Claude rattled the thirty-odd graduated metal funnels which he was trying to fit together in their proper sequence. "Well, if this is labour-saving"

The younger boy giggled and ran upstairs for his panama hat. He never quarrelled. Mrs. Wheeler sometimes said it was wonderful, how much Ralph would take from Claude.

After Ralph and his mother had gone off in the car, Mr. Wheeler drove to see his German neighbour, Gus Yoeder, who had just bought a blooded bull. Dan and Jerry were pitching horseshoes down behind the barn. Claude told Mahailey he was going to the cellar to put up the swinging shelf she had been wanting, so that the rats couldn't get at her vegetables.

"Thank you, Mr. Claude. I don't know what does make the rats so bad. The cats catches one most every day, too."

"I guess they come up from the barn. I've got a nice wide board down at the garage for your shelf." The cellar was cemented, cool and dry, with deep closets for canned fruit and flour and groceries, bins for coal and cobs, and a dark-room full of photographer's apparatus. Claude took his place at the carpenter's bench under one of the square windows. Mysterious objects stood about him in the grey twilight; electric batteries, old bicycles and typewriters, a machine for making cement fence-posts, a vulcanizer, a stereopticon with a broken lens. The mechanical toys Ralph could not operate successfully, as well as those he had got tired of, were stored away here. If they were left in the barn, Mr. Wheeler saw them too often, and sometimes, when they happened to be in his way, he made sarcastic comments. Claude had begged his mother to let him pile this lumber into a wagon and dump it into some washout hole along the creek; but Mrs. Wheeler said he must not think of such a thing; it would hurt Ralph's feelings. Nearly every time Claude went into the cellar, he made a desperate resolve to clear the place out some day, reflecting bitterly that the money this wreckage cost would have put a boy through college decently.

While Claude was planing off the board he meant to suspend from the joists, Mahailey left her work and came down to watch him. She made some pretence of hunting for pickled onions, then seated herself upon a cracker box; close at hand there was a plush "spring-rocker" with one arm gone, but it wouldn't have been her idea of good manners to sit there.

Her eyes had a kind of sleepy contentment in them as she followed Claude's motions. She watched him as if he were a baby playing. Her hands lay comfortably in her lap.

"Mr. Ernest ain't been over for a long time. He ain't mad about nothin', is he?"

"Oh, no! He's awful busy this summer. I saw him in town yesterday. We went to the circus together."

Mahailey smiled and nodded. "That's nice. I'm glad for you two boys to have a good time. Mr. Ernest's a nice boy; I always liked him first rate. He's a little feller, though. He ain't big like you, is he? I guess he ain't as tall as Mr. Ralph, even."

"Not quite," said Claude between strokes. "He's strong, though, and gets through a lot of work."

"Oh, I know! I know he is. I know he works hard. All them foreigners works hard, don't they, Mr. Claude? I reckon he liked the circus. Maybe they don't have circuses like our'n, over where he come from."

Claude began to tell her about the clown elephant and the trained dogs, and she sat listening to him with her pleased, foolish smile; there was something wise and far-seeing about her smile, too.

Mahailey had come to them long ago, when Claude was only a few months old. She had been brought West by a shiftless Virginia family which went to pieces and scattered under the rigours of pioneer farm-life. When the mother of the family died, there was nowhere for Mahailey to go, and Mrs. Wheeler took her in. Mahailey had no one to take care of her, and Mrs. Wheeler had no one to help her with the work; it had turned out very well.

Mahailey had had a hard life in her young days, married to a savage mountaineer who often abused her and never provided for her. She could remember times when she sat in the cabin, beside an empty meal-barrel and a cold iron pot, waiting for "him" to bring home a squirrel he had shot or a chicken he had stolen. Too often he brought nothing but a jug of mountain whiskey and a pair of brutal fists. She thought herself well off now, never to have to beg for food or go off into the woods to gather firing, to be sure of a warm bed and shoes and decent clothes. Mahailey was one of eighteen children; most of them grew up lawless or half-witted, and two of her brothers, like her husband, ended their lives in jail. She had never been sent to school, and could not read or write. Claude, when he was a little boy, tried to teach her to read, but what she learned one night she had forgotten by the next. She could count, and tell the time of day by the clock, and she was very proud of knowing the alphabet and of being able to spell out letters on the flour sacks and coffee packages. "That's a big A." she would murmur, "and that there's a little a."

Mahailey was shrewd in her estimate of people, and Claude thought her judgment sound in a good many things. He knew she sensed all the shades of personal feeling, the accords and antipathies in the household, as keenly as he did, and he would have hated to lose her good opinion. She consulted him in all her little difficulties. If the leg of the kitchen table got wobbly, she knew he would put in new screws for her. When she broke a handle off her rolling pin, he put on another, and he fitted a haft to her favourite butcher-knife after every one else said it must be thrown away. These objects, after they had been mended, acquired a new value in her eyes, and she liked to work with them. When Claude helped her lift or carry anything, he never avoided touching her, this she felt deeply. She suspected that Ralph was a little ashamed of her, and would prefer to have some brisk young thing about the kitchen.

On days like this, when other people were not about, Mahailey liked to talk to Claude about the things they did together when he was little; the Sundays when they used to wander along the creek, hunting for wild grapes and watching the red squirrels; or trailed across the high pastures to a wild-plum thicket at the north end of the Wheeler farm. Claude could remember warm spring days when the plum bushes were all in blossom and Mahailey used to lie down under them and sing to herself, as if the honey-heavy sweetness made her drowsy; songs without words, for the most part, though he recalled one mountain dirge which said over and over, "And they laid Jesse James in his grave."

IV.

THE TIME WAS APPROACHING for Claude to go back to the struggling denominational college on the outskirts of the state capital, where he had already spent two dreary and unprofitable winters.

"Mother," he said one morning when he had an opportunity to speak to her alone, "I wish you would let me quit the Temple, and go to the State University."

She looked up from the mass of dough she was kneading.

"But why, Claude?"

"Well, I could learn more, for one thing. The professors at the Temple aren't much good. Most of them are just preachers who couldn't make a living at preaching."

The look of pain that always disarmed Claude came instantly into his mother's face. "Son, don't say such things. I can't believe but teachers are more interested in their students when they are concerned for their spiritual development, as well as the mental. Brother Weldon said many of the professors at the State University are not Christian men; they even boast of it, in some cases."

"Oh, I guess most of them are good men, all right; at any rate they know their subjects. These little pin-headed preachers like Weldon do a lot of harm, running about the country talking. He's sent around to pull in students for his own school. If he didn't get them he'd lose his job. I wish he'd never got me. Most of the fellows who flunk out at the State come to us, just as he did."

"But how can there be any serious study where they give so much time to athletics and frivolity? They pay their football coach a larger salary than their President. And those fraternity houses are places where boys learn all sorts of evil. I've heard that dreadful things go on in them sometimes. Besides, it would take more money, and you couldn't live as cheaply as you do at the Chapins'."

Claude made no reply. He stood before her frowning and pulling at a calloused spot on the inside of his palm. Mrs. Wheeler looked at him wistfully. "I'm sure you must be able to study better in a quiet, serious atmosphere," she said.

He sighed and turned away. If his mother had been the least bit unctuous, like Brother Weldon, he could have told her many enlightening facts. But she was so trusting and childlike, so faithful by nature and so ignorant of life as he knew it, that it was hopeless to argue with her. He could shock her and make her fear the world even more than she did, but he could never make her understand.

His mother was old-fashioned. She thought dancing and card-playing dangerous pastimes—only rough people did such things when she was a girl in Vermont—and "worldliness" only another word for wickedness. According to her conception of education, one should learn, not think; and above all, one must not enquire. The history of the human race, as it lay behind one, was already explained; and so was its destiny, which lay before. The mind should remain obediently within the theological concept of history.

Nat Wheeler didn't care where his son went to school, but he, too, took it for granted that the religious institution was cheaper than the State University; and that because the students there looked shabbier they were less likely to become too knowing, and to be offensively intelligent at home. However, he referred the matter to Bayliss one day when he was in town.

"Claude's got some notion he wants to go to the State University this winter."

Bayliss at once assumed that wise, better-be-prepared-for-the-worst expression which had made him seem shrewd and seasoned from boyhood. "I don't see any point in changing unless he's got good reasons."

"Well, he thinks that bunch of parsons at the Temple don't make first-rate teachers."

"I expect they can teach Claude quite a bit yet. If he gets in with that fast football crowd at the State, there'll be no holding him." For some reason Bayliss detested football. "This athletic business is a good deal over-done. If Claude wants exercise, he might put in the fall wheat."

That night Mr. Wheeler brought the subject up at supper, questioned Claude, and tried to get at the cause of his discontent. His manner was jocular, as usual, and Claude hated any public discussion of his personal affairs. He was afraid of his father's humour when it got too near him.

Claude might have enjoyed the large and somewhat gross cartoons with which Mr. Wheeler enlivened daily life, had they been of any other authorship. But he unreasonably wanted his father to be the most dignified, as he was certainly the handsomest and most intelligent, man in the community. Moreover, Claude couldn't bear ridicule very well. He squirmed before he was hit; saw it coming, invited it. Mr. Wheeler had observed this trait in him when he was a little chap, called it false pride, and often purposely outraged his feelings to harden him, as he had hardened Claude's mother, who was afraid of everything but schoolbooks and prayer-meetings when he first married her. She was still more or less bewildered, but she had long ago got over any fear of him and any dread of living with him. She accepted everything about her husband as part of his rugged masculinity, and of that she was proud, in her quiet way.

Claude had never quite forgiven his father for some of his practical jokes. One warm spring day, when he was a boisterous little boy of five, playing in and out of the house, he heard his mother entreating Mr. Wheeler to go down to the orchard and pick the cherries from a tree that hung loaded. Claude remembered that she persisted rather complainingly, saying that the cherries were too high for her to reach, and that even if she had a ladder it would hurt her back. Mr. Wheeler was always annoyed if his wife referred to any physical weakness, especially if she complained about her back. He got up and went out. After a while he returned. "All right now, Evangeline," he called cheerily as he passed through the kitchen. "Cherries won't give you any trouble. You and Claude can run along and pick 'em as easy as can be."

Mrs. Wheeler trustfully put on her sunbonnet, gave Claude a little pail and took a big one herself, and they went down the pasture hill to the orchard, fenced in on the low land by the creek. The ground had been ploughed that spring to make it hold moisture, and Claude was running happily along in one of the furrows, when he looked up and beheld a sight he could never forget. The beautiful, round-topped cherry tree, full of green leaves and red fruit,—his father had sawed it through! It lay on the ground beside its bleeding stump. With one scream Claude became a little demon. He threw away his tin pail, jumped about howling and kicking the loose earth with his copper-toed shoes, until his mother was much more concerned for him than for the tree.

"Son, son," she cried, "it's your father's tree. He has a perfect right to cut it down if he wants to. He's often said the trees were too thick in here. Maybe it will be better for the others."

"'Tain't so! He's a damn fool, damn fool!" Claude bellowed, still hopping and kicking, almost choking with rage and hate.

His mother dropped on her knees beside him. "Claude, stop! I'd rather have the whole orchard cut down than hear you say such things."

After she got him quieted they picked the cherries and went back to the house. Claude had promised her that he would say nothing, but his father must have noticed the little boy's angry eyes fixed upon him all through dinner, and his expression of scorn. Even then his flexible lips were only too well adapted to hold the picture of that feeling. For days afterward Claude went down to the orchard and watched the tree grow sicker, wilt and wither away. God would surely punish a man who could do that, he thought.

A violent temper and physical restlessness were the most conspicuous things about Claude when he was a little boy. Ralph was docile, and had a precocious sagacity for keeping out of trouble. Quiet in manner, he was fertile in devising mischief, and easily persuaded his older brother, who was always looking for something to do, to execute his plans. It was usually Claude who was caught red-handed. Sitting mild and contemplative on his quilt on the floor, Ralph would whisper to Claude that it might be amusing to climb up and take the clock from the shelf, or to operate the sewing-machine. When they were older, and played out of doors, he had only to insinuate that Claude was afraid, to make him try a frosted axe with his tongue, or jump from the shed roof.

The usual hardships of country boyhood were not enough for Claude; he imposed physical tests and penances upon himself. Whenever he burned his finger, he followed Mahailey's advice and held his hand close to the stove to "draw out the fire." One year he went to school all winter in his jacket, to make himself tough. His mother would button him up in his overcoat and put his dinner-pail in his hand and start him off. As soon as he got out of sight of the house, he pulled off his coat, rolled it under his arm, and scudded along the edge of the frozen fields, arriving at the frame schoolhouse panting and shivering, but very well pleased with himself.

V.

CLAUDE WAITED for his elders to change their mind about where he should go to school; but no one seemed much concerned, not even his mother.

Two years ago, the young man whom Mrs. Wheeler called "Brother Weldon" had come out from Lincoln, preaching in little towns and country churches, and recruiting students for the institution at which he taught in the winter. He had convinced Mrs. Wheeler that his college was the safest possible place for a boy who was leaving home for the first time.

Claude's mother was not discriminating about preachers. She believed them all chosen and sanctified, and was never happier than when she had one in the house to cook for and wait upon. She made young Mr. Weldon so comfortable that he remained under her roof for several weeks, occupying the spare room, where he spent the mornings in study and meditation. He appeared regularly at mealtime to ask a blessing upon the food and to sit with devout, downcast eyes while the chicken was being dismembered. His top-shaped head hung a little to one side, the thin hair was parted precisely over his high forehead and brushed in little ripples. He was soft spoken and apologetic in manner and took up as little room as possible. His meekness amused Mr. Wheeler, who liked to ply him with food and never failed to ask him gravely "what part of the chicken he would prefer," in order to hear him murmur, "A little of the white meat, if you please," while he drew his elbows close, as if he were adroitly sliding over a dangerous place. In the afternoon Brother Weldon usually put on a fresh lawn necktie and a hard, glistening straw hat which left a red streak across his forehead, tucked his Bible under his arm, and went out to make calls. If he went far, Ralph took him in the automobile.

Claude disliked this young man from the moment he first met him, and could scarcely answer him civilly. Mrs. Wheeler, always absent-minded, and now absorbed in her cherishing care of the visitor, did not notice Claude's scornful silences until Mahailey, whom such things never escaped, whispered to her over the stove one day: "Mr. Claude, he don't like the preacher. He just ain't got no use fur him, but don't you let on."

As a result of Brother Weldon's sojourn at the farm, Claude was sent to the Temple College. Claude had come to believe that the things and people he most disliked were the ones that were to shape his destiny.

When the second week of September came round, he threw a few clothes and books into his trunk and said good-bye to his mother and Mahailey. Ralph took him into Frankfort to catch the train for Lincoln. After settling himself in the dirty day-coach, Claude fell to meditating upon his prospects. There was a Pullman car on the train, but to take a Pullman for a daylight journey was one of the things a Wheeler did not do.

Claude knew that he was going back to the wrong school, that he was wasting both time and money. He sneered at himself for his lack of spirit. If he had to do with strangers, he told himself, he could take up his case and fight for it. He could not assert himself against his father or mother, but he could be bold enough with the rest of the world. Yet, if this were true, why did he continue to live with the tiresome Chapins? The Chapin household consisted of a brother and sister. Edward Chapin was a man of twenty-six, with an old, wasted face,—and he was still going to school, studying for the ministry. His sister Annabelle kept house for him; that is to say, she did whatever housework was done. The brother supported himself and his sister by getting odd jobs from churches and religious societies; he "supplied" the pulpit when a minister was ill, did secretarial work for the college and the Young Men's Christian Association. Claude's weekly payment for room and board, though a small sum, was very necessary to their comfort.

Chapin had been going to the Temple College for four years, and it would probably take him two years more to complete the course. He conned his book on trolley-cars, or while he waited by the track on windy corners, and studied far into the night. His natural stupidity must have been something quite out of the ordinary; after years of reverential study, he could not read the Greek Testament without a lexicon and grammar at his elbow. He gave a great deal of time to the practice of elocution and oratory. At certain hours their frail domicile—it had been thinly built for the academic poor and sat upon concrete blocks in lieu of a foundation—re-echoed with his hoarse, overstrained voice, declaiming his own orations or those of Wendell Phillips.

Annabelle Chapin was one of Claude's classmates. She was not as dull as her brother; she could learn a conjugation and recognize the forms when she met with them again. But she was a gushing, silly girl, who found almost everything in their grubby life too good to be true; and she was, unfortunately, sentimental about Claude. Annabelle chanted her lessons over and over to herself while she cooked and scrubbed. She was one of those people who can make the finest things seem tame and flat merely by alluding to them. Last winter she had recited the odes of Horace about the house—it was exactly her notion of the student-like thing to do—until Claude feared he would always associate that poet with the heaviness of hurriedly prepared luncheons.

Mrs. Wheeler liked to feel that Claude was assisting this worthy pair in their struggle for an education; but he had long ago decided that since neither of the Chapins got anything out of their efforts but a kind of messy inefficiency, the struggle might better have been relinquished in the beginning. He took care of his own room; kept it bare and habitable, free from Annabelle's attentions and decorations. But the flimsy pretences of light-housekeeping were very distasteful to him. He was born with a love of order, just as he was born with red hair. It was a personal attribute.

The boy felt bitterly about the way in which he had been brought up, and about his hair and his freckles and his awkwardness. When he went to the theatre in Lincoln, he took a seat in the gallery, because he knew that he looked like a green country boy. His clothes were never right. He bought collars that were too high and neckties that were too bright, and hid them away in his trunk. His one experiment with a tailor was unsuccessful. The tailor saw at once that his stammering client didn't know what he wanted, so he persuaded him that as the season was spring he needed light checked trousers and a blue serge coat and vest. When Claude wore his new clothes to St. Paul's church on Sunday morning, the eyes of every one he met followed his smart legs down the street. For the next week he observed the legs of old men and young, and decided there wasn't another pair of checked pants in Lincoln. He hung his new clothes up in his closet and never put them on again, though Annabelle Chapin watched for them wistfully. Nevertheless, Claude thought he could recognize a well-dressed man when he saw one. He even thought he could recognize a well-dressed woman. If an attractive woman got into the street car when he was on his way to or from Temple Place, he was distracted between the desire to look at her and the wish to seem indifferent.

Claude is on his way back to Lincoln, with a fairly liberal allowance which does not contribute much to his comfort or pleasure. He has no friends or instructors whom he can regard with admiration, though the need to admire is just now uppermost in his nature. He is convinced that the people who might mean something to him will always misjudge him and pass him by. He is not so much afraid of loneliness as he is of accepting cheap substitutes; of making excuses to himself for a teacher who flatters him, of waking up some morning to find himself admiring a girl merely because she is accessible. He has a dread of easy compromises, and he is terribly afraid of being fooled.

VI.

THREE MONTHS LATER, on a grey December day, Claude was seated in the passenger coach of an accommodation freight train, going home for the holidays. He had a pile of books on the seat beside him and was reading, when the train stopped with a jerk that sent the volumes tumbling to the floor. He picked them up and looked at his watch. It was noon. The freight would lie here for an hour or more, until the east-bound passenger went by. Claude left the car and walked slowly up the platform toward the station. A bundle of little spruce trees had been flung off near the freight office, and sent a smell of Christmas into the cold air. A few drays stood about, the horses blanketed. The steam from the locomotive made a spreading, deep-violet stain as it curled up against the grey sky.

Claude went into a restaurant across the street and ordered an oyster stew. The proprietress, a plump little German woman with a frizzed bang, always remembered him from trip to trip. While he was eating his oysters she told him that she had just finished roasting a chicken with sweet potatoes, and if he liked he could have the first brown cut off the breast before the train-men came in for dinner. Asking her to bring it along, he waited, sitting on a stool, his boots on the lead-pipe foot-rest, his elbows on the shiny brown counter, staring at a pyramid of tough looking bun-sandwiches under a glass globe.

"I been lookin' for you every day," said Mrs. Voigt when she brought his plate. "I put plenty good gravy on dem sweet pertaters, ja."

"Thank you. You must be popular with your boarders."

She giggled. "Ja, all de train men is friends mit me. Sometimes dey bring me a liddle Schweizerkase from one of dem big saloons in Omaha what de Cherman beobles batronize. I ain't got no boys mein own self, so I got to fix up liddle tings for dem boys, eh?"

She stood nursing her stumpy hands under her apron, watching every mouthful he ate so eagerly that she might have been tasting it herself. The train crew trooped in, shouting to her and asking what there was for dinner, and she ran about like an excited little hen, chuckling and cackling. Claude wondered whether working-men were as nice as that to old women the world over. He didn't believe so. He liked to think that such geniality was common only in what he broadly called "the West." He bought a big cigar, and strolled up and down the platform, enjoying the fresh air until the passenger whistled in.

After his freight train got under steam he did not open his books again, but sat looking out at the grey homesteads as they unrolled before him, with their stripped, dry cornfields, and the great ploughed stretches where the winter wheat was asleep. A starry sprinkling of snow lay like hoar-frost along the crumbly ridges between the furrows.

Claude believed he knew almost every farm between Frankfort and Lincoln, he had made the journey so often, on fast trains and slow. He went home for all the holidays, and had been again and again called back on various pretexts; when his mother was sick, when Ralph overturned the car and broke his shoulder, when his father was kicked by a vicious stallion. It was not a Wheeler custom to employ a nurse; if any one in the household was ill, it was understood that some member of the family would act in that capacity.

Claude was reflecting upon the fact that he had never gone home before in such good spirits. Two fortunate things had happened to him since he went over this road three months ago.

As soon as he reached Lincoln in September, he had matriculated at the State University for special work in European History. The year before he had heard the head of the department lecture for some charity, and resolved that even if he were not allowed to change his college, he would manage to study under that man. The course Claude selected was one upon which a student could put as much time as he chose. It was based upon the reading of historical sources, and the Professor was notoriously greedy for full notebooks. Claude's were of the fullest. He worked early and late at the University Library, often got his supper in town and went back to read until closing hour. For the first time he was studying a subject which seemed to him vital, which had to do with events and ideas, instead of with lexicons and grammars. How often he had wished for Ernest during the lectures! He could see Ernest drinking them up, agreeing or dissenting in his independent way. The class was very large, and the Professor spoke without notes,—he talked rapidly, as if he were addressing his equals, with none of the coaxing persuasiveness to which Temple students were accustomed. His lectures were condensed like a legal brief, but there was a kind of dry fervour in his voice, and when he occasionally interrupted his exposition with purely personal comment, it seemed valuable and important.

Claude usually came out from these lectures with the feeling that the world was full of stimulating things, and that one was fortunate to be alive and to be able to find out about them. His reading that autumn actually made the future look brighter to him; seemed to promise him something. One of his chief difficulties had always been that he could not make himself believe in the importance of making money or spending it. If that were all, then life was not worth the trouble.

The second good thing that had befallen him was that he had got to know some people he liked. This came about accidentally, after a football game between the Temple eleven and the State University team—merely a practice game for the latter. Claude was playing half-back with the Temple. Toward the close of the first quarter, he followed his interference safely around the right end, dodged a tackle which threatened to end the play, and broke loose for a ninety yard run down the field for a touchdown. He brought his eleven off with a good showing. The State men congratulated him warmly, and their coach went so far as to hint that if he ever wanted to make a change, there would be a place for him on the University team.

Claude had a proud moment, but even while Coach Ballinger was talking to him, the Temple students rushed howling from the grandstand, and Annabelle Chapin, ridiculous in a sport suit of her own construction, bedecked with the Temple colours and blowing a child's horn, positively threw herself upon his neck. He disengaged himself, not very gently, and stalked grimly away to the dressing shed.... What was the use, if you were always with the wrong crowd?

Julius Erlich, who played quarter on the State team, took him aside and said affably: "Come home to supper with me tonight, Wheeler, and meet my mother. Come along with us and dress in the Armory. You have your clothes in your suitcase, haven't you?"

"They're hardly clothes to go visiting in," Claude replied doubtfully.

"Oh, that doesn't matter! We're all boys at home. Mother wouldn't mind if you came in your track things."

Claude consented before he had time to frighten himself by imagining difficulties. The Erlich boy often sat next him in the history class, and they had several times talked together. Hitherto Claude had felt that he "couldn't make Erlich out," but this afternoon, while they dressed after their shower, they became good friends, all in a few minutes. Claude was perhaps less tied-up in mind and body than usual. He was so astonished at finding himself on easy, confidential terms with Erlich that he scarcely gave a thought to his second-day shirt and his collar with a broken edge,—wretched economies he had been trained to observe.

They had not walked more than two blocks from the Armory when Julius turned in at a rambling wooden house with an unfenced, terraced lawn. He led Claude around to the wing, and through a glass door into a big room that was all windows on three sides, above the wainscoting. The room was full of boys and young men, seated on long divans or perched on the arms of easy chairs, and they were all talking at once. On one of the couches a young man in a smoking jacket lay reading as composedly as if he were alone.

"Five of these are my brothers," said his host, "and the rest are friends."

The company recognized Claude and included him in their talk about the game. When the visitors had gone, Julius introduced his brothers. They were all nice boys, Claude thought, and had easy, agreeable manners. The three older ones were in business, but they too had been to the game that afternoon. Claude had never before seen brothers who were so outspoken and frank with one another. To him they were very cordial; the one who was lying down came forward to shake hands, keeping the place in his book with his finger.

On a table in the middle of the room were pipes and boxes of tobacco, cigars in a glass jar, and a big Chinese bowl full of cigarettes. This provisionment seemed the more remarkable to Claude because at home he had to smoke in the cowshed. The number of books astonished him almost as much; the wainscoting all around the room was built up in open bookcases, stuffed with volumes fat and thin, and they all looked interesting and hard-used. One of the brothers had been to a party the night before, and on coming home had put his dress-tie about the neck of a little plaster bust of Byron that stood on the mantel. This head, with the tie at a rakish angle, drew Claude's attention more than anything else in the room, and for some reason instantly made him wish he lived there.

Julius brought in his mother, and when they went to supper Claude was seated beside her at one end of the long table. Mrs. Erlich seemed to him very young to be the head of such a family. Her hair was still brown, and she wore it drawn over her ears and twisted in two little horns, like the ladies in old daguerreotypes. Her face, too, suggested a daguerreotype; there was something old-fashioned and picturesque about it. Her skin had the soft whiteness of white flowers that have been drenched by rain. She talked with quick gestures, and her decided little nod was quaint and very personal. Her hazel-coloured eyes peered expectantly over her nose-glasses, always watching to see things turn out wonderfully well; always looking for some good German fairy in the cupboard or the cake-box, or in the steaming vapor of wash-day.

The boys were discussing an engagement that had just been announced, and Mrs. Erlich began to tell Claude a long story about how this brilliant young man had come to Lincoln and met this beautiful young girl, who was already engaged to a cold and academic youth, and how after many heart-burnings the beautiful girl had broken with the wrong man and become betrothed to the right one, and now they were so happy, and every one, she asked Claude to believe, was equally happy! In the middle of her narrative Julius reminded her smilingly that since Claude didn't know these people, he would hardly be interested in their romance, but she merely looked at him over her nose-glasses and said, "And is that so, Herr Julius!" One could see that she was a match for them.

The conversation went racing from one thing to another. The brothers began to argue hotly about a new girl who was visiting in town; whether she was pretty, how pretty she was, whether she was naive. To Claude this was like talk in a play. He had never heard a living person discussed and analysed thus before. He had never heard a family talk so much, or with anything like so much zest. Here there was none of the poisonous reticence he had always associated with family gatherings, nor the awkwardness of people sitting with their hands in their lap, facing each other, each one guarding his secret or his suspicion, while he hunted for a safe subject to talk about. Their fertility of phrase, too, astonished him; how could people find so much to say about one girl? To be sure, a good deal of it sounded far-fetched to him, but he sadly admitted that in such matters he was no judge. When they went back to the living room Julius began to pick out airs on his guitar, and the bearded brother sat down to read. Otto, the youngest, seeing a group of students passing the house, ran out on to the lawn and called them in,—two boys, and a girl with red cheeks and a fur stole. Claude had made for a corner, and was perfectly content to be an on-looker, but Mrs. Erlich soon came and seated herself beside him. When the doors into the parlour were opened, she noticed his eyes straying to an engraving of Napoleon which hung over the piano, and made him go and look at it. She told him it was a rare engraving, and she showed him a portrait of her great-grandfather, who was an officer in Napoleon's army. To explain how this came about was a long story.

As she talked to Claude, Mrs. Erlich discovered that his eyes were not really pale, but only looked so because of his light lashes. They could say a great deal when they looked squarely into hers, and she liked what they said. She soon found out that he was discontented; how he hated the Temple school, and why his mother wished him to go there.

When the three who had been called in from the sidewalk took their leave, Claude rose also. They were evidently familiars of the house, and their careless exit, with a gay "Good-night, everybody!" gave him no practical suggestion as to what he ought to say or how he was to get out. Julius made things more difficult by telling him to sit down, as it wasn't time to go yet. But Mrs. Erlich said it was time; he would have a long ride out to Temple Place.

It was really very easy. She walked to the door with him and gave him his hat, patting his arm in a final way. "You will come often to see us. We are going to be friends." Her forehead, with its neat curtains of brown hair, came something below Claude's chin, and she peered up at him with that quaintly hopeful expression, as if—as if even he might turn out wonderfully well! Certainly, nobody had ever looked at him like that before.

"It's been lovely," he murmured to her, quite without embarrassment, and in happy unconsciousness he turned the knob and passed out through the glass door.

While the freight train was puffing slowly across the winter country, leaving a black trail suspended in the still air, Claude went over that experience minutely in his mind, as if he feared to lose something of it on approaching home. He could remember exactly how Mrs. Erlich and the boys had looked to him on that first night, could repeat almost word for word the conversation which had been so novel to him. Then he had supposed the Erlichs were rich people, but he found out afterwards that they were poor. The father was dead, and all the boys had to work, even those who were still in school. They merely knew how to live, he discovered, and spent their money on themselves, instead of on machines to do the work and machines to entertain people. Machines, Claude decided, could not make pleasure, whatever else they could do. They could not make agreeable people, either. In so far as he could see, the latter were made by judicious indulgence in almost everything he had been taught to shun.

Since that first visit, he had gone to the Erlichs', not as often as he wished, certainly, but as often as he dared. Some of the University boys seemed to drop in there whenever they felt like it, were almost members of the family; but they were better looking than he, and better company. To be sure, long Baumgartner was an intimate of the house, and he was a gawky boy with big red hands and patched shoes; but he could at least speak German to the mother, and he played the piano, and seemed to know a great deal about music.

Claude didn't wish to be a bore. Sometimes in the evening, when he left the Library to smoke a cigar, he walked slowly past the Erlichs' house, looking at the lighted windows of the sitting-room and wondering what was going on inside. Before he went there to call, he racked his brain for things to talk about. If there had been a football game, or a good play at the theatre, that helped, of course.

Almost without realizing what he was doing, he tried to think things out and to justify his opinions to himself, so that he would have something to say when the Erlich boys questioned him. He had grown up with the conviction that it was beneath his dignity to explain himself, just as it was to dress carefully, or to be caught taking pains about anything. Ernest was the only person he knew who tried to state clearly just why he believed this or that; and people at home thought him very conceited and foreign. It wasn't American to explain yourself; you didn't have to! On the farm you said you would or you wouldn't; that Roosevelt was all right, or that he was crazy. You weren't supposed to say more unless you were a stump speaker,—if you tried to say more, it was because you liked to hear yourself talk. Since you never said anything, you didn't form the habit of thinking. If you got too much bored, you went to town and bought something new.

But all the people he met at the Erlichs' talked. If they asked him about a play or a book and he said it was "no good," they at once demanded why. The Erlichs thought him a clam, but Claude sometimes thought himself amazing. Could it really be he, who was airing his opinions in this indelicate manner? He caught himself using words that had never crossed his lips before, that in his mind were associated only with the printed page. When he suddenly realized that he was using a word for the first time, and probably mispronouncing it, he would become as much confused as if he were trying to pass a lead dollar, would blush and stammer and let some one finish his sentence for him.

Claude couldn't resist occasionally dropping in at the Erlichs' in the afternoon; then the boys were away, and he could have Mrs. Erlich to himself for half-an-hour. When she talked to him she taught him so much about life. He loved to hear her sing sentimental German songs as she worked; "Spinn, spinn, du Tochter mein." He didn't know why, but he simply adored it! Every time he went away from her he felt happy and full of kindness, and thought about beech woods and walled towns, or about Carl Schurz and the Romantic revolution.

He had been to see Mrs. Erlich just before starting home for the holidays, and found her making German Christmas cakes. She took him into the kitchen and explained the almost holy traditions that governed this complicated cookery. Her excitement and seriousness as she beat and stirred were very pretty, Claude thought. She told off on her fingers the many ingredients, but he believed there were things she did not name: the fragrance of old friendships, the glow of early memories, belief in wonder-working rhymes and songs. Surely these were fine things to put into little cakes! After Claude left her, he did something a Wheeler didn't do; he went down to O street and sent her a box of the reddest roses he could find. In his pocket was the little note she had written to thank him.

VII.

It was beginning to grow dark when Claude reached the farm. While Ralph stopped to put away the car, he walked on alone to the house. He never came back without emotion, —try as he would to pass lightly over these departures and returns which were all in the day's work. When he came up the hill like this, toward the tall house with its lighted windows, something always clutched at his heart. He both loved and hated to come home. He was always disappointed, and yet he always felt the rightness of returning to his own place. Even when it broke his spirit and humbled his pride, he felt it was right that he should be thus humbled. He didn't question that the lowest state of mind was the truest, and that the less a man thought of himself, the more likely he was to be correct in his estimate.

Approaching the door, Claude stopped a moment and peered in at the kitchen window. The table was set for supper, and Mahailey was at the stove, stirring something in a big iron pot; cornmeal mush, probably,—she often made it for herself now that her teeth had begun to fail. She stood leaning over, embracing the pot with one arm, and with the other she beat the stiff contents, nodding her head in time to this rotary movement. Confused emotions surged up in Claude. He went in quickly and gave her a bearish hug.

Her face wrinkled up in the foolish grin he knew so well. "Lord, how you scared me, Mr. Claude! A little more'n I'd 'a' had my mush all over the floor. You lookin' fine, you nice boy, you!"

He knew Mahailey was gladder to see him come home than any one except his mother. Hearing Mrs. Wheeler's wandering, uncertain steps in the enclosed stairway, he opened the door and ran halfway up to meet her, putting his arm about her with the almost painful tenderness he always felt, but seldom was at liberty to show. She reached up both hands and stroked his hair for a moment, laughing as one does to a little boy, and telling him she believed it was redder every time he came back.

"Have we got all the corn in, Mother?"

"No, Claude, we haven't. You know we're always behindhand. It's been fine, open weather for husking, too. But at least we've got rid of that miserable Jerry; so there's something to be thankful for. He had one of his fits of temper in town one day, when he was hitching up to come home, and Leonard Dawson saw him beat one of our horses with the neck-yoke. Leonard told your father, and spoke his mind, and your father discharged Jerry. If you or Ralph had told him, he most likely wouldn't have done anything about it. But I guess all fathers are the same." She chuckled confidingly, leaning on Claude's arm as they descended the stairs.

"I guess so. Did he hurt the horse much? Which one was it?"

"The little black, Pompey. I believe he is rather a mean horse. The men said one of the bones over the eye was broken, but he would probably come round all right."

"Pompey isn't mean; he's nervous. All the horses hated Jerry, and they had good reason to." Claude jerked his shoulders to shake off disgusting recollections of this mongrel man which flashed back into his mind. He had seen things happen in the barn that he positively couldn't tell his father. Mr. Wheeler came into the kitchen and stopped on his way upstairs long enough to say, "Hello, Claude. You look pretty well."

"Yes, sir. I'm all right, thank you."

"Bayliss tells me you've been playing football a good deal."

"Not more than usual. We played half a dozen games; generally got licked. The State has a fine team, though."

"I ex-pect," Mr. Wheeler drawled as he strode upstairs.

Supper went as usual. Dan kept grinning and blinking at Claude, trying to discover whether he had already been informed of Jerry's fate. Ralph told him the neighbourhood gossip: Gus Yoeder, their German neighbour, was bringing suit against a farmer who had shot his dog. Leonard Dawson was going to marry Susie Grey. She was the girl on whose account Leonard had slapped Bayliss, Claude remembered.

After supper Ralph and Mr. Wheeler went off in the car to a Christmas entertainment at the country schoolhouse. Claude and his mother sat down for a quiet talk by the hard-coal burner in the living room upstairs. Claude liked this room, especially when his father was not there. The old carpet, the faded chairs, the secretary book-case, the spotty engraving with all the scenes from Pilgrim's Progress that hung over the sofa,—these things made him feel at home. Ralph was always proposing to re-furnish the room in Mission oak, but so far Claude and his mother had saved it.

Claude drew up his favourite chair and began to tell Mrs. Wheeler about the Erlich boys and their mother. She listened, but he could see that she was much more interested in hearing about the Chapins, and whether Edward's throat had improved, and where he had preached this fall. That was one of the disappointing things about coming home; he could never interest his mother in new things or people unless they in some way had to do with the church. He knew, too, she was always hoping to hear that he at last felt the need of coming closer to the church. She did not harass him about these things, but she had told him once or twice that nothing could happen in the world which would give her so much pleasure as to see him reconciled to Christ. He realized, as he talked to her about the Erlichs, that she was wondering whether they weren't very "worldly" people, and was apprehensive about their influence on him. The evening was rather a failure, and he went to bed early.

Claude had gone through a painful time of doubt and fear when he thought a great deal about religion. For several years, from fourteen to eighteen, he believed that he would be lost if he did not repent and undergo that mysterious change called conversion. But there was something stubborn in him that would not let him avail himself of the pardon offered. He felt condemned, but he did not want to renounce a world he as yet knew nothing of. He would like to go into life with all his vigour, with all his faculties free. He didn't want to be like the young men who said in prayer-meeting that they leaned on their Saviour. He hated their way of meekly accepting permitted pleasures.

In those days Claude had a sharp physical fear of death. A funeral, the sight of a neighbour lying rigid in his black coffin, overwhelmed him with terror. He used to lie awake in the dark, plotting against death, trying to devise some plan of escaping it, angrily wishing he had never been born. Was there no way out of the world but this? When he thought of the millions of lonely creatures rotting away under ground, life seemed nothing but a trap that caught people for one horrible end. There had never been a man so strong or so good that he had escaped. And yet he sometimes felt sure that he, Claude Wheeler, would escape; that he would actually invent some clever shift to save himself from dissolution. When he found it, he would tell nobody; he would be crafty and secret. Putrefaction, decay.... He could not give his pleasant, warm body over to that filthiness! What did it mean, that verse in the Bible, "He shall not suffer His holy one to see corruption"?

If anything could cure an intelligent boy of morbid religious fears, it was a denominational school like that to which Claude had been sent. Now he dismissed all Christian theology as something too full of evasions and sophistries to be reasoned about. The men who made it, he felt sure, were like the men who taught it. The noblest could be damned, according to their theory, while almost any mean-spirited parasite could be saved by faith. "Faith," as he saw it exemplified in the faculty of the Temple school, was a substitute for most of the manly qualities he admired. Young men went into the ministry because they were timid or lazy and wanted society to take care of them; because they wanted to be pampered by kind, trusting women like his mother.

Though he wanted little to do with theology and theologians, Claude would have said that he was a Christian. He believed in God, and in the spirit of the four Gospels, and in the Sermon on the Mount. He used to halt and stumble at "Blessed are the meek," until one day he happened to think that this verse was meant exactly for people like Mahailey; and surely she was blessed!

VIII.

ON THE SUNDAY after Christmas Claude and Ernest were walking along the banks of Lovely Creek. They had been as far as Mr. Wheeler's timber claim and back. It was like an autumn afternoon, so warm that they left their overcoats on the limb of a crooked elm by the pasture fence. The fields and the bare tree-tops seemed to be swimming in light. A few brown leaves still clung to the bushy trees along the creek. In the upper pasture, more than a mile from the house, the boys found a bittersweet vine that wound about a little dogwood and covered it with scarlet berries. It was like finding a Christmas tree growing wild out of doors. They had just been talking about some of the books Claude had brought home, and his history course. He was not able to tell Ernest as much about the lectures as he had meant to, and he felt that this was more Ernest's fault than his own; Ernest was such a literal-minded fellow. When they came upon the bittersweet, they forgot their discussion and scrambled down the bank to admire the red clusters on the woody, smoke-coloured vine, and its pale gold leaves, ready to fall at a touch. The vine and the little tree it honoured, hidden away in the cleft of a ravine, had escaped the stripping winds, and the eyes of schoolchildren who sometimes took a short cut home through the pasture. At its roots, the creek trickled thinly along, black between two jagged crusts of melting ice.

When they left the spot and climbed back to the level, Claude again felt an itching to prod Ernest out of his mild and reasonable mood.

"What are you going to do after a while, Ernest? Do you mean to farm all your life?"

"Naturally. If I were going to learn a trade, I'd be at it before now. What makes you ask that?"

"Oh, I don't know! I suppose people must think about the future sometime. And you're so practical."

"The future, eh?" Ernest shut one eye and smiled. "That's a big word. After I get a place of my own and have a good start, I'm going home to see my old folks some winter. Maybe I'll marry a nice girl and bring her back."

"Is that all?"

"That's enough, if it turns out right, isn't it?"

"Perhaps. It wouldn't be for me. I don't believe I can ever settle down to anything. Don't you feel that at this rate there isn't much in it?"

"In what?"

"In living at all, going on as we do. What do we get out of it? Take a day like this: you waken up in the morning and you're glad to be alive; it's a good enough day for anything, and you feel sure something will happen. Well, whether it's a workday or a holiday, it's all the same in the end. At night you go to bed—nothing has happened."

"But what do you expect? What can happen to you, except in your own mind? If I get through my work, and get an afternoon off to see my friends like this, it's enough for me."

"Is it? Well, if we've only got once to live, it seems like there ought to be something—well, something splendid about life, sometimes."

Ernest was sympathetic now. He drew nearer to Claude as they walked along and looked at him sidewise with concern. "You Americans are always looking for something outside yourselves to warm you up, and it is no way to do. In old countries, where not very much can happen to us, we know that,—and we learn to make the most of little things."

"The martyrs must have found something outside themselves. Otherwise they could have made themselves comfortable with little things."

"Why, I should say they were the ones who had nothing but their idea! It would be ridiculous to get burned at the stake for the sensation. Sometimes I think the martyrs had a good deal of vanity to help them along, too."

Claude thought Ernest had never been so tiresome. He squinted at a bright object across the fields and said cuttingly, "The fact is, Ernest, you think a man ought to be satisfied with his board and clothes and Sundays off, don't you?"

Ernest laughed rather mournfully. "It doesn't matter much what I think about it; things are as they are. Nothing is going to reach down from the sky and pick a man up, I guess."

Claude muttered something to himself, twisting his chin about over his collar as if he had a bridle-bit in his mouth.

The sun had dropped low, and the two boys, as Mrs. Wheeler watched them from the kitchen window, seemed to be walking beside a prairie fire. She smiled as she saw their black figures moving along on the crest of the hill against the golden sky; even at that distance the one looked so adaptable, and the other so unyielding. They were arguing, probably, and probably Claude was on the wrong side.

IX.

AFTER THE VACATION Claude again settled down to his reading in the University Library. He worked at a table next the alcove where the books on painting and sculpture were kept. The art students, all of whom were girls, read and whispered together in this enclosure, and he could enjoy their company without having to talk to them. They were lively and friendly; they often asked him to lift heavy books and portfolios from the shelves, and greeted him gaily when he met them in the street or on the campus, and talked to him with the easy cordiality usual between boys and girls in a co-educational school. One of these girls, Miss Peachy Millmore, was different from the others,—different from any girl Claude had ever known. She came from Georgia, and was spending the winter with her aunt on B street.

Although she was short and plump, Miss Millmore moved with what might be called a "carriage," and she had altogether more manner and more reserve than the Western girls. Her hair was yellow and curly,—the short ringlets about her ears were just the colour of a new chicken. Her vivid blue eyes were a trifle too prominent, and a generous blush of colour mantled her cheeks. It seemed to pulsate there,-one had a desire to touch her cheeks to see if they were hot. The Erlich brothers and their friends called her "the Georgia peach." She was considered very pretty, and the University boys had rushed her when she first came to town. Since then her vogue had somewhat declined.

Miss Millmore often lingered about the campus to walk down town with Claude. However he tried to adapt his long stride to her tripping gait, she was sure to get out of breath. She was always dropping her gloves or her sketchbook or her purse, and he liked to pick them up for her, and to pull on her rubbers, which kept slipping off at the heel. She was very kind to single him out and be so gracious to him, he thought. She even coaxed him to pose in his track clothes for the life class on Saturday morning, telling him that he had "a magnificent physique," a compliment which covered him with confusion. But he posed, of course.

Claude looked forward to seeing Peachy Millmore, missed her if she were not in the alcove, found it quite natural that she should explain her absences to him,—tell him how often she washed her hair and how long it was when she uncoiled it.

One Friday in February Julius Erlich overtook Claude on the campus and proposed that they should try the skating tomorrow.

"Yes, I'm going out," Claude replied. "I've promised to teach Miss Millmore to skate. Won't you come along and help me?"

Julius laughed indulgently. "Oh, no! Some other time. I don't want to break in on that."

"Nonsense! You could teach her better than I."

"Oh, I haven't the courage!"

"What do you mean?"

"You know what I mean."

"No, I don't. Why do you always laugh about that girl, anyhow?"

Julius made a little grimace. "She wrote some awfully slushy letters to Phil Bowen, and he read them aloud at the frat house one night."

"Didn't you slap him?" Claude demanded, turning red.

"Well, I would have thought I would," said Julius smiling, "but I didn't. They were too silly to make a fuss about. I've been wary of the Georgia peach ever since. If you touched that sort of peach ever so lightly, it might remain in your hand."

"I don't think so," replied Claude haughtily. "She's only kind-hearted."

"Perhaps you're right. But I'm terribly afraid of girls who are too kindhearted," Julius confessed. He had wanted to drop Claude a word of warning for some time.

Claude kept his engagement with Miss Millmore. He took her out to the skating pond several times, indeed, though in the beginning he told her he feared her ankles were too weak. Their last excursion was made by moonlight, and after that evening Claude avoided Miss Millmore when he could do so without being rude. She was attractive to him no more. It was her way to subdue by clinging contact. One could scarcely call it design; it was a degree less subtle than that. She had already thus subdued a pale cousin in Atlanta, and it was on this account that she had been sent North. She had, Claude angrily admitted, no reserve,—though when one first met her she seemed to have so much. Her eager susceptibility presented not the slightest temptation to him. He was a boy with strong impulses, and he detested the idea of trifling with them. The talk of the disreputable men his father kept about the place at home, instead of corrupting him, had given him a sharp disgust for sensuality. He had an almost Hippolytean pride in candour.

X.

THE ERLICH FAMILY LOVED ANNIVERSARIES, birthdays, occasions. That spring Mrs. Erlich's first cousin, Wilhelmina Schroeder-Schatz, who sang with the Chicago Opera Company, came to Lincoln as soloist for the May Festival. As the date of her engagement approached, her relatives began planning to entertain her. The Matinee Musical was to give a formal reception for the singer, so the Erlichs decided upon a dinner. Each member of the family invited one guest, and they had great difficulty in deciding which of their friends would be most appreciative of the honour. There were to be more men than women, because Mrs. Erlich remembered that cousin Wilhelmina had never been partial to the society of her own sex.

One evening when her sons were revising their list, Mrs. Erlich reminded them that she had not as yet named her guest. "For me," she said with decision, "you may put down Claude Wheeler."

This announcement was met with groans and laughter.

"You don't mean it, Mother," the oldest son protested. "Poor old Claude wouldn't know what it was all about,—and one stick can spoil a dinner party."

Mrs. Erlich shook her finger at him with conviction. "You will see; your cousin Wilhelmina will be more interested in that boy than in any of the others!"

Julius thought if she were not too strongly opposed she might still yield her point. "For one thing, Mother, Claude hasn't any dinner clothes," he murmured. She nodded to him. "That has been attended to, Herr Julius. He is having some made. When I sounded him, he told me he could easily afford it."

The boys said if things had gone as far as that, they supposed they would have to make the best of it, and the eldest wrote down "Claude Wheeler" with a flourish.

If the Erlich boys were apprehensive, their anxiety was nothing to Claude's. He was to take Mrs. Erlich to Madame Schroeder-Schatz's recital, and on the evening of the concert, when he appeared at the door, the boys dragged him in to look him over. Otto turned on all the lights, and Mrs. Erlich, in her new black lace over white satin, fluttered into the parlour to see what figure her escort cut.

Claude pulled off his overcoat as he was bid, and presented himself in the sooty blackness of fresh broadcloth. Mrs. Erlich's eyes swept his long black legs, his smooth shoulders, and lastly his square red head, affectionately inclined toward her. She laughed and clapped her hands.

"Now all the girls will turn round in their seats to look, and wonder where I got him!"

Claude began to bestow her belongings in his overcoat pockets; opera glasses in one, fan in another. She put a lorgnette into her little bag, along with her powder-box, handkerchief and smelling salts,—there was even a little silver box of peppermint drops, in case she might begin to cough. She drew on her long gloves, arranged a lace scarf over her hair, and at last was ready to have the evening cloak which Claude held wound about her. When she reached up and took his arm, bowing to her sons, they laughed and liked Claude better. His steady, protecting air was a frame for the gay little picture she made.

The dinner party came off the next evening. The guest of honour, Madame Wilhelmina Schroeder-Schatz, was some years younger than her cousin, Augusta Erlich. She was short, stalwart, with an enormous chest, a fine head, and a commanding presence. Her great contralto voice, which she used without much discretion, was a really superb organ and gave people a pleasure as substantial as food and drink. At dinner she sat on the right of the oldest son. Claude, beside Mrs. Erlich at the other end of the table, watched attentively the lady attired in green velvet and blazing rhinestones.

After dinner, as Madame Schroeder-Schatz swept out of the dining room, she dropped her cousin's arm and stopped before Claude, who stood at attention behind his chair.

"If Cousin Augusta can spare you, we must have a little talk together. We have been very far separated," she said.

She led Claude to one of the window seats in the living-room, at once complained of a draft, and sent him to hunt for her green scarf. He brought it and carefully put it about her shoulders; but after a few moments, she threw it off with a slightly annoyed air, as if she had never wanted it. Claude with solicitude reminded her about the draft.

"Draft?" she said lifting her chin, "there is no draft here."

She asked Claude where he lived, how much land his father owned, what crops they raised, and about their poultry and dairy. When she was a child she had lived on a farm in Bavaria, and she seemed to know a good deal about farming and live-stock. She was disapproving when Claude told her they rented half their land to other farmers. "If I were a young man, I would begin to acquire land, and I would not stop until I had a whole county," she declared. She said that when she met new people, she liked to find out the way they made their living; her own way was a hard one.

Later in the evening Madame Schroeder-Schatz graciously consented to sing for her cousins. When she sat down to the piano, she beckoned Claude and asked him to turn for her. He shook his head, smiling ruefully.

"I'm sorry I'm so stupid, but I don't know one note from another."

She tapped his sleeve. "Well, never mind. I may want the piano moved yet; you could do that for me, eh?"

When Madame Schroeder-Schatz was in Mrs. Erlich's bedroom, powdering her nose before she put on her wraps, she remarked, "What a pity, Augusta, that you have not a daughter now, to marry to Claude Melnotte. He would make you a perfect son-in-law."

"Ah, if I only had!" sighed Mrs. Erlich.

"Or," continued Madame Schroeder-Schatz, energetically pulling on her large carriage shoes, "if you were but a few years younger, it might not yet be too late. Oh, don't be a fool, Augusta! Such things have happened, and will happen again. However, better a widow than to be tied to a sick man—like a stone about my neck! What a husband to go home to! and I a woman in full vigour. Jas ist ein Kreuz ich trage!" She smote her bosom, on the left side.

Having put on first a velvet coat, then a fur mantle, Madame Schroeder-Schatz moved like a galleon out into the living room and kissed all her cousins, and Claude Wheeler, good-night.

XI.

ONE WARM AFTERNOON in May Claude sat in his upstairs room at the Chapins', copying his thesis, which was to take the place of an examination in history. It was a criticism of the testimony of Jeanne d'Arc in her nine private examinations and the trial in ordinary. The Professor had assigned him the subject with a flash of humour. Although this evidence had been pawed over by so many hands since the fifteenth century, by the phlegmatic and the fiery, by rhapsodists and cynics, he felt sure that Wheeler would not dismiss the case lightly.

Indeed, Claude put a great deal of time and thought upon the matter, and for the time being it seemed quite the most important thing in his life. He worked from an English translation of the Proces, but he kept the French text at his elbow, and some of her replies haunted him in the language in which they were spoken. It seemed to him that they were like the speech of her saints, of whom Jeanne said, "the voice is beautiful, sweet and low, and it speaks in the French tongue." Claude flattered himself that he had kept all personal feeling out of the paper; that it was a cold estimate of the girl's motives and character as indicated by the consistency and inconsistency of her replies; and of the change wrought in her by imprisonment and by "the fear of the fire."

When he had copied the last page of his manuscript and sat contemplating the pile of written sheets, he felt that after all his conscientious study he really knew very little more about the Maid of Orleans than when he first heard of her from his mother, one day when he was a little boy. He had been shut up in the house with a cold, he remembered, and he found a picture of her in armour, in an old book, and took it down to the kitchen where his mother was making apple pies. She glanced at the picture, and while she went on rolling out the dough and fitting it to the pans, she told him the story. He had forgotten what she said,—it must have been very fragmentary,—but from that time on he knew the essential facts about Joan of Arc, and she was a living figure in his mind. She seemed to him then as clear as now, and now as miraculous as then.

It was a curious thing, he reflected, that a character could perpetuate itself thus; by a picture, a word, a phrase, it could renew itself in every generation and be born over and over again in the minds of children. At that time he had never seen a map of France, and had a very poor opinion of any place farther away than Chicago; yet he was perfectly prepared for the legend of Joan of Arc, and often thought about her when he was bringing in his cobs in the evening, or when he was sent to the windmill for water and stood shaking in the cold while the chilled pump brought it slowly up. He pictured her then very much as he did now; about her figure there gathered a luminous cloud, like dust, with soldiers in it… the banner with lilies… a great church… cities with walls.

On this balmy spring afternoon, Claude felt softened and reconciled to the world. Like Gibbon, he was sorry to have finished his labour,—and he could not see anything else as interesting ahead. He must soon be going home now. There would be a few examinations to sit through at the Temple, a few more evenings with the Erlichs, trips to the Library to carry back the books he had been using,—and then he would suddenly find himself with nothing to do but take the train for Frankfort.

He rose with a sigh and began to fasten his history papers between covers. Glancing out of the window, he decided that he would walk into town and carry his thesis, which was due today; the weather was too fine to sit bumping in a street car. The truth was, he wished to prolong his relations with his manuscript as far as possible.

He struck off by the road,—it could scarcely be called a street, since it ran across raw prairie land where the buffalo-peas were in blossom. Claude walked slower than was his custom, his straw hat pushed back on his head and the blaze of the sun full in his face. His body felt light in the scented wind, and he listened drowsily to the larks, singing on dried weeds and sunflower stalks. At this season their song is almost painful to hear, it is so sweet. He sometimes thought of this walk long afterward; it was memorable to him, though he could not say why.

On reaching the University, he went directly to the Department of European History, where he was to leave his thesis on a long table, with a pile of others. He rather dreaded this, and was glad when, just as he entered, the Professor came out from his private office and took the bound manuscript into his own hands, nodding cordially.

"Your thesis? Oh yes, Jeanne d'Arc. The Proces. I had forgotten. Interesting material, isn't it?" He opened the cover and ran over the pages. "I suppose you acquitted her on the evidence?"

Claude blushed. "Yes, sir."

"Well, now you might read what Michelet has to say about her. There's an old translation in the Library. Did you enjoy working on it?"

"I did, very much." Claude wished to heaven he could think of something to say.

"You've got a good deal out of your course, altogether, haven't you? I'll be interested to see what you do next year. Your work has been very satisfactory to me." The Professor went back into his study, and Claude was pleased to see that he carried the manuscript with him and did not leave it on the table with the others.

XII.

BETWEEN HAYING and harvest that summer Ralph and Mr. Wheeler drove to Denver in the big car, leaving Claude and Dan to cultivate the corn. When they returned Mr. Wheeler announced that he had a secret. After several days of reticence, during which he shut himself up in the sitting-room writing letters, and passed mysterious words and winks with Ralph at table, he disclosed a project which swept away all Claude's plans and purposes.

On the return trip from Denver Mr. Wheeler had made a detour down into Yucca county, Colorado, to visit an old friend who was in difficulties. Tom Wested was a Maine man, from Wheeler's own neighbourhood. Several years ago he had lost his wife. Now his health had broken down, and the Denver doctors said he must retire from business and get into a low altitude. He wanted to go back to Maine and live among his own people, but was too much discouraged and frightened about his condition even to undertake the sale of his ranch and live stock. Mr. Wheeler had been able to help his friend, and at the same time did a good stroke of business for himself. He owned a farm in Maine, his share of his father's estate, which for years he had rented for little more than the up-keep. By making over this property, and assuming certain mortgages, he got Wested's fine, well-watered ranch in exchange. He paid him a good price for his cattle, and promised to take the sick man back to Maine and see him comfortably settled there. All this Mr. Wheeler explained to his family when he called them up to the living room one hot, breathless night after supper. Mrs. Wheeler, who seldom concerned herself with her husband's business affairs, asked absently why they bought more land, when they already had so much they could not farm half of it.

"Just like a woman, Evangeline, just like a woman!" Mr. Wheeler replied indulgently. He was sitting in the full glare of the acetylene lamp, his neckband open, his collar and tie on the table beside him, fanning himself with a palm-leaf fan. "You might as well ask me why I want to make more money, when I haven't spent all I've got."

He intended, he said, to put Ralph on the Colorado ranch and "give the boy some responsibility." Ralph would have the help of Wested's foreman, an old hand in the cattle business, who had agreed to stay on under the new management. Mr. Wheeler assured his wife that he wasn't taking advantage of poor Wested; the timber on the Maine place was really worth a good deal of money; but because his father had always been so proud of his great pine woods, he had never, he said, just felt like turning a sawmill loose in them. Now he was trading a pleasant old farm that didn't bring in anything for a grama-grass ranch which ought to turn over a profit of ten or twelve thousand dollars in good cattle years, and wouldn't lose much in bad ones. He expected to spend about half his time out there with Ralph. "When I'm away," he remarked genially, "you and Mahailey won't have so much to do. You can devote yourselves to embroidery, so to speak."

"If Ralph is to live in Colorado, and you are to be away from home half of the time, I don't see what is to become of this place," murmured Mrs. Wheeler, still in the dark.

"Not necessary for you to see, Evangeline," her husband replied, stretching his big frame until the rocking chair creaked under him. "It will be Claude's business to look after that."

"Claude?" Mrs. Wheeler brushed a lock of hair back from her damp forehead in vague alarm.

"Of course." He looked with twinkling eyes at his son's straight, silent figure in the corner. "You've had about enough theology, I presume? No ambition to be a preacher? This winter I mean to turn the farm over to you and give you a chance to straighten things out. You've been dissatisfied with the way the place is run for some time, haven't you? Go ahead and put new blood into it. New ideas, if you want to; I've no objection. They're expensive, but let it go. You can fire Dan if you want, and get what help you need."

Claude felt as if a trap had been sprung on him. He shaded his eyes with his hand. "I don't think I'm competent to run the place right," he said unsteadily.

"Well, you don't think I am either, Claude, so we're up against it. It's always been my notion that the land was made for man, just as it's old Dawson's that man was created to work the land. I don't mind your siding with the Dawsons in this difference of opinion, if you can get their results."

Mrs. Wheeler rose and slipped quickly from the room, feeling her way down the dark staircase to the kitchen. It was dusky and quiet there. Mahailey sat in a corner, hemming dish-towels by the light of a smoky old brass lamp which was her own cherished luminary. Mrs. Wheeler walked up and down the long room in soft, silent agitation, both hands pressed tightly to her breast, where there was a physical ache of sympathy for Claude.

She remembered kind Tom Wested. He had stayed over night with them several times, and had come to them for consolation after his wife died. It seemed to her that his decline in health and loss of courage, Mr. Wheeler's fortuitous trip to Denver, the old pine-wood farm in Maine; were all things that fitted together and made a net to envelop her unfortunate son. She knew that he had been waiting impatiently for the autumn, and that for the first time he looked forward eagerly to going back to school. He was homesick for his friends, the Erlichs, and his mind was all the time upon the history course he meant to take.

Yet all this would weigh nothing in the family councils probably he would not even speak of it—and he had not one substantial objection to offer to his father's wishes. His disappointment would be bitter. "Why, it will almost break his heart," she murmured aloud. Mahailey was a little deaf and heard nothing. She sat holding her work up to the light, driving her needle with a big brass thimble, nodding with sleepiness between stitches. Though Mrs. Wheeler was scarcely conscious of it, the old woman's presence was a comfort to her, as she walked up and down with her drifting, uncertain step.

She had left the sitting-room because she was afraid Claude might get angry and say something hard to his father, and because she couldn't bear to see him hectored. Claude had always found life hard to live; he suffered so much over little things,-and she suffered with him. For herself, she never felt disappointments. Her husband's careless decisions did not disconcert her. If he declared that he would not plant a garden at all this year, she made no protest. It was Mahailey who grumbled. If he felt like eating roast beef and went out and killed a steer, she did the best she could to take care of the meat, and if some of it spoiled she tried not to worry. When she was not lost in religious meditation, she was likely to be thinking about some one of the old books she read over and over. Her personal life was so far removed from the scene of her daily activities that rash and violent men could not break in upon it. But where Claude was concerned, she lived on another plane, dropped into the lower air, tainted with human breath and pulsating with poor, blind, passionate human feelings.

It had always been so. And now, as she grew older, and her flesh had almost ceased to be concerned with pain or pleasure, like the wasted wax images in old churches, it still vibrated with his feelings and became quick again for him. His chagrins shrivelled her. When he was hurt and suffered silently, something ached in her. On the other hand, when he was happy, a wave of physical contentment went through her. If she wakened in the night and happened to think that he had been happy lately, she would lie softly and gratefully in her warm place.

"Rest, rest, perturbed spirit," she sometimes whispered to him in her mind, when she wakened thus and thought of him. There was a singular light in his eyes when he smiled at her on one of his good days, as if to tell her that all was well in his inner kingdom. She had seen that same look again and again, and she could always remember it in the dark,—a quick blue flash, tender and a little wild, as if he had seen a vision or glimpsed bright uncertainties.

XIII.

THE NEXT FEW weeks were busy ones on the farm. Before the wheat harvest was over, Nat Wheeler packed his leather trunk, put on his "store clothes," and set off to take Tom Welted back to Maine. During his absence Ralph began to outfit for life in Yucca county. Ralph liked being a great man with the Frankfort merchants, and he had never before had such an opportunity as this. He bought a new shot gun, saddles, bridles, boots, long and short storm coats, a set of furniture for his own room, a fireless cooker, another music machine, and had them shipped to Colorado. His mother, who did not like phonograph music, and detested phonograph monologues, begged him to take the machine at home, but he assured her that she would be dull without it on winter evenings. He wanted one of the latest make, put out under the name of a great American inventor.

Some of the ranches near Wested's were owned by New York men who brought their families out there in the summer. Ralph had heard about the dances they gave, and he way counting on being one of the guests. He asked Claude to give him his dress suit, since Claude wouldn't be needing it any more.

"You can have it if you want it," said Claude indifferently "But it won't fit you."

"I'll take it in to Fritz and have the pants cut off a little and the shoulders taken in," his brother replied lightly.

Claude was impassive. "Go ahead. But if that old Dutch man takes a whack at it, it will look like the devil."

"I think I'll let him try. Father won't say anything about what I've ordered for the house, but he isn't much for glad rags, you know." Without more ado he threw Claude's black clothes into the back seat of the Ford and ran into town to enlist the services of the German tailor.

Mr. Wheeler, when he returned, thought Ralph had been rather free in expenditures, but Ralph told him it wouldn't do to take over the new place too modestly. "The ranchers out there are all high-fliers. If we go to squeezing nickels, they won't think we mean business."

The country neighbours, who were always amused at the Wheelers' doings, got almost as much pleasure out of Ralph's lavishness as he did himself. One said Ralph had shipped a new piano out to Yucca county, another heard he had ordered a billiard table. August Yoeder, their prosperous German neighbour, asked grimly whether he could, maybe, get a place as hired man with Ralph. Leonard Dawson, who was to be married in October, hailed Claude in town one day and shouted;

"My God, Claude, there's nothing left in the furniture store for me and Susie! Ralph's bought everything but the coffins. He must be going to live like a prince out there."

"I don't know anything about it," Claude answered coolly. "It's not my enterprise."

"No, you've got to stay on the old place and make it pay the debts, I understand." Leonard jumped into his car, so that Claude wouldn't have a chance to reply.

Mrs. Wheeler, too, when she observed the magnitude of these preparations, began to feel that the new arrangement was not fair to Claude, since he was the older boy and much the steadier. Claude had always worked hard when he was at home, and made a good field hand, while Ralph had never done much but tinker with machinery and run errands in his car. She couldn't understand why he was selected to manage an undertaking in which so much money was invested.

"Why, Claude," she said dreamily one day, "if your father were an older man, I would almost think his judgment had begun to fail. Won't we get dreadfully into debt at this rate?"

"Don't say anything, Mother. It's Father's money. He shan't think I want any of it."

"I wish I could talk to Bayliss. Has he said anything?"

"Not to me, he hasn't."

Ralph and Mr. Wheeler took another flying trip to Colorado, and when they came back Ralph began coaxing his mother to give him bedding and table linen. He said he wasn't going to live like a savage, even in the sand hills. Mahailey was outraged to see the linen she had washed and ironed and taken care of for so many years packed into boxes. She was out of temper most of the time now, and went about muttering to herself.

The only possessions Mahailey brought with her when she came to live with the Wheelers, were a feather bed and three patchwork quilts, interlined with wool off the backs of Virginia sheep, washed and carded by hand. The quilts had been made by her old mother, and given to her for a marriage portion. The patchwork on each was done in a different design; one was the popular "log-cabin" pattern, another the "laurel-leaf," the third the "blazing star." This quilt Mahailey thought too good for use, and she had told Mrs. Wheeler that she was saving it "to give Mr. Claude when he got married."

She slept on her feather bed in winter, and in summer she put it away in the attic. The attic was reached by a ladder which, because of her weak back, Mrs. Wheeler very seldom climbed. Up there Mahailey had things her own way, and thither she often retired to air the bedding stored away there, or to look at the pictures in the piles of old magazines. Ralph facetiously called the attic "Mahailey's library."

One day, while things were being packed for the western ranch, Mrs. Wheeler, going to the foot of the ladder to call Mahailey, narrowly escaped being knocked down by a large feather bed which came plumping through the trap door. A moment later Mahailey herself descended backwards, holding to the rungs with one hand, and in the other arm carrying her quilts.

"Why, Mahailey," gasped Mrs. Wheeler. "It's not winter yet; whatever are you getting your bed for?"

"I'm just a-goin' to lay on my fedder bed," she broke out, "or direc'ly I won't have none. I ain't a-goin' to have Mr. Ralph carryin' off my quilts my mudder pieced fur me."

Mrs. Wheeler tried to reason with her, but the old woman took up her bed in her arms and staggered down the hall with it, muttering and tossing her head like a horse in fly-time.

That afternoon Ralph brought a barrel and a bundle of straw into the kitchen and told Mahailey to carry up preserves and canned fruit, and he would pack them. She went obediently to the cellar, and Ralph took off his coat and began to line the barrel with straw. He was some time in doing this, but still Mahailey had not returned. He went to the head of the stairs and whistled.

"I'm a-comin', Mr. Ralph, I'm a-comin'! Don't hurry me, I don't want to break nothin'."

Ralph waited a few minutes. "What are you doing down there, Mahailey?" he fumed. "I could have emptied the whole cellar by this time. I suppose I'll have to do it myself."

"I'm a-comin'. You'd git yourself all dusty down here." She came breathlessly up the stairs, carrying a hamper basket full of jars, her hands and face streaked with black.

"Well, I should say it is dusty!" Ralph snorted. "You might clean your fruit closet once in awhile, you know, Mahailey. You ought to see how Mrs. Dawson keeps hers. Now, let's see." He sorted the jars on the table. "Take back the grape jelly. If there's anything I hate, it's grape jelly. I know you have lots of it, but you can't work it off on me. And when you come up, don't forget the pickled peaches. I told you particularly, the pickled peaches!"

"We ain't got no pickled peaches." Mahailey stood by the cellar door, holding a corner of her apron up to her chin, with a queer, animal look of stubbornness in her face.

"No pickled peaches? What nonsense, Mahailey! I saw you making them here, only a few weeks ago."

"I know you did, Mr. Ralph, but they ain't none now. I didn't have no luck with my peaches this year. I must 'a' let the air git at 'em. They all worked on me, an' I had to throw 'em out."

Ralph was thoroughly annoyed. "I never heard of such a thing, Mahailey! You get more careless every year. Think of wasting all that fruit and sugar! Does mother know?"

Mahailey's low brow clouded. "I reckon she does. I don't wase your mudder's sugar. I never did wase nothin'," she muttered. Her speech became queerer than ever when she was angry.

Ralph dashed down the cellar stairs, lit a lantern, and searched the fruit closet. Sure enough, there were no pickled peaches. When he came back and began packing his fruit, Mahailey stood watching him with a furtive expression, very much like the look that is in a chained coyote's eyes when a boy is showing him off to visitors and saying he wouldn't run away if he could.

"Go on with your work," Ralph snapped. "Don't stand there watching me!"

That evening Claude was sitting on the windmill platform, down by the barn, after a hard day's work ploughing for winter wheat. He was solacing himself with his pipe. No matter how much she loved him, or how sorry she felt for him, his mother could never bring herself to tell him he might smoke in the house. Lights were shining from the upstairs rooms on the hill, and through the open windows sounded the singing snarl of a phonograph. A figure came stealing down the path. He knew by her low, padding step that it was Mahailey, with her apron thrown over her head. She came up to him and touched him on the shoulder in a way which meant that what she had to say was confidential.

"Mr. Claude, Mr. Ralph's done packed up a barr'l of your mudder's jelly an' pickles to take out there."

"That's all right, Mahailey. Mr. Wested was a widower, and I guess there wasn't anything of that sort put up at his place."

She hesitated and bent lower. "He asked me fur them pickled peaches I made fur you, but I didn't give him none. I hid 'em all in my old cook-stove we done put down cellar when Mr. Ralph bought the new one. I didn't give him your mudder's new preserves, nudder. I give him the old last year's stuff we had left over, and now you an' your mudder'll have plenty."

Claude laughed. "Oh, I don't care if Ralph takes all the fruit on the place, Mahailey!"

She shrank back a little, saying confusedly, "No, I know you don't, Mr. Claude. I know you don't."

"I surely ought not to take it out on her," Claude thought, when he saw her disappointment. He rose and patted her on the back. "That's all right, Mahailey. Thank you for saving the peaches, anyhow."

She shook her finger at him. "Don't you let on!"

He promised, and watched her slipping back over the zigzag path up the hill.

XIV.

RALPH and his father moved to the new ranch the last of August, and Mr. Wheeler wrote back that late in the fall he meant to ship a carload of grass steers to the home farm to be fattened during the winter. This, Claude saw, would mean a need for fodder. There was a fifty-acre corn field west of the creek,—just on the sky-line when one looked out from the west windows of the house. Claude decided to put this field into winter wheat, and early in September he began to cut and bind the corn that stood upon it for fodder. As soon as the corn was gathered, he would plough up the ground, and drill in the wheat when he planted the other wheat fields.

This was Claude's first innovation, and it did not meet with approval. When Bayliss came out to spend Sunday with his mother, he asked her what Claude thought he was doing, anyhow. If he wanted to change the crop on that field, why didn't he plant oats in the spring, and then get into wheat next fall? Cutting fodder and preparing the ground now, would only hold him back in his work. When Mr. Wheeler came home for a short visit, he jocosely referred to that quarter as "Claude's wheat field."

Claude went ahead with what he had undertaken to do, but all through September he was nervous and apprehensive about the weather. Heavy rains, if they came, would make him late with his wheat-planting, and then there would certainly be criticism. In reality, nobody cared much whether the planting was late or not, but Claude thought they did, and sometimes in the morning he awoke in a state of panic because he wasn't getting ahead faster. He had Dan and one of August Yoeder's four sons to help him, and he worked early and late. The new field he ploughed and drilled himself. He put a great deal of young energy into it, and buried a great deal of discontent in its dark furrows. Day after day he flung himself upon the land and planted it with what was fermenting in him, glad to be so tired at night that he could not think.

Ralph came home for Leonard Dawson's wedding, on the first of October. All the Wheelers went to the wedding, even Mahailey, and there was a great gathering of the country folk and townsmen.

After Ralph left, Claude had the place to himself again, and the work went on as usual. The stock did well, and there were no vexatious interruptions. The fine weather held, and every morning when Claude got up, another gold day stretched before him like a glittering carpet, leading…? When the question where the days were leading struck him on the edge of his bed, he hurried to dress and get down-stairs in time to fetch wood and coal for Mahailey. They often reached the kitchen at the same moment, and she would shake her finger at him and say, "You come down to help me, you nice boy, you!" At least he was of some use to Mahailey. His father could hire one of the Yoeder boys to look after the place, but Mahailey wouldn't let any one else save her old back.

Mrs. Wheeler, as well as Mahailey, enjoyed that fall. She slept late in the morning, and read and rested in the afternoon. She made herself some new house-dresses out of a grey material Claude chose. "It's almost like being a bride, keeping house for just you, Claude," she sometimes said.

Soon Claude had the satisfaction of seeing a blush of green come up over his brown wheat fields, visible first in the dimples and little hollows, then flickering over the knobs and levels like a fugitive smile. He watched the green blades coming every day, when he and Dan went afield with their wagons to gather corn. Claude sent Dan to shuck on the north quarter, and he worked on the south. He always brought in one more load a day than Dan did,—that was to be expected. Dan explained this very reasonably, Claude thought, one afternoon when they were hooking up their teams.

"It's all right for you to jump at that corn like you was a-beating carpets, Claude; it's your corn, or anyways it's your Paw's. Them fields will always lay betwixt you and trouble. But a hired man's got no property but his back, and he has to save it. I figure that I've only got about so many jumps left in me, and I ain't a-going to jump too hard at no man's corn."

"What's the matter? I haven't been hinting that you ought to jump any harder, have I?"

"No, you ain't, but I just want you to know that there's reason in all things." With this Dan got into his wagon and drove off. He had probably been meditating upon this declaration for some time.

That afternoon Claude suddenly stopped flinging white ears into the wagon beside him. It was about five o'clock, the yellowest hour of the autumn day. He stood lost in a forest of light, dry, rustling corn leaves, quite hidden away from the world. Taking off his husking-gloves, he wiped the sweat from his face, climbed up to the wagon box, and lay down on the ivory-coloured corn. The horses cautiously advanced a step or two, and munched with great content at ears they tore from the stalks with their teeth.

Claude lay still, his arms under his head, looking up at the hard, polished blue sky, watching the flocks of crows go over from the fields where they fed on shattered grain, to their nests in the trees along Lovely Creek. He was thinking about what Dan had said while they were hitching up. There was a great deal of truth in it, certainly. Yet, as for him, he often felt that he would rather go out into the world and earn his bread among strangers than sweat under this half-responsibility for acres and crops that were not his own. He knew that his father was sometimes called a "land hog" by the country people, and he himself had begun to feel that it was not right they should have so much land,—to farm, or to rent, or to leave idle, as they chose. It was strange that in all the centuries the world had been going, the question of property had not been better adjusted. The people who had it were slaves to it, and the people who didn't have it were slaves to them.

He sprang down into the gold light to finish his load. Warm silence nestled over the cornfield. Sometimes a light breeze rose for a moment and rattled the stiff, dry leaves, and he himself made a great rustling and crackling as he tore the husks from the ears.

Greedy crows were still cawing about before they flapped homeward. When he drove out to the highway, the sun was going down, and from his seat on the load he could see far and near. Yonder was Dan's wagon, coming in from the north quarter; over there was the roof of Leonard Dawson's new house, and his windmill, standing up black in the declining day. Before him were the bluffs of the pasture, and the little trees, almost bare, huddled in violet shadow along the creek, and the Wheeler farm-house on the hill, its windows all aflame with the last red fire of the sun.

XV.

CLAUDE DREADED the inactivity of the winter, to which the farmer usually looks forward with pleasure. He made the Thanksgiving football game a pretext for going up to Lincoln,—went intending to stay three days and stayed ten. The first night, when he knocked at the glass door of the Erlichs' sitting-room and took them by surprise, he thought he could never go back to the farm. Approaching the house on that clear, frosty autumn evening, crossing the lawn strewn with crackling dry leaves, he told himself that he must not hope to find things the same. But they were the same. The boys were lounging and smoking about the square table with the lamp on it, and Mrs. Erlich was at the piano, playing one of Mendelssohn's "Songs Without Words." When he knocked, Otto opened the door and called:

"A surprise for you, Mother! Guess who's here."

What a welcome she gave him, and how much she had to tell him! While they were all talking at once, Henry, the oldest son, came downstairs dressed for a Colonial ball, with satin breeches and stockings and a sword. His brothers began to point out the inaccuracies of his costume, telling him that he couldn't possibly call himself a French emigré unless he wore a powdered wig. Henry took a book of memoirs from the shelf to prove to them that at the time when the French emigrés were coming to Philadelphia, powder was going out of fashion.

During this discussion, Mrs. Erlich drew Claude aside and told him in excited whispers that her cousin Wilhelmina, the singer, had at last been relieved of the invalid husband whom she had supported for so many years, and now was going to marry her accompanist, a man much younger than herself.

After the French emigré had gone off to his party, two young instructors from the University dropped in, and Mrs. Erlich introduced Claude as her "landed proprietor" who managed a big ranch out in one of the western counties. The instructors took their leave early, but Claude stayed on. What was it that made life seem so much more interesting and attractive here than elsewhere? There was nothing wonderful about this room; a lot of books, a lamp... comfortable, hard-used furniture, some people whose lives were in no way remarkable—and yet he had the sense of being in a warm and gracious atmosphere, charged with generous enthusiasms and ennobled by romantic friendships. He was glad to see the same pictures on the wall; to find the Swiss wood-cutter on the mantel, still bending under his load of faggots; to handle again the heavy brass paper-knife that in its time had cut so many interesting pages. He picked it up from the cover of a red book lying there,-one of Trevelyan's volumes on Garibaldi, which Julius told him he must read before he was another week older.

The next afternoon Claude took Mrs. Erlich to the football game and came home with the family for dinner. He lingered on day after day, but after the first few evenings his heart was growing a little heavier all the time. The Erlich boys had so many new interests he couldn't keep up with them; they had been going on, and he had been standing still. He wasn't conceited enough to mind that. The thing that hurt was the feeling of being out of it, of being lost in another kind of life in which ideas played but little part. He was a stranger who walked in and sat down here; but he belonged out in the big, lonely country, where people worked hard with their backs and got tired like the horses, and were too sleepy at night to think of anything to say. If Mrs. Erlich and her Hungarian woman made lentil soup and potato dumplings and Wiener-Schnitzel for him, it only made the plain fare on the farm seem the heavier.

When the second Friday came round, he went to bid his friends good-bye and explained that he must be going home tomorrow. On leaving the house that night, he looked back at the ruddy windows and told himself that it was goodbye indeed, and not, as Mrs. Erlich had fondly said, auf wiedersehen. Coming here only made him more discontented with his lot; his frail claim on this kind of life existed no longer. He must settle down into something that was his own, take hold of it with both hands, no matter how grim it was. The next day, during his journey out through the bleak winter country, he felt that he was going deeper and deeper into reality.

Claude had not written when he would be home, but on Saturday there were always some of the neighbours in town. He rode out with one of the Yoeder boys, and from their place walked on the rest of the way. He told his mother he was glad to be back again. He sometimes felt as if it were disloyal to her for him to be so happy with Mrs. Erlich. His mother had been shut away from the world on a farm for so many years; and even before that, Vermont was no very stimulating place to grow up in, he guessed. She had not had a chance, any more than he had, at those things which make the mind more supple and keep the feeling young.

The next morning it was snowing outside, and they had a long, pleasant Sunday breakfast. Mrs. Wheeler said they wouldn't try to go to church, as Claude must be tired. He worked about the place until noon, making the stock comfortable and looking after things that Dan had neglected in his absence. After dinner he sat down at the secretary and wrote a long letter to his friends in Lincoln. Whenever he lifted his eyes for a moment, he saw the pasture bluffs and the softly falling snow. There was something beautiful about the submissive way in which the country met winter. It made one contented,—sad, too. He sealed his letter and lay down on the couch to read the paper, but was soon asleep.

When he awoke the afternoon was already far gone. The clock on the shelf ticked loudly in the still room, the coal stove sent out a warm glow. The blooming plants in the south bow-window looked brighter and fresher than usual in the soft white light that came up from the snow. Mrs. Wheeler was reading by the west window, looking away from her book now and then to gaze off at the grey sky and the muffled fields. The creek made a winding violet chasm down through the pasture, and the trees followed it in a black thicket, curiously tufted with snow. Claude lay for some time without speaking, watching his mother's profile against the glass, and thinking how good this soft, clinging snow-fall would be for his wheat fields.

"What are you reading, Mother?" he asked presently.

She turned her head toward him. "Nothing very new. I was just beginning 'Paradise Lost' again. I haven't read it for a long while."

"Read aloud, won't you? Just wherever you happen to be. I like the sound of it."

Mrs. Wheeler always read deliberately, giving each syllable its full value. Her voice, naturally soft and rather wistful, trailed over the long measures and the threatening Biblical names, all familiar to her and full of meaning.

"A dungeon horrible, on all sides round
As one great furnace flamed; yet from the flames
No light, but rather darkness visible
Served only to discover sights of woe."

Her voice groped as if she were trying to realize something. The room was growing greyer as she read on through the turgid catalogue of the heathen gods, so packed with stories and pictures, so unaccountably glorious. At last the light failed, and Mrs. Wheeler closed the book.

"That's fine," Claude commented from the couch. "But Milton couldn't have got along without the wicked, could he?"

Mrs. Wheeler looked up. "Is that a joke?" she asked slyly.

"Oh no, not at all! It just struck me that this part is so much more interesting than the books about perfect innocence in Eden."

"And yet I suppose it shouldn't be so," Mrs. Wheeler said slowly, as if in doubt.

Her son laughed and sat up, smoothing his rumpled hair. "The fact remains that it is, dear Mother. And if you took all the great sinners out of the Bible, you'd take out all the interesting characters, wouldn't you?"

"Except Christ," she murmured.

"Yes, except Christ. But I suppose the Jews were honest when they thought him the most dangerous kind of criminal."

"Are you trying to tangle me up?" his mother inquired, with both reproach and amusement in her voice.

Claude went to the window where she was sitting, and looked out at the snowy fields, now becoming blue and desolate as the shadows deepened. "I only mean that even in the Bible the people who were merely free from blame didn't amount to much."

"Ah, I see!" Mrs. Wheeler chuckled softly. "You are trying to get me back to Faith and Works. There's where you always balked when you were a little fellow. Well, Claude, I don't know as much about it as I did then. As I get older, I leave a good deal more to God. I believe He wants to save whatever is noble in this world, and that He knows more ways of doing it than I." She rose like a gentle shadow and rubbed her cheek against his flannel shirt-sleeve, murmuring, "I believe He is sometimes where we would least expect to find Him,—even in proud, rebellious hearts."

For a moment they clung together in the pale, clear square of the west window, as the two natures in one person sometimes meet and cling in a fated hour.

XVI.

RALPH and his father came home to spend the holidays, and on Christmas day Bayliss drove out from town for dinner. He arrived early, and after greeting his mother in the kitchen, went up to the sitting-room, which shone with a holiday neatness, and, for once, was warm enough for Bayliss,—having a low circulation, he felt the cold acutely. He walked up and down, jingling the keys in his pockets and admiring his mother's winter chrysanthemums, which were still blooming. Several times he paused before the old-fashioned secretary, looking through the glass doors at the volumes within. The sight of some of those books awoke disagreeable memories. When he was a boy of fourteen or fifteen, it used to make him bitterly jealous to hear his mother coaxing Claude to read aloud to her. Bayliss had never been bookish. Even before he could read, when his mother told him stories, he at once began to prove to her how they could not possibly be true. Later he found arithmetic and geography more interesting than "Robinson Crusoe." If he sat down with a book, he wanted to feel that he was learning something. His mother and Claude were always talking over his head about the people in books and stories.

Though Bayliss had a sentimental feeling about coming home, he considered that he had had a lonely boyhood. At the country school he had not been happy; he was the boy who always got the answers to the test problems when the others didn't, and he kept his arithmetic papers buttoned up in the inside pocket of his little jacket until he modestly handed them to the teacher, never giving a neighbour the benefit of his cleverness. Leonard Dawson and other lusty lads of his own age made life as terrifying for him as they could. In winter they used to throw him into a snow-drift, and then run away and leave him. In summer they made him eat live grasshoppers behind the schoolhouse, and put big bull-snakes in his dinner pail to surprise him. To this day, Bayliss liked to see one of those fellows get into difficulties that his big fists couldn't get him out of.

It was because Bayliss was quick at figures and undersized for a farmer that his father sent him to town to learn the implement business. From the day he went to work, he managed to live on his small salary. He kept in his vest pocket a little day-book wherein he noted down all his expenditures,—like the millionaire about whom the Baptist preachers were never tired of talking,-and his offering to the contribution box stood out conspicuous in his weekly account.

In Bayliss' voice, even when he used his insinuating drawl and said disagreeable things, there was something a little plaintive; the expression of a deep-seated sense of injury. He felt that he had always been misunderstood and underestimated. Later after he went into business for himself, the young men of Frankfort had never urged him to take part in their pleasures. He had not been asked to join the tennis club or the whist club. He envied Claude his fine physique and his unreckoning, impulsive vitality, as if they had been given to his brother by unfair means and should rightly have been his.

Bayliss and his father were talking together before dinner when Claude came in and was so inconsiderate as to put up a window, though he knew his brother hated a draft. In a moment Bayliss addressed him without looking at him:

"I see your friends, the Erlichs, have bought out the Jenkinson company, in Lincoln; at least, they've given their notes."

Claude had promised his mother to keep his temper today, "Yes, I saw it in the paper. I hope they'll succeed."

"I doubt it." Bayliss shook his head with his wisest look. "I understand they've put a mortgage on their home. That old woman will find herself without a roof one of these days."

"I don't think so. The boys have wanted to go into business together for a long while. They are all intelligent and industrious; why shouldn't they get on?" Claude flattered himself that he spoke in an easy, confidential way.

Bayliss screwed up his eyes. "I expect they're too fond of good living. They'll pay their interest, and spend whatever's left entertaining their friends. I didn't see the young fellow's name in the notice of incorporation, Julius, do they call him?"

"Julius is going abroad to study this fall. He intends to be a professor."

"What's the matter with him? Does he have poor health?"

At this moment the dinner bell sounded, Ralph ran down from his room where he had been dressing, and they all descended to the kitchen to greet the turkey. The dinner progressed pleasantly. Bayliss and his father talked politics, and Ralph told stories about his neighbours in Yucca county. Bayliss was pleased that his mother had remembered he liked oyster stuffing, and he complimented her upon her mince pies. When he saw her pour a second cup of coffee for herself and for Claude at the end of dinner, he said, in a gentle, grieved tone, "I'm sorry to see you taking two, Mother."

Mrs. Wheeler looked at him over the coffee-pot with a droll, guilty smile. "I don't believe coffee hurts me a particle, Bayliss."

"Of course it does; it's a stimulant." What worse could it be, his tone implied! When you said anything was a "stimulant," you had sufficiently condemned it; there was no more noxious word.

Claude was in the upper hall, putting on his coat to go down to the barn and smoke a cigar, when Bayliss came out from the sitting-room and detained him by an indefinite remark.

"I believe there's to be a musical show in Hastings Saturday night."

Claude said he had heard something of the sort.

"I was thinking," Bayliss affected a careless tone, as if he thought of such things every day, "that we might make a party and take Gladys and Enid. The roads are pretty good."

"It's a hard drive home, so late at night," Claude objected. Bayliss meant, of course, that Claude should drive the party up and back in Mr. Wheeler's big car. Bayliss never used his glistening Cadillac for long, rough drives.

"I guess Mother would put us up overnight, and we needn't take the girls home till Sunday morning. I'll get the tickets."

"You'd better arrange it with the girls, then. I'll drive you, of course, if you want to go."

Claude escaped and went out, wishing that Bayliss would do his own courting and not drag him into it. Bayliss, who didn't know one tune from another, certainly didn't want to go to this concert, and it was doubtful whether Enid Royce would care much about going. Gladys Farmer was the best musician in Frankfort, and she would probably like to hear it.

Claude and Gladys were old friends, from their High School days, though they hadn't seen much of each other while he was going to college. Several times this fall Bayliss had asked Claude to go somewhere with him on a Sunday, and then stopped to "pick Gladys up," as he said. Claude didn't like it. He was disgusted, anyhow, when he saw that Bayliss had made up his mind to marry Gladys. She and her mother were so poor that he would probably succeed in the end, though so far Gladys didn't seem to give him much encouragement. Marrying Bayliss, he thought, would be no joke for any woman, but Gladys was the one girl in town whom he particularly ought not to marry. She was as extravagant as she was poor. Though she taught in the Frankfort High School for twelve hundred a year, she had prettier clothes than any of the other girls, except Enid Royce, whose father was a rich man. Her new hats and suede shoes were discussed and criticized year in and year out. People said if she married Bayliss Wheeler, he would soon bring her down to hard facts. Some hoped she would, and some hoped she wouldn't. As for Claude, he had kept away from Mrs. Farmer's cheerful parlour ever since Bayliss had begun to drop in there. He was disappointed in Gladys. When he was offended, he seldom stopped to reason about his state of feeling. He avoided the person and the thought of the person, as if it were a sore spot in his mind.

XVII.

IT HAD BEEN Mr. Wheeler's intention to stay at home until spring, but Ralph wrote that he was having trouble with his foreman, so his father went out to the ranch in February. A few days after his departure there was a storm which gave people something to talk about for a year to come.

The snow began to fall about noon on St. Valentine's day, a soft, thick, wet snow that came down in billows and stuck to everything. Later in the afternoon the wind rose, and wherever there was a shed, a tree, a hedge, or even a clump of tall weeds, drifts began to pile up. Mrs. Wheeler, looking anxiously out from the sitting-room windows, could see nothing but driving waves of soft white, which cut the tall house off from the rest of the world.

Claude and Dan, down in the corral, where they were provisioning the cattle against bad weather, found the air so thick that they could scarcely breathe; their ears and mouths and nostrils were full of snow, their faces plastered with it. It melted constantly upon their clothing, and yet they were white from their boots to their caps as they worked,—there was no shaking it off. The air was not cold, only a little below freezing. When they came in for supper, the drifts had piled against the house until they covered the lower sashes of the kitchen windows, and as they opened the door, a frail wall of snow fell in behind them. Mahailey came running with her broom and pail to sweep it up.

"Ain't it a turrible storm, Mr. Claude? I reckon poor Mr. Ernest won't git over tonight, will he? You never mind, honey; I'll wipe up that water. Run along and git dry clothes on you, an' take a bath, or you'll ketch cold. Th' ole tank's full of hot water for you." Exceptional weather of any kind always delighted Mahailey.

Mrs. Wheeler met Claude at the head of the stairs. "There's no danger of the steers getting snowed under along the creek, is there?" she asked anxiously.

"No, I thought of that. We've driven them all into the little corral on the level, and shut the gates. It's over my head down in the creek bottom now. I haven't a dry stitch on me. I guess I'll follow Mahailey's advice and get in the tub, if you can wait supper for me."

"Put your clothes outside the bathroom door, and I'll see to drying them for you."

"Yes, please. I'll need them tomorrow. I don't want to spoil my new corduroys. And, Mother, see if you can make Dan change. He's too wet and steamy to sit at the table with. Tell him if anybody has to go out after supper, I'll go."

Mrs. Wheeler hurried down stairs. Dan, she knew, would rather sit all evening in wet clothes than take the trouble to put on dry ones. He tried to sneak past her to his own quarters behind the wash-room, and looked aggrieved when he heard her message.

"I ain't got no other outside clothes, except my Sunday ones," he objected.

"Well, Claude says he'll go out if anybody has to. I guess you'll have to change for once, Dan, or go to bed without your supper." She laughed quietly at his dejected expression as he slunk away.

"Mrs. Wheeler," Mahailey whispered, "can't I run down to the cellar an' git some of them nice strawberry preserves? Mr. Claude, he loves 'em on his hot biscuit. He don't eat the honey no more; he's got tired of it."

"Very well. I'll make the coffee good and strong; that will please him more than anything."

Claude came down feeling clean and warm and hungry. As he opened the stair door he sniffed the coffee and frying ham, and when Mahailey bent over the oven the warm smell of browning biscuit rushed out with the heat. These combined odours somewhat dispersed Dan's gloom when he came back in squeaky Sunday shoes and a bunglesome cut-away coat. The latter was not required of him, but he wore it for revenge.

During supper Mrs. Wheeler told them once again how, long ago when she was first married, there were no roads or fences west of Frankfort. One winter night she sat on the roof of their first dugout nearly all night, holding up a lantern tied to a pole to guide Mr. Wheeler home through a snowstorm like this.

Mahailey, moving about the stove, watched over the group at the table. She liked to see the men fill themselves with food-though she did not count Dan a man, by any means, and she looked out to see that Mrs. Wheeler did not forget to eat altogether, as she was apt to do when she fell to remembering things that had happened long ago. Mahailey was in a happy frame of mind because her weather predictions had come true; only yesterday she had told Mrs. Wheeler there would be snow, because she had seen snowbirds. She regarded supper as more than usually important when Claude put on his "velvet close," as she called his brown corduroys.

After supper Claude lay on the couch in the sitting room, while his mother read aloud to him from "Bleak House,"—one of the few novels she loved. Poor Jo was drawing toward his end when Claude suddenly sat up. "Mother, I believe I'm too sleepy. I'll have to turn in. Do you suppose it's still snowing?"

He rose and went to look out, but the west windows were so plastered with snow that they were opaque. Even from the one on the south he could see nothing for a moment; then Mahailey must have carried her lamp to the kitchen window beneath, for all at once a broad yellow beam shone out into the choked air, and down it millions of snowflakes hurried like armies, an unceasing progression, moving as close as they could without forming a solid mass. Claude struck the frozen window-frame with his fist, lifted the lower sash, and thrusting out his head tried to look abroad into the engulfed night. There was a solemnity about a storm of such magnitude; it gave one a feeling of infinity. The myriads of white particles that crossed the rays of lamplight seemed to have a quiet purpose, to be hurrying toward a definite end. A faint purity, like a fragrance almost too fine for human senses, exhaled from them as they clustered about his head and shoulders. His mother, looking under his lifted arm, strained her eyes to see out into that swarming movement, and murmured softly in her quavering voice:

"Ever thicker, thicker, thicker,
Froze the ice on lake and river;
Ever deeper, deeper, deeper,
Fell the snow o'er all the landscape."

XVIII.

Claude's bedroom faced the east. The next morning, when he looked out of his windows, only the tops of the cedars in the front yard were visible. Hurriedly putting on his clothes he ran to the west window at the end of the hall; Lovely Creek, and the deep ravine in which it flowed, had disappeared as if they had never been. The rough pasture was like a smooth field, except for humps and mounds like haycocks, where the snow had drifted over a post or a bush.

At the kitchen stairs Mahailey met him in gleeful excitement. "Lord 'a' mercy, Mr. Claude, I can't git the storm door open. We're snowed in fas'." She looked like a tramp woman, in a jacket patched with many colours, her head tied up in an old black "fascinator," with ravelled yarn hanging down over her face like wild locks of hair. She kept this costume for calamitous occasions; appeared in it when the water-pipes were frozen and burst, or when spring storms flooded the coops and drowned her young chickens.

The storm door opened outward. Claude put his shoulder to it and pushed it a little way. Then, with Mahailey's fireshovel he dislodged enough snow to enable him to force back the door. Dan came tramping in his stocking-feet across the kitchen to his boots, which were still drying behind the stove. "She's sure a bad one, Claude," he remarked, blinking.

"Yes. I guess we won't try to go out till after breakfast. We'll have to dig our way to the barn, and I never thought to bring the shovels up last night."

"Th' ole snow shovels is in the cellar. I'll git 'em."

"Not now, Mahailey. Give us our breakfast before you do anything else."

Mrs. Wheeler came down, pinning on her little shawl, her shoulders more bent than usual. "Claude," she said fearfully, "the cedars in the front yard are all but covered. Do you suppose our cattle could be buried?"

He laughed. "No, Mother. The cattle have been moving around all night, I expect."

When the two men started out with the wooden snow shovels, Mrs. Wheeler and Mahailey stood in the doorway, watching them. For a short distance from the house the path they dug was like a tunnel, and the white walls on either side were higher than their heads. On the breast of the hill the snow was not so deep, and they made better headway. They had to fight through a second heavy drift before they reached the barn, where they went in and warmed themselves among the horses and cows. Dan was for getting next a warm cow and beginning to milk.

"Not yet," said Claude. "I want to have a look at the hogs before we do anything here."

The hog-house was built down in a draw behind the barn. When Claude reached the edge of the gully, blown almost bare, he could look about him. The draw was full of snow, smooth... except in the middle, where there was a rumpled depression, resembling a great heap of tumbled bed-linen.

Dan gasped. "God a' mighty, Claude, the roof's fell in! Them hogs'll be smothered."

"They will if we don't get at them pretty quick. Run to the house and tell Mother. Mahailey will have to milk this morning, and get back here as fast as you can."

The roof was a flat thatch, and the weight of the snow had been too much for it. Claude wondered if he should have put on a new thatch that fall; but the old one wasn't leaky, and had seemed strong enough.

When Dan got back they took turns, one going ahead and throwing out as much snow as he could, the other handling the snow that fell back. After an hour or so of this work, Dan leaned on his shovel.

"We'll never do it, Claude. Two men couldn't throw all that snow out in a week. I'm about all in."

"Well, you can go back to the house and sit by the fire," Claude called fiercely. He had taken off his coat and was working in his shirt and sweater. The sweat was rolling from his face, his back and arms ached, and his hands, which he couldn't keep dry, were blistered. There were thirty-seven hogs in the hog-house.

Dan sat down in the hole. "Maybe if I could git a drink of water, I could hold on a-ways," he said dejectedly.

It was past noon when they got into the shed; a cloud of steam rose, and they heard grunts. They found the pigs all lying in a heap at one end, and pulled the top ones off alive and squealing. Twelve hogs, at the bottom of the pile, had been suffocated. They lay there wet and black in the snow, their bodies warm and smoking, but they were dead; there was no mistaking that.

Mrs. Wheeler, in her husband's rubber boots and an old overcoat, came down with Mahailey to view the scene of disaster.

"You ought to git right at them hawgs an' butcher 'em today," Mahailey called down to the men. She was standing on the edge of the draw, in her patched jacket and ravelled hood. Claude, down in the hole, brushed the sleeve of his sweater across his streaming face. "Butcher them?" he cried indignantly. "I wouldn't butcher them if I never saw meat again."

"You ain't a-goin' to let all that good hawg-meat go to wase, air you, Mr. Claude?" Mahailey pleaded. "They didn't have no sickness nor nuthin'. Only you'll have to git right at 'em, or the meat won't be healthy."

"It wouldn't be healthy for me, anyhow. I don't know what I will do with them, but I'm mighty sure I won't butcher them."

"Don't bother him, Mahailey," Mrs. Wheeler cautioned her. "He's tired, and he has to fix some place for the live hogs."

"I know he is, mam, but I could easy cut up one of them hawgs myself. I butchered my own little pig onct, in Virginia. I could save the hams, anyways, and the spare-ribs. We ain't had no spare-ribs for ever so long."

What with the ache in his back and his chagrin at losing the pigs, Claude was feeling desperate. "Mother," he shouted, "if you don't take Mahailey into the house, I'll go crazy!"

That evening Mrs. Wheeler asked him how much the twelve hogs would have been worth in money. He looked a little startled.

"Oh, I don't know exactly; three hundred dollars, anyway."

"Would it really be as much as that? I don't see how we could have prevented it, do you?" Her face looked troubled.

Claude went to bed immediately after supper, but he had no sooner stretched his aching body between the sheets than he began to feel wakeful. He was humiliated at losing the pigs, because they had been left in his charge; but for the loss in money, about which even his mother was grieved, he didn't seem to care. He wondered whether all that winter he hadn't been working himself up into a childish contempt for money-values.

When Ralph was home at Christmas time, he wore on his little finger a heavy gold ring, with a diamond as big as a pea, surrounded by showy grooves in the metal. He admitted to Claude that he had won it in a poker game. Ralph's hands were never free from automobile grease—they were the red, stumpy kind that couldn't be kept clean. Claude remembered him milking in the barn by lantern light, his jewel throwing off jabbing sparkles of colour, and his fingers looking very much like the teats of the cow. That picture rose before him now, as a symbol of what successful farming led to.

The farmer raised and took to market things with an intrinsic value; wheat and corn as good as could be grown anywhere in the world, hogs and cattle that were the best of their kind. In return he got manufactured articles of poor quality; showy furniture that went to pieces, carpets and draperies that faded, clothes that made a handsome man look like a clown. Most of his money was paid out for machinery,—and that, too, went to pieces. A steam thrasher didn't last long; a horse outlived three automobiles.

Claude felt sure that when he was a little boy and all the neighbours were poor, they and their houses and farms had more individuality. The farmers took time then to plant fine cottonwood groves on their places, and to set osage orange hedges along the borders of their fields. Now these trees were all being cut down and grubbed up. Just why, nobody knew; they impoverished the land... they made the snow drift... nobody had them any more. With prosperity came a kind of callousness; everybody wanted to destroy the old things they used to take pride in. The orchards, which had been nursed and tended so carefully twenty years ago, were now left to die of neglect. It was less trouble to run into town in an automobile and buy fruit than it was to raise it.

The people themselves had changed. He could remember when all the farmers in this community were friendly toward each other; now they were continually having lawsuits. Their sons were either stingy and grasping, or extravagant and lazy, and they were always stirring up trouble. Evidently, it took more intelligence to spend money than to make it.

When he pondered upon this conclusion, Claude thought of the Erlichs. Julius could go abroad and study for his doctor's degree, and live on less than Ralph wasted every year. Ralph would never have a profession or a trade, would never do or make anything the world needed.

Nor did Claude find his own outlook much better. He was twenty-one years old, and he had no skill, no training,—no ability that would ever take him among the kind of people he admired. He was a clumsy, awkward farmer boy, and even Mrs. Erlich seemed to think the farm the best place for him. Probably it was; but all the same he didn't find this kind of life worth the trouble of getting up every morning. He could not see the use of working for money, when money brought nothing one wanted. Mrs. Erlich said it brought security. Sometimes he thought this security was what was the matter with everybody; that only perfect safety was required to kill all the best qualities in people and develop the mean ones.

Ernest, too, said "it's the best life in the world, Claude."

But if you went to bed defeated every night, and dreaded to wake in the morning, then clearly it was too good a life for you. To be assured, at his age, of three meals a day and plenty of sleep, was like being assured of a decent burial. Safety, security; if you followed that reasoning out, then the unborn, those who would never be born, were the safest of all; nothing could happen to them.

Claude knew, and everybody else knew, seemingly, that there was something wrong with him. He had been unable to conceal his discontent. Mr. Wheeler was afraid he was one of those visionary fellows who make unnecessary difficulties for themselves and other people. Mrs. Wheeler thought the trouble with her son was that he had not yet found his Saviour. Bayliss was convinced that his brother was a moral rebel, that behind his reticence and his guarded manner he concealed the most dangerous opinions. The neighbours liked Claude, but they laughed at him, and said it was a good thing his father was well fixed. Claude was aware that his energy, instead of accomplishing something, was spent in resisting unalterable conditions, and in unavailing efforts to subdue his own nature. When he thought he had at last got himself in hand, a moment would undo the work of days; in a flash he would be transformed from a wooden post into a living boy. He would spring to his feet, turn over quickly in bed, or stop short in his walk, because the old belief flashed up in him with an intense kind of hope, an intense kind of pain,—the conviction that there was something splendid about life, if he could but find it.

XIX.

The weather, after the big storm, behaved capriciously. There was a partial thaw which threatened to flood everything,—then a hard freeze. The whole country glittered with an icy crust, and people went about on a platform of frozen snow, quite above the level of ordinary life. Claude got out Mr. Wheeler's old double sleigh from the mass of heterogeneous objects that had for years lain on top of it, and brought the rusty sleighbells up to the house for Mahailey to scour with brick dust. Now that they had automobiles, most of the farmers had let their old sleighs go to pieces. But the Wheelers always kept everything.

Claude told his mother he meant to take Enid Royce for a sleigh-ride. Enid was the daughter of Jason Royce, the grain merchant, one of the early settlers, who for many years had run the only grist mill in Frankfort county. She and Claude were old playmates; he made a formal call at the millhouse, as it was called, every summer during his vacation, and often dropped in to see Mr. Royce at his town office.

Immediately after supper, Claude put the two wiry little blacks, Pompey and Satan, to the sleigh. The moon had been up since long before the sun went down, had been hanging pale in the sky most of the afternoon, and now it flooded the snow-terraced land with silver. It was one of those sparkling winter nights when a boy feels that though the world is very big, he himself is bigger; that under the whole crystalline blue sky there is no one quite so warm and sentient as himself, and that all this magnificence is for him. The sleighbells rang out with a kind of musical lightheartedness, as if they were glad to sing again, after the many winters they had hung rusty and dustchoked in the barn.

The mill road, that led off the highway and down to the river, had pleasant associations for Claude. When he was a youngster, every time his father went to mill, he begged to go along. He liked the mill and the miller and the miller's little girl. He had never liked the miller's house, however, and he was afraid of Enid's mother. Even now, as he tied his horses to the long hitch-bar down by the engine room, he resolved that he would not be persuaded to enter that formal parlour, full of new-looking, expensive furniture, where his energy always deserted him and he could never think of anything to talk about. If he moved, his shoes squeaked in the silence, and Mrs. Royce sat and blinked her sharp little eyes at him, and the longer he stayed, the harder it was to go.

Enid herself came to the door.

"Why, it's Claude!" she exclaimed. "Won't you come in?"

"No, I want you to go riding. I've got the old sleigh out. Come on, it's a fine night!"

"I thought I heard bells. Won't you come in and see Mother while I get my things on?"

Claude said he must stay with his horses, and ran back to the hitch-bar. Enid didn't keep him waiting long; she wasn't that kind. She came swiftly down the path and through the front gate in the Maine seal motor-coat she wore when she drove her coupe in cold weather.

"Now, which way?" Claude asked as the horses sprang forward and the bells began to jingle.

"Almost any way. What a beautiful night! And I love your bells, Claude. I haven't heard sleighbells since you used to bring me and Gladys home from school in stormy weather. Why don't we stop for her tonight? She has furs now, you know!" Here Enid laughed. "All the old ladies are so terribly puzzled about them; they can't find out whether your brother really gave them to her for Christmas or not. If they were sure she bought them for herself, I believe they'd hold a public meeting."

Claude cracked his whip over his eager little blacks. "Doesn't it make you tired, the way they are always nagging at Gladys?"

"It would, if she minded. But she's just as serene! They must have something to fuss about, and of course poor Mrs. Farmer's back taxes are piling up. I certainly suspect Bayliss of the furs."

Claude did not feel as eager to stop for Gladys as he had been a few moments before. They were approaching the town now, and lighted windows shone softly across the blue whiteness of the snow. Even in progressive Frankfort, the street lights were turned off on a night so glorious as this. Mrs. Farmer and her daughter had a little white cottage down in the south part of the town, where only people of modest means lived. "We must stop to see Gladys' mother, if only for a minute," Enid said as they drew up before the fence. "She is so fond of company." Claude tied his team to a tree, and they went up to the narrow, sloping porch, hung with vines that were full of frozen snow.

Mrs. Farmer met them; a large, rosy woman of fifty, with a pleasant Kentucky voice. She took Enid's arm affectionately, and Claude followed them into the long, low sitting-room, which had an uneven floor and a lamp at either end, and was scantily furnished in rickety mahogany. There, close beside the hard-coal burner, sat Bayliss Wheeler. He did not rise when they entered, but said, "Hello, folks," in a rather sheepish voice. On a little table, beside Mrs. Farmer's workbasket, was the box of candy he had lately taken out of his overcoat pocket, still tied up with its gold cord. A tall lamp stood beside the piano, where Gladys had evidently been practising. Claude wondered whether Bayliss actually pretended to an interest in music! At this moment Gladys was in the kitchen, Mrs. Farmer explained, looking for her mother's glasses, mislaid when she was copying a recipe for a cheese soufflé.

"Are you still getting new recipes, Mrs. Farmer?" Enid asked her. "I thought you could make every dish in the world already."

"Oh, not quite!" Mrs. Farmer laughed modestly and showed that she liked compliments. "Do sit down, Claude," she besought of the stiff image by the door. "Daughter will be here directly."

At that moment Gladys Farmer appeared.

"Why, I didn't know you had company, Mother," she said, coming in to greet them.

This meant, Claude supposed, that Bayliss was not company. He scarcely glanced at Gladys as he took the hand she held out to him.

One of Gladys' grandfathers had come from Antwerp, and she had the settled composure, the full red lips, brown eyes, and dimpled white hands which occur so often in Flemish portraits of young women. Some people thought her a trifle heavy, too mature and positive to be called pretty, even though they admired her rich, tulip-like complexion. Gladys never seemed aware that her looks and her poverty and her extravagance were the subject of perpetual argument, but went to and from school every day with the air of one whose position is assured. Her musicianship gave her a kind of authority in Frankfort.

Enid explained the purpose of their call. "Claude has got out his old sleigh, and we've come to take you for a ride. Perhaps Bayliss will go, too?"

Bayliss said he guessed he would, though Claude knew there was nothing he hated so much as being out in the cold. Gladys ran upstairs to put on a warm dress, and Enid accompanied her, leaving Mrs. Farmer to make agreeable conversation between her two incompatible guests.

"Bayliss was just telling us how you lost your hogs in the storm, Claude. What a pity!" she said sympathetically. Yes, Claude thought, Bayliss wouldn't be at all reticent about that incident!

"I suppose there was really no way to save them," Mrs. Farmer went on in her polite way;

her voice was low and round, like her daughter's, different from the high, tight Western voice. "So I hope you don't let yourself worry about it."

"No, I don't worry about anything as dead as those hogs were. What's the use?" Claude asked boldly.

"That's right," murmured Mrs. Farmer, rocking a little in her chair. "Such things will happen sometimes, and we ought not to take them too hard. It isn't as if a person had been hurt, is it?"

Claude shook himself and tried to respond to her cordiality, and to the shabby comfort of her long parlour, so evidently doing its best to be attractive to her friends. There weren't four steady legs on any of the stuffed chairs or little folding tables she had brought up from the South, and the heavy gold moulding was half broken away from the oil portrait of her father, the judge. But she carried her poverty lightly, as Southern people did after the Civil War, and she didn't fret half so much about her back taxes as her neighbours did. Claude tried to talk agreeably to her, but he was distracted by the sound of stifled laughter upstairs. Probably Gladys and Enid were joking about Bayliss' being there. How shameless girls were, anyhow!

People came to their front windows to look out as the sleigh dashed jingling up and down the village streets. When they left town, Bayliss suggested that they drive out past the Trevor place. The girls began to talk about the two young New Englanders, Trevor and Brewster, who had lived there when Frankfort was still a tough little frontier settlement. Every one was talking about them now, for a few days ago word had come that one of the partners, Amos Brewster, had dropped dead in his law office in Hartford. It was thirty years since he and his friend, Bruce Trevor, had tried to be great cattle men in Frankfort county, and had built the house on the round hill east of the town, where they wasted a great deal of money very joyously. Claude's father always declared that the amount they squandered in carousing was negligible compared to their losses in commendable industrial endeavour. The country, Mr. Wheeler said, had never been the same since those boys left it. He delighted to tell about the time when Trevor and Brewster went into sheep. They imported a breeding ram from Scotland at a great expense, and when he arrived were so impatient to get the good of him that they turned him in with the ewes as soon as he was out of his crate. Consequently all the lambs were born at the wrong season; came at the beginning of March, in a blinding blizzard, and the mothers died from exposure. The gallant Trevor took horse and spurred all over the county, from one little settlement to another, buying up nursing bottles and nipples to feed the orphan lambs.

The rich bottom land about the Trevor place had been rented out to a truck gardener for years now; the comfortable house with its billiard-room annex—a wonder for that part of the country in its day—remained closed, its windows boarded up. It sat on the top of a round knoll, a fine cottonwood grove behind it. Tonight, as Claude drove toward it, the hill with its tall straight trees looked like a big fur cap put down on the snow.

"Why hasn't some one bought that house long ago and fixed it up?" Enid remarked. "There is no building site around here to compare with it. It looks like the place where the leading citizen of the town ought to live."

"I'm glad you like it, Enid," said Bayliss in a guarded voice. "I've always had a sneaking fancy for the place myself. Those fellows back there never wanted to sell it. But now the estate's got to be settled up. I bought it yesterday. The deed is on its way to Hartford for signature."

Enid turned round in her seat. "Why Bayliss, are you in earnest? Think of just buying the Trevor place off-hand, as if it were any ordinary piece of real estate! Will you make over the house, and live there some day?"

"I don't know about living there. It's too far to walk to my business, and the road across this bottom gets pretty muddy for a car in the spring."

"But it's not far, less than a mile. If I once owned that spot, I'd surely never let anybody else live there. Even Carrie remembers it. She often asks in her letters whether any one has bought the Trevor place yet."

Carrie Royce, Enid's older sister, was a missionary in China.

"Well," Bayliss admitted, "I didn't buy it for an investment, exactly. I paid all it was worth."

Enid turned to Gladys, who was apparently not listening. "You'd be the one who could plan a mansion for Trevor Hill, Gladys. You always have such original ideas about houses."

"Yes, people who have no houses of their own often seem to have ideas about building," said Gladys quietly. "But I like the Trevor place as it is. I hate to think that one of them is dead. People say they did have such good times up there."

Bayliss grunted. "Call it good times if you like. The kids were still grubbing whiskey bottles out of the cellar when I first came to town. Of course, if I decide to live there, I'll pull down that old trap and put up something modern." He often took this gruff tone with Gladys in public.

Enid tried to draw the driver into the conversation. "There seems to be a difference of opinion here, Claude."

"Oh," said Gladys carelessly, "it's Bayliss' property, or soon will be. He will build what he likes. I've always known somebody would get that place away from me, so I'm prepared."

"Get it away from you?" muttered Bayliss, amazed.

"Yes. As long as no one bought it and spoiled it, it was mine as much as it was anybody's."

"Claude," said Enid banteringly, "now both your brothers have houses. Where are you going to have yours?"

"I don't know that I'll ever have one. I think I'll run about the world a little before I draw my plans," he replied sarcastically.

"Take me with you, Claude!" said Gladys in a tone of sudden weariness. From that spiritless murmur Enid suspected that Bayliss had captured Gladys' hand under the buffalo robe.

Grimness had settled down over the sleighing party. Even Enid, who was not highly sensitive to unuttered feelings, saw that there was an uncomfortable constraint. A sharp wind had come up. Bayliss twice suggested turning back, but his brother answered, "Pretty soon," and drove on. He meant that Bayliss should have enough of it. Not until Enid whispered reproachfully, "I really think you ought to turn; we're all getting cold," did he realize that he had made his sleighing party into a punishment! There was certainly nothing to punish Enid for; she had done her best, and had tried to make his own bad manners less conspicuous. He muttered a blundering apology to her when he lifted her from the sleigh at the mill house. On his long drive home he had bitter thoughts for company.

He was so angry with Gladys that he hadn't been able to bid her good-night. Everything she said on the ride had nettled him. If she meant to marry Bayliss, then she ought to throw off this affectation of freedom and independence. If she did not mean to, why did she accept favours from him and let him get into the habit of walking into her house and putting his box of candy on the table, as all Frankfort fellows did when they were courting? Certainly she couldn't make herself believe that she liked his society!

When they were classmates at the Frankfort High School, Gladys was Claude's aesthetic proxy. It wasn't the proper thing for a boy to be too clean, or too careful about his dress and manners. But if he selected a girl who was irreproachable in these respects, got his Latin and did his laboratory work with her, then all her personal attractions redounded to his credit. Gladys had seemed to appreciate the honour Claude did her, and it was not all on her own account that she wore such beautifully ironed muslin dresses when they went on botanical expeditions.

Driving home after that miserable sleigh-ride, Claude told himself that in so far as Gladys was concerned he could make up his mind to the fact that he had been "stung" all along. He had believed in her fine feelings; believed implicitly. Now he knew she had none so fine that she couldn't pocket them when there was enough to be gained by it. Even while he said these things over and over, his old conception of Gladys, down at the bottom of his mind, remained persistently unchanged. But that only made his state of feeling the more painful. He was deeply hurt,—and for some reason, youth, when it is hurt, likes to feel itself betrayed.

2

ENID

I.

ONE AFTERNOON that spring Claude was sitting on the long flight of granite steps that leads up to the State House in Denver. He had been looking at the collection of Cliff Dweller remains in the Capitol, and when he came out into the sunlight the faint smell of fresh-cut grass struck his nostrils and persuaded him to linger. The gardeners were giving the grounds their first light mowing. All the lawns on the hill were bright with daffodils and hyacinths. A sweet, warm wind blew over the grass, drying the waterdrops. There had been showers in the afternoon, and the sky was still a tender, rainy blue, where it showed through the masses of swiftly moving clouds.

Claude had been away from home for nearly a month. His father had sent him out to see Ralph and the new ranch, and from there he went on to Colorado Springs and Trinidad. He had enjoyed travelling, but now that he was back in Denver he had that feeling of loneliness which often overtakes country boys in a city; the feeling of being unrelated to anything, of not mattering to anybody. He had wandered about Colorado Springs wishing he knew some of the people who were going in and out of the houses; wishing that he could talk to some of those pretty girls he saw driving their own cars about the streets, if only to say a few words. One morning when he was walking out in the hills a girl passed him, then slowed her car to ask if she could give him a lift. Claude would have said that she was just the sort who would never stop to pick him up, yet she did, and she talked to him pleasantly all the way back to town. It was only twenty minutes or so, but it was worth everything else that happened on his trip. When she asked him where she should put him down, he said at the Antlers, and blushed so furiously that she must have known at once he wasn't staying there.

He wondered this afternoon how many discouraged young men had sat here on the State House steps and watched the sun go down behind the mountains. Every one was always saying it was a fine thing to be young; but it was a painful thing, too. He didn't believe older people were ever so wretched. Over there, in the golden light, the mass of mountains was splitting up into four distinct ranges, and as the sun dropped lower the peaks emerged in perspective, one behind the other. It was a lonely splendour that only made the ache in his breast the stronger. What was the matter with him, he asked himself entreatingly. He must answer that question before he went home again.

The statue of Kit Carson on horseback, down in the Square, pointed Westward; but there was no West, in that sense, any more. There was still South America; perhaps he could find something below the Isthmus. Here the sky was like a lid shut down over the world; his mother could see saints and martyrs behind it.

Well, in time he would get over all this, he supposed. Even his father had been restless as a young man, and had run away into a new country. It was a storm that died down at last,—but what a pity not to do anything with it! A waste of power—for it was a kind of power; he sprang to his feet and stood frowning against the ruddy light, so deep in his struggling thoughts that he did not notice a man, mounting from the lower terraces, who stopped to look at him.

The stranger scrutinized Claude with interest. He saw a young man standing bareheaded on the long flight of steps, his fists clenched in an attitude of arrested action,—his sandy hair, his tanned face, his tense figure copper-coloured in the oblique rays. Claude would have been astonished if he could have known how he seemed to this stranger.

II.

THE NEXT MORNING Claude stepped off the train at Frankfort and had his breakfast at the station before the town was awake. His family were not expecting him, so he thought he would walk home and stop at the mill to see Enid Royce. After all, old friends were best.

He left town by the low road that wound along the creek. The willows were all out in new yellow leaves, and the sticky cotton-wood buds were on the point of bursting. Birds were calling everywhere, and now and then, through the studded willow wands, flashed the dazzling wing of a cardinal.

All over the dusty, tan-coloured wheatfields there was a tender mist of green,—millions of little fingers reaching up and waving lightly in the sun. To the north and south Claude could see the corn-planters, moving in straight lines over the brown acres where the earth had been harrowed so fine that it blew off in clouds of dust to the roadside. When a gust of wind rose, gay little twisters came across the open fields, corkscrews of powdered earth that whirled through the air and suddenly fell again. It seemed as if there were a lark on every fence post, singing for everything that was dumb; for the great ploughed lands, and the heavy horses in the rows, and the men guiding the horses.

Along the roadsides, from under the dead weeds and wisps of dried bluestem, the dandelions thrust up their clean, bright faces. If Claude happened to step on one, the acrid smell made him think of Mahailey, who had probably been out this very morning, gouging the sod with her broken butcher knife and stuffing dandelion greens into her apron. She always went for greens with an air of secrecy, very early, and sneaked along the roadsides stooping close to the ground, as if she might be detected and driven away, or as if the dandelions were wild things and had to be caught sleeping.

Claude was thinking, as he walked, of how he used to like to come to mill with his father. The whole process of milling was mysterious to him then; and the mill house and the miller's wife were mysterious; even Enid was, a little—until he got her down in the bright sun among the cat-tails. They used to play in the bins of clean wheat, watch the flour coming out of the hopper and get themselves covered with white dust.

Best of all he liked going in where the water-wheel hung dripping in its dark cave, and quivering streaks of sunlight came in through the cracks to play on the green slime and the spotted jewel-weed growing in the shale. The mill was a place of sharp contrasts; bright sun and deep shade, roaring sound and heavy, dripping silence. He remembered how astonished he was one day, when he found Mr. Royce in gloves and goggles, cleaning the millstones, and discovered what harmless looking things they were. The miller picked away at them with a sharp hammer until the sparks flew, and Claude still had on his hand a blue spot where a chip of flint went under the skin when he got too near.

Jason Royce must have kept his mill going out of sentiment, for there was not much money in it now. But milling had been his first business, and he had not found many things in life to be sentimental about. Sometimes one still came upon him in dusty miller's clothes, giving his man a day off. He had long ago ceased to depend on the risings and fallings of Lovely Creek for his power, and had put in a gasoline engine. The old dam now lay "like a holler tooth," as one of his men said, grown up with weeds and willow-brush.

Mr. Royce's family affairs had never gone as well as his business. He had not been blessed with a son, and out of five daughters he had succeeded in bringing up only two. People thought the mill house damp and unwholesome. Until he built a tenant's cottage and got a married man to take charge of the mill, Mr. Royce was never able to keep his millers long. They complained of the gloom of the house, and said they could not get enough to eat. Mrs. Royce went every summer to a vegetarian sanatorium in Michigan, where she learned to live on nuts and toasted cereals. She gave her family nourishment, to be sure, but there was never during the day a meal that a man could look forward to with pleasure, or sit down to with satisfaction. Mr. Royce usually dined at the hotel in town. Nevertheless, his wife was distinguished for certain brilliant culinary accomplishments. Her bread was faultless. When a church supper was toward, she was always called upon for her wonderful mayonnaise dressing, or her angel-food cake,—sure to be the lightest and spongiest in any assemblage of cakes.

A deep preoccupation about her health made Mrs. Royce like a woman who has a hidden grief, or is preyed upon by a consuming regret. It wrapped her in a kind of insensibility. She lived differently from other people, and that fact made her distrustful and reserved. Only when she was at the sanatorium, under the care of her idolized doctors, did she feel that she was understood and surrounded by sympathy.

Her distrust had communicated itself to her daughters and in countless little ways had coloured their feelings about life. They grew up under the shadow of being "different," and formed no close friendships. Gladys Farmer was the only Frankfort girl who had ever gone much to the mill house. Nobody was surprised when Caroline Royce, the older daughter, went out to China to be a missionary, or that her mother let her go without a protest. The Royce women were strange, anyhow, people said; with Carrie gone, they hoped Enid would grow up to be more like other folk. She dressed well, came to town often in her car, and was always ready to work for the church or the public library.

Besides, in Frankfort, Enid was thought very pretty,—in itself a humanizing attribute. She was slender, with a small, well-shaped head, a smooth, pale skin, and large, dark, opaque eyes with heavy lashes. The long line from the lobe of her ear to the tip of her chin gave her face a certain rigidity, but to the old ladies, who are the best critics in such matters, this meant firmness and dignity. She moved quickly and gracefully, just brushing things rather than touching them, so that there was a suggestion of flight about her slim figure, of gliding away from her surroundings. When the Sunday School gave tableaux vivants, Enid was chosen for Nydia, the blind girl of Pompeii, and for the martyr in "Christ or Diana." The pallor of her skin, the submissive inclination of her forehead, and her dark, unchanging eyes, made one think of something "early Christian."

On this May morning when Claude Wheeler came striding up the mill road, Enid was in the yard, standing by a trellis for vines built near the fence, out from under the heavy shade of the trees. She was raking the earth that had been spaded up the day before, and making furrows in which to drop seeds. From the turn of the road, by the knotty old willows, Claude saw her pink starched dress and little white sun-bonnet. He hurried forward.

"Hello, are you farming?" he called as he came up to the fence.

Enid, who was bending over at that moment, rose quickly, but without a start. "Why, Claude! I thought you were out West somewhere. This is a surprise!" She brushed the earth from her hands and gave him her limp white fingers. Her arms, bare below the elbow, were thin, and looked cold, as if she had put on a summer dress too early.

"I just got back this morning. I'm walking out home. What are you planting?"

"Sweet peas."

"You always have the finest ones in the country. When I see a bunch of yours at church or anywhere, I always know them."

"Yes, I'm quite successful with my sweet peas," she admitted. "The ground is rich down here, and they get plenty of sun."

"It isn't only your sweet peas. Nobody else has such lilacs or rambler roses, and I expect you have the only wistaria vine in Frankfort county."

"Mother planted that a long while ago, when she first moved here. She is very partial to wistaria. I'm afraid we'll lose it, one of these hard winters."

"Oh, that would be a shame! Take good care of it. You must put in a lot of time looking after these things, anyway." He spoke admiringly.

Enid leaned against the fence and pushed back her little bonnet. "Perhaps I take more interest in flowers than I do in people. I often envy you, Claude; you have so many interests."

He coloured. "I? Good gracious, I don't have many! I'm an awfully discontented sort of fellow. I didn't care about going to school until I had to stop, and then I was sore because I couldn't go back. I guess I've been sulking about it all winter."

She looked at him with quiet astonishment. "I don't see why you should be discontented; you're so free."

"Well, aren't you free, too?"

"Not to do what I want to. The only thing I really want to do is to go out to China and help Carrie in her work. Mother thinks I'm not strong enough. But Carrie was never very strong here. She is better in China, and I think I might be."

Claude felt concern. He had not seen Enid since the sleigh-ride, when she had been gayer than usual. Now she seemed sunk in lassitude. "You must get over such notions, Enid. You don't want to go wandering off alone like that. It makes people queer. Isn't there plenty of missionary work to be done right here?"

She sighed. "That's what everybody says. But we all of us have a chance, if we'll take it. Out there they haven't. It's terrible to think of all those millions that live and die in darkness."

Claude glanced up at the sombre mill house, hidden in cedars,—then off at the bright, dusty fields. He felt as if he were a little to blame for Enid's melancholy. He hadn't been very neighbourly this last year. "People can live in darkness here, too, unless they fight it. Look at me. I told you I've been moping all winter. We all feel friendly enough, but we go plodding on and never get together. You and I are old friends, and yet we hardly ever see each other.

Mother says you've been promising for two years to run up and have a visit with her. Why don't you come? It would please her."

"Then I will. I've always been fond of your mother." She paused a moment, absently twisting the strings of her bonnet, then twitched it from her head with a quick movement and looked at him squarely in the bright light. "Claude, you haven't really become a free-thinker, have you?"

He laughed outright. "Why, what made you think I had?"

"Everybody knows Ernest Havel is, and people say you and he read that kind of books together."

"Has that got anything to do with our being friends?"

"Yes, it has. I couldn't feel the same confidence in you. I've worried about it a good deal."

"Well, you just cut it out. For one thing, I'm not worth it," he said quickly.

"Oh, yes, you are! If worrying would do any good—" she shook her head at him reproachfully.

Claude took hold of the fence pickets between them with both hands. "It will do good! Didn't I tell you there was missionary work to be done right here? Is that why you've been so stand-offish with me the last few years, because you thought I was an atheist?"

"I never, you know, liked Ernest Havel," she murmured.

When Claude left the mill and started homeward he felt that he had found something which would help him through the summer. How fortunate he had been to come upon Enid alone and talk to her without interruption,—without once seeing Mrs. Royce's face, always masked in powder, peering at him from behind a drawn blind. Mrs. Royce had always looked old, even long ago when she used to come into church with her little girls,—a tiny woman in tiny high-heeled shoes and a big hat with nodding plumes, her black dress covered with bugles and jet that glittered and rattled and made her seem hard on the outside, like an insect.

Yes, he must see to it that Enid went about and saw more of other people. She was too much with her mother, and with her own thoughts. Flowers and foreign missions—her garden and the great kingdom of China; there was something unusual and touching about her preoccupations. Something quite charming, too. Women ought to be religious; faith was the natural fragrance of their minds. The more incredible the things they believed, the more lovely was the act of belief. To him the story of "Paradise Lost" was as mythical as the "Odyssey"; yet when his mother read it aloud to him, it was not only beautiful but true. A woman who didn't have holy thoughts about mysterious things far away would be prosaic and commonplace, like a man.

III.

DURING THE NEXT few weeks Claude often ran his car down to the mill house on a pleasant evening and coaxed Enid to go into Frankfort with him and sit through a moving picture show, or to drive to a neighbouring town. The advantage of this form of companionship was that it did not put too great a strain upon one's conversational powers. Enid could be admirably silent, and she was never embarrassed by either silence or speech. She was cool and sure of herself under any circumstances, and that was one reason why she drove a car so well,—much better than Claude, indeed.

One Sunday, when they met after church, she told Claude that she wanted to go to Hastings to do some shopping, and they arranged that he should take her on Tuesday in his father's big car. The town was about seventy miles to the northeast and, from Frankfort, it was an inconvenient trip by rail.

On Tuesday morning Claude reached the mill house just as the sun was rising over the damp fields. Enid was on the front porch waiting for him, wearing a blanket coat over her spring suit. She ran down to the gate and slipped into the seat beside him.

"Good morning, Claude. Nobody else is up. It's going to be a glorious day, isn't it?"

"Splendid. A little warm for this time of year. You won't need that coat long."

For the first hour they found the roads empty. All the fields were grey with dew, and the early sunlight burned over everything with the transparent brightness of a fire that has just been kindled. As the machine noiselessly wound off the miles, the sky grew deeper and bluer, and the flowers along the roadside opened in the wet grass. There were men and horses abroad on every hill now. Soon they began to pass children on the way to school, who stopped and waved their bright dinner pails at the two travellers. By ten o'clock they were in Hastings.

While Enid was shopping, Claude bought some white shoes and duck trousers. He felt more interest than usual in his summer clothes. They met at the hotel for lunch, both very hungry and both satisfied with their morning's work. Seated in the dining room, with Enid opposite him, Claude thought they did not look at all like a country boy and girl come to town, but like experienced people touring in their car.

"Will you make a call with me after dinner?" she asked while they were waiting for their dessert.

"Is it any one I know?"

"Certainly. Brother Weldon is in town. His meetings are over, and I was afraid he might be gone, but he is staying on a few days with Mrs. Gleason. I brought some of Carrie's letters along for him to read."

Claude made a wry face. "He won't be delighted to see me. We never got on well at school. He's a regular muff of a teacher, if you want to know," he added resolutely.

Enid studied him judicially. "I'm surprised to hear that; he's such a good speaker. You'd better come along. It's so foolish to have a coolness with your old teachers."

An hour later the Reverend Arthur Weldon received the two young people in Mrs. Gleason's half-darkened parlour, where he seemed quite as much at home as that lady herself. The hostess, after chatting cordially with the visitors for a few moments, excused herself to go to a P. E. O. meeting. Every one rose at her departure, and Mr. Weldon approached Enid, took her hand, and stood looking at her with his head inclined and his oblique smile. "This is an unexpected pleasure, to see you again, Miss Enid. And you, too, Claude," turning a little toward the latter. "You've come up from Frankfort together this beautiful day?" His tone seemed to say, "How lovely for you!"

He directed most of his remarks to Enid and, as always, avoided looking at Claude except when he definitely addressed him.

"You are farming this year, Claude? I presume that is a great satisfaction to your father. And Mrs. Wheeler is quite well?"

Mr. Weldon certainly bore no malice, but he always pronounced Claude's name exactly like the word "Clod," which annoyed him. To be sure, Enid pronounced his name in the same way, but either Claude did not notice this, or did not mind it from her. He sank into a deep, dark sofa, and sat with his driving cap on his knee while Brother Weldon drew a chair up to the one open window of the dusky room and began to read Carrie Royce's letters. Without being asked to do so, he read them aloud, and stopped to comment from time to time. Claude observed with disappointment that Enid drank in all his platitudes just as Mrs.

Wheeler did. He had never looked at Weldon so long before. The light fell full on the young man's pear-shaped head and his thin, rippled hair. What in the world could sensible women like his mother and Enid Royce find to admire in this purring, white-necktied fellow? Enid's dark eyes rested upon him with an expression of profound respect. She both looked at him and spoke to him with more feeling than she ever showed toward Claude.

"You see, Brother Weldon," she said earnestly, "I am not naturally much drawn to people. I find it hard to take the proper interest in the church work at home. It seems as if I had always been holding myself in reserve for the foreign field,—by not making personal ties, I mean. If Gladys Farmer went to China, everybody would miss her. She could never be replaced in the High School. She has the kind of magnetism that draws people to her. But I have always been keeping myself free to do what Carrie is doing. There I know I could be of use."

Claude saw it was not easy for Enid to talk like this. Her face looked troubled, and her dark eyebrows came together in a sharp angle as she tried to tell the young preacher exactly what was going on in her mind. He listened with his habitual, smiling attention, smoothing the paper of the folded letter pages and murmuring, "Yes, I understand. Indeed, Miss Enid?"

When she pressed him for advice, he said it was not always easy to know in what field one could be most useful; perhaps this very restraint was giving her some spiritual discipline that she particularly needed. He was careful not to commit himself, not to advise anything unconditionally, except prayer.

"I believe that all things are made clear to us in prayer, Miss Enid."

Enid clasped her hands; her perplexity made her features look sharper. "But it is when I pray that I feel this call the strongest. It seems as if a finger were pointing me over there. Sometimes when I ask for guidance in little things, I get none, and only get the feeling that my work lies far away, and that for it, strength would be given me. Until I take that road, Christ withholds himself."

Mr. Weldon answered her in a tone of relief, as if something obscure had been made clear. "If that is the case, Miss Enid, I think we need have no anxiety. If the call recurs to you in prayer, and it is your Saviour's will, then we can be sure that the way and the means will be revealed. A passage from one of the Prophets occurs to me at this moment; 'And behold a way shall be opened up before thy feet; walk thou in it.' We might say that this promise was originally meant for Enid Royce! I believe God likes us to appropriate passages of His word personally." This last remark was made playfully, as if it were a kind of Christian Endeavour jest. He rose and handed Enid back the letters. Clearly, the interview was over.

As Enid drew on her gloves she told him that it had been a great help to talk to him, and that he always seemed to give her what she needed. Claude wondered what it was. He hadn't seen Weldon do anything but retreat before her eager questions. He, an "atheist," could have given her stronger reinforcement.

Claude's car stood under the maple trees in front of Mrs. Gleason's house. Before they got into it, he called Enid's attention to a mass of thunderheads in the west.

"That looks to me like a storm. It might be a wise thing to stay at the hotel tonight."

"Oh, no! I don't want to do that. I haven't come prepared."

He reminded her that it wouldn't be impossible to buy whatever she might need for the night.

"I don't like to stay in a strange place without my own things," she said decidedly.

"I'm afraid we'll be going straight into it. We may be in for something pretty rough,—but it's as you say." He still hesitated, with his hand on the door.

"I think we'd better try it," she said with quiet determination. Claude had not yet learned that Enid always opposed the unexpected, and could not bear to have her plans changed by people or circumstances.

For an hour he drove at his best speed, watching the clouds anxiously. The table-land, from horizon to horizon, was glowing in sunlight, and the sky itself seemed only the more brilliant for the mass of purple vapours rolling in the west, with bright edges, like new-cut lead. He had made fifty odd miles when the air suddenly grew cold, and in ten minutes the whole shining sky was blotted out. He sprang to the ground and began to jack up his wheels. As soon as a wheel left the earth, Enid adjusted the chain. Claude told her he had never got the chains on so quickly before. He covered the packages in the back seat with an oilcloth and drove forward to meet the storm.

The rain swept over them in waves, seemed to rise from the sod as well as to fall from the clouds. They made another five miles, ploughing through puddles and sliding over liquefied roads. Suddenly the heavy car, chains and all, bounded up a two-foot bank, shot over the sod a dozen yards before the brake caught it, then swung a half-circle and stood still. Enid sat calm and motionless.

Claude drew a long breath. "If that had happened on a culvert, we'd be in the ditch with the car on top of us. I simply can't control the thing. The whole top soil is loose, and there's nothing to hold to. That's Tommy Rice's place over there. We'd better get him to take us in for the night."

"But that would be worse than the hotel," Enid objected. "They are not very clean people, and there are a lot of children."

"Better be crowded than dead," he murmured. "From here on, it would be a matter of luck. We might land anywhere."

"We are only about ten miles from your place. I can stay with your mother tonight."

"It's too dangerous, Enid. I don't like the responsibility. Your father would blame me for taking such a chance."

"I know, it's on my account you're nervous." Enid spoke reasonably enough. "Do you mind letting me drive for awhile? There are only three bad hills left, and I think I can slide down them sideways; I've often tried it."

Claude got out and let her slip into his seat, but after she took the wheel he put his hand on her arm. "Don't do anything so foolish," he pleaded.

Enid smiled and shook her head. She was amiable, but inflexible.

He folded his arms. "Go on."

He was chafed by her stubbornness, but he had to admire her resourcefulness in handling the car. At the bottom of one of the worst hills was a new cement culvert, overlaid with liquid mud, where there was nothing for the chains to grip. The car slid to the edge of the culvert and stopped on the very brink. While they were ploughing up the other side of the hill, Enid remarked; "It's a good thing your starter works well; a little jar would have thrown us over."

They pulled up at the Wheeler farm just before dark, and Mrs. Wheeler came running out to meet them with a rubber coat over her head.

"You poor drowned children!" she cried, taking Enid in her arms. "How did you ever get home? I so hoped you had stayed in Hastings."

"It was Enid who got us home," Claude told her. "She's a dreadfully foolhardy girl, and somebody ought to shake her, but she's a fine driver."

Enid laughed as she brushed a wet lock back from her forehead. "You were right, of course; the sensible thing would have been to turn in at the Rice place; only I didn't want to."

Later in the evening Claude was glad they hadn't. It was pleasant to be at home and to see Enid at the supper table, sitting on his father's right and wearing one of his mother's new grey house-dresses. They would have had a dismal time at the Rices', with no beds to sleep in except such as were already occupied by Rice children. Enid had never slept in his mother's guest room before, and it pleased him to think how comfortable she would be there.

At an early hour Mrs. Wheeler took a candle to light her guest to bed; Enid passed near Claude's chair as she was leaving the room. "Have you forgiven me?" she asked teasingly.

"What made you so pig-headed? Did you want to frighten me? or to show me how well you could drive?"

"Neither. I wanted to get home. Good-night."

Claude settled back in his chair and shaded his eyes. She did feel that this was home, then. She had not been afraid of his father's jokes, or disconcerted by Mahailey's knowing grin. Her ease in the household gave him unaccountable pleasure. He picked up a book, but did not read. It was lying open on his knee when his mother came back half an hour later.

"Move quietly when you go upstairs, Claude. She is so tired that she may be asleep already."

He took off his shoes and made his ascent with the utmost caution.

IV.

Ernest Havel was cultivating his bright, glistening young cornfield one summer morning, whistling to himself an old German song which was somehow connected with a picture that rose in his memory. It was a picture of the earliest ploughing he could remember.

He saw a half-circle of green hills, with snow still lingering in the clefts of the higher ridges; behind the hills rose a wall of sharp mountains, covered with dark pine forests. In the meadows at the foot of that sweep of hills there was a winding creek, with polled willows in their first yellow-green, and brown fields. He himself was a little boy, playing by the creek and watching his father and mother plough with two great oxen, that had rope traces fastened to their heads and their long horns. His mother walked barefoot beside the oxen and led them; his father walked behind, guiding the plough. His father always looked down. His mother's face was almost as brown and furrowed as the fields, and her eyes were pale blue, like the skies of early spring. The two would go up and down thus all morning without speaking, except to the oxen. Ernest was the last of a long family, and as he played by the creek he used to wonder why his parents looked so old.

Leonard Dawson drove his car up to the fence and shouted, waking Ernest from his revery. He told his team to stand, and ran out to the edge of the field.

"Hello, Ernest," Leonard called. "Have you heard Claude Wheeler got hurt day before yesterday?"

"You don't say so! It can't be anything bad, or they'd let me know."

"Oh, it's nothing very bad, I guess, but he got his face scratched up in the wire quite a little. It was the queerest thing I ever saw. He was out with the team of mules and a heavy plough, working the road in that deep cut between their place and mine. The gasoline motor-truck came along, making more noise than usual, maybe. But those mules know a motor truck, and what they did was pure cussedness. They begun to rear and plunge in that deep cut. I was working my corn over in the field and shouted to the gasoline man to stop, but he didn't hear me. Claude jumped for the critters' heads and got 'em by the bits, but by that time he was all tangled up in the lines. Those damned mules lifted him off his feet and started to run. Down the draw and up the bank and across the fields they went, with that big plough-blade jumping three or four feet in the air every clip. I was sure it would cut one of the mules open, or go clean through Claude. It would have got him, too, if he hadn't kept his hold on the bits. They carried him right along, swinging in the air, and finally ran him into the barb-wire fence and cut his face and neck up."

"My goodness! Did he get cut bad?"

"No, not very, but yesterday morning he was out cultivating corn, all stuck up with court plaster. I knew that was a fool thing to do; a wire cut's nasty if you get overheated out in the dust. But you can't tell a Wheeler anything. Now they say his face has swelled and is hurting him terrible, and he's gone to town to see the doctor. You'd better go over there tonight, and see if you can make him take care of himself."

Leonard drove on, and Ernest went back to his team. "It's queer about that boy," he was thinking. "He's big and strong, and he's got an education and all that fine land, but he don't seem to fit in right." Sometimes Ernest thought his friend was unlucky. When that idea occurred to him, he sighed and shook it off. For Ernest believed there was no help for that; it was something rationalism did not explain.

The next afternoon Enid Royce's coupe drove up to the Wheeler farmyard. Mrs. Wheeler saw Enid get out of her car and came down the hill to meet her, breathless and distressed. "Oh, Enid! You've heard of Claude's accident? He wouldn't take care of himself, and now he's got erysipelas. He's in such pain, poor boy!"

Enid took her arm, and they started up the hill toward the house. "Can I see Claude, Mrs. Wheeler? I want to give him these flowers."

Mrs. Wheeler hesitated. "I don't know if he will let you come in, dear. I had hard work persuading him to see Ernest for a few moments last night. He seems so low-spirited, and he's sensitive about the way he's bandaged up. I'll go to his room and ask him."

"No, just let me go up with you, please. If I walk in with you, he won't have time to fret about it. I won't stay if he doesn't wish it, but I want to see him."

Mrs. Wheeler was alarmed at this suggestion, but Enid ignored her uncertainty. They went up to the third floor together, and Enid herself tapped at the door.

"It's I, Claude. May I come in for a moment?"

A muffled, reluctant voice answered. "No. They say this is catching, Enid. And anyhow, I'd rather you didn't see me like this."

Without waiting she pushed open the door. The dark blinds were down, and the room was full of a strong, bitter odor. Claude lay flat in bed, his head and face so smothered in surgical cotton that only his eyes and the tip of his nose were visible. The brown paste with which his features were smeared oozed out at the edges of the gauze and made his dressings look untidy. Enid took in these details at a glance.

"Does the light hurt your eyes? Let me put up one of the blinds for a moment, because I want you to see these flowers. I've brought you my first sweet peas."

Claude blinked at the bunch of bright colours she held out before him. She put them up to his face and asked him if he could smell them through his medicines. In a moment he ceased to feel embarrassed. His mother brought a glass bowl, and Enid arranged the flowers on the little table beside him.

"Now, do you want me to darken the room again?"

"Not yet. Sit down for a minute and talk to me. I can't say much because my face is stiff."

"I should think it would be! I met Leonard Dawson on the road yesterday, and he told me how you worked in the field after you were cut. I would like to scold you hard, Claude."

"Do. It might make me feel better." He took her hand and kept her beside him a moment. "Are those the sweet peas you were planting that day when I came back from the West?"

"Yes. Haven't they done well to blossom so early?"

"Less than two months. That's strange," he sighed.

"Strange? What?"

"Oh, that a handful of seeds can make anything so pretty in a few weeks, and it takes a man so long to do anything and then it's not much account."

"That's not the way to look at things," she said reprovingly.

Enid sat prim and straight on a chair at the foot of his bed. Her flowered organdie dress was very much like the bouquet she had brought, and her floppy straw hat had a big lilac bow. She began to tell Claude about her father's several attacks of erysipelas. He listened but absently. He would never have believed that Enid, with her severe notions of decorum, would come into his room and sit with him like this. He noticed that his mother was quite as much astonished as he. She hovered about the visitor for a few moments, and then, seeing that Enid was quite at her ease, went downstairs to her work. Claude wished that Enid would not talk at all, but would sit there and let him look at her. The sunshine she had let into the room, and her tranquil, fragrant presence, soothed him. Presently he realized that she was asking him something.

"What is it, Enid? The medicine they give me makes me stupid. I don't catch things."

"I was asking whether you play chess."

"Very badly."

"Father says I play passably well. When you are better you must let me bring up my ivory chessmen that Carrie sent me from China. They are beautifully carved. And now it's time for me to go."

She rose and patted his hand, telling him he must not be foolish about seeing people. "I didn't know you were so vain. Bandages are as becoming to you as they are to anybody. Shall I pull the dark blind again for you?"

"Yes, please. There won't be anything to look at now."

"Why, Claude, you are getting to be quite a ladies' man!"

Something in the way Enid said this made him wince a little. He felt his burning face grow a shade warmer. Even after she went downstairs he kept wishing she had not said that.

His mother came to give him his medicine. She stood beside him while he swallowed it. "Enid Royce is a real sensible girl—" she said as she took the glass. Her upward inflection expressed not conviction but bewilderment.

Enid came every afternoon, and Claude looked forward to her visits restlessly; they were the only pleasant things that happened to him, and made him forget the humiliation of his poisoned and disfigured face. He was disgusting to himself; when he touched the welts on his forehead and under his hair, he felt unclean and abject. At night, when his fever ran high, and the pain began to tighten in his head and neck, it wrought him to a distressing pitch of excitement. He fought with it as one bulldog fights with another. His mind prowled about among dark legends of torture,—everything he had ever read about the Inquisition, the rack and the wheel.

When Enid entered his room, cool and fresh in her pretty summer clothes, his mind leaped to meet her. He could not talk much, but he lay looking at her and breathing in a sweet contentment. After awhile he was well enough to sit up half-dressed in a steamer chair and play chess with her.

One afternoon they were by the west window in the sitting-room with the chess board between them, and Claude had to admit that he was beaten again.

"It must be dull for you, playing with me," he murmured, brushing the beads of sweat from his forehead. His face was clean now, so white that even his freckles had disappeared, and his hands were the soft, languid hands of a sick man.

"You will play better when you are stronger and can fix your mind on it," Enid assured him. She was puzzled because Claude, who had a good head for some things, had none at all for chess, and it was clear that he would never play well.

"Yes," he sighed, dropping back into his chair, "my wits do wander. Look at my wheatfield, over there on the skyline. Isn't it lovely? And now I won't be able to harvest it. Sometimes I wonder whether I'll ever finish anything I begin."

Enid put the chessmen back into their box. "Now that you are better, you must stop feeling blue. Father says that with your trouble people are always depressed."

Claude shook his head slowly, as it lay against the back of the chair. "No, it's not that. It's having so much time to think that makes me blue. You see, Enid, I've never yet done anything that gave me any satisfaction. I must be good for something. When I lie still and think, I wonder whether my life has been happening to me or to somebody else. It doesn't seem to have much connection with me. I haven't made much of a start."

"But you are not twenty-two yet. You have plenty of time to start. Is that what you are thinking about all the time!" She shook her finger at him.

"I think about two things all the time. That is one of them." Mrs. Wheeler came in with Claude's four o'clock milk; it was his first day downstairs.

When they were children, playing by the mill-dam, Claude had seen the future as a luminous vagueness in which he and Enid would always do things together. Then there came a time when he wanted to do everything with Ernest, when girls were disturbing and a bother, and he pushed all that into the distance, knowing that some day he must reckon with it again.

Now he told himself he had always known Enid would come back; and she had come on that afternoon when she entered his drug-smelling room and let in the sunlight. She would have done that for nobody but him. She was not a girl who would depart lightly from conventions that she recognized as authoritative. He remembered her as she used to march up to the platform for Children's Day exercises with the other little girls of the infant class; in her stiff white dress, never a curl awry or a wrinkle in her stocking, keeping her little comrades in order by the acquiescent gravity of her face, which seemed to say, "How pleasant it is to do thus and to do Right!"

Old Mr. Smith was the minister in those days,—a good man who had been much tossed about by a stormy and temperamental wife—and his eyes used to rest yearningly upon little Enid Royce, seeing in her the promise of "virtuous and comely Christian womanhood," to use one of his own phrases. Claude, in the boys' class across the aisle, used to tease her and try to distract her, but he respected her seriousness.

When they played together she was fair-minded, didn't whine if she got hurt, and never claimed a girl's exemption from anything unpleasant. She was calm, even on the day when she fell into the mill-dam and he fished her out; as soon as she stopped choking and coughing up muddy water, she wiped her face with her little drenched petticoats, and sat shivering and saying over and over, "Oh, Claude, Claude!" Incidents like that one now seemed to him significant and fateful.

When Claude's strength began to return to him, it came overwhelmingly. His blood seemed to grow strong while his body was still weak, so that the in-rush of vitality shook him. The desire to live again sang in his veins while his frame was unsteady. Waves of youth swept over him and left him exhausted. When Enid was with him these feelings were never so strong; her actual presence restored his equilibrium—almost. This fact did not perplex him; he fondly attributed it to something beautiful in the girl's nature,—a quality so lovely and subtle that there is no name for it.

During the first days of his recovery he did nothing but enjoy the creeping stir of life. Respiration was a soft physical pleasure. In the nights, so long he could not sleep them through, it was delightful to lie upon a cloud that floated lazily down the sky. In the depths of this lassitude the thought of Enid would start up like a sweet, burning pain, and he would drift out into the darkness upon sensations he could neither prevent nor control. So long as he could plough, pitch hay, or break his back in the wheatfield, he had been master; but now he was overtaken by himself. Enid was meant for him and she had come for him; he would never let her go. She should never know how much he longed for her. She would be slow to feel even a little of what he was feeling; he knew that. It would take a long while. But he would be infinitely patient, infinitely tender of her. It should be he who suffered, not she. Even in his dreams he never wakened her, but loved her while she was still and unconscious like a statue. He would shed love upon her until she warmed and changed without knowing why.

Sometimes when Enid sat unsuspecting beside him, a quick blush swept across his face and he felt guilty toward her, meek and humble, as if he must beg her forgiveness for something. Often he was glad when she went away and left him alone to think about her. Her presence brought him sanity, and for that he ought to be grateful. When he was with her, he thought how she was to be the one who would put him right with the world and make him fit into the life about him. He had troubled his mother and disappointed his father, His marriage would be the first natural, dutiful, expected thing he had ever done. It would be the beginning of usefulness and content; as his mother's oft-repeated Psalm said, it would restore his soul. Enid's willingness to listen to him he could scarcely doubt. Her devotion to him during his illness was probably regarded by her friends as equivalent to an engagement.

V.

Claude's first trip to Frankfort was to get his hair cut. After leaving the barber-shop he presented himself, glistening with bayrum, at Jason Royce's office. Mr. Royce, in the act of closing his safe, turned and took the young man by the hand.

"Hello, Claude, glad to see you around again! Sickness can't do much to a husky young farmer like you. With old fellows, it's another story. I'm just starting off to have a look at my alfalfa, south of the river. Get in and go along with me."

They went out to the open car that stood by the sidewalk, and when they were spinning along between fields of ripening grain Claude broke the silence. "I expect you know what I want to see you about, Mr. Royce?"

The older man shook his head. He had been preoccupied and grim ever since they started.

"Well," Claude went on modestly, "it oughtn't to surprise you to hear that I've set my heart on Enid. I haven't said anything to her yet, but if you're not against me, I'm going to try to persuade her to marry me."

"Marriage is a final sort of thing, Claude," said Mr. Royce. He sat slumping in his seat, watching the road ahead of him with intense abstraction, looking more gloomy and grizzled than usual. "Enid is a vegetarian, you know," he remarked unexpectedly.

Claude smiled. "That could hardly make any difference to me, Mr. Royce."

The other nodded slightly. "I know. At your age you think it doesn't. Such things do make a difference, however." His lips closed over his half-dead cigar, and for some time he did not open them.

"Enid is a good girl," he said at last. "Strictly speaking, she has more brains than a girl needs. If Mrs. Royce had another daughter at home, I'd take Enid into my office. She has good judgment. I don't know but she'd run a business better than a house." Having got this out, Mr. Royce relaxed his frown, took his cigar from his mouth, looked at it, and put it back between his teeth without relighting it.

Claude was watching him with surprise. "There's no question about Enid, Mr. Royce. I didn't come to ask you about her," he exclaimed. "I came to ask if you'd be willing to have me for a son-in-law. I know, and you know, that Enid could do a great deal better than to marry me. I surely haven't made much of a showing, so far."

"Here we are," announced Mr. Royce. "I'll leave the car under this elm, and we'll go up to the north end of the field and have a look."

They crawled under the wire fence and started across the rough ground through a field of purple blossoms. Clouds of yellow butterflies darted up before them. They walked jerkily, breaking through the sun-baked crust into the soft soil beneath. Mr. Royce lit a fresh cigar, and as he threw away the match let his hand drop on the young man's shoulder. "I always envied your father. You took my fancy when you were a little shaver, and I used to let you in to see the water-wheel. When I gave up water power and put in an engine, I said to myself: 'There's just one fellow in the country will be sorry to see the old wheel go, and that's Claude Wheeler.'"

"I hope you don't think I'm too young to marry," Claude said as they tramped on.

"No, it's right and proper a young man should marry. I don't say anything against marriage," Mr. Royce protested doggedly. "You may find some opposition in Enid's missionary motives. I don't know how she feels about that now. I don't enquire. I'd be pleased to see her get rid of such notions. They don't do a woman any good."

"I want to help her get rid of them. If it's all right with you, I hope I can persuade Enid to marry me this fall."

Jason Royce turned his head quickly toward his companion, studied his artless, hopeful countenance for a moment, and then looked away with a frown.

The alfalfa field sloped upward at one corner, lay like a bright green-and-purple handkerchief thrown down on the hillside. At the uppermost angle grew a slender young cottonwood, with leaves as light and agitated as the swarms of little butterflies that hovered above the clover. Mr. Royce made for this tree, took off his black coat, rolled it up, and sat down on it in the flickering shade. His shirt showed big blotches of moisture, and the sweat was rolling in clear drops along the creases in his brown neck. He sat with his hands clasped over his knees, his heels braced in the soft soil, and looked blankly off across the field. He found himself absolutely unable to touch upon the vast body of experience he wished to communicate to Claude. It lay in his chest like a physical misery, and the desire to speak struggled there. But he had no words, no way to make himself understood. He had no argument to present. What he wanted to do was to hold up life as he had found it, like a picture, to his young friend; to warn him, without explanation, against certain heart-breaking disappointments. It could not be done, he saw. The dead might as well try to speak to the living as the old to the young. The only way that Claude could ever come to share his secret, was to live. His strong yellow teeth closed tighter and tighter on the cigar, which had gone out like the first. He did not look at Claude, but while he watched the wind plough soft, flowery roads in the field, the boy's face was clearly before him, with its expression of reticent pride melting into the desire to please, and the slight stiffness of his shoulders, set in a kind of stubborn loyalty. Claude lay on the sod beside him, rather tired after his walk in the sun, a little melancholy, though he did not know why.

After a long while Mr. Royce unclasped his broad, thick-fingered miller's hands, and for a moment took out the macerated cigar. "Well, Claude," he said with determined cheerfulness, "we'll always be better friends than is common between father and son-in-law. You'll find out that pretty nearly everything you believe about life—about marriage, especially—is lies. I don't know why people prefer to live in that sort of a world, but they do."

VI.

AFTER HIS INTERVIEW with Mr. Royce, Claude drove directly to the mill house. As he came up the shady road, he saw with disappointment the flash of two white dresses instead of one, moving about in the sunny flower garden. The visitor was Gladys Farmer. This was her vacation time. She had walked out to the mill in the cool of the morning to spend the day with Enid. Now they were starting off to gather water-cresses, and had stopped in the garden to smell the heliotrope. On this scorching afternoon the purple sprays gave out a fragrance that hung over the flower-bed and brushed their cheeks like a warm breath. The girls looked up at the same moment and recognized Claude. They waved to him and hurried down to the gate to congratulate him on his recovery. He took their little tin pails and followed them around the old dam-head and up a sandy gorge, along a clear thread of water that trickled into Lovely Creek just above the mill. They came to the gravelly hill where the stream took its source from a spring hollowed out under the exposed roots of two elm trees. All about the spring, and in the sandy bed of the shallow creek, the cresses grew cool and green.

Gladys had strong feelings about places. She looked around her with satisfaction. "Of all the places where we used to play, Enid, this was my favourite," she declared.

"You girls sit up there on the elm roots," Claude suggested. "Wherever you put your foot in this soft gravel, water gathers. You'll spoil your white shoes. I'll get the cress for you."

"Stuff my pail as full as you can, then," Gladys called as they sat down. "I wonder why the Spanish dagger grows so thick on this hill, Enid? These plants were old and tough when we were little. I love it here."

She leaned back upon the hot, glistening hill-side. The sun came down in red rays through the elm-tops, and all the pebbles and bits of quartz glittered dazzlingly. Down in the stream bed the water, where it caught the light, twinkled like tarnished gold. Claude's sandy head and stooping shoulders were mottled with sunshine as they moved about over the green patches, and his duck trousers looked much whiter than they were. Gladys was too poor to travel, but she had the good fortune to be able to see a great deal within a few miles of Frankfort, and a warm imagination helped her to find life interesting. She did, as she confided to Enid, want to go to Colorado; she was ashamed of never having seen a mountain.

Presently Claude came up the bank with two shining, dripping pails. "Now may I sit down with you for a few minutes?"

Moving to make room for him beside her, Enid noticed that his thin face was heavily beaded with perspiration. His pocket handkerchief was wet and sandy, so she gave him her own, with a proprietary air. "Why, Claude, you look quite tired! Have you been over-doing? Where were you before you came here?"

"I was out in the country with your father, looking at his alfalfa."

"And he walked you all over the field in the hot sun, I suppose?"

Claude laughed. "He did."

"Well, I'll scold him tonight. You stay here and rest. I am going to drive Gladys home."

Gladys protested, but at last consented that they should both drive her home in Claude's car. They lingered awhile, however, listening to the soft, amiable bubbling of the spring; a wise, unobtrusive voice, murmuring night and day, continually telling the truth to people who could not understand it.

When they went back to the house Enid stopped long enough to cut a bunch of heliotrope for Mrs. Farmer,—though with the sinking of the sun its rich perfume had already vanished. They left Gladys and her flowers and cresses at the gate of the white cottage, now half hidden by gaudy trumpet vines.

Claude turned his car and went back along the dim, twilight road with Enid. "I usually like to see Gladys, but when I found her with you this afternoon, I was terribly disappointed for a minute. I'd just been talking with your father, and I wanted to come straight to you. Do you think you could marry me, Enid?"

"I don't believe it would be for the best, Claude." She spoke sadly.

He took her passive hand. "Why not?"

"My mind is full of other plans. Marriage is for most girls, but not for all."

Enid had taken off her hat. In the low evening light Claude studied her pale face under her brown hair. There was something graceful and charming about the way she held her head, something that suggested both submissiveness and great firmness. "I've had those far-away dreams, too, Enid; but now my thoughts don't get any further than you. If you could care ever so little for me to start on, I'd be willing to risk the rest." She sighed. "You know I care for you. I've never made any secret of it. But we're happy as we are, aren't we?"

"No, I'm not. I've got to have some life of my own, or I'll go to pieces. If you won't have me, I'll try South America,—and I won't come back until I am an old man and you are an old woman."

Enid looked at him, and they both smiled.

The mill house was black except for a light in one upstairs window. Claude sprang out of his car and lifted Enid gently to the ground. She let him kiss her soft cool mouth, and her long lashes. In the pale, dusty dusk, lit only by a few white stars, and with the chill of the creek already in the air, she seemed to Claude like a shivering little ghost come up from the rushes where the old mill-dam used to be. A terrible melancholy clutched at the boy's heart. He hadn't thought it would be like this. He drove home feeling weak and broken. Was there nothing in the world outside to answer to his own feelings, and was every turn to be fresh disappointment? Why was life so mysteriously hard? This country itself was sad, he thought, looking about him,-and you could no more change that than you could change the story in an unhappy human face. He wished to God he were sick again; the world was too rough a place to get about in.

There was one person in the world who felt sorry for Claude that night. Gladys Farmer sat at her bedroom window for a long while, watching the stars and thinking about what she had seen plainly enough that afternoon. She had liked Enid ever since they were little girls,—and knew all there was to know about her. Claude would become one of those dead people that moved about the streets of Frankfort; everything that was Claude would perish, and the shell of him would come and go and eat and sleep for fifty years. Gladys had taught the children of many such dead men. She had worked out a misty philosophy for herself, full of strong convictions and confused figures. She believed that all things which might make the world beautiful—love and kindness, leisure and art—were shut up in prison, and that successful men like Bayliss Wheeler held the keys. The generous ones, who would let these things out to make people happy, were somehow weak, and could not break the bars. Even her own little life was squeezed into an unnatural shape by the domination of people like Bayliss. She had not dared, for instance, to go to Omaha that spring for the three performances of the Chicago Opera Company. Such an extravagance would have aroused a corrective spirit in all her friends, and in the schoolboard as well; they would probably have decided not to give her the little increase in salary she counted upon having next year.

There were people, even in Frankfort, who had imagination and generous impulses, but they were all, she had to admit, inefficient—failures. There was Miss Livingstone, the fiery, emotional old maid who couldn't tell the truth; old Mr. Smith, a lawyer without clients, who read Shakespeare and Dryden all day long in his dusty office; Bobbie Jones, the effeminate drug clerk, who wrote free verse and "movie" scenarios, and tended the sodawater fountain.

Claude was her one hope. Ever since they graduated from High School, all through the four years she had been teaching, she had waited to see him emerge and prove himself. She wanted him to be more successful than Bayliss AND STILL BE CLAUDE. She would have made any sacrifice to help him on. If a strong boy like Claude, so well endowed and so fearless, must fail, simply because he had that finer strain in his nature,—then life was not worth the chagrin it held for a passionate heart like hers.

At last Gladys threw herself upon the bed. If he married Enid, that would be the end. He would go about strong and heavy, like Mr. Royce; a big machine with the springs broken inside.

VII.

CLAUDE WAS WELL ENOUGH to go into the fields before the harvest was over. The middle of July came, and the farmers were still cutting grain. The yield of wheat and oats was so heavy that there were not machines enough to thrash it within the usual time. Men had to await their turn, letting their grain stand in shock until a belching black engine lumbered into the field. Rains would have been disastrous; but this was one of those "good years" which farmers tell about, when everything goes well. At the time they needed rain, there was plenty of it; and now the days were miracles of dry, glittering heat.

Every morning the sun came up a red ball, quickly drank the dew, and started a quivering excitement in all living things. In great harvest seasons like that one, the heat, the intense light, and the important work in hand draw people together and make them friendly. Neighbours helped each other to cope with the burdensome abundance of man-nourishing grain; women and children and old men fell to and did what they could to save and house it. Even the horses had a more varied and sociable existence than usual, going about from one farm to another to help neighbour horses drag wagons and binders and headers. They nosed the colts of old friends, ate out of strange mangers, and drank, or refused to drink, out of strange water-troughs. Decrepit horses that lived on a pension, like the Wheelers' stiff-legged Molly and Leonard Dawson's Billy with the heaves—his asthmatic cough could be heard for a quarter of a mile—were pressed into service now. It was wonderful, too, how well these invalided beasts managed to keep up with the strong young mares and geldings; they bent their willing heads and pulled as if the chafing of the collar on their necks was sweet to them.

The sun was like a great visiting presence that stimulated and took its due from all animal energy. When it flung wide its cloak and stepped down over the edge of the fields at evening, it left behind it a spent and exhausted world. Horses and men and women grew thin, seethed all day in their own sweat. After supper they dropped over and slept anywhere at all, until the red dawn broke clear in the east again, like the fanfare of trumpets, and nerves and muscles began to quiver with the solar heat.

For several weeks Claude did not have time to read the newspapers; they lay about the house in bundles, unopened, for Nat Wheeler was in the field now, working like a giant. Almost every evening Claude ran down to the mill to see Enid for a few minutes; he did not get out of his car, and she sat on the old stile, left over from horse-back days, while she chatted with him. She said frankly that she didn't like men who had just come out of the harvest field, and Claude did not blame her. He didn't like himself very well after his clothes began to dry on him. But the hour or two between supper and bed was the only time he had to see anybody. He slept like the heroes of old; sank upon his bed as the thing he desired most on earth, and for a blissful moment felt the sweetness of sleep before it overpowered him. In the morning, he seemed to hear the shriek of his alarm clock for hours before he could come up from the deep places into which he had plunged. All sorts of incongruous adventures happened to him between the first buzz of the alarm and the moment when he was enough awake to put out his hand and stop it. He dreamed, for instance, that it was evening, and he had gone to see Enid as usual. While she was coming down the path from the house, he discovered that he had no clothes on at all! Then, with wonderful agility, he jumped over the picket fence into a clump of castor beans, and stood in the dusk, trying to cover himself with the leaves, like Adam in the garden, talking commonplaces to Enid through chattering teeth, afraid lest at any moment she might discover his plight.

Mrs. Wheeler and Mahailey always lost weight in thrashing time, just as the horses did; this year Nat Wheeler had six hundred acres of winter wheat that would run close upon thirty bushels to the acre. Such a harvest was as hard on the women as it was on the men. Leonard Dawson's wife, Susie, came over to help Mrs. Wheeler, but she was expecting a baby in the fall, and the heat proved too much for her. Then one of the Yoeder daughters came; but the methodical German girl was so distracted by Mahailey's queer ways that Mrs. Wheeler said it was easier to do the work herself than to keep explaining Mahailey's psychology. Day after day ten ravenous men sat down at the long dinner table in the kitchen. Mrs. Wheeler baked pies and cakes and bread loaves as fast as the oven would hold them, and from morning till night the range was stoked like the fire-box of a locomotive. Mahailey wrung the necks of chickens until her wrist swelled up, as she said, "like a puff-adder."

By the end of July the excitement quieted down. The extra leaves were taken out of the dining table, the Wheeler horses had their barn to themselves again, and the reign of terror in the henhouse was over.

One evening Mr. Wheeler came down to supper with a bundle of newspapers under his arm. "Claude, I see this war scare in Europe has hit the market. Wheat's taken a jump. They're paying eighty-eight cents in Chicago. We might as well get rid of a few hundred bushel before it drops again. We'd better begin hauling tomorrow. You and I can make two trips a day over to Vicount, by changing teams,—there's no grade to speak of."

Mrs. Wheeler, arrested in the act of pouring coffee, sat holding the coffee-pot in the air, forgetting she had it. "If this is only a newspaper scare, as we think, I don't see why it should affect the market," she murmured mildly. "Surely those big bankers in New York and Boston have some way of knowing rumour from fact."

"Give me some coffee, please," said her husband testily. "I don't have to explain the market, I've only got to take advantage of it."

"But unless there's some reason, why are we dragging our wheat over to Vicount? Do you suppose it's some scheme the grain men are hiding under a war rumour? Have the financiers and the press ever deceived the public like this before?"

"I don't know a thing in the world about it, Evangeline, and I don't suppose. I telephoned the elevator at Vicount an hour ago, and they said they'd pay me seventy cents, subject to change in the morning quotations. Claude," with a twinkle in his eye, "you'd better not go to mill tonight. Turn in early. If we are on the road by six tomorrow, we'll be in town before the heat of the day."

"All right, sir. I want to look at the papers after supper. I haven't read anything but the headlines since before thrashing. Ernest was stirred up about the murder of that Grand Duke and said the Austrians would make trouble. But I never thought there was anything in it."

"There's seventy cents a bushel in it, anyway," said his father, reaching for a hot biscuit.

"If there's that much, I'm somehow afraid there will be more," said Mrs. Wheeler thoughtfully. She had picked up the paper fly-brush and sat waving it irregularly, as if she were trying to brush away a swarm of confusing ideas.

"You might call up Ernest, and ask him what the Bohemian papers say about it," Mr. Wheeler suggested.

Claude went to the telephone, but was unable to get any answer from the Havels. They had probably gone to a barn dance down in the Bohemian township. He went upstairs and sat down before an armchair full of newspapers; he could make nothing reasonable out of the smeary telegrams in big type on the front page of the Omaha World Herald. The German army was entering Luxembourg; he didn't know where Luxembourg was, whether it was a city or a country; he seemed to have some vague idea that it was a palace! His mother had gone up to "Mahailey's library," the attic, to hunt for a map of Europe,—a thing for which Nebraska farmers had never had much need. But that night, on many prairie homesteads, the women, American and foreign-born, were hunting for a map.

Claude was so sleepy that he did not wait for his mother's return. He stumbled upstairs and undressed in the dark. The night was sultry, with thunder clouds in the sky and an unceasing play of sheet-lightning all along the western horizon. Mosquitoes had got into his room during the day, and after he threw himself upon the bed they began sailing over him with their high, excruciating note. He turned from side to side and tried to muffle his ears with the pillow. The disquieting sound became merged, in his sleepy brain, with the big type on the front page of the paper; those black letters seemed to be flying about his head with a soft, high, sing-song whizz.

VIII.

Late in the afternoon of the sixth of August, Claude and his empty wagon were bumping along the level road over the flat country between Vicount and the Lovely Creek valley. He had made two trips to town that day. Though he had kept his heaviest team for the hot afternoon pull, his horses were too tired to be urged off a walk. Their necks were marbled with sweat stains, and their flanks were plastered with the white dust that rose at every step. Their heads hung down, and their breathing was deep and slow. The wood of the green-painted wagon seat was blistering hot to the touch. Claude sat at one end of it, his head bared to catch the faint stir of air that sometimes dried his neck and chin and saved him the trouble of pulling out a handkerchief. On every side the wheat stubble stretched for miles and miles. Lonely straw stacks stood up yellow in the sun and cast long shadows. Claude peered anxiously along the distant locust hedges which told where the road ran. Ernest Havel had promised to meet him somewhere on the way home. He had not seen Ernest for a week: since then Time had brought prodigies to birth.

At last he recognized the Havels' team along way off, and he stopped and waited for Ernest beside a thorny hedge, looking thoughtfully about him. The sun was already low. It hung above the stubble, all milky and rosy with the heat, like the image of a sun reflected in grey water. In the east the full moon had just risen, and its thin silver surface was flushed with pink until it looked exactly like the setting sun. Except for the place each occupied in the heavens, Claude could not have told which was which. They rested upon opposite rims of the world, two bright shields, and regarded each other, as if they, too, had met by appointment.

Claude and Ernest sprang to the ground at the same instant and shook hands, feeling that they had not seen each other for a long while.

"Well, what do you make of it, Ernest?"

The young man shook his head cautiously, but replied no further. He patted his horses and eased the collars on their necks.

"I waited in town for the Hastings paper," Claude went on impatiently. "England declared war last night."

"The Germans," said Ernest, "are at Liege. I know where that is. I sailed from Antwerp when I came over here."

"Yes, I saw that. Can the Belgians do anything?"

"Nothing." Ernest leaned against the wagon wheel and drawing his pipe from his pocket slowly filled it. "Nobody can do anything. The German army will go where it pleases."

"If it's as bad as that, why are the Belgians putting up a fight?"

"I don't know. It's fine, but it will come to nothing in the end. Let me tell you something about the German army, Claude."

Pacing up and down beside the locust hedge, Ernest rehearsed the great argument; preparation, organization, concentration, inexhaustible resources, inexhaustible men. While he talked the sun disappeared, the moon contracted, solidified, and slowly climbed the pale sky. The fields were still glimmering with the bland reflection left over from daylight, and the distance grew shadowy,—not dark, but seemingly full of sleep.

"If I were at home," Ernest concluded, "I would be in the Austrian army this minute. I guess all my cousins and nephews are fighting the Russians or the Belgians already. How would you like it yourself, to be marched into a peaceful country like this, in the middle of harvest, and begin to destroy it?"

"I wouldn't do it, of course. I'd desert and be shot."

"Then your family would be persecuted. Your brothers, maybe even your father, would be made orderlies to Austrian officers and be kicked in the mouth."

"I wouldn't bother about that. I'd let my male relatives decide for themselves how often they would be kicked."

Ernest shrugged his shoulders. "You Americans brag like little boys; you would and you wouldn't! I tell you, nobody's will has anything to do with this. It is the harvest of all that has been planted. I never thought it would come in my life-time, but I knew it would come."

The boys lingered a little while, looking up at the soft radiance of the sky. There was not a cloud anywhere, and the low glimmer in the fields had imperceptibly changed to full, pure moonlight. Presently the two wagons began to creep along the white road, and on the backless seat of each the driver sat drooping forward, lost in thought. When they reached the corner where Ernest turned south, they said goodnight without raising their voices. Claude's horses went on as if they were walking in their sleep. They did not even sneeze at the low cloud of dust beaten up by their heavy foot-falls,—the only sounds in the vast quiet of the night.

Why was Ernest so impatient with him, Claude wondered. He could not pretend to feel as Ernest did. He had nothing behind him to shape his opinions or colour his feelings about what was going on in Europe; he could only sense it day by day. He had always been taught that the German people were pre-eminent in the virtues Americans most admire; a month ago he would have said they had all the ideals a decent American boy would fight for. The invasion of Belgium was contradictory to the German character as he knew it in his friends and neighbours. He still cherished the hope that there had been some great mistake; that this splendid people would apologize and right itself with the world.

Mr. Wheeler came down the hill, bareheaded and coatless, as Claude drove into the barnyard. "I expect you're tired. I'll put your team away. Any news?"

"England has declared war."

Mr. Wheeler stood still a moment and scratched his head. "I guess you needn't get up early tomorrow. If this is to be a sure enough war, wheat will go higher. I've thought it was a bluff until now. You take the papers up to your mother."

IX.

Enid and Mrs. Royce had gone away to the Michigan sanatorium where they spent part of every summer, and would not be back until October. Claude and his mother gave all their attention to the war despatches. Day after day, through the first two weeks of August, the bewildering news trickled from the little towns out into the farming country.

About the middle of the month came the story of the fall of the forts at Liege, battered at for nine days and finally reduced in a few hours by siege guns brought up from the rear,—guns which evidently could destroy any fortifications that ever had been, or ever could be constructed. Even to these quiet wheat-growing people, the siege guns before Liege were a menace; not to their safety or their goods, but to their comfortable, established way of thinking. They introduced the greater-than-man force which afterward repeatedly brought into this war the effect of unforeseeable natural disaster, like tidal waves, earthquakes, or the eruption of volcanoes.

On the twenty-third came the news of the fall of the forts at Namur; again giving warning that an unprecedented power of destruction had broken loose in the world. A few days later the story of the wiping out of the ancient and peaceful seat of learning at Louvain made it clear that this force was being directed toward incredible ends. By this time, too, the papers were full of accounts of the destruction of civilian populations. Something new, and certainly evil, was at work among mankind. Nobody was ready with a name for it. None of the well-worn words descriptive of human behaviour seemed adequate. The epithets grouped about the name of "Attila" were too personal, too dramatic, too full of old, familiar human passion.

One afternoon in the first week of September Mrs. Wheeler was in the kitchen making cucumber pickles, when she heard Claude's car coming back from Frankfort. In a moment he entered, letting the screen door slam behind him, and threw a bundle of mail on the table.

"What do you, think, Mother? The French have moved the seat of government to Bordeaux! Evidently, they don't think they can hold Paris."

Mrs. Wheeler wiped her pale, perspiring face with the hem of her apron and sat down in the nearest chair. "You mean that Paris is not the capital of France any more? Can that be true?"

"That's what it looks like. Though the papers say it's only a precautionary measure."

She rose. "Let's go up to the map. I don't remember exactly where Bordeaux is. Mahailey, you won't let my vinegar burn, will you?"

Claude followed her to the sitting-room, where her new map hung on the wall above the carpet lounge. Leaning against the back of a willow rocking-chair, she began to move her hand about over the brightly coloured, shiny surface, murmuring, "Yes, there is Bordeaux, so far to the south; and there is Paris."

Claude, behind her, looked over her shoulder. "Do you suppose they are going to hand their city over to the Germans, like a Christmas present? I should think they'd burn it first, the way the Russians did Moscow. They can do better than that now, they can dynamite it!"

"Don't say such things." Mrs. Wheeler dropped into the deep willow chair, realizing that she was very tired, now that she had left the stove and the heat of the kitchen. She began weakly to wave the palm leaf fan before her face. "It's said to be such a beautiful city. Perhaps the Germans will spare it, as they did Brussels. They must be sick of destruction by now. Get the encyclopaedia and see what it says. I've left my glasses downstairs."

Claude brought a volume from the bookcase and sat down on the lounge. He began: "Paris, the capital city of France and the Department of the Seine,—shall I skip the history?"

"No. Read it all."

He cleared his throat and began again: "At its first appearance in history, there was nothing to foreshadow the important part which Paris was to play in Europe and in the world," etc.

Mrs. Wheeler rocked and fanned, forgetting the kitchen and the cucumbers as if they had never been. Her tired body was resting, and her mind, which was never tired, was occupied with the account of early religious foundations under the Merovingian kings. Her eyes were always agreeably employed when they rested upon the sunburned neck and catapult shoulders of her red-headed son.

Claude read faster and faster until he stopped with a gasp.

"Mother, there are pages of kings! We'll read that some other time. I want to find out what it's like now, and whether it's going to have any more history." He ran his finger up and down the columns. "Here, this looks like business.

"Defences: Paris, in a recent German account of the greatest fortresses of the world, possesses three distinct rings of defences"—here he broke off. "Now what do you think of that? A German account, and this is an English book! The world simply made a mistake about the Germans all along. It's as if we invited a neighbour over here and showed him our cattle and barns, and all the time he was planning how he would come at night and club us in our beds."

Mrs. Wheeler passed her hand over her brow. "Yet we have had so many German neighbours, and never one that wasn't kind and helpful."

"I know it. Everything Mrs. Erlich ever told me about Germany made me want to go there. And the people that sing all those beautiful songs about women and children went into Belgian villages and—"

"Don't, Claude!" his mother put out her hands as if to push his words back. "Read about the defences of Paris; that's what we must think about now. I can't but believe there is one fort the Germans didn't put down in their book, and that it will stand. We know Paris is a wicked city, but there must be many God-fearing people there, and God has preserved it all these years. You saw in the paper how the churches are full all day of women praying." She leaned forward and smiled at him indulgently. "And you believe those prayers will accomplish nothing, son?"

Claude squirmed, as he always did when his mother touched upon certain subjects.

"Well, you see, I can't forget that the Germans are praying, too. And I guess they are just naturally more pious than the French." Taking up the book he began once more: "In the low ground again, at the narrowest part of the great loop of the Marne," etc.

Claude and his mother had grown familiar with the name of that river, and with the idea of its strategic importance, before it began to stand out in black headlines a few days later.

The fall ploughing had begun as usual. Mr. Wheeler had decided to put in six hundred acres of wheat again. Whatever happened on the other side of the world, they would need bread. He took a third team himself and went into the field every morning to help Dan and Claude. The neighbours said that nobody but the Kaiser had ever been able to get Nat Wheeler down to regular work.

Since the men were all afield, Mrs. Wheeler now went every morning to the mailbox at the crossroads, a quarter of a mile away, to get yesterday's Omaha and Kansas City papers which the carrier left. In her eagerness she opened and began to read them as she turned homeward, and her feet, never too sure, took a wandering way among sunflowers and buffaloburrs. One morning, indeed, she sat down on a red grass bank beside the road and read all the war news through before she stirred, while the grasshoppers played leap-frog over her skirts, and the gophers came out of their holes and blinked at her. That noon, when she saw Claude leading his team to the water tank, she hurried down to him without stopping to find her bonnet, and reached the windmill breathless.

"The French have stopped falling back, Claude. They are standing at the Marne. There is a great battle going on. The papers say it may decide the war. It is so near Paris that some of the army went out in taxi-cabs." Claude drew himself up. "Well, it will decide about Paris, anyway, won't it? How many divisions?"

"I can't make out. The accounts are so confusing. But only a few of the English are there, and the French are terribly outnumbered. Your father got in before you, and he has the papers upstairs."

"They are twenty-four hours old. I'll go to Vicount tonight after I'm done work, and get the Hastings paper."

In the evening, when he came back from town, he found his father and mother waiting up for him. He stopped a moment in the sitting-room. "There is not much news, except that the battle is on, and practically the whole French army is engaged. The Germans outnumber them five to three in men, and nobody knows how much in artillery. General Joffre says the French will fall back no farther." He did not sit down, but went straight upstairs to his room.

Mrs. Wheeler put out the lamp, undressed, and lay down, but not to sleep. Long afterward, Claude heard her gently closing a window, and he smiled to himself in the dark. His mother, he knew, had always thought of Paris as the wickedest of cities, the capital of a frivolous, wine-drinking, Catholic people, who were responsible for the massacre of St. Bartholomew and for the grinning atheist, Voltaire. For the last two weeks, ever since the French began to fall back in Lorraine, he had noticed with amusement her growing solicitude for Paris.

It was curious, he reflected, lying wide awake in the dark: four days ago the seat of government had been moved to Bordeaux,—with the effect that Paris seemed suddenly to have become the capital, not of France, but of the world! He knew he was not the only farmer boy who wished himself tonight beside the Marne. The fact that the river had a pronounceable name, with a hard Western "r" standing like a keystone in the middle of it, somehow gave one's imagination a firmer hold on the situation. Lying still and thinking fast, Claude felt that even he could clear the bar of French "politeness"—so much more terrifying than German bullets—and slip unnoticed into that outnumbered army. One's manners wouldn't matter on the Marne tonight, the night of the eighth of September, 1914. There was nothing on earth he would so gladly be as an atom in that wall of flesh and blood that rose and melted and rose again before the city which had meant so much through all the centuries—but had never meant so much before. Its name had come to have the purity of an abstract idea. In great sleepy continents, in land-locked harvest towns, in the little islands of the sea, for four days men watched that name as they might stand out at night to watch a comet, or to see a star fall.

X.

It was Sunday afternoon and Claude had gone down to the mill house, as Enid and her mother had returned from Michigan the day before. Mrs. Wheeler, propped back in a rocking chair, was reading, and Mr. Wheeler, in his shirt sleeves, his Sunday collar unbuttoned, was sitting at his walnut secretary, amusing himself with columns of figures. Presently he rose and yawned, stretching his arms above his head.

"Claude thinks he wants to begin building right away, up on the quarter next the timber claim. I've been figuring on the lumber. Building materials are cheap just now, so I suppose I'd better let him go ahead."

Mrs. Wheeler looked up absently from the page. "Why, I suppose so."

Her husband sat down astride a chair, and leaning his arms on the back of it, looked at her. "What do you think of this match, anyway? I don't know as I've heard you say."

"Enid is a good, Christian girl..." Mrs. Wheeler began resolutely, but her sentence hung in the air like a question.

He moved impatiently. "Yes, I know. But what does a husky boy like Claude want to pick out a girl like that for? Why, Evangeline, she'll be the old woman over again!"

Apparently these misgivings were not new to Mrs. Wheeler, for she put out her hand to stop him and whispered in solemn agitation, "Don't say anything! Don't breathe!"

"Oh, I won't interfere! I never do. I'd rather have her for a daughter-in-law than a wife, by a long shot. Claude's more of a fool than I thought him." He picked up his hat and strolled down to the barn, but his wife did not recover her composure so easily. She left the chair where she had hopefully settled herself for comfort, took up a feather duster and began moving distractedly about the room, brushing the surface of the furniture. When the war news was bad, or when she felt troubled about Claude, she set to cleaning house or overhauling the closets, thankful to be able to put some little thing to rights in such a disordered world.

As soon as the fall planting was done, Claude got the well borers out from town to drill his new well, and while they were at work he began digging his cellar. He was building his house on the level stretch beside his father's timber claim because, when he was a little boy, he had thought that grove of trees the most beautiful spot in the world. It was a square of about thirty acres, set out in ash and box-elder and cotton-woods, with a thick mulberry hedge on the south side. The trees had been neglected of late years, but if he lived up there he could manage to trim them and care for them at odd moments.

Every morning now he ran up in the Ford and worked at his cellar. He had heard that the deeper a cellar was, the better it was; and he meant that this one should be deep enough. One day Leonard Dawson stopped to see what progress he was making. Standing on the edge of the hole, he shouted to the lad who was sweating below.

"My God, Claude, what do you want of a cellar as deep as that? When your wife takes a notion to go to China, you can open a trap-door and drop her through!"

Claude flung down his pick and ran up the ladder. "Enid's not going to have notions of that sort," he said wrathfully.

"Well, you needn't get mad. I'm glad to hear it. I was sorry when the other girl went. It always looked to me like Enid had her face set for China, but I haven't seen her for a good while,—not since before she went off to Michigan with the old lady."

After Leonard was gone, Claude returned to his work, still out of humour. He was not altogether happy in his mind about Enid. When he went down to the mill it was usually Mr. Royce, not Enid, who sought to detain him, followed him down the path to the gate and seemed sorry to see him go. He could not blame Enid with any lack of interest in what he was doing. She talked and thought of nothing but the new house, and most of her suggestions were good. He often wished she would ask for something unreasonable and extravagant. But she had no selfish whims, and even insisted that the comfortable upstairs sleeping room he had planned with such care should be reserved for a guest chamber.

As the house began to take shape, Enid came up often in her car, to watch its growth, to show Claude samples of wallpapers and draperies, or a design for a window-seat she had cut from some magazine. There could be no question of her pride in every detail. The disappointing thing was that she seemed more interested in the house than in him. These months when they could be together as much as they pleased, she treated merely as a period of time in which they were building a house.

Everything would be all right when they were married, Claude told himself. He believed in the transforming power of marriage, as his mother believed in the miraculous effects of conversion. Marriage reduced all women to a common denominator; changed a cool, self-satisfied girl into a loving and generous one. It was quite right that Enid should be unconscious now of everything that she was to be when she was his wife. He told himself he wouldn't want it otherwise.

But he was lonely, all the same. He lavished upon the little house the solicitude and cherishing care that Enid seemed not to need. He stood over the carpenters urging the greatest nicety in the finish of closets and cupboards, the convenient placing of shelves, the exact joining of sills and casings. Often he stayed late in the evening, after the workmen with their noisy boots had gone home to supper. He sat down on a rafter or on the skeleton of the upper porch and quite lost himself in brooding, in anticipation of things that seemed as far away as ever. The dying light, the quiet stars coming out, were friendly and sympathetic. One night a bird flew in and fluttered wildly about among the partitions, shrieking with fright before it darted out into the dusk through one of the upper windows and found its way to freedom.

When the carpenters were ready to put in the staircase, Claude telephoned Enid and asked her to come and show them just what height she wanted the steps made. His mother had always had to climb stairs that were too steep. Enid stopped her car at the Frankfort High School at four o'clock and persuaded Gladys Farmer to drive out with her.

When they arrived they found Claude working on the lattice enclosure of the back porch. "Claude is like Jonah," Enid laughed. "He wants to plant gourd vines here, so they will run over the lattice and make shade. I can think of other vines that might be more ornamental."

Claude put down his hammer and said coaxingly: "Have you ever seen a gourd vine when it had something to climb on, Enid? You wouldn't believe how pretty they are; big green leaves, and gourds and yellow blossoms hanging all over them at the same time. An old German woman who keeps a lunch counter at one of those stations on the road to

Lincoln has them running up her back porch, and I've wanted to plant some ever since I first saw hers."

Enid smiled indulgently. "Well, I suppose you'll let me have clematis for the front porch, anyway? The men are getting ready to leave, so we'd better see about the steps."

After the workmen had gone, Claude took the girls upstairs by the ladder. They emerged from a little entry into a large room which extended over both the front and back parlours. The carpenters called it "the pool hall". There were two long windows, like doors, opening upon the porch roof, and in the sloping ceiling were two dormer windows, one looking north to the timber claim and the other south toward Lovely Creek. Gladys at once felt a singular pleasantness about this chamber, empty and unplastered as it was. "What a lovely room!" she exclaimed.

Claude took her up eagerly. "Don't you think so? You see it's my idea to have the second floor for ourselves, instead of cutting it up into little boxes as people usually do. We can come up here and forget the farm and the kitchen and all our troubles. I've made a big closet for each of us, and got everything just right. And now Enid wants to keep this room for preachers!"

Enid laughed. "Not only for preachers, Claude. For Gladys, when she comes to visit us—you see she likes it—and for your mother when she comes to spend a week and rest. I don't think we ought to take the best room for ourselves."

"Why not?" Claude argued hotly. "I'm building the whole house for ourselves. Come out on the porch roof, Gladys. Isn't this fine for hot nights? I want to put a railing round and make this into a balcony, where we can have chairs and a hammock."

Gladys sat down on the low window-sill. "Enid, you'd be foolish to keep this for a guest room. Nobody would ever enjoy it as much as you would. You can see the whole country from here."

Enid smiled, but showed no sign of relenting. "Let's wait and watch the sun go down. Be careful, Claude. It makes me nervous to see you lying there."

He was stretched out on the edge of the roof, one leg hanging over, and his head pillowed on his arm. The flat fields turned red, the distant windmills flashed white, and little rosy clouds appeared in the sky above them.

"If I make this into a balcony," Claude murmured, "the peak of the roof will always throw a shadow over it in the afternoon, and at night the stars will be right overhead. It will be a fine place to sleep in harvest time."

"Oh, you could always come up here to sleep on a hot night," Enid said quickly.

"It wouldn't be the same."

They sat watching the light die out of the sky, and Enid and Gladys drew close together as the coolness of the autumn evening came on. The three friends were thinking about the same thing; and yet, if by some sorcery each had begun to speak his thoughts aloud, amazement and bitterness would have fallen upon all. Enid's reflections were the most blameless. The discussion about the guest room had reminded her of Brother Weldon. In September, on her way to Michigan with Mrs. Royce, she had stopped for a day in Lincoln to take counsel with Arthur Weldon as to whether she ought to marry one whom she described to him as "an unsaved man." Young Mr. Weldon approached this subject with a cautious tread, but when he learned that the man in question was Claude Wheeler, he became more partisan than was his wont. He seemed to think that her marrying Claude was the one way to reclaim him, and did not hesitate to say that the most important service devout girls could perform for the church was to bring promising young men to its support. Enid had been almost certain that Mr. Weldon would approve her course before she consulted him, but his concurrence always gratified her pride. She told him that when she had a home of her own she would expect him to spend a part of his summer vacation there, and he blushingly expressed his willingness to do so.

Gladys, too, was lost in her own thoughts, sitting with that ease which made her seem rather indolent, her head resting against the empty window frame, facing the setting sun. The rosy light made her brown eyes gleam like old copper, and there was a moody look in them, as if in her mind she were defying something. When he happened to glance at her, it occurred to Claude that it was a hard destiny to be the exceptional person in a community, to be more gifted or more intelligent than the rest. For a girl it must be doubly hard. He sat up suddenly and broke the long silence.

"I forgot, Enid, I have a secret to tell you. Over in the timber claim the other day I started up a flock of quail. They must be the only ones left in all this neighbourhood, and I doubt if they ever come out of the timber. The bluegrass hasn't been mowed in there for years,—not since I first went away to school, and maybe they live on the grass seeds. In summer, of course, there are mulberries."

Enid wondered whether the birds could have learned enough about the world to stay hidden in the timber lot. Claude was sure they had.

"Nobody ever goes near the place except Father; he stops there sometimes. Maybe he has seen them and never said a word. It would be just like him." He told them he had scattered shelled corn in the grass, so that the birds would not be tempted to fly over into Leonard Dawson's cornfield. "If Leonard saw them, he'd likely take a shot at them."

"Why don't you ask him not to?" Enid suggested.

Claude laughed. "That would be asking a good deal. When a bunch of quail rise out of a cornfield they're a mighty tempting sight, if a man likes hunting. We'll have a picnic for you when you come out next summer, Gladys. There are some pretty places over there in the timber."

Gladys started up. "Why, it's night already! It's lovely here, but you must get me home, Enid."

They found it dark inside. Claude took Enid down the ladder and out to her car, and then went back for Gladys. She was sitting on the floor at the top of the ladder. Giving her his hand he helped her to rise.

"So you like my little house," he said gratefully.

"Yes. Oh, yes!" Her voice was full of feeling, but she did not exert herself to say more. Claude descended in front of her to keep her from slipping. She hung back while he led her through confusing doorways and helped her over the piles of laths that littered the floors. At the edge of the gaping cellar entrance she stopped and leaned wearily on his arm for a moment. She did not speak, but he understood that his new house made her sad; that she, too, had come to the place where she must turn out of the old path. He longed to whisper to her and beg her not to marry his brother. He lingered and hesitated, fumbling in the dark. She had his own cursed kind of sensibility; she would expect too much from life and be disappointed. He was reluctant to lead her out into the chilly evening without some word of entreaty. He would willingly have prolonged their passage,— through many rooms and corridors. Perhaps, had that been possible, the strength in him would have found what it was seeking; even in this short interval it had stirred and made itself felt, had uttered a confused appeal. Claude was greatly surprised at himself.

XI.

Enid decided that she would be married in the first week of June. Early in May the plasterers and painters began to be busy in the new house. The walls began to shine, and Claude went about all day, oiling and polishing the hard-pine floors and wainscoting. He hated to have anybody step on his floors. He planted gourd vines about the back porch, set out clematis and lilac bushes, and put in a kitchen garden. He and Enid were going to Denver and Colorado Springs for their wedding trip, but Ralph would be at home then, and he had promised to come over and water the flowers and shrubs if the weather was dry.

Enid often brought her work and sat sewing on the front porch while Claude was rubbing the woodwork inside the house, or digging and planting outside. This was the best part of his courtship. It seemed to him that he had never spent such happy days before. If Enid did not come, he kept looking down the road and listening, went from one thing to another and made no progress. He felt full of energy, so long as she sat there on the porch, with lace and ribbons and muslin in her lap. When he passed by, going in or out, and stopped to be near her for a moment, she seemed glad to have him tarry. She liked him to admire her needlework, and did not hesitate to show him the featherstitching and embroidery she was putting on her new underclothes. He could see, from the glances they exchanged, that the painters thought this very bold behaviour in one so soon to be a bride. He thought it very charming behaviour himself, though he would never have expected it of Enid. His heart beat hard when he realized how far she confided in him, how little she was afraid of him! She would let him linger there, standing over her and looking down at her quick fingers, or sitting on the ground at her feet, gazing at the muslin pinned to her knee, until his own sense of propriety told him to get about his work and spare the feelings of the painters.

"When are you going over to the timber claim with me?" he asked, dropping on the ground beside her one warm, windy afternoon. Enid was sitting on the porch floor, her back against a pillar, and her feet on one of those round mats of pursley that grow over hard-beaten earth. "I've found my flock of quail again. They live in the deep grass, over by a ditch that holds water most of the year. I'm going to plant a few rows of peas in there, so they'll have a feeding ground at home. I consider Leonard's cornfield a great danger. I don't know whether to take him into my confidence or not."

"You've told Ernest Havel, I suppose?"

"Oh, yes!" Claude replied, trying not to be aware of the little note of acrimony in her voice. "He's perfectly safe. That place is a paradise for birds. The trees are full of nests. You can stand over there in the morning and hear the young robins squawking for their breakfast. Come up early tomorrow morning and go over with me, won't you? But wear heavy shoes; it's wet in the long grass."

While they were talking a sudden whirlwind swept round the corner of the house, caught up the little mound of folded lace corset-covers and strewed them over the dusty yard. Claude ran after them with Enid's flowered workbag and thrust them into it as he came upon one after another, fluttering in the weeds. When he returned, Enid had folded her needle-case and was putting on her hat. "Thank you," she said with a smile. "Did you find everything?"

"I think so." He hurried toward the car to hide his guilty face. One little lace thing he had not put into the bag, but had thrust into his pocket.

The next morning Enid came up early to hear the birds in the timber.

XII.

On the night before his wedding Claude went to bed early. He had been dashing about with Ralph all day in the car, making final preparations, and was worn out. He fell asleep almost at once. The women of the household could not so easily forget the great event of tomorrow. After the supper dishes were washed, Mahailey clambered up to the attic to get the quilt she had so long been saving for a wedding present for Claude. She took it out of the chest, unfolded it, and counted the stars in the pattern—counting was an accomplishment she was proud of—before she wrapped it up. It was to go down to the mill house with the other presents tomorrow. Mrs. Wheeler went to bed many times that night. She kept thinking of things that ought to be looked after; getting up and going to make sure that Claude's heavy underwear had been put into his trunk, against the chance of cold in the mountains; or creeping downstairs to see that the six roasted chickens which were to help out at the wedding supper were securely covered from the cats. As she went about these tasks, she prayed constantly. She had not prayed so long and fervently since the battle of the Marne.

Early the next morning Ralph loaded the big car with the presents and baskets of food and ran down to the Royces'. Two motors from town were already standing in the mill yard; they had brought a company of girls who came with all the June roses in Frankfort to trim the house for the wedding. When Ralph tooted his horn, half-a-dozen of them ran out to greet him, reproaching him because he had not brought his brother along. Ralph was immediately pressed into service. He carried the step-ladder wherever he was told, drove nails, and wound thorny sprays of rambler roses around the pillars between the front and back parlours, making the arch under which the ceremony was to take place.

Gladys Farmer had not been able to leave her classes at the High School to help in this friendly work, but at eleven o'clock a livery automobile drove up, laden with white and pink peonies from her front yard, and bringing a box of hothouse flowers she had ordered for Enid from Hastings. The girls admired them, but declared that Gladys was extravagant, as usual; the flowers from her own yard would really have been enough. The car was driven by a lank, ragged boy who worked about the town garage, and who was called "Silent Irv," because nobody could ever get a word out of him. He had almost no voice at all,—a thin little squeak in the top of his throat, like the gasping whisper of a medium in her trance state. When he came to the front door, both arms full of peonies, he managed to wheeze out:

"These are from Miss Farmer. There are some more down there."

The girls went back to his car with him, and he took out a square box, tied up with white ribbons and little silver bells, containing the bridal bouquet.

"How did you happen to get these?" Ralph asked the thin boy. "I was to go to town for them."

The messenger swallowed. "Miss Farmer told me if there were any other flowers at the station marked for here, I should bring them along."

"That was nice of her." Ralph thrust his hand into his trousers pocket. "How much? I'll settle with you before I forget."

A pink flush swept over the boy's pale face,—a delicate face under ragged hair, contracted by a kind of shrinking unhappiness. His eyes were always half-closed, as if he did not want to see the world around him, or to be seen by it. He went about like somebody in a dream. "Miss Farmer," he whispered, "has paid me."

"Well, she thinks of everything!" exclaimed one of the girls. "You used to go to school to Gladys, didn't you, Irv?"

"Yes, mam." He got into his car without opening the door, slipping like an eel round the steering-rod, and drove off.

The girls followed Ralph up the gravel walk toward the house. One whispered to the others: "Do you suppose Gladys will come out tonight with Bayliss Wheeler? I always thought she had a pretty warm spot in her heart for Claude, myself."

Some one changed the subject. "I can't get over hearing Irv talk so much. Gladys must have put a spell on him."

"She was always kind to him in school," said the girl who had questioned the silent boy. "She said he was good in his studies, but he was so frightened he could never recite. She let him write out the answers at his desk."

Ralph stayed for lunch, playing about with the girls until his mother telephoned for him. "Now I'll have to go home and look after my brother, or he'll turn up tonight in a striped shirt."

"Give him our love," the girls called after him, "and tell him not to be late."

As he drove toward the farm, Ralph met Dan, taking Claude's trunk into town. He slowed his car. "Any message?" he called.

Dan grinned. "Naw. I left him doin' as well as could be expected."

Mrs. Wheeler met Ralph on the stairs. "He's up in his room. He complains his new shoes are too tight. I think it's nervousness. Perhaps he'll let you shave him; I'm sure he'll cut himself. And I wish the barber hadn't cut his hair so short, Ralph. I hate this new fashion of shearing men behind the ears. The back of his neck is the ugliest part of a man." She spoke with such resentment that Ralph broke into a laugh.

"Why, Mother, I thought all men looked alike to you! Anyhow, Claude's no beauty."

"When will you want your bath? I'll have to manage so that everybody won't be calling for hot water at once." She turned to Mr. Wheeler who sat writing a check at the secretary. "Father, could you take your bath now, and be out of the way?"

"Bath?" Mr. Wheeler shouted, "I don't want any bath! I'm not going to be married tonight. I guess we don't have to boil the whole house for Enid."

Ralph snickered and shot upstairs. He found Claude sitting on the bed, with one shoe off and one shoe on. A pile of socks lay scattered on the rug. A suitcase stood open on one chair and a black travelling bag on another.

"Are you sure they're too small?" Ralph asked.

"About four sizes."

"Well, why didn't you get them big enough?"

"I did. That shark in Hastings worked off another pair on me when I wasn't looking. That's all right," snatching away the shoe his brother had picked up to examine. "I don't care, so long as I can stand in them. You'd better go telephone the depot and ask if the train's on time."

"They won't know yet. It's seven hours till it's due."

"Then telephone later. But find out, somehow. I don't want to stand around that station, waiting for the train."

Ralph whistled. Clearly, his young man was going to be hard to manage. He proposed a bath as a soothing measure. No, Claude had had his bath. Had he, then, packed his suitcase?

"How the devil can I pack it when I don't know what I'm going to put on?"

"You'll put on one shirt and one pair of socks. I'm going to get some of this stuff out of the way for you." Ralph caught up a handful of socks and fell to sorting them. Several had bright red spots on the toe. He began to laugh.

"I know why your shoe hurts, you've cut your foot!"

Claude sprang up as if a hornet had stung him. "Will you get out of here," he shouted, "and let me alone?"

Ralph vanished. He told his mother he would dress at once, as they might have to use force with Claude at the last moment. The wedding ceremony was to be at eight, supper was to follow, and Claude and Enid were to leave Frankfort at 10:25, on the Denver express. At six o'clock, when Ralph knocked at his brother's door, he found him shaved and brushed, and dressed, except for his coat. His tucked shirt was not rumpled, and his tie was properly knotted. Whatever pain they concealed, his patent leather shoes were smooth and glistening and resolutely pointed.

"Are you packed?" Ralph asked in astonishment.

"Nearly. I wish you'd go over things and make them look a little neater, if you can. I'd hate to have a girl see the inside of that suitcase, the way it is. Where shall I put my cigars? They'll make everything smell, wherever I put them. All my clothes seem to smell of cooking, or starch, or something. I don't know what Mahailey does to them," he ended bitterly.

Ralph looked outraged. "Well, of all ingratitude! Mahailey's been ironing your damned old shirts for a week!"

"Yes, yes, I know. Don't rattle me. I forgot to put any handkerchiefs in my trunk, so you'll have to get the whole bunch in somewhere."

Mr. Wheeler appeared in the doorway, his Sunday black trousers gallowsed up high over a white shirt, wafting a rich odor of bayrum from his tumbled hair. He held a thin folded paper delicately between his thick fingers.

"Where is your bill-book, son?"

Claude caught up his discarded trousers and extracted a square of leather from the pocket. His father took it and placed the bit of paper inside with the bank notes. "You may want to pick up some trifle your wife fancies," he said. "Have you got your railroad tickets in here? Here is your trunk check Dan brought back. Don't forget, I've put it in with your tickets and marked it C. W., so you'll know which is your check and which is Enid's."

"Yes, sir. Thank you, sir."

Claude had already drawn from the bank all the money he would need. This additional bank check was Mr. Wheeler's admission that he was sorry for some sarcastic remarks he had made a few days ago, when he discovered that Claude had reserved a stateroom on the Denver express. Claude had answered curtly that when Enid and her mother went to Michigan they always had a stateroom, and he wasn't going to ask her to travel less comfortably with him.

At seven o'clock the Wheeler family set out in the two cars that stood waiting by the windmill. Mr. Wheeler drove the big Cadillac, and Ralph took Mahailey and Dan in the Ford. When they reached the mill house the outer yard was already black with motors, and the porch and parlours were full of people talking and moving about.

Claude went directly upstairs. Ralph began to seat the guests, arranging the folding chairs in such a way as to leave a passage from the foot of the stairs to the floral arch he had constructed that morning. The preacher had his Bible in his hand and was standing under the light, hunting for his chapter. Enid would have preferred to have Mr. Weldon come down from Lincoln to marry her, but that would have wounded Mr. Snowberry deeply. After all, he was her minister, though he was not eloquent and persuasive like Arthur Weldon. He had fewer English words at his command than most human beings, and even those did not come to him readily. In his pulpit he sought for them and struggled with them until drops of perspiration rolled from his forehead and fell upon his coarse, matted brown beard. But he believed what he said, and language was so little an accomplishment with him that he was not tempted to say more than he believed. He had been a drummer boy in the Civil War, on the losing side, and he was a simple, courageous man.

Ralph was to be both usher and best man. Gladys Farmer could not be one of the bridesmaids because she was to play the wedding march. At eight o'clock Enid and Claude came downstairs together, conducted by Ralph and followed by four girls dressed in white, like the bride. They took their places under the arch before the preacher. He began with the chapter from Genesis about the creation of man, and Adam's rib, reading in a laboured manner, as if he did not quite know why he had selected that passage and was looking for something he did not find. His nose-glasses kept falling off and dropping upon the open book. Throughout this prolonged fumbling Enid stood calm, looking at him respectfully, very pretty in her short veil. Claude was so pale that he looked unnatural,—nobody had ever seen him like that before. His face, between his very black clothes and his smooth, sandy hair, was white and severe, and he uttered his responses in a hollow voice. Mahailey, at the back of the room, in a black hat with green gooseberries on it, was standing, in order to miss nothing. She watched Mr. Snowberry as if she hoped to catch some visible sign of the miracle he was performing. She always wondered just what it was the preacher did to make the wrongest thing in the world the rightest thing in the world.

When it was over, Enid went upstairs to put on her travelling dress, and Ralph and Gladys began seating the guests for supper. Just twenty minutes later Enid came down and took her place beside Claude at the head of the long table. The company rose and drank the bride's health in grape-juice punch. Mr. Royce, however, while the guests were being seated, had taken Mr. Wheeler down to the fruit cellar, where the two old friends drank off a glass of well-seasoned Kentucky whiskey, and shook hands. When they came back to the table, looking younger than when they withdrew, the preacher smelled the tang of spirits and felt slighted. He looked disconsolately into his ruddy goblet and thought about the marriage at Cana. He tried to apply his Bible literally to life and, though he didn't dare breathe it aloud in these days, he could never see why he was better than his Lord.

Ralph, as master of ceremonies, kept his head and forgot nothing. When it was time to start, he tapped Claude on the shoulder, cutting his father short in one of his best stories. Contrary to custom, the bridal couple were to go to the station unaccompanied, and they vanished from the head of the table with only a nod and a smile to the guests. Ralph hurried them into the light car, where he had already stowed Enid's hand luggage. Only wizened little Mrs. Royce slipped out from the kitchen to bid them good-bye.

That evening some bad boys had come out from town and strewn the road near the mill with dozens of broken glass bottles, after which they hid in the wild plum bushes to wait for the fun. Ralph's was the first car out, and though his lights glittered on this bed of jagged glass, there was no time to stop; the road was ditched on either side, so he had to drive straight ahead, and got into Frankfort on flat tires. The express whistled just as he pulled up at the station. He and Claude caught up the four pieces of hand luggage and put them in the stateroom. Leaving Enid there with the bags, the two boys went to the rear platform of the observation car to talk until the last moment. Ralph checked off on his fingers the list of things he had promised Claude to attend to. Claude thanked him feelingly. He felt that without Ralph he could never have got married at all. They had never been such good friends as during the last fortnight.

The wheels began to turn. Ralph gripped Claude's hand, ran to the front of the car and stepped off. As Claude passed him, he stood waving his handkerchief,—a rather funny figure under the station lights, in his black clothes and his stiff straw hat, his short legs well apart, wearing his incurably jaunty air.

The train glided quietly out through the summer darkness, along the timbered river valley. Claude was alone on the back platform, smoking a nervous cigar. As they passed the deep cut where Lovely Creek flowed into the river, he saw the lights of the mill house flash for a moment in the distance. The night air was still; heavy with the smell of sweet clover that grew high along the tracks, and of wild grapevines wet with dew. The conductor came to ask for the tickets, saying with a wise smile that he had been hunting for him, as he didn't like to trouble the lady.

After he was gone, Claude looked at his watch, threw away the end of his cigar, and went back through the Pullman cars. The passengers had gone to bed; the overhead lights were always turned low when the train left Frankfort. He made his way through the aisles of swaying green curtains, and tapped at the door of his state room. It opened a little way, and Enid stood there in a white silk dressing-gown with many ruffles, her hair in two smooth braids over her shoulders.

"Claude," she said in a low voice, "would you mind getting a berth somewhere out in the car tonight? The porter says they are not all taken. I'm not feeling very well. I think the dressing on the chicken salad must have been too rich."

He answered mechanically. "Yes, certainly. Can't I get you something?"

"No, thank you. Sleep will do me more good than anything else. Good-night."

She closed the door, and he heard the lock slip. He stood looking at the highly polished wood of the panel for a moment, then turned irresolutely and went back along the slightly swaying aisle of green curtains. In the observation car he stretched himself out upon two wicker chairs and lit another cigar. At twelve o'clock the porter came in.

"This car is closed for the night, sah. Is you the gen'leman from the stateroom in fourteen? Do you want a lower?"

"No, thank you. Is there a smoking car?"

"They is the day-coach smokah, but it ain't likely very clean at this time o' night."

"That's all right. It's forward?" Claude absently handed him a coin, and the porter conducted him to a very dirty car where the floor was littered with newspapers and cigar stumps, and the leather cushions were grey with dust. A few desperate looking men lay about with their shoes off and their suspenders hanging down their backs. The sight of them reminded Claude that his left foot was very sore, and that his shoes must have been hurting him for some time. He pulled them off, and thrust his feet, in their silk socks, on the opposite seat.

On that long, dirty, uncomfortable ride Claude felt many things, but the paramount feeling was homesickness. His hurt was of a kind that made him turn with a sort of aching cowardice to the old, familiar things that were as sure as the sunrise. If only the sagebrush plain, over which the stars were shining, could suddenly break up and resolve itself into the windings of Lovely Creek, with his father's house on the hill, dark and silent in the summer night! When he closed his eyes he could see the light in his mother's window; and, lower down, the glow of Mahailey's lamp, where she sat nodding and mending his old shirts. Human love was a wonderful thing, he told himself, and it was most wonderful where it had least to gain.

By morning the storm of anger, disappointment, and humiliation that was boiling in him when he first sat down in the observation car, had died out. One thing lingered; the peculiarly casual, indifferent, uninterested tone of his wife's voice when she sent him away. It was the flat tone in which people make commonplace remarks about common things.

Day broke with silvery brightness on the summer sage. The sky grew pink, the sand grew gold. The dawn-wind brought through the windows the acrid smell of the sagebrush: an odour that is peculiarly stimulating in the early morning, when it always seems to promise freedom… large spaces, new beginnings, better days.

The train was due in Denver at eight o'clock. Exactly at seven thirty Claude knocked at Enid's door,—this time firmly. She was dressed, and greeted him with a fresh, smiling face, holding her hat in her hand.

"Are you feeling better?" he asked.

"Oh, yes! I am perfectly all right this morning. I've put out all your things for you, there on the seat."

He glanced at them. "Thank you. But I won't have time to change, I'm afraid."

"Oh, won't you? I'm so sorry I forgot to give you your bag last night. But you must put on another necktie, at least. You look too much like a groom."

"Do I?" he asked, with a scarcely perceptible curl of his lip.

Everything he needed was neatly arranged on the plush seat; shirt, collar, tie, brushes, even a handkerchief. Those in his pockets were black from dusting off the cinders that blew in all night, and he threw them down and took up the clean one. There was a damp spot on it, and as he unfolded it he recognized the scent of a cologne Enid often used. For some reason this attention unmanned him. He felt the smart of tears in his eyes, and to hide them bent over the metal basin and began to scrub his face. Enid stood behind him, adjusting her hat in the mirror.

"How terribly smoky you are, Claude. I hope you don't smoke before breakfast?"

"No. I was in the smoking car awhile. I suppose my clothes got full of it."

"You are covered with dust and cinders, too!" She took the clothes broom from the rack and began to brush him.

Claude caught her hand. "Don't, please!" he said sharply. "The porter can do that for me."

Enid watched him furtively as he closed and strapped his suitcase. She had often heard that men were cross before breakfast.

"Sure you've forgotten nothing?" he asked before he closed her bag.

"Yes. I never lose things on the train,—do you?"

"Sometimes," he replied guardedly, not looking up as he snapped the catch.

❧ 3 ☙

SUNRISE ON THE PRAIRIE

I.

CLAUDE WAS to continue farming with his father, and after he returned from his wedding journey, he fell at once to work. The harvest was almost as abundant as that of the summer before, and he was busy in the fields six days a week.

One afternoon in August he came home with his team, watered and fed the horses in a leisurely way, and then entered his house by the back door. Enid, he knew, would not be there. She had gone to Frankfort to a meeting of the Anti-Saloon League. The Prohibition party was bestirring itself in Nebraska that summer, confident of voting the State dry the following year, which purpose it triumphantly accomplished.

Enid's kitchen, full of the afternoon sun, glittered with new paint, spotless linoleum, and blue-and-white cooking vessels. In the dining-room the cloth was laid, and the table was neatly set for one. Claude opened the icebox, where his supper was arranged for him; a dish of canned salmon with a white sauce; hardboiled eggs, peeled and lying in a nest of lettuce leaves; a bowl of ripe tomatoes, a bit of cold rice pudding; cream and butter. He placed these things on the table, cut some bread, and after carelessly washing his face and hands, sat down to eat in his working shirt. He propped the newspaper against a red glass water pitcher and read the war news while he had his supper. He was annoyed when he heard heavy footsteps coming around the house. Leonard Dawson stuck his head in at the kitchen door, and Claude rose quickly and reached for his hat; but Leonard came in, uninvited, and sat down. His brown shirt was wet where his suspenders gripped his shoulders, and his face, under a wide straw hat which he did not remove, was unshaven and streaked with dust.

"Go ahead and finish your supper," he cried. "Having a wife with a car of her own is next thing to having no wife at all. How they do like to roll around! I've been mighty blamed careful to see that Susie never learned to drive a car. See here, Claude, how soon do you figure you'll be able to let me have the thrasher? My wheat will begin to sprout in the shock pretty soon. Do you reckon your father would be willing to work on Sunday, if I helped you, to let the machine off a day earlier?"

"I'm afraid not. Mother wouldn't like it. We never have done that, even when we were crowded."

"Well, I think I'll go over and have a talk with your mother. If she could look inside my wheat shocks, maybe I could convince her it's pretty near a case of your neighbour's ox falling into a pit on the Sabbath day."

"That's a good idea. She's always reasonable."

Leonard rose. "What's the news?"

"The Germans have torpedoed an English passenger ship, the Arabic; coming this way, too."

"That's all right," Leonard declared. "Maybe Americans will stay at home now, and mind their own business. I don't care how they chew each other up over there, not a bit! I'd as soon one got wiped off the map as another."

"Your grandparents were English people, weren't they?"

"That's a long while ago. Yes, my grandmother wore a cap and little white curls, and I tell Susie I wouldn't mind if the baby turned out to have my grandmother's skin. She had the finest complexion I ever saw."

As they stepped out of the back door, a troop of white chickens with red combs ran squawking toward them. It was the hour at which the poultry was usually fed. Leonard stopped to admire them. "You've got a fine lot of hens. I always did like white leghorns. Where are all your roosters?"

"We've only got one. He's shut up in the coop. The brood hens are setting. Enid is going to try raising winter frys."

"Only one rooster? And may I ask what these hens do?"

Claude laughed. "They lay eggs, just the same,—better. It's the fertile eggs that spoil in warm weather."

This information seemed to make Leonard angry. "I never heard of such damned nonsense," he blustered. "I raise chickens on a natural basis, or I don't raise 'em at all." He jumped into his car for fear he would say more.

When he got home his wife was lifting supper, and the baby sat near her in its buggy, playing with a rattle. Dirty and sweaty as he was, Leonard picked up the clean baby and began to kiss it and smell it, rubbing his stubbly chin in the soft creases of its neck. The little girl was beside herself with delight.

"Go and wash up for supper, Len," Susie called from the stove. He put down the baby and began splashing in the tin basin, talking with his eyes shut.

"Susie, I'm in an awful temper. I can't stand that damned wife of Claude's!"

She was spearing roasting ears out of a big iron pot and looked up through the steam. "Why, have you seen her? I was listening on the telephone this morning and heard her tell Bayliss she would be in town until late." "Oh, yes! She went to town all right, and he's over there eating a cold supper by himself. That woman's a fanatic. She ain't content with practising prohibition on humankind; she's begun now on the hens." While he placed the chairs and wheeled the baby up to the table, he explained Enid's method of raising poultry to his wife. She said she really didn't see any harm in it.

"Now be honest, Susie; did you ever know hens would keep on laying without a rooster?"

"No, I didn't, but I was brought up the old-fashioned way. Enid has poultry books and garden books, and all such things. I don't doubt she gets good ideas from them. But anyhow, you be careful. She's our nearest neighbour, and I don't want to have trouble with her."

"I'll have to keep out of her way, then. If she tries to do any missionary work among my chickens, I'll tell her a few home truths her husband's too bashful to tell her. It's my opinion she's got that boy cowed already."

"Now, Len, you know she won't bother your chickens. You keep quiet. But Claude does seem to sort of avoid people," Susie admitted, filling her husband's plate again. "Mrs. Joe Havel says Ernest don't go to Claude's any more. It seems Enid went over there and wanted Ernest to paste some Prohibition posters about fifteen million drunkards on their barn, for an example to the Bohemians. Ernest wouldn't do it, and told her he was going to vote for saloons, and Enid was quite spiteful, Mrs. Havel said. It's too bad, when those boys were such chums. I used to like to see them together." Susie spoke so kindly that her husband shot her a quick glance of shy affection.

"Do you suppose Claude relished having that preacher visiting them, when they hadn't been married two months? Sitting on the front porch in a white necktie every day, while Claude was out cutting wheat?"

"Well, anyhow, I guess Claude had more to eat when Brother Weldon was staying there. Preachers won't be fed on calories, or whatever it is Enid calls 'em," said Susie, who was given to looking on the bright side of things. "Claude's wife keeps a wonderful kitchen; but so could I, if I never cooked any more than she does."

Leonard gave her a meaning look. "I don't believe you would live with the sort of man you could feed out of a tin can."

"No, I don't believe I would." She pushed the buggy toward him. "Take her up, Daddy. She wants to play with you."

Leonard set the baby on his shoulder and carried her off to show her the pigs. Susie kept laughing to herself as she cleared the table and washed the dishes; she was much amused by what her husband had told her.

Late that evening, when Leonard was starting for the barn to see that all was well before he went to bed, he observed a discreet black object rolling along the highroad in the moonlight, a red spark winking in the rear. He called Susie to the door.

"See, there she goes; going home to report the success of the meeting to Claude. Wouldn't that be a nice way to have your wife coming in?"

"Now, Leonard, if Claude likes it—"

"Likes it?" Big Leonard drew himself up. "What can he do, poor kid? He's stung!"

II.

After Leonard left him, Claude cleared away the remains of his supper and watered the gourd vine before he went to milk. It was not really a gourd vine at all, but a summer-squash, of the crook-necked, warty, orange-coloured variety, and it was now full of ripe squashes, hanging by strong stems among the rough green leaves and prickly tendrils. Claude had watched its rapid growth and the opening of its splotchy yellow blossoms, feeling grateful to a thing that did so lustily what it was put there to do. He had the same feeling for his little Jersey cow, which came home every night with full udders and gave down her milk willingly, keeping her tail out of his face, as only a well disposed cow will do.

His milking done, he sat down on the front porch and lit a cigar. While he smoked, he did not think about anything but the quiet and the slow cooling of the atmosphere, and how good it was to sit still. The moon swam up over the bare wheat fields, big and magical, like a great flower. Presently he got some bath towels, went across the yard to the windmill, took off his clothes, and stepped into the tin horse tank. The water had been warmed by the sun all afternoon, and was not much cooler than his body. He stretched himself out in it, and resting his head on the metal rim, lay on his back, looking up at the moon. The sky was a midnight-blue, like warm, deep, blue water, and the moon seemed to lie on it like a water-lily, floating forward with an invisible current. One expected to see its great petals open.

For some reason, Claude began to think about the far-off times and countries it had shone upon. He never thought of the sun as coming from distant lands, or as having taken part in human life in other ages. To him, the sun rotated about the wheatfields. But the moon, somehow, came out of the historic past, and made him think of Egypt and the Pharaohs, Babylon and the hanging gardens. She seemed particularly to have looked down upon the follies and disappointments of men; into the slaves' quarters of old times, into prison windows, and into fortresses where captives languished.

Inside of living people, too, captives languished. Yes, inside of people who walked and worked in the broad sun, there were captives dwelling in darkness, never seen from birth to death. Into those prisons the moon shone, and the prisoners crept to the windows and looked out with mournful eyes at the white globe which betrayed no secrets and comprehended all. Perhaps even in people like Mrs. Royce and his brother Bayliss there was something of this sort—but that was a shuddery thought. He dismissed it with a quick movement of his hand through the water, which, disturbed, caught the light and played black and gold, like something alive, over his chest. In his own mother the imprisoned spirit was almost more present to people than her corporeal self. He had so often felt it when he sat with her on summer nights like this. Mahailey, too, had one, though the walls of her prison were so thick —and Gladys Farmer. Oh, yes, how much Gladys must have to tell this perfect confidant! The people whose hearts were set high needed such intercourse—whose wish was so beautiful that there were no experiences in this world to satisfy it. And these children of the moon, with their unappeased longings and futile dreams, were a finer race than the children of the sun. This conception flooded the boy's heart like a second moonrise, flowed through him indefinite and strong, while he lay deathly still for fear of losing it.

At last the black cubical object which had caught Leonard Dawson's wrathful eye, came rolling along the highroad. Claude snatched up his clothes and towels, and without waiting to make use of either, he ran, a white man across a bare white yard. Gaining the shelter of the house, he found his bathrobe, and fled to the upper porch, where he lay down in the hammock. Presently he heard his name called, pronounced as if it were spelled "Clod." His wife came up the stairs and looked out at him. He lay motionless, with his eyes closed. She went away. When all was quiet again he looked off at the still country, and the moon in the dark indigo sky. His revelation still possessed him, making his whole body sensitive, like a tightly strung bow. In the morning he had forgotten, or was ashamed of what had seemed so true and so entirely his own the night before. He agreed, for the most part, that it was better not to think about such things, and when he could he avoided thinking.

III.

AFTER THE HEAVY work of harvest was over, Mrs. Wheeler often persuaded her husband, when he was starting off in his buckboard, to take her as far as Claude's new house. She was glad Enid didn't keep her parlour dark, as Mrs. Royce kept hers. The doors and windows were always open, the vines and the long petunias in the window-boxes waved in the breeze, and the rooms were full of sunlight and in perfect order. Enid wore white dresses about her work, and white shoes and stockings. She managed a house easily and systematically. On

Monday morning Claude turned the washing machine before he went to work, and by nine o'clock the clothes were on the line. Enid liked to iron, and Claude had never before in his life worn so many clean shirts, or worn them with such satisfaction. She told him he need not economize in working shirts; it was as easy to iron six as three.

Although within a few months Enid's car travelled more than two thousand miles for the Prohibition cause, it could not be said that she neglected her house for reform. Whether she neglected her husband depended upon one's conception of what was his due. When Mrs. Wheeler saw how well their little establishment was conducted, how cheerful and attractive Enid looked when one happened to drop in there, she wondered that Claude was not happy. And Claude himself wondered. If his marriage disappointed him in some respects, he ought to be a man, he told himself, and make the best of what was good in it. If his wife didn't love him, it was because love meant one thing to him and quite another thing to her. She was proud of him, was glad to see him when he came in from the fields, and was solicitous for his comfort. Everything about a man's embrace was distasteful to Enid; something inflicted upon women, like the pain of childbirth,— for Eve's transgression, perhaps.

This repugnance was more than physical; she disliked ardour of any kind, even religious ardour. She had been fonder of Claude before she married him than she was now; but she hoped for a readjustment. Perhaps sometime she could like him again in exactly the same way. Even Brother Weldon had hinted to her that for the sake of their future tranquillity she must be lenient with the boy. And she thought she had been lenient. She could not understand his moods of desperate silence, the bitter, biting remarks he sometimes dropped, his evident annoyance if she went over to join him in the timber claim when he lay there idle in the deep grass on a Sunday afternoon.

Claude used to lie there and watch the clouds, saying to himself, "It's the end of everything for me." Other men than he must have been disappointed, and he wondered how they bore it through a lifetime. Claude had been a well behaved boy because he was an idealist; he had looked forward to being wonderfully happy in love, and to deserving his happiness. He had never dreamed that it might be otherwise.

Sometimes now, when he went out into the fields on a bright summer morning, it seemed to him that Nature not only smiled, but broadly laughed at him. He suffered in his pride, but even more in his ideals, in his vague sense of what was beautiful. Enid could make his life hideous to him without ever knowing it. At such times he hated himself for accepting at all her grudging hospitality. He was wronging something in himself.

In her person Enid was still attractive to him. He wondered why she had no shades of feeling to correspond to her natural grace and lightness of movement, to the gentle, almost wistful attitudes of body in which he sometimes surprised her. When he came in from work and found her sitting on the porch, leaning against a pillar, her hands clasped about her knees, her head drooping a little, he could scarcely believe in the rigidity which met him at every turn. Was there something repellent in him? Was it, after all, his fault?

Enid was rather more indulgent with his father than with any one else, he noticed. Mr. Wheeler stopped to see her almost every day, and even took her driving in his old buckboard. Bayliss came out from town to spend the evening occasionally. Enid's vegetarian suppers suited him, and as she worked with him in the Prohibition campaign, they always had business to discuss. Bayliss had a social as well as a hygienic prejudice against alcohol, and he hated it less for the harm it did than for the pleasure it gave. Claude consistently refused to take any part in the activities of the Anti-Saloon League, or to distribute what Bayliss and Enid called "our literature."

In the farming towns the term "literature" was applied only to a special kind of printed matter; there was Prohibition literature, Sex-Hygiene literature, and, during a scourge of cattle disease, there was Hoof-and-Mouth literature. This special application of the word didn't bother Claude, but his mother, being an old-fashioned school-teacher, complained about it.

Enid did not understand her husband's indifference to a burning question, and could only attribute it to the influence of Ernest Havel. She sometimes asked Claude to go with her to one of her committee meetings. If it was a Sunday, he said he was tired and wanted to read the paper. If it was a week-day, he had something to do at the barn, or meant to clear out the timber claim. He did, indeed, saw off a few dead limbs, and cut down a tree the lightning had blasted. Further than that he wouldn't have let anybody clear the timber lot; he would have died defending it.

The timber claim was his refuge. In the open, grassy spots, shut in by the bushy walls of yellowing ash trees, he felt unmarried and free; free to smoke as much as he liked, and to read and dream. Some of his dreams would have frozen his young wife's blood with horror —and some would have melted his mother's heart with pity. To lie in the hot sun and look up at the stainless blue of the autumn sky, to hear the dry rustle of the leaves as they fell, and the sound of the bold squirrels leaping from branch to branch; to lie thus and let his imagination play with life—that was the best he could do. His thoughts, he told himself, were his own. He was no longer a boy. He went off into the timber claim to meet a young man more experienced and interesting than himself, who had not tied himself up with compromises.

IV.

From her upstairs window Mrs. Wheeler could see Claude moving back and forth in the west field, drilling wheat. She felt lonely for him. He didn't come home as often as he might. She had begun to wonder whether he was one of those people who are always discontented; but whatever his disappointments were, he kept them locked in his own breast. One had to learn the lessons of life. Nevertheless, it made her a little sad to see him so settled and indifferent at twenty-three.

After watching from the window for a few moments, she turned to the telephone and called up Claude's house, asking Enid whether she would mind if he came there for dinner. "Mahailey and I get lonesome with Mr. Wheeler away so much," she added.

"Why, no, Mother Wheeler, of course not." Enid spoke cheerfully, as she always did. "Have you any one there you can send over to tell him?"

"I thought I would walk over myself, Enid. It's not far, if I take my time."

Mrs. Wheeler left the house a little before noon and stopped at the creek to rest before she climbed the long hill. At the edge of the field she sat down against a grassy bank and waited until the horses came tramping up the long rows. Claude saw her and pulled them in.

"Anything wrong, Mother?" he called.

"Oh, no! I'm going to take you home for dinner with me, that's all. I telephoned Enid." He unhooked his team, and he and his mother started down the hill together, walking behind the horses. Though they had not been alone like this for a long while, she felt it best to talk about impersonal things.

"Don't let me forget to give you an article about the execution of that English nurse."

"Edith Cavell? I've read about it," he answered listlessly. "It's nothing to be surprised at. If they could sink the Lusitania, they could shoot an English nurse, certainly."

"Someway I feel as if this were different," his mother murmured. "It's like the hanging of John Brown. I wonder they could find soldiers to execute the sentence."

"Oh, I guess they have plenty of such soldiers!"

Mrs. Wheeler looked up at him. "I don't see how we can stay out of it much longer, do you? I suppose our army wouldn't be a drop in the bucket, even if we could get it over. They tell us we can be more useful in our agriculture and manufactories than we could by going into the war. I only hope it isn't campaign talk. I do distrust the Democrats."

Claude laughed. "Why, Mother, I guess there's no party politics in this."

She shook her head. "I've never yet found a public question in which there wasn't party politics. Well, we can only do our duty as it comes to us, and have faith. This field finishes your fall work?"

"Yes. I'll have time to do some things about the place, now. I'm going to make a good ice-house and put up my own ice this winter."

"Were you thinking of going up to Lincoln, for a little?"

"I guess not."

Mrs. Wheeler sighed. His tone meant that he had turned his back on old pleasures and old friends.

"Have you and Enid taken tickets for the lecture course in Frankfort?"

"I think so, Mother," he answered a little impatiently. "I told her she could attend to it when she was in town some day."

"Of course," his mother persevered, "some of the programs are not very good, but we ought to patronize them and make the best of what we have."

He knew, and his mother knew, that he was not very good at that. His horses stopped at the water tank. "Don't wait for me. I'll be along in a minute." Seeing her crestfallen face, he smiled. "Never mind, Mother, I can always catch you when you try to give me a pill in a raisin. One of us has to be pretty smart to fool the other."

She blinked up at him with that smile in which her eyes almost disappeared. "I thought I was smart that time!"

It was a comfort, she reflected, as she hurried up the hill, to get hold of him again, to get his attention, even.

While Claude was washing for dinner, Mahailey came to him with a page of newspaper cartoons, illustrating German brutality. To her they were all photographs,—she knew no other way of making a picture.

"Mr. Claude," she asked, "how comes it all them Germans is such ugly lookin' people? The Yoeders and the German folks round here ain't ugly lookin'."

Claude put her off indulgently. "Maybe it's the ugly ones that are doing the fighting, and the ones at home are nice, like our neighbours."

"Then why don't they make their soldiers stay home, an' not go breakin' other people's things, an' turnin' 'em out of their houses," she muttered indignantly. "They say little babies was born out in the snow last winter, an' no fires for their mudders nor nothin'. 'Deed, Mr. Claude, it wasn't like that in our war; the soldiers didn't do nothin' to the women an' chillun. Many a time our house was full of Northern soldiers, an' they never so much as broke a piece of my mudder's chiney."

"You'll have to tell me about it again sometime, Mahailey. I must have my dinner and get back to work. If we don't get our wheat in, those people over there won't have anything to eat, you know."

The picture papers meant a great deal to Mahailey, because she could faintly remember the Civil War. While she pored over photographs of camps and battlefields and devastated villages, things came back to her; the companies of dusty Union infantry that used to stop to drink at her mother's cold mountain spring. She had seen them take off their boots and wash their bleeding feet in the run. Her mother had given one louse-bitten boy a clean shirt, and she had never forgotten the sight of his back, "as raw as beef where he'd scratched it." Five of her brothers were in the Confederate army. When one was wounded in the second battle of Bull Run, her mother had borrowed a wagon and horses, gone a three days' journey to the field hospital, and brought the boy home to the mountain. Mahailey could remember how her older sisters took turns pouring cold spring water on his gangrenous leg all day and all night. There were no doctors left in the neighbourhood, and as nobody could amputate the boy's leg, he died by inches. Mahailey was the only person in the Wheeler household who had ever seen war with her own eyes, and she felt that this fact gave her a definite superiority.

V.

CLAUDE HAD BEEN MARRIED a year and a half. One December morning he got a telephone message from his father-in-law, asking him to come in to Frankfort at once. He found Mr. Royce sunk in his desk-chair, smoking as usual, with several foreign-looking letters on the table before him. As he took these out of their envelopes and sorted the pages, Claude noticed how unsteady his hands had become.

One letter, from the chief of the medical staff in the mission school where Caroline Royce taught, informed Mr. Royce that his daughter was seriously ill in the mission hospital. She would have to be sent to a more salubrious part of the country for rest and treatment, and would not be strong enough to return to her duties for a year or more. If some member of her family could come out to take care of her, it would relieve the school authorities of great anxiety. There was also a letter from a fellow teacher, and a rather incoherent one from Caroline herself. After Claude finished reading them, Mr. Royce pushed a box of cigars toward him and began to talk despondently about missionaries.

"I could go to her," he complained, "but what good would that do? I'm not in sympathy with her ideas, and it would only fret her. You can see she's made her mind up not to come home. I don't believe in one people trying to force their ways or their religion on another. I'm not that kind of man." He sat looking at his cigar. After a long pause he broke out suddenly, "China has been drummed into my ears. It seems like a long way to go to hunt for trouble, don't it? A man hasn't got much control over his own life, Claude. If it ain't poverty or disease that torments him, it's a name on the map. I could have made out pretty well, if it hadn't been for China, and some other things.... If Carrie'd had to teach for her clothes and help pay off my notes, like old man Harrison's daughters, like enough she'd have stayed at home. There's always something. I don't know what to say about showing these letters to Enid."

"Oh, she will have to know about it, Mr. Royce. If she feels that she ought to go to Carrie, it wouldn't be right for me to interfere."

Mr. Royce shook his head. "I don't know. It don't seem fair that China should hang over you, too."

When Claude got home he remarked as he handed Enid the letters, "Your father has been a good deal upset by this. I never saw him look so old as he did today."

Enid studied their contents, sitting at her orderly little desk, while Claude pretended to read the paper.

"It seems clear that I am the one to go," she said when she had finished.

"You think it's necessary for some one to go? I don't see it."

"It would look very strange if none of us went," Enid replied with spirit.

"How, look strange?"

"Why, it would look to her associates as if her family had no feeling."

"Oh, if that's all!" Claude smiled perversely and took up his paper again. "I wonder how it will look to people here if you go off and leave your husband?"

"What a mean thing to say, Claude!" She rose sharply, then hesitated, perplexed. "People here know me better than that. It isn't as if you couldn't be perfectly comfortable at your mother's." As he did not glance up from his paper, she went into the kitchen.

Claude sat still, listening to Enid's quick movements as she opened up the range to get supper. The light in the room grew greyer. Outside the fields melted into one another as evening came on. The young trees in the yard bent and whipped about under a bitter north wind. He had often thought with pride that winter died at his front doorstep; within, no draughty halls, no chilly corners. This was their second year here. When he was driving home, the thought that he might be free of this house for a long while had stirred a pleasant excitement in him; but now, he didn't want to leave it. Something grew soft in him. He wondered whether they couldn't try again, and make things go better. Enid was singing in the kitchen in a subdued, rather lonely voice. He rose and went out for his milking coat and pail. As he passed his wife by the window, he stopped and put his arm about her questioningly.

She looked up. "That's right. You're feeling better about it, aren't you? I thought you would. Gracious, what a smelly coat, Claude! I must find another for you."

Claude knew that tone. Enid never questioned the rightness of her own decisions. When she made up her mind, there was no turning her. He went down the path to the barn with his hands stuffed in his trousers pockets, his bright pail hanging on his arm. Try again—what was there to try? Platitudes, littleness, falseness.... His life was choking him, and he hadn't the courage to break with it. Let her go! Let her go when she would!... What a hideous world to be born into! Or was it hideous only for him? Everything he touched went wrong under his hand—always had.

When they sat down at the supper table in the back parlour an hour later, Enid looked worn, as if this time her decision had cost her something. "I should think you might have a restful winter at your mother's," she began cheerfully. "You won't have nearly so much to look after as you do here. We needn't disturb things in this house. I will take the silver down to Mother, and we can leave everything else just as it is. Would there be room for my car in your father's garage? You might find it a convenience."

"Oh, no! I won't need it. I'll put it up at the mill house," he answered with an effort at carelessness.

All the familiar objects that stood about them in the lamplight seemed stiller and more solemn than usual, as if they were holding their breath.

"I suppose you had better take the chickens over to your mother's," Enid continued evenly. "But I shouldn't like them to get mixed with her Plymouth Rocks; there's not a dark feather among them now. Do ask Mother Wheeler to use all the eggs, and not to let my hens set in the spring."

"In the spring?" Claude looked up from his plate.

"Of course, Claude. I could hardly get back before next fall, if I'm to be of any help to poor Carrie. I might try to be home for harvest, if that would make it more convenient for you." She rose to bring in the dessert.

"Oh, don't hurry on my account!" he muttered, staring after her disappearing figure.

Enid came back with the hot pudding and the after-dinner coffee things. "This has come on us so suddenly that we must make our plans at once," she explained. "I should think your mother would be glad to keep Rose for us; she is such a good cow. And then you can have all the cream you want."

He took the little gold-rimmed cup she held out to him. "If you are going to be gone until next fall, I shall sell Rose," he announced gruffly.

"But why? You might look a long time before you found another like her."

"I shall sell her, anyhow. The horses, of course, are Father's; he paid for them. If you clear out, he may want to rent this place. You may find a tenant in here when you get back from China." Claude swallowed his coffee, put down the cup, and went into the front parlour, where he lit a cigar. He walked up and down, keeping his eyes fixed upon his wife, who still sat at the table in the circle of light from the hanging lamp. Her head, bent forward a little, showed the neat part of her brown hair. When she was perplexed, her face always looked sharper, her chin longer.

"If you've no feeling for the place," said Claude from the other room, "you can hardly expect me to hang around and take care of it. All the time you were campaigning, I played housekeeper here."

Enid's eyes narrowed, but she did not flush. Claude had never seen a wave of colour come over his wife's pale, smooth cheeks.

"Don't be childish. You know I care for this place; it's our home. But no feeling would be right that kept me from doing my duty. You are well, and you have your mother's house to go to. Carrie is ill and among strangers."

She began to gather up the dishes. Claude stepped quickly out into the light and confronted her. "It's not only your going. You know what's the matter with me. It's because you want to go. You are glad of a chance to get away among all those preachers, with their smooth talk and make-believe."

Enid took up the tray. "If I am glad, it's because you are not willing to govern our lives by Christian ideals. There is something in you that rebels all the time. So many important questions have come up since our marriage, and you have been indifferent or sarcastic about every one of them. You want to lead a purely selfish life."

She walked resolutely out of the room and shut the door behind her. Later, when she came back, Claude was not there. His hat and coat were gone from the hat rack; he must have let himself out quietly by the front door. Enid sat up until eleven and then went to bed.

In the morning, on coming out from her bedroom, she found Claude asleep on the lounge, dressed, with his overcoat on. She had a moment of terror and bent over him, but she could not detect any smell of spirits. She began preparations for breakfast, moving quietly.

Having once made up her mind to go out to her sister, Enid lost no time. She engaged passage and cabled the mission school. She left Frankfort the week before Christmas. Claude and Ralph took her as far as Denver and put her on a trans-continental express. When Claude came home, he moved over to his mother's, and sold his cow and chickens to Leonard Dawson. Except when he went to see Mr. Royce, he seldom left the farm now, and he avoided the neighbours. He felt that they were discussing his domestic affairs,—as, of course, they were. The Royces and the Wheelers, they said, couldn't behave like anybody else, and it was no use their trying. If Claude built the best house in the neighbourhood, he just naturally wouldn't live in it. And if he had a wife at all, it was like him to have a wife in China!

One snowy day, when nobody was about, Claude took the big car and went over to his own place to close the house for the winter and bring away the canned fruit and vegetables left in the cellar. Enid had packed her best linen in her cedar chest and had put the kitchen and china closets in scrupulous order before she went away. He began covering the upholstered chairs and the mattresses with sheets, rolled up the rugs, and fastened the windows securely. As he worked, his hands grew more and more numb and listless, and his heart was like a lump of ice. All these things that he had selected with care and in which he had taken such pride, were no more to him now than the lumber piled in the shop of any second-hand dealer.

How inherently mournful and ugly such objects were, when the feeling that had made them precious no longer existed! The debris of human life was more worthless and ugly than the dead and decaying things in nature. Rubbish... junk... his mind could not picture anything that so exposed and condemned all the dreary, weary, ever-repeated actions by which life is continued from day to day. Actions without meaning.... As he looked out and saw the grey landscape through the gently falling snow, he could not help thinking how much better it would be if people could go to sleep like the fields; could be blanketed down under the snow, to wake with their hurts healed and their defeats forgotten. He wondered how he was to go on through the years ahead of him, unless he could get rid of this sick feeling in his soul.

At last he locked the door, put the key in his pocket, and went over to the timber claim to smoke a cigar and say goodbye to the place. There he soberly walked about for more than an hour, under the crooked trees with empty birds' nests in their forks. Every time he came to a break in the hedge, he could see the little house, giving itself up so meekly to solitude. He did not believe that he would ever live there again. Well, at any rate, the money his father had put into the place would not be lost; he could always get a better tenant for having a comfortable house there. Several of the boys in the neighbourhood were planning to be married within the year. The future of the house was safe. And he? He stopped short in his walk; his feet had made an uncertain, purposeless trail all over the white ground. It vexed him to see his own footsteps. What was it—what WAS the matter with him? Why, at least, could he not stop feeling things, and hoping? What was there to hope for now?

He heard a sound of distress, and looking back, saw the barn cat, that had been left behind to pick up her living. She was standing inside the hedge, her jet black fur ruffled against the wet flakes, one paw lifted, mewing miserably. Claude went over and picked her up.

"What's the matter, Blackie? Mice getting scarce in the barn? Mahailey will say you are bad luck. Maybe you are, but you can't help it, can you?" He slipped her into his overcoat pocket. Later, when he was getting into his car, he tried to dislodge her and put her in a basket, but she clung to her nest in his pocket and dug her claws into the lining. He laughed. "Well, if you are bad luck, I guess you are going to stay right with me!"

She looked up at him with startled yellow eyes and did not even mew.

VI.

MRS. WHEELER WAS afraid that Claude might not find the old place comfortable, after having had a house of his own. She put her best rocking chair and a reading lamp in his bedroom. He often sat there all evening, shading his eyes with his hand, pretending to read. When he stayed downstairs after supper, his mother and Mahailey were grateful. Besides collecting war pictures, Mahailey now hunted through the old magazines in the attic for pictures of

China. She had marked on her big kitchen calendar the day when Enid would arrive in Hong-Kong.

"Mr. Claude," she would say as she stood at the sink washing the supper dishes, "it's broad daylight over where Miss Enid is, ain't it? Cause the world's round, an' the old sun, he's a-shinin' over there for the yaller people."

From time to time, when they were working together, Mrs. Wheeler told Mahailey what she knew about the customs of the Chinese. The old woman had never had two impersonal interests at the same time before, and she scarcely knew what to do with them. She would murmur on, half to Claude and half to herself: "They ain't fightin' over there where Miss Enid is, is they? An' she won't have to wear their kind of clothes, cause she's a white woman. She won't let 'em kill their girl babies nor do such awful things like they always have, an' she won't let 'em pray to them stone iboles, cause they can't help 'em none. I 'spect Miss Enid'll do a heap of good, all the time."

Behind her diplomatic monologues, however, Mahailey had her own ideas, and she was greatly scandalized at Enid's departure. She was afraid people would say that Claude's wife had "run off an' lef' him," and in the Virginia mountains, where her social standards had been formed, a husband or wife thus deserted was the object of boisterous ridicule. She once stopped Mrs. Wheeler in a dark corner of the cellar to whisper, "Mr. Claude's wife ain't goin' to stay off there, like her sister, is she?"

If one of the Yoeder boys or Susie Dawson happened to be at the Wheelers' for dinner, Mahailey never failed to refer to Enid in a loud voice. "Mr. Claude's wife, she cuts her potatoes up raw in the pan an' fries 'em. She don't boil 'em first like I do. I know she's an awful good cook, I know she is." She felt that easy references to the absent wife made things look better.

Ernest Havel came to see Claude now, but not often. They both felt it would be indelicate to renew their former intimacy. Ernest still felt aggrieved about his beer, as if Enid had snatched the tankard from his lips with her own corrective hand. Like Leonard, he believed that Claude had made a bad bargain in matrimony; but instead of feeling sorry for him, Ernest wanted to see him convinced and punished. When he married Enid, Claude had been false to liberal principles, and it was only right that he should pay for his apostasy. The very first time he came to spend an evening at the Wheelers' after Claude came home to live, Ernest undertook to explain his objections to Prohibition. Claude shrugged his shoulders.

"Why not drop it? It's a matter that doesn't interest me, one way or the other."

Ernest was offended and did not come back for nearly a month—not, indeed, until the announcement that Germany would resume unrestricted submarine warfare made every one look questioningly at his neighbour.

He walked into the Wheelers' kitchen the night after this news reached the farming country, and found Claude and his mother sitting at the table, reading the papers aloud to each other in snatches. Ernest had scarcely taken a seat when the telephone bell rang. Claude answered the call.

"It's the telegraph operator at Frankfort," he said, as he hung up the receiver. "He repeated a message from Father, sent from Wray: 'Will be home day after tomorrow. Read the papers.' What does he mean? What does he suppose we are doing?"

"It means he considers our situation very serious. It's not like him to telegraph except in case of illness." Mrs. Wheeler rose and walked distractedly to the telephone box, as if it might further disclose her husband's state of mind.

"But what a queer message! It was addressed to you, too, Mother, not to me."

"He would know how I feel about it. Some of your father's people were seagoing men, out of Portsmouth. He knows what it means when our shipping is told where it can go on the ocean, and where it cannot. It isn't possible that Washington can take such an affront for us. To think that at this time, of all times, we should have a Democratic administration!"

Claude laughed. "Sit down, Mother. Wait a day or two. Give them time."

"The war will be over before Washington can do anything, Mrs. Wheeler," Ernest declared gloomily, "England will be starved out, and France will be beaten to a standstill. The whole German army will be on the Western front now. What could this country do? How long do you suppose it takes to make an army?"

Mrs. Wheeler stopped short in her restless pacing and met his moody glance. "I don't know anything, Ernest, but I believe the Bible. I believe that in the twinkling of an eye we shall be changed!"

Ernest looked at the floor. He respected faith. As he said, you must respect it or despise it, for there was nothing else to do.

Claude sat leaning his elbows on the table. "It always comes back to the same thing, Mother. Even if a raw army could do anything, how would we get it over there? Here's one naval authority who says the Germans are turning out submarines at the rate of three a day. They probably didn't spring this on us until they had enough built to keep the ocean clear."

"I don't pretend to say what we could accomplish, son. But we must stand somewhere, morally. They have told us all along that we could be more helpful to the Allies out of the war than in it, because we could send munitions and supplies. If we agree to withdraw that aid, where are we? Helping Germany, all the time we are pretending to mind our own business! If our only alternative is to be at the bottom of the sea, we had better be there!"

"Mother, do sit down! We can't settle it tonight. I never saw you so worked up."

"Your father is worked up, too, or he would never have sent that telegram." Mrs. Wheeler reluctantly took up her workbasket, and the boys talked with their old, easy friendliness.

When Ernest left, Claude walked as far as the Yoeders' place with him, and came back across the snow-drifted fields, under the frosty brilliance of the winter stars. As he looked up at them, he felt more than ever that they must have something to do with the fate of nations, and with the incomprehensible things that were happening in the world. In the ordered universe there must be some mind that read the riddle of this one unhappy planet, that knew what was forming in the dark eclipse of this hour. A question hung in the air; over all this quiet land about him, over him, over his mother, even. He was afraid for his country, as he had been that night on the State House steps in Denver, when this war was undreamed of, hidden in the womb of time.

Claude and his mother had not long to wait. Three days later they knew that the German ambassador had been dismissed, and the American ambassador recalled from Berlin. To older men these events were subjects to think and converse about; but to boys like Claude they were life and death, predestination.

VII.

ONE STORMY MORNING Claude was driving the big wagon to town to get a load of lumber. The roads were beginning to thaw out, and the country was black and dirty looking. Here and there on the dark mud, grey snow crusts lingered, perforated like honeycomb, with wet weedstalks sticking up through them. As the wagon creaked over the high ground just above Frankfort, Claude noticed a brilliant new flag flying from the schoolhouse cupola. He had never seen the flag before when it meant anything but the Fourth of July, or a political rally.

Today it was as if he saw it for the first time; no bands, no noise, no orators; a spot of restless colour against the sodden March sky.

He turned out of his way in order to pass the High School, drew up his team, and waited a few minutes until the noon bell rang. The older boys and girls came out first, with a flurry of raincoats and umbrellas. Presently he saw Gladys Farmer, in a yellow "slicker" and an oilskin hat, and waved to her. She came up to the wagon.

"I like your decoration," he said, glancing toward the cupola.

"It's a silk one the Senior boys bought with their athletic money. I advised them not to run it up in this rain, but the class president told me they bought that flag for storms."

"Get in, and I'll take you home."

She took his extended hand, put her foot on the hub of the wheel, and climbed to the seat beside him. He clucked to his team.

"So your High School boys are feeling war-like these days?"

"Very. What do you think?"

"I think they'll have a chance to express their feelings."

"Do you, Claude? It seems awfully unreal."

"Nothing else seems very real, either. I'm going to haul out a load of lumber, but I never expect to drive a nail in it. These things don't matter now. There is only one thing we ought to do, and only one thing that matters; we all know it."

"You feel it's coming nearer every day?"

"Every day."

Gladys made no reply. She only looked at him gravely with her calm, generous brown eyes. They stopped before the low house where the windows were full of flowers. She took his hand and swung herself to the ground, holding it for a moment while she said good-bye. Claude drove back to the lumber yard. In a place like Frankfort, a boy whose wife was in China could hardly go to see Gladys without causing gossip.

VIII.

DURING THE BLEAK month of March Mr. Wheeler went to town in his buckboard almost every day. For the first time in his life he had a secret anxiety. The one member of his family who had never given him the slightest trouble, his son Bayliss, was just now under a cloud.

Bayliss was a Pacifist, and kept telling people that if only the United States would stay out of this war, and gather up what Europe was wasting, she would soon be in actual possession of the capital of the world. There was a kind of logic in Bayliss' utterances that shook Nat Wheeler's imperturbable assumption that one point of view was as good as another. When Bayliss fought the dram and the cigarette, Wheeler only laughed. That a son of his should turn out a Prohibitionist, was a joke he could appreciate. But Bayliss' attitude in the present crisis disturbed him. Day after day he sat about his son's place of business, interrupting his arguments with funny stories. Bayliss did not go home at all that month. He said to his father, "No, Mother's too violent. I'd better not."

Claude and his mother read the papers in the evening, but they talked so little about what they read that Mahailey inquired anxiously whether they weren't still fighting over yonder. When she could get Claude alone for a moment, she pulled out Sunday supplement pictures of the devastated countries and asked him to tell her what was to become of this family, photographed among the ruins of their home; of this old woman, who sat by the roadside with her bundles. "Where's she goin' to, anyways? See, Mr. Claude, she's got her iron cookpot, pore old thing, carryin' it all the way!"

Pictures of soldiers in gas-masks puzzled her; gas was something she hadn't learned about in the Civil War, so she worked it out for herself that these masks were worn by the army cooks, to protect their eyes when they were cutting up onions! "All them onions they have to cut up, it would put their eyes out if they didn't wear somethin'," she argued.

On the morning of the eighth of April Claude came downstairs early and began to clean his boots, which were caked with dry mud. Mahailey was squatting down beside her stove, blowing and puffing into it. The fire was always slow to start in heavy weather. Claude got an old knife and a brush, and putting his foot on a chair over by the west window, began to scrape his shoe. He had said good-morning to Mahailey, nothing more. He hadn't slept well, and was pale.

"Mr. Claude," Mahailey grumbled, "this stove ain't never drawed good like my old one Mr. Ralph took away from me. I can't do nothin' with it. Maybe you'll clean it out for me next Sunday."

"I'll clean it today, if you say so. I won't be here next Sunday. I'm going away."

Something in his tone made Mahailey get up, her eyes still blinking with the smoke, and look at him sharply. "You ain't goin' off there where Miss Enid is?" she asked anxiously.

"No, Mahailey." He had dropped the shoebrush and stood with one foot on the chair, his elbow on his knee, looking out of the window as if he had forgotten himself. "No, I'm not going to China. I'm going over to help fight the Germans."

He was still staring out at the wet fields. Before he could stop her, before he knew what she was doing, she had caught and kissed his unworthy hand.

"I knowed you would," she sobbed. "I always knowed you would, you nice boy, you! Old Mahail' knowed!"

Her upturned face was working all over; her mouth, her eyebrows, even the wrinkles on her low forehead were working and twitching. Claude felt a tightening in his throat as he tenderly regarded that face; behind the pale eyes, under the low brow where there was not room for many thoughts, an idea was struggling and tormenting her. The same idea that had been tormenting him.

"You're all right, Mahailey," he muttered, patting her back and turning away. "Now hurry breakfast."

"You ain't told your mudder yit?" she whispered.

"No, not yet. But she'll be all right, too." He caught up his cap and went down to the barn to look after the horses.

When Claude returned, the family were already at the breakfast table. He slipped into his seat and watched his mother while she drank her first cup of coffee. Then he addressed his father.

"Father, I don't see any use of waiting for the draft. If you can spare me, I'd like to get into a training camp somewhere. I believe I'd stand a chance of getting a commission."

"I shouldn't wonder." Mr. Wheeler poured maple syrup on his pancakes with a liberal hand. "How do you feel about it, Evangeline?"

Mrs. Wheeler had quietly put down her knife and fork. She looked at her husband in vague alarm, while her fingers moved restlessly about over the tablecloth.

"I thought," Claude went on hastily, "that maybe I would go up to Omaha tomorrow and find out where the training camps are to be located, and have a talk with the men in charge of the enlistment station. Of course," he added lightly, "they may not want me. I haven't an idea what the requirements are."

"No, I don't understand much about it either." Mr. Wheeler rolled his top pancake and conveyed it to his mouth. After a moment of mastication he said, "You figure on going tomorrow?"

"I'd like to. I won't bother with baggage—some shirts and underclothes in my suitcase. If the Government wants me, it will clothe me."

Mr. Wheeler pushed back his plate. "Well, now I guess you'd better come out with me and look at the wheat. I don't know but I'd best plough up that south quarter and put it in corn. I don't believe it will make anything much."

When Claude and his father went out of the door, Dan sprang up with more alacrity than usual and plunged after them. He did not want to be left alone with Mrs. Wheeler. She remained sitting at the foot of the deserted breakfast table. She was not crying. Her eyes were utterly sightless. Her back was so stooped that she seemed to be bending under a burden. Mahailey cleared the dishes away quietly.

Out in the muddy fields Claude finished his talk with his father. He explained that he wanted to slip away without saying good-bye to any one. "I have a way, you know," he said, flushing, "of beginning things and not getting very far with them. I don't want anything said about this until I'm sure. I may be rejected for one reason or another."

Mr. Wheeler smiled. "I guess not. However, I'll tell Dan to keep his mouth shut. Will you just go over to Leonard Dawson's and get that wrench he borrowed? It's about noon, and he'll likely be at home." Claude found big Leonard watering his team at the windmill. When Leonard asked him what he thought of the President's message, he blurted out at once that he was going to Omaha to enlist. Leonard reached up and pulled the lever that controlled the almost motionless wheel.

"Better wait a few weeks and I'll go with you. I'm going to try for the Marines. They take my eye."

Claude, standing on the edge of the tank, almost fell backward. "Why, what—what for?"

Leonard looked him over. "Good Lord, Claude, you ain't the only fellow around here that wears pants! What for? Well, I'll tell you what for," he held up three large red fingers threateningly; "Belgium, the Lusitania, Edith Cavell. That dirt's got under my skin. I'll get my corn planted, and then Father'll look after Susie till I come back."

Claude took a long breath. "Well, Leonard, you fooled me. I believed all this chaff you've been giving me about not caring who chewed up who."

"And no more do I care," Leonard protested, "not a damn! But there's a limit. I've been ready to go since the Lusitania. I don't get any satisfaction out of my place any more. Susie feels the same way."

Claude looked at his big neighbour. "Well, I'm off tomorrow, Leonard. Don't mention it to my folks, but if I can't get into the army, I'm going to enlist in the navy. They'll always take an able-bodied man. I'm not coming back here." He held out his hand and Leonard took it with a smack.

"Good luck, Claude. Maybe we'll meet in foreign parts. Wouldn't that be a joke! Give my love to Enid when you write. I always did think she was a fine girl, though I disagreed with her on Prohibition." Claude crossed the fields mechanically, without looking where he went. His power of vision was turned inward upon scenes and events wholly imaginary as yet.

IX.

ONE BRIGHT JUNE day Mr. Wheeler parked his car in a line of motors before the new pressed-brick Court house in Frankfort. The Court house stood in an open square, surrounded by a grove of cotton-woods. The lawn was freshly cut, and the flower beds were blooming. When Mr. Wheeler entered the courtroom upstairs, it was already half-full of farmers and townspeople, talking in low tones while the summer flies buzzed in and out of the open windows. The judge, a one-armed man, with white hair and side-whiskers, sat at his desk, writing with his left hand. He was an old settler in Frankfort county, but from his frockcoat and courtly manners you might have thought he had come from Kentucky yesterday instead of thirty years ago. He was to hear this morning a charge of disloyalty brought against two German farmers. One of the accused was August Yoeder, the Wheelers' nearest neighbour, and the other was Troilus Oberlies, a rich German from the northern part of the county.

Oberlies owned a beautiful farm and lived in a big white house set on a hill, with a fine orchard, rows of beehives, barns, granaries, and poultry yards. He raised turkeys and tumbler-pigeons, and many geese and ducks swam about on his cattleponds. He used to boast that he had six sons, "like our German Emperor." His neighbours were proud of his place, and pointed it out to strangers. They told how Oberlies had come to Frankfort county a poor man, and had made his fortune by his industry and intelligence. He had twice crossed the ocean to re-visit his fatherland, and when he returned to his home on the prairies he brought presents for every one; his lawyer, his banker, and the merchants with whom he dealt in Frankfort and Vicount. Each of his neighbours had in his parlour some piece of woodcarving or weaving, or some ingenious mechanical toy that Oberlies had picked up in Germany. He was an older man than Yoeder, wore a short beard that was white and curly, like his hair, and though he was low in stature, his puffy red face and full blue eyes, and a certain swagger about his carriage, gave him a look of importance. He was boastful and quick-tempered, but until the war broke out in Europe nobody had ever had any trouble with him. Since then he had constantly found fault and complained,—everything was better in the Old Country.

Mr. Wheeler had come to town prepared to lend Yoeder a hand if he needed one. They had worked adjoining fields for thirty years now. He was surprised that his neighbour had got into trouble. He was not a blusterer, like Oberlies, but a big, quiet man, with a serious, large-featured face, and a stern mouth that seldom opened. His countenance might have been cut out of red sandstone, it was so heavy and fixed. He and Oberlies sat on two wooden chairs outside the railing of the judge's desk.

Presently the judge stopped writing and said he would hear the charges against Troilus Oberlies. Several neighbours took the stand in succession; their complaints were confused and almost humorous. Oberlies had said the United States would be licked, and that would be a good thing; America was a great country, but it was run by fools, and to be governed by Germany was the best thing that could happen to it. The witness went on to say that since Oberlies had made his money in this country—

Here the judge interrupted him. "Please confine yourself to statements which you consider disloyal, made in your presence by the defendant." While the witness proceeded, the judge took off his glasses and laid them on the desk and began to polish the lenses with a silk handkerchief, trying them, and rubbing them again, as if he desired to see clearly.

A second witness had heard Oberlies say he hoped the German submarines would sink a few troopships; that would frighten the Americans and teach them to stay at home and mind their own business. A third complained that on Sunday afternoons the old man sat on his front porch and played Die Wacht am Rhein on a slide-trombone, to the great annoyance of his neighbours. Here Nat Wheeler slapped his knee with a loud guffaw, and a titter ran through the courtroom. The defendant's puffy red cheeks seemed fashioned by his Maker to give voice to that piercing instrument.

When asked if he had anything to say to these charges, the old man rose, threw back his shoulders, and cast a defiant glance at the courtroom. "You may take my property and imprison me, but I explain nothing, and I take back nothing," he declared in a loud voice.

The judge regarded his inkwell with a smile. "You mistake the nature of this occasion, Mr. Oberlies. You are not asked to recant. You are merely asked to desist from further disloyal utterances, as much for your own protection and comfort as from consideration for the feelings of your neighbours. I will now hear the charges against Mr. Yoeder."

Mr. Yoeder, a witness declared, had said he hoped the United States would go to Hell, now that it had been bought over by England. When the witness had remarked to him that if the Kaiser were shot it would end the war, Yoeder replied that charity begins at home, and he wished somebody would put a bullet in the President.

When he was called upon, Yoeder rose and stood like a rock before the judge. "I have nothing to say. The charges are true. I thought this was a country where a man could speak his mind."

"Yes, a man can speak his mind, but even here he must take the consequences. Sit down, please." The judge leaned back in his chair, and looking at the two men in front of him, began with deliberation: "Mr. Oberlies, and Mr. Yoeder, you both know, and your friends and neighbours know, why you are here. You have not recognized the element of appropriateness, which must be regarded in nearly all the transactions of life; many of our civil laws are founded upon it. You have allowed a sentiment, noble in itself, to carry you away and lead you to make extravagant statements which I am confident neither of you mean. No man can demand that you cease from loving the country of your birth; but while you enjoy the benefits of this country, you should not defame its government to extol another. You both admit to utterances which I can only adjudge disloyal. I shall fine you each three hundred dollars; a very light fine under the circumstances. If I should have occasion to fix a penalty a second time, it will be much more severe."

After the case was concluded, Mr. Wheeler joined his neighbour at the door and they went downstairs together.

"Well, what do you hear from Claude?" Mr. Yoeder asked.

"He's still at Fort R—. He expects to get home on leave before he sails. Gus, you'll have to lend me one of your boys to cultivate my corn. The weeds are getting away from me."

"Yes, you can have any of my boys,—till the draft gets 'em," said Yoeder sourly.

"I wouldn't worry about it. A little military training is good for a boy. You fellows know that." Mr. Wheeler winked, and Yoeder's grim mouth twitched at one corner.

That evening at supper Mr. Wheeler gave his wife a full account of the court hearing, so that she could write it to Claude. Mrs. Wheeler, always more a school-teacher than a housekeeper, wrote a rapid, easy hand, and her long letters to Claude reported all the neighbourhood doings. Mr. Wheeler furnished much of the material for them. Like many long-married men he had fallen into the way of withholding neighbourhood news from his wife. But since Claude went away he reported to her everything in which he thought the boy would be interested. As she laconically said in one of her letters:

"Your father talks a great deal more at home than formerly, and sometimes I think he is trying to take your place."

X.

On the first day of July Claude Wheeler found himself in the fast train from Omaha, going home for a week's leave. The uniform was still an unfamiliar sight in July, 1917. The first draft was not yet called, and the boys who had rushed off and enlisted were in training camps far away. Therefore a redheaded young man with long straight legs in puttees, and broad, energetic, responsible-looking shoulders in close-fitting khaki, made a conspicuous figure among the passengers. Little boys and young girls peered at him over the tops of seats, men stopped in the aisle to talk to him, old ladies put on their glasses and studied his clothes, his bulky canvas hold-all, and even the book he kept opening and forgetting to read.

The country that rushed by him on each side of the track was more interesting to his trained eye than the pages of any book. He was glad to be going through it at harvest,—the season when it is most itself. He noted that there was more corn than usual,—much of the winter wheat had been weather killed, and the fields were ploughed up in the spring and replanted in maize. The pastures were already burned brown, the alfalfa was coming green again after its first cutting. Binders and harvesters were abroad in the wheat and oats, gathering the soft-breathing billows of grain into wide, subduing arms. When the train slowed down for a trestle in a wheat field, harvesters in blue shirts and overalls and wide straw hats stopped working to wave at the passengers. Claude turned to the old man in the opposite seat. "When I see those fellows, I feel as if I'd wakened up in the wrong clothes."

His neighbour looked pleased and smiled. "That the kind of uniform you're accustomed to?"

"I surely never wore anything else in the month of July," Claude admitted. "When I find myself riding along in a train, in the middle of harvest, trying to learn French verbs, then I know the world is turned upside down, for a fact!"

The old man pressed a cigar upon him and began to question him. Like the hero of the Odyssey upon his homeward journey, Claude had often to tell what his country was, and who were the parents that begot him. He was constantly interrupted in his perusal of a French phrase-book (made up of sentences chosen for their usefulness to soldiers,—such as; "Non, jamais je ne regarde les femmes") by the questions of curious strangers. Presently he gathered up his luggage, shook hands with his neighbour, and put on his hat—the same old Stetson, with a gold cord and two hard tassels added to its conical severity. "I get off at this station and wait for the freight that goes down to Frankfort; the cotton-tail, we call it."

The old man wished him a pleasant visit home, and the best of luck in days to come. Every one in the car smiled at him as he stepped down to the platform with his suitcase in one hand and his canvas bag in the other. His old friend, Mrs. Voigt, the German woman, stood out in front of her restaurant, ringing her bell to announce that dinner was ready for travellers. A crowd of young boys stood about her on the sidewalk, laughing and shouting in disagreeable, jeering tones. As Claude approached, one of them snatched the bell from her hand, ran off across the tracks with it, and plunged into a cornfield. The other boys followed, and one of them shouted, "Don't go in there to eat, soldier. She's a German spy, and she'll put ground glass in your dinner!"

Claude swept into the lunch room and threw his bags on the floor. "What's the matter, Mrs. Voigt? Can I do anything for you?"

She was sitting on one of her own stools, crying piteously, her false frizzes awry. Looking up, she gave a little screech of recognition. "Oh, I tank Gott it was you, and no more trouble coming! You know I ain't no spy nor nodding, like what dem boys say. Dem young fellers is dreadful rough mit me. I sell dem candy since dey was babies, an' now dey turn on me like dis. Hindenburg, dey calls me, and Kaiser Bill!" She began to cry again, twisting her stumpy little fingers as if she would tear them off.

"Give me some dinner, ma'am, and then I'll go and settle with that gang. I've been away for a long time, and it seemed like getting home when I got off the train and saw your squaw vines running over the porch like they used to."

"Ya? You remember dat?" she wiped her eyes. "I got a pot-pie today, and green peas, chust a few, out of my own garden."

"Bring them along, please. We don't get anything but canned stuff in camp."

Some railroad men came in for lunch. Mrs. Voigt beckoned Claude off to the end of the counter, where, after she had served her customers, she sat down and talked to him, in whispers.

"My, you look good in dem clothes," she said patting his sleeve. "I can remember some wars, too; when we got back dem provinces what Napoleon took away from us, Alsace and Lorraine. Dem boys is passed de word to come and put tar on me some night, and I am skeered to go in my bet. I chust wrap in a quilt and sit in my old chair."

"Don't pay any attention to them. You don't have trouble with the business people here, do you?"

"No-o, not troubles, exactly." She hesitated, then leaned impulsively across the counter and spoke in his ear. "But it ain't all so bad in de Old Country like what dey say. De poor people ain't slaves, and dey ain't ground down like what dey say here. Always de forester let de poor folks come into de wood and carry off de limbs dat fall, and de dead trees. Und if de rich farmer have maybe a liddle more manure dan he need, he let de poor man come and take some for his land. De poor folks don't git such wages like here, but dey lives chust as comfortable. Und dem wooden shoes, what dey makes such fun of, is cleaner dan what leather is, to go round in de mud and manure. Dey don't git so wet and dey don't stink so."

Claude could see that her heart was bursting with homesickness, full of tender memories of the far-away time and land of her youth. She had never talked to him of these things before, but now she poured out a flood of confidences about the big dairy farm on which she had worked as a girl; how she took care of nine cows, and how the cows, though small, were very strong,—drew a plough all day and yet gave as much milk at night as if they had been browsing in a pasture! The country people never had to spend money for doctors, but cured all diseases with roots and herbs, and when the old folks had the rheumatism they took "one of dem liddle jenny-pigs" to bed with them, and the guinea-pig drew out all the pain.

Claude would have liked to listen longer, but he wanted to find the old woman's tormentors before his train came in. Leaving his bags with her, he crossed the railroad tracks, guided by an occasional teasing tinkle of the bell in the cornfield. Presently he came upon the gang, a dozen or more, lying in a shallow draw that ran from the edge of the field out into an open pasture. He stood on the edge of the bank and looked down at them, while he slowly cut off the end of a cigar and lit it. The boys grinned at him, trying to appear indifferent and at ease.

"Looking for any one, soldier?" asked the one with the bell.

"Yes, I am. I'm looking for that bell. You'll have to take it back where it belongs. You every one of you know there's no harm in that old woman."

"She's a German, and we're fighting the Germans, ain't we?"

"I don't think you'll ever fight any. You'd last about ten minutes in the American army. You're not our kind. There's only one army in the world that wants men who'll bully old women. You might get a job with them."

The boys giggled. Claude beckoned impatiently. "Come along with that bell, kid."

The boy rose slowly and climbed the bank out of the gully. As they tramped back through the cornfield, Claude turned to him abruptly. "See here, aren't you ashamed of yourself?"

"Oh, I don't know about that!" the boy replied airily, tossing the bell up like a ball and catching it.

"Well, you ought to be. I didn't expect to see anything of this kind until I got to the front. I'll be back here in a week, and I'll make it hot for anybody that's been bothering her." Claude's train was pulling in, and he ran for his baggage. Once seated in the "cotton-tail," he began going down into his own country, where he knew every farm he passed,—knew the land even when he did not know the owner, what sort of crops it yielded, and about how much it was worth. He did not recognize these farms with the pleasure he had anticipated, because he was so angry about the indignities Mrs. Voigt had suffered. He was still burning with the first ardour of the enlisted man. He believed that he was going abroad with an expeditionary force that would make war without rage, with uncompromising generosity and chivalry.

Most of his friends at camp shared his Quixotic ideas. They had come together from farms and shops and mills and mines, boys from college and boys from tough joints in big cities; sheepherders, street car drivers, plumbers' assistants, billiard markers. Claude had seen hundreds of them when they first came in; "show men" in cheap, loud sport suits, ranch boys in knitted waistcoats, machinists with the grease still on their fingers, farm-hands like Dan, in their one Sunday coat. Some of them carried paper suitcases tied up with rope, some brought all they had in a blue handkerchief. But they all came to give and not to ask, and what they offered was just themselves; their big red hands, their strong backs, the steady, honest, modest look in their eyes. Sometimes, when he had helped the medical examiner, Claude had noticed the anxious expression in the faces of the long lines of waiting men. They seemed to say, "If I'm good enough, take me. I'll stay by." He found them like that to work with; serviceable, good-natured, and eager to learn. If they talked about the war, or the enemy they were getting ready to fight, it was usually in a facetious tone; they were going to "can the Kaiser," or to make the Crown Prince work for a living. Claude, loved the men he trained with,—wouldn't choose to live in any better company.

The freight train swung into the river valley that meant home,—the place the mind always came back to, after its farthest quest. Rapidly the farms passed; the haystacks, the cornfields, the familiar red barns—then the long coal sheds and the water tank, and the train stopped.

On the platform he saw Ralph and Mr. Royce, waiting to welcome him. Over there, in the automobile, were his father and mother, Mr. Wheeler in the driver's seat. A line of motors stood along the siding. He was the first soldier who had come home, and some of the townspeople had driven down to see him arrive in his uniform. From one car Susie Dawson waved to him, and from another Gladys Farmer. While he stopped and spoke to them, Ralph took his bags.

"Come along, boys," Mr. Wheeler called, tooting his horn, and he hurried the soldier away, leaving only a cloud of dust behind.

Mr. Royce went over to old man Dawson's car and said rather childishly, "It can't be that Claude's grown taller? I suppose it's the way they learn to carry themselves. He always was a manly looking boy."

"I expect his mother's a proud woman," said Susie, very much excited. "It's too bad Enid can't be here to see him. She would never have gone away if she'd known all that was to happen."

Susie did not mean this as a thrust, but it took effect. Mr. Royce turned away and lit a cigar with some difficulty. His hands had grown very unsteady this last year, though he insisted that his general health was as good as ever. As he grew older, he was more depressed by the conviction that his women-folk had added little to the warmth and comfort of the world. Women ought to do that, whatever else they did. He felt apologetic toward the Wheelers and toward his old friends. It seemed as if his daughters had no heart.

XI.

Camp habits persisted. On his first morning at home Claude came downstairs before even Mahailey was stirring, and went out to have a look at the stock. The red sun came up just as he was going down the hill toward the cattle corral, and he had the pleasant feeling of being at home, on his father's land. Why was it so gratifying to be able to say "our hill," and "our creek down yonder"? to feel the crunch of this particular dried mud under his boots?

When he went into the barn to see the horses, the first creatures to meet his eye were the two big mules that had run away with him, standing in the stalls next the door. It flashed upon Claude that these muscular quadrupeds were the actual authors of his fate. If they had not bolted with him and thrown him into the wire fence that morning, Enid would not have felt sorry for him and come to see him every day, and his life might have turned out differently. Perhaps if older people were a little more honest, and a boy were not taught to idealize in women the very qualities which can make him utterly unhappy—But there, he had got away from those regrets. But wasn't it just like him to be dragged into matrimony by a pair of mules!

He laughed as he looked at them. "You old devils, you're strong enough to play such tricks on green fellows for years to come. You're chock full of meanness!"

One of the animals wagged an ear and cleared his throat threateningly. Mules are capable of strong affections, but they hate snobs, are the enemies of caste, and this pair had always seemed to detect in Claude what his father used to call his "false pride." When he was a young lad they had been a source of humiliation to him, braying and balking in public places, trying to show off at the lumber yard or in front of the post office.

At the end manger Claude found old Molly, the grey mare with the stiff leg, who had grown a second hoof on her off forefoot, an achievement not many horses could boast of. He was sure she recognized him; she nosed his hand and arm and turned back her upper lip, showing her worn, yellow teeth.

"Mustn't do that, Molly," he said as he stroked her. "A dog can laugh, but it makes a horse look foolish. Seems to me Dan might curry you about once a week!" He took a comb from its niche behind a joist and gave her old coat a rubbing. Her white hair was flecked all over with little rust-coloured dashes, like India ink put on with a fine brush, and her mane and tail had turned a greenish yellow. She must be eighteen years old, Claude reckoned, as he polished off her round, heavy haunches. He and Ralph used to ride her over to the Yoeders' when they were barefoot youngsters, guiding her with a rope halter, and kicking at the leggy colt that was always running alongside.

When he entered the kitchen and asked Mahailey for warm water to wash his hands, she sniffed him disapprovingly.

"Why, Mr. Claude, you've been curryin' that old mare, and you've got white hairs all over your soldier-clothes. You're jist covered!"

If his uniform stirred feeling in people of sober judgment, over Mahailey it cast a spell. She was so dazzled by it that all the time Claude was at home she never once managed to examine it in detail. Before she got past his puttees, her powers of observation were befogged by excitement, and her wits began to jump about like monkeys in a cage. She had expected his uniform to be blue, like those she remembered, and when he walked into the kitchen last night she scarcely knew what to make of him. After Mrs. Wheeler explained to her that American soldiers didn't wear blue now, Mahailey repeated to herself that these brown clothes didn't show the dust, and that Claude would never look like the bedraggled men who used to stop to drink at her mother's spring.

"Them leather leggins is to keep the briars from scratchin' you, ain't they? I 'spect there's an awful lot of briars over there, like them long blackberry vines in the fields in Virginia. Your madder says the soldiers git lice now, like they done in our war. You jist carry a little bottle of coal-oil in your pocket an' rub it on your head at night. It keeps the nits from hatchin'."

Over the flour barrel in the corner Mahailey had tacked a Red Cross poster; a charcoal drawing of an old woman poking with a stick in a pile of plaster and twisted timbers that had once been her home. Claude went over to look at it while he dried his hands.

"Where did you get your picture?"

"She's over there where you're goin', Mr. Claude. There she is, huntin' for somethin' to cook with; no stove nor no dishes nor nothin'—everything all broke up. I reckon she'll be mighty glad to see you comin'."

Heavy footsteps sounded on the stairs, and Mahailey whispered hastily, "Don't forgit about the coal-oil, and don't you be lousy if you can help it, honey." She considered lice in the same class with smutty jokes,—things to be whispered about.

After breakfast Mr. Wheeler took Claude out to the fields, where Ralph was directing the harvesters. They watched the binder for a while, then went over to look at the haystacks and alfalfa, and walked along the edge of the cornfield, where they examined the young ears. Mr. Wheeler explained and exhibited the farm to Claude as if he were a stranger; the boy had a curious feeling of being now formally introduced to these acres on which he had worked every summer since he was big enough to carry water to the harvesters. His father told him how much land they owned, and how much it was worth, and that it was unencumbered except for a trifling mortgage he had given on one quarter when he took over the Colorado ranch.

"When you come back," he said, "you and Ralph won't have to hunt around to get into business. You'll both be well fixed. Now you'd better go home by old man Dawson's and drop in to see Susie. Everybody about here was astonished when Leonard went." He walked with Claude to the corner where the Dawson land met his own. "By the way," he said as he turned back, "don't forget to go in to see the Yoeders sometime. Gus is pretty sore since they had him up in court. Ask for the old grandmother. You remember she never learned any English. And now they've told her it's dangerous to talk German, she don't talk at all and hides away from everybody. If I go by early in the morning, when she's out weeding the garden, she runs and squats down in the gooseberry bushes till I'm out of sight."

Claude decided he would go to the Yoeders' today, and to the Dawsons' tomorrow. He didn't like to think there might be hard feeling toward him in a house where he had had so many good times, and where he had often found a refuge when things were dull at home. The Yoeder boys had a music-box long before the days of Victrolas, and a magic lantern, and the old grandmother made wonderful shadow-pictures on a sheet, and told stories about them. She used to turn the map of Europe upside down on the kitchen table and showed the children how, in this position, it looked like a jungfrau; and recited a long German rhyme which told how Spain was the maiden's head, the Pyrenees her lace ruff, Germany her heart and bosom, England and Italy were two arms, and Russia, though it looked so big, was only a hoopskirt. This rhyme would probably be condemned as dangerous propaganda now!

As he walked on alone, Claude was thinking how this country that had once seemed little and dull to him, now seemed large and rich in variety. During the months in camp he had been wholly absorbed in new work and new friendships, and now his own neighbourhood came to him with the freshness of things that have been forgotten for a long while,—came together before his eyes as a harmonious whole. He was going away, and he would carry the whole countryside in his mind, meaning more to him than it ever had before. There was Lovely Creek, gurgling on down there, where he and Ernest used to sit and lament that the book of History was finished; that the world had come to avaricious old age and noble enterprise was dead for ever. But he was going away....

That afternoon Claude spent with his mother. It was the first time she had had him to herself. Ralph wanted terribly to stay and hear his brother talk, but understanding how his mother felt, he went back to the wheat field. There was no detail of Claude's life in camp so trivial that Mrs. Wheeler did not want to hear about it. She asked about the mess, the cooks, the laundry, as well as about his own duties. She made him describe the bayonet drill and explain the operation of machine guns and automatic rifles.

"I hardly see how we can bear the anxiety when our transports begin to sail," she said thoughtfully. "If they can once get you all over there, I am not afraid; I believe our boys are as good as any in the world. But with submarines reported off our own coast, I wonder how the Government can get our men across safely. The thought of transports going down with thousands of young men on board is something so terrible—" she put her hands quickly over her eyes.

Claude, sitting opposite his mother, wondered what it was about her hands that made them so different from any others he had ever seen. He had always known they were different, but now he must look closely and see why. They were slender, and always white, even when the nails were stained at preserving time. Her fingers arched back at the joints, as if they were shrinking from contacts. They were restless, and when she talked often brushed her hair or her dress lightly. When she was excited she sometimes put her hand to her throat, or felt about the neck of her gown, as if she were searching for a forgotten brooch. They were sensitive hands, and yet they seemed to have nothing to do with sense, to be almost like the groping fingers of a spirit.

"How do you boys feel about it?"

Claude started. "About what, Mother? Oh, the transportation! We don't worry about that. It's the Government's job to get us across. A soldier mustn't worry about anything except what he's directly responsible for. If the Germans should sink a few troop ships, it would be unfortunate, certainly, but it wouldn't cut any figure in the long run. The British are perfecting an enormous dirigible, built to carry passengers. If our transports are sunk, it will only mean delay. In another year the Yankees will be flying over. They can't stop us."

Mrs. Wheeler bent forward. "That must be boys' talk, Claude. Surely you don't believe such a thing could be practicable?"

"Absolutely. The British are depending on their aircraft designers to do just that, if everything else fails. Of course, nobody knows yet how effective the submarines will be in our case."

Mrs. Wheeler again shaded her eyes with her hand. "When I was young, back in Vermont, I used to wish that I had lived in the old times when the world went ahead by leaps and bounds. And now, I feel as if my sight couldn't bear the glory that beats upon it. It seems as if we would have to be born with new faculties, to comprehend what is going on in the air and under the sea."

XII.

THE AFTERNOON SUN was pouring in at the back windows of Mrs. Farmer's long, uneven parlour, making the dusky room look like a cavern with a fire at one end of it. The furniture was all in its cool, figured summer cretonnes. The glass flower vases that stood about on little tables caught the sunlight and twinkled like tiny lamps. Claude had been sitting there for a long while, and he knew he ought to go. Through the window at his elbow he could see rows of double hollyhocks, the flat leaves of the sprawling catalpa, and the spires of the tangled mint bed, all transparent in the gold-powdered light. They had talked about everything but the thing he had come to say. As he looked out into the garden he felt that he would never get it out. There was something in the way the mint bed burned and floated that made one a fatalist,—afraid to meddle. But after he was far away, he would regret; uncertainty would tease him like a splinter in his thumb.

He rose suddenly and said without apology: "Gladys, I wish I could feel sure you'd never marry my brother."

She did not reply, but sat in her easy chair, looking up at him with a strange kind of calmness.

"I know all the advantages," he went on hastily, "but they wouldn't make it up to you. That sort of a—compromise would make you awfully unhappy. I know."

"I don't think I shall ever marry Bayliss," Gladys spoke in her usual low, round voice, but her quick breathing showed he had touched something that hurt. "I suppose I have used him. It gives a school-teacher a certain prestige if people think she can marry the rich bachelor of the town whenever she wants to. But I am afraid I won't marry him,—because you are the member of the family I have always admired."

Claude turned away to the window. "A fine lot I've been to admire," he muttered.

"Well, it's true, anyway. It was like that when we went to High School, and it's kept up. Everything you do always seems exciting to me."

Claude felt a cold perspiration on his forehead. He wished now that he had never come. "But that's it, Gladys. What HAVE I ever done, except make one blunder after another?"

She came over to the window and stood beside him. "I don't know; perhaps it's by their blunders that one gets to know people,—by what they can't do. If you'd been like all the rest, you could have got on in their way. That was the one thing I couldn't have stood."

Claude was frowning out into the flaming garden. He had not heard a word of her reply. "Why didn't you keep me from making a fool of myself?" he asked in a low voice.

"I think I tried—once. Anyhow, it's all turning out better than I thought. You didn't get stuck here. You've found your place. You're sailing away. You've just begun."

"And what about you?"

She laughed softly. "Oh, I shall teach in the High School!"

Claude took her hands and they stood looking searchingly at each other in the swimming golden light that made everything transparent. He never knew exactly how he found his hat and made his way out of the house. He was only sure that Gladys did not accompany him to the door. He glanced back once, and saw her head against the bright window.

She stood there, exactly where he left her, and watched the evening come on, not moving, scarcely breathing. She was thinking how often, when she came downstairs, she would see him standing here by the window, or moving about in the dusky room, looking at last as he ought to look,—like his convictions and the choice he had made. She would never let this house be sold for taxes now. She would save her salary and pay them off. She could never like any other room so well as this. It had always been a refuge from Frankfort; and now there would be this vivid, confident figure, an image as distinct to her as the portrait of her grandfather upon the wall.

XIII.

SUNDAY WAS Claude's last day at home, and he took a long walk with Ernest and Ralph. Ernest would have preferred to lose Ralph, but when the boy was out of the harvest field he stuck to his brother like a burr. There was something about Claude's new clothes and new manner that fascinated him, and he went through one of those sudden changes of feeling that often occur in families. Although they had been better friends ever since Claude's wedding, until now Ralph had always felt a little ashamed of him. Why, he used to ask himself, wouldn't Claude "spruce up and be somebody"? Now, he was struck by the fact that he was somebody.

On Monday morning Mrs. Wheeler wakened early, with a faintness in her chest. This was the day on which she must acquit herself well. Breakfast would be Claude's last meal at home. At eleven o'clock his father and Ralph would take him to Frankfort to catch the train. She was longer than usual in dressing. When she got downstairs Claude and Mahailey were already talking. He was shaving in the washroom, and Mahailey stood watching him, a side of bacon in her hand.

"You tell 'em over there I'm awful sorry about them old women, with their dishes an' their stove all broke up."

"All right. I will." Claude scraped away at his chin.

She lingered. "Maybe you can help 'em mend their things, like you do mine fur me," she suggested hopefully.

"Maybe," he murmured absently. Mrs. Wheeler opened the stair door, and Mahailey dodged back to the stove.

After breakfast Dan went out to the fields with the harvesters. Ralph and Claude and Mr. Wheeler were busy with the car all morning.

Mrs. Wheeler kept throwing her apron over her head and going down the hill to see what they were doing. Whether there was really something the matter with the engine, or whether the men merely made it a pretext for being together and keeping away from the house, she did not know. She felt that her presence was not much desired, and at last she went upstairs and resignedly watched them from the sitting-room window. Presently she heard Ralph run up to the third storey. When he came down with Claude's bags in his hands, he stuck his head in at the door and shouted cheerfully to his mother:

"No hurry. I'm just taking them down so they'll be ready."

Mrs. Wheeler ran after him, calling faintly, "Wait, Ralph! Are you sure he's got everything in? I didn't hear him packing."

"Everything ready. He says he won't have to go upstairs again. He'll be along pretty soon. There's lots of time." Ralph shot down through the basement.

Mrs. Wheeler sat down in her reading chair. They wanted to keep her away, and it was a little selfish of them. Why couldn't they spend these last hours quietly in the house, instead of dashing in and out to frighten her? Now she could hear the hot water running in the kitchen; probably Mr. Wheeler had come in to wash his hands. She felt really too weak to get up and go to the west window to see if he were still down at the garage. Waiting was now a matter of seconds, and her breath came short enough as it was.

She recognized a heavy, hob-nailed boot on the stairs, mounting quickly. When Claude entered, carrying his hat in his hand, she saw by his walk, his shoulders, and the way he held his head, that the moment had come, and that he meant to make it short. She rose, reaching toward him as he came up to her and caught her in his arms. She was smiling her little, curious intimate smile, with half-closed eyes.

"Well, is it good-bye?" she murmured. She passed her hands over his shoulders, down his strong back and the close-fitting sides of his coat, as if she were taking the mould and measure of his mortal frame. Her chin came just to his breast pocket, and she rubbed it against the heavy cloth. Claude stood looking down at her without speaking a word. Suddenly his arms tightened and he almost crushed her.

"Mother!" he whispered as he kissed her. He ran downstairs and out of the house without looking back.

She struggled up from the chair where she had sunk and crept to the window; he was vaulting down the hill as fast as he could go. He jumped into the car beside his father. Ralph was already at the wheel, and Claude had scarcely touched the cushions when they were off. They ran down the creek and over the bridge, then up the long hill on the other side. As they neared the crest of the hill, Claude stood up in the car and looked back at the house, waving his cone-shaped hat. She leaned out and strained her sight, but her tears blurred everything. The brown, upright figure seemed to float out of the car and across the fields, and before he was actually gone, she lost him. She fell back against the windowsill, clutching her temples with both hands, and broke into choking, passionate speech. "Old eyes," she cried, "why do you betray me? Why do you cheat me of my last sight of my splendid son!"

4

THE VOYAGE OF THE ANCHISES

I.

A LONG TRAIN of crowded cars, the passengers all of the same sex, almost of the same age, all dressed and hatted alike, was slowly steaming through the green sea-meadows late on a summer afternoon. In the cars, incessant stretching of cramped legs, shifting of shoulders, striking of matches, passing of cigarettes, groans of boredom; occasionally concerted laughter about nothing. Suddenly the train stops short. Clipped heads and tanned faces pop out at every window. The boys begin to moan and shout; what is the matter now?

The conductor goes through the cars, saying something about a freight wreck on ahead; he has orders to wait here for half an hour. Nobody pays any attention to him. A murmur of astonishment rises from one side of the train. The boys crowd over to the south windows. At last there is something to look at,—though what they see is so strangely quiet that their own exclamations are not very loud.

Their train is lying beside an arm of the sea that reaches far into the green shore. At the edge of the still water stand the hulls of four wooden ships, in the process of building. There is no town, there are no smoke-stacks—very few workmen. Piles of lumber lie about on the grass. A gasoline engine under a temporary shelter is operating a long crane that reaches down among the piles of boards and beams, lifts a load, silently and deliberately swings it over to one of the skeleton vessels, and lowers it somewhere into the body of the motionless thing. Along the sides of the clean hulls a few riveters are at work; they sit on suspended planks, lowering and raising themselves with pulleys, like house painters. Only by listening very closely can one hear the tap of their hammers. No orders are shouted, no thud of heavy machinery or scream of iron drills tears the air. These strange boats seem to be building themselves.

Some of the men got out of the cars and ran along the tracks, asking each other how boats could be built off in the grass like this. Lieutenant Claude Wheeler stretched his legs upon the opposite seat and sat still at his window, looking down on this strange scene. Shipbuilding, he had supposed, meant noise and forges and engines and hosts of men. This was like a dream. Nothing but green meadows, soft grey water, a floating haze of mist a little rosy from the sinking sun, spectre-like seagulls, flying slowly, with the red glow tinging their wings—and those four hulls lying in their braces, facing the sea, deliberating by the sea.

Claude knew nothing of ships or shipbuilding, but these craft did not seem to be nailed together,—they seemed all of a piece, like sculpture. They reminded him of the houses not made with hands; they were like simple and great thoughts, like purposes forming slowly here in the silence beside an unruffled arm of the Atlantic. He knew nothing about ships, but he didn't have to; the shape of those hulls—their strong, inevitable lines—told their story, WAS their story; told the whole adventure of man with the sea.

Wooden ships! When great passions and great aspirations stirred a country, shapes like these formed along its shores to be the sheath of its valour. Nothing Claude had ever seen or heard or read or thought had made it all so clear as these untried wooden bottoms. They were the very impulse, they were the potential act, they were the "going over," the drawn arrow, the great unuttered cry, they were Fate, they were tomorrow!...

The locomotive screeched to her scattered passengers, like an old turkey-hen calling her brood. The soldier boys came running back along the embankment and leaped aboard the train. The conductor shouted they would be in Hoboken in time for supper.

II.

IT WAS midnight when the men had got their supper and began unrolling their blankets to sleep on the floor of the long dock waiting-rooms,—which in other days had been thronged by people who came to welcome home-coming friends, or to bid them God-speed to foreign shores. Claude and some of his men had tried to look about them; but there was little to be seen. The bow of a boat, painted in distracting patterns of black and white, rose at one end of the shed, but the water itself was not visible. Down in the cobble-paved street below they watched for awhile the long line of drays and motor trucks that bumped all night into a vast cavern lit by electricity, where crates and barrels and merchandise of all kinds were piled, marked American Expeditionary Forces; cases of electrical machinery from some factory in Ohio, parts of automobiles, gun-carriages, bath-tubs, hospital supplies, bales of cotton, cases of canned food, grey metal tanks full of chemical fluids. Claude went back to the waiting room, lay down and fell asleep with the glare of an arc-light shining full in his face.

He was called at four in the morning and told where to report to headquarters. Captain Maxey, stationed at a desk on one of the landings, explained to his lieutenants that their company was to sail at eight o'clock on the Anchises. It was an English boat, an old liner pulled off the Australian trade, that could carry only twenty-five hundred men. The crew was English, but part of the stores,—the meat and fresh fruit and vegetables,—were furnished by the United States Government. The Captain had been over the boat during the night, and didn't like it very well. He had expected to be scheduled for one of the fine big Hamburg-American liners, with dining-rooms finished in rosewood, and ventilation plants and cooling plants, and elevators running from top to bottom like a New York office building. "However," he said, "we'll have to make the best of it. They're using everything that's got a bottom now."

The company formed for roll-call at one end of the shed, with their packs and rifles. Breakfast was served to them while they waited. After an hour's standing on the concrete, they saw encouraging signs. Two gangplanks were lowered from the vessel at the end of the slip, and up each of them began to stream a close brown line of men in smart service caps.

They recognized a company of Kansas Infantry, and began to grumble because their own service caps hadn't yet been given to them; they would have to sail in their old Stetsons. Soon they were drawn into one of the brown lines that went continuously up the gangways, like belting running over machinery. On the deck one steward directed the men down to the hold, and another conducted the officers to their cabins. Claude was shown to a four-berth state-room. One of his cabin mates, Lieutenant Fanning, of his own company, was already there, putting his slender luggage in order. The steward told them the officers were breakfasting in the dining saloon.

By seven o'clock all the troops were aboard, and the men were allowed on deck. For the first time Claude saw the profile of New York City, rising thin and gray against an opal-coloured morning sky. The day had come on hot and misty. The sun, though it was now high, was a red ball, streaked across with purple clouds. The tall buildings, of which he had heard so much, looked unsubstantial and illusionary,—mere shadows of grey and pink and blue that might dissolve with the mist and fade away in it. The boys were disappointed. They were Western men, accustomed to the hard light of high altitudes, and they wanted to see the city clearly; they couldn't make anything of these uneven towers that rose dimly through the vapour. Everybody was asking questions. Which of those pale giants was the Singer Building? Which the Woolworth? What was the gold dome, dully glinting through the fog? Nobody knew. They agreed it was a shame they could not have had a day in New York before they sailed away from it, and that they would feel foolish in Paris when they had to admit they had never so much as walked up Broadway. Tugs and ferry boats and coal barges were moving up and down the oily river, all novel sights to the men. Over in the Canard and French docks they saw the first examples of the "camouflage" they had heard so much about; big vessels daubed over in crazy patterns that made the eyes ache, some in black and white, some in soft rainbow colours.

A tug steamed up alongside and fastened. A few moments later a man appeared on the bridge and began to talk to the captain. Young Fanning, who had stuck to Claude's side, told him this was the pilot, and that his arrival meant they were going to start. They could see the shiny instruments of a band assembling in the bow.

"Let's get on the other side, near the rail if we can," said Fanning. "The fellows are bunching up over here because they want to look at the Goddess of Liberty as we go out. They don't even know this boat turns around the minute she gets into the river. They think she's going over stern first!"

It was not easy to cross the deck; every inch was covered by a boot. The whole superstructure was coated with brown uniforms; they clung to the boat davits, the winches, the railings and ventilators, like bees in a swarm. Just as the vessel was backing out, a breeze sprang up and cleared the air. Blue sky broke overhead, and the pale silhouette of buildings on the long island grew sharp and hard. Windows flashed flame-coloured in their grey sides, the gold and bronze tops of towers began to gleam where the sunlight struggled through. The transport was sliding down toward the point, and to the left the eye caught the silver cobweb of bridges, seen confusingly against each other.

"There she is!" "Hello, old girl!" "Good-bye, sweetheart!"

The swarm surged to starboard. They shouted and gesticulated to the image they were all looking for,—so much nearer than they had expected to see her, clad in green folds, with the mist streaming up like smoke behind. For nearly every one of those twenty-five hundred boys, as for Claude, it was their first glimpse of the Bartholdi statue. Though she was such a definite image in their minds, they had not imagined her in her setting of sea and sky, with the shipping of the world coming and going at her feet, and the moving cloud masses behind her. Post-card pictures had given them no idea of the energy of her large gesture, or how her heaviness becomes light among the vapourish elements. "France gave her to us," they kept saying, as they saluted her. Before Claude had got over his first thrill, the Kansas band in the bow began playing "Over There." Two thousand voices took it up, booming out over the water the gay, indomitable resolution of that jaunty air.

A Staten Island ferry-boat passed close under the bow of the transport. The passengers were office-going people, on their way to work, and when they looked up and saw these hundreds of faces, all young, all bronzed and grinning, they began to shout and wave their handkerchiefs. One of the passengers was an old clergyman, a famous speaker in his day, now retired, who went over to the City every morning to write editorials for a church paper. He closed the book he was reading, stood by the rail, and taking off his hat began solemnly to quote from a poet who in his time was still popular. "Sail on," he quavered,

"Thou, too, sail on, O Ship of State,
Humanity, with all its fears,
With all its hopes of future years,
Is hanging breathless on thy fate."

As the troop ship glided down the sea lane, the old man still watched it from the turtle-back. That howling swarm of brown arms and hats and faces looked like nothing, but a crowd of American boys going to a football game somewhere. But the scene was ageless; youths were sailing away to die for an idea, a sentiment, for the mere sound of a phrase... and on their departure they were making vows to a bronze image in the sea.

III.

ALL THE FIRST morning Tod Fanning showed Claude over the boat,—not that Fanning had ever been on anything bigger than a Lake Michigan steamer, but he knew a good deal about machinery, and did not hesitate to ask the deck stewards to explain anything he didn't know. The stewards, indeed all the crew, struck the boys as an unusually good-natured and obliging set of men.

The fourth occupant of number 96, Claude's cabin, had not turned up by noon, nor had any of his belongings, so the three who had settled their few effects there began to hope they would have the place to themselves. It would be crowded enough, at that. The third bunk was assigned to an officer from the Kansas regiment, Lieutenant Bird, a Virginian, who had been working in his uncle's bank in Topeka when he enlisted. He and Claude sat together at mess. When they were at lunch, the Virginian said in his very gentle voice:

"Lieutenant, I wish you'd explain Lieutenant Fanning to me. He seems very immature. He's been telling me about a submarine destroyer he's invented, but it looks to me like foolishness."

Claude laughed. "Don't try to understand Fanning. Just let him sink in, and you'll come to like him. I used to wonder how he ever got a commission. You never can tell what crazy thing he'll do."

Fanning had, for instance, brought on board a pair of white flannel pants, his first and only tailor-made trousers, because he had a premonition that the boat would make a port and that he would be asked to a garden party! He had a way of using big words in the wrong place, not because he tried to show off, but because all words sounded alike to him. In the first days of their acquaintance in camp he told Claude that this was a failing he couldn't help, and that it was called "anaesthesia." Sometimes this failing was confusing; when Fanning sententiously declared that he would like to be on hand when the Crown Prince settled his little account with Plato, Claude was perplexed until subsequent witticisms revealed that the boy meant Pluto.

At three o'clock there was a band concert on deck. Claude fell into talk with the bandmaster, and was delighted to find that he came from Hillport, Kansas, a town where Claude had once been with his father to buy cattle, and that all his fourteen men came from Hillport. They were the town band, had enlisted in a body, had gone into training together, and had never been separated. One was a printer who helped to get out the Hillport Argus every week, another clerked in a grocery store, another was the son of a German watch repairer, one was still in High School, one worked in an automobile livery. After supper Claude found them all together, very much interested in their first evening at sea, and arguing as to whether the sunset on the water was as fine as those they saw every night in Hillport. They hung together in a quiet, determined way, and if you began to talk to one, you soon found that all the others were there.

When Claude and Fanning and Lieutenant Bird were undressing in their narrow quarters that night, the fourth berth was still unclaimed. They were in their bunks and almost asleep, when the missing man came in and unceremoniously turned on the light. They were astonished to see that he wore the uniform of the Royal Flying Corps and carried a cane. He seemed very young, but the three who peeped out at him felt that he must be a person of consequence. He took off his coat with the spread wings on the collar, wound his watch, and brushed his teeth with an air of special personal importance. Soon after he had turned out the light and climbed into the berth over Lieutenant Bird, a heavy smell of rum spread in the close air.

Fanning, who slept under Claude, kicked the sagging mattress above him and stuck his head out. "Hullo, Wheeler! What have you got up there?"

"Nothing."

"Nothing smells pretty good to me. I'll have some with anybody that asks me."

No response from any quarter. Bird, the Virginian, murmured, "Don't make a row," and they went to sleep.

In the morning, when the bath steward came, he edged his way into the narrow cabin and poked his head into the berth over Bird's. "I'm sorry, sir, I've made careful search for your luggage, and it's not to be found, sir."

"I tell you it must be found," fumed a petulant voice overhead. "I brought it over from the St. Regis myself in a taxi. I saw it standing on the pier with the officers' luggage,—a black cabin trunk with V.M. lettered on both ends. Get after it."

The steward smiled discreetly. He probably knew that the aviator had come on board in a state which precluded any very accurate observation on his part. "Very well, sir. Is there anything I can get you for the present?"

"You can take this shirt out and have it laundered and bring it back to me tonight. I've no linen in my bag."

"Yes, sir."

Claude and Fanning got on deck as quickly as possible and found scores of their comrades already there, pointing to dark smudges of smoke along the clear horizon. They knew that these vessels had come from unknown ports, some of them far away, steaming thither under orders known only to their commanders. They would all arrive within a few hours of each other at a given spot on the surface of the ocean. There they would fall into place, flanked by their destroyers, and would proceed in orderly formation, without changing their relative positions. Their escort would not leave them until they were joined by gunboats and destroyers off whatever coast they were bound for,—what that coast was, not even their own officers knew as yet.

Later in the morning this meeting was actually accomplished. There were ten troop ships, some of them very large boats, and six destroyers. The men stood about the whole morning, gazing spellbound at their sister transports, trying to find out their names, guessing at their capacity. Tanned as they already were, their lips and noses began to blister under the fiery sunlight. After long months of intensive training, the sudden drop into an idle, soothing existence was grateful to them. Though their pasts were neither long or varied, most of them, like Claude Wheeler, felt a sense of relief at being rid of all they had ever been before and facing something absolutely new. Said Tod Fanning, as he lounged against the rail, "Whoever likes it can run for a train every morning, and grind his days out in a Westinghouse works; but not for me any more!"

The Virginian joined them. "That Englishman ain't got out of bed yet. I reckon he's been liquouring up pretty steady. The place smells like a bar. The room steward was just coming out, and he winked at me. He was slipping something in his pocket, looked like a banknote."

Claude was curious, and went down to the cabin. As he entered, the air-man, lying half-dressed in his upper berth, raised himself on one elbow and looked down at him. His blue eyes were contracted and hard, his curly hair disordered, but his cheeks were as pink as a girl's, and the little yellow humming-bird moustache on his upper lip was twisted sharp.

"You're missing fine weather," said Claude affably.

"Oh, there'll be a great deal of weather before we get over, and damned little of anything else!" He drew a bottle from under his pillow. "Have a nip?"

"I don't mind if I do," Claude put out his hand.

The other laughed and sank back on his pillow, drawling lazily, "Brave boy! Go ahead; drink to the Kaiser."

"Why to him in particular?"

"It's not particular. Drink to Hindenburg, or the High Command, or anything else that got you out of the cornfield. That's where they did get you, didn't they?"

"Well, it's a good guess, anyhow. Where did they get you?"

"Crystal Lake, Iowa. I think that was the place." He yawned and folded his hands over his stomach.

"Why, we thought you were an Englishman."

"Not quite. I've served in His Majesty's army two years, though."

"Have you been flying in France?"

"Yes. I've been back and forth all the time, England and France. Now I've wasted two months at Fort Worth. Instructor. That's not my line. I may have been sent over as a reprimand. You can't tell about my Colonel, though; may have been his way of getting me out of danger."

Claude glanced up at him, shocked at such an idea.

The young man in the berth smiled with listless compassion. "Oh, I don't mean Bosch planes! There are dangers and dangers. You'll find you got bloody little information about this war, where they trained you. They don't communicate any details of importance. Going?"

Claude hadn't intended to, but at this suggestion he pulled back the door.

"One moment," called the aviator. "Can't you keep that long-legged ass who bunks under you quiet?"

"Fanning? He's a good kid. What's the matter with him?"

"His general ignorance and his insufferably familiar tone," snapped the other as he turned over.

Claude found Fanning and the Virginian playing checkers, and told them that the mysterious air-man was a fellow countryman. Both seemed disappointed.

"Pshaw!" exclaimed Lieutenant Bird.

"He can't put on airs with me, after that," Fanning declared. "Crystal Lake! Why it's no town at all!"

All the same, Claude wanted to find out how a youth from Crystal Lake ever became a member of the Royal Flying Corps. Already, from among the hundreds of strangers, half-a-dozen stood out as men he was determined to know better. Taking them altogether the men were a fine sight as they lounged about the decks in the sunlight, the petty rivalries and jealousies of camp days forgotten. Their youth seemed to flow together, like their brown uniforms. Seen in the mass like this, Claude thought, they were rather noble looking fellows. In so many of the faces there was a look of fine candour, an expression of cheerful expectancy and confident goodwill.

There was on board a solitary Marine, with the stripes of Border service on his coat. He had been sick in the Navy Hospital in Brooklyn when his regiment sailed, and was now going over to join it. He was a young fellow, rather pale from his recent illness, but he was exactly Claude's idea of what a soldier ought to look like. His eye followed the Marine about all day.

The young man's name was Albert Usher, and he came from a little town up in the Wind River mountains, in Wyoming, where he had worked in a logging camp. He told Claude these facts when they found themselves standing side by side that evening, watching the broad purple sun go down into a violet coloured sea.

It was the hour when the farmers at home drive their teams in after the day's work. Claude was thinking how his mother would be standing at the west window every evening now, watching the sun go down and following him in her mind. When the young Marine came up and joined him, he confessed to a pang of homesickness.

"That's a kind of sickness I don't have to wrastle with," said Albert Usher. "I was left an orphan on a lonesome ranch, when I was nine, and I've looked out for myself ever since."

Claude glanced sidewise at the boy's handsome head, that came up from his neck with clean, strong lines, and thought he had done a pretty good job for himself. He could not have said exactly what it was he liked about young Usher's face, but it seemed to him a face that had gone through things,—that had been trained down like his body, and had developed a definite character. What Claude thought due to a manly, adventurous life, was really due to well-shaped bones; Usher's face was more "modelled" than most of the healthy countenances about him.

When questioned, the Marine went on to say that though he had no home of his own, he had always happened to fall on his feet, among kind people. He could go back to any house in Pinedale or Du Bois and be welcomed like a son.

"I suppose there are kind women everywhere," he said, "but in that respect Wyoming's got the rest of the world beat. I never felt the lack of a home. Now the U. S. Marines are my family. Wherever they are, I'm at home."

"Were you at Vera Cruz?" Claude asked.

"I guess! We thought that was quite a little party at the time, but I suppose it will seem small potatoes when we get over there. I'm figuring on seeing some first-rate scrapping. How long have you been in the army?"

"Year ago last April. I've had hard luck about getting over. They kept me jumping about to train men."

"Then yours is all to come. Are you a college graduate?"

"No. I went away to school, but I didn't finish."

Usher frowned at the gilded path on the water where the sun lay half submerged, like a big, watchful eye, closing. "I always wanted to go to college, but I never managed it. A man in Laramie offered to stake me to a course in the University there, but I was too restless. I guess I was ashamed of my handwriting." He paused as if he had run against some old regret. A moment later he said suddenly, "Can you parlez-vous?"

"No. I know a few words, but I can't put them together."

"Same here. I expect to pick up some. I pinched quite a little Spanish down on the Border."

By this time the sun had disappeared, and all over the west the yellow sky came down evenly, like a gold curtain, on the still sea that seemed to have solidified into a slab of dark blue stone,—not a twinkle on its immobile surface. Across its dusky smoothness were two long smears of pale green, like a robin's egg.

"Do you like the water?" Usher asked, in the tone of a polite host. "When I first shipped on a cruiser I was crazy about it. I still am. But, you know, I like them old bald mountains back in Wyoming, too. There's waterfalls you can see twenty miles off from the plains; they look like white sheets or something, hanging up there on the cliffs. And down in the pine woods, in the cold streams, there's trout as long as my fore-arm."

That evening Claude was on deck, almost alone; there was a concert down in the ward room. To the west heavy clouds had come up, moving so low that they flapped over the water like a black washing hanging on the line.

The music sounded well from below. Four Swedish boys from the Scandinavian settlement at Lindsborg, Kansas, were singing "Long, Long Ago." Claude listened from a sheltered spot in the stern. What were they, and what was he, doing here on the Atlantic? Two years ago he had seemed a fellow for whom life was over; driven into the ground like a post, or like those Chinese criminals who are planted upright in the earth, with only their heads left out for birds to peck at and insects to sting. All his comrades had been tucked away in prairie towns, with their little jobs and their little plans. Yet here they were, attended by unknown ships called in from the four quarters of the earth. How had they come to be worth the watchfulness and devotion of so many men and machines, this extravagant consumption of fuel and energy? Taken one by one, they were ordinary fellows like himself. Yet here they were. And in this massing and movement of men there was nothing mean or common; he was sure of that. It was, from first to last, unforeseen, almost incredible. Four years ago, when the French were holding the Marne, the wisest men in the world had not conceived of this as possible; they had reckoned with every fortuity but this. "Out of these stones can my Father raise up seed unto Abraham."

Downstairs the men began singing "Annie Laurie." Where were those summer evenings when he used to sit dumb by the windmill, wondering what to do with his life?

IV.

THE MORNING of the third day; Claude and the Virginian and the Marine were up very early, standing in the bow, watching the Anchises mount the fresh blowing hills of water, her prow, as it rose and fell, always a dull triangle against the glitter. Their escorts looked like dream ships, soft and iridescent as shell in the pearl-coloured tints of the morning. Only the dark smudges of smoke told that they were mechanical realities with stokers and engines.

While the three stood there, a sergeant brought Claude word that two of his men would have to report at sick-call. Corporal Tannhauser had had such an attack of nose-bleed during the night that the sergeant thought he might die before they got it stopped. Tannhauser was up now, and in the breakfast line, but the sergeant was sure he ought not to be. This Fritz Tannhauser was the tallest man in the company, a German-American boy who, when asked his name, usually said that his name was Dennis and that he was of Irish descent. Even this morning he tried to joke, and pointing to his big red face told Claude he thought he had measles. "Only they ain't German measles, Lieutenant," he insisted.

Medical inspection took a long while that morning. There seemed to be an outbreak of sickness on board. When Claude brought his two men up to the Doctor, he told them to go below and get into bed. As they left he turned to Claude.

"Give them hot tea, and pile army blankets on them. Make them sweat if you can." Claude remarked that the hold wasn't a very cheerful place for sick men.

"I know that, Lieutenant, but there are a number of sick men this morning, and the only other physician on board is the sickest of the lot. There's the ship's doctor, of course, but he's only responsible for the crew, and so far he doesn't seem interested. I've got to overhaul the hospital and the medical stores this morning."

"Is there an epidemic of some sort?"

"Well, I hope not. But I'll have plenty to do today, so I count on you to look after those two." The doctor was a New Englander who had joined them at Hoboken. He was a brisk, trim man, with piercing eyes, clean-cut features, and grey hair just the colour of his pale face. Claude felt at once that he knew his business, and he went below to carry out instructions as well as he could.

When he came up from the hold, he saw the aviator—whose name, he had learned, was Victor Morse—smoking by the rail. This cabin-mate still piqued his curiosity.

"First time you've been up, isn't it?"

The aviator was looking at the distant smoke plumes over the quivering, bright water. "Time enough. I wish I knew where we are heading for. It will be awfully awkward for me if we make a French port."

"I thought you said you were to report in France."

"I am. But I want to report in London first." He continued to gaze off at the painted ships. Claude noticed that in standing he held his chin very high. His eyes, now that he was quite sober, were brilliantly young and daring; they seemed scornful of things about him. He held himself conspicuously apart, as if he were not among his own kind.

Claude had seen a captured crane, tied by its leg to a hencoop, behave exactly like that among Mahailey's chickens; hold its wings to its sides, and move its head about quickly and glare.

"I suppose you have friends in London?" he asked.

"Rather!" the aviator replied with feeling.

"Do you like it better than Paris?"

"I shouldn't imagine anything was much better than London. I've not been in Paris; always went home when I was on leave. They work us pretty hard. In the infantry and artillery our men get only a fortnight off in twelve months. I understand the Americans have leased the Riviera,—recuperate at Nice and Monte Carlo. The only Cook's tour we had was Gallipoli," he added grimly.

Victor had gone a good way toward acquiring an English accent, the boys thought. At least he said 'necess'ry' and 'dysent'ry' and called his suspenders 'braces'. He offered Claude a cigarette, remarking that his cigars were in his lost trunk.

"Take one of mine. My brother sent me two boxes just before we sailed. I'll put a box in your bunk next time I go down. They're good ones."

The young man turned and looked him over with surprise. "I say, that's very decent of you! Yes, thank you, I will."

Claude had tried yesterday, when he lent Victor some shirts, to make him talk about his aerial adventures, but upon that subject he was as close as a clam. He admitted that the long red scar on his upper arm had been drilled by a sharpshooter from a German Fokker, but added hurriedly that it was of no consequence, as he had made a good landing. Now, on the strength of the cigars, Claude thought he would probe a little further. He asked whether there was anything in the lost trunk that couldn't be replaced, anything "valuable."

"There's one thing that's positively invaluable; a Zeiss lens, in perfect condition. I've got several good photographic outfits from time to time, but the lenses are always cracked by heat,—the things usually come down on fire. This one I got out of a plane I brought down up at Bar-le-Duc, and there's not a scratch on it; simply a miracle."

"You get all the loot when you bring down a machine, do you?" Claude asked encouragingly.

"Of course. I've a good collection; altimeters and compasses and glasses. This lens I always carry with me, because I'm afraid to leave it anywhere."

"I suppose it makes a fellow feel pretty fine to bring down one of those German planes."

"Sometimes. I brought down one too many, though; it was very unpleasant." Victor paused, frowning. But Claude's open, credulous face was too much for his reserve. "I brought down a woman once. She was a plucky devil, flew a scouting machine and had bothered us a bit, going over our lines. Naturally, we didn't know it was a woman until she came down. She was crushed underneath things. She lived a few hours and dictated a letter to her people. I went out and dropped it inside their lines. It was nasty business. I was quite knocked out. I got a fortnight's leave in London, though. Wheeler," he broke out suddenly, "I wish I knew we were going there now!"

"I'd like it well enough if we were."

Victor shrugged. "I should hope so!" He turned his chin in Claude's direction. "See here, if you like, I'll show you London! It's a promise. Americans never see it, you know. They sit in a Y. hut and write to their Pollyannas, or they go round hunting for the Tower. I'll show you a city that's alive; that is, unless you've a preference for museums."

His listener laughed. "No, I want to see life, as they say."

"Umph! I'd like to set you down in some places I can think of. Very well, I invite you to dine with me at the Savoy, the first night we're in London. The curtain will rise on this world for you. Nobody admitted who isn't in evening dress. The jewels will dazzle you. Actresses, duchesses, all the handsomest women in Europe."

"But I thought London was dark and gloomy since the war."

Victor smiled and teased his small straw-coloured moustache with his thumb and middle finger. "There are a few bright spots left, thank you!" He began to explain to a novice what life at the front was really like. Nobody who had seen service talked about the war, or thought about it; it was merely a condition under which they lived. Men talked about the particular regiment they were jealous of, or the favoured division that was put in for all the show fighting. Everybody thought about his own game, his personal life that he managed to keep going in spite of discipline; his next leave, how to get champagne without paying for it, dodging the guard, getting into scrapes with women and getting out again. "Are you quick with your French?" he asked.

Claude grinned. "Not especially."

"You'd better brush up on it if you want to do anything with French girls. I hear your M.P.'s are very strict. You must be able to toss the word the minute you see a skirt, and make your date before the guard gets onto you."

"I suppose French girls haven't any scruples?" Claude remarked carelessly.

Victor shrugged his narrow shoulders. "I haven't found that girls have many, anywhere. When we Canadians were training in England, we all had our week-end wives. I believe the girls in Crystal Lake used to be more or less fussy,—but that's long ago and far away. You won't have any difficulty."

When Victor was in the middle of a tale of amorous adventure, a little different from any Claude had ever heard, Tod Fanning joined them. The aviator did not acknowledge the presence of a new listener, but when he had finished his story, walked away with his special swagger, his eyes fixed upon the distance.

Fanning looked after him with disgust. "Do you believe him? I don't think he's any such heart-smasher. I like his nerve, calling you `Leftenant'! When he speaks to me he'll have to say Lootenant, or I'll spoil his beauty."

That day the men remembered long afterward, for it was the end of the fine weather, and of those first long, carefree days at sea. In the afternoon Claude and the young Marine, the Virginian and Fanning, sat together in the sun watching the water scoop itself out in hollows and pile itself up in blue, rolling hills. Usher was telling his companions a long story about the landing of the Marines at Vera Cruz.

"It's a great old town," he concluded. "One thing there I'll never forget. Some of the natives took a few of us out to the old prison that stands on a rock in the sea. We put in the whole day there, and it wasn't any tourist show, believe me! We went down into dungeons underneath the water where they used to keep State prisoners, kept them buried alive for years. We saw all the old instruments of torture; rusty iron cages where a man couldn't lie down or stand up, but had to sit bent over till he grew crooked. It made you feel queer when you came up, to think how people had been left to rot away down there, when there was so much sun and water outside. Seems like something used to be the matter with the world." He said no more, but Claude thought from his serious look that he believed he and his countrymen who were pouring overseas would help to change all that.

V.

THAT NIGHT THE VIRGINIAN, who berthed under Victor Morse, had an alarming attack of nose-bleed, and by morning he was so weak that he had to be carried to the hospital. The Doctor said they might as well face the facts; a scourge of influenza had broken out on board, of a peculiarly bloody and malignant type.[1] Everybody was a little frightened. Some of the officers shut themselves up in the smoking-room, and drank whiskey and soda and played poker all day, as if they could keep contagion out.

Lieutenant Bird died late in the afternoon and was buried at sunrise the next day, sewed up in a tarpaulin, with an eighteen pound shell at his feet. The morning broke brilliantly clear and bitter cold. The sea was rolling blue walls of water, and the boat was raked by a wind as sharp as ice. Excepting those who were sick, the boys turned out to a man. It was the first burial at sea they had ever witnessed, and they couldn't help finding it interesting. The

Chaplain read the burial service while they stood with uncovered heads. The Kansas band played a solemn march, the Swedish quartette sang a hymn. Many a man turned his face away when that brown sack was lowered into the cold, leaping indigo ridges that seemed so destitute of anything friendly to human kind. In a moment it was done, and they steamed on without him.

The glittering walls of water kept rolling in, indigo, purple, more brilliant than on the days of mild weather. The blinding sunlight did not temper the cold, which cut the face and made the lungs ache. Landsmen began to have that miserable sense of being where they were never meant to be. The boys lay in heaps on the deck, trying to keep warm by hugging each other close. Everybody was seasick. Fanning went to bed with his clothes on, so sick he couldn't take off his boots. Claude lay in the crowded stern, too cold, too faint to move. The sun poured over them like flame, without any comfort in it. The strong, curling, foam-crested waves threw off the light like millions of mirrors, and their colour was almost more than the eye could bear. The water seemed denser than before, heavy like melted glass, and the foam on the edges of each blue ridge looked sharp as crystals. If a man should fall into them, he would be cut to pieces.

The whole ocean seemed suddenly to have come to life, the waves had a malignant, graceful, muscular energy, were animated by a kind of mocking cruelty. Only a few hours ago a gentle boy had been thrown into that freezing water and forgotten. Yes, already forgotten; every one had his own miseries to think about.

Late in the afternoon the wind fell, and there was a sinister sunset. Across the red west a small, ragged black cloud hurried,—then another, and another. They came up out of the sea, —wild, witchlike shapes that travelled fast and met in the west as if summoned for an evil conclave. They hung there against the afterglow, distinct black shapes, drawing together, devising something. The few men who were left on deck felt that no good could come out of a sky like that. They wished they were at home, in France, anywhere but here.

VI.

THE NEXT MORNING Doctor Trueman asked Claude to help him at sick call. "I've got a bunch of sergeants taking temperatures, but it's too much for one man to oversee. I don't want to ask anything of those dude officers who sit in there playing poker all the time. Either they've got no conscience, or they're not awake to the gravity of the situation."

The Doctor stood on deck in his raincoat, his foot on the rail to keep his equilibrium, writing on his knee as the long string of men came up to him. There were more than seventy in the line that morning, and some of them looked as if they ought to be in a drier place. Rain beat down on the sea like lead bullets. The old Anchises floundered from one grey ridge to another, quite alone. Fog cut off the cheering sight of the sister ships. The doctor had to leave his post from time to time, when seasickness got the better of his will. Claude, at his elbow, was noting down names and temperatures. In the middle of his work he told the sergeants to manage without him for a few minutes. Down near the end of the line he had seen one of his own men misconducting himself, snivelling and crying like a baby,—a fine husky boy of eighteen who had never given any trouble. Claude made a dash for him and clapped him on the shoulder.

"If you can't stop that, Bert Fuller, get where you won't be seen. I don't want all these English stewards standing around to watch an American soldier cry. I never heard of such a thing!"

"I can't help it, Lieutenant," the boy blubbered. "I've kept it back just as long as I can. I can't hold in any longer!"

"What's the matter with you? Come over here and sit down on this box and tell me."

Private Fuller willingly let himself be led, and dropped on the box. "I'm so sick, Lieutenant!"

"I'll see how sick you are." Claude stuck a thermometer into his mouth, and while he waited, sent the deck steward to bring a cup of tea. "Just as I thought, Fuller. You've not half a degree of fever. You're scared, and that's all. Now drink this tea. I expect you didn't eat any breakfast."

"No, sir. I can't eat the awful stuff on this boat."

"It is pretty bad. Where are you from?"

"I'm from P-P-Pleasantville, up on the P-P-Platte," the boy gulped, and his tears began to flow afresh.

"Well, now, what would they think of you, back there? I suppose they got the band out and made a fuss over you when you went away, and thought they were sending off a fine soldier. And I've always thought you'd be a first rate soldier. I guess we'll forget about this. You feel better already, don't you?"

"Yes, sir. This tastes awful good. I've been so sick to my stomach, and last night I got pains in my chest. All my crowd is sick, and you took big Tannhauser, I mean Corporal, away to the hospital. It looks like we're all going to die out here."

"I know it's a little gloomy. But don't you shame me before these English stewards." "I won't do it again, sir," he promised.

When the medical inspection was over, Claude took the Doctor down to see Fanning, who had been coughing and wheezing all night and hadn't got out of his berth. The examination was short. The Doctor knew what was the matter before he put the stethoscope on him. "It's pneumonia, both lungs," he said when they came out into the corridor. "I have one case in the hospital that will die before morning."

"What can you do for him, Doctor?"

"You see how I'm fixed; close onto two hundred men sick, and one doctor. The medical supplies are wholly inadequate. There's not castor oil enough on this boat to keep the men clean inside. I'm using my own drugs, but they won't last through an epidemic like this. I can't do much for Lieutenant Fanning. You can, though, if you'll give him the time. You can take better care of him right here than he could get in the hospital. We haven't an empty bed there."

Claude found Victor Morse and told him he had better get a berth in one of the other staterooms. When Victor left with his belongings, Fanning stared after him. "Is he going?"

"Yes. It's too crowded in here, if you've got to stay in bed."

"Glad of it. His stories are too raw for me. I'm no sissy, but that fellow's a regular Don Quixote."

Claude laughed. "You mustn't talk. It makes you cough."

"Where's the Virginian?"

"Who, Bird?" Claude asked in astonishment,—Fanning had stood beside him at Bird's funeral. "Oh, he's gone, too. You sleep if you can."

After dinner Doctor Trueman came in and showed Claude how to give his patient an alcohol bath. "It's simply a question of whether you can keep up his strength. Don't try any of this greasy food they serve here. Give him a raw egg beaten up in the juice of an orange every two hours, night and day. Waken him out of his sleep when it's time, don't miss a single two-hour period. I'll write an order to your table steward, and you can beat the eggs up here in your cabin. Now I must go to the hospital. It's wonderful what those band boys are doing there. I begin to take some pride in the place. That big German has been asking for you. He's in a very bad way."

As there were no nurses on board, the Kansas band had taken over the hospital. They had been trained for stretcher and first aid work, and when they realized what was happening on the Anchises, the bandmaster came to the Doctor and offered the services of his men. He chose nurses and orderlies, divided them into night and day shifts.

When Claude went to see his Corporal, big Tannhauser did not recognize him. He was quite out of his head and was conversing with his own family in the language of his early childhood. The Kansas boys had singled him out for special attention. The mere fact that he kept talking in a tongue forbidden on the surface of the seas, made him seem more friendless and alone than the others.

From the hospital Claude went down into the hold where half-a-dozen of his company were lying ill. The hold was damp and musty as an old cellar, so steeped in the smells and leakage of innumerable dirty cargoes that it could not be made or kept clean. There was almost no ventilation, and the air was fetid with sickness and sweat and vomit. Two of the band boys were working in the stench and dirt, helping the stewards. Claude stayed to lend a hand until it was time to give Fanning his nourishment. He began to see that the wrist watch, which he had hitherto despised as effeminate and had carried in his pocket, might be a very useful article. After he had made Fanning swallow his egg, he piled all the available blankets on him and opened the port to give the cabin an airing. While the fresh wind blew in, he sat down on the edge of his berth and tried to collect his wits. What had become of those first days of golden weather, leisure and good-comradeship? The band concerts, the Lindsborg Quartette, the first excitement and novelty of being at sea: all that had gone by like a dream.

That night when the Doctor came in to see Fanning, he threw his stethoscope on the bed and said wearily, "It's a wonder that instrument doesn't take root in my ears and grow there." He sat down and sucked his thermometer for a few minutes, then held it out for inspection. Claude looked at it and told him he ought to go to bed.

"Then who's to be up and around? No bed for me, tonight. But I will have a hot bath by and by."

Claude asked why the ship's doctor didn't do anything and added that he must be as little as he looked.

"Chessup? No, he's not half bad when you get to know him. He's given me a lot of help about preparing medicines, and it's a great assistance to talk the cases over with him. He'll do anything for me except directly handle the patients. He doesn't want to exceed his authority. It seems the English marine is very particular about such things. He's a Canadian, and he graduated first in his class at Edinburgh. I gather he was frozen out in private practice. You see, his appearance is against him. It's an awful handicap to look like a kid and be as shy as he is."

The Doctor rose, shored up his shoulders and took his bag. "You're looking fine yourself, Lieutenant," he remarked. "Parents both living? Were they quite young when you were born? Well, then their parents were, probably. I'm a crank about that. Yes, I'll get my bath pretty soon, and I will lie down for an hour or two. With those splendid band boys running the hospital, I get a little lee-way."

Claude wondered how the Doctor kept going. He knew he hadn't had more than four hours sleep out of the last forty-eight, and he was not a man of rugged constitution. His bath steward was, as he said, his comfort. Hawkins was an old fellow who had held better positions on better boats,—yes, in better times, too. He had first gone to sea as a bath steward, and now, through the fortunes of war, he had come back where he began,—not a good place for an old man. His back was bent meekly, and he shuffled along with broken arches. He looked after the comfort of all the officers, and attended the doctor like a valet; got out his clean linen, persuaded him to lie down and have a hot drink after his bath, stood on guard at his door to take messages for him in the short hours when he was resting. Hawkins had lost two sons in the war and he seemed to find a solemn consolation in being of service to soldiers. "Take it a bit easy now, sir. You'll 'ave it 'ard enough over there," he used to say to one and another.

At eleven o'clock one of the Kansas men came to tell Claude that his Corporal was going fast. Big Tannhauser's fever had left him, but so had everything else. He lay in a stupor. His congested eyeballs were rolled back in his head and only the yellowish whites were visible. His mouth was open and his tongue hung out at one side. From the end of the corridor Claude had heard the frightful sounds that came from his throat, sounds like violent vomiting, or the choking rattle of a man in strangulation,—and, indeed, he was being strangled. One of the band boys brought Claude a camp chair, and said kindly, "He doesn't suffer. It's mechanical now. He'd go easier if he hadn't so much vitality. The Doctor says he may have a few moments of consciousness just at the last, if you want to stay."

"I'll go down and give my private patient his egg, and then I'll come back." Claude went away and returned, and sat dozing by the bed. After three o'clock the noise of struggle ceased; instantly the huge figure on the bed became again his good-natured corporal. The mouth closed, the glassy jellies were once more seeing, intelligent human eyes. The face lost its swollen, brutish look and was again the face of a friend. It was almost unbelievable that anything so far gone could come back. He looked up wistfully at his Lieutenant as if to ask him something. His eyes filled with tears, and he turned his head away a little.

"Mein' arme Mutter!" he whispered distinctly.

A few moments later he died in perfect dignity, not struggling under torture, but consciously, it seemed to Claude,—like a brave boy giving back what was not his to keep.

Claude returned to his cabin, roused Fanning once more, and then threw himself upon his tipping bunk. The boat seemed to wallow and sprawl in the waves, as he had seen animals do on the farm when they gave birth to young. How helpless the old vessel was out here in the pounding seas, and how much misery she carried! He lay looking up at the rusty water pipes and unpainted joinings. This liner was in truth the "Old Anchises"; even the carpenters who made her over for the service had not thought her worth the trouble, and had done their worst by her. The new partitions were hung to the joists by a few nails.

Big Tannhauser had been one of those who were most anxious to sail. He used to grin and say, "France is the only climate that's healthy for a man with a name like mine." He had waved his good-bye to the image in the New York harbour with the rest, believed in her like the rest. He only wanted to serve. It seemed hard.

When Tannhauser first came to camp he was confused all the time, and couldn't remember instructions. Claude had once stepped him out in front of the line and reprimanded him for not knowing his right side from his left. When he looked into the case, he found that the fellow was not eating anything, that he was ill from homesickness. He was one of those farmer boys who are afraid of town. The giant baby of a long family, he had never slept away from home a night in his life before he enlisted.

Corporal Tannhauser, along with four others, was buried at sunrise. No band this time; the chaplain was ill, so one of the young captains read the service. Claude stood by watching until the sailors shot one sack, longer by half a foot than the other four, into a lead-coloured chasm in the sea. There was not even a splash. After breakfast one of the Kansas orderlies called him into a little cabin where they had prepared the dead men for burial. The Army regulations minutely defined what was to be done with a deceased soldier's effects. His uniform, shoes, blankets, arms, personal baggage, were all disposed of according to instructions. But in each case there was a residue; the dead man's toothbrushes, his razors, and the photographs he carried upon his person. There they were in five pathetic little heaps; what should be done with them?

Claude took up the photographs that had belonged to his corporal; one was a fat, foolish-looking girl in a white dress that was too tight for her, and a floppy hat, a little flag pinned on her plump bosom. The other was an old woman, seated, her hands crossed in her lap. Her thin hair was drawn back tight from a hard, angular face—unmistakably an Old-World face—and her eyes squinted at the camera. She looked honest and stubborn and unconvinced, he thought, as if she did not in the least understand.

"I'll take these," he said. "And the others—just pitch them over, don't you think?"

VII.

B COMPANY'S FIRST OFFICER, Captain Maxey, was so seasick throughout the voyage that he was of no help to his men in the epidemic. It must have been a frightful blow to his pride, for nobody was ever more anxious to do an officer's whole duty.

Claude had known Harris Maxey slightly in Lincoln; had met him at the Erlichs' and afterward kept up a campus acquaintance with him. He hadn't liked Maxey then, and he didn't like him now, but he thought him a good officer. Maxey's family were poor folk from Mississippi, who had settled in Nemaha county, and he was very ambitious, not only to get on in the world, but, as he said, to "be somebody." His life at the University was a feverish pursuit of social advantages and useful acquaintances. His feeling for the "right people" amounted to veneration. After his graduation, Maxey served on the Mexican Border. He was a tireless drill master, and threw himself into his duties with all the energy of which his frail physique was capable. He was slight and fair-skinned; a rigid jaw threw his lower teeth out beyond the upper ones and made his face look stiff. His whole manner, tense and nervous, was the expression of a passionate desire to excel.

Claude seemed to himself to be leading a double life these days. When he was working over Fanning, or was down in the hold helping to take care of the sick soldiers, he had no time to think,—did mechanically the next thing that came to hand. But when he had an hour to himself on deck, the tingling sense of ever-widening freedom flashed up in him again. The weather was a continual adventure; he had never known any like it before. The fog, and rain, the grey sky and the lonely grey stretches of the ocean were like something he had imagined long ago—memories of old sea stories read in childhood, perhaps—and they kindled a warm spot in his heart. Here on the Anchises he seemed to begin where childhood had left off. The ugly hiatus between had closed up. Years of his life were blotted out in the fog. This fog which had been at first depressing had become a shelter; a tent moving through space, hiding one from all that had been before, giving one a chance to correct one's ideas about life and to plan the future. The past was physically shut off; that was his illusion. He had already travelled a great many more miles than were told off by the ship's log. When Bandmaster Fred Max asked him to play chess, he had to stop a moment and think why it was that game had such disagreeable associations for him. Enid's pale, deceptive face seldom rose before him unless some such accident brought it up. If he happened to come upon a group of boys talking about their sweethearts and war-brides, he listened a moment and then moved away with the happy feeling that he was the least married man on the boat.

There was plenty of deck room, now that so many men were ill either from seasickness or the epidemic, and sometimes he and Albert Usher had the stormy side of the boat almost to themselves. The Marine was the best sort of companion for these gloomy days; steady, quiet, self-reliant. And he, too, was always looking forward. As for Victor Morse, Claude was growing positively fond of him. Victor had tea in a special corner of the officers' smoking-room every afternoon—he would have perished without it—and the steward always produced some special garnishes of toast and jam or sweet biscuit for him. Claude usually managed to join him at that hour.

On the day of Tannhauser's funeral he went into the smoking-room at four. Victor beckoned the steward and told him to bring a couple of hot whiskeys with the tea. "You're very wet, you know, Wheeler, and you really should. There," he said as he put down his glass, "don't you feel better with a drink?"

"Very much. I think I'll have another. It's agreeable to be warm inside."

"Two more, steward, and bring me some fresh lemon." The occupants of the room were either reading or talking in low tones. One of the Swedish boys was playing softly on the old piano. Victor began to pour the tea. He had a neat way of doing it, and today he was especially solicitous. "This Scotch mist gets into one's bones, doesn't it? I thought you were looking rather seedy when I passed you on deck."

"I was up with Tannhauser last night. Didn't get more than an hour's sleep," Claude murmured, yawning.

"Yes, I heard you lost your big corporal. I'm sorry. I've had bad news, too. It's out now that we're to make a French port. That dashes all my plans. However, c'est la guerre!" He pushed back his cup with a shrug. "Take a turn outside?"

Claude had often wondered why Victor liked him, since he was so little Victor's kind. "If it isn't a secret," he said, "I'd like to know how you ever got into the British army, anyway."

As they walked up and down in the rain, Victor told his story briefly. When he had finished High School, he had gone into his father's bank at Crystal Lake as bookkeeper. After banking hours he skated, played tennis, or worked in the strawberry-bed, according to the season. He bought two pairs of white pants every summer and ordered his shirts from Chicago and thought he was a swell, he said. He got himself engaged to the preacher's daughter. Two years ago, the summer he was twenty, his father wanted him to see Niagara Falls; so he wrote a modest check, warned his son against saloons—Victor had never been inside one—against expensive hotels and women who came up to ask the time without an introduction, and sent him off, telling him it wasn't necessary to fee porters or waiters. At Niagara Falls, Victor fell in with some young Canadian officers who opened his eyes to a great many things. He went over to Toronto with them. Enlistment was going strong, and he saw an avenue of escape from the bank and the strawberry bed. The air force seemed the most brilliant and attractive branch of the service. They accepted him, and here he was.

"You'll never go home again," Claude said with conviction. "I don't see you settling down in any little Iowa town."

"In the air service," said Victor carelessly, "we don't concern ourselves about the future. It's not worth while." He took out a dull gold cigarette case which Claude had noticed before.

"Let me see that a minute, will you? I've often admired it. A present from somebody you like, isn't it?"

A twitch of feeling, something quite genuine, passed over the air-man's boyish face, and his rather small red mouth compressed sharply. "Yes, a woman I want you to meet. Here," twitching his chin over his high collar, "I'll write Maisie's address on my card: `Introducing Lieutenant Wheeler, A.E.F.' That's all you'll need. If you should get to London before I do, don't hesitate. Call on her at once. Present this card, and she'll receive you."

Claude thanked him and put the card in his pocketbook, while Victor lit a cigarette. "I haven't forgotten that you're dining with us at the Savoy, if we happen in London together. If I'm there, you can always find me. Her address is mine. It will really be a great thing for you to meet a woman like Maisie. She'll be nice to you, because you're my friend." He went on to say that she had done everything in the world for him; had left her husband and given up her friends on his account. She now had a studio flat in Chelsea, where she simply waited his coming and dreaded his going. It was an awful life for her. She entertained other officers, of course, old acquaintances; but it was all camouflage. He was the man.

Victor went so far as to produce her picture, and Claude gazed without knowing what to say at a large moon-shaped face with heavy-lidded, weary eyes,—the neck clasped by a pearl collar, the shoulders bare to the matronly swell of the bosom. There was not a line or wrinkle in that smooth expanse of flesh, but from the heavy mouth and chin, from the very shape of the face, it was easy to see that she was quite old enough to be Victor's mother. Across the photograph was written in a large splashy hand, 'A mon aigle!' Had Victor been delicate enough to leave him in any doubt, Claude would have preferred to believe that his relations with this lady were wholly of a filial nature.

"Women like her simply don't exist in your part of the world," the aviator murmured, as he snapped the photograph case. "She's a linguist and musician and all that. With her, everyday living is a fine art. Life, as she says, is what one makes it. In itself, it's nothing. Where you came from it's nothing—a sleeping sickness."

Claude laughed. "I don't know that I agree with you, but I like to hear you talk."

"Well; in that part of France that's all shot to pieces, you'll find more life going on in the cellars than in your home town, wherever that is. I'd rather be a stevedore in the London docks than a banker-king in one of your prairie States. In London, if you're lucky enough to have a shilling, you can get something for it."

"Yes, things are pretty tame at home," the other admitted.

"Tame? My God, it's death in life! What's left of men if you take all the fire out of them? They're afraid of everything. I know them; Sunday-school sneaks, prowling around those little towns after dark!" Victor abruptly dismissed the subject. "By the way, you're pals with the doctor, aren't you? I'm needing some medicine that is somewhere in my lost trunk. Would you mind asking him if he can put up this prescription? I don't want to go to him myself. All these medicos blab, and he might report me. I've been lucky dodging medical inspections. You see, I don't want to get held up anywhere. Tell him it's not for you, of course."

When Claude presented the piece of blue paper to Doctor Trueman, he smiled contemptuously. "I see; this has been filled by a London chemist. No, we have nothing of this sort." He handed it back. "Those things are only palliatives. If your friend wants that, he needs treatment,—and he knows where he can get it."

Claude returned the slip of paper to Victor as they left the dining-room after supper, telling him he hadn't been able to get any.

"Sorry," said Victor, flushing haughtily. "Thank you so much!"

VIII.

TOD FANNING HELD out better than many of the stronger men; his vitality surprised the doctor. The death list was steadily growing; and the worst of it was that patients died who were not very sick. Vigorous, clean-blooded young fellows of nineteen and twenty turned over and died because they had lost their courage, because other people were dying,—because death was in the air. The corridors of the vessel had the smell of death about them. Doctor Trueman said it was always so in an epidemic; patients died who, had they been isolated cases, would have recovered.

"Do you know, Wheeler," the doctor remarked one day when they came up from the hospital together to get a breath of air, "I sometimes wonder whether all these inoculations they've been having, against typhoid and smallpox and whatnot, haven't lowered their vitality. I'll go off my head if I keep losing men! What would you give to be out of it all, and safe back on the farm?" Hearing no reply, he turned his head, peered over his raincoat collar, and saw a startled, resisting look in the young man's blue eyes, followed by a quick flush.

"You don't want to be back on the farm, do you! Not a little bit! Well, well; that's what it is to be young!" He shook his head with a smile which might have been commiseration, might have been envy, and went back to his duties.

Claude stayed where he was, drawing the wet grey air into his lungs and feeling vexed and reprimanded. It was quite true, he realized; the doctor had caught him. He was enjoying himself all the while and didn't want to be safe anywhere. He was sorry about Tannhauser and the others, but he was not sorry for himself. The discomforts and misfortunes of this voyage had not spoiled it for him. He grumbled, of course, because others did. But life had never seemed so tempting as it did here and now. He could come up from heavy work in the hospital, or from poor Fanning and his everlasting eggs, and forget all that in ten minutes. Something inside him, as elastic as the grey ridges over which they were tipping, kept bounding up and saying: "I am all here. I've left everything behind me. I am going over."

Only on that one day, the cold day of the Virginian's funeral, when he was seasick, had he been really miserable. He must be heartless, certainly, not to be overwhelmed by the sufferings of his own men, his own friends—but he wasn't. He had them on his mind and did all he could for them, but it seemed to him just now that he took a sort of satisfaction in that, too, and was somewhat vain of his usefulness to Doctor Trueman. A nice attitude! He awoke every morning with that sense of freedom and going forward, as if the world were growing bigger each day and he were growing with it. Other fellows were sick and dying, and that was terrible,—but he and the boat went on, and always on.

Something was released that had been struggling for a long while, he told himself. He had been due in France since the first battle of the Marne; he had followed false leads and lost precious time and seen misery enough, but he was on the right road at last, and nothing could stop him. If he hadn't been so green, so bashful, so afraid of showing what he felt, and so stupid at finding his way about, he would have enlisted in Canada, like Victor, or run away to France and joined the Foreign Legion. All that seemed perfectly possible now. Why hadn't he?

Well, that was not "the Wheelers' way." The Wheelers were terribly afraid of poking themselves in where they weren't wanted, of pushing their way into a crowd where they didn't belong. And they were even more afraid of doing anything that might look affected or "romantic." They couldn't let themselves adopt a conspicuous, much less a picturesque course of action, unless it was all in the day's work. Well, History had condescended to such as he; this whole brilliant adventure had become the day's work. He had got into it after all, along with Victor and the Marine and other fellows who had more imagination and self-confidence in the first place. Three years ago he used to sit moping by the windmill because he didn't see how a Nebraska farmer boy had any "call," or, indeed, any way, to throw himself into the struggle in France. He used enviously to read about Alan Seeger and those fortunate American boys who had a right to fight for a civilization they knew.

But the miracle had happened; a miracle so wide in its amplitude that the Wheelers,—all the Wheelers and the roughnecks and the low-brows were caught up in it. Yes, it was the rough-necks' own miracle, all this; it was their golden chance. He was in on it, and nothing could hinder or discourage him unless he were put over the side himself—which was only a way of joking, for that was a possibility he never seriously considered. The feeling of purpose, of fateful purpose, was strong in his breast.

IX.

"Look at this, Doctor!" Claude caught Dr. Trueman on his way from breakfast and handed him a written notice, signed D. T. Micks, Chief Steward. It stated that no more eggs or oranges could be furnished to patients, as the supply was exhausted.

The doctor squinted at the paper. "I'm afraid that's your patient's death warrant. You'll never be able to keep him going on anything else. Why don't you go and talk it over with Chessup? He's a resourceful fellow. I'll join you there in a few minutes."

Claude had often been to Dr. Chessup's cabin since the epidemic broke out,-rather liked to wait there when he went for medicines or advice. It was a comfortable, personal sort of place with cheerful chintz hangings. The walls were lined with books, held in place by sliding wooden slats, padlocked at the ends. There were a great many scientific works in German and English; the rest were French novels in paper covers. This morning he found Chessup weighing out white powders at his desk. In the rack over his bunk was the book with which he had read himself to sleep last night; the title, "Un Crime d'Amour," lettered in black on yellow, caught Claude's eye. The doctor put on his coat and pointed his visitor to the jointed chair in which patients were sometimes examined. Claude explained his predicament.

The ship's doctor was a strange fellow to come from Canada, the land of big men and rough. He looked like a schoolboy, with small hands and feet and a pink complexion. On his left cheekbone was a large brown mole, covered with silky hair, and for some reason that seemed to make his face effeminate. It was easy to see why he had not been successful in private practice. He was like somebody trying to protect a raw surface from heat and cold; so cursed with diffidence, and so sensitive about his boyish appearance that he chose to shut himself up in an oscillating wooden coop on the sea. The long run to Australia had exactly suited him. A rough life and the pounding of bad weather had fewer terrors for him than an office in town, with constant exposure to human personalities.

"Have you tried him on malted milk?" he asked, when Claude had told him how Farming's nourishment was threatened.

"Dr. Trueman hasn't a bottle left. How long do you figure we'll be at sea?"

"Four days; possibly five."

"Then Lieutenant Wheeler will lose his pal," said Dr. Trueman, who had just come in.

Chessup stood for a moment frowning and pulling nervously at the brass buttons on his coat. He slid the bolt on his door and turning to his colleague said resolutely: "I can give you some information, if you won't implicate me. You can do as you like, but keep my name out of it. For several hours last night cases of eggs and boxes of oranges were being carried into the Chief Steward's cabin by a flunky of his from the galley. Whatever port we make, he can get a shilling each for the fresh eggs, and perhaps sixpence for the oranges. They are your property, of course, furnished by your government; but this is his customary perquisite. I've been on this boat six years, and it's always been so. About a week before we make port, the choicest of the remaining stores are taken to his cabin, and he disposes of them after we dock. I can't say just how he manages it, but he does. The skipper may know of this custom, and there may be some reason why he permits it. It's not my business to see anything. The Chief Steward is a powerful man on an English vessel. If he has anything against me, sooner or later he can lose my berth for me. There you have the facts."

"Have I your permission to go to the Chief Steward?" Dr. Trueman asked.

"Certainly not. But you can go without my knowledge. He's an ugly man to cross, and he can make it uncomfortable for you and your patients."

"Well, we'll say no more about it. I appreciate your telling me, and I will see that you don't get mixed up in this. Will you go down with me to look at that new meningitis case?"

Claude waited impatiently in his stateroom for the doctor's return. He didn't see why the Chief Steward shouldn't be exposed and dealt with like any other grafter. He had hated the man ever since he heard him berating the old bath steward one morning. Hawkins had made no attempt to defend himself, but stood like a dog that has been terribly beaten, trembling all over, saying "Yes, sir. Yes, sir," while his chief gave him a cold cursing in a low, snarling voice. Claude had never heard a man or even an animal addressed with such contempt. The Steward had a cruel face,—white as cheese, with limp, moist hair combed back from a high forehead,—the peculiarly oily hair that seems to grow only on the heads of stewards and waiters. His eyes were exactly the shape of almonds, but the lids were so swollen that the dull pupil was visible only through a narrow slit. A long, pale moustache hung like a fringe over his loose lips.

When Dr. Trueman came back from the hospital, he declared he was now ready to call on Mr. Micks. "He's a nasty looking customer, but he can't do anything to me."

They went to the Chief Steward's cabin and knocked.

"What's wanted?" called a threatening voice.

The doctor made a grimace to his companion and walked in. The Steward was sitting at a big desk, covered with account books. He turned in his chair. "I beg your pardon," he said coldly, "I do not see any one here. I will be—"

The doctor held up his hand quickly. "That's all right, Steward. I'm sorry to intrude, but I've something I must say to you in private. I'll not detain you long." If he had hesitated for a moment, Claude believed the Steward would have thrown him out, but he went on rapidly. "This is Lieutenant Wheeler, Mr. Micks. His fellow officer lies very ill with pneumonia in stateroom 96. Lieutenant Wheeler has kept him alive by special nursing. He is not able to retain anything in his stomach but eggs and orange juice. If he has these, we may be able to keep up his strength till the fever breaks, and carry him to a hospital in France. If we can't get them for him, he will be dead within twenty-four hours. That's the situation."

The steward rose and turned out the drop-light on his desk. "Have you received notice that there are no more eggs and oranges on board? Then I am afraid there is nothing I can do for you. I did not provision this ship."

"No. I understand that. I believe the United States Government provided the fruit and eggs and meat. And I positively know that the articles I need for my patient are not exhausted. Without going into the matter further, I warn you that I'm not going to let a United States officer die when the means of saving him are procurable. I'll go to the skipper, I'll call a meeting of the army officers on board. I'll go any length to save this man."

"That is your own affair, but you will not interfere with me in the discharge of my duties. Will you leave my cabin?"

"In a moment, Steward. I know that last night a number of cases of eggs and oranges were carried into this room. They are here now, and they belong to the A.E.F. If you will agree to provision my man, what I know won't go any further. But if you refuse, I'll get this matter investigated. I won't stop till I do."

The Steward sat down, and took up a pen. His large, soft hand looked cheesy, like his face. "What is the number of the cabin?" he asked indifferently.

"Ninety-six."

"Exactly what do you require?"

"One dozen eggs and one dozen oranges every twenty-four hours, to be delivered at any time convenient to you."

"I will see what I can do."

The Steward did not look up from his writing pad, and his visitors left as abruptly as they had come.

At about four o'clock every morning, before even the bath stewards were on duty, there was a scratching at Claude's door, and a covered basket was left there by a messenger who was unwashed, half-naked, with a sacking apron tied round his middle and his hairy chest splashed with flour. He never spoke, had only one eye and an inflamed socket. Claude learned that he was a half-witted brother of the Chief Steward, a potato peeler and dish-washer in the galley.

Four day after their interview with Mr. Micks, when they were at last nearing the end of the voyage, Doctor Trueman detained Claude after medical inspection to tell him that the Chief Steward had come down with the epidemic. "He sent for me last night and asked me to take his case,—won't have anything to do with Chessup. I had to get Chessup's permission. He seemed very glad to hand the case over to me."

"Is he very bad?"

"He hasn't a look-in, and he knows it. Complications; chronic Bright's disease. It seems he has nine children. I'll try to get him into a hospital when we make port, but he'll only live a few days at most. I wonder who'll get the shillings for all the eggs and oranges he hoarded away. Claude, my boy," the doctor spoke with sudden energy, "if I ever set foot on land again, I'm going to forget this voyage like a bad dream. When I'm in normal health, I'm a Presbyterian, but just now I feel that even the wicked get worse than they deserve."

A day came at last when Claude was wakened from sleep by a sense of stillness. He sprang up with a dazed fear that some one had died; but Fanning lay in his berth, breathing quietly.

Something caught his eye through the porthole,—a great grey shoulder of land standing up in the pink light of dawn, powerful and strangely still after the distressing instability of the sea. Pale trees and long, low fortifications... close grey buildings with red roofs... little sailboats bounding seaward... up on the cliff a gloomy fortress.

He had always thought of his destination as a country shattered and desolated, —"bleeding France"; but he had never seen anything that looked so strong, so self-sufficient, so fixed from the first foundation, as the coast that rose before him. It was like a pillar of eternity. The ocean lay submissive at its feet, and over it was the great meekness of early morning.

This grey wall, unshaken, mighty, was the end of the long preparation, as it was the end of the sea. It was the reason for everything that had happened in his life for the last fifteen months. It was the reason why Tannhauser and the gentle Virginian, and so many others who had set out with him, were never to have any life at all, or even a soldier's death. They were merely waste in a great enterprise, thrown overboard like rotten ropes. For them this kind release,—trees and a still shore and quiet water,—was never, never to be. How long would their bodies toss, he wondered, in that inhuman kingdom of darkness and unrest?

He was startled by a weak voice from behind.

"Claude, are we over?"

"Yes, Fanning. We're over."

---

1. The actual outbreak of influenza on transports carrying United States troops is here anticipated by several months.

5

BIDDING THE EAGLES OF THE WEST FLY ON

I.

AT NOON that day Claude found himself in a street of little shops, hot and perspiring, utterly confused and turned about. Truck drivers and boys on bell less bicycles shouted at him indignantly, furiously. He got under the shade of a young plane tree and stood close to the trunk, as if it might protect him. His greatest care, at any rate, was off his hands. With the help of Victor Morse he had hired a taxi for forty francs, taken Fanning to the base hospital, and seen him into the arms of a big orderly from Texas. He came away from the hospital with no idea where he was going—except that he wanted to get to the heart of the city. It seemed, however, to have no heart; only long, stony arteries, full of heat and noise. He was still standing there, under his plane tree, when a group of uncertain, lost-looking brown figures, headed by Sergeant Hicks, came weaving up the street; nine men in nine different attitudes of dejection, each with a long loaf of bread under his arm. They hailed Claude with joy, straightened up, and looked as if now they had found their way! He saw that he must be a plane tree for somebody else.

Sergeant Hicks explained that they had been trudging about the town, looking for cheese. After sixteen days of heavy, tasteless food, cheese was what they all wanted. There was a grocery store up the street, where there seemed to be everything else. He had tried to make the old woman understand by signs.

"Don't these French people eat cheese, anyhow? What's their word for it, Lieutenant? I'm damned if I know, and I've lost my phrase book. Suppose you could make her understand?"

"Well, I'll try. Come along, boys."

Crowding close together, the ten men entered the shop. The proprietress ran forward with an exclamation of despair. Evidently she had thought she was done with them, and was not pleased to see them coming back. When she paused to take breath, Claude took off his hat respectfully, and performed the bravest act of his life; uttered the first phrase-book sentence he had ever spoken to a French person. His men were at his back; he had to say something or run, there was no other course. Looking the old woman in the eye, he steadily articulated:

"Avez-vous du fromage, Madame?" It was almost inspiration to add the last word, he thought; and when it worked, he was as much startled as if his revolver had gone off in his belt.

"Du fromage?" the shop woman screamed. Calling something to her daughter, who was at the desk, she caught Claude by the sleeve, pulled him out of the shop, and ran down the street with him. She dragged him into a doorway darkened by a long curtain, greeted the proprietress, and then pushed the men after their officer, as if they were stubborn burros.

They stood blinking in the gloom, inhaling a sour, damp, buttery, smear-kase smell, until their eyes penetrated the shadows and they saw that there was nothing but cheese and butter in the place. The shopkeeper was a fat woman, with black eyebrows that met above her nose; her sleeves were rolled up, her cotton dress was open over her white throat and bosom. She began at once to tell them that there was a restriction on milk products; every one must have cards; she could not sell them so much. But soon there was nothing left to dispute about. The boys fell upon her stock like wolves. The little white cheeses that lay on green leaves disappeared into big mouths. Before she could save it, Hicks had split a big round cheese through the middle and was carving it up like a melon. She told them they were dirty pigs and worse than the Boches, but she could not stop them.

"What's the matter with Mother, Lieutenant? What's she fussing about? Ain't she here to sell goods?"

Claude tried to look wiser than he was. "From what I can make out, there's some sort of restriction; you aren't allowed to buy all you want. We ought to have thought about that; this is a war country. I guess we've about cleaned her out."

"Oh, that's all right," said Hicks wiping his clasp-knife. "We'll bring her some sugar tomorrow. One of the fellows who helped us unload at the docks told me you can always quiet 'em if you give 'em sugar."

They surrounded her and held out their money for her to take her pay. "Come on, ma'm, don't be bashful. What's the matter, ain't this good money?"

She was distracted by the noise they made, by their bronzed faces with white teeth and pale eyes, crowding so close to her. Ten large, well-shaped hands with straight fingers, the open palms full of crumpled notes.... Holding the men off under the pretence of looking for a pencil, she made rapid calculations. The money that lay in their palms had no relation to these big, coaxing, boisterous fellows; it was a joke to them; they didn't know what it meant in the world. Behind them were shiploads of money, and behind the ships....

The situation was unfair. Whether she took much or little out of their hands, couldn't possibly matter to the Americans, couldn't even dash their good humour. But there was a strain on the cheesewoman, and the standards of a lifetime were in jeopardy. Her mind mechanically fixed upon two-and-a-half; she would charge them two-and-a-half times the market price of the cheese. With this moral plank to cling to, she made change with conscientious accuracy and did not keep a penny too much from anybody. Telling them what big stupids they were, and that it was necessary to learn to count in this world, she urged them out of her shop. She liked them well enough, but she did not like to do business with them. If she didn't take their money, the next one would. All the same, fictitious values were distasteful to her, and made everything seem flimsy and unsafe.

Standing in her doorway, she watched the brown band go ambling down the street; as they passed in front of the old church of St. Jacques, the two foremost stumbled on a sunken step that was scarcely above the level of the pavement. She laughed aloud. They looked back and waved to her. She replied with a smile that was both friendly and angry. She liked them, but not the legend of waste and prodigality that ran before them—and followed after. It was superfluous and disintegrating in a world of hard facts. An army in which the men had meat for breakfast, and ate more every day than the French soldiers at the front got in a week! Their moving kitchens and supply trains were the wonder of France. Down below Arles, where her husband's sister had married, on the desolate plain of the Crau, their tinned provisions were piled like mountain ranges, under sheds and canvas. Nobody had ever seen so much food before; coffee, milk, sugar, bacon, hams; everything the world was famished for. They brought shiploads of useless things, too. And useless people. Shiploads of women who were not nurses; some said they came to dance with the officers, so they would not be ennuyés.

All this was not war,—any more than having money thrust at you by grown men who could not count, was business. It was an invasion, like the other. The first destroyed material possessions, and this threatened everybody's integrity. Distaste of such methods, deep, recoiling distrust of them, clouded the cheesewoman's brow as she threw her money into the drawer and turned the key on it.

As for the doughboys, having once stubbed their toes on the sunken step, they examined it with interest, and went in to explore the church. It was in their minds that they must not let a church escape, any more than they would let a Boche escape. Within they came upon a bunch of their shipmates, including the Kansas band, to whom they boasted that their Lieutenant could "speak French like a native."

The Lieutenant himself thought he was getting on pretty well, but a few hours later his pride was humbled. He was sitting alone in a little triangular park beside another church, admiring the cropped locust trees and watching some old women who were doing their mending in the shade. A little boy in a black apron, with a close-shaved, bare head, came along, skipping rope. He hopped lightly up to Claude and said in a most persuasive and confiding voice,

"Voulez-vous me dire l'heure, s'il vous plaît, M'sieu' l' soldat?"

Claude looked down into his admiring eyes with a feeling of panic. He wouldn't mind being dumb to a man, or even to a pretty girl, but this was terrible. His tongue went dry, and his face grew scarlet. The child's expectant gaze changed to a look of doubt, and then of fear. He had spoken before to Americans who didn't understand, but they had not turned red and looked angry like this one; this soldier must be ill, or wrong in his head. The boy turned and ran away.

Many a serious mishap had distressed Claude less. He was disappointed, too. There was something friendly in the boy's face that he wanted... that he needed. As he rose he ground his heel into the gravel. "Unless I can learn to talk to the CHILDREN of this country," he muttered, "I'll go home!"

II.

CLAUDE SET OFF TO find the Grand Hotel, where he had promised to dine with Victor Morse. The porter there spoke English. He called a red-headed boy in a dirty uniform and told him to take the American to vingt-quatre. The boy also spoke English. "Plenty money in New York, I guess! In France, no money." He made their way, through musty corridors and up slippery staircases, as long as possible, shrewdly eyeing the visitor and rubbing his thumb nervously against his fingers all the while.

"Vingt-quatre, twen'y-four," he announced, rapping at a door with one hand and suggestively opening the other. Claude put something into it—anything to be rid of him.

Victor was standing before the fireplace. "Hello, Wheeler, come in. Our dinner will be served up here. It's big enough, isn't it? I could get nothing between a coop, and this at fifteen dollars a day."

The room was spacious enough for a banquet; with two huge beds, and great windows that swung in on hinges, like doors, and that had certainly not been washed since before the war. The heavy red cotton-brocade hangings and lace curtains were stiff with dust, the thick carpet was strewn with cigarette-ends and matches. Razor blades and "Khaki Comfort" boxes lay about on the dresser, and former occupants had left their autographs in the dust on the table. Officers slept there, and went away, and other officers arrived,—and the room remained the same, like a wood in which travellers camp for the night. The valet de chambre carried away only what he could use; discarded shirts and socks and old shoes. It seemed a rather dismal place to have a party.

When the waiter came, he dusted off the table with his apron and put on a clean cloth, napkins, and glasses. Victor and his guest sat down under an electric light bulb with a broken shade, around which a silent halo of flies moved unceasingly. They did not buzz, or dart aloft, or descend to try the soup, but hung there in the center of the room as if they were a part of the lighting system. The constant attendance of the waiter embarrassed Claude; he felt as if he were being watched.

"By the way," said Victor while the soup plates were being removed, "what do you think of this wine? It cost me thirty francs the bottle."

"It tastes very good to me," Claude replied. "But then, it's the first champagne I've ever drunk."

"Really?" Victor drank off another glass and sighed. "I envy you. I wish I had it all to do over. Life's too short, you know."

"I should say you had made a good beginning. We're a long way from Crystal Lake."

"Not far enough." His host reached across the table and filled Claude's empty glass. "I sometimes waken up with the feeling I'm back there. Or I have bad dreams, and find myself sitting on that damned stool in the glass cage and can't make my books balance; I hear the old man coughing in his private room, the way he coughs when he's going to refuse a loan to some poor devil who needs it. I've had a narrow escape, Wheeler; 'as a brand from the burning'. That's all the Scripture I remember."

The bright red spots on Victor's cheeks, his pale forehead and brilliant eyes and saucy little moustaches seemed to give his quotation a peculiar vividness. Claude envied him. It must be great fun to take up a part and play it to a finish; to believe you were making yourself over, and to admire the kind of fellow you made. He, too, in a way, admired Victor, —though he couldn't altogether believe in him.

"You'll never go back," he said, "I wouldn't worry about that."

"Take it from me, there are thousands who will never go back! I'm not speaking of the casualties. Some of you Americans are likely to discover the world this trip... and it'll make the hell of a lot of difference! You boys never had a fair chance. There's a conspiracy of Church and State to keep you down. I'm going off to play with some girls tonight, will you come along?"

Claude laughed. "I guess not."

"Why not? You won't be caught, I guarantee."

"I guess not." Claude spoke apologetically. "I'm going out to see Fanning after dinner."

Victor shrugged. "That ass!" He beckoned the waiter to open another bottle and bring the coffee. "Well, it's your last chance to go nutting with me." He looked intently at Claude and lifted his glass. "To the future, and our next meeting!" When he put down his empty goblet he remarked, "I got a wire through today; I'm leaving tomorrow."

"For London?"

"For Verdun."

Claude took a quick breath. Verdun... the very sound of the name was grim, like the hollow roll of drums. Victor was going there tomorrow. Here one could take a train for Verdun, or thereabouts, as at home one took a train for Omaha. He felt more "over" than he had done before, and a little crackle of excitement went all through him. He tried to be careless:

"Then you won't get to London soon?"

"God knows," Victor answered gloomily. He looked up at the ceiling and began to whistle softly an engaging air. "Do you know that? It's something Maisie often plays; 'Roses of Picardy.' You won't know what a woman can be till you meet her, Wheeler."

"I hope I'll have that pleasure. I was wondering if you'd forgotten her for the moment. She doesn't object to these diversions?"

Victor lifted his eyebrows in the old haughty way. "Women don't require that sort of fidelity of the air service. Our engagements are too uncertain."

Half an hour later Victor had gone in quest of amorous adventure, and Claude was wandering alone in a brightly lighted street full of soldiers and sailors of all nations. There were black Senegalese, and Highlanders in kilts, and little lorry-drivers from Siam,—all moving slowly along between rows of cabarets and cinema theatres. The wide-spreading branches of the plane trees met overhead, shutting out the sky and roofing in the orange glare. The sidewalks were crowded with chairs and little tables, at which marines and soldiers sat drinking schnapps and cognac and coffee. From every doorway music-machines poured out jazz tunes and strident Sousa marches. The noise was stupefying. Out in the middle of the street a band of bareheaded girls, hardy and tough looking; were following a string of awkward Americans, running into them, elbowing them, asking for treats, crying, "You dance me Fausse-trot, Sammie?"

Claude stationed himself before a movie theatre, where the sign in electric lights read, "Amour, quand tu nous tiens!" and stood watching the people. In the stream that passed him, his eye lit upon two walking arm-in-arm, their hands clasped, talking eagerly and unconscious of the crowd,—different, he saw at once, from all the other strolling, affectionate couples.

The man wore the American uniform; his left arm had been amputated at the elbow, and he carried his head awry, as if he had a stiff neck. His dark, lean face wore an expression of intense anxiety, his eyebrows twitched as if he were in constant pain. The girl, too, looked troubled. As they passed him, under the red light of the Amour sign, Claude could see that her eyes were full of tears. They were wide, blue eyes, innocent looking, and she had the prettiest face he had seen since he landed. From her silk shawl, and little bonnet with blue strings and a white frill, he thought she must be a country girl. As she listened to the soldier, with her mouth half-open, he saw a space between her two front teeth, as with children whose second teeth have just come. While they pushed along in the crowd she looked up intently at the man beside her, or off into the blur of light, where she evidently saw nothing. Her face, young and soft, seemed new to emotion, and her bewildered look made one feel that she did not know where to turn.

Without realizing what he did, Claude followed them out of the crowd into a quiet street, and on into another, even more deserted, where the houses looked as if they had been asleep a long while. Here there were no street lamps, not even a light in the windows, but natural darkness; with the moon high overhead throwing sharp shadows across the white cobble paving. The narrow street made a bend, and he came out upon the church he and his comrades had entered that afternoon. It looked larger by night, and but for the sunken step, he might not have been sure it was the same. The dark neighbouring houses seemed to lean toward it, the moonlight shone silver-grey upon its battered front.

The two walking before him ascended the steps and withdrew into the deep doorway, where they clung together in an embrace so long and still that it was like death. At last they drew shuddering apart. The girl sat down on the stone bench beside the door. The soldier threw himself upon the pavement at her feet, and rested his head on her knee, his one arm lying across her lap.

In the shadow of the houses opposite, Claude kept watch like a sentinel, ready to take their part if any alarm should startle them. The girl bent over her soldier, stroking his head so softly that she might have been putting him to sleep; took his one hand and held it against her bosom as if to stop the pain there. Just behind her, on the sculptured portal, some old bishop, with a pointed cap and a broken crozier, stood, holding up two fingers.

III.

THE NEXT MORNING when Claude arrived at the hospital to see Fanning, he found every one too busy to take account of him. The courtyard was full of ambulances, and a long line of camions waited outside the gate. A train-load of wounded Americans had come in, sent back from evacuation hospitals to await transportation home.

As the men were carried past him, he thought they looked as if they had been sick a long while—looked, indeed, as if they could never get well. The boys who died on board the Anchises had never seemed as sick as these did. Their skin was yellow or purple, their eyes were sunken, their lips sore. Everything that belonged to health had left them, every attribute of youth was gone. One poor fellow, whose face and trunk were wrapped in cotton, never stopped moaning, and as he was carried up the corridor he smelled horribly. The Texas orderly remarked to Claude, "In the beginning that one only had a finger blown off; would you believe it?"

These were the first wounded men Claude had seen. To shed bright blood, to wear the red badge of courage,—that was one thing; but to be reduced to this was quite another. Surely, the sooner these boys died, the better.

The Texan, passing with his next load, asked Claude why he didn't go into the office and wait until the rush was over. Looking in through the glass door, Claude noticed a young man writing at a desk enclosed by a railing. Something about his figure, about the way he held his head, was familiar. When he lifted his left arm to prop open the page of his ledger, it was a stump below the elbow. Yes, there could be no doubt about it; the pale, sharp face, the beak nose, the frowning, uneasy brow. Presently, as if he felt a curious eye upon him, the young man paused in his rapid writing, wriggled his shoulders, put an iron paperweight on the page of his book, took a case from his pocket and shook a cigarette out on the table. Going up to the railing, Claude offered him a cigar. "No, thank you. I don't use them any more. They seem too heavy for me." He struck a match, moved his shoulders again as if they were cramped, and sat down on the edge of his desk.

"Where do these wounded men come from?" Claude asked. "I just got in on the Anchises yesterday."

"They come from various evacuation hospitals. I believe most of them are the Belleau Wood lot."

"Where did you lose your arm?"

"Cantigny. I was in the First Division. I'd been over since last September, waiting for something to happen, and then got fixed in my first engagement."

"Can't you go home?"

"Yes, I could. But I don't want to. I've got used to things over here. I was attached to Headquarters in Paris for awhile."

Claude leaned across the rail. "We read about Cantigny at home, of course. We were a good deal excited; I suppose you were?"

"Yes, we were nervous. We hadn't been under fire, and we'd been fed up on all that stuff about it's taking fifty years to build a fighting machine. The Hun had a strong position; we looked up that long hill and wondered how we were going to behave." As he talked the boy's eyes seemed to be moving all the time, probably because he could not move his head at all. After blowing out deep clouds of smoke until his cigarette was gone, he sat down to his ledger and frowned at the page in a way which said he was too busy to talk.

Claude saw Dr. Trueman standing in the doorway, waiting for him. They made their morning call on Fanning, and left the hospital together. The Doctor turned to him as if he had something on his mind.

"I saw you talking to that wry-necked boy. How did he seem, all right?"

"Not exactly. That is, he seems very nervous. Do you know anything about him?"

"Oh, yes! He's a star patient here, a psychopathic case. I had just been talking to one of the doctors about him, when I came out and saw you with him. He was shot in the neck at Cantigny, where he lost his arm. The wound healed, but his memory is affected; some nerve cut, I suppose, that connects with that part of his brain. This psychopath, Phillips, takes a great interest in him and keeps him here to observe him. He's writing a book about him. He says the fellow has forgotten almost everything about his life before he came to France. The queer thing is, it's his recollection of women that is most affected. He can remember his father, but not his mother; doesn't know if he has sisters or not,—can remember seeing girls about the house, but thinks they may have been cousins. His photographs and belongings were lost when he was hurt, all except a bunch of letters he had in his pocket. They are from a girl he's engaged to, and he declares he can't remember her at all; doesn't know what she looks like or anything about her, and can't remember getting engaged. The doctor has the letters. They seem to be from a nice girl in his own town who is very ambitious for him to make the most of himself. He deserted soon after he was sent to this hospital, ran away. He was found on a farm out in the country here, where the sons had been killed and the people had sort of adopted him. He'd quit his uniform and was wearing the clothes of one of the dead sons. He'd probably have got away with it, if he hadn't had that wry neck. Some one saw him in the fields and recognized him and reported him. I guess nobody cared much but this psychopathic doctor; he wanted to get his pet patient back. They call him 'the lost American' here."

"He seems to be doing some sort of clerical work," Claude observed discreetly.

"Yes, they say he's very well educated. He remembers the books he has read better than his own life. He can't recall what his home town looks like, or his home. And the women are clear wiped out, even the girl he was going to marry."

Claude smiled. "Maybe he's fortunate in that."

The Doctor turned to him affectionately, "Now Claude, don't begin to talk like that the minute you land in this country."

Claude walked on past the church of St. Jacques. Last night already seemed like a dream, but it haunted him. He wished he could do something to help that boy; help him get away from the doctor who was writing a book about him, and the girl who wanted him to make the most of himself; get away and be lost altogether in what he had been lucky enough to find. All day, as Claude came and went, he looked among the crowds for that young face, so compassionate and tender.

IV.

Deeper and deeper into flowery France! That was the sentence Claude kept saying over to himself to the jolt of the wheels, as the long troop train went southward, on the second day after he and his company had left the port of debarkation. Fields of wheat, fields of oats, fields of rye; all the low hills and rolling uplands clad with harvest. And everywhere, in the grass, in the yellowing grain, along the road-bed, the poppies spilling and streaming. On the second day the boys were still calling to each other about the poppies; nothing else had so entirely surpassed their expectations. They had supposed that poppies grew only on battle fields, or in the brains of war correspondents. Nobody knew what the cornflowers were, except Willy Katz, an Austrian boy from the Omaha packing-houses, and he knew only an objectionable name for them, so he offered no information. For a long time they thought the red clover blossoms were wild flowers,—they were as big as wild roses. When they passed the first alfalfa field, the whole train rang with laughter; alfalfa was one thing, they believed, that had never been heard of outside their own prairie states.

All the way down, Company B had been finding the old things instead of the new,—or, to their way of thinking, the new things instead of the old. The thatched roofs they had so counted upon seeing were few and far between. But American binders, of well-known makes, stood where the fields were beginning to ripen,—and they were being oiled and put in order, not by "peasants," but by wise-looking old farmers who seemed to know their business. Pear trees, trained like vines against the wall, did not astonish them half so much as the sight of the familiar cottonwood, growing everywhere. Claude thought he had never before realized how beautiful this tree could be. In verdant little valleys, along the clear rivers, the cottonwoods waved and rustled; and on the little islands, of which there were so many in these rivers, they stood in pointed masses, seemed to grip deep into the soil and to rest easy, as if they had been there for ever and would be there for ever more. At home, all about Frankfort, the farmers were cutting down their cottonwoods because they were "common," planting maples and ash trees to struggle along in their stead. Never mind; the cottonwoods were good enough for France, and they were good enough for him! He felt they were a real bond between him and this people.

When B Company had first got their orders to go into a training camp in north central France, all the men were disappointed. Troops much rawer than they were being rushed to the front, so why fool around any longer? But now they were reconciled to the delay. There seemed to be a good deal of France that wasn't the war, and they wouldn't mind travelling about a little in a country like this. Was the harvest always a month later than at home, as it seemed to be this year? Why did the farmers have rows of trees growing along the edges of every field—didn't they take the strength out of the soil? What did the farmers mean by raising patches of mustard right along beside other crops? Didn't they know that mustard got into wheat fields and strangled the grain?

The second night the boys were to spend in Rouen, and they would have the following day to look about. Everybody knew what had happened at Rouen—if any one didn't, his neighbours were only too eager to inform him! It had happened in the market-place, and the market-place was what they were going to find.

Tomorrow, when it came, proved to be black and cold, a day of pouring rain. As they filed through the narrow, crowded streets, that harsh Norman city presented no very cheering aspect. They were glad, at last, to find the waterside, to go out on the bridge and breathe the air in the great open space over the river, away from the clatter of cart-wheels and the hard voices and crafty faces of these townspeople, who seemed rough and unfriendly. From the bridge they looked up at the white chalk hills, the tops a blur of intense green under the low, lead-coloured sky. They watched the fleets of broad, deep-set river barges, coming and going under their feet, with tilted smokestacks. Only a little way up that river was Paris, the place where every doughboy meant to go; and as they leaned on the rail and looked down at the slow-flowing water, each one had in his mind a confused picture of what it would be like. The Seine, they felt sure, must be very much wider there, and it was spanned by many bridges, all longer than the bridge over the Missouri at Omaha. There would be spires and golden domes past counting, all the buildings higher than anything in Chicago, and brilliant —dazzlingly brilliant, nothing grey and shabby about it like this old Rouen. They attributed to the city of their desire incalculable immensity, bewildering vastness, Babylonian hugeness and heaviness—the only attributes they had been taught to admire.

Late in the morning Claude found himself alone before the Church of St. Ouen. He was hunting for the Cathedral, and this looked as if it might be the right place. He shook the water from his raincoat and entered, removing his hat at the door. The day, so dark without, was darker still within;... far away, a few scattered candles, still little points of light... just before him, in the grey twilight, slender white columns in long rows, like the stems of silver poplars.

The entrance to the nave was closed by a cord, so he walked up the aisle on the right, treading softly, passing chapels where solitary women knelt in the light of a few tapers. Except for them, the church was empty... empty. His own breathing was audible in this silence. He moved with caution lest he should wake an echo.

When he reached the choir he turned, and saw, far behind him, the rose window, with its purple heart. As he stood staring, hat in hand, as still as the stone figures in the chapels, a great bell, up aloft, began to strike the hour in its deep, melodious throat; eleven beats, measured and far apart, as rich as the colours in the window, then silence... only in his memory the throbbing of an undreamed-of quality of sound. The revelations of the glass and the bell had come almost simultaneously, as if one produced the other; and both were superlatives toward which his mind had always been groping,—or so it seemed to him then.

In front of the choir the nave was open, with no rope to shut it off. Several straw chairs were huddled on a flag of the stone floor. After some hesitation he took one, turned it round, and sat down facing the window. If some one should come up to him and say anything, anything at all, he would rise and say, "Pardon, Monsieur; je ne sais pas c'est defendu." He repeated this to himself to be quite sure he had it ready.

On the train, coming down, he had talked to the boys about the bad reputation Americans had acquired for slouching all over the place and butting in on things, and had urged them to tread lightly, "But Lieutenant," the kid from Pleasantville had piped up, "isn't this whole Expedition a butt-in? After all, it ain't our war." Claude laughed, but he told him he meant to make an example of the fellow who went to rough-housing.

He was well satisfied that he hadn't his restless companions on his mind now. He could sit here quietly until noon, and hear the bell strike again. In the meantime, he must try to think: This was, of course, Gothic architecture; he had read more or less about that, and ought to be able to remember something. Gothic… that was a mere word; to him it suggested something very peaked and pointed,—sharp arches, steep roofs. It had nothing to do with these slim white columns that rose so straight and far,—or with the window, burning up there in its vault of gloom….

While he was vainly trying to think about architecture, some recollection of old astronomy lessons brushed across his brain,—something about stars whose light travels through space for hundreds of years before it reaches the earth and the human eye. The purple and crimson and peacock-green of this window had been shining quite as long as that before it got to him…. He felt distinctly that it went through him and farther still… as if his mother were looking over his shoulder. He sat solemnly through the hour until twelve, his elbows on his knees, his conical hat swinging between them in his hand, looking up through the twilight with candid, thoughtful eyes.

When Claude joined his company at the station, they had the laugh on him. They had found the Cathedral,—and a statue of Richard the Lion-hearted, over the spot where the lion-heart itself was buried; "the identical organ," fat Sergeant Hicks assured him. But they were all glad to leave Rouen.

V.

B COMPANY REACHED the training camp at S— thirty-six men short: twenty-five they had buried on the voyage over, and eleven sick were left at the base hospital. The company was to be attached to a battalion which had already seen service, commanded by Lieutenant Colonel Scott. Arriving early in the morning, the officers reported at once to Headquarters. Captain Maxey must have suffered a shock when the Colonel rose from his desk to acknowledge his salute, then shook hands with them all around and asked them about their journey. The Colonel was not a very martial figure; short, fat, with slouching shoulders, and a lumpy back like a sack of potatoes. Though he wasn't much over forty, he was bald, and his collar would easily slip over his head without being unbuttoned. His little twinkling eyes and good-humoured face were without a particle of arrogance or official dignity.

Years ago, when General Pershing, then a handsome young Lieutenant with a slender waist and yellow moustaches, was stationed as Commandant at the University of Nebraska, Walter Scott was an officer in a company of cadets the Lieutenant took about to military tournaments. The Pershing Rifles, they were called, and they won prizes wherever they went. After his graduation, Scott settled down to running a hardware business in a thriving Nebraska town, and sold gas ranges and garden hose for twenty years. About the time Pershing was sent to the Mexican border, Scott began to think there might eventually be something in the wind, and that he would better get into training. He went down to Texas with the National Guard. He had come to France with the First Division, and had won his promotions by solid, soldierly qualities.

"I see you're an officer short, Captain Maxey," the Colonel remarked at their conference. "I think I've got a man here to take his place. Lieutenant Gerhardt is a New York man, came over in the band and got transferred to infantry. He has lately been given a commission for good service. He's had some experience and is a capable fellow." The Colonel sent his orderly out to bring in a young man whom he introduced to the officers as Lieutenant David Gerhardt.

Claude had been ashamed of Tod Fanning, who was always showing himself a sap-head, and who would never have got a commission if his uncle hadn't been a Congressman. But the moment he met Lieutenant Gerhardt's eye, something like jealousy flamed up in him. He felt in a flash that he suffered by comparison with the new officer; that he must be on his guard and must not let himself be patronized.

As they were leaving the Colonel's office together, Gerhardt asked him whether he had got his billet. Claude replied that after the men were in their quarters, he would look out for something for himself.

The young man smiled. "I'm afraid you may have difficulty. The people about here have been overworked, keeping soldiers, and they are not willing as they once were. I'm with a nice old couple over in the village. I'm almost sure I can get you in there. If you'll come along, we'll speak to them, before some one else is put off on them."

Claude didn't want to go, didn't want to accept favours,—nevertheless he went. They walked together along a dusty road that ran between half-ripe wheat fields, bordered with poplar trees. The wild morning-glories and Queen Anne's lace that grew by the road-side were still shining with dew. A fresh breeze stirred the bearded grain, parting it in furrows and fanning out streaks of crimson poppies. The new officer was not intrusive, certainly. He walked along, whistling softly to himself, seeming quite lost in the freshness of the morning, or in his own thoughts. There had been nothing patronizing in his manner so far, and Claude began to wonder why he felt ill at ease with him. Perhaps it was because he did not look like the rest of them. Though he was young, he did not look boyish. He seemed experienced; a finished product, rather than something on the way. He was handsome, and his face, like his manner and his walk, had something distinguished about it. A broad white forehead under reddish brown hair, hazel eyes with no uncertainty in their look, an aquiline nose, finely cut, —a sensitive, scornful mouth, which somehow did not detract from the kindly, though slightly reserved, expression of his face.

Lieutenant Gerhardt must have been in this neighbourhood for some time; he seemed to know the people. On the road they passed several villagers; a rough looking girl taking a cow out to graze, an old man with a basket on his arm, the postman on his bicycle; they all spoke to Claude's companion as if they knew him well.

"What are these blue flowers that grow about everywhere?" Claude asked suddenly, pointing to a clump with his foot.

"Cornflowers," said the other. "The Germans call them Kaiser-blumen."

They were approaching the village, which lay on the edge of a wood,—a wood so large one could not see the end of it; it met the horizon with a ridge of pines. The village was but a single street. On either side ran clay-coloured walls, with painted wooden doors here and there, and green shutters. Claude's guide opened one of these gates, and they walked into a little sanded garden; the house was built round it on three sides. Under a cherry tree sat a woman in a black dress, sewing, a work table beside her.

She was fifty, perhaps, but though her hair was grey she had a look of youthfulness; thin cheeks, delicately flushed with pink, and quiet, smiling, intelligent eyes. Claude thought she looked like a New England woman,—like the photographs of his mother's cousins and schoolmates. Lieutenant Gerhardt introduced him to Madame Joubert. He was quite disheartened by the colloquy that followed. Clearly his new fellow officer spoke Madame Joubert's perplexing language as readily as she herself did, and he felt irritated and grudging as he listened. He had been hoping that, wherever he stayed, he could learn to talk to the people a little; but with this accomplished young man about, he would never have the courage to try. He could see that Mme. Joubert liked Gerhardt, liked him very much; and all this, for some reason, discouraged him.

Gerhardt turned to Claude, speaking in a way which included Madame Joubert in the conversation, though she could not understand it: "Madame Joubert will let you come, although she has done her part and really doesn't have to take any one else in. But you will be so well off here that I'm glad she consents. You will have to share my room, but there are two beds. She will show you."

Gerhardt went out of the gate and left him alone with his hostess. Her mind seemed to read his thoughts. When he uttered a word, or any sound that resembled one, she quickly and smoothly made a sentence of it, as if she were quite accustomed to talking in this way and expected only monosyllables from strangers. She was kind, even a little playful with him; but he felt it was all good manners, and that underneath she was not thinking of him at all. When he was alone in the tile-floored sleeping room upstairs, unrolling his blankets and arranging his shaving things, he looked out of the window and watched her where she sat sewing under the cherry tree. She had a very sad face, he thought; it wasn't grief, nothing sharp and definite like sorrow. It was an old, quiet, impersonal sadness,—sweet in its expression, like the sadness of music.

As he came out of the house to start back to the barracks, he bowed to her and tried to say, "Au revoir, Madame. Jusq' au ce soir." He stopped near the kitchen door to look at a many-branched rose vine that ran all over the wall, full of cream-coloured, pink-tipped roses, just a shade stronger in colour than the clay wall behind them. Madame Joubert came over and stood beside him, looking at him and at the rosier, "Oui, c'est joli, n'est-ce pas?" She took the scissors that hung by a ribbon from her belt, cut one of the flowers and stuck it in his buttonhole. "Voilà." She made a little flourish with her thin hand.

Stepping into the street, he turned to shut the wooden door after him, and heard a soft stir in the dark tool-house at his elbow. From among the rakes and spades a child's frightened face was staring out at him. She was sitting on the ground with her lap full of baby kittens. He caught but a glimpse of her dull, pale face.

VI.

THE NEXT MORNING Claude awoke with such a sense of physical well-being as he had not had for a long time. The sun was shining brightly on the white plaster walls and on the red tiles of the floor. Green jalousies, half-drawn, shaded the upper part of the two windows. Through their slats, he could see the forking branches of an old locust tree that grew by the gate. A flock of pigeons flew over it, dipping and mounting with a sharp twinkle of silver wings. It was good to lie again in a house that was cared for by women. He must have felt that even in his sleep, for when he opened his eyes he was thinking about Mahailey and breakfast and summer mornings on the farm. The early stillness was sweet, and the feeling of dry, clean linen against his body. There was a smell of lavender about his warm pillow. He lay still for fear of waking Lieutenant Gerhardt. This was the sort of peace one wanted to enjoy alone. When he rose cautiously on his elbow and looked at the other bed, it was empty. His companion must have dressed and slipped out when day first broke. Somebody else who liked to enjoy things alone; that looked hopeful. But now that he had the place to himself, he decided to get up. While he was dressing he could see old M. Joubert down in the garden, watering the plants and vines, raking the sand fresh and smooth, clipping off dead leaves and withered flowers and throwing them into a wheelbarrow. These people had lost both their sons in the war, he had been told, and now they were taking care of the property for their grandchildren,—two daughters of the elder son. Claude saw Gerhardt come into the garden, and sit down at the table under the trees, where they had their dinner last night. He hurried down to join him. Gerhardt made room for him on the bench.

"Do you always sleep like that? It's an accomplishment. I made enough noise when I dressed,—kept dropping things, but it never reached you."

Madame Joubert came out of the kitchen in a purple flowered morning gown, her hair in curl-papers under a lace cap. She brought the coffee herself, and they sat down at the unpainted table without a cloth, and drank it out of big crockery bowls. They had fresh milk with it,—the first Claude had tasted in a long while, and sugar which Gerhardt produced from his pocket. The old cook had her coffee sitting in the kitchen door, and on the step, at her feet, sat the strange, pale little girl.

Madame Joubert amiably addressed herself to Claude; she knew that Americans were accustomed to a different sort of morning repast, and if he wished to bring bacon from the camp, she would gladly cook it for him. She had even made pancakes for officers who stayed there before. She seemed pleased, however, to learn that Claude had had enough of these things for awhile. She called David by his first name, pronouncing it the French way, and when Claude said he hoped she would do as much for him, she said, Oh, yes, that his was a very good French name, "mais un peu, un peu… romanesque," at which he blushed, not quite knowing whether she were making fun of him or not.

"It is rather so in English, isn't it?" David asked.

"Well, it's a sissy name, if you mean that."

"Yes, it is, a little," David admitted candidly. The day's work on the parade ground was hard, and Captain Maxey's men were soft, felt the heat,—didn't size up well with the Kansas boys who had been hardened by service. The Colonel wasn't pleased with B Company and detailed them to build new barracks and extend the sanitation system. Claude got out and worked with the men. Gerhardt followed his example, but it was easy to see that he had never handled lumber or tin-roofing before. A kind of rivalry seemed to have sprung up between him and Claude, neither of them knew why.

Claude could see that the sergeants and corporals were a little uncertain about Gerhardt. His laconic speech, never embroidered by the picturesque slang they relished, his gravity, and his rare, incredulous smile, alike puzzled them. Was the new officer a dude? Sergeant Hicks asked of his chum, Dell Able. No, he wasn't a dude. Was he a swellhead? No, not at all; but he wasn't a good mixer. He was "an Easterner"; what more he was would develop later. Claude sensed something unusual about him. He suspected that Gerhardt knew a good many things as well as he knew French, and that he tried to conceal it, as people sometimes do when they feel they are not among their equals; this idea nettled him. It was Claude who seized the opportunity to be patronizing, when Gerhardt betrayed that he was utterly unable to select lumber by given measurements.

The next afternoon, work on the new barracks was called off because of rain. Sergeant Hicks set about getting up a boxing match, but when he went to invite the lieutenants, they had both disappeared. Claude was tramping toward the village, determined to get into the big wood that had tempted him ever since his arrival.

The highroad became the village street, and then, at the edge of the wood, became a country road again. A little farther on, where the shade grew denser, it split up into three wagon trails, two of them faint and little used. One of these Claude followed. The rain had dwindled to a steady patter, but the tall brakes growing up in the path splashed him to the middle, and his feet sank in spongy, mossy earth. The light about him, the very air, was green. The trunks of the trees were overgrown with a soft green moss, like mould. He was wondering whether this forest was not always a damp, gloomy place, when suddenly the sun broke through and shattered the whole wood with gold. He had never seen anything like the quivering emerald of the moss, the silky green of the dripping beech tops. Everything woke up; rabbits ran across the path, birds began to sing, and all at once the brakes were full of whirring insects.

The winding path turned again, and came out abruptly on a hillside, above an open glade piled with grey boulders. On the opposite rise of ground stood a grove of pines, with bare, red stems. The light, around and under them, was red like a rosy sunset. Nearly all the stems divided about half-way up into two great arms, which came together again at the top, like the pictures of old Grecian lyres.

Down in the grassy glade, among the piles of flint boulders, little white birches shook out their shining leaves in the lightly moving air. All about the rocks were patches of purple heath; it ran up into the crevices between them like fire. On one of these bald rocks sat Lieutenant Gerhardt, hatless, in an attitude of fatigue or of deep dejection, his hands clasped about his knees, his bronze hair ruddy in the sun. After watching him for a few minutes, Claude descended the slope, swishing the tall ferns.

"Will I be in the way?" he asked as he stopped at the foot of the rocks.

"Oh, no!" said the other, moving a little and unclasping his hand.

Claude sat down on a boulder. "Is this heather?" he asked. "I thought I recognized it, from 'Kidnapped.' This part of the world is not as new to you as it is to me."

"No. I lived in Paris for several years when I was a student."

"What were you studying?"

"The violin."

"You are a musician?" Claude looked at him wonderingly.

"I was," replied the other with a disdainful smile, languidly stretching out his legs in the heather.

"That seems too bad," Claude remarked gravely.

"What does?"

"Why, to take fellows with a special talent. There are enough of us who haven't any."

Gerhardt rolled over on his back and put his hands under his head. "Oh, this affair is too big for exceptions; it's universal. If you happened to be born twenty-six years ago, you couldn't escape. If this war didn't kill you in one way, it would in another." He told Claude he had trained at Camp Dix, and had come over eight months ago in a regimental band, but he hated the work he had to do and got transferred to the infantry.

When they retraced their steps, the wood was full of green twilight. Their relations had changed somewhat during the last half hour, and they strolled in confidential silence up the home like street to the door of their own garden.

Since the rain was over, Madame Joubert had laid the cloth on the plank table under the cherry tree, as on the previous evenings. Monsieur was bringing the chairs, and the little girl was carrying out a pile of heavy plates. She rested them against her stomach and leaned back as she walked, to balance them. She wore shoes, but no stockings, and her faded cotton dress switched about her brown legs. She was a little Belgian refugee who had been sent there with her mother. The mother was dead now, and the child would not even go to visit her grave. She could not be coaxed from the court-yard into the quiet street. If the neighbour children came into the garden on an errand, she hid herself. She would have no playmates but the cat; and now she had the kittens in the tool house.

Dinner was very cheerful that evening. M. Joubert was pleased that the storm had not lasted long enough to hurt the wheat. The garden was fresh and bright after the rain. The cherry tree shook down bright drops on the tablecloth when the breeze stirred. The mother cat dozed on the red cushion in Madame Joubert's sewing chair, and the pigeons fluttered down to snap up earthworms that wriggled in the wet sand. The shadow of the house fell over the dinner-table, but the tree-tops stood up in full sunlight, and the yellow sun poured on the earth wall and the cream-coloured roses. Their petals, ruffled by the rain, gave out a wet, spicy smell.

M. Joubert must have been ten years older than his wife. There was a great contentment in his manner and a pleasant sparkle in his eye. He liked the young officers. Gerhardt had been there more than two weeks, and somewhat relieved the stillness that had settled over the house since the second son died in hospital. The Jouberts had dropped out of things. They had done all they could do, given all they had, and now they had nothing to look forward to,—except the event to which all France looked forward. The father was talking to Gerhardt about the great sea-port the Americans were making of Bordeaux; he said he meant to go there after the war, to see it all for himself.

Madame Joubert was pleased to hear that they had been walking in the wood. And was the heather in bloom? She wished they had brought her some. Next time they went, perhaps. She used to walk there often. Her eyes seemed to come nearer to them, Claude thought, when she spoke of it, and she evidently cared a great deal more about what was blooming in the wood than about what the Americans were doing on the Garonne. He wished he could talk to her as Gerhardt did. He admired the way she roused herself and tried to interest them, speaking her difficult language with such spirit and precision. It was a language that couldn't be mumbled; that had to be spoken with energy and fire, or not spoken at all. Merely speaking that exacting tongue would help to rally a broken spirit, he thought.

The little maid who served them moved about noiselessly. Her dull eyes never seemed to look; yet she saw when it was time to bring the heavy soup tureen, and when it was time to take it away. Madame Joubert had found that Claude liked his potatoes with his meat—when there was meat—and not in a course by themselves. She had each time to tell the little girl to go and fetch them. This the child did with manifest reluctance,—sullenly, as if she were being forced to do something wrong. She was a very strange little creature, altogether. As the two soldiers left the table and started for the camp, Claude reached down into the tool house and took up one of the kittens, holding it out in the light to see it blink its eyes. The little girl, just coming out of the kitchen, uttered a shrill scream, a really terrible scream, and squatted down, covering her face with her hands. Madame Joubert came out to chide her.

"What is the matter with that child?" Claude asked as they hurried out of the gate. "Do you suppose she was hurt, or abused in some way?"

"Terrorized. She often screams like that at night. Haven't you heard her? They have to go and wake her, to stop it. She doesn't speak any French; only Walloon. And she can't or won't learn, so they can't tell what goes on in her poor little head."

In the two weeks of intensive training that followed, Claude marvelled at Gerhardt's spirit and endurance. The muscular strain of mimic trench operations was more of a tax on him than on any of the other officers. He was as tall as Claude, but he weighed only a hundred and forty-six pounds, and he had not been roughly bred like most of the others. When his fellow officers learned that he was a violinist by profession, that he could have had a soft job as interpreter or as an organizer of camp entertainments, they no longer resented his reserve or his occasional superciliousness. They respected a man who could have wriggled out and didn't.

VII.

ON THE MARCH AT LAST; through a brilliant August day Colonel Scott's battalion was streaming along one of the dusty, well-worn roads east of the Somme, their railway base well behind them. The way led through rolling country; fields, hills, woods, little villages shattered but still habitable, where the people came out to watch the soldiers go by.

The Americans went through every village in march step, colours flying, the band playing, "to show that the morale was high," as the officers said. Claude trudged on the outside of the column,—now at the front of his company, now at the rear,—wearing a stoical countenance, afraid of betraying his satisfaction in the men, the weather, the country.

They were bound for the big show, and on every hand were reassuring signs: long lines of gaunt, dead trees, charred and torn; big holes gashed out in fields and hillsides, already half concealed by new undergrowth; winding depressions in the earth, bodies of wrecked motor-trucks and automobiles lying along the road, and everywhere endless straggling lines of rusty barbed-wire, that seemed to have been put there by chance,—with no purpose at all.

"Begins to look like we're getting in, Lieutenant," said Sergeant Hicks, smiling behind his salute.

Claude nodded and passed forward.

"Well, we can't arrive any too soon for us, boys?" The Sergeant looked over his shoulder, and they grinned, their teeth flashing white in their red, perspiring faces. Claude didn't wonder that everybody along the route, even the babies, came out to see them; he thought they were the finest sight in the world. This was the first day they had worn their tin hats; Gerhardt had shown them how to stuff grass and leaves inside to keep their heads cool. When they fell into fours, and the band struck up as they approached a town, Bert Fuller, the boy from Pleasantville on the Platte, who had blubbered on the voyage over, was guide right, and whenever Claude passed him his face seemed to say, "You won't get anything on me in a hurry, Lieutenant!"

They made camp early in the afternoon, on a hill covered with half-burned pines. Claude took Bert and Dell Able and Oscar the Swede, and set off to make a survey and report the terrain.

Behind the hill, under the burned edge of the wood, they found an abandoned farmhouse and what seemed to be a clean well.

It had a solid stone curb about it, and a wooden bucket hanging by a rusty wire. When the boys splashed the bucket about, the water sent up a pure, cool breath. But they were wise boys, and knew where dead Prussians most loved to hide. Even the straw in the stable they regarded with suspicion, and thought it would be just as well not to bed anybody there.

Swinging on to the right to make their circuit, they got into mud; a low field where the drain ditches had been neglected and had overflowed. There they came upon a pitiful group of humanity, bemired. A woman, ill and wretched looking, sat on a fallen log at the end of the marsh, a baby in her lap and three children hanging about her. She was far gone in consumption; one had only to listen to her breathing and to look at her white, perspiring face to feel how weak she was. Draggled, mud to the knees, she was trying to nurse her baby, half hidden under an old black shawl. She didn't look like a tramp woman, but like one who had once been able to take proper care of herself, and she was still young. The children were tired and discouraged. One little boy wore a clumsy blue jacket, made from a French army coat. The other wore a battered American Stetson that came down over his ears. He carried, in his two arms, a pink celluloid clock. They all looked up and waited for the soldiers to do something.

Claude approached the woman, and touching the rim of his helmet, began: "Bonjour, Madame. Qu'est que c'est?"

She tried to speak, but went off into a spasm of coughing, only able to gasp, "'Toinette, 'Toinette!"

'Toinette stepped quickly forward. She was about eleven, and seemed to be the captain of the party. A bold, hard little face with a long chin, straight black hair tied with rags, uneasy, crafty eyes; she looked much less gentle and more experienced than her mother. She began to explain, and she was very clever at making herself understood. She was used to talking to foreign soldiers,—spoke slowly, with emphasis and ingenious gestures.

She, too, had been reconnoitering. She had discovered the empty farmhouse and was trying to get her party there for the night. How did they come here? Oh, they were refugees. They had been staying with people thirty kilometers from here. They were trying to get back to their own village. Her mother was very sick, presque morte and she wanted to go home to die. They had heard people were still living there; an old aunt was living in their own cellar, —and so could they if they once got there. The point was, and she made it over and over, that her mother wished to die chez elle, comprenez-vous? They had no papers, and the French soldiers would never let them pass, but now that the Americans were here they hoped to get through; the Americans were said to be toujours gentils.

While she talked in her shrill, clicking voice, the baby began to howl, dissatisfied with its nourishment. The little girl shrugged. "Il est toujours en colère," she muttered. The woman turned it around with difficulty—it seemed a big, heavy baby, but white and sickly—and gave it the other breast. It began sucking her noisily, rooting and sputtering as if it were famished. It was too painful, it was almost indecent, to see this exhausted woman trying to feed her baby. Claude beckoned his men away to one side, and taking the little girl by the hand drew her after them.

"Il faut que votre mère—se reposer," he told her, with the grave caesural pause which he always made in the middle of a French sentence. She understood him. No distortion of her native tongue surprised or perplexed her. She was accustomed to being addressed in all persons, numbers, genders, tenses; by Germans, English, Americans. She only listened to hear whether the voice was kind, and with men in this uniform it usually was kind.

Had they anything to eat? "Vous avez quelque chose à manger?"

"Rien. Rien du tout."

Wasn't her mother "trop malade à marcher?"

She shrugged; Monsieur could see for himself.

And her father?

He was dead; "mort à la Marne, en quatorze."

"At the Marne?" Claude repeated, glancing in perplexity at the nursing baby. Her sharp eyes followed his, and she instantly divined his doubt. "The baby?" she said quickly. "Oh, the baby is not my brother, he is a Boche."

For a moment Claude did not understand. She repeated her explanation impatiently, something disdainful and sinister in her metallic little voice. A slow blush mounted to his forehead.

He pushed her toward her mother, "Attendez là."

"I guess we'll have to get them over to that farmhouse," he told the men. He repeated what he had got of the child's story. When he came to her laconic statement about the baby, they looked at each other. Bert Fuller was afraid he might cry again, so he kept muttering, "By God, if we'd a-got here sooner, by God if we had!" as they ran back along the ditch.

Dell and Oscar made a chair of their crossed hands and carried the woman, she was no great weight. Bert picked up the little boy with the pink clock; "Come along, little frog, your legs ain't long enough."

Claude walked behind, holding the screaming baby stiffly in his arms. How was it possible for a baby to have such definite personality, he asked himself, and how was it possible to dislike a baby so much? He hated it for its square, tow-thatched head and bloodless ears, and carried it with loathing... no wonder it cried! When it got nothing by screaming and stiffening, however, it suddenly grew quiet; regarded him with pale blue eyes, and tried to make itself comfortable against his khaki coat. It put out a grimy little fist and took hold of one of his buttons. "Kamerad, eh?" he muttered, glaring at the infant. "Cut it out!"

Before they had their own supper that night, the boys carried hot food and blankets down to their family.

VIII.

FOUR O'CLOCK... a summer dawn... his first morning in the trenches.

Claude had just been along the line to see that the gun teams were in position. This hour, when the light was changing, was a favourite time for attack. He had come in late last night, and had everything to learn. Mounting the firestep, he peeped over the parapet between the sandbags, into the low, twisting mist. Just then he could see nothing but the wire entanglement, with birds hopping along the top wire, singing and chirping as they did on the wire fences at home. Clear and flute-like they sounded in the heavy air,—and they were the only sounds. A little breeze came up, slowly clearing the mist away. Streaks of green showed through the moving banks of vapour. The birds became more agitated. That dull stretch of grey and green was No Man's Land. Those low, zigzag mounds, like giant molehills protected by wire hurdles, were the Hun trenches; five or six lines of them. He could easily follow the communication trenches without a glass. At one point their front line could not be more than eighty yards away, at another it must be all of three hundred. Here and there thin columns of smoke began to rise; the Hun was getting breakfast; everything was comfortable and natural. Behind the enemy's position the country rose gradually for several miles, with ravines and little woods, where, according to his map, they had masked artillery. Back on the hills were ruined farmhouses and broken trees, but nowhere a living creature in sight. It was a dead, nerveless countryside, sunk in quiet and dejection. Yet everywhere the ground was full of men. Their own trenches, from the other side, must look quite as dead. Life was a secret, these days.

It was amazing how simply things could be done. His battalion had marched in quietly at midnight, and the line they came to relieve had set out as silently for the rear. It all took place in utter darkness. Just as B Company slid down an incline into the shallow rear trenches, the country was lit for a moment by two star shells, there was a rattling of machine guns, German Maxims,—a sporadic crackle that was not followed up. Filing along the communication trenches, they listened anxiously; artillery fire would have made it bad for the other men who were marching to the rear. But nothing happened. They had a quiet night, and this morning, here they were!

The sky flamed up saffron and silver. Claude looked at his watch, but he could not bear to go just yet. How long it took a Wheeler to get round to anything! Four years on the way; now that he was here, he would enjoy the scenery a bit, he guessed. He wished his mother could know how he felt this morning. But perhaps she did know. At any rate, she would not have him anywhere else. Five years ago, when he was sitting on the steps of the Denver State House and knew that nothing unexpected could ever happen to him… suppose he could have seen, in a flash, where he would be today? He cast a long look at the reddening, lengthening landscape, and dropped down on the duckboard.

Claude made his way back to the dugout into which he and Gerhardt had thrown their effects last night. The former occupants had left it clean. There were two bunks nailed against the side walls,—wooden frames with wire netting over them, covered with dry sandbags. Between the two bunks was a soap-box table, with a candle stuck in a green bottle, an alcohol stove, a bainmarie, and two tin cups. On the wall were coloured pictures from Jugend, taken out of some Hun trench.

He found Gerhardt still asleep on his bed, and shook him until he sat up.

"How long have you been out, Claude? Didn't you sleep?"

"A little. I wasn't very tired. I suppose we could heat shaving water on this stove; they've left us half a bottle of alcohol. It's quite a comfortable little hole, isn't it?"

"It will doubtless serve its purpose," David remarked dryly. "So sensitive to any criticism of this war! Why, it's not your affair; you've only just arrived."

"I know," Claude replied meekly, as he began to fold his blankets. "But it's likely the only one I'll ever be in, so I may as well take an interest."

THE NEXT AFTERNOON four young men, all more or less naked, were busy about a shell-hole full of opaque brown water. Sergeant Hicks and his chum, Dell Able, had hunted through half the blazing hot morning to find a hole not too scummy, conveniently, and even picturesquely situated, and had reported it to the Lieutenants. Captain Maxey, Hicks said, could send his own orderly to find his own shell-hole, and could take his bath in private. "He'd never wash himself with anybody else," the Sergeant added. "Afraid of exposing his dignity!"

Bruger and Hammond, the two second Lieutenants, were already out of their bath, and reclined on what might almost be termed a grassy slope, examining various portions of their body with interest. They hadn't had all their clothes off for some time, and four days of marching in hot weather made a man anxious to look at himself.

"You wait till winter," Gerhardt told them. He was still splashing in the hole, up to his armpits in muddy water. "You won't get a wash once in three months then. Some of the Tommies told me that when they got their first bath after Vimy, their skins peeled off like a snake's. What are you doing with my trousers, Bruger?"

"Hunting for your knife. I dropped mine yesterday, when that shell exploded in the cut-off. I darned near dropped my old nut!"

"Shucks, that wasn't anything. Don't keep blowing about it—shows you're a greenhorn."

Claude stripped off his shirt and slid into the pool beside Gerhardt. "Gee, I hit something sharp down there! Why didn't you fellows pull out the splinters?"

He shut his eyes, disappeared for a moment, and came up sputtering, throwing on the ground a round metal object, coated with rust and full of slime. "German helmet, isn't it? Phew!" He wiped his face and looked about suspiciously.

"Phew is right!" Bruger turned the object over with a stick. "Why in hell didn't you bring up the rest of him? You've spoiled my bath. I hope you enjoy it."

Gerhardt scrambled up the side. "Get out, Wheeler! Look at that," he pointed to big sleepy bubbles, bursting up through the thick water. "You've stirred up trouble, all right! Something's going very bad down there."

Claude got out after him, looking back at the activity in the water. "I don't see how pulling out one helmet could stir the bottom up so. I should think the water would keep the smell down."

"Ever study chemistry?" Bruger asked scornfully. "You just opened up a graveyard, and now we get the exhaust. If you swallowed any of that German cologne—Oh, you should worry!"

Lieutenant Hammond, still barelegged, with his shirt tied over his shoulders, was scratching in his notebook. Before they left he put up a placard on a split stick.

No Public Bathing!! Private Beach
C. Wheeler, Co. B. 2-th Inf'ty.

THE FIRST LETTERS FROM HOME! The supply wagons brought them up, and every man in the Company got something except Ed Drier, a farm-hand from the Nebraska sand hills, and Willy Katz, the tow-headed Austrian boy from the South Omaha packing-houses. Their comrades were sorry for them. Ed didn't have any "folks" of his own, but he had expected letters all the same. Willy was sure his mother must have written. When the last ragged envelope was given out and he turned away empty-handed, he murmured, "She's Bohunk, and she don't write so good. I guess the address wasn't plain, and some fellow in another comp'ny has got my letter."

No second class matter was sent up,—the boys had hoped for newspapers from home to give them a little war news, since they never got any here. Dell Able's sister, however, had enclosed a clipping from the Kansas City Star; a long account by one of the British war correspondents in Mesopotamia, describing the hardships the soldiers suffered there; dysentery, flies, mosquitoes, unimaginable heat. He read this article aloud to a group of his friends as they sat about a shell-hole pool where they had been washing their socks. He had just finished the story of how the Tommies had found a few mud huts at the place where the original Garden of Eden was said to have been,—a desolate spot full of stinging insects—when Oscar Petersen, a very religious Swedish boy who was often silent for days together, opened his mouth and said scornfully,

"That's a lie!"

Dell looked up at him, annoyed by the interruption. "How do you know it is?"

"Because; the Lord put four cherubims with swords to guard the Garden, and there ain't no man going to find it. It ain't intended they should. The Bible says so."

Hicks began to laugh. "Why, that was about six thousand years ago, you cheese! Do you suppose your cherubims are still there?"

"'Course they are. What's a thousand years to a cherubim? Nothin'!"

The Swede rose and sullenly gathered up his socks.

Dell Able looked at his chum. "Ain't he the complete bonehead? Solid ivory!"

Oscar wouldn't listen further to a "pack of lies" and walked off with his washing.

BATTALION HEADQUARTERS WAS NEARLY HALF a mile behind the front line, part dugout, part shed, with a plank roof sodded over. The Colonel's office was partitioned off at one end; the rest of the place he gave over to the officers for a kind of club room. One night Claude went back to make a report on the new placing of the gun teams. The young officers were sitting about on soap boxes, smoking and eating sweet crackers out of tin cases. Gerhardt was working at a plank table with paper and crayons, making a clean copy of a rough map they had drawn up together that morning, showing the limits of fire. Noise didn't fluster him; he could sit among a lot of men and write as calmly as if he were alone.

There was one officer who could talk all the others down, wherever he was; Captain Barclay Owens, attached from the Engineers. He was a little stumpy thumb of a man, only five feet four, and very broad,—a dynamo of energy. Before the war he was building a dam in Spain, "the largest dam in the world," and in his excavations he had discovered the ruins of one of Julius Caesar's fortified camps. This had been too much for his easily-inflamed imagination. He photographed and measured and brooded upon these ancient remains. He was an engineer by day and an archaeologist by night. He had crates of books sent down from Paris,—everything that had been written on Caesar, in French and German; he engaged a young priest to translate them aloud to him in the evening. The priest believed the American was mad.

When Owens was in college he had never shown the least interest in classical studies, but now it was as if he were giving birth to Caesar. The war came along, and stopped the work on his dam. It also drove other ideas into his exclusively engineering brains. He rushed home to Kansas to explain the war to his countrymen.. He travelled about the West, demonstrating exactly what had happened at the first battle of the Marne, until he had a chance to enlist.

In the Battalion, Owens was called "Julius Caesar," and the men never knew whether he was explaining the Roman general's operations in Spain, or Joffre's at the Marne, he jumped so from one to the other. Everything was in the foreground with him; centuries made no difference. Nothing existed until Barclay Owens found out about it. The men liked to hear him talk. Tonight he was walking up and down, his yellow eyes rolling, a big black cigar in his hand, lecturing the young officers upon French characteristics, coaching and preparing them. It was his legs that made him so funny; his trunk was that of a big man, set on two short stumps.

"Now you fellows don't want to forget that the night-life of Paris is not a typical thing at all; that's a show got up for foreigners.... The French peasant, he's a thrifty fellow.... This red wine's all right if you don't abuse it; take it two-thirds water and it keeps off dysentery.... You don't have to be rough with them, simply firm. Whenever one of them accosts me, I follow a regular plan; first, I give her twenty-five francs; then I look her in the eye and say, 'My girl, I've got three children, three boys.' She gets the point at once; never fails. She goes away ashamed of herself."

"But that's so expensive! It must keep you poor, Captain Owens," said young Lieutenant Hammond innocently. The others roared.

Claude knew that David particularly detested Captain Owens of the Engineers, and wondered that he could go on working with such concentration, when snatches of the Captain's lecture kept breaking through the confusion of casual talk and the noise of the phonograph. Owens, as he walked up and down, cast furtive glances at Gerhardt. He had got wind of the fact that there was something out of the ordinary about him.

The men kept the phonograph going; as soon as one record buzzed out, somebody put in another. Once, when a new tune began, Claude saw David look up from his paper with a curious expression. He listened for a moment with a half-contemptuous smile, then frowned and began sketching in his map again. Something about his momentary glance of recognition made Claude wonder whether he had particular associations with the air,—melancholy, but beautiful, Claude thought. He got up and went over to change the record himself this time. He took out the disk, and holding it up to the light, read the inscription:

"Meditation from Thais—Violin solo—David Gerhardt."

When they were going back along the communication trench in the rain, wading single file, Claude broke the silence abruptly. "That was one of your records they played tonight, that violin solo, wasn't it?"

"Sounded like it. Now we go to the right. I always get lost here."

"Are there many of your records?"

"Quite a number. Why do you ask?"

"I'd like to write my mother. She's fond of good music. She'll get your records, and it will sort of bring the whole thing closer to her, don't you see?"

"All right, Claude," said David good-naturedly. "She will find them in the catalogue, with my picture in uniform alongside. I had a lot made before I went out to Camp Dix. My own mother gets a little income from them. Here we are, at home." As he struck a match two black shadows jumped from the table and disappeared behind the blankets. "Plenty of them around, these wet nights. Get one? Don't squash him in there. Here's the sack."

Gerhardt held open the mouth of a gunny sack, and Claude thrust the squirming corner of his blanket into it and vigorously trampled whatever fell to the bottom. "Where do you suppose the other is?" "He'll join us later. I don't mind the rats half so much as I do Barclay Owens. What a sight he would be with his clothes off! Turn in; I'll go the rounds." Gerhardt splashed out along the submerged duckboard. Claude took off his shoes and cooled his feet in the muddy water. He wished he could ever get David to talk about his profession, and wondered what he looked like on a concert platform, playing his violin.

IX.

THE FOLLOWING NIGHT, Claude was sent back to Division Head-quarters at Q— with information the Colonel did not care to commit to paper. He set off at ten o'clock, with Sergeant Hicks for escort. There had been two days of rain, and the communication trenches were almost knee-deep in water. About half a mile back of the front line, the two men crawled out of the ditch and went on above ground. There was very little shelling along the front that night. When a flare went up, they dropped and lay on their faces, trying, at the same time, to get a squint at what was ahead of them.

The ground was rough, and the darkness thick; it was past midnight when they reached the east-and-west road—usually full of traffic, and not entirely deserted even on a night like this. Trains of horses were splashing through the mud, with shells on their backs, empty supply wagons were coming back from the front. Claude and Hicks paused by the ditch, hoping to get a ride. The rain began to fall with such violence that they looked about for shelter. Stumbling this way and that, they ran into a big artillery piece, the wheels sunk over the hubs in a mud-hole.

"Who's there?" called a quick voice, unmistakably British.

"American infantrymen, two of us. Can we get onto one of your trucks till this lets up?"

"Oh, certainly! We can make room for you in here, if you're not too big. Speak quietly, or you'll waken the Major." Giggles and smothered laughter; a flashlight winked for a moment and showed a line of five trucks, the front and rear ones covered with tarpaulin tents. The voices came from the shelter next the gun. The men inside drew up their legs and made room for the strangers; said they were sorry they hadn't anything dry to offer them except a little rum. The intruders accepted this gratefully.

The Britishers were a giggly lot, and Claude thought, from their voices, they must all be very young. They joked about their Major as if he were their schoolmaster. There wasn't room enough on the truck for anybody to lie down, so they sat with their knees under their chins and exchanged gossip. The gun team belonged to an independent battery that was sent about over the country, "wherever needed." The rest of the battery had got through, gone on to the east, but this big gun was always getting into trouble; now something had gone wrong with her tractor and they couldn't pull her out. They called her "Jenny," and said she was taken with fainting fits now and then, and had to be humoured. It was like going about with your grandmother, one of the invisible Tommies said, "she is such a pompous old thing!" The Major was asleep on the rear truck; he was going to get the V.C. for sleeping. More giggles.

No, they hadn't any idea where they were going; of course, the officers knew, but artillery officers never told anything. What was this country like, anyhow? They were new to this part, had just come down from Verdure.

Claude said he had a friend in the air service up there; did they happen to know anything about Victor Morse?

Morse, the American ace? Hadn't he heard? Why, that got into the London papers. Morse was shot down inside the Hun line three weeks ago. It was a brilliant affair. He was chased by eight Boche planes, brought down three of them, put the rest to flight, and was making for base, when they turned and got him. His machine came down in flames and he jumped, fell a thousand feet or more.

"Then I suppose he never got his leave?" Claude asked.

They didn't know. He got a fine citation.

The men settled down to wait for the weather to improve or the night to pass. Some of them fell into a doze, but Claude felt wide awake. He was wondering about the flat in Chelsea; whether the heavy-eyed beauty had been very sorry, or whether she was playing "Roses of Picardy" for other young officers. He thought mournfully that he would never go to London now. He had quite counted on meeting Victor there some day, after the Kaiser had been properly disposed of. He had really liked Victor. There was something about that fellow… a sort of debauched baby, he was, who went seeking his enemy in the clouds. What other age could have produced such a figure? That was one of the things about this war; it took a little fellow from a little town, gave him an air and a swagger, a life like a movie-film, —and then a death like the rebel angels.

A man like Gerhardt, for instance, had always lived in a more or less rose-colored world; he belonged over here, really. How could he know what hard moulds and crusts the big guns had broken open on the other side of the sea? Who could ever make him understand how far it was from the strawberry bed and the glass cage in the bank, to the sky-roads over Verdure?

By three o'clock the rain had stopped. Claude and Hicks set off again, accompanied by one of the gun team who was going back to get help for their tractor. As it began to grow light, the two Americans wondered more and more at the extremely youthful appearance of their companion. When they stopped at a shell-hole and washed the mud from their faces, the English boy, with his helmet off and the weather stains removed, showed a countenance of adolescent freshness, almost girlish; cheeks like pink apples, yellow curls above his forehead, long, soft lashes.

"You haven't been over very long, have you?" Claude asked in a fatherly tone, as they took the road again.

"I came out in 'sixteen. I was formerly in the infantry."

The Americans liked to hear him talk; he spoke very quickly, in a high, piping voice.

"How did you come to change?"

"Oh, I belonged to one of the Pal Battalions, and we got cut to pieces. When I came out of hospital, I thought I'd try another branch of the service, seeing my pals were gone."

"Now, just what is a Pal Battalion?" drawled Hicks. He hated all English words he didn't understand, though he didn't mind French ones in the least.

"Fellows who signed up together from school," the lad piped.

Hicks glanced at Claude. They both thought this boy ought to be in school for some time yet, and wondered what he looked like when he first came over.

"And you got cut up, you say?" he asked sympathetically.

"Yes, on the Somme. We had rotten luck. We were sent over to take a trench and couldn't. We didn't even get to the wire. The Hun was so well prepared that time, we couldn't manage it. We went over a thousand, and we came back seventeen."

"A hundred and seventeen?"

"No, seventeen."

Hicks whistled and again exchanged looks with Claude. They could neither of them doubt him. There was something very unpleasant about the idea of a thousand fresh-faced schoolboys being sent out against the guns. "It must have been a fool order," he commented. "Suppose there was some mistake at Headquarters?"

"Oh, no, Headquarters knew what it was about! We'd have taken it, if we'd had any sort of luck. But the Hun happened to be full of fight. His machine guns did for us."

"You were hit yourself?" Claude asked him.

"In the leg. He was popping away at me all the while, but I wriggled back on my tummy. When I came out of the hospital my leg wasn't strong, and there's less marching in the artillery.

"I should think you'd have had about enough."

"Oh, a fellow can't stay out after all his chums have been killed! He'd think about it all the time, you know," the boy replied in his clear treble.

Claude and Hicks got into Headquarters just as the cooks were turning out to build their fires. One of the Corporals took them to the officers' bath,—a shed with big tin tubs, and carried away their uniforms to dry them in the kitchen. It would be an hour before the officers would be about, he said, and in the meantime he would manage to get clean shirts and socks for them.

"Say, Lieutenant," Hicks brought out as he was rubbing himself down with a real bath towel, "I don't want to hear any more about those Pal Battalions, do you? It gets my goat. So long as we were going to get into this, we might have been a little more previous. I hate to feel small." "Guess we'll have to take our medicine," Claude said dryly, "There wasn't anywhere to duck, was there? I felt like it. Nice little kid. I don't believe American boys ever seem as young as that."

"Why, if you met him anywhere else, you'd be afraid of using bad words before him, he's so pretty! What's the use of sending an orphan asylum out to be slaughtered? I can't see it," grumbled the fat sergeant. "Well, it's their business. I'm not going to let it spoil my breakfast. Suppose we'll draw ham and eggs, Lieutenant?"

X.

After breakfast Claude reported to Headquarters and talked with one of the staff Majors. He was told he would have to wait until tomorrow to see Colonel James, who had been called to Paris for a general conference. He had left in his car at four that morning, in response to a telephone message.

"There's not much to do here, by way of amusement," said the Major. "A movie show tonight, and you can get anything you want at the estaminet,—the one on the square, opposite the English tank, is the best. There are a couple of nice Frenchwomen in the Red Cross barrack, up on the hill, in the old convent garden. They try to look out for the civilian population, and we're on good terms with them. We get their supplies through with our own, and the quartermaster has orders to help them when they run short. You might go up and call on them. They speak English perfectly."

Claude asked whether he could walk in on them without any kind of introduction.

"Oh, yes, they're used to us! I'll give you a card to Mlle. Olive, though. She's a particular friend of mine. There you are: 'Mlle. Olive de Courcy, introducing, etc.' And, you understand," here he glanced up and looked Claude over from head to foot, "she's a perfect lady."

Even with an introduction, Claude felt some hesitancy about presenting himself to these ladies. Perhaps they didn't like Americans; he was always afraid of meeting French people who didn't. It was the same way with most of the fellows in his battalion, he had found; they were terribly afraid of being disliked. And the moment they felt they were disliked, they hastened to behave as badly as possible, in order to deserve it; then they didn't feel that they had been taken in—the worst feeling a doughboy could possibly have!

Claude thought he would stroll about to look at the town a little. It had been taken by the Germans in the autumn of 1914, after their retreat from the Marne, and they had held it until about a year ago, when it was retaken by the English and the Chasseurs d'Alpins. They had been able to reduce it and to drive the Germans out, only by battering it down with artillery; not one building remained standing.

Ruin was ugly, and it was nothing more, Claude was thinking, as he followed the paths that ran over piles of brick and plaster. There was nothing picturesque about this, as there was in the war pictures one saw at home. A cyclone or a fire might have done just as good a job. The place was simply a great dump-heap; an exaggeration of those which disgrace the outskirts of American towns. It was the same thing over and over; mounds of burned brick and broken stone, heaps of rusty, twisted iron, splintered beams and rafters, stagnant pools, cellar holes full of muddy water. An American soldier had stepped into one of those holes a few nights before, and been drowned.

This had been a rich town of eighteen thousand inhabitants; now the civilian population was about four hundred. There were people there who had hung on all through the years of German occupation; others who, as soon as they heard that the enemy was driven out, came back from wherever they had found shelter. They were living in cellars, or in little wooden barracks made from old timbers and American goods boxes. As he walked along, Claude read familiar names and addresses, painted on boards built into the sides of these frail shelters: "From Emery Bird, Thayer Co. Kansas City, Mo." "Daniels and Fisher, Denver, Colo." These inscriptions cheered him so much that he began to feel like going up and calling on the French ladies.

The sun had come out hot after three days of rain. The stagnant pools and the weeds that grew in the ditches gave out a rank, heavy smell. Wild flowers grew triumphantly over the piles of rotting wood and rusty iron; cornflowers and Queen Anne's lace and poppies; blue and white and red, as if the French colours came up spontaneously out of the French soil, no matter what the Germans did to it.

Claude paused before a little shanty built against a half-demolished brick wall. A gilt cage hung in the doorway, with a canary, singing beautifully. An old woman was working in the garden patch, picking out bits of brick and plaster the rain had washed up, digging with her fingers around the pale carrot-tops and neat lettuce heads. Claude approached her, touched his helmet, and asked her how one could find the way to the Red Cross.

She wiped her hands on her apron and took him by the elbow. "Vous savez le tank Anglais? Non? Marie, Marie!"

(He learned afterward that every one was directed to go this way or that from a disabled British tank that had been left on the site of the old town hall.)

A little girl ran out of the barrack, and her grandmother told her to go at once and take the American to the Red Cross. Marie put her hand in Claude's and led him off along one of the paths that wound among the rubbish. She took him out of the way to show him a church,—evidently one of the ruins of which they were proudest,—where the blue sky was shining through the white arches. The Virgin stood with empty arms over the central door; a little foot sticking to her robe showed where the infant Jesus had been shot away.

"Le bébé est cassé, mais il a protégé sa mère," Marie explained with satisfaction. As they went on, she told Claude that she had a soldier among the Americans who was her friend. "Il est bon, il est gai, mon soldat," but he sometimes drank too much alcohol, and that was a bad habit. Perhaps now, since his comrade had stepped into a cellar hole Monday night while he was drunk, and had been drowned, her "Sharlie" would be warned and would do better. Marie was evidently a well brought up child. Her father, she said, had been a schoolmaster. At the foot of the convent hill, she turned to go home. Claude called her back and awkwardly tried to give her some money, but she thrust her hands behind her and said resolutely, "Non, merci. Je n'ai besoin de rien," and then ran away down the path.

As he climbed toward the top of the hill he noticed that the ground had been cleaned up a bit. The path was clear, the bricks and hewn stones had been piled in neat heaps, the broken hedges had been trimmed and the dead parts cut away. Emerging at last into the garden, he stood still for wonder; even though it was in ruins, it seemed so beautiful after the disorder of the world below.

The gravel walks were clean and shining. A wall of very old boxwoods stood green against a row of dead Lombardy poplars. Along the shattered side of the main building, a pear tree, trained on wires like a vine, still flourished,—full of little red pears. Around the stone well was a shaven grass plot, and everywhere there were little trees and shrubs, which had been too low for the shells to hit,—or for the fire, which had seared the poplars, to catch. The hill must have been wrapped in flames at one time, and all the tall trees had been burned.

The barrack was built against the walls of the cloister,—three arches of which remained, like a stone wing to the shed of planks. On a ladder stood a one-armed young man, driving nails very skillfully with his single hand. He seemed to be making a frame projection from the sloping roof, to support an awning. He carried his nails in his mouth. When he wanted one, he hung his hammer to the belt of his trousers, took a nail from between his teeth, stuck it into the wood, and then deftly rapped it on the head. Claude watched him for a moment, then went to the foot of the ladder and held out his two hands. "Laissez-moi," he exclaimed.

The one aloft spat his nails out into his palm, looked down, and laughed. He was about Claude's age, with very yellow hair and moustache and blue eyes. A charming looking fellow.

"Willingly," he said. "This is no great affair, but I do it to amuse myself, and it will be pleasant for the ladies." He descended and gave his hammer to the visitor. Claude set to work on the frame, while the other went under the stone arches and brought back a roll of canvas,—part of an old tent, by the look of it.

"Un héritage des Boches," he explained unrolling it upon the grass. "I found it among their filth in the cellar, and had the idea to make a pavilion for the ladies, as our trees are destroyed." He stood up suddenly. "Perhaps you have come to see the ladies?"

"Plus tard."

Very well, the boy said, they would get the pavilion done for a surprise for Mlle. Olive when she returned. She was down in the town now, visiting the sick people. He bent over his canvas again, measuring and cutting with a pair of garden shears, moving round the green plot on his knees, and all the time singing. Claude wished he could understand the words of his song.

While they were working together, tying the cloth up to the frame, Claude, from his elevation, saw a tall girl coming slowly up the path by which he had ascended. She paused at the top, by the boxwood hedge, as if she were very tired, and stood looking at them. Presently she approached the ladder and said in slow, careful English, "Good morning. Louis has found help, I see."

Claude came down from his perch.

"Are you Mlle. de Courcy? I am Claude Wheeler. I have a note of introduction to you, if I can find it."

She took the card, but did not look at it. "That is not necessary. Your uniform is enough. Why have you come?"

He looked at her in some confusion. "Well, really, I don't know! I am just in from the front to see Colonel James, and he is in Paris, so I must wait over a day. One of the staff suggested my coming up here—I suppose because it is so nice!" he finished ingenuously.

"Then you are a guest from the front, and you will have lunch with Louis and me. Madame Barre is also gone for the day. Will you see our house?" She led him through the low door into a living room, unpainted, uncarpeted, light and airy. There were coloured war posters on the clean board walls, brass shell cases full of wild flowers and garden flowers, canvas camp-chairs, a shelf of books, a table covered by a white silk shawl embroidered with big butterflies. The sunlight on the floor, the bunches of fresh flowers, the white window curtains stirring in the breeze, reminded Claude of something, but he could not remember what.

"We have no guest room," said Mlle. de Courcy. "But you will come to mine, and Louis will bring you hot water to wash."

In a wooden chamber at the end of the passage, Claude took off his coat, and set to work to make himself as tidy as possible. Hot water and scented soap were in themselves pleasant things. The dresser was an old goods box, stood on end and covered with white lawn. On it there was a row of ivory toilet things, with combs and brushes, powder and cologne, and a pile of white handkerchiefs fresh from the iron. He felt that he ought not to look about him much, but the odor of cleanness, and the indefinable air of personality, tempted him. In one corner, a curtain on a rod made a clothes-closet; in another was a low iron bed, like a soldier's, with a pale blue coverlid and white pillows. He moved carefully and splashed discreetly. There was nothing he could have damaged or broken, not even a rug on the plank floor, and the pitcher and hand-basin were of iron; yet he felt as if he were imperiling something fragile.

When he came out, the table in the living room was set for three. The stout old dame who was placing the plates paid no attention to him,—seemed, from her expression, to scorn him and all his kind. He withdrew as far as possible out of her path and picked up a book from the table, a volume of Heine's Reisebilder in German.

Before lunch Mlle. de Courcy showed him the store room in the rear, where the shelves were stocked with rows of coffee tins, condensed milk, canned vegetables and meat, all with American trade names he knew so well; names which seemed doubly familiar and "reliable" here, so far from home. She told him the people in the town could not have got through the winter without these things. She had to deal them out sparingly, where the need was greatest, but they made the difference between life and death. Now that it was summer, the people lived by their gardens; but old women still came to beg for a few ounces of coffee, and mothers to get a can of milk for the babies.

Claude's face glowed with pleasure. Yes, his country had a long arm. People forgot that; but here, he felt, was some one who did not forget. When they sat down to lunch he learned that Mlle. de Courcy and Madame Barre had been here almost a year now; they came soon after the town was retaken, when the old inhabitants began to drift back. The people brought with them only what they could carry in their arms.

"They must love their country so much, don't you think, when they endure such poverty to come back to it?" she said. "Even the old ones do not often complain about their dear things—their linen, and their china, and their beds. If they have the ground, and hope, all that they can make again. This war has taught us all how little the made things matter. Only the feeling matters."

Exactly so; hadn't he been trying to say this ever since he was born? Hadn't he always known it, and hadn't it made life both bitter and sweet for him? What a beautiful voice she had, this Mlle. Olive, and how nobly it dealt with the English tongue. He would like to say something, but out of so much... what? He remained silent, therefore, sat nervously breaking up the black war bread that lay beside his plate.

He saw her looking at his hand, felt in a flash that she regarded it with favour, and instantly put it on his knee, under the table.

"It is our trees that are worst," she went on sadly. "You have seen our poor trees? It makes one ashamed for this beautiful part of France. Our people are more sorry for them than to lose their cattle and horses."

Mlle. de Courcy looked over-taxed by care and responsibility, Claude thought, as he watched her. She seemed far from strong. Slender, grey-eyed, dark-haired, with white transparent skin and a too ardent colour in her lips and cheeks,—like the flame of a feverish activity within. Her shoulders drooped, as if she were always tired. She must be young, too, though there were threads of grey in her hair,—brushed flat and knotted carelessly at the back of her head.

After the coffee, Mlle. de Courcy went to work at her desk, and Louis took Claude to show him the garden. The clearing and trimming and planting were his own work, and he had done it all with one arm. This autumn he would accomplish much more, for he was stronger now, and he had the habitude of working single-handed. He must manage to get the dead trees down; they distressed Mademoiselle Olive. In front of the barrack stood four old locusts; the tops were naked forks, burned coal-black, but the lower branches had put out thick tufts of yellow-green foliage, so vigorous that the life in the trunks must still be sound. This fall, Louis said, he meant to get some strong American boys to help him, and they would saw off the dead limbs and trim the tops flat over the thick boles. How much it must mean to a man to love his country like this, Claude thought; to love its trees and flowers; to nurse it when it was sick, and tend its hurts with one arm. Among the flowers, which had come back self-sown or from old roots, Claude found a group of tall, straggly plants with reddish stems and tiny white blossoms,—one of the evening primrose family, the Gaura, that grew along the clay banks of Lovely Creek, at home. He had never thought it very pretty, but he was pleased to find it here. He had supposed it was one of those nameless prairie flowers that grew on the prairie and nowhere else.

When they went back to the barrack, Mlle. Olive was sitting in one of the canvas chairs Louis had placed under the new pavilion.

"What a fine fellow he is!" Claude exclaimed, looking after him.

"Louis? Yes. He was my brother's orderly. When Emile came home on leave he always brought Louis with him, and Louis became like one of the family. The shell that killed my brother tore off his arm. My mother and I went to visit him in the hospital, and he seemed ashamed to be alive, poor boy, when my brother was dead. He put his hand over his face and began to cry, and said, 'Oh, Madame, il était toujours plus chic que moi!'"

Although Mlle. Olive spoke English well, Claude saw that she did so only by keeping her mind intently upon it. The stiff sentences she uttered were foreign to her nature; her face and eyes ran ahead of her tongue and made one wait eagerly for what was coming. He sat down in a sagging canvas chair, absently twisting a sprig of Gaura he had pulled.

"You have found a flower?" She looked up.

"Yes. It grows at home, on my father's farm."

She dropped the faded shirt she was darning. "Oh, tell me about your country! I have talked to so many, but it is difficult to understand. Yes, tell me about that!"

Nebraska—What was it? How many days from the sea, what did it look like? As he tried to describe it, she listened with half-closed eyes. "Flat-covered with grain-muddy rivers. I think it must be like Russia. But your father's farm; describe that to me, minutely, and perhaps I can see the rest."

Claude took a stick and drew a square in the sand: there, to begin with, was the house and farmyard; there was the big pasture, with Lovely Creek flowing through it; there were the wheatfields and cornfields, the timber claim; more wheat and corn, more pastures. There it all was, diagrammed on the yellow sand, with shadows gliding over it from the half-charred locust trees. He would not have believed that he could tell a stranger about it in such detail. It was partly due to his listener, no doubt; she gave him unusual sympathy, and the glow of an unusual mind. While she bent over his map, questioning him, a light dew of perspiration gathered on her upper lip, and she breathed faster from her effort to see and understand everything. He told her about his mother and his father and Mahailey; what life was like there in summer and winter and autumn—what it had been like in that fateful summer when the Hun was moving always toward Paris, and on those three days when the French were standing at the Marne; how his mother and father waited for him to bring the news at night, and how the very cornfields seemed to hold their breath.

Mlle. Olive sank back wearily in her chair. Claude looked up and saw tears sparkling in her brilliant eyes. "And I myself," she murmured, "did not know of the Marne until days afterward, though my father and brother were both there! I was far off in Brittany, and the trains did not run. That is what is wonderful, that you are here, telling me this! We, we were taught from childhood that some day the Germans would come; we grew up under that threat. But you were so safe, with all your wheat and corn. Nothing could touch you, nothing!"

Claude dropped his eyes. "Yes," he muttered, blushing, "shame could. It pretty nearly did. We are pretty late." He rose from his chair as if he were going to fetch something.... But where was he to get it from? He shook his head. "I am afraid," he said mournfully, "there is nothing I can say to make you understand how far away it all seemed, how almost visionary. It didn't only seem miles away, it seemed centuries away."

"But you do come,—so many, and from so far! It is the last miracle of this war. I was in Paris on the fourth day of July, when your Marines, just from Belleau Wood, marched for your national fete, and I said to myself as they came on, 'That is a new man!' Such heads they had, so fine there, behind the ears. Such discipline and purpose. Our people laughed and called to them and threw them flowers, but they never turned to look... eyes straight before. They passed like men of destiny." She threw out her hands with a swift movement and dropped them in her lap. The emotion of that day came back in her face. As Claude looked at her burning cheeks, her burning eyes, he understood that the strain of this war had given her a perception that was almost like a gift of prophecy.

A woman came up the hill carrying a baby. Mlle. de Courcy went to meet her and took her into the house. Claude sat down again, almost lost to himself in the feeling of being completely understood, of being no longer a stranger. In the far distance the big guns were booming at intervals. Down in the garden Louis was singing. Again he wished he knew the words of Louis' songs. The airs were rather melancholy, but they were sung very cheerfully. There was something open and warm about the boy's voice, as there was about his face-something blond, too. It was distinctly a bland voice, like summer wheatfields, ripe and waving. Claude sat alone for half an hour or more, tasting a new kind of happiness, a new kind of sadness. Ruin and new birth; the shudder of ugly things in the past, the trembling image of beautiful ones on the horizon; finding and losing; that was life, he saw.

When his hostess came back, he moved her chair for her out of the creeping sunlight. "I didn't know there were any French girls like you," he said simply, as she sat down.

She smiled. "I do not think there are any French girls left. There are children and women. I was twenty-one when the war came, and I had never been anywhere without my mother or my brother or sister. Within a year I went all over France alone; with soldiers, with Senegalese, with anybody. Everything is different with us." She lived at Versailles, she told him, where her father had been an instructor in the Military School. He had died since the beginning of the war. Her grandfather was killed in the war of 1870. Hers was a family of soldiers, but not one of the men would be left to see the day of victory.

She looked so tired that Claude knew he had no right to stay. Long shadows were falling in the garden. It was hard to leave; but an hour more or less wouldn't matter. Two people could hardly give each other more if they were together for years, he thought.

"Will you tell me where I can come and see you, if we both get through this war?" he asked as he rose.

He wrote it down in his notebook.

"I shall look for you," she said, giving him her hand.

There was nothing to do but to take his helmet and go. At the edge of the hill, just before he plunged down the path, he stopped and glanced back at the garden lying flattened in the sun; the three stone arches, the dahlias and marigolds, the glistening boxwood wall. He had left something on the hilltop which he would never find again.

The next afternoon Claude and his sergeant set off for the front. They had been told at Headquarters that they could shorten their route by following the big road to the military cemetery, and then turning to the left. It was not advisable to go the latter half of the way before nightfall, so they took their time through the belt of straggling crops and hayfields.

When they struck the road they came upon a big Highlander sitting in the end of an empty supply wagon, smoking a pipe and rubbing the dried mud out of his kilts. The horses were munching in their nose-bags, and the driver had disappeared. The Americans hadn't happened to meet with any Highlanders before, and were curious. This one must be a good fighter, they thought; a brawny giant with a bulldog jaw, and a face as red and knobby as his knees. More because he admired the looks of the man than because he needed information, Hicks went up and asked him if he had noticed a military cemetery on the road back. The Kilt nodded.

"About how far back would you say it was?"

"I wouldn't say at all. I take no account of their kilometers," he replied dryly, rubbing away at his skirt as if he had it in a washtub.

"Well, about how long will it take us to walk it?"

"That I couldn't say. A Scotsman would do it in an hour."

"I guess a Yankee can do it as quick as a Scotchman, can't be?" Hicks asked jovially.

"That I couldn't say. You've been four years gettin' this far, I know verra well."

Hicks blinked as if he had been hit. "Oh, if that's the way you talk—"

"That's the way I do," said the other sourly.

Claude put out a warning hand. "Come on, Hicks. You'll get nothing by it." They went up the road very much disconcerted. Hicks kept thinking of things he might have said. When he was angry, the Sergeant's forehead puffed up and became dark red, like a young baby's. "What did you call me off for?" he sputtered.

"I don't see where you'd have come out in an argument, and you certainly couldn't have licked him."

They turned aside at the cemetery to wait until the sun went down. It was unfenced, unsodded, and a wagon trail ran through the middle, bisecting the square. On one side were the French graves, with white crosses; on the other side the German graves, with black crosses. Poppies and cornflower ran over them. The Americans strolled about, reading the names. Here and there the soldier's photograph was nailed upon his cross, left by some comrade to perpetuate his memory a little longer.

The birds, that always came to life at dusk and dawn, began to sing, flying home from somewhere. Claude and Hicks sat down between the mounds and began to smoke while the sun dropped. Lines of dead trees marked the red west. This was a dreary stretch of country, even to boys brought up on the flat prairie. They smoked in silence, meditating and waiting for night. On a cross at their feet the inscription read merely:

Soldat Inconnu, Mort pour La France.

A very good epitaph, Claude was thinking. Most of the boys who fell in this war were unknown, even to themselves. They were too young. They died and took their secret with them,—what they were and what they might have been. The name that stood was La France. How much that name had come to mean to him, since he first saw a shoulder of land bulk up in the dawn from the deck of the Anchises. It was a pleasant name to say over in one's mind, where one could make it as passionately nasal as one pleased and never blush.

Hicks, too, had been lost in his reflections. Now he broke the silence. "Somehow, Lieutenant, 'mort' seems deader than 'dead.' It has a coffinish sound. And over there they're all 'tod,' and it's all the same damned silly thing. Look at them set out here, black and white, like a checkerboard. The next question is, who put 'em here, and what's the good of it?"

"Search me," the other murmured absently.

Hicks rolled another cigarette and sat smoking it, his plump face wrinkled with the gravity and labour of his cerebration. "Well," he brought out at last, "we'd better hike. This afterglow will hang on for an hour,—always does, over here."

"I suppose we had." They rose to go. The white crosses were now violet, and the black ones had altogether melted in the shadow. Behind the dead trees in the west, a long smear of red still burned. To the north, the guns were tuning up with a deep thunder. "Somebody's getting peppered up there. Do owls always hoot in graveyards?"

"Just what I was wondering, Lieutenant. It's a peaceful spot, otherwise. Good-night, boys," said Hicks kindly, as they left the graves behind them.

They were soon finding their way among shell holes, and jumping trench-tops in the dark,-beginning to feel cheerful at getting back to their chums and their own little group. Hicks broke out and told Claude how he and Dell Able meant to go into business together when they got home; were going to open a garage and automobile-repair shop. Under their talk, in the minds of both, that lonely spot lingered, and the legend: *Soldat Inconnu, Mort pour La France.*

XI.

After four days' rest in the rear, the Battalion went to the front again in new country, about ten kilometers east of the trench they had relieved before. One morning Colonel Scott sent for Claude and Gerhardt and spread his maps out on the table.

"We are going to clean them out there in F 6 tonight, and straighten our line. The thing that bothers us is that little village stuck up on the hill, where the enemy machine guns have a strong position. I want to get them out of there before the Battalion goes over. We can't spare too many men, and I don't like to send out more officers than I can help; it won't do to reduce the Battalion for the major operation. Do you think you two boys could manage it with a hundred men? The point is, you will have to be out and back before our artillery begins at three o'clock."

Under the hill where the village stood, ran a deep ravine, and from this ravine a twisting water course wound up the hillside. By climbing this gully, the raiders should be able to fall on the machine gunners from the rear and surprise them. But first they must get across the open stretch, nearly one and a half kilometers wide, between the American line and the ravine, without attracting attention. It was raining now, and they could safely count on a dark night.

The night came on black enough. The Company crossed the open stretch without provoking fire, and slipped into the ravine to wait for the hour of attack, A young doctor, a Pennsylvanian, lately attached to the staff, had volunteered to come with them, and he arranged a dressing station at the bottom of the ravine, where the stretchers were left. They were to pick up their wounded on the way back. Anything left in that area would be exposed to the artillery fire later on.

At ten o'clock the men began to ascend the water-course, creeping through pools and little waterfalls, making a continuous spludgy sound, like pigs rubbing against the sty. Claude, with the head of the column, was just pulling out of the gully on the hillside above the village, when a flare went up, and a volley of fire broke from the brush on the up-hill side of the water-course; machine guns, opening on the exposed line crawling below. The Hun had been warned that the Americans were crossing the plain and had anticipated their way of approach. The men in the gully were trapped; they could not retaliate with effect, and the bullets from the Maxims bounded on the rocks about them like hail. Gerhardt ran along the edge of the line, urging the men not to fall back and double on themselves, but to break out of the gully on the downhill side and scatter.

Claude, with his group, started back. "Go into the brush and get 'em! Our fellows have got no chance down there. Grenades while they last, then bayonets. Pull your plugs and don't hold on too long."

They were already on the run, charging the brush. The Hun gunners knew the hill like a book, and when the bombs began bursting among them, they took to trails and burrows. "Don't follow them off into the rocks," Claude kept calling. "Straight ahead! Clear everything to the ravine."

As the German gunners made for cover, the firing into the gully stopped, and the arrested column poured up the steep defile after Gerhardt.

Claude and his party found themselves back at the foot of the hill, at the edge of the ravine from which they had started. Heavy firing on the hill above told them the rest of the men had got through. The quickest way back to the scene of action was by the same water-course they had climbed before. They dropped into it and started up. Claude, at the rear, felt the ground rise under him, and he was swept with a mountain of earth and rock down into the ravine.

He never knew whether he lost consciousness or not. It seemed to him that he went on having continuous sensations. The first, was that of being blown to pieces; of swelling to an enormous size under intolerable pressure, and then bursting. Next he felt himself shrink and tingle, like a frost-bitten body thawing out. Then he swelled again, and burst. This was repeated, he didn't know how often. He soon realized that he was lying under a great weight of earth; his body, not his head. He felt rain falling on his face. His left hand was free, and still attached to his arm. He moved it cautiously to his face. He seemed to be bleeding from the nose and ears. Now he began to wonder where he was hurt; he felt as if he were full of shell splinters. Everything was buried but his head and left shoulder. A voice was calling from somewhere below.

"Are any of you fellows alive?"

Claude closed his eyes against the rain beating in his face. The same voice came again, with a note of patient despair.

"If there's anybody left alive in this hole, won't he speak up? I'm badly hurt myself."

That must be the new doctor; wasn't his dressing station somewhere down here? Hurt, he said. Claude tried to move his legs a little. Perhaps, if he could get out from under the dirt, he might hold together long enough to reach the doctor. He began to wriggle and pull. The wet earth sucked at him; it was painful business. He braced himself with his elbows, but kept slipping back.

"I'm the only one left, then?" said the mournful voice below.

At last Claude worked himself out of his burrow, but he was unable to stand. Every time he tried to stand, he got faint and seemed to burst again. Something was the matter with his right ankle, too—he couldn't bear his weight on it. Perhaps he had been too near the shell to be hit; he had heard the boys tell of such cases. It had exploded under his feet and swept him down into the ravine, but hadn't left any metal in his body. If it had put anything into him, it would have put so much that he wouldn't be sitting here speculating. He began to crawl down the slope on all fours. "Is that the Doctor? Where are you?"

"Here, on a stretcher. They shelled us. Who are you? Our fellows got up, didn't they?"

"I guess most of them did. What happened back here?"

"I'm afraid it's my fault," the voice said sadly. "I used my flash light, and that must have given them the range. They put three or four shells right on top of us. The fellows that got hurt in the gully kept stringing back here, and I couldn't do anything in the dark. I had to have a light to do anything. I just finished putting on a Johnson splint when the first shell came. I guess they're all done for now."

"How many were there?"

"Fourteen, I think. Some of them weren't much hurt. They'd all be alive, if I hadn't come out with you."

"Who were they? But you don't know our names yet, do you? You didn't see Lieutenant Gerhardt among them?"

"Don't think so."

"Nor Sergeant Hicks, the fat fellow?"

"Don't think so."

"Where are you hurt?"

"Abdominal. I can't tell anything without a light. I lost my flash light. It never occurred to me that it could make trouble; it's one I use at home, when the babies are sick," the doctor murmured.

Claude tried to strike a match, with no success. "Wait a minute, where's your helmet?" He took off his metal hat, held it over the doctor, and managed to strike a light underneath it. The wounded man had already loosened his trousers, and now he pulled up his bloody shirt. His groin and abdomen were torn on the left side. The wound, and the stretcher on which he lay, supported a mass of dark, coagulated blood that looked like a great cow's liver.

"I guess I've got mine," the Doctor murmured as the match went out.

Claude struck another. "Oh, that can't be! Our fellows will be back pretty soon, and we can do something for you."

"No use, Lieutenant. Do you suppose you could strip a coat off one of those poor fellows? I feel the cold terribly in my intestines. I had a bottle of French brandy, but I suppose it's buried."

Claude stripped off his own coat, which was warm on the inside, and began feeling about in the mud for the brandy. He wondered why the poor man wasn't screaming with pain. The firing on the hill had ceased, except for the occasional click of a Maxim, off in the rocks somewhere. His watch said 12:10; could anything have miscarried up there?

Suddenly, voices above, a clatter of boots on the shale. He began shouting to them.

"Coming, coming!" He knew the voice. Gerhardt and his rifles ran down into the ravine with a bunch of prisoners. Claude called to them to be careful. "Don't strike a light! They've been shelling down here."

"All right are you, Wheeler? Where are the wounded?"

"There aren't any but the Doctor and me. Get us out of here quick. I'm all right, but I can't walk."

They put Claude on a stretcher and sent him ahead. Four big Germans carried him, and they were prodded to a lope by Hicks and Dell Able. Four of their own men took up the doctor, and Gerhardt walked beside him. In spite of their care, the motion started the blood again and tore away the clots that had formed over his wounds. He began to vomit blood and to strangle. The men put the stretcher down. Gerhardt lifted the Doctor's head. "It's over," he said presently. "Better make the best time you can."

They picked up their load again. "Them that are carrying him now won't jolt him," said Oscar, the pious Swede.

B Company lost nineteen men in the raid. Two days later the Company went off on a ten-day leave. Claude's sprained ankle was twice its natural size, but to avoid being sent to the hospital he had to march to the railhead. Sergeant Hicks got him a giant shoe he found stuck on the barbed wire entanglement. Claude and Gerhardt were going off on their leave together.

XII.

A rainy autumn night; Papa Joubert sat reading his paper. He heard a heavy pounding on his garden gate. Kicking off his slippers, he put on the wooden sabots he kept for mud, shuffled across the dripping garden, and opened the door into the dark street. Two tall figures with rifles and kits confronted him. In a moment he began embracing them, calling to his wife:

"Nom de diable, Maman, c'est David, David et Claude, tous les deux!"

Sorry-looking soldiers they appeared when they stood in the candlelight, plastered with clay, their metal hats shining like copper bowls, their clothes dripping pools of water upon the flags of the kitchen floor. Mme. Joubert kissed their wet cheeks, and Monsieur, now that he could see them, embraced them again. Whence had they come, and how had it fared with them, up there? Very well, as anybody could see. What did they want first,—supper, perhaps? Their room was always ready for them; and the clothes they had left were in the big chest.

David explained that their shirts had not once been dry for four days; and what they most desired was to be dry and to be clean. Old Martha, already in bed, was routed out to heat water. M. Joubert carried the big washtub upstairs. Tomorrow for conversation, he said; tonight for repose. The boys followed him and began to peel off their wet uniforms, leaving them in two sodden piles on the floor. There was one bath for both, and they threw up a coin to decide which should get into the warm water first. M. Joubert, seeing Claude's fat ankle strapped up in adhesive bandages, began to chuckle. "Oh, I see the Boche made you dance up there!"

When they were clad in clean pyjamas out of the chest, Papa Joubert carried their shirts and socks down for Martha to wash. He returned with the big meat platter, on which was an omelette made of twelve eggs and stuffed with bacon and fried potatoes. Mme. Joubert brought the three-story earthen coffee-pot to the door and called, "Bon appetit!" The host poured the coffee and cut up the loaf with his clasp knife. He sat down to watch them eat. How had they found things up there, anyway? The Boches polite and agreeable as usual? Finally, when there was not a crumb of anything left, he poured for each a little glass of brandy, "pour cider la digestion," and wished them good-night. He took the candle with him.

Perfect bliss, Claude reflected, as the chill of the sheets grew warm around his body, and he sniffed in the pillow the old smell of lavender. To be so warm, so dry, so clean, so beloved! The journey down, reviewed from here, seemed beautiful. As soon as they had got out of the region of martyred trees, they found the land of France turning gold. All along the river valleys the poplars and cottonwoods had changed from green to yellow,—evenly coloured, looking like candle flames in the mist and rain. Across the fields, along the horizon they ran, like torches passed from hand to hand, and all the willows by the little streams had become silver. The vineyards were green still, thickly spotted with curly, blood-red branches. It all flashed back beside his pillow in the dark: this beautiful land, this beautiful people, this beautiful omelette; gold poplars, blue-green vineyards, wet, scarlet vine leaves, rain dripping into the court, fragrant darkness… sleep, stronger than all.

XIII.

THE WOODLAND PATH was deep in leaves. Claude and David were lying on the dry, springy heather among the flint boulders. Gerhardt, with his Stetson over his eyes, was presumably asleep. They were having fine weather for their holiday. The forest rose about this open glade like an amphitheatre, in golden terraces of horse chestnut and beech. The big nuts dropped velvety and brown, as if they had been soaked in oil, and disappeared in the dry leaves below. Little black yew trees, that had not been visible in the green of summer, stood out among the curly yellow brakes. Through the grey netting of the beech twigs, stiff holly bushes glittered.

It was the Wheeler way to dread false happiness, to feel cowardly about being fooled. Since he had come back, Claude had more than once wondered whether he took too much for granted and felt more at home here than he had any right to feel. The Americans were prone, he had observed, to make themselves very much at home, to mistake good manners for good-will. He had no right to doubt the affection of the Jouberts, however; that was genuine and personal,—not a smooth surface under which almost any shade of scorn might lie and laugh… was not, in short, the treacherous "French politeness" by which one must not let oneself be taken in. Merely having seen the season change in a country gave one the sense of having been there for a long time. And, anyway, he wasn't a tourist. He was here on legitimate business.

Claude's sprained ankle was still badly swollen. Madame Joubert was sure he ought not to move about on it at all, begged him to sit in the garden all day and nurse it. But the surgeon at the front had told him that if he once stopped walking, he would have to go to the hospital. So, with the help of his host's best holly-wood cane, he limped out into the forest every day. This afternoon he was tempted to go still farther. Madame Joubert had told him about some caves at the other end of the wood, underground chambers where the country people had gone to live in times of great misery, long ago, in the English wars. The English wars; he could not remember just how far back they were,—but long enough to make one feel comfortable. As for him, perhaps he would never go home at all. Perhaps, when this great affair was over, he would buy a little farm and stay here for the rest of his life. That was a project he liked to play with. There was no chance for the kind of life he wanted at home, where people were always buying and selling, building and pulling down. He had begun to believe that the Americans were a people of shallow emotions. That was the way Gerhardt had put it once; and if it was true, there was no cure for it. Life was so short that it meant nothing at all unless it were continually reinforced by something that endured; unless the shadows of individual existence came and went against a background that held together. While he was absorbed in his day dream of farming in France, his companion stirred and rolled over on his elbow.

"You know we are to join the Battalion at A—. They'll be living like kings there. Hicks will get so fat he'll drop over on the march. Headquarters must have something particularly nasty in mind; the infantry is always fed up before a slaughter. But I've been thinking; I have some old friends at A—. Suppose we go on there a day early, and get them to take us in? It's a fine old place, and I ought to go to see them. The son was a fellow student of mine at the

Conservatoire. He was killed the second winter of the war. I used to go up there for the holidays with him; I would like to see his mother and sister again. You've no objection?"

Claude did not answer at once. He lay squinting off at the beech trees, without moving. "You always avoid that subject with me, don't you?" he said presently.

"What subject?"

"Oh, anything to do with the Conservatoire, or your profession."

"I haven't any profession at present. I'll never go back to the violin."

"You mean you couldn't make up for the time you'll lose?"

Gerhardt settled his back against a rock and got out his pipe. "That would be difficult; but other things would be harder. I've lost much more than time."

"Couldn't you have got exemption, one way or another?"

"I might have. My friends wanted to take it up and make a test case of me. But I couldn't stand for it. I didn't feel I was a good enough violinist to admit that I wasn't a man. I often wish I had been in Paris that summer when the war broke out; then I would have gone into the French army on the first impulse, with the other students, and it would have been better."

David paused and sat puffing at his pipe. Just then a soft movement stirred the brakes on the hillside. A little barefoot girl stood there, looking about. She had heard voices, but at first did not see the uniforms that blended with the yellow and brown of the wood. Then she saw the sun shining on two heads; one square, and amber in colour,—the other reddish bronze, long and narrow. She took their friendliness for granted and came down the hill, stopping now and again to pick up shiny horse chestnuts and pop them into a sack she was dragging. David called to her and asked her whether the nuts were good to eat.

"Oh, non!" she exclaimed, her face expressing the liveliest terror, "pour les cochons!" These inexperienced Americans might eat almost anything. The boys laughed and gave her some pennies, "pour les cochons aussi." She stole about the edge of the wood, stirring among the leaves for nuts, and watching the two soldiers.

Gerhardt knocked out his pipe and began to fill it again. "I went home to see my mother in May, of 1914. I wasn't here when the war broke out. The Conservatoire closed at once, so I arranged a concert tour in the States that winter, and did very well. That was before all the little Russians went over, and the field wasn't so crowded. I had a second season, and that went well. But I was getting more nervous all the time; I was only half there." He smoked thoughtfully, sitting with folded arms, as if he were going over a succession of events or states of feeling. "When my number was drawn, I reported to see what I could do about getting out; I took a look at the other fellows who were trying to squirm, and chucked it. I've never been sorry. Not long afterward, my violin was smashed, and my career seemed to go along with it."

Claude asked him what he meant.

"While I was at Camp Dix, I had to play at one of the entertainments. My violin, a Stradivarius, was in a vault in New York. I didn't need it for that concert, any more than I need it at this minute; yet I went to town and brought it out. I was taking it up from the station in a military car, and a drunken taxi driver ran into us. I wasn't hurt, but the violin, lying across my knees, was smashed into a thousand pieces. I didn't know what it meant then; but since, I've seen so many beautiful old things smashed... I've become a fatalist."

Claude watched his brooding head against the grey flint rock.

"You ought to have kept out of the whole thing. Any army man would say so."

David's head went back against the boulder, and he threw one of the, chestnuts lightly into the air. "Oh, one violinist more or less doesn't matter! But who is ever going back to anything? That's what I want to know!"

Claude felt guilty; as if David must have guessed what apostasy had been going on in his own mind this afternoon. "You don't believe we are going to get out of this war what we went in for, do you?" he asked suddenly.

"Absolutely not," the other replied with cool indifference.

"Then I certainly don't see what you're here for!"

"Because in 1917 I was twenty-four years old, and able to bear arms. The war was put up to our generation. I don't know what for; the sins of our fathers, probably. Certainly not to make the world safe for Democracy, or any rhetoric of that sort. When I was doing stretcher work, I had to tell myself over and over that nothing would come of it, but that it had to be. Sometimes, though, I think something must.... Nothing we expect, but something unforeseen." He paused and shut his eyes. "You remember in the old mythology tales how, when the sons of the gods were born, the mothers always died in agony? Maybe it's only Semele I'm thinking of. At any rate, I've sometimes wondered whether the young men of our time had to die to bring a new idea into the world... something Olympian. I'd like to know. I think I shall know. Since I've been over here this time, I've come to believe in immortality. Do you?"

Claude was confused by this quiet question. "I hardly know. I've never been able to make up my mind."

"Oh, don't bother about it! If it comes to you, it comes. You don't have to go after it. I arrived at it in quite the same way I used to get things in art,—knowing them and living on them before I understood them. Such ideas used to seem childish to me." Gerhardt sprang up. "Now, have I told you what you want to know about my case?" He looked down at Claude with a curious glimmer of amusement and affection. "I'm going to stretch my legs. It's four o'clock."

He disappeared among the red pine stems, where the sunlight made a rose-colored lake, as it used to do in the summer... as it would do in all the years to come, when they were not there to see it, Claude was thinking. He pulled his hat over his eyes and went to sleep.

The little girl on the edge of the beech wood left her sack and stole quietly down the hill. Sitting in the heather and drawing her feet up under her, she stayed still for a long time, and regarded with curiosity the relaxed, deep breathing body of the American soldier.

The next day was Claude's twenty-fifth birthday, and in honour of that event Papa Joubert produced a bottle of old Burgundy from his cellar, one of a few dozens he had laid in for great occasions when he was a young man.

During that week of idleness at Madame Joubert's, Claude often thought that the period of happy "youth," about which his old friend Mrs. Erlich used to talk, and which he had never experienced, was being made up to him now. He was having his youth in France. He knew that nothing like this would ever come again; the fields and woods would never again be laced over with this hazy enchantment. As he came up the village street in the purple evening, the smell of wood-smoke from the chimneys went to his head like a narcotic, opened the pores of his skin, and sometimes made the tears come to his eyes. Life had after all turned out well for him, and everything had a noble significance. The nervous tension in which he had lived for years now seemed incredible to him... absurd and childish, when he thought of it at all. He did not torture himself with recollections. He was beginning over again.

One night he dreamed that he was at home; out in the ploughed fields, where he could see nothing but the furrowed brown earth, stretching from horizon to horizon. Up and down it moved a boy, with a plough and two horses. At first he thought it was his brother Ralph; but on coming nearer, he saw it was himself,—and he was full of fear for this boy. Poor Claude, he would never, never get away; he was going to miss everything! While he was struggling to speak to Claude, and warn him, he awoke.

In the years when he went to school in Lincoln, he was always hunting for some one whom he could admire without reservations; some one he could envy, emulate, wish to be. Now he believed that even then he must have had some faint image of a man like Gerhardt in his mind. It was only in war times that their paths would have been likely to cross; or that they would have had anything to do together... any of the common interests that make men friends.

XIV.

GERHARDT AND CLAUDE Wheeler alighted from a taxi before the open gates of a square-roofed, solid-looking house, where all the shutters on the front were closed, and the tops of many trees showed above the garden wall. They crossed a paved court and rang at the door. An old valet admitted the young men, and took them through a wide hall to the salon, which opened on the garden. Madame and Mademoiselle would be down very soon. David went to one of the long windows and looked out. "They have kept it up, in spite of everything. It was always lovely here."

The garden was spacious,—like a little park. On one side was a tennis court, on the other a fountain, with a pool and water-lilies. The north wall was hidden by ancient yews; on the south two rows of plane trees, cut square, made a long arbour. At the back of the garden there were fine old lindens. The gravel walks wound about beds of gorgeous autumn flowers; in the rose garden, small white roses were still blooming, though the leaves were already red.

Two ladies entered the drawing-room. The mother was short, plump, and rosy, with strong, rather masculine features and yellowish white hair. The tears flashed into her eyes as David bent to kiss her hand, and she embraced him and touched both his cheeks with her lips.

"Et vous, vous aussi!" she murmured, touching the coat of his uniform with her fingers. There was but a moment of softness. She gathered herself up like an old general, Claude thought, as he stood watching the group from the window, drew her daughter forward, and asked David whether he recognized the little girl with whom he used to play. Mademoiselle Claire was not at all like her mother; slender, dark, dressed in a white costume de tennis and an apple green hat with black ribbons, she looked very modern and casual and unconcerned. She was already telling David she was glad he had arrived early, as now they would be able to have a game of tennis before tea. Maman would bring her knitting to the garden and watch them. This last suggestion relieved Claude's apprehension that he might be left alone with his hostess. When David called him and presented him to the ladies, Mlle. Claire gave him a quick handshake, and said she would be very glad to try him out on the court as soon as she had beaten David. They would find tennis shoes in their room,—a collection of shoes, for the feet of all nations; her brother's, some that his Russian friend had forgotten when he hurried off to be mobilized, and a pair lately left by an English officer who was quartered on them. She and her mother would wait in the garden. She rang for the old valet.

The Americans found themselves in a large room upstairs, where two modern iron beds stood out conspicuous among heavy mahogany bureaus and desks and dressing-tables, stuffed chairs and velvet carpets and dull red brocade window hangings. David went at once into the little dressing-room and began to array himself for the tennis court. Two suits of flannels and a row of soft shirts hung there on the wall.

"Aren't you going to change?" he asked, noticing that Claude stood stiff and unbending by the window, looking down into the garden. "Why should I?" said Claude scornfully. "I don't play tennis. I never had a racket in my hand."

"Too bad. She used to play very well, though she was only a youngster then." Gerhardt was regarding his legs in trousers two inches too short for him. "How everything has changed, and yet how everything is still the same! It's like coming back to places in dreams."

"They don't give you much time to dream, I should say!" Claude remarked.

"Fortunately!"

"Explain to the girl that I don't play, will you? I'll be down later."

"As you like."

Claude stood in the window, watching Gerhardt's bare head and Mlle. Claire's green hat and long brown arm go bounding about over the court.

When Gerhardt came to change before tea, he found his fellow officer standing before his bag, which was open, but not unpacked.

"What's the matter? Feeling shellshock again?"

"Not exactly." Claude bit his lip. "The fact is, Dave, I don't feel just comfortable here. Oh, the people are all right. But I'm out of place. I'm going to pull out and get a billet somewhere else, and let you visit your friends in peace. Why should I be here? These people don't keep a hotel."

"They very nearly do, from what they've been telling me. They've had a string of Scotch and English quartered on them. They like it, too,-or have the good manners to pretend they do. Of course, you'll do as you like, but you'll hurt their feelings and put me in an awkward position. To be frank, I don't see how you can go away without being distinctly rude."

Claude stood looking down at the contents of his bag in an irresolute attitude. Catching a glimpse of his face in one of the big mirrors, Gerhardt saw that he looked perplexed and miserable. His flash of temper died, and he put his hand lightly on his friend's shoulder.

"Come on, Claude! This is too absurd. You don't even have to dress, thanks to your uniform,—and you don't have to talk, since you're not supposed to know the language. I thought you'd like coming here. These people have had an awfully rough time; can't you admire their pluck?"

"Oh, yes, I do! It's awkward for me, though." Claude pulled off his coat and began to brush his hair vigorously. "I guess I've always been more afraid of the French than of the Germans. It takes courage to stay, you understand. I want to run."

"But why? What makes you want to?"

"Oh, I don't know! Something in the house, in the atmosphere."

"Something disagreeable?"

"No. Something agreeable."

David laughed. "Oh, you'll get over that!"

They had tea in the garden, English fashion—English tea, too, Mlle. Claire informed them, left by the English officers.

At dinner a third member of the family was introduced, a little boy with a cropped head and big black eyes. He sat on Claude's left, quiet and shy in his velvet jacket, though he followed the conversation eagerly, especially when it touched upon his brother Rene, killed at Verdun in the second winter of the war. The mother and sister talked about him as if he were living, about his letters and his plans, and his friends at the Conservatoire and in the

Army. Mlle. Claire told Gerhardt news of all the girl students he had known in Paris: how this one was singing for the soldiers; another, when she was nursing in a hospital which was bombed in an air raid, had carried twenty wounded men out of the burning building, one after another, on her back, like sacks of flour. Alice, the dancer, had gone into the English Red Cross and learned English. Odette had married a New Zealander, an officer who was said to be a cannibal; it was well known that his tribe had eaten two Auvergnat missionaries. There was a great deal more that Claude could not understand, but he got enough to see that for these women the war was France, the war was life, and everything that went into it. To be alive, to be conscious and have one's faculties, was to be in the war.

After dinner, when they went into the salon, Madame Fleury asked David whether he would like to see Rene's violin again, and nodded to the little boy. He slipped away and returned carrying the case, which he placed on the table. He opened it carefully and took off the velvet cloth, as if this was his peculiar office, then handed the instrument to Gerhardt.

David turned it over under the candles, telling Madame Fleury that he would have known it anywhere, Rene's wonderful Amati, almost too exquisite in tone for the concert hall, like a woman who is too beautiful for the stage. The family stood round and listened to his praise with evident satisfaction. Madame Fleury told him that Lucien was très sérieux with his music, that his master was well pleased with him, and when his hand was a little larger he would be allowed to play upon Rene's violin. Claude watched the little boy as he stood looking at the instrument in David's hands; in each of his big black eyes a candle flame was reflected, as if some steady fire were actually burning there.

"What is it, Lucien?" his mother asked.

"If Monsieur David would be so good as to play before I must go to bed—" he murmured entreatingly.

"But, Lucien, I am a soldier now. I have not worked at all for two years. The Amati would think it had fallen into the hands of a Boche."

Lucien smiled. "Oh, no! It is too intelligent for that. A little, please," and he sat down on a footstool before the sofa in confident anticipation.

Mlle. Claire went to the piano. David frowned and began to tune the violin. Madame Fleury called the old servant and told him to light the sticks that lay in the fireplace. She took the arm-chair at the right of the hearth and motioned Claude to a seat on the left. The little boy kept his stool at the other end of the room. Mlle. Claire began the orchestral introduction to the Saint-Saens concerto.

"Oh, not that!" David lifted his chin and looked at her in perplexity.

She made no reply, but played on, her shoulders bent forward. Lucien drew his knees up under his chin and shivered. When the time came, the violin made its entrance. David had put it back under his chin mechanically, and the instrument broke into that suppressed, bitter melody.

They played for a long while. At last David stopped and wiped his forehead. "I'm afraid I can't do anything with the third movement, really."

"Nor can I. But that was the last thing Rene played on it, the night before he went away, after his last leave." She began again, and David followed. Madame Fleury sat with half-closed eyes, looking into the fire. Claude, his lips compressed, his hands on his knees, was watching his friend's back. The music was a part of his own confused emotions. He was torn between generous admiration, and bitter, bitter envy. What would it mean to be able to do anything as well as that, to have a hand capable of delicacy and precision and power? If he had been taught to do anything at all, he would not be sitting here tonight a wooden thing amongst living people. He felt that a man might have been made of him, but nobody had taken the trouble to do it; tongue-tied, foot-tied, hand-tied. If one were born into this world like a bear cub or a bull calf, one could only paw and upset things, break and destroy, all one's life.

Gerhardt wrapped the violin up in its cloth. The little boy thanked him and carried it away. Madame Fleury and her daughter wished their guests goodnight.

David said he was warm, and suggested going into the garden to smoke before they went to bed. He opened one of the long windows and they stepped out on the terrace. Dry leaves were rustling down on the walks; the yew trees made a solid wall, blacker than the darkness. The fountain must have caught the starlight; it was the only shining thing,—a little clear column of twinkling silver. The boys strolled in silence to the end of the walk.

"I guess you'll go back to your profession, all right," Claude remarked, in the unnatural tone in which people sometimes speak of things they know nothing about.

"Not I. Of course, I had to play for them. Music has always been like a religion in this house. Listen," he put up his hand; far away the regular pulsation of the big guns sounded through the still night. "That's all that matters now. It has killed everything else."

"I don't believe it." Claude stopped for a moment by the edge of the fountain, trying to collect his thoughts. "I don't believe it has killed anything. It has only scattered things." He glanced about hurriedly at the sleeping house, the sleeping garden, the clear, starry sky not very far overhead. "It's men like you that get the worst of it," he broke out. "But as for me, I never knew there was anything worth living for, till this war came on. Before that, the world seemed like a business proposition."

"You'll admit it's a costly way of providing adventure for the young," said David drily.

"Maybe so; all the same..."

Claude pursued the argument to himself long after they were in their luxurious beds and David was asleep. No battlefield or shattered country he had seen was as ugly as this world would be if men like his brother Bayliss controlled it altogether. Until the war broke out, he had supposed they did control it; his boyhood had been clouded and enervated by that belief. The Prussians had believed it, too, apparently. But the event had shown that there were a great many people left who cared about something else.

The intervals of the distant artillery fire grew shorter, as if the big guns were tuning up, choking to get something out. Claude sat up in his bed and listened. The sound of the guns had from the first been pleasant to him, had given him a feeling of confidence and safety; tonight he knew why. What they said was, that men could still die for an idea; and would burn all they had made to keep their dreams. He knew the future of the world was safe; the careful planners would never be able to put it into a strait-jacket,—cunning and prudence would never have it to themselves. Why, that little boy downstairs, with the candlelight in his eyes, when it came to the last cry, as they said, could "carry on" for ever! Ideals were not archaic things, beautiful and impotent; they were the real sources of power among men. As long as that was true, and now he knew it was true—he had come all this way to find out—he had no quarrel with Destiny. Nor did he envy David. He would give his own adventure for no man's. On the edge of sleep it seemed to glimmer, like the clear column of the fountain, like the new moon,—alluring, half-averted, the bright face of danger.

XV.

When Claude and David rejoined their Battalion on the 20th of September, the end of the war looked as far away as ever. The collapse of Bulgaria was unknown to the American army, and their acquaintance with European affairs was so slight that this would have meant very little to them had they heard of it. The German army still held the north and east of France, and no one could say how much vitality was left in that sprawling body.

The Battalion entrained at Arras. Lieutenant Colonel Scott had orders to proceed to the railhead, and then advance on foot into the Argonne.

The cars were crowded, and the railway journey was long and fatiguing. They detrained at night, in the rain, at what the men said seemed to be the jumping off place. There was no town, and the railway station had been bombed the day before, by an air fleet out to explode artillery ammunition. A mound of brick, and holes full of water told where it had been. The Colonel sent Claude out with a patrol to find some place for the men to sleep. The patrol came upon a field of straw stacks, and at the end of it found a black farmhouse.

Claude went up and hammered on the door. Silence. He kept hammering and calling, "The Americans are here!" A shutter opened. The farmer stuck his head out and demanded gruffly what was wanted; "What now?"

Claude explained in his best French that an American battalion had just come in; might they sleep in his field if they did not destroy his stacks?

"Sure," replied the farmer, and shut the window.

That one word, coming out of the dark in such an unpromising place, had a cheering effect upon the patrol, and upon the men, when it was repeated to them. "Sure, eh?" They kept laughing over it as they beat about the field and dug into the straw. Those who couldn't burrow into a stack lay down in the muddy stubble. They were asleep before they could feel sorry for themselves.

The farmer came out to offer his stable to the officers, and to beg them not on any account to make a light. They had never been bothered here by air raids until yesterday, and it must be because the Americans were coming and were sending in ammunition.

Gerhardt, who was called to talk to him, told the farmer the Colonel must study his map, and for that the man took them down into the cellar, where the children were asleep. Before he lay down on the straw bed his orderly had made for him, the Colonel kept telling names and kilometers off on his fingers. For officers like Colonel Scott the names of places constituted one of the real hardships of the war. His mind worked slowly, but it was always on his job, and he could go without sleep for more hours together than any of his officers. Tonight he had scarcely lain down, when a sentinel brought in a runner with a message. The Colonel had to go into the cellar again to read it. He was to meet Colonel Harvey at Prince Joachim farm, as early as possible tomorrow morning. The runner would act as guide.

The Colonel sat with his eye on his watch, and interrogated the messenger about the road and the time it would take to get over the ground. "What's Fritz's temper up here, generally speaking?"

"That's as it happens, sir. Sometimes we nab a night patrol of a dozen or fifteen and send them to the rear under a one-man guard. Then, again, a little bunch of Heinies will fight like the devil. They say it depends on what part of Germany they come from; the Bavarians and Saxons are the bravest."

Colonel Scott waited for an hour, and then went about, shaking his sleeping officers.

"Yes, sir." Captain Maxey sprang to his feet as if he had been caught in a disgraceful act. He called his sergeants, and they began to beat the men up out of the strawstacks and puddles. In half an hour they were on the road.

This was the Battalion's first march over really bad roads, where walking was a question of pulling and balancing. They were soon warm, at any rate; it kept them sweating. The weight of their equipment was continually thrown in the wrong place. Their wet clothing dragged them back, their packs got twisted and cut into their shoulders. Claude and Hicks began wondering to each other what it must have been like in the real mud, up about Ypres and Passchendaele, two years ago. Hicks had been training at Arras last week, where a lot of Tommies were "resting" in the same way, and he had tales to tell.

The Battalion got to Joachim farm at nine o'clock. Colonel Harvey had not yet come up, but old Julius Caesar was there with his engineers, and he had a hot breakfast ready for them. At six o'clock in the evening they took the road again, marching until daybreak, with short rests. During the night they captured two Hun patrols, a bunch of thirty men. At the halt for breakfast, the prisoners wanted to make themselves useful, but the cook said they were so filthy the smell of them would make a stew go bad. They were herded off by themselves, a good distance from the grub line.

It was Gerhardt, of course, who had to go over and question them. Claude felt sorry for the prisoners; they were so willing to tell all they knew, and so anxious to make themselves agreeable; began talking about their relatives in America, and said brightly that they themselves were going over at once, after the war—seemed to have no doubt that everybody would be glad to see them!

They begged Gerhardt to be allowed to do something. Couldn't they carry the officers' equipment on the march? No, they were too buggy; they might relieve the sanitary squad. Oh, that they would gladly do, Herr Offizier!

The plan was to get to Rupprecht trench and take it before nightfall. It was easy taking—empty of everything but vermin and human discards; a dozen crippled and sick, left for the enemy to dispose of, and several half-witted youths who ought to have been locked up in some institution. Fritz had known what it meant when his patrols did not come back. He had evacuated, leaving behind his hopelessly diseased, and as much filth as possible. The dugouts were fairly dry, but so crawling with vermin that the Americans preferred to sleep in the mud, in the open.

After supper the men fell on their packs and began to lighten them, throwing away all that was not necessary, and much that was. Many of them abandoned the new overcoats that had been served out at the railhead; others cut off the skirts and made the coats into ragged jackets. Captain Maxey was horrified at these depredations, but the Colonel advised him to shut his eyes. "They've got hard going before them; let them travel light. If they'd rather stand the cold, they've got a right to choose."

XVI.

THE BATTALION HAD TWENTY-FOUR HOURS' rest at Rupprecht trench, and then pushed on for four days and nights, stealing trenches, capturing patrols, with only a few hours' sleep,—snatched by the roadside while their food was being prepared. They pushed hard after a retiring foe, and almost outran themselves. They did outrun their provisions; on the fourth night, when they fell upon a farm that had been a German Headquarters, the supplies that were to meet them there had not come up, and they went to bed supperless.

This farmhouse, for some reason called by the prisoners Frau Hulda farm, was a nest of telephone wires; hundreds of them ran out through the walls, in all directions. The Colonel cut those he could find, and then put a guard over the old peasant who had been left in charge of the house, suspecting that he was in the pay of the enemy.

At last Colonel Scott got into the Headquarters bed, large and lumpy,—the first one he had seen since he left Arras. He had not been asleep more than two hours, when a runner arrived with orders from the Regimental Colonel. Claude was in a bed in the loft, between Gerhardt and Bruger. He felt somebody shaking him, but resolved that he wouldn't be disturbed and went on placidly sleeping. Then somebody pulled his hair,—so hard that he sat up. Captain Maxey was standing over the bed.

"Come along, boys. Orders from Regimental Headquarters. The Battalion is to split here. Our Company is to go on four kilometers tonight, and take the town of Beaufort."

Claude rose. "The men are pretty well beat out, Captain Maxey, and they had no supper."

"That can't be helped. Tell them we are to be in Beaufort for breakfast."

Claude and Gerhardt went out to the barn and roused Hicks and his pal, Dell Able. The men were asleep in dry straw, for the first time in ten days. They were completely worn out, lost to time and place. Many of them were already four thousand miles away, scattered among little towns and farms on the prairie. They were a miserable looking lot as they got together, stumbling about in the dark.

After the Colonel had gone over the map with Captain Maxey, he came out and saw the Company assembled. He wasn't going with them, he told them, but he expected them to give a good account of themselves. Once in Beaufort, they would have a week's rest; sleep under cover, and live among people for awhile.

The men took the road, some with their eyes shut, trying to make believe they were still asleep, trying to have their agreeable dreams over again, as they marched. They did not really waken up until the advance challenged a Hun patrol, and sent it back to the Colonel under a one-man guard. When they had advanced two kilometers, they found the bridge blown up. Claude and Hicks went in one direction to look for a ford, Bruger and Dell Able in the other, and the men lay down by the roadside and slept heavily. Just at dawn they reached the outskirts of the village, silent and still.

Captain Maxey had no information as to how many Germans might be left in the town. They had occupied it ever since the beginning of the war, and had used it as a rest camp. There had never been any fighting there.

At the first house on the road, the Captain stopped and pounded. No answer.

"We are Americans, and must see the people of the house. If you don't open, we must break the door."

A woman's voice called; "There is nobody here. Go away, please, and take your men away. I am sick."

The Captain called Gerhardt, who began to explain and reassure through the door. It opened a little way, and an old woman in a nightcap peeped out. An old man hovered behind her. She gazed in astonishment at the officers, not understanding. These were the first soldiers of the Allies she had ever seen. She had heard the Germans talk about Americans, but thought it was one of their lies, she said. Once convinced, she let the officers come in and replied to their questions.

No, there were no Boches left in her house. They had got orders to leave day before yesterday, and had blown up the bridge. They were concentrating somewhere to the east. She didn't know how many were still in the village, nor where they were, but she could tell the Captain where they had been. Triumphantly she brought out a map of the town—lost, she said with a meaning smile, by a German officer—on which the billets were marked.

With this to guide them, Captain Maxey and his men went on up the street. They took eight prisoners in one cellar, seventeen in another. When the villagers saw the prisoners bunched together in the square, they came out of their houses and gave information. This cleaning up, Bert Fuller remarked, was like taking fish from the Platte River when the water was low, simply pailing them out! There was no sport in it.

At nine o'clock the officers were standing together in the square before the church, checking off on the map the houses that had been searched. The men were drinking coffee, and eating fresh bread from a baker's shop. The square was full of people who had come out to see for themselves. Some believed that deliverance had come, and others shook their heads and held back, suspecting another trick. A crowd of children were running about, making friends with the soldiers. One little girl with yellow curls and a clean white dress had attached herself to Hicks, and was eating chocolate out of his pocket. Gerhardt was bargaining with the baker for another baking of bread. The sun was shining, for a change,—everything was looking cheerful. This village seemed to be swarming with girls; some of them were pretty, and all were friendly. The men who had looked so haggard and forlorn when dawn overtook them at the edge of the town, began squaring their shoulders and throwing out their chests. They were dirty and mud-plastered, but as Claude remarked to the Captain, they actually looked like fresh men.

Suddenly a shot rang out above the chatter, and an old woman in a white cap screamed and tumbled over on the pavement,—rolled about, kicking indecorously with both hands and feet. A second crack,—the little girl who stood beside Hicks, eating chocolate, threw out her hands, ran a few steps, and fell, blood and brains oozing out in her yellow hair. The people began screaming and running. The Americans looked this way and that; ready to dash, but not knowing where to go. Another shot, and Captain Maxey fell on one knee, blushed furiously and sprang up, only to fall again,—ashy white, with the leg of his trousers going red.

"There it is, to the left!" Hicks shouted, pointing. They saw now. From a closed house, some distance down a street off the square, smoke was coming. It hung before one of the upstairs windows. The Captain's orderly dragged him into a wineshop. Claude and David, followed by the men, ran down the street and broke in the door. The two officers went through the rooms on the first floor, while Hicks and his lot made straight for an enclosed stairway at the back of the house. As they reached the foot of the stairs, they were met by a volley of rifle shots, and two of the men tumbled over. Four Germans were stationed at the head of the steps.

The Americans scarcely knew whether their bullets or their bayonets got to the Huns first; they were not conscious of going up, till they were there. When Claude and David reached the landing, the squad were wiping their bayonets, and four grey bodies were piled in the corner.

Bert Fuller and Dell Able ran down the narrow hallway and threw open the door into the room on the street. Two shots, and Dell came back with his jaw shattered and the blood spouting from the left side of his neck. Gerhardt caught him, and tried to close the artery with his fingers.

"How many are in there, Bert?" Claude called.

"I couldn't see. Look out, sir! You can't get through that door more than two at a time!"

The door still stood open, at the end of the corridor. Claude went down the steps until he could sight along the floor of the passage, into the front room. The shutters were closed in there, and the sunlight came through the slats. In the middle of the floor, between the door and the windows, stood a tall chest of drawers, with a mirror attached to the top. In the narrow space between the bottom of this piece of furniture and the floor, he could see a pair of boots. It was possible there was but one man in the room, shooting from behind his movable fort,—though there might be others hidden in the corners.

"There's only one fellow in there, I guess. He's shooting from behind a big dresser in the middle of the room. Come on, one of you, we'll have to go in and get him."

Willy Katz, the Austrian boy from the Omaha packing house, stepped up and stood beside him.

"Now, Willy, we'll both go in at once; you jump to the right, and I to the left,—and one of us will jab him. He can't shoot both ways at once. Are you ready? All right—Now!"

Claude thought he was taking the more dangerous position himself, but the German probably reasoned that the important man would be on the right. As the two Americans dashed through the door, he fired. Claude caught him in the back with his bayonet, under the shoulder blade, but Willy Katz had got the bullet in his brain, through one of his blue eyes. He fell, and never stirred. The German officer fired his revolver again as he went down, shouting in English, English with no foreign accent,

"You swine, go back to Chicago!" Then he began choking with blood.

Sergeant Hicks ran in and shot the dying man through the temples. Nobody stopped him.

The officer was a tall man, covered with medals and orders; must have been very handsome. His linen and his hands were as white as if he were going to a ball. On the dresser were the files and paste and buffers with which he had kept his nails so pink and smooth. A ring with a ruby, beautifully cut, was on his little finger. Bert Fuller screwed it off and offered it to Claude. He shook his head. That English sentence had unnerved him. Bert held the ring out to Hicks, but the Sergeant threw down his revolver and broke out:

"Think I'd touch anything of his? That beautiful little girl, and my buddy—He's worse than dead, Dell is, worse!" He turned his back on his comrades so that they wouldn't see him cry.

"Can I keep it myself, sir?" Bert asked.

Claude nodded. David had come in, and was opening the shutters. This officer, Claude was thinking, was a very different sort of being from the poor prisoners they had been scooping up like tadpoles from the cellars. One of the men picked up a gorgeous silk dressing gown from the bed, another pointed to a dressing-case full of hammered silver. Gerhardt said it was Russian silver; this man must have come from the Eastern front. Bert Fuller and Nifty Jones were going through the officer's pockets. Claude watched them, and thought they did about right. They didn't touch his medals; but his gold cigarette case, and the platinum watch still ticking on his wrist,—he wouldn't have further need for them. Around his neck, hung by a delicate chain, was a miniature case, and in it was a painting,—not, as Bert romantically hoped when he opened it, of a beautiful woman, but of a young man, pale as snow, with blurred forget-me-not eyes.

Claude studied it, wondering. "It looks like a poet, or something. Probably a kid brother, killed at the beginning of the war."

Gerhardt took it and glanced at it with a disdainful expression. "Probably. There, let him keep it, Bert." He touched Claude on the shoulder to call his attention to the inlay work on the handle of the officer's revolver.

Claude noticed that David looked at him as if he were very much pleased with him,—looked, indeed, as if something pleasant had happened in this room; where, God knew, nothing had; where, when they turned round, a swarm of black flies was quivering with greed and delight over the smears Willy Katz' body had left on the floor. Claude had often observed that when David had an interesting idea, or a strong twinge of recollection, it made him, for the moment, rather heartless. Just now he felt that Gerhardt's flash of high spirits was in some way connected with him. Was it because he had gone in with Willy? Had David doubted his nerve?

XVII.

WHEN THE SURVIVORS of Company B are old men, and are telling over their good days, they will say to each other, "Oh, that week we spent at Beaufort!" They will close their eyes and see a little village on a low ridge, lost in the forest, overgrown with oak and chestnut and black walnut… buried in autumn colour, the streets drifted deep in autumn leaves, great branches interlacing over the roofs of the houses, wells of cool water that tastes of moss and tree roots. Up and down those streets they will see figures passing; themselves, young and brown and clean-limbed; and comrades, long dead, but still alive in that far-away village. How they will wish they could tramp again, nights on days in the mud and rain, to drag sore feet into their old billets at Beaufort! To sink into those wide feather beds and sleep the round of the clock while the old women washed and dried their clothes for them; to eat rabbit stew and pommes frites in the garden,—rabbit stew made with red wine and chestnuts. Oh, the days that are no more!

As soon as Captain Maxey and the wounded men had been started on their long journey to the rear, carried by the prisoners, the whole company turned in and slept for twelve hours —all but Sergeant Hicks, who sat in the house off the square, beside the body of his chum.

The next day the Americans came to life as if they were new men, just created in a new world. And the people of the town came to life… excitement, change, something to look forward to at last! A new flag, le drapeau étoilé, floated along with the tricolour in the square. At sunset the soldiers stood in formation behind it and sang "The Star Spangled Banner" with uncovered heads. The old people watched them from the doorways. The Americans were the first to bring "Madelon" to Beaufort. The fact that the village had never heard this song, that the children stood round begging for it, "Chantez-vous la Madelon!" made the soldiers realize how far and how long out of the world these villagers had been. The German occupation was like a deafness which nothing pierced but their own arrogant martial airs.

Before Claude was out of bed after his first long sleep, a runner arrived from Colonel Scott, notifying him that he was in charge of the Company until further orders. The German prisoners had buried their own dead and dug graves for the Americans before they were sent off to the rear. Claude and David were billeted at the edge of the town, with the woman who had given Captain Maxey his first information, when they marched in yesterday morning. Their hostess told them, at their mid-day breakfast, that the old dame who was shot in the square, and the little girl, were to be buried this afternoon. Claude decided that the Americans might as well have their funeral at the same time. He thought he would ask the priest to say a prayer at the graves, and he and David set off through the brilliant, rustling autumn sunshine to find the Cure's house. It was next the church, with a high-walled garden behind it. Over the bell-pull in the outer wall was a card on which was written, "Tirez fort."

The priest himself came out to them, an old man who seemed weak like his doorbell. He stood in his black cap, holding his hands against his breast to keep them from shaking, and looked very old indeed,—broken, hopeless, as if he were sick of this world and done with it. Nowhere in France had Claude seen a face so sad as his. Yes, he would say a prayer. It was better to have Christian burial, and they were far from home, poor fellows! David asked him whether the German rule had been very oppressive, but the old man did not answer clearly, and his hands began to shake so uncontrollably over his cassock that they went away to spare him embarrassment.

"He seems a little gone in the head, don't you think?" Claude remarked.

"I suppose the war has used him up. How can he celebrate mass when his hands quiver so?" As they crossed the church steps, David touched Claude's arm and pointed into the square. "Look, every doughboy has a girl already! Some of them have trotted out fatigue caps! I supposed they'd thrown them all away!"

Those who had no caps stood with their helmets under their arms, in attitudes of exaggerated gallantry, talking to the women,—who seemed all to have errands abroad. Some of them let the boys carry their baskets. One soldier was giving a delighted little girl a ride on his back.

After the funeral every man in the Company found some sympathetic woman to talk to about his fallen comrades. All the garden flowers and bead wreaths in Beaufort had been carried out and put on the American graves. When the squad fired over them and the bugle sounded, the girls and their mothers wept. Poor Willy Katz, for instance, could never have had such a funeral in South Omaha.

The next night the soldiers began teaching the girls to dance the "Pas Seul" and the "Fausse Trot." They had found an old violin in the town; and Oscar, the Swede, scraped away on it. They danced every evening. Claude saw that a good deal was going on, and he lectured his men at parade. But he realized that he might as well scold at the sparrows. Here was a village with several hundred women, and only the grandmothers had husbands. All the men were in the army; hadn't even been home on leave since the Germans first took the place. The girls had been shut up for four years with young men who incessantly coveted them, and whom they must constantly outwit. The situation had been intolerable—and prolonged. The Americans found themselves in the position of Adam in the garden.

"Did you know, sir," said Bert Fuller breathlessly as he overtook Claude in the street after parade, "that these lovely girls had to go out in the fields and work, raising things for those dirty pigs to eat? Yes, sir, had to work in the fields, under German sentinels; marched out in the morning and back at night like convicts! It's sure up to us to give them a good time now."

One couldn't walk out of an evening without meeting loitering couples in the dusky streets and lanes. The boys had lost all their bashfulness about trying to speak French. They declared they could get along in France with three verbs, and all, happily, in the first conjugation: manger, aimer, payer,—quite enough! They called Beaufort "our town," and they were called "our Americans." They were going to come back after the war, and marry the girls, and put in waterworks!

"Chez-moi, sir!" Bill Gates called to Claude, saluting with a bloody hand, as he stood skinning rabbits before the door of his billet. "Bunny casualties are heavy in town this week!"

"You know, Wheeler," David remarked one morning as they were shaving, "I think Maxey would come back here on one leg if he knew about these excursions into the forest after mushrooms."

"Maybe."

"Aren't you going to put a stop to them?"

"Not I!" Claude jerked, setting the corners of his mouth grimly. "If the girls, or their people, make complaint to me, I'll interfere. Not otherwise. I've thought the matter over."

"Oh, the girls—" David laughed softly. "Well, it's something to acquire a taste for mushrooms. They don't get them at home, do they?"

When, after eight days, the Americans had orders to march, there was mourning in every house. On their last night in town, the officers received pressing invitations to the dance in the square. Claude went for a few moments, and looked on. David was dancing every dance, but Hicks was nowhere to be seen. The poor fellow had been out of everything. Claude went over to the church to see whether he might be moping in the graveyard.

There, as he walked about, Claude stopped to look at a grave that stood off by itself, under a privet hedge, with withered leaves and a little French flag on it. The old woman with whom they stayed had told them the story of this grave.

The Cure's niece was buried there. She was the prettiest girl in Beaufort, it seemed, and she had a love affair with a German officer and disgraced the town. He was a young Bavarian, quartered with this same old woman who told them the story, and she said he was a nice boy, handsome and gentle, and used to sit up half the night in the garden with his head in his hands—homesick, lovesick. He was always after this Marie Louise; never pressed her, but was always there, grew up out of the ground under her feet, the old woman said. The girl hated Germans, like all the rest, and flouted him. He was sent to the front. Then he came back, sick and almost deaf, after one of the slaughters at Verdun, and stayed a long while. That spring a story got about that some woman met him at night in the German graveyard. The Germans had taken the land behind the church for their cemetery, and it joined the wall of the Cure's garden. When the women went out into the fields to plant the crops, Marie Louise used to slip away from the others and meet her Bavarian in the forest. The girls were sure of it now; and they treated her with disdain. But nobody was brave enough to say anything to the Cure. One day, when she was with her Bavarian in the wood, she snatched up his revolver from the ground and shot herself. She was a Frenchwoman at heart, their hostess said.

"And the Bavarian?" Claude asked David later. The story had become so complicated he could not follow it.

"He justified her, and promptly. He took the same pistol and shot himself through the temples. His orderly, stationed at the edge of the thicket to keep watch, heard the first shot and ran toward them. He saw the officer take up the smoking pistol and turn it on himself. But the Kommandant couldn't believe that one of his officers had so much feeling. He held an enquête, dragged the girl's mother and uncle into court, and tried to establish that they were in conspiracy with her to seduce and murder a German officer. The orderly was made to tell the whole story; how and where they began to meet. Though he wasn't very delicate about the details he divulged, he stuck to his statement that he saw Lieutenant Muller shoot himself with his own hand, and the Kommandant failed to prove his case. The old Cure had known nothing of all this until he heard it aired in the military court. Marie Louise had lived in his house since she was a child, and was like his daughter. He had a stroke or something, and has been like this ever since. The girl's friends forgave her, and when she was buried off alone by the hedge, they began to take flowers to her grave. The Kommandant put up an affiche on the hedge, forbidding any one to decorate the grave. Apparently, nothing during the German occupation stirred up more feeling than poor Marie Louise."

It would stir anybody, Claude reflected. There was her lonely little grave, the shadow of the privet hedge falling across it. There, at the foot of the Cure's garden, was the German cemetery, with heavy cement crosses,—some of them with long inscriptions; lines from their poets, and couplets from old hymns. Lieutenant Muller was there somewhere, probably. Strange, how their story stood out in a world of suffering. That was a kind of misery he hadn't happened to think of before; but the same thing must have occurred again and again in the occupied territory. He would never forget the Cure's hands, his dim, suffering eyes.

Claude recognized David crossing the pavement in front of the church, and went back to meet him.

"Hello! I mistook you for Hicks at first. I thought he might be out here." David sat down on the steps and lit a cigarette.

"So did I. I came out to look for him."

"Oh, I expect he's found some shoulder to cry on. Do you realize, Claude, you and I are the only men in the Company who haven't got engaged? Some of the married men have got engaged twice. It's a good thing we're pulling out, or we'd have banns and a bunch of christenings to look after." "All the same," murmured Claude, "I like the women of this country, as far as I've seen them." While they sat smoking in silence, his mind went back to the quiet scene he had watched on the steps of that other church, on his first night in France; the country girl in the moonlight, bending over her sick soldier.

When they walked back across the square, over the crackling leaves, the dance was breaking up. Oscar was playing "Home, Sweet Home," for the last waltz.

"Le dernier baiser," said David. "Well, tomorrow we'll be gone, and the chances are we won't come back this way."

XVIII.

"WITH US IT'S always a feast or a famine," the men groaned, when they sat down by the road to munch dry biscuit at noon. They had covered eighteen miles that morning, and had still seven more to go. They were ordered to do the twenty-five miles in eight hours. Nobody had fallen out yet, but some of the boys looked pretty well wilted. Nifty Jones said he was done for. Sergeant Hicks was expostulating with the faint-hearted. He knew that if one man fell out, a dozen would.

"If I can do it, you can. It's worse on a fat man like me. This is no march to make a fuss about. Why, at Arras I talked with a little Tommy from one of those Pal Battalions that got slaughtered on the Somme. His battalion marched twenty-five miles in six hours, in the heat of July, into certain death. They were all kids out of school, not a man of them over five-foot-three, called them the 'Bantams.' You've got to hand it to them, fellows."

"I'll hand anything to anybody, but I can't go no farther on these," Jones muttered, nursing his sore feet.

"Oh, you! We're going to heave you onto the only horse in the Company. The officers, they can walk!"

When they got into Battalion lines there was food ready for them, but very few wanted it. They drank and lay down in the bushes. Claude went at once to Headquarters and found Barclay Owens, of the Engineers, with the Colonel, who was smoking and studying his maps as usual.

"Glad to see you, Wheeler. Your men ought to be in good shape, after a week's rest. Let them sleep now. We've got to move out of here before midnight, to relieve two Texas battalions at Moltke trench. They've taken the trench with heavy casualties and are beat out; couldn't hold it in case of counter-attack. As it's an important point, the enemy will try to recover it. I want to get into position before daylight, so he won't know fresh troops are coming in. As ranking officer, you are in charge of the Company."

"Very well, sir. I'll do my best."

"I'm sure you will. Two machine gun teams are going up with us, and some time tomorrow a Missouri battalion comes up to support. I'd have had you over here before, but I only got my orders to relieve yesterday. We may have to advance under shell fire. The enemy has been putting a lot of big stuff over; he wants to cut off that trench."

Claude and David got into a fresh shell hole, under the half-burned scrub, and fell asleep. They were awakened at dusk by heavy artillery fire from the north.

At ten o'clock the Battalion, after a hot meal, began to advance through almost impassable country. The guns must have been pounding away at the same range for a long while; the ground was worked and kneaded until it was soft as dough, though no rain had fallen for a week. Barclay Owens and his engineers were throwing down a plank road to get food and the ammunition wagons across. Big shells were coming over at intervals of twelve minutes. The intervals were so regular that it was quite possible to get forward without damage. While B Company was pulling through the shell area, Colonel Scott overtook them, on foot, his orderly leading his horse.

"Know anything about that light over there, Wheeler?" he asked. "Well, it oughtn't to be there. Come along and see."

The light was a mere match-head down in the ground, Claude hadn't noticed it before. He followed the Colonel, and when they reached the spark they found three officers of A Company crouching in a shell crater, covered with a piece of sheet-iron.

"Put out that light," called the Colonel sharply. "What's the matter, Captain Brace?"

A young man rose quickly. "I'm waiting for the water, sir. It's coming up on mules, in petrol cases, and I don't want to get separated from it. The ground's so bad here the drivers are likely to get lost."

"Don't wait more than twenty minutes. You must get up and take your position on time, that's the important thing, water or no water."

As the Colonel and Claude hurried back to overtake the Company, five big shells screamed over them in rapid succession. "Run, sir," the orderly called. "They're getting on to us; they've shortened the range."

"That light back there was just enough to give them an idea," the Colonel muttered.

The bad ground continued for about a mile, and then the advance reached Headquarters, behind the eighth trench of the great system of trenches. It was an old farmhouse which the Germans had made over with reinforced concrete, lining it within and without, until the walls were six feet thick and almost shell-proof, like a pill-box. The Colonel sent his orderly to enquire about A Company. A young Lieutenant came to the door of the farmhouse.

"A Company is ready to go into position, sir. I brought them up."

"Where is Captain Brace, Lieutenant?"

"He and both our first lieutenants were killed, Colonel. Back in that hole. A shell fell on them not five minutes after you were talking to them."

"That's bad. Any other damage?"

"Yes, sir. There was a cook wagon struck at the same time; the first one coming along Julius Caesar's new road. The driver was killed, and we had to shoot the horses. Captain Owens, he near got scalded with the stew."

The Colonel called in the officers one after another and discussed their positions with them.

"Wheeler," he said when Claude's turn came, "you know your map? You've noticed that sharp loop in the front trench, in H 2; the Boar's Head, I believe they call it. It's a sort of spear point that reaches out toward the enemy, and it will be a hot place to hold. If I put your company in there, do you think you can do the Battalion credit in case of a counter attack?"

Claude said he thought so.

"It's the nastiest bit of the line to hold, and you can tell your men I pay them a compliment when I put them there."

"All right, sir. They'll appreciate it."

The Colonel bit off the end of a fresh cigar. "They'd better, by thunder! If they give way and let the Hun bombers in, it will let down the whole line. I'll give you two teams of Georgia machine guns to put in that point they call the Boar's Snout. When the Missourians come up tomorrow, they'll go in to support you, but until then you'll have to take care of the loop yourselves. I've got an awful lot of trench to hold, and I can't spare you any more men."

The Texas men whom the Battalion came up to relieve had been living for sixty hours on their iron rations, and on what they could pick off the dead Huns. Their supplies had been shelled on the way, and nothing had got through to them. When the Colonel took Claude and Gerhardt forward to inspect the loop that B Company was to hold, they found a wallow, more like a dump heap than a trench. The men who had taken the position were almost too weak to stand. All their officers had been killed, and a sergeant was in command. He apologized for the condition of the loop.

"Sorry to leave such a mess for you to clean up, sir, but we got it bad in here. He's been shelling us every night since we drove him out. I couldn't ask the men to do anything but hold on."

"That's all right. You beat it, with your boys, quick! My men will hand you out some grub as you go back."

The battered defenders of the Boar's Head stumbled past them through the darkness into the communication. When the last man had filed out, the Colonel sent for Barclay Owens. Claude and David tried to feel their way about and get some idea of the condition the place was in. The stench was the worst they had yet encountered, but it was less disgusting than the flies; when they inadvertently touched a dead body, clouds of wet, buzzing flies flew up into their faces, into their eyes and nostrils. Under their feet the earth worked and moved as if boa constrictors were wriggling down there soft bodies, lightly covered. When they had found their way up to the Snout they came upon a pile of corpses, a dozen or more, thrown one on top of another like sacks of flour, faintly discernible in the darkness. While the two officers stood there, rumbling, squirting sounds began to come from this heap, first from one body, then from another—gases, swelling in the liquefying entrails of the dead men. They seemed to be complaining to one another; glup, glup, glup.

The boys went back to the Colonel, who was standing at the mouth of the communication, and told him there was nothing much to report, except that the burying squad was needed badly.

"I expect!" The Colonel shook his head. When Barclay Owens arrived, he asked him what could be done here before daybreak. The doughty engineer felt his way about as Claude and Gerhardt had done; they heard him coughing, and beating off the flies. But when he came back he seemed rather cheered than discouraged.

"Give me a gang to get the casualties out, and with plenty of quick-lime and concrete I can make this loop all right in four hours, sir," he declared.

"I've brought plenty of lime, but where'll you get your concrete?"

"The Hun left about fifty sacks of it in the cellar, under your Headquarters. I can do better, of course, if I have a few hours more for my concrete to dry."

"Go ahead, Captain." The Colonel told Claude and David to bring their men up to the communication before light, and hold them ready. "Give Owens' cement a chance, but don't let the enemy put over any surprise on you."

The shelling began again at daybreak; it was hardest on the rear trenches and the three-mile area behind. Evidently the enemy felt sure of what he had in Moltke trench; he wanted to cut off supplies and possible reinforcements. The Missouri battalion did not come up that day, but before noon a runner arrived from their Colonel, with information that they were hiding in the wood. Five Boche planes had been circling over the wood since dawn, signalling to the enemy Headquarters back on Dauphin Ridge; the Missourians were sure they had avoided detection by lying close in the under-brush. They would come up in the night. Their linemen were following the runner, and Colonel Scott would be in telephone communication with them in half an hour.

When B Company moved into the Boar's Head at one o'clock in the afternoon, they could truthfully say that the prevailing smell was now that of quick-lime. The parapet was evenly built up, the firing step had been partly restored, and in the Snout there were good emplacements for the machine guns. Certain unpleasant reminders were still to be found if one looked for them. In the Snout a large fat boot stuck stiffly from the side of the trench. Captain Ovens explained that the ground sounded hollow in there, and the boot probably led back into a dugout where a lot of Hun bodies were entombed together. As he was pressed for time, he had thought best not to look for trouble. In one of the curves of the loop, just at the top of the earth wall, under the sand bags, a dark hand reached out; the five fingers, well apart, looked like the swollen roots of some noxious weed. Hicks declared that this object was disgusting, and during the afternoon he made Nifty Jones and Oscar scrape down some earth and make a hump over the paw. But there was shelling in the night, and the earth fell away.

"Look," said Jones when he wakened his Sergeant. "The first thing I seen when daylight come was his old fingers, wigglin' in the breeze. He wants air, Heinie does; he won't stay covered."

Hicks got up and re-buried the hand himself, but when he came around with Claude on inspection, before breakfast, there were the same five fingers sticking out again. The Sergeant's forehead puffed up and got red, and he swore that if he found the man who played dirty jokes, he'd make him eat this one.

The Colonel sent for Claude and Gerhardt to come to breakfast with him. He had been talking by telephone with the Missouri officers and had agreed that they should stay back in the bush for the present. The continual circling of planes over the wood seemed to indicate that the enemy was concerned about the actual strength of Moltke trench. It was possible their air scouts had seen the Texas men going back,—otherwise, why were they holding off?

While the Colonel and the officers were at breakfast, a corporal brought in two pigeons he had shot at dawn. One of them carried a message under its wing. The Colonel unrolled a strip of paper and handed it to Gerhardt.

"Yes, sir, it's in German, but it's code stuff. It's a German nursery rhyme. Those reconnoitering planes must have dropped scouts on our rear, and they are sending in reports. Of course, they can get more on us than the air men can. Here, do you want these birds, Dick?"

The boy grinned. "You bet I do, sir! I may get a chance to fry 'em, later on."

After breakfast the Colonel went to inspect B Company in the Boar's Head. He was especially pleased with the advantageous placing of the machine guns in the Snout. "I expect you'll have a quiet day," he said to the men, "but I wouldn't like to promise you a quiet night. You'll have to be very steady in here; if Fritz takes this loop, he's got us, you understand."

They had, indeed, a quiet day. Some of the men played cards, and Oscar read his Bible. The night, too, began well. But at four fifteen everybody was roused by the gas alarm. Gas shells came over for exactly half an hour. Then the shrapnel broke loose; not the long, whizzing scream of solitary shells, but drum-fire, continuous and deafening. A hundred electrical storms seemed raging at once, in the air and on the ground. Balls of fire were rolling all over the place. The range was a little long for the Boar's Head, they were not getting the worst of it; but thirty yards back everything was torn to pieces. Claude didn't see how anybody could be left alive back there. A single twister had killed six of his men at the rear of the loop, where they were shovelling to keep the communication clear. Captain Owns' neat earthworks were being badly pounded.

Claude and Gerhardt were consulting together when the smoke and darkness began to take on the livid colour that announced the coming of daybreak. A messenger ran in from the Colonel; the Missourians had not yet come up, and his telephone communication with them was cut off. He was afraid they had got lost in the bombardment. "The Colonel says you are to send two men back to bring them up; two men who can take charge if they're stampeded."

When the messenger shouted this order, Gerhardt and Hicks looked at each other quickly, and volunteered to go.

Claude hesitated. Hicks and David waited for no further consent; they ran down the communication and disappeared.

Claude stood in the smoke that was slowly growing greyer, and looked after them with the deepest stab of despair he had ever known. Only a man who was bewildered and unfit to be in command of other men would have let his best friend and his best officer take such a risk. He was standing there under shelter, and his two friends were going back through that curtain of flying steel, toward the square from which the lost battalion had last reported. If he knew them, they would not lose time following the maze of trenches; they were probably even now out on the open, running straight through the enemy barrage, vaulting trench tops.

Claude turned and went back into the loop. Well, whatever happened, he had worked with brave men. It was worth having lived in this world to have known such men. Soldiers, when they were in a tight place, often made secret propositions to God; and now he found himself offering terms: If They would see to it that David came back, They could take the price out of him. He would pay. Did They understand?

An hour dragged by. Hard on the nerves, waiting. Up the communication came a train with ammunition and coffee for the loop. The men thought Headquarters did pretty well to get hot food to them through that barrage. A message came up in the Colonel's hand:

"Be ready when the barrage stops."

Claude took this up and showed it to the machine gunners in the Snout. Turning back, he ran into Hicks, stripped to his shirt and trousers, as wet as if he had come out of the river, and splashed with blood. His hand was wrapped up in a rag. He put his mouth to Claude's ear and shouted: "We found them. They were lost. They're coming. Send word to the Colonel."

"Where's Gerhardt?"

"He's coming; bringing them up. God, it's stopped!"

The bombardment ceased with a suddenness that was stupefying. The men in the loop gasped and crouched as if they were falling from a height. The air, rolling black with smoke and stifling with the smell of gases and burning powder, was still as death. The silence was like a heavy anaesthetic.

Claude ran back to the Snout to see that the gun teams were ready. "Wake up, boys! You know why we're here!"

Bert Fuller, who was up in the look-out, dropped back into the trench beside him. "They're coming, sir."

Claude gave the signal to the machine guns. Fire opened all along the loop. In a moment a breeze sprang up, and the heavy smoke clouds drifted to the rear. Mounting to the firestep, he peered over. The enemy was coming on eight deep, on the left of the Boar's Head, in long, waving lines that reached out toward the main trench. Suddenly the advance was checked.

The files of running men dropped behind a wrinkle in the earth fifty yards forward and did not instantly re-appear. It struck Claude that they were waiting for something; he ought to be clever enough to know for what, but he was not. The Colonel's line man came up to him.

"Headquarters has a runner from the Missourians. They'll be up in twenty minutes. The Colonel will put them in here at once. Till then you must manage to hold."

"We'll hold. Fritz is behaving queerly. I don't understand his tactics..."

While he was speaking, everything was explained. The Boar's Snout spread apart with an explosion that split the earth, and went up in a volcano of smoke and flame. Claude and the Colonel's messenger were thrown on their faces. When they got to their feet, the Snout was a smoking crater full of dead and dying men. The Georgia gun teams were gone.

It was for this that the Hun advance had been waiting behind the ridge. The mine under the Snout had been made long ago, probably, on a venture, when the Hun held Moltke trench for months without molestation. During the last twenty-four hours they had been getting their explosives in, reasoning that the strongest garrison would be placed there.

Here they were, coming on the run. It was up to the rifles. The men who had been knocked down by the shock were all on their feet again. They looked at their officer questioningly, as if the whole situation had changed. Claude felt they were going soft under his eyes. In a moment the Hun bombers would be in on them, and they would break. He ran along the trench, pointing over the sand bags and shouting, "It's up to you, it's up to you!"

The rifles recovered themselves and began firing, but Claude felt they were spongy and uncertain, that their minds were already on the way to the rear. If they did anything, it must be quick, and their gun-work must be accurate. Nothing but a withering fire could check.... He sprang to the firestep and then out on the parapet. Something instantaneous happened; he had his men in hand.

"Steady, steady!" He called the range to the rifle teams behind him, and he could see the fire take effect. All along the Hun lines men were stumbling and falling. They swerved a little to the left; he called the rifles to follow, directing them with his voice and with his hands. It was not only that from here he could correct the range and direct the fire; the men behind him had become like rock. That line of faces below; Hicks, Jones, Fuller, Anderson, Oscar.... Their eyes never left him. With these men he could do anything.

The right of the Hun line swerved out, not more than twenty yards from the battered Snout, trying to run to shelter under that pile of debris and human bodies. A quick concentration of rifle fire depressed it, and the swell came out again toward the left. Claude's appearance on the parapet had attracted no attention from the enemy at first, but now the bullets began popping about him; two rattled on his tin hat, one caught him in the shoulder. The blood dripped down his coat, but he felt no weakness. He felt only one thing; that he commanded wonderful men. When David came up with the supports he might find them dead, but he would find them all there. They were there to stay until they were carried out to be buried. They were mortal, but they were unconquerable.

The Colonel's twenty minutes must be almost up, he thought. He couldn't take his eyes from the front line long enough to look at his wrist watch.... The men behind him saw Claude sway as if he had lost his balance and were trying to recover it. Then he plunged, face down, outside the parapet. Hicks caught his foot and pulled him back. At the same moment the Missourians ran yelling up the communication. They threw their machine guns up on the sand bags and went into action without an unnecessary motion.

Hicks and Bert Fuller and Oscar carried Claude forward toward the Snout, out of the way of the supports that were pouring in. He was not bleeding very much. He smiled at them as if he were going to speak, but there was a weak blankness in his eyes. Bert tore his shirt open;

three clean bullet holes. By the time they looked at him again, the smile had gone… the look that was Claude had faded. Hicks wiped the sweat and smoke from his officer's face. "Thank God I never told him," he said. "Thank God for that!"

Bert and Oscar knew what Hicks meant. Gerhardt had been blown to pieces at his side when they dashed back through the enemy barrage to find the Missourians. They were running together across the open, not able to see much for smoke. They bumped into a section of wire entanglement, left above an old trench. David cut round to the right, waving Hicks to follow him. The two were not ten yards apart when the shell struck. Then Sergeant Hicks ran on alone.

XIX.

THE SUN IS SINKING LOW, a transport is steaming slowly up the narrows with the tide. The decks are covered with brown men. They cluster over the superstructure like bees in swarming time. Their attitudes are relaxed and lounging. Some look thoughtful, some well contented, some are melancholy, and many are indifferent, as they watch the shore approaching. They are not the same men who went away.

Sergeant Hicks was standing in the stern, smoking, reflecting, watching the twinkle of the red sunset upon the cloudy water. It is more than a year since he sailed for France. The world has changed in that time, and so has he.

Bert Fuller elbowed his way up to the Sergeant. "The doctor says Colonel Maxey is dying, He won't live to get off the boat, much less to ride in the parade in New York tomorrow."

Hicks shrugged, as if Maxey's pneumonia were no affair of his. "Well, we should worry! We've left better officers than him over there."

"I'm not saying we haven't. But it seems too bad, when he's so strong for fuss and feathers. He's been sending cables about that parade for weeks."

"Huh!" Hicks elevated his eyebrows and glanced sidewise in disdain. Presently he sputtered, squinting down at the glittering water, "Colonel Maxey, anyhow! Colonel for what Claude and Gerhardt did, I guess!" Hicks and Bert Fuller have been helping to keep the noble fortress of Ehrenbreitstein. They have always hung together and are usually quarrelling and grumbling at each other when they are off duty. Still, they hang together. They are the last of their group. Nifty Jones and Oscar, God only knows why, have gone on to the Black Sea.

During the year they were in the Rhine valley, Bert and Hicks were separated only once, and that was when Hicks got a two weeks' leave and, by dint of persevering and fatiguing travel, went to Venice. He had no proper passport, and the consuls and officials to whom he had appealed in his difficulties begged him to content himself with something nearer. But he said he was going to Venice because he had always heard about it. Bert Fuller was glad to welcome him back to Coblentz, and gave a "wine party" to celebrate his return. They expect to keep an eye on each other. Though Bert lives on the Platte and Hicks on the Big Blue, the automobile roads between those two rivers are excellent.

Bert is the same sweet-tempered boy he was when he left his mother's kitchen; his gravest troubles have been frequent betrothals. But Hicks' round, chubby face has taken on a slightly cynical expression,—a look quite out of place there. The chances of war have hurt his feelings… not that he ever wanted anything for himself. The way in which glittering honours bump down upon the wrong heads in the army, and palms and crosses blossom on the wrong breasts, has, as he says, thrown his compass off a few points.

What Hicks had wanted most in this world was to run a garage and repair shop with his old chum, Dell Able. Beaufort ended all that. He means to conduct a sort of memorial shop, anyhow, with "Hicks and Able" over the door. He wants to roll up his sleeves and look at the logical and beautiful inwards of automobiles for the rest of his life.

As the transport enters the North River, sirens and steam whistles all along the water front begin to blow their shrill salute to the returning soldiers. The men square their shoulders and smile knowingly at one another; some of them look a little bored. Hicks slowly lights a cigarette and regards the end of it with an expression which will puzzle his friends when he gets home.

By the banks of Lovely Creek, where it began, Claude Wheeler's story still goes on. To the two old women who work together in the farmhouse, the thought of him is always there, beyond everything else, at the farthest edge of consciousness, like the evening sun on the horizon.

Mrs. Wheeler got the word of his death one afternoon in the sitting-room, the room in which he had bade her good-bye. She was reading when the telephone rang.

"Is this the Wheeler farm? This is the telegraph office at Frankfort. We have a message from the War Department,—" the voice hesitated. "Isn't Mr. Wheeler there?"

"No, but you can read the message to me."

Mrs. Wheeler said, "Thank you," and hung up the receiver. She felt her way softly to her chair. She had an hour alone, when there was nothing but him in the room,—but him and the map there, which was the end of his road. Somewhere among those perplexing names, he had found his place.

Claude's letters kept coming for weeks afterward; then came the letters from his comrades and his Colonel to tell her all.

In the dark months that followed, when human nature looked to her uglier than it had ever done before, those letters were Mrs. Wheeler's comfort. As she read the newspapers, she used to think about the passage of the Red Sea, in the Bible; it seemed as if the flood of meanness and greed had been held back just long enough for the boys to go over, and then swept down and engulfed everything that was left at home. When she can see nothing that has come of it all but evil, she reads Claude's letters over again and reassures herself; for him the call was clear, the cause was glorious. Never a doubt stained his bright faith. She divines so much that he did not write. She knows what to read into those short flashes of enthusiasm; how fully he must have found his life before he could let himself go so far—he, who was so afraid of being fooled! He died believing his own country better than it is, and France better than any country can ever be. And those were beautiful beliefs to die with. Perhaps it was as well to see that vision, and then to see no more. She would have dreaded the awakening,—she sometimes even doubts whether he could have borne at all that last, desolating disappointment. One by one the heroes of that war, the men of dazzling soldiership, leave prematurely the world they have come back to. Airmen whose deeds were tales of wonder, officers whose names made the blood of youth beat faster, survivors of incredible dangers,—one by one they quietly die by their own hand. Some do it in obscure lodging houses, some in their office, where they seemed to be carrying on their business like other men. Some slip over a vessel's side and disappear into the sea. When Claude's mother hears of these things, she shudders and presses her hands tight over her breast, as if she had him there. She feels as if God had saved him from some horrible suffering, some horrible end. For as she reads, she thinks those slayers of themselves were all so like him; they were the ones who had hoped extravagantly,—who in order to do what they did had to hope extravagantly, and to believe passionately. And they found they had hoped and believed too much. But one she knew, who could ill bear disillusion… safe, safe.

Mahailey, when they are alone, sometimes addresses Mrs. Wheeler as "Mudder"; "Now, Mudder, you go upstairs an' lay down an' rest yourself." Mrs. Wheeler knows that then she is thinking of Claude, is speaking for Claude. As they are working at the table or bending over the oven, something reminds them of him, and they think of him together, like one person: Mahailey will pat her back and say, "Never you mind, Mudder; you'll see your boy up yonder." Mrs. Wheeler always feels that God is near,—but Mahailey is not troubled by any knowledge of interstellar spaces, and for her He is nearer still,—directly overhead, not so very far above the kitchen stove.